APPLYING

IFRS®
Standards

FOURTH EDITION

RUTH **PICKER**
EY

KERRY **CLARK**
EY

JOHN **DUNN**
University of Strathclyde

DAVID **KOLITZ**
University of Exeter Business School

GILAD **LIVNE**
University of Exeter Business School

JANICE **LOFTUS**
University of Adelaide

LEO **VAN DER TAS**
EY
Tilburg University

WILEY

Copyright © 2016 John Wiley & Sons, Ltd
Copyright © 2013 Ruth Picker, Ken Leo, Janice Loftus, Victoria Wise, Kerry Clark
Copyright © 2009 Keith Alfredson, Ken Leo, Ruth Picker, Janice Loftus, Kerry Clark, Victoria Wise
Copyright © 2007, 2005 Keith Alfredson, Ken Leo, Ruth Picker, Paul Pacter, Jennie Radford, Victoria Wise

All effort has been made to trace and acknowledge ownership of copyright. The publisher would be glad to hear from any copyright holders whom it has not been possible to contact.

Cover image credit: © Val_Iva/Shutterstock.com

Registered office

John Wiley & Sons Ltd, The Atrium, Southern Gate, Chichester, West Sussex, PO19 8SQ, United Kingdom

For details of our global editorial offices, for customer services and for information about how to apply for permission to reuse the copyright material in this book please see our website at www.wiley.com.

The rights of the authors of this work has been asserted in accordance with the UK Copyright, Designs and Patents Act 1988.

All rights reserved. No part of this publication may be reproduced, stored in a retrieval system, or transmitted, in any form or by any means, electronic, mechanical, photocopying, recording or otherwise, except as permitted by the UK Copyright, Designs and Patents Act 1988, without the prior permission of the publisher.

Wiley publishes in a variety of print and electronic formats and by print-on-demand. Some material included with standard print versions of this book may not be included in e-books or in print-on-demand. If this book refers to media such as a CD or DVD that is not included in the version you purchased, you may download this material at http://booksupport.wiley.com. For more information about Wiley products, visit www.wiley.com.

Disclaimer: To the extent permitted by applicable law, the publisher, the authors, the International Accounting Standards Board (IASB) and the IFRS Foundation expressly disclaim all liability howsoever arising from this publication or any translation thereof whether in contract, tort or otherwise (including, but not limited to, liability for any negligent act or omission) to any person in respect of any claims or losses of any nature including direct, indirect, incidental or consequential loss, punitive damages, penalties or costs. Any and all implied warranties — including but not limited to — implied warranties of satisfactory quality, fitness for a particular purpose, non-infringement and accuracy are excluded to the extent that they may be excluded as a matter of law. Information contained in this publication does not constitute advice, should therefore not be used as a basis for making decisions and should not be substituted for the services of an appropriately qualified professional. For further information on financial reporting, reference must be made to the IFRS Standards as issued by the IASB.

Content provided by IFRS is copyright © IFRS Foundation, used under licence. All rights reserved. Reproduction and use rights are strictly limited. For further details with regard to publication and copyright matters, please contact the Foundation at (licenses@ifrs.org).

The following trademarks are the registered trademarks of The International Financial Reporting Standards Foundation: ⬛️❉IFRS˙

The IFRS Foundation logo, the IASB logo, the IFRS for SMEs logo, the 'Hexagon Device', 'IFRS Foundation', 'eIFRS', 'IAS' 'IASB', 'IFRS for SMEs', 'IASs', 'IFRS', 'IFRSs', 'International Accounting Standards', 'International Financial Reporting Standards', 'IFRIC' 'SIC' and 'IFRS Taxonomy'.

Further details of the Trade Marks including details of countries where the Trade Marks are registered or applied for are available from the Foundation on request.

Library of Congress Cataloging-in-Publication Data

Names: Picker, Ruth.
Title: Applying IFRS / Ruth Picker,
    Ernst & Young, Kerry Clark, Ernst & Young, John Dunn, University of
    Strathclyde, David Kolitz, University of Exeter Business School, Gilad
    Livne, University of Exeter Business School, Janice Loftus, The University
    of Adelaide, Leo van der Tas, Ernst & Young.
Description: Fourth edition. | Chichester, West Sussex, United Kingdom: John
    Wiley & Sons, [2016] | Includes bibliographical references and index.
Identifiers: LCCN 2015048910 | ISBN 9781119159223 (pbk.)
Subjects: LCSH: Accounting—Standards. | Financial statements—Standards.
Classification: LCC HF5626 .P45 2016 | DDC 657/.30218—dc23 LC record available at http://lccn.loc.gov/2015048910

ISBN 9781119159223 (pbk)
ISBN 9781119250777 (ebk)

A catalogue record for this book is available from the British Library

Set in 9.5pt/ITC Giovanni Std by Aptara Inc., India

EY is delighted to support *Applying IFRS Standards*, fourth edition. With International Financial Reporting Standards (IFRS®) now being mandated, or permitted, for the financial reporting of listed entities in most parts of the world, it has become the global language of accounting. This means that comparing financial statements from companies across the globe has become much easier, fostering capital markets and reducing the cost of capital. It also has led to reductions in training costs and greater mobility of accounting staff and professionals across countries. You, as accountancy students and professionals, will benefit greatly from being able to carry your knowledge and experience from country to country without always having to study local accounting standards each time you cross a border.

Business and capital markets are developing continuously. So must financial reporting. The International Accounting Standards Board (IASB®), the IFRS Standards setter, recently issued a number of important new standards. The new IFRS 9 *Financial Instruments* addresses the issues that arose during the global credit crisis and, among others, answers calls for better loan loss provisions by banks and more practical hedge accounting rules. IFRS 15 *Revenue from Contracts with Customers* modernises and greatly enhances the guidance on revenue recognition. Both new standards are covered in this new edition of *Applying IFRS Standards* as well as the key highlights of the new standard for lease accounting.

Applying IFRS Standards aims to help you master the complex world of IFRS Standards; as such, it is truly global in the wealth of insights and examples it provides, as well as abstracts from financial statements of companies across the globe. I am sure this book will be instructive not only to those learning about financial reporting standards for the first time, but also to accountancy professionals keeping abreast of developments in IFRS Standards and trying to find their way in applying IFRS Standards to transactions and events.

Now that IFRS Standards have been adopted in most parts of the world, it is important to interpret and apply the standards consistently to make it a truly single global set of accounting standards. I hope and trust this book will help in achieving a common and consistent understanding and application of IFRS Standards.

Leo van der Tas
Global Leader — IFRS Services, Global Professional Practice
EY
London

May 2016

BRIEF CONTENTS

Part 1 **CONCEPTUAL FRAMEWORK   1**

    1   The IASB and its *Conceptual Framework*   **3**

Part 2 **ELEMENTS   19**

    2   Owners' equity: share capital and reserves   21

    3   Fair value measurement   49

    4   Revenue from contracts with customers   73

    5   Provisions, contingent liabilities and contingent assets   95

    6   Income taxes   123

    7   Financial instruments   155

    8   Share-based payment   199

    9   Inventories   219

    10   Employee benefits   245

    11   Property, plant and equipment   275

    12   Leases   321

    13   Intangible assets   355

    14   Business combinations   379

    15   Impairment of assets   417

Online chapter A   Exploration for and evaluation of mineral resources

Online chapter B   Agriculture

PART 3 **PRESENTATION AND DISCLOSURES   447**

    16   Financial statement presentation   449

    17   Statement of cash flows   485

    18   Operating segments   517

    19   Other key notes disclosures   537

PART 4 **ECONOMIC ENTITIES   559**

    20   Consolidation: controlled entities   561

    21   Consolidation: wholly owned subsidiaries   577

    22   Consolidation: intragroup transactions   605

    23   Consolidation: non-controlling interest   635

    24   Translation of the financial statements of foreign entities   679

Online chapter C   Associates and joint ventures

Online chapter D   Joint arrangements

CONTENTS

Preface ix
About the authors xi
List of Acronyms xiii

Part 1

CONCEPTUAL FRAMEWORK 1

1 The IASB and its *Conceptual Framework* 3
1.1 The International Accounting Standards Board (IASB®) 4
1.2 The purpose of a conceptual framework 6
1.3 Qualitative characteristics of useful financial information 7
1.4 Going concern assumption 9
1.5 Definition of elements in financial statements 10
1.6 Recognition of elements of financial statements 12
1.7 Measurement of the elements of financial statements 13
1.8 Concepts of capital 14
1.9 Future developments 14
Summary 15
Discussion questions 15
References 15
Exercises 15
Academic perspective 17

Part 2

ELEMENTS 19

2 Owners' equity: share capital and reserves 21
2.1 Equity 22
2.2 For-profit companies 23
2.3 Key features of the corporate structure 23
2.4 Different forms of share capital 24
2.5 Contributed equity: issue of share capital 26
2.6 Contributed equity: subsequent movements in share capital 28
2.7 Share capital: subsequent decreases in share capital 32
2.8 Reserves 34
2.9 Disclosure 38
Summary 40
Discussion questions 40
References 40
Exercises 40
Academic perspective 46

3 Fair value measurement 49
3.1 Introduction 50
3.2 The definition of fair value 51
3.3 The fair value framework 53
3.4 Application to non-financial assets 59

3.5 Application to liabilities 62
3.6 Application to measurement of an entity's own equity 65
3.7 Application to financial instruments with offsetting positions 65
3.8 Disclosure 65
Summary 68
Discussion questions 68
References 68
Exercises 69
Academic perspective 71

4 Revenue from contracts with customers 73
4.1 Introduction 74
4.2 Scope 74
4.3 Identify the contract with the customer 75
4.4 Identify the performance obligations 76
4.5 Determine the transaction price 78
4.6 Allocate the transaction price 81
4.7 Satisfaction of performance obligations 82
4.8 Contract costs 84
4.9 Other application issues 85
4.10 Presentation and disclosures 87
Summary 89
Discussion questions 89
References 90
Exercises 90
Academic perspective 92

5 Provisions, contingent liabilities and contingent assets 95
5.1 Introduction to IAS 37 96
5.2 Scope 96
5.3 Definition of a provision 97
5.4 Distinguishing provisions from other liabilities 97
5.5 Definition of a contingent liability 97
5.6 Distinguishing a contingent liability from a provision 98
5.7 The recognition criteria for provisions 98
5.8 Measurement of provisions 100
5.9 Application of the definitions, recognition and measurement rules 104
5.10 Contingent assets 111
5.11 Disclosure 111
5.12 Comparison between IFRS 3 and IAS 37 in respect of contingent liabilities 113
5.13 Expected future developments 115
Summary 115
Discussion questions 116
References 116
Exercises 116
Academic perspective 120

6 Income taxes 123

6.1 The nature of income tax 124
6.2 Differences between accounting profit and taxable profit 124
6.3 Accounting for income taxes 126
6.4 Calculation of current tax 127
6.5 Recognition of current tax 131
6.6 Payment of tax 131
6.7 Tax losses 132
6.8 Calculation of deferred tax 133
6.9 Recognition of deferred tax liabilities and deferred tax assets 139
6.10 Change of tax rates 142
6.11 Other issues 142
6.12 Presentation in the financial statements 143
6.13 Disclosures 144
Summary 148
Discussion questions 148
References 148
Exercises 148
Academic perspective 153

7 Financial instruments 155

7.1 Introduction 156
7.2 What is a financial instrument? 158
7.3 Financial assets and financial liabilities 159
7.4 Distinguishing financial liabilities from equity instruments 160
7.5 Compound financial instruments 163
7.6 Interest, dividends, gains and losses 164
7.7 Financial assets and financial liabilities: scope 164
7.8 Derivatives and embedded derivatives 166
7.9 Financial assets and financial liabilities: categories of financial instruments 168
7.10 Financial assets and financial liabilities: recognition criteria 171
7.11 Financial assets and financial liabilities: measurement 171
7.12 Financial assets and financial liabilities: offsetting 181
7.13 Hedge accounting 181
7.14 Disclosures 188
Summary 194
Discussion questions 194
References 194
Exercises 194
Academic perspective 197

8 Share-based payment 199

Introduction 200
8.1 Application and scope 200
8.2 Cash-settled and equity-settled share-based payment transactions 201
8.3 Recognition 201
8.4 Equity-settled share-based payment transactions 202
8.5 Vesting 204
8.6 Treatment of a reload feature 207

8.7 Modifications to terms and conditions on which equity instruments were granted 208
8.8 Cash-settled share-based payment transactions 209
8.9 Disclosure 212
Summary 214
Discussion questions 214
References 214
Exercises 214
Academic perspective 217

9 Inventories 219

9.1 The nature of inventories 220
9.2 Measurement of inventory upon initial recognition 221
9.3 Determination of cost 221
9.4 Accounting for inventory 224
9.5 End-of-period accounting 227
9.6 Assigning costs to inventory on sale 231
9.7 Net realisable value 234
9.8 Recognition as an expense 236
9.9 Disclosure 236
Summary 237
Discussion questions 237
References 238
Exercises 238
Academic perspective 243

10 Employee benefits 245

10.1 Introduction to accounting for employee benefits 246
10.2 Scope and purpose of IAS 19 246
10.3 Defining employee benefits 246
10.4 Short-term employee benefits 246
10.5 Post-employment benefits 253
10.6 Accounting for defined contribution post-employment plans 254
10.7 Accounting for defined benefit post-employment plans 255
10.8 Other long-term employee benefits 263
10.9 Termination benefits 266
Summary 268
Discussion questions 268
References 268
Exercises 269
Academic perspective 273

11 Property, plant and equipment 275

11.1 The nature of property, plant and equipment 276
11.2 Initial recognition of property, plant and equipment 277
11.3 Initial measurement of property, plant and equipment 278
11.4 Measurement subsequent to initial recognition 283
11.5 The cost model 283
11.6 The revaluation model 289
11.7 Choosing between the cost model and the revaluation model 299

11.8 Derecognition   300

11.9 Disclosure   301

11.10 Investment properties   303

Summary   305

Discussion questions   312

References   313

Exercises   313

Academic perspective   319

12 Leases   321

Introduction   322

12.1 What is a lease?   322

12.2 Classification of leases   323

12.3 Classification guidance   324

12.4 Accounting for finance leases by lessees   330

12.5 Accounting for finance leases by lessors   336

12.6 Accounting for finance leases by manufacturer or dealer lessors   341

12.7 Accounting for operating leases   342

12.8 Accounting for sale and leaseback transactions   346

12.9 Changes to the leasing standards   348

Summary   349

Discussion questions   349

Exercises   349

Academic perspective   354

13 Intangible assets   355

Introduction   356

13.1 The nature of intangible assets   358

13.2 Recognition and initial measurement   360

13.3 Measurement subsequent to initial recognition   364

13.4 Retirements and disposals   367

13.5 Disclosure   367

Summary   371

Discussion questions   372

References   373

Exercises   373

Academic perspective   376

14 Business combinations   379

14.1 The nature of a business combination   380

14.2 Accounting for a business combination — basic principles   381

14.3 Accounting in the records of the acquirer   383

14.4 Recognition and measurement of assets acquired and liabilities assumed   383

14.5 Goodwill and gain on bargain purchase   385

14.6 Shares acquired in the acquiree   392

14.7 Accounting in the records of the acquiree   392

14.8 Subsequent adjustments to the initial accounting for a business combination   395

14.9 Disclosure — business combinations   398

Summary   400

Discussion questions   406

References   406

Exercises   407

Academic perspective   414

15 Impairment of assets   417

15.1 Introduction to IAS 36   418

15.2 When to undertake an impairment test   418

15.3 Impairment test for an individual asset   420

15.4 Cash-generating units — excluding goodwill   426

15.5 Cash-generating units and goodwill   430

15.6 Reversal of an impairment loss   432

15.7 Disclosure   433

Summary   434

Discussion questions   438

References   438

Exercises   439

Academic perspective   444

Online chapter A   *Exploration for and evaluation of mineral resources*

Online chapter B   *Agriculture*

Part 3

PRESENTATION AND DISCLOSURES   447

16 Financial statement presentation   449

Introduction   450

16.1 Components of financial statements   450

16.2 General principles of financial statements   451

16.3 Statement of financial position   452

16.4 Statement of profit or loss and other comprehensive income   457

16.5 Statement of changes in equity   463

16.6 Notes   466

16.7 Accounting policies, changes in accounting estimates and errors   468

16.8 Events after the reporting period   473

Summary   475

Discussion questions   475

References   476

Exercises   476

Academic perspective   482

17 Statement of cash flows   485

Introduction and scope   486

17.1 Purpose of a statement of cash flows   486

17.2 Defining cash and cash equivalents   486

17.3 Classifying cash flow activities   487

17.4 Format of the statement of cash flows   489

17.5 Preparing a statement of cash flows   491

17.6 Other disclosures   506

Summary   509

Discussion questions   509

References   509

Exercises   509

Academic perspective   515

18 Operating segments   517

18.1 Objectives of financial reporting by segments   518

18.2 Scope   518

18.3 A controversial standard 518

18.4 Identifying operating segments 520

18.5 Identifying reportable segments 522

18.6 Applying the definition of reportable segments 524

18.7 Disclosure 524

18.8 Applying the disclosures in practice 527

18.9 Results of the post-implementation review of IFRS 8 531

Summary 532

Discussion questions 532

References 532

Exercises 532

Academic perspective 535

19 Other key notes disclosures 537

Introduction 538

19.1 Related party disclosures 538

19.2 Earnings per share 543

Summary 554

Discussion questions 554

References 555

Exercises 555

Academic perspective 557

Part 4

ECONOMIC ENTITIES 559

20 Consolidation: controlled entities 561

Introduction 562

20.1 Consolidated financial statements 562

20.2 Control as the criterion for consolidation 564

20.3 Preparation of consolidated financial statements 569

20.4 Business combinations and consolidation 570

20.5 Disclosure 572

Summary 574

Discussion questions 574

Exercises 575

21 Consolidation: wholly owned subsidiaries 577

21.1 The consolidation process 578

21.2 Consolidation worksheets 579

21.3 The acquisition analysis: determining goodwill or bargain purchase 580

21.4 Worksheet entries at the acquisition date 583

21.5 Worksheet entries subsequent to the acquisition date 588

21.6 Revaluations in the records of the subsidiary at acquisition date 595

21.7 Disclosure 595

Summary 598

Discussion questions 598

Exercises 598

22 Consolidation: intragroup transactions 605

Introduction 606

22.1 Rationale for adjusting for intragroup transactions 606

22.2 Transfers of inventory 607

22.3 Intragroup services 613

22.4 Intragroup dividends 614

22.5 Intragroup borrowings 616

Summary 617

Discussion questions 625

Exercises 626

23 Consolidation: non-controlling interest 635

23.1 Non-controlling interest explained 636

23.2 Effects of an NCI on the consolidation process 638

23.3 Calculating the NCI share of equity 644

23.4 Adjusting for the effects of intragroup transactions 656

23.5 Gain on bargain purchase 658

Summary 660

Discussion questions 672

Exercises 672

24 Translation of the financial statements of foreign entities 679

24.1 Translation of a foreign subsidiary's statements 680

24.2 Functional and presentation currencies 680

24.3 The rationale underlying the functional currency choice 680

24.4 Identifying the functional currency 683

24.5 Translation into the functional currency 684

24.6 Changing the functional currency 689

24.7 Translation into the presentation currency 689

24.8 Consolidating foreign subsidiaries — where local currency is the functional currency 691

24.9 Consolidating foreign subsidiaries — where functional currency is that of the parent entity 698

24.10 Net investment in a foreign operation 699

24.11 Disclosure 700

Summary 700

Discussion questions 701

References 701

Exercises 701

Online chapter C Associates and joint ventures

Online chapter D Joint arrangements

Glossary 707

Index 717

With International Financial Reporting Standards (IFRS®) now being mandated for listed companies in 100+ countries across the globe, it has become a truly global set of standards for financial reporting. IFRS Standards have also become the example for national accounting standards. The credit crisis has shown that a stable, globally accepted set of financial reporting standards is important to maintain transparency in financial communication by companies to their constituents.

An understanding of the IFRS Standards is therefore paramount for all those involved in financial reporting or preparing to attain such a role. It provides not just technical knowledge and in-depth understanding of the financial reporting process, but does so in a global business environment. *Applying IFRS Standards*, fourth edition, has been written to meet the needs of accountancy students and practitioners in understanding the complexities of IFRS Standards.

This publication is the fourth edition of the book. It has now established itself as a text that is used by academics and practitioners throughout the world. We have welcomed the comments and suggestions received from various people and have tried to ensure that these are reflected in this edition.

What's new in this edition?

The fourth edition addresses the major changes to a number of accounting standards and the release of new IFRS Standards, in particular:
- the IASB's *Conceptual Framework for Financial Reporting*
- IFRS 9 *Financial Instruments*
- IFRS 15 *Revenue from Contracts with Customers*
- IFRS 16 *Leases*.

The chapters covering these topics reflect these changes and discuss the consequences.

An important new feature has been introduced for the first time in this edition. Academic perspectives can be found at the end of all chapters in the first three parts of the book (i.e. chapters 1 to 19). These academic perspectives summarise and highlight certain findings from published research in accounting and other fields that pertain to a chapter's topic. Referring to these Perspectives should give the reader a basic understanding of questions that accounting researchers have attempted to address. Note, however, that the academic perspectives do not furnish a comprehensive review of related literature. Rather, they provide a starting point for further reading and exploration of relevant academic research.

Applying IFRS Standards fourth edition, also comes equipped with discussion questions and exercises at the end of each chapter, specifically designed to test the reader's understanding of the content. A wealth of additional learning materials can also be found at **www.wiley.com/college/picker**, including:
- Four additional chapters entitled: Exploration for and evaluation of mineral resources; Agriculture; Associates and joint ventures; Joint arrangements
- Instructor slides
- Testbank
- Additional exercises
- Solutions manual
- Access to the IFRS Learning Resources

In writing this book, we have endeavoured to ensure that the following common themes flow throughout the text:
- *Accounting standards are underpinned by a conceptual framework.* Accounting standards are not simply a rulebook to be learnt by heart. An understanding of the conceptual basis of accounting, and the rationale behind the principles espoused in particular standards, is crucial to their consistent application in a variety of practical applications.
- *The International Accounting Standards Board (IASB®) financial reporting standards are principles-based.* Although a specific standard is a stand-alone document, the principles in any standard relate to and are interpreted in conjunction with other standards. To appreciate the application of a specific standard, an understanding of the reasoning within other standards is required. We have endeavoured where applicable to refer to other accounting standards that are connected in principle and application. In particular, extensive references are made to the Basis for Conclusions documents accompanying each standard issued by the IASB. This material, although not integral to the standards, explains the reasoning process used by the IASB and provides indicators of changes in direction being proposed by the IASB.
- *Accounting standards have a practical application.* The end product of the standard-setting process must be applied by accounting practitioners in a variety of organisational structures and practical settings. While a theoretical understanding of a standard is important, practitioners should be able to apply the relevant standard. The author of each chapter has demonstrated the practical application of the

accounting standards by providing case studies, examples and journal entries (where relevant). The references to practical situations require the reader to pay close attention to the detailed information discussed, given that such a detailed examination is essential to an understanding of the standards. Having only a broad overview of the basic principles is insufficient.

Writing a book like this is impossible without the help and input from many people. Much of the knowledge and insights reflected in this book have been gained through discussions and debates with many colleagues and with staff associated with the standard-setting bodies, particularly at the IASB. We thank them for sharing their perspectives and experience. We would like to thank the following people in particular. A team of people from EY's Global IFRS team in London, consisting of Angela Covic, Pieter Dekker, Steinar Kvifte, Victoria O'Leary, Alexandra Poddubnaya, Serene Seah-Tan and Charlene Teo, wrote and reviewed individual chapters of the book. Richard Barker from Saïd Business School, Oxford University reviewed the chapters in Part 4. Erik Roelofsen from Rotterdam School of Management, Erasmus University Rotterdam and PwC reviewed the Academic Perspectives. Elisabetta Barone from Brunel Business School updated the testbank. We would also like to thank Natalie Forde from Cardiff Business School and other anonymous reviewers who have provided valuable feedback and recommendations during the development of the fourth edition. In addition, we extend our thanks to the people at Wiley and professional freelancers for their help realising this edition, including Juliet Booker, Steve Hardman, Georgia King, Joyce Poh and Joshua Poole as well as Jennifer Mair and Paul Stringer. Last but not least, writing a book takes huge commitment, and this has left less time for family and friends. We thank them also for their support and understanding.

Finally, in a time when the world, with its increasing sophistication, seems to produce situations and pronouncements that have added complexity, we hope that this book assists in the lifelong learning process that ourselves and the readers of this book are continuously engaged in.

Ruth Picker
Kerry Clark
John Dunn
David Kolitz
Gilad Livne
Janice Loftus
Leo van der Tas

May 2016

Ruth Picker

Ruth Picker BA, FCA, FSIA, FCPA, was Global Leader, Global IFRS Services, Global Professional Practice, with EY between 2009 and 2013. Ruth has over 30 years' experience with EY and has held various leadership roles during this time. Up until June 2009, Ruth was Managing Partner — Melbourne and the Oceania Team Leader of Climate Change and Sustainability Services. Prior to this role, Ruth was a senior partner in the Technical Consulting Group, Global IFRS and the firm's Professional Practice Director (PPD) responsible for directing the firm's accounting and auditing policies with the ultimate authority on accounting and auditing issues.

Ruth's authoritative insight and understanding of accounting policy and regulation was acknowledged through her appointment to the International Financial Reporting Interpretations Committee (IFRIC®), the official interpretative arm of the International Accounting Standards Board (IASB®). She was a member of IFRIC between 2006 and 2013.

Ruth has conducted numerous 'Directors' Schools' for listed company boards. These schools were designed by Ruth and are aimed at enhancing the financial literacy of listed company board members.

She is a frequent speaker and author on accounting issues and has been actively involved in the Australian accounting standard-setting process, being a past member and former deputy chair of the Australian Accounting Standards Board (AASB) and having served on the Urgent Issues Group for 3 years. She has been a long-standing lecturer and Task Force member for the Securities Institute of Australia, serving that organisation for 17 years.

Her written articles have been published in numerous publications, and she is frequently quoted in the media on accounting and governance issues.

Kerry Clark

Kerry Clark BCom, CA, CPA, is an Associate Partner in EY's Financial Accounting Advisory Services team in Calgary, Canada. Kerry provides accounting guidance to clients and staff advising on various financial reporting matters under International Financial Reporting Standards (IFRS® Standards) and United States generally accepted accounting principles and has over 25 years of experience with EY.

Kerry is a member of CPA Canada's Oil and Gas Industry Task Force, the Canadian Association of Petroleum Producers' IFRS Committee, EY's internal expert network on the new revenue recognition and leases standards and EY's Global Oil and Gas Industry Network.

Kerry's accounting experience spans a variety of industries, with a specific focus over the past several years on financial reporting issues in the energy industries, including oil and gas, infrastructure and utilities in Canada. Prior to this Kerry was a key member of EY's Technical Consulting Group, Global IFRS based in Melbourne, Australia, where she was responsible for advising clients on the application of IFRS Standards to complex transactions with a specific focus on the communications, entertainment and technology industry sectors.

Kerry frequently assists clients in understanding the financial reporting implications of complex transactions such as complicated infrastructure construction and partnership arrangements, leases, acquisitions and joint arrangements. She has been involved in the authoring of many EY publications and *Charter* magazine articles and assisted Ruth Picker in conducting 'Directors' Schools' for listed company boards. She has also spoken on accounting issues in many different forums in both Canada and Australia.

John Dunn

John Dunn is a lecturer at the University of Strathclyde in Glasgow, where he teaches financial accounting and auditing. He has published widely on those topics and others. He is a qualified accountant with extensive experience of examining for professional bodies.

David Kolitz

David Kolitz, BComm (Natal), BCom (Hons) (SA), MCom (Wits) is Senior Lecturer in the Business School at the University of Exeter. He was previously Associate Professor and Assistant Dean in the Faculty of Commerce, Law and Management at the University of the Witwatersrand, Johannesburg. He is an experienced accounting academic and the lead author/co-author of three other books in the area of Financial Accounting.

Gilad Livne

Gilad Livne, PhD, CPA, is a professor of accounting at the University of Exeter Business School. Previously Gilad served on the accounting faculty of the London Business School and Cass Business School. Gilad received his MSc and PhD in accounting at the University of California at Berkeley, and BA (Accounting and Economics) in Tel Aviv University.

Gilad's teaching involves financial statement analysis, international accounting as well as advanced financial accounting courses. Gilad has taught on Undergraduate, MBA, Executive MBA, Sloan, Ph.D., and MSc programmes. In addition to teaching at Cass and LBS, Gilad has also taught at HEC (Paris), New Economic School (Moscow), Lancaster University, University of Lausanne (Switzerland), Oulu University (Finland) and on various company-specific programmes. Gilad has also consulted and appeared on TV and various radio programmes.

Gilad's research looks into auditor independence, international accounting, fair value accounting, and compensation. Gilad currently serves on a number of editorial boards of accounting journals. His research has been published in several journals including *European Accounting Review, Journal of Banking and Finance, Journal of Business Finance and Accounting, Journal of Corporate Finance*, and *Review of Accounting Studies*.

Janice Loftus

Janice Loftus BBus, MCom (Hons) FCPA is an associate professor in accounting at the University of Adelaide, Australia. Her teaching interests are in the area of financial accounting and she has written several study guides for distance learning programmes. Janice's research interests are in the areas of financial reporting and social and environmental reporting. She co-authored Accounting Theory Monograph 11 on solvency and cash condition with Professor M.C. Miller. She has numerous publications on international financial reporting standards, risk reporting, solvency, earnings management, social and environmental reporting, and developments in standard setting in Australian and international journals. Janice co-authored *Financial Reporting, Understanding Australian Accounting Standards* and *Accounting: Building Business Skills* published by John Wiley & Sons Australia. Prior to embarking on an academic career, Janice held several senior accounting positions in Australian and multinational corporations.

Leo van der Tas

Leo van der Tas (PhD, RA) is the Global IFRS Leader at EY in London since 2013, before which he was the Global IFRS Technical Director at EY in London. In that role he is responsible for the IFRS Standards policy of EY and consistency of IFRS Standards implementation within the EY network. He is senior technical partner at EY in the Netherlands. He was a member of the IFRIC (and predecessor Standing Interpretations Committee of the IASB) between 1997 and 2006 and a member of the IFRS Foundation Advisory Council between 2009 and 2013.

Leo has been part-time full professor of financial reporting at Tilburg University, the Netherlands, since 2010 and before that part-time full professor at Erasmus University Rotterdam, the Netherlands, since 1993. He chaired the committee for permanent education in financial reporting of the Dutch Institute of Accountants (NIVRA) until 2010.

Leo has been a member of the Consultative Working Group of the Standing Corporate Reporting Committee of the European Securities and Market Authority (ESMA) in Paris, France, since 2010. From 2007 to 2012 he was a member of the Advisory Committee on Financial Reporting of the Netherlands Authority for the Financial Markets (AFM) in Amsterdam, the Netherlands.

He has published many books and articles in the area of international accounting and is a frequent speaker and teacher on the subject.

He was seconded to the European Commission in Brussels, Belgium, for a period of 2 years to assist in the development of the Commission's policy in the area of European accounting harmonisation.

ACRONYMS

AFS	Available-for-sale
AGM	Annual general meeting
ASC	Accounting Standards Codification
BCVR	Business combinations value reserve
CEO	Chief Executive Officer
CGU	Cash-generating unit
CODM	Chief Operating Decision Maker
COO	Chief Operating Officer
DBL(A)	Defined benefit liability (asset)
DBO	Defined benefit obligation
ED	Exposure draft
EFRAG	European Financial Reporting Advisory Group
EPS	Earnings per share
FAS	Financial Accounting Standards
FASB	US Financial Accounting Standards Board
FIFO	First-in, first-out
FV	Fair value
FVOCI	Fair value through other comprehensive income
FVPL	Fair value through profit or loss
GAAP	US generally accepted accounting principles
IAS®	International Accounting Standards
IASB®	International Accounting Standards Board
IASC	International Accounting Standards Committee, predecessor of the IASB
IDC	Initial direct costs
IFRIC®	International Financial Reporting Interpretations Committee, now the IFRS® Interpretations Committee
IFRS®	International Financial Reporting Standards
IPO	Initial public offering
LIBOR	London interbank offered rate
MLP	Minimum lease payments
NCI	Non-controlling interest
OCI	Other comprehensive income
PV	Present value
R&D	Research and development
ROA	Return on assets
SAC	Standards Advisory Council
SARs	Share appreciation rights
SFAS	US Statement of Financial Accounting Standards
SPPI	Solely payments of principal and interest
TSR	Total shareholder return
US GAAP	see GAAP

Part 1

Conceptual Framework

1 The IASB and its *Conceptual Framework*   3

1
The IASB and its *Conceptual Framework*

After studying this chapter, you should be able to:

1 describe the organisational structure of the key players in setting International Financial Reporting Standards (IFRS® Standards)

2 describe the purpose of a conceptual framework — who uses it and why

3 explain the qualitative characteristics that make information in financial statements useful

4 discuss the going concern assumption underlying the preparation of financial statements

5 define the basic elements in financial statements — assets, liabilities, equity, income and expenses

6 explain the principles for recognising the elements of financial statements

7 distinguish between alternative bases for measuring the elements of financial statements

8 outline concepts of capital.

INTRODUCTION

The purpose of this book is to identify and explain the major concepts and principles of International Financial Reporting Standards (IFRS® Standards) and to help you develop skills in applying them in business contexts. You may be familiar with the accounting treatment for various transactions, such as the purchase of inventory. The text will build on that knowledge and consider the principles and techniques required or permitted by IFRS Standards in accounting for a range of transactions, events and circumstances.

This first chapter provides an outline of the International Accounting Standards Board (IASB®) and its role in setting international accounting standards, which are generally referred to as IFRS Standards. It also explains that the IASB develops those IFRS Standards on the basis of some fundamental principles. While IFRSs take precedence, the concepts and principles expounded in the *Conceptual Framework for Financial Reporting* (the *Conceptual Framework*) are generally reflected in the requirements of IFRS Standards. IFRS Standards are principles-based standards, rather than rules-based standards, even though the volume of guidance under IFRS Standards has expanded considerably over the years. This means that *professional judgement* is needed in applying IFRS Standards as they rely more on concepts and principles, such as a requirement that a value be measured reliably, rather than on objective prescriptions, such as quantitative tests for classification of leases. The *Conceptual Framework* establishes the qualitative characteristics financial information needs to have in order to be useful, as well as definitions and recognition criteria for the elements of financial statements. These principles underlie the exercise of professional judgement in applying IFRS Standards. The *Conceptual Framework* is also an important source of guidance to standard setters in the development of new standards and to preparers of financial statements in the absence of an applicable accounting standard. Accordingly, study of the *Conceptual Framework* provides a useful foundation to understanding and applying IFRS Standards.

1.1 THE INTERNATIONAL ACCOUNTING STANDARDS BOARD (IASB)

The purpose of this section is to provide an understanding of the structure of the IASB and its role in the determination of IFRS Standards. Much of this information has been obtained from the website of the IASB, www.ifrs.org. To keep up to date with what the IASB is doing, this website should be regularly visited.

1.1.1 Formation of the IASB

In 1972, at the 10th World Congress of Accountants in Sydney, Australia, a proposal was put forward for the establishment of an International Accounting Standards Committee (IASC). In 1973, the IASC was formed by 16 national professional accountancy bodies from nine countries — Canada, the United Kingdom, the United States, Australia, France, Germany, Japan, the Netherlands and Mexico. By December 1998, the membership of the IASC had expanded and the committee had completed its core set of accounting standards.

However, the IASC was seen as having a number of shortcomings:
- It had weak relationships with national standard setters; this was due in part to the fact that the representatives on the IASC were not representative of the national standard setters but rather of national professional accounting bodies.
- There was a lack of convergence between the IASC standards and those adopted in major countries, even after 25 years of trying.
- The board was only part time.
- The board lacked resources and technical support.

In 1998, the committee responsible for overseeing the operations of the IASC began a review of the IASC's operations. The results of the review were recommendations that the IASC be replaced with a smaller, full-time International Accounting Standards Board. In 1999, the IASC board approved the constitutional changes necessary for the restructuring of the IASC. A new International Accounting Standards Committee Foundation was established and its trustees appointed. By early 2001, the members of the IASB and the Standards Advisory Council (SAC) were appointed, as were technical staff to assist the IASB.

The IASB initially adopted the International Accounting Standards (IAS® Standards), with some modifications, as issued by the IASC (e.g. IAS 2 *Inventories*). As standards were revised or newly issued by the IASB, they were called International Financial Reporting Standards (e.g. IFRS 8 *Operating Segments*). So the term International Financial Reporting Standards includes both IFRS Standards and IAS Standards.

1.1.2 The standard-setting structure of the IASB

Available on the IASB website is a document entitled *IASB and the IASC Foundation: Who We Are and What We Do*. This document is available in ten languages. The IASB is an independent standard-setting board. The IFRS Interpretations Committee (formerly IFRIC) issues interpretations of and guidance on the requirements of IFRS Standards in relation to accounting for specific transactions or events. Compliance with IFRS Standards includes compliance with IFRIC® Interpretations.

The IASB and IFRS Interpretations Committee are appointed and overseen by a geographically and professionally diverse group of trustees (IFRS Foundation Trustees) who are publicly accountable to a monitoring board made up of public authorities, which currently comprises representatives from the Japanese and, US capital market regulators and IOSCO (International Organization of Securities Commissions), as well as a representative from the European Commission. The IFRS Foundation Trustees appoint an IFRS Advisory Council, which provides strategic advice to the IASB and informs the IFRS Foundation Trustees. This structure can be seen diagrammatically in figure 1.1.

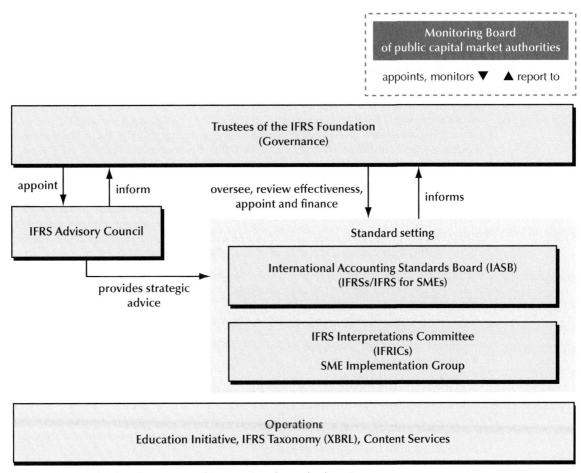

FIGURE 1.1 Institutional structure of international standard setting
Source: IASB (2016).

As of July 2015, the Constitution envisages that the IASB comprises 16 members but the actual number of members is currently 14. The IFRS Foundation has issued a proposal to reduce the number of IASB Board members to 13. The members are experts with a mix of recent practical experience in setting accounting standards, preparing, auditing, or using financial statements and accounting education. While the mix of members is not based on geographical criteria, the trustees endeavour to ensure that the IASB is not dominated by any particular constituency or geographical interest.

The trustees approved the publication of the booklet *IASB and IFRS Interpretations Committee Due Process Handbook* in 2013. It is available on the IASB's website. The due process for issuing IFRSs comprises the following six stages:

1. *Setting the agenda.* The IASB considers the relevance and reliability of the information that could be provided, the existing guidance (if any), the potential for enhanced convergence of accounting practice, the quality of the standard to be developed and any resource constraints.
2. *Planning the project.* The IASB decides whether it should undertake the project by itself or jointly with another standard setter such as the US Financial Accounting Standards Board (FASB).
3. *Developing and publishing the discussion paper.* The IASB may issue a discussion paper; however, this is not mandatory.
4. *Developing and publishing the exposure draft (ED).* The IASB must issue an ED. This is a mandatory step.
5. *Developing and publishing the standard.* The IASB may re-expose an ED, particularly where there are major changes since the ED was first released in stage 4.

As part of stages 4 and 5, the IASB may hold regular meetings with interested parties, including other standard-setting bodies, to help understand unanticipated issues related to the practical implementation and potential impact of the ED or IFRS respectively.

6. *Procedures involving consultation and evaluation after an IFRS has been issued.* The IASB may carry out post-implementation reviews of each new IFRS.

The IASB has full discretion over its technical agenda and over the assignment of projects, potentially to national standard setters. In preparing the IFRSs, the IASB has complete responsibility for all technical matters including the preparation and issuance of standards and exposure drafts, including any dissenting opinions on these, as well as final approval of interpretations developed by the IFRS Interpretations Committee.

IASB meetings are normally held every month and last between three and five days. The meetings are open to the public. Interested parties can attend the meetings in person, or may listen and view the meeting via the IASB webcast. Subsequent to each meeting, the decisions are summarised in the form of a publication called *IASB Update* which is available on the IASB website.

1.1.3 IFRS Interpretations Committee

The IFRS Interpretations Committee reviews newly identified financial reporting issues that are not specifically dealt with in IFRSs, and issues for which unsatisfactory or conflicting interpretations have emerged or may emerge. The IFRS Interpretations Committee endeavours to reach a consensus on appropriate accounting treatment and provides authoritative guidance on the issue concerned. The interpretations issued by the committee are referred to as IFRIC Interpretations, taking their name from the previous name given to the committee, the International Financial Reporting Interpretations Committee (IFRIC). When approved by the IASB, IFRIC Interpretations have equivalent status to standards issued by the IASB; that is, although IFRIC Interpretations are not accounting standards, they form part of IFRSs such that compliance with IFRSs means compliance with both accounting standards issued by the IASB and IFRIC Interpretations approved by the IASB. More recently the IFRS Interpretations Committee has been asked by the IASB to help with the drafting of minor amendments to standards and with the Annual Improvement Projects. The latter are annual packages of changes to standards that are minor or narrow in scope.

1.1.4 Advisory bodies

The IASB has formal advisory bodies that provide a means for the Board to consult and engage with interested parties from a range of backgrounds and geographical areas. These advisory bodies include the:
- IFRS Advisory Council
- Capital Markets Advisory Committee
- Emerging Economies Group
- Global Preparers Forum
- SME Interpretations Group.

Working groups may be established for major projects to provide the IASB with access to additional expertise as required; for example, the Employee Benefits Working Group and the Insurance Working Group. Further information about advisory bodies, including reports and summaries of discussions, can be obtained from the IASB's website.

1.2 THE PURPOSE OF A CONCEPTUAL FRAMEWORK

In 1989, the IASC, the predecessor to the IASB, adopted the *Framework for the Preparation and Presentation of Financial Statements* (the *Framework*). The *Framework* borrowed heavily from the Statements of Financial Accounting Concepts developed by the FASB in the 1970s. This document was superseded by the *Conceptual Framework for Financial Reporting* (the *Conceptual Framework*) in 2010, developed jointly by the IASB and the FASB.

The purpose of a conceptual framework is to provide a coherent set of principles:
- to assist standard setters to develop a consistent set of accounting standards for the preparation of financial statements
- to assist preparers of financial statements in the application of accounting standards and in dealing with topics that are not the subject of an existing applicable accounting standard
- to assist auditors in forming an opinion about compliance with accounting standards
- to assist users in the interpretation of information in financial statements.

The *Conceptual Framework* issued by the IASB provides guidance to preparers in the application of IFRSs. The role of the *Conceptual Framework* in providing guidance for dealing with accounting issues that are not addressed by an IFRS is explicitly reinforced in IFRSs. IAS 8 *Accounting Policies, Changes in Accounting Estimates and Errors* requires preparers to consider the definitions, recognition criteria and measurement concepts in the *Conceptual Framework* when developing accounting policies for transactions, events or conditions in the absence of an IFRS that specifically applies or that applies to similar circumstances. *The requirements of IAS 8 are considered in more detail in chapter 16.*

Based upon feedback from the agenda consultation in 2011 it became clear to the IASB that an update of the *Conceptual Framework* was needed. A discussion paper was issued in 2013 and an exposure draft in 2015. In the remainder of the chapter the existing *Conceptual Framework* is described. *An overview of proposed changes can be found in section 1.9.*

This chapter is based upon the IASB's current *Conceptual Framework* which is rather patchy as it comprises four chapters, two of which (chapters 1 and 3) are final, one (chapter 2) is work in progress, and one (chapter 4) comprises the leftover bits of the old *Framework* that have not been amended yet:
- Chapter 1: The objective of general purpose financial reporting
- Chapter 2: The reporting entity (in progress, to be added by the IASB)
- Chapter 3: The qualitative characteristics of useful financial reporting
- Chapter 4: The *Framework* (1989): the remaining text (comprising underlying assumption, definition and recognition of elements of financial statements, measurement and concepts of capital).

1.2.1 The objective of financial reporting

The IASB's *Conceptual Framework* deals only with the objective of general purpose financial reporting; that is, financial reporting intended to meet the information needs common to a range of users who are unable to command the preparation of reports tailored to satisfy their own particular needs.

Paragraph OB2 of the IASB *Conceptual Framework* states the objective of general purpose financial reporting:

> The objective of general purpose financial reporting is to provide financial information about the reporting entity that is useful to present and potential equity investors, lenders and other creditors in making decisions about providing resources to the entity. Those decisions involve buying, selling or holding equity and debt instruments, and providing or settling loans and other forms of credit.

This objective reflects several value judgements made by the IASB about the role of financial statements, which are described in the *Basis for Conclusions on Chapter 1: The objective of general purpose financial reporting*. The Basis for Conclusions includes the following arguments:
- Financial statements should reflect the perspective of the entity rather than the perspective of the entity's equity investors. The focus is then on the entity's resources and the changes in them rather than on the shareholders as owners of the entity. Shareholders are providers of resources as are those who provide credit resources to the entity. Under the entity perspective, the reporting entity is deemed to have substance of its own, separate from that of its owners (paragraph BC1.8).
- The key users of financial statements are capital providers — existing and potential investors and lenders. An entity obtains economic resources from capital providers in exchange for claims on those resources. Because of these claims, capital providers have the most critical and immediate need for economic information about the entity. These parties also have common information needs. The focus on these users of information, as opposed to other potential users such as government, regulatory bodies, employees and customers, is a narrowing of the user groups in comparison to the groups considered in the former version of the IASB *Conceptual Framework* (paragraphs BC1.9–1.12).

Before the objective of general purpose financial reporting can be implemented in practice, the basic qualitative characteristics of financial reporting information need to be specified. Further, it is necessary to define the basic elements — assets, liabilities, equity, income and expenses — used in financial statements.

1.2.2 The reporting entity

Chapter 2 of the *Conceptual Framework* is reserved for the reporting entity. In March 2010, the IASB released an exposure draft titled *Exposure Draft ED/2010/2 Conceptual Framework for Financial Reporting — The Reporting Entity*. However, before finalising this chapter, the Board decided to include it in the exposure draft of a new *Conceptual Framework*, which was released in 2015 *(refer to section 1.9)*.

1.3 QUALITATIVE CHARACTERISTICS OF USEFUL FINANCIAL INFORMATION

What characteristics should financial information have in order to be included in general purpose financial reporting? The following section discusses both the qualitative characteristics of useful information and the constraint on providing useful information. The qualitative characteristics are divided into fundamental qualitative characteristics and enhancing qualitative characteristics.

1.3.1 Fundamental qualitative characteristics

For financial information to be decision useful, it must possess two fundamental qualitative characteristics:
- relevance
- faithful representation.

Relevance

Paragraphs QC6 to QC10 of the IASB's *Conceptual Framework* elaborate on the qualitative characteristic of *relevance*. Information is relevant if:

- it is capable of making a difference in the decisions made by the capital providers as users of financial information
- it has predictive value, confirmatory value or both. Predictive value occurs where the information is useful as an input into the users' decision models and affects their expectations about the future. Confirmatory value arises where the information provides feedback that confirms or changes past or present expectations based on previous evaluations
- it is capable of making a difference whether the users use it or not. It is not necessary that the information has actually made a difference in the past or will make a difference in the future.

Information about the financial position and past performance is often used as the basis for predicting future financial position and performance and other matters in which users are directly interested, such as future dividends and wage payments, future share prices, and the ability of the reporting entity to pay its debts when they fall due. The predictive ability of information may be improved if unusual or infrequent transactions and events are reported separately in the statement of profit or loss and other comprehensive income.

Materiality is an entity-specific aspect of the relevance of information. Information is *material* if its omission or misstatement could influence the decisions that users make about a specific reporting entity (paragraph QC11).

Small expenditures for non-current assets (e.g. tools) are often expensed immediately rather than depreciated over their useful lives to save the clerical costs of recording depreciation and because the effects on performance and financial position measures over their useful lives are not large enough to affect decisions. Another example of the application of materiality is the common practice by large companies of rounding amounts to the nearest thousand units of currency (e.g. euros or dollars) in their financial statements.

Materiality is a relative matter — what is material for one entity may be immaterial for another. A $10 000 error may not be important in the financial statements of a multimillion-dollar company, but it may be critical to a small business. The materiality of an item may depend not only on its relative size but also on its nature. For example, the discovery of a $10 000 bribe may be a material event even for a large company. Judgements as to the materiality of an item or event are often difficult. Management make judgements based on their knowledge of the company and on past experience. Auditors make their own judgements about materiality when auditing the financial statements.

Faithful representation

Paragraphs QC12 to QC16 of the IASB's *Conceptual Framework* elaborate on the concept of faithful representation. Faithful representation is attained when the depiction of an economic phenomenon is complete, neutral, and free from material error. This results in the depiction of the economic substance of the underlying transaction. Note the following in relation to these characteristics:

- A depiction is *complete* if it includes all information necessary for faithful representation.
- *Neutrality* is the absence of bias intended to attain a predetermined result. Providers of information should not influence the making of a decision or judgement to achieve a predetermined result.
- As information is provided under conditions of uncertainty and judgements must be made, there is not necessarily certainty about the information provided. It may be necessary to disclose information about the degree of uncertainty in the information in order that the disclosure attains faithful representation.

As explained in paragraph BC3.23 of the *Basis for Conclusions on Chapter 3: Qualitative characteristics of useful financial information*, the boards noted that there are various notions as to what is meant by reliability. The boards believe that the term 'faithful representation' provides a better understanding of the quality of information required (paragraph BC3.24).

The two fundamental qualitative characteristics of financial information may give rise to conflicting guidance on how to account for phenomena. For example, the measurement base that provides the most relevant information about an asset will not always provide the most faithful representation. The *Conceptual Framework* (paragraphs QC17–QC18) explains how to apply the fundamental qualitative characteristics. Once the criterion of relevance is applied to information to determine which economic information should be contained in the financial statements, the criterion of faithful representation is applied to determine how to depict those phenomena in the financial statements. The two characteristics work together. Either irrelevance (the economic phenomenon is not connected to the decision to be made) or unfaithful representation (the depiction is incomplete, biased or contains error) results in information that is not decision useful.

1.3.2 Enhancing qualitative characteristics

The *Conceptual Framework* (paragraph QC19) identifies four enhancing qualitative characteristics:

- comparability
- verifiability
- timeliness
- understandability.

These characteristics are *complementary* to the fundamental characteristics. The enhancing characteristics distinguish *more useful* information from *less useful* information. In relation to these enhancing qualities, note:

- *Comparability* is the quality of information that enables users to identify similarities in and differences between two sets of economic phenomena. Making decisions about one entity may be enhanced if comparable information is available about similar entities; for example, if profit per share is calculated using the same accounting policies.
- *Verifiability* is a quality of information that helps assure users that information faithfully represents the economic phenomena that it purports to represent. Verifiability is achieved if different independent observers could reach the same general conclusions that the information represents the economic phenomena or that a particular recognition or measurement model has been appropriately applied.
- *Timeliness* means having information available to decision makers before it loses its capacity to influence decisions. If such capacity is lost, then the information loses its relevance. Information may continue to be timely after it has been initially provided, for example, in trend analysis.
- *Understandability* is the quality of information that enables users to comprehend its meaning. Information may be more understandable if it is classified, characterised and presented clearly and concisely. Users of financial statements are assumed to have a reasonable knowledge of business and economic activities and to be able to read a financial report.

Alternative accounting policies exist in the treatment of many items, such as property, plant and equipment; investment properties; and financial instruments. The IASB have expressed their position regarding the consistency of accounting methods in accounting standard IAS 8 *Accounting Policies, Changes in Accounting Estimates and Errors*, which states that an entity must select and apply its accounting policies in a consistent manner from one period to another. Consistency of practices between entities is also desired. Any change made in an accounting policy by an entity must be disclosed by stating the nature of the change, the reasons the change provides reliable and more relevant information, and the effect of the change in monetary terms on each financial statement item affected. For example, a change in policies may be disclosed in a note such as this:

> During the year, the company changed from the first-in first-out to the weighted average cost method of accounting for inventory because the weighted average cost method provides a more relevant measure of the entity's financial performance. The effect of this change was to increase cost of sales by $460 000 for the current financial year.

Note that the need for consistency does not require a given accounting method to be applied throughout the entity. An entity may very well use different inventory methods for different types of inventory and different depreciation methods for different kinds of non-current assets. *(Different inventory costing and depreciation methods are discussed in chapters 9 and 11, respectively.)* Furthermore, the need for consistency should not be allowed to hinder the introduction of better accounting methods. Consistency from year to year or entity to entity is not an end in itself, but a means for achieving greater comparability in the presentation of information in general purpose financial reporting. The need for comparability should not be confused with mere uniformity or consistency. It is not appropriate for an entity to continue to apply an accounting policy if the policy is not in keeping with the qualitative characteristics of relevance and faithful representation.

1.3.3 Cost constraint on useful financial reporting

Paragraphs QC35 to QC37 of the *Conceptual Framework* note that cost is the constraint that limits the information provided by financial reporting. The provision of information incurs *costs*. The benefits of supplying information should always be greater than the costs. Costs include costs of collecting and processing information, costs of verifying information, and costs of disseminating information. The non-provision of information also imposes costs on the users of financial information as they seek alternative sources of information.

1.4 GOING CONCERN ASSUMPTION

The *Conceptual Framework* retains the going concern assumption. Financial statements are prepared under the assumption that the entity will continue to operate for the foreseeable future. Past experience indicates that the continuation of operations in the future is highly probable for most entities. Thus, it is assumed that an entity will continue to operate at least long enough to carry out its existing commitments. This assumption is called the *going concern assumption* or sometimes the *continuity assumption*.

Adoption of the going concern assumption has important implications in accounting. For example, it is an assumption used by some to justify the use of historical costs in accounting for non-current assets and for the systematic allocation of their costs to depreciation expense over their useful lives. Because it is assumed that the assets will not be sold in the near future but will continue to be used in operating activities, current market values of the assets are sometimes assumed to be of little importance. If the entity continues to use the assets, fluctuations in their market values cause no gain or loss; nor do they increase or decrease the usefulness of the assets. The going concern assumption also supports the inclusion of some assets, such as prepaid expenses and acquired goodwill, in the statement of financial position (balance sheet) even though they may have little, if any, sales value.

If management intends to liquidate the entity or to cease trading, or has no realistic alternative than to do so, the going concern assumption is set aside. In that case the financial statements are prepared on a different basis, but IFRS provides no guidance on what that basis would be. Paragraph 25 of IAS 1 *Presentation of Financial Statements* prescribes disclosures when an entity does not prepare financial statements on a going concern basis, including the basis on which it prepared the financial statements *(see chapter 16)*.

1.5 DEFINITION OF ELEMENTS IN FINANCIAL STATEMENTS

The *Conceptual Framework* identifies and defines the elements of financial statements; namely assets, liabilities, equity, income and expenses.

1.5.1 Assets

An *asset* is defined in paragraph 4.4(a) of the *Conceptual Framework* as:

> a resource controlled by the entity as a result of past events and from which future economic benefits are expected to flow to the entity.

This definition identifies three essential characteristics of an asset:

1. The resource must contain *future economic benefits*; that is, it must have the potential to contribute, directly or indirectly, to the flow of cash and cash equivalents to the entity. An asset can cause future economic benefits to flow to the entity in a number of ways:
   - it can be exchanged for another asset
   - it can be used to settle a liability
   - it can be used singly or in combination with other assets to produce goods or services to be sold by the entity.
2. The entity must have *control* over the future economic benefits in such a way that the entity has the capacity to benefit from the asset in the pursuit of the entity's objectives, and can deny or regulate the access of others to those benefits.
3. There must have been a *past event*; that is, an event or events giving rise to the entity's control over the future economic benefits must have occurred.

An asset may have other characteristics, but the *Conceptual Framework* does not consider them essential for an asset to exist. For instance, assets are normally acquired at a cost incurred by the entity, but it is not essential that a cost is incurred in order to determine the existence of an asset. Similarly, it is not essential that an asset is tangible, that is, has a physical form (see paragraph 4.11 of the *Conceptual Framework*). Assets such as brands, copyrights and patents represent future economic benefits without the existence of any physical substance. Such assets may be classified as intangible assets. Furthermore, assets can be exchanged normally for other assets, but this does not make exchangeability an essential characteristic of an asset. Finally, it is not essential that an asset is legally owned by the reporting entity. Control by the entity often results from legal ownership, but the absence of legal rights or ownership does not preclude the existence of control; for example, a lease (see paragraph 4.12 of the *Conceptual Framework*).

1.5.2 Liabilities

A *liability* is defined in paragraph 4.4(b) of the *Conceptual Framework* as:

> a present obligation of the entity arising from past events, the settlement of which is expected to result in an outflow from the entity of resources embodying economic benefits.

There are a number of important aspects concerning this definition:
- A legal debt constitutes a liability, but a liability is not restricted to being a legal debt. Its essential characteristic is the existence of a *present obligation*, being a duty or responsibility of the entity to act or perform in a certain way. A present obligation may arise as an obligation imposed by notions of equity or fairness (referred to as an 'equitable' obligation), and by custom or normal business practices (referred to as a 'constructive' obligation), as well as those resulting from legally enforceable contracts. For example, an entity may decide as a matter of policy to rectify faults in its products even after the warranty period has expired. Hence, the amounts that are expected to be spent in respect of goods already sold are liabilities.

  It is not sufficient for an entity merely to have an intention to sacrifice economic benefits in the future. A present obligation needs to be distinguished from a future commitment. A decision by management to buy an asset in the future does not give rise to a present obligation. An obligation normally arises when the asset is delivered, or the entity has entered into an irrevocable agreement to buy the asset, with a substantial penalty if the agreement is revoked.

- A liability must result in the *giving up of resources* embodying economic benefits that require settlement in the future. The entity must have little, if any, discretion in avoiding this sacrifice. This settlement in the future may be required on demand, at a specified date, or when a specified event occurs. Thus, a guarantee under a loan agreement is regarded as giving rise to a liability in that a sacrifice is required when a specified event occurs, for example, default under the loan.
  Settlement of a present obligation may occur in a number of ways:
  – by paying cash
  – by transferring other assets
  – by providing services
  – by replacing that obligation with another obligation
  – by converting that obligation to equity
  – by a creditor waiving or forfeiting their rights.
- A final characteristic of a liability is that it must have resulted from a *past transaction* or event. For example, the acquisition of goods and the work done by staff give rise to accounts payable and wages payable respectively. Wages to be paid to staff for work they will do in the future is not a liability as there is no past transaction or event and no present obligation.

1.5.3 Equity

Paragraph 4.4(c) of the *Conceptual Framework* defines *equity* as:

> the residual interest in the assets of the entity after deducting all its liabilities.

Defining equity in this manner shows clearly that it cannot be defined independently of the other elements in the statement of financial position. The characteristics of equity are as follows:
- Equity is a residual, that is, something left over. In other words:

$$\text{Equity} = \text{Assets} - \text{Liabilities}$$

- Equity increases as a result of profitable operations, that is, the excesses of income over expenses, and by contributions by owners. Similarly, equity is diminished by unprofitable operations and by distributions to owners (drawings and dividends).
- Equity is influenced by the measurement system adopted for assets and liabilities and by the concepts of capital and capital maintenance adopted in the preparation of general purpose financial statements. (These aspects are discussed later in the chapter.)
- Equity may be subclassified in the statement of financial position, for example, into contributed funds from owners, retained earnings, other reserves representing appropriations of retained earnings, and reserves representing capital maintenance adjustments.

1.5.4 Income

The *Conceptual Framework* defines *income* in paragraph 4.25(a) as:

> Increases in economic benefits during the accounting period in the form of inflows or enhancements of assets or decreases of liabilities that result in increases in equity, other than those relating to contributions from equity participants.

Note that this definition of income is linked to the definitions of assets and liabilities. The definition of income is wide in its scope, in that income in the form of inflows or enhancements of assets can arise from providing goods or services, investing in or lending to another entity, holding and disposing of assets, and receiving contributions such as grants and donations. To qualify as income, the inflows or enhancements of assets must have the effect of increasing equity, excluding capital contributions by owners. Depending on the concept of capital maintenance used *(see section 1.8)*, certain increases in equity from revaluations of assets must be excluded from income as well.

Another important aspect of the definition is that, if income arises as a result of an increase in economic benefits, it is necessary for the entity to *control* that increase in economic benefits. If control does not exist, then no asset exists. Income arises once control over the increase in economic benefits has been achieved and an asset exists, provided there is no equivalent increase in liabilities. For example, in the case of magazine subscriptions received in advance, no income exists on receipt of the cash because an equivalent obligation has also arisen for services to be performed through supply of magazines to subscribers in the future.

Income can also exist through a reduction in liabilities that increases the entity's equity. An example of a liability reduction is if a liability of the entity is 'forgiven'. Income arises as a result of that forgiveness, unless the forgiveness of the debt constitutes a contribution by owners.

Under the *Conceptual Framework*, income encompasses both revenue and gains. A definition of *revenue* is contained in paragraph 7 of IAS 18 *Revenue* as follows:

> [T]he gross inflow of economic benefits during the period arising in the course of the ordinary activities of an entity when those inflows result in increases in equity, other than increases relating to contributions from equity participants.

Thus revenue represents income which has arisen from 'the ordinary activities of an entity'. On the other hand, *gains* represent income that does not necessarily arise from the ordinary activities of the entity; for example, gains on the disposal of non-current assets or on the revaluation of marketable securities. Gains are usually disclosed in the statement of profit or loss and other comprehensive income net of any related expenses, whereas revenues are reported at a gross amount. As revenues and gains are both income, there is no need to regard them as separate elements under the *Conceptual Framework*.

1.5.5 Expenses

Paragraph 4.25(b) of the *Conceptual Framework* contains the following definition of *expenses*:

> Expenses are decreases in economic benefits during the accounting period in the form of outflows or depletions of assets or incurrences of liabilities that result in decreases in equity, other than those relating to distributions to equity participants.

To qualify as an expense, a reduction in an asset or an increase in a liability must have the effect of decreasing the entity's equity. The purchase of an asset does not decrease equity and therefore does not create an expense. An expense arises whenever the economic benefits in the asset are consumed, expire or are lost. Like income, the definition of expenses is expressed in terms of changes in assets, liabilities and equity. This concept of expense is broad enough to encompass items that have typically been reported in financial statements as 'losses', for example, losses on foreign currency transactions, losses from fire, flood, and so on, or losses on the abandonment of a research project. Losses are expenses that may not arise in the ordinary course of the entity's activities.

1.6 RECOGNITION OF ELEMENTS OF FINANCIAL STATEMENTS

There are recognition criteria to be followed in the preparation and presentation of financial statements in practice. These criteria have been set down as part of the *Conceptual Framework*. *Recognition* means the process of incorporating in the statement of financial position or statement of profit or loss and other comprehensive income an item that meets the definition of an element. In other words, it involves the inclusion of cash amounts in the entity's accounting system. Note that an item must satisfy the definition of an element before it is 'recognised'.

1.6.1 Asset recognition

The *Conceptual Framework* states in paragraph 4.44 that an asset should be recognised in the statement of financial position when it is probable that the future economic benefits will flow to the entity and the asset has a cost or other value that can be measured reliably. Here, emphasis is placed on criteria for determining *when to record* an asset in the entity's accounting records. An asset is to be recognised only when both the probability and the reliable measurement criteria are satisfied. The term 'probability' refers to the degree of certainty that the future economic benefits will flow to the entity. The benefits should be more likely rather than less likely. For example, some development costs are not recognised as an asset because it is not 'probable' that future economic benefits will eventuate.

Even if such probability of future benefits is high, recognition of an asset cannot occur unless some cost or other value is capable of reliable measurement. Without such a measurement, the qualitative characteristic of 'reliability' will not be achieved. In practice, reliable measurement of internally generated goodwill has been difficult, and therefore such goodwill has not been recognised as an asset. Similarly, reliable measurement of an entity's mineral reserves is difficult. It is argued in the *Conceptual Framework* that assets that cannot be measured reliably may nevertheless be disclosed in notes to the financial statements, particularly if knowledge of the item is considered relevant to evaluating the entity's financial position, performance and cash flows.

1.6.2 Liability recognition

Paragraph 4.46 of the *Conceptual Framework* establishes criteria for the recognition of a liability in an entity's accounting records. A liability is recognised in the statement of financial position when it is probable that an outflow of resources embodying economic benefits will result from settling the present obligation and the amount at which the settlement will take place can be measured reliably.

As with the recognition of assets, 'probable' means that the chance of the outflow of economic benefits being required is likely. The additional need for reliable measurement is an attempt to measure, in monetary terms, the amount of economic benefits that will be sacrificed to satisfy the obligation. Any liabilities that are not recognised in the accounting records because they do not satisfy the recognition criteria may be disclosed in notes to the financial statements, if considered relevant. *Further discussion of the recognition of liabilities is provided in chapter 5.*

1.6.3 Income recognition

In accordance with paragraph 4.47 of the *Conceptual Framework*, income is recognised in the statement of profit or loss and other comprehensive income when an increase in future economic benefits relating to an increase in an asset or a decrease in a liability can be measured reliably. As with the recognition criteria for assets and liabilities, probability of occurrence and reliability of measurement are presented as the two criteria for income recognition in paragraph 4.38. For many entities, the majority of income in the form of revenues results from the provision of goods and services during the reporting period. There is little uncertainty that the income has been earned since the entity has received cash or has an explicit claim against an external party as a result of a past transaction. However, the absence of an exchange transaction often raises doubts as to whether the income has achieved the required degree of certainty. In situations of uncertainty, the *Conceptual Framework* requires the income to be recognised as long as it is 'probable' that it has occurred and the amount can be measured reliably.

As stated previously, income includes both revenues and gains. The standard setters have provided further requirements for the recognition of revenues in accounting standard IAS 18 *Revenue*, which deals with the recognition of different types of revenue that can arise in an entity. The standard requires all revenue recognised in the entity's financial statements to be measured at the fair value of the consideration received or receivable. Separate recognition criteria are then provided for each different category of revenue. *See chapter 4 for a detailed discussion of revenue recognition.*

1.6.4 Expense recognition

Just as the income recognition criteria have been developed in the *Conceptual Framework* as a guide to the timing of income recognition, the expense recognition criteria have been developed to guide the timing of expense recognition. The *Conceptual Framework* defines expenses in terms of decreases in future economic benefits in the form of reductions in assets or increases in liabilities of the entity *(see the definition of expenses in section 1.5.5)*. In addition to the probability criteria for expense recognition, the *Conceptual Framework* states that expenses are recognised in the statement of profit or loss and other comprehensive income when a decrease in future economic benefits related to a decrease in an asset or an increase in a liability can be measured reliably (paragraph 4.49). This means that an expense is recognised simultaneously with a decrease in an asset or an increase in a liability. An expense is also recognised in the statement of profit or loss and other comprehensive income when the entity incurs a liability without the recognition of any asset, for example, wages payable.

In years past, the process of recognising expenses was referred to as a 'matching process', whereby an attempt was made to associate each cost with the income recognised in the current period. Costs that were 'associated' with the revenue were then said to be 'matched' and written off to expenses. This idea of matching expenses with income has been dropped in the *Conceptual Framework* in favour of assessing the probability of a decrease in economic benefits that can be measured reliably. Matching is no longer the expense recognition criterion under the *Conceptual Framework*.

1.7 MEASUREMENT OF THE ELEMENTS OF FINANCIAL STATEMENTS

Paragraph 4.54 of the *Conceptual Framework* states:

> Measurement is the process of determining the monetary amounts at which the elements of the financial statements are to be recognised and carried in the balance sheet [statement of financial position] and income statement [statement of profit or loss and other comprehensive income].

Because the concepts of equity, income and expenses are highly dependent on the concepts of assets and liabilities, measurement of the former depends on measurement of the latter. In other words, emphasis is placed on measuring assets and liabilities; the measurement of equity, income and expenses then follows. Measurement is very important in accounting in that it is the process by which valuations are placed on all elements reported in financial statements. Measurements can have an important effect on the economic decisions made by users of those financial statements. The *Conceptual Framework* (paragraph 4.55) points out that a number of different measurement bases may be used for assets, liabilities, income and expenses in varying degrees and in varying combinations in financial statements. They include the following, the most common of which, in practice, is the historical cost basis:

- *Historical cost.* Under the *historical cost* measurement basis, an asset is recorded at the amount of cash or cash equivalents paid or the fair value of the consideration given to acquire it at its acquisition date. Liabilities are recorded at the amount of the proceeds received in exchange for an obligation, or at the amount of cash to be paid out in order to satisfy the liability in the normal course of business.
- *Current cost.* For an asset, *current cost* represents the amount of cash or cash equivalents that would be paid if the same or equivalent asset was acquired currently. A liability is recorded at the amount of cash or cash equivalents needed to settle the obligation currently.

- *Realisable or settlement value.* For an asset, the *realisable value* is the amount of cash or cash equivalents that could be obtained currently by selling the asset in an orderly disposal, or in the normal course of business. The settlement amount of a liability is the amount of cash or cash equivalents expected to be paid to satisfy the obligation in the normal course of business.
- *Present value.* The present value of an asset means the discounted future net cash inflows or net cash savings that are expected to arise in the normal course of business. The present value of a liability is the discounted future net cash outflows that are expected to settle the obligation in the normal course of business.

In relation to measurement principles, the *Conceptual Framework* merely describes practice rather than establishing any principles that should be applied in the measurement of elements of financial statements. The measurement basis most commonly adopted by entities is the historical cost basis, although over time the IASB has increasingly allowed or mandated the use of fair values. Realisable value is mainly used to perform impairment tests under the historical cost method and for the measurement of certain types of inventory such as agricultural or extractive inventory. There is little use of current cost (replacement cost) in financial statements. The fact that fair value as measurement basis is not even mentioned in the *Conceptual Framework* reflects the need to revise and update this chapter of the *Conceptual Framework*. The use of *fair value*, which is defined as 'the price that would be received to sell an asset or paid to transfer a liability in an orderly transaction between market participants at the measurement date' (IFRS 13 *Fair Value Measurement* paragraph 9) is also referred to in many accounting standards.

1.8 CONCEPTS OF CAPITAL

Scant attention has been given to the concept of capital in accounting in the last 35 years, but it was a topic that received considerable focus during the current value debates of the 1960s to the early 1980s. It was argued then, and now, that before an entity can determine its income for any period, it must adopt not only a measurement basis for assets and liabilities, but also a concept of capital. Two main concepts of capital are discussed in the *Conceptual Framework*, namely financial capital and physical capital.

Under the *financial capital* concept, capital is synonymous with the net assets or equity of the entity, measured either in terms of the actual amount of currency by subtracting the total of liabilities from assets, or in terms of the purchasing power of the amount recorded as equity. Profit exists only after the entity has maintained its capital, measured as either the financial amount of equity at the beginning of the period, adjusted for dividends and contributions or the purchasing power of financial amount of equity at the beginning of the period.

Under the *physical capital* concept, capital is seen not so much as the equity recorded by the entity but as the operating capability of the entity's assets. Profit exists only after the entity has set aside enough capital to maintain the operating capability of its assets.

A number of different accounting systems have been devised in the past to provide alternatives to the conventional historical cost system, which is the system predominantly used in practice. These alternatives, which represent different combinations of the measurement of assets and liabilities and the concept of capital maintenance, include:

- the *general price level accounting system*, which had its origins in Germany after World War I when inflation reached excessive levels — this system modifies the conventional historical cost system for the effects of inflation and therefore follows a financial capital concept
- *current value systems*, which attempt to measure the changes in the current values of assets and liabilities — these systems include measures of the current buying or input prices of net assets, and/or measures of the current selling or realisable values of net assets. Capital may be measured as either financial or physical.

1.9 FUTURE DEVELOPMENTS

In 2015 the IASB released an exposure draft for a new *Conceptual Framework*. With these proposals the IASB responds to a widely felt need to fill the gaps in the *Conceptual Framework*, make it more robust and update it for developments that have taken place in thinking about financial reporting. This did not take place without controversy. In 2010 the IASB had decided to remove the notions of stewardship and prudence from the *Conceptual Framework*. Stewardship was not considered necessary as the information needs to assess stewardship were considered no different from the information needs for other economic decisions of users, in particular investors. Prudence was believed to be implying some bias in making judgements and therefore difficult to reconcile with a fundamental qualitative characteristic of financial information, i.e. faithful representation. The proposed *Conceptual Framework*, however, brings back both notions, after heavy lobbying from some constituents. Arguments provided to bring back stewardship are that there may well be information needs specific to stewardship that are not necessarily covered by other economic decisions of investors, such as buy, hold and sell decisions. The notion of prudence is brought back in, but with a very specific meaning, i.e. that caution must be exercised when making judgements under conditions of uncertainty and it is necessary to achieve neutrality. The proposed *Conceptual Framework* also:

- provides guidance on the reporting entity and acknowledges the need for combined financial statements
- contains new definitions of asset and liability
- includes some concepts of measurement
- still distinguishes profit and loss and other comprehensive income without providing the concept of how to distinguish between the two or whether and when to reclassify amounts in other comprehensive income to profit and loss (also referred to as 'recycling').

SUMMARY

This chapter has provided an overview of the structure of the IASB and the process of setting IFRSs, including IFRIC Interpretations. The adoption of IFRSs in many parts of the world has increased the importance of developments in international standards setting.

The *Conceptual Framework* describes the basic concepts that underlie financial statements prepared in conformity with IFRSs. It serves as a guide to the standard setters in developing accounting standards and in resolving accounting issues that are not addressed directly in an accounting standard.

The *Conceptual Framework* identifies the principal classes of users of an entity's general purpose financial statements and states that the objective of financial statements is to provide information — about the financial position, performance and changes in financial position of an entity — that is useful to existing and potential investors, lenders and other creditors in making decisions about providing resources to the entity. It specifies the fundamental qualities that make financial information useful, namely relevance and faithful representation. The usefulness of financial information is enhanced by comparability, verifiability, timeliness and understandability, and constrained by cost.

The *Conceptual Framework* also defines the basic elements in financial statements (assets, liabilities, equity, income and expenses) and discusses the criteria for recognising them. The *Conceptual Framework* identifies alternative measurement bases used in practice and describes alternative concepts of capital maintenance.

Discussion questions

1. Describe the standard-setting process of the IASB.
2. Identify the potential benefits of a globally accepted set of accounting standards.
3. Outline the fundamental qualitative characteristics of financial reporting information to be considered when preparing general purpose financial statements.
4. Discuss the importance of the going concern assumption to the practice of accounting.
5. Discuss the essential characteristics of an asset as described in the *Conceptual Framework*.
6. Discuss the essential characteristics of a liability as described in the *Conceptual Framework*.
7. Discuss the difference, if any, between income, revenue and gains.
8. Distinguish between the financial and physical concepts of capital and their implications for the measurement of profit.

References

IFRS Foundation 2013, *IASB and IFRS Interpretations Committee Due Process Handbook*, www.ifrs.org.
IFRS Foundation and International Accounting Standards Board 2015, *IASB and the IASC Foundation: Who We Are and What We Do*, www.ifrs.org.
International Accounting Standards Board 2016, *Conceptual Framework for Financial Reporting*, www.ifrs.org.

Exercises

STAR RATING ★ BASIC ★★ MODERATE ★★★ DIFFICULT

| Exercise 1.1 | MEASURING INVENTORIES OF GOLD AND SILVER |

★ IAS 2 *Inventories* allows producers of gold and silver to measure inventories of these commodities at selling price even before they have sold them, which means a profit is recognised at production. In nearly all other industries, however, profit is recognised only when the inventories are sold to outside customers. What concepts in the *Conceptual Framework* might the standard setters have considered with regard to accounting for gold and silver production?

Exercise 1.2	RECOGNISING A LOSS FROM A LAWSUIT

★ The law in your community requires store owners to shovel snow and ice from the pavement in front of their shops. You failed to do that, and a pedestrian slipped and fell, resulting in serious and costly injury. The pedestrian has sued you. Your lawyers say that while they will vigorously defend you in the lawsuit, you should expect to lose $25 000 to cover the injured party's costs. A court decision, however, is not expected for at least a year. What aspects of the *Conceptual Framework* might help you in deciding the appropriate accounting for this situation?

Exercise 1.3	NEED FOR THE CONCEPTUAL FRAMEWORK VS. INTERPRETATIONS

★ Applying the *Conceptual Framework* is subjective and requires judgement. Would the IASB be better off to abandon the *Conceptual Framework* entirely and instead rely on a very active interpretations committee that develops detailed guidance in response to requests from constituents?

Exercise 1.4	ASSESSING PROBABILITIES IN ACCOUNTING RECOGNITION

★ The *Conceptual Framework* defines an asset as a resource from which future economic benefits are expected to flow. 'Expected' means it is not certain, and involves some degree of probability. At the same time the *Conceptual Framework* establishes, as a criterion for recognising an asset, that 'it is probable that any future economic benefit associated with the item will flow to or from the entity.' Again, an assessment of probability is required. Is there a redundancy, or possibly some type of inconsistency, in including the notion of probability in both the asset definition and recognition criteria?

Exercise 1.5	PURCHASE ORDERS

★ An airline places a non-cancellable order for a new aeroplane with one of the major commercial aircraft manufacturers at a fixed price, with delivery in 30 months and payment in full to be made on delivery.
(a) Under the *Conceptual Framework*, do you think the airline should recognise any asset or liability at the time it places the order?
(b) One year later, the price of this aeroplane model has risen by 5%, but the airline had locked in a fixed, lower price. Under the *Conceptual Framework*, do you think the airline should recognise any asset (and gain) at the time when the price of the aeroplane rises? If the price fell by 5% instead of rising, do you think the airline should recognise any liability (and loss) under the *Conceptual Framework*?

Exercise 1.6	DEFINITIONS OF ELEMENTS AND RECOGNITION CRITERIA

★ Explain how you would account for the following items/situations, justifying your answer by reference to the *Conceptual Framework*'s definitions and recognition criteria:
(a) A trinket of sentimental value only.
(b) You are guarantor for your friend's bank loan:
  (i) You have no reason to believe your friend will default on the loan.
  (ii) As your friend is in serious financial difficulties, you think it likely that he will default on the loan.
(c) You receive 1000 shares in X Ltd, trading at $4 each, as a gift from a grateful client.
(d) The panoramic view of the coast from your café's windows, which you are convinced attracts customers to your café.
(e) The court has ordered your firm to repair the environmental damage it caused to the local river system. You have no idea how much this repair work will cost.

Exercise 1.7	ASSETS

★ Lampeter Cosmetics has spent $220 000 this year on a project to develop a new range of chemical-free cosmetics. As yet, it is too early for Lampeter Cosmetics' management to be able to predict whether this project will prove to be commercially successful. Explain whether Lampeter Cosmetics should recognise this expenditure as an asset, justifying your answer by reference to the *Conceptual Framework* asset definition and recognition criteria.

Exercise 1.8	ASSET DEFINITION AND RECOGNITION

★ On 28 May 2013, $20 000 cash was stolen from Ming Lee Ltd's night safe. Explain how Ming Lee should account for this event, justifying your answer by reference to relevant *Conceptual Framework* definitions and recognition criteria.

ACADEMIC PERSPECTIVE — CHAPTER 1

The *Conceptual Framework* highlights the decision useful-ness property of accounting numbers and identifies certain underlying qualities that enhance it. It is therefore an important question, in the light of the large resources society expends on accounting regulation and profession, whether published financial statements do in fact provide useful information. In attempting to address this question, accounting research largely has focused on the 'value relevance' property of accounting numbers as a way to operationalise criteria such as relevance and faithful representation (or, as previously known, reliability). There may be a number of ways to assess the value relevance and reliability of specific numbers or disclosures, but a popular approach in the archival empirical academic literature has been to examine the association between specific disclosures and stock prices or stock returns. Extensive reviews that go well beyond the scope of this section are offered by, for example, Barth et al. (2001) and Kothari (2001).

Modern empirical accounting research traces its origin to the seminal paper of Ball and Brown (1968) which shows that stock returns and earnings surprises tend to move in the same direction. From this evidence one can infer that earnings and share prices impound similar information, although causality (i.e., whether accounting numbers shape stock prices and trading decisions) is more difficult to show. Beaver's (1968) seminal paper on trading volume around earnings announcements provides more persuasive evidence that earnings announcements furnish useful *news* to market participants. Specifically, he documents a spike in trading activity around earnings announcements, suggesting information conveyed in these announcements leads investors to revise their prior beliefs and hence trade. Notwithstanding the centrality of the value relevance strand in accounting research, it is not without shortcomings. Criticisms of the value relevance literature can be found in Holthausen and Watts (2001) and the interested reader should bear these in mind. In particular, many academics stress the role of accounting in contracting, such as in debt and compensation. However, contracting is not a consideration in the *Conceptual Framework*.

Of the extensive research that links earnings to stock prices and returns, we mention here only a few important papers. Kormendi and Lipe (1987) link returns to earnings surprises (or, earnings innovations) by regressing stock returns on earnings surprises. The coefficient on the earnings surprise is called the earnings response coefficient (ERC). If the surprise is permanent *and* value relevant, then $1 of a surprise should translate into more than $1 of return. Kormendi and Lipe (1987) show that greater earnings persistence translates to a larger ERC.

Using changes in earnings as a proxy for new information can shed light on how informative earnings are when they are announced. Because earnings may not be timely, in the sense that news from other sources is already impounded in prices before the earnings are announced (Beaver et al. 1980), changes in annual or quarterly earnings may be only weakly related to returns. Therefore, a smaller earnings response coefficient may indicate a lack of timeliness (rather than weaker persistence), which is an enhancing qualitative

characteristic of accounting information. The relatively small magnitude observed for earnings response coefficients from the extant research (Kothari, 2001) may be then attributed to the fact that earnings lag behind share prices. Another, not mutually exclusive, explanation for the low magnitude of the earnings response coefficient is that the quality of accounting standards is poor (Lev and Zarowin, 1999).

Research that followed includes Easton and Harris (1991) who refine the specification used in Kormendi and Lipe (1987) to show that prices and returns are also related to earnings levels as well as earnings changes. Kothari and Sloan (1992) argue that the earnings response coefficient is a function of news about future growth in earnings that is contained in current earnings. As is suggested by Kormendi and Lipe (1987), the earnings response coefficient may also be smaller when earnings changes are transitory. In particular, losses are transitory because they cannot continue for a long time; in such a case the reporting entity will go out of business or be purchased by another company. Hayn (1995) provides evidence on the earnings response coefficient in loss firms that is consistent with this idea.

Surprisingly, only in recent years have accounting researchers started to look at the value relevance of earnings in the much larger debt markets. Easton et al. (2009) find that bond returns and earnings are positively associated, and more so for negative earnings surprises. This is explained by the sensitivity of investors in bonds to bad news, as this may affect the return on their investments (whereas increases in firm value normally benefit equity investors). They also find that trading activity in bonds increases around earnings announcements, evidence that extends the findings of Beaver (1968) to debt markets. Overall, therefore, the accounting literature has provided evidence that accounting numbers are capable of, and likely are, providing information that is useful to investors.

The qualitative characteristic that received most scrutiny in more recent accounting research is probably faithful representation. Faithful representation requires the accounting treatment to be unbiased and neutral. In particular, it negates the concept of conservatism that requires estimates to be cautious in that, if a range of estimates is available for an item of assets or income, a lower estimate should be selected. The opposite holds for liabilities and expenses. It should be noted that historically conservatism has been one of the fundamental principles in accounting (Watts, 2003) and the requirement for neutral and unbiased treatment is very new. That many standards, old and new, are nevertheless conservative may be surprising given standard setters' insistence on neutrality as per the *Conceptual Framework* of 2010 (although this may change in the future). However, as Watts (2003) argues, conservatism reduces political cost for standard setters and so when they promulgate specific standards they still require conservatism in measurement procedures. Consistent with this argument, Barker and McGeachin (2015) find many examples in accounting standards promulgated by the IASB that show that IAS and IFRS are, in practice, conservative. Basu (1997) operationalised the concept of conservatism to predict that bad news is incorporated into earnings at a faster rate than good news. Employing negative share returns as a proxy for bad news he finds that in a regression of earnings on returns and negative returns the coefficient on negative returns is positively associated with earnings. This implies that negative returns (bad news) reduce earnings more than positive returns (good news) increase earnings, thus confirming his conjecture. Basu (1997) has been a highly influential paper. It has spawned a very large number of studies that investigate the relation between conservatism and an array of economic phenomena. As of writing this section, Basu (1997) has been cited more than 3000 times (source: Google Scholar).

Other qualitative characteristics may be less amenable to empirical research. For example, only recently have accounting researchers attempted to look at the economic consequences of comparability. De Franco et al. (2011) propose a novel approach to the operationalisation of comparability. The underlying concept in their paper is that two accounting systems are comparable if the same economic event maps into earnings in a similar way. They employ time series of earnings and stock returns for each firm in their sample to regress the former on the latter. The regression coefficients are then used to calculate expected earnings given an economic event, which is proxied by returns. Comparability is defined with respect to the difference between expected earnings between any two firms within the same industry and financial year assuming both firms experience the same return. The smaller the absolute difference, the greater the comparability. Employing this measure De Franco et al. (2011) show that analyst following increases in comparability of one firm's earnings to other firms. This suggests that comparability reduces barriers for analysts.

References

Ball, R., and P. Brown, 1968. An empirical evaluation of accounting income numbers. *Journal of Accounting Research*, 159–178.

Barker, R., and McGeachin, A., 2015. An analysis of concepts and evidence on the question of whether IFRS should be conservative. *Abacus*, 51(2), 169–207.

Barth, M.E., Beaver, W.H., and Landsman, W.R., 2001. The relevance of the value relevance literature for financial accounting standard setting: another view. *Journal of Accounting and Economics*, 31(1), 77–104.

Basu, S., 1997. The conservatism principle and the asymmetric timeliness of earnings. *Journal of Accounting and Economics*, 24(1), 3–37.

Beaver, W., 1968. The information content of annual earnings announcements. *Journal of Accounting Research*, Supplement, 67–92.

Beaver, W., Lambert, R., and Morse, D., 1980. The information content of security prices. *Journal of Accounting and Economics*, 2(1), 3–28.

De Franco, G., Kothari S.P., and Verdi, R.S., 2011. The benefits of financial statement comparability. *Journal of Accounting Research*, 49(4), 895–931.

Easton, P., and Harris, T., 1991. Earnings as an explanatory variable for returns. *Journal of Accounting Research*, 19–36.

Easton, P., Monahan, S., and Vasvari, F., 2009. Initial evidence on the role of accounting earnings in the bond market. *Journal of Accounting Research*, 47(3), 721–766.

Hayn, C., 1995. The information content of losses. *Journal of Accounting and Economics*, 20(2), 125–153.

Holthausen, R.W., and Watts, R.L., 2001. The relevance of the value relevance literature for financial accounting standard setting. *Journal of Accounting and Economics*, 31(1), 3–75.

Kormendi, R., and Lipe, R., 1987. Earnings innovations, earnings persistence and stock returns. *Journal of Business*, 60(3), 23–345.

Kothari, S.P., 2001. Capital markets research in accounting. *Journal of Accounting and Economics*, 31(1), 105–231.

Kothari, S.P., and Sloan, R., 1992. Information in prices about future earnings: implications for earnings response coefficients. *Journal of Accounting and Economics*, 15(2), 143–171.

Lev, B., and Zarowin, P., 1999. The boundaries of financial reporting and how to extend them. *Journal of Accounting Research*, 37(2), 353–385.

Watts, R., 2003. Conservatism in accounting part I: Explanations and implications. *Accounting Horizons*, 17(3), 207–221.

Part 2

Elements

2 Owners' equity: share capital and reserves   21

3 Fair value measurement   49

4 Revenue from contracts with customers   73

5 Provisions, contingent liabilities and contingent assets   95

6 Income taxes   123

7 Financial instruments   155

8 Share-based payment   199

9 Inventories   219

10 Employee benefits   245

11 Property, plant and equipment   275

12 Leases   321

13 Intangible assets   355

14 Business combinations   379

15 Impairment of assets   417

Visit the companion website to access additional chapters online at: **www.wiley.com/college/picker**

Online chapter A Exploration for and evaluation of mineral resources

Online chapter B Agriculture

2 Owners' equity: share capital and reserves

ACCOUNTING STANDARDS IN FOCUS

IAS 1 *Presentation of Financial Statements*

IAS 32 *Financial Instruments: Presentation*

LEARNING OBJECTIVES

After studying this chapter, you should be able to:

1. describe the essence of the equity section in the statement of financial position
2. describe in general terms what a for-profit company is
3. outline the key features of the corporate structure
4. discuss the different forms of share capital
5. account for the issue of both no-par and par value shares
6. account for share placements, rights issues, options, and bonus issues
7. discuss the rationale behind and accounting treatment of share buy-backs
8. outline the nature of reserves and account for movements in retained earnings, including dividends
9. prepare note disclosures in relation to equity, as well as a statement of changes in equity.

2.1 EQUITY

The purpose of this chapter is to introduce the element of equity in financial statements, describe its various components and the accounting for transactions that give rise to these components.

Equity is part of the statement of financial position, or balance sheet. From an algebraic standpoint it is the difference between total assets and liabilities. The IASB®'s *Conceptual Framework* (IASB 2010 paragraph 4.4(c)) defines it as a residual, implying shareholders' financial interest in a company is confined to the excess, if any, of its assets over its liabilities.[1] This definition largely stems from the notion that shareholders' claims on a firm's assets are typically inferior to other stakeholders' rights (e.g. creditors). It is important to note that the figure for equity reported in the balance sheet is based on accounting conventions (as explained throughout this book) and is typically quite different from the real worth of the company to its owners.[2]

The main components of the equity section of the statement of financial position are contributed capital (e.g. share capital) and reserves (e.g. retained earnings). The specific element of capital will differ depending on the nature of the organisation, whether a sole proprietorship, partnership or company. Reserves comprise equity attributable to the owners of the entity other than amounts directly contributed by the owners. An example of the equity section of the statement of financial position of a for-profit entity is shown in figure 2.1. It contains an extract from the consolidated balance sheet of Tesco as at 22 February 2014. The accounts were prepared in accordance with IFRS® Standards. Note that the sum of share capital and share premium represents the amount of cash the company raised upon issuing its shares. For example, total share capital and premium for Tesco as at 22 February 2014 is £5485m. An alternative term to 'share premium' that is used, in particular by US firms, is 'additional paid-in capital'. The second component, the reserves, is all the other line items, with the exception of non-controlling interest. In the case of Tesco 2014 total reserves is £9230m. US firms do not use the term 'retained earnings'; instead they use 'accumulated other comprehensive income'. Non-controlling interests represents the ownership interests of non-Tesco shareholders in other companies that Tesco controls, but does not hold 100% of the voting rights. *(This is discussed in detail in Chapter 23.)*

	22 February 2014 £m	23 February 2014 £m
Share capital	405	403
Share premium	5 080	5 020
All other reserves	(498)	685
Retained earnings	9 728	10 535
Equity attributable to owners of the parent	14 715	16 643
Non-controlling interests	7	18
Total equity	14 722	16 661

FIGURE 2.1 Owners' equity of Tesco
Source: Tesco plc (2014, p. 71).

In contrast to a multi-shareholders company like Tesco, with a *sole proprietor*, having a single owner means there is little reason for distinguishing between capital (potentially the initial investment in the business) and profits retained in the business for investment purposes. Nevertheless, many single-owned companies could still adopt a similar presentation.

Traditionally with *partnerships*, the rights and responsibilities of the partners are specified in a partnership agreement. This document details how the profits or losses of the partnership are to be divided between the partners, including rules relating to distributions on dissolution of the partnership. In accounting for partnerships, a distinction is generally made for each partner between a capital account, to which amounts invested by a partner are credited, and a current account or retained earnings account, to which a partner's share of profits are credited and from which any drawings are debited. As with a sole proprietorship, there generally is no real distinction between capital contributed and profits retained (unless there is some other specification in the partnership agreement, which is unlikely). Both amounts represent the ongoing investment by the partners. On dissolution of the partnership, the distribution to partners is unaffected by whether an equity balance is capital or retained earnings.

With *companies*, the focus of this chapter, the situation is different because their formation is generally governed by legislation, and there is normally a clear distinction made between contributed capital and profits retained in the entity. For example, the amount of dividend a company can pay may be restricted to what is reported in retained earnings.

---

[1] See also chapter 1.
[2] IAS 1 employs the term 'owners' to mean 'shareholders'. In this chapter, the two terms are used interchangeably.

2.2 FOR-PROFIT COMPANIES

Generally, companies can be distinguished by the nature of the ownership, and the rights and responsibilities of the shareholders. In particular, some companies are not-for-profit and some are for-profit. The focus of this chapter, however, is on for-profit companies.

For-profit companies may be:

- listed — their shares are traded on a stock exchange
- unlisted — the shares are traded through brokers and financial institutions
- limited by guarantee — the members undertake to contribute a guaranteed amount in the event of the company going into liquidation
- unlimited — members are liable for all the debts of the company
- no-liability — members are not required to pay any calls on their shares if they do not wish to continue being shareholders in the company.

The exact rights and responsibilities of shareholders in relation to the different forms of companies will differ according to the relevant companies legislation and other laws specific to the country or countries in which the company operates.

Many global companies list on a number of stock exchanges. Nokia, for example, is now quoted on the NASDAQ, OMX Helsinki and the New York Stock Exchange, but in the past was also listed in Stockholm (Stockholmsborsen) and Frankfurt (Wertpapierborse).

2.3 KEY FEATURES OF THE CORPORATE STRUCTURE

The choice of the company as the preferred form of organisational structure brings with it certain advantages, such as limited liability to shareholders. It also comes with certain disadvantages, such as making the entity subject to increasing government regulation including the forced and detailed disclosure of information about the company. Some features of the company structure that affect the subsequent accounting for a company are described below.

2.3.1 The use of share capital

The ownership rights in a company are generally represented by shares; that is, the share capital of a company comprises a number of units or shares. Each share represents a proportional right to the net assets of the company and, within a class of shares, all shares have the same equal rights. These shares are generally transferable between parties. As a result, markets have been established to provide investors with an ability to trade in shares. A further advantage of transferability is that a change in ownership by one shareholder selling shares to a new investor does not have an effect on the continued existence and operation of the company.

Besides the right to share equally in the net assets, and hence the profits or losses of a company, each share typically has other rights, including:

- *the right to vote for directors of the company.* This establishes the right of shareholders to have a say as owners in the strategic direction of the company. Where there are a large number of owners in a company, there is generally a separation between ownership and management. The shareholders thus employ professional managers (the directors) to manage the organisation; these managers then provide periodic reports to the shareholders on the financial performance and position of the company. Some directors are executive directors, being employed as executives in the company, while others have non-executive roles. The directors are elected at the annual general meeting of the company, and shareholders exercise their voting rights to elect the directors. The shareholders may vote in person, or by proxy. In relation to the latter, a shareholder may authorise another party to vote on their behalf at the meeting; the other party could be the chairperson of the company's board.
- *the right to share in assets on the winding-up or liquidation of the company.* The rights and responsibilities of shareholders in the event of liquidation are generally covered in legislation specific to each country, as are the rights of creditors to receive payment in preference to shareholders. However, if upon liquidation the assets are insufficient to pay the outstanding liabilities, shareholders of limited liability companies will receive no consideration for their shares *(also see section 2.3.2)*.
- *the right to share proportionately in any new issues of shares of the same class.* This right is sometimes referred to as the pre-emptive right. It ensures that a shareholder is able to retain the same proportionate ownership in a company, and that this ownership percentage cannot be diluted by the company issuing new shares to other investors, possibly at prices lower than the current fair value. However, the directors may be allowed to make limited placements of shares under certain conditions.

2.3.2 Limited liability

When shares are issued, the maximum amount payable by each shareholder is set. Even if a company incurs losses or goes into liquidation, the company cannot require a shareholder to provide additional capital. In some countries, shares are issued with a specific amount stated on the share certificate, this amount being called the par value of the share. For example, a company may issue 1 million shares each with a par value of $1. The company then receives share capital of $1 million.

Par value shares may also be issued at a premium. For example, where a company requires share capital of $2 million, 1 million $1 shares may be issued at a premium of $1 per share; in this case, each shareholder is required to pay $2 per share. Similarly, par value shares may be issued at a discount. For example, where a company issues $1 shares at a discount of 20c, the company requires each shareholder to initially pay 80c per share. The only real purpose of the par value is to establish the maximum liability of the shareholder in relation to the company, and so owners may be required to contribute a further 20c per share upon liquidation, or at a later stage, as agreed with the company. Legislation in some countries restricts the issue of shares at a discount, and also establishes the subsequent uses of any share premium received on a share.

Note that the par value does not represent a fair or market value of the share. At the issue date, it would be expected that the par value, plus the premium or minus the discount, would represent the market value of the share. In some countries the use of par value shares has been replaced by the issue of shares at a specified price with no par value. For example, a company may issue 1000 shares in 2012 at $3 per share, and in 2015 it may issue another 1000 shares at $5 per share. At the end of 2015, the company then has 2000 shares and a share capital of $8000. The issue price becomes irrelevant subsequent to the issue. The variables are the number of shares issued and the amount of share capital in total. The liability of each shareholder is limited to the issue price of the shares at the time of issue.

The feature of limited liability protects shareholders by limiting the contribution required of them, which in turn places limitations on the ability of creditors to access funds for the repayment of company debts. To protect creditors, many countries have enacted legislation that prohibits companies from distributing capital to shareholders in the form of dividends. Dividends are then payable only from retained profits, not out of capital *(see section 2.8.1)*. Other forms of legislation require that assets exceed liabilities immediately before a dividend is 'declared'.

2.4 DIFFERENT FORMS OF SHARE CAPITAL

Shares are issued with specific rights attached. Shares are then given different names to signify differences in rights.

2.4.1 Ordinary shares

The most common form of share capital is the ordinary share or common stock. These shares have no specific rights to any distributions of profit by the company, and ordinary shareholders are often referred to as 'residual' equity holders in that these shareholders obtain what is left after all other parties' claims have been met. An example of a company that has only one class of share is Nokia and each share entitles its holder to one vote (Nokia Corporation 2013, p. 16). Further information on its shares as at 31 December 2009 to 2013 was provided in its 2013 annual report in the notes to the financial statements of the parent company. Part of this information is shown in figure 2.2.

FIGURE 2.2 Share capital, Nokia Corporation

Shares and share capital

Nokia has one class of shares. Each Nokia share entitles the holder to one vote at General Meetings of Nokia.

On December 31, 2013, the share capital of Nokia Corporation was EUR 245 896 461.96 and the total number of shares issued was 3 744 994 342. On December 31, 2013, the total number of shares included 32 567 617 shares owned by Group companies representing approximately 0.9% of the share capital and the total voting rights.

Under the Articles of Association of Nokia, Nokia Corporation does not have minimum or maximum share capital or a par value of a share.

FIGURE 2.2 *(continued)*

Share capital and shares December 31, 2013	2013	2012	2011	2010	2009
Share capital, EURm	**246**	246	266	246	246
Shares (1000)	**3 744 994**	3 744 956	3 744 956	3 744 956	3 744 956
Shares owned by the Group (1 000)	**32 568**	33 971	34 767	35 826	36 694
Number of shares excluding shares owned by the Group (1 000)	**3 712 427**	3 710 985	3 710 189	3 709 130	3 708 262
Average number of shares excluding shares owned by the Group during the year (1 000), basic	**3 712 079**	3 710 845	3 709 947	3 708 816	3 705 116
Average number of shares excluding shares owned by the Group during the year (1 000), diluted	**3 712 079**	3 710 845	3 709 947	3 713 250	3 721 072
Number of registered shareholders[1]	**225 587**	250 799	229 096	191 790	156 081

[1] Each account operator is included in the figure as only one registered shareholder.

Key ratios December 31, 2013, IFRS (calculation see page 98)	2013	2012	2011	2010	2009
Earnings per share for profit attributable to equity holders of the parent, EUR					
Earnings per share, basic	**−0.17**	−0.84	−0.31	0.50	0.24
Earnings per share, diluted	**−0.17**	−0.84	−0.31	0.50	0.24
P/E ratio	**neg.**	neg.	neg.	15.48	37.17
(Nominal) dividend per share, EUR[1]	**0.37**	0.00	0.20	0.40	0.40
Total dividends paid, EURm[2]	**1 386**	0.00	749	1 498	1 498
Payout ratio	**neg.**	0.00	neg.	0.80	1.67
Dividend yield, %	**6.36**	0.00	5.30	5.17	4.48
Shareholders' equity per share, EUR[3]	**1.74**	2.14	3.20	3.88	3.53
Market capitalization, EURm[3]	**21 606**	10 873	13 987	28 709	33 078

[1] Dividend to be proposed by the Board of Directors for fiscal year 2013 for shareholders' approval at the Annual General Meeting convening on June 17, 2014.
[2] Calculated for all the shares of the company as of the applicable year-end.
[3] Shares owned by the Group companies are not included.

Source: Nokia Corporation (2013, p. 90).

Returns to shareholders

As already noted, the shareholders of ordinary shares have no specific rights to dividends, being residual equity holders. Whether a dividend is paid depends on the decisions made by the directors. Regulations in some countries may specify from which equity accounts the dividends can be paid, or whether the company has to meet solvency tests before paying dividends. In some cases, the directors may be allowed to propose a dividend at year-end, but this proposal may have to be approved by the shareholders in the annual general meeting.

2.4.2 Preference shares

Another form of share capital is the preference share. As the name implies, holders of preference shares generally have a preferential right to dividends over the ordinary shareholders. Note firstly that the name of the instrument does not necessarily indicate the rights associated with that instrument. *As is discussed in chapter 7,* some preference shares are in substance not equity but liabilities, or they may be compound instruments being partially debt and partially equity, sometimes referred to as hybrid, or compound, securities. Secondly, the rights of preference shareholders may be very diverse. Some preference shares have a fixed dividend; for example, a company may issue preference shares at $10 each with a 4% dividend per annum, thus entitling the shareholder to a 40c dividend per annum. Other common features of preference shares are:

- *cumulative versus non-cumulative shares.* Where a preference share is cumulative, if a dividend is not declared in a particular year, the right to the dividend is not lost but carries over to a subsequent year. The dividends are said to be in arrears. With non-cumulative shares, if a dividend is not paid in a particular year, the right to that dividend is lost.
- *participating versus non-participating shares.* A participating share gives the holder the right to share in extra dividends. For example, if a company has issued 8% participating preference shares and it pays a 10% dividend to the ordinary shareholders, the preference shareholders may be entitled to a further 2% dividend.
- *convertible versus non-convertible shares.* Convertible preference shares may give the holder the right to convert the preference shares into ordinary shares. The right to convert may be at the option of the holder of the shares or at the option of the company itself. *As explained in chapter 7,* convertible preference shares may need to be classified into debt and equity components.
- *redeemable preference shares.* Redeemable preference shares are shares that may be converted into cash under certain pre-specified conditions. *As explained in chapter 7,* if the terms of the issue are such that the shares are redeemed at the discretion of the shareholder, the issue of the preference shares is treated as a liability. However, if the terms are such that the decision to redeem is at the issuer's discretion, it will be reported as equity.

2.5 CONTRIBUTED EQUITY: ISSUE OF SHARE CAPITAL

Once a business has decided to form a public company, it will commence the procedures necessary to issue shares to the public. The initial offering of shares to the public to invest in the new company is called an initial public offering (IPO). To arrange the sale of the shares, the business that wishes to float the company usually employs a promoter, such as a stockbroker or a financial institution, with expert knowledge of the legal requirements and experience in this area. Once the promoter and the managers of the business agree on the structure of the new company, a prospectus is drawn up and lodged with the regulating authority. The prospectus contains information about the current status of the business and its future prospects.

In order to ensure that the statements in the prospectus are accurate, a process of due diligence is undertaken by an accounting firm. To ensure that the sale of shares is successful, an underwriter may be employed. The role of the underwriter is to advise on such matters as the pricing of the issue, the timing of the issue and how the issue will be marketed. One of the principal reasons for using an underwriter is to ensure that all the shares are sold, as the underwriter agrees to acquire all shares that are not taken up by the public.

2.5.1 Issue costs

The costs of issuing the shares can then be quite substantial and could amount to 10% of the amount raised. The costs include those associated with preparing and printing the relevant documentation and marketing the share issue, as well as the fees charged by the various experts consulted which could include accountants, lawyers and taxation specialists. Accounting for these costs is covered in paragraph 37 of IAS 32 *Financial Instruments: Presentation.* It requires the offsetting issuance cost from the proceeds of the issued share capital, unless the issue is aborted, in which case the costs are expensed.

The costs are then treated as a reduction in share capital such that the amount shown in share capital immediately after the share issue is the net amount available to the company for operations. *The accounting for share issue costs is demonstrated in the next section.*

Any costs associated with the formation of the company that cannot be directly related to the issue of the shares, such as registration of the company name, are expensed as the cost is incurred. These outlays do not meet the definition of an asset as there are no expected future economic benefits associated with these outlays that can be controlled by the company.

As discussed in 2.3.2, shares may be issued with a stated par value, or as no-par shares. Shares with stated par value may be issued at a premium, or a discount. *These possibilities are illustrated next.*

2.5.2 Issue of no-par shares

Illustrative example 2.1 shows the recording of issuing no-par shares.

ILLUSTRATIVE EXAMPLE 2.1 Issue of no-par shares

Quebec Ltd issues 500 no-par shares for cash at $10 each, incurring share issue costs of $450. Quebec Ltd records on its share register the number of shares issued, and makes the following journal entry:

Cash	Dr	5 000	
Share Capital	Cr		5 000
(Issue of 500 $10 shares)			
Share Capital	Dr	450	
Cash	Cr		450
(Share issue costs)			

2.5.3 Issue of par value shares

When shares certificates specify the par value, the share issue proceeds are compared to the par value. If proceeds exceed par value, shares are said to be issued at a premium. If proceeds fall below par value, then they are issued at a discount.

Shares issued at a premium

Where shares are issued at a premium, the excess over the par value is credited to an equity account which may be called share premium, additional paid-in capital, or share capital in excess of par. The share premium is then a component of contributed equity.

ILLUSTRATIVE EXAMPLE 2.2 Issue of par value shares at a premium

Bhutan Ltd issues 5000 shares of $1 par value at a premium of $2 per share. Issuance costs (lawyers, accountants, registration, etc.) amount to $500. The journal entry is:

Cash	Dr	14 500	
Share Capital	Cr		5 000
Share Premium	Cr		9 500
(Issue of shares at a premium after deducting issuance costs)			

Shares issued at a discount

Where shares are issued at a discount, the account used in relation to the discount can be the same as that used for a premium, or it can be a separate discount account. The accounting treatment will vary depending on the regulations governing discounts in particular jurisdictions.

ILLUSTRATIVE EXAMPLE 2.3 Issue of par value shares at a discount

Iran Ltd issues 5000 shares of $2 par value at a 50c discount. Issuance costs are $500. The net cash received therefore is $7000 (5000 × $1.5 − $500). The journal entry is:

Cash	Dr	7 000	
Discount on Shares	Dr	3 000	
Share Capital	Cr		10 000
(Issue of shares at a discount)			

2.5.4 Oversubscriptions

An issue of shares by a company may be so popular that it is oversubscribed (see illustrative example 2.4); that is, there are more applications for shares than shares to be issued. Some investors may then receive an allotment of fewer shares than they applied for, or may not be allotted any shares at all. In most cases, therefore, excess application monies are simply refunded to the applicants.

China Ltd was incorporated on 1 July 2015. The directors offered to the general public 100 000 ordinary shares for subscription at an issue price of $2. The company received applications for 200 000 shares and collected $400 000. The directors then decided to issue 150 000 shares, returning the balance of application money to the unsuccessful applicants.

The appropriate journal entries are:

Cash	Dr	400 000	
Application Reserve (Equity)	Cr		400 000
(Money received on application)			
Application Reserve	Dr	300 000	
Share Capital	Cr		300 000
(Issue of shares)			
Application Reserve	Dr	100 000	
Cash	Cr		100 000
(Refund of excess application money)			

2.6 CONTRIBUTED EQUITY: SUBSEQUENT MOVEMENTS IN SHARE CAPITAL

Having floated the company, the directors may at a later stage decide to make changes to the share capital. For example, at its annual general meeting in March 2011, Pöyry plc, a global consulting and engineering company based in Finland, authorised its Board of Directors to issue new shares. This authorisation is shown in figure 2.3.

Authorisation to issue shares

The Annual General Meeting (AGM) on 10 March 2008 authorised the Board of Directors to decide to issue new shares and to convey the Company's own shares held by the Company in one or more tranches. The share issue can be carried out as a share issue against payment or without consideration on terms to be determined by the Board of Directors and in relation to a share issue against payment at a price to be determined by the Board of Directors.

A maximum of 11 600 000 new shares can be issued. A maximum of 5 800 000 own shares held by the Company can be conveyed. The authorisation is in force for three years from the decision of the AGM.

At the end of 2010 totally 226 727 shares have been issued. After these directed share issues, the maximum number of shares that may be conveyed is 5 573 273 shares.

The Board of Directors proposes that the General Meeting on 10 March 2011 authorise to decide to issue new shares and to convey the Company's own shares held by the Company in one or more tranches. The share issue can be carried out as a share issue against payment or without consideration on terms to be determined by the Board of Directors and in relation to a share issue against payment at a price to determined by the Board of Directors. A maximum of 11 800 000 new shares can be issued. A maximum of 5 900 000 own shares held by the company can be conveyed. The authorisation shall be effective for a period of 18 months.

FIGURE 2.3 An authorisation to increase share capital, Pöyry plc
Source: Pöyry plc (2011, p. 65).

The example in figure 2.3 shows an authorisation for an increase in share capital, but share capital may be either increased or decreased. This section of the chapter discusses the methods a company may use to increase its share capital. *Section 2.7 examines how a company may decrease its share capital.*

2.6.1 Placements of shares

Rather than issue new shares through an issue to the public or current shareholders, the company may decide to place the shares with specific investors such as life insurance companies and pension funds. The advantages to the company of a placement of shares are:
• *speed* — a placement can be effected in a short period of time

- *price* — because a placement is made to other than existing shareholders, and to a market that is potentially more informed and better funded, the issue price of the new shares may be closer to the market price at the date of issue
- *direction* — the shares may be placed with investors who approve of the direction of the company, or who will not interfere in the formation of company policies
- *prospectus* — in some cases, a placement can occur without the need for a detailed prospectus to be prepared.

There are potential disadvantages to the existing shareholders from private placements in that the current shareholders will have their interest in the company diluted as a result of the placement. In some countries, the securities regulations place limits on the amounts of placements of shares without the approval of existing shareholders. Further disadvantages to current shareholders can occur if the company places the shares at a large discount. Again, securities laws are generally enacted to ensure that management cannot abuse the placement process and that current shareholders are protected.

ILLUSTRATIVE EXAMPLE 2.5 Placement of shares

Thailand Ltd placed 5000 no-par ordinary shares at $5 each with Turkey Ltd.
The entry in the journals of Thailand Ltd is:

Cash	Dr	25 000	
Share Capital	Cr		25 000
(Placement of shares)			

2.6.2 Rights issues

A rights issue is an issue of new shares with the terms of issue giving existing shareholders the right to an additional number of shares in proportion to their current shareholding; that is, the shares are offered pro rata. For example, an offer could be made to each shareholder to buy two new shares on the basis of every 10 shares currently held. If all the existing shareholders exercise their rights and take up the shares, there is no change in each shareholder's percentage ownership interest in the company. Rights issues are typical in the context of protecting shareholders from involuntary dilution of their interest, and may also be offered below market price to encourage shareholders' participation. This was the case for Santander, as well as other banks, which in the height of the financial crisis in 2008–09 was forced to support its equity by a large share issue through a deeply discounted rights issue (*Santander's Rushed Rights Issue is Raising Hackles*, FT.com, 20 November 2008).

Rights issues may be tradeable or non-tradeable. If tradeable, existing shareholders may sell their rights to the new shares to another party during the offer period. If the rights are non-tradeable, a shareholder is not allowed to sell their rights to the new shares and must either accept or reject the offer to acquire new shares in the company.

ILLUSTRATIVE EXAMPLE 2.6 Rights issue

Pakistan Ltd planned to raise $3.6 million from shareholders through a renounceable one-for-six rights issue. The terms of the issue were 6 million no-par shares to be issued at 60c each, applications to be received by 15 April 2015. The rights issue was fully taken up. The shares were issued on 20 April 2015.
The journal entries in the company's records are passed when the rights are exercised:

April 20	Cash	Dr	3 600 000	
	Share Capital	Cr		3 600 000
	(Issue of shares)			

2.6.3 Options

Companies often provide their employees with share-based compensation. In particular, under some of these arrangements employees are issued shares, or options to shares, that replace cash payment. This may involve entries to owners' equity that may increase share premium account or a specific reserve. *Chapter 8 discusses the specific requirements for such arrangements.*

More generally, a company-issued share option is an instrument that gives the holder the right but not the obligation to buy a certain number of shares in the company by a specified date at a stated price. For example, a company could issue options that give an investor the right to acquire shares in the company at $2 each, with the options having to be exercised before 31 December 2017. The option holder is taking a risk in that the share price may not reach $2 (the option is 'out of the money') or the share price may exceed $2 (the option is 'in the money').

When the options are issued, the issuing entity will receive an initial amount of cash that corresponds to the fair value of the option at that time. Where the option holder exercises the option, the company increases its share capital as it issues the shares to the option holder.

To illustrate: assume Beckham Inc. company issues 100 options on 30 June 2016 at $0.25 each to two investors in equal amounts (i.e. 50 options each). Each option entitles the investors to acquire a share in the company at a price of $3. The current market price of the company shares is $2.80. Assume that on 30 November 2016 the share price reaches $4 and the investor exercises the option. The journal entries required are shown below. The par value of each share is $1.[3]

June 30	Cash	Dr	25	
	Equity*	Cr		25
	(100 options issued at 25c each)			
November 30	Cash	Dr	300	
	Equity	Dr	25	
	Share Capital	Cr		100
	Share Premium	Cr		225
	(Exercise of options issued)			

*This account may be called 'Options Reserve' or simply 'Other Equity'.

Options generally have to be exercised by a specific date. Assume that in the case of Beckham Inc. the options had to be exercised by 31 December 2016, and only one investor exercised their rights to acquire shares. The journal entries required are:

December 31	Cash	Dr	150	
	Equity	Dr	12.5	
	Share Capital	Cr		50
	Share Premium	Cr		112.5
	(Issue of shares on exercise of options)			

Note that the issue price of those options exercised is treated as part of share capital; in essence, the investor who exercises the option is paying $3.25 ($0.25 + $3.0) in total for each share (and a total of $50 \times \$3.25 = \$162.5$). Also note the specific use of accounts in this example. However, these accounts may not always be the appropriate ones across all legal jurisdictions and the choice of which accounts are used may also be affected by taxation implications.

For the options that were not exercised, the entity could transfer the equity balance of $12.5 to share premium or a reserve account including retained earnings. Again, legal and taxation implications should be considered in choosing the appropriate accounts to be used. For the example above where the holder of 50 options did not exercise those options, the journal entry required when the options lapse would be:

	Equity	Dr	12.5	
	Share Premium	Cr		12.5
	(Transfer of lapsed options)			

[3] This is an example of 'gross-settled' share options (i.e. when the option is exercised the full amount of shares is issued). Option contracts that are 'cash-settled' are treated as a derivative liability, and hence are not recognised in equity. If the contract is net 'equity-settled' the initial amount raised is treated as a liability, which is subsequently adjusted to changes in the fair value of the option. Upon exercise, the entity issues shares so as to settle the balance. For example, if the share price on exercise day is $4, then the total value of outstanding options is $100 (($4 − $3) × 100), and hence the liability on that day stands at $100. When 25 ($100/$4) new shares are issued to settle the balance, the issuer debits the liability $100, and credits share capital $25 and share premium $75.

2.6.4 Share warrants and compound securities

Other forms of option are company-issued warrants and embedded options to convert debt to equity in a compound debt-equity instrument. While an option is a freestanding equity instrument, a warrant or an embedded option in a convertible bond is generally attached to another form of financing. For example, embedded options may be attached to an issue of debt, and warrants may be given as an incentive to acquire a large parcel of shares in a future capital raising activity. Warrants may be detachable or non-detachable, but typically upon exercise require the holder to contribute further funds. If warrants are non-detachable, then they cannot be traded separately from the shares or debt package to which they were attached. In either case the warrant or conversion option has a value that needs to be recorded in equity, although where in equity is not generally prescribed. *The measurement and accounting for convertible bonds is described in chapter 7.*

2.6.5 Bonus issues (or stock dividend)

A bonus issue is an issue of shares to existing shareholders in proportion to their current shareholdings at no cost to the shareholders. The company uses its reserves balances or retained earnings to make the issue. The bonus issue is a transfer from one equity account to another, so it does not increase or decrease the equity of the company. Instead, it increases the share capital and decreases another equity account of the company.

The standards do not provide guidance as to how a bonus issue should be measured. Reference to fair value of the bonus issue may be unwarranted, as firm valuation remains intact. Furthermore when *all* shareholders receive *equal* bonus (on a pro rata basis), each shareholder's wealth is unaffected although the value of each share is smaller following the bonus. This suggests that the charge to the other equity account should be recoded at the par value. To illustrate: assume a company has a share capital consisting of 500 000 shares, $1 par value each. If it makes a 1-for-20 bonus issue from its retained earnings, it will issue 25 000 shares pro rata to its current shareholders. The journal entry required is:

Retained Earnings	Dr	25 000	
Share Capital	Cr		25 000
(Bonus issue of 25 000 shares from retained earnings)			

Nevertheless, in the case where a company assigns a value to the stock dividend that exceeds the par value, perhaps by reference to the prevailing share price, the charge to retained earnings, or any other permissible reserve, will be higher, with a balancing entry to the share premium account. Considering the previous example, assume the share bonus is valued at $100 000. Then the journal entry for issuing 25 000 bonus shares is:

Retained Earnings	Dr	100 000	
Share Capital	Cr		25 000
Share Premium	Cr		75 000
(Bonus issue of 25 000 shares at $100 000 from retained earnings)			

Depending on prevailing law, companies may use other equity accounts instead of retained earnings. In the example above, issuing the stock dividend at par value could be charged against the share premium account:

Share Premium	Dr	25 000	
Share Capital	Cr		25 000
(Bonus issue of 25 000 shares from retained earnings)			

On occasions where the debit to the share premium account exceeds its opening balance, the difference between the 25 000 and the opening balance may be debited to retained earnings, or any other reserve account permitted by the relevant country's regulations. *(See section 2.8 for the discussion of reserves.)*

2.6.6 Share split

Rewarding shareholders with bonus shares has the effect of reducing the value of each share, and consequently increases the liquidity and ease with which these shares can be exchanged or traded. A similar effect on share value is reached via share splits. A share split involves increasing the number of shares outstanding while proportionally reducing the par value of each share. For example, if a company has 10 000 shares outstanding at 90c each, and carries out a 3-for-1 split, it will report after the split 30 000 shares at 30c each. Total share capital is therefore unchanged and, unlike a share bonus, no charge is required to any other equity account.

2.6.7 Share-based transactions

A company may acquire assets, including other entities, with the consideration for the acquisition being shares in the company itself. *Accounting for this form of transaction is covered in chapter 14. Accounting for share-based payments is covered in chapter 8.*

2.7 SHARE CAPITAL: SUBSEQUENT DECREASES IN SHARE CAPITAL

A company may decrease the number of shares issued by buying back some of its own shares. The extent to which a company may buy back its own shares and the frequency with which it may do so are generally governed by specific laws within a jurisdiction as well as the company's own charter. A key feature of such regulations is the protection of creditors, as the company is reducing equity by using cash that otherwise would have been available to repay creditors. Companies may undertake a share buy-back to:
- increase earnings-per-share (EPS)
- manage the capital structure by reducing equity
- most efficiently return surplus funds held by the company to shareholders, rather than pay a dividend or reinvest in other ventures.

Repurchased shares are called treasury shares. IAS 32 (paragraph 33) requires that the amount spent on buying back treasury shares is deducted from equity. The standard, however, does not prescribe which element of equity should be reduced.

Consider Harlem Inc. which has issued 500 000 shares at $1 par value each over a period of years. Further assume the total equity of Harlem Inc. consists of:

Share Capital	$ 500 000
Share Premium	270 000
Retained Earnings	230 000
	$1 000 000

If Harlem Inc. now buys back 50 000 shares for $2.20 per share, the amount of treasury shares is $110 000. This is recorded as follows:

Treasury Shares	Dr	110 000	
Cash	Cr		110 000
(Share buy-back 50 000 shares at $2.20 per share)			

The equity section will now report:

Share Capital	$ 500 000
Share Premium	270 000
Retained Earnings	230 000
Treasury Shares	(110 000)
	$ 890 000

Note that the treasury shares account is a contra-equity account, as it appears in equity, but with a negative sign.

Following the repurchase, treasury shares may be (i) kept by the company; (ii) reissued and (iii) cancelled. The accounting treatment for these different possibilities is described below.

2.7.1 Treasury shares kept in the company

As long as the treasury shares are kept in the company, the equity reports a deduction of $110 000, as illustrated above. Treasury shares are not regarded as issued for the purpose of voting, dividends and other rights that come along with ordinary shares.

2.7.2 Treasury shares are reissued

Companies may reuse treasury shares to satisfy demand for options that have been exercised (e.g. in employee share option schemes), or resell them in the open market or to other investors. Since the proceeds on such resell may differ from the original cost of the treasury shares, a gain or a loss may arise. However, IAS 32 (paragraph 33) disallows the recognition of such gain or loss in the income statement. Instead, it should be recognised directly in reserves.

Assume Harlem Inc. resells on the open market 10 000 treasury shares at $3 each. This generates a gain of $0.80 per share, or a total gain of $8000. A typical entry to record this would be:

Cash	Dr	30 000	
Treasury Shares	Cr		22 000
Share Premium	Cr		8 000
(Resell of 10 000 treasury shares at $3.00 per share)			

If, on the other hand, Harlem Inc. resells 10 000 treasury shares at $1.40 a share, a loss of $8000 is generated. This will be recorded as follows:

Cash	Dr	14 000	
Share Premium	Dr	8 000	
Treasury Shares	Cr		22 000
(Re-sell of 10 000 treasury shares at $1.40 per share)			

Again, on occasions where the debit to the share premium account exceeds its opening balance, the difference may be debited to retained earnings, or any other reserve account permitted by the relevant country's regulations. *(See section 2.8 for the discussion of reserves.)*

2.7.3 Treasury shares are cancelled

A repurchase of shares that is followed by a cancellation is equivalent from an economic perspective to a redistribution of wealth to owners. According to this view, when treasury shares are cancelled, a suitable reduction to retained earnings should be made. However, depending on the legal jurisdiction, other distributable reserves can be used *(see section 2.8 for the discussion of reserves in equity)*. In addition, the original share capital should be cancelled. Assume that prior to the purchase of the 100 000 treasury shares Harlem Inc. also had an asset revaluation surplus reserve of $20 000 that can be used for this purpose. The cancellation of 50 000 shares is therefore recorded as:

Share Capital	Dr	50 000	
Share Premium	Dr	27 000	
Revaluation Surplus	Dr	20 000	
Retained Earnings	Dr	13 000	
Treasury Shares	Cr		110 000
(Cancellation of 50 000 treasury shares with $1 par value each that were purchased at $2.20 each)			

Corporate law in some countries requires the maintenance of capital, as a means of protecting creditors (this is the case, for example, in the UK). This implies that a new non-distributable reserve in equity is also established at the amount of cancelled share capital. Employing the previous example, this can be recorded as follows:

Share Capital	Dr	50 000	
Share Premium	Dr	27 000	
Revaluation Reserve	Dr	20 000	
Retained Earnings	Dr	63 000	
Capital Redemption Reserve	Cr		50 000
Treasury Shares	Cr		110 000
(Cancellation of 50 000 treasury shares with $1 par value each that were purchased at $2.20 each)			

Creditors' protection is obtained through the larger debit to retained earnings, implying Harlem Inc.'s ability to further pay cash dividends in the future is reduced (by an additional $50 000).

An example of a repurchase of shares is that undertaken by Pöyry plc in 2011. The authorisation for the company to acquire its own shares is shown in figure 2.4.

Authorisation to acquire the company's own shares

The AGM on 11 March 2010 authorised the Board of Directors to decide on acquiring maximum of 5 800 000 own shares with distributable funds. The company's own shares can be acquired in accordance with the decision of the Board of Directors either through public trading or by public offer at their market price at the time of purchase.

The authorisation is effective for a period of 18 months. The Board has not exercised the authorisation during 2010.

The Board of Directors proposes that the General Meeting on 10 March 2011 authorise the Board of Directors to decide on the acquisition of a maximum of 5 900 000 of the Company's own shares by using distributable funds. It is proposed that the authorisation be effective for a period of 18 months. The authorisation granted to the Board of Directors regarding acquisition of the Company's own shares in the previous Annual General Meeting shall expire simultaneously.

FIGURE 2.4 Repurchase of shares, Pöyry plc
Source: Pöyry plc (2011, p. 65).

In Nokia's 2013 balance sheet *(see figure 2.2)*, the treasury shares are shown as a reduction in total equity because the share capital of the entity has effectively been reduced by the repurchase of the shares.

2.8 RESERVES

'Reserves' is the generic term for all equity accounts other than contributed equity. A major component is the retained earnings account. This account accumulates the sum of the periodic income earned by an entity, and certain other comprehensive income (OCI). IAS 1 requires entities to prepare a Statement of Comprehensive Income that lists both periodic income and items of OCI *(see chapter 16)*. OCI includes all income items that certain accounting standards require (or allow) to flow directly through equity, net of related tax effects. Some notable examples of OCI are:

- remeasurements of financial assets not held for trading and cash flow value hedges (IFRS 9 — *see chapter 7*)
- remeasurement of defined benefit pension plans (IAS 19 (Revised) — *see chapter 10*)
- revaluation of property, plant and equipment (IAS 16 — *see chapter 11*)
- particular foreign exchange differences (IAS 21 — *see chapter 24*).

However, not all income items recognized in OCI need to be incorporated into retained earnings. They may be incorporated into a separate reserve, *as discussed in section 2.8.2.*

Retained earnings is the primary account from which distributions to owners are made in the form of dividends. Hence, in general, the retained earnings account will accumulate comprehensive income (that is not recognised in other reserves) earned over the life of the entity.

2.8.1 Retained earnings

'Retained earnings' has the same meaning as 'retained profits' and 'accumulated profit or loss'. The key change in this account is the addition of the comprehensive income or loss for the current period. The main other movements in the retained earnings account are:

- dividends declared
- cancellation of shares *(see section 2.7.3)*
- transfers to and from reserves
- changes in accounting policy and errors (see IAS 8 *Accounting Policies, Changes in Accounting Estimates and Errors, discussed in detail in chapter 16*).

Cash dividends. Cash dividends are a distribution from the company to its owners in the form of cash. It is generally the case, under companies legislation, that dividends can be paid only from profits, and not from capital. In some jurisdictions, companies must comply with a solvency test before paying dividends. The purpose in both situations is to protect the creditors, as any money paid to shareholders is money unavailable for paying creditors.

Scrip dividends. Companies often give shareholders a choice between cash dividend and receiving more shares in an equivalent value to the cash dividend. As an example, Sean plc declares a 10c per share dividend during 2015. The market value of its 1m shares is $10m at the time of the declaration. The par value of each share is $1. As the total cash dividend amounts to $100 000, the dividend is equal to 1%

of the market value of its equity ($0.1 × 1m/$10m). Hence, Sean plc offers a 1-for-100 scrip alternative. Assuming 50% of shareholders opt for the scrip alternative, Sean plc would record these entries:

2015	Retained Earnings	Dr	100 000	
	Dividends Payable	Cr		100 000
	(Declaration of dividend of $100 000)			
	Dividends Payable	Dr	100 000	
	Cash	Cr		50 000
	Share Capital	Cr		5 000
	Retained Earnings	Cr		45 000
	(Payment of dividend and issue of 5 000 new shares)			

The scrip alternative can be thought of as equivalent to a share bonus. Hence, if the share premium account can be used for the share bonus, it is possible to record the following entries when the dividend is paid and new shares are issued:

2015	Dividends Payable	Dr	100 000	
	Share Premium	Dr	5 000	
	Cash	Cr		50 000
	Share Capital	Cr		5 000
	Retained Earnings	Cr		50 000
	(Payment of dividend and issue of 5 000 new shares)			

Note that in this case retained earnings are reduced only by the amount of cash dividend.

ILLUSTRATIVE EXAMPLE 2.7 Scrip dividend

Banco Santander SA declared a scrip dividend on 10 April 2015. The terms of the dividend scheme were as follows. On the announcement date the number of outstanding shares of Santander was 14 060 585 886 and it offered the right to receive one share per 46 shares held. This ratio was based on cash equivalent of €2 165 000 000 (or €0.154 per share). Santander determined that the relevant share price was €7.076; hence the scrip ratio is 2 165 000 000/(7.076 × 14 060 585 886) = 1:46 (rounded).

If all shareholders took the scrip alternative, a total of 305 664 910 (= 14 060 585 886/46) new shares would have been issued. The par value of each share is €0.50, implying a maximum increase in share capital of €152 832 455. Santander announced it will use its share premium account to charge the €152 832 455.

Santander also offered to buy back the rights from its shareholders at 7.076/(1 + 46) = €0.151 each.

Source: www.santander.com

Interim and final dividends. Dividends are sometimes divided into interim and final dividends. Interim dividends are paid during the financial year, while final dividends are declared by the directors at financial year-end for payment sometime after the end of the reporting period. In some companies, the eventual payment of the final dividends is subject to approval of the dividend by the annual general meeting. With the final dividend, there is some debate as to when the company should raise a liability for the dividend, particularly where payment of the dividend is subject to shareholder approval. Some would argue that until approval is received there is only a contingent liability, the entity not having a present obligation to pay the dividend until approval is received. Others argue that there is a constructive obligation existing at year-end and, given customary business practice, the entity has a liability at the end of the reporting period.

In this regard, paragraphs 12 and 13 of IAS 10 *Events after the Reporting Period* state:

12. If an entity declares dividends to holders of equity instruments (as defined in IAS 32 *Financial Instruments: Presentation*) after the reporting period, the entity shall not recognise those dividends as a liability at the end of the reporting period.
13. If dividends are declared after the reporting period but before the financial statements are authorised for issue, the dividends are not recognised as a liability at the end of the reporting period because no obligation exists at that time. Such dividends are disclosed in the notes in accordance with IAS 1 *Presentation of Financial Statements*.

If the dividends are not declared at the end of the reporting period, no liability is recognised at the end of the reporting period. When shareholder approval is required for dividends declared prior to the end of the reporting period, a liability should be recognised only once the annual general meeting approves the dividends, because before that date the entity does not have a present obligation. Until that occurs, the declared dividend is only a contingent liability. *(See chapter 5 for further discussion on provisions and contingencies.)* It is expected that companies that prefer to raise a liability at year-end will change their regulations or constitution so that dividends can be declared without the need for shareholder approval.

ILLUSTRATIVE EXAMPLE 2.8 Interim and final dividends

During the period ending 30 June 2015, the following events occurred in relation to Oman Ltd.

2014	
Sept. 25	Annual general meeting approves the final dividend of $10 000.
Sept. 30	Oman Ltd pays the final dividend to shareholders.

2015	
Jan. 10	Oman Ltd pays an interim dividend of $8 000.
June 30	Oman Ltd declares a final dividend of $12 000, this dividend requiring shareholder approval at the next AGM.

Required

Prepare the journal entries to record the dividend transactions of Oman Ltd.

Solution

2014				
Sept. 25	Retained Earnings	Dr	10 000	
	Dividends Payable	Cr		10 000
	(Dividend of $10 000 authorised by annual meeting)			
Sept. 30	Dividends Payable	Dr	10 000	
	Cash	Cr		10 000
	(Payment of dividend)			
2015				
Jan. 10	Retained Earnings	Dr	8 000	
	Cash	Cr		8 000
	(Payment of interim dividend)			

No entry is required in relation to the final dividend of $12 000. A contingent liability would be recorded in the notes to the 2015 financial statements.

2.8.2 Other components of equity

In section 2.7 we encountered two special reserves: treasury shares (a contra-equity account) and capital redemption reserve. Some additional examples of reserves other than retained earnings are shown below.

Asset revaluation reserve

IAS 16 *Property, Plant and Equipment* allows entities a choice in the measurement of these assets. In particular, entities may choose between measuring the assets at cost (the cost model) or at fair value (the revaluation model). If the fair value basis is chosen, revaluation increases are recognised in other comprehensive income and accumulated in equity via an asset revaluation surplus. *(Details of the accounting under a fair value basis for property, plant and equipment are covered in chapter 11.)*

An asset revaluation surplus, may be used for payment of dividends or be transferred to other reserve accounts including retained earnings, depending on a jurisdiction's specific laws. Amounts recognised directly in the asset revaluation surplus cannot subsequently be recognised in profit or loss for the period even when the revalued asset is disposed of.

Foreign currency translation differences

Foreign currency translation differences arise when foreign operations are translated from one currency into another currency for presentation purposes. *(Details of the establishment of this account can be found in chapter 24.)* The changes in wealth as a result of the translation process are thereby not taken through profit or loss for the period, and are recognised in profit or loss only if and when the investor disposes of its interest in the foreign operation.

Fair value differences

Under IFRS 9 *Financial Instruments*, at initial recognition, financial assets and liabilities are measured at fair value. Paragraph 5.7.5 of IFRS 9 permits an entity to make an irrevocable election to present in other comprehensive income changes in the fair value of an investment in an equity instrument that is not held for trading. Because IFRS 9 (paragraph B5.7.1) does not allow such gains and losses to be transferred into profit and loss, they should be recorded in other reserves, or directly in retained earnings.

ILLUSTRATIVE EXAMPLE 2.9 Reserves

As an example of the disclosure of reserves, the note disclosure provided by Qantas in its 2011 annual report is shown in figure 2.5.

23. Capital and reserves	Qantas Group	
Reserves	**2011 $m**	**2010 $m**
Employee compensation reserve	65	53
Hedge reserve	80	85
Foreign currency translation reserve	(60)	(29)
	85	109

Nature and purpose of reserves
Employee compensation reserve
The fair value of equity plans granted is recognised in the employee compensation reserve over the vesting period. This reserve will be reversed against treasury shares when the underlying shares vest and transfer to the employee. No gain or loss is recognised in the Consolidated Income Statement on the purchase, sale, issue or cancellation of Qantas' own equity instruments.

Hedge reserve
The hedge reserve comprises the effective portion of the cumulative net change in the fair value of cash flow hedging instruments related to future forecast transactions.

Foreign currency translation reserve
The foreign currency translation reserve comprises all foreign exchange differences arising from the translation of the Financial Statements of foreign controlled entities and associates, as well as from the translation of liabilities that form part of the Qantas Group's net investment in a foreign controlled entity.

FIGURE 2.5 Disclosure of reserves
Source: Qantas (2011, p. 81).

As illustrated earlier in the chapter, entities may make transfers between various reserves. For example, share premium may be used to issue bonus shares. Asset revaluation surplus can be transferred gradually to retained earnings, when the depreciation on the underlying asset exceeds the historical-cost depreciation. It may also be transferred into retained earnings when the underlying asset is sold.

ILLUSTRATIVE EXAMPLE 2.10 Reserve transfers

During the period ending 30 June 2015, the following events occurred in relation to the company Malaysia Ltd:

Jan. 1	$10 000 transferred from retained earnings to general reserve
Feb. 18	$4 000 transferred from asset revaluation surplus to retained earnings
June 15	Bonus share dividend of $50 000, half from general reserve and half from retained earnings

Required

Prepare the journal entries to record these transactions.

Solution

2015				
Jan. 1	Retained Earnings	Dr	10 000	
	General Reserve	Cr		10 000
	(Transfer from retained earnings to general reserves)			
Feb. 18	Asset Revaluation Surplus	Dr	4 000	
	Retained Earnings	Cr		4 000
	(Transfer from asset revaluation surplus)			
June 15	General Reserve	Dr	25 000	
	Retained Earnings	Dr	25 000	
	Share Capital	Cr		50 000
	(Bonus issue of shares)			

2.9 DISCLOSURE

Disclosures in relation to equity are detailed in IAS 1 *Presentation of Financial Statements*. The disclosures relate to specific items of equity as well as the preparation of a statement of changes in equity.

2.9.1 Specific disclosures

IAS 1 provides several disclosure requirements regarding the equity section in the balance sheet. The main ones appear in paragraphs 54, 79, 106, 136, 137 and 138 and require disclosures regarding:

1. The amount of non-controlling interest within the equity section (paragraph 54(q))
2. The amount of issued capital and reserves attributed to parent company (paragraph 54(r)).
3. By class of shares: The number of shares authorised for issue; the number of shares issued, distinguishing between those that are fully paid and those that are not; whether shares have par value (and how much) or not; explaining the change during the year in the number of shares outstanding; the contractual arrangements concerning the shares, including any rights and restrictions; treasury shares and description of each reserve included in the equity section (paragraph 79).
4. Statement of changes in equity, *as discussed in section 2.9.2* (paragraph 106).
5. Puttable instruments classified as equity, including amounts and explanations as to the entity's objectives in respect to these instruments and expected cash flows (paragraph 136A).
6. The amounts of dividends proposed or declared, inclusive of preference dividend, which have not been recognised as a liability (paragraph 137).

2.9.2 Statement of changes in equity

Paragraph 106 of IAS 1 requires the preparation of a statement of changes in equity. This paragraph requires the statement to show the following:

(a) total comprehensive income for the period, showing separately the total amounts attributable to owners of the parent and to non-controlling interests;
(b) for each component of equity, the effects of retrospective application or retrospective restatement recognised in accordance with IAS 8; and
(c) [deleted]
(d) for each component of equity, a reconciliation between the carrying amount at the beginning and the end of the period, separately disclosing changes resulting from:
   (i) profit or loss;
   (ii) other comprehensive income; and
   (iii) transactions with owners in their capacity as owners, showing separately contributions by and distributions to owners and changes in ownership interests in subsidiaries that do not result in a loss of control.

These requirements can be met in a number of ways, including using a columnar format. The statement of changes in equity must contain the information in paragraph 106 of IAS 1. The information required by paragraph 107 in relation to dividends may be included in the statement of changes in equity or disclosed in the notes.

Figure 2.6, the statement of changes in equity disclosed in the 2014 annual report of Diageo plc, demonstrates a columnar format for this statement.

Retained earnings/(deficit)

£m	Share capital	Share premium	Capital redemption reserve	Hedging and exchange reserve	Own shares	Other retained earnings	Total	Equity attributable to parent company shareholders	Non-controlling interest	Total equity
At 30 June 2012 (restated)	797	1 344	3 146	67	(2 257)	2 491	234	5 588	1 204	6 792
Total comprehensive income				(59)		2 606	2 606	2 547	134	2 681
Employee share scheme					25	(34)	(9)	(9)		(9)
Share-based incentive plans						45	45	45		45
Share-based incentive plans in respect of associates						2	2	2		2
Tax on share-based incentive plans						30	30	30		30
Acquisitions						0	0	0	(21)	(21)
Change in fair value of put options						(7)	(7)	(7)		(7)
Purchase of non-controlling interests						(100)	(100)	(100)	(100)	(200)
Dividends paid						(1 125)	(1 125)	(1 125)	(100)	(1 225)
Transfers						65	65	65	(65)	0
At 30 June 2013 (restated)	797	1 344	3 146	8	(2 232)	3 973	1 741	7 036	1 052	8 088
Total comprehensive income				(911)		2 025	2 025	1 114	(187)	927
Employee share scheme					(48)	(67)	(115)	(115)		(115)
Share-based incentive plans						37	37	37		37
Share-based incentive plans in respect of associates						3	3	3		3
Tax on share-based incentive plans						1	1	1		1
Shares issued		1					0	1		1
Acquisitions						0	0	0	8	8
Change in fair value of put options						0	0	0		0
Purchase of non-controlling interests						(7)	(7)	(7)		(7)
Dividends paid						(19)	(19)	(19)	(18)	(37)
Transfers						(1 228)	(1 228)	(1 228)	(88)	(1 316)
At 30 June 2014	797	1 345	3 146	(903)	(2 280)	4 718	2 438	6 823	767	7 590

FIGURE 2.6 Statement of changes in equity for Diageo plc
Source: Diageo plc (2014, pp. 91).

SUMMARY

The corporate form of organisational structure is a popular one in many countries, particularly because of the limited liability protection that it affords to shareholders. These companies' operations are financed by a mixture of equity and debt. In this chapter the focus is on the equity of a corporate entity. The components of equity recognised generally by companies are share capital, other reserves and retained earnings. Share capital in particular is affected by a variety of financial instruments developed in the financial markets, offering investors instruments with an array of risk–return alternatives. Each of these equity alternatives has its own accounting implications. The existence of reserves is driven by traditional accounting as well as the current restrictions in some accounting standards for some wealth increases to be recognised directly in equity rather than in current income. Even though definite distinctions are made between the various components of equity, it needs to be recognised that they are all equity and differences relate to jurisdictional differences in terms of restrictions on dividend distribution, taxation effects and rights of owners. IAS 1 requires detailed disclosures in relation to each of the components of equity.

Discussion questions

1. Discuss the nature of a reserve. How do reserves differ from the other main components of equity?
2. A company announces a final dividend at the end of the financial year. Discuss whether a dividend payable should be recognised.
3. The telecommunications industry in a particular country has been a part of the public sector. As a part of its privatisation agenda, the government decided to establish a limited liability company called Telecom Plus, with the issue of 10 million $3 shares. These shares were to be offered to the citizens of the country. The terms of issue were such that investors had to pay $2 on application and the other $1 per share would be called at a later time. Discuss:
   (a) the nature of the limited liability company, and in particular the financial obligations of acquirers of shares in the company
   (b) the journal entries that would be required if applications were received for 11 million shares.
4. Why would a company wish to buy back its own shares? Discuss.
5. A company has a share capital consisting of 100 000 shares issued at $2 per share, and 50 000 shares issued at $3 per share. Discuss the effects on the accounts if:
   (a) the company buys back 20 000 shares at $4 per share
   (b) the company buys back 20 000 shares at $2.50 per share.
6. A company has a share capital consisting of 100 000 shares having a par value of $1 per share and issued at a premium of $1 per share, and 50 000 shares issued at $2 par and $1 premium. Discuss the effects on the accounts if:
   (a) the company buys back 20 000 shares at $4 per share
   (b) the company buys back 20 000 shares at $2.50 per share.
7. What is a rights issue? Distinguish between a tradeable and a non-tradeable issue.
8. What is a private placement of shares? Outline its advantages and disadvantages.
9. Discuss whether it is necessary to distinguish between the different components of equity rather than just having a single number for shareholders' equity.
10. For what reasons may a company make an appropriation of its retained earnings?

References

Diageo plc 2014, *Annual Report 2014*, Diageo, http://www.diageo.com/en-row/investor/Pages/financialreports.aspx.
International Accounting Standards Board 2010, *Conceptual Framework for Financial Reporting*, www.ifrs.org.
Nokia Corporation 2013, *Annual Report 2013*, Nokia Corporation, Finland, www.nokia.com.
Pöyry plc 2011, *Annual Report 2010*, Pöyry plc, Finland, www.poyry.com.
Qantas 2011, *Annual Report 2011*, Qantas Airways Limited, Australia, www.qantas.com.au.
Santander 2015, *Material Fact: Information on Dividendo Eleccion*, www.santander.com.
Tesco plc 2014, *Annual Report 2014*, Tesco, http://www.tescoplc.com/index.asp?pageid=548.

Exercises

STAR RATING ★ BASIC ★★ MODERATE ★★★ DIFFICULT

| Exercise 2.1 | RESERVES AND DIVIDENDS |

★ Prepare journal entries to record the following unrelated transactions of a public company:
(a) payment of interim dividend of €30 000
(b) transfer of €52 000 from the asset revaluation surplus to the general reserve
(c) transfer of €34 000 from the general reserve to retained earnings
(d) issue of 240 000 bonus shares, fully paid, at €2 per share from the general reserve.

Exercise 2.2 | **RIGHTS ISSUE**

★ Property Ltd had share capital of 1 million $1 shares, fully paid. As it needed finance for certain construction projects, the company's management decided to make a non-tradeable rights issue to existing shareholders of 200 000 new shares at an issue price of $5 per share. The rights issue was to be fully underwritten by Brokers Ltd. The prospectus was issued on 15 February 2016 and applications closed on 15 March 2016. Costs associated with the rights issue and the eventual issue of the shares were $10 000.
(a) If 80% of the rights were exercised by the due date, provide journal entries made by Property Ltd in relation to the rights issue and the eventual share issue.
(b) If the rights issue was not underwritten and any unexercised rights lapsed, what would be the required journal entries?

Exercise 2.3 | **SHARE ISSUE, OPTIONS**

★ Jordan Ltd has the following shareholders' equity at 1 January 2016:

Share capital — 500 000 shares	£1 240 000
Asset revaluation surplus	350 000
Retained earnings	110 000

On 1 March the company decided to make a public share issue to raise £600 000 for new capital development. The company issued a prospectus inviting applications for 200 000 £3 shares, payable in full on application. Shareholders who acquired more than 10 000 shares were allowed to buy options at 50 cents each. These options enabled the owner to buy shares in Jordan Ltd at £3.50 each, the acquisition having to occur before 31 December 2016.

By 25 March the company had received applications for 250 000 shares and for 20 000 options. The shares and options were allotted on 2 April, and money returned to unsuccessful applicants on the same day. All applicants who acquired options also received shares.

By 31 December 2016, the company's share price had reached £3.75. Holders of 18 000 options exercised their options in December. The remaining options lapsed.

Required

Prepare the journal entries in the records of Jordan Ltd in relation to the equity transactions in 2016.

Exercise 2.4 | **ISSUE OF ORDINARY AND PREFERENCE SHARES**

★★ Prepare journal entries to record the following transactions for Kahuna Ltd:

2016	
April 1	A prospectus was issued inviting applications for 100 000 ordinary shares at an issue price of €1.50, fully payable on application. The prospectus also offered 100 000 10% preference shares at an issue price of €2, fully payable on application. The issue was underwritten at a commission of €4500, being €500 relating to the issue of ordinary shares and the balance for preference shares. All unsuccessful application monies were to be returned to the applicants.
April 10	Applications closed with the ordinary issue oversubscribed by 40 000 shares and the preference shares undersubscribed by 15 000 shares.
April 15	100 000 ordinary shares were allotted and applications for 40 000 shares were rejected and money refunded. 100 000 preference shares were also allotted.
April 20	The underwriter paid for the shares allocated to her, less the commission due.

Exercise 2.5 | **SHARE ISSUE, OPTIONS**

★★ On 30 June 2015, the equity accounts of Boron Ltd consisted of:

175 000 'A' ordinary shares, issued at $2.50 each, fully paid	$437 500
50 000 6% cumulative preference shares, issued at $3 and paid to $2	100 000
Options (20 000 at 56c each)	11 200
Accumulated losses	(6 250)

As the company had incurred a loss for the year ended 30 June 2015, no dividends were declared for that year. The options were exercisable between 1 March 2016 and 30 April 2016. Each option allowed the holder to buy one 'A' ordinary share for $4.50.

The following transactions and events occurred during the year ended 30 June 2016:

2015	
July 25	The directors made the final call of $1 on the preference shares.
Aug. 31	All call monies were received except those owing on 7500 preference shares.
Sept. 7	The directors resolved to forfeit 7500 preference shares for non-payment of the call. The constitution of the company directs that forfeited amounts are not to be refunded to shareholders. The shares will not be reissued.
Nov. 1	The company issued a prospectus offering 30 000 'B' ordinary shares payable in two instalments: $3 on application and $2 on 30 November 2015. The offer closed on 30 November.
Nov. 30	Applications for 40 000 'B' ordinary shares were received.
Dec. 1	The directors resolved to allot the 'B' ordinary shares pro rata with all applicants receiving 75% of the shares applied for. Excess application monies were allowed to be held. The shares were duly allotted.
Dec. 5	Share issue costs of $5200 were paid.
2016	
April 30	The holders of 15 000 options applied to purchase shares. All monies were sent with the applications. All remaining options lapsed. The shares were duly issued.

Required

Prepare general journal entries to record the above transactions.

Exercise 2.6   **BUY-BACK OF SHARES**

★★   Victor Ltd decided to repurchase 10% of its ordinary shares under a buy-back scheme for £5.60 per share. At the date of the buy-back, the equity of Victor Ltd consisted of:

Share capital — 4 million shares fully paid	£4 000 000
General reserve	600 000
Retained earnings	1 100 000

The costs of the buy-back scheme amounted to £3500.

Required

(a) Prepare the journal entries to account for the buy-back. Explain the reasons for the entries made.
(b) Assume that the buy-back price per share was equal to 70p per share. Prepare journal entries to record the buy-back, and explain your answer.
(c) Assume that, instead of the share capital shown above, Victor Ltd had issued 1 million shares at a par value of £1 and a share premium of £3 per share. Rework your answers to (a) assuming the repurchased shares were subsequently cancelled (ignore costs of buy-back scheme).

Exercise 2.7   **SHARES, OPTIONS, DIVIDENDS AND RESERVE TRANSFERS**

★★★   The equity of Mondegreen Inc. at 30 June 2015 consisted of:

400 000 ordinary 'A' shares issued at $2.00, fully paid	$800 000
300 000 ordinary 'B' shares issued at $2.00, called to $1.20	360 000
50 000 6% non-cumulative preference shares issued at $1.50, fully paid	75 000
Share options issued at 60c, fully paid	24 000
Retained earnings	318 000

The options were exercisable before 28 February 2016. Each option entitled the holder to acquire two ordinary 'C' shares at $1.80 per share, the amount payable on notification to exercise the option.

The following transactions occurred during the year ended 30 June 2016:

2015 Sept. 15	The preference dividend and the final ordinary dividend of 16c per fully paid share, both declared on 30 June 2015, were paid. (Dividend is paid only with respect to capital paid.) The directors do not need any other party to authorise the payment of dividends.
Nov. 1	A one-for-five tradeable rights offer was made to ordinary 'A' shareholders at an issue price of $1.90 per share. The expiry date on the offer was 30 November 2015. The issue was underwritten at a commission of $3000.
Nov. 30	Holders of 320 000 shares accepted the rights offer, paying the required price per share, with the renounced rights being taken up by the underwriter. Ordinary 'A' shares were duly issued.
Dec. 10	Money due from the underwriter was received.
2016 Jan. 10	The directors transferred $35 000 from retained earnings to a general reserve.
Feb. 28	As a result of options being exercised, 70 000 ordinary 'C' shares were issued. Unexercised options lapsed.
April 30	The directors made a call on the ordinary 'B' shares for 80c per share. Call money was payable by 31 May.
May 31	All call money was received except for that due on 15 000 shares.
June 18	Shares on which the final call was unpaid were transferred to treasury shares reserve.
June 26	Treasury shares were reissued for $1.80 per share. The called balance of the 15 000 B shares was returned to the former shareholders, less the 20c shortfall per share.
June 27	Refund paid to former holders of cancelled shares.
June 30	The directors declared a 20c per share final dividend to be paid on 15 September 2016.

Required

(a) Prepare general journal entries to record the above transactions.
(b) Prepare the equity section of the statement of financial position as at 30 June 2016.

Exercise 2.8   DIVIDENDS, SHARE ISSUES, SHARE BUY-BACKS, OPTIONS AND MOVEMENTS IN RESERVES

★★★   Hide Ltd, a company whose principal interests are in the manufacture of fine leather shoes and hand-bags, was formed on 1 January 2013. Prior to the 2016 period, Hide Ltd had issued 110 000 ordinary shares:
- 95 000 €30 shares were issued for cash on 1 January 2013
- 5000 shares were exchanged on 1 February 2014 for a patent that had a fair value at date of exchange of €240 000
- 10 000 shares were issued on 13 November 2015 for €50 per share.

At 1 January 2016, Hide Ltd had a balance in its retained earnings account of €750 000, while the general reserve and the asset revaluation surplus had balances of €240 000 and €180 000, respectively. The purpose of the general reserve is to reflect the need for the company to regularly replace certain pieces of the shoe-making machinery to reflect technological changes.

During the 2016 financial year, the following transactions occurred:

Feb. 15	Hide Ltd paid a €25 000 dividend that had been declared in December 2015. Liabilities for dividends are recognised when they are declared by the company.
May 10	10 000 shares at €55 per share were offered to the general public. These were fully subscribed and issued on 20 June 2016. On the same date, another 15 000 shares were placed with major investors at €55 per share.

June 25	The company paid a €20 000 interim dividend.
June 30	The company revalued land by €30 000, increasing the asset revaluation surplus by €21 000 and the deferred tax liability by €9000.
July 1	The company early adopted IFRS 4 in relation to insurance. The transitional liability on initial adoption was €55 000 more than the liability recognised under the previous accounting standard. This amount was recognised directly in retained earnings.
July 22	Hide Ltd repurchased 5000 shares on the open market for €56 per share. The repurchase was accounted for as treasury shares.
Nov. 16	Hide Ltd declared a 1-for-20 bonus issue to shareholders on record at 1 October 2016. The general reserve was used to fund this bonus issue.
Dec. 1	The company issued 100 000 options at 20c each, each option entitling the holder to acquire an ordinary share in Hide Ltd at a price of €60 per share, the options to be exercised by 31 December 2016. No options had been exercised by 31 December 2016.
Dec. 31	Hide Ltd calculated that its profit for the 2016 year was €150 000. It declared a €30 000 final dividend (which was authorise for payment on that day), transferred €40 000 to the general reserve, and transferred €30 000 from the asset revaluation surplus to retained earnings.

Share issue costs amount to 10% of the worth of any share issue.

Required

(a) Prepare the general journal entries to record the above transactions.
(b) Prepare the statement of changes in equity for Hide Ltd for the year ended 31 December 2016.

Exercise 2.9   **DIVIDENDS, SHARE-ISSUES, OPTIONS, RESERVE TRANSFERS**

★★★   Mercury plc's equity as at 30 June 2016 was as follows:

120 000 ordinary 'A' shares, issued at £1.10, fully paid	£ 132 000
150 000 ordinary 'B' shares, issued at £1.20, called to 70p	105 000
100 000 8% cumulative preference shares, issued at £1, fully paid	100 000
Calls in advance (30 000 shares)	15 000
Share issue costs	(11 200)
General reserve	160 000
Retained earnings	158 000
Total equity	£ 658 800

The general journal is used for all entries.
The following events occurred after 30 June 2016:

2016 Sep. 30	The final 10p per share ordinary dividend and the preference dividend, both declared on 25 June 2016, were approved and paid.
Oct. 31	A prospectus was issued inviting offers to acquire one option for every two ordinary 'A' shares held at a price of 80p per option, payable by 30 November 2016. Each option entitles the holder to one ordinary 'A' share at a price of 70p per share and is exercisable in November 2014. Any options not exercised by 30 November 2018 will lapse.
Nov. 30	Offers and monies were received for 50 000 options, and these were issued.
2017 Jan. 15	The final call on ordinary 'B' shares was made, payable by 15 February 2017. The call takes into account that 15 000 were already paid in advance.
Feb. 15	All call monies were received.
April 20	50 000 preference shares were repurchased at £1.10 per share. Following the repurchase Mercury wrote down Preference Share Capital by £50 000 and charged Retained Earnings by the balance. Mercury does not need to establish a capital redemption reserve.

June 30	The profit for the year was £44 000. The directors decided to transfer £20 000 from the general reserve to retained profits and declared a 10p per share dividend and the preference dividend, both payable on 30 September 2017. The dividend has not yet been approved by the annual general meeting (AGM).
Sept. 30	The final ordinary and preference dividends declared on 30 June 2017 were approved and paid.
Dec. 15	A 5p per share interim ordinary dividend was declared and paid.
2018 Jan. 31	The directors made a one-for-five tradeable rights offer to ordinary 'B' shareholders at an issue price of £1.50 per share. The offer's expiry date was 28 February 2018.
Feb. 28	Holders of 120 000 shares accepted the rights offer. Shares were issued, with monies payable by 15 March 2018.
Mar. 15	All monies were received.
June 30	Profit for the year was £56 000. The directors, in lieu of declaring a final dividend, made a 1-for-10 bonus issue from the general reserve to all shareholders. Ordinary 'A' shares were valued at £1.20 each, ordinary 'B' shares were valued at £1.60 each and preference shares were valued at £1.15 each.
Nov. 30	Holders of 40 000 options exercised their options, and 40 000 ordinary 'A' shares were issued. Monies were payable by 20 December 2018.
Dec. 20	All monies were received.
2019 Jan. 10	A 5p per share interim ordinary dividend was declared and paid.
June 30	Profit for the year was £48 000. The directors declared a 10p per share final dividend and the preference dividend, both payable on 30 September 2019. The dividend has not yet been approved by the AGM.

Required

(a) Prepare general journal entries and closing entries to record the above transactions and events.
(b) Prepare reconciliations for the following accounts for the period 30 June 2016 to 30 June 2019:
  • Share capital (Ordinary 'A')
  • Share capital (Ordinary 'B')
  • Share capital (Preference).

Equity transactions can be broadly classified into one of the following three categories: (1) issue of shares, inclusive of employee share options; (2) share buy-back and (3) cash dividends. Starting with new share issues the academic literature has been largely concerned with attempts by managers to influence share prices and hence proceeds by the means of earnings management and abnormal accruals.[1] However, the academic literature has provided conflicting evidence as to the relation between abnormal accruals (a measure of earnings management) and pricing of new share issues. One strand of the literature argues that earnings in initial public offerings (IPOs) are inflated by managers because they attempt to increase IPO proceeds or IPO valuation. Teoh et al. (1998b) provide evidence suggesting that IPO managers inflate earnings and that the market is misled by this. They reach this conclusion from observing subsequent poor share price performance for earnings-inflating firms. Teoh and Wong (2002) report that analysts systematically fail to detect earnings management in IPOs and seasoned equity offerings (SEOs) and this may be a contributing factor to the post-issue share performance. Teoh et al. (1998a) examine SEOs and find evidence consistent with naive reaction of equity investors to earnings management pre-SEO. Shivakumar (2000), in contrast, shows that stock returns at the time when firms announce SEOs are negatively related to previously announced abnormal accruals. His evidence thus suggests that the SEO announcement prompts investors to revise their assessment of prior earnings, but also suggests that earnings management misleads market participants, at least for some time. A different view developed in the literature suggests that only strong IPOs inflate earnings as a costly signal of quality (Fan, 2007). According to this theory, earnings management is priced. However, this is not because investors are misled, rather because they understand that only good firms can inflate earnings and sustain the potential cost of litigation that earnings inflation may entail.

When firms issue share options they typically do so in the context of employee compensation, in particular CEO compensation. This practice is commonly known as employee stock options, or ESOP. One typical feature of ESOP is that the exercise price is set equal to the share price on the grant day. The lower the exercise price, the greater the scope for managers to make a gain on their options when they are exercised. Yermack (1997) finds evidence of positive abnormal stock returns in the two days following the grant of ESOP. He argues that this is consistent with managers that time the terms of the ESOP to gain from lower share price, and hence exercise price. Aboody and Kasznik (2000) further show that managers delay voluntary disclosure of good news but advance disclosure of bad news before the grant day. Both studies therefore support the notion that managers manipulate the terms of the ESOP.

Returning money to shareholders can be done via either share buy-back or cash dividend. Skinner (2008) estimates that both methods were of similar magnitude in the mid-2000s, whereas share buy-back used to be smaller in magnitude in earlier years. Recently, the fraction of firms that only pay dividend has become very small. Skinner (2008) further reports that share buy-back programmes respond to variations in earnings more than cash dividends do. That is, dividends are quite 'sticky' and are largely unrelated to profitability.

Accounting researchers have been in particular interested in understanding what dividend and share buy-back programmes imply about past and future earnings and whether the information content in share buy-back or dividend announcements is incremental to the information content of earnings. With respect to share buy-back programmes the literature has distinguished between two forms. The first is called share repurchase tender offer. Here the firm asks shareholders to submit their offer as to how many shares they are willing to sell back to the firm and at what price. The firm then decides which offers to accept. The second method is an open-market buy-back programme. Under this method the company announces its plan to buy shares on the open market and, occasionally, how much cash is set aside for this purpose. Bartov (1991) claims that tender offers command a greater amount of cash that is distributed back to shareholders and hence the information content of these announcements may differ. For open-market offers he finds that earnings announced by repurchasing firms *before* tender offers outperform analyst expectations more than earnings announced by non-purchasing firms. Hertzel and Jain (1991) examine tender offers and find that analysts revise their forecasts of future (short-term) earnings upwards for firms announcing repurchases. Taken together these studies suggest that share buy-back programmes are triggered by strong performance in the past but also indicate managers' expectations about future performance. These findings notwithstanding, it is not clear why managers engage in share buy-back programmes in practice. Survey evidence indicates that managers buy-back shares when they feel the share price is too low, or as a means to increase earnings per share, not necessarily to convey information about future earnings (Brav et al., 2005).

The Academic Perspective of chapter 1 discusses the information content, or value relevance, of earnings. A similar issue arises with dividends — are they informative? Furthermore, are they informative *incrementally* to earnings? One concern about the informativeness of dividends is that, unlike share repurchases, they are very 'sticky' and do not change much, suggesting they do not normally convey much news. Additionally, managers are reluctant to reduce dividends because they expect negative market reaction (Brav et al., 2005). To investigate the information content of dividends Aharony and Swary (1980) investigate quarterly dividend and earnings announcements made on different dates (i.e., not concurrently). Most dividend announcements follow earnings announcements, but consistent with dividend 'stickiness,' only 13% of sample firms change their dividends. The authors find that firms announcing dividend increases (decreases) experience positive (negative) abnormal stock

---

[1] Earnings management refers to selection by managers of accounting policies, estimates and other assessments with the intention of meeting certain objectives.

returns (returns that are measured relative to the overall market return) on the announcement date. They also find that this was the case regardless of whether the dividend announcement preceded or followed the earnings announcement. Therefore they conclude that changes in dividends do convey information incrementally to earnings. Healy and Palepu (1988) take this line of inquiry further by looking at specific type of changes: dividend initiations and omissions. They find that companies that start paying dividends experienced earnings growth prior and after the dividend initiation. The opposite holds for firms that omit dividend payments. They also find that initiations and omissions provide incremental predictive power for future earnings over and above changes in prior earnings. However, some of these results were contested in subsequent studies (see Lie, 2005 for a summary of the follow-up literature as well as some more recent evidence).

Another form of dividend is stock dividend, or share bonus. However, unlike normal dividends (or share buyback), share bonus does not use cash and so the value of the company should remain unaffected, ignoring relatively minor administrative expenses. The same argument holds for stock splits. Nevertheless, this practice is not unusual and therefore begs the question: why do companies engage in it? Intrigued by evidence that such share issues are rewarded by capital markets, Lakonishok and Lev (1987) look at this question from the perspective of earnings growth. They find that firms that split their shares experienced a robust earnings growth in the 5-year period before the split. But this does not hold for firms using share dividends. Further examining stock returns they conclude that the aim of stock split is to bring high stock prices to a normal level. Asquith et al. (1989) provide additional evidence suggesting that share split announcements are perceived by the market to be associated with permanent earnings growth rather than a transitory one. This suggests that managers can communicate their positive outlook of firm performance via splits.

References

Aboody, D., and Kasznik, R., 2002. CEO stock option awards and the timing of corporate voluntary disclosures. *Journal of Accounting and Economics* 29, 73–100.

Aharony, J., and Swary, I., 1980. Quarterly dividend and earnings announcements and stockholders'

returns: an empirical analysis. *Journal of Finance*, 35, 1–12.

Asquith, P., Healy, P., and Palepu, K., 1989. Earnings and stock splits. *The Accounting Review*, 64(3), 387–403.

Bartov, E., 1991. Open-market stock repurchases as signals for earnings and risk changes. *Journal of Accounting and Economics*, 14, 275–294.

Brav, A., Graham, J. R., Harvey, C. R., and Michaely, R., 2005. Payout policy in the 21st century. *Journal of Financial Economics*, 77, 483–527.

Fan, Q., 2007. Earnings management and ownership retention for initial public offering firms: Theory and evidence. *The Accounting Review*, 82, 27–64.

Healy, P.M., and Palepu, K.G., 1988. Earnings information conveyed by dividend initiations and omissions. *Journal of Financial Economics*, 21, 149–175.

Hertzel, M., and Jain, P., 1991. Earnings and risk changes around stock repurchase tender offers. *Journal of Accounting and Economics*, 11, 253–274.

Lakonishok, J., and Lev, B., 1987. Stock splits and stock dividends: Why, who, and when. *The Journal of Finance*, 42(4), 913–932.

Lie, E., 2005. Operating performance following dividend decreases and omissions. *Journal of Corporate Finance*, 12, 27–53.

Shivakumar, L., 2000. Do firms mislead investors by overstating earnings before seasoned equity offerings? *Journal of Accounting and Economics*, 29(3), 339–371.

Skinner, D. J., 2008. The evolving relation between earnings, dividends, and stock repurchases. *Journal of Financial Economics*, 87, 582–609.

Teoh, S. H., Welch I., and Wong, T. J., 1998a. Earnings management and the underperformance of seasoned equity offerings. *Journal of Financial Economics*, 50, 63–99.

Teoh, S. H., Welch I., and Wong, T. J., 1998b. Earnings management and the long-run market performance of initial public offerings. *Journal of Finance*, 53(6), 1935–1974.

Teoh, S. H., and Wong, T. J., 2002. Why new issues and high-accrual firms underperform: The role of analysts' credulity. *Review of Financial Studies*, 15(3), 863–900.

Yermack, D., 1997. Good timing: CEO stock option awards and company news announcements. *The Journal of Finance*, 52, 449–476.

3

Fair value measurement

ACCOUNTING STANDARDS IN FOCUS

IFRS 13 *Fair Value Measurement*

LEARNING OBJECTIVES

After studying this chapter, you should be able to:

1. explain the need for an accounting standard on fair value measurement
2. understand the key characteristics of the term 'fair value'
3. understand the key concepts used in the fair value framework
4. explain the steps in determining the fair value of non-financial assets
5. understand how to measure the fair value of liabilities
6. explain how to measure the fair value of an entity's own equity instruments
7. discuss issues relating to the measurement of the fair value of financial instruments
8. prepare the disclosures required by IFRS 13 *Fair Value Measurement*.

3.1 INTRODUCTION

3.1.1 The need for a standard on fair value

Under accounting standards issued by the International Accounting Standards Board (IASB®), there are various ways in which assets are required to be measured. Many standards specify how assets are to be initially recognised, and some standards specify or give choices on measurement subsequent to initial recognition. The two main measures used are cost and fair value, for example:

- Paragraph 15 of IAS 16 *Property, Plant and Equipment* requires an item of property, plant and equipment that qualifies for recognition as an asset to be measured initially at its cost.
- Paragraph 24 of IAS 38 *Intangible Assets* requires intangible assets to be measured initially at cost.
- Paragraph 43 of IAS 39 *Financial Instruments: Recognition and Measurement* requires financial assets to be measured at fair value.
- Both IAS 16 and IAS 38 allow entities the choice, subsequent to initial recognition, of measuring assets using the cost model or the revaluation model.

Other measurement methods used in accounting standards include net realisable value, fair value less costs of disposal, recoverable amount and value in use.

In relation to the measurement of liabilities, IAS 39 requires financial liabilities to be measured at fair value, while non-financial liabilities are measured, in accordance with paragraph 36 of IAS 37 *Provisions, Contingent Liabilities and Contingent Assets*, at the best estimate of the expenditure required to settle the present obligation.

Prior to 2011, many accounting standards defined the term 'fair value' as:

> The amount for which an asset could be exchanged, or a liability settled, between knowledgeable, willing parties in an arm's length transaction.

Various accounting standards also provided guidance on the measurement of fair value, such as IAS 38 *Intangible Assets*, which provided a hierarchy of fair value measurement, and IAS 40 *Investment Property*, which contained a discussion of the meaning of 'a transaction between knowledgeable, willing parties'. However, despite this, there was generally limited guidance in IFRS® Standards on how to measure fair value and, in some cases, the guidance was conflicting. To remedy this, the IASB undertook a convergence project with the US FASB. In May 2009, the IASB issued the exposure draft *Fair Value Measurement*.

Three reasons for issuing the exposure draft were given in the Introduction:

(a) to establish a single source of guidance for all fair value measurements required or permitted by IFRSs to reduce complexity and improve consistency in their application;
(b) to clarify the definition of fair value and related guidance in order to communicate the measurement objective more clearly;
(c) to enhance disclosures about fair value to enable users of financial statements to assess the extent to which fair value is used and to inform them about the inputs used to derive those fair values.

Some constituents noted that if the IASB were to advocate its fair value approach on the grounds of relevance, this position is only tenable if the meaning of fair value is both clear and unambiguous and if the fair value of an asset and liability can be measured with sufficient reliability to justify its use as the primary basis of asset and liability measurement. An accounting standard on fair value measurement would hopefully allay such concerns about the use of fair value to measure assets and liabilities.

In preparing a separate accounting standard on the measurement of fair value, the IASB was *not* proposing to introduce new requirements for the use of fair value as the required measurement method or to eliminate current practicability exceptions to the measurement of fair value, such as that in IAS 41 *Agriculture*.

The Boards' joint discussions resulted in the issuance of IFRS 13 *Fair Value Measurement*, in May 2011, and amendments to ASC (Accounting Standards Codification) 820 and created a generally uniform framework for applying fair value measurement in both IFRS and US GAAP.

3.1.2 The objectives of IFRS 13

A primary goal of IFRS 13 is to increase the consistency and comparability of fair value measurements used in financial reporting. The objectives of IFRS 13 are succinctly stated in paragraph 1:

- to define fair value
- to set out in a single standard a framework for measuring fair value
- to require disclosures about fair value measurement.

3.1.3 When does IFRS 13 apply?

IFRS 13 applies whenever another accounting standard requires or permits the measurement or disclosure (i.e. those items that are not measured at fair value, but whose fair value is required to be disclosed) of fair value or measures based on fair value (e.g. fair value less costs of disposal). It also specifies when and what information about fair value measurement is to be disclosed.

IFRS 13 does not apply to share-based payment transactions within IFRS 2 *Share-based Payment;* leasing transactions within the scope of IAS 17 *Leases;* and measurements that have similarities to, but are not, fair value, such as net realisable value in IAS 2 *Inventories* or value in use in IAS 36 *Impairment of Assets.*

3.2 THE DEFINITION OF FAIR VALUE

Fair value is defined in Appendix A of IFRS 13 as:

> The price that would be received to sell an asset or paid to transfer a liability in an orderly transaction between market participants at the measurement date.

The definition of fair value in IFRS 13 is not significantly different from previous definitions in IFRS — that is, 'the amount for which an asset could be exchanged, or a liability settled, between knowledgeable, willing parties in an arm's length transaction'. In both definitions the measurement of fair value is not based on an actual transaction, but a hypothetical one. In addition, it assumes an orderly transaction, not a forced transaction or a distress sale.

So, why change the definition of fair value? Paragraph BC30 provides three reasons:

1. The previous definition did not specify whether an entity was buying or selling the asset. As such, it was uncertain whether fair value was an exit (selling) price or an entry (buying) price. The new definition requires the use of an exit price.
2. In the previous definition, it was unclear what was meant by 'settling' a liability with knowledgeable parties. Does this mean the creditor or other parties? The new definition requires measurement by reference to the transfer of a liability to a party who may not be the creditor.
3. There was no explicit statement in the previous definition as to whether the exchange or settlement took place at the measurement date or at some other date. The new definition specifies that fair value is the price at the measurement date.

In addition, the revised definition clarifies that fair value is a market-based measurement, not an entity-specific measurement, and, as such, is determined based on the assumptions that market participants would use in pricing the asset or liability (paragraph BC31).

3.2.1 Current exit price

Exit price is defined in Appendix A of IFRS 13 as follows:

> The price that would be received to sell an asset or paid to transfer a liability.

Paragraph 57 of IFRS 13 notes that, when an entity acquires an asset or assumes a liability in an exchange transaction, the transaction price is the amount paid by the entity. This is an *entry* price. In contrast, the fair value of the asset or liability is the price that would be received to sell the asset or paid to transfer the liability. This is an *exit* price.

Importantly, the definition of fair value is that it is an exit price based on the perspective of the entity that holds the asset or owes the liability.

An exit price is based on expectations about the future cash flows that will be generated by the asset subsequent to the sale of the asset or transfer of the liability. These cash flows may be generated from use of the asset or from sale of the asset by the acquiring entity. Even if the entity holding the asset intends to use it rather than sell it, fair value is measured as an exit price by reference to the sale of the asset to a market participant who will use the asset or sell it.

Similarly, with a liability, an entity may continue to hold a liability until settlement or transfer the liability to another entity. The fair value in both cases is based on market participants' expectations about cash outflows by the entity.

According to paragraph BC44 of the Basis for Conclusions to IFRS 13, the IASB concluded that a current entry price and a current exit price will be equal when they relate to the same asset or liability on the same date in the same form in the same market. However, valuation experts informed the IASB that, in a business combination, an exit price for an asset or liability acquired or assumed might differ from an exchange price — entry or exit — if:

- an entity's intended use for an acquired asset is different from its highest and best use
- a liability is measured on the basis of settling it with the creditor rather than transferring it to a third party.

The equivalence of exit prices and entry prices was questioned by Ernst & Young (2009, p. 5) in their response to the IASB exposure draft:

> The ED seems to minimise any distinction between measurements based on entry prices versus exit prices, based on a belief that a current entry price and a current exit price are equal when they relate to the same asset or liability in the same market. In our view, this conclusion is only true for assets and liabilities that trade in active markets, as it takes competitive market forces to derive a single price. The price in a principal-to-principal

transaction that occurs outside of an active market is the result of a unique negotiation between buyer and seller, considering the specific attributes of both parties in the transaction, but not other market participants. As such, an entity may negotiate a different price in a transaction to sell the asset to one party than it would pay to buy the same asset from another party. In practice, we believe many constituents relate an entry price notion as more akin to an entity-specific measurement, whereas exit price is clearly a market-based measurement. The Board should consider such limitations when it evaluates the decision usefulness of fair value measures versus other measurement objectives, such as value in use.

This distinction between an entry price and exit price is significant and can have important implications for the initial recognition of assets and liabilities at fair value. Prior to the issuance of IFRS 13, it was common for entities to use the transaction price as fair value of an asset or liability on its initial recognition. Therefore, an entity must determine whether the transaction price represents the fair value of an asset or liability at initial recognition and paragraph B4 of IFRS 13 provides certain factors that an entity should consider in making this determination.

3.2.2 Orderly transactions

The definition of fair value requires that an asset be sold or a liability transferred in an orderly transaction. An orderly transaction is not a forced or distressed sale, such as occurs in liquidations. It assumes that, before the measurement date, there is sufficient time and exposure to a market to allow the usual marketing activities to take place for that transaction.

Fair value is measured by considering a hypothetical transaction in a market. To determine that fair value, the entity will make observations in current markets. The markets to be observed must be those containing orderly transactions. Prices of goods sold in a liquidation or 'fire sale' are not appropriate to include in the measurement. Similarly, prices between entities that are not at arm's length are not prices from orderly transactions.

While fair value assumes an orderly transaction, in practice entities may need to consider prices from such transactions or from markets where there has been a decline in trading. An example relates to 2011 trading activity for Greek sovereign bonds. During that calendar year, the economic situation in Greece had deteriorated and some had questioned whether the Greek sovereign bonds were still being actively traded.

IFRS 13 is clear that fair value remains a market-based exit price that considers the current market conditions as at the measurement date, even if there has been a significant decrease in the volume and level of activity for the asset or liability (paragraph 15). Therefore, paragraphs B37–B47 of Appendix B provide guidance to assist entities in measuring fair value when the volume or level of activity for an asset or a liability has significantly decreased.

3.2.3 Transaction and transportation costs

Both transaction and transport costs affect the determination of the fair value of an asset or liability. However, the price used to measure fair value is not adjusted for transaction costs, but would consider transportation costs.

Transaction costs are the incremental direct costs, that are essential to the transaction, to sell an asset or transfer a liability and are defined as the costs that would be incurred in the principal (or most advantageous) market and are directly attributable to the sale or transfer. Similar to other requirements, incremental costs are those that would not otherwise have been incurred had the entity not decided to enter into the transaction to sell or transfer.

Transportation costs are those that would be incurred to move the asset to the principal (or most advantageous) market.

As discussed in section 3.3.2, when determining the most advantageous market (in the absence of a principal market), an entity takes into consideration the transaction costs and transportation costs it would incur to sell the asset or transfer the liability. However, the price in that market that is used to measure the fair value of an asset or liability is not adjusted for transaction costs. The reason for this is that transaction costs are not considered to be a characteristic of the asset or liability. Instead they are specific to a transaction and will change from transaction to transaction.

An asset may have to be transported from its present location to the principal (or most advantageous) market. As the location of an asset or a liability is a characteristic of the asset or liability, it will have a different fair value because of associated transport costs. For example, if an entity located in a capital city is considering buying a vehicle, then a vehicle located in a country town has a different fair value compared to one located in the capital city because of the transport costs associated with moving the vehicle from the country town. A price in the principal (or most advantageous) market is then adjusted for the transport costs. In contrast, transaction costs, such as registration costs, are not a characteristic of the asset. Illustrative example 3.1 shows how transport costs and transaction costs are considered in the measurement of fair value.

ILLUSTRATIVE EXAMPLE 3.1 Transaction costs and transport costs

Entity A holds a physical commodity measured at fair value in its warehouse in Europe. For this commodity, the London exchange is determined to be the principal market as it represents the market with the greatest volume and level of activity for the asset that the entity can reasonably access.

The exchange price for the asset is £25. However, the contracts traded on the exchange for this commodity require physical delivery to London. Entity A determines that it would cost £5 to transport the physical commodity to London and the broker's commission would be £3 to transact on the London exchange.

Since location is a characteristic of the asset and transportation to the principal market is required, the fair value of the physical commodity would be £20 — the price in the principal market for the asset £25, less transportation costs of £5. The £3 broker commission represents a transaction cost; therefore, no adjustment is made to the price in the principal market used to measure fair value.

Source: Adapted from EY, *International GAAP 2015*, Volume 1, Chapter 14 *Fair value measurement*, Section 9.2, Example 14.10, p. 973.

3.3 THE FAIR VALUE FRAMEWORK

In addition to providing a single definition of fair value, IFRS 13 includes a framework for applying this definition to financial reporting. Many of the key concepts used in the fair value framework are interrelated and their interaction needs to be considered in the context of the entire approach.

When measuring fair value, paragraph B2 of IFRS 13 requires an entity to determine all of the following:
- the particular asset or liability that is the subject of the measurement (consistent with its unit of account) — *see section 3.3.1*.
- for a non-financial asset, the valuation premise that is appropriate for the measurement (consistent with its highest and best use) — *see section 3.4*.
- the principal (or most advantageous) market for the asset or liability — *see section 3.3.2*.
- the valuation technique(s) appropriate for the measurement, considering the available inputs that represent market participants assumptions and their categorisation within the fair value hierarchy — *see sections 3.3.3 to 3.3.5*.

IFRS 13 provides specific requirements to assist entities in applying its fair value framework to:

(a) non-financial assets;
(b) liabilities and an entity's own equity instruments; and
(c) financial instruments with offsetting risks.

This application guidance is discussed in sections 3.4 to 3.7.

3.3.1 What is the particular asset or liability that is the subject of the measurement?

Paragraph 11 of IFRS 13 clarifies that in order to measure fair value for a particular asset or liability, an entity must take into account those characteristics that exist at the measurement date that a market participant would consider when pricing the asset or liability. Some of the key questions that need to be asked when determining the asset or liability to be measured are:
- *What is the unit of account? Is the asset a stand-alone asset or is it a group of assets?* The unit of account defines what is to be measured. Other standards specify this — that is, the level at which an asset or liability is aggregated or disaggregated for financial reporting purposes (Appendix A of IFRS 13). For example, where a fair value is being calculated for impairment purposes, the assets being valued may be a single asset or a cash generating unit, as defined in IAS 36. Similarly, if the fair value relates to a business, the definition of a business in IFRS 3 *Business Combinations* would need to be considered.
- *Are there any restrictions on sale or use of the asset or transfer of the liability?* There may be legal limits on the use of the asset (e.g. patents, licences or expiry dates of related lease contracts). A restriction that would transfer with the asset in an assumed sale would generally be a characteristic of the asset that market participants would consider. However, a restriction that is specific to the entity that holds the asset would not transfer with the asset and, therefore, would not be considered. A liability or an entity's own equity instrument may be subject to restrictions that prevent its transfer. IFRS 13 does not allow an entity to include a separate input (or an adjustment to other inputs) for such restrictions because the effect will either implicitly or explicitly be included in other inputs.
- *What is the condition of the asset?* Many of the factors that are considered in depreciating an asset will be of relevance, such as remaining useful life, physical condition, expected usage, and technical or commercial obsolescence.

- *What is the location of the asset?* If the location of a non-financial asset is different from the market in which it would hypothetically be sold, the asset would need to be transported in order to sell it. In such cases, location is considered a characteristic of the asset and the costs to transport the asset to market would be deducted from the price received in order to measure fair value.

A further consideration relates to whether or not the size of an entity's holding can be considered. Assume, for example, that an entity holds 100 shares that it needs to measure at fair value. The unit of account is the individual financial instrument. So, in order to measure fair value, does the entity use the price to sell a single share or the block of 100 shares? In general, the price per unit would be expected to fall if a large volume of the units were being sold as a package. This is referred to as a 'block discount' arising because the volume is a 'blockage factor'. Paragraph 69 prohibits the use of a blockage factor, arguing that a blockage factor is not relevant. As noted in paragraph BC42 of the Basis for Conclusions on IFRS 13, the transaction being considered between the market participants is a hypothetical transaction, and as such, the determination of fair value does not consider any entity-specific factors that might influence the transaction. The size of an entity's holding is entity-specific. Therefore, fair value must be measured based on the unit of account of the asset or liability being measured.

In addition to the above, for non-financial assets, an entity must consider the highest and best use of the asset and the valuation premise. *This is discussed further in section 3.4.*

3.3.2 What is the principal (or most advantageous) market for the asset?

When measuring fair value, an entity is required to assume that the hypothetical transaction to sell the asset or transfer the liability takes place either (paragraph 16):

(a) in the *principal market* for the asset or liability; or
(b) in the absence of a principal market, in the *most advantageous market* for the asset or liability.

Appropriately determining the relevant exit market is important because an entity needs to determine the market participants to whom it would sell the asset or transfer the liability, *as is discussed in section 3.3.3.*

IFRS 13 is clear that, if there is a principal market for the asset or liability, the fair value measurement represents the price in that market at the measurement date (regardless of whether that price is directly observable or estimated using another valuation technique). The price in the principal market must be used even if the price in a different market is potentially more advantageous (paragraph 18).

Appendix A contains a definition of principal market, as follows:

The market with the greatest volume and level of activity for the asset or liability.

The principal market is, therefore, the deepest and most liquid market for the non-financial asset. However, an entity need not make an exhaustive search of all markets in order to determine which market is the principal market. IFRS 13 presumes that the market in which the entity usually enters to sell this type of asset or liability is the principal market, unless evidence to the contrary exists (paragraph 17).

Where there is no principal market, the entity needs to determine the most advantageous market.

The determination of the most advantageous market is based on a comparison of the amounts that would be received from transacting for the asset or liability in a number of markets. The most advantageous market is the one that offers the highest return when selling an asset or requires the lowest payment when transferring a liability, after taking into consideration transportation and transaction costs. Illustrative example 3.2 provides an example of determining the principal market and the most advantageous market.

ILLUSTRATIVE EXAMPLE 3.2 Principal market and most advantageous market

The following three markets exist for Entity A's fleet of vehicles. Entity A has the ability to transact in all three markets. The entity has 100 vehicles (same make, model and mileage) that it needs to measure at fair value. Volumes and prices in the respective markets are as follows:

Market	Price	The entity's volume for the asset in the market (based on history and/or intent)	Total market-based volume for the asset	Transportation costs	Transaction costs
A	£27 000	60%	15%	£3 500	£1 100
B	£25 000	25%	75%	£2 300	£900
C	£23 000	15%	10%	£900	£800

Based on this information, Market B would be the principal market as this is the market in which the majority of transactions for the asset occur. As such, the fair value of the 100 vehicles as at the measurement date would be £2.27 million (£22 700 = £25 000 per car – transportation costs of £2300). Actual sales of the assets in either Market A or C would result in a gain or loss to the entity, i.e. when compared to the fair value of £25 000.

If none of the markets is the principal market for the asset, the fair value of the asset would be measured using the price in the most advantageous market.

The most advantageous market is the one that maximises the amount that would be received to sell the asset, after considering transaction costs and transportation costs (i.e. the net amount that would be received in the respective markets).

In Market A, the net amount received by the entity is £22 400 (= £27 000 – £3500 – £1100).

In Market B, the net amount received by the entity is £21 800 (= £25 000 – £2300 – £900).

In Market C, the net amount received by the entity is £21 300 (= £23 000 – £900 – £800).

Since the net amount that would be received is higher in Market A, that is the most advantageous market for the entity. Therefore, the fair value of each vehicle is £23 500, being the amount received net of transportation costs. Please note that although transaction costs are used to determine the most advantageous market, they are not used in the measurement of fair value.

Source: Adapted from EY, *International GAAP 2015*, Volume 1, Chapter 14 *Fair value measurement*, Section 6.1.2, Example 14.16, p. 955.

The principal (or most advantageous) market is considered from the perspective of the reporting entity, which means that it could be different for different entities. An entity may also be able to access different markets at different points of time — that is, not all markets are always accessible to the entity. The principal (or most advantageous) market must be one that the entity can access at the measurement date (paragraph 19).

The IASB reasoned that the principal market was the most liquid market and provided the most representative input for a fair value measurement (paragraph BC52 of the Basis for Conclusions to IFRS 13). The IASB also believed that most entities made operational decisions based upon an objective of maximisation of profits; therefore entities would choose the most advantageous market in which to conduct operations. The most advantageous market would then often be the market that the entity usually enters, or expects to enter.

In some cases, there may be no observable market in which transactions take place for an asset or liability — for example, a patent or a trademark. Where this occurs, an entity must assume that a transaction takes place at the measurement date. The assumed transaction establishes a basis for estimating the price to sell the asset or transfer the liability.

3.3.3 Who are the market participants?

Market participants are 'buyers and sellers in the principal (or most advantageous) market for the asset or liability' (IFRS 13 Appendix A). IFRS 13 assumes they have all of the following characteristics:

- *They are independent of each other, that is, they are not related parties.* As a result, the hypothetical transaction is assumed to take place between market participants at the measurement date, not between the reporting entity and another market participant. While market participants are not related parties, the standard does allow the price in a related party transaction to be used as an input in a fair value measurement provided the entity has evidence the transaction was entered into at market terms.
- *They are knowledgeable, having a reasonable understanding about the asset or liability using all available information.* Market participants should have sufficient knowledge before transacting. However, this knowledge does not necessarily need to come from publicly available information. It could be obtained in the course of a normal due diligence process.
- *They are able and willing to enter into a transaction for the asset or liability.* When determining potential market participants, certain characteristics should be considered, including the legal capability and the operating or financial capacity of an entity to purchase the asset or assume the liability. As well as being able to transact, market participants must be willing to do so. That is, they are motivated but not forced or otherwise compelled to transact.

When measuring fair value, an entity is required to use the assumptions that market participants would use when pricing the asset or liability. Fair value is not the value specific to the reporting entity and it is not the specific value to any one market participant that may have a greater incentive to transact than other market participants. The reporting entity should consider those factors that market participants, in general, would consider.

There is no need to identify specific market participants. The focus should be on the characteristics of the participants (paragraph 22). For example, it is not necessary to identify, say, ArcelorMittal S.A. or Nippon Steel & Sumitomo Metal Corporation as potential market participants; rather, the entity would identify market participants as large steel producers and consider the characteristics of such producers.

Determining these characteristics takes into consideration factors that are specific to the asset or liability *(see section 3.3.1)*; the principal (or most advantageous) market *(see section 3.3.2)*; and the market participants in that market (paragraph 23).

The proposal that the fair value should not be an entity-specific value was questioned by Nestlé in its response to the IASB on its exposure draft. Nestlé (2009, p. 3) made the following comment:

> Such a market-based measurement method should be driven by the market in which the entity operates. We consequently believe that the entity being a market participant itself must consider assumptions that other market participants would use in pricing the asset or liability in addition to its own entity-specific assumptions.

Ernst & Young (2009, pp. 4–5) in its response to the IASB exposure draft noted that it was important to consider the trade-off between relevance and reliability in assessing the measurement of fair value:

> [W]e believe that choosing a measurement basis for any asset or liability includes evaluating the balance between the relevance of the information provided and its reliability with respect to fair value. Such an assessment includes weighing the relevance of market participant assumptions versus entity-specific assumptions in predicting expected future cash inflows and outflows associated with an asset or liability. This evaluation also includes assessing the trade-off between the potential for management bias in entity-specific assumptions versus the subjectivity of market-based assumptions for assets and liabilities without an active market.

3.3.4 What are the appropriate valuation techniques for the measurement?

Having determined the nature of the asset being valued (including additional considerations for non-financial assets, *discussed in section 3.4 below*) and the principal (or most advantageous) market (the exit market) in which the asset would be sold or liability transferred, the next step is to determine the appropriate valuation technique(s) and inputs *(see section 3.3.5)* to use to estimate the exit price.

The appropriateness of a valuation technique and inputs may vary depending on the level of activity in the exit market. However, the objective of a fair value measurement does not change depending on the level of activity or the valuation technique(s) used (paragraph 62).

The following three possible valuation approaches are noted in paragraph 62. Within the application of each of these approaches, there may be a number of possible valuation techniques.

- The *market approach*: based on market transactions involving identical or similar assets or liabilities.
- The *income approach*: based on future amounts (e.g. cash flows or income and expenses) that are converted (discounted) to a single present amount. The fair value is based upon market expectations about future cash flows, or income and expenses associated with that asset. Present value techniques are an example of techniques used in applying the income approach. The fair value of an asset is then not based on an observed market price but rather is generated by discounting the expected earnings from the use of the asset by a market participant. Paragraphs B13–B30 of Appendix B provide details about present value techniques.
- The *cost approach*: based on the amount required to replace the service capacity of an asset (often referred to as current replacement cost). This may involve consideration of the amount to be paid for a new asset, with this amount then adjusted for both physical deterioration and technological obsolescence.

IFRS 13 does not propose a hierarchy of valuation techniques (with the exception of the requirement to measure identical financial instruments that trade in active markets at price multiplied by quantity $(P \times Q)$). Instead, it prioritises the inputs used in the application of these techniques *(see section 3.3.5)*. Some valuation techniques are better in some circumstances than in others. Significant judgement is required in selecting the appropriate valuation technique for the situation. Sufficient knowledge of the asset or liability and an adequate level of expertise regarding the valuation techniques is also needed. However, some guidance in the choice of technique is provided in IFRS 13:

- The technique must be appropriate to the circumstances (paragraph 61).
- There must be sufficient data available to apply the technique (paragraph 61).
- The technique must maximise the use of observable inputs and minimise the use of unobservable inputs (paragraph 61).
- In some cases, multiple techniques may be appropriate. This is likely to result in a range of possible values. Therefore, an entity must evaluate the reasonableness of the range and select the point within the range that is most representative of fair value in the circumstances (paragraph 63). This could include weighting the results. However, evaluating the range does not necessarily require calibration of the approaches (i.e. the results from different approaches do not have to be equal). Paragraph 40 indicates that a wide range of fair value measurements may indicate that further analysis is needed.
- Valuation techniques used to measure fair value must be consistently applied. Paragraph 65 provides examples of situations where a change in technique may be appropriate, such as when new markets develop or new information becomes available.

Use of different valuation techniques is shown in illustrative example 3.3.

ILLUSTRATIVE EXAMPLE 3.3 Valuation techniques

MediaCo is a newspaper and magazine publishing company. It previously acquired another publishing company that had two weekly newspapers and five monthly magazines. As a result of a sustained decline in circulation for the two newspapers, MediaCo tests the related cash-generating units (including the newspaper mastheads) for impairment in accordance with IAS 36 and measures the fair value less costs of disposal.

MediaCo concludes the market and income approaches could be applied as follows:
- The market approach is applied by using prices for comparable business combinations, adjusted for differences between those business combinations and each cash-generating unit (including location, circulation) and changes in market conditions since those business combinations took place.
- The income approach is applied using a present value technique. The expected cash flows reflect market participants' expectations were a buyer to operate each cash-generating unit, in light of anticipated market conditions, including expectations about future circulation.

3.3.5 Which inputs should be used when measuring fair value?

Selecting inputs

According to Appendix A of IFRS 13, inputs are:

> The assumptions that market participants would use when pricing the asset or liability, including assumptions about risk, such as the following:
>
> (a) the risk inherent in a particular valuation technique used to measure fair value (such as a pricing model); and
> (b) the risk inherent in the inputs to the valuation technique.
>
> Inputs may be observable or unobservable.

Observable inputs are defined in Appendix A as:

> Inputs that are developed using market data, such as publicly available information about actual events or transactions, and reflect the assumptions that market participants would use when pricing the asset or liability.

Unobservable inputs are defined in Appendix A as:

> Inputs for which market data are not available and that are developed using the best information available about the assumptions that market participants would use when pricing the asset or liability.

Regardless of the selected valuation technique, the inputs an entity uses must be consistent with the characteristics of the asset or liability that market participants would take into account. In addition, inputs exclude premiums or discounts that reflect size as a characteristic of the entity's holding, as these are not a characteristic of the item being measured (for example, blockage factors, *see section 3.3.1*), and any other premiums or discounts that are inconsistent with the unit of account (paragraph 69).

Regardless of the technique used, an entity must maximise the use of observable inputs and minimise the use of unobservable inputs. Therefore, for example, an income approach valuation technique that maximises the use of observable inputs and minimises the use of unobservable inputs may provide a better measure of fair value than a market valuation technique that requires significant adjustment using unobservable inputs.

Inputs based on bid and ask prices

Some input measures are based on market prices where there are both bid prices — the price a dealer is willing to pay — and ask prices — the price a dealer is willing to sell. An example is a foreign exchange dealer who is willing to exchange one currency for another, such as exchanging Euros for Japanese Yen. In such cases paragraph 70 of IFRS 13 states that the price within a bid–ask spread that is most representative of fair value should be used to measure fair value. Paragraph 71 notes that mid-market pricing (that is, using the mid-point in the bid–ask spread), or another pricing convention that is used by market participants, may be used as a practical expedient.

Fair value hierarchy — prioritising inputs

To achieve consistency and comparability in the measurement of fair values, IFRS 13 provides a hierarchy of inputs showing which inputs are considered to be given higher priority in determining a fair value measurement.

Four important points critical to understanding the uses of these inputs are:

1. The inputs are prioritised into three levels — Level 1, Level 2 and Level 3.
2. The fair value hierarchy gives the highest priority to quoted market prices in active markets for identical assets and liabilities and the lowest priority to unobservable inputs (paragraph 72).
3. Where observable inputs are used, they must be *relevant* observable inputs (paragraph 67). As noted in paragraph BC151 of the Basis for Conclusions, some respondents to the IASB expressed concerns about being required to use observable inputs during the global financial crisis that started in 2007 when the available observable inputs were not representative of the asset or liability being measured at fair value. Observability is, therefore, not the only criterion applied when selecting inputs; the inputs must be relevant as well as observable. Market conditions may require adjustments to be made to current observable inputs in measuring fair value.
4. The availability of inputs and their relative subjectivity potentially affects the selection of the valuation technique; however, the fair value hierarchy prioritises the *inputs* to the valuation techniques, not the techniques themselves.

IFRS 13 also distinguishes between where an individual input may fall within the fair value hierarchy and where the entire measurement is categorised for disclosure purposes. *The latter is discussed in section 3.8.1.*

Level 1 inputs

Level 1 inputs are defined in Appendix A as:

> Quoted prices (unadjusted) in active markets for identical assets or liabilities that the entity can access at the measurement date.

An active market is defined in Appendix A as follows:

> A market in which transactions for the asset or liability take place with sufficient frequency and volume to provide pricing information on an ongoing basis.

Observable markets in which debt instruments, equity instruments or commodities are regularly traded on a securities exchange would likely be active markets. However, the above definitions make it clear that pricing needs to be for *identical* items. Assets such as vehicles, intangibles and buildings, and many liabilities may be similar, but will not be identical. Therefore, it is unlikely that Level 1 inputs would be available for such items.

As noted in paragraph 77, a quoted price in an active market for the identical asset or liability provides the most reliable evidence of fair value. As a result, IFRS 13 requires this price (without adjustment) to be used whenever available (also known as price multiplied by quantity, or $P \times Q$). Adjustments to this price are only permitted in the limited circumstances specified in paragraph 79 of IFRS 13.

A market may no longer be considered active if:

- there has been a significant decrease in the volume and level of activity for the asset or liability when compared with normal market activity
- there are few recent transactions
- price quotations are not based on current information
- price quotations vary substantially over time or among market-makers.

Level 2 inputs

Level 2 inputs are any inputs, other than Level 1 inputs, that are directly or indirectly observable.

These inputs, like Level 1 inputs, are observable. According to paragraph 82, level 2 inputs include:

- quoted prices for similar assets or liabilities in active markets
- quoted prices for identical or similar assets or liabilities in markets that are not active
- inputs, other than quoted prices, that are observable for the asset or liability, such as interest rates and yield curves
- inputs that are derived from, or corroborated, by observable market data by correlation or other means.

It may be necessary to make adjustments to Level 2 inputs. For example, in relation to quoted prices for similar assets, these may have to be adjusted for the condition of the assets or the location of the assets..

Paragraph B35 in Appendix B contains examples of Level 2 inputs:

- *Finished goods inventory at a retail outlet:* Level 2 inputs include either a price to customers in a retail market or a wholesale price to retailers in a wholesale market, adjusted for differences between the condition and location of the inventory item and the comparable (i.e. similar) inventory items.
- *Building held and used:* A Level 2 input would be the price per square metre for the building derived from observable market data, or derived from prices in observed transactions involving comparable buildings in similar locations.
- *Cash-generating unit:* A Level 2 input may involve obtaining a multiple of earnings or revenue from observable market data by observing transactions of similar businesses.

In all cases, the examples refer to market data or to prices being observable either directly (that is, the price itself is available) or indirectly (that is, price is derived from observable information).

Level 3 inputs

Level 3 inputs are those that are unobservable.

While Level 1 and Level 2 inputs are based on observable market data, Level 3 inputs are unobservable. The data used may be that of the entity itself, which may be adjusted for factors that market participants would build into the valuation, or to eliminate the effect of variables that are specific to this entity, but not relevant to other market participants.

Examples of Level 3 inputs include:

- *Cash-generating unit:* A Level 3 input would include a financial forecast of cash flow or earnings based on the entity's own data.
- *Trademark:* A Level 3 input would be to measure the expected royalty rate that could be obtained by allowing other entities to use the trademark to produce the products covered by the trademark.
- *Accounts receivable:* A Level 3 input would be to measure the asset based upon the amount expected to be recovered based upon the entity's historical record of recoverability of accounts receivable.

In illustrative example 3.4, an example is given where different valuation techniques could be used to measure the fair value of an asset, with a consideration of the level of inputs that might be used.

ILLUSTRATIVE EXAMPLE 3.4 Valuation techniques and inputs used

Van Hoff revalues its buildings, which are held and used, in accordance with IAS 16. All three valuation approaches could be applied to measure fair value. Van Hoff would evaluate the results of using these valuation techniques. It would consider the relevance, reliability and subjectivity of the information used in the valuations and the range of values given by the three techniques in order to select the point within the range that is most representative of fair value in the circumstances.

Market approach

Van Hoff applies the market approach using observable prices for comparable buildings in similar locations adjusted for differences between the buildings, including its location and condition. The prices for comparable buildings are Level 2 inputs. Both observable information (e.g. square-metres, age of the building) and unobservable information was used to determine the adjustments to the prices for comparable buildings. As such, the adjustments were generally Level 3 inputs.

Income approach

Van Hoff uses a present value technique using expected cash flows that reflect what market participants would expect to receive from renting the building to tenants. Van Hoff derives the price per square metre for the building and expected incentives to entice new tenants from observable market data, which are Level 2 inputs. Adjustments are made for differences in location and condition of the building. The expected cash flows also include market participants' expectations about costs to maintain the building, which Van Hoff estimates based on its own data, which are Level 3 inputs. The discount rate used is based on the risk-free rate, which is observable, but is adjusted for the premium a market participant would require to accept the uncertainty related to purchasing and renting the building. As such, the discount rate is a Level 3 input.

Cost approach

Van Hoff estimates the amount that would currently be required to construct a substitute building. Adjustments would be necessary for the effects of location and condition of the building. The inputs used are a mix of Level 2 and Level 3 inputs. Some inputs are based on observable market data; for example, costs related to materials and labour. Inputs related to estimated physical obsolescence to reflect the current condition of the building are derived from Van Hoff's own data, which is unobservable.

3.4 APPLICATION TO NON-FINANCIAL ASSETS

In addition to the general fair value framework *(discussed in section 3.3)*, the fair value of a non-financial asset must take into consideration the highest and best use of the asset from a market participant perspective. The highest and best use determines the valuation premise. *These concepts are discussed in sections 3.4.1 and 3.4.2.*

Paragraph BC63 of the Basis for Conclusions to IFRS 13 clarifies that the concepts of highest and best use and valuation premise in IFRS 13 are only relevant for non-financial assets (and not liabilities or financial assets). This is because:

- Financial assets have specific contractual terms; they do not have alternative uses. Changing the characteristics (i.e. contractual terms) of the financial asset causes the item to become a different asset and the objective of a fair value measurement is to measure the asset as it exists as at the measurement date.

- The different ways by which an entity may relieve itself of a liability (e.g. repayment) are not alternative uses. In addition, entity-specific advantages (or disadvantages) that enable an entity to fulfil a liability more or less efficiently than other market participants are not considered in a fair value measurement.

3.4.1 What is the highest and best use of a non-financial asset?

Unlike liabilities and financial assets, a non-financial asset may have several uses. The way in which the reporting entity uses a non-financial asset may not be the way market participants would use the asset. As such, the standard requires that the fair value of a non-financial asset be measured by considering the highest and best use from a market participant perspective. Highest and best use is defined in Appendix A of IFRS 13 as:

> The use of a non-financial asset by market participants that would maximise the value of the asset or the group of assets and liabilities (e.g. a business) within which the asset would be used.

Highest and best use is a valuation concept that considers how market participants would use a non-financial asset in order to maximise its benefit or value. This may come from its use: (a) in combination with other assets (or with other assets and liabilities); or (b) on a stand-alone basis. This establishes the valuation premise to be used to measure the fair value of that asset (paragraph 31).

According to paragraph 28 of IFRS 13, the highest and best use must be:

- *Physically possible*, taking into account the physical characteristics of the asset.
- *Legally permissible*, considering any legal restrictions (e.g. zoning regulations on the use of property). A use of a non-financial asset need not be legal (or have legal approval) at the measurement date, but it must not be legally prohibited in the jurisdiction (paragraph BC69).
- *Financially feasible*, in that the use of the asset must result in the market participant obtaining an appropriate return from the asset.

IFRS 13 presumes that an entity's current use of an asset is its highest and best use, unless market or other factors suggest that a different use by market participants would maximise the value of that asset (paragraph 29). On 2 November 2009, at the IASB roundtable held at the FASB offices in Norwalk in the United States, one participant argued that it is rare that the highest and best use of a commodity would be something other than its actual current use in its current form, citing that an entity with crude oil should not have to look to all the different potential uses of that oil such as refined oil, gasoline, and electricity through oil-burning plants.

Importantly, the highest and best use is determined from a market participant perspective. Therefore, despite the presumption, the highest and best use may not be the entity's current use. For example, an entity may have acquired a trademark that competes with its own trademark and chooses not to use it. If market participants would use the trademark, the current use may not be the highest and best use. Care is needed when the highest and best use is in combination with other non-financial assets to ensure that consistent assumptions are made about the highest and best use (*see illustrative example 3.6 in section 3.4.2*).

If the highest and best use of the asset is something other than its current use:

- Any costs to transform the non-financial asset (e.g. obtaining a new zoning permit or converting the asset to the alternative use) and profit expectations from a market participant's perspective are also considered in the fair value measurement.
- An entity must disclose that fact and its basis.

3.4.2 What is the valuation premise?

Depending on its highest and best use, the fair value of the non-financial asset will either be measured assuming market participants would purchase the asset to benefit from the use or sale of the asset on a stand-alone basis or in combination with other assets (or other assets and liabilities) — that is, the asset's valuation premise.

Decisions concerning the highest and best use of an asset and the relevant valuation premise are considered in illustrative examples 3.5 and 3.6.

Stand-alone valuation premise

As noted in paragraph 31(b) of IFRS 13, under this premise, the fair value of the asset is the price that would be received in a current transaction to sell the asset to market participants *who would use the asset on a stand-alone basis*.

In-combination valuation premise

When a fair value is measured under this premise, the highest and best use of the asset is where the market participants obtain maximum value through using the asset *in combination with other assets and liabilities*.

Paragraph 31(a) states that, under this premise, the fair value is measured on the basis of the price that would be received in a current transaction to sell the asset such that the purchaser could use it with other assets and liabilities as a group and that those assets and liabilities (complementary assets and liabilities) would be available to market participants. The transaction is for the individual asset, consistent with its unit of account. The fair value measurement assumes that the complementary assets and liabilities would be available to market participants. For example, as noted in paragraph B3(c) of Appendix B *Application guidance* of IFRS 13, if the asset is work-in-progress that would be converted into finished goods, in determining the fair value of the work-in-progress, it is assumed that the market participants already have or would be able to acquire any necessary machinery for that conversion process.

The fair value is what the market participants would pay for the asset being measured knowing that they can use it with those complementary assets. For some specialised assets, the market price may not capture the value the asset contributes to the group of complementary assets and liabilities because the market price would be for an unmodified, stand-alone asset. As noted in paragraph BC79 of the Basis for Conclusions on IFRS 13, the IASB recognised that in some cases an entity will need to measure fair value using another valuation technique, such as an income approach, or the cost to replace or recreate the asset.

A further question considered by the IASB was whether the exit price for specialised equipment is equal to its scrap value (paragraph BC78 of the Basis for Conclusions on IFRS 13). An item of specialised equipment would generally be used in conjunction with other assets; hence the valuation premise would be in-use rather than in-exchange. The exit price is then based on the sale of the specialised equipment to market participants who will use the specialised equipment in conjunction with other assets to obtain a return. The in-use valuation premise assumes there are market participants who will use the asset in combination with other assets and that those assets are available to them (paragraph 31 of IFRS 13). This means the answer to the question raised would generally be no.

Under IAS 36 *Impairment of Assets*, recoverable amount is determined as the higher of value in use and fair value less costs of disposal. It should be noted that there is a difference between value in use and a fair value measure determined under the in-use valuation premise as the objective of each of those measures is different. Value in use measures the expected cash flows an entity expects to receive from using those assets. This is an entity-specific value. In contrast, fair value measured under the in-use premise is based on the cash flows that market participants would expect to receive from using the asset. However, the two measures may often be the same if determined as a market-based value.

ILLUSTRATIVE EXAMPLE 3.5 Determining highest and best use and valuation premise

Addison owns 100 restaurants in a large city. Each restaurant's land and buildings are accounted for using the revaluation model in IAS 16. Addison has no intention to sell. However, in the past it has sold the land and buildings and the buyers have either also used them as restaurants or converted them into grocery stores.

To measure the fair value, it is necessary to determine the highest and best use of the restaurants, from a market participant perspective, and the valuation premise. The highest and best use of each parcel of land and the building thereon may be to:

(a) continue using them (in combination with each other and other assets) as a restaurant. The fair value would be determined on the basis of the price that Addison would receive to sell the land and building to market participants, assuming that these market participants would use them in conjunction with their other assets as a group and that these assets are available to the market participants.

(b) convert the building into a grocery store. The fair value would be determined on the basis of the price that would be received to sell the land and building to market participants who would convert the building. This price would take into consideration the conversion costs that market participants would incur before being able to use the building as a grocery store.

ILLUSTRATIVE EXAMPLE 3.6 Consistent assumptions about highest and best use and valuation premise in an asset group

A wine producer owns and manages a vineyard and produces its own wine on site. The vines are measured at fair value less costs to sell in accordance with IAS 41 at the end of each reporting period. The grapes are measured at the point of harvest at fair value less costs to sell in accordance with IAS 41 (being its 'cost' when transferred to IAS 2). Before harvest, the grapes are considered part of the vines. The wine producer elects to measure its land using IAS 16's revaluation model (fair value less any subsequent accumulated depreciation and accumulated impairment). All other non-financial assets are measured at cost.

At the end of the reporting period, the entity assesses the highest and best use of the vines and the land from the perspective of market participants. The vines and land could continue to be used, in combination with the entity's other assets and liabilities, to produce and sell its wine (i.e. its current use). Alternatively, the land could be converted into residential property. Conversion would include removing the vines and plant and equipment from the land.

Scenario A

The entity determines that the highest and best use of these assets is in combination as a vineyard (that is, its current use). The entity must make consistent assumptions for assets in the group (for which highest and best use is relevant, i.e. non-financial assets). Therefore, the highest and best use of all non-financial assets in the group is to produce and sell wine, even if conversion into residential property might yield a higher value for the land on its own.

Scenario B

The entity determines that the highest and best use of these assets is to convert the land into residential property, even if the current use might yield a higher value for the vines on their own. The entity would need to consider what a market participant would do to convert the land, which could include the cost of rezoning, selling cuttings from the vines or simply removing the vines, and the sale of the buildings and equipment either individually or as an asset group.

Since the highest and best use of these assets is not their current use in this scenario, the entity would disclose that fact, as well as the reason why those assets are being used in a manner that differs from their highest and best use.

Source: EY, *International GAAP 2015*, Volume 1, Chapter 14 *Fair value measurement*, Section 10.2.2, Example 14.13, p. 981.

3.5 APPLICATION TO LIABILITIES

The objective of a fair value measurement of a liability is to estimate the price that would be paid to transfer the liability between market participants at the measurement date under current market conditions. In all cases, an entity must maximise the use of relevant observable inputs and minimise the use of unobservable inputs.

This section applies to both financial and non-financial liabilities.

3.5.1 Settlement versus transfer

Prior to the issuance of IFRS 13, the measurement of a liability was commonly based on the amount required to *settle* the present obligation. As per its definition in IFRS 13, fair value is the amount paid to *transfer* a liability. The fair value measurement thus assumes that the liability is transferred to another market participant at the measurement date. According to paragraph 34(a) of IFRS 13, the transfer of a liability assumes:

> A liability would remain outstanding and the market participant transferee would be required to fulfil the obligation. The liability would not be settled with the counterparty or otherwise extinguished on the measurement date.

The liability is assumed to continue (i.e. it is not settled or extinguished), and the market participant to whom the liability is transferred would be required to fulfil the obligation. The IASB considered the settlement versus transfer in developing IFRS 13. In paragraph BC82 of the Basis for Conclusions on IFRS 13, the IASB explains that the thought-process to determine a settlement amount is similar to determining an amount at which to transfer a liability. This is because both settlement and transfer of a liability reflect all costs incurred, whether direct or indirect, and the entity faces the same risks as a market participant transferee. Despite this, the IASB concluded that the transfer notion was necessary in a fair value measurement. Importantly, it captures market participants' expectations (e.g. about the liquidity and uncertainty), which may not be captured by a settlement notion because it may incorporate entity-specific factors.

The clarification in IFRS 13 that fair value is not based on the price to settle a liability with the existing counterparty, but rather to transfer it to a market participant of equal credit standing, also affects the assumptions about the principal (or most advantageous) market and the market participants in the exit market for the liability.

3.5.2 Non-performance risk

In addition to the fair value framework *discussed in section 3.3*, when an entity measures the fair value of a liability it also considers the effect of non-performance risk. Non-performance risk is defined in Appendix A as:

> The risk that an entity will not fulfil an obligation. Non-performance risk includes, but may not be limited to, the entity's own credit risk.

Non-performance is discussed in paragraphs 42–44 of IFRS 13. When measuring the fair value of a liability, it is necessary to consider the effect of an entity's own credit risk and any other risk factors that may influence the likelihood that the obligation will not be fulfilled (paragraph 43). The requirement that non-performance risk remains unchanged before and after the transfer implies that the liability is hypothetically transferred to a market participant of equal credit standing. Illustrative example 3.7 demonstrates the valuation of liabilities with a consideration of non-performance risk.

ILLUSTRATIVE EXAMPLE 3.7 Valuation of liabilities and non-performance risk

Shore Ltd issues a zero coupon loan of €5000 to Cove Bank with a 5-year term. At the time, it has an AA credit rating and can borrow at 5% p.a. One year later, Shore Ltd issues another zero coupon loan of €5000 to Cove Bank with a 5-year term. Due to a change in credit standing, it must now borrow at 7% p.a.

Shore Ltd measures both liabilities at fair value at initial recognition. The fair value of the first loan is €3918, being the present value of the payment in 5 years' time discounted at 5% p.a. A year later Shore Ltd determines that the fair value of the second loan is €3565, being the present value of the second loan in 5 years' time discounted at 7% p.a. As a result, the fair value of each liability reflects the credit standing of the entity at initial recognition.

Some respondents to the IASB questioned the decision to take non-performance risk into consideration when valuing a liability (paragraph BC95 of the Basis for Conclusions on IFRS 13). The problem they saw was that a change in an entity's credit standing — whether deterioration or improvement — would affect the fair value of the liability. This would lead to gains and losses being recognised in profit or loss for the period, potentially affecting the usefulness of the reported numbers. Furthermore, counterintuitively, a deterioration in the credit standing of the entity could lead to gains being recognised in profit or loss (*this is considered in illustrative example 3.8 in section 3.5.3*). However, the IASB noted that this issue was beyond the scope of the fair value measurement project.

3.5.3 Approaches to measuring the fair value of a liability

Where there is a quoted price for an identical or similar liability, an entity uses that price to measure fair value. However, in many cases, there will be no quoted prices available for the transfer of an instrument that is identical or similar to an entity's liability, particularly as liabilities are generally not transferred. For example, this might be the case for debt obligations that are legally restricted from being transferred or for decommissioning liabilities that the entity does not intend to transfer. In such situations, an entity must determine whether the identical item is held by another party as an asset:

- *If the identical item is held by another party as an asset* — measure fair value from the perspective of a market participant that holds the asset
- *If the identical item is not held by another party as an asset* — measure the fair value using a valuation technique from the perspective of a market participant that owes the liability.

In most circumstances, a liability will be *held as an asset* by another entity — for example, a loan is recognised as a payable by one entity, the recipient of the loan, and a receivable by another entity, the lender. From the standard setter's perspective, the fair value of a liability generally equals the fair value of a properly defined corresponding asset. However, paragraph 39 of IFRS 13 does provide guidance on when adjustments to that price may be needed.

Paragraph 38 of IFRS 13 states that measurement of the corresponding asset should be in the following descending order of preference:

- the quoted price of the asset in an active market
- the quoted price for the asset in a market that is not active
- a valuation under a technique such as:
  - an income approach: present value techniques could be used based on the expected future cash flows a market participant would expect to receive from holding the liability as an asset
  - a market approach: the measure would be based on quoted prices for similar liabilities held by other parties as assets.

Illustrative example 3.8 demonstrates a situation where an entity uses a valuation technique under a market approach to measure the fair value of a liability. *Refer to Example 13 of IFRS 13 for an illustration of an entity using an income approach to measure the fair value of a liability.*

ILLUSTRATIVE EXAMPLE 3.8 Liability held as an asset

On 1 January 2016, Urban Ltd issued at par $5 million exchange-traded 4-year fixed rate corporate bonds with annual coupon payments of 7.5%.

On 30 June 2016, the instrument is trading as an asset in an active market at $1015 per $1000 of par value after payment of accrued interest. On 31 December 2016, the quoted price is $830 per $1000 of par value after payment of accrued interest. The decrease in the quoted price is partly caused by concerns about the entity's ability to pay. Urban Ltd determines there are no factors (e.g. third-party credit enhancements) that are included in the quoted price for the asset that would not be included in the price of the liability. Therefore, no adjustments are needed to the quoted price for the asset.

Urban Ltd uses the quoted price for the asset as its initial input into the fair value measurement of the bond. This results in a fair value of $5 075 000 (= $1015/$1000 = $5 000 000) at 30 June 2016 and $4 150 000 (= $830/$1000 = $5 000 000) at 31 December 2016. *As noted in section 3.5.2*, counterintuitively a worsening of Urban Ltd's credit standing leads to a decrease in the fair value of the liability and a gain recognised in profit or loss.

For some liabilities, the corresponding *asset is not held* by another entity, such as in the case of an entity that must decommission an oil platform when drilling ceases. The entity measuring the fair value of a liability must, therefore, use a valuation technique from the perspective of a market participant that owes the liability (paragraph 40). In such cases a present value technique could be applied, as is shown in illustrative example 3.9. This illustrative example also highlights the elements that are captured by using a present value technique (paragraph B13 of IFRS 13), being:
• an estimate of future cash flows
• expectations about variations in the amount and timing of the cash flows representing the uncertainty inherent in the cash flows
• the time value of money, represented by a risk-free interest rate
• a risk premium, being the price for bearing the uncertainty inherent in the cash flows
• other factors that market participants would take into account
• for a liability, non-performance risk.

ILLUSTRATIVE EXAMPLE 3.9 Present value technique: decommissioning liability

On 1 January 2015, BigOil Ltd assumed a decommissioning liability in a business combination. The entity is legally required to dismantle and remove an offshore oil platform at the end of its useful life, which is estimated to be 10 years.

If BigOil Ltd were contractually allowed to transfer its decommissioning liability to a market participant, market participant would need to take into account the following inputs:
• labour costs — these would be developed on the basis of current market wages, adjusted for expected wage increases with the final amount to be determined on a probability-weighted basis allocation of overhead costs
• compensation for undertaking the activity, including a reasonable profit margin and a premium for undertaking the risks involved effects of inflation time value of money, represented by the risk-free rate
• non-performance risk relating to the risk that BigOil Ltd will not fulfil the obligation, including BigOil Ltd's own credit risk.

The risk-free rate of interest for a 10-year maturity at 1 January 2015 is 5%. BigOil Ltd adjusts that rate by 3.5% to reflect its risk of non-performance including its credit risk. Hence, the interest rate used in the present value calculation is 8.5%.

The fair value of the decommissioning liability at 1 January 2015 determined using the present value technique is $194 879, calculated as follows:

Expected labour costs	$131 250
Allocated overhead and equipment costs	$105 000
Contractor's profit margin (20% of total costs of $236 250)	$47 250
Expected cash flows before inflation adjustment	$283 500
Inflation factor (4% for 10 years)	1.4802
Expected cash flows adjusted for inflation	$419 637
Market risk premium (0.05 × $419 637)	$20 982
Expected cash flows adjusted for market risk	$440 619
Expected present value using a discount rate of 8.5% for 10 years	$194 879

Source: Adapted from IASB 2011, IFRS 13 *Fair Value Measurement*, Illustrative Examples, Example 11 — Decommissioning liability, pp. 17–20.

3.6 APPLICATION TO MEASUREMENT OF AN ENTITY'S OWN EQUITY

The fair value of an entity's own equity instruments may need to be measured, for example, when an entity undertakes a business combination and issues its own equity instruments as part of the consideration for the exchange. Depending on the facts and circumstances, an instrument may be classified as either a liability or equity instrument (in accordance with other standards) for accounting purposes. Therefore, in developing the requirements in IFRS 13 for measuring the fair value of liabilities and an entity's own equity, paragraph BC106 in the Basis for Conclusions notes that the Boards concluded the requirements should generally be consistent with those for liabilities. Therefore, in general, the principles set out in *section 3.5* (in relation to liabilities) also apply to an entity's own equity instruments, except for the requirement to consider non-performance risk, which does not apply directly to an entity's own equity.

A fair value measurement assumes that an entity's own equity instruments are transferred to a market participant at the measurement date. Paragraph 34(b) of IFRS 13 notes that the transfer assumes the following:

> An entity's own equity instrument would remain outstanding and the market participant transferee would take on the rights and responsibilities associated with the instrument. The instrument would not be cancelled or otherwise extinguished on the measurement date.

In order to exit from its own equity, an entity would need to either cancel the share or repurchase the share. Since it cannot consider cancelling its own equity, an entity will likely need to measure the fair value of its own equity instruments from the perspective of a market participant that holds the corresponding instrument as an asset — for example, shareholders. *See section 3.5 for a discussion on measuring the fair value of a liability by reference to the corresponding asset.*

3.7 APPLICATION TO FINANCIAL INSTRUMENTS WITH OFFSETTING POSITIONS

Financial instruments consist of both financial assets and financial liabilities. IAS 32 *Financial Instruments: Presentation* contains definitions of these terms. An entity may hold both financial assets and financial liabilities and, as such, be exposed to both market risk (e.g. interest rate risk, currency risk or other price risk) and to the credit risk of each of its counterparties. Entities may manage some or all of these financial instruments as a group (or portfolio), having a net exposure to a particular risk(s).

In such a situation, IFRS 13 allows entities to make an accounting policy choice to measure the fair value of a group of financial assets and liabilities based on the price that would be received to sell a net long position or transfer a net short position for a particular risk exposure (portfolio approach, paragraph 48). Paragraph 49 provides conditions under which the portfolio approach may be applied, including that an entity must manage the group of financial assets and liabilities on a net exposure basis as a part of its documented risk management strategy. The criteria must be met both initially and on an ongoing basis.

3.8 DISCLOSURE

3.8.1 Categorisation within the fair value hierarchy for disclosure purposes

IFRS 13 requires a fair value measurement *in its entirety to be categorised within the hierarchy* for disclosure purposes. Inputs used in a valuation technique may be within different levels in the fair value hierarchy *(as discussed in section 3.3.5)*. Therefore, the observability of a fair value measurement needs to reflect the observability of the various inputs used. Categorisation within the hierarchy is, therefore, based on the *lowest* level input that is significant to the entire measurement (paragraph 73). A valuation technique that relies solely on a Level 1 input ($P \times Q$) produces a fair value measurement categorised within Level 1. However, if a measurement uses even a single Level 3 input that is significant to the measurement in its entirety, the fair value measurement would be categorised within Level 3.

3.8.2 The disclosure requirements

The disclosure requirements in IFRS 13 apply to fair value measurements recognised in the statement of financial position after initial recognition and disclosures of fair value, with limited exceptions. The standard establishes a set of broad disclosure objectives and provides the minimum disclosures an entity must make. The disclosures are designed to provide users of financial statements with additional transparency regarding:
- the extent to which fair value is used to measure assets and liabilities;
- the valuation techniques, inputs and assumptions used in measuring fair value; and
- the effect of Level 3 fair value measurements on profit or loss (or other comprehensive income).

The minimum requirements vary depending on whether the fair value measurements are recurring or non-recurring and their categorisation within the fair value hierarchy (i.e. Level 1, 2, or 3). More disclosure is required for fair value measurements categorised in Level 3 of the fair value hierarchy than for those categorised in Levels 1 or 2.

'Recurring' fair value measurements are those that other IFRSs require or permit in the statement of financial position at the end of the period. 'Non-recurring' fair value measurements are those that other IFRSs require or permit in particular circumstances — for example, under the application of IFRS 5 *Non-current Assets Held for Sale and Discontinued Operations* in relation to non-current assets held for sale. Disclosures must be presented by class of asset or liability. The appropriate classes may depend on the entity's specific facts and circumstances and the needs of users of its financial statements.

In order for users of the financial statements to be able to assess the relevance of the fair value information provided, IFRS 13 requires the disclosure of information that assists users in understanding:

- *An entity's policies and processes with regard to measuring fair value* — for example, its accounting policy choice with respect to financial instruments with offsetting positions. Another example is the valuation processes used for fair value measurements categorised within *Level 3* of the fair value hierarchy, *which is illustrated in Figure 3.1.*
- *The specific assets and liabilities for which fair value is being measured* — for example, the reason for the measurement (if non-recurring); and the reason why the *current use* of a non-financial asset differs from its *highest and best use* (if applicable).
- *How fair value was measured* — for example, the fair value of the asset or liability; valuation technique(s) used; and the inputs used. For fair value measurements categorised within Level 3, an entity must disclose quantitative information about the significant unobservable inputs used in the fair value measurement.
- *The likelihood that fair value could change (i.e. the sensitivity)* — for example, quantitative and qualitative information about the sensitivity of the measurement to changes in inputs for any fair value measurement categorised within Level 3 of the fair value hierarchy.
- *The reasons for changes in fair value between periods* — examples of such disclosures include a reconciliation from the opening balances to the closing balances for fair value measurements categorised within *Level 3* of the fair value hierarchy, including what caused any change. In addition, disclosure is required of changes in valuation techniques used, as well as transfers between levels within the fair value hierarchy for recurring fair value measurements, along with the reasons for those transfers.

Many of these disclosure requirements apply regardless of whether the fair value measurement is recognised in the financial statements or only disclosed. Figures 3.1 and 3.2 provide illustrations of the type of information required for fair value measurements categorised within Level 3.

All fair value methods are considered to be able to provide reliable measures of fair value; however, users need disclosures about the methods, inputs used and the fair value in order to assess the extent of subjectivity of the techniques used. Irrespective of the frequency at which the measurements are made, the disclosures under IFRS 13 are intended to provide financial statement users with additional insight into the relative subjectivity of various fair value measurements and enhance their ability to broadly assess an entity's quality of earnings.

FIGURE 3.1 Disclosure requirements — valuation processes used for fair value measurements categorised within Level 3

> **Note 22 Fair value measurement [extract]**
>
> **(b) Valuation governance**
>
> The Company's fair value measurement and model governance framework includes numerous controls and other procedural safeguards that are intended to maximize the quality of fair value measurements reported in the financial statements. New products and valuation techniques must be reviewed and approved by key stakeholders from risk and finance control functions. Responsibility for the ongoing measurement of financial and non-financial instruments at fair value resides with the business divisions, but is validated by risk and finance control functions, which are independent of the business divisions. In carrying out their valuation responsibilities, the businesses are required to consider the availability and quality of external market information and to provide justification and rationale for their fair value estimates.
>
> Independent price verification is performed by the finance function to evaluate the business divisions' pricing input assumptions and modeling approaches. By benchmarking the business's fair value estimates with observable market prices and other independent sources, the degree of valuation uncertainty embedded in these measurements is assessed and managed as required in the governance framework. Fair value measurement models are assessed for their ability to value specific products in the principal markets of the product itself as well as the principal market for the main valuation input parameters to the model.
>
> An independent model review group evaluates the Company's valuation models on a regular basis, or if established triggers occur, and approves them for valuing specific products. As a result of the valuation controls employed, valuation adjustments may be made to the business's estimate of fair value to align with independent market information and accounting standards (refer to Note 12d Valuation adjustments for more information).
>
> *Source:* UBS Ltd, *Annual Report* and Financial Statements for the year ended 31 December 2013 (Note 22(b), p. 34).

FIGURE 3.2 Disclosure requirements — fair value measurements categorised within Level 3

26. Derivative financial instruments [extract]
Level 3 derivatives

The following table shows the changes during the year in the net fair value of derivatives held for trading purposes within level 3 of the fair value hierarchy.

	$ million				
	Oil price	Natural gas price	Power price	Other	Total
Net fair value of contracts at 1 January 2013	105	304	(43)	71	437
Gains (losses) recognized in the income statement	(47)	62	81	—	96
Purchases	110	1	—	—	111
New contracts	—	—	—	475	475
Settlements	(143)	(52)	10	(71)	(256)
Transfers out of level 3	(43)	(1)	36	—	(8)
Exchange adjustments	—	(1)	2	—	1
Net fair value of contracts at 31 December 2013	(18)	313	86	475	856

	$ million				
	Oil price	Natural gas price	Power price	Other	Total
Net fair value of contracts at 1 January 2012	162	408	13	—	583
Gains (losses) recognized in the income statement	30	4	(4)	—	30
New contracts	—	—	—	71	71
Settlements	(87)	(56)	—	—	(143)
Transfers into level 3	—	(19)	—	—	(19)
Transfers out of level 3	—	(33)	(51)	—	(84)
Exchange adjustments	—	—	(1)	—	(1)
Net fair value of contracts at 31 December 2012	105	304	(43)	71	437

US natural gas price derivatives are valued using observable market data for maturities up to 60 months in basis locations that trade at a premium or discount to the NYMEX Henry Hub price, and using internally developed price curves based on economic forecasts for periods beyond that time. At 31 December 2013, the US natural gas derivatives in level 3 of the fair value hierarchy had a net fair value of $351 million. Of this amount, $71 million (asset of $598 million and liability of $527 million) depends on level 3 inputs, with the remainder valued using level 2 inputs. The significant unobservable inputs for fair value measurements categorized within level 3 of the fair value hierarchy for the year ended 31 December 2013 are presented below.

	Unobservable inputs	Range $/mmBtu	Weighted average $/mmBtu
Natural gas price contracts	Long-dated market price	3.15–6.71	4.63

If the natural gas prices after 2018 were 10% higher (lower), this would result in a decrease (increase) in derivative assets of $82 million, and decrease (increase) in derivative liabilities of $78 million, and a net decrease (increase) in profit before tax of $4 million.

Source: BP plc, *Annual Report* and Form-20-F (2013, Note 26, pp. 174–175).

SUMMARY

The debate over the best measurement method for assets and liabilities is not a new one. Discussions of the decision usefulness of various models of current value accounting have occupied many pages in accounting journals and were the focus of the research of many academics. Historically, accounting standards have relied primarily on the use of historical cost, but the use of fair values has become increasingly common, particularly with the focus on financial instruments. The standard setters therefore decided that it was time to produce an accounting standard on fair value measurement, with the focus on how to measure fair value rather than on when to use those fair values. This has resulted in the issue of IFRS 13 by the IASB.

IFRS 13 contains a definition of fair value that seeks to clarify questions raised in the application of the definition in previous standards. A key feature of the definition is that fair value is a current exit price, rather than an entry price.

The fair value framework in IFRS 13 is based on a number of key concepts including unit of account, exit price, valuation premise, highest and best use, principal market, market participant assumptions and the fair value hierarchy. The requirements incorporate financial theory and valuation techniques, but are focused solely on how these concepts are to be applied when determining fair value for financial reporting purposes. Critical to the measurement process are the assumptions that market participants make when using a valuation technique. The assumptions or inputs are classified into three levels, the classification being based on the use of observable and unobservable inputs. In choosing a valuation technique an entity should seek to maximise the number of observable inputs used.

A key element of IFRS 13 is the requirement to disclose sufficient information about the fair value measures used. Users of financial statements should be able to assess the methods and inputs used to develop the fair value measurements and the effects on income.

Discussion questions

1. Name three current accounting standards that permit or require the use of fair values.
2. What are the main objectives of IFRS 13?
3. What are the key elements of the definition of 'fair value'?
4. How does the definition of fair value differ from that used in previous accounting standards?
5. How does entry price differ from exit price?
6. Is the reporting entity a market participant?
7. Does the measurement of fair value take into account transport costs and transaction costs? Explain.
8. What are the key steps in measuring fair value?
9. Explain the difference between the current use of an asset and the highest and best use of that asset.
10. Explain the difference between the in-combination valuation premise and the stand-alone valuation premise.
11. What is the difference between the principal market for an asset or liability and its most advantageous market?
12. What valuation techniques are available to measure fair value?
13. Explain the fair value hierarchy.
14. Explain the different levels of fair value inputs.
15. How does the measurement of the fair value of a liability differ from that of an asset?

References

Benston, G. J. 2008, 'The shortcomings of fair value accounting described in SFAS 157', *Journal of Accounting and Public Policy*, 27(2), March–April, pp. 101–14.

Chasan, E. 2008, 'Is fair value accounting really fair?', Reuters, www.reuters.com, 26 February.

Ernst & Young 2009, *Invitation to Comment — Fair Value Measurement*, www.ifrs.org.

IASB 2009, IASB *Fair Value Measurements Roundtable Summary*, www.iasplus.com.

Nestlé 2009, *Comments on Exposure Draft ED/2009/5/Fair Value Measurement*, www.ifrs.org.

Royal Dutch Shell 2009, *Exposure Draft 2009/5 Fair Value Measurements*, www.ifrs.org.

Exercises

Exercise 3.1 VALUATION PREMISE FOR MEASUREMENT OF FAIR VALUE

★ Heel Ltd conducts a business that makes women's shoes. It operates a factory in an inner suburb of a large European city. The factory contains a large amount of equipment that is used in the manufacture of shoes. Heel Ltd owns both the factory and the land on which the factory stands. The land was acquired in 2005 for €200 000 and the factory was built in that year at a cost of €520 000. Both assets are recorded at cost, with the factory having a carrying amount at 30 June 2016 of €260 000.

In recent years there has been a property boom in the city with residential house prices doubling such that the average price of a house is approximately €500 000. A recent valuation of the land on which the factory stands was performed by a property valuation group and based on recent sales of land in the area. It valued the land at €1 000 000. The land is now considered prime real estate given its proximity to the city centre and, with its superb river views, its suitability for building executive apartments. It would cost €100 000 to demolish the factory to make way for these apartments to be built. It is estimated that to build a new factory on the current site would cost around €780 000.

The directors of Heel Ltd want to measure both the factory and the land at fair value as at 30 June 2016.

Required

Discuss how you would measure these fair values.

Exercise 3.2 HIGHEST AND BEST USE

★ BGW Ltd is in the business of bottling wine, particularly for small wineries that cannot afford sophisticated technical equipment and want to concentrate on the growing of the grapes themselves. One of the key features of the bottles that are used by BGW Ltd is that, for the bottles used for white wine and champagne, they have an built-in insulation device that is successful in keeping the contents of the bottle cold, with the temperature being unaffected by the bottle being held in the hand.

In January 2014, Solar-Blue, a company experimenting with energy sources useful in combating climate change, produced a device which, when attached to the outside of a container, could display the actual temperature of the liquid inside. The temperature was displayed by the highlighting of certain colours on the device. Exactly how this device could be attached to wine bottles had yet to be specifically determined. However, BGW Ltd believed that its employees had the skills that would enable the company to determine the feasibility of such a project. Whether the costs of attaching the device to wine bottles would be prohibitive was also unknown.

As BGW Ltd was concerned that competing wine bottling companies may acquire the device from Solar-Blue, it paid €7 100 000 for the exclusive rights to use the device with bottles.

The accountant wants to measure the fair value of the asset acquired.

Required

Discuss the process of determining this fair value.

Exercise 3.3 CHARACTERISTICS OF AN ASSET

★ Mr Merman owned a large house on a sizeable piece of land in London. The property had been in his family since around 1889. Mr Merman was 92 years old and was incapable of taking care of the large property. He wanted to move into a retirement village and so sold his property to the MedSea Group which was an association of doctors. The doctors wanted to use the house for their medical practice as it was centrally situated, had many rooms and had a charming 'old-world' atmosphere that would make patients feel comfortable.

The house was surrounded by a large group of trees that had been planted by the Merman family over the years. The trees covered a large portion of the land. MedSea did not want to make large alterations to the house as it was suitable for a doctors' surgery. Only minor alterations to the inside of the house and some maintenance to the exterior were required. However, MedSea wanted to divide the land and sell the portion adjacent to the house; the portion currently being covered in trees. The property sold would be very suitable for up-market apartment blocks.

One of the conditions of the sale of the property to MedSea was that, while Mr Merman remained alive, the trees on the property could not be cut down as it would have caused him great distress to see such alterations to the family home. This clause in the contract would restrict the building of the apartment blocks. However, this restriction would not be enforceable on subsequent buyers of the property if MedSea wanted to sell the property in the future. A further issue affecting the building of the apartment blocks was that across one corner of the block there was a gas pipeline that was a part of the city infrastructure for the supply of gas facilities to London residents.

Required

Outline any provisions in IFRS 13 that relate to consideration of restrictions on the measurement of fair values of assets, and how in the situation described above the restrictions would affect the measurement of the fair value of the property by MedSea.

Exercise 3.4 | ASSETS WITHOUT AN ACTIVE MARKET

★ Emily Chasan (2008) reported:

> 'It's ridiculous to apply fair value accounting to assets that have no market,' said Christopher Whalen, managing director of risk research firm Institutional Risk Analytics. 'All this volatility we now have in financial reporting and disclosure, it's just absolute madness.'
>
> 'Investors as a group have to get a better understanding of what the volatility means,' said Ed Nusbaum, chief executive of accounting firm Grant Thornton. 'They want to live in a perfect world. They'd like complete transparency and no surprises. But I think it's unlikely that the big write-downs that we've seen will reverse.'

Required

Discuss the issues associated with fair value accounting for assets without an active market.

Exercise 3.5 | EXIT PRICES AS FAIR VALUE FOR CLASSES OF ASSETS

★ In its response to the IASB exposure draft, the G100 in Australia stated:

> The G100 does not believe that an exit price based measure of fair value is appropriate for all classes of assets. While such a measure may be appropriate for financial instruments we do not believe that an exit price based measure provides useful information for certain classes of non-financial assets such as property, plant and equipment where an entity-specific measure may be more appropriate.

Required

Discuss the use of entity-specific information in the generation of fair value numbers under IFRS 13.

Exercise 3.6 | MEASUREMENT OF FAIR VALUE

★ The use of fair value to measure assets and liabilities inevitably results in fluctuations in profit or loss, which can be large. Users of financial statements, therefore, need information that clearly explains the source of these fluctuations — whether they are realised or unrealised, based on objective or subjective information, real transactions and market activity or estimates.

Required

Discuss how IFRS 13 attempts to overcome these issues when providing information to users of financial statements.

Exercise 3.7 | MANAGEMENT BIAS ON FAIR VALUE MEASUREMENT

★ One of the concerns associated with fair value measurement is that management bias may affect the reliability of the information. IFRS 13 requires that fair values be based on market-based assumptions rather than entity-specific assumptions in order to overcome this issue.

Required

Compare the potential for management bias when making market-based or entity-specific assumptions.

Fair value measurement has increasingly replaced the historical cost measurement basis in past two decades. One major concern for academic research against this background has been whether fair value accounting is value relevant and sufficiently reliable. Historical cost accounting (HCA) is typically verifiable as it is based on past evidence (e.g., an invoice confirming the purchase cost of an asset). In contrast, by construction, fair value accounting is based on unrealised gains or losses. Moreover, fair value measurement may be based on unobservable and subjective inputs, as is the case, for example, with Level 3 inputs. Landsman (2007) provides a good discussion on the value relevance and reliability of fair value accounting, although his review of related empirical research precedes more recent rules and studies. Beatty and Liao's (2014) review of accounting in banks is also a very useful source of detailed discussion of issues related to fair value accounting.

Since the use of fair value accounting is more pronounced in financial firms, such as banks, early research has examined the value relevance of fair value accounting mostly in banks. Barth (1994) finds that fair value gains and losses on investment securities provide incremental explanatory power for stock returns over that of historical cost gains and losses. Nelson (1996) examines fair value disclosures in banks' financial statements but fails to find evidence that these disclosures are value relevant over historical cost measures. In contrast Eccher et al. (1996) and Barth et al. (1996) find that fair value disclosures are incorporated into share prices. More recently Livne et al. (2011)examine assets that are *recognised* and measured at fair value. Their evidence suggests that the unrealised component of fair values of investment securities is positively associated with stock returns, but the historical cost component is not.

This result is intriguing because the unrealised component is precisely the part in the fair value measure that may be susceptible to managerial discretion and manipulation. Evans et al. (2014) provide evidence that the unrealised component in fair value measurement has predictive ability with respect to future income and cash flows. This may explain the association of unrealised gains and losses with returns in that investors use this information to value shares. Consistent with the evidence in Livne et al. (2011), Evans et al. (2014) also show that unrealised gains and losses are associated with market value of equity. Beaver and Venkatachalam (2003) find that whether the discretionary component in fair value measurement (i.e., the unrealised gain or loss) is value relevant is dependent on managers' reporting incentives. They provide some evidence suggesting that when the discretionary component is measured in opportunistic fashion, investors find it less relevant than when opportunism does not play a role.

Does this evidence then suggest that historical cost accounting is not useful? An answer for this can be found by taking advantage of the accounting rules for available-for-sale (AFS) securities. These require that gains and losses arising upon the disposal of AFS assets are recorded on historical cost basis. But, at the same time AFS securities are measured on the balance sheet at fair value. If historical cost accounting is superfluous when fair value accounting is used, then it is not expected that historical cost measures of realised gains and losses would be value relevant incrementally over fair value measures of the underlying assets. Dong et al. (2014), however,

show that these historical cost measures are incrementally value relevant. They conclude that historical cost measures can still be value relevant when fair value accounting is used.

IFRS 13, and FAS 157 in the US, set fair value hierarchy as described in this chapter. Several researchers have conjectured that the value relevance and reliability of fair value decreases from Level 1 to Level 3. However, the evidence on this is quite mixed. Song et al. (2010) examine quarterly reports of banks in 2008 and find evidence consistent with this conjecture. In contrast, Altamuro and Zhang (2013) examine mortgage services rights that are fair-valued and find that Level 3 is more value relevant.

The relevance and reliability of Level 2 and Level 3 may be a function of both noisy inputs, as well as managerial discretion. Altamuro and Zhang (2013) argue that managers can convey useful information using their discretion in Level 3 reporting and that this effect may be more pronounced when the underlying asset is not traded in an active market. Song et al. (2010) find that the value relevance of Level 3 fair values increases with the strength of corporate governance. Taken together, this suggests that opportunism plays a role but can be constrained by board monitoring.

Relying on markets to supply objective inputs into fair value measurement can introduce noise even absent discretion and corporate governance effects. Banks often rely on market-based indices when valuing mortgage portfolios. Stanton and Wallace (2011) show that the pricing of a leading default risk index used by many banks in marking-to-market loan portfolios was inconsistent with reasonable assumptions about future default rates. They argue that, consequently, certain banks that relied on this index wrote off billions of dollars' worth of assets during the financial crisis, potentially unnecessarily.

The above-mentioned research is mostly focused on fair value accounting for financial assets and liabilities. However, fair value accounting is also employed in non financial assets (see also the Academic Perspective to chapter 11). Aboody et al. (1999) examine revaluations of property plant and equipment under UK GAAP (prior to IFRS adoption in 2005). They provide evidence that the revalued balances of these assets are positively associated with share prices and that changes in revaluation amounts are positively associated with stock returns. They also provide evidence suggesting that revaluations predict future performance. Liang and Riedl (2014) examine the value relevance of unrealised gains and losses recorded when investment properties are measured at fair value. They find that analyst forecasts of EPS are less accurate when investment properties are measured at fair value than when they are measured at historical cost. However, analysts are better able to forecast the balance sheet for firms employing the fair value model.

References

Aboody, D., Barth., M., and Kasznik, R., 1999. Revaluations of fixed assets and future firm performance: Evidence from the UK. *Journal of Accounting and Economics*, 26, 149–178.

Altamuro, A., and Zhang, H., 2013. The financial reporting of fair value based on managerial inputs versus market inputs: Evidence from mortgage servicing rights. *Review of Accounting Studies*,18, 833–858.

Barth, M., 1994. Fair Value accounting: Evidence from investment securities and the market valuation of banks. *The Accounting Review*, 69, 1–25.

Barth, M., Beaver, W., and Landsman, W., 1996. Value-relevance of banks' fair value disclosures under SFAS No. 107. *The Accounting Review*, 71, 513–537.

Beatty, A., and Liao, S., 2014. Financial accounting in the banking industry: A review of the empirical literature. *Journal of Accounting and Economics*, 58, 339–383.

Beaver, W., and Venkatachalam, M., 2003. Differential pricing of components of bank loan fair values. *Journal of Accounting, Auditing and Finance*, 18, 41–67.

Dong, M., Ryan, S., and Zhang, X.-J., 2014. Preserving amortized costs within a fair-value-accounting framework: Reclassification of gains and losses on available-for-sale securities upon realization. *Review of Accounting Studies*, 19, 242–280.

Eccher, E., Ramesh, K., and Thiagarajan, S., 1996. Fair value disclosures by bank holding companies. *Journal of Accounting and Economics*, 22, 79–117.

Evans, M.E., Hodder, L., and Hopkins, P.E., 2014. The predictive ability of fair values for future financial performance of commercial banks and the relation of predictive ability to banks' share prices. *Contemporary Accounting Research*, 31, 13–44.

Landsman, W., 2007. Is fair value accounting information relevant and reliable? Evidence from capital market research. *Accounting and Business Research*, 37, 19–30.

Liang., L., and Riedl, E., 2014. The effect of fair value versus historical cost reporting model on analyst forecast accuracy. *The Accounting Review*, 89, 1151–1177.

Livne, G., Markarian, G., and Milne, A., 2011. Bankers' compensation and fair value accounting. *Journal of Corporate Finance*, 17, 1096–1115.

Nelson, K.K., 1996. Fair value accounting for commercial banks: An empirical analysis of SFAS No. 107. *The Accounting Review*, 161–182.

Song, C., Thomas, W., and Yi, H., 2010. Value relevance of FAS 157 fair value hierarchy information and the impact of corporate governance mechanisms. *The Accounting Review*, 85, 1375–1410.

Stanton, R., and Wallace, N., 2011. The Bear's Lair: Index credit defaults waps and the subprime mortgage crisis. *Review of Financial Studies*, 24, 3250–3280.

4

Revenue from contracts with customers

ACCOUNTING STANDARDS IN FOCUS

IFRS 15 *Revenue from Contracts with Customers*

LEARNING OBJECTIVES

After studying this chapter, you should be able to:

1. discuss the background behind the issuance of IFRS 15
2. identify the types of contracts that are within the scope of IFRS 15
3. apply the five-step model for measuring and recognising revenue under IFRS 15
4. understand how to account for contract related costs
5. identify other significant application issues associated with IFRS 15
6. explain the presentation and disclosure requirements of IFRS 15.

4.1 INTRODUCTION

The International Accounting Standards Board (IASB®) issued IFRS 15 *Revenue from Contracts with Customers* ('IFRS 15' or 'the standard') in May 2014. The standard was developed jointly with the US FASB (collectively, 'the Boards'). The US FASB issued its new revenue standard at the same time that the IASB issued IFRS 15. The new revenue standards issued by the Boards are largely converged and will supersede virtually all revenue recognition requirements currently in IFRS® Standards and US GAAP.

Noting several concerns with existing requirements for revenue recognition under both IFRS Standards and US GAAP, the Boards jointly developed a revenue standard that would:

- remove inconsistencies and weaknesses in the current revenue recognition literature;
- provide a more robust framework for addressing revenue recognition issues;
- improve comparability of revenue recognition practices across the various industries, entities, jurisdictions and capital markets;
- provide a single reference point in order to reduce the volume of the relevant standards and interpretations that entities will need to refer to; and
- provide more useful information to users through enhanced disclosure requirements.

IFRS 15 outlines the accounting treatment for all revenue arising from contracts with customers and provides a model for the measurement and recognition of gains and losses on the sale of certain non-financial assets, such as intangible assets, property, plant or equipment or investment properties. IFRS 15 replaces all of the existing revenue standards and interpretations in IFRS Standards, including IAS 11 *Construction Contracts*, IAS 18 *Revenue*, IFRS Interpretations Committee (IFRIC®) Interpretation 13 *Customer Loyalty Programmes*, IFRIC Interpretation 15 *Agreements for the Construction of Real Estate*, IFRIC Interpretation 18 *Transfers of Assets from Customers* and Standing Interpretations Committee (SIC®) Interpretation 31 *Revenue–Barter Transactions Involving Advertising Services*.

The core principle of IFRS 15 is that an entity will recognise revenue at an amount that reflects the consideration to which the entity expects to be entitled in exchange for transferring goods or services to a customer, which requires entities to apply a five-step model as follows:

1. Identify the contract(s) with a customer *(discussed in section 4.3)*.
2. Identify the performance obligations in the contract *(discussed in section 4.4)*.
3. Determine the transaction price *(discussed in section 4.5)*.
4. Allocate the transaction price to the performance obligations in the contract *(discussed in section 4.6)*.
5. Recognise revenue when (or as) the entity satisfies a performance obligation *(discussed in section 4.7)*.

For the purposes of first-time adoption of IFRS 15, entities can choose to apply either a fully retrospective approach for all periods presented in the period of adoption (with some limited relief provided) or a modified retrospective approach. At the time of writing this chapter, IFRS 15 is mandatorily effective for annual periods beginning on or after 1 January 2017[1] with early adoption permitted.

4.2 SCOPE

All contracts with customers to provide goods or services in the ordinary course of business are included within the scope of IFRS 15, except for the following contracts and arrangements:

- lease contracts accounted for under IAS 17 *Leases*;
- insurance contracts accounted for under IFRS 4 *Insurance Contracts*;
- financial instruments and other contractual rights or obligations accounted for under IFRS 9 *Financial Instruments* or IAS 39 *Financial Instruments: Recognition and Measurement*, IFRS 10 *Consolidated Financial Statements*, IFRS 11 *Joint Arrangements*, IAS 27 *Separate Financial Statements* and IAS 28 *Investments in Associates and Joint Ventures*; and
- non-monetary exchanges between entities in the same line of business to facilitate sales to customers or potential customers.

Entities will have to evaluate their relationship with the counterparty to the contract in order to determine whether a vendor–customer relationship exists, which may be particularly judgemental for certain arrangements. For example, some collaboration arrangements are more akin to a partnership, while others represent a vendor–customer relationship. Only transactions that are with a customer are within the scope of IFRS 15.

Entities may enter into transactions that are partially within the scope of IFRS 15 and partially within the scope of other standards. In these situations, the standard requires that an entity apply the requirements in the other standard(s) first, to separate and measure the different parts in the contract, before applying the requirements in IFRS 15.

---

[1] In September 2015, the IASB issued *Effective Date of IFRS 15*, which amends IFRS 15 to defer the effective date of the standard by one year (i.e. for annual periods beginning on or after 1 January 2018).

4.3 IDENTIFY THE CONTRACT WITH THE CUSTOMER

An entity must identify the contract, or contracts, to provide goods and services to customers as the first step in the model in IFRS 15. Any contracts that create enforceable rights and obligations fall within the scope of the standard. Such contracts may be written, oral or implied through an entity's customary business practice and this may impact an entity's determination of when an arrangement meets the definition of a contract with a customer. Since enforceability is driven by the laws within the jurisdiction, the assessment of whether there are legally enforceable rights and obligations will depend on the facts and circumstances.

Take, for example, an entity that has an established business practice of starting performance based on oral agreements with its customers. The entity may assess that such oral agreements result in a contract as defined in IFRS 15 and therefore account for a contract as soon as performance begins, instead of delaying until there is a signed agreement. Certain arrangements may require a written agreement to comply with jurisdictional law or trade regulation. In those cases, the assessment may differ and a contract may exist only when there is a written document.

4.3.1 Arrangements that meet the definition of a contract

To help entities determine whether (and when) their arrangements with customers are contracts within the scope of the standard, the Boards provided five criteria that must be met at the commencement of the arrangement. Once the criteria are met, an entity would apply the five-step model in IFRS 15 to account for the contract and it is not required to reassess these criteria unless there is a significant change in facts and circumstances.

Paragraph 9 of IFRS 15 provides five criteria, as summarised below:
(a) the contract is approved by all parties, whether in writing, orally or in accordance with other customary business practices, and the parties are committed to carrying out their respective obligations;
(b) the entity can identify the rights of each party with regard to the goods or services that are to be transferred under the contract;
(c) the entity can identify the payment terms for the goods or services to be transferred;
(d) the contract has commercial substance; and
(e) collectability of the amount of consideration that an entity will be entitled to in exchange for the goods and services that will be transferred to the customer is probable.

The purpose of these criteria is to help an entity assess whether a contract with its customer is genuine and entered into for a valid business purpose. If the criteria are not met, then the arrangement is not considered a revenue contract under IFRS 15. *Instead, the requirements discussed in section 4.3.2 must be applied.* Entities are required to continue assessing the criteria throughout the term of the arrangement to determine if they are subsequently met.

4.3.2 Arrangements that do not meet the definition of a contract

Paragraph 15 of IFRS 15 indicates that when a contract with a customer does not meet the criteria for a revenue contract *(i.e. the criteria discussed in section 4.3.1)* and an entity receives consideration from the customer, the entity can only recognise the consideration received as revenue when such amounts are non-refundable and either of the following events has occurred:
(a) the entity has completed performing all of its obligations under the contract and has received all, or substantially all, of the consideration promised by the customer; or
(b) the contract has been terminated.

The standard goes on to specify that an entity must recognise any consideration received from a customer as a liability until one of the events described above occurs or until the contract meets the criteria to be accounted for within the revenue model.

4.3.3 Contracts that are combined

In some cases, entities have to combine individual contracts entered into at, or near, the same time with the same customer if they meet one or more of the following criteria in paragraph 17 of IFRS 15:
(a) the contracts are negotiated as a package with the intent of meeting a singular business purpose (e.g. where a contract would be loss-making without taking into account the consideration received under another contract);
(b) the amount of consideration that a customer has to pay in one contract is impacted by the price or performance of the other contract (e.g. where failure to perform under one contract affects the amount paid under another contract); or
(c) some or all of the goods or services promised in the individual contracts form a single performance obligation (e.g. a contract for the sale of specialised equipment and a second contract entered into at the same time with the same customer for significant customisation and modification of that specialised equipment may give rise to a single performance obligation).

Note that only contracts entered into at or near the same time are assessed under the contract combination requirements. Arrangements entered into at a much later date that were not anticipated at the start of the contract or implied based on the entity's customary business practices may be accounted for as contract modifications, *which are discussed in section 4.9.1.*

4.4 IDENTIFY THE PERFORMANCE OBLIGATIONS

Once an entity has identified the contract with the customer, the second step in the model requires an entity to identify the promised goods and services in the contract. This assessment is performed at the commencement of the contract.

The entity has to determine which of the promised goods or services (individually or as a bundle of promised goods or services) will be treated as separate performance obligations. Under IFRS 15, a promised good or service that is not distinct on its own must be combined with other goods or services until a distinct bundle of goods or services is formed. Each separate performance obligation is an individual unit of account for purposes of applying the standard. These concepts are discussed further below.

4.4.1 Separate performance obligations

Paragraph 26 of IFRS 15 provides a non-exhaustive list of examples of promised goods or services that may be identified in a contract. Such promised goods or services are accounted for as separate performance obligations if they are distinct (either by themselves or as part of a bundle of goods and services) or they are part of a series of distinct goods and services that are substantially the same and have the same pattern of transfer to the customer *(see section 4.4.2).*

In assessing whether a promised good or service (or a bundle of goods and services) is distinct, an entity has to meet both of the criteria below:
• the goods or services are capable of being distinct; and
• the goods or services are distinct when considered in the context of the entire contract.

Capable of being distinct

A good or service is capable of being distinct if the customer can benefit from it (i.e. it could be used, consumed, sold for an amount greater than scrap value or otherwise held in a way that generates economic benefits). In assessing this, an entity considers the individual characteristics of the good or service, rather than how a customer may use the good or service.

A customer may be able to benefit from some goods or services on their own or in conjunction with other readily available resources. Readily available resources are goods and services that may be sold separately by the entity (or another entity) or that the customer has already obtained from the entity (including goods or services that have already been transferred to the customer under the contract) or from other transactions or events. Separately selling a good or service on a regular basis indicates that a customer can benefit from that good or service on its own or with readily available resources.

Distinct within the context of the contract

The second criterion requires that the entity considers whether the good or service is separable from other promises in the contract. The standard provides a non-exhaustive list of indicators that an entity's promise to transfer a good or service to a customer is separately identifiable. The indicators are summarised as follows:
(a) The entity is not using the good or service as an input into a single process or project that is the output of the contract. That is, the entity is not providing a significant integration service.
(b) The good or service does not significantly modify or customise other promised goods and services in the contract.
(c) The good or service is not highly dependent on, or highly interrelated with, other promised goods or services in the contract. For example, if a customer could decide not to purchase a particular good or service and it would not significantly impact the customer's decision to purchase the other promised goods or services in the contract, this might indicate that the good or service is not highly dependent on or highly interrelated with those other promised goods or services.

If a promised good or service is not distinct, an entity is required to combine that good or service with other promised goods or services until it identifies a bundle of goods or services that is distinct. As a consequence, an entity may end up accounting for all the goods or services promised in a contract as a single performance obligation if the bundle of promised goods and services is the only distinct item identified.

Illustrative example 4.1 demonstrates how an entity might apply the two-step process for determining whether promised goods or services in a contract are distinct and how an entity might bundle inseparable goods and services.

Entity Z is a software development company that provides hosting services to a variety of consumer products entities. Entity Z offers a hosted inventory management software product that requires the customer to purchase hardware from Entity Z. In addition, customers may purchase professional services from Entity Z to migrate historical data and create interfaces with existing back office accounting systems. Entity Z always delivers the hardware first, followed by professional services and finally, the ongoing hosting services.

Scenario A – All goods and services sold separately

Entity Z determines that all of the individual goods and services in the contract are capable of being distinct because the entity regularly sells each element of the contract separately. Entity Z also determines that the goods and services are separable from other promises in the contract (i.e. distinct within the context of the contract), because it is not providing a significant service of integrating the goods and services and the level of customisation is not significant. Furthermore, because the customer could purchase (or not purchase) each good and service without significantly affecting the other goods and services purchased, the goods and services are not highly dependent on, or highly interrelated with, each other. Accordingly, the hardware, professional services and hosting services are each accounted for as separate performance obligations.

Scenario B – Hardware not sold separately

Entity Z determines that the professional services are distinct because it frequently sells those services on a stand-alone basis (e.g. Entity Z also performs professional services related to hardware and software it does not sell). Furthermore, the entity determines that the hosting services are distinct because it also sells those services on a stand-alone basis. For example, customers that have completed their initial contractual term and elect each month to continue purchasing the hosting services are purchasing those services on a stand-alone basis. The hardware, however, is always sold in a package with the professional and hosting services and the customer cannot use the hardware on its own or with resources that are readily available to it. Therefore, Entity Z determines the hardware is not distinct.

Entity Z must determine which promised goods and services in the contract to bundle with the hardware. Entity Z likely would conclude that because the hardware is integral to the delivery of the hosted software, the hardware and hosting services should be accounted for as one performance obligation, and the professional services, which are distinct, would be a separate performance obligation.

Source: Ernst & Young (2015, p. 1959).

4.4.2 Series of distinct goods and services that are substantially the same and have the same pattern of transfer

Even if a good or service is determined to be distinct, if it is part of a series of goods or services that are substantially the same and have the same pattern of transfer, that series of goods or services must be treated as a single performance obligation when both of the following criteria are met:
- each distinct good or service in the series is a performance obligation that would be satisfied over time *(see section 4.7.1)* if it were accounted for separately; and
- the measure used to assess the entity's progress toward satisfaction of the performance obligation is the same for each distinct good or service in the series *(see section 4.7.2)*.

4.4.3 Customer options for additional goods or services

Some entities frequently give customers the option to purchase additional goods or services ('customer options'). These additional goods or services may be priced at a discount or may even be free of charge. Customer options also come in many forms, including sales incentives, customer award credits (e.g. frequent flyer programmes offered by airlines), contract renewal options (e.g. waiver of certain fees, reduced future rates) or other discounts on future goods or services.

IFRS 15 indicates that a customer option is a separate performance obligation only if it provides the customer with a material right that the customer would not have received without entering into the contract (e.g. a discount that exceeds the range of discounts typically given for those goods or services to that class of customer in that geographical area or market). The purpose of this requirement is for entities to identify and account for options that customers are essentially paying for as part of the current transaction.

If the discounted price of the customer option reflects the stand-alone selling price *(see section 4.6.1)*, separate from any existing relationship or contract, the entity is deemed to have made a marketing offer rather than having granted a material right. This is the case even if the customer option can only be exercised because the customer entered into the earlier transaction.

4.5 DETERMINE THE TRANSACTION PRICE

The third step in the model requires an entity to determine the transaction price. This is the amount of consideration to which an entity expects to be entitled in exchange for transferring promised goods or services to a customer, which excludes amounts collected on behalf of third parties (e.g. some sales taxes). In determining the transaction price, the entity has to consider the contractual terms and its customary business practices.

In many cases, the transaction price can be readily determined because the entity receives a fixed payment when it transfers promised goods or services to the customer (e.g. the sale of goods in a retail store). Determining the transaction price can be more challenging in other situations, such as:
• when the transaction price is variable
• when a customer pays for the goods or services before or after the entity's performance
• when a customer pays in a form other than cash, or
• when the entity pays consideration to the customer.
    The effects of these items on the determination of the transaction price are discussed in sections 4.5.1 to 4.5.4.

Determining the transaction price is an important step in the model because this amount is subsequently allocated to the identified performance obligations in the fourth step of the model. It is also the amount that will be recognised as revenue as those performance obligations are satisfied.

4.5.1 Variable consideration

Paragraph 50 of IFRS 15 requires that if the consideration promised in a contract includes a variable amount, the entity must estimate the amount of consideration to which it will be entitled and include that amount in the transaction price, subject to a constraint (which is discussed further below).

Variable consideration may include discounts, rebates, refunds, credits, price concessions, incentives, performance bonuses, penalties or other similar items. If an entity's entitlement to the consideration is contingent on the occurrence or non-occurrence of a future event, the transaction price is considered to be variable. An example of this is when a portion of the transaction price depends on an entity meeting specified performance conditions and there is uncertainty about the outcome and therefore whether the entity will receive that amount of consideration.

Estimating variable consideration

An entity is required to estimate the variable consideration using either an 'expected value' or a 'most likely amount' approach. An entity has to decide which approach better predicts the amount of consideration to which it expects it will be entitled and apply that approach. That is, an entity will need to select the method not based on a 'free choice' but rather on what is most suitable given the specific facts and circumstances. In some cases, an entity may have to use different approaches (i.e. expected value or most likely amount) for estimating different types of variable consideration within a single contract.

The selected method(s) must be applied consistently throughout the contract and an entity will have to update the estimated transaction price at the end of each reporting period. Furthermore, an entity is required to apply the selected approach consistently to similar types of contracts.

The expected value approach is based on probability weighting the possible outcomes of a contract. As a result, it may better predict the expected consideration when an entity has a large number of contracts with similar characteristics. Using the most likely amount approach, an entity will select the amount that is most likely to be received considering the range of possible amounts. The most likely amount approach may be the better method to use when there are a limited number of possible amounts expected (e.g. a contract in which an entity is entitled to receive all or none of a specified commission payment, but not a portion of that commission).

When applying either of these approaches, all information (historical, current and forecast) that is reasonably available to the entity must be considered.

Constraining the cumulative amount of revenue recognised

As mentioned earlier, after estimating the amount of variable consideration, an entity must apply the 'constraint' to the estimated amount. The constraint is aimed at preventing revenue from being overstated. To include variable consideration in the estimated transaction price, the entity has to conclude that it is 'highly probable' that a significant revenue reversal will not occur in future periods when the uncertainties related to the variability are subsequently resolved. This conclusion involves considering both the likelihood and magnitude of a potential revenue reversal. In assessing the magnitude, an entity needs to consider if the potential revenue reversal is 'significant' relative to total contract revenue, rather than just the variable consideration. The estimate of the variable consideration (which is subject to the effect of the constraint) included in the transaction price is updated throughout the contractual period to reflect the conditions that exist at the end of each reporting period.

Illustrative example 4.2 provides an example of estimating the variable consideration using the 'expected value' and the 'most likely amount' approaches, and the effect of the constraint on both approaches.

Scenario A

Entity A provides transportation to theme park customers to and from accommodation in the area under a 1 year agreement. It is required to provide scheduled transportation throughout the year for a fixed fee of $400 000 annually. Entity A also is entitled to performance bonuses for on-time performance and average customer wait times. Its performance may yield a bonus from $0 to $600 000 under the contract. Based on its history with the theme park, customer travel patterns and its current expectations, Entity A estimates the probabilities for different amounts of bonus within the range as follows:

Bonus amount	Probability of outcome
$0	30%
$200 000	30%
$400 000	35%
$600 000	5%

Analysis

Expected value

Because Entity A believes that there is no one amount within the range that is most likely to be received, Entity A determines that the expected value approach is most appropriate to use. As a result, Entity A estimates variable consideration to be $230 000 (($200 000 × 30%) + ($400 000 × 35%) + ($600 000 × 5%)) before considering the effect of the constraint.

Assume that Entity A is a calendar year-end entity and it entered into the contract with the theme park during its second quarter. Customer wait times were slightly above average during the second quarter. Based on this experience, Entity A determines that it is highly probable that a significant revenue reversal for $200 000 of variable consideration will not occur. Therefore, after applying the constraint, Entity A only includes $200 000 in its estimated transaction price. At the end of its third quarter, Entity A updates its analysis and expected value calculation. The updated analysis again results in estimated variable consideration of $230 000, with a probability outcome of 75%. Based on analysis of the factors in paragraph 57 of IFRS 15 and in light of slightly better-than-expected average customer wait times during the third quarter, Entity A determines that it is probable that a significant revenue reversal for the entire $230 000 estimated transaction price would not be subject to a significant revenue reversal. Entity A updates its estimate to include the entire $230 000 in the transaction price. Entity A will continue to update its estimate of the transaction price at each subsequent reporting period.

Scenario B

Assume the same facts as in Scenario A, except that the potential bonus will be one of four stated amounts: $0, $200 000, $400 000 or $600 000. Based on its history with the theme park and customer travel patterns, Entity A estimates the probabilities for each bonus amount as follows:

Bonus amount	Probability of outcome
$0	30%
$200 000	30%
$400 000	35%
$600 000	5%

Analysis

Expected value

Entity A determined that the expected value approach was the most appropriate to use when estimating its variable consideration. Under that approach, it estimates the variable consideration is $230 000. Entity A must then consider the effect of the constraint on the amount of variable consideration included in the transaction price. Entity A notes that, because there are only four potential outcomes under the contract, the constraint essentially limits the amount of revenue Entity A can recognise to one of the stated bonus amounts. In this example, Entity A would be limited to including $200 000 in the estimated transaction price until it became highly probable that the next bonus level (i.e. $400 000) would be achieved. This is because any amount over $200 000 would be subject to subsequent reversal, unless $400 000 was received.

Most likely amount

As there are only a limited number of outcomes for the amount of bonus that can be received, Entity A is concerned that a probability-weighted estimate may result in an amount that is not a potential outcome. Therefore, Entity A determines that estimating the transaction price by identifying the most likely outcome would be the best predictor.

The standard is not clear about how an entity would determine the most likely amount when there are more than two potential outcomes and none of the potential outcomes is significantly more likely than the others. A literal reading of the standard might suggest that, in this example, Entity A would select $400 000 because that is the amount with the highest estimated probability. However, Entity A must then apply a constraint on the amount of variable consideration included in the transaction price.

To include $400 000 in the estimated transaction price, Entity A has to believe it is highly probable that the bonus amount will be at least $400 000. Based on the listed probabilities above, however, Entity A believes it is only 40% likely to receive a bonus of at least $400 000 (i.e. 35% + 5%) and 70% likely it will receive a bonus of at least $200 000 (i.e. 30% + 35% + 5%). As a result, Entity A would include only $200 000 in its estimate of the transaction price.

Source: Ernst & Young (2015, pp. 1973–1974).

4.5.2 Significant financing component

For some transactions, customers may pay in advance or in arrears of the goods or services being transferred to them. When the customer pays before (or after) the goods or services are provided, the entity is effectively receiving financing from (or providing financing to) the customer. Paragraph 60 of IFRS 15 requires that the entity adjusts the transaction price for the effects of the time value of money if either the customer or the entity is provided with a significant financing benefit due to the timing of payments.

As a practical expedient, an entity is only required to assess whether the arrangement contains a significant financing component when the period between the customer's payment and the entity's transfer of the goods or services is greater than 1 year. This assessment, performed at the commencement of the contract, will likely require entities to exercise significant judgement. Furthermore, a financing component only affects the transaction price when it is considered significant to the contract.

For contracts with a significant financing component, the transaction price is calculated by discounting the amount of promised consideration, using the same discount rate that an entity would use if it were to enter into a separate financing transaction with the customer. Using a risk-free rate or a rate that is explicitly specified in the contract that does not reflect the borrower's credit characteristics would not be acceptable. An entity does not need to update the discount rate for changes in circumstances or interest rates after the commencement of the contract.

4.5.3 Non-cash consideration

A customer might pay in cash or in forms other than cash (e.g. goods, services, equity shares). Paragraph 66 of IFRS 15 requires an entity to include the fair value of any non-cash consideration it receives (or expects to receive) in the transaction price. An entity applies the requirements of IFRS 13 *Fair Value Measurement* when measuring the fair value of any non-cash consideration. If an entity cannot reasonably estimate the fair value of non-cash consideration, it measures the non-cash consideration indirectly by reference to the estimated stand-alone selling price of the promised goods or services.

The fair value of non-cash consideration may change because of the occurrence (or non-occurrence) of a future event (e.g. performance considerations that affect the amount of consideration) or because of the form of consideration (e.g. shares in which the share price may change). Under IFRS 15, an entity has to consider constraining the non-cash consideration using the requirements for constraining variable consideration *(as discussed in section 4.5.1)*, if the amount may vary for reasons other than the form of consideration (i.e. there is uncertainty as to whether the entity will receive the non-cash consideration).

4.5.4 Consideration paid or payable to a customer

It is common for entities to make payments to their customers or, in some cases, to other parties that purchase the entity's goods or services from the customer (e.g. customers of a reseller or distributor). Such payments might be explicitly stated in the contract or implied by the entity's customary business practice.

In addition, the term 'payments' does not only refer to cash payments. Paragraph 70 of IFRS 15 provides that consideration paid or payable can also be in the form of non-cash items (e.g. discounts, coupons, vouchers) that a customer can apply against amounts owed to the entity.

To determine the appropriate accounting treatment, an entity would need to assess the purpose of the payments. That is, an entity must first determine whether the consideration paid or payable to a customer is:

- a payment for a distinct good or service *(see discussion in section 4.4.1)*; or
- to reduce the transaction price; or
- a combination of both.

If the consideration paid or payable to a customer is a payment for a distinct good or service from the customer, an entity accounts for the purchase of the good or service like any other purchase from a supplier. Otherwise, such payments are accounted for as a reduction to the transaction price and recognised at the later of when the entity:

- transfers the promised goods or services to the customer; or
- pays or promises to pay the consideration.

In some cases, the payments could be for both a distinct good or service and to reduce the transaction price. If the payments to the customer exceed the fair value of the distinct good or service received from the customer, the excess is accounted for as a reduction of the transaction price. If the fair value of the good or service received from the customer cannot be reasonably estimated, the entire payment to the customer is accounted for as a reduction of the transaction price.

Furthermore, the consideration paid or payable to a customer may be fixed or variable in amount (e.g. in the form of a discount or refund for goods or services provided). If the discount or refund is subject to variability, an entity would estimate it using either of the two approaches *discussed in section 4.5.1* and apply the constraint to the estimate to determine the effect of the discount or refund on the transaction price or related revenues.

4.6 ALLOCATE THE TRANSACTION PRICE

In the fourth step of the model, IFRS 15 requires an entity to allocate the transaction price to each performance obligation that has been identified. In this step, an entity allocates the transaction price to each identified performance obligation based on the proportion of the stand-alone selling price of that performance obligation to the sum of the total stand-alone selling prices of all performance obligations. This is known as the relative stand-alone selling price method. Under this method, any discount within the contract will be allocated proportionally to all of the separate performance obligations in the contract.

There are two exceptions to using the relative stand-alone selling price method:

- An entity will allocate variable consideration to one or more (but not all) performance obligations, or one or more (but not all) distinct goods or services promised in a series of distinct goods or services that forms part of a single performance obligation *(as discussed in section 4.4.2)*, in a contract in some situations.
- An entity will allocate a discount in an arrangement to one or more (but not all) performance obligations in a contract, if specified criteria are met.

4.6.1 Stand-alone selling prices

In applying the relative stand-alone selling price method, an entity must first determine the stand-alone selling price for each identified performance obligation. The stand-alone selling price is the price at which a good or service is, or would be, sold separately by the entity. This price is determined by the entity at the commencement of the contract and is not typically updated subsequently. However, if the contract is modified and that modification is not treated as a separate contract, the entity would update its estimate of the stand-alone selling price at the time of the modification *(see section 4.9.1)*.

Under IFRS 15, an entity should use the observable price of a good or service sold separately, when it is readily available. In situations in which there is no observable stand-alone selling price, the entity must estimate the stand-alone selling price. Paragraph 79 of IFRS 15 highlights the following methods, which may be, but are not required to be, used:

- **Adjusted market assessment approach** — this approach considers the amount that the market is willing to pay for a good or service and focuses primarily on external factors rather than entity-specific factors.
- **Expected cost plus margin approach** — this approach is based primarily on internal factors (e.g. incurred costs). However, it factors in a margin that the entity believes the market would be willing to pay, not the margin that an entity would like to get.
- **Residual approach** — this approach allows an entity that can estimate the stand-alone selling prices for one or more, but not all, promised goods or service to allocate the remaining transaction price to the goods or services for which it could not reasonably make an estimate, provided certain criteria are met. However, the use of this approach may be limited because it requires that the selling price of the goods or services be either highly variable or uncertain because the goods or services have not yet been sold.

An entity is required to consider all reasonably available information (including market conditions, entity-specific factors and information about the customer or class of customer) when determining the estimated stand-alone selling price. The standard requires an entity to make as much use of observable inputs as reasonably possible and to apply estimation methods consistently to similar circumstances. This will require an entity to consider a variety of data sources.

4.6.2 Application of the relative stand-alone selling price method

Under the relative stand-alone selling price method, once the stand-alone selling price of each performance obligation is determined, the entity will then allocate the transaction price to each performance obligation based on the proportion of the stand-alone selling price of each performance obligation to the sum of the stand-alone selling prices of all the performance obligations in the contract. Illustrative example 4.3 shows a relative stand-alone selling price allocation.

ILLUSTRATIVE EXAMPLE 4.3 Relative stand-alone selling price allocation

Manufacturing Co. entered into a contract with a customer to sell a machine for £100 000. The total contract price included installation of the machine and a 2 year extended warranty. Assume that Manufacturing Co. determined there were three performance obligations and the stand-alone selling prices of those performance obligations were as follows: machine — £75 000, installation services — £14 000 and extended warranty — £20 000.

The aggregate of the stand-alone selling prices (£109 000) exceeds the total transaction price of £100 000, indicating there is a discount inherent in the contract. That discount must be allocated to each of the individual performance obligations based on the relative stand-alone selling price of each performance obligation. Therefore, the amount of the £100 000 transaction price is allocated to each performance obligation as follows:

Machine	—	£68 807 (£75 000 × (£100 000/£109 000))
Installation	—	£12 844 (£14 000 × (£100 000/£109 000))
Warranty	—	£18 349 (£20 000 × (£100 000/£109 000))

The entity would recognise as revenue the amount allocated to each performance obligation when (or as) each performance obligation is satisfied.

Source: Ernst & Young (2015, p. 1997).

4.7 SATISFACTION OF PERFORMANCE OBLIGATIONS

Under IFRS 15, revenue can only be recognised when an entity satisfies an identified performance obligation by transferring a promised good or service to a customer. A good or service is considered transferred when the customer obtains control over the promised good or service (i.e. the customer can direct the use of, and receive benefits from, the good or service, or prevent others from doing the same).

For each performance obligation identified in the contract, an entity must determine at the commencement of the contract, whether the performance obligation will be satisfied over time or at a point in time. If a performance obligation does not meet the criteria to be satisfied over time, it is presumed to be satisfied at a point in time. These concepts are explored further in the following sections.

4.7.1 Performance obligations satisfied over time

Paragraph 35 of IFRS 15 provides the criteria to help an entity determine if a performance obligation is satisfied over time. An entity has to meet one of the following criteria in order to recognise revenue over time:
(a) the benefits provided by the entity's performance are simultaneously received and consumed by the customer;
(b) the customer controls an asset that is being created or enhanced by the entity's performance; or
(c) the asset created has no alternative use to the entity and there is an enforceable right to payment for the work performed to date.

Illustrative example 4.4 demonstrates the application of each of the above criteria:

ILLUSTRATIVE EXAMPLE 4.4 Application of the criteria for recognition over time

Scenario A — Customer simultaneously receives and consumes the benefits

Sparkle and Co. enters into a contract to provide weekly cleaning services to a customer for 2 years.

The promised cleaning services are accounted for as a single performance obligation *as discussed in section 4.4.2*. The performance obligation is satisfied over time because the customer simultaneously receives and consumes the benefits of Sparkle and Co.'s cleaning services as and when Sparkle and Co. performs. The fact that another entity would not need to re-perform the cleaning services that Sparkle

---

and Co. has provided to date also demonstrates that the customer simultaneously receives and consumes the benefits of Sparkle and Co.'s performance as Sparkle and Co. performs. As such, Sparkle and Co. recognises revenue over time by measuring its progress towards satisfaction of that performance obligation *as discussed in section 4.7.2.*

Scenario B — Customer controls asset as it is created or enhanced

Sakalian enters into an agreement to build an integrated IT system that interfaces sales, procurement and accounting functions. Sakalian is expected to take 1 year to complete the work.

During the development of the integrated system, Sakalian works extensively with the customer to design and configure the system as well as to run tests to check its operability. All work is being performed at the customer's site so that throughout the different stages of development, the customer takes ownership and physical possession of the integrated system as it is being built.

Because the customer controls the integrated IT system as it is built, Sakalian determines that the performance obligation is satisfied over time (i.e. the control over the asset is transferred over time), rather than at a point in time.

Scenario C — Asset with no alternative use and right to payment

Novak Ltd enters into a contract to construct a highly customised piece of equipment subject to specifications provided by the customer. If the customer were to terminate the contract for reasons other than Novak Ltd's failure to perform as promised, the contract requires the customer to compensate Novak Ltd for its costs incurred plus a 10% margin. The 10% margin approximates the profit margin that Novak Ltd earns from similar contracts.

In the event of contract cancellation, the contract also contains an enforceable restriction on Novak Ltd's ability to direct the equipment (regardless of the extent of completion) for another use, such as selling the equipment to another customer. As a result, the equipment does not have an alternative use to Novak Ltd.

Furthermore, Novak Ltd has an enforceable right to payment for its performance completed to date for its costs plus a reasonable margin, which approximates the profit margin in other contracts.

As a result, Novak Ltd recognises revenue over time by measuring the progress towards satisfaction of the performance obligation *as discussed in section 4.7.2.*

If a performance obligation is satisfied over time, an entity would recognise revenue over time by using a method that best reflects its progress in satisfying that performance obligation *(see section 4.7.2).*

4.7.2 Measure of progress

When an entity has determined that a performance obligation is satisfied over time, paragraph 40 of IFRS 15 requires an entity to select a single revenue recognition method to measure the entity's progress in transferring the promised goods or services over time. In selecting the method that best reflects the transfer of the promised goods or services, the entity considers both the nature of the goods or services and the work to be performed by the entity. The selected method must be applied consistently to similar performance obligations and in similar circumstances, and the standard does not allow a change in methods. That is, a performance obligation is accounted for under the method the entity selects until it has been fully satisfied. However, the standard does require an entity to update its estimates related to the measure of progress selected at each reporting date. The effect of changes in the measure of progress is accounted for as a change in estimate under IAS 8 *Accounting Policies, Changes in Accounting Estimates and Errors.*

There are two methods for recognising revenue on arrangements involving the transfer of goods and services over time:

- **Output methods** — measure the value of goods or services transferred to date relative to the remaining goods or services promised under the agreement (e.g. surveys of performance completed to date, appraisals of results achieved, milestones reached, time elapsed and units produced or units delivered).
- **Input methods** — measure the inputs/efforts put in by the entity relative to the total expected inputs needed to transfer the promised goods or services to the customer (e.g. resources consumed, labour hours expended, costs incurred, time elapsed or machine hours used). Using a straight-line basis to recognise revenue is appropriate only if the entity's efforts or inputs are expended evenly throughout the period that an entity performs.

If an entity does not have a reasonable basis to measure its progress, revenue is not recognised until the entity is able to measure its progress. However, in cases in which the entity is not able to reasonably estimate the amount of profit but is able to determine that a loss will not be incurred, the entity will recognise revenue but only up to the amount of the costs incurred, until the outcome/profit can be reasonably estimated.

4.7.3 Performance obligation satisfied at a point in time

For performance obligations in which control is not transferred over time, control is transferred at a point in time. In many situations, the determination of the point at which control is transferred is relatively straightforward. However, there are instances when this determination could be more complicated. To help entities determine the point in time when a customer obtains control of a particular good or service, the standard provides a non-exhaustive list of indicators of the transfer of control, as follows:

(a) The entity has a present right to payment for the asset.
(b) The asset's legal title is held by the customer.
(c) Physical possession of the asset has been transferred by the entity.
(d) The significant risks and rewards of ownership of the asset reside with the customer.
(e) There is customer acceptance of the asset.

These indicators are not individually determinative and no one indicator is more important than the others. Rather, an entity must consider all relevant facts and circumstances to determine when control has been transferred. Furthermore, this list of indicators is not intended to be a 'checklist'. That is, an entity does not need to meet all of these indicators to determine that the customer has gained control. Rather, they are just some common factors that are often present when a customer has obtained control of an asset.

4.8 CONTRACT COSTS

IFRS 15 requires an entity to capitalise, as an asset, two types of costs relating to a contract with a customer:
- any incremental costs to obtain the contract that would otherwise not have been incurred, if the entity expects to recover them;
- costs incurred to fulfil a contract with the customer, if certain criteria are met.
  We will discuss these two types of costs further in section 4.8.1.

Any capitalised contract costs are then amortised on a systematic basis that reflects the pattern of transfer of the related promised goods or services to the customer. Entities will also have to assess any capitalised contract costs for impairment at the end of each reporting period. *See further discussion in section 4.8.2.*

4.8.1 Contract costs to be capitalised

Incremental costs to obtain a contract

Under IFRS 15, the costs that an entity incurs in order to obtain a contract are capitalised only if they are incremental and expected to be recoverable. This means that the costs need to be either explicitly reimbursable under the contract or implicitly recoverable through the margin inherent in the contract. Costs that would have been incurred regardless of whether the contract is obtained or those costs that are not directly related to obtaining a contract would not be capitalisable.

To illustrate this distinction, consider the following examples:
- Sales commissions paid to an employee if a contract with a customer is successfully won would likely meet the requirements for capitalisation.
- Bonuses paid to an employee based on quantitative or qualitative metrics that are unrelated to winning a contract (e.g. profitability, earnings per share, performance evaluations) would likely not meet the criteria for capitalisation.

If the amortisation period of the incremental costs would be 1 year or less, an entity can choose to expense these costs immediately, as a practical expedient, instead of capitalising such costs.

Costs to fulfil a contract

Entities may incur some costs as they fulfil a contract. An entity will first have to determine if such contract fulfilment costs are within the scope of other standards (e.g. IAS 2 *Inventories*, IAS 16 *Property, Plant and Equipment*, IAS 38 *Intangible Assets*). The requirements of IFRS 15 will apply only if such costs do not fall within the scope of other standards.

Under IFRS 15, the costs incurred to fulfil a contract are capitalised only if all the following conditions are met:

(a) they are directly related to a specific contract or to a specific anticipated contract (e.g. direct labour, direct materials);
(b) they generate or enhance resources of the entity that will be used in satisfying (or in continuing to satisfy) performance obligations in the future; and
(c) they are expected to be recovered (*see discussion on incremental costs to obtain a contract*).

If the above criteria are not met, an entity will expense the contract fulfilment costs as they are incurred. In assessing the above criteria, an entity must consider its specific facts and circumstances.

Criterion (a) above indicates that such costs may be incurred even before the related contract is finalised. However, such costs need to be associated with a specifically identifiable anticipated contract in order to be capitalisable.

4.8.2 Amortisation and impairment of contract costs

An entity has to amortise any capitalised contract costs and recognise the expense in the statement of profit or loss. *As discussed earlier in the introduction to section 4.8,* an entity amortises the capitalised contract costs on a systematic basis that reflects the pattern of transfer of the related promised goods or services to the customer.

In some cases, the capitalised costs may relate to multiple goods and services that are transferred under multiple contracts. Entities will need to consider this aspect when determining the amortisation period to apply. Entities are also required to update the amortisation period to reflect a significant change in the expected timing of transfer to the customer of the goods or services to which the asset relates. Such a change would need to be treated as a change in accounting estimate under IAS 8.

Capitalised contract costs must continue to be recoverable throughout the arrangement. As such, any contract costs asset recognised under IFRS 15 is subject to an impairment assessment at the end of each reporting period. An impairment loss is recognised in the statement of profit or loss for the difference between:

- the carrying amount of the capitalised contract costs; and
- the remaining amount of consideration that an entity expects to receive in exchange for providing the associated goods and services, less the remaining costs that relate directly to providing those good and services.

4.9 OTHER APPLICATION ISSUES

4.9.1 Contract modifications

Paragraph 18 of IFRS 15 states that:

A contract modification is a change in the scope or price (or both) of a contract that is approved by the parties to the contract. In some industries and jurisdictions, a contract modification may be described as a change order, a variation or an amendment. A contract modification exists when the parties to a contract approve a modification that either creates new or changes existing enforceable rights and obligations of the parties to the contract. A contract modification could be approved in writing, by oral agreement or implied by customary business practices. If the parties to the contract have not approved a contract modification, an entity shall continue to apply this Standard to the existing contract until the contract modification is approved.

As evident in the definition, an approved contract modification can be explicit or implicit; however, as long as it results in enforceable changes to the rights and obligations of the parties involved in the contract, it would need to be accounted for.

Once an entity has determined that a contract has been modified, the entity has to determine the appropriate accounting treatment under IFRS 15. Certain modifications are treated as separate, stand-alone contracts, while others are combined with the existing contract and accounted for together. Two criteria must be met for a modification to be treated as a separate contract:

(a) The scope of the contract increases because of the promise of additional goods or services that are distinct from those already promised in the original contract.

This assessment is done in accordance with IFRS 15's requirements for determining whether promised goods and services are distinct *as discussed in section 4.4.1.* Although a contract modification may add a new good or service that would be distinct in a stand-alone transaction, the new good or service may not be distinct when it is considered within the context of a contract modification. Furthermore, only modifications that add distinct goods or services to the arrangement can be treated as separate contracts. Arrangements that reduce the amount of promised goods or services or change the scope of the original promised goods or services cannot, by their very nature, be considered separate contracts. Instead, they would be considered modifications of the original contract.

(b) The expected amount of consideration for the additional promised goods or services reflects the entity's stand-alone selling price(s) of those goods or services.

However, when determining the stand-alone selling price, entities have some flexibility to adjust that price, depending on the facts and circumstances. For example, a discount may be given to a customer who decides to purchase additional goods and the discount relates to selling-related costs that are only incurred for new customers. In this example, the entity may determine that the adjusted selling price meets the stand-alone selling price requirement, even though the discounted price is less than the stand-alone selling price of that good or service for a new customer.

If the two criteria are not met, the contract modification would be accounted for as a change to the original contract (i.e. not accounted for as a separate contract). Such types of contract modifications (which may include changes that modify or remove previously agreed-upon goods and services) may be accounted for in any of the following three ways depending on the specific facts and circumstances:

1. **Termination of the old contract and the creation of a new contract.**

This accounting treatment applies if the remaining goods or services after the contract modification are distinct from the goods or services transferred on or before the contract modification. Under this approach, an entity does not adjust the revenue previously recognised. Instead, the remaining portion of the original contract and the modification are accounted for, together, on a prospective basis by allocating the total remaining consideration to the remaining performance obligations.

2. Continuation of the original contract.

This accounting treatment applies if the remaining goods and services to be provided after the contract modification are not distinct from those already provided. That is, the remaining goods or services constitute part of a single performance obligation that is partially satisfied at the date of modification. Under this approach, the entity adjusts the revenue previously recognised, either up or down, for any changes to the transaction price and the measure of progress as a result of the contract modification, on a cumulative catch-up basis.

3. Modification of the existing contract and the creation of a new contract.

This accounting treatment is a combination of the two above treatments. In this case, an entity does not adjust the revenue previously recognised for the goods or services already transferred that are distinct from the modified goods or services.

However, for the transferred goods or services that are not distinct from the modified goods or services, the entity would have to adjust the revenue previously recognised, either up or down, for any changes to the estimated transaction price and the measure of progress as a result of the contract modification, on a cumulative catch-up basis.

4.9.2 Licences of intellectual property

The standard provides separate application guidance specific to licences of intellectual property ('licences') that will apply to licences for any of the following: software and technology, media and entertainment (e.g. motion pictures and music), franchises, patents, trademarks and copyrights.

Determining whether a licence is distinct

The application guidance on licences applies to distinct licences regardless of whether they are promised explicitly or implicitly in the contract. In many transactions, licences may be sold together with other goods or services. In these circumstances, the entity needs to assess whether the licence is a separate performance obligation (i.e. whether the benefit derived from the licence can only be obtained when it is used together with another good or service or whether it can be of use to the customer on its own) *as discussed in section 4.4.1.*

If the licence is distinct, the entity then has to determine the nature of its promise to the customer (discussed further below) to determine if the licence revenue is recognised over time or at a point in time.

If the licence is not distinct, then an entity would look to the other requirements in IFRS 15 to account for the combined performance obligation that includes the licence. However, in some cases, it could be necessary for an entity to consider the nature of the entity's promise in granting a licence (discussed further below) even when the licence is not distinct (e.g. when the licence is the primary or dominant component of a combined performance obligation) in order to appropriately determine whether the performance obligation is satisfied over time or at a point in time and/or to determine the appropriate measure of progress.

Determining the nature of the entity's promise

For distinct licences (and in some cases, combined performance obligations for which the licence is the primary or dominant component), an entity must determine whether the licence is a 'right to access' or a 'right to use'.

If the entity has promised a customer a right to access the intellectual property (including any updates) throughout the licence period, revenue is recognised over time. In making this assessment as to whether the nature of the promise is a right to access, all of the following criteria must be met:

(a) the entity is required to (or the customer reasonably expects that the entity will) perform activities that significantly affect the intellectual property to which the licence relates;

(b) the customer is directly exposed to any affects (both positive and negative) of those activities in (a) as a result of the rights granted under the licence; and

(c) the activities in (a) do not transfer any goods or services to the customer.

If the licensed intellectual property does not have the above characteristics, the nature of the entity's promise will be a right to use (i.e. the customer is granted the use of the intellectual property as it exists at the point in time in which the licence is granted). Therefore the revenue for a right to use licence is recognised at a point in time.

It is critical for an entity to assess the above criteria and judgement will be required to assess whether a customer has a reasonable expectation that the entity will perform the relevant activities. For example, the existence of a shared economic interest between the parties (e.g. sales or usage-based royalties which are discussed further below) may be an indicator that the customer has a reasonable expectation for the entity to perform such activities. These activities need not be specifically linked to the contract but they can be part of an entity's ongoing business activities and customary business practices.

Sales or usage-based royalties on licences of intellectual property

IFRS 15 includes an exception in which sales-based or usage-based royalties on licences of intellectual property are excluded from the estimate of variable consideration. Under the standard, these amounts are recognised only at the later of:
- when the subsequent sale or usage occurs; or
- the performance obligation to which some or all of the sales-based or usage-based royalty has been allocated is wholly or partially satisfied.

This exception is applicable to all licences of intellectual property, regardless of whether they have been determined to be distinct. However, the exception is not applicable to all arrangements involving sales or usage-based royalties. It only applies to sales- or usage-based royalties related to licences of intellectual property.

4.9.3 Principal versus agent considerations

In arrangements that have three or more parties, an entity will have to determine whether it is acting as a principal or an agent in order to determine the amount of revenue to which it is entitled. To make this determination, the entity must conclude whether the nature of its promise to the customer is to provide the specified goods and services itself (i.e. it is a principal) or if its promise is to arrange for another to provide those goods or services (i.e. it is an agent).

When the entity is the principal in the arrangement, the revenue recognised is the gross amount to which the entity expects to be entitled. When the entity is the agent, the revenue recognised is the net amount that the entity is entitled to retain in return for its services as the agent (e.g. its commission).

Given that the identification of the principal and agent in a contract is not always straightforward, IFRS 15 provides the following indicators to help entities assess if there is an agency relationship:
(a) the entity does not have the primary responsibility of fulfilling the contract
(b) the entity has no inventory risk over the goods transferred (or to be transferred)
(c) the entity does not have discretion in establishing prices for the other party's goods or services
(d) the entity's consideration is in the form of a commission
(e) the entity is not exposed to customer credit risk for the amount due in exchange for the other party's goods or services.

After an entity identifies its promise and determines whether it is the principal or the agent, the entity recognises the revenue to which it is entitled when it satisfies that performance obligation (*see section 4.7*).

4.10 PRESENTATION AND DISCLOSURES

4.10.1 Presentation of contract assets, contract liabilities and revenue

Under the standard, when either party to a contract performs, a contract asset or contract liability must be recognised in the statement of financial position.

A contract liability arises if the customer performs first (e.g. by prepaying the promised consideration before the promised goods or services are transferred). Conversely, a contract asset represents an entity's conditional right to consideration from the customer when it satisfies a performance obligation under the contract. This conditional right may be because the entity must first satisfy another performance obligation in the contract before it is entitled to invoice the customer. When the entity's right to collect the consideration becomes unconditional (i.e. there is nothing other than the passage of time before the customer pays the entity), a receivable is recognised in place of the contract asset.

The standard does not require entities to specifically use the terms 'contract assets' or 'contract liabilities'. However, the standard does require that the unconditional rights to consideration (i.e. receivables) be clearly distinguished from the conditional rights to receive consideration (i.e. contract assets). After initial recognition, receivables and contract assets are subject to an impairment assessment in accordance with IFRS 9 or IAS 39.

Other assets, such as capitalised contract costs (*see section 4.8*), are required to be presented separately from contract assets and contract liabilities in the statement of financial position, if they are material. In addition, revenue from contracts with customers is required to be separately presented or disclosed from other sources of revenue.

4.10.2 Disclosure objective and general requirements

The overall disclosure objective is set out in paragraph 110 of IFRS 15:

> The objective of the disclosure requirements is for an entity to disclose sufficient information to enable users of financial statements to understand the nature, amount, timing and uncertainty of revenue and cash flows arising from contracts with customers.

As a result, qualitative and quantitative information about the following must be disclosed:

(a) contracts with customers *(see section 4.10.3)*;
(b) the significant judgements, and changes in the judgements, made in applying the standard *(see section 4.10.4)*; and
(c) any assets recognised from the costs to obtain or fulfil a contract with a customer *(see section 4.10.5)*.

Entities are required to ensure that useful information is not obscured by either the inclusion of a large amount of insignificant detail or the aggregation of items that have substantially different characteristics.

The disclosures are required for (and as at) each annual period for which a statement of comprehensive income and a statement of financial position are presented. The standard also requires information on disaggregated revenue in both an entity's annual and interim financial statements *(see section 4.10.3)*.

4.10.3 Disclosures on contracts with customers

These disclosures comprise information on disaggregation of revenue, contract asset and liability balances and an entity's performance obligations.

The main purpose of the disaggregated revenue disclosures is to illustrate how the nature, amount, timing and uncertainty about revenue and cash flows are affected by economic factors. Entities would have to determine how they should present the disaggregated revenue information according to their facts and circumstances because the standard does not specify how revenue should be disaggregated. However, the application guidance suggests categories, including: by major product line, by country or region, by type of customer, by type of contract or by contract duration.

Furthermore, an entity is required to disclose:

- the opening and closing balances of receivables, contract assets and contract liabilities from contracts with customers, if not otherwise separately presented or disclosed;
- revenue recognised in the reporting period that was included in the contract liability balance at the beginning of the period; and
- revenue recognised in the reporting period from performance obligations satisfied (or partially satisfied) in previous periods (e.g. changes in transaction price).

In addition, an entity is required to explain the interaction between the revenue recognised and significant movements in the contract asset and the contract liability balances during the reporting period. This requires both qualitative and quantitative information to be disclosed, such as how the timing of satisfaction of the entity's performance obligations relates to the typical timing of payment and the effect that those factors have on the contract asset and the contract liability balances.

Illustrative example 4.5 shows how an entity may fulfil these requirements:

ILLUSTRATIVE EXAMPLE 4.5 Disclosure of contract balances

Cheng Ltd discloses trade receivables separately in the statement of financial position. In order to comply with the remainder of the required disclosures pertaining to contract assets and liabilities, Cheng Ltd includes the following information in the notes to the financial statements:

	2019	2018	2017
Contract asset	€1 500	€2 250	€1 800
Contract liability	€ (200)	€ (850)	€ (500)

	2019	2018	2017
Revenue recognised in the period from:			
Amounts included in contract liability at the beginning of the period	€ 650	€ 200	€ 100
Performance obligations satisfied in previous periods	€ 200	€ 125	€ 200

We receive payments from customers based on a billing schedule, as established in our contracts. The contract asset relates to costs incurred to perform in advance of scheduled billing. The contract liability relates to payments received in advance of performance under the contract. Changes in the contract asset and liability are due to our performance under the contract. In addition, a contract asset decreased in 2018 due to a contract asset impairment of €400 relating to an early cancellation of a contract with a customer.

Note that IFRS 15 requires the disclosure of opening and closing balances for contract assets and liabilities and, as such, the balances presented for 2017 reflect the opening balances for 2018. There may be alternative approaches to presenting such information.

Source: Adapted from Ernst & Young (2015, p. 2048).

Separate disclosure of an entity's remaining performance obligations is also required, as well as the amount of the transaction price allocated to the remaining performance obligations and an explanation of the expected timing of recognition for those amount(s). This disclosure can be provided on either a quantitative basis (e.g. amounts to be recognised in given time bands, such as between 1 and 2 years or between 2 and 3 years) or by disclosing a mix of quantitative and qualitative information.

Note that there is a practical expedient exempting an entity from making these particular disclosures if the remaining performance obligation is for contracts with an original expected duration of less than 1 year or the entity is recognising revenue based on invoiced amounts.

4.10.4 Significant judgements

IFRS 15 requires an entity to disclose the significant accounting estimates and judgements made in applying Steps 3 to 5 of the model in IFRS 15 *(see section 4.1)*. These requirements are in addition to the requirements in IAS 1 *Presentation of Financial Statements*.

Entities will need to exercise significant judgement when applying the model in IFRS 15, such as when estimating the variable consideration included in the transaction price and application of the constraint (Step 3), when estimating the stand-alone selling prices used to allocate the transaction price (Step 4) and when measuring obligations for returns, refunds and other similar obligations. Paragraph 126 of IFRS 15 requires entities to disclose qualitative information about the methods, inputs and assumptions used in all of the above judgements in their annual financial statements.

IFRS 15 also requires entities to provide disclosures about the significant judgements made in determining when performance obligations are satisfied. For performance obligations that are satisfied over time, entities must disclose the output or input method used to recognise revenue and how the selected method reflects the pattern of goods or services that are transferred.

For performance obligations satisfied at a point in time, entities must disclose the significant judgements made in determining the point at which the entity transfers control of the promised goods or services to the customer.

4.10.5 Assets recognised from the costs to obtain or fulfil a contract

IFRS 15 requires entities to disclose information on contract costs that are capitalised to help users understand the amounts and types of costs that have been capitalised, the amortisation methods applied or any impairment losses that have been recognised. The information includes an explanation of any judgements made in applying the requirements under IFRS 15.

4.10.6 Practical expedients

In addition, IFRS 15 has several practical expedients that entities can elect to use. If either or both of the practical expedients relating to a significant financing component *(see section 4.5.2)* or incremental costs of obtaining a contract *(see section 4.8.1)* are applied, the entity must disclose this fact.

SUMMARY

IFRS 15 is a new standard specifying the accounting treatment for all revenue arising from contracts with customers and, at the time of writing this chapter, is effective for annual reporting periods beginning on or after 1 January 2018. It applies to all entities that enter into contracts to provide goods or services to their customers, unless the contracts are within the scope of other IFRS Standards. The standard outlines the principles an entity must apply to measure and recognise revenue and the related cash flows. Under the standard, an entity applies the five-step model outlined in *sections 4.3 to 4.7* to recognise revenue at an amount that reflects the consideration to which the entity expects to be entitled in exchange for transferring goods or services to a customer.

At the time of writing, entities had not yet adopted this standard and therefore there were no examples of its use in practice. As a result, additional implementation issues are likely to arise as entities begin to apply the standard and practice may evolve during that process.

Discussion questions

1. What are the main accounting issues associated with the recognition of revenue and how does IFRS 15 address those?
2. What is the five-step model in connection with revenue recognition?
3. What is the distinction between revenue and income?

4. Why might it be necessary to combine individual contracts?
5. Describe some common forms of variable consideration.
6. Explain the disclosure objectives and general requirements of IFRS 15.

References

Ernst & Young 2015, *International GAAP 2015, Volume 2*, Chapter 29: Revenue from contracts with customers (IFRS 15). Chichester: John Wiley & Sons.

Exercises

STAR RATING ★ BASIC ★★ MODERATE ★★★ DIFFICULT

| Exercise 4.1 | SCOPE OF IFRS 15 |

★ List the criteria that must be met in order to determine whether an arrangement with a customer is a contact within the scope of IFRS 15.

| Exercise 4.2 | IDENTIFYING THE CONTRACT (1) |

★ A car dealership has cars available that can be used by potential customers for test drives (`demonstration cars'). The cars are used for more than one year and then sold as used cars. The dealership sells both new and used cars.

Required

Is the sale of a demonstration car accounted for as revenue or as a gain?

| Exercise 4.3 | IDENTIFYING THE CONTRACT (2) |

★★ A seller's practice is to obtain written and customer-signed sales agreements. It delivers a product to a customer without a signed agreement, based on a request by the customer to fulfil an urgent need.

Required

Can an enforceable contract exist if the seller has not obtained a signed agreement in accordance with its customary business practice?

| Exercise 4.4 | IDENTIFYING THE CONTRACT (3) |

★★ A service provider has a 12-month agreement to provide a customer with services for which the customer pays $1,000 per month. The agreement does not include any provisions for automatic extensions, and it expires on 30 November 2018. The two parties sign a new agreement on 28 February 2019 that requires the customer to pay $1,250 per month in fees, retroactive to 1 December 2018.
The customer continued to pay $1,000 per month during December, January and February, and the service provider continued to provide services during that period. There are no performance issues being disputed between the parties in the expired period, only negotiation of rates under the new contract.

Required

Does a contract exist in December, January and February (prior to the new agreement being signed)?

| Exercise 4.5 | COMBINED CONTRACT — CONTRACT MODIFICATION (1) |

★★ A manufacturer enters into an arrangement with a customer to sell 100 items of goods for $10,000 ($100 per item). The goods are distinct and are transferred to the customer over a six-month period. The parties modify the contract in the fourth month to sell an additional 20 items for $95 each. The price of the additional goods represents the stand-alone selling price on the modification date.

Required

Should the manufacturer account for the modification as a separate contract?

| Exercise 4.6 | COMBINED CONTRACT — CONTRACT MODIFICATION (2) |

★★ Entity A enters into a three-year service contract with a customer for $450,000 ($150,000 per year). The stand-alone selling price for one year of service at inception of the contract is $150,000 per year. Entity D accounts for the contract as a series of distinct services.

At the end of the second year, the parties agree to modify the contract as follows:
1. the fee for the third year is reduced to $120,000; and
2. the customer agrees to extend the contract for another three years for $300,000 ($100,000 per year). The stand-alone selling price for one year of service at the time of modification is $120,000.

Required

How should entity D account for the modification?

| Exercise 4.7 | MULTIPLE-ELEMENT ARRANGEMENT |

★★ Company A provides a bundled service offering to Customer B. It charges Customer B $35 000 for initial connection to its network and two ongoing services — access to the network for 1 year and 'on-call trouble-shooting' advice for that year.

Customer B pays the $35 000 upfront, on 1 July 2015. Company A determines that, if it were to charge a separate fee for each service if sold separately, the fee would be:

Connection fee	$ 5 000
Access fee	$12 000
Troubleshooting	$23 000

The end of Company A's reporting period is 30 June.

Required

Prepare the journal entries to record this transaction in accordance with IFRS 15 for the year ended 30 June 2016, assuming Company A applies the relative fair value approach. Show all workings.

Perhaps no other line-item in the income statement invites as much scrutiny as the top line of sales (or, revenues). Wagenhofer (2014)[1] states that 'Revenue is one of the most important measures of companies' financial performance'. He bases this assertion, in part, on reference to analysts' view of revenues as hard to manipulate, persistent and more responsive to underlying changes in the business environment than expenses.

If revenues possess these properties, we would expect them to be more value relevant than other numbers in the financial statements. Ertimur et al. (2003) analyse market reaction to earnings surprises. They claim that expenses reported in the income statement aggregate variety of expense types, which makes this information harder to analyse than revenues. Consistent with this argument they find that surprises in revenues are incorporated into prices with a larger magnitude than surprises in expenses. Jegadeesh and Livnat (2006) extend this line of research. They examine the relation between both earnings surprises and revenue surprises on one hand and current and future stock return on the other hand. They are motivated by the question of whether any reaction to earnings surprises is driven by news about revenue growth or contraction of costs (or vice versa). They show that both earnings surprises and revenue surprises are associated with current and future stock returns. However, the association with current returns is considerably weaker for revenue surprises. At the same time, future stock returns are more closely associated with current revenue surprises than current earnings surprises. This suggests that market participants may under-react to the information content in the revenue surprises.

A fundamental property of accrual accounting is the matching between revenues and expenses and costs. The Conceptual Framework (IASB, 2010, section 4.50) describes the process of matching as follows: 'Expenses are recognised in the income statement on the basis of a direct association between the costs incurred and the earning of specific items of income'. This implies that expenses follow revenues. Accounting researchers have been therefore interested in understanding this process and whether the quality of matching has improved over time. This question is of high relevance given the force with which standard setters have embarked on improving existing standards and issuing new ones over time. Dichev and Tang (2008) argue that more recent standards deviate from the tradition of matching as income is progressively based on changes in the balance sheet. Dichev and Tang (2008) develop a simple model for matching. Based on this model they posit that poor matching is manifested in lower correlation between revenues and expenses, higher variability of earnings and lower persistence. They then examine a long period (1967–2003) and find lower association between current expenses and current revenues for the sub-period of 1986–2003 than the earlier period of 1967–1985. Moreover, consistent with Givoly and Hayn (2000), they find evidence of early recognition of expenses in the latter sub-period, which is indicative

of increasing conservatism. In addition Dichev and Tang (2008) find that earnings persistence declined in the latter period relative to the earlier period.

While Dichev and Tang's (2008) paper is consistent with the notion of poorer matching in recent years, a limitation of their study is the way they define expenses. Specifically, expenses are captured as the difference between revenues and profits. Hence, their study is silent on which expense line-item contributes the most to the documented decline in matching. Donelson et al. (2011) take up this task by looking at cost of goods sold; selling, general, and administrative expense; depreciation; taxes; other income/expenses and special items. Their evidence suggests that the decline in the association between revenues and expenses is mostly attributable to special items. Special items include a variety of 'one-off' events, such as impairments and restructuring charges. Once these one-off items are excluded, Donelson et al. (2011) find no evidence of poorer matching in recent years.

Contrary to what some may believe, revenues may be susceptible to earnings manipulations. In particular, the US Securities and Exchange Commission (SEC) raised the concern that firms advance recognition of revenues. As a result, the SEC issued in 1999 Staff Accounting Bulletin (SAB) No. 101. The essence of this pronouncement is the tightening of revenue recognition criteria to reduce the incidence of premature revenue recognition. To the extent that the new regulation was effective, it is expected that firms that had to adopt SAB 101 would exhibit evidence of greater earnings management before adoption than after it. Altamuro et al. (2005) investigate this hypothesis. They find evidence suggesting that firms that adopted SAB 101 managed earnings more prior to adoption and less subsequently. This is supportive for the motivation behind the SEC's decision to pass SAB 101. This also speaks to the success of this promulgation. To provide further support for this result and remove suspicion it only captures time effect, Altamuro et al. (2005) compare earnings management in firms that were unaffected by SAB 101 around adoption time. Unlike firms subject to SAB 101, unaffected firms do not exhibit a decline in earnings management following the enactment of SAB 101.

References

Altamuro, J., Beatty, A.L., and Weber, J., 2005. The effects of accelerated revenue recognition on earnings management and earnings informativeness: Evidence from SEC Staff Accounting Bulletin No. 101. *The Accounting Review*, 80, 373–401.

Dichev, I.D., and Tang, V.W., 2008. Matching and the changing properties of accounting earnings over the last 40 years. *The Accounting Review*, 83, 1425–1460.

Donelson, D.C., Jennings, R., and McInnis, J., 2011. Changes over time in the revenue–expense relation: Accounting or economics? *The Accounting Review*, 86, 945–974.

---

[1]This paper provides a more extensive review of the literature and is recommended for the interested reader.

Ertimur, Y., Livnat, J., and Martikainen, M., 2003. Differential market reactions to revenue and expense surprises. *Review of Accounting Studies*, 8, 185–211.

Givoly, D., and Hayn, C., 2000. The changing time-series properties of earnings, cash flows and accruals: Has financial reporting become more conservative? *Journal of Accounting and Economics*, 29, 287–320.

IASB, 2010. *The Conceptual Framework for Financial Reporting*. London: IASB.

Jegadeesh, N., and Livnat, J., 2006. Revenue surprises and stock returns. *Journal of Accounting and Economics*, 41, 147–171.

Securities and Exchange Commission (SEC), 1999. Revenue recognition. Staff Accounting Bulletin No. 101. Washington DC: Government Printing Office.

Wagenhofer A., 2014. The role of revenue recognition in performance reporting. *Accounting and Business Research*, 44, 349–379.

5 Provisions, contingent liabilities and contingent assets

ACCOUNTING STANDARDS IN FOCUS

IAS 37 *Provisions, Contingent Liabilities and Contingent Assets*

LEARNING OBJECTIVES

After studying this chapter, you should be able to:

1. describe the background to IAS 37
2. identify which items are included within the scope of the standard
3. outline the concept of a provision
4. discuss how to distinguish provisions from other liabilities
5. outline the concept of a contingent liability
6. describe how to distinguish a provision from a contingent liability
7. explain when a provision should be recognised
8. explain how a provision, once recognised, should be measured
9. apply the definitions, recognition and measurement criteria for provisions and contingent liabilities to practical situations
10. outline the concept of a contingent asset
11. describe the disclosure requirements for provisions, contingent liabilities and contingent assets
12. compare the requirements of IFRS 3 regarding contingent liabilities with those of IAS 37
13. explain the expected future developments for IAS 37.

5.1 INTRODUCTION TO IAS 37

IAS 37 deals with the recognition, measurement and presentation of provisions, contingent liabilities and contingent assets. In 2005, the International Accounting Standards Board (IASB®) added a project on amending IAS 37 to its agenda and subsequently issued an exposure draft in June 2005. After obtaining and considering feedback from constituents, the IASB issued a second exposure draft in January 2010. However, the project was suspended, pending the outcome of the Board's 2011 consultation on its future agenda.

The IASB decided in May 2012 to initiate a research programme which includes the topic of non-financial liabilities. At the time of writing, the IASB has issued an exposure draft proposing the revision of its *Conceptual Framework*. One of the proposed changes is the revised definition of a liability *(see chapter 1)*.

Therefore, IAS 37 remains largely unchanged since its original issue date of 1998 by the IASC. This chapter addresses the standard and its related interpretations in effect at 1 January 2015.

The standard:

- defines provisions and specifies recognition criteria and measurement requirements for the recognition of provisions in financial statements
- defines contingent liabilities and contingent assets and prohibits their recognition in the financial statements but requires their disclosure when certain conditions are met
- requires that where provisions are measured using estimated cash flows the cash flows be discounted to their present value at the reporting date and specifies the discount rate to be used for this purpose
- prohibits providing for future operating losses
- defines onerous contracts and requires the estimated net loss under onerous contracts to be provided for
- specifies recognition criteria for restructuring provisions and identifies the types of costs that may be included in restructuring provisions
- requires extensive disclosures relating to provisions, recoveries, contingent liabilities and contingent assets.

5.2 SCOPE

IAS 37 prescribes the accounting and disclosure for all provisions, contingent liabilities and contingent assets except:

(a) those resulting from financial instruments *(see chapter 7)* and those arising in insurance entities from contracts with policy holders

(b) those resulting from executory contracts, except where the contract is onerous (Executory contracts are contracts under which neither party has performed any of its obligations or both parties have partially performed their obligations to an equal extent.)

(c) those specifically covered by another IAS®/IFRS® Standard. For example, certain types of provisions are also addressed in standards on:

- income taxes *(see IAS 12 Income Taxes, covered in chapter 6)*
- leases *(see IAS 17 Leases, covered in chapter 12. However, as IAS 17 contains no specific requirements to deal with operating leases that have become onerous, IAS 37 applies to such cases.)*
- employee benefits *(see IAS 19 Employee Benefits)*
- insurance contracts *(see IFRS 4 Insurance Contracts).*

Some amounts sometimes described as provisions may relate to the recognition of revenue; for example, where an entity gives guarantees in exchange for a fee. This may also be described as 'deferred revenue'. IAS 37 does not address the recognition of revenue. IFRS 15 *Revenue from Contracts with Customers* identifies the circumstances in which revenue is recognised and provides practical guidance on the application of the recognition criteria *(see chapter 4)*.

Sometimes the term 'provision' is also used in the context of items such as depreciation, impairment of assets and doubtful debts. These are adjustments to the carrying amounts of assets and are not addressed in IAS 37. *Refer to IAS 36 Impairment of Assets, which is covered in chapter 15.*

Other standards specify whether expenditures are treated as assets or as expenses. These issues are not addressed in IAS 37. However, this issue has been discussed by the IFRS Interpretations Committee in the context of levies imposed by governments. The Committee spent considerable time debating this issue and eventually decided not to address this in IFRIC 21 *Levies, which is covered in section 5.9.5.* Accordingly, IAS 37 neither prohibits nor requires capitalisation of the costs recognised when a provision is made. Refer to IAS 38 *Intangible Assets,* which deals partly with this issue, *and is covered in chapter 13.*

IAS 37 applies to provisions for restructuring (including discontinued operations). Where a restructuring meets the definition of a discontinued operation, additional disclosures may be required by IFRS 5 *Non-current Assets Held for Sale and Discontinued Operations.* IFRS 3 *Business Combinations* deals with accounting for restructuring provisions arising in business combinations. This chapter covers the relevant requirements of IFRS 3 *in section 5.12.*

5.3 DEFINITION OF A PROVISION

Paragraph 4.4 of the current *Conceptual Framework for Financial Reporting* (*Conceptual Framework*) defines a liability as:

> a present obligation of the entity arising from past events, the settlement of which is expected to result in an outflow from the entity of resources embodying economic benefits.

This definition is repeated in paragraph 10 of IAS 37.

A provision is a subset of liabilities (i.e. it is a type of liability) which is of uncertain timing or amount in accordance with paragraph 10 of IAS 37.

It is this *uncertainty* that distinguishes provisions from other liabilities.

The current *Conceptual Framework* states that an essential characteristic of a liability is that the entity has a present obligation. An obligation is a duty or responsibility to act or perform in a certain way. Obligations may be legally enforceable as a consequence of a binding contract, for example. This is normally the case with amounts payable for goods or services received, which are described as 'payables' or 'trade creditors'. However, legal enforceability is not a necessary requirement to demonstrate the existence of a liability. An entity may have a constructive obligation, arising from normal business practice or custom, to act in an equitable manner. Determining whether a constructive obligation exists is often more difficult than identifying a legal obligation. A constructive obligation is defined as an obligation that derives from an entity's actions where an established pattern of past practice (including published or sufficiently specific current statements) indicates to other parties that the entity will accept certain responsibilities, consequently creating a reasonable expectation from those parties that the entity will discharge those responsibilities (IAS 37 paragraph 10).

A present obligation exists only where the entity has no realistic alternative but to settle the obligation (*Conceptual Framework* paragraph 4.16).

For example, assume that an entity makes a public announcement that it will match the financial assistance provided by other entities to victims of a natural disaster and, because of past practice and moral considerations, has no realistic alternative but to provide the assistance. In this case the events have already taken place — the natural disaster — and the public announcement is the obligating event.

Importantly, a decision by the entity's management or governing body does not, in itself, create a constructive obligation. This is because the management or governing body retains the ability to reverse that decision. A present obligation would come into existence when the decision was communicated publicly to those affected by it. This would result in the valid expectation that the entity would fulfil the obligation, thus leaving the entity with little or no discretion to avoid the outflow of economic benefits.

5.4 DISTINGUISHING PROVISIONS FROM OTHER LIABILITIES

A provision may arise from either a legal or constructive obligation. As stated previously, the key distinguishing factor is the uncertainty relating to either the timing of settlement or the amount to be settled.

Paragraph 11 of IAS 37 illustrates the distinction between liabilities and provisions. The first example used for the illustration is trade payables to suppliers, which are certain in both timing and amount. The second example used is accruals, such as accrued vacation pay, which may not be as certain in terms of timing and amount, but the uncertainty is generally much less than for provisions. Accruals are generally reported as part of trade and other payables, whereas provisions are reported separately.

Note, however, that employee benefits are addressed specifically by IAS 19 *Employee Benefits*, and are not included in the scope of IAS 37, *as mentioned in section 5.2*.

Some examples of typical provisions include provisions for warranty, restructuring provisions and provisions for onerous contracts. These are discussed in more detail later in this chapter.

5.5 DEFINITION OF A CONTINGENT LIABILITY

A contingent liability is defined in the standard as:

(a) a possible obligation that arises from past events and whose existence will be confirmed only by the occurrence or non-occurrence of one or more uncertain future events not wholly within the control of the entity; or

(b) a present obligation that arises from past events but is not recognised because:
  (i) it is not probable that an outflow of resources embodying economic benefits will be required to settle the obligation; or
  (ii) the amount of the obligation cannot be measured with sufficient reliability.

The definition of a contingent liability is interesting because it encompasses two distinctly different concepts. The first, part (a) of the definition, is the concept of a *possible* obligation. This seemingly fails one of the essential characteristics of a liability — the requirement for the existence of a present obligation. If there is no present obligation, only a possible one, there is no liability. Hence, part (a) of the definition does not meet the definition of a liability which may lead one to argue that the term 'contingent *liability*' is misleading, because items falling into category (a) are not liabilities by definition.

Part (b) of the definition, on the other hand, deals with liabilities that fail the recognition criteria. They are present obligations, so they meet the essential requirements of the definition of liabilities, but they do not meet the recognition criteria (probability of outflow of economic benefits and reliability of measurement).

However, the definition needs to be considered together with the criteria for recognising a provision in the standard. A possible obligation whose existence is yet to be confirmed does not meet the definition of a liability; and a present obligation in respect of which an outflow of resources is not probable, or which cannot be measured reliably, does not qualify for recognition. On that basis a contingent liability under IAS 37 means one of the following:

- an obligation that is estimated to have less than a 50% likelihood of existing (i.e. it does not meet the definition of a liability). Where it is more likely than not that a present obligation exists at the end of the reporting period, a provision is recognised (see IAS 37 paragraph 16(a)). Where it is more likely than not that no present obligation exists, a contingent liability is disclosed (unless the possibility is remote); or
- a present obligation that has less than a 50% likelihood of requiring an outflow of economic benefits (i.e. it meets the definition of a liability but does not meet the recognition criteria). Where it is not probable that there will be an outflow of resources, an entity discloses a contingent liability (unless the possibility is remote); or
- a present obligation for which a sufficiently reliable estimate cannot be made (i.e. it meets the definition of a liability but does not meet the recognition criteria). In these rare circumstances, a liability cannot be recognised and it is disclosed as a contingent liability (see IAS 37 paragraph 26).

5.6 DISTINGUISHING A CONTINGENT LIABILITY FROM A PROVISION

As mentioned previously, contingent liabilities are not recognised in the financial statements but must be disclosed in the financial statements unless the possibility of an outflow in settlement is remote. All provisions can be seen as being 'contingent', however, as they are uncertain in timing or amount. However, in the context of this standard, the term 'contingent' specifically refers to liabilities and assets that are not recognised because their existence can only be confirmed by the occurrence or non-occurrence of one or more uncertain future events that are not wholly within the control of the entity. A contingent liability in IAS 37 also refers to a liability that does not meet the recognition criteria.

Illustrative example 5.1 illustrates the difference between a contingent liability and a provision.

ILLUSTRATIVE EXAMPLE 5.1 Example of the difference between a provision and a contingent liability

Legal proceedings against Lemon Pharma Co. started after several people became ill, possibly as a result of taking the health supplements manufactured and sold by Lemon. Lemon disputes any liability and, up to the authorised date of issue of its financial statements for 31 December 2015, its lawyers have advised that it is probable that Lemon will not be found liable. However, when Lemon prepares its financial statements for 31 December 2016, its lawyers advise that, owing to the developments in the case, it is probable that Lemon will be found liable and a reliable estimate of the amount of damages can be made.

For 31 December 2015, no provision is recognised and the matter is disclosed as a contingent liability unless the probability of any outflow is regarded as remote. On the basis of the evidence available when the financial statements were approved, there is no obligation as a result of a past event.

For 31 December 2016, a provision is recognised for the best estimate of the amount required to settle the obligation. The fact that an outflow of economic benefits is now believed to be probable and a reliable estimate can be made means that this is no longer a contingent liability, but a provision.

5.7 THE RECOGNITION CRITERIA FOR PROVISIONS

The recognition criteria for provisions are the same as those for liabilities as set out in the *Conceptual Framework*. IAS 37 also includes part of the definition of a liability in its recognition criteria for provisions (part (a) of the recognition criteria below).

Paragraph 14 of IAS 37 requires a provision to be recognised when:

(a) an entity has a present obligation (legal or constructive) as a result of a past event;
(b) it is probable that an outflow of resources embodying economic benefits will be required to settle the obligation; and
(c) a reliable estimate can be made of the amount of the obligation.
If these conditions are not met, no provision shall be recognised.

The concept of probability is discussed in the *Conceptual Framework* and deals essentially with the likelihood of something eventuating. If it is more likely than not to eventuate, IAS 37 regards the outflow as probable. Probability is assessed for each obligation separately, unless the obligations form a group of similar obligations (such as product warranties) in which case the probability that an outflow will be required in settlement is determined by assessing the class of obligations as a whole.

In instances of rare cases where it is unclear whether a present obligation exists, a past event is deemed to give rise to a present obligation if, taking account of all available evidence, it is more likely than not that a present obligation exists at the end of the reporting period, For example in a law suit, it may be disputed either whether certain events have occurred or whether those events result in a present obligation. In such a circumstance, an entity determines whether a present obligation exists at the end of the reporting period by taking all available evidence into account, including, for example, the opinion of experts. The evidence considered includes any additional evidence provided by events after the end of the reporting period. On the basis of such evidence, where it is more likely than not that a present obligation exists at the end of the reporting period, a provision is recognised, provided the recognition criteria are met. Alternatively, if it is more likely that no present obligation exists at the end of the reporting period, the entity discloses a contingent liability, unless the possibility of an outflow of resources embodying economic benefits is remote, in which case no disclosure is made.

A past event that leads to a present obligation is called an obligating event. *As discussed in the section on constructive obligations,* for an event to be an obligating event the entity must have no realistic alternative to settling the obligation created by the event. In the case of a legal obligation this is because the settlement of the obligation can be enforced by law. In the case of a constructive obligation the event needs to create a valid expectation in other parties that the entity will discharge the obligation.

Reliable estimation is the final criterion for recognition of a provision. Although the use of estimates is a necessary part of the preparation of financial statements, in the case of provisions the uncertainty associated with reliable measurement is greater than for other liabilities. Accordingly, IAS 37 goes on to give more detailed guidance on measurement of provisions, *which we will discuss later in the chapter.* However, it is expected that except in very rare cases an entity will be able to determine a reliable estimate of the obligation.

Note the use of the concept of 'probability' in the recognition criteria for liabilities, including provisions, contrasted with the use of the concept of 'possibility' in determining whether or not a contingent liability should be disclosed. Paragraph 86 of IAS 37 requires contingent liabilities to be disclosed in the financial statements 'unless the possibility of an outflow in settlement is remote'. IAS 37 interprets 'probable' as meaning more likely than not to occur (IAS 37 paragraph 23). IAS 37 does not, however, provide any further guidance on what it means by 'possibility'. In plain English terms, 'probability' addresses the likelihood of whether or not something will happen, whereas 'possibility' has a broader meaning — virtually anything is possible, but how probable is it? Given this distinction, we should assume that the intention of IAS 37 is that most contingent liabilities should be disclosed and that only in very rare circumstances is no disclosure appropriate.

Contingent liabilities need to be continually assessed to determine whether or not they have become actual liabilities. This is done by considering whether the recognition criteria for liabilities have been met. If it becomes probable that an outflow of economic benefits will be required for an item previously dealt with as a contingent liability, a provision is recognised in the financial statements in the period in which the change in probability occurs (IAS 37 paragraph 30).

5.7.1 Putting it all together — a useful decision tree

In sections 5.3 to 5.7 we discussed the definitions of provisions and contingent liabilities, the recognition criteria for provisions and when a contingent liability must be disclosed. The decision tree (figure 5.1) summarises this discussion. The decision tree is based on Appendix B of IAS 37 but has been modified to aid understanding.

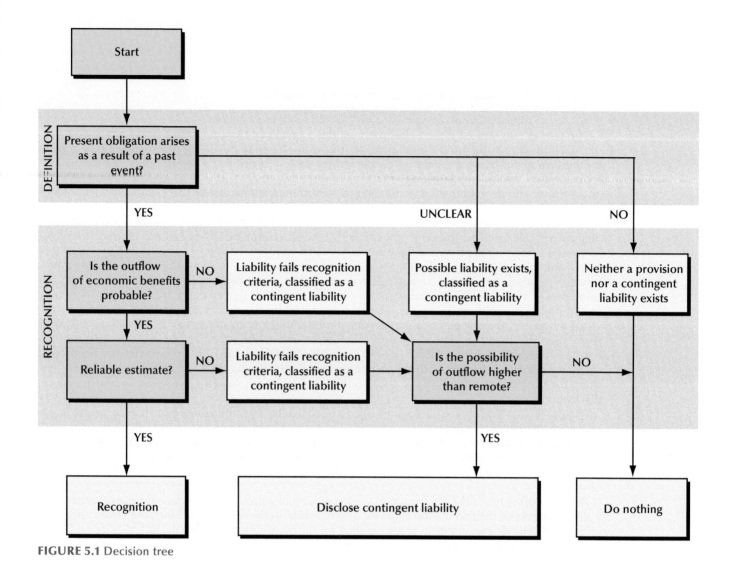

FIGURE 5.1 Decision tree

5.8 MEASUREMENT OF PROVISIONS

5.8.1 Best estimate

When measuring a provision, the amount recognised should be the *best estimate* of the consideration required to settle the present obligation at the end of the reporting period (IAS 37 paragraph 36). This amount is often expressed as the amount which represents, as closely as possible, what the entity would rationally pay to settle the present obligation at the end of the reporting period or to provide consideration to a third party to assume it. The fact that it is difficult to measure the provision and that estimates have to be used does not mean that the provision is not reliably measurable.

The standard provides guidance on estimation of a provision which involves a large population of items. In such circumstances, the obligation is estimated using the expected value method, i.e. weighting all possible outcomes by their associated probabilities. For example, in January 20X1 Taiwan Imports sells 10 000 units of good Y with a 1-year warranty which covers manufacturing defects that become apparent within the first 12 months after purchase. If minor defects are detected, repair costs of $200 per unit of good Y would result. If major defects are detected, repair costs of $1000 per unit of good Y would result. Taiwan Import's past experience and future expectations indicate that, for the coming year, 85% of the goods sold will have no defects, 10% of the goods sold will have minor defects and 5% of the goods sold will have major defects. Therefore Taiwan Imports assesses the probability of an outflow for the warranty obligations as a whole. The expected value of the cost of repairs will be (85% of nil) + (10% of ($200 × 10 000)) + (5% of ($1000 × 10 000)) = $700 000.

In situations where there is only one single obligation to measure, the individual most likely outcome may be the best estimate of the liability. However, the entity has to consider other possible outcomes as well. Where other possible outcomes are either mostly higher or mostly lower than the most likely outcome, the best estimate will be a higher or lower amount. For example, if an entity has to rectify a serious fault in a major plant that it has constructed for a customer, the individual most likely outcome may be for the repair to succeed at the first attempt at a cost of €100 000, but a provision for a larger amount is made if there is a significant chance that further attempts might be necessary.

The provision is measured before tax. Any tax consequences are accounted for in accordance with IAS 12 *Income Taxes*.

The need to use judgement in determining the best estimate is clearly evident. Judgement is used in assessing, inter alia:

- what the likely consideration required to settle the obligation will be
- when the consideration is likely to be settled
- whether there are various scenarios that are likely to arise
- what the probability of those various scenarios arising will be.

The distinguishing characteristic of provisions — the uncertainty relating to either the timing of settlement or the amount to be settled — is clearly illustrated in the above discussion. Because of the extent of judgement required in measuring provisions, auditors focus more on auditing provisions than on other normal liabilities such as trade creditors and accruals. This is particularly the case if a change in one of the assumptions, such as the probability of a particular scenario eventuating or the likely consideration required to settle the obligation, could have a significant impact on the amount recognised as a provision and thus on the financial statements.

5.8.2 Risks and uncertainties

IAS 37 paragraph 42 requires that the risks and uncertainties surrounding the events and circumstances should be taken into account in reaching the best estimate of a provision. The standard also requires a risk adjustment to be made when measuring liabilities. However, uncertainty is not a justifiable reason for making excessive provisions or deliberately overstating liabilities.

Furthermore, disclosure of the uncertainties surrounding the amount or timing of expected outflows is required by paragraph 85(b) of the standard.

5.8.3 Present value

Provisions are required to be *discounted to present value* where the effect of discounting is material (IAS 37 paragraph 45). IAS 37 (paragraph 47) requires that the discount rate used must be a pre-tax rate that reflects current market assessments of the time value of money and the *risks specific to the liability*. Where future cash flow estimates have been adjusted for risk, the discount rate should not reflect this risk — otherwise the effect of risk would be double-counted.

In practical terms it is often difficult to determine reliably a liability-specific discount rate. Usually entities use a rate available for a liability with similar terms and conditions or, if a similar liability is not available, a risk-free rate for a liability with the same term (e.g. a government bond[1] with a 5-year term may be used as the basis for a company's specific liability with a 5-year term) and this rate is then adjusted for the risks pertaining to the liability in question.

The mechanism for risk-adjusting a discount rate may seem counterintuitive at first as a risk-adjusted rate for a liability would be a *lower* rate than the risk-free rate. This is demonstrated and further explained in illustrative example 5.2.

ILLUSTRATIVE EXAMPLE 5.2 Calculation of a risk-adjusted rate

A company has a provision for which the expected value of the cash outflow in 3 years' time is £150 and the risk-free rate is 5%. However, the possible outcomes from which the expected value has been determined lie within a range between £100 and £200. The company is risk-averse and would settle instead for a certain payment of, say, £160 in 3 years' time rather than be exposed to the risk of the actual outcome being as high as £200. The effect of risk in calculating present value can be expressed as either:

(a) discounting the risk-adjusted cash flow of £160 at the risk-free (unadjusted) rate of 5%, giving a present value of £138; or

(b) discounting the expected cash flow (which is unadjusted for risk) of £150 at a risk-adjusted rate that will give the present value of £138, i.e. a rate of 2.8%.

As can be seen from this example, the risk-adjusted discount rate is a lower rate than the unadjusted (risk-free) discount rate. This may seem counterintuitive initially, because the experience of most borrowers is that lenders will charge a higher rate of interest on loans that are assessed to be higher risk to the lender. However, in the case of a provision a risk premium is being suffered to eliminate the possibility of the

---

[1] Assumed to be risk-free although this may not always be the case.

actual cost being higher (thereby capping a liability), whereas in the case of a loan receivable a premium is required to compensate the lender for taking on the risk of not recovering its full value (setting a floor for the value of the lender's financial asset). In both cases the actual cash flows incurred by the paying entity are higher to reflect a premium for risk. In other words, the discount rate for an asset is increased to reflect the risk of recovering less and the discount rate for a liability is reduced to reflect the risk of paying more.

Source: Ernst & Young (2015, p. 1772).

Perhaps an easier way to factor in risk is to use it in assessing the probability of outcomes (*as discussed in section 5.8.1*) and then use a risk-free rate in discounting the cash flows. Paragraph 83 of IAS 19 *Employee Benefits* requires the discount rate for long-term employee benefit obligations to be determined by reference to market yields at the end of the reporting period on high-quality corporate bonds or, where there is no deep market in such bonds, the market yield on government bonds. The currency and term of the corporate bonds or government bonds should be consistent with the currency and estimated term of the employee benefit obligations. Although there may be some debate about how to determine the risk-free rate, market yields on high-quality corporate bonds or government bonds could serve as a reasonable basis for assessing the risk-free rate.

Illustrative example 5.3 shows the way a provision should be measured, taking into account risks and the time value of money.

ILLUSTRATIVE EXAMPLE 5.3 Measuring a provision

Iconic plc estimates that the expected cash outflows to settle its warranty obligations at the end of the reporting period are as follows. (Note that the probability of cash outflows has already been adjusted for risk and, accordingly, no further adjustment for risk is made to the discount rate.) Iconic plc has used a discount rate based on government bonds with the same term and currency as the expected cash outflows as a proxy for the risk-free rate.

Expected cash outflow	Timing	Discount rate	Present value of cash outflow
£400 000	In 1 year	6.0%	£377 358
100 000	In 2 years	6.5%	88 166
20 000	In 3 years	6.9%	16 371
Present value			481 895

5.8.4 Future events

Anticipated future events expected to affect the amount required to settle the entity's present obligation must be reflected in the amount provided, when there is reliable evidence that they will occur. For example, an entity may believe that the cost of cleaning up a site at the end of its life will be reduced by future changes in technology. The amount recognised reflects a reasonable expectation of technically qualified, objective observers, taking account of all available evidence as to the technology that will be available at the time of the clean-up. Therefore, it is appropriate to include, for example, expected cost reductions associated with increased experience in applying existing technology or the expected cost of applying existing technology to a larger or more complex clean-up operation than has previously been carried out.

5.8.5 Expected disposal of assets

Gains from the expected disposal of assets must not be taken into account when measuring the amount of a provision (IAS 37 paragraph 51), even if the expected disposal is closely linked to the event giving rise to the provision. Rather, when the gain on disposal is made, it should be recognised at that time, in accordance with the relevant IFRS. Therefore, it is clear that only expected cash *outflows* must be taken into account in measuring the provision. Any cash inflows are treated separately from the measurement of the provision.

5.8.6 Reimbursements

When some of the amount required to settle a provision is expected to be recovered from a third party, IAS 37 requires that the recovery be recognised as an asset, but only when it is *virtually certain* that the reimbursement will be received if the entity settles the obligation (paragraph 53). This differs from the normal asset recognition criteria, which require that the inflow of future economic benefits be *probable*. Presumably, the standard setters were concerned with recognition of an uncertain asset related to a liability of uncertain timing and amount, and therefore decided to make the recognition criteria stricter for these types of assets to avoid variability in the balance sheet. When such an asset is recognised, the amount should not exceed the amount of the provision. No 'netting off' is allowed in the statement of financial position, with any asset classified separately from any provision in accordance with paragraph 53 of IAS 37. However, IAS 37 allows the income from the asset to be set off against the expense relating to the provision in the income statement.

5.8.7 Changes in provisions and use of provisions

IAS 37 requires provisions to be reviewed at the end of each reporting period and adjusted to reflect the current best estimate. If it is no longer probable that an outflow of resources embodying economic benefits will be required to settle the obligation, the provision should be reversed (IAS 37 paragraph 59).

Where discounting is used, the carrying amount of a provision increases in each period to reflect the passage of time. This increase is recognised as borrowing cost. This is similar to the way finance lease liabilities are accounted for under IAS 17 *Leases, as shown in chapter 12*.

A provision should be used only for expenditures for which the provision was originally recognised. Illustrative example 5.4 shows how a provision is accounted for where discounting is applied and where the provision is adjusted to reflect the current best estimate.

ILLUSTRATIVE EXAMPLE 5.4 Accounting for a provision

Weber AG estimates that it will be required to pay €100 000 in 3 years' time to settle a warranty obligation. The risk-free discount rate applied is 5.5%. The probability of cash outflows has been assessed (i.e. adjusted for risk) in determining the €100 000.

The following table shows how the provision is accreted over the 3 years:

A. Year	B. Present value at the beginning of the year	C. Interest expense at 5.5% (B × 5.5%)	D. Cash flows	E. Present value at the end of the year (B + C − D)
1	85 161	4 683	—	89 844
2	89 844	4 942	—	94 786
3	94 786	5 214	(100 000)	—

Journal entries are as follows:

On initial recognition in year 1:			
Warranty Expense	Dr	85 161	
Warranty Provision	Cr		85 161
On recognition of interest in year 1:			
Interest Expense	Dr	4 683	
Warranty Provision	Cr		4 683
On recognition of interest in year 2:			
Interest Expense	Dr	4 942	
Warranty Provision	Cr		4 942
On recognition of interest in year 3:			
Interest Expense	Dr	5 214	
Warranty Provision	Cr		5 214
On settlement of provision, end of year 3:			
Warranty Provision	Dr	100 000	
Cash	Cr		100 000

Now assume the same facts as above except that, at the end of year 2, Weber AG re-estimates the amount to be paid to settle the obligation at the end of year 3 to be €90 000. The appropriate discount rate remains at 5.5%.

The present value of €90 000 at the end of year 2 is €85 306. Company A thus adjusts the provision by €9480 (€94 786 – €85 306) to reflect the revised estimated cash flows.

Journal entries are as follows:

Revision of estimate at end of year 2:			
Warranty Provision	Dr	9 480	
Warranty Expense (statement of comprehensive income)	Cr		9 480
On recognition of interest in year 3:			
Interest Expense (€85 306 × 5.5% rounded)	Dr	4 694	
Warranty Provision	Cr		4 694
On settlement of provision, end of year 3:			
Warranty Provision	Dr	90 000	
Cash	Cr		90 000

The re-estimated cash flows are adjusted against the warranty expense recorded in the statement of comprehensive income, while the unwinding of the discount continues to be recorded as interest expense (IAS 37 paragraph 60). Any change in the discount rate used would also be adjusted against interest expense.

5.9 APPLICATION OF THE DEFINITIONS, RECOGNITION AND MEASUREMENT RULES

5.9.1 Future operating losses

IAS 37 disallows recognition of provisions for future operating losses (paragraph 63). Even if a sacrifice of future economic benefits is expected, a provision for future operating losses is not recognised because a past event creating a present obligation has not occurred. This is because the entity's management will generally have the ability to avoid incurring future operating losses by either disposing of or restructuring the operation in question. An expectation of future operating losses may, however, be an indicator that an asset is impaired and the requirements of IAS 36 *Impairment of Assets* should be applied.

5.9.2 Onerous contracts

IAS 37 defines an onerous contract as a contract in which the unavoidable costs of meeting the obligations under the contract exceed the economic benefits expected to be received under it.

If an entity is a party to an onerous contract, a provision for the present obligation under the contract must be recognised (IAS 37 paragraph 66). The reason these losses should be provided for is that the entity is contracted to fulfil the contract. Therefore an onerous contract gives rise to a present obligation.

Examples of onerous contracts include:
- where an electricity supplier has entered into a contract to supply electricity at a price lower than the price at which it is contracted to receive
- where a manufacturer has entered into a supply contract to provide goods to a customer at a price below its costs of production.

IAS 37 does not go into a lot of detail regarding onerous contracts. Judgement has to be applied on a case-by-case basis to assess whether or not individual contracts qualify as onerous contracts under the standard.

For the purpose of raising a provision in respect of an onerous contract, the amount to be recognised is the least net cost of exiting the contract; that is, the lesser of:
- the cost of fulfilling the contract, and
- any compensation or penalties arising from failure to fulfil the contract.

IAS 37 also requires that before a separate provision is made for an onerous contract, an entity must first recognise any impairment loss that has occurred on assets dedicated to that contract. This is shown in illustrative example 5.5.

Alpha Ltd enters into a supply agreement with Beta Ltd on 1 January 2015. The agreement states that Alpha Ltd must supply Beta Ltd with 100 chairs at a price of $150 per chair. The agreement also states that if Alpha Ltd cannot deliver the chairs on time and under the terms of the contract it must pay Beta Ltd a penalty of $12 000. The delivery date is 31 March 2015. Alpha Ltd commences manufacturing the chairs on 1 March and experiences a series of production problems that result in the cost to produce each chair totalling $200 as at 31 March 2015. As at 31 March, Alpha Ltd identifies an onerous contract in accordance with IAS 37 because the costs of fulfilling the contract (100 × $200 = $20 000) exceed the agreed amount to be received (100 × $150 = $15 000). The cost of the chairs is recognised as inventory as at 31 March 2015. Assuming the end of Alpha Ltd's reporting period is 31 March, it must first recognise an impairment loss on the inventory. This would be calculated and recorded as $5000 (lower of cost and net realisable value (ignoring costs to sell) under IAS 2 *Inventories* — *see chapter 9*). Once this impairment loss has been recognised, there is no amount to be recorded as a provision under the onerous contract. However, if Alpha Ltd had not yet recorded any costs as inventory it would need to determine what amount to recognise as a provision for the onerous contract. This would be the lesser of the penalty required to be paid to Beta Ltd ($12 000) and the cost of fulfilling the contract ($5000, which is only to the extent that costs are not covered by related revenues). Thus, Alpha Ltd would record a provision of $5000.

5.9.3 Restructuring provisions

Perhaps one of the more controversial aspect of IAS 37 is the recognition criteria for restructuring provisions. IFRS 3 *Business Combinations* addresses restructuring provisions arising as part of a business combination, whereas IAS 37 addresses restructuring provisions arising other than as part of a business combination. Although the fundamental criteria are consistent, i.e. only liabilities for restructuring or exit activities that meet the definition of a liability at acquisition date are recognised as liabilities, see IFRS 3 *Basis for Conclusions BC132*, IFRS 3 has more prescriptive requirements than IAS 37. For ease of discussion, both types of restructuring provision are discussed here.

During the 1990s, standard setters in various jurisdictions set tougher rules on when a restructuring provision could be recognised, particularly when the provision related to the acquisition of a business. The reason for stricter requirements was the tendency for companies to create restructuring provisions deliberately to avoid the recognition of an expense in future periods. Illustrative example 5.6 demonstrates this point.

Assume Presto SpA acquires Costa SpA on 1 February 2013. The identifiable net assets and liabilities of Costa SpA are €400 million and Presto SpA pays €500 million cash as purchase consideration. The goodwill arising on acquisition is thus €100 million. Presto SpA then decides to create a restructuring provision of €60 million for future possible restructuring activities related to Costa SpA. Presto SpA records the following additional entry as part of its acquisition accounting entries:

Goodwill	Dr	60 m	
Restructuring Provision	Cr		60 m

Why does Presto SpA have an incentive to record this entry? The entry increases the amount recorded as goodwill, and in the 1990s goodwill was required to be amortised in most jurisdictions. Why would Presto SpA want to expose itself to future goodwill amortisation? The answer is that because the restructuring provision was recorded directly against goodwill, an expense for the restructuring will *never* be recorded. When Presto SpA incurs the expenditure in the future, the outflows will be recorded against the provision. Presto SpA would likely have been able to highlight goodwill amortisation as a separate item either in its statement of comprehensive income or the attached notes, and thus would have been satisfied that the amortisation expense was effectively quarantined from the rest of its reported profit. The benefit for Presto SpA was that the restructuring expense never affected its profit, and thus the creation of the restructuring provision as part of the acquisition entries protected Presto SpA's future profits.

Examples of restructurings include:

(a) sale or termination of a line of business;
(b) the closure of business locations in a country or region or the relocation of business activities from one country or region to another;
(c) changes in management structure, for example, eliminating a layer of management; and
(d) fundamental reorganisations that have a material effect on the nature and focus of the entity's operations.

In broad terms, to be able to raise a restructuring provision, three conditions need to be met. First, the entity must have a *present obligation (either legal or constructive)* to restructure such that it cannot realistically avoid going ahead with the restructuring and thus incurring the costs involved. Second, only costs that are *directly and necessarily* caused by the restructuring and *not associated with the ongoing activities* of the entity may be included in a restructuring provision. Third, if the restructuring involves the sale of an operation, no obligation is deemed to arise for the sale of an operation until the entity is committed to the sale by a *binding sale agreement*.

Each of these requirements is considered in more detail below.

Present obligation

Usually management initiates a restructuring and thus it is uncommon that a legal obligation will exist for a restructuring. IAS 37 therefore focuses on the conditions that need to be met for a constructive obligation to exist.

In respect of restructuring provisions, a constructive obligation to restructure arises only when an entity:

(a) has a detailed formal plan for the restructuring identifying at least:
  (i) the business or part of a business concerned;
  (ii) the principal locations affected;
  (iii) the location, function, and approximate number of employees who will be compensated for terminating their services;
  (iv) the expenditures that will be undertaken; and
  (v) when the plan will be implemented; and
(b) has raised a valid expectation in those affected that it will carry out the restructuring by starting to implement that plan or announcing its main features to those affected by it *(see IAS 37 paragraph 72)*.

Therefore, we see that the entity needs to have a *detailed formal plan* and must have raised a *valid expectation* in those affected.

Recording restructuring provisions

Where a provision for restructuring costs arises on the acquisition of an entity, judgement is required as to whether the restructuring activities form part of the liabilities assumed in accounting for the business combination. Illustrative example 5.7 demonstrates this issue further.

ILLUSTRATIVE EXAMPLE 5.7 Recognition or otherwise of a restructuring liability as part of a business combination

The acquirer and the acquiree (or the vendors of the acquiree) enter into an arrangement before the acquisition that requires the acquiree to restructure its workforce or activities. They intend to develop the main features of a plan that involve terminating or reducing its activities and to announce the plan's main features to those affected by it so as to raise a valid expectation that the plan will be implemented. The combination is contingent on the plan being implemented.

Does such a restructuring plan that the acquiree puts in place simultaneously with the business combination, i.e. the plan is effective upon the change in control, but was implemented by or at the request of the acquirer, qualify for inclusion as part of the liabilities assumed in accounting for the business combination?

The facts to be analysed are:

(a) *the reason:* a restructuring plan implemented at the request of the acquirer is presumably arranged primarily for the benefit of the acquirer or the combined entity because of the possible redundancy expected to arise from the combination of activities of the acquirer with activities of the acquiree, e.g. capacity redundancy leading to closure of the acquiree's facilities;
(b) *who initiated:* if such a plan is the result of a request of the acquirer, it means that the acquirer is expecting future economic benefits from the arrangement and the decision to restructure;
(c) *the timing:* the restructuring plan is usually discussed during the negotiations; therefore, it is contemplated in the perspective of the future combined entity.

Accordingly, a restructuring plan that is implemented as a result of an arrangement between the acquirer and the acquiree is not a liability of the acquiree as at the date of acquisition and cannot be part of the accounting for the business combination under the acquisition method.

Does the answer differ if the combination is not contingent on the plan being implemented?

The answer applies regardless of whether the combination is contingent on the plan being implemented or not. A plan initiated by the acquirer will most likely not make commercial sense from the acquiree's perspective absent the business combination. For example, there are retrenchments of staff whose position will only truly become redundant once the entities are combined. In that case, this is an arrangement to be accounted for separately rather than as part of the business combination exchange. This arrangement may also indicate that control of the acquiree has already passed to the acquirer as otherwise there would be little reason for the acquiree to enter into an arrangement that makes little or no commercial sense to it.

Source: Ernst & Young (2015).

Looking at the discussion in IAS 37 in more detail, in order to satisfy the 'valid expectation' test in IAS 37, an entity needs to have started to implement the detailed formal plan or announced the main features to those affected by it. An entity can do this in the following ways:

- By the entity having already entered into firm contracts to carry out parts of the restructuring. These contracts would be of such a nature that they effectively force the entity to carry out the restructuring. This would be the case if they contained severe penalty provisions or the costs of not fulfilling the contract were so high that it would effectively leave the entity with no alternative but to proceed.
- By starting to implement the detailed restructuring. This could include, for example, selling assets, notifying customers that supplies will be discontinued, notifying suppliers that orders will be ceasing, dismantling plant and equipment, and terminating employees' service.
- By announcing the main features of the plan to those affected by it (or their representatives). There may be a number of ways in which such an announcement could be made. It could be through written communication, meetings or discussions with the affected parties.

It is important that the communication is made in such a way that it raises a valid expectation in the affected parties such that they can be expected to act as a result of the communication, and by them doing so the entity would be left with no realistic alternative but to go ahead with the restructuring. For example, affected employees would start looking for other employment and customers would seek alternative sources of supply.

Qualifying restructuring costs

The second requirement for recognition of a restructuring provision is that the provision can include only costs that are directly and necessarily caused by the restructuring and not associated with the ongoing activities of the entity (IAS 37 paragraph 80).

Examples of the types of costs that would be included in a restructuring provision include the costs of terminating leases and other contracts as a direct result of the restructuring; costs of operations conducted in effecting the restructuring, such as employee remuneration while they are engaged in such tasks as dismantling plant, disposing of surplus stocks and fulfilling contractual obligations; and costs of making employees redundant.

Paragraph 81 of IAS 37 specifically indicates that the types of costs excluded from provisions for restructuring would be the costs of retraining or relocating the continuing staff, marketing costs and costs related to investment in new systems and distribution networks. These types of costs relate to the future conduct of the entity and do not relate to present obligations.

These requirements relating to the types of costs that qualify as restructuring costs apply equally to internal restructurings as well as to restructurings occurring as part of an acquisition.

It is important to note that, although certain costs have occurred only because of restructuring (i.e. they would not have had to be incurred had the restructuring not taken place), this fact alone does not qualify them for recognition as restructuring costs. They also have to be costs that are not associated with the ongoing activities of the entity.

Binding sale agreement

The final requirement for recognition of a restructuring provision is that if the restructuring involves the sale of an operation, no obligation is deemed to arise for the sale until the entity is committed to the sale by a binding sale agreement (IAS 37 paragraph 78). It is because, before there is a binding sale agreement, an entity could change its mind or take another course of action if a purchaser cannot be found on acceptable terms. For the treatment of non-current assets held for sale and discontinued operations, refer to IFRS 5 *Non-current Assets Held for Sale and Discontinued Operations* for further guidance.

5.9.4 Decommissioning provisions

When an entity is required to remove an asset at the end of its useful life and to restore the site where it was located, these decommissioning costs are required to be provided for (see IAS 37 IE Example 3). A provision is required to be recognised at the time the asset is being constructed as the environmental damage requiring restoration in the future presumably starts at that point in time.

Using IE Example 3 from IAS 37, recognition of the provision starts at construction of the oil rig, to reflect the need to reverse the damage caused. The total decommissioning cost as well as its timing is estimated and subsequently discounted to its present value. This initial estimate of the costs to remove the asset is added to the cost of the asset. Thereafter, the asset is depreciated over its useful life, while interest is accrued on the provision, with the accrual shown as a finance cost.

For changes in estimates of the decommissioning provision, IAS 37 lacks relevant guidance, therefore IFRIC 1 *Changes in Existing Decommissioning, Restoration and Similar Liabilities* was issued in May 2004 to rectify this.

IFRIC 1 addresses:

(a) a change in the estimated outflow of resources embodying economic benefits (e.g. cash flows) required to settle the obligation;

(b) change in the current market-based discount rate (including changes in time value of money and risks specific to the liability); and

(c) an increase that reflects the passage of time (i.e. the unwinding of the discount).

For a change caused by (a) or (b), the adjustment is first taken to the carrying amount of the asset to which it relates. If the adjustment gives rise to an addition to cost, the entity should test the new carrying amount for impairment. Reductions that are over and above the remaining carrying amount of the asset are recognised immediately in the income statement. The adjusted depreciable amount of the asset is then depreciated prospectively over its remaining useful life (see IFRIC 1 *paragraphs IE1–4*).

A change caused by (c) above, the periodic unwinding of the discount, is recognised in profit or loss as a finance cost as it occurs.

5.9.5 Levies

As a result of economic events in recent years, levies (e.g. bank levies) have become more common as governments try to generate income from other sources. Issues have arisen regarding timing of when such liabilities should be recognised, in which the obligation to pay depended upon participation in a particular market on a specified date. IFRIC 21 *Levies* was issued in May 2013 to address these concerns.

The types and mechanisms of levies can be complex. The concerns regarding timing of recognition of levies mainly surfaced as a result of how bank levies across various jurisdictions were calculated and measured. Typically, a bank levy is calculated based on the closing balances of the respective figures as stipulated by legislation, at the last day of the annual reporting period. The question is whether the bank would be able to estimate and accrue for the levy as it operates throughout the year.

IFRIC 21 clarifies that although an entity (such as the bank) could be economically compelled to continue operations, that does not mean the bank would have a constructive obligation to pay the levy, before the obligating event to pay the levy occurs. Coming back to the bank levy example, assuming that in accordance with legislation, the levy is only payable if the bank is operating as a bank at the last day of the reporting period, the activity that triggers payment of the levy does not occur till that last day. Therefore no provision is recognised till that point in time.

In circumstances where a levy is payable progressively, for example as a company generates revenue, the company would be able to recognise liability over a period of time on that basis. This is because the obligating event is the activity that generates revenue. If an obligation to pay a levy is triggered in full as soon as a minimum threshold is reached, such as when the entity commences generating sales or achieves a certain level of revenue, the liability is recognised in full on the first day that the entity reaches that threshold. Table 5.1 summarises the illustrative examples that accompany IFRIC 21.

TABLE 5.1 IFRIC 21 examples		
Illustrative examples	Obligating event	Recognition of liability
Levy triggered progressively as revenue is generated in a specified period.	Generation of revenue in the specified period.	Recognise progressively. A liability must be recognised progressively because, at any point in time during the specified period, the entity has a present obligation to pay a levy on revenues generated to date.
Levy triggered in full as soon as revenue is generated in one period, based on revenues from a previous period.	First generation of revenue in subsequent period.	Full recognition at that point in time. Where an entity generates revenue in one period, which serves as the basis for measuring the amount of the levy, the entity does not become liable for the levy, and therefore cannot recognise a liability, until it first starts generating revenue in the subsequent period.

TABLE 5.1 *(continued)*

Illustrative examples	Obligating event	Recognition of liability
Levy triggered in full if the entity operates as a bank at the end of the annual reporting period.	Operating as a bank at the end of the reporting period.	Full recognition at the end of the annual reporting period. Before the end of the annual reporting period, the entity has no present obligation to pay a levy, even if it is economically compelled to continue operating as a bank in the future. The liability is recognised only at the end of the annual reporting period.
Levy triggered if revenues are above a minimum specified threshold (e.g. when a certain level of revenue has been achieved).	Reaching the specified minimum threshold.	Recognise an amount consistent with the obligation at that point of time. A liability is recognised only at the point that the specified minimum threshold is reached. For example, a levy is triggered when an entity generates revenues above specified thresholds: 0% for the first $50 million and 2% above $50 million. In this example, no liability is accrued until the entity's revenues reach the revenue threshold of $50 million.

Source: Ernst & Young (2015).

5.9.6 Other applications

Illustrative examples 5.8 to 5.15, sourced from IAS 37 and modified to aid understanding, illustrate the applications of the recognition requirements of IAS 37.

ILLUSTRATIVE EXAMPLE 5.8 Warranties

Eastern Systems gives warranties at the time of sale to purchasers of its product. Under the terms of the contract for sale Eastern Systems undertakes to make good, by repair or replacement, manufacturing defects that become apparent within 3 years from the date of sale. On past experience, it is probable (that is, more likely than not) that there will be some claims under the warranties.

In these circumstances the obligating event is the sale of the product with a warranty, which gives rise to a legal obligation. Because it is more likely than not that there will be an outflow of resources for some claims under the warranties as a whole, a provision is recognised for the best estimate of the costs of making good under the warranty for those products sold before the end of the reporting period.

ILLUSTRATIVE EXAMPLE 5.9 Legal obligation

Hadafa Petrochemical in the oil industry causes contamination but cleans up only when required to do so under the laws of the particular country in which it operates. One country in which it operates has had no legislation requiring cleaning up, and the entity has been contaminating land in that country for several years. At 31 December 2015, it is virtually certain that a draft law requiring a clean-up of land already contaminated will be enacted shortly after the year end.

In these circumstances, the virtual certainty of new legislation being enacted means that Hadafa has a present legal obligation as a result of the past event (contamination of the land), requiring a provision to be recognised.

Conch in the oil industry causes contamination and operates in a country where there is no environmental legislation. However, Conch has a widely published environmental policy in which it undertakes to clean up all contamination that it causes. Conch has a record of honouring this published policy.

In these circumstances a provision is still required because Conch has created a valid expectation that it will clean up the land, meaning that Conch has a present constructive obligation as a result of past contamination. It is therefore clear that where an entity causes environmental damage and has a present legal or constructive obligation to make it good, it is probable that an outflow of resources will be required to settle the obligation, and a reliable estimate can be made of the amount, a provision will be required.

Pearl operates an offshore oilfield where its licensing agreement requires it to remove the oil rig at the end of production and restore the seabed. Of the eventual costs, 90% relate to the removal of the oil rig and restoration of damage caused by building it, and 10% arise through the extraction of oil. At the end of the reporting period, the rig has been constructed but no oil has been extracted.

A provision is recognised at the time of constructing the oil rig (obligating event) in relation to the eventual costs that relate to its removal and the restoration of damage caused by building it. Additional provisions are recognised over the life of the oil field to reflect the need to reverse damage caused during the extraction of oil. A provision is recognised for the best estimate of 90% of the eventual costs that relate to the removal of the oil rig and restoration of damage caused by building it. These costs are included as part of the cost of the oil rig. The 10% of costs that arise through the extraction of oil are recognised as a liability when the oil is extracted.

Under new legislation, Karachi Ltd is required to fit smoke filters to its factories by 30 June 20X3. Karachi Ltd has not fitted the smoke filters.

(a) At the end of the reporting period, 31 December 20X2:

No event has taken place to create an obligation. Only once the smoke filters are fitted or the legislation takes effect will there be a present obligation as a result of a past event, either for the cost of fitting smoke filters or for fines under the legislation.

(b) At the end of the reporting period, 31 December 20X3:

There is still no obligating event to justify provision for the cost of fitting the smoke filters required under the legislation because the filters have not been fitted. However, an obligation may exist as at the reporting date to pay fines or penalties under the legislation because Karachi Ltd is operating its factory in a non-compliant way. However, a provision would only be recognised for the best estimate of any fines and penalties if, as at 31 December 20X3, it is determined to be more likely than not that such fines and penalties will be imposed.

Indonesian Clothing Inc. operates profitably from a factory that it has leased under an operating lease. During December 20X3 Indonesian Clothing Inc. relocates its operations to a new factory. The lease on the old factory continues for the next 4 years, it cannot be cancelled and the factory cannot be re-let to another user.

In these circumstances, the obligating event is the signing of the lease contract (a legal obligation) and when the lease becomes onerous, an outflow of resources embodying economic benefits is probable. Accordingly, a provision is recognised for the best estimate of the unavoidable lease payments.

ILLUSTRATIVE EXAMPLE 5.14 Provision not recognised

Some assets require, in addition to routine maintenance, substantial expenditure every few years for major refits or refurbishment and the replacement of major components. IAS 16 *Property, Plant and Equipment* gives guidance on allocating expenditure on an asset to its component parts where these components have different useful lives or provide benefits in a different pattern.

An aircraft has an air-conditioning and pressurisation system that needs to be replaced every 5 years for technical reasons. At the end of the reporting period, the system has been in use for 3 years.

In these circumstances, a provision for the cost of replacing the system is not recognised because, at the end of the reporting period, no obligation to replace the system exists independently of the entity's future actions. Even the intention to incur the expenditure depends upon the entity deciding to continue operating the system or to replace the system. Instead of a provision being recognised, the initial cost of the system is treated as a significant part of the aircraft and depreciated over a period of 5 years. The replacement costs are then capitalised when incurred and depreciated over the next 5 years.

ILLUSTRATIVE EXAMPLE 5.15 Cost identified as separate

Sunshine Air is required by law to overhaul its aircraft once every 3 years.

Even with the legal requirement to perform the overhaul, there is no obligating event until the 3-year period has elapsed. As with the previous example, no obligation exists independently of Sunshine Air's future actions. Sunshine Air could avoid the cost of the overhaul by selling the aircraft before the 3-year period has elapsed. Instead of a provision being recognised, the overhaul cost is identified as a separate part of the aircraft asset under IAS 16 and is depreciated over 3 years.

5.10 CONTINGENT ASSETS

A contingent asset is a possible asset that arises from past events and whose existence will be confirmed only by the occurrence or non-occurrence of one or more uncertain future events not wholly within the control of the entity (IAS 37 paragraph 10). IAS 37 does not allow the recognition of a contingent asset and disclosures are required when an inflow of benefits is probable.

An example of a contingent asset would be the possible receipt of damages arising from a court case, which has been decided in favour of the entity as at the end of the reporting period. The hearing to determine damages, however, will be held after the end of the reporting period. The outcome of the hearing is outside the control of the entity, but the receipt of damages is probable because the case has been decided in the entity's favour. The asset meets the definition of a contingent asset because it is possible that the entity will receive the damages and the hearing is outside its control. In addition, the contingent asset is disclosed because it is probable that the damages (the inflow of economic benefits) will flow to the entity.

5.11 DISCLOSURE

The disclosure requirements of IAS 37 are self-explanatory and are described in paragraphs 84 to 92 of the standard.

Note that the disclosures required for contingent liabilities and assets would involve judgement and estimation. Many analysts consider the contingent liabilities note to be one of the most important notes provided by a company because it helps the analyst in making decisions about the likely consequences for the company and is useful in providing an overall view of the company's exposures. Therefore, the use of the exemption for non-disclosure of information, which would prejudice an entity's position in a dispute with other parties as permitted in paragraph 92, should be treated with caution because it could be interpreted as a deliberate concealing of the company's exposures.

An example of extensive disclosures of provisions, related assumptions and contingent liabilities is included in the annual report of Bayer AG, a global enterprise based in Germany, reporting under IFRS Standards (see note 4). Figure 5.2 is an extract from the contingencies note (note 31) and the first part of the note on legal risks (note 32). Students should refer to the annual report at www.bayer.com for the full note 32.

FIGURE 5.2 Example of disclosures of contingencies

31. Contingencies and other financial commitments

The following warranty contracts, guarantees and other contingent liabilities existed at the end of the reporting period:

Contingent Liabilities	31 Dec. 2013	31 Dec. 2014
	€ million	€ million
Warranties	107	95
Guarantees	140	144
Other contingent liabilities	467	339
Total	714	578

The guarantees mainly comprise a declaration issued by Bayer AG to the trustees of the UK pension plans guaranteeing the pension obligations of Bayer Public Limited Company and Bayer CropScience Limited. Under the declaration, Bayer AG — in addition to the two companies — undertakes to make further payments into the plans upon receipt of a payment request from the trustees. The net liability with respect to these defined benefit plans as of 31 December 2014 amounted to €144 million (2013: €100 million).

The potential payment claims related to the partial exemption from the surcharge levied under the German Renewable Energy Act that were included in other contingent liabilities in 2013 no longer exist following the conclusion of the EU state-aid proceedings in 2014 (2013: €172 million).

Other financial commitments

The other financial commitments were as follows:

Other financial commitments	31 Dec. 2013	31 Dec. 2014
	€ million	€ million
Operating leases	596	671
Orders already placed under purchase agreements	365	476
Unpaid portion of the effective initial fund	1 005	1 005
Potential payment obligations under R&D collaboration agreements	2 106	2 427
Revenue-based milestone payment commitments	2 191	2 169
Total	6 263	6 748

The non-discounted future minimum lease payments relating to operating leases totalled €671 million (2013: €596 million). The maturities of the respective payment obligations were as follows:

Operating Leases			
Maturing in	31 Dec. 2013	Maturing in	31 Dec. 2014
	€ million		€ million
2014	174	2015	174
2015	144	2016	125
2016	81	2017	98
2017	66	2018	70
2018	42	2019	59
2019 or later	89	2020 or later	145
Total	596	Total	671

FIGURE 5.2 *(continued)*

Financial commitments resulting from orders already placed under purchase agreements related to planned or ongoing capital expenditure projects totalled €476 million (2013: €365 million).

The Bayer Group has entered into cooperation agreements with third parties under which it has agreed to fund various research and development projects or has assumed other payment obligations based on the achievement of certain milestones or other specific conditions. If all of these payments have to be made, their maturity distribution as of 31 December 2014 was expected to be as set forth in the following table. The amounts shown represent the maximum payments to be made, and it is unlikely that they will all fall due. Since the achievement of the conditions for payment is highly uncertain, both the amounts and the dates of the actual payments may vary considerably from those stated in the table.

Potential payment obligations under R&D collaboration agreements			
Maturing in	31 Dec. 2013	Maturing in	31 Dec. 2014
	€ million		€ million
2014	155	2015	155
2015	181	2016	198
2016	144	2017	164
2017	113	2018	130
2018	95	2019	203
2019 or later	1 418	2020 or later	1 577
Total	2 106	Total	2 427

In addition to the above commitments, there were also revenue-based milestone payment commitments totalling €2169 million (2013: €2191 million), of which €2157 million (2013: €2090 million) were not expected to fall due until 2020 (2013: 2019) or later. These commitments are also highly uncertain.

Should the achievement of the milestones or specific conditions become sufficiently probable, a provision or other liability is recognised in the statement of financial position, and this may also lead to the recognition of an intangible asset in the same amount. The above table includes neither current revenue-based royalty payments nor future payments that are probable and therefore already reflected in the statement of financial position.

32. Legal risks

As a global company with a diverse business portfolio, the Bayer Group is exposed to numerous legal risks, particularly in the areas of product liability, competition and antitrust law, patent disputes, tax assessments and environmental matters. The outcome of any current or future proceedings cannot normally be predicted. It is therefore possible that legal or regulatory judgments or future settlements could give rise to expenses that are not covered, or not fully covered, by insurers' compensation payments and could significantly affect our revenues and earnings.

Source: Bayer AG (*Annual Report 2014*, pp. 320–326).

The legal proceedings (which includes product-related proceedings, competition law, patent disputes and tax proceedings) were also listed in Bayer AG's note 32.

5.12 COMPARISON BETWEEN IFRS 3 AND IAS 37 IN RESPECT OF CONTINGENT LIABILITIES

IFRS 3 *Business Combinations*, as revised in 2008, contains a number of requirements that are inconsistent with IAS 37. However, *as discussed in section 5.9.3*, the requirements in respect of restructuring provisions are consistent with IAS 37. The two areas of difference are in respect of contingent liabilities acquired in a business combination and contingent consideration.

5.12.1 Contingent liabilities acquired in a business combination

As discussed in section 5.6, IAS 37 does not allow contingent liabilities to be recognised in the statement of financial position. Instead, they are disclosed if certain conditions are met. However, IFRS 3 (paragraph 23) states that the requirements of IAS 37 *do not apply* in determining which contingent liabilities to recognise at the acquisition date. Instead, the acquirer *must* recognise contingent liabilities assumed in a business combination — just as it must recognise all other liabilities assumed in a business combination. The only conditions for recognising the contingent liability are:

(a) it must be a present obligation arising from past events
(b) its fair value can be measured reliably.

Condition (a) means that contingent liabilities falling within part (a) of the contingent liability definition (i.e. a possible obligation — *see section 5.5*) are not recognised in a business combination — only those that fall within part (b) of the definition are eligible for recognition (i.e. there is a present obligation) provided their value can be reliably measured *(see chapter 3 Fair Value Measurement which covers the requirements with respect to measuring fair value for liabilities)*. This means that an acquirer must identify which contingent liabilities of the acquiree are present obligations that failed the recognition criteria from the perspective of the acquiree but which can be assigned a fair value by the acquirer. This is shown in illustrative example 5.16.

ILLUSTRATIVE EXAMPLE 5.16 Contingent liabilities in a business combination

Assume that an acquiree had identified damages payable in a lawsuit as a present obligation because it had lost the case, but it did not record the contingent liability as a liability because it could not reliably measure the amount payable. In this case, the acquirer would need to estimate the fair value of the amount payable and recognise it as one of the liabilities assumed in the business combination.

5.12.2 Contingent consideration in a business combination

Sometimes an acquirer may enter into an agreement with the vendor of the acquiree that entitles the vendor to additional consideration if certain conditions are met in the future. This is referred to as contingent consideration. IFRS 3 paragraph 39 requires the acquirer to include the acquisition-date fair value of that contingent consideration as part of the consideration transferred in exchange for the acquiree. This means that the acquirer must make an estimate, if necessary, to determine the fair value and would record a liability for the amount of the contingency. This is demonstrated in illustrative example 5.17. The classification of a contingent consideration obligation that meets the definition of a financial instrument as either a financial liability or equity is based on the definitions in IAS 32 *Financial Instruments: Presentation*.

ILLUSTRATIVE EXAMPLE 5.17 Accounting for contingent consideration in a business combination

Sporty Co. acquires 100% of Pluto Co. from Venus Co. The purchase consideration is comprised of cash of $1 500 000 plus an agreement to pay a further $200 000 in cash to Venus Co. if Pluto Co. achieves certain profit targets within 3 years of the acquisition date. The fair value of the identifiable assets and liabilities of Pluto Co. acquired is $1 200 000. Sporty Co. estimates the acquisition-date fair value of the contingent consideration to be $140 000 based on its expectations of Pluto Co.'s future performance and the time value of money. Sporty Co. thus records the following journal entry at the date of acquisition *(see chapter 14 for more details on how to account for a business combination)*:

Net Assets of Pluto Co.	Dr	1 200 000	
Goodwill	Dr	440 000	
Cash	Cr		1 500 000
Liability to Pay Venus Co.	Cr		140 000

Note that if the contingent consideration was not recorded (i.e. if the requirements of IAS 37 were followed) goodwill would be lower. Companies wishing to minimise the amount of goodwill arising on acquisition would thus want to record a lower amount for contingent consideration.

Table 5.2 summarises the similarities and differences between IFRS 3 and IAS 37.

TABLE 5.2 Similarities and differences between IFRS 3 and IAS 37			
	IAS 37	IFRS 3	Same/Different
Contingent liabilities — part (a) of the definition of a contingent liability	Possible liabilities are not recognised by the entity	Possible liabilities are not recognised by the acquirer	Same
Contingent liabilities — part (b) of the definition of a contingent liability	A present obligation that fails *either* of the recognition criteria must not be recognised by the entity	A present obligation whose fair value can be reliably measured must be recognised by the acquirer	Different
Contingent consideration	Contingent consideration is not specifically addressed, but applying the definition of a contingent liability would likely result in no amount being recognised by the entity	Contingent consideration must be recognised by the acquirer at its acquisition-date fair value	Different
Restructuring provisions	A restructuring provision is recognised by the entity only if the criteria in IAS 37 are met	A restructuring provision is recognised by the *acquiree* only if the criteria in IAS 37 are met	Same

5.13 EXPECTED FUTURE DEVELOPMENTS

In June 2005, the IASB issued an exposure draft proposing significant changes to IAS 37 as part of its programme to amend IFRS 3 *(see chapter 14)*. The exposure draft proposed amendments to the title of IAS 37 (to 'Non-financial Liabilities'), new definitions of contingencies, and new recognition and measurement criteria. The proposed changes are so far-reaching that they attracted widespread concern by respondents to the exposure draft. In 2012, the project on non-financial liabilities was paused and removed from the Board's active agenda. However, it has since been added back onto the work plan as a short- and medium-term research project. At the time of writing, the IASB has indicated that progress of this project is dependent on the developments of the *Conceptual Framework*. Therefore it is not yet clear what the direction and scope of the project will be.

SUMMARY

IAS 37 deals with the recognition, measurement and presentation of provisions and contingent assets and contingent liabilities. The standard contains specific requirements regarding the recognition of restructuring provisions and onerous contracts.

The standard:
- defines provisions and specifies recognition criteria and measurement requirements for the recognition of provisions in financial statements
- defines contingent liabilities and contingent assets and prohibits their recognition in the financial statements but requires their disclosure when certain conditions are met
- requires that where provisions are measured using estimated cash flows, that the cash flows be discounted to their present value at the reporting date and specifies the discount rate to be used for this purpose
- prohibits providing for future operating losses
- defines onerous contracts and requires the estimated net loss under onerous contracts to be provided for
- specifies recognition criteria for restructuring provisions and identifies the types of costs that may be included in restructuring provisions
- requires extensive disclosures relating to provisions, recoveries, contingent liabilities and contingent assets.

The standard differs from IFRS 3 *Business Combinations* in respect of the recognition of contingent liabilities and contingent consideration. However, it is consistent with IFRS 3 in respect of restructuring provisions.

Discussion questions

1. How is present value related to the concept of a liability?
2. Define (a) a contingency and (b) a contingent liability.
3. What are the characteristics of a provision?
4. Define a constructive obligation.
5. What is the key characteristic of a present obligation?
6. What are the recognition criteria for provisions?
7. At what point would a contingent liability become a provision?
8. Compare and contrast the requirements of IFRS 3 and IAS 37 in respect of restructuring provisions and contingent liabilities.

References

Bayer AG 2014, *Annual Report 2014*, Bayer AG, Germany, www.bayer.com.
Ernst & Young 2011, *International GAAP 2011*, Chichester: John Wiley & Sons, Inc.
Ernst & Young 2015, *International GAAP 2015*, Chichester: John Wiley & Sons, Inc.

Exercises

STAR RATING ★ BASIC ★★ MODERATE ★★★ DIFFICULT

Exercise 5.1 | **RECOGNISING A PROVISION**

★ When should liabilities for each of the following items be recorded in the accounts of the business entity?
(a) Acquisition of goods by purchase on credit
(b) Salaries
(c) Annual bonus paid to management
(d) Dividends

Exercise 5.2 | **RECOGNISING A PROVISION**

★ The government introduces a number of changes to the value added tax system. As a result of these changes, Company A, a manufacturing company, will need to retrain a large proportion of its administrative and sales workforce in order to ensure continued compliance with the new taxation regulations. At the end of the reporting period, no retraining of staff has taken place.

Required

Should Company A provide for the costs of the staff training at the end of the reporting period?

Exercise 5.3 | **RECOGNISING A PROVISION**

★★ Company B, a listed company, provides food to function centres that host events such as weddings and engagement parties. After an engagement party held by one of Company B's customers in June 2016, 100 people became seriously ill, possibly as a result of food poisoning from products sold by Company B. Legal proceedings were commenced seeking damages from Company B, which disputed liability by claiming that the function centre was at fault for handling the food incorrectly. Up to the date of authorisation for issue of the financial statements for the year to 30 June 2016, Company B's lawyers advised that it was probable that Company B would not be found liable. However, two weeks after the financial statements were published, Company B's lawyers advised that, owing to developments in the case, it was probable that Company B would be found liable and the estimated damages would be material to the company's reported profits.

Required

Should Company B recognise a liability for damages in its financial statements at 30 June 2016? How should it deal with the information it receives two weeks after the financial statements are published?

Exercise 5.4 | **DISTINGUISHING BETWEEN LIABILITIES, PROVISIONS AND CONTINGENT LIABILITIES**

★★ Identify whether each of the following would be a liability, a provision or a contingent liability, or none of the above, in the financial statements of Company A as at the end of its reporting period of 30 June 2016. Assume that Company A's financial statements are authorised for issue on 24 August 2016.
(a) An amount of $35 000 owing to Company Z for services rendered during May 2016.
(b) Long service leave, estimated to be $500 000, owing to employees in respect of past services.

(c) Costs of $26 000 estimated to be incurred for relocating employee D from Company A's head office location to another city. The staff member will physically relocate during July 2016.

(d) Provision of $50 000 for the overhaul of a machine. The overhaul is needed every 5 years and the machine was 5 years old as at 30 June 2016.

(e) Damages awarded against Company A resulting from a court case decided on 26 June 2016. The judge has announced that the amount of damages will be set at a future date, expected to be in September 2016. Company A has received advice from its lawyers that the amount of the damages could be anything between $20 000 and $7 million.

Exercise 5.5

RECOGNISING A PROVISION

★★ In each of the following scenarios, explain whether or not Company G would be required to recognise a provision.

(a) As a result of its plastics operations, Company G has contaminated the land on which it operates. There is no legal requirement to clean up the land, and Company G has no record of cleaning up land that it has contaminated.

(b) As a result of its plastics operations, Company G has contaminated the land on which it operates. There is a legal requirement to clean up the land.

(c) As a result of its plastics operations, Company G has contaminated the land on which it operates. There is no legal requirement to clean up the land, but Company G has a long record of cleaning up land that it has contaminated.

Exercise 5.6

CALCULATION OF A PROVISION

★★ In May 2013, Company A relocated employee R from Company A's head office to an office in another city. As at 30 June 2013, the end of Company A's reporting period, the costs were estimated to be $40 000. Analysis of the costs is as follows:

Costs for shipping goods	$ 3 000
Airfare	6 000
Temporary accommodation costs (May and June)	8 000
Temporary accommodation costs (July and August)	9 000
Reimbursement for lease break costs (paid in July; lease was terminated in May)	2 000
Reimbursement for cost-of-living increases (for the period 15 May 2013 to 15 May 2014)	12 000

Required

Calculate the provision for relocation costs for Company A's financial statements as at 30 June 2013. Assume that IAS 37 applies to this provision and that the effect of discounting is immaterial.

Exercise 5.7

COMPREHENSIVE PROBLEM

★★★ ChubbyChocs Ltd, a listed company, is a manufacturer of confectionery and biscuits. The end of its reporting period is 30 June. Relevant extracts from its financial statements at 30 June 2014 are shown below

Current liabilities		
Provisions		
Provision for warranties		$270 000
Non-current liabilities		
Provisions		
Provision for warranties		160 715
Non-current assets		
Plant and equipment		
At cost	$2 000 000	
Accumulated depreciation	600 000	
Carrying amount	1 400 000	

Plant and equipment has a useful life of 10 years and is depreciated on a straight-line basis.

> **Note 36 — Contingent liabilities**
> ChubbyChocs is engaged in litigation with various parties in relation to allergic reactions to traces of peanuts alleged to have been found in packets of fruit gums. ChubbyChocs strenuously denies the allegations and, as at the date of authorising the financial statements for issue, is unable to estimate the financial effect, if any, of any costs or damages that may be payable to the plaintiffs.

The provision for warranties at 30 June 2014 was calculated using the following assumptions (there was no balance carried forward from the prior year):

Estimated cost of repairs — products with minor defects	$1 000 000
Estimated cost of repairs — products with major defects	$6 000 000
Expected % of products sold during FY 2014 having no defects in FY 2015	80%
Expected % of products sold during FY 2014 having minor defects in FY 2015	15%
Expected % of products sold during FY 2014 having major defects in FY 2015	5%
Expected timing of settlement of warranty payments — those with minor defects	All in FY 2015
Expected timing of settlement of warranty payments — those with major defects	40% in FY 2015, 60% in FY 2016
Discount rate	6%. The effect of discounting for FY 2015 is considered to be immaterial

During the year ended 30 June 2015, the following occurred:
1. In relation to the warranty provision of $430 715 at 30 June 2014, $200 000 was paid out of the provision. Of the amount paid, $150 000 was for products with minor defects and $50 000 was for products with major defects, all of which related to amounts that had been expected to be paid in the 2015 financial year.
2. In calculating its warranty provision for 30 June 2015, ChubbyChocs made the following adjustments to the assumptions used for the prior year:

Estimated cost of repairs — products with minor defects	No change
Estimated cost of repairs — products with major defects	$5 000 000
Expected % of products sold during FY 2015 having no defects in FY 2016	85%
Expected % of products sold during FY 2015 having minor defects in FY 2016	12%
Expected % of products sold during FY 2015 having major defects in FY 2016	3%
Expected timing of settlement of warranty payments — those with minor defects	All in FY 2016
Expected timing of settlement of warranty payments — those with major defects	20% in FY 2016, 80% in FY 2017
Discount rate	No change. The effect of discounting for FY 2016 is considered to be immaterial

3. ChubbyChocs determined that part of its plant and equipment needed an overhaul — the conveyer belt on one of its machines would need to be replaced in about May 2016 at an estimated cost of $250 000. The carrying amount of the conveyer belt at 30 June 2014 was $140 000. Its original cost was $200 000.
4. ChubbyChocs was unsuccessful in its defence of the peanut allergy case and was ordered to pay $1 500 000 to the plaintiffs. As at 30 June 2015, ChubbyChocs had paid $800 000.

5. ChubbyChocs commenced litigation against one of its advisers for negligent advice given on the original installation of the conveyer belt referred to in (3) above. In April 2015 the court found in favour of ChubbyChocs. The hearing for damages had not been scheduled as at the date the financial statements for 2015 were authorised for issue. ChubbyChocs estimated that it would receive about $425 000.
6. ChubbyChocs signed an agreement with BankSweet to the effect that ChubbyChocs would guarantee a loan made by BankSweet to ChubbyChocs' subsidiary, CCC Ltd. CCC's loan with BankSweet was $3 200 000 as at 30 June 2015. CCC was in a strong financial position at 30 June 2015.

Required

Prepare the relevant extracts from the financial statements (including the notes) of ChubbyChocs Ltd as at 30 June 2015, in compliance with IAS 37 and related International Financial Reporting Standards. Include comparative figures where required. Show all workings separately. Perform your workings in the following order:
(a) Calculate the warranty provision as at 30 June 2014. This should agree with the financial statements provided in the question.
(b) Calculate the warranty provision as at 30 June 2015.
(c) Calculate the movement in the warranty provision for the year.
(d) Calculate the prospective change in depreciation required as a result of the shortened useful life of the conveyer belt.
(e) Determine whether the unpaid amount owing as a result of the peanut allergy case is a liability or a provision.
(f) Determine whether the receipt of damages for the negligent advice meets the definition of an asset or a contingent asset.
(g) Determine whether the bank guarantee meets the definition of a provision or a contingent liability.
(h) Prepare the financial statement disclosures.

As pointed out in the chapter, one of the main types of provision is the provision for restructuring costs. The requirements of IAS 37 with respect to restructuring likely had been influenced by some high profile abuses of previous rules (e.g., the case of W.R. Grace & Co. and Lucent Technologies in the late 1990s). But what is the evidence as to how prone is the restructuring provision to earnings management? Nelson et al. (2002) surveyed over 250 auditors working in Big audit firms about their experience with earnings management. One interesting insight that emerged from this survey is that provisions are most susceptible to earnings management. By initially inflating the provision managers create a 'cookie jar' that can be used later to support future earnings. Consistent with this, Gu and Chen's (2004) analysis of non-recurring items indicates that restructuring charges are the leading type among such items.

Moehrle (2002) examines the financials of 121 firms who reversed their restructuring charges (reversing firms) to understand the motivation for the reversal. Reversed charges work to increase reported profit and hence may be opportunistically used by managers to meet market expectations. Consistent with this conjecture, he finds that reversing firms experience pre-reversal negative earnings, and pre-reversal earnings that fall short of analyst expectations. This evidence is consistent with 'cookie jar' earnings management that enables managers to reverse the charge when managers need to boost reported income to meet certain profit targets.

Environmental liabilities and environmental-related disclosures received considerable attention in the accounting literature. Firms that contaminate sites they use for their plants and operations need to estimate the 'clean-up' costs that will be needed after cessation of activity and accrue a provision. Barth and McNichols (1994) is one of the earliest studies of this provision. They provide evidence that suggests that clean-up provisions are understated. In a follow-up paper Barth et al. (1997) examine the determinants of the disclosures of clean-up provisions. They provide evidence that indicates that several factors influence these disclosures including, the regulatory environment, manager's information, and threat of litigation. Lawrence and Khurana (1997) investigate the accrual of clean-up provisions in US municipalities. They find that two thirds of sample municipalities fail to accrue clean-up provisions and provide adequate disclosures.

Provisions need to be accrued and recognised, provided the resource outflow is probable, whereas (unrecognised) contingent liabilities arise when the outflow is only possible. For both accrued provisions and contingent liabilities there are additional disclosure requirements regarding expected amounts and timing. A powerful disincentive to provide detailed disclosures is present in the case of legal provisions. This is because disclosed information can be used by the opposing litigating party. Desir et al. (2010) examine 51 cases in which companies disclose details regarding the resolution of litigation cases. While 47 of these companies mention the exposure in the statements immediately preceding the loss resolution, only 24 quantify the magnitude of the expected loss. Nevertheless, only 31 firms accrue the loss beforehand. This evidence in Desir et al. (2010) is consistent with resistance of managers to disclose potentially harmful information. This conclusion is reinforced by Hennes's (2014) study of 212 resolved employee discrimination lawsuits.

There is little evidence on other types of provisions. A recent study by Cohen et al. (2011) looks at the provision for warranty cost. They posit that this provision can convey to the market managers' information about the underlying product quality. Specifically, employing signalling theory they argue greater warranty expense and larger provisions indicate better product quality and hence better future sales and return on assets. They provide evidence that is consistent with this view. In addition, they find that the market regards this provision similar to other liabilities. Finally, they provide evidence suggesting that the warranty provision is used opportunistically by managers of underperforming firms.

The accrual of a provision is dependent on how managers and auditors interpret the concept of 'probable' outflow. This can be quite subjective and prior accounting and psychology research reviewed in Amer et al. (1995) suggests probability measures vary quite significantly across individuals. Specifically, Amer et al. (1995) examine whether the meaning of 'probable' varies across loss contexts, an outcome that was not intended by standard setters. In particular, in experimental setting auditor-subjects were asked to assess risk of default of a customer of a hypothetical audit client. The subjects were also given background information about the health of the industry in which the hypothetical client operates in addition to information about the client's customer. The main finding was that the threshold for 'probable' was higher when industry conditions were good than when they were poorer (0.75 vs. 0.68). Hence Amer et al. (1995) conclude that auditors' interpretation of what is probable may be sensitive to the context in which the assessment is applied.

Aharony and Dotan (2004) explore whether analysts and managers similarly interpret 'remote' and 'probable'. They analysed about 300 questionnaires sent to managers, analysts and auditors in the US. They report that analysts regard an outflow event as 'remote' when the probability is up to 0.17, on average. Mangers' probability assessment of a remote event is higher, at 0.20, on average. Analysts quantify 'probable' as an event whose chance is 0.67, on average, while managers assign it 0.75, on average. Auditors provide estimates that are identical to those of managers, on average. These findings suggest that managers' and auditors' threshold for accruing a provision are higher than market perceptions and that they tend to under-report loss events by arguing they are remote.

References

Aharony, J., and Dotan, A., 2004. A comparative analysis of auditor, manager and financial analyst interpretations of SFAS 5 Disclosure Guidelines. *Journal of Business Finance & Accounting*, 31, 475–504.

Amer, T., Hackenbrack, K., and Nelson, M.W., 1995. Context-dependence of auditors' interpretations of the SFAS No. 5 probability expressions. *Contemporary Accounting Research*, 12(1), 25–39.

Barth, M.E., and McNichols, M.C., 1994. Estimation and market valuation of environmental liabilities relating to Superfund sites. *Journal of Accounting Research*, 32 (Supplement), 177–209.

Barth, M.E., McNichols, M.C., Wilson, G.P., 1997. Factors influencing firms' disclosures about environmental liabilities. *Review of Accounting Studies*, 2(1), 35–64.

Cohen, D., Darrough, M.N., Huang, R., and Zach, T., 2011. Warranty reserve: Contingent liability, information signal, or earnings management tool?. *The Accounting Review*, 86(2), 569–604.

Desir, R., Fanning, K., and Pfeiffer, R.J., 2010. Are revisions to SFAS No. 5 needed? *Accounting Horizons*, 24(4), 525–545.

Gu, Z., and Chen, T., 2004. Analysts' treatment of nonrecurring items in street earnings. *Journal of Accounting and Economics*, 38 (Conference Issue), 129–170.

Hennes, K.M., 2014. Disclosure of contingent legal liabilities. *Journal of Accounting and Public Policy*, 33(1), 32–50.

Lawrence, C.M., and Khurana, I.K., 1997. Superfund liabilities and governmental reporting entities: An empirical analysis. *Journal of Accounting and Public Policy*, 16(2), 155–186.

Moehrle, S.R., 2002. Do firms use restructuring charge reversals to meet earnings targets? *The Accounting Review*, 77(2), 397–413.

Nelson, M.W., Elliott, J.A., and Tarpley, R.L., 2002. Evidence from auditors about managers' and auditors' earnings management decisions. *The Accounting Review*, 77(s-1), 175–202.

6 Income taxes

ACCOUNTING STANDARDS IN FOCUS

IAS 12 *Income Taxes*

LEARNING OBJECTIVES

After studying this chapter, you should be able to:

1. understand the nature of income tax
2. understand differences in accounting treatments and taxation treatments for a range of transactions
3. explain the concept of tax-effect accounting
4. calculate and account for current taxation expense
5. discuss the recognition requirements for current tax
6. account for the payment of tax
7. explain the nature of and accounting for tax losses
8. calculate and account for movements in deferred taxation accounts
9. apply the recognition criteria for deferred tax items
10. account for changes in tax rates
11. account for amendments to prior year taxes and identify other issues
12. explain the presentation requirements of IAS 12
13. implement the disclosure requirements of IAS 12.

6.1 THE NATURE OF INCOME TAX

Income taxes are levied by governments on income earned by individuals and entities in order to raise money to fund the provision of government services and infrastructure. The percentage payable and the determination of taxable profit are governed by income tax legislation administered by a dedicated government body. Tax payable is normally determined annually with the lodgement of a taxation document, although some jurisdictions may require payment by instalment, with estimates of tax payable being made on a periodic basis.

This chapter analyses the accounting standard IAS 12 *Income Taxes*. According to paragraph 1 of IAS 12, the standard applies in accounting for income taxes, including all domestic and foreign taxes based on taxable profits. It also applies to withholding taxes that are payable by a subsidiary, associate or joint arrangement on distributions to a reporting entity. The standard does not deal with methods of accounting for government grants or investment tax credits, but it does deal with accounting for tax effects arising in respect of such transactions.

At first glance, accounting for income tax appears to be a simple matter of calculating the liability owing, recognising the liability and expense, and recording the eventual payment of the amount outstanding. Such a simplistic approach applies only if accounting profit is the same amount as taxable profit and the respective profits have been determined by the same rules. Because this is generally not the case, accounting for income taxes can be a complicated exercise; hence the need for an accounting standard.

In each country there are different legal requirements for calculating taxable profit. It is not the purpose of this chapter to deal with these requirements. Instead the focus is on the differences between the way in which income and expense are measured for accounting purposes and how they are measured for tax purposes. In general, it is assumed for simplicity that income and expense for tax purposes are based on cash flow in contrast to the use of the accrual method for accounting purposes. It is also assumed in this chapter that the company tax rate is 30%.

6.2 DIFFERENCES BETWEEN ACCOUNTING PROFIT AND TAXABLE PROFIT

Accounting profit is defined in IAS 12, paragraph 5, as 'profit or loss for a period before deducting tax expense', profit or loss being the excess (or deficiency) of income less expenses for that period. Such income and expenses would be determined and recognised in accordance with accounting standards and the *Conceptual Framework*. Taxable profit is defined in the same paragraph as the profit for a period, determined in accordance with the rules established by the taxation authorities, upon which income taxes are payable. Taxable profit is thus the excess of taxable income over taxation deductions allowable against that income. Thus, accounting profit and taxable profit — because they are determined by different principles and rules — are unlikely to be the same figure in any one period. Tax expense cannot be determined by simply multiplying the accounting profit by the applicable taxation rate. Instead, accounting for income taxes involves identifying and accounting for the differences between accounting profit and taxable profit. These differences arise from a number of common transactions and may be either permanent or temporary in nature.

6.2.1 Permanent differences

Permanent differences between accounting profit and taxable profit arise when the treatment of a transaction by taxation legislation and accounting standards is such that amounts recognised as part of accounting profit are never recognised as part of taxable profit, or vice versa. In some jurisdictions, for example, entities are allowed to deduct from their taxable income more than 100% of expenditure incurred on certain research and development activities undertaken during the taxation period. As a result of this extra deduction, taxable profit for the period is lower than accounting profit, and the extra amount is never recognised as an expense for accounting purposes. Other examples of permanent differences include income never subject to taxation such as dividend income, and expenditure incurred by an entity that will never be an allowable deduction such as entertainment expenditure. Where such differences exist, taxable profit will never equal accounting profit. No accounting requirements other than disclosure exist for these permanent differences *(see section 6.13)*.

6.2.2 Temporary differences

Temporary differences between accounting profit and taxable profit arise when the period in which revenues and expenses are recognised for accounting purposes is different from the period in which such revenues and expenses are treated as taxable income and allowable deductions for tax purposes. Interest revenue recognised on an accrual basis, for example, may not be taxable income until it is received as cash. Similarly, insurance paid in advance may be tax-deductible when paid but is not recognised in calculating accounting profit as an expense until a later period. The key feature of these differences is that they are temporary, because sooner or later the amount of interest revenue will equal the amount of taxable interest income, and the amount deducted against taxable income for insurance will equal the insurance expense offset against accounting income. However, in any one individual accounting/taxation period, these amounts will differ when calculating accounting profit and taxable profit respectively.

Differences that result in the entity paying more tax in the future (e.g. when interest is recognised for accounting purposes in a period before it is received and included in taxable income) are known as taxable temporary differences. Differences that result in the entity recovering tax via additional deductible expenses in the future (e.g. when accrued expenses are recognised for accounting purposes in a period before they are paid and included as a tax deduction) are known as deductible temporary differences. The existence of such temporary differences means that income tax payable that is calculated on taxable profit will vary in the current period from that based on accounting profit, but tax payments will eventually catch up. This is demonstrated in illustrative example 6.1.

ILLUSTRATIVE EXAMPLE 6.1 Reversal of temporary difference

Assume that the accounting profit of Aster Ltd for the year ended 30 June 2013 was £150 000, including £5600 in interest revenue of which only £4000 had been received in cash. The company income tax rate is 30%.

If tax is not payable on interest until it has been received in cash, the company's taxable profit will differ from its accounting profit, and a taxable temporary difference will exist in respect of the £1600 interest receivable. If accounting profit for the next year is also £150 000 and the outstanding interest is received in August 2013, tax payable for the years ending 30 June 2013 and 2014 is calculated as follows:

	2013	2014
Accounting profit	£150 000	£150 000
Temporary difference:		
Interest revenue not taxable for year ended 2013	(1 600)	
Interest revenue taxable for year ended June 2014		1 600
Taxable profit	£148 400	£151 600
Tax payable (30%)	44 520	45 480

Note that tax of £90 000, which is equal to 30% of £300 000 (being 2 × £150 000), is paid over the 2 years. The temporary difference created in 2013 is reversed in 2014. The same process occurs with all temporary differences although it may take a number of periods for a complete reversal to occur.

Appendix A to IAS 12 gives examples of temporary differences arising from different treatments of transactions for accounting and taxation purposes, some of which are listed below. These examples are not all-inclusive, so the relevant taxation legislation for specific jurisdictions should be consulted to determine if additional differences exist.

Circumstances that give rise to taxable temporary differences
Such circumstances include the following:
1. Interest revenue is received in arrears and is included in accounting profit on a time-apportionment basis but is included in taxable profit on a cash basis.
2. Revenue from the sale of goods is included in accounting profit when goods are delivered but is included in taxable profit only when cash is collected.
3. Depreciation of an asset is accelerated for tax purposes (the taxation depreciation rate is greater than the accounting rate).
4. Development costs are capitalised and amortised to the statement of profit or loss and other comprehensive income but are deducted in determining taxable profit in the period in which they are incurred.
5. Prepaid expenses have already been deducted on a cash basis in determining the taxable profit of the current or previous periods.
6. Depreciation of an asset is not deductible for tax purposes and no deduction will be available for tax purposes when the asset is sold or scrapped *(see section 6.9)*.
7. Financial assets or investment property are carried at fair value, which exceeds cost, but no equivalent adjustment is made for tax purposes.

8. An entity revalues property, plant and equipment, but no equivalent adjustment is made for tax purposes.
9. Impairment of goodwill is not deductible in determining taxable profit, and the cost of the goodwill would not be deductible on disposal of the business *(see section 6.9)*.

The tax treatment of temporary differences arising from fair value accounting and revaluation to fair value (items 7 and 8) are discussed and illustrated later in the book *(see section 11.6.1)*.

Circumstances that give rise to deductible temporary differences
Such circumstances include the following:
1. Retirement benefit costs are deducted in determining accounting profit because service is provided by the employee, but are not deducted in determining taxable profit until the entity pays either retirement benefits or contributions to a fund. Similar temporary differences arise in relation to other accrued expenses — such as product warranties, leave entitlements and interest — which are deductible on a cash basis in determining taxable profit.
2. Accumulated depreciation of an asset in the financial statements is greater than the cumulative depreciation allowed up to the end of the reporting period for tax purposes. That is, the accounting depreciation rate is greater than the allowable taxation depreciation rate.
3. The cost of inventories sold before the end of the reporting period is deducted in determining accounting profit when goods or services are delivered, but is deducted in determining taxable profit only when cash is collected.
4. The net realisable value *(see chapter 9)* of an item of inventory, or the recoverable amount *(see chapter 11)* of an item of property, plant and equipment, is less than the previous carrying amount. The entity therefore reduces the carrying amount of the asset, but that reduction is ignored for tax purposes until the asset is sold.
5. Research costs (or organisation or other start-up costs) are recognised as an expense in determining accounting profit, but are not permitted as a deduction in determining taxable profit until a later period.
6. Income is deferred in the statement of financial position but has already been included in taxable profit in current or prior periods (for example, subscriptions received in advance).
7. A government grant that is included in the statement of financial position as deferred income will not be taxable in a future period *(see section 6.9)*.
8. Financial assets or investment property is carried at fair value, which is less than cost, but no equivalent adjustment is made for tax purposes. (Temporary differences arising in these circumstances are beyond the scope of this chapter.)

In summary, income tax payable in any one period is affected by differences between items used to determine accounting profit and taxable profit. Some revenue items are not taxable, have already been taxed or will not be taxed until some future period(s). Some expense items are not deductible, have already been deducted or may be deducted in some future period(s). Additionally, extra deductions for which no expense will ever be incurred may be allowable under taxation legislation. The illustrative examples, exercises and problems in this chapter assume that the revenue from selling goods and services is taxable irrespective of whether cash has been received for the sale, and that the cost of sales is an allowable deduction irrespective of whether cash has been paid to acquire those goods.

6.3 ACCOUNTING FOR INCOME TAXES

As the objective paragraph of IAS 12 points out:

> The principal issue in accounting for income taxes is how to account for the current and future tax consequences of:
> (a) the future recovery (settlement) of the carrying amount of assets (liabilities) that are recognised in an entity's statement of financial position; and
> (b) transactions and other events of the current period that are recognised in an entity's financial statements.

IAS 12 requires the tax consequences of transactions and other events to be accounted for in the same manner and the same period as the transactions themselves. Thus, if a transaction is recognised in profit or loss for the period, so too is the related tax payable or tax benefit. Similarly, if a transaction is adjusted directly to equity, so too is the related tax effect. Differing accounting and taxation rules *(as discussed in section 6.2)* mean that the actual payment (deduction) of tax relating to revenue (expense) items may take place in both current and/or future accounting periods but IAS 12, paragraph 58, requires that the total income tax expense relating to transactions is recorded in the current year irrespective of when it will be paid or deducted.

To illustrate: an entity recognises interest revenue of £21 000 for the year ended 30 June 2014. Of this amount, £15 000 has been received in cash and a receivable asset has been raised for the remaining £6000. Tax legislation regards interest revenue as taxable only when it has been received. Therefore, the entity will pay tax of £4500 (£15 000 × 30%) in the current year and tax of £1800 (£6000 × 30%) in the following year when the £6000 is received.

If the entity were to record only the current tax payable amount as income tax expense, the profit for the year would be overstated by £1800 (£4500 current tax as opposed to £6300 tax expense on £21 000 of interest revenue). To ensure that the profit after-tax figure for the year is both relevant and reliable, IAS 12 requires the entity to record an income tax expense of £6300 (£21 000 × 30%) for the current year in respect to the interest revenue. This comprises a current tax liability amount of £4500 and a deferred tax (future) liability of £1800.

The need to recognise both current and future tax consequences of current year transactions means that each transaction has two tax effects:

1. tax payable on profit earned for the year may be reduced or increased because the transaction is not taxable or deductible in the current year
2. future tax payable may be reduced or increased when that transaction becomes taxable or deductible.

If only current tax payable is recorded as an expense, then the profit for the current year will be understated or overstated by the amount of tax or benefit to be paid or received in future years. Similarly, in the years that the tax or benefit on these transactions is paid or received, income tax expense will include amounts relating to prior periods and therefore be understated or overstated. As IAS 12 requires income tax expense to reflect all tax effects of transactions entered into during the year regardless of when the effects occur, two calculations are required at the end of the reporting period:

• the calculation of current tax liability, which determines the amount of tax payable for the period
• the calculation of movements in deferred tax effects relating to assets and liabilities recognised in the statement of financial position, which determines the net effect of deferred taxes and deductions arising from transactions during the year.

Acknowledging the current and future tax consequences of all items recognised in the statement of financial position (subject to certain exceptions) should make the information about the tax implications of an entity's operations and financial position more relevant and reliable.

6.4 CALCULATION OF CURRENT TAX

Current tax is the recognition of taxes payable to the taxation authorities in respect of a particular period. The current tax calculation involves identifying differences between accounting revenues and taxable income, and between accounting expenses and allowable deductions, for transactions during the year, as well as reversing temporary differences from prior years that occur in the current period. Accounting profit for the period is adjusted by these differences to calculate taxable profit, which is then multiplied by the current tax rate to determine current tax payable.

When selecting the tax rate to apply, the requirements of IAS 12 paragraph 46, must be considered. This paragraph states:

> Current tax liabilities (assets) for the current and prior periods shall be measured at the amount expected to be paid to (recovered from) the taxation authorities, using the tax rates (and tax laws) that have been enacted or substantively enacted by the end of the reporting period.

Therefore, if a tax rate has changed — or, in some jurisdictions, if a change has been announced — the rate applicable to the taxable profit for the period must be applied.

Identifying permanent and temporary differences in the current year's profit is a relatively simple exercise. All revenues and expenses are reviewed for amounts that are not taxable or deductible. Identifying reversals of prior year temporary differences may require referring back to prior year worksheets, transactions posted to asset and liability accounts during the current year, or reconstructions of ledger accounts. (The latter method is used in this chapter.) Such reversals include, where applicable, accrued expenses that have been paid and are now deductible, bad debts written off and now deductible, accrued revenue that has been received and is now taxable, and prepaid expenses deducted in a prior period but now expensed in accounting profit.

Once the differences have been isolated, there are two ways that the current tax could be determined: (1) the net differences could be adjusted against accounting profit to derive taxable profit, or (2) the gross amounts of items with differences could be added back or deducted against accounting profit. (The latter method is adopted in this chapter.) A worksheet is used to perform this reconciliation between accounting profit and taxable profit using the following formula:

Accounting profit (loss)
 + (–) accounting expenses not deductible for tax
 + (–) accounting expenses where the amount differs from deductible amounts
 + (–) taxable income where the amount differs from accounting revenue
 – (+) accounting revenues not subject to taxation
 – (+) accounting revenue where the amount differs from taxable income
 – (+) deductible amounts where the amount differs from accounting expense
= taxable profit

The current tax rate is then applied to taxable profit to derive the current tax payable (illustrative example 6.2).

Iris Ltd's accounting profit for the year ended 30 June 2013 was £250 450. Included in this profit were the following items of income and expense:

Amortisation — development project	£30 000
Impairment of goodwill expense	7 000
Depreciation — equipment (15%)	40 000
Entertainment expense	12 450
Insurance expense	24 000
Doubtful debts expense	14 000
Loss on sale of equipment	6 667
Rent revenue	25 000
Annual leave expense	54 000

At 30 June 2013, the company's draft statement of financial position showed the following balances:

	30 June 2013	30 June 2012
Assets		
Cash	£ 55 000	£ 65 000
Accounts receivable	295 000	277 000
Allowance for doubtful debts	(16 000)	(18 000)
Inventories	162 000	185 000
Prepaid insurance	30 000	25 000
Rent receivable	3 500	5 500
Development project	120 000	—
Accumulated amortisation	(30 000)	—
Equipment	200 000	266 667
Accumulated depreciation	(90 000)	(80 000)
Goodwill	35 000	35 000
Accumulated impairment expense	(14 000)	(7 000)
Deferred tax asset	?	24 900
Liabilities		
Accounts payable	310 500	294 000
Provision for annual leave	61 000	65 000
Mortgage loan	100 000	150 000
Deferred tax liability	?	57 150
Current tax liability	?	12 500

Additional information
1. Taxation legislation allows Iris Ltd to deduct 125% of the £120 000 spent on development during the year.
2. Iris Ltd has capitalised development expenditure relating to a filter project and amortises the balance over the period of expected benefit (4 years).
3. The taxation depreciation rate for equipment is 20%.
4. The equipment sold on 30 June 2013 cost £66 667 when it was purchased 3 years ago.
5. Neither entertainment expenditure nor goodwill impairment expense is deductible for taxation purposes.
6. The insurance and annual leave expenses are deductible when paid.
7. The rent revenue is taxable when received.
8. The company income tax rate is 30%.

Calculation of current tax payable

Before completing the worksheet, all differences between accounting and taxation figures must be identified:

1. Development project

There are two differences here: a permanent difference arising from the extra 25% deduction allowed by tax legislation, and a temporary difference arising from the treatment of the development costs. For accounting purposes, the £120 000 has been capitalised and will be amortised over 4 years; for tax purposes, the entire expenditure is deductible in the current year. The tax deduction for development is therefore: £150 000 (being £120 000 + [25% × £120 000]).

2. Impairment of goodwill expense

No tax deduction is allowed for impairment expense, so the taxation deduction is nil. Paragraph 21 of IAS 12 does not permit the recognition of the deferred tax liability arising from the taxable temporary difference created (see section 6.9). Therefore, a permanent difference exists.

3. Depreciation expense — equipment

Because equipment is being depreciated at a faster rate for taxation purposes, a temporary taxable difference will exist. The amount of depreciation deductible is £53 333.40 (being £266 667 × 20%).

4. Entertainment expense

No deduction is allowed for entertainment expenditure, so the taxation deduction is nil and there is a permanent difference between accounting profit and taxable profit.

5. Insurance expense

Insurance expenditure is deductible when paid. The existence of a prepaid insurance asset account in the statement of financial position indicates that the insurance payment and insurance expense figures are different. It is therefore necessary to reconstruct the asset account to identify if any part of the expense has already been deducted for taxation purposes. This is done as follows:

Prepaid Insurance			
Balance b/d	£25 000	Insurance Expense	£24 000
Bank (Insurance Paid)	29 000	Balance c/d	30 000
	54 000		54 000

The insurance paid figure of £29 000 represents the deduction allowable in determining taxable profit. The expense figure of £24 000 shows that the payment made includes £5000 for insurance cover for the next accounting period. When this amount is expensed, no deduction will be available against taxable profit.

6. Allowance for doubtful debts

If, under taxation legislation, no deduction is allowed for bad debts until they have been written off, the taxation amount for doubtful debts will be nil. The draft statement of financial position shows that an allowance was raised in the previous year, so any debts written off against that allowance are deductible in the current year. To determine the amount (if any) of that write-off, the ledger account is reconstructed as follows:

Allowance for Doubtful Debts			
Balance b/d	£16 000	Doubtful Debts Expense	£14 000
Bad Debts Written Off	16 000	Balance c/d	18 000
	32 000		32 000

The allowable deduction for bad debts written off is therefore £16 000.

7. Loss on sale of equipment

The gain or loss on the sale of equipment is different for accounting and taxation purposes, and is calculated as shown in the following table.

	Accounting	Taxation
Cost	£66 667	£66 667
Accumulated depreciation	30 000	40 000
Carrying amount	36 667	26 667
Proceeds	30 000	30 000
Gain (loss)	£ (6 667)	£ 3 333

The difference in the loss or gain on sale is caused by the different depreciation rates for accounting and tax purposes, resulting in different carrying amounts. When preparing the current tax worksheet, the accounting effect is reversed and the taxation effect is included, in this case, the accounting loss of £6667 is added and the taxation gain is also added.

8. Rent revenue

Rent revenue is taxable when received. The presence in the statement of financial position of a rent receivable asset indicates that part of the revenue has not yet been received as cash and is not taxable in the current year. A temporary difference therefore exists in respect of rent, as demonstrated by reconstructing the ledger account:

Rent Receivable			
Balance b/d	£ 5 500	Cash received	£27 000
Rent Revenue	25 000	Balance	3 500
	30 500		30 500

In this instance, the cash received figure represents rent received for two different accounting periods: £5500 outstanding at the end of the prior year, and £21 500 for the current year. Thus, the taxable amount combines the reversal of last year's temporary difference and the tax payable on the current year's income. A temporary difference still exists for the £3500 rent for this year not yet received in cash.

9. Annual leave expense
The annual leave expense is deductible when paid in cash. The provision for annual leave indicates the existence of unpaid leave and therefore a taxation temporary difference. This is demonstrated by reconstructing the ledger account.

Provision for Annual Leave			
Leave paid	£ 58 000	Balance b/d	£ 65 000
Balance c/d	61 000	Leave Expense	54 000
	119 000		119 000

The reconstruction reveals a payment of £58 000, which is deductible in the current year and represents a partial reversal of the temporary difference related to the opening balance. As none of the current year expense has been paid, no deduction is available this year and a further temporary difference is created.

This chapter assumes that sales revenue and cost of sales are taxable/deductible even when not received/paid in cash, so there are no differences with respect to the accounts receivable or accounts payable balances. If different assumptions applied, then the amounts of cash received for sales and cash paid for inventory would need to be determined in order to calculate the current tax payable.

Figure 6.1 contains the current worksheet used to calculate the current tax liability for Iris Ltd.

IRIS LTD Current Tax Worksheet for the year ended 30 June 2013		
Accounting profit		£ 250 450
Add:		
Amortisation of development expenditure	£ 30 000	
Impairment of goodwill expense	7 000	
Depreciation expense – equipment	40 000	
Entertainment expense	12 450	
Insurance expense	24 000	
Doubtful debts expense	14 000	
Accounting loss on sale of equipment	6 667	
Taxation gain on sale of equipment	3 333	
Annual leave expense	54 000	
Rent received	27 000	218 450
		495 567
Deduct:		468 900
Rent revenue	25 000	
Bad debts written off	16 000	
Insurance paid	29 000	
Development costs paid	150 000	
Annual leave paid	58 000	
Depreciation of equipment for tax	53 333	(331 333)
Taxable profit		137 567
Current liability @ 30%		£ 41 270

FIGURE 6.1 Completed current tax worksheet for Iris Ltd

6.5 RECOGNITION OF CURRENT TAX

Paragraph 12 of IAS 12 states:

> Current tax for current and prior periods shall, to the extent unpaid, be recognised as a liability. If the amount already paid in respect of current and prior periods exceeds the amount due for those periods, the excess shall be recognised as an asset.

Additionally, paragraph 58 of the standard requires current tax to be recognised as income or an expense and included in the profit or loss for the period, except to the extent that the tax relates to a transaction recognised directly in equity or to a business combination. Therefore, the following journal entry is required to recognise the current tax payable for Iris Ltd at 30 June 2013:

30 June 2013			
Income Tax Expense (Current)	Dr	41 270	
Current Tax Liability	Cr		41 270
(Recognition of current tax liability)			

6.6 PAYMENT OF TAX

Taxation legislation may require taxation debts to be paid annually upon lodgement of a taxation return or at some specified time after lodgement (such as on receipt of an assessment notice, or at a set date or time). Alternatively, the taxation debt may be paid by instalment throughout the taxation year. In some jurisdictions, payments in advance relating to next year's estimated taxable profit may be required. Where one annual payment is required, the entry is:

Current Tax Liability	Dr	41 270	
Cash	Cr		41 270
(Payment of current liability)			

If payment by instalment is required, the process is a little more complicated. To pay by instalment, an estimate of taxable profit needs to be made; hence the reference in paragraph 12 of IAS 12 to amounts paid in excess of the amount due. To illustrate the process of payment by instalment, assume that Iris Ltd (from illustrative example 6.2) has to pay tax quarterly and has paid the following amounts for the first three quarters of the 2012–13 taxation year:

28 October 2012	£ 9 420
28 January 2013	10 380
28 April 2013	10 750

The journal entry to record the first payment is:

Current Tax Liability	Dr	9 420	
Cash	Cr		9 420
(Payment of first quarterly taxation instalment)			

Similar entries are passed at 28 January 2013 and 28 April 2013. At 30 June 2013, because the tax liability has been partially paid, an adjustment is required on the current tax worksheet to determine the balance of tax owing in relation to the 2012–13 year (see below).

IRIS LTD Current Tax Worksheet (extract) for the year ended 30 June 2013	
Taxable profit	£ 137 567
Tax payable @ 30%	41 270
Less: Tax already paid (£9 420 + £10 380 + £10 750)	(30 550)
Current tax liability	10 720

The effect of the adjusting journal entry is to change the debit balance of £30 550 in the current tax liability account (caused by the instalment payments) into a credit balance of £10 720, representing the amount owing to the tax authority :

30 June 2013		
Income Tax Expense (Current)	Dr	41 270
Current Tax Liability	Cr	
(Recognition of current tax liability)		41 270

6.7 TAX LOSSES

Tax losses are created when allowable deductions exceed taxable income. IAS 12 envisages three possible treatments for tax losses: they may be carried forward, carried back, or simply lost. Where taxation legislation allows tax losses to be carried forward and deducted against future taxable profits, the carry-forward may be either indefinite or for a limited number of years. Other restrictions — such as requiring losses to be deducted against non-taxable income on recoupment — may also apply. Carry-forward tax losses create a deductible temporary difference and therefore a deferred tax asset in that the company will pay less tax on future taxable profits. *The recognition of a deferred tax asset for tax losses is discussed in detail in section 6.9.2.*

ILLUSTRATIVE EXAMPLE 6.3 Creation and recoupment of carry-forward tax losses

The following information relates to Poppy Ltd for the year ended 30 June 2014:

Accounting loss on income statement	£ 7 600
Depreciation expense	14 700
Depreciation deductible for tax	20 300
Entertainment expense (not tax-deductible)	10 000
Income tax rate	30%

The calculation of the tax loss appears below:

POPPY LTD Current Tax Worksheet (extract) for the year ended 30 June 2014	
Accounting loss	£ (7 600)
Add:	
Depreciation expense	14 700
Entertainment expense	10 000
	17 100
Deduct:	
Depreciation deduction for tax	(20 300)
Tax loss	(3 200)
Deferred tax asset @ 30%	£ 960

Assuming that recognition criteria are met, the adjusting journal entry is:

30 June 2014		
Deferred Tax Asset (Tax Losses)	Dr	960
Income Tax Expense	Cr	
(Recognition of deferred tax asset from tax loss)		960

If Poppy Ltd then makes a taxable profit of £23 600 for the year ending 30 June 2015, the loss is recouped as follows:

POPPY LTD
Current Tax Worksheet (extract)
for the year ended 30 June 2015

Taxable profit before tax loss	£23 600
Tax loss recouped	(3 200)
Taxable profit	20 400
Current tax liability @ 30%	£ 6 120

The adjusting journal entry is:

30 June 2015			
Income Tax Expense (Current)	Dr	7 080	
Deferred Tax Asset (Tax Losses)	Cr		960
Current Tax Liability	Cr		6 120
(Recognition of current tax liability and reversal of deferred tax asset from tax loss)			

6.8 CALCULATION OF DEFERRED TAX

As already explained, IAS 12 adopts the philosophy that the tax consequences of transactions that occur during a period should be recognised in income tax expense for that period. Where a transaction has two effects, both have to be recognised. The existence of temporary differences between accounting profit and taxable profit was identified *earlier in the chapter*. These temporary differences result in the carrying amounts of an entity's assets and liabilities being different from the amounts that would arise if a statement of financial position was prepared for the taxation authority. The latter are referred to as the tax base of an entity's assets and liabilities. At the end of the reporting period, a comparison of an entity's carrying amounts of assets and liabilities and their tax bases will reveal the temporary differences that exist, and adjustments will then be made to deferred assets and liabilities. (The reference to 'deferred' tax adjustments comes from the fact that assets and liabilities reflect future inflows and outflows to an entity. The deferred tax balances are related to these future flows, and hence are deferred to the future rather than affecting current tax.) For assets such as goodwill and entertainment costs payable, differences between their tax bases and carrying amounts may be caused by permanent differences. Such differences will not give rise to deferred tax adjustments.

The following steps are required to calculate deferred tax:

1. Determine the carrying amounts of items recognised in the statement of financial position.
2. Determine the tax bases of the items recognised by identifying the taxable and deductible temporary differences relating to the future tax consequences of each item.
3. Calculate and recognise the deferred tax assets and liabilities arising from these temporary differences after taking into account any relevant recognition exceptions *(see section 6.8.5)* and offset considerations *(see section 6.12.1)*.
4. Recognise the net movement in deferred tax assets and liabilities during the period as deferred tax expense or income in profit or loss (unless an accounting standard requires recognition directly in equity or as part of a business combination).

The first three steps are carried out on a worksheet. The final step requires an adjusting journal entry.

6.8.1 Determining carrying amounts

Carrying amounts are asset and liability balances net of valuation allowances, accumulated depreciation, amortisation and impairment losses (for example, accounts receivable less allowance for doubtful debts).

6.8.2 Determining tax bases

Tax bases need to be calculated for assets and liabilities.

Tax bases of assets

The economic benefits embodied in an asset are normally taxable when recovered by an entity through the use or sale of that asset. The entity may then be able to deduct all or part of the cost or carrying amount of the asset against those taxable amounts when determining taxable profits.

Paragraph 7 of IAS 12 describes the tax base of an asset as:

> the amount that will be deductible for tax purposes against any taxable economic benefits that will flow to an entity when it recovers the carrying amount of the asset. If those economic benefits will not be taxable, the tax base of the asset is equal to its carrying amount.

The following formula can be applied to derive the tax base from the carrying amount of the asset:

$$\text{Carrying amount} - \text{Future taxable amounts} + \text{Future deductible amounts} = \text{Tax base}$$

Figure 6.2 contains examples of the calculation of tax bases for assets.

	Carrying amount	Future taxable amounts*	Future deductible amounts	Tax base
Prepayments £3 000: fully deductible for tax when paid	£ 3 000	£(3 000)	£ 0	£ 0
Trade receivables of £52 000 less £2 000 allowance for doubtful debts: sales revenue is already included in taxable profit	50 000	0	2 000	52 000
Plant and equipment costing £10 000 has a carrying value of £5 400: accumulated tax depreciation is £6 500	5 400	(5 400)	3 500**	3 500
Loan receivable £25 000: loan repayment will have no tax consequences	25 000	0	0	25 000
Interest receivable £1 000: recognised as revenue but not taxable until received	1 000	(1 000)	0	0

* Future taxable amounts are equal to carrying amounts unless economic benefits have already been included in taxable profit.

** The deductible amount represents the original cost of the asset less the accumulated depreciation based on taxation depreciation rates (being £10 000 − £6 500 = £3 500).

FIGURE 6.2 Calculation of the tax base of assets

Figure 6.2 illustrates the following situations:

- Where the future benefits are taxable, the carrying amount equals the future taxable amount. Hence, the tax base equals the future deductible amount. This can be seen in figure 6.2 for prepayments, plant and equipment, and interest receivable.
- Where there are no future taxable amounts, generally the deductible amount is zero and the tax base equals the carrying amount. In figure 6.2, this applies to the loan receivable. An exception is trade receivables where, although the future taxable amount is zero, the future deductible amount is not zero because of the existence of doubtful debts. In this case, the tax base equals the sum of the carrying amount and the future deductible amount.

Tax bases of liabilities

Liabilities, other than those relating to unearned revenue, do not create taxable amounts. Instead, settlement gives rise to deductible items.

Paragraph 8 of IAS 12 describes the tax base of a liability as:

> its carrying amount, less any amount that will be deductible for tax purposes in respect of that liability in future periods. In the case of revenue which is received in advance, the tax base of the resulting liability is its carrying amount, less any amount of the revenue that will not be taxable in future periods.

The following formula can be applied to derive the tax base from the carrying amount of the liability:

$$\text{Carrying amount} + \text{Future taxable amounts} - \text{Future deductible amounts} = \text{Tax base}$$

Figure 6.3 contains examples of the calculation of the tax base for liabilities.

	Carrying amount	Future taxable amounts	Future deductible amounts	Tax base
Provision for annual leave £3 900: not deductible for tax until paid	£ 3 900	£ 0	£(3 900)	£ 0
Trade payables £34 000: expense already deducted from taxable income	34 000	0	0	34 000
Subscription revenue received in advance £500: taxed when received	(500)	(500)	0	0
Loan payable £20 000: loan repayment will have no tax consequences	20 000	0	0	20 000
Accrued expenses £6 700: deductible when paid in cash	6 700	0	(6 700)	0
Accrued penalties £700: not tax-deductible	700	0	0	700

FIGURE 6.3 Calculation of the tax base of liabilities

Figure 6.3 illustrates two situations:
- Where the carrying amount equals the future deductible amount, the tax base is zero. This applies to provisions for annual leave and accrued expenses.
- Where there is no future deductible amount, the carrying amount equals the tax base. This applies to trade payables and the loan payable.

Some items may have a tax base but are not recognised as assets and liabilities in the statement of financial position. Paragraph 9 of IAS 12 provides the example of research costs that are recognised as an expense in determining accounting profit in the period in which they are incurred but are not allowed as a deduction in determining taxable profit until a later period. Additionally, under paragraph 52 the manner in which an asset/liability is recovered/settled may affect the tax base of that asset/liability in some jurisdictions.

6.8.3 Calculating temporary differences

When the carrying amount of an asset or liability is different from its tax base, a temporary difference exists. Temporary differences effectively represent the expected net future taxable amounts arising from the recovery of assets and the settlement of liabilities at their carrying amounts. Therefore, a temporary difference cannot exist where there are no future tax consequences from the realisation or settlement of an asset or liability at its carrying value.

Taxable temporary differences

A taxable temporary difference exists when the future taxable amount of an asset or liability exceeds any future deductible amounts. This is demonstrated in illustrative example 6.4.

ILLUSTRATIVE EXAMPLE 6.4 Calculation of a taxable temporary difference

An asset, which cost 150, has an accumulated depreciation of 50.
Accumulated depreciation for tax purposes is 90 and the tax rate is 25%.

Carrying amount	= 100
Future taxable amount	= 100
Future deductible amount	= 60
Tax base	= 100 − 100 + 60
	= 60 (= 150 cost less 90 tax depreciation)

Because the future taxable amount is greater than the future deductible amount, a temporary taxable difference exists. In other words, the expectation is that the entity will pay income taxes in the future, when it recovers the carrying amount of the asset, because it expects to earn 100 but receive a tax deduction of 60. The entity has a liability to pay tax on that extra 40. As the payment occurs in the future, the liability is referred to as a 'deferred tax liability'.

Source: Adapted from IAS 12, paragraph 16.

Deductible temporary differences

A deductible temporary difference exists when the future taxable amount of an asset or liability is less than any future deductible amounts. This is demonstrated in illustrative example 6.5.

ILLUSTRATIVE EXAMPLE 6.5 Calculation of a deductible temporary difference

Dalal Inc. recognises a liability of 100 for accrued product warranty costs. For tax purposes, the product warranty costs will not be deductible until Dalal Inc. pays claims. The tax rate is 25%.

Carrying amount	= 100
Future taxable amount	= 0
Future deductible amount	= 100
Tax base	= 100 + 0 − 100
	= 0

As the future deductible amount is greater than the future taxable amount, a deductible temporary difference exists. In other words, in settling the liability for its carrying amount, Dalal Inc. will reduce its future tax profits and hence its future tax payments. Dalal Inc. then has an expected benefit relating to the future tax deduction. As the benefits are to be received in the future, the asset raised is referred to as a 'deferred tax asset'.

Source: Adapted from IAS 12, paragraph 25.

6.8.4 Calculating deferred tax liabilities and deferred tax assets

Paragraphs 15 and 24 of IAS 12 require (with some exceptions) that a deferred tax liability and a deferred tax asset be recognised for all taxable temporary differences and all deductible temporary differences, and that a total be determined for taxable temporary differences and for deductible temporary differences. An appropriate tax rate can then be applied to these totals to derive the balance of deferred tax liability and deferred tax asset at the end of the period. Paragraph 47 of the standard specifies that:

> Deferred tax assets and liabilities shall be measured at the tax rates that are expected to apply to the period when the asset is realised or the liability is settled, based on tax rates (and tax laws) that have been enacted or substantively enacted by the end of the reporting period.

Thus, if the tax rate is currently 30% but will rise to 32% in the next reporting period, deferred amounts should be measured at 32%. Should a change be enacted (or substantively enacted) between the end of the reporting period and the time of completion of the financial statements, no adjustment needs to be made to the tax balances recognised. However, disclosure of any material impacts should be made by note in compliance with IAS 10 *Events after the Reporting Period*.

Different tax rates may be required when temporary differences are expected to reverse in different periods and a change of tax rate is probable, or when temporary differences relate to different taxation jurisdictions. Additionally, consideration should be given to the manner in which an asset/liability is recovered/settled in jurisdictions where the manner of recovery/settlement determines the applicable tax rate (IAS 12 paragraph 52).

Before determining the amounts of deferred tax liabilities and deferred tax assets, consideration must be given to the recognition criteria mandated by the accounting standard. *(See section 6.9.)*

6.8.5 Excluded differences

A deferred tax liability is usually recognised on taxable temporary differences, but if the taxable temporary difference meets the criteria in paragraph 15 of IAS 12, it is exempt from deferred tax. Likewise, a deferred tax asset is normally recognised on deductible temporary differences, but if this difference meets the criteria in paragraph 24 of IAS 12, it may also be exempt from deferred tax.

Paragraph 15 states that a *deferred tax liability* shall be recognised for all *taxable* temporary differences, *except* where the deferred tax liability arises from:

(a) goodwill; or
(b) the initial recognition of an asset or liability, which
  (i) did not arise through a business combination, and which
  (ii) at the time of the transaction, affects neither accounting profit nor taxable profit.

Paragraph 24 states that a *deferred tax asset* shall be recognised for all *deductible* temporary differences, *except* where the deferred tax asset arises from the initial recognition of an asset or liability, which:

(a) did not arise through a business combination, and
(b) at the time of the transaction, affects neither accounting profit nor taxable profit.

Goodwill

Goodwill is the excess of the cost of the business combination over the acquirer's interest in the net fair value of the identifiable assets, liabilities and contingent liabilities *(see chapter 14)*. A taxable temporary difference is created because the tax base of goodwill is always nil. IAS 12 does not permit the recognition of the deferred tax liability relating to goodwill, because goodwill is a residual amount and recognising the deferred tax amount would increase the carrying amount of goodwill (IAS 12 paragraph 21).

Initial recognition of an asset or liability

The tax base and carrying amount of an asset are usually the same on initial recognition but in the case of a non-deductible asset, such as land, a temporary difference arises on initial recognition. Consider the example of a non-deductible asset that is not acquired through a business combination. A non-deductible asset is an asset whose cost is not allowed as a deduction when calculating taxable profits and therefore the tax base on date of purchase is zero. A taxable temporary difference will arise on the initial recognition, being the difference between the carrying amount on date of purchase (the asset's cost) and its tax base (zero).

The initial recognition, in other words, the purchase, does not affect accounting profit or taxable profit. Thus, although a deferred tax liability is normally recognised on taxable temporary differences, no deferred tax is recognised on this taxable temporary difference since it meets the requirements of paragraph 12 of IAS 12 to be exempt from deferred tax.

6.8.6 Deferred tax worksheet

A deferred tax worksheet is shown in illustrative example 6.6. The purpose of the deferred tax worksheet is to calculate the movements in the deferred tax asset and the deferred tax liability accounts during the current period. Determining the temporary differences relating to assets and liabilities allows the closing balances of the deferred tax accounts to be calculated. A consideration of the beginning balances and movements during the year allows the calculation of the adjustments required to achieve those closing balances. All assets and liabilities may be included in the worksheet; alternatively, only those expected to have different accounting and tax bases could be shown.

ILLUSTRATIVE EXAMPLE 6.6 Deferred tax worksheet

Using the information provided in illustrative example 6.2, the deferred tax worksheet for Iris Ltd is shown in figure 6.4.

IRIS LTD Deferred Tax Worksheet as at 30 June 2013						
	Carrying amount	Future taxable amount	Future deductible amount	Tax base	Taxable temporary differences	Deductible temporary differences
Relevant assets						
Receivables[1]	£279 000	£ 0	£16 000	£295 000		£16 000
Prepaid insurance[2]	30 000	(30 000)	0	0	£ 30 000	
Rent receivable[3]	3 500	(3 500)	0	0	3 500	
Development project[4]	90 000	(90 000)	0	0	90 000	
Equipment[5]	110 000	(110 000)	80 000	80 000	30 000	
Goodwill[6]	21 000	(21 000)	0	0	21 000	
Relevant liabilities						
Provision for annual leave[7]	61 000	0	(61 000)	0		61 000
Total temporary differences						174 500	77 000
Excluded differences[8]					(21 000)	—
Temporary differences					153 500	77 000
Deferred tax liability[9]					46 050	
Deferred tax asset[9]						23 100
Beginning balances[10]					(17 150)	(24 900)
Movement during year[11]					—	—
Adjustment[10]					28 900 Cr	(1 800) Cr

FIGURE 6.4 Deferred tax worksheet for Iris Ltd

1. The carrying amount of receivables £279 000 (£295 000 – 16 000) represents the cash that the company expects to receive after allowing for any doubtful debts. Tax on this amount has already been paid via sales revenue recognised in the current year, so the future taxable amount is zero. The allowance for doubtful debts raised as an expense in the current year is not deductible against taxable profit until the debts actually go 'bad' and are written out of the accounts receivable balance. Thus, there is a future deduction of £5000 available. The tax base for receivables is £283 000, being the total of all debts outstanding at 30 June 2013 (doubtful or otherwise). Because the future deductible amount is greater than the future taxable amount, a deductible temporary difference of £5000 exists in respect of receivables.

2. The prepaid insurance asset represents the future benefit of insurance cover at 30 June 2013. The recovery of these benefits results in the flow of taxable economic benefits to Iris Ltd, giving a future taxable amount of £30 000. This amount was paid in the year ended 30 June 2013 and was allowed as a deduction against the taxable profit for that year. This means that no deduction is available when the £30 000 is expensed in the year ended 30 June 2014, giving a tax base for the asset of £0. As the future taxable amount exceeds the future deductible amount, a taxable temporary difference of £30 000 exists in respect of prepaid insurance.

3. The rent receivable asset represents monies to be received at 30 June 2013. The recovery of these benefits results in the flow of taxable economic benefits to Iris Ltd. Hence, a future taxable amount of £3500 exists. As this is a revenue item, no future deduction is available and the tax base is £0. As the future taxable amount exceeds the future deductible amount, a taxable temporary difference of £3500 exists in respect of the rent receivable.

4. The development project asset represents the future economic benefits expected to arise from development work undertaken in the current year. When those benefits are received, they are taxable. The total expenditure on development was deducted from taxable profit in the current year, so no future deduction is available. The tax base is £0 as the cash paid has already reduced taxable profit in the current year. As the future taxable amount exceeds the future deductible amount, a taxable temporary difference of £90 000 exists in respect of the development project.

5. The carrying amount of equipment represents the future economic benefits expected to be received from that asset over the remainder of its useful life, £110 000 (£200 000 – £90 000). When those benefits are received, they are taxable. Iris Ltd will be able to claim a deduction against those taxable benefits, but only to the extent of the tax base of the asset. As the depreciation rate for tax purposes is greater than the accounting rate, the future deduction is only £80 000, being the original cost of £200 000 less £120 000 (i.e. 3 years' accumulated depreciation at 20% per annum). As the future taxable amount exceeds the future deductible amount, a taxable temporary difference of £30 000 exists in respect of equipment.

6. The carrying amount of goodwill represents the future economic benefits expected to be received. Those benefits are taxable when received but, unlike equipment, no deduction against the benefits is available. The tax base of goodwill is £0 as taxation law does not allow a deduction for any amounts paid to acquire goodwill. As the future taxable amount exceeds the future deductible amount, a taxable temporary difference of £21 000 exists in respect of goodwill (however, see exemption in 8 below).

7. The provision for annual leave represents leave accrued by employees as at the end of the reporting period. As the leave represents future payments, there is no future taxable amount. When those payments are made, they are fully deductible against taxable profit. The tax base at 30 June 2013 is £0 because leave payments are only deductible in the year of payment. As the future deductible amount exceeds the future taxable amount, a deductible temporary difference of £61 000 exists in respect of the annual leave provision.

8. The adjustment for excluded differences recognises that IAS 12 (paragraphs 15 and 24) has prohibited the recognition of deferred tax amounts relating to certain temporary differences (see section 6.9.2). Paragraph 15 prohibits the recognition of the taxable temporary difference relating to goodwill, so it is removed from the total temporary differences existing at 30 June 2013.

9. The deferred tax liability figure of £46 050 is the future tax payable as a result of the existence of taxable temporary differences of £153 500. The deferred tax asset figure of £23 100 is the future deductions available as a result of the existence of deductible temporary differences of £77 000. These figures represent the closing balances of the deferred tax accounts.

10. Deferred tax amounts may accumulate over time; for example, the taxable temporary difference for equipment represents 3 years' differentials between accounting and taxation depreciation charges. This means that the deferred tax accounts have an opening balance representing prior year differences. If no adjustment is made for the opening balance, the deferred tax amounts are overstated. Accordingly, the opening balances are deducted from the total balances in order to determine the adjustment necessary to account for changes (additions and reversals) to deferred tax items during the current year. These adjustments are shown on the last line of the worksheet and form the basis of the adjusting journal entry for deferred tax. Positive figures are increases and negative figures are decreases in the account balances.

11. Normally, the deferred tax accounts are only adjusted at the end of each reporting period after the worksheet has been completed. Occasionally, however, adjustments are made to the deferred accounts during the year so the 'movements' line is used to adjust for such changes. Adjustments could be made for:
  - recoupment of prior year tax losses *(see section 6.7)*
  - a change in tax rates *(see section 6.10)*
  - an amendment to a prior year tax return *(see section 6.11)*
  - revaluation of property, plant and equipment items *(see section 6.11.2)*
  - business combinations *(see section 6.11.3)*.

The flowcharts in figure 6.5 below summarise the measurement of deferred tax items according to IAS 12. While the flowcharts show the steps in the calculation of deferred tax items, they do not present the steps in determining whether the resultant deferred tax assets or deferred tax liabilities will be recognised. The criteria for the recognition of deferred tax assets and deferred tax liabilities are considered next, *in section 6.9.*

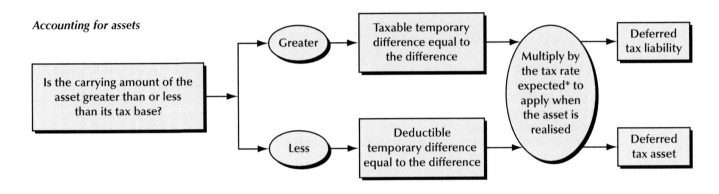

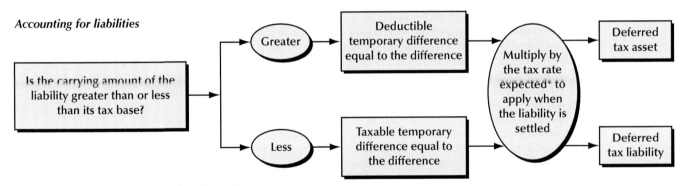

FIGURE 6.5 Accounting for deferred tax items
Note: *refers to the present tax rate or tax laws (tax rates) that have been enacted or substantively enacted by reporting date.
Source: CPA Australia (2010, p. 2).

6.9 RECOGNITION OF DEFERRED TAX LIABILITIES AND DEFERRED TAX ASSETS

The existence of temporary taxable and deductible differences may not result in the recognition of deferred tax assets and liabilities. Paragraphs 15 and 24 of IAS 12 specify recognition criteria that must be met before recognition occurs.

6.9.1 Deferred tax liabilities

Deferred tax liabilities must be recognised for all taxable temporary differences (except as outlined below). A liability is recognised when it is probable that an outflow of resources embodying economic benefits will result from the settlement of a present obligation, and the amount at which the settlement will take place can be measured reliably (*Conceptual Framework* paragraph 4.46). There is no need to explicitly consider the recognition criteria for a deferred tax liability, because it is always probable that resources will flow from the entity to pay the tax associated with taxable temporary differences. As the carrying amount of the asset or liability giving rise to the taxable temporary difference is recovered or settled, the temporary difference will reverse and give rise to taxable amounts in future periods.

6.9.2 Deferred tax assets

Deferred tax assets must be recognised for all deductible temporary differences (subject to certain exceptions) and from the carry forward of tax losses, but only to the extent that it is probable that future taxable profits will be available against which the temporary differences can be utilised.

An asset is recognised when it is probable that the future economic benefits will flow to the entity, and the asset has a cost or value that can be measured reliably (*Conceptual Framework* paragraph 4.44). According to paragraph 4.40 of the *Conceptual Framework*, probability refers to the degree of uncertainty about whether the future economic benefits associated with the asset will flow to the entity. This probability must be assessed using the best evidence available based on the conditions at the end of the reporting period. The reversal of deductible temporary differences results in deductions against the taxable profits of future periods. Economic benefits in the form of reductions in tax payments will flow to the entity only if it earns sufficient taxable profits against which the deductions can be offset. Therefore, an entity recognises deferred tax assets only when it is probable that taxable profits will be available against which the deductible temporary differences can be utilised (IAS 12 paragraph 27). The realisation of a deferred tax asset would be probable where:

- there are sufficient taxable temporary differences relating to the same taxation authority and the same taxable entity that are expected to reverse in the same period as the deductible temporary differences, or in periods to which a tax loss arising from the deferred tax asset can be carried back or forward (paragraph 28)
- there would be taxable temporary differences arising if unrecognised increases in the fair values of assets were recognised
- it is probable that there will be other sufficient taxable profits arising in future periods against which to utilise the deductions
- other factors indicate that it is probable that the deductions can be realised.

If there are insufficient taxable temporary differences available against which to offset the deductible temporary differences, an entity can recognise a deferred tax asset only to the extent that sufficient taxable profits will be made in the future or that tax planning opportunities are available to create future taxable profits (IAS 12 paragraph 29).

A history of accounting losses, or the existence of unused tax losses, provides evidence that future taxable profits are unlikely to be available for the utilisation of deductible temporary differences. In these circumstances, the recognition of deferred tax assets would require either the existence of sufficient taxable temporary differences or convincing evidence that future taxable profits will be earned. In assessing the likelihood that tax losses will be utilised, the entity should consider whether:

- future budgets indicate that there will be sufficient taxable income derived in the foreseeable future
- the losses arise from causes that are unlikely to recur in the foreseeable future
- actions can be taken to create taxable amounts in the future
- there are existing contracts or sales backlogs that will produce taxable amounts
- there are new developments or favourable opportunities likely to give rise to taxable amounts
- there is a strong history of earnings other than those giving rise to the loss, and the loss was an aberration and not a continuing condition.

Where, on the balance of the evidence available, it is not probable that deductible temporary differences will be utilised in the future, no deferred tax asset is recognised. This probability assessment must also be applied to deferred tax assets that have previously been recognised and, if it is no longer probable that the benefits of such assets will flow to the entity, the carrying amount must be derecognised by passing the following entry:

30 June			
Income Tax Expense	Dr	xxx	
Deferred Tax Asset	Cr		xxx
(Derecognition of deferred tax assets where recovery is no longer probable)			

At the end of each reporting period, the entity should reassess the probability of recovery of all unrecognised deferred tax assets; it should recognise these assets to the extent that it is now probable that future taxable profit will allow the deduction of the temporary difference on its reversal. Changes in trading conditions, new taxation legislation, or a business combination may all contribute to improving the chance of recovering the deferred tax benefits. Paragraph 60 of IAS 12 requires that any adjustment to deferred tax be recognised in the statement of comprehensive income except to the extent that it relates to items previously charged or credited to equity.

Using the figures calculated in illustrative example 6.6 and assuming that the recognition criteria for deferred tax assets can be met, the adjusting journal for deferred tax movements is:

30 June 2013			
Income Tax Expense	Dr	30 700	
Deferred Tax Asset	Cr		1 800
Deferred Tax Liability	Cr		28 900
(Recognition of movements in deferred tax balances for the year)			

These movements can be checked back to the current worksheet as follows:
- Deferred tax assets arise in respect of doubtful debts and annual leave. In the current year, additional deductions of £2000 (doubtful debts) and £4000 (leave) are received. This indicates that more deductible temporary differences had been reversed than had been created, resulting in a decrease of £6000 in future deductions and a £1800 decrease in the deferred tax asset.
- Deferred tax liabilities arise in respect of development expenditure, equipment, insurance and rent. In the current year, additional deductions of £90 000 (development), £13 333 (depreciation) and £5000 (insurance) are offset by additional taxable amounts of £10 000 (sale of equipment) and £2000 (rent revenue), giving a net extra increase in taxable temporary differences and a £28 900 increase in the deferred tax liability.

The posting of this entry results in the deferred tax ledger accounts appearing as follows:

Deferred Tax Asset

1/7/12	Balance b/d	24 900	30/6/13	Income Tax Expense	1 800
			30/6/13	Balance c/d	23 100
		24 900			24 900
1/7/13	Balance b/d	23 100			

Deferred Tax Liability

30/6/13	Balance c/d	46 050	1/7/12	Balance b/d	17 150
			30/6/13	Income Tax Expense	28 900
		46 050			46 050
			1/7/13	Balance b/d	46 050

If the two taxation adjusting journals — current and deferred — are combined, then the total income tax expense recorded for the year ended 2013 by Iris Ltd is:

Income Tax Expense (Current) (see section 6.5)	£ 41 270
Income Tax Expense (Deferred) (see above)	30 700
Total	£ 71 970

This figure represents the total tax consequences of the transactions recorded in profit or loss for the year. It can be checked in this way: The accounting profit for the year is £250 450. All items of revenue and expense are taxable or deductible with the exception of goodwill impairment and entertainment expense. The development expenditure during the year gave rise to an 'extra' deduction of £30 000 against taxable profit. If the accounting profit adjusted for these permanent differences is multiplied by the tax rate, the result represents the total tax payable above (both now and in the future):

Accounting profit	£250 450
Add: Non-deductible amortisation	7 000
Add: Non-deductible entertainment expense	12 450
Less: Additional deduction for development	(30 000)
Taxable net profit	239 900
Tax @ 30%	£ 71 970

6.10 CHANGE OF TAX RATES

When a new tax rate is enacted (or substantively enacted), the new rate should be applied in calculating the current tax liability and adjustments to deferred tax accounts during the year. It should also be applied to the deferred amounts recognised in prior years. A journal adjustment must be passed to increase or reduce the carrying amounts of deferred tax assets and liabilities, in order to reflect the new value of future taxable or deductible amounts. Paragraph 60 of IAS 12 requires the net amount arising from the restatement of deferred tax balances to be recognised in the statement of comprehensive income, except to the extent that the deferred tax amounts relate to items previously charged or credited to equity.

ILLUSTRATIVE EXAMPLE 6.8 Change of tax rate

As at 30 June 2013, the balances of deferred tax accounts for Carnation Ltd were:

Deferred Tax Asset	£29 600
Deferred Tax Liability	(72 800)

In September 2013, the government reduced the company tax rate from 40 pence to 30 pence in the pound, effective from 1 July 2013. The recorded deferred tax balances represent the tax effect of future taxable amounts and future deductible amounts at 40 pence in the pound, so they are now overstated and must be adjusted as follows:

	Deferred tax asset	Deferred tax liability
Opening balance	£29 600	£ 72 800
Adjustment for change in tax rate: ([40 − 30]/40)	(7 400)	(18 200)
Restated balance	£22 200	£ 54 600

The adjusting journal entry is:

Deferred Tax Liability	Dr	18 200	
Deferred Tax Asset	Cr		7 400
Income Tax Expense	Cr		10 800
(Recognition of the impact of a change of tax rate on deferred tax amounts)			

6.11 OTHER ISSUES

6.11.1 Amended prior year tax figures

In taxation jurisdictions where entities self-assess their taxable profit, it is possible that the taxation authority will amend that assessment by changing the amount of taxable or deductible items. This amendment could result in the entity being liable to pay extra tax or becoming eligible for a taxation refund. Upon receipt of an amended assessment, the entity should analyse the reason for the adjustment and consider whether both current and deferred tax are affected. For example, if an entity has used an incorrect taxation depreciation rate, then the amendment to the correct rate will change both the prior year taxable profit and future taxable profits across the economic life of the depreciable asset. If only current tax for the previous year has changed, the following journal entry would be passed:

Income Tax Expense	Dr	xxx	
Current Tax Liability	Cr		xxx
(Amendment to prior year current tax on receipt of amended assessment)			

If the amendment also changes a deferred item, the new temporary difference will need to be calculated and the carry-forward balance adjusted accordingly. In the depreciation example used above, the adjustment (assuming the accounting depreciation rate is lower than the rate used to calculate taxable profit) is:

Income Tax Expense	Dr	xxx	
Deferred Tax Liability	Cr		xxx
Current Tax Liability	Cr		xxx
(Amendment to prior year current tax and deferred tax liability on receipt of amended assessment)			

Any amendment to the deferred tax liability or the deferred tax asset arising from amended assessments would appear on the deferred tax worksheet as a 'movement' adjustment.

6.11.2 Items recognised outside profit or loss

In general, the amount of current and deferred tax arising in a period must be recognised outside profit or loss if the tax relates to items that are recognised outside profit or loss (IAS 12 paragraph 61A). Examples of items that are recognised in other comprehensive income are:
- revaluation of items of property, plant and equipment to fair value *(see chapter 11)*. At the time of revaluation, an adjustment may be required to be made to the balance of the deferred tax liability account. For example, if an item of plant is revalued upwards from £100 to £200 and the tax rate is 30%, the entity would pass the following journal entry:

Plant	Dr	100	
(Revaluation of plant)			
Deferred Tax Liability	Cr		30
Asset Revaluation Surplus	Cr		70
(Revaluation of plant, recognition of deferred tax liability and accumulation of net revaluation gain in equity)			

- exchange differences arising on the translation of the financial statements of a foreign entity *(see chapter 24)*.

6.11.3 Deferred tax arising from a business combination

The amount of deferred tax arising in relation to the acquisition of an entity or business is recognised (subject to the recognition criteria) and included as part of identifiable assets acquired and liabilities assumed when determining the goodwill or gain on bargain purchase arising on acquisition. *(Further discussion of the determination of goodwill and gain on bargain purchase can be found in chapter 14.)* When a deferred tax asset of the acquiree not recognised at the date of a business combination is subsequently recognised by the acquirer, the resulting deferred tax income is recognised in the statement of profit or loss and other comprehensive income. Additionally, paragraph 68 of IAS 12 requires that the amount of goodwill recognised on acquisition must be adjusted to the amount that would be recorded had the deferred tax asset been recognised on acquisition.

6.12 PRESENTATION IN THE FINANCIAL STATEMENTS

IAS 12 specifies the way in which tax items (revenues, expenses, assets and liabilities) are to be presented in the financial statements, including the circumstances in which items can be offset.

6.12.1 Tax assets and tax liabilities

Tax assets and tax liabilities must be classified as current and non-current as required by IAS 1 *Presentation of Financial Statements* (paragraph 60) and presented in the statement of financial position in accordance with IAS 1 paragraphs 54(n), 54(o) and 56. Paragraph 71 of IAS 12 allows current tax assets and current tax liabilities to be offset only when the entity has a legally enforceable right to offset the amount, and intends either to settle on a net basis or to realise the asset and settle the liability simultaneously. A legal right to set off the accounts would normally exist where the accounts relate to income taxes levied by the same taxing authority.

Deferred tax assets and deferred tax liabilities can be offset only if a legally enforceable right to offset current amounts exists; and the deferred items relate to income taxes levied by the same taxing authority on the same taxable entity, or on different taxable entities which intend either to settle on a net basis or to realise the asset and settle the liability simultaneously in each future period in which significant deferred amounts will reverse (IAS 12 paragraph 74).

Consequently, entities operating in a single country will normally offset both current and deferred tax assets and liabilities, and show only a net current tax liability or asset and a net deferred asset or liability.

6.12.2 Tax expense

The tax expense (or income) related to profit or loss for the period is required to be presented in the statement of profit or loss and other comprehensive income (IAS 12 paragraph 77).

6.13 DISCLOSURES

Paragraphs 79–82A of IAS 12 contain the required disclosures relating to income taxes. These disclosures are very detailed, and provide significant additional information about the makeup of income tax expense (or income), and both taxable and deductible temporary differences. Paragraph 79 requires the tax expense figure shown in the statement of profit or loss and other comprehensive income to be broken down into its various components (examples of which are listed in paragraph 80), such as current tax expense and deferred tax arising from temporary differences. Paragraph 81 requires a wide range of disclosures including tax relating to equity and discontinued operations, changes in tax rates, and unrecognised deferred tax assets and liabilities.

Paragraph 81 also requires two detailed reconciliations to be prepared:

- Paragraph 81(c) requires entities to disclose 'an explanation of the relationship between tax expense (income) and accounting profit'. This essentially reconciles expected tax — accounting profit multiplied by tax rate — to the actual tax expense recognised. The reconciliation enables financial statement users to understand why the relationship between accounting profit and income tax expense is unusual, the factors causing the variance, and factors that could affect the relationship in the future. Entities are allowed to reconcile in either or both of the following ways:
  - a numerical reconciliation between tax expense and expected tax
  - a numerical reconciliation between the average effective tax rate (tax expense divided by the accounting profit) and the applicable tax rate.

  Irrespective of the reconciliation method used, entities must disclose the basis on which the applicable tax rate is computed.
- Paragraph 81(g) requires disclosure of the following information for deferred tax items recognised in the statement of financial position:

  in respect of each type of temporary difference, and in respect of each type of unused tax loss and unused tax credit:

  (i) the amount of the deferred tax assets and liabilities recognised in the statement of financial position for each period presented; and
  (ii) the amount of the deferred tax income or expense recognised in profit or loss, if this is not apparent from the changes in the amounts recognised in the statement of financial position.

Normally, the second part of the paragraph 81(g) disclosure is required only if a change in tax rate or legislation has occurred during the year, or if some other event causes an adjustment to a deferred account during the period.

When an entity has suffered tax losses in either the current or previous period, and recognised a deferred tax asset related to those losses that is dependent on earning future taxable profits in excess of those arising on the reversal of taxable temporary differences, paragraph 82 requires disclosure of the amount of the deferred tax asset and the nature of the evidence supporting its recognition.

Paragraph 82A applies only in those jurisdictions where tax rates vary according to the quantum of profit or retained earnings distributed as dividends. In this situation, paragraph 82A requires the entity to disclose the nature and amounts (to the extent practicable) of the potential income tax consequences that would result from the payment of dividends to its shareholders.

Figure 6.6 provides an illustration of the disclosures required by IAS 12.

FIGURE 6.6 Illustrative disclosures required by IAS 12

Note 4: Income tax expense	Notes	2016 £	2015 £	IAS 12 paragraph
Major components of income tax expense				79
Current tax expense		126 600	117 600	80(a)
Deferred tax from origination and reversal of temporary differences		(20 250)	11 320	80(c)
Deferred tax relating to tax rate change		250	—	80(d)
Benefit from unrecognised tax loss used to reduce current tax expense		(1 500)	—	80(e)
Income tax expense		105 100	128 920	80(f)

FIGURE 6.6 *(continued)*

Note 4: Income tax expense	Notes	2016 £	2015 £	IAS 12 paragraph
Tax relating to items charged (credited) direct to equity				
Deferred tax relating to revaluation of land		12 500	—	80(h)
Reconciliation of tax expense to prima facie tax on accounting profit				81(b)
The applicable tax rate is the company income tax rate of 30% (2012: 40%)				81(c)(i)
The prima facie tax on accounting profit differs from the tax expense provided in the accounts as follows:				
Accounting profit		402 000	397 000	
Prima facie tax at 30% (2012: 40%)		120 600	158 800	
Tax effect of non-deductible expenses				
Goodwill impairment		3 900	5 200	
Non-taxable revenue		(1 500)	(2 000)	
Entertainment		3 600	2 300	
		126 600	164 300	
Increase in beginning deferred taxes resulting from reduction in tax rate		250	—	
Reduction in current tax from recoupment of tax losses		(1 500)	—	
Tax effect of net movements in items giving rise to:*				
Deferred tax assets		(8 250)	3 200	
Deferred tax liabilities		(12 000)	(38 580)	
Tax expense		105 100	128 920	81(d)
Change in tax rate				
As of 1 July 2012, the company tax rate changed from 40% to 30%				81(d)
Unrecognised deferred tax assets				
Tax losses in respect of which deferred tax has not been recognised as it is not probable that benefits will be received		20 000	40 000	81(e)
Unrecognised deferred tax liabilities				
Aggregate of temporary differences associated with investments in subsidiaries for which deferred tax liabilities have not been recognised		16 000	16 000	81(f)
Deferred tax assets and liabilities				
The following items have given rise to deferred tax assets:				
Accounts receivable		12 000	15 000	
Employee entitlements		24 000	22 000	
Total deferred tax assets		36 000	37 000	
The following items have given rise to deferred tax liabilities:				
Land		12 500	—	
Plant and equipment		15 000	36 000	
Total deferred tax liabilities		27 500	36 000	
Offset of deferred tax asset against liability		36 000	37 000	
Net deferred tax asset (liability)		8 500	(1 000)	81(g) (i)

* These figures represent the net effect of movements in assets and liabilities during the year which have increased or decreased current tax. The details can be found in disclosures required by paragraph 81(g)(ii).

(continued)

FIGURE 6.6 *(continued)*

Note 4: Income tax expense	Notes	2016 £	2015 £	IAS 12 paragraph
Deferred tax expenses (income) recognised in the statement of comprehensive income for each type of temporary difference*				
Deferred tax expense in relation to:				
Plant and equipment		(12 000)	(38 580)	
Total deferred tax expense		(12 000)	(38 580)	
Deferred tax income in relation to:				
Accounts receivable		750	1 200	
Employee entitlements		7 500	2 000	
Total deferred tax income		8 250	3 200	*81(g) (ii)*

* This disclosure is required only if the movements in deferred items cannot readily be ascertained from other disclosures made with respect to deferred assets and liabilities. This is the case in this situation because the change in tax rate adjustments has obscured the movements in deferred items.

FIGURE 6.7 Income tax notes to the consolidated financial statements of Marks & Spencer

7 Income tax expense

A. Taxation charge

	2014 £m	2013 (restated)[1] £m
Current tax		
UK corporation tax on profits for the year at 23% (last year 24%)		
– current year	97.1	125.5
– adjustments in respect of prior years	(55.8)	(24.6)
UK current tax	41.3	100.9
Overseas current taxation		
– current year	14.5	12.8
– adjustments in respect of prior years	(2.7)	3.8
Total current taxation	53.1	117.5
Deferred tax		
– origination and reversal of temporary differences	17.7	(6.6)
– adjustments in respect of prior years	26.2	(2.8)
– changes in tax rate	(22.6)	(5.7)
Total deferred tax (see note 23)	21.3	(15.1)
Total income tax expense	74.4	102.4

1. Restatement relates to the adoption of the revised IAS 19 'Employee Benefits' (see note 1).

B. Taxation reconciliation

The effective tax rate was 12.8% (last year 18.7%) and is reconciled below:

	2014 £m	2013 (restated)[1] £m
Profit before tax	580.4	547.2
Notional taxation at the standard UK corporation tax rate of 23% (last year 24%)	133.5	131.5
Depreciation and other amounts in relation to fixed assets that do not qualify for tax relief	4.3	3.0
Other income and expenses that are not taxable or allowable for tax purposes	(5.4)	(8.1)
Retranslation of deferred tax balances due to the change in statutory UK tax rates	(22.5)	(5.4)
Overseas profits taxed at rates different to those of the UK	(3.7)	(4.0)
Overseas tax losses where there is no relief anticipated in the foreseeable future	8.7	9.3
Adjustments to current and deferred tax charges in respect of prior periods	(6.4)	(3.2)

FIGURE 6.7 *(continued)*

B. Taxation reconciliation *(continued)*

	2014 £m	2013 (restated)[1] £m
Adjustments to underlying profit:		
– international store review charges where no tax relief is available	4.9	–
– property disposal gain covered by other losses arising in the year	(13.0)	–
– deferred tax rate change benefit	–	(0.3)
Non-underlying adjustment to current and deferred tax charges in respect of prior periods	(26.0)	(20.4)
Total income tax expense	74.4	102.4

1. Restatement relates to the adoption of the revised IAS 19 'Employee Benefits' (see note 1).

After excluding non-underlying items the underlying effective tax rate was 18.8% (last year 22.7%).

The non-underlying adjustment to the tax charge in respect of prior periods arises from the successful outcome of litigation in relation to the Group's claim for UK tax relief of losses of its former European subsidiaries (£18.5m, last year £nil) and release of provisions following settlement of historic disputes with the tax authorities (£7.5m, last year £20.4m).

On 2 July 2013, the Finance Bill received its final reading in the House of Commons and so the previously announced reduced rates of corporation tax of 21% from 1 April 2014 to 31 March 2015 and 20% from 1 April 2015 onwards were substantively enacted. The Group has remeasured its UK deferred tax assets and liabilities at the end of the reporting period at 20%, which has resulted in the recognition of a deferred tax credit of £22.5m in the income statement (reducing the total effective tax rate by 3.9%), and the recognition of a deferred tax credit of £11.3m in other comprehensive income.

23 Deferred tax

Deferred tax is provided under the balance sheet liability method using a tax rate of 20% (last year 23%) for UK differences and local tax rates for overseas differences. Details of the changes to the UK corporation tax rate and the impact on the Group are described in note 7.

The movements in deferred tax assets and liabilities (after offsetting balances within the same jurisdiction as permitted by IAS 12 – 'Income Taxes') during the year are shown below.

	Fixed assets temporary differences £m	Capital allowances in excess of depreciation £m	Pension temporary differences (restated)[1] £m	Other short-term temporary differences £m	Total UK deferred tax (restated)[1] £m	Overseas deferred tax £m	Total (restated)[1] £m
At 1 April 2012	(58.2)	(100.6)	(38.9)	6.5	(191.2)	(14.9)	(206.1)
Credited/(charged) to the income statement	5.7	10.0	(2.6)	0.7	13.8	1.3	15.1
Credited/(charged) to equity/other comprehensive income	–	–	(55.1)	(0.7)	(55.8)	6.2	(49.6)
At 30 March 2013	(52.5)	(90.6)	(96.6)	6.5	(233.2)	(7.4)	(240.6)
At 31 March 2013	(52.5)	(90.6)	(96.6)	6.5	(233.2)	(7.4)	(240.6)
Credited/(charged) to the income statement	3.2	(9.3)	(0.8)	(12.5)	(19.4)	(1.9)	(21.3)
Credited/(charged) to equity/other comprehensive income	–	–	0.1	20.9	21.0	(1.7)	19.3
At 29 March 2014	(49.3)	(99.9)	(97.3)	14.9	(231.6)	(11.0)	(242.6)

1. Restatement relates to the adoption of the revised IAS 19 'Employee Benefits' (see note 1).

Other short-term temporary differences relate mainly to employee share options and financial instruments.

The deferred tax liability on land and buildings temporary differences is reduced by the benefit of capital losses with a tax value of £46.5m (last year £62.0m). Due to uncertainty over their future use, no benefit has been recognised in respect of unexpired trading losses carried forward in overseas jurisdictions with a tax value of £38.7m (last year £30.8m).

No deferred tax has been recognised in respect of undistributed earnings of overseas subsidiaries and joint ventures, as no material liability is expected to arise on distribution of these earnings under applicable tax legislation.

Source: Marks & Spencer plc (2014, pp. 100, 101, 119).

SUMMARY

This chapter analyses the content of IAS 12 *Income Taxes* and provides guidance on its implementation. The principal issue in accounting for taxes is how to account for the current and future tax consequences of transactions and other events of the current period. The accounting standard requires entities to recognise (with limited exceptions) deferred tax liabilities and deferred tax assets when the recovery or settlement of an asset or liability will result in larger or smaller tax payments than would occur if such settlement or recovery had no tax consequence. The tax consequences of transactions are to be accounted for in the same way as the transaction to which they are related. Therefore, for transactions recognised in the statement of profit or loss and other comprehensive income, all related tax effects are also recognised in the statement of profit or loss and other comprehensive income. Where a transaction requires a direct adjustment to equity, so do any tax effects. Deferred tax assets, particularly those relating to tax losses, are recognised only if it is probable that the entity will have sufficient taxable profit in the future against which the tax benefit can be offset. All deferred tax liabilities must be recognised in full. IAS 12 requires extensive disclosures to be made in relation to both current and deferred tax items.

Discussion questions

1. What is the main principle of tax-effect accounting as outlined in IAS 12?
2. Explain the meaning of a temporary difference as it relates to deferred tax calculations and give three examples.
3. Explain how accounting profit and taxable profit differ, and how each is treated when accounting for income taxes.
4. In tax-effect accounting, the creation of temporary differences between the carrying amount and the tax base for assets and liabilities leads to the establishment of deferred tax assets and liabilities in the accounting records. List examples of temporary differences that create:
   (a) deferred tax assets
   (b) deferred tax liabilities.
5. In IAS 12, criteria are established for the recognition of a deferred tax asset and a deferred tax liability. Identify these criteria, and discuss any differences between the criteria for assets and those for liabilities.

References

CPA Australia 2010, *International Financial Reporting Standards Fact Sheet — IAS 12 Income Taxes*, CPA Australia, February, www.cpaaustralia.com.au.

International Accounting Standards Board 2014, IAS 12 *Income Taxes*, www.ifrs.org.

Marks & Spencer plc 2014, *Annual Report*, http://corporate.marksandspencer.com/investors/reports-results-and-presentations.

Exercises

STAR RATING ★ BASIC ★★ MODERATE ★★★ DIFFICULT

Exercise 6.1 | **TAX EFFECTS OF A TEMPORARY DIFFERENCE**

★ The following information was extracted from the records of Protea Ltd for the year ended 30 June 2013:

PROTEA LTD Deferred Tax Worksheet (extract) as at 30 June 2013						
	Carrying amount	Future Taxable amount	Future deductible amount	Tax base	Taxable temporary differences	Deductible temporary differences
Relevant assets Equipment	£75 000	£(75 000)	£120 000	£120 000		£45 000

The equipment cost £300 000 and is depreciated at 25% p.a. straight-line for accounting purposes, but the allowable rate for taxation is 20% p.a.

Required

Assuming that no equipment is purchased or sold during the years ended 30 June 2014 and 30 June 2015, calculate:
(a) the accounting expense and tax deduction for each year
(b) the impact of depreciation on the taxable profit for each year
(c) the movement in the temporary difference balance for each year.

CALCULATION OF CURRENT TAX

★ Thistle Ltd made an accounting profit before tax of £40 000 for the year ended 30 June 2014. Included in the accounting profit were the following items of revenue and expense.

Donations to political parties (non-deductible)	5 000
Depreciation — machinery (20%)	15 000
Annual leave expense	5 600
Rent revenue	12 000

For tax purposes the following applied:

Depreciation rate for machinery	25%
Annual leave paid	6 500
Rent received	10 000
Income tax rate	30%

Required

1. Calculate the current tax liability for the year ended 30 June 2014, and prepare the adjusting journal entry.
2. Explain your treatment of rent items in your answer to requirement 1.

CALCULATION OF DEFERRED TAX

★ The following information was extracted from the records of Orchid Ltd for the year ended 30 June 2014:

ORCHID LTD Statement of Financial Position (extract) as at 30 June 2014		
Assets		
Accounts receivable	£25 000	
Allowance for doubtful debts	(2 000)	£23 000
Machines	100 000	
Accumulated depreciation — machines	(25 000)	75 000
Liabilities		
Interest payable		1 000

Additional information
(a) The accumulated depreciation for tax purposes at 30 June 2014 was £50 000.
(b) The tax rate is 30%.

Required

Prepare a deferred tax worksheet to identify the temporary differences arising in respect of the assets and liabilities in the statement of financial position, and to calculate the balance of the deferred tax liability and deferred tax asset accounts at 30 June 2014. Assume the opening balance of the deferred tax accounts was £0.

CURRENT AND DEFERRED TAX

★ Myrtle Ltd has determined its accounting profit before tax for the year ended 30 June 2013 to be £256 700. Included in this profit are the items of revenue and expense shown below.

Royalty revenue (non-taxable)	£8 000
Proceeds on sale of building	75 000
Entertainment expense	1 700
Depreciation expense — buildings	7 600
Depreciation expense — plant	22 500
Carrying amount of building sold	70 000
Doubtful debts expense	4 100
Annual leave expense	46 000
Insurance expense	4 200
Development expense	15 000

The company's draft statement of financial position at 30 June 2013 showed the following assets and liabilities:

Assets		
Cash		£2 500
Accounts receivable	£21 500	
Less: Allowance for doubtful debts	(4 100)	17 400
Inventory		31 600
Prepaid insurance		4 500
Land		75 000
Buildings	170 000	
Less: Accumulated depreciation	(59 500)	110 500
Plant	150 000	
Less: Accumulated depreciation	(67 500)	82 500
Deferred tax asset (opening balance)		9 600
		333 600
Liabilities		
Accounts payable		25 000
Provision for annual leave		10 000
Deferred tax liability (opening balance)		6 000
Loan		140 000
		£181 000

Additional information
(a) Quarterly income tax instalments paid during the year were:

28 October 2012	£ 18 000
28 January 2013	17 500
28 April 2013	18 000

with the final balance due on 28 July 2013.
(b) The tax depreciation rate for plant (which cost £150 000 3 years ago) is 20%. Depreciation on buildings is not deductible for taxation purposes.
(c) The building sold during the year had cost £100 000 when acquired 6 years ago. The company depreciates buildings at 5% p.a., straight-line. Any gain (loss) on sale of buildings is not taxable (i.e. not deductible).
(d) During the year, the following cash amounts were paid:

Annual leave	£52 000
Insurance	3 700

(e) Bad debts of £3500 were written off against the allowance for doubtful debts during the year.
(f) The £15 000 spent (and expensed) on development during the year is not deductible for tax purposes until 30 June 2014.
(g) Myrtle Ltd has tax losses amounting to £12 500 carried forward from prior years.
(h) The company tax rate is 30%.

Required

1. Determine the balance of any current and deferred tax assets and liabilities for Myrtle Ltd as at 30 June 2013.
2. Prepare any necessary journal entries.

CALCULATION OF CURRENT TAX LIABILITY AND ADJUSTING JOURNAL ENTRY

★ The profit before tax, as reported in the statement of profit or loss and other comprehensive income of Violet for the year ended 30 June 2014, amounted to £60 000, including the following revenue and expense items:

Rent revenue	£3 000
Government grant received (non-taxable)	1 000
Bad debts expense	6 000
Depreciation of plant	5 000
Annual leave expense	3 000
Entertainment costs (non-deductible)	1 800
Depreciation of buildings (non-deductible)	800

The statement of financial position of the company at 30 June 2014 showed the following net assets.

	2014	2013
Assets		
Cash	8 000	8 500
Inventory	17 000	15 500
Receivables	50 000	48 000
Allowance for doubtful debts	(5 500)	(4 000)
Office supplies	2 500	2 200
Plant	50 000	50 000
Accumulated depreciation	(26 000)	(21 000)
Buildings	30 000	30 000
Accumulated depreciation	(14 800)	(14 000)
Goodwill (net)	(7 000)	(7 000)
Deferred tax asset	?	4 050
Liabilities		
Accounts payable	29 000	26 000
Provision for long-service leave	6 000	4 500
Provision for annual leave	4 000	3 000
Rent received in advance	2 500	2 000
Deferred tax liability	?	3 150

Additional information
(a) Accumulated depreciation of plant for tax purposes was £31 500 at 30 June 2013, and depreciation for tax purposes for the year ended 30 June 2014 amounted to £7500.
(b) The tax rate is 30%.

Required

Prepare a worksheet to calculate taxable profit and the company's current tax liability as at 30 June 2014, and prepare the end of reporting period adjustment journal.

CREATION AND REVERSAL OF TEMPORARY DIFFERENCES

★★ The following are all independent situations. Prepare the journal entries for deferred tax on the creation or reversal of any temporary differences. Explain in each case the nature of the temporary difference. Assume a tax rate of 30%.

1. The entity has an allowance for doubtful debts of £10 000 at the end of the current year relating to accounts receivable of £125 000. The prior year balances for these accounts were £8500 and £97500 respectively. During the current year, debts worth £9250 were written off as uncollectable.
2. The entity sold a vehicle at the end of the current year for £15 000. The vehicle cost £100 000 when purchased 3 years ago, and had a carrying amount of £25 000 when sold. The taxation depreciation rate for equipment of this type is 33%.
3. The entity has recognised an interest receivable asset with a beginning balance of £17 000 and an ending balance of £19 500 for the current year. During the year, interest of £127 000 was received in cash.
4. At the end of the current year, the entity has recognised a liability of £4000 in respect of outstanding fines for non-compliance with safety legislation. Such fines are not tax-deductible.

CREATION AND REVERSAL OF A TEMPORARY DIFFERENCE

★★ Rose Ltd purchased equipment on 1 July 2011 at a cost of £25 000. The equipment had an expected economic life of 5 years and was to be depreciated on a straight-line basis. The taxation depreciation rate for equipment of this type is 15% p.a. straight-line. On 30 June 2013, Rose Ltd reassessed the remaining economic life of the equipment from 3 years to 2 years, and the accounting depreciation charge was adjusted accordingly. The equipment was sold on 30 June 2014 for £15 000. The company tax rate is 30%.

Required

For each of the years ended 30 June 2012, 2013 and 2014, calculate the carrying amount and the tax base of the asset and determine the appropriate deferred tax entry. Explain your answer.

CALCULATION OF DEFERRED TAX, AND ADJUSTMENT ENTRY

★★★ The following information was extracted from the records of Bulb Ltd as at 30 June 2013:

Asset (liability)	Carrying amount	Tax base
Accounts receivable	£150 000	£175 000
Motor vehicles	(165 000)	125 000
Provision for warranty	(12 000)	0
Deposits received in advance	(15 000)	0

The depreciation rates for accounting and taxation are 15% and 25% respectively. Deposits are taxable when received, and warranty costs are deductible when paid. An allowance for doubtful debts of £25 000 has been raised against accounts receivable for accounting purposes, but such debts are deductible only when written off as uncollectable.

Required

1. Calculate the temporary differences for Bulb Ltd as at 30 June 2013. Justify your classification of each difference as either a deductible temporary difference or a taxable temporary difference.
2. Prepare the journal entry to record deferred tax for the year ended 30 June 2013 assuming no deferred items had been raised in prior years.

Accounting researchers have been interested in whether differences between taxable profit and pre-tax profit (the accounting measure of profit before tax) provide information that is useful to investors. Additionally, accounting research has hypothesised that a greater book–tax difference may indicate poorer earnings quality and/or manipulation of recorded tax expense (Hanlon, 2005).

Within research that looks at the usefulness of tax accounting, Amir et al. (1997) examine the pricing implications of six types of deferred tax assets and liabilities in 1992–1994. These include assets and liabilities created with respect to temporary differences in depreciation, losses carried forward, restructuring charges, environmental charges, employee benefits and valuation allowance (also see below). They find consistent evidence that deferred tax assets for employee benefit and restructuring charges are positively related to stock prices. This is consistent with these assets representing anticipated reduction in future cash payment for tax. They, however, find mixed evidence with respect to the other types of deferred tax assets and liabilities. Lev and Nissim (2004) explore if taxable income can help predict growth to assess the usefulness of tax accounting. They find that the ratio of taxable income to book income is positively associated with measures of future growth, suggesting that tax-based calculation of income can assist investors in predicting growth. They also find that this ratio and earnings-to-price are negatively related, consistent with notion that earnings are more highly priced when taxable earnings are higher.

Laux (2013) extends Amir et al. (1997) by examining directly whether deferred tax assets (liabilities) predict reductions (increases) in future cash payments to tax authorities. He argues that this depends on the timing of the recognition of revenues and expenses in pre-tax income relative to taxable income. Specifically, he predicts lower future tax payments if expenses and revenues are first recognised in pre-tax income, and only later in taxable income (e.g., warranty expense). In contrast, he predicts no effect on future tax payments if the recognition of revenues and expenses in taxable income precedes recognition in pre-tax income (e.g., as in the case of unearned revenues and accelerated tax depreciation). His findings are consistent with these predictions. Laux (2013) also examines the valuation implications of the two categories of the timeliness of recognition of expenses and revenues. He finds that only expenses and revenues that are first recognised in pre-tax income are value relevant. Additionally, and similarly to Amir et al. (1997), he finds that deferred tax liabilities related to depreciation are not positively associated with stock prices. This is consistent with the possibility that these liabilities do not reverse and so do not trigger additional cash payments. This will be the case, for example, in growing firms who increase the depreciable asset base over time. As the asset base grows, origination of new deferred tax liabilities exceeds the reversal of old liabilities, implying no cash is returned to the tax authorities.

Accounting for taxes may speak as to the quality of underlying reported earnings. Specifically, deferred taxes may be indicative of managerial discretion in accruals, since this discretion typically does not affect current tax liability. Phillips et al. (2003) therefore conjecture that higher deferred tax expense is associated with more earnings management. Consistent with this, they find that companies are more likely to avoid earnings declines, and avoid losses when they show higher deferred tax expense. Ayers et al. (2010) examine the implications of book–tax differences for credit ratings. They find that larger changes in the difference between pre-tax income and taxable income are associated with lower credit ratings. They interpret this result as follows. As the amount by which book income exceeds tax income increases, credit analysts interpret this as poor earnings quality, which in turn suggests greater credit risk. This risk may stem from the lower earnings persistence that is documented by Hanlon (2005) for firms with large book–tax differences.

Deferred taxes themselves can be subject to manipulation. IAS 12 and US GAAP allow for partial recognition of deferred tax *assets*, to the extent that managers do not believe these assets will be recoverable. The accounting item that reduces the carrying amount of deferred tax asset under partial provisioning is often called valuation allowance. By changing their assessment of the valuation allowance managers can influence reported earnings. However, Bauman et al. (2001) do not find evidence consistent with this conjecture from contextual analysis of Fortune 500 firms. Miller and Skinner (1998) find that the valuation allowance is largely related to losses carried forward that may not be utilised. This is consistent with the view that the allowance is correctly stated, on average. Nevertheless, Schrand and Wong (2003) provide some evidence that banks in a strong financial position tend to have higher valuation allowance, suggesting they opportunistically create hidden reserves.

IAS 12 has removed much discretion that was previously available to companies under local standards. Specifically, in the UK, before 2005, both deferred tax assets and liabilities were recorded only to the extent that managers believed that a reversal would take place (see illustrative example 6.1 in this chapter). That is, partial recognition was allowed for both deferred tax liabilities and deferred tax assets. Gordon and Joos (2004) examine how this discretion was used by UK managers and find that it was mostly deployed in highly leveraged firms who report larger unrecognised deferred tax liabilities. This enabled them to reduce the overall reported leverage of their firms, suggesting the allowance was measured opportunistically. The implication is that removing the level of discretion allowed by the new standard may have improved the quality of tax accounting.

References

Amir, E., Kirschenheiter, M., and Willard, K., 1997. The valuation of deferred taxes. *Contemporary Accounting Research*, 14(4), 597–622.

Ayers, B. C., Laplante, S. K., and McGuire, S. T., 2010. Credit ratings and taxes: The effect of book–tax differences on ratings changes. *Contemporary Accounting Research*, 27(2), 359–402.

Bauman, C. C., Bauman, M. P., and Halsey, R. F., 2001. Do firms use the deferred tax asset valuation allowance to manage earnings? *Journal of the American Taxation Association*, 23(s-1), 27–48.

Gordon, E. A., and Joos, P. R., 2004. Unrecognized deferred taxes: evidence from the UK. *The Accounting Review*, 79(1), 97–124.

Hanlon, M., 2005. The persistence and pricing of earnings, accruals and cash flows when firms have large book–tax differences. *The Accounting Review*, 80(1), 137–166.

Laux, R. C., 2013. The association between deferred tax assets and liabilities and future tax payments. *The Accounting Review*, 88(4), 1357–1383.

Lev, B., and Nissim. D., 2004. Taxable income, future earnings and equity values. *The Accounting Review*, 79(4), 1039–1074.

Miller, G. S., and Skinner, D. J., 1998. Determinants of the valuation allowance for deferred tax assets under SFAS No. 109. *The Accounting Review*, 73(2), 213–233.

Phillips, J., Pincus, M., and Rego, S. O., 2003. Earnings management: New evidence based on deferred tax expense. *The Accounting Review*, 78(2), 491–521.

Schrand, C. M., and Wong, M. H., 2003. Earnings management using the valuation allowance for deferred tax assets under SFAS No. 109. *Contemporary Accounting Research*, 20(3), 579–611.

7 Financial instruments

ACCOUNTING STANDARDS IN FOCUS

IAS 32 *Financial Instruments: Presentation*

IFRS 7 *Financial Instruments: Disclosures*

IFRS 9 *Financial Instruments*

LEARNING OBJECTIVES

After studying this chapter, you should be able to:

1. describe the background to the development of accounting standards on financial instruments

2. define a financial instrument

3. outline and apply the definitions of financial assets and financial liabilities

4. distinguish between equity instruments and financial liabilities

5. explain the concept of a compound financial instrument

6. determine the classification of revenues and expenses arising from financial instruments

7. describe the scope of IFRS 9

8. explain the concept of an embedded derivative

9. distinguish between the categories of financial instruments specified in IFRS 9

10. apply the recognition criteria for financial instruments

11. understand and apply the measurement criteria for each category of financial instrument

12. determine when financial assets and financial liabilities may be offset

13. outline the rules of hedge accounting set out in IFRS 9 and be able to apply the rules to simple common cash flow and fair value hedges.

14. describe the main disclosure requirements of IFRS 7.

7.1 INTRODUCTION

Accounting for financial instruments was the most controversial area in the development of the International Accounting Standards Board's (IASB®) 'stable platform' of standards adopted in 2005. Indeed, the controversy surrounding IAS 39 *Financial Instruments: Recognition and Measurement* in particular almost derailed the IASB's plans for adopting IFRS® Standards in Europe for financial years beginning on or after 1 January 2005. As late as 30 June 2004, IAS 39 had still not been completed because changes continued to be proposed or made in response to lobbying from various European interested parties, notably the banks. The controversial aspects of the standards at that time were largely related to hedge accounting. The controversy continued during the financial crisis of 2008 and put the IASB under enormous pressure to amend IAS 39. In this case there was pressure to allow entities to move away from using a fair value measurement basis and to change the requirements for impairment of financial assets. As a result, the IASB amended the reclassification rules of IAS 39 and then very quickly started work on a new standard to replace IAS 39. This standard, IFRS 9 *Financial Instruments*, was issued in phases between November 2009 and July 2014. IFRS 9 is expected to be endorsed by the European Commission in the first half of 2016 and so this chapter focuses on IFRS 9.

Figure 7.1 provides an extract from the Report of the Financial Crisis Advisory Group[1], which illustrates the controversy and complexity surrounding the accounting for financial instruments at the time of the 2008 financial crisis.

In response to the financial crisis in 2008, the IASB commenced its work on IFRS 9 in November 2008 and issued the complete version of IFRS 9 in July 2014. IFRS 9 introduced a new classification and measurement approach for financial assets, a forward-looking expected credit loss model, an improved hedge accounting model and a better approach to deal with the so-called 'own credit' issue *(see section 7.9.2)*. These changes were made to address the concerns that the Group of Twenty (G-20, an international forum for the governments and central bank governors from 20 major economies), the Financial Crisis Advisory Group and others had raised.

FIGURE 7.1 Effective financial reporting

Report of the Financial Crisis Advisory Group

While the post-mortems are still being written, it seems clear that accounting standards were not a root cause of the financial crisis. At the same time, it is clear that the crisis has exposed weaknesses in accounting standards and their application. These weaknesses reduced the credibility of financial reporting, which in part contributed to the general loss of confidence in the financial system. The weaknesses primarily involved (1) the difficulty of applying fair value ('mark-to-market') accounting in illiquid markets; (2) the delayed recognition of losses associated with loans, structured credit products, and other financial instruments by banks, insurance companies and other financial institutions; (3) issues surrounding the broad range of off-balance-sheet financing structures, especially in the US; and (4) the extraordinary complexity of accounting standards for financial instruments, including multiple approaches to recognizing asset impairment. Some of these weaknesses also highlighted areas in which International Financial Reporting Standards ('IFRS') and US generally accepted accounting principles ('US GAAP') diverged.

In the early part of the crisis, the principal criticism of financial reporting focused on fair value accounting. This criticism contended that fair value accounting contributed to the pro-cyclicality of the financial system. Prior to the crisis, it is argued, fair value accounting led to significant overstatement of profits; however, during the crisis, it was supposed to have led to a severe overstatement of losses and the consequent 'destruction of capital'. Thus, the argument went, a vicious cycle ensued: falling asset prices led to accounting write-downs; the write-downs led to forced asset sales by institutions needing to meet capital adequacy requirements; and the forced sales exacerbated the fall in asset prices. In the US, moreover, critics singled out the other-than-temporary impairment standards for available-for-sale and held-to-maturity securities as being particularly 'destructive' because institutions were forced to take charges against earnings as a consequence of what they believed to be temporary 'market irrationality'.

Proponents of fair value accounting do not deny that indeed mark-to-market accounting shows the fluctuations of the market, but they maintain that these cycles are a fact of life and that the use of fair value accounting does not exacerbate these cycles. Moreover, they argue that fair value accounting standards provided 'early warning' signals by revealing the market's discomfort with inflated asset values. In their view, this contributed to a more timely recognition of problems and mitigation of the crisis.

---

[1] Report of the Financial Crisis Advisory Group, 28 July 2009.

FIGURE 7.1 (continued)

Whatever the final outcome of the debate over fair value accounting, it is unlikely that, on balance, accounting standards led to an understatement of the value of financial assets. While the crisis may have led to some understatement of the value of mark-to-market assets, it is important to recognize that, in most countries, a majority of bank assets are still valued at historic cost using the amortized cost basis. Those assets are not marked to market and are not adjusted for market liquidity. By now it seems clear that the overall value of these assets has not been understated — but overstated. The incurred loss model for loan loss provisioning and difficulties in applying the model — in particular, identifying appropriate trigger points for loss recognition — in many instances has delayed the recognition of losses on loan portfolios. (The results of the US stress tests seem to bear this out.) Moreover, the off-balance-sheet standards, and the way they were applied, may have obscured losses associated with securitizations and other complex structured products. Thus, the overall effect of the current mixed attribute model by which assets of financial institutions have been measured, coupled with the obscurity of off-balance sheet exposures, has probably been to understate the losses that were embedded in the system.

Even if the overall effect of accounting standards may not have been pro-cyclical, we consider it imperative that the weaknesses in the current standards be addressed as a matter of urgency. Improvements in accounting standards cannot 'cure' the financial crisis by resolving underlying economic and governance issues (for example, the massive overleveraging of the global economy, excessive risk taking, and the undercapitalization of the banking sector). However, as demonstrated by the positive market reaction to disclosure of the results of the US stress tests, improvements in standards that enhance transparency and reduce complexity can help restore the confidence of financial market participants and thereby serve as a catalyst for increased financial stability and sound economic growth. Conversely, any changes in financial reporting that reduce transparency and allow the impact of the crisis to be obscured would likely have the opposite effect, by further reducing the confidence of market participants and thereby prolonging the crisis or by laying the foundation for future problems.

Source: Financial Crisis Advisory Group (2009).

Although the IASB worked closely with the US FASB in the initial stages of the development of IFRS 9, the efforts to develop a converged standard were ultimately unsuccessful. So unlike IAS 39 — which was largely based on the similar FASB standard in the United States, Statement of Financial Accounting Standards No. 133 (SFAS 133) *Accounting for Derivative Instruments and Hedging Activities* — IFRS 9 differs in important respects from the accounting prescribed by the FASB.

IAS 32 sets out the definitions of financial instruments, financial assets and financial liabilities, the distinction between financial liabilities and equity instruments, and originally prescribed detailed disclosures. The standard was developed before IAS 39 because consensus on the recognition, derecognition, measurement and hedging rules for financial instruments was difficult to achieve. Therefore, the standard setters first established classification and disclosure rules, anticipating that increased disclosure by reporting entities would provide more information, not only for users, but also for the standard setters. Increased disclosure helps to provide standard setters with information that assists in developing further standards.

In 2006, IAS 32 was renamed *Financial Instruments: Presentation* and a new standard, IFRS 7 *Financial Instruments: Disclosures*, was introduced, applicable to annual periods beginning on or after 1 January 2007. IFRS 7 contains many of the disclosure requirements that were originally in IAS 32 and IAS 30 *Disclosures in the Financial Statements of Banks and Similar Financial Institutions*. It also introduced a number of new requirements.

Because IFRS 9, IAS 32 and IFRS 7 are complex standards, this chapter provides an overall explanation of the requirements. It emphasises those areas most commonly affecting the majority of reporting entities, and places less emphasis on specialised areas.

Each standard is addressed separately in this chapter.

IAS 32, IFRS 7 and IFRS 9 each contain Application Guidance, which is abbreviated in this chapter as AG. IFRS 7 and IFRS 9 also contain Implementation Guidance.

The main definitions and accounting requirements of IAS 32 are covered *in sections 7.2 to 7.6*, while its requirements on offsetting are dealt with *in section 7.12*. The IFRS 9 requirements on accounting for financial assets, financial liabilities and derivatives and its recognition, measurement and hedge accounting requirements are covered *in sections 7.7 to 7.13*. Finally, the disclosure requirements of IFRS 7 are covered *in section 7.14*.

7.2 WHAT IS A FINANCIAL INSTRUMENT?

7.2.1 Definition of a financial instrument

IAS 32, paragraph 11, defines a financial instrument as:

> any contract that gives rise to a financial asset of one entity and a financial liability or equity instrument of another entity.

Financial assets and financial liabilities are terms defined in IAS 32 (*see sections 7.3.1 and 7.3.2*). Financial assets are defined from the perspective of the *holder* of the instrument, whereas financial liabilities and equity instruments are defined from the perspective of the *issuer* of the instrument.

An equity instrument is defined in paragraph 11 as:

> any contract that evidences a residual interest in the assets of an entity after deducting all of its liabilities.

The most common type of equity instrument is an ordinary share of a company. The holder of the shares is not entitled to any fixed return on or of its investment; instead, the holder receives the residual after all liabilities have been settled. This applies both to periodic returns (where dividends are paid after interest on liabilities has been paid) and capital returns (when a company is wound up, all liabilities are settled before shareholders are entitled to any return of their investment).

7.2.2 Two sides to the story

Note that the definition of a financial instrument is two-sided — the contract must always give rise to a financial asset of one party, with a corresponding financial liability or equity instrument of another party. For example, a contract that gives the seller of a product the right to receive cash from the purchaser creates a receivable for the seller (a financial asset) and a payable for the purchaser (a financial liability).

7.2.3 Common types of financial instruments

Financial instruments include primary instruments such as cash, receivables, investments and payables, as well as derivative financial instruments such as financial options and forward exchange contracts. Derivative financial instruments, or derivatives, are instruments that *derive* their value from another underlying item such as a share price or an interest rate. (*The definition of a derivative is discussed in section 7.8.*)

7.2.4 Contracts to buy or sell non-financial instruments

Financial instruments do *not* include non-financial assets such as property, plant and equipment, or non-financial liabilities such as provisions for restoration. Contracts to buy or sell non-financial items are also usually not financial instruments. Many commodity contracts fall into this category (contracts to buy or sell oil, cotton, wheat and so on). These commodity contracts are thus outside the scope of IAS 32. However, reporting entities with commodity contracts that are within the scope of IFRS 9 should follow the disclosure requirements of IFRS 7. Certain commodity contracts are, however, included within the scope of IAS 32. These include contracts to buy or sell non-financial items that can be settled net (in cash) or by exchanging financial instruments, or in which the non-financial item is readily convertible into cash. Contracts to buy or sell gold might fall into the latter category and so might be caught by IAS 32 and IFRS 9.

7.2.5 Other items that are *not* financial instruments

Note also that the definition of a financial instrument requires there to be a contractual right or obligation. Therefore, liabilities or assets that are not contractual — such as income taxes that are created as a result of statutory requirements imposed by governments, or constructive obligations as defined in IAS 37 *Provisions, Contingent Liabilities and Contingent Assets (see chapter 5)* — are not financial instruments.

In addition, certain financial assets and liabilities are outside the scope of IAS 32. These include employee benefits accounted for under IAS 19, and investments in subsidiaries, associates and joint ventures that are accounted for under IFRS 10 *Consolidated Financial Statements*, IAS 27 *Separate Financial Statements*, IAS 28 *Investments in Associates and Joint Ventures* and IFRS 11 *Joint Arrangements*.

7.3 FINANCIAL ASSETS AND FINANCIAL LIABILITIES

7.3.1 Financial assets

A financial asset is defined in paragraph 11 of IAS 32 as follows:

> any asset that is:
>
> (a) cash;
> (b) an equity instrument of another entity;
> (c) a contractual right:
>   (i) to receive cash or another financial asset from another entity; or
>   (ii) to exchange financial assets or financial liabilities with another entity under conditions that are potentially favourable to the entity; or
> (d) a contract that will or may be settled in the entity's own equity instruments and meets certain additional conditions.

Examples of common financial assets in each of the categories of the definition include:

(a) cash — either cash on hand or the right of the depositor to obtain cash from the financial institution with which it has deposited the cash
(b) an equity instrument of another entity — ordinary shares held in another entity
(c) a contractual right
    (i) to receive cash or another financial asset — trade accounts receivable, notes receivable, loans receivable
    (ii) to exchange under potentially favourable conditions — an option held by the holder to purchase shares in a specified company at less than the market price.

Part (d) of the definition was added in response to issues arising from the classification of certain complex financial instruments as liabilities or equity. The IASB considered that to treat any transaction settled in the entity's own shares as an equity instrument would not deal adequately with transactions in which an entity is using its own shares as 'currency' (e.g. where it has an obligation to pay a fixed or determinable amount that is settled in a variable number of its own shares). In such transactions the counterparty bears no share price risk, and is therefore not in the same position as a 'true' equity shareholder. *(Liability/equity classification is discussed in section 7.4.)*

7.3.2 Financial liabilities

A financial liability is defined in paragraph 11 of IAS 32 as follows:

> any liability that is:
>
> (a) a contractual obligation:
>   (i) to deliver cash or another financial asset to another entity; or
>   (ii) to exchange financial assets or financial liabilities with another entity under conditions that are potentially unfavourable to the entity; or
> (b) a contract that will or may be settled in the entity's own equity instruments and meets certain additional conditions.

Examples of common financial liabilities in each of the categories of the definition include:

(a) a contractual obligation
    (i) to deliver cash or another financial asset — trade accounts payable, notes payable, loans payable
    (ii) to exchange under potentially unfavourable conditions — an option written (i.e. issued) by the issuer to sell shares in a specified company at less than the market price.

Part (b) of the definition was added in response to issues arising from the classification of certain complex financial instruments as liabilities or equity, *as discussed in section 7.3.1. (Liability/equity classification is discussed in section 7.4.)*

Table 7.1 contains a summary of common financial instruments.

TABLE 7.1 Summary of common financial instruments

Financial assets	Financial liabilities	Equity instruments
Cash	Bank overdraft	Ordinary shares
Accounts receivable	Accounts payable	Certain preference shares
Notes receivable	Notes payable	
Loans receivable	Loans payable	
Derivatives with potentially favourable exchange conditions	Derivatives with potentially unfavourable exchange conditions	
	Certain preference shares	

7.4 DISTINGUISHING FINANCIAL LIABILITIES FROM EQUITY INSTRUMENTS

IAS 32 is very prescriptive in the way it distinguishes between financial liabilities and equity instruments. This area, commonly known as the debt versus equity distinction, is of great concern to many reporting entities because instruments classified as liabilities rather than equity affect:

- a company's gearing and solvency ratios
- debt covenants with financial institutions (usually a requirement that specified financial ratios of the borrower do not exceed predetermined thresholds; if they do exceed the thresholds, the financial institution has a right to require repayment of the loan)
- whether periodic payments on these instruments are treated as interest (affecting profit or loss) or dividends (not affecting profit or loss)
- regulatory requirements for capital adequacy (banks and other financial institutions are required by their regulators to maintain a certain level of capital, which is calculated by reference to assets and equity).

Accordingly, reporting entities are often motivated, when raising funds, to issue instruments that are classified as equity for accounting purposes. In the years since IAS 32 was first issued, many complex instruments were devised by market participants specifically to achieve equity classification under IAS 32. Some of these instruments were liabilities in substance but were able to be classified technically as equity, notwithstanding a 'substance over form' test in IAS 32. As a result, the IASB amended IAS 32 to create specific rules designed to address these complex instruments. Unfortunately, the rules are now quite complicated, so this section will address the key principles of liability versus equity classification only.

7.4.1 The rules

IAS 32, paragraph 15, states:

> The issuer of a financial instrument shall classify the instrument, or its component parts, on initial recognition as a financial liability, a financial asset or an equity instrument in accordance with the substance of the contractual arrangement and the definitions of a financial liability, a financial asset and an equity instrument.

To avoid any doubt, paragraph 16 goes on to repeat and clarify the definition of a financial liability. It states that an instrument shall be classified as an equity instrument if, and only if, *both* conditions (a) and (b) below are met:

(a) The instrument includes no contractual obligation:
  (i) to deliver cash or another financial asset to another entity; or
  (ii) to exchange financial assets or financial liabilities with another entity under conditions that are potentially unfavourable to the issuer.
(b) If the instrument will or may be settled in the issuer's own equity instruments, it is:
  (i) a non-derivative that includes no contractual obligation for the issuer to deliver a variable number of its own equity instruments; or
  (ii) a derivative that will be settled only by the issuer exchanging a fixed amount of cash or another financial asset for a fixed number of its own equity instruments.

Part (a) is clearly referring to the definition of a financial liability. The rules in part (b) are trying to establish who bears 'equity risk' in complex transactions where an entity issues a financial instrument that will or may be settled in its own shares.

The concept of equity risk is useful for both part (b) of the test and generally in determining whether an instrument is equity or a liability. Note, however, that part (a) of the test turns only on whether or not the issuer has a contractual obligation.

Part (a) of the equity/liability test: contractual obligation

The examples in figure 7.2 apply part (a) of the equity/liability test, together with the equity risk concept.

FIGURE 7.2 Applying part (a) of the equity/liability test

Example 1: Ordinary shares

Company A wants to raise funds of $1 million. It does so by issuing ordinary shares to the public. The holders of those shares are exposed to equity risk (they are not entitled to any fixed return on or of their investment, and receive the residual left over after all liabilities have been settled) in respect of both periodic payments and capital returns. If there is no profit after interest on liabilities and other contractual obligations have been paid, then there are no dividends. If, on winding up, there are no assets after all liabilities have been settled, there is nothing returned to the shareholders.

This is the fundamental nature of equity risk. The ordinary shares issued by Company A are equity instruments of Company A. Under part (a) of the test, Company A has no contractual obligation to its ordinary shareholders.

FIGURE 7.2 (continued)

Company A would record the following journal entry on initial recognition:

Cash (financial asset)	Dr	1 000 000	
Ordinary Share Capital (equity)	Cr		1 000 000

Example 2: Non-cumulative, non-redeemable preference shares

Company A decides to issue preference shares instead of ordinary shares. It issues 1 million preference shares for $1 each. Each preference shareholder is entitled to a non-cumulative dividend of 5% annually. (A non-cumulative dividend means that, if in any year a dividend is not paid, the shareholder forfeits it.) The preference shareholders rank ahead of ordinary shareholders on the winding up of the company. The preference shares are non-redeemable (the holders of the shares cannot get their money back).

Under part (a) of the test, Company A has no contractual obligation to the preference shareholders, either to pay dividends or to return the cash. Therefore, the preference shares are equity instruments of Company A. In addition, applying the concept of equity risk reveals that the preference shareholders are exposed to equity risk, although it is lower than for the ordinary shareholders.

Company A would record the following journal entry on initial recognition:

Cash (financial asset)	Dr	1 000 000	
Preference Share Capital (equity)	Cr		1 000 000

Example 3: Cumulative preference shares redeemable by the holder

Company A issues 1 million preference shares for $1 each, and each preference shareholder is entitled to a cumulative dividend of 5% annually. The preference share-holders rank ahead of ordinary shareholders on the winding-up of the company. The preference shares are redeemable for cash at the option of the holder.

Under part (a) of the test, Company A now has a contractual obligation to the preference shareholders — both in respect of dividends and to return the cash. Company A must pay the dividends and, if in any period it cannot pay, it must make up the payment with the next dividend. Furthermore, Company A must repay the money whenever the holder demands repayment. Therefore, the preference shares are financial liabilities of Company A. In addition, applying the concept of equity risk reveals that the preference shareholders are not exposed to equity risk – they are guaranteed a periodic return of 5% and they can require that their cash be returned. They bear a similar risk as would a lender to Company A, although a lender may rank ahead of cumulative preference shareholders in the winding-up of the company. A lender's risk is generally credit risk (the risk that Company A will fail to discharge its obligations) and liquidity risk (the risk that Company A will fail to raise funds to enable it to redeem the liability on demand).

Company A would record the following journal entry on initial recognition:

Cash (financial asset)	Dr	1 000 000	
Preference Share Liability (financial liability)	Cr		1 000 000

Paragraph 17 of IAS 32 reiterates that a critical feature in differentiating a financial liability from an equity instrument is the existence of a contractual obligation of the issuer. Paragraph 18 then goes on to state that the substance of a financial instrument, rather than its legal form, governs its classification on the entity's statement of financial position. Some financial instruments, *such as the preference shares in example 3 of figure 7.2*, take the legal form of equity but are liabilities in substance. Sometimes the combined features result in the financial instrument being split into its component parts *(see section 7.5)*.

Another example of a financial instrument whose legal form may be equity but whose accounting classification is a financial liability is a puttable instrument. A puttable instrument gives the holder the right to put the instrument back to the issuer for cash or another financial asset. This is so even when the amount of cash/other financial asset is determined based on an index or another amount that may increase or decrease. For example, certain mutual funds, unit trusts and partnerships provide their unit holders or members with a right to redeem their interests in the issuer at any time for cash equal to their proportionate share of the net asset value of the issuer. In 2008, the IASB amended IAS 32 to modify the definition of a financial liability so that such puttable instruments would not automatically result in liability classification.

Paragraphs 19 and 20 of IAS 32 explain that an entity has a contractual obligation to deliver cash/other financial assets notwithstanding:
- any restrictions on the entity's ability to meet its obligation (such as access to foreign currency)
- that the obligation may be conditional on the counterparty exercising its redemption right (*as in example 3 of figure 7.2* — redemption is at the option of the holder and therefore could be considered

to be conditional on the holder exercising its right to redeem. However, this does not negate the fact that the issuer has a contractual obligation to redeem the shares, because it cannot avoid its obligation should it be required to redeem by the holder)

- that the financial instrument does not explicitly establish a contractual obligation to deliver cash/other financial assets. A contractual obligation may be implied in the terms and conditions of the instrument. However, the guidance in paragraph 20 should be read in a narrow way given the guidance on preference shares. Paragraph AG26 states that non-redeemable preference shares are equity instruments, notwithstanding a term that prevents ordinary share dividends from being paid if the preference share dividend is not paid, or from being paid on the issuer's expectation of profit or loss for a period. A fairly common term in certain non-redeemable preference shares is that the dividend is 'discretionary' but, if the preference dividend is not paid, then ordinary dividends cannot be paid. If these terms exist in the preference shares of highly profitable companies, one could argue under paragraph 20 that the implicit terms and conditions of the preference shares require the dividend to be paid. However, paragraph AG26 states that such conditions do not create a financial liability of the issuer.

Part (b) of the equity/liability test: settlement in the entity's own equity instruments

Paragraph 21 of IAS 32 states that a contract is not an equity instrument solely because it may result in the receipt or delivery of the entity's own equity instruments. As noted earlier in this section, such an instrument can be classified as an equity instrument under paragraph 16(b) of IAS 32 only if it is:

(i) a non-derivative that includes no contractual obligation for the issuer to deliver a variable number of its own equity instruments; or

(ii) a derivative that will be settled only by the issuer exchanging a fixed amount of cash or another financial asset for a fixed number of its own equity instruments.

Part (i) will be examined first. Assume listed Company A has an obligation to deliver to Party B as many of Company A's own ordinary shares as will equal $100 000. The number of shares that Company A will have to issue will vary depending on the market price of its own shares. If Company A's shares are each worth $1 at the date of settlement of the contract, it will have to deliver 100 000 shares. If Company A's shares are each worth $0.50 at the date of settlement of the contract, it will have to deliver 200 000 shares. Company A has a contractual obligation at all times to deliver $100 000 to Party B; that is, the value is fixed, and so the number of shares to be delivered will vary. Therefore, Company A's financial instrument fails the test in part (i) and the instrument is a financial liability. Applying the concept of equity risk, the holder of the financial instrument (Party B) is not exposed to equity risk because it will always receive $100 000 regardless of the market price of Company A's shares. A true equity risk-taker will be exposed to share price fluctuations — this reflects the residual nature of an equity risk-taker's investment.

Now examine part (ii). Assume listed Company A issues a share option to Party B that entitles Party B to buy 100 000 shares in Company A at $1 each in 3 months' time. This financial instrument meets the conditions for equity classification under part (ii) because it is a derivative that will be settled by issuing a fixed number of shares for a fixed amount. Assume that, at the date of the grant of the option, Company A's share price is $1. If in 3 months' time Company A's share price exceeds $1, Party B will exercise its option and Company A must issue its shares to Party B for $100 000. If, however, in 3 months' time Company A's share price falls below $1, Party B will not exercise its option and Company A will not issue any shares. Applying the concept of equity risk reveals that the holder of the financial instrument (Party B) is exposed to equity risk because it is not guaranteed to receive $100 000 in value. Whether or not it receives $100 000 is entirely dependent on the market price of Company A's shares. As a true equity risk-taker, it is exposed to share price fluctuations; this reflects the residual nature of an equity risk-taker's investment. Party B will have paid a premium to Company A for the option. Paragraph 22 of IAS 32 states that this premium is added directly to Company A's equity, consistent with the classification of the instrument as an equity instrument.

7.4.2 Contingent settlement provisions and settlement options

Sometimes, when a financial instrument requires an entity to deliver cash/other financial assets, the terms of settlement are dependent on the occurrence or non-occurrence of uncertain future events that are beyond the control of both the issuer and the holder. Examples of such events include changes in a share market index, the consumer price index or the issuer's future revenues. The issuer of such an instrument does not have the unconditional right to avoid delivering the cash/other financial assets, so paragraph 25 of IAS 32 requires such instruments to be classified as financial liabilities unless they meet certain rare exceptions. For example, assume that Company A issues preference shares to Party B, the terms of which entitle Party B to redeem the preference shares for cash if Company A's revenues fall below a specified level. Because neither Company A nor Party B can control the level of Company A's revenues, the settlement provision is considered to be contingent. However, because Company A cannot avoid repaying Party B should Company A's revenues fall below the specified level, Company A does not have an unconditional right to avoid repayment. Thus the preference shares are a financial liability of Company A.

Some financial instruments contain a choice of settlement. For example, preference shares may be redeemed for cash or for the issuer's ordinary shares. Sometimes the choice is the issuer's; sometimes it is the holder's. Paragraph 26 of IAS 32 requires that, when a *derivative* financial instrument gives one party a choice over how it is settled, it is a financial asset or a financial liability unless all of the settlement alternatives would result in it being an equity instrument. An example is a share option that the issuer can decide to settle net in cash or by exchanging its own shares for cash. Because not all of the settlement options would result in an equity instrument being issued, the option must be classified as a financial asset or liability. Note that the likely outcome is not taken into account; the fact that cash settlement may be required is sufficient to create a financial asset or liability.

Paragraph 26 does not address *non-derivative* financial instruments. Therefore, where a non-derivative financial instrument such as a preference share may be redeemed for cash or for the issuer's own ordinary shares, paragraph 26 does not apply. Instead, paragraph 16 would be applied to determine whether or not there is (a) a contractual obligation to deliver cash/other financial assets, or (b) a contractual obligation to deliver a variable number of the issuer's ordinary shares. Note that both (a) and (b) must be answered with a 'no' for equity classification to apply. So, for example, if the *issuer* of the preference share has the option to redeem for cash or for a variable number of its ordinary shares, the first question to ask is: Does the issuer have a contractual obligation to deliver cash? If redemption is at the issuer's option, the issuer has *no* contractual obligation to redeem *at all* and therefore arguably the second question about the number of ordinary shares is irrelevant. Indeed, paragraph 16(b) asks whether or not the issuer has a contractual obligation to deliver a variable number of its own shares and, since redemption is at the issuer's option, it has no such contractual obligation, even though the number of shares that potentially will be issued is variable. Therefore, all other things being equal, the preference shares will be classified as equity. On the other hand, if redemption is at the *holder's* option, the instrument would be classified as a liability, because the issuer has a contractual obligation to deliver cash/other financial assets or ordinary shares because the holder has the right to call for redemption. This is so even if the number of ordinary shares is fixed, because the holder's right to redeem for cash means that paragraph 16(a) is met.

7.5 COMPOUND FINANCIAL INSTRUMENTS

Paragraph 28 of IAS 32 requires an issuer of a non-derivative financial instrument to determine whether it contains both a liability and an equity component. Such components must be classified separately as financial liabilities, financial assets or equity instruments.

Paragraph 29 goes on to explain that this means that an entity recognises separately the components of a financial instrument that (a) creates a financial liability of the entity, and (b) grants an option to the holder of the instrument to convert it into an equity instrument of the entity. A common example of such a financial instrument is a convertible bond or note that entitles the holder to convert the note into a fixed number of ordinary shares of the issuer. From the perspective of the *issuer*, such an instrument comprises two components: (a) a financial liability, being a contractual obligation to deliver cash/other financial assets in the form of interest payments and redemption of the note; and (b) an equity instrument, being an option issued to the holder entitling it to the right, for a specified period of time, to convert the note into a fixed number of ordinary shares of the issuer. Note that the number of shares to be issued must be fixed, otherwise the option would not meet the definition of an equity instrument under paragraph 16(b) *as discussed in section 7.4.1.*

Classification of the liability and equity components is made on initial recognition of the financial instrument and is not revised as a result of a change in the likelihood that the conversion option may be exercised. This is because, until such time as the conversion option is either exercised or lapses, the issuer has a contractual obligation to make future payments.

How does the issuer measure the separate liability and equity components? Paragraphs 31 and 32 of IAS 32 prescribe that the financial liability must be calculated first, with the equity component by definition being the residual. The example in figure 7.3 illustrates how this is done.

FIGURE 7.3 A convertible note, allocating the components between liability and equity

> **Example 4: Compound financial instrument — a convertible note**
>
> Company A issues 2000 convertible notes on 1 July 2013. The notes have a 3-year term and are issued at par with a face value of €1000 per note, giving total proceeds at the date of issue of €2 million. The notes pay interest at 6% annually in arrears. The holder of each note is entitled to convert the note into 250 ordinary shares of Company A at any time up to maturity.
>
> When the notes are issued, the prevailing market interest rate for similar debt (similar term, similar credit status of issuer and similar cash flows) without conversion options is 9%. This rate is higher than the convertible note's rate because the holder of the convertible note is prepared to accept a lower interest rate given the implicit value of its conversion option.

(continued)

FIGURE 7.3 *(continued)*

The issuer calculates the contractual cash flows using the market interest rate (9%) to work out the value of the holder's option, as follows:

Present value of the principal: €2 million payable in 3 years' time:	€ 1 544 367
Present value of the interest: €120 000 (€2 million × 6%) payable annually in arrears for 3 years	€ 303 755
Total liability component	€ 1 848 122
Equity component (by deduction)	€ 151 878
Proceeds of the note issue	€ 2 000 000

The journal entries at the date of issue are as follows:

Cash	Dr	2 000 000	
Financial Liability	Cr		1 848 122
Equity	Cr		151 878

The equity component is not remeasured and thus remains at €151 878 until the note is either converted or redeemed. The liability component accrues interest of 9% until it is redeemed or converted. If the note is converted, the remaining liability component is transferred to equity. If the note is not converted at the end of the 3-year term, the carrying amount has accreted up to €2 000 000 and the notes will be redeemed at €2 000 000. The equity component remains in equity.

Source: Adapted from IAS 32, Illustrative Example 9, paragraphs IE35–IE36.

7.6 INTEREST, DIVIDENDS, GAINS AND LOSSES

IAS 32 requires the statement of profit or loss and other comprehensive income classification of items relating to financial instruments to match their statement of financial position classification. Thus, statement of profit or loss and other comprehensive income items relating to financial liabilities and financial assets are classified as income or expenses, or gains or losses. These are usually interest expense, interest income and dividend income. Distributions to holders of equity instruments are debited directly to equity. Usually these are dividends. These principles also apply to the component parts of a compound financial instrument.

Table 7.2 summarises these principles.

TABLE 7.2 Classification of revenues, expenses and equity distributions

Statement of financial position classification	Statement of profit or loss and other comprehensive income classification	Statement of changes in equity
Equity instrument		Dividends distributed
Financial liability	Interest expense	
Financial asset	Interest income, dividend income	

The transaction costs of an equity transaction are deducted from equity, but only to the extent to which they are incremental costs directly attributable to the equity transaction that otherwise would have been avoided. Examples of such costs include registration and other regulatory fees, legal and accounting fees and stamp duties. These costs are required to be shown separately under IAS 1 *Presentation of Financial Statements.*

7.7 FINANCIAL ASSETS AND FINANCIAL LIABILITIES: SCOPE

The objective of IFRS 9 is to set principles for financial reporting of financial assets and financial liabilities that is relevant and useful to users in assessing the amounts, timing and uncertainty of an entity's future cash flows. As the standard is very complex, particularly in its application to financial institutions, this chapter addresses only the more common applications of IFRS 9 and provides a general understanding of its requirements.

IFRS 9 applies to all entities and to all types of financial instruments, subject to a list of exceptions that in themselves are complicated. Therefore, the following is only an overview of the exceptions:

1. Investments in subsidiaries, associates and joint ventures that are accounted for under IFRS 10, IAS 27 or IAS 28. However, certain investments in such entities may be accounted for under IFRS 9 if so permitted

by IFRS 10, IAS 27 or IAS 28. For example, IAS 27 permits investments in subsidiaries, associates and joint ventures to be carried at fair value under IFRS 9 in the investor's separate financial statements.

2. Rights and obligations under leases to which IAS 17 *Leases* applies. However, certain lease receivables and finance lease payables are subject to the derecognition and impairment provisions of IFRS 9. Also, embedded derivatives in leases are subject to IFRS 9.

3. Employers' rights and obligations under employee benefit plans to which IAS 19 *Employee Benefits* applies.

4. Rights and obligations arising under insurance contracts, with certain exceptions. Insurance contracts are covered by their own standard, but contracts issued by insurers that are not insurance contracts (such as investment contracts) are covered by IFRS 9. Contracts that require a payment based on climatic, geological or other physical variables are commonly used as insurance policies and payment is made based on the amount of loss to the insured entity. These contracts are caught by the standard on insurance contracts and are outside the scope of IFRS 9 under this exemption. However, if the payment under the contract is unrelated to the insured entity's loss, then IFRS 9 applies. IFRS 9 also covers embedded derivatives in such contracts.

5. Financial instruments issued by the entity that meet the definition of an equity instrument in IAS 32. This applies only to the issuer of the equity instrument. The holder of such an instrument will have a financial asset that is covered by IFRS 9.

6. Financial guarantee contracts, such as letters of credit, that provide for specified payments to be made to reimburse the holder of the contract for a loss it incurs because a specified debtor fails to make payment when due under a debt instrument are measured either under IFRS 4 *Insurance Contracts* or IFRS 9 at the election of the issuer.

7. Loan commitments that cannot be settled net in cash or another financial instrument, unless the loan commitment is measured at fair value through profit or loss *(see section 7.9)* under IFRS 9, in which case it is covered by IFRS 9. Loan commitments outside the scope of IFRS 9 are still subject to the impairment requirements *(see section 7.11.5)* of the standard.

8. Contracts between an acquirer and a vendor in a business combination to buy or sell an acquiree at a future date.

9. Financial instruments to which IFRS 2 *Share-based Payment* applies.

10. Rights to payments to reimburse the entity for expenditure it is required to make to settle a liability that it recognises as a liability under IAS 37.

11. Financial instruments within the scope of IFRS 15 *Revenue from Contracts with Customers*, except those for which that standard specifies they should be accounted for under IFRS 9.

As discussed in section 7.2.4, contracts to buy or sell non-financial items are generally not financial instruments. Certain commodity contracts are, however, included within the scope of IAS 32. These include contracts to buy or sell non-financial items that can be settled net (in cash) or by exchanging financial instruments, or in which the non-financial item is readily convertible into cash.

7.7.1 'Own use' contracts

Contracts to buy or sell non-financial items do not generally meet the definition of a financial instrument. However, many such contracts are standardised in form and traded on organised markets in much the same way as some derivative financial instruments. The ability to buy or sell such a contract for cash, the ease with which it may be bought or sold, and the possibility of negotiating a cash settlement of the obligation to receive or deliver the commodity, do not alter the fundamental character of the contract in a way that creates a financial instrument. However, the IASB believes that there are many circumstances where these contracts should be accounted for as if they were financial instruments.

Accordingly, the provisions of IFRS 9 are normally applied to those contracts — effectively as if the contracts were financial instruments — to buy or sell non-financial items (1) that can be settled net in cash or another financial instrument, (2) that can be settled by exchanging financial instruments or (3) in which the non-financial instrument is readily convertible to cash. However, there is an exception for what are commonly termed 'normal' purchases and sales or 'own use' contracts.

The provisions of IFRS 9 are not to be applied to those contracts to buy or sell non-financial items that can be settled net if they were entered into and continue to be held for the purpose of the receipt or delivery of the non-financial item in accordance with the entity's expected purchase, sale or usage requirements (a 'normal' purchase or sale). For example, an entity that enters into a contract to purchase 1000 kg of copper in accordance with its expected usage requirements would not account for such a contract as a derivative under IFRS 9, even if it could be settled net in cash.

IFRS 9 includes a fair value option for those so-called 'own use' contracts. At inception of a contract, an entity may make an irrevocable designation to measure an own use contract at fair value through profit or loss even if it was entered into for the purpose of the receipt or delivery of the non-financial item in accordance with the entity's expected purchase, sale or usage requirement. However, such designation is only allowed if it eliminates or significantly reduces an accounting mismatch.

7.8 DERIVATIVES AND EMBEDDED DERIVATIVES

The concept of a derivative may appear daunting because there are numerous derivative financial instruments in the market that seem complex and difficult to understand. However, as already noted, fundamentally all derivatives simply derive their value from another underlying item such as a share price or an interest rate. Derivative financial instruments create rights and obligations that have the effect of transferring between the parties to the instrument one or more of the financial risks inherent in an underlying primary financial instrument. On inception, derivative financial instruments give one party a contractual right to exchange financial assets or financial liabilities with another party under conditions that are potentially favourable, while the other party has a contractual obligation to exchange under potentially unfavourable conditions.

Figure 7.4 illustrates an option contract as an example of a derivative.

An option contract

Party A buys an option that entitles it to purchase 1000 shares in Company Z at £3 a share, at any time in the next 6 months. The shares in Company Z are the underlying financial instruments from which the option derives its value. The option is thus the derivative financial instrument. The amount of £3 a share is called the exercise price of the option.

Party B sells the option to Party A. Party A is called the holder of the option, and Party B is called the writer of the option. Party A will usually pay an amount called a premium to purchase the option. The amount of the premium is less than what Party A would have to pay for the shares in Company Z.

Assume that at the date of the option contract the market price of shares in Company Z is £2.60.

The financial instrument created by this transaction is a contractual right of Party A to purchase the 1000 shares in Company Z at £3 a share (a financial asset of Party A), and a contractual obligation of Party B to sell the shares in Company Z to Party A at £3 a share (a financial liability of Party B). Party A's right is a financial asset because it has the right to exchange under potentially favourable conditions to itself. Thus, if the share price of Company Z rises above £3, Party A will exercise its option and require Party B to deliver the shares at £3 a share. Party A will have benefited from this transaction by acquiring the shares in Company Z at less than the market price. Conversely, Party B's obligation is a financial liability because it has the obligation to exchange under potentially unfavourable conditions to itself. Thus, if the shares in Company Z rise to £3.20, Party A will purchase the shares from Party B for £3000. If Party A had had to purchase the shares on the market, it would have paid £3200.

Party B may have made a loss from this transaction, depending on whether it already held the shares in Company Z, or had to go out and buy them for £3200 and then sell them to Party A for £3000, or had entered into other derivative contracts with other parties enabling it to purchase the shares at less than £3000.

What if the share price in Company Z never exceeds £3 over the 6-month term of the option? In this case, Party A will not exercise the option and the option will lapse. The option is termed 'out of the money' from Party A's perspective — it has no value to Party A because the exercise price is higher than the market price. Once the share price rises above £3, the option is termed 'in the money'. Party A is not compelled to exercise its option, even if it is in the money. From Party A's perspective, it has a right to exercise the option should it so choose. However, if Party A exercises its option, Party B is then compelled to deliver the shares under its contractual obligation.

IAS 32 notes that the nature of the holder's right and of the writer's obligation is not affected by the likelihood that the option will be exercised.

FIGURE 7.4 How an option contract works

In simple terms, parties to derivative financial instruments are taking bets on what will happen to the underlying financial instrument in the future. In the example in figure 7.4, Party A was taking a bet that the share price in Company Z would rise above £3 within 6 months, and Party B was taking a bet that it would not. Party B would most likely hedge its bet by doing something to protect itself should the market price rise above £3. It could do this by entering into another derivative with another party, enabling Party B to purchase shares from that other party at £3. Often a chain of derivative financial instruments will be created in this way. Party A will probably not know anything about the chain created. *(Hedging is discussed in section 7.13.)*

IAS 32 does not prescribe recognition and measurement rules for derivatives; these are addressed in IFRS 9. Instead, IAS 32 includes derivatives in the definition of financial instruments. Other types of derivatives include interest rate swaps, forward exchange contracts and futures contracts.

7.8.1 Three required characteristics

Appendix A of IFRS 9 defines a derivative. Derivatives derive their value from another underlying item such as a share price or an interest rate. The definition requires all of the following three characteristics to be met:

- its value must change in response to a change in an underlying variable such as a specified interest rate, price, or foreign exchange rate
- it must require no initial net investment or an initial net investment that is smaller than would be required for other types of contracts with similar responses to changes in market factors
- it is settled at a future date.

7.8.2 Examples of derivatives

Typical examples of derivatives are futures and forward, swap and option contracts. A derivative usually has a notional amount, which is an amount of currency, a number of shares or other units specified in a contract. However, a derivative does not require the holder or writer to invest or receive the notional amount at the inception of the contract. In the example in figure 7.4, where Party A buys an option that entitles it to purchase 1000 shares in Company Z at £3 a share at any time in the next 6 months, the 1000 shares is the notional amount. However, a notional amount is not an essential feature of a derivative. For example, a contract may require a fixed payment of £2000 if a specified interest rate increases by a specified percentage. Such a contract is a derivative even though there is no notional amount.

Many option contracts require a premium to be paid to the writer of the option. The premium is less than what would be required to purchase the underlying shares or other underlying financial instruments and thus option contracts meet the definition of a derivative.

7.8.3 Embedded derivatives

Derivatives may exist on a stand-alone basis, or they may be embedded in other financial instruments. An embedded derivative is a component of a hybrid contract that also includes a non-derivative host contract, with the effect that some of the cash flows of the combined instrument vary in a way similar to a stand-alone instrument (IFRS 9 paragraph 4.3.1). An embedded derivative cannot be contractually detached from the host contract, nor can it have a different counterparty from that of the host instrument, as it would otherwise be considered a separate financial instrument.

Separation of embedded derivatives

A derivative should not be separated from the host contract if it is embedded in an asset host that is within the scope of IFRS 9. Instead, an entity should apply the IFRS 9 requirements to such hybrid financial assets in their entirety. Note that the guidance on embedded derivatives still applies to financial *liabilities* scoped within IFRS 9.

If an embedded derivative is separated, it is generally required to be measured at fair value. If fair value of the separated derivative cannot be reliably measured, then the entire hybrid contract must be measured at fair value through profit or loss (IFRS 9 paragraph 4.3.6).

For all embedded derivatives other than those where the host is an asset scoped within IFRS 9, paragraph 4.3.3 of IFRS 9 requires them to be separated from the host contract if, and only if, the following three conditions are met:

- the economic characteristics and risks of the embedded derivative are not closely related to the economic characteristics and risks of the host contract
- a separate instrument with the same terms as the embedded derivative would meet the definition of a derivative
- the hybrid contract is not measured at fair value through profit or loss. This means that a derivative embedded in a hybrid contract measured at fair value through profit or loss is not separated, even if it could be separated, as the separated embedded derivative would be required to be measured at fair value through profit or loss anyway.

The following are examples of instruments scoped within IFRS 9 where the economic characteristics and risks of the embedded derivative are not closely related to the economic characteristics and risks of the host contract (and therefore the embedded derivative must be separated):

- a put option embedded in a debt instrument that allows the holder to require the issuer to reacquire the instrument for an amount of cash that varies on the basis of the change in an equity or commodity price or index. This is because the host is a debt instrument and the variables are not related to the debt instrument
- an option to extend the remaining term to maturity of a debt instrument without a concurrent adjustment to the market rate of interest at the time of the extension
- equity-indexed interest or principal payments embedded in a host debt instrument or insurance contract by which the amount of interest or principal is indexed to a share price
- commodity-indexed interest or principal payments embedded in a host debt instrument or insurance contract by which the amount of interest or principal is indexed to the price of the commodity (such as gold).

A common example of an underlying contract not scoped within IFRS 9 where entities need to determine whether an embedded derivative needs to be separated is one where an entity enters into a purchase of sale contract in a currency other than its functional currency. IFRS 9 stipulates that the embedded foreign currency derivative in the host contract is only closely related to the host contract if (i) the host contract is not leveraged and (ii) does not contain option features and (iii) is denominated in either (a) the currency of one of the counterparties to the contract or (b) the currency in which the price of the related good or service is routinely denominated such as the USD for oil, or (c) a currency that is commonly used in the specific economic environment.

IFRS 9 contains further examples of such instruments. In addition, it also gives examples of instruments where the economic characteristics and risks of the embedded derivative are closely related to the economic characteristics and risks of the host contract. These examples are very prescriptive and not clearly principle-based.

7.9 FINANCIAL ASSETS AND FINANCIAL LIABILITIES: CATEGORIES OF FINANCIAL INSTRUMENTS

7.9.1 Financial assets

During the credit crisis commentators argued that IAS 39 contained too many categories of financial assets, that were not geared to the various business models, in particular of banks, and was not flexible enough to allow preparers to reclassify, for example when their business model changes. Some also argued that IAS 39 was biased towards the fair value model rather than the cost model.

In response to this feedback the IASB issued an initial proposal with only three categories of financial assets, no options and rigid criteria to classify financial assets which included the business model test. In the course of the consideration of these proposals though, several options and additional categories were introduced and the criteria for classification were changed, including an additional business model to accommodate the insurance sector. The categories and the criteria for classification in the final standard are described below.

IFRS 9 has the following measurement categories for financial assets:
- Debt instruments at amortised cost.
- Debt instruments at fair value through other comprehensive income (FVOCI) with cumulative gains and losses reclassified to profit or loss upon derecognition.
- Equity instruments designated as measured at FVOCI with gains and losses remaining in other comprehensive income (OCI) without subsequent reclassification to profit or loss.
- Debt instruments, derivatives and equity instruments at fair value through profit or loss (FVPL).

The classification is based on both the entity's business model for managing the financial assets and the contractual cash flow characteristics of the financial asset, as set out in figure 7.5.

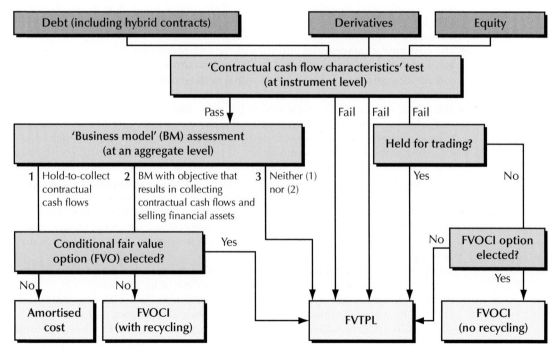

FIGURE 7.5 The categories of financial assets

Table 7.3 sets out the requirements of IFRS 9 in further detail.

TABLE 7.3 The categories of financial assets			
Category	Characteristics of the instrument	Business model and other requirements	Examples
Debt instruments measured at amortised cost	The asset's contractual cash flows represent 'solely payments of principle and interest' (SPPI)	The asset is held within a 'hold to collect' business model whose objective is to collect contractual cash flows	Commercial bill investments; government bonds; corporate bonds; accounts receivable; mortgage loans
Debt instruments at fair value through other comprehensive income	The asset's contractual cash flows represent 'solely payments of principal and interest'	Held within a 'hold to collect and sell' business model whose objective is achieved by both collecting contractual cash flows and selling financial assets	Commercial bill investments; government bonds; corporate bonds; mortgage loans
Equity instruments designated as measured at FVOCI	Equity instrument	Designation of the equity instrument not held for trading as measured at FVOCI with gains and losses remaining in other comprehensive income	Shares
Debt instruments, derivatives and equity instruments at fair value through profit or loss	Any financial asset	Debt instruments that fail the business model tests above Debt instruments that are designated at fair value through profit or loss because it reduces or eliminates a measurement or recognition inconsistency Equity instruments that are not designated as measured at FVOCI	Commercial bill investments; government bonds; corporate bonds Share portfolio held for short-term gains Forward exchange contracts; interest rate swaps; call options

Business models

An entity's business model for managing financial assets is a matter of fact typically observable through particular activities that the entity undertakes to achieve its stated objectives. An entity will need to use judgement to assess its business model for managing financial assets and that assessment is not determined by a single factor or activity. Rather, the entity must consider all relevant evidence that is available at the date of the assessment.

The business model assessment is not an instrument-by-instrument assessment, but it takes place at a higher level of aggregation, which is the level at which the key decision makers manage groups or portfolios of financial assets to achieve the business objective. IFRS 9 distinguishes between three types of business model:

1. In a 'hold to collect' business model, management's objective is to collect the instrument's contractual cash flows. Although IFRS 9 is slightly vague about the role of sales, expected future sales are the key determining factor and past sales are of relevance only as a source of evidence. Portfolios in which the expected sales are more than infrequent and significant in value do not meet the criteria of a 'hold to collect' business model. A typical example of such a business model is a liquidity buffer portfolio where an entity only sells assets in rare 'stress case' scenarios.
2. In the 'hold to collect and sell' business model, the entity's key management personnel have made a decision that both collecting contractual cash flows and selling are fundamental to achieving the objective of the business model. For example, the objective of the business model may be to manage everyday liquidity needs, to achieve a particular interest yield profile or to match the duration of financial assets to the duration of the liabilities that those assets are funding. To achieve these objectives, the entity will both collect contractual cash flows and sell the financial assets. This business model will typically involve greater frequency and value of sales than the 'hold to collect' business model.

3. In other business models, financial assets are held for trading or are managed on a fair value basis. In each case, the entity manages the financial assets with the objective of realising cash flows through the sale of the assets and the entity's objective will typically result in active buying and selling. Although the entity might hold certain assets for longer periods, this, however, is purely incidental and not essential to this business model.

Cash flow characteristics

The assessment of the characteristics of the contractual cash flows is done at the individual financial asset level and aims to identify whether the contractual cash flows are solely payments of principal and interest (SPPI) on the principal amount outstanding. For the purposes of the SPPI test, interest is typically the compensation for the time value of money and credit risk, but may also include consideration for other basic lending risks (e.g. liquidity risk) and costs (e.g. servicing or administrative costs) associated with holding the financial asset for a period of time, as well as a profit margin.

The SPPI test is designed to screen out financial assets for which the application of the effective interest method either is not viable from a purely mechanical standpoint (e.g. a share where the cash flows simply cannot be reflected by the effective interest method) or does not provide useful information about the uncertainty, timing and amount of the financial asset's contractual cash flows (e.g. a debt instrument that is linked to a commodity price where variability of cash flows is largely caused by the change in the commodity price). Accordingly, the SPPI test is based on the premise that the application of the effective interest method only provides useful information when the variability in the contractual cash flows arises to maintain the holder's return in line with a basic lending arrangement.

Sometimes, contractual provisions may modify the cash flows of an instrument so that it does not give rise only to a straightforward repayment of principal and interest. However, financial assets may still meet the SPPI test if:

- the contractual cash flow characteristic has only a *de minimis* (i.e. very minor) effect on the contractual cash flows of the financial asset
- the contractual cash flow characteristic is *not genuine*, i.e. it affects the instrument's contractual cash flows only on the occurrence of an event that is extremely rare, highly abnormal and very unlikely to occur
- the entity can determine, quantitatively or qualitatively, that the contractual cash flows that have a modified time value of money element of interest (e.g. a 6-month loan that pays 12-month LIBOR has such an element) do not differ significantly from the cash flows on a benchmark instrument that represent solely payments of principal and interest on the principal outstanding), or
- the interest rate is set by government or a regulatory authority. In such a case, the interest rate may be considered a proxy for the time value of money element for applying the contractual cash flow characteristics test if that regulated interest rate meets certain conditions.

Many financial assets have characteristics that could cause them to fail the SPPI test, even though they arise in the course of regular lending operations in the economy. Therefore, the IASB included detailed guidance in IFRS 9 — that deals with contingent events affecting cash flows, prepayment and extension options, contractually linked instruments and non-recourse lending — in order to limit the circumstances in which these instruments would have to be measured at fair value.

7.9.2 Financial liabilities

IFRS 9 has the following measurement categories for financial liabilities:
- Financial liabilities at amortised cost.
- Financial liabilities at fair value through profit or loss.

The classification of financial liabilities under IFRS 9 does not follow the approach for the classification of financial assets, but follows the approach set out in Table 7.4.

TABLE 7.4 The categories of financial liabilities

Category	Characteristics of the instrument	Other requirements	Examples
Financial liabilities at fair value through profit or loss	Financial liabilities	Financial liabilities that meet the definition of held for trading Financial liabilities that are designated at fair value through profit or loss because it reduces or eliminates a measurement or recognition inconsistency	Bond issues; short positions in trading; derivatives
Financial liabilities at amortised cost	Financial liabilities	Financial liabilities that do not fall into the above category	Bond issues; trade creditors

Note that derivative financial liabilities are deemed to meet the definition of held for trading and are measured at fair value through profit or loss.

For financial liabilities that do not meet the definition of held for trading, but are designated as at fair value through profit or loss, the element of gains or losses attributable to changes in the entity's own credit risk is normally recognised in OCI. This avoids the counterintuitive effect of a deterioration of an entity's credit standing resulting in a gain recognised in profit and loss *(see section 3.5 on fair value measurement)*. However, if this creates or enlarges an accounting mismatch in profit or loss, gains and losses must be entirely presented in profit or loss.

7.10 FINANCIAL ASSETS AND FINANCIAL LIABILITIES: RECOGNITION CRITERIA

IFRS 9 states that an entity shall recognise a financial asset or a financial liability in its statement of financial position when, and only when, the entity becomes a party to the contractual provisions of the instrument. The standard provides examples of applying the recognition criteria, as follows:

- Unconditional receivables and payables are recognised as assets or liabilities when the entity becomes a party to the contract and, consequently, has a legal right to receive or a legal obligation to pay cash. Normal trade debtors and trade creditors would fall into this category.
- Assets to be acquired and liabilities to be incurred under a firm commitment to purchase or sell goods or services are generally not recognised until at least one of the parties has performed under the agreement. However, this is subject to the rules set out in the scope paragraph of IFRS 9 *(discussed in section 7.7)*. Thus, if a firm commitment to buy or sell non-financial items is within the scope of IFRS 9, its net fair value is recognised as an asset or liability on the commitment date.
- A forward contract within the scope of the standard is also recognised as an asset or liability at the commitment date. When an entity becomes party to a forward contract, the rights and obligations at the commitment date are often equal, so that the net fair value of the forward is zero.
  Note the following:
- Option contracts within the scope of the standard are recognised as assets or liabilities when the holder or writer becomes a party to the contract.
- Planned future transactions, no matter how likely, are not assets and liabilities because the entity has not become a party to a contract.

7.11 FINANCIAL ASSETS AND FINANCIAL LIABILITIES: MEASUREMENT

The measurement rules in IFRS 9 address:
1. initial measurement
2. subsequent measurement
3. reclassifications
4. gains and losses
5. impairment and uncollectability of financial assets.

The rules are applied distinctly to each of the categories of financial instruments *discussed in section 7.9*.

7.11.1 Initial measurement

Paragraph 5.1.1 of IFRS 9 requires that, on initial recognition, financial assets and financial liabilities must be measured at fair value. Fair value is defined by IFRS 13 as:

> the price that would be received to sell an asset or paid to transfer a liability in an orderly transaction between market participants at the measurement date.

The concept of fair value is discussed in chapter 3.

In addition, paragraph 5.1.1 requires that transaction costs directly attributable to the acquisition or issue of the financial asset or liability must be added to or deducted from the fair value, except for financial assets and liabilities measured at fair value through profit or loss. Transaction costs are defined in IFRS 9 as:

> incremental costs that are directly attributable to the acquisition, issue or disposal of a financial asset or financial liability (see paragraph B5.4.8). An incremental cost is one that would not have been incurred if the entity had not acquired, issued or disposed of the financial instrument.

Paragraph B5.4.8 of IFRS 9 provides further guidance. Examples of transaction costs include fees and commissions paid to agents, advisers, brokers and dealers; levies by regulatory agencies and securities exchanges; and transfer taxes and duties (such as stamp duties). Transaction costs do not include debt premiums or discounts, financing costs or internal administrative or holding costs.

The fair value of a financial instrument on initial recognition is normally the transaction price (the fair value of the consideration given or received). However, if part of the consideration given or received is for something other than the financial instrument, then the fair value must be estimated using valuation techniques. For example, if a company provides an interest-free loan to its employees, part of the consideration is given in the form of recognition of employee services or loyalty rather than for the entire loan itself. The fair value of the loan must be calculated by discounting the future cash flows using a market rate of interest for a similar loan (similar as to currency, term and credit rating). Any additional amount lent is accounted for as an expense unless it qualifies for recognition as some other type of asset. Figure 7.6 provides an example.

Initial measurement of an interest-free loan

Company Z provides interest-free loans to 10 employees for a 5-year term, payable at the end of 5 years. The total loan amount is $200 000. A market rate of interest for a similar 5-year loan is 5%.

The present value of this receivable, being the future cash flows discounted at 5%, is approximately $157 000. Therefore, $43 000 is an employee expense to Company Z. Depending on the terms of the loan, this employee expense is either recognised immediately (e.g. if the employee can continue to benefit from the interest free loan even if he/she stops providing employee services), or deferred over the period that the employee is required to provide employee services to continue to benefit from the interest-free loan (e.g. if the loan needs to be repaid immediately on termination of employment).

Company Z would record the following journal entries:

Loans Receivable	Dr	157 000	
(Deferred) Expenses	Dr	43 000	
Cash	Cr		200 000

FIGURE 7.6 Initial measurement of an interest-free loan

7.11.2 Subsequent measurement

Subsequent measurement depends on whether or not the item is a financial asset or financial liability, and on which of the categories applies.

Financial assets are measured as follows:

1. At amortised cost — debt instruments measured at amortised cost.
2. At fair value —
   (i) Debt instruments at fair value through other comprehensive income
   (ii) Equity instruments designated as measured at fair value through other comprehensive income
   (iii) Debt instruments, derivatives and equity instruments at fair value through profit or loss.

If any of these financial assets are hedged items, they are subject to the hedge accounting measurement rules (see section 7.13).

Amortised cost is defined in IFRS 9 as follows:

> The amount at which the financial asset or financial liability is measured at initial recognition minus the principal repayments, plus or minus the cumulative amortisation using the effective interest method of any difference between that initial amount and the maturity amount and, for financial assets, adjusted for any loss allowance.

The effective interest method calculates the amortised cost of a financial asset or a financial liability and allocates interest revenue or interest expense in profit or loss over the relevant period. The effective interest rate is defined by IFRS 9 as:

> The rate that exactly discounts estimated future cash payments or receipts through the expected life of the financial asset or financial liability to the gross carrying amount of a financial asset [which is the asset's amortised cost before deducting any loss allowance] or to the amortised cost of a financial liability.

The effective interest rate must be calculated considering all contractual terms of the instrument. It includes all fees, transaction costs, premiums and discounts.

Illustrative example 7.1 provides an example of how amortised cost is calculated.

ILLUSTRATIVE EXAMPLE 7.1 Calculation of amortised cost (based on IFRS 9, Implementation Guidance B.26)

Cape Ventures purchases a debt instrument at 1 January 2016 with a 5-year term for its fair value of $1000 (including transaction costs). The instrument has a principal amount of $1250 (the amount payable on redemption) and carries fixed interest of 4.7% annually. The annual cash interest income is thus $59 ($1250 × 0.047). Using a financial calculator, the effective interest rate is calculated as 10%. The debt instrument is classified as at amortised cost.

The following table sets out the cash flows and interest income for each period, using the effective interest rate of 10%:

A. Year	B. Amortised cost at beginning of year	C. Interest income (B × 10%)	D. Cash flows	E. Amortised cost at end of year (B + C − D)
2016	1 000	100	59	1 041
2017	1 041	104	59	1 086
2018	1 086	109	59	1 136
2019	1 136	113	59	1 190
2020	1 190	119	59 + 1 250	−

The journal entries to record this transaction on initial recognition and throughout the life of the instrument are as follows:

On initial recognition at 1 January 2016:

Debt instrument measured at amortised cost	Dr	1 000
Cash	Cr	1 000

On recognition of interest in 2016:

Debt instrument measured at amortised cost	Dr	41
Cash	Dr	59
Interest Income	Cr	100

On recognition of interest in 2017:

Debt instrument measured at amortised cost	Dr	45
Cash	Dr	59
Interest Income	Cr	104

On recognition of interest in 2018:

Debt instrument measured at amortised cost	Dr	50
Cash	Dr	59
Interest Income	Cr	109

On recognition of interest in 2019:

Debt instrument measured at amortised cost	Dr	54
Cash	Dr	59
Interest Income	Cr	113

On recognition of interest in 2020:

Debt instrument measured at amortised cost	Dr	60
Cash	Dr	59
Interest Income	Cr	119

On redemption of investment at 31 December 2020:

Cash	Dr	1 250
Debt instrument measured at amortised cost	Cr	1 250

Financial liabilities are measured subsequent to initial recognition at amortised cost except for those designated as 'at fair value through profit or loss', which must be measured at fair value (IFRS 9 paragraph 4.2.2). There are four exceptions to this rule:

1. Financial liabilities arising in certain circumstances when a financial asset is transferred under the derecognition rules. These are outside the scope of this chapter.
2. Financial guarantee contracts (*see section 7.7*). These are initially measured at fair value and subsequently at the *higher* of:
   (i) the amount determined in accordance with the IFRS 9 requirements on impairment (*see section 7.11.5*) and
   (ii) the amount initially recognised less, where appropriate, cumulative amortisation recognised in accordance with IFRS 15 *Revenue from Contracts with Customers.*

   A common example of a financial guarantee contract is when a parent company guarantees the debts of its subsidiary to an external financier. The parent undertakes to pay the financier in the event that the subsidiary is unable to pay.
3. Commitments to provide a loan at a below-market interest rate. The measurement rules are the same as for (2) above.
4. Contingent consideration recognised in a business combination should be measured at fair value with changes recognised in profit or loss.

If any of these financial liabilities are hedged items, they are subject to the hedge accounting measurement rules (*see section 7.13*). If any of the financial liabilities are measured at fair value, an entity would need to apply the specific requirements for effect of its own credit risk (*see section 7.9.2*).

Illustrative example 7.2 provides an example of a financial liability measured at amortised cost.

ILLUSTRATIVE EXAMPLE 7.2 A financial liability measured at amortised cost

Lenglen enters into an agreement with Bartoli to lend it $1 million on 1 January 2016. Bartoli incurs transaction costs of $25 000. The interest to be paid is 5% for each of the first 2 years and 7% for each of the next 2 years, annually in arrears. The loan must be repaid after 4 years. The annual cash interest expense is thus $50 000 ($1 million × 0.05) for each of the first 2 years and $70 000 ($1 million × 0.07) for each of the next 2 years. Using a financial calculator, the effective interest rate is calculated as 6.67%. Bartoli measures the financial liability at fair value on initial recognition and subsequently at amortised cost in accordance with IFRS 9.

The following table sets out the cash flows and interest expense for each period, using the effective interest rate of 6.67%.

A. Year	B. Amortised cost at beginning of year	C. Interest income (B × 6.67%)	D. Cash flows	E. Amortised cost at end of year (B + C − D)
2016	975 000	65 014	50 000	990 014
2017	990 014	66 015	50 000	1 006 029
2018	1 066 029	67 083	70 000	1 003 112
2019	1 003 112	66 888	70 000 + 1 000 000	–

The journal entries to record this transaction on initial recognition and throughout the life of the instrument in the books of Bartoli are as follows:

On initial recognition in 2016:

Cash	Dr	975 000	
Bond – Liability	Dr	25 000	
Bond – Liability	Cr		1 000 000

On recognition of interest in 2016:

Interest Expense	Dr	65 014	
Bond – Liability	Cr		15 014
Cash	Cr		50 000

On recognition of interest in 2017:

Interest Expense	Dr	65 015	
Bond – Liability	Cr		16 015
Cash	Cr		50 000

On recognition of interest in 2018:

Interest Expense	Dr	67 083	
Bond – Liability	Dr	2 917	
Cash	Cr		70 000

On recognition of interest in 2019:

Interest Expense	Dr	66 888	
Bond – Liability	Dr	3 112	
Cash	Cr		70 000

On repayment of liability in 2019:

Interest Expense	Dr	0	
Bond – Liability	Dr	1 000 000	
Cash	Cr		1 000 000

7.11.3 Reclassifications

IFRS 9 contains various prescriptive rules on the reclassification of financial instruments. The rules are aimed at preventing inconsistent gain or loss recognition and the use of arbitrage between the categories. In summary:

- In certain rare circumstances when an entity changes its business model for managing financial assets, non-derivative debt assets are required to be reclassified between the amortised cost, fair value through profit or loss, and fair value through other comprehensive income categories. Changes in the business model for managing financial assets are expected to be very rare and occur for example when an entity acquires a new business or disposes of an existing business. A business model may develop over time in a way that it no longer meets the requirements of the initial measurement category. Those cases are not reclassifications and existing assets remain in the old category while new assets are classified taking into consideration the new business model.
- Equity instruments measured at fair value through other comprehensive income and financial liabilities should not be reclassified.
- The following changes in circumstances are not reclassifications:
  - when an item is designated as (or ceases to be) an effective hedging instrument in a cash flow hedge or net investment hedge
  - changes in measurement in accordance with the guidance on designation of credit exposure as measured at fair value through profit or loss *(see section 7.13.5)*.

7.11.4 Gains and losses

A gain or loss on a financial asset or financial liability that is measured at fair value is recognised in profit or loss unless:

1. it is part of a hedge relationship
2. it is an investment in an equity instrument for which the gains and losses are recognised in other comprehensive income
3. it is a financial liability for which the entity is required to present the effects of changes in own credit risk in other comprehensive income, or
4. it is a debt instrument at fair value through other comprehensive income — a gain or loss is recognised in profit or loss when the financial asset is derecognised, reclassified to measurement at fair value through profit or loss, through the amortisation process or in order to recognise impairment gains or losses.

A gain or loss on a financial instrument that is measured at amortised cost and is not part of a hedging relationship should be recognised in profit or loss when:
1. financial assets are derecognised, reclassified to measurement at fair value through profit or loss, through the amortisation process or in order to recognise impairment gains or losses
2. financial liabilities are derecognised through the amortisation process.

7.11.5 Impairment and uncollectability of financial assets

Background

In April 2009, *as mentioned in section 7.1*, the leaders of the G-20 called upon accounting standard setters to strengthen accounting recognition of loan-loss provisions by incorporating a broader range of credit information. During the financial crisis, the delayed recognition of credit losses associated with loans and other financial instruments was identified as a weakness in existing accounting standards. This is primarily because the impairment requirements under IAS 39 were based on an 'incurred loss model', i.e. credit losses were not recognised until a credit loss event occurs. The IASB has sought to address the concerns about the delayed recognition of credit losses by introducing in IFRS 9 a forward-looking expected credit loss model.

The expected credit loss model applies to:
- financial debt assets measured at amortised cost or at fair value through other comprehensive income under IFRS 9 (which include debt instruments such as loans, debt securities and trade receivables)
- loan commitments and financial guarantee contracts that are not accounted for at fair value through profit or loss under IFRS 9
- contracts assets under the revenue standard IFRS 15
- lease receivables under IAS 17.

General approach

Under the general approach, entities must recognise expected credit losses in two stages. For credit exposures where there has not been a significant increase in credit risk since initial recognition (Stage 1), entities are required to provide for credit losses that result from default events 'that are possible' within the next 12 months. For those credit exposures where there has been a significant increase in credit risk since initial recognition (Stage 2), a loss allowance is required for credit losses expected over the remaining life of the exposure irrespective of the timing of the default.

An entity should determine whether the risk of a default occurring over the expected life of the financial instrument has increased significantly between the date of initial recognition and the reporting date. In making that assessment, an entity should not consider collateral as this only affects the expected credit loss but not the risk of a default occurring. An entity should make this assessment considering all reasonable and supportable information (including forward-looking information) that is available without undue cost or effort. IFRS 9 provides a non-exhaustive list of information — such as external market indicators, internal factors and borrower-specific information — that may be relevant in making the assessment. Some factors and indicators may not be identifiable at the level of individual financial instruments and should be assessed at a higher level of aggregation (e.g. portfolio level).

If financial assets become credit-impaired (Stage 3), interest revenue would be calculated by applying the effective interest rate to the amortised cost (net of loss allowance) rather than the gross carrying amount. Financial assets are assessed as credit-impaired using the following criteria in Appendix A of IFRS 9:

(a) significant financial difficulty of the borrower
(b) a breach of contract or default in interest or principal payments
(c) a lender granting concessions related to the borrower's financial difficulty that the lender would not otherwise consider
(d) it becoming probable that a borrower will enter bankruptcy or other financial reorganisation (such as administration)
(e) the disappearance of an active market for the financial asset because of financial difficulties
(f) the purchase or origination of a financial asset at a deep discount that reflects the incurred credit losses.

IFRS 9 does not define 'default', but is clear that default is broader than failure to pay and entities would need to consider other qualitative indicators of default (e.g. covenant breaches). IFRS 9 requires an entity to apply a definition of 'default' that is consistent with the definition used for internal credit risk management purposes. However, there is a presumption that default does not occur later than when a financial asset is 90 days past due unless an entity can demonstrate that a more lagging default criterion is more appropriate.

Figure 7.7 provides an overview of the three stages of the model, the recognition of expected credit losses and the presentation of interest revenue.

← Change in credit quality since initial recognition →		
Stage 1 Performing Initial recognition	Stage 2 Underperforming Assets with a significant increase in credit risk	Stage 3 Non-performing Credit-impaired assets
Recognition of expected credit losses		
12-month expected credit losses	Lifetime expected credit losses	Lifetime expected credit losses
Interest revenue		
Effective interest on gross carrying amount	Effective interest on gross carrying amount	Effective interest on amortised cost (net of loss allowance)

FIGURE 7.7 Overview of the model

When applying the general approach, a number of operational simplifications and presumptions are available to help entities assess significant increases in credit risk since initial recognition:
• If a financial instrument has low credit risk (equivalent to investment grade quality), then an entity may assume that no significant increases in credit risk have occurred.
• If forward-looking information (either on an individual or collective basis) is not available, there is a rebuttable presumption that credit risk has increased significantly when contractual payments are more than 30 days past due.
• The change in risk of a default occurring in the next 12 months may often be used as an approximation for the change in risk of a default occurring over the remaining life.

Simplified approach
IFRS 9 also provides a simplified approach that does not require the tracking of changes in credit risk, but instead requires the recognition of lifetime expected credit losses at all times.

The simplified approach must be applied to trade receivables or contract assets that do not contain a significant financing component. However, for trade receivables or contract assets that contain a significant financing component, and for lease receivables, entities have an accounting policy choice to apply either the simplified approach or the general approach. Entities may want to apply the general approach despite its complexity, because it would result in a lower loss allowance for receivables with a term of less than 12 months. This accounting policy choice should be applied consistently, but can be applied independently to trade receivables, contract assets and lease receivables.

Purchased or originated credit-impaired financial assets
The general approach does not apply to financial assets for which there is evidence of impairment upon purchase or origination. Instead of recognising a separate loss allowance, the expected credit loss would be reflected in a (higher) credit-adjusted effective interest rate. Subsequently, entities would recognise in profit or loss the amount of any change in lifetime expected credit loss as an impairment gain or loss.

Measurement of expected credit losses
Lifetime expected credit losses should be estimated based on the present value of all cash shortfalls over the remaining life of the financial instrument. The 12-month expected credit losses are also based on the present value of cash shortfalls over the remaining life of the financial instruments, but only take into account the shortfalls resulting from default events that are expected to occur within the 12 months after the reporting date.

In measuring expected credit losses, entities would need to take into account:
• The period over which to estimate expected credit losses: entities would consider the maximum contractual period (including extension options). However, for revolving credit facilities (e.g. credit cards and overdrafts), this period extends beyond the contractual period over which the entities are exposed to credit risk and the expected credit losses would not be mitigated by credit risk management actions. This is to be calculated based on historical experience.
• Probability-weighted outcomes: although entities do not need to identify every possible scenario, they will need to take into account the possibility that a credit loss occurs, no matter how low that possibility is. This is not the same as the most likely outcome or a single best estimate.
• Time value of money: for financial assets, the expected credit losses are discounted to the reporting date using the effective interest rate that is determined at initial recognition and may be approximated. For loan commitments and financial guarantee contracts, the effective interest rate of the resulting asset

will be applied and if this is not determinable, then the current rate representing the risk of the cash flows is used.

- Reasonable and supportable information: entities need to consider information that is reasonably available at the reporting date about past events, current conditions and forecasts of future economic conditions.

The expected credit loss calculation considers the amount and the timing of payments, which means that a credit loss arises even if an entity expects to be paid in full but later than when those payments are contractually due.

Impairment losses are recognised as follows in the statement of financial position for the different categories of financial assets:

(a) Debt instruments measured at amortised cost — an entity should recognise a loss allowance in its statement of financial position that reduces the carrying amount of these financial instruments.

(b) Debt instruments measured at fair value through other comprehensive income — an entity should recognise the loss allowance in other comprehensive income and not reduce the carrying amount of the financial asset in the statement of financial position.

The impairment rules do not apply to equity instruments designated as measured at fair value through other comprehensive income and they do not apply to debt instruments, derivatives and equity instruments at fair value through profit or loss.

Illustrative example 7.3 demonstrates the calculation of an impairment loss for a debt instrument measured at amortised cost.

ILLUSTRATIVE EXAMPLE 7.3 12-month expected credit loss measurement for a debt instrument measured at amortised cost

Nurul Bank originates 2000 loans with a total gross carrying amount of €50 000 000. Nurul Bank segments its portfolio into two borrower groups (Groups Bagus and Roti) based on shared credit risk characteristics at initial recognition. Group Bagus comprises 1000 loans with a gross carrying amount per client of €20 000, for a total gross carrying amount of €20 000 000. Group Roti comprises 1000 loans with a gross carrying amount per client of €30 000, for a total gross carrying amount of €30 000 000. There are no transaction costs and the loan contracts include no options (for example, prepayment or call options), premiums or discounts, points paid, or other fees.

Nurul Bank measures expected credit losses based on a loss rate approach for Groups Bagus and Roti. In order to develop its loss rates, Nurul Bank considers samples of its own historical default and loss experience for those types of loans. In addition, Nurul Bank considers forward-looking information, and updates its historical information for current economic conditions as well as reasonable and supportable forecasts of future economic conditions. Historically, for a population of 1000 loans in each group, Group Bagus's loss rates are 0.3%, based on four defaults, and historical loss rates for Group Roti are 0.15%, based on two defaults.

	Number of clients in sample	Estimated per client gross carrying amount at default	Total estimated gross carrying amount at default	Historic per annum average defaults	Estimated total gross carrying amount at default	Present value of observed loss	Loss rate
Group	A	B	C = A × B	D	E = B × D	F	G = F ÷ C
Bagus	1 000	€20 000	€20 000 000	4	€80 000	€60 000	0.30%
Roti	1 000	€30 000	€30 000 000	2	€60 000	€45 000	0.15%
			€50 000 000			€105 000	

Nurul Bank would account for the following journal entry when it originates the loans that are measured at amortised cost as follows:

Investment in debt instrument	Dr	49 895 000	
Impairment loss (profit or loss)	Dr	105 000	
Cash	Cr		50 000 000

The expected credit losses should be discounted using the effective interest rate; however, for the purposes of this example, the present value of the observed loss is assumed.

At the reporting date, Nurul Bank expects an increase in defaults over the next 12 months compared to the historical rate. As a result, Nurul Bank estimates five defaults in the next 12 months for loans in Group Bagus and three for loans in Group Roti. It estimates that the present value of the observed credit loss per client will remain consistent with the historical loss per client.

Based on the expected life of the loans, Nurul Bank determines that the expected increase in defaults does not represent a significant increase in credit risk since initial recognition for the portfolios. Based on its forecasts, Nurul Bank measures the loss allowance at an amount equal to 12-month expected credit losses on the 1000 loans in each group amounting to €75 000 and €67 500 respectively. This equates to a loss rate in the first year of 0.375% for Group Bagus and 0.225% for Group Roti.

	Number of clients in sample	Estimated per client gross carrying amount at default	Total estimated gross carrying amount at default	Expected defaults	Estimated total gross carrying amount at default	Present value of observed loss	Loss rate
Group	A	B	C = A × B	D	E = B × D	F	G = F ÷ C
Bagus	1 000	€20 000	€20 000 000	5	€100 000	€75 000	0.375%
Roti	1 000	€30 000	€30 000 000	3	€90 000	€67 500	0.225%
			€50 000 000			€142 500	

Nurul Bank uses the loss rates of 0.375% and 0.225% respectively to estimate 12-month expected credit losses on new loans in Group Bagus and Group Roti originated during the year and for which credit risk has not increased significantly since initial recognition.

Nurul Bank would account for the increase in the 12-month expected credit losses on the debt instruments as follows:

Impairment loss (profit or loss)	Dr	37 500	
Investment in debt	Cr		37 500
instrument			

Illustrative example 7.4 shows the calculation of an impairment loss on a debt instrument measured at fair value through other comprehensive income.

ILLUSTRATIVE EXAMPLE 7.4 Impairment loss on a debt instrument measured at fair value through other comprehensive income

Branislava Ventures purchases a debt instrument with a fair value of £1 000 000 on 15 December 2016 and measures the debt instrument at fair value through other comprehensive income (FVOCI). The instrument has an interest rate of 5% over the contractual term of 10 years, and has a 5% effective interest rate. At initial recognition Branislava Ventures determines that the asset is not purchased or originated credit-impaired.

Branislava Ventures would account for the following journal entry to recognise the investment in the debt instrument measured at fair value through other comprehensive income:

Investment in debt instrument	Dr	1 000 000	
Cash	Cr		1 000 000

On 31 December 2016 (the reporting date), the fair value of the debt instrument has decreased to £950 000 because of changes in market interest rates. Branislava Ventures determines that there has not been a significant increase in credit risk since initial recognition and that expected credit losses should be measured at an amount equal to 12-month expected credit losses, which amounts to £30 000. For simplicity, journal entries for the receipt of interest revenue are not provided.

Branislava Ventures would account for the recognition of the 12-month expected credit losses and other fair value changes on the debt instrument as follows:

Impairment loss (profit or loss)	Dr	30 000	
Other comprehensive income	Dr	20 000	
Investment in debt instrument	Cr		50 000

Disclosure would be provided about the accumulated impairment amount of £30 000.

On 1 January 2017, Branislava Ventures decides to sell the debt instrument for £950 000, which is its fair value at that date. Branislava Ventures would derecognise the fair value through other comprehensive income asset and recycle amounts accumulated in other comprehensive income to profit or loss (i.e. £20 000) as follows:

Cash	Dr	950 000	
Investment in debt instrument	Cr		950 000
Loss (profit or loss)	Dr	20 000	
Other comprehensive income	Cr		20 000

7.11.6 Summary of the measurement rules of IFRS 9

Table 7.5 summarises the measurement rules of IFRS 9 *discussed earlier in this section.*

TABLE 7.5 Summary of the measurement rules in IFRS 9

Category of financial asset/liability	Initial measurement	Subsequent measurement	Reclassifications	Gains and losses	Impairment
Debt instruments measured at amortised cost	Fair value plus transaction costs	Amortised cost	Only when an entity changes its business model	Recognised in profit or loss, unless a hedged item	Changes in the expected credit loss allowance recognised in profit or loss
Debt instruments at fair value through other comprehensive income	Fair value plus transaction costs	Fair value	Only when an entity changes its business model	Recognised in other comprehensive income, but recycled to profit or loss upon derecognition	Changes in the expected credit loss allowance recognised in profit or loss with offset in other comprehensive income
Equity instruments designated as measured at FVOCI	Fair value	Fair value	Not permitted	Recognised in other comprehensive income without recycling to profit or loss	Not applicable
Debt instruments, derivatives and equity instruments at fair value through profit or loss	Fair value	Fair value	Debt instruments: only when an entity changes its business model. Other instruments: not permitted	Recognised in profit or loss, unless a hedging instrument or hedged item	Not applicable
Financial liabilities at fair value through profit or loss	Fair value	Fair value	Not permitted	Recognised in profit or loss, unless a hedging instrument or hedged item	Not applicable
Financial liabilities at amortised cost	Fair value less transaction costs	Amortised cost	Not permitted	Recognised in profit or loss, unless a hedged item	Not applicable

7.12 FINANCIAL ASSETS AND FINANCIAL LIABILITIES: OFFSETTING

Often two entities may have both financial assets and financial liabilities in relation to each other. For example, a customer may have returned some goods to a supplier and expects repayment (financial asset) from the supplier while at the same time receiving invoices for new deliveries from the same supplier (financial liability). Or an entity may have multiple accounts with the same bank, some of which may have a debit balance (financial asset) while others may have a credit balance (financial liability). In those cases the question arises whether those financial assets and financial liabilities can be presented net (offset). This of course may be relevant for important key ratios such as solvency and liquidity ratios.

Paragraph 42 of IAS 32 states that a financial asset and a financial liability shall be offset and the net amount presented when, and only when, an entity:

(a) currently has a legally enforceable right to set off the recognised amounts; and
(b) intends either to settle on a net basis, or to realise the asset and settle the liability simultaneously.

The underlying rationale of this requirement is that when an entity has the right to receive or pay a single net amount and intends to do so, it has effectively only a single financial asset or financial liability.

Note that the right of set-off must be legally enforceable and therefore usually stems from a written contract between two parties. In rare cases, there may be an agreement between three parties allowing a debtor to apply an amount due from a third party against the amount due to a creditor. Assume, for example, that Company A owes Company B £1000, and Company Z owes Company A £1000. Company A has therefore recorded in its books the following:

| Amount Receivable from Company Z | Dr | 1 000 | |
| Amount Owing to Company B | Cr | | 1 000 |

Provided there is a legal right of set-off allowing Company A to offset the amount owing to Company B against the amount owed by Company Z, the amounts may be offset in Company A's accounts. Both Company B and Company Z must be parties to this legal right of set-off with Company A.

The conditions for offsetting are strict and essentially require written legal contracts resulting in net cash settlement. Many arrangements that create 'synthetic' (manufactured) offsetting do not result in offsetting under IAS 32, which also provides examples of common cases where offsetting is not permitted.

7.13 HEDGE ACCOUNTING

Entities enter into hedge arrangements for economic reasons; namely, to protect themselves from the types of risks *discussed in section 7.14* — currency risk, interest rate risk, other price risk and so on. Entities often enter into derivative and other contracts to manage these risk exposures. Hedging can be seen, therefore, as a risk management activity that changes an entity's risk profile. However, application of the normal IFRS® Standards accounting requirements to those risk management activities often results in accounting mismatches, when the gains or losses on a hedging instrument and hedged items are not recognised in the same period. The idea of hedge accounting is to reduce this mismatch by changing either the measurement or recognition of the hedged exposure, or the accounting for the hedging instrument.

Although the basic idea is simple, the development of hedge accounting standards raises difficult questions about when hedge accounting is more appropriate than the normal IFRS Standards accounting. In practice, this meant that some of the requirements in IAS 39 were arguably arbitrary and did not allow hedge accounting for certain risk management activities that are commonly applied by entities. Consequently, many entities would report 'accounting' hedges in their financial statements that did not correspond to the hedges that were entered into for risk management purposes, which was unhelpful for preparers and users alike.

The objective of the hedge accounting requirements in IFRS 9 is to present in the financial statements the effect of an entity's risk management activities. That is, hedge accounting under IFRS 9 is intended to align the accounting more closely to risk management. While the hedge accounting rules in IFRS 9 are less restrictive than those in IAS 39, the fact remains that hedge accounting is only permitted if all the qualifying criteria are met *(see section 7.13.3)*. Consequently, an entity would not apply hedge accounting to risk management activities that either do not meet the qualifying criteria or that are not designated by the entity as accounting hedges. A number of important concepts need to be understood:

1. the hedging instrument
2. the hedged item
3. the conditions for hedge accounting and the three types of hedges
4. the hedge ratio, rebalancing and discontinuation.

7.13.1 The hedging instrument

A financial instrument must meet the following essential criteria for it to be classified as a hedging instrument:

1. It must be designated as such. This means that management must document the details of the hedging instrument and the item it is hedging, at the inception of the hedge.
2. It must be a derivative, non-derivative financial asset or non-derivative financial liability measured at fair value through profit or loss to be designated as a hedging instrument, unless criteria 3 is met. However, financial liabilities for which changes in the credit risk are presented in other comprehensive income cannot be a hedging instrument.
3. It is hedging foreign currency exchange risk, in which case it can be a non-derivative.
4. At the inception of the hedging relationship, there is formal designation and documentation of the hedging relationship and the entity's risk management objective and strategy for undertaking the hedge.
5. It must be with a party external to the reporting entity — external to the consolidated group or individual entity being reported on. There is one exception to this rule in respect of intragroup monetary items when certain conditions are met.
6. It cannot be split into component parts, except for separating the time value and intrinsic value in an option contract, and the interest element and spot price in a forward contract.
7. A proportion of the entire hedging instrument, such as 50% of the notional amount, may be designated as the hedging instrument. However, a hedging relationship may not be designated for only a portion of the period during which the hedging instrument remains outstanding.
8. A single hedging instrument may be designated as a hedging instrument of more than one type of risk, if there is a specific designation of the hedging instrument and of the different risk positions as hedged items. Those hedged items can be in different hedging relationships.

IFRS 9 contains further detailed guidance, which is not discussed here in detail, that must be complied with and that further restricts which financial instruments can be treated as hedging instrument.

Examples of hedging instruments are forward foreign currency exchange contracts, interest rate swaps and futures contracts. Written options cannot be hedging instruments of the writer, unless they are designated as a hedge of a purchased option.

7.13.2 The hedged item

IFRS 9 defines the following terms:

- A *hedged item* can be a recognised asset or liability, an unrecognised firm commitment, a highly probable forecast transaction or a net investment in a foreign operation.
- A *forecast transaction* is an uncommitted but anticipated future transaction (e.g. expected future sales or purchases).
- A *firm commitment* is a binding agreement for the exchange of a specified quantity of resources at a specified price on a specified future date or dates (e.g. a purchase order to buy a machine for $50 000 in 3 months' time).

A hedged item:
1. can be a single item, a group of items or a component of such item(s)
2. can be a combination of a derivative with a hedged item as described above
3. must be reliably measurable
4. must arise from a transaction with a party external to the reporting entity (i.e. an entity that is not consolidated by the reporting entity), subject to certain exceptions regarding intragroup foreign currency balances
5. can be a risk component of financial item (e.g. only the interest, currency or credit risk on a bond) or a risk component of a non-financial item (e.g. fuel price component in an electricity purchase contract), subject to certain conditions
6. can be a net nil position (i.e. on a group basis the hedged items themselves offset the risk being managed), subject to certain conditions
7. can be a 'layer' of an overall group of items (e.g. the bottom €60 million of a €100 million fixed rate loan), subject to certain conditions.

IFRS 9 contains further detailed requirements, which are not discussed here specifically, that restrict which exposures can be treated as hedged items.

7.13.3 The conditions for hedge accounting and the three types of hedges

Hedge accounting recognises the offsetting effects on profit or loss of changes in the fair values of the hedging instrument and the hedged item. Paragraph 6.4.1 of IFRS 9 sets out the following conditions that must be met in order for hedge accounting to be applied:

1. At the inception of the hedge, there must be formal designation and documentation of the hedging relationship and the entity's risk-management objective and strategy for undertaking the hedge. That documentation must include identification of:

- the hedging instrument
- the hedged item
- the nature of the risk being hedged
- how the entity will assess hedge effectiveness.

2. The hedging relationship consists only of eligible hedging instruments and eligible hedged items *as described in sections 7.13.1 and 7.13.2.*
3. The hedging relationship should meet the following hedge effectiveness requirements: .
    (a) there is an economic relationship between the hedged item and the hedging instrument
    (b) credit risk does not dominate the value changes that result from that economic relationship
    (c) the hedge ratio of the hedging relationship is the same as that resulting from the quantity of the hedged item that the entity actually hedges and the quantity of the hedging instrument that the entity actually uses to hedge that quantity of hedged item.

The three types of hedging relationships are:
- fair value hedge
- cash flow hedge
- hedge of a net investment in a foreign operation as defined in IAS 21. This is accounted for in a similar manner to cash flow hedges, but will not be discussed further in this chapter.

Note the following points:
- A fair value hedge is a hedge of the exposure to changes in fair value of an asset, liability or unrecognised firm commitment.
- A cash flow hedge is a hedge of the exposure to variability in cash flows of a recognised asset or liability, or a highly probable forecast transaction.
- Paragraph 6.5.4 of IFRS 9 states that a hedge of the foreign currency risk of a firm commitment may be accounted for as either a fair value hedge or a cash flow hedge.
- A simple way of remembering the difference between the two types of hedge is that a cash flow hedge locks in future cash flows, whereas a fair value hedge does not.
- The most commonly occurring hedge transactions for average reporting entities are interest rate hedges and foreign currency hedges.

As an example of a simple cash flow hedge, assume that Company B has a borrowing with lender Bank L that carries a variable rate of interest. Company B is worried about its exposure to future increases in the variable rate of interest and decides to enter into an interest rate swap with Bank S. The borrowing is the hedged item, and the risk being hedged is interest rate risk. Under the interest rate swap, Bank S pays Company B the variable interest rate, and Company B pays Bank S a specified fixed interest rate. The interest rate swap is the hedging instrument. The net cash flows for Company B are its payments of a fixed interest rate, so it has locked in its cash flows. This is therefore a cash flow hedge, assuming all the required criteria of IAS 39 are met. Figure 7.8 illustrates this example of a simple cash flow hedge.

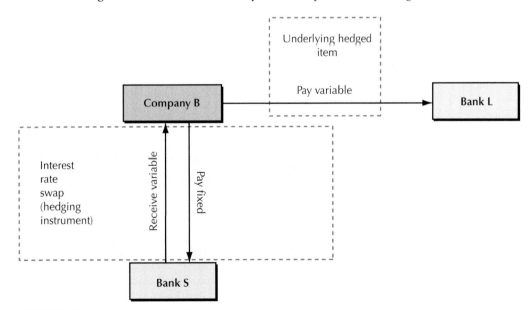

FIGURE 7.8 A simple cash flow hedge

There is no exchange of principal in an interest rate swap — the cash flows are simply calculated using the principal as the basis for the calculation. For the example illustrated in figure 7.8, assume that the hedged item is a borrowing of $100 000 with a variable interest rate, currently 5%. The fixed rate under the interest rate swap is 6%. For the relevant period, Company B will pay Bank L $100 000 × 5% = $5000. Under the swap, Company B will pay a net $1000 (receive $100 000 × 5% and pay $100 000 × 6%).

Thus, Company B's net cash outflow is $5000 + $1000 = $6000, which is the fixed rate. Note that Bank L is not a party to the swap — it continues to receive payments from Company B under its borrowing arrangement. Company B has locked in its cash flows at $6000, and has certainty that this is what it will pay over the term of the swap. Currently the cash flows are higher than what it would pay under a variable rate, but Company B has entered into the swap in the expectation that the variable rate will rise.

Table 7.6 sets out the main requirements for fair value hedges and cash flow hedges.

TABLE 7.6 Summary of the main requirements of IFRS 9 for fair value hedges and cash flow hedges

	Fair value hedge	Cash flow hedge
Hedged item	Fair value exposures in a recognised asset or liability or unrecognised firm commitment	Cash flow variability exposures in a recognised asset or liability or highly probable forecast transaction
Gain or loss on hedging instrument	Recognised immediately in profit or loss. If hedging an equity instrument at fair value through other comprehensive income then recognise in other comprehensive income	Fully effective portion recognised directly in other comprehensive income. Ineffective portion recognised immediately in profit or loss
Gain or loss on hedged item	Generally, adjust hedged item and recognise in profit or loss. This applies even if the hedged item is otherwise measured at cost However, if the hedged item is an equity instrument at fair value through other comprehensive income then recognise entire gain or loss on hedged risk in other comprehensive income	Not applicable because the exposure being hedged is future cash flows that are not recognised
Hedge ineffectiveness is recorded in profit or loss	Automatically, since the entire gain or loss on both the hedged item and the hedging instrument is recorded in profit or loss	Must be calculated and separated from the amount recorded in equity
Timing of recycling of hedge gains/losses in equity to profit or loss	Not applicable	Hedge of a forecast transaction that subsequently results in the recognition of a *financial* asset or financial liability: during the periods in which said asset/liability affects profit or loss, e.g. when the interest income or expense is recognised Hedge of a forecast transaction that subsequently results in the recognition of a *non-financial* asset or non-financial liability: include immediately in the initial cost of said asset/ liability If the amount is an unrecoverable loss then the entity should recognise that loss immediately in profit or loss

A simple fair value hedge is demonstrated in illustrative example 7.5.

ILLUSTRATIVE EXAMPLE 7.5 A simple fair value hedge

Onur Holding has an investment in a debt instrument classified as at fair value through other comprehensive income. The cost of the investment on 1 July 2016 was $250 000. On 1 September 2016, Onur Holding enters into a derivative futures contract to hedge the fair value of the investment. All the conditions for hedge accounting are met, and the hedge qualifies as a fair value hedge because it is a hedge of an exposure to changes in the fair value of a recognised asset. At the next reporting date, 30 September 2016, the fair value of the investment (hedged item) was $230 000, based on quoted market bid prices. The fair value of the derivative (hedging instrument) at that date was $18 000. Onur Holding would record the journal entries shown below.

On initial recognition of the investment 1 July 2016:

Debt instrument at fair value through other comprehensive income	Dr	250 000	
Cash	Cr		250 000

On entering into the futures contract 1 September 2016:
No entries because the net fair value is zero.
On remeasurement at 30 September 2016:

Expense (profit or loss)	Dr	20 000	
Debt instrument at fair value through other comprehensive income	Cr		20 000
Futures Contract	Dr	18 000	
Income (profit or loss)	Cr		18 000

The hedge continues to meet the criteria in IFRS 9, so the hedge accounting may continue. The net effect of the hedge is that Onur Holding records a net loss in profit or loss of $2000. The ineffective portion of the hedge ($2000) is recorded automatically in profit or loss. Note that the decline in fair value of the debt instrument at fair value through other comprehensive income is recorded in profit or loss, even though the normal accounting for such investments is to recognise fair value changes directly in equity. This exception is made specifically for hedge accounting, to enable the matching effect of the hedging instrument with the hedged item in profit or loss to occur.

A cash flow hedge of a firm commitment is demonstrated in illustrative example 7.6.

ILLUSTRATIVE EXAMPLE 7.6 Cash flow hedge of a firm commitment

On 30 June 2016, King Kong enters into a forward exchange contract to receive foreign currency (FC) of 100 000 and deliver local currency (LC) of 109 600 on 30 June 2017. It designates the forward exchange contract as a hedging instrument in a cash flow hedge of a firm commitment to purchase a specified quantity of paper on 31 March 2017, and the resulting payable. Payment for the paper is due on 30 June 2017. All hedge accounting conditions in IFRS 9 are met.

Note that a hedge of foreign currency risk in a firm commitment may be either a cash flow hedge or a fair value hedge. King Kong has elected to account for it as a cash flow hedge. Under IFRS 9, King Kong is required to adjust the cost of non-financial items acquired as a result of hedged forecast transactions.

The following table sets out the spot rate, forward rate and fair value of the forward contract at relevant dates.

Date	Spot rate	Forward rate to 30 June 2017	Fair value of forward contract
30 June 2016	1.072	1.096	—
31 December 2016	1.080	1.092	(388)[1]
31 March 2017	1.074	1.076	(1 971)
30 June 2017	1.072	—	(2 400)

1. This can be calculated if the applicable yield curve in the local currency is known. Assuming the rate is 6%, the fair value is calculated as follows: $([1.092 \times 100\,000] - 109\,600)/1.06(6/12)$.

Journal entries are shown below:
At 30 June 2016:

Forward Contract	Dr	LC0	
Cash	Cr		LC0
(Initial recognition of forward contract)			

No entries because on initial recognition, the forward contract has a fair value of zero.
At 31 December 2016:

Other comprehensive income	Dr	LC388	
Forward Contract (liability)	Cr		LC388
(Recording the change in the fair value of the forward contract)			

At 31 March 2017:

Other comprehensive income	Dr	LC1 583	
Forward Contract (liability)	Cr		LC1 583
(Recording the change in the fair value of the forward contract)			
Paper (purchase price)	Dr	LC107 400	
Paper (hedging loss)	Dr	LC1 971	
Other comprehensive income	Cr		LC1 971
Payable	Cr		LC107 400

The last entry recognises the purchase of the paper at the spot rate (1.074 × FC100 000), and removes the cumulative loss that has been recognised in equity and includes it in the initial measurement of the purchased paper. The paper is thus recognised effectively at the forward rate, and the hedge has been 100% effective.

The purchase of paper is no longer a forecast transaction once King Kong has recognised the paper and the payable. If King Kong wants to continue hedge accounting after 31 March 2017, it would need to account for a fair value hedge of the resulting payable as illustrated below.
At 30 June 2017:

Payable	Dr	LC107 400	
Cash	Cr		LC107 200
Profit or Loss	Cr		LC200
(Recording settlement of the payable at the spot rate and associated exchange gain)			
Profit or Loss	Dr	LC429	
Forward Contract	Cr		LC429
(Recording loss on forward contract between 1 April 2017 and 30 June 2017)			
Forward Contract	Dr	LC2 400	
Cash	Cr		LC2 400
(Recording net settlement of forward contract)			

The forward contract has been effective in hedging the commitment and the payable up to this date. King Kong accounts for the loss on the contract in profit or loss because it is applying fair value hedge accounting to the forward contract and the payable.

If this transaction had been designated as a fair value hedge from the outset, then the entries recorded in equity for the cash flow hedge would instead be recorded as an asset or liability. IFRS 9 would then require the initial carrying amount of the asset acquired to be adjusted for the cumulative amount recognised in the statement of financial position. The adjusted journal entries would be as follows:
At 31 December 2016:

Asset	Dr	LC388	
Forward Contract (liability)	Cr		LC388
(Recording change in fair value of forward contract)			

At 31 March 2017:

Asset	Dr	LC1 583	
Forward Contract (liability)	Cr		LC1 583
(Recording change in fair value of forward contract)			
Paper (purchase price)	Dr	LC107 400	
Paper (hedging loss)	Dr	LC1 971	
Asset	Cr		LC1 971
Payable	Cr		LC107 400
(Recording purchase of paper and transferring cumulative amount recognised as an asset to the cost of the paper)			

At 30 June 2017, there would not be any difference and King Kong would record the same fair value hedge journals as shown above.

7.13.4 Hedge ratio, rebalancing and discontinuation

IFRS 9 does not require a retrospective quantitative effectiveness assessment (i.e. was the hedge effective in the past?), but that does not mean that hedge accounting continues regardless of how effective a hedge is. A prospective effectiveness assessment is still required, in a similar manner as at the inception of the hedging relationship and on an ongoing basis, as a minimum at each reporting date. This process involves the steps shown in figure 7.9.

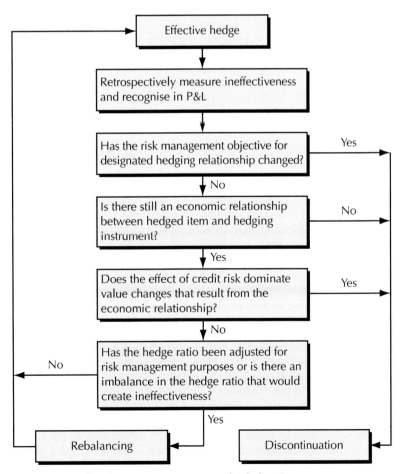

FIGURE 7.9 Effectiveness assessment and rebalancing

An entity first has to assess whether the risk management objective for the hedging relationship has changed. A change in risk management objective is a matter of fact that triggers discontinuation of the hedge relationship. Accordingly, a hedge relationship cannot be de-designated without an underlying change in risk management. An entity would also have to discontinue hedge accounting if it turns out that there is no longer an economic relationship (e.g. the hedging instrument or hedged item was sold) because in that case there would not be a hedge to account for. The same is true for the impact of credit risk; if credit risk is now dominating the hedging relationship, then the entity has to discontinue hedge accounting. When an entity discontinues hedge accounting then any gain or loss on cash flow hedges deferred in other comprehensive income must be recycled to profit or loss.

The hedge ratio is the ratio between the amount of hedged item and the amount of hedging instrument. For many hedging relationships, the hedge ratio would be 1:1 as the underlying of the hedging instrument perfectly matches the designated hedged risk.

If the hedge ratio has been adjusted for risk management purposes or if it turns out that the hedged item and hedging instrument do not move in relation to each other as expected (i.e. there is an imbalance in the hedge ratio) then the hedge ratio may need to be adjusted to reflect this. In that case, the entity has to assess whether it expects this to continue to be the case going forward. If so, the entity is likely to rebalance the hedge ratio to reflect the change in the relationship between the underlying items.

Rebalancing can be achieved by: increasing the volume of the hedged item, increasing the volume of the hedging instrument, decreasing the volume of the hedged item, or decreasing the volume of the hedging instrument. Rebalancing under IFRS 9 allows entities to refine their hedge ratio without having to account for a discontinuation of the entire hedge relationship, but it may result in a partial discontinuation if the hedged volume is reduced.

7.13.5 Alternatives to hedge accounting

IFRS 9 offers two important alternatives to hedge accounting. The first alternative is that IFRS 9 extends the fair value through profit or loss option to contracts that meet the 'own use' scope exception *(see section 7.7)* if this eliminates or significantly reduces an accounting mismatch. In other words, by measuring 'own use' contracts at fair value, it would be possible to reduce the measurement mismatch with derivatives and other financial instruments that are also measured at fair value. This would alleviate the need for hedge accounting.

The second alternative applies to the many financial institutions that hedge the credit risk arising from loans or loan commitments using credit default swaps. This would often result in an accounting mismatch, as loans and loan commitments are typically not accounted for at fair value through profit or loss. The simplest accounting would be to designate the credit risk as a risk component in a hedging relationship. However, the IASB noted that due to the difficulty in isolating the credit risk as a separate risk it does not meet the eligibility criteria for risk components. As a result, the accounting mismatch creates profit or loss volatility.

Under IFRS 9, an entity undertaking economic credit risk hedging may elect to account for a debt instrument (such as a loan or a bond), a loan commitment or a financial guarantee contract, at fair value through profit or loss. This election can only be made if the asset referenced by the credit derivative has the same issuer and subordination as the hedged exposure (i.e. both the issuer's name and seniority of the exposure match). The accounting for the credit derivative would not change, i.e. it would continue to be accounted at fair value through profit or loss. Consequently, even though it is not equivalent to fair value hedge accounting, this accounting does address several concerns of entities that use credit default swaps for hedging credit exposures.

 ### 7.14 DISCLOSURES

IFRS 7 contains many pages dealing with disclosures, but only relatively few 'black letter' requirements. This chapter does not address these requirements in detail, and readers are expected to have a general understanding of the requirements only.

The purpose of the disclosure requirements is to provide information to enhance understanding of the significance of financial instruments to an entity's financial position, performance and cash flows; and to assist in assessing the amounts, timing and certainty of future cash flows associated with those instruments.

Transactions in financial instruments may result in an entity assuming or transferring to another party one or more of the financial risks described in Table 7.7. The purpose of the required disclosures is to assist users in assessing the extent of such risks related to financial instruments.

TABLE 7.7 Financial risks pertaining to financial instruments

Type of risk	Description
Credit risk	The risk that one party to a financial instrument will fail to discharge an obligation and cause the other party to incur a financial loss.
Liquidity risk	The risk that an entity will encounter difficulty in meeting obligations associated with financial liabilities. This is also known as funding risk. For example, as a financial liability approaches its redemption date, the issuer may experience liquidity risk if its available financial assets are insufficient to meet its obligations.
Market risk	• *Currency risk* — the risk that the value of a financial instrument will fluctuate because of changes in foreign exchange rates. • *Interest rate risk* — the risk that the value of a financial instrument will fluctuate because of changes in market interest rates. For example, the issuer of a financial liability that carries a fixed rate of interest is exposed to decreases in market interest rates, such that the issuer of the liability is paying a higher rate of interest than the market rate. • *Other price risk* — the risk that the value of a financial instrument will fluctuate as a result of changes in market prices (other than those arising from interest rate risk or currency risk).

IFRS 7 applies to all entities for all types of financial instruments, other than those specifically excluded from its scope. Scope exclusions include:
- interest in subsidiaries, associates and joint ventures accounted for under IFRS 10, IAS 27, or IAS 28
- employers' rights and obligations arising from employee benefit plans, to which IAS 19 *Employee Benefits* applies
- insurance contracts as defined in IFRS 4 *Insurance Contracts*
- share-based payment transactions to which IFRS 2 *Share-based Payment* applies.

IFRS 7 applies to both recognised and unrecognised financial instruments. For example, loan commitments not within the scope of IFRS 9 are within the scope of IFRS 7.

IFRS 7 requires disclosure of financial instruments grouped by class. A class of financial instrument is a lower level of aggregation than a category, such as 'available-for-sale' or 'loans and receivables' *(see section 7.9)*. For example, government debt securities, equity securities, or asset-backed securities could all be considered classes of financial instruments.

IFRS 7 is divided into three main sections. The first section requires disclosure of the significance of financial instruments for financial position and performance. These disclosures are grouped into:
1. statement of financial position
2. statement of other comprehensive income
3. other disclosures.

The second section requires disclosure about the nature and extent of risks arising from financial instruments. These include both quantitative and qualitative disclosures. The risks are grouped into the three categories noted above, that is, market risk, credit risk and liquidity risk. These risk disclosures shall be given either in the financial statements or incorporated by cross-reference from the financial statements to some other statement, such as a management commentary or risk report.

The third section requires disclosure about financial assets transferred to another entity.

Examples of the types of disclosures required in each of the sections are provided in Tables 7.8 and 7.9.

TABLE 7.8 Significance of financial instruments for financial position and performance

Statement of financial position

Overall requirement	Summary of details required
Categories of financial assets and financial liabilities (paragraph 8)	• The carrying amount of specified categories, as defined in IFRS 9, for example, financial assets measured at fair value through profit or loss and financial assets measured at amortised cost.

(continued)

TABLE 7.8 *(continued)*

Overall requirement	Summary of details required
Financial assets or financial liabilities at fair value through profit or loss (paragraphs 9, 10, 10A and 11)	• An entity that designates a *financial asset* as measured at fair value through profit or loss should disclose specified details including the maximum exposure to credit risk, the amount by which credit derivatives mitigate that exposure, the amount of fair value changes attributable to changes in credit risk and the change in the fair value of any credit derivative or similar instruments. • An entity that designates a *financial liability* at fair value through profit or loss should disclose specified details including the change in fair value that is attributable to changes in the credit risk, and the difference between the carrying amount of the liability and the amount the entity would be contractually required to pay at maturity.
Investments in equity instruments designated at fair value through other comprehensive income (paragraphs 11A and 11B)	• An entity that designates investments in equity instruments to be measured at fair value through other comprehensive income should disclose specified details including which investments have been designated and the reason for doing so, fair value of each investment, the related dividends received, and the cumulative gain or loss upon and reason for any disposal of such investments.
Reclassification (paragraph 12B, 12C and 12D)	• Disclosure is required of the circumstances around any change in business model that lead to a reclassification of financial assets and information about the financial performance of those reclassified assets after the reclassification.
Offsetting financial assets and financial liabilities (paragraphs 13A to 13F)	• Specified disclosures are required for all recognised financial instruments that are set off in accordance with IAS 32, such that users of the financial statements can assess the (potential) effect of netting arrangements on the entity's financial position.
Collateral (paragraphs 14 and 15)	• Collateral given: an entity must disclose the carrying amount of financial assets it has pledged as collateral (security) for liabilities or contingent liabilities. The terms and conditions of the pledge must also be disclosed. • Collateral received: specified details must be disclosed where an entity holds collateral (of financial and non-financial assets) and is permitted to sell or repledge that collateral.
Allowance for credit losses (paragraph 16A)	• The loss allowance related to financial assets measured at fair value through other comprehensive income should be disclosed.
Compound financial instruments with multiple embedded derivatives (paragraph 17)	• Disclosure is required of the existence of such features in compound financial instruments.
Defaults and breaches (paragraphs 18 and 19)	• For loans payable, disclosure is required of any defaults during the period, the carrying amount of loans payable in default at the end of the reporting period and whether the default was remedied before the financial statements were authorised for issue.
Statement of other comprehensive income	
Items of income, expense, gains or losses (paragraphs 20 and 20A)	• Net gains or losses for each category of financial asset and financial liability. • Total interest income and total interest expense for financial assets or liabilities that are not at fair value through profit or loss. • Fee income and expense arising from financial assets or liabilities not at fair value through profit or loss, and from trust and other fiduciary activities. • Analysis of gains and of losses recognised in the statement of comprehensive income that resulted from the derecognition of financial assets measured at amortised cost.

TABLE 7.9 Significance of financial instruments for other disclosures

Other disclosures

Overall requirement	Summary of details required
Accounting policies (paragraph 21)	• Disclose relevant accounting policies. Where the accounting methods are prescribed in the relevant standards (e.g. in IFRS 9) then the entity should not repeat these but rather disclose where it has applied choices available.

Hedge accounting (paragraphs 21A to 21D, 23A to 23F and 24A to 24G)	• Disclose the risk management strategy, how it is applied to each risk category, a description of the hedging instruments used, the determination of the economic relationship between the hedged item and hedging instrument, and qualitative or quantitative information about how risk components were determined.
	• Disclose information about the terms and conditions of the hedging instruments and how hedging activities affect the amount, timing and uncertainty of future cash flows.
	• Tabular information about the effects of hedge accounting on the financial position and performance, which includes specified details separately by risk category and by type of hedge (i.e. fair value hedges, cash flow hedges and hedges of net investments in foreign operations) about:
	  • carrying amounts, presentation, change in fair value and nominal amounts of the items designated as hedging instruments;
	  • carrying amounts, presentation and accumulated fair value changes of the items designated as hedged items and information about hedge ineffectiveness.

Credit exposure measured at fair value through profit or loss (paragraph 24G)	• For financial instruments designated as measured at fair value through profit or loss because a credit derivative is used to manage the credit risk of that financial instrument, disclosure is required of specified information about the credit derivative, the amount recognised in profit or loss upon designation of the financial instrument and information about discontinuation of the treatment.
Fair value (paragraphs 25–30)	• For each class of financial assets and liabilities, disclose the fair value of that class in a way that permits it to be compared with its carrying amount. • Other details are required in respect of gains or losses arising on initial recognition of certain financial instruments.

It should be noted that IFRS 7 does not prescribe how statement of profit or loss and other comprehensive income amounts are determined. For example, interest income on financial instruments carried at fair value through profit or loss may be included in total interest income or it may be included in net gains or losses for that category.

Table 7.10 shows the disclosure requirements for the risks arising from financial instruments. These disclosures are intended to allow users of financial statements to assess the nature and extent of the risk that an entity is exposed to at the balance sheet date.

TABLE 7.10 Nature and extent of risks arising from financial instruments

Overall requirement	Summary of details required
For each type of risk (credit risk, liquidity risk and market risk) disclose . . . (paragraph 33)	(a) the exposures to risk and how they arise (b) the entity's objectives, policies and processes for managing the risk and the methods used to measure the risk (c) any changes in (a) or (b) from the previous period. The policies and processes an entity uses would normally include the structure and organisation of its risk management function, the policies for hedging or otherwise mitigating risks, processes for monitoring hedge effectiveness, and policies and processes for avoiding large concentrations of risk.

(continued)

TABLE 7.10 *(continued)*

Overall requirement	Summary of details required
For each type of risk (credit risk, liquidity risk and market risk) disclose . . . (paragraph 34)	(a) summary quantitative data about its exposure to that risk at the end of the reporting period. This disclosure must be based on the information provided internally to key management personnel of the entity (as defined in IAS 24 *Related Party Disclosures*) (b) the disclosures required by paragraphs 35A–42 (see below) to the extent not provided in (a) (c) concentrations of risk if not apparent from (a) and (b). Concentrations of risk arise from financial instruments that have similar characteristics and that are affected similarly by changes in economic or other conditions. For example, a risk concentration may be by geographic area, by industry or by currency.
Credit risk	
Scope and objectives (paragraphs 35A–35E)	The credit risk disclosures apply to the financial instruments to which the impairment requirements of IFRS 9 are applied. The objective of the credit risk disclosures is to enable users to understand the effect on the amount, timing and uncertainty of future cash flows by requiring: • information about credit risk management practices • quantitative and qualitative information • information about the entity's credit risk exposure.
Credit risk management practices (paragraphs 35F and 35G)	Disclose information about credit risk management practices and how they relate to the recognition and measurement of expected credit losses (including the methods, assumptions and information used to measure those losses). For example, an entity should disclose: • how it determined whether the credit risk of financial instruments has increased significantly since initial recognition • its definition of default • how it determined that financial assets are credit-impaired • the basis of inputs and assumptions and estimation techniques • how forward-looking information has been incorporated.
Quantitative and qualitative information about amounts arising from expected credit losses (paragraphs 35H–35L)	Disclose quantitative and qualitative information that allows users of financial statements to evaluate the amounts in the financial statements arising from expected credit losses, including changes in the amount of those losses and the reasons for those changes.
Credit risk exposure (paragraphs 35M, 35N and 36)	Disclose information about the entity's credit risk exposure; that is, the credit risk inherent in its financial assets and commitments to extend credit, including significant credit risk concentrations.
Collateral and other credit enhancements obtained (paragraph 38)	Specified details are required to be disclosed when an entity obtains financial or non-financial assets during the period by taking possession of collateral it holds as security.
Liquidity risk	
Liquidity risk . . . (paragraph 39)	(a) a maturity analysis for financial liabilities that shows the remaining contractual maturities (b) a description of how the entity manages the liquidity risk inherent in (a). An entity must use judgement to determine the appropriate time bands for a maturity analysis, that is, for when amounts fall due. For example, an entity might determine that the following time bands are appropriate: • not later than 1 month • between 1 month and 3 months • between 3 months and 6 months • later than 6 months.

TABLE 7.10 *(continued)*

Overall requirement	Summary of details required
	The amounts disclosed in the maturity analysis must be the contractual undiscounted cash flows. This could be problematic for liabilities that mature later than 1 year because the amounts disclosed in the note would likely not reconcile to the statement of financial position where the discounted amount would be shown.
	Examples of how an entity might manage liquidity risk include: • having access to undrawn loan commitments • holding readily liquid financial assets that can be sold to meet liquidity needs • having diverse funding sources.
Market risk	
Market risk — sensitivity analysis (paragraphs 40 and 41)	An entity must disclose: (a) for each type of market risk (i.e. currency risk, interest rate risk and other price risk) a sensitivity analysis showing how profit or loss or equity would have been affected by changes in the relevant risk variables that were reasonably possible at the end of the reporting period (b) the methods and assumptions used in preparing the sensitivity analysis (c) changes from the previous period in the methods and assumptions used.
	For example, if an entity has a floating interest rate (i.e. variable) liability at the end of the year, the entity would disclose the effect on interest expense for the current year if interest rates had varied by reasonably possible amounts.
	This effect could be disclosed as a range. For example, the entity could state that had the interest rate varied by between 0.25% and 0.5% then total interest expense would have increased by an amount of between $xx and $xy.
	If an entity prepares a sensitivity analysis that analyses the interdependencies between market risk variables (e.g. between interest rate risk and currency risk) then it need not make the disclosures in (a) but must rather disclose its own interdependent risk analysis.

Table 7.11 shows the disclosure requirements for financial assets transferred to another entity. The purpose of the required disclosures is to assist users in assessing the extent of such risks related to financial instruments.

TABLE 7.11 Transfers of financial assets

Overall requirement	Summary of details required
Transfers of financial assets (paragraphs 42A to 42C and 42H)	Disclose specified information for all transferred financial assets that are not derecognised and for any continuing involvement in a transferred asset existing at the reporting date.
	The objective of these requirements is to provide information that enables users of financial statements to understand the relationship between transferred financial assets that are not derecognised in their entirety and the associated liabilities. In addition, users should be able to evaluate the nature of, and risks associated with, an entity's continuing involvement in derecognised financial assets.
Transferred financial assets that are not derecognised in their entirety (paragraph 42D)	Disclose information such as, for example, the nature of the transferred assets, the nature of the risks and rewards of ownership to which the reporting entity is exposed, and a description of the nature of the relationship between the transferred assets and the associated liabilities.
Transferred financial assets that are derecognised in their entirety (paragraphs 42E–42G)	For transferred financial assets derecognised in their entirety but where the entity has continuing involvement in those assets, disclosure of certain specified qualitative and quantitative information is required for each type of continuing involvement.

SUMMARY

IAS 32 defines financial instruments, financial assets, financial liabilities and derivatives and distinguishes between financial liabilities and equity instruments. IFRS 7 prescribes disclosures. IAS 32 sets prescriptive rules for distinguishing financial liabilities from equity instruments, and for accounting for compound financial instruments that have elements of both. It requires that interest, dividends, gains and losses be accounted for consistent with the statement of financial position classification of the related financial assets and financial liabilities. It also sets prescriptive requirements for offsetting a financial asset and a financial liability.

IFRS 9 requires all financial instruments including derivatives to be initially recorded at fair value. It defines an embedded derivative and establishes rules for separating an embedded derivative from the host contract. It creates four categories of financial instruments. Each category has its own rules for measurement, including initial and subsequent measurement, reclassifications, gains and losses and impairment.

IFRS 9 permits hedge accounting provided that strict criteria are met. These include meeting specified conditions before hedge accounting can be applied, meeting the definition of a hedging instrument and a hedged item, and identifying which of the three types of hedge the hedge transaction meets. IFRS 9 prescribes when hedge accounting must be rebalanced or discontinued and how this must be accounted for. It also contains rules for the derecognition of financial instruments, but these are not addressed in this chapter.

IFRS 9 is a new standard that was developed to address the criticisms raised during the financial crisis in 2008. Even though IFRS 9 offers many improvements over its predecessor standard, IAS 39, accounting for financial instruments remains controversial.

Discussion questions

1. Discuss the concept of 'equity risk' and how it is useful in determining whether a financial instrument is a financial liability or an equity instrument of the issuer.
2. Explain how IAS 32 distinguishes between financial liabilities and equity instruments.
3. Explain the conditions that must be met in order to apply hedge accounting.
4. Describe the main characteristics of a derivative. What is meant by an underlying?
5. Identify the main criticisms of accounting for financial instruments that emerged during the financial crisis. To what extent had the IASB addressed these by the end of 2011?

References

Financial Crisis Advisory Group 2009, *Report of the Financial Crisis Advisory Group*, 28 July, www.ifrs.org.

Exercises

STAR RATING ★ BASIC ★★ MODERATE ★★★ DIFFICULT

Exercise 7.1 | **SCOPE OF IAS 32**

★ Which of the following are financial instruments (i.e. a financial asset, financial liability, or equity instrument in another entity) within the scope of IAS 32? Give reasons for your answer.
(a) Cash
(b) Investment in a debt instrument
(c) Investment in a subsidiary
(d) Provision for restoration of a mine site
(e) Buildings owned by the reporting entity
(f) Forward contract entered into by a bread manufacturer to buy wheat
(g) Forward contract entered into by a gold producer to hedge the future sales of gold
(h) General sales tax payable

Exercise 7.2 | **DISTINGUISHING FINANCIAL LIABILITIES FROM EQUITY INSTRUMENTS (1)**

★ Company A issues 100 000 $1 convertible notes. The notes pay interest at 7%. The market rate for similar debt without the conversion option is 9%. The note is not redeemable, but it converts at the option of the holder into however many shares that will have a value of exactly $100 000.

Required

Determine whether this financial instrument should be classified as a financial liability or equity instrument of Company A. Give reasons for your answer.

Exercise 7.3 — DISTINGUISHING FINANCIAL LIABILITIES FROM EQUITY INSTRUMENTS (2)

★★ Company A issues 100 000 $1 redeemable convertible notes. The notes pay interest at 5%. They convert at any time at the option of the holder into 100 000 ordinary shares. The notes are redeemable at the option of the holder for cash after 5 years. Market rates for similar notes without the conversion option are 7%.

Required

Determine whether this financial instrument should be classified as a financial liability or equity instrument of Company A. Give reasons for your answer.

Exercise 7.4 — CATEGORISING COMMON FINANCIAL INSTRUMENTS UNDER IAS 32

★★ Categorise each of the following common financial instruments as financial assets, financial liabilities or equity instruments — of the issuer or the holder, as specified.
(a) Loans receivable (holder)
(b) Loans payable (issuer)
(c) Ordinary shares of the issuer
(d) The holder's investment in the ordinary shares in part (c)
(e) Redeemable preference shares of the issuer, redeemable at any time at the option of the holder
(f) The holder's investment in the preference shares in part (e)

Exercise 7.5 — BUSINESS MODEL ASSESSMENT (1)

★ Describe some of the indicators that management might find helpful to consider in assessing the business model for each portfolio that it has identified.

Exercise 7.6 — BUSINESS MODEL ASSESSMENT (2)

★★ What is the impact on the business model if cash flows are realised in a way that is different from the entity's expectations when performing the initial business model assessment?

Exercise 7.7 — BUSINESS MODEL ASSESSMENT (3)

★★ (a) An entity anticipates capital expenditure in a few years. The entity invests its excess cash in financial assets, so that it can fund the expenditure when the need arises. The entity will hold the financial assets to collect the contractual cash flows and, when an opportunity arises, it will sell financial assets to re-invest the cash in financial assets with a higher return. The managers responsible for the portfolio are remunerated based on the overall return generated by the portfolio.
(b) A financial institution holds financial assets to meet its everyday liquidity needs. The entity holds financial assets to collect contractual cash flows, and it sells financial assets to re-invest in higher-yielding financial assets or to better match the duration of its liabilities. In the past, this strategy has resulted in frequent sales activity, and such sales have been significant in value. This activity is expected to continue in the future. What is the business model for the financial assets?

Exercise 7.8 — AMORTISED COST, JOURNAL ENTRIES

★★★ Company B issues a bond with a face value of $500 000 on 1 July 2016. Transaction costs incurred amount to $12 000. The bond pays interest at 6% per annum, in arrears. The bond must be repaid after 5 years.

Required

Prepare the journal entries to record this transaction on initial recognition and throughout the life of the bond in the books of Company B.

Exercise 7.9 — SUBSEQUENT MEASUREMENT AT AMORTISED COST

★★ On 1 January 2015, entity A originates a 10-year 7% $1m loan. The loan carries an annual interest rate of 7% payable at the end of each year, and it is repayable at par at the end of 2024. Entity A charges a 1.25% ($12,500) non-refundable loan origination fee to the borrower, and it also incurs $25,000 in direct loan origination costs.

The contract specifies that the borrower has an option to pre-pay the instrument and that no penalty will be charged for pre-payment. The contract meets the SPPI criteria. At inception, the entity expects the borrower not to pre-pay.

What is the carrying amount on initial recognition, and what impact does the pre-payment feature have on the amortised cost calculations?

| SUBSEQUENT MEASUREMENT AT AMORTISED COST

★★★ On 1 January 2015, entity A originates a 10-year 7% $1m loan. The loan is repaid in equal annual payments of $142,378, through to the maturity date at 31 December 2024. Entity A charges a 1.25% ($12,500) non-refundable loan origination fee to the borrower, and it also incurs $25,000 in direct loan origination costs.

The contract specifies that the borrower has an option to pre-pay the instrument and that no penalty will be charged for pre-payment. The contract meets the SPPI criteria. At inception, the entity expects the borrower not to pre-pay.

What is the carrying amount on initial recognition, and what impact does the pre-payment feature have?

Since several categories of financial instruments are measured at fair value, the Academic Perspective of chapter 3 should be read in conjunction with this section. This review therefore concerns several other key areas, including loan losses, hedge accounting, debt–equity classification and securitisation of financial instruments.

The measurement and disclosure of accrued losses on loans and receivables has attracted significant interest in accounting research. This is an important issue especially for the banking sector. This is because banks carry large amounts of loans and receivables in their balance sheets owing to their lending activities. One would expect that greater loan losses are negatively related to stock prices and future cash flows. The empirical evidence, however, suggests otherwise. In particular, Beaver et al. (1989) examine the relation between the market-to-book ratio (a measure of the excess of market value of equity over book value of equity) and the allowance for doubtful debt. They find that the two are positively related. A possible explanation of this is that in taking larger loan losses banks signal to investors they acknowledge underlying problems and are ready to tackle them. Wahlen (1994) finds that larger than expected loan losses are associated with future earnings before loan losses. This suggests that managers recognise more losses in the current period when they anticipate better future performance. Wahlen (1994) also performs market-based tests and finds a positive relation between stock returns and unexpected loan losses. This supports the notion that investors also expect better future performance when recorded losses exceed expectations. Beaver and Engel (1996) decompose the allowance for loan losses into discretionary and non-discretionary components and examine their pricing implications. Specifically, they regress the allowance on a number of factors they argue should explain the amount recognised. The predicted amount, which is taken from the regression line is regarded as the non-discretionary element and the residual the discretionary element. They predict that the 'nondiscretionary portion of the allowance is negatively priced because it reflects an impairment of the loan assets'. In contrast, the discretionary component should be unrelated to stock price, if it conveys no news. Alternatively, if it conveys some news, it should be positively related to prices. They report results that are consistent with these conjectures, implying that managers use the discretion that is available to them to convey useful information.

Hedging can be used by managers to reduce undesirable effects of volatility in earnings on their capacity to borrow by reducing bankruptcy risk. The incentive to hedge, however, may be affected by accounting rules. Specifically, hedge accounting may have two countervailing effects on hedging activity. On one hand, beyond the specific measurement rules, they require disclosure, which in turn improves the information environment and makes the statements clearer to investors (DeMarzo and Duffie, 1995). Better information can therefore enable investors to appreciate the reduction in risk and encourage hedging. On the other hand, too restrictive rules may discourage economically desirable hedging, if it does not qualify to be presented as such. Lins et al. (2011) provide survey-based evidence that introducing fair value measurement to derivative transactions both reduced speculative hedging, consistent with the theoretical prediction of Melumad et al. (1999), as well as economically desired hedging. Panaretou et al. (2013) show that the adoption of the more transparent and stricter IFRS Standards hedge rules in the UK resulted in lower information asymmetry.

The equity-or-debt classification of financial instruments would not be thought to have any real effects. Hopkins (1996) challenges this view. He conducts an experiment in which analysts are presented with different classifications of mandatorily redeemable preference shares (MRPS). Based on past empirical evidence that shows that issuing new shares reduces stock prices, but new debt does not, he conjectures and finds evidence that MRPS presented in equity cause subjects to assign lower stock price than the alternative classification as liability. Levi and Segal (2014) identify another real effect. They document that firms issued fewer MRPS following the change in US GAAP that required firms to classify MRPS as a liability rather than equity. De Jong et al. (2006) show that following the adoption of IFRS in the Netherlands, Dutch companies repurchased MRPS or changed their terms.

During the financial crisis of 2008 the IASB amended IAS 39 to allow firms to retroactively reclassify financial assets that previously were measured at fair value to amortized cost, provided they can maintain a long position. The reclassification criteria were much stricter prior to the crisis. Many banks had taken the option up, as it allowed them to avoid reporting the adverse consequences of falling asset prices. Lim et al. (2013) find that this retroactive classification resulted in a loss of reliable information, as judged by decline in analyst forecast accuracy and an increase forecast dispersion.

Securitisation has been subjected to academic scrutiny because the accounting for derecognition of financial assets involves managerial discretion. Specifically, when an entity sells its receivables, but retains some cash flow streams, accounting rules require a gain or loss to be recorded based on the fair value of the retained cash flow streams. Dechow et al. (2010) examine whether such fair value gains tend to be higher in circumstances where managers face stronger incentives to inflate reported profit. They identify a sample of 305 firms that reported derecognition gains or losses. In this sample a higher pre-securitisation profit is inversely related to derecognition profit. In other words, firms whose pre-securitisation income is low tend to record higher gains from securitisation. The retained interest in securitised assets may also affect the selling entity's risk. Barth et al. (2012) examine the relation between bond rating (and yields) and retained interest in securitised assets and find that it is negative (positive). This suggests that securitisation increases default risk. This suggests that managers of securitising firms should employ high discount factors in calculating the gain or loss on derecognition. However this does not seem to be the case. Dechow et al. (2010) provide evidence that suggests managers of gain-reporting firms in fact employ *low* discount rates as it enables them to inflate earnings.

References

Barth, M. E., Ormazabal, G., and Taylor, D. J. 2012. Asset securitizations and credit risk. *The Accounting Review*, 87(2), 423–448.

Beaver, W., Eger, C., Ryan, S., and Wolfson, M. 1989. Financial reporting, supplemental disclosures, and bank share prices. *Journal of Accounting Research*, 157–178.

Beaver, W., and Engel, E. 1996. Discretionary behavior with respect to allowances for loan losses and the behavior of security prices. *Journal of Accounting and Economics*, 22(1), 177–206.

Dechow, P. M., Myers, L. A., and Shakespeare, C. 2010. Fair value accounting and gains from asset securitizations: A convenient earnings management tool with compensation side-benefits. *Journal of Accounting and Economics*, 49(1), 2–25.

De Jong, A., Rosellón, M., and Verwijmeren, P. 2006. The economic consequences of IFRS: The impact of IAS 32 on preference shares in the Netherlands. *Accounting in Europe*, 3(1), 169–185.

DeMarzo, P. M., and Duffie, D. 1995. Corporate incentives for hedging and hedge accounting. *Review of Financial Studies*, 8(3), 743–771.

Hopkins, P. E. 1996. The effect of financial statement classification of hybrid financial instruments on financial analysts' stock price judgments. *Journal of Accounting Research*, 33–50.

Levi, S., and Segal, B. 2014. The impact of debt–equity reporting classifications on the firm's decision to issue hybrid securities. *European Accounting Review*, 24(4), 801–822.

Lim, C. Y., Lim, C. Y., and Lobo, G. J. 2013. IAS 39 reclassification choice and analyst earnings forecast properties. *Journal of Accounting and Public Policy*, 32(5), 342–356.

Lins, K. V., Servaes, H., and Tamayo, A. 2011. Does fair value reporting affect risk management? International survey evidence. *Financial Management*, 40(3), 525–551.

Melumad, N. D., Weyns, G., and Ziv, A. 1999. Comparing alternative hedge accounting standards: Shareholders' perspective. *Review of Accounting Studies*, 4(3–4), 265–292.

Panaretou, A., Shackleton, M. B., and Taylor, P. A. 2013. Corporate risk management and hedge accounting. *Contemporary Accounting Research*, 30(1), 116–139.

Wahlen, J. M. 1994. The nature of information in commercial bank loan loss disclosures. *The Accounting Review*, 69(3), 455–478.

8 Share-based payment

ACCOUNTING STANDARDS IN FOCUS

IFRS 2 *Share-based Payment*

LEARNING OBJECTIVES

After studying this chapter, you should be able to:

1. explain the objective and scope of IFRS 2
2. distinguish between cash-settled and equity-settled share-based payment transactions
3. demonstrate how equity-settled and cash-settled share-based payment transactions are recognised
4. explain how equity-settled share-based payment transactions are measured
5. explain the concept of vesting through differentiating between vesting and non-vesting conditions
6. explain the concept of a share option reload feature
7. explain how modifications to granted equity instruments are treated
8. demonstrate how cash-settled share-based payment transactions are measured
9. describe and apply the disclosure requirements of IFRS 2.

INTRODUCTION

The purpose of this chapter is to examine share-based payments. The IFRS® Standard covering share-based payments is IFRS 2 *Share-based Payment*. Under IFRS 2, all transactions with employees or other parties — whether to be settled in cash (or settled in other assets) or settled in the equity instruments of an entity — must now be recognised in the entity's financial statements. The standard adopts the view that all share-based payment transactions ultimately lead to expense recognition, and entities must reflect the effects of such transactions in their profit or loss.

Organisations use various mechanisms to encourage their managers and employees to make decisions that improve the returns to shareholders, including offering remuneration that is linked to the share price of the organisation. This reflects a view that the behaviour of employees can be directed and controlled through the use of remuneration and other similar incentives. It is theorised that remuneration incentives linked to accounting and other performance measures will encourage managers and employees to take decisions and actions that positively impact the financial performance of the organisation and, in turn, the interests of shareholders of the organisation.

Share plans and share option plans are a common feature of remuneration for directors, senior managers and executives, and many other employees as a means of aligning employees' interests with those of the shareholders, and encouraging employee retention. Share plans reward employees by giving them shares or cash payments linked to the share price. Share option plans give the right to buy shares at a fixed price, which means that the option will expire worthless if the share price is below the exercise price at maturity. The value of the right to buy will increase as the share price increases once that price has been exceeded. Both types of plan reassure the shareholders that the directors and other employees have a direct financial interest in the share price increasing. The plans also provide an indirect incentive to remain with the company because rights to shares and share options rarely 'vest' until an agreed period, usually 3 years or more, have passed from the date on which the rights are 'granted'. Thus, an employee who resigns will almost certainly sacrifice the value of at least 2 years' worth of rights under any share plan or share option plan that is in place.

Most countries require quoted companies to publish details of their executive remuneration schemes. For example, the remuneration report provided by the Australian arm of Woolworths (Woolworths Limited) in its 2014 annual report provides more than 20 pages of disclosure and comment on the company's remuneration policies. These are prefaced by a statement of Woolworths Limited's reward principles (see figure 8.1).

Reward principles

- Align reward to shareholder value creation
- Attract, motivate and retain key talent with market competitive reward
- Provide demanding measures for high performance, which link reward to the Company's strategic and financial outcomes
- Deliver reward that is differentiated by business and individual performance

FIGURE 8.1 Woolworths Limited's reward principles
Source: Woolworths Ltd (2014, p. 46).

Companies have been criticised over the size of executive remuneration, for failing to align executive incentives more closely with shareholder returns, and for using short terms (1 to 3 years) for share incentives to vest rather than longer-term incentives (5 to 10 years). A review of Woolworths Limited's approach shows the inclusion of a long-term incentive component in its remuneration strategy. Companies have also been criticised for failure to disclose details of their executive performance hurdles, such as return on equity rates, which they usually justify on the basis of commercial sensitivity. *Details of required disclosures and examples of actual disclosures are presented in section 8.9.*

Some entities may also issue shares or share options to pay for the purchase of property or for professional advice or services. Before the issue of IFRS 2, there was no requirement to identify the expenses associated with this type of transaction or to measure and recognise such transactions in the financial statements of an entity. Accounting standard setters have decided that recognising the cost of share-based payments in the financial statements of entities should improve the relevance, reliability and comparability of financial information and help users of financial information to understand the economic transactions affecting entities.

8.1 APPLICATION AND SCOPE

IFRS 2 applies to share-based payment transactions. The standard was first issued with an effective date for financial statements covering periods beginning on or after 1 January 2005. IFRS 2 has since been amended for vesting conditions and cancellations, with an effective date for these amendments of

1 January 2009. Equity instruments issued in a business combination in exchange for control of the acquiree are not within the scope of IFRS 2; they are accounted for under IFRS 3 *Business Combinations*. However, IFRS 2 applies to the cancellation, replacement or modification of share-based payments arising because of a business combination or restructuring.

Also excluded under paragraph 6 of IFRS 2 are share-based payments in which the entity receives or acquires goods or services under a contract within the scope of paragraphs 8–10 of IAS 32 *Financial Instruments: Presentation* or paragraphs 2.4–2.7 of IFRS 9 *Financial Instruments*.

8.2 CASH-SETTLED AND EQUITY-SETTLED SHARE-BASED PAYMENT TRANSACTIONS

IFRS 2 applies to share-based payments in which an entity acquires or receives goods or services. Goods can include inventory, consumables, property, plant or equipment, intangibles and other non-financial forms of assets; services, such as the provision of labour, are usually consumed immediately.

Measurement principles and specific requirements for three forms of share-based payments are dealt with in IFRS 2. These three forms are defined in paragraph 2 and Appendix A to IFRS 2 and are summarised as follows:

1. *equity-settled* share-based payment transactions, in which the entity receives goods or services as consideration for its own equity instruments (including shares or share options)
2. *cash-settled* share-based payment transactions, in which the entity acquires goods or services by incurring liabilities to transfer cash or other assets to the supplier (counterparty) for amounts that are based on the value (price) of the shares or other equity instruments of the entity
3. *other* transactions in which the entity receives or acquires goods or services, and the terms of the arrangement provide either the entity or the counterparty of the goods or services with a choice of settling the transaction in cash (or other assets) or equity instruments.

The accounting treatment for these transactions differs depending on the form of settlement. The three forms and the essential features of share-based payment transactions are summarised in table 8.1.

TABLE 8.1 Form and features of share-based payment transactions

Form	Features
Equity-settled share-based payment	Entity receives goods or services as consideration for its own equity instruments
Cash-settled share-based payment	Entity acquires goods or services by incurring liabilities for amounts based on the value of its own equities
Other	Entity receives or acquires goods or services and the entity, or the counterparty, has the choice of whether the transaction is settled in cash or equity

Any transfers of an entity's equity instruments by its shareholders to parties that have supplied goods or services to the entity are considered, under paragraph 3A of IFRS 2, to be share-based payments (unless the transfer is clearly for a purpose other than payment for goods or services supplied to the entity). This treatment also applies to transfers of equity instruments of the entity's parent, or equity instruments of another entity in the same group as the entity, to parties that have supplied goods or services.

A transaction with an employee who holds equity instruments of the employing entity is not within the scope of IFRS 2 (paragraph 4). If, for example, the employee holds equity in the employer and is granted the right to acquire additional equity at a price that is less than fair value (e.g. a rights issue), the granting or exercise of that right by the employee is not governed by IFRS 2.

8.3 RECOGNITION

Paragraph 7 of IFRS 2 requires goods or services received in a share-based payment transaction to be recognised when they are received. A corresponding increase in equity must be recognised if the goods or services were received in an equity-settled share-based payment transaction. An increase in a liability must be recognised if the goods or services were acquired in a cash-settled share-based payment.

Usually an expense arises from the consumption of goods or services. For example, as services are normally consumed immediately, an expense is recognised as the service is rendered. If goods are consumed over a period of time or, as in the case of inventories, sold at a later date, an expense will not be recognised until the goods are consumed or sold. Sometimes it may be necessary to recognise an expense before the goods or services are consumed or sold because they do not qualify for recognition as assets. For example, this may occur if goods are acquired as part of the research phase of a project. Even though the goods may not have been consumed, they will not qualify for recognition as assets under other accounting standards. When the goods or services received in a share-based payment do not qualify for recognition as an asset, they must be expensed (IFRS 2 paragraph 8).

A share-based payment transaction would, depending on the principles for asset or liability recognition, be recognised in journal entries as shown below.

Asset or Expense	Dr	YYY	
Equity	Cr		XXX
(Recognition of an equity-settled share-based payment)			
Asset or Expense	Dr	XXX	
Liability	Cr		XXX
(Recognition of a cash-settled share-based payment)			

A significant feature of IFRS 2 is the accounting treatment it applies to transactions settled in cash, which is different to the treatment it applies to equity-settled transactions. If a share-based payment is settled in cash, the general principle employed in IFRS 2 is that the goods or services received and the liability incurred are measured at the fair value of the liability (IFRS 2 paragraph 10). The fair value of the liability must be remeasured at the end of each reporting period and at the date of settlement, and any changes in fair value are recognised in profit or loss (IFRS 2 paragraph 30). For share-based payment transactions that are equity-settled, the general principle is that the goods or services received and the corresponding increase in equity are measured at the date the goods or services are received, using the fair value of those goods or services. If the fair value cannot be measured reliably, the goods or services are measured indirectly by reference to the fair value of the equity instruments granted.

Under this approach a differential accounting treatment of changes in the fair value of equity instruments occurs, based on whether a transaction is classified as a liability or as equity. The fair value of transactions classified as equity is measured at the date the goods or services are received and subsequent value changes are ignored. In contrast, the fair value of transactions classified as liabilities (debt) are adjusted to fair value at the end of each reporting period and the resulting profit or loss is included in income.

8.4 EQUITY-SETTLED SHARE-BASED PAYMENT TRANSACTIONS

The goods or services received in equity-settled share-based payments and the corresponding increase in equity must be measured at the fair value of the goods or services unless that fair value cannot be estimated reliably (IFRS 2 paragraph 10). For transactions with parties other than employees, there is a rebuttable presumption in IFRS 2 (paragraph 13) that the fair value of goods or services can be estimated reliably. In the unusual cases where the fair value cannot be reliably estimated, paragraph 10 requires that the goods or services and the corresponding increase in equity are to be measured indirectly by reference to the fair value of the equity instruments granted at the date the goods are obtained or the service is rendered.

It is normally considered that the fair value of services received in transactions with employees cannot be reliably measured. Thus, the fair value of the services received from employees is measured by reference to the equity instruments granted. In summary, under IFRS 2, equity-settled share-based payments are measured and recognised as follows:

Asset or Expense	Dr	Fair value of goods or
Equity	Cr	services received or acquired
(Recognition of a share-based payment in which fair value of goods or services can be reliably estimated)		
Asset or Expense	Dr	Fair value of the equity
Equity	Cr	instruments granted
(Recognition of a share-based payment where fair value of goods or services cannot be reliably estimated)		

8.4.1 Transactions in which services are received

Certain conditions may need to be satisfied before the counterparty in a share-based payment transaction becomes entitled to receive cash (or other assets) or equity instruments of the entity. When the conditions have been satisfied, the counterparty's entitlement is said to have 'vested'. Under a share-based payment arrangement, a counterparty's right to receive cash, other assets or equity instruments of the entity vests when the counterparty's entitlement is no longer conditional on the satisfaction of any vesting conditions (IFRS 2 Appendix A).

If the equity instruments vest immediately, the counterparty is not required to serve a specified period of service before becoming unconditionally entitled to the equity instruments (IFRS 2 paragraph 14). On grant date, the services received are recognised in full together with a corresponding increase in equity. However, if the equity instruments do not vest until a period of service has been completed, under paragraph 15 the services and the corresponding increase in equity are accounted for across the vesting period as the services are rendered.

The granting of equity instruments in the form of share options to employees conditional on completing a 2-year period of service accounted for over the 2-year vesting period is demonstrated in illustrative example 8.1.

ILLUSTRATIVE EXAMPLE 8.1 Recognition of share options as services are rendered across the vesting period

Wang Ltd grants 100 share options to each of its 50 employees. Each grant is conditional upon the employee working for Wang Ltd for the next 2 years. It is assumed that each employee will satisfy the vesting conditions. At grant date, the fair value of each share option is estimated as $25.

According to IFRS 2, paragraph 15(a), Wang Ltd will recognise the following amounts during the vesting period for the services received from the employees as consideration for the share options granted.

Year	Calculation	Remuneration expense for period $	Cumulative remuneration expense $
1	(100 × 50 options) × $25 × 1/2 years	62 500	62 500
2	(100 × 50 options) × $25 − $62 500	62 500	125 000

8.4.2 Transactions measured by reference to the fair value of the equity instruments granted

Determining the fair value of equity instruments granted

Paragraph 11 of IFRS 2 states that, if share-based payments are with employees and others providing similar services, it is not usually possible to measure the fair value of services received. If it is not possible to reliably estimate the value of goods or services received, then the transaction is measured by reference to the fair value of the equity instruments granted. If market prices are not available, or if the equity instruments are subject to terms and conditions that do not apply to traded equity instruments, then a valuation technique must be used to estimate what the price of the equity instruments would have been, in an arm's length transaction, on the measurement date.

While IFRS 2 (Appendix B11–41) discusses the inputs to option-pricing models such as the Black–Scholes–Merton formula, the choice of model is left to the entity. The valuation technique chosen must be consistent with generally accepted valuation methodologies for pricing financial instruments. It must also incorporate the terms and conditions of the equity instruments (e.g. whether or not an employee is entitled to receive dividends during the vesting period), and any other factors and assumptions that knowledgeable, willing market participants would consider in setting the price (IFRS 2 paragraph 17). For instance, many employee share options have long lives, and they are usually exercisable after the vesting period and before the end of the option's life. Option-pricing models calculate a theoretical price by using key determinants of the options.

Appendix B6 of IFRS 2 supplies the following list of factors that option-pricing models take into account as a minimum:
- exercise price of the option
- life of the option
- current price of the underlying shares
- expected volatility of the share price
- dividends expected on the shares
- risk-free interest rate for the life of the option.

Expected volatility is a measure of the amount by which a price is expected to fluctuate during a period. The value of the option is generally greater if the share price is more volatile. High volatility implies that future share price movements are likely to be large. A large increase in the share price will make the option far more valuable than a small increase and so the upside risk is valuable to the option's holder. If the share price falls below the striking price then it makes no difference to the option's holder whether it is slightly lower or significantly lower. Volatility is typically expressed in annualised terms, for example, daily, weekly or monthly price observations. Often there is likely to be a range of reasonable expectations about future volatility, dividends and exercise date behaviour. If so, an expected value would be calculated by weighting each amount within the range by its associated probability of occurrence.

Expectations about the future are generally based on experience and modified if the future is reasonably expected to differ from the past. For instance, if an entity with two distinctly different lines of business disposes of the one that was significantly less risky than the other, historical volatility may not be the best information on which to base reasonable expectations for the future. In other circumstances, historical information may not be available. For example, unlisted entities will have no historical share price data; likewise, newly listed entities will have little share price data available.

Whether expected dividends should be taken into account when measuring the fair value of shares or options granted depends on whether the counterparty is entitled to dividends. Generally, the assumption about expected dividends is based on publicly available information.

The risk-free interest rate is the implied yield currently available on zero-coupon government issues of the country in whose currency the exercise price is expressed, with a remaining term equal to the expected term of the option (IFRS 2 Appendix B37). It may be necessary to use an appropriate substitute if no such government issues exist or if circumstances indicate that the implied yield on zero-coupon government issues is not representative of the risk-free interest rate (e.g. in high inflation economies).

Woolworths Limited (introduced earlier the chapter) discloses its use of an option pricing model in the determination of the fair value of options and performance rights. The company distinguishes vesting conditions that are based on earnings per share (EPS) measures from those that are based on total shareholder return (TSR). The company uses the Black–Scholes option pricing model to deal with the valuation of rights arising under EPS and Monte Carlo simulation for the valuation of TSR-related rights. The detailed application of both Black–Scholes and Monte Carlo simulation would be difficult to explain in further detail, so little more is said. These are, however, well-established and supported models that enable Woolworths to base valuations on the assumptions that have to be made in the valuation process. Thus, shareholders are alerted to the fact that the valuations are matters of judgement, but that there is a clear structure in place for drawing a final conclusion.

8.5 VESTING

8.5.1 Treatment of vesting conditions

If a grant of equity instruments is conditional on satisfying certain vesting conditions such as remaining in the entity's employment for a specified period of time, then the vesting conditions are not taken into account when estimating the fair value of the equity instruments. Instead, the vesting conditions are accounted for by adjusting the number of equity instruments included in the measurement of the transaction amount. Thus, the amount recognised for goods or services received as consideration for the equity instrument is based on the number of equity instruments that eventually vest. On a cumulative basis, this means that if a vesting condition is not satisfied then no amount is recognised for goods or services received.

In a situation where employees leave during the vesting period, the number of equity instruments expected to vest varies. This is demonstrated in illustrative example 8.2.

ILLUSTRATIVE EXAMPLE 8.2 Grant where the number of equity instruments expected to vest varies

Seers Company grants 100 share options to each of its 50 employees. Each grant is conditional on the employee working for the company for the next 3 years. The fair value of each share option is estimated as $25. On the basis of a weighted average probability, the company estimates that 10% of its employees will leave during the 3-year period and therefore forfeit their rights to the share options.

During the year immediately following grant date (year 1) three employees leave, and at the end of year 1 the company revised its estimate of total employee departures over the full 3-year period from 10% (five employees) to 16% (eight employees).

During year 2 a further two employees leave, and the company revised its estimate of total employee departures across the 3-year period down to 12% (six employees). During year 3 a further employee leaves, making a total of six (3 + 2 + 1) employees who have departed. A total of 4400 share options (44 employees × 100 options per employee) vested at the end of year 3.

Year	Calculation	Remuneration expense for period $	Cumulative remuneration expense $
1	(5000 options × 84%) × $25 × 1/3 years	35 000	35 000
2	([5000 options × 88%] × $25 × 2/3 years) − $35 000	38 333	73 333
3	(4400 options × $25) − $73 333	36 667	110 000

Source: Adapted from IFRS 2, IG11.

In addition to continuing in service with the entity, employees may be granted equity instruments that are conditional on the achievement of a performance condition. Where the length of the vesting period varies according to when the performance condition is satisfied, the estimated length of the vesting period, at grant date, is based on the most likely outcome of the performance condition (IFRS 2 paragraph 15(b)).

A grant of shares with a performance condition linked to the level of an entity's earnings and in which the length of the vesting period varies is demonstrated in illustrative example 8.3.

ILLUSTRATIVE EXAMPLE 8.3 Grant with a performance condition linked to earnings

At the beginning of year 1, Benning Ltd grants 100 shares to each of its 50 employees, conditional on the employee remaining in the company's employ during the 3-year vesting period. The shares have a fair value of $20 per share at grant date. No dividends are expected to be paid over the 3-year period. Additionally, the vesting conditions allow the shares to vest at the end of:
- year 1 if the company's earnings have increased by more than 18%
- year 2 if earnings have increased by more than 13% averaged across the 2-year period
- year 3 if earnings have increased by more than 10% averaged across the 3-year period.

By the end of year 1, Benning Ltd's earnings have increased by only 14% and three employees have left. The company expects that earnings will continue to increase at a similar rate in year 2 and the shares will vest at the end of year 2. It also expects that a further three employees will leave during year 2, and therefore that 44 employees will vest in 100 shares each at the end of year 2.

Year	Calculation	Remuneration expense for period $	Cumulative remuneration expense $
1	(44 employees × 100 shares) × $20 × 1/2 years	44 000	44 000

By the end of year 2 the company's earnings have increased by only 10%, resulting in an average of only 12% ([14% + 10%]/2) and so the shares do not vest. Two employees left during the year. The company expects that another two employees will leave during year 3 and that its earnings will increase by at least 6%, thereby achieving the average of 10% per year.

Year	Calculation	Remuneration expense for period $	Cumulative remuneration expense $
2	([43 employees × 100 shares] × $20 × 2/3 years) − $44 000	13 333	57 333

Another three employees leave during year 3 and the company's earnings have increased by 8%, resulting in an average increase of 10.67% over the 3-year period. Therefore, the performance condition has been satisfied. The 42 remaining employees (50 − [3 + 2 + 3]) are entitled to receive 100 shares each at the end of year 3.

Year	Calculation	Remuneration expense for period $	Cumulative remuneration expense $
3	([42 employees × 100 shares] × $20) − $57 333	26 667	84 000

Source: Adapted from IFRS 2, IG12.

An entity may also grant equity instruments to its employees with a performance condition, and where the exercise price varies. This particular situation is demonstrated in illustrative example 8.4.

Because the exercise price varies depending on the outcome of a performance condition that is not a market condition, the effect of the performance condition (in this case, the possibility that the exercise price might be either $40 or $30) is not taken into account when estimating the fair value of the share options at grant date. Instead, the entity estimates the fair value of the share options at grant date and ultimately revises the transaction amount to reflect the outcome of the performance condition.

ILLUSTRATIVE EXAMPLE 8.4 Grant of equity instruments where the exercise price varies

At the beginning of year 1 Phillipe Ltd granted 5000 share options with an exercise price of $40 to a senior executive, conditional upon the executive remaining with the company until the end of year 3. The exercise price drops to $30 if Phillipe Ltd's earnings increase by an average of 10% per year over the 3-year period. On grant date the estimated fair value of the share options with an exercise price of $40 is $12 per option and, if the exercise price is $30, the estimated fair value of the options is $16 per option.

During year 1 the company's earnings increased by 12% and they are expected to continue to increase at this rate over the next 2 years. During year 2 the company's earnings increased by 13% and the company continued to expect that the earnings target would be achieved. During year 3 the company's earnings increased by only 3%. The earnings target was therefore not achieved and so the 5000 vested share options will have an exercise price of $40. The executive completed 3 years' service and so satisfied the service condition.

Year	Calculation	Remuneration expense for period $	Cumulative remuneration expense $
1	5000 options × $16 × 1/3 years	26 667	26 667
2	(5000 options × $16 × 2/3 years) − $26 667	26 666	53 333
3	(5000 options × $12) − $53 333	6 667	60 000

Source: Adapted from IFRS 2, IG12.

Paragraph 21 of IFRS 2 requires that market conditions (such as a target share price) be taken into account when estimating the fair value of equity instruments. The goods or services received from a counterparty that satisfies all other vesting conditions (such as remaining in service for a specified period of time) are recognised whether or not the market condition is satisfied.

A grant of equity instruments with a market condition is demonstrated in illustrative example 8.5.

ILLUSTRATIVE EXAMPLE 8.5 Grant with a market condition

At the beginning of year 1 Smallville Ltd grants 5000 share options to a senior executive, conditional on that executive remaining in the company's employ until the end of year 3. The share options cannot be exercised unless the share price has increased from $15 at the beginning of year 1 to above $25 at the end of year 3. If the share price is above $25 at the end of year 3, the share options can be exercised at any time during the next 7 years (that is, by the end of year 10). The company applies an option-pricing model that takes into account the possibility that the share price will exceed $25 at the end of year 3 and the possibility that the share price will not exceed $25 at the end of year 3. It estimates the fair value of the share options with this embedded market condition to be $9 per option. The executive completes 3 years' service with Smallville Ltd.

Year	Calculation	Remuneration expense for period $	Cumulative remuneration expense $
1	5000 options × $9 × 1/3 years	15 000	15 000
2	(5000 options × $9 × 2/3 years) − $15 000	15 000	30 000
3	(5000 options × $9) − $30 000	15 000	45 000

Source: Adapted from IFRS 2, IG13.

As noted earlier, because the executive has satisfied the service condition, the company is required to recognise these amounts irrespective of the outcome of the market condition.

8.5.2 Treatment of non-vesting conditions

Vesting conditions comprise service and performance conditions only, and other features of a share-based payment are not vesting conditions.

All non-vesting conditions are taken into account when estimating the fair value of equity instruments granted (paragraph 21A). Under this provision, for grants of equity with non-vesting conditions, an entity must recognise the goods or services received from a counterparty that satisfy all vesting conditions that are not market conditions (such as services from an employee who remains in service for a specified period of time). This applies whether or not the non-vesting conditions are satisfied.

The process of determining whether or not a condition is a non-vesting condition, or a service or performance condition, is illustrated in the flowchart in figure 8.2.

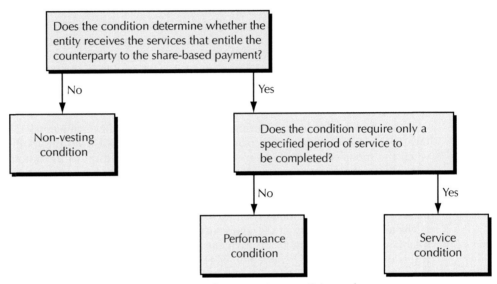

FIGURE 8.2 Distinguishing vesting and non-vesting conditions
Source: Adapted from Australian Accounting Standards Board (AASB) 2008–1, IG11.

8.6 TREATMENT OF A RELOAD FEATURE

Employee share options often include features that are not found in exchange-traded options. One such feature is a *reload* which entitles the employee to be automatically granted new options when the previously granted options are exercised using shares rather than cash to satisfy the exercise price. Although a reload feature can add considerably to an option's value, it is not considered feasible to value the reload feature at grant date. Under paragraph 22 of IFRS 2, a reload feature is not taken into account when estimating the fair value of the options granted at measurement date. Instead, a reload feature is accounted for as a new option if and when a reload option is subsequently granted.

After vesting date

Having recognised the goods or services received and a corresponding increase in equity, paragraph 23 of IFRS 2 prevents an entity from making a subsequent adjustment to total equity after vesting date. For example, if an amount is recognised for services received from an employee, it may not be reversed if the vested equity instruments are later forfeited or, in the case of share options, if the options are not subsequently exercised. This restriction applies only to total equity; it does not preclude an entity from transferring amounts from one component of equity to another.

If the fair value of the equity instruments cannot be estimated reliably

In the event that the fair value of equity instruments cannot be reliably estimated, they must instead be measured at their intrinsic value (IFRS 2 paragraph 24(a)). Intrinsic value is measured at the date goods are obtained or services are rendered, at the end of each subsequent reporting period, and at the date of final settlement. Any change in intrinsic value must be recognised in profit or loss. For a grant of share options, the share-based payment arrangement is finally settled when the options are exercised, forfeited, or when they lapse. The amount to be recognised for goods or services is based on the number of equity instruments that ultimately vest or are exercised. The estimate must be revised if subsequent information indicates that the number of share options expected to vest differs from previous estimates. On vesting date, the estimate is then revised to equal the number of equity instruments that ultimately vest.

8.7 MODIFICATIONS TO TERMS AND CONDITIONS ON WHICH EQUITY INSTRUMENTS WERE GRANTED

An entity might choose to modify the terms and conditions on which it granted equity instruments. For example, it might change (reprice/retest) the exercise price of share options previously granted to employees at prices that were higher than the current price of the entity's shares. It might accelerate the vesting of share options to make the options more favourable to employees; or it might remove or alter a performance condition. If the exercise price of options is modified, the fair value of the options changes. A reduction in the exercise price would increase the fair value of share options. Irrespective of any modifications to the terms and conditions on which equity instruments are granted, paragraph 27 of IFRS 2 requires the services received, measured at the grant-date fair value of the equity instruments, to be recognised unless those equity instruments do not vest.

The incremental effects of modifications that increase the total fair value of the share-based payment arrangement, or that are otherwise beneficial to the employee, must also be recognised. The incremental fair value is the difference between the fair value of the modified equity instrument and that of the original equity instrument, both estimated at the date of modification (IFRS 2 Appendix B43(a)). Similarly, if the modification increases the number of equity instruments granted, the fair value of the additional equity instruments, measured at the date of modification, must be included in the amount recognised for services received.

If the modification occurs during the vesting period, the incremental fair value is included in the measurement of the amount recognised for services received from the modification date until the date when the modified equity instruments vest. This is in addition to the amount based on the grant-date fair value of the original equity instruments that is recognised over the remainder of the original vesting period. If the modification occurs after the vesting date, the incremental fair value is recognised immediately, or over the vesting period if the employee is required to complete an additional period of service before becoming unconditionally entitled to the modified equity instruments.

The terms or conditions of the equity instruments granted may be modified in a manner that reduces the total fair value of the share-based payment arrangement or that is not otherwise beneficial to the employee. If this occurs, then IFRS 2 (Appendix B44) requires the services received as consideration to be accounted for as if that modification had not occurred (i.e. the decrease in fair value is not to be taken into account).

Illustrative example 8.6 demonstrates the accounting treatment of a repricing modification to the terms and conditions of share options.

ILLUSTRATIVE EXAMPLE 8.6 Grant of equity instruments that are subsequently repriced

Merton Ltd grants 100 share options to each of its 50 employees, conditional upon the employee remaining in service over the next 3 years. The company estimates that the fair value of each option is $15. On the basis of a weighted average probability, the company also estimates that 10 employees will leave during the 3-year vesting period and therefore forfeit their rights to the share options.

A Four employees leave during year 1, and the company estimates that a further seven employees will leave during years 2 and 3. By the end of year 1 the company's share price has dropped, and it decides to reprice the share options. The repriced share options will vest at the end of year 3. At the date of repricing, Merton Ltd estimates that the fair value of each of the original share options is $5 and the fair value of each repriced share option is $8. The incremental value is $3 per share option, and this amount is recognised over the remaining 2 years of the vesting period along with the remuneration expense based on the original option value of $15.

Year	Calculation	Remuneration expense for period $	Cumulative remuneration expense $
A 1	(50 − 11) employees × 100 options × $15 × 1/3 years	19 500	19 500

B During year 2, a further four employees leave, and the company estimates that another four employees will leave during year 3 to bring the total expected employee departures over the 3-year vesting period to 12 employees.

Year		Calculation	Remuneration expense for period $	Cumulative remuneration expense $
B	2	([50 − 12] employees × 100 options) × ([$15 × 2/3 years] + [$3 × 1/2 years]) − $19 500	24 200	43 700

C A further three employees leave during year 3. For the remaining 39 employees (50 − [4 + 4 + 3]), the share options vested at the end of year 3.

Year		Calculation	Remuneration expense for period $	Cumulative remuneration expense $
C	3	([50 − 11] employees × 100 options × [$15 + $3]) − $43 700	26 500	70 200

Source: Adapted from IFRS 2, IG15.

8.7.1 Repurchases

If vested equity instruments are repurchased, IFRS 2 (paragraph 29) specifies that the payment made to the employee is accounted for as a deduction from equity. If the payment exceeds the fair value of the equity instruments repurchased, the excess is recognised as an expense.

8.8 CASH-SETTLED SHARE-BASED PAYMENT TRANSACTIONS

Paragraphs 30–33 of IFRS 2 set out the requirements for share-based payments in which an entity incurs a liability for goods or services received, based on the price of its own equity instruments. These are known as cash-settled share-based payments. The fair value of the liability involved is remeasured at the end of each reporting period and the date of settlement, and any changes in the fair value are recognised in profit or loss for the period. In contrast, the fair value of equity-settled share-based payments is determined at grant date, and remeasurement of the granted equity instruments at the end of each subsequent reporting period and settlement date does not occur.

Examples of cash-settled share-based payments included in paragraph 31 of IFRS 2 are share appreciation rights that might be granted to an employee as part of a remuneration package. Share appreciation rights entitle the holder to a future cash payment (rather than an equity instrument) based on increases in the share price. Another example is where an employee is granted rights to shares that are redeemable, providing the employee with a right to receive a future cash payment.

There is a presumption in IFRS 2 that the services rendered by employees in exchange for the share appreciation rights have been received. Where share appreciation rights vest immediately, the services and the associated liability must also be recognised immediately. Where the share appreciation rights do not vest until the employees have completed a specified period of service, the services received and the associated liability to pay for those services are recognised as the service is rendered. The liability is measured, initially and at the end of each reporting period until settled, at the fair value of the share appreciation rights by applying an option-pricing model that takes into account the terms and conditions on which share appreciation rights were granted, and the extent to which employees have rendered service (paragraph 33).

Illustrative example 8.7 provides an example of the accounting treatment for cash-settled share appreciation rights.

ILLUSTRATIVE EXAMPLE 8.7 Cash-settled share appreciation rights

Brierley Ltd grants 100 share appreciation rights (SARs) to each of its 50 employees, conditional upon the employee staying with the company for the next 3 years. The company estimates the fair value of the SARs at the end of each year as shown below. The intrinsic values of the SARs at the date of exercise (which equal the cash paid out) at the end of years 3, 4 and 5 are also shown. All SARs held by employees remaining at the end of year 3 will vest.

Year	Fair value	Intrinsic value
1	$14.40	
2	$15.50	
3	$18.20	$15.00
4	$21.40	$20.00
5		$25.00

A   During year 1, three employees leave and the company estimates that six more will leave during years 2 and 3.

B   Four employees leave during year 2, and the company estimates that three more will leave during year 3.

Year	Calculation	Expense $	Liability $
A 1	(50 − 9) employees × 100 SARs × $14.40 × 1/3 years	19 680	19 680
B 2	([50 − 10] employees × 100 SARs × $15.50 × 2/3 years) − $19 680	21 653	41 333

C   Two employees leave during year 3.
D   At the end of year 3, 15 employees have exercised their SARs.
E   Another 14 employees exercise their SARs at the end of year 4.
F   The remaining 12 employees exercise their SARs at the end of year 5.

Year	Calculation	Expense $	Liability $
C 3 D	([50 − 9 − 15] employees × 100 SARs × $18.20) − $41 333 15 employees × 100 SARs × $15	5 987 22 500	47 320
E 4	([26 − 14] employees × 100 SARs × $21.40) − $47 320 14 employees × 100 SARs × $20	(21 640) 28 000	25 680
F 5	(0 employees × 100 SARs × $25) − $25 680 12 employees × 100 SARs × $25	(25 680) 30 000	0
	Total	80 500	

Source: Adapted from IFRS 2, IG19.

8.8.1 Share-based payment transactions with cash alternatives

Some share-based payments may provide either the entity or the counterparty with the choice of having the transaction settled in cash (or other assets) or the issue of equity instruments. If the entity has incurred a liability to settle in cash or other assets, the transaction is treated as a cash-settled share-based payment. If no liability has been incurred, paragraph 34 of IFRS 2 requires that the transaction be treated as an equity-settled share-based payment.

Share-based payment transactions where the counterparty has settlement choice

If the counterparty to a share-based payment has the right to choose whether a transaction is settled in cash or equity instruments, a compound financial instrument has been created that includes a debt component and an equity component. The debt component represents the counterparty's right to demand a cash settlement, and the equity component represents the counterparty's right to demand settlement in equity instruments.

IFRS 2 (paragraphs 35, 36) requires that transactions with employees be measured at fair value on measurement date, by taking into account the terms and conditions on which rights to cash and equity were granted. For transactions with others in which the fair value of goods or services is measured directly, the equity component is measured as the difference between the fair value of the goods or services received and the fair value of the debt component at the date they are received. The fair value of the debt component is measured before the fair value of the equity component (paragraph 37), as the counterparty must forfeit the right to receive cash in order to receive equity instruments. The measurement of compound financial instruments with employees (and other counterparties) is summarised in table 8.2.

TABLE 8.2 Measurement of compound financial instruments

Counterparty	Measurement approach
Employees	Measure fair value (FV) of the debt component then FV of the equity component, at measurement date, taking into account the terms and conditions on which rights to cash or equity were granted
Parties other than employees	Equity component is the difference between FV of goods or services received and FV of the debt component, at the date the goods or services are received

The goods or services received in respect of each component of the compound financial instrument must be accounted for separately. For the debt component, the goods or services and a liability to pay for them is recognised as the counterparty supplies the goods or services, in the same manner as other cash-settled share-based payments. For the equity component, the goods or services received and the increase in equity are recognised as the counterparty supplies the goods or services, in the same manner as other equity-settled share-based payments.

At settlement date, the liability must be remeasured to fair value (IFRS 2 paragraph 39). If equity instruments are issued rather than a cash settlement paid, the liability must be transferred directly to equity as consideration for the equity instruments. If the counterparty takes cash settlement, the payment is applied in settlement of the liability. Any equity component previously recognised remains within equity although it can be transferred within equity.

A grant of shares with a cash alternative subsequently added that provides an employee with a settlement choice is demonstrated in illustrative example 8.8.

ILLUSTRATIVE EXAMPLE 8.8 Grant of shares with a cash alternative subsequently added

At the beginning of year 1, Scotland Ltd granted 10 000 shares with a fair value of $24 per share to a senior manager, conditional on the manager remaining in the company's employ for 3 years. By the end of year 2 the share price had dropped to $15 per share. At that date the company added a cash alternative to the grant, giving the manager the right to choose whether to receive the 10 000 shares or cash equal to the value of the shares on vesting date. On vesting date the share price had dropped to $12.

Year	Calculation	Asset/expense $	Equity $	Liability $
1	10 000 shares × $24 × 1/3 years	80 000	80 000	

The addition of the cash alternative at the end of year 2 created an obligation to settle in cash. Scotland Ltd must recognise the liability to settle in cash based on the fair value of the shares at the modification date and the extent to which the specified services have been received. The liability must be remeasured at the end of each subsequent reporting period and at the date of settlement.

Year	Calculation	Asset/expense $	Equity $	Liability $
2	(10 000 shares × $24 × 2/3 years) − $80 000 10 000 shares × $15 × 2/3 years	80 000	80 000 (100 000)	100 000*

Year	Calculation	Asset/expense $	Equity $	Liability $
3	(10 000 shares × $24) − $160 000 (10 000 shares × $12) − $150 000	80 000 (30 000)	30 000	50 000* (30 000)
	Total	210 000	90 000	120 000**

* At the date of modification when the cash alternative is added the total liability is $150 000 ($15 x 10 000 shares). At this date a potential liability must be recognised.
** Total liability at date of settlement is $120 000 ($12 x 10 000 shares).

Source: Adapted from IFRS 2, IG15.

Share-based payment transactions where the entity has settlement choice

Where an entity has a choice of settling in cash or equity instruments, it must determine whether it has a present obligation to settle in cash. Paragraph 41 of IFRS 2 states that an entity has a present obligation to settle in cash if the choice of settlement in equity instruments has no commercial substance (perhaps the entity is legally prohibited from issuing shares), it has a past practice or a stated policy of settling in cash, or if it generally settles in cash whenever the counterparty asks for cash settlement. If a present obligation exists, the transaction must be accounted for as a cash-settled share-based payment. If a present obligation to settle in cash does not exist, the transaction is accounted for as an equity-settled arrangement.

On settlement, if the entity elects to settle in cash, paragraph 43(a) of IFRS 2 requires the cash payment to be accounted for as the repurchase of an equity interest, resulting in a deduction from equity. Where there is an equity settlement, no further accounting adjustments are required. If, on settlement, the entity selects the settlement alternative with the higher fair value, an additional expense for the excess value given must be recognised. The excess value is either the difference between the cash paid and the fair value of the equity instruments that would have been issued, or the difference between the fair value of the equity instruments issued and the amount of cash that would have been paid, whichever is applicable.

8.9 DISCLOSURE

The global financial crisis which emerged in 2008 has resulted in much criticism about the inadequacy of disclosure in regard to performance hurdles and incentives used in share-based payment transactions. Corporate executives, on the other hand, complain about the onerous reporting and disclosure requirements necessary under the accounting rules. One difficulty faced by regulators is how to reduce the volume of required information yet still retain meaningful and useful disclosure.

Paragraphs 44–52 of IFRS 2 prescribe various disclosures relating to share-based payments. The objective of these disclosures is to provide significant additional information to assist financial statement users to understand the nature and extent of share-based payment arrangements that existed during the reporting period. The three principles that underpin the disclosures required by IFRS 2 are shown in table 8.3.

TABLE 8.3 Principles underpinning the disclosures in IFRS 2	
Disclosure principle	**IFRS 2 paragraph**
The nature and extent of the share-based payment arrangements.	44
How the fair value of goods or services received, or the fair value of equity instruments granted during the period, was determined.	46
The effect of share-based payment transactions on the entity's profit or loss for the period and on its financial position.	50

Paragraph 45 of IFRS 2 specifies the disclosures necessary to give effect to the principle in paragraph 44 as including at least the following:
- a description of each type of share-based payment arrangement that existed at any time during the period, including the general terms and conditions of each arrangement, such as vesting requirements, the maximum term of options granted, and the methods of settlement.

An entity with substantially similar types of share-based payments may aggregate this information unless separate disclosure of each arrangement is necessary to enable users to understand the nature and extent of the arrangements.

Other specific disclosures required by paragraph 45 are the number and weighted average exercise prices of share options for options that:
- are outstanding at the beginning of the period
- are granted during the period
- are forfeited during the period
- are exercised during the period

- have expired during the period
- are outstanding at the end of the period
- are exercisable at the end of the period.

In relation to share options exercised during the period, the weighted average share price at the date of exercise must be disclosed. If the options were exercised on a regular basis throughout the period, the weighted average share price during the period may be disclosed instead. For share options outstanding at the end of the period, the range of exercise prices and weighted average remaining contractual life must be disclosed. If the range of exercise prices is wide, the outstanding options must be divided into ranges that are meaningful for assessing the number and timing of additional shares that may be issued and the cash that may be received upon exercise of those options.

If the fair value of goods or services received as consideration for equity instruments of the entity has been measured indirectly by reference to the fair value of the equity instruments granted, the following information must be disclosed (paragraph 47):
- the weighted average fair value of share options granted during the period, at the measurement date, and information on how the fair value was measured including:
  - the option-pricing model used and the inputs to that model including the weighted average share price, exercise price, expected volatility, option life, expected dividends, the risk-free interest rate, and any other inputs to the model including the assumptions made to incorporate the effects of expected early exercise
  - how expected volatility was determined, including an explanation of the extent to which expected volatility was based on historical volatility
  - whether, and how many, other features of the option grant (such as a market condition) were incorporated into the measurement of fair value
- for equity instruments other than share options granted during the period, the number and weighted average fair value at the measurement date, and information on how that fair value was measured, including:
  - if not measured on the basis of an observable market price, how fair value was determined
  - whether and how expected dividends were incorporated
  - whether and how any other features of the equity instruments were incorporated
- for share-based payment arrangements that were modified during the period:
  - an explanation of the modifications
  - the incremental fair value granted as a result of the modifications and information on how the incremental fair value granted was measured.

If the entity has measured the fair value of goods or services received during the period directly, it is required to disclose how that fair value was determined (e.g. at market price).

If the entity has rebutted the assumption that the fair value of goods or services received can be estimated reliably, it is required to disclose that fact (paragraph 49) together with an explanation of why the presumption was rebutted.

Paragraph 51 gives effect to the principle that an entity must disclose information that enables financial statement users to understand the effect of share-based payments on the entity's profit or loss for the period and on its financial position. This paragraph requires disclosure of at least the following:
- the total expense recognised for the period arising from share-based payments in which the goods or services received did not qualify for recognition as assets, including separate disclosure of that portion of the total expense that arises from transactions accounted for as equity-settled share-based payments
- for liabilities arising from share-based payment transactions:
  - the total carrying amount at the end of the period
  - the total intrinsic value at the end of the period of liabilities for which the counterparty's right to cash or other assets had vested by the end of the period.

Finally, paragraph 52 requires the disclosure of such other additional information as may be needed to enable the users of the financial statements to understand the nature and extent of the share-based payment arrangements; how the fair value of goods or services received, or the fair value of equity instruments granted, was determined; and the effect of share-based payments on the entity's profit or loss and on its financial position.

A review of the corporate annual reports shows the large volume of space devoted to share-based payment disclosure. For example, it has already been stated that Woolworth Limited's 2014 remuneration report covers more than 20 pages, much of which relates to share-based payments. In addition, there is an extensive note to the consolidated financial statements that adds a further 8 pages of disclosure.

SUMMARY

IFRS 2 deals with the recognition and measurement of share-based payment transactions. Share-based payments are arrangements in which an entity receives or acquires goods or services as consideration for, or based on the price of (respectively) its own equity instruments. The main features of the standard are that it:

- requires financial statement recognition of the goods or services acquired or received under share-based payment arrangements, regardless of whether the settlement is cash or equity or whether the counterparty is an employee or another party.
- employs the general principle for cash-settled transactions that the goods or services received and the liability incurred are measured at the fair value of the liability; and, until it is settled, the fair value of the liability is remeasured at the end of each reporting period and at the date of settlement and any changes in fair value are recognised in profit or loss.
- employs the general principle for equity-settled transactions that the goods or services received and the corresponding increase in equity are measured at the grant date, and at the fair value of the goods or services received; and if the fair value cannot be measured reliably, the goods or services are measured indirectly by reference to the fair value of the equity instruments granted.
- allows an entity to choose appropriate option-valuation models to determine fair values and to tailor those models to suit the entity's specific circumstances.
- includes a lengthy set of disclosure requirements aimed at enabling financial statement users to understand the nature, extent and effect of share-based payments, and how the fair value of goods or services received or equity instruments granted was determined.

Discussion questions

1. Why do standard setters formulate rules on the measurement and recognition of share-based payment transactions?
2. What is the difference between equity-settled and cash-settled share-based payment transactions?
3. What is the different accounting treatment for instruments classified as debt and those classified as equity?
4. Outline the accounting treatment for the recognition of an equity-settled share-based payment transaction.
5. Explain when a counterparty's entitlement to receive equity instruments of an entity vests.
6. What are the minimum factors required under IFRS 2 to be taken into account in option-pricing models?
7. Distinguish between vesting and non-vesting conditions.
8. Explain what the 'retesting' of share options means.
9. Explain the measurement approach for cash-settled share-based payment transactions.
10. Are the following statements true or false?
    (a) Goods or services received in a share-based payment transaction must be recognised when they are received.
    (b) Historical volatility provides the best basis for forming reasonable expectations of the future price of share options.
    (c) Share appreciation rights entitle the holder to a future equity instrument based on the profitability of the issuer.

References

International Accounting Standards Board 2009, *IFRS 2 Share-based Payments*, IFRS Foundation, London, www.ifrs.org.

Woolworths Ltd 2014, *Annual Report 2014*, Woolworths Limited, Australia, www.woolworthslimited.com.au.

Exercises

STAR RATING ★ BASIC ★★ MODERATE ★★★ DIFFICULT

Exercise 8.1	SCOPE OF IFRS 2

★ Which of the following is a share-based payment transaction within the scope of IFRS 2? Give reasons for your answer.

(a) Goods acquired from a supplier (counterparty) by incurring a liability based on the market price of the goods
(b) An invoiced amount for professional advice provided to an entity, charged at an hourly rate, and to be settled in cash
(c) Services provided by an employee to be settled in equity instruments of the entity
(d) Supply of goods in return for cash or equity instruments at the discretion of the counterparty
(e) Dividend payment to employees who are holders of an entity's shares

Exercise 8.2
★ EQUITY-SETTLED SHARE-BASED PAYMENT TRANSACTIONS

On 1 January 2016, Park Ltd announces a grant of 250 share options to each of its 20 senior executives. The grant is conditional on the employee continuing to work for Park Ltd for the next 3 years. The fair value of each share option is estimated to be $14. On the basis of a weighted average probability, Park Ltd estimates that 10% of its senior executives will leave during the vesting period.

Required

Prepare a schedule setting out the annual and cumulative remuneration expense to be recognised by Park Ltd for services rendered as consideration for the share options granted.

Exercise 8.3
★★ ACCOUNTING FOR A GRANT WHERE THE NUMBER OF EQUITY INSTRUMENTS EXPECTED TO VEST VARIES

Tiger Ltd grants 80 share options to each of its 200 employees. Each grant is conditional on the employee working for the company for the 3 years following the grant date. On grant date, the fair value of each share option is estimated to be $12. On the basis of a weighted average probability, the company estimates that 20% of its employees will leave during the 3-year vesting period.

During year 1, 15 employees leave and the company revises its estimate of total employee departures over the full 3-year period from 20% to 22%.

Required

Prepare a schedule setting out the annual and cumulative remuneration expense for year 1.

Exercise 8.4
★★ ACCOUNTING FOR A GRANT OF SHARE OPTIONS WHERE THE EXERCISE PRICE VARIES

At the beginning of 2015, Whistler Ltd grants 3000 employee share options with an exercise price of $45 to its newly appointed chief executive officer, conditional on the executive remaining in the company's employ for the next 3 years. The exercise price drops to $35 if Whistler Ltd's earnings increase by an average of 10% per year over the 3-year period. On grant date, the estimated fair value of the employee share options with an exercise price of $35 is $22 per option. If the exercise price is $45, the options have an estimated fair value of $17 each.

During 2015, Whistler Ltd's earnings increased by 8% and are expected to continue to increase at this rate over the next 2 years.

Required

Prepare a schedule setting out the annual remuneration expense to be recognised by Whistler Ltd and the cumulative remuneration expense for 2015.

Exercise 8.5
★★ ACCOUNTING FOR A GRANT WITH A MARKET CONDITION

At the beginning of 2016, Bay Ltd grants 10 000 share options to a senior marketing executive, conditional on that executive remaining in the company's employ until the end of 2018. The share options cannot be exercised unless the share price has increased from $20 at the beginning of 2016 to above $30 at the end of 2018. If the share price is above $30 at the end of 2016, the share options can be exercised at any time during the following 5 years. Bay Ltd applies a binomial option-pricing model that takes into account the possibility that the share price will exceed $30 at the end of 2018 and the possibility that the share price will not exceed $30 at the end of 2018. The fair value of the share options with this market condition is estimated to be $14 per option.

Required

Calculate the annual and cumulative remuneration expense to be recognised by Bay Ltd for 2016.

Exercise 8.6
★★★ SHARE-BASED PAYMENT WITH A NON-VESTING CONDITION

An employee is offered the opportunity to contribute 10% of his annual salary of $3000 across the next 2 years to a plan under which he receives share options. The employee's accumulated contributions to the plan may be used to exercise the options at the end of the 2-year period. The estimated annual expense for this share-based payment arrangement is $200.

Required

Prepare the necessary journal entry or entries to recognise this arrangement at the end of the first year.

ACCOUNTING FOR CASH-SETTLED SHARE-BASED PAYMENT TRANSACTIONS

★★★ Abernethy Ltd grants 1000 share appreciation rights (SARs) to 10 senior managers, to be taken in cash within 2 years of vesting date on condition that the managers do not leave in the next 3 years. The SARs vest at the end of year 3. Abernethy Ltd estimates the fair value of the SARs at the end of each year in which a liability exists as shown below. The intrinsic value of the SARs at the date of exercise at the end of year 3 is also shown.

Year	Fair value	Intrinsic value	Number of managers who exercised their SARs
1	$ 4.40		
2	$ 5.50		
3	$10.20	$9.00	4

During year 1, one employee leaves and Abernethy Ltd estimates that a further two will leave before the end of year 3. One employee leaves during year 2 and the corporation estimates that another employee will depart during year 3. One employee leaves during year 3. At the end of year 3, four employees exercise their SARs.

Required

Prepare a schedule setting out the expense and liability that Abernethy Ltd must recognise at the end of each of the first 3 years.

Share-based payments received attention in academic research almost exclusively with respect to share-based compensation. One strand in this research challenges the accounting treatment of expensing this form of compensation and whether the use of fair value is relevant and reliable. A second strand has tried to understand the economic consequences of share-based compensation. A third strand reviewed here concerns how share-based compensation may affect earnings management.

In contrast to ordinary salary expense, share-based compensation has the important element of incentive that aligns employee interest with that of shareholders. That is, share-based payments carry both cost and value to issuing employers (Hall and Murphy, 2002). It is therefore interesting to find if investors agree with the treatment of expensing. An argument against expensing and in favour of recognition of an (intangible) asset is that share-based compensation may generate benefits (or, value) that exceed its cost. In addition, unlike cash payments, the related expense is measured by reference to fair values, which raises a concern whether the recorded amount is sufficiently reliable. Bell et al. (2002) examine how investors perceive share-based expense in a sample of 85 profitable firms. They find that market value of equity is positively related to the share-based compensation. Hanlon et al. (2003) argue that the positive effects documented by Bell et al. (2002) arise only in certain circumstances. They posit that share-based compensation is positively related to future performance only when firms issue employee stock options that are at a level that is appropriate for their underlying economic conditions and corporate governance mechanisms. Consistent with this prediction, Hanlon et al. (2003) find positive (negative) association with future performance for share-based compensation that is determined by (deviates from) these fundamentals. These two studies therefore suggest that the benefits of share-based compensation exceed the costs, at least in certain circumstances. Aboody (1996) examines the relation between the value of outstanding stock options and share prices. He finds a negative relation, suggesting options are net cost to employers. This evidence therefore justifies expensing. However, he also finds a positive relation when options are measured closer to the grant date. One interpretation of this is that benefits exceed costs at the outset, but are then incorporated into earnings and prices faster than the cost. In an attempt to separate between the incentive and cost effect Aboody et al. (2004) proxy for the benefit effect by using analyst predictions of future growth. Once controlling for growth, they find that share-based expense is negatively related to stock prices and stock returns, as would be expected from an expense. Hence, from this strand of research we get mixed evidence as to whether share-based compensation is a net expense or net benefit. Nevertheless, establishing the above relations (whether positive or negative) suggests that share-based compensation is useful and reliable.

Dechow et al. (1996) turn attention to the economic consequences of share-based compensation. Many opponents to the treatment of expensing argue that this could limit their access to equity and debt markets, which in turn would negatively affect their performance. In 1993 the FASB issued its Exposure Draft proposing the expense of employee stock options. Dechow et al. (1996) argue that if adverse consequences to the expensing are present, then one should find support in the behaviour of stock prices of firms that issue large amounts of employee stock options. They therefore examine stock returns around events that increased the probability of adopting the new expensing rule. However, their analysis fails to find a more pronounced effect on stock prices for firms that issue more employee stock options. They therefore conclude that markets did not anticipate any adverse real effect of the new accounting rule.

Another economic consequence of share-based payment is its scope to motivate risk-averse managers to engage in more risky projects for the benefit of well-diversified investors. Rajgopal and Shevlin (2002) test this theory in the Oil and Gas industry. They find a positive link between share-based compensation to managers and exploration activity, their proxy to managerial risk-taking. Cheng (2004) finds that share-based compensation encourages managers to engage in research and development (R&D) activity. Because R&D may be quite risky in nature (Kothari et al., 2002; Amir et al., 2007), this provides additional evidence as to the positive link between share-based compensation and risk-taking.

While share-based compensation works to align the incentives of managers with those of shareholders, managers may feel they are over-exposed to the specific risk of the company they run. To remedy this, they may want to diversify by selling vested options and shares (Ofek and Yermack, 2007). This, in turn, may provide them the incentive to manage earnings prior to the sale of their shares to positively affect share price. To explore this possibility, Cheng and Warfield (2005) examine the propensity of earnings to meet certain targets, such as analyst forecasts. They find that firms that award high levels of share-based compensation to their managers are more likely to meet or beat analyst forecasts. Additionally they find that managers that meet or beat analyst forecasts tend to sell more shares afterward than managers that do not meet analyst forecasts. Bergstresser and Philippon (2006) provide complementary evidence. They find that managers whose overall compensation is more sensitive to changes in stock prices typically managers that are awarded large share-based compensation, tend to manage accruals to a greater degree.

References

Aboody, D. 1996. Market valuation of employee stock options. *Journal of Accounting and Economics*, 22(1), 357–391.

Aboody, D., Barth, M. E., and Kasznik, R. 2004. SFAS No. 123 stock-based compensation expense and equity market values. *The Accounting Review*, 79(2), 251–275.

Amir, E., Guan, Y., and Livne, G. 2007. The association of R&D and capital expenditures with subsequent earnings variability. *Journal of Business Finance & Accounting*, 34(1–2), 222–246.

Bell, T. B., Landsman, W. R., Miller, B. L., and Yeh, S. 2002. The valuation implications of employee stock option accounting for profitable computer software firms. *The Accounting Review*, 77(4), 971–996.

Bergstresser, D., and Philippon, T. 2006. CEO incentives and earnings management. *Journal of Financial Economics*, 80(3), 511–529.

Cheng, Q., and Warfield, T. D. 2005. Equity incentives and earnings management. *The accounting review*, 80(2), 441–476.

Cheng, S. 2004. R&D expenditures and CEO compensation. *The Accounting Review*, 79(2), 305–328.

Dechow, P. M., Hutton, A. P., and Sloan, R. G. 1996. Economic consequences of accounting for stock-based compensation. *Journal of Accounting Research*, 34, 1–20.

Hall, B. J., and Murphy, K. J. 2002. Stock options for undiversified executives. *Journal of Accounting and Economics*, 33, 3–42.

Hanlon, M., Rajgopal, S., and Shevlin, T. 2003. Are executive stock options associated with future earnings? *Journal of Accounting and Economics*, 36(1), 3–43.

Kothari, S. P., Laguerre, T. E., and Leone, A. J. 2002. Capitalization versus expensing: Evidence on the uncertainty of future earnings from capital expenditures versus R&D outlays. *Review of Accounting Studies*, 7(4), 355–382.

Ofek, E., and Yermack, D. 2000. Taking stock: Equity-based compensation and the evolution of managerial ownership. *The Journal of Finance*, 55(3), 1367–1384.

Rajgopal, S., and Shevlin, T. 2002. Empirical evidence on the relation between stock option compensation and risk taking. *Journal of Accounting and Economics*, 33(2), 145–171.

9 Inventories

ACCOUNTING STANDARDS IN FOCUS

IAS 2 *Inventories*

LEARNING OBJECTIVES

After studying this chapter, you should be able to:

1. discuss the nature of inventories
2. explain how to measure inventories
3. explain what is included in the cost of inventory
4. account for inventory transactions using both the periodic and the perpetual methods
5. explain and apply end-of-period procedures for inventory under both periodic and perpetual methods
6. explain why cost flow assumptions are required and apply both FIFO and weighted average cost formulas
7. explain the net realisable value basis of measurement and account for adjustments to net realisable value
8. identify the amounts to be recognised as inventory expenses
9. implement the disclosure requirements of IAS 2.

9.1 THE NATURE OF INVENTORIES

For retail and manufacturing entities inventory is one of the most important assets, and may make up a significant proportion of current assets. The cost of sales during the period is normally the largest expense of such entities.

The main accounting standard analysed in this chapter is IAS 2 *Inventories*. The standard was originally issued in December 1993 when it replaced IAS 2 *Valuation and Presentation of Inventories in the Context of the Historical Cost System* (issued in October 1975) and has been amended several times.

According to paragraph 2 of IAS 2, the standard applies to all inventories except financial instruments and biological assets related to agricultural activity and agricultural produce at the point of harvest (IAS 41 *Agriculture*). Work in progress would be scoped in IFRS 15 *Revenue from Contracts with Customers* unless it gives rise to inventories (or assets within the scope of another standard).

Paragraph 6 of IAS 2 defines inventories as follows:

Inventories are assets:
(a) held for sale in the ordinary course of business;
(b) in the process of production for such sale; or
(c) in the form of materials or supplies to be consumed in the production process or in the rendering of services.

Note the following points:

1. The assets are held for sale in the ordinary course of business. The accounting standards do not define 'ordinary', but IFRS 5 *Non-current Assets Held for Sale and Discontinued Operations* requires that non-current assets held for sale are to be distinguished from inventories. This indicates that the term 'inventories' should be applied only to those assets that are always intended for sale or use in producing saleable goods or services.

2. Accounting for assets held for use by the entity is covered by other accounting standards according to their nature. IAS 16 *Property, Plant and Equipment* covers tangible assets such as production equipment; IAS 38 *Intangible Assets* covers intangible assets such as patents.

3. Supplies or materials such as stationery would not be treated as inventories unless they are held for sale or are used in producing goods for sale.

4. In accordance with IAS 16 paragraph 8, spare parts, standby equipment and servicing equipment are classified as inventory unless they meet the definition of property, plant and equipment. This standard clearly envisages that spare parts as inventory are those items consumed regularly during the production process, such as bobbin winders on commercial sewing machines.

5. 'In the case of a service provider, inventories include the costs of the service . . . for which the entity has not yet recognised the related revenue' (IAS 2 paragraph 8).

6. The assets are current assets if they satisfy the following criteria set out in paragraph 66 of IAS 1 *Presentation of Financial Statements*:
   • the asset is expected to be realised in, or is intended for sale or consumption in the entity's normal operating cycle
   • it is held primarily for the purpose of being traded
   • it is expected to realise the asset within 12 months after the reporting period, or
   • it is cash or a cash equivalent as defined in IAS 7 *Statement of Cash Flows* unless the asset is restricted from being exchanged or used to settle a liability for at least 12 months after the reporting period.

'The operating cycle of an entity is the time between the acquisition of assets for processing and their realisation in cash or cash equivalents' (IAS 1 paragraph 68). In some industries, such as retailing, the operating cycle may be very short, but for others, like winemaking, the operating cycle could cover a number of years. When the entity's operating cycle is not clearly identifiable, its duration is assumed to be 12 months (IAS 1 paragraph 68).

To illustrate: Nokia Group, based in Finland, prepares its financial statements in accordance with International Financial Reporting Standards (IFRS® Standards). The extract from Nokia's notes to the consolidated financial statements at 31 December 2014, as shown in figure 9.1, indicates what is contained in inventories.

In this chapter, accounting for inventory is considered as follows:
• initial recognition of inventory — determining the cost of inventory acquired or made
• recording of inventory transactions using either the periodic or perpetual inventory methods, including end-of-period procedures and adjustments
• assignment of costs to inventory using the first-in, first-out (FIFO) or weighted average cost formulas
• measurement subsequent to initial recognition — determining the amount at which the asset is reported subsequent to acquisition, including any write-down to net realisable value.

21 INVENTORIES	2014 EURm	2013 EURm
Continuing operations		
Raw materials, supplies and other	228	147
Work in progress	441	136
Finished goods	606	521
Total	1 275	804

FIGURE 9.1 Extract from the consolidated financial statements of Nokia
Source: Nokia 2015 (*Nokia in* 2014, p. 163).

9.2 MEASUREMENT OF INVENTORY UPON INITIAL RECOGNITION

According to paragraph 9 of IAS 2, 'Inventories shall be measured at the lower of cost and net realisable value.' As the purpose of acquiring or manufacturing inventory items is to sell them at a profit, inventory will initially be recognised at cost. Two specific industry groups have been exempted from applying the lower of cost and net realisable value rule, namely:

(a) producers of agricultural and forest products, agricultural produce after harvest and minerals and mineral products, to the extent that they are measured at net realisable value in accordance with well-established practices in those industries . . .

(b) commodity broker-traders who measure their inventories at fair value less costs to sell . . . (IAS 2 paragraph 3)

In these cases, movements in net realisable value or fair value less costs to sell incurred during the period are recognised in profit or loss. Where inventories in these industries are measured by reference to historical cost, the lower of cost and net realisable value rule mandated by paragraph 9 would still apply.

In both cases, the standard stresses that these inventories are only scoped out from the measurement requirements of IAS 2; the standard's other requirements, such as disclosure, continue to apply.

9.3 DETERMINATION OF COST

The first step in accounting for inventory is its initial recognition at cost. IAS 2, paragraph 10, specifies three components of cost:

- costs of purchase
- costs of conversion
- other costs incurred in bringing the inventories to their present location and condition.

Costs of conversion appear only in manufacturing entities where raw materials and other supplies are purchased and then converted to other products.

9.3.1 Costs of purchase

Paragraph 11 of IAS 2 states that 'the costs of purchase of inventories comprise the purchase price, import duties and other taxes (other than those subsequently recoverable by the entity from the taxing authorities), and transport, handling and other costs directly attributable to the acquisition of finished goods, materials and services. Trade discounts, rebates and other similar items are deducted in determining the costs of purchase.'

Transaction taxes

Many countries levy taxes on transactions involving the exchange of goods and services, and require entities engaging in such activities to collect and remit the tax to the government. If such a 'goods and services tax' or 'value added tax' exists, care must be taken to exclude these amounts from the costs of purchase if they are recoverable by the entity from the taxing authorities.

Trade and cash discounts

Trade discounts are reductions in selling prices granted to customers. Such discounts may be granted as an incentive to buy, as a means to quit ageing inventory or as a reward for placing large orders for goods. Because the discount reduces the purchase cost, it is deducted when determining the cost of inventory.

Cash or settlement discounts are offered as incentives for early payment of amounts owing on credit sales. Credit terms appear on invoices or contracts and often take the form '2/7, n/30', which means that the buyer will receive a 2% discount if the invoice is paid within 7 days of the invoice date or will get 30 days to pay without discount. Some entities may also impose an interest penalty for late payment. In November 2004, the International Financial Reporting Interpretations Committee (IFRIC®) issued an agenda decision that 'settlement discounts should be deducted from the cost of inventories'. The tentative agenda decision also clarified that 'rebates that specifically and genuinely refund selling expenses would not to be deducted from the cost of inventories' (*IASB*, 2004).

Deferred payment terms

Where an item of inventory is acquired for cash or short term credit, determination of the purchase price is relatively straightforward. In the case that some or all of the cash payment is deferred, as noted in paragraph 18 of IAS 2, the purchase cost contains a financing element — the difference between the amount paid and a purchase on normal credit terms — which must be recognised as interest expense over the period of deferral.

9.3.2 Costs of conversion

IAS 2, paragraph 12, identifies costs of conversion as being the costs directly related to the units of production, such as direct labour, plus a systematic allocation of fixed and variable production overheads that are incurred in converting materials into finished goods. Variable production overheads are indirect costs of production that vary directly with the volume of production and are allocated to each unit of production on the basis of actual use of production facilities. Fixed overheads, such as depreciation of production machinery, remain relatively constant regardless of the volume of production and are allocated to the cost of inventory on the basis of normal production capacity. Where a production process simultaneously produces one or more products, the costs of conversion must be allocated between products on a systematic and rational basis (IAS 2 paragraphs 12–14).

Costing methodologies are a managerial accounting issue and outside the scope of this book.

9.3.3 Other costs

Other costs can be included only if they are 'incurred in bringing the inventories to their present location and condition' (IAS 2 paragraph 15). Such costs could include specific design expenses incurred in producing goods for individual customers. IAS 23 *Borrowing Costs* allows borrowing costs such as interest to be included in the cost of inventories, but only where such inventories are a qualifying asset; that is, one which 'takes a substantial period of time to get ready for its intended use or sale' (IAS 23 paragraph 5). Inventory items would rarely meet this criterion.

9.3.4 Excluded costs

The following costs are specifically listed in paragraph 16 of IAS 2 as costs that cannot be included in the cost of inventories and must be recognised as expenses when incurred:
- abnormal amounts of wasted materials, labour or other production costs
- storage costs, unless necessary in the production process before a further production stage
- administrative overheads that do not contribute to bringing inventories to their present location and condition
- selling costs.

9.3.5 Cost of inventories of a service provider

Service providers, such as cleaners, would normally measure any inventories at the cost of production. Because a service is being provided, such costs would consist primarily of labour and other personnel costs for those employees directly engaged in providing the service. The costs of supervisory personnel and directly attributable overheads may also be included, but paragraph 19 of IAS 2 prohibits the inclusion of labour and other costs relating to sales and general administrative personnel. Profit margins or non-attributable overheads that are built into the prices charged by service providers cannot be included into the cost of inventories.

Such inventory assets would be recognised only for services 'in-progress' at the end of the reporting period for which the service provider has not as yet recognised any revenue (e.g. where a catering firm has provided meals for 10 days as at the end of the reporting period, but bills the client on a fortnightly basis).

Western Ltd, an Australian company, received the following invoice from De Ferrari Garments Ltd, an Italian garment manufacturer.

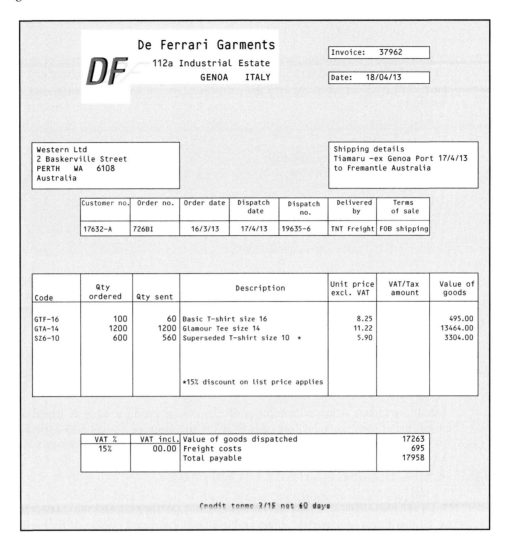

De Ferrari Garments
112a Industrial Estate
GENOA   ITALY

Invoice: 37962
Date: 18/04/13

Western Ltd
2 Baskerville Street
PERTH   WA   6108
Australia

Shipping details
Tiamaru —ex Genoa Port 17/4/13
to Fremantle Australia

Customer no.	Order no.	Order date	Dispatch date	Dispatch no.	Delivered by	Terms of sale
17632−A	726BI	16/3/13	17/4/13	19635−6	TNT Freight	FOB shipping

Code	Qty ordered	Qty sent	Description	Unit price excl. VAT	VAT/Tax amount	Value of goods
GTF−16	100	60	Basic T-shirt size 16	8.25		495.00
GTA−14	1200	1200	Glamour Tee size 14	11.22		13464.00
SZ6−10	600	560	Superseded T-shirt size 10 ★	5.90		3304.00
			★15% discount on list price applies			

VAT %	VAT incl.		
15%	00.00	Value of goods dispatched	17263
		Freight costs	695
		Total payable	17958

Credit terms 3/15 net 60 days

The goods arrived at Fremantle port on 29 May 2013 and were held in a bond store pending payment of import duties and taxes. After the payment of storage costs of A$145, import duty at 1.5% of the total value of goods in Australian dollars, goods and services tax (GST) of 10% and local freight charges of A$316, the goods were finally delivered to Western Ltd's warehouse on 6 June 2013. The invoice was received on 8 June and a liability of $A23 628.95 recorded using the exchange rate of A$1 — €0.76 at that date. The invoice was paid in full on 8 July by the remittance of $A23 322.08 (at an exchange rate of A$1 = €0.77). Western Ltd paid A$167 to acquire the euros. Upon receipt of the goods, Western Ltd attaches its own logo to the T-shirts and repackages them for sale. The cost of this further processing is A$2.54 per T-shirt.

Problem

What is the cost of this inventory?

Solution

The cost of inventory would include the following amounts:

Purchase price	€17 263.00
Shipping costs	695.00
	€17 958.00
Conversion to Australian dollars:	
€17 958 ÷ 0.76	23 628.95
Storage costs − bond store	145.00

Import duty ($22 714.47 × 1.5%)	340.72
Freight costs	316.00
Foreign exchange commission	167.00
Logo and repackaging (1820 items × $2.54)	4 622.80
Total cost	A$ 29 220.47

Where a cost per unit for each type of T-shirt is required, some method of allocating the 'generic' costs of shipping, storage, freight and foreign exchange commission would need to be employed. In this case, such costs could be allocated on a per garment basis. For example, the cost per unit for the Basic T-shirts would be:

	A$
Purchase price (€8.25 ÷ A$0.76)	10.86
Import duty (1.5% ÷ $10.86)	0.16
Shipping and other costs*	0.85
Logo and repackaging	2.54
Cost per unit	$14.41

*(A$145 + 316 + 167 + [€695 ÷ 0.76] = A$1542.47/1820 garments = A$0.85 per garment)

Note that the exchange gain of $306.87 arising from the change in euro–dollar exchange rates between the recognition of the liability and its payment cannot be incorporated in the calculation of cost as it is not associated with the acquisition transaction. Additionally, the GST of 10% payable is not included as it is a transaction tax receivable by Western Ltd against GST collected on sale of inventory.

9.3.6 Cost of agricultural produce harvested from biological assets

IAS 41 *Agriculture* requires inventories of agricultural produce, such as wheat and oranges, to be initially measured at their fair value less costs to sell at the point of harvest. IAS 2, paragraph 20, deems this value to be the cost for the purposes of applying the requirements of the inventory standard.

9.3.7 Cost measurement techniques

Techniques for the measurement of cost, such as the standard cost method or the retail method, may be used for convenience as long as the resulting values approximate cost. Manufacturing entities determine a 'standard' cost of materials, direct and indirect labour and overheads for each product based on normal levels of efficiency and capacity utilisation. Adjustments are made at the end of the reporting period to account for variances between standard and actual costs. The retail method is used to measure inventories of large numbers of rapidly changing items with similar margins for which it is impractical to use other costing methods. Supermarket and department store chains most often employ this method of approximating cost. Cost is determined by reducing the sales value of the inventory by an appropriate percentage gross margin or an average percentage margin. In applying this method, care must be taken to ensure that gross margins are adjusted for goods that have been discounted below their original selling price.

9.4 ACCOUNTING FOR INVENTORY

There are two main methods of accounting for inventory: the periodic method and the perpetual method.

9.4.1 Periodic method

Under the periodic method, the amount of inventory is determined periodically (normally annually) by conducting a physical count and multiplying the number of units by a cost per unit to value the inventory on hand. This amount is then recognised as a current asset. This balance remains unchanged until the next count is taken. Purchases and returns of inventory during the reporting period are posted directly to expense accounts. Cost of sales during the year is determined as follows:

> Cost of sales = Opening inventory + Purchases + Freight inwards − Purchase returns − Cash discounts received − Closing inventory

Accounting for inventory using the periodic method is cost effective and easy to apply, but its major disadvantage is that the exact quantity and cost of inventory cannot be determined on a day-to-day basis, and this might result in lost sales or unhappy customers. Additionally, it is not possible to identify stock losses or posting errors, resulting in accounting figures that might be inaccurate or misleading.

9.4.2 Perpetual method

Under the perpetual method, inventory records are updated each time a transaction involving inventory takes place. Thus, up-to-date information about the quantity and cost of inventory on hand will always be available, enabling the entity to provide better customer service and maintain better control over this essential asset. This system is more complicated and expensive than the periodic method, but, with the advent of user-friendly computerised accounting packages and point-of-sale machines linked directly to accounting records, most businesses today can afford to and do use the perpetual method.

The perpetual method requires a subsidiary ledger to be maintained, either manually or on computer, with a separate record for each inventory item detailing all movements in both quantity and cost. This subsidiary record is linked to the general ledger account for inventory, and regular reconciliations are carried out to ensure the accuracy and completeness of the accounting records. *This reconciliation process is discussed in section 9.5.*

ILLUSTRATIVE EXAMPLE 9.2 Comparing the periodic and the perpetual inventory methods

Kotka Ltd sells garden furniture settings. This example illustrates the journal entries necessary to record the normal inventory transactions that would occur during an accounting period, and the reporting of gross profit from the sale of inventory under both accounting systems.

The inventory account in the general ledger of Kotka Ltd at the beginning of the year under both methods is shown below.

Inventory		
1/1/14 Balance b/d	6 700	
(10 units @ $670)		

The following transactions took place during the year:
(a) Purchased 354 settings (FOB shipping) at $670 each on credit terms of 2/10, *n*/30 from Grimstad Pty Ltd
(b) Sold, on credit, 352 settings for $975 each.
(c) Returned four settings to the supplier.
(d) Seven settings were returned by customers.

The journal entries necessary to record these transactions under both inventory accounting methods are shown below.

KOTKA LTD
Journal entries

Perpetual inventory method   *Periodic inventory method*

(a) Purchased 354 settings (FOB shipping) at $670 each on credit terms of 2/10, *n*/30 from Grimstad Pty Ltd.

	Dr	Cr		Dr	Cr
Inventory	237 180		Purchases	237 180	
A/cs Payable		237 180	A/cs Payable		237 180

(b) Sold, on credit, 352 settings for $975 each.

	Dr	Cr		Dr	Cr
A/cs Receivable	343 200		A/cs Receivable	343 200	
Sales Revenue		343 200	Sales Revenue		343 200
Cost of Sales	235 840				
Inventory		235 840			

(c) Returned four settings to the supplier.

	Dr	Cr		Dr	Cr
A/cs Payable	2 680		A/cs Payable	2 680	
Inventory		2 680	Purchase Returns		2 680

(d) Seven settings were returned by customers.

	Dr	Cr		Dr	Cr
Sales Returns	6 825		Sales Returns	6 825	
A/cs Receivable		6 825	A/cs Receivable		6 825
Inventory	4 690				
Cost of Sales		4 690			

Important differences to note between the two methods of accounting for inventory are as follows:
- Purchases are posted directly to the asset account under the perpetual method, and are posted to expense accounts under the periodic method.
- When goods are sold, a second entry is necessary under the perpetual method to transfer the cost of those goods from the inventory account to the expense account, cost of sales.
- When goods are returned to suppliers, the return is adjusted directly to inventory under the perpetual method, and is posted to a purchase returns account under the periodic method.
- When goods are returned from customers, a second journal entry is necessary under the perpetual method to transfer the cost of these goods out of the cost of sales account and back into the inventory account.
- Under the periodic method, freight is normally posted to a separate account. Under the perpetual method, freight is included in the cost of inventory.
- If inventory items being returned to the supplier have been paid for, an accounts receivable account would be opened pending a cash refund from the supplier.
- If sales returns have been paid for, an accounts payable entry would be raised to recognise the need to refund cash to the customer.
- Under the periodic method, cash settlement discounts would be posted to a separate ledger account. Under the perpetual method, settlement discounts would be deducted from the cost of inventory.

After posting the journal entries, the general ledger account would appear as shown below.

Perpetual inventory method

Inventory

1/1/14	Balance b/d	6 700	Cost of Sales	235 840
	A/cs Payable	237 180	A/cs Payable	2 680
	Cost of Sales	4 690	Balance c/d	10 050
		248 570		248 570
	Balance b/d	10 050		

Periodic inventory method

Inventory

1/1/14	Balance b/d	6 700		

Assuming that the physical count at the end of the reporting period found 15 settings on hand at a cost of $670 each, the gross profit earned on these would be determined as follows:

KOTKA LTD	
Determination of Gross Profit	

Perpetual inventory method

Sales revenue	343 200
Less: Sales returns and allowances	(6 825)
Net sales revenue	336 375
Cost of sales	(231 150)
Gross profit	$ 105 225

Periodic inventory method

Sales revenue		343 200
Less: Sales returns		(6 825)
Net sales revenue		336 375
Cost of sales		
Opening inventory	6 700	
Add: Purchases	237 180	
	243 880	
Less: Purchase returns	(2 680)	
Goods available for sale	241 200	
Less: Closing inventory	(10 050)	
Cost of sales		(231 150)
Gross profit		$ 105 225

Note that, in this example, the same gross profit is reported irrespective of the inventory recording method adopted. However, where adjustments are made for damaged or lost inventory, the gross profit will be different under the perpetual method.

9.5 END-OF-PERIOD ACCOUNTING

To ensure that reported figures for inventory, cost of sales and other expenses are accurate and complete, certain procedures must be carried out at the end of each accounting period. It is essential that good internal controls are in place to ensure that inventory is protected from fraud or loss and that inventory figures are complete and accurate. This section examines the physical count, end-of-year cut-off and essential reconciliation procedures.

9.5.1 Physical count

Under the periodic method, inventory must be counted at the end of each accounting period to determine the carrying value of closing inventory. Periodic counts are made under the perpetual method to verify the accuracy of recorded quantities for each inventory item, although not necessarily at the end of the reporting period, if inventory differences are historically found to be immaterial.

The way in which the physical count is conducted will depend on the type of inventory and the accounting system of the entity. Stockpiled inventory such as mineral sands may require the use of surveyors to measure quantities on hand and assay tests to determine mineral content.

The following are some steps that are generally taken to ensure the accuracy of a physical count:

• The warehouse, retail store or storage facility should be arranged so as to facilitate counting and clearly segregate non-inventory items.
• Cut-off procedures should be put in place and final numbers of important documents such as dispatch notes and invoices are recorded. *(Cut-off procedures are discussed in greater detail in section 9.5.2.)*
• Prenumbered count sheets, tags or cards should be produced detailing inventory codes and descriptions. A supervisor should record all numbers used and account for spoiled documents to ensure that the count details are complete. Alternatively, where inventory items have bar codes, electronic scanners can be used to record the count.
• Counting should be done in teams of at least two people: one counter and one checker. All team members should sign the count records.
• Any damaged or incomplete items located during the count should be clearly listed on the count records.
• The supervisor should ensure that all goods have been counted before the count sheets are collected.

Perpetual method

Once the physical count is complete, under the perpetual method the quantities on hand are then compared to recorded quantities and all discrepancies investigated. Recording errors cause discrepancies; for example, the wrong code number or quantity might have been entered, or a transaction might not have been processed in the correct period. Alternatively, discrepancies may reveal losses of goods caused by damage or fraud. Recording errors can be corrected, but the value of goods that have been lost should be written off using the following entry:

Inventory Losses	Dr	5 000	
Inventory	Cr		5 000
(Recognition of inventory losses during the period)			

Unless they are immaterial, inventory losses must be disclosed separately in the notes to the financial statements *(see section 9.9)*.

Periodic method

Once the count is completed, under this method the count quantities are then assigned with a cost and the carrying value of inventory is recorded. This adjustment can be done in a number of ways, but the simplest is to post the following two journal entries:

Opening Inventory (Cost of Sales)	Dr	79 600	
Inventory	Cr		79 600
(Transfer of opening balance to expense)			

Inventory	Dr	87 100	
Closing Inventory (Cost of Sales)	Cr		87 100
(Recognition of final inventory balance)			

Under the periodic method, inventory losses and fraud cannot be identified and recorded as a separate expense. The movement in inventory balances plus the cost of purchases is presumed to represent the cost of sales during the reporting period.

9.5.2 Cut-off procedures

Under both periodic and perpetual methods there is a need to ensure that, when a physical count is conducted, there is a proper cut-off of the record keeping so that the accounting records reflect the results of the physical count and include all transactions relevant to the accounting period, while excluding those that belong to other periods. For all inventory transactions (sales, purchases and returns), it is possible for inventory records to be updated before transaction details are posted to the general ledger accounts. For example, goods are normally entered into inventory records when the goods are received, but accounts payable records will not record the liability until the invoice arrives because shipping documents may not record price details. Under the periodic method, there is a need to ensure a proper cut-off between the general ledger recording of goods received, shipped and returned, and the inventory counted. Under the perpetual method, there is a need to ensure that all inventory movements are properly recorded in the perpetual records, so a valid comparison is made between inventory counted and the perpetual record quantities. Further, if the perpetual method is not integrated with the general ledger, there is also a need to ensure a proper cut-off between the general ledger and the perpetual records. Thus, at the end of the reporting period it is essential that proper cut-off procedures be implemented.

The following cut-off errors could arise:
- Goods have been received into inventory, but the purchase invoice has not been processed.
- Goods have been returned to a supplier, and deleted from inventory, but the credit note has not been processed.
- Goods have been sold and dispatched to a customer, but the invoice has not been raised.
- Goods have been returned by a customer, but the credit note has not been issued.

If inventory movements have been processed before invoices and credit notes, adjusting entries are needed to bring both sides of the transaction into the same accounting period.

9.5.3 Goods in transit

Accounting for goods in transit at the end of the reporting period will depend upon the terms of trade. Where goods are purchased on an FOB shipping basis, the goods belong to the purchaser from the time they are shipped, and should be included in inventory/accounts payable at the end of the reporting period. All such purchases in transit will need to be identified and the following adjusting journal entry posted:

Goods in Transit (Inventory)	Dr	1 500	
Accounts Payable	Cr		1 500
(Recognition of inventory in transit at the end of the reporting period)			

If goods are purchased on FOB destination terms, no adjustment will be required because the goods still legally belong to the supplier.

If goods are sold on FOB destination terms, they belong to the entity until they arrive at the customer's premises. Because the sale will have been recorded in the current year, the following adjusting entries will be required to remove that sale and reinstate the inventory:

Inventory	Dr	3 000	
Cost of Sales	Cr		3 000
(Reversal of sale for goods in transit at the end of the reporting period)			

Sales Revenue	Dr	4 500	
Accounts Receivable	Cr		4 500
(Reversal of sale for goods in transit at the end of the reporting period)			

9.5.4 Consignment inventory

Care must be taken in the treatment of consignment inventory. Under a consignment arrangement, an agent (the consignee) agrees to sell goods on behalf of the consignor on a commission basis. The transfer of goods to the consignee is not a legal sale/purchase transaction. Legal ownership remains with the consignor until the agent sells the goods to a third party. Steps must be taken to ensure that goods held on consignment are not included in the physical count. Equally, goods owned by the entity that are held by consignees must be added to the physical count.

9.5.5 Control account/subsidiary ledger reconciliation

This end-of-period procedure is required only under the perpetual method. The general ledger account balance must be reconciled with the total of the subsidiary ledger (manual or computerised). Recording errors and omissions will cause the reconciliation process to fail. Any material discrepancies should be investigated and corrected. This process will identify only amounts that have not been posted to both records; it cannot identify errors within the subsidiary records, such as posting a purchase to the wrong inventory item code. However, the physical count/recorded figure reconciliation will isolate these errors.

ILLUSTRATIVE EXAMPLE 9.3 End-of-period adjustments

Bob Smith, trading as Honefoss Pty Ltd, completed his first year of trading as a toy wholesaler on 31 December 2014. He is worried about his end-of-year physical and cut-off procedures.

The inventory ledger account balance at 31 December 2014, under the perpetual inventory method, was £78 700. His physical count, however, revealed the cost of inventory on hand at 31 December 2014 to be only £73 400. While Bob expected a small inventory shortfall due to breakage and petty theft, he considered this shortfall to be excessive.

Upon investigating reasons for the inventory 'shortfall', Bob discovered the following:
- Goods costing £800 were sold on credit to R Finn for £1300 on 27 December 2014 on FOB destination terms. The goods were still in transit at 31 December 2014. Honefoss Pty Ltd recorded the sale on 27 December 2014 and did not include these goods in the physical count.
- Included in the physical count were £2200 of goods held on consignment.
- Goods costing £910 were purchased on credit from Lapua Ltd on 23 December 2014 and received on 28 December 2014. The purchase was unrecorded at 31 December 2014, but the goods were included in the physical count.
- Goods costing £400 were purchased on credit from Kuovola Supplies on 22 December 2014 on FOB shipping terms. The goods were delivered to the transport company on 27 December 2014. The purchase was recorded on 27 December 2014, but, as the goods had not yet arrived, Honefoss Pty Ltd did not include these goods in the physical count.
- At 31 December 2014 Honefoss Pty Ltd had unsold goods costing £3700 out on consignment. These goods were not included in the physical count.
- Goods costing £2100 were sold on credit to Vetlonda Ltd for £3200 on 24 December 2014 on FOB shipping terms. The goods were shipped on 28 December 2014. The sale was unrecorded at 31 December 2014 and Honefoss Pty Ltd did not include these goods in the physical count.
- Goods costing £1500 had been returned to Ruovesi Garments on 31 December 2014. A credit note was received from the supplier on 5 January 2015. No payment had been made for the goods prior to their return.

These transactions and events must be analysed to determine if adjustments are required to the ledger accounts (general and subsidiary) and/or the physical count records as follows:

Workings

	Recorded balance £	Physical count £
Balance prior to adjustment	78 700	73 400
Add: Goods sold, FOB destination and in transit at 31 December	800	800
Less: Goods held on consignment	—	(2 200)
Add: Unrecorded purchase	910	—
Add: Goods purchased, FOB shipping and in transit at 31 December	—	400
Add: Goods out on consignment	—	3 700
Less: Unrecorded sale	(2 100)	—
Less: Unrecorded purchase returns	(1 500)	—
	£76 810	£76 100

If, after all adjustments are made, the recorded balance cannot be reconciled to the physical count, the remaining discrepancy is presumed to represent inventory losses and a final adjustment is made as follows:

Adjusted balances	76 810	76 100
Inventory shortfall	(710)	—
	£76 100	£76 100

The following journal entries are necessary on 31 December 2014 to correct errors and adjust the inventory ledger accounts:

HONEFOSS PTY LTD General Journal		
2014		
31 December		
Sales Revenue	Dr	1 300	
Accounts Receivable (R Finn)	Cr		1 300
(Correction of sale recorded incorrectly)			
Inventory (Item X)	Dr	800	
Cost of Sales	Cr		800
(Correction of sale recorded incorrectly)			
Inventory (Item Y)	Dr	910	
Accounts Payable (Lapua Ltd)	Cr		910
(Correction of unrecorded purchase)			
Accounts Receivable (Vetlonda Ltd)	Dr	3 200	
Sales Revenue	Cr		3 200
(Correction of unrecorded sale)			
Cost of Sales	Dr	2 100	
Inventory (Item Z)	Cr		2 100
(Correction of unrecorded sale)			
Accounts Payable (Ruovesi Garments)	Dr	1 500	
Inventory (Item W)	Cr		1 500
(Correction of unrecorded purchase return)			
Inventory Losses and Write-Downs	Dr	710	
Inventory	Cr		710
(Unexplained variance (physical/records) written off)			

9.6 ASSIGNING COSTS TO INVENTORY ON SALE

The nature of inventory held by an entity does not affect its initial recognition at cost, but has a significant impact when that inventory is sold. As shown in illustrative example 9.2, under the perpetual system the cost of inventory items is transferred to a 'Cost of Sales' expense account on sale, and under the periodic system a 'Cost of Sales' figure is calculated at the end of the reporting period. This is an easy task if the nature of inventory is such that it is possible to clearly identify the exact inventory item that has been sold and its cost, but what if it is not possible to identify exactly the cost of the item sold? How can you measure the cost of a tonne of wheat when it is extracted from a stockpile consisting of millions of tonnes acquired at different prices over the accounting period?

IAS 2 addresses this problem by mandating two different rules for the assigning of cost to inventory items sold.

The rules differ depending on the nature of inventory held. Paragraph 23 of IAS 2 states that:

> The cost of inventories of items that are not ordinarily interchangeable and goods or services produced and segregated for specific projects shall be assigned by using specific identification of their individual costs.

Thus, if the inventory held consists of items that can be individually identified because of their unique nature or by some other means, or cannot be individually identified, but have been acquired for a specific project, then the exact cost of the item sold must be recorded as cost of sales expense.

Paragraph 25 of IAS 2 states that:

> The cost of inventories, other than those dealt with in paragraph 23, shall be assigned by using the first-in, first-out (FIFO) or weighted average cost formula.

This means that, where a specific cost cannot be identified because of the nature of the item sold, then some method has to be adopted to estimate that cost. This process is known as 'assigning' cost. Most inventory items fall into this category; for example, identical items of food and clothing and bulk items like oil and minerals. There are many methods of assigning a cost to inventory items sold, but IAS 2 restricts entities to a choice between two methods — FIFO and weighted average.

9.6.1 First-in, first-out (FIFO) cost formula

The FIFO formula assumes that items of inventory that were purchased or produced first are sold first, and the items remaining in inventory at the end of the period are those most recently purchased or produced (IAS 2 paragraph 27). Thus, more recent purchase costs are assigned to the inventory asset account, and older costs are assigned to the cost of sales expense account.

Consider this example: there are 515 Blu-ray players on hand at 31 December 2014, and recent purchase invoices showed the following costs:

28 December	180 players at €49.00
15 December	325 players at €48.50
30 November	200 players at €47.00

The value of ending inventory is found by starting with the most recent purchase and working backwards until all items on hand have been priced (on the assumption that it is not known when any particular Blu-ray player was sold). The value of ending inventory would be €25052.50 (being 180 players at €49 + 325 players at €48.50 + 10 players at €47).

Many proponents of the FIFO method argue that this method best reflects the physical movement of inventory, particularly perishable goods or those subject to changes in fashion or rapid obsolescence (as in the case of Blu-ray players). If the oldest goods are normally sold first, then the oldest costs should be assigned to expense.

9.6.2 Weighted average cost formula

Under the weighted average cost formula, the cost of each item sold is determined from the cost of similar items purchased or produced during the period. The average may be calculated on a periodic basis (weighted average), or as each additional shipment is received (moving average).

Using a periodic basis, the cost of inventory on hand at the beginning of the period plus all inventory purchased during the year is divided by the total number of items available for sale during the period (opening quantity plus purchased quantity). This produces the cost per unit. For example: inventory on hand at 1 January 2015 was valued at £3439.78, consisting of 134 units at an average of £25.67 each. During the year the following purchases were made:

200 units at £27.50	= £5 500.00
175 units at £28.35	= £4 961.25
300 units at £29.10	= £8 730.00
120 units at £29.00	= £3 480.00

At the end of the year, the weighted average cost of inventory would be calculated as:

£3439.78 + £5500.00 + £4961.25 + £8730.00 + £3480.00 = £26 111.03 ÷ 929 units = £28.11 per unit

Using the *moving weighted average method*, the average unit cost is recalculated each time there is an inventory purchase or purchase return. This is demonstrated in illustrative example 9.4.

ILLUSTRATIVE EXAMPLE 9.4 Application of cost formulas

The following information has been extracted from the records of Savonlinna Parts about one of its products. Savonlinna Parts uses the perpetual inventory method and its reporting period ends on 31 December.

		No. of units	Unit cost $	Total cost $
2014				
01/01	Beginning balance	800	7.00	5 600
06/01	Purchased	300	7.05	2 115
05/02	Sold @ $12.00 per unit	1 000		
19/03	Purchased	1 100	7.35	8 085
24/03	Purchase returns	80	7.35	588
10/04	Sold @ $12.10 per unit	700		
22/06	Purchased	8 400	7.50	63 000
31/07	Sold @ $13.25 per unit	1 800		
04/08	Sales returns @ $13.25 per unit	20		
04/09	Sold @ $13.50 per unit	3 500		
06/10	Purchased	500	8.00	4 000
27/11	Sold @ $15.00 per unit	3 100		

Required

1. Calculate the cost of inventory on hand at 31 December 2014 and the cost of sales for the year ended 31 December 2014, assuming:
   (a) the FIFO cost flow assumption
   (b) the moving average cost flow assumption (round the average unit costs to the nearest cent, and round the total cost amounts to the nearest dollar).
2. Prepare the trading section of the statement of profit or loss and other comprehensive income for the year ended 31 December 2014, assuming:
   (a) the FIFO cost flow assumption
   (b) the moving average cost flow assumption.

Part 1. (a) First-in, first-out cost formula

		Purchases			Cost of sales			Balance[1]		
Date	Details	No. units	Unit cost	Total cost	No. units	Unit cost	Total cost	No. units	Unit cost	Total cost
01/01	Inventory balance							800	7.00	5 600
06/01	Purchases	300	7.05	2 115				800	7.00	5 600
								300	7.05	2 115
05/02	Sales				800	7.00	5 600			
					200	7.05	1 410	100	7.05	705

Date	Details	No. units	Unit cost	Total cost	No. units	Unit cost	Total cost	No. units	Unit cost	Total cost
19/03	Purchases	1 100	7.35	8 085				100 1 100	7.05 7.35	705 8 085
24/03	Purchase returns	(80)	7.35	(588)				100 1 020	7.05 7.35	705 7 497
10/04	Sales				100 600	7.05 7.35	705 4 410	420	7.35	3 087
22/06	Purchases	8 400	7.50	63 000				420 8 400	7.35 7.50	3 087 63 000
31/07	Sales				420 1 380	7.35 7.50	3 087 10 350	7 020	7.50	52 650
04/08	Sales returns[2]				(20)	7.50	(150)	7 040	7.50	52 800
04/09	Sales				3 500	7.50	26 250	3 540	7.50	26 550
06/10	Purchases	500	8.00	4 000				3 540 500	7.50 8.00	26 550 4 000
22/11	Sales				3 100	7.50	23 250	440 500	7.50 8.00	3 300 4 000
				76 612			74 912			

Notes:
1. As it is assumed the earliest purchases are sold first, a separate balance of each purchase at a different price must be maintained.
2. The principle of 'last-out, first-in' is applied to sales returns.

Part 1. (b) Moving average cost formula

		Purchases			Cost of sales[1]			Balance		
Date	Details	No. units	Unit cost	Total cost	No. units	Unit cost	Total cost	No. units	Unit cost[2]	Total cost
01/01	Inventory balance							800	7.00	5 600
06/01	Purchases	300	7.05	2 115				1 100	7.01	7 715
05/02	Sales				1 000	7.01	7 010	100	7.01	705
19/03	Purchases	1 100	7.35	8 085				1 200	7.33	8 790
24/03	Purchase returns	(80)	7.35	(588)				1 120	7.32	8 202
10/04	Sales				700	7.32	5 124	420	7.32	3 078
01/01	Inventory balance	8 400	7.50	63 000				8 820	7.49	66 078
06/01	Purchases				1 800	7.49	13 482	7 020	7.49	52 596
05/02	Sales				(20)	7.49	(150)	7 040	7.49	52 746
19/03	Purchases				3 500	7.49	26 215	3 540	7.49	26 531
24/03	Purchase returns	500	8.00	4 000				4 040	7.56	30 531
10/04	Sales				3 100	7.56	23 436	940	7.56	7 095
				76 612			75 117			

Notes:
1. The 'average' cost on the date of sale is applied to calculate the 'cost of sales'.
2. The average cost per unit is recalculated each time there is a purchase or a purchase return at a different cost.

Part 2

	SAVONLINNA PARTS Statement of Profit or Loss and Other Comprehensive Income (extract) for the year ended 31 December 2014		
	FIFO **$**	**Moving** **average** **$**
Sales revenue	138 070	138 070
Less: Sales returns	(265)	(265)
Net sales	137 805	137 805
Less: Cost of sales	(74 912)	(75 117)
Gross profit	$ 62 893	$ 62 688

Because the purchase price has been rising throughout the year, using the FIFO formula produces a lower cost of sales (higher gross profit) and a higher inventory balance than the moving average formula.

9.6.3 Which cost formula to use?

The choice of method is a matter for management judgement and depends upon the nature of the inventory, the information needs of management and financial statement users, and the cost of applying the formulas. For example, the weighted average method is easy to apply and is particularly suited to inventory where homogeneous products are mixed together, like iron ore or spring water. On the other hand, first-in, first-out may be a better reflection of the actual physical movement of goods, such as those with use-by dates where the first produced must be sold first to avoid loss due to obsolescence, spoilage or legislative restrictions. Entities with diversified operations may use both methods because they carry different types of inventory. Using diverse methods is acceptable under IAS 2, but paragraph 26 cautions that 'a difference in geographical location of inventories (or in the respective tax rules), by itself, is not sufficient to justify the use of different cost formulas'. The nature of the inventory itself should determine the choice of formula.

9.6.4 Consistent application of costing methods

Once a cost formula has been selected, management cannot randomly switch from one formula to another. Because the choice of method can have a significant impact on an entity's reported profit and asset figures, particularly in times of volatile prices, indiscriminate changes in formulas could result in the reporting of financial information that is neither comparable nor reliable. Accordingly, paragraph 13 of IAS 8 *Accounting Policies, Changes in Accounting Estimates and Errors* requires that 'accounting policies be consistently applied to ensure comparability of financial information. Changes in accounting policies are allowed (IAS 8 paragraph 14) only when required by an accounting standard or where the change results in reporting more relevant and reliable financial information.' Therefore, unless the nature of inventory changes, it is unlikely that the cost formulas will change. Paragraph 19 of IAS 2 requires voluntary changes in accounting policies to be applied retrospectively, i.e. the information is presented as if the new accounting policy had always been applied. Hence, a change from one method to another would require adjustments to the financial statements to show the information as if the new method had always been applied. Adjustments can be taken through the opening balance of retained earnings. Comparative information would also need to be restated.

9.7 NET REALISABLE VALUE

As the measurement rule mandated by IAS 2 for inventories is the 'lower of cost and net realisable value' (paragraph 9), an estimate of net realisable value must be made to determine if inventory must be written down. Normally, this estimate is done at the end of the reporting period, but, where management become aware during the reporting period that goods or services can no longer be sold at a price above cost, inventory values should be written down to net realisable value. The rationale for this measurement rule, according to paragraph 28 of IAS 2, is that 'assets should not be carried in excess of amounts expected to be realised from their sale or use'.

Net realisable value is the net amount that an entity expects to realise from the sale of inventory in the ordinary course of business. It is defined in paragraph 6 of IAS 2 as 'the estimated selling price in the ordinary course of business less the estimated costs of completion and the estimated costs necessary to make the sale'. Net realisable value is specific to an individual entity and is not necessarily equal to fair value less selling costs. Fair value is defined as 'the price that would be received to sell an asset or paid to transfer a liability in an orderly transaction between market participants at the measurement date. (See IFRS 13 *Fair Value Measurement*.)' (IAS 2 paragraph 6).

Net realisable value may fall below cost for a number of reasons including:
- a fall in selling price (e.g. fashion garments)
- physical deterioration of inventories (e.g. fruit and vegetables)
- product obsolescence (e.g. computers and electrical equipment)
- a decision, as part of an entity's marketing strategy, to manufacture and sell products for the time being at a loss (e.g. new products)
- miscalculations or other errors in purchasing or production (e.g. over-stocking)
- an increase in the estimated costs of completion or the estimated costs of making the sale (e.g. air-conditioning plants).

9.7.1 Estimating net realisable value

Estimates of net realisable value must be based on the most reliable evidence available at the time the estimate is made (normally the end of the reporting period) of the amount that the inventories are expected to realise. Thus, estimates must be made of:
- expected selling price
- estimated costs of completion (if any)
- estimated selling costs.

These estimates take into consideration fluctuations of price or cost occurring after the end of the reporting period to the extent that such events confirm conditions existing at the end of the reporting period. The purpose for which inventory is held should be taken into account when reviewing net realisable values. For example, the net realisable value of inventory held to satisfy firm sales or service contracts is based on the contract price. If the sales contracts are for less than the inventory quantities held, the net realisable value of the excess is based on general selling prices. Estimated selling costs include all costs likely to be incurred in securing and filling customer orders such as advertising costs, sales personnel salaries and operating costs, and the costs of storing and shipping finished goods.

It is possible to use formulas based on predetermined criteria to initially estimate net realisable value. These formulas normally take into account, as appropriate, the age, past movements, expected future movements and estimated scrap values of the inventories. However, the results must be reviewed in the light of any special circumstances not anticipated in the formulas, such as changes in the current demand for inventories or unexpected obsolescence.

9.7.2 Materials and other supplies

IAS 2, paragraph 32, states that 'materials and other supplies held for use in the production of inventories are not written down below cost if the finished goods in which they will be incorporated are expected to be sold at or above cost'. When the sale of finished goods is not expected to recover the costs, then materials are to be written down to net realisable value. IAS 2 suggests that the replacement cost of the materials or other supplies is probably the best measure of their net realisable value.

9.7.3 Write-down to net realisable value

Inventories are usually written down to net realisable value on an item-by-item basis. Paragraph 29 of IAS 2 states that 'it is not appropriate to write inventories down on the basis of a classification of inventory, for example, finished goods, or all the inventories in a particular operating segment'. Where it is not practical to separately evaluate the net realisable value of each item within a product line, the write-down may be applied on a group basis provided that the products have similar purposes or end uses, and are produced and marketed in the same geographical area. IAS 2 generally requires that service providers apply the measurement rule only on an item-by-item basis, as each service ordinarily has a separate selling price.

The journal entry to process the write-down would be:

Inventory Write-Down Expense	Dr	800	
Inventory	Cr		800
(Write-down to net realisable value)			

9.7.4 Reversal of prior write-down to net realisable value

If the circumstances that previously caused inventories to be written down below cost change, or if a new assessment confirms that net realisable value has increased, the amount of a previous write-down can be reversed (subject to an upper limit of the original write-down). This could occur if an item of inventory written down to net realisable value because of falling sales prices is still on hand at the end of a subsequent period and its selling price has recovered.

The journal entry to process the reversal would be:

Inventory	Dr	800	
Inventory Write-Down Expense	Cr		800
(Write-up to revised net realisable value)			

ILLUSTRATIVE EXAMPLE 9.5 Application of measurement rule

Vastervick Pty Ltd retails gardening equipment and has four main product lines: mowers, vacuum blowers, edgers and garden tools. At 31 December 2014, cost and net realisable values for each line were as shown below.

Application of lower of cost and net realisable value measurement rule

Inventory item	Quantity	Cost per unit €	NRV per unit €	Lower of cost and NRV €
Mowers	16	215.80	256.00	3 452.80
Vacuum blowers	113	62.35	60.00	6 780.00
Edgers	78	27.40	36.00	2 137.20
Garden tools	129	12.89	11.00	1 419.00
Inventory at the lower of cost and net realisable value				€13 789.00

The following journal entry would be required to adjust inventory values to net realisable value:

31 December 2014			
Inventory Write-Down Expense	Dr	509.36	
Inventory	Cr		509.36
(Write-down to net realisable value — vacuum blowers €265.55 (113 × €2.35) and garden tools €243.81 (129 × €1.89))			

9.8 RECOGNITION AS AN EXPENSE

Paragraph 34 of IAS 2 requires the following items to be recognised as expenses:
- carrying amount of inventories in the period in which the related revenue is recognised, in other words, cost of sales
- write-down of inventories to net realisable value and all losses
- reversals of write-downs to net realisable value (reduction of the expense).

The only exception to this rule relates to inventory items allocated to other asset accounts, e.g. used by an entity as components in self-constructed property, plant or equipment. The cost of these items would be capitalised and recognised as an expense via depreciation.

9.9 DISCLOSURE

Paragraph 36 of IAS 2 contains the required disclosures relating to inventories. Before preparing the disclosure note, inventories on hand will need to be classified into categories because paragraph 36(b) requires 'the carrying amount in classifications appropriate to the entity' to be disclosed. Common classifications suggested in paragraph 37 are 'merchandise, production supplies, materials, work in progress and finished goods'. Figure 9.2 provides an illustration of the disclosures required by IAS 2.

	IAS 2 Paragraph
Note 1: Summary of accounting policies (extract)	
Inventories	
Inventories are valued at the lower of cost and net realisable value.	36(a)
Costs incurred in bringing each product to its present location and condition are accounted for as follows:	9–10
• raw materials: purchase cost on a first-in, first-out basis	25
• finished goods and work in progress: cost of direct materials and labour and a proportion of manufacturing overheads based on the normal operating capacity, but excluding borrowing costs	12–13
• production supplies: purchase cost on a weighted average cost basis.	25
Net realisable value is the estimated selling price in the ordinary course of business, less estimated costs of completion and the estimated costs necessary to make the sale.	6

Note 6: Inventories

	2014 €'000	2013 €'000	
			36(b)
Raw materials	1 257	1 840	
Work in progress	649	721	
Finished goods	3 932	4 278	
Production supplies	385	316	
Total inventories at the lower of cost and net realisable value	6 223	7 155	
In respect to inventory, the following items have been recognised as expenses during the period:			
Cost of sales	11 674	10 543	36(d)
Write-down to net realisable value	26	18	36(e)
Reversal of write-down[(a)]	(3)	—	36(f)
(a) A prior year write-down was reversed during the current period as a result of an increase in selling price for that inventory item.			36(g)
Inventory with a carrying amount of €570 000 has been pledged as security for loans to the company.			36(h)

FIGURE 9.2 An example of illustrative disclosures required by IAS 2

SUMMARY

The purpose of this chapter is to analyse the content of IAS 2 *Inventories* and provide guidance on its implementation. The principal issue in accounting for inventories is the determination of cost and its subsequent recognition as an expense, including any write-down to net realisable value (IAS 2 paragraph 1). One key decision in recognising inventory is the selection of an appropriate method for allocating costs between individual items of inventory to determine the cost of sales and the cost of inventory on hand. Following the initial recognition of the inventory, cost must be compared to net realisable value, and the value of inventory written down where net realisable value falls below cost. IAS 2 requires disclosures to be made in relation to the inventories held by an entity and the accounting policies adopted with respect to these assets.

Discussion questions

1. Define 'cost' as applied to the valuation of inventory.
2. What is meant by the term 'net realisable value'? Is this the same as fair value? If not, why not?
3. In what circumstances must assumptions be made in order to assign a cost to inventory items when they are sold?
4. Compare and contrast the impact on the reported profit and asset value for an accounting period of the first-in, first-out method and the weighted average method.
5. Why is the lower of cost and net realisable value rule used in the accounting standard? Is it permissible to revalue inventory upwards? If so, when?
6. What impact do the terms of trade have on the determination of the quantity and value of inventory on hand where goods are in transit at the end of the reporting period?

References

IASB 2004, *IFRIC Update*, November, www.ifrs.org.
Nokia 2015, *Nokia in 2014*, Nokia Corporation, Finland, www.nokia.com.

Exercises

STAR RATING ★ BASIC ★★ MODERATE ★★★ DIFFICULT

Exercise 9.1 CONSIGNMENT OF INVENTORY

★ Arend al Ltd reported in a recent financial statement that approximately $12 million of merchandise was received on consignment. Should the company recognise this amount on its statement of financial position? Explain.

Exercise 9.2 SELECTION OF COST ASSUMPTION

★ Under what circumstances would each of the following inventory cost methods be appropriate?
(a) Specific identification
(b) Last-in, first-out
(c) Average cost
(d) First-in, first-out
(e) Retail inventory

Exercise 9.3 DETERMINING INVENTORY COST AND COST OF SALES (PERIODIC)

★ *Select the correct answer. Show any workings required and provide reasons to justify your choice.*
1. The cost of inventory on hand at 1 January 2013 was $25 000 and at 31 December 2013 was $35 000. Inventory purchases for the year amounted to $160 000, freight outwards expense was $500, and purchase returns were $1400. What was the cost of sales for the year ended 31 December 2013?
(a) $148 100
(c) $149 100
(b) $148 600
(d) $150 000

The following inventory information relates to K Rauma, who uses a periodic inventory system and rounds the average unit cost to the nearest dollar:

Beginning inventory	10 units @ average cost of $25 each = $250
January purchase	10 units @ $24 each
July purchase	39 units @ $26 each
October purchase	20 units @ $24 each
Ending inventory	25 units

What is the cost of ending inventory using the weighted average costing method?
(a) $625
(c) $618.75
(b) $620
(d) $610

Exercise 9.4 ASSIGNMENT OF COST (PERIODIC AND PERPETUAL)

★ *Select the correct answer. Show any workings required and provide reasons to justify your choice.*
Malmo Ltd's inventory transactions for April 2014 are shown below.

Date	Purchases			Cost of sales			Balance		
	No. units	Unit cost	Total cost	No. units	Unit cost	Total cost	No. units	Unit cost	Total cost
April 1							20	$8.00	$160.00
4	90	$8.40	$756.00						
7	100	$8.60	$860.00						
10				50					
13	(20)	$8.60	($172.00)						
18				70					
21				(5)					
29				40					

1. If Malmo Ltd uses the perpetual inventory system with the moving average cost flow method, the 18 April sale would be costed at what unit cost?
   - (a) $8.60
   - (b) $8.46
   - (c) $8.44
   - (d) $8.42
2. If Malmo Ltd uses the periodic inventory system with the FIFO cost flow method, what would be the cost of sales for April?
   - (a) $1303.00
   - (b) $1508.60
   - (c) $1310.00
   - (d) $1324.00
3. If Malmo Ltd uses the perpetual inventory system with the FIFO cost flow method, the 21 April sale return (relating to the 18 April sale) would be costed at what unit cost?
   - (a) $8.00
   - (b) $8.60
   - (c) $8.40
   - (d) $8.50
4. If Malmo Ltd uses the periodic method with the weighted average cost flow method, what would be the value of closing inventory at 30 April 2011? (Round average cost to the nearest cent.)
   - (a) $295.40
   - (b) $301.00
   - (c) $253.20
   - (d) $297.50

Exercise 9.5 END-OF-PERIOD ADJUSTMENTS

★★ An extract from Uppsala Ltd's unadjusted trial balance as at 30 June 2013 appears below. Uppsala Ltd's reporting period ends on 30 June and uses the perpetual method to record inventory transactions.

	$	$
Inventory	194 400	
Sales		631 770
Sales returns	6 410	
Cost of sales	468 640	
Inventory losses	12 678	

Additional information
- On 24 June 2013, Uppsala Ltd recorded a $1320 credit sale of goods costing $1200. These goods, which were sold on FOB destination terms and were in transit at 30 June 2013, were included in the physical count.
- Inventory on hand at 30 June 2013 (determined via physical count) had a cost of $195 600 and a net realisable value of $194 740.

Required
1. Prepare any adjusting journal entries required on 30 June 2013.
2. Prepare the trading section of the statement of profit or loss and other comprehensive income for the year ended 30 June 2013.

Exercise 9.6 APPLYING THE LOWER OF COST AND NRV RULE

★★ The following information relates to the inventory on hand at 30 June 2013 held by Vaasa Ltd.

Item No.	Quantity	Cost per unit $	Cost to replace $	Estimated selling price $	Cost of completion and disposal $
A1458	600	2.30	2.41	3.75	0.49
A1965	815	3.40	3.26	3.50	0.55
B6730	749	7.34	7.35	10.00	0.95
D0943	98	1.23	1.14	1.00	0.12
G8123	156	3.56	3.56	5.70	0.67
W2167	1 492	6.12	6.15	7.66	0.36

Required

Calculate the value of inventory on hand at 30 June 2013 in accordance with the requirements of IAS 2.

Exercise 9.7 END-OF-REPORTING-PERIOD ADJUSTMENTS

★★ Norway Outfitters sells outdoor adventure equipment. The entity uses the perpetual inventory method to account for inventory transactions and assigns costs using the moving average method. All purchases and sales are made on FOB destination, 30-day credit terms.

At 30 June 2014, the balance of the inventory control account in the general ledger was $248 265 after the special journal totals were posted but before the balance-date adjusting entries were prepared and posted.

A physical count showed goods worth $256 100 to be on hand. Investigations of the discrepancy between the general ledger account balance and the count total revealed the following:
- Damaged ropes worth $1200 were returned to the supplier on 29 June, but this transaction has not yet been recorded.
- During the stocktake, staff found that a box of leather gloves worth $595 had suffered water damage during a recent storm. The gloves were damaged beyond repair and so were not included in the count, but they are still recorded in the inventory records.
- Equipment worth $1500, which was sold for $2500 on 29 June, was still in transit to the customer on 30 June. The sale was recorded on 29 June and the equipment was not included in the physical count.
- An error occurred when posting the purchase journal totals for May 2014. The correct total of $25 100 was erroneously posted as $21 500.
- The physical count included goods worth $7600 that were being held on consignment for All Weather Gear Pty Ltd.
- An all-terrain kit worth $1570 was returned by a customer on 28 June. The sales return transaction was correctly journalised and posted to the ledgers, but the kit was not returned to the warehouse and therefore was not included in the physical count.

Required

Adjust and reconcile the inventory control ledger account balance to the physical account (adjusted as necessary).

Exercise 9.8 ALLOCATING COST (WEIGHTED AVERAGE), REPORTING GROSS PROFIT AND APPLYING THE NRV RULE

★★ Oslo Ltd wholesales bicycles. It uses the perpetual inventory method and allocates cost to inventory on a moving average basis. The company's reporting period ends on 31 March. At 1 March 2014, inventory on hand consisted of 350 bicycles at $82 each and 43 bicycles at $85 each. During the month ended 31 March 2014, the following inventory transactions took place (all purchase and sales transactions are on credit):

March	1	Sold 300 bicycles for $120 each.
	3	Five bicycles were returned by a customer. They had originally cost $82 each and were sold for $120 each.
	9	Purchased 55 bicycles at $91 each.
	10	Purchased 76 bicycles at $96 each.
	15	Sold 86 bicycles for $135 each.
	17	Returned one damaged bicycle to the supplier. This bicycle had been purchased on 9 March.
	22	Sold 60 bicycles for $125 each.
	26	Purchased 72 bicycles at $98 each.
	29	Two bicycles, sold on 22 March, were returned by a customer. The bicycles were badly damaged so it was decided to write them off. They had originally cost $91 each.

Required

1. Calculate the cost of inventory on hand at 31 March 2014 and the cost of sales for the month of March. (Round the average unit cost to the nearest cent, and round the total cost amounts to the nearest dollar.)

2. Show the Inventory general ledger control account (in T-format) as it would appear at 31 March 2014.
3. Calculate the gross profit on sales for the month of March 2014.

ALLOCATING COST (FIFO), REPORTING GROSS PROFIT AND APPLYING THE NRV RULE

★★★ Stockholm Ltd wholesales bicycles. It uses the perpetual inventory method and allocates cost to inventory on a first-in, first-out basis. The company's reporting period ends on 31 March. At 1 March 2013, inventory on hand consisted of 350 bicycles at $82 each and 43 bicycles at $85 each. During the month ended 31 March 2013, the following inventory transactions took place (all purchase and sales transactions are on credit):

March	1	Sold 300 bicycles for $120 each.
	3	Five bicycles were returned by a customer. They had originally cost $82 each and were sold for $120 each.
	9	Purchased 55 bicycles at $91 each.
	10	Purchased 76 bicycles at $96 each.
	15	Sold 86 bicycles for $135 each.
	17	Returned one damaged bicycle to the supplier. This bicycle had been purchased on 9 March.
	22	Sold 60 bicycles for $125 each.
	26	Purchased 72 bicycles at $98 each.
	29	Two bicycles, sold on 22 March, were returned by a customer. The bicycles were badly damaged so it was decided to write them off. They had originally cost $91 each.

Required

1. Calculate the cost of inventory on hand at 31 March 2013 and the cost of sales for the month of March.
2. Show the Inventory general ledger control account (in T-format) as it would appear at 31 March 2013.
3. Calculate the gross profit on sales for the month of March 2013.
4. IAS 2 requires inventories to be measured at the lower of cost and net realisable value. Identify three reasons why the net realisable value of the bicycles on hand at 31 March 2013 may be below their cost.
5. If the net realisable value is below cost, what action should Stockholm Ltd take?

ASSIGNING COSTS AND END-OF-PERIOD ADJUSTMENTS

★★★ Lund Retailing Ltd is a food wholesaler that supplies independent grocery stores. The company operates a perpetual inventory system, with the first-in, first-out method used to assign costs to inventory items. Freight costs are not included in the calculation of unit costs. Transactions and other related information regarding two of the items (baked beans and plain flour) carried by Lund Ltd are given below for June 2013, the last month of the company's reporting period.

	Baked beans	Plain flour
Unit of packaging	Case containing 25 × 410 g cans	Box containing 12 × 4 kg bags
Inventory @ 1 June 2013	350 cases @ $19.60	625 boxes @ $38.40
Purchases	10 June: 200 cases @ $19.50 plus freight of $135 19 June: 470 cases @ $19.70 per case plus freight of $210	3 June: 150 boxes @ $38.45 15 June: 200 boxes @ $38.45 29 June: 240 boxes @ $39.00
Purchase terms	2/10, n/30, FOB shipping	n/30, FOB destination
June sales	730 cases @ $28.50	950 boxes @ 40.00

Returns and allowances	A customer returned 50 cases that had been shipped in error. The customer's account was credited for $1425.	As the June 15 purchase was unloaded, 10 boxes were discovered damaged. A credit of $384.50 was received by Lund Retailing Ltd.
Physical count at 30 June 2013	326 cases on hand	15 boxes on hand
Explanation of variance	No explanation found — assumed stolen	Boxes purchased on 29 June still in transit on 30 June
Net realisable value at 30 June 2013	$29.00 per case	$38.50 per box

Required

1. Calculate the number of units in inventory and the FIFO unit cost for baked beans and plain flour as at 30 June 2013 (show all workings).
2. Calculate the total dollar amount of the inventory for baked beans and plain flour, applying the lower of cost and net realisable rule on an item-by-item basis. Prepare any necessary journal entries (show all workings).

There is only scant literature on inventories and IAS 2, perhaps because the accounting treatment is not controversial. The main research interest therefore rests with the information content of inventory and inventory changes. There is also some research into earnings management through production costs.

Starting with the information role of inventory, Lev and Thiagarajan (1993) postulate that increases in inventory above the level of increases in sales serve as a fundamental signal to investors. Specifically, they argue that when inventory increases more than sales do, this is likely associated with unwarranted inventory buildup. One consequence of this is that future sales will decline as managers will have to offer discounts to customers. Alternatively, such an increase is likely to be followed by inventory write-offs. At the same time, over-production of inventory may entail a positive effect on current earnings in manufacturing firms. This is because overhead costs are allocated to a larger number of units, and hence reduces the per-unit cost of sales. Lev and Thiagarajan (1993) show that inventory buildup is negatively associated with stock returns. This is consistent with market participants regarding inventory buildup as a negative signal. Abarbanell and Bushee's (1997) formally show that Lev and Thiagarajan's (1993) conjecture about the negative association between inventory buildup and future earnings is borne out in the data. However, they do not find that financial analysts revise their predictions in line with the empirical evidence. This raises a concern that financial analysts do not fully appreciate the consequences of inventory buildup. Abarbanell and Bushee's (1998) subsequent analysis employs the same fundamental signal as Lev and Thiagarajan (1993), but this time to show it can help form a profitable buy-and-hold strategy. Specifically, a portfolio that takes a long (short) position in firms with increases in inventory below (above) the levels of increase in sales generates positive returns.

Thomas and Zhang (2002) link inventory changes to another important empirical finding that was previously established by Sloan (1996). Sloan (1996) finds that accruals are inversely related to future stock returns. This suggests that market participants do not fully understand the reversal property of accruals. Thomas and Zhang (2002) investigate if this is primarily caused by inventory changes. They find that both inventory and other components of accruals explain this phenomenon. However, the contribution of changes in inventory is the largest.

Roychowdhury (2006) examines real earnings management, which he defines as 'manipulating real activities to avoid reporting annual losses'. This contrasts with manipulating accruals, which is the convention in accounting research for earnings management. One of the real activities subject to such manipulations is overproduction of inventory. As Lev and Thiagarajan (1993) note, this can help reduce

cost of sales, and hence improve reported profitability. Roychowdhury (2006) estimates production costs as cost of goods sold plus the change in inventory. He focuses on firms who report the smallest profit among available observations during the 1987–2001 period. Based on past research these are firms suspected of using earnings management to avoid losses (e.g., Burgstahler and Dichev, 1997). Consistent with his conjecture that real earnings management takes place in inventory production cost, he finds that suspect firms are characterised by high production costs, low operating cash flows, and lower level of accruals than non-suspect firms.

Gunny (2010) extends this line of research to examine future operating performance of firms that engage in real earnings management to meet earnings benchmarks. She argues that engaging in real earnings management may serve as a signal about future performance. She finds that firms that overproduce to avoid reporting losses show higher return on equity and operating cash flows in the subsequent year than firms that report small losses while not engaging in real earnings management. The conclusion therefore is that real earnings management to meet earnings benchmarks indicates better future performance.

References

Abarbanell, J., and Bushee. B. 1997. Fundamental analysis, future earnings, and stock prices. *Journal of Accounting Research*, 35, 1–24.

Abarbanell, J., and Bushee. B. 1998. Abnormal returns to a fundamental analysis strategy. *The Accounting Review*, 73, 19–45.

Burgstahler, D., and Dichev, I., 1997. Earnings management to avoid earnings decreases and losses. *Journal of Accounting and Economics* 24, 99–126.

Gunny, K. A. 2010. The relation between earnings management using real activities manipulation and future performance: Evidence from meeting earnings benchmarks. *Contemporary Accounting Research*, 27(3), 855–888.

Lev, B., and Thiagarajan, R. 1993. Fundamental information analysis. *Journal of Accounting Research*, 31, 190–215.

Roychowdhury, S. 2006. Earnings management through real activities manipulation. *Journal of Accounting and Economics*, 42(3), 335–70.

Sloan, R. G. 1996. Do stock prices fully reflect information in accruals and cash flows about future earnings? *The Accounting Review*, 71, 289–315.

Thomas, J. K., and Zhang, H., 2002. Inventory changes and future returns. *Review of Accounting Studies*, 7(2–3), 163–187.

10 Employee benefits

ACCOUNTING STANDARDS IN FOCUS

IAS 19 *Employee Benefits*

LEARNING OBJECTIVES

After studying this chapter, you should be able to:

1. outline the principles applied in accounting for employee benefits

2. discuss the scope and purpose of IAS 19

3. discuss the definition of employee benefits

4. prepare journal entries to account for short-term liabilities for employee benefits, such as wages and salaries, sick leave and annual leave

5. compare defined benefit and defined contribution post-employment benefit plans

6. prepare entries to account for expenses, assets and liabilities arising from defined contribution post-employment plans

7. prepare entries to record expenses, assets and liabilities arising from defined benefit post-employment plans

8. explain how to measure and record other long-term liabilities for employment benefits, such as long service leave

9. explain when a liability should be recognised for termination benefits and how it should be measured.

10.1 INTRODUCTION TO ACCOUNTING FOR EMPLOYEE BENEFITS

Employee benefits typically constitute a significant component of an entity's expenses, particularly in the services sector. For example, HSBC Holdings plc reports in its 2014 financial statements that 'total operating expenses' of US$41 249 million include 'employee compensation and benefits' of US$20 366 million. Employees are remunerated for the services they provide. Employee remuneration is not limited to wages, which may be paid weekly, fortnightly or monthly, but often includes entitlements to be paid, such as sick leave, annual leave, long service leave and post-employment benefits, such as pension plans. The measurement of short-term liabilities for employee benefits, such as sick leave and annual leave, is relatively straightforward. However, the measurement of other types of employee benefits, including post-employment benefits, other long-term benefits, such as long service leave, and termination benefits, is more complex because it requires estimation and present value calculations.

10.2 SCOPE AND PURPOSE OF IAS 19

IAS 19 *Employee Benefits* applies to all employee benefits except those to which IFRS 2 *Share-based Payment* applies. Employee benefits arise from formal employment contracts between an entity and its individual employees. Employee benefits also include requirements specified by legislation or industry arrangements for employers to contribute to an industry, state or national plan. Informal practices that generate a constructive obligation, such as payment of annual bonuses, also fall within the scope of employee benefits under IAS 19. Share-based employee benefits are beyond the scope of IAS 19. *Chapter 8 considers share-based payments, including share-based employee remuneration.*

The purpose of IAS 19 is to prescribe the recognition, measurement and disclosure requirements for expenses, assets and liabilities arising from services provided by employees. Liabilities arise when employees provide services in exchange for benefits to be provided later by the employer. Accounting for employee benefits is complicated because some benefits may be provided many years after employees have provided services. The measurement of liabilities for employee benefits is made more difficult because the payment of some employee benefits for past services may be conditional upon the continuation of employment.

10.3 DEFINING EMPLOYEE BENEFITS

Paragraph 8 of IAS 19 defines employee benefits as including all types of consideration that the employer may give in exchange for services provided by employees or for the termination of employment. Employee benefits are usually paid to employees but the term also includes amounts paid to their dependants or to other parties.

Wages, salaries and other employee benefits are usually recognised as expenses. However, the costs of employee benefits may be allocated to assets in accordance with other accounting standards. For example, the cost of labour used in the manufacture of inventory is included in the cost of inventory in accordance with IAS 2 *Inventories*. The cost of an internally generated intangible asset recognised in accordance with IAS 38 *Intangible Assets*, such as the development of a new production process, includes the cost of employee benefits for staff, such as engineers, employed in generating the new production process.

10.4 SHORT-TERM EMPLOYEE BENEFITS

Short-term employee benefits are expected to be settled wholly within 1 year after the end of the annual reporting period in which the employee renders the service. Examples of short-term employee benefits include wages, salaries, bonuses and profit-sharing arrangements. They also include various forms of paid leave entitlements for which employees may be eligible. Sick leave and annual leave are common forms of paid leave entitlements. IAS 19 refers to various forms of leave entitlements as paid absences.

Short-term employee benefits also include non-monetary benefits, which are often referred to as 'fringe benefits'. Non-monetary benefits include the provision of health insurance, housing and motor vehicles. An entity may offer non-monetary benefits to attract staff. For example, a mining company may provide housing to employees where there are no major towns located near its mining sites. Non-monetary benefits may also arise from salary sacrifice arrangements, otherwise referred to as salary packaging. A salary sacrifice arrangement involves the employee electing to forgo some of his or her salary or wages in return for other benefits, such as a motor vehicle, provided by the employer.

10.4.1 Payroll

The subsystem for regular recording and payment of employee benefits is referred to as the payroll. The payroll involves:

- recording the amount of wages or salaries for the pay period
- updating personnel records for the appointment of new employees
- updating personnel records for the termination of employment contracts
- calculating the amount to be paid to each employee, net of deductions
- remitting payment of net wages or salaries to employees
- remitting payment of deductions to various external parties
- complying with regulatory requirements, such as reporting to taxation authorities.

Entities may process several payrolls. For example, an entity may process a payroll each fortnight for employees who are paid on a fortnightly basis and process a separate monthly payroll for employees paid on a monthly basis.

In return for providing services to the employer, employees regularly receive benefits, or remuneration, in the form of wages or salaries. Employers are typically required to deduct income tax from employees' wages and salaries. Thus the employee receives a payment that is net of tax, and the employer subsequently pays the amount of income tax to the taxation authority.

Employers may offer a service of deducting other amounts from employees' wages and salaries and paying other parties on their behalf. For example, the employer may deduct union membership fees from employees' wages and make payments to the various unions on behalf of the employees.

Payments made on behalf of an employee from amounts deducted from the employee's wages or salaries form part of the entity's wages and salaries expense. As these amounts are typically remitted in the month following the payment of wages and salaries, they represent a short-term liability for employee benefits at the end of each month.

Paragraph 11(a) of IAS 19 requires short-term employee benefits for services rendered during the period to be recognised as a liability after deducting any amounts already paid. Short-term liabilities for employee benefits must be measured at the nominal (undiscounted) amount that the entity expects to pay.

10.4.2 Accounting for the payroll

Illustrative example 10.1 demonstrates accounting for the payroll, including deductions from employees' remuneration, the remittance of payroll deductions and the measurement of resulting liabilities at the end of the period.

ILLUSTRATIVE EXAMPLE 10.1 Accounting for the payroll

Pacific Inc. pays its managers on a monthly basis. All managerial salaries are recognised as expenses. Pacific Inc.'s employees can elect to have their monthly health insurance premiums deducted from their salaries and paid to their health insurance fund on their behalf. Pacific Inc. also operates a giving scheme under which employees can elect to have donations to nominated charities deducted from their salaries and wages and remitted on their behalf to the selected charities. Figure 10.1 summarises the managerial payrolls for May and June 2016.

	$	May 2016 $	$	June 2016 $
Gross payroll for the month		2 400 000		2 500 000
Deductions payable to:				
Taxation authority	530 000		600 000	
Total Care Health Fund	40 000		40 000	
National Health Fund	32 000		32 500	
UNICEF	7 000		7 000	
Total deductions for the month		609 000		679 500
Net salaries paid		1 791 000		1 820 500

FIGURE 10.1 Summary of Pacific Inc.'s payroll.

Each time the monthly payroll is processed, the cost of the salaries is charged to expense accounts and a liability is accrued for the gross wages payable. Payments of net wages and salaries and remittance of payroll deductions to taxation authorities and other parties reduce the payroll liability account.

The managerial payroll is processed on the second Monday of the month and net salaries are paid to employees on the following Tuesday. During May, managers earned salaries of $2.4 million. After deducting amounts for income tax, contributions to health funds and donations, Pacific Inc. paid its managers a net amount of $1 791 000 during May. All of the deductions are paid to the various external bodies in the following month. Health insurance deductions are remitted on the first Friday of the following month. Thus, the deductions for health insurance and union subscriptions for the May payroll are remitted on Friday 3 June. Income tax withheld is remitted on the 20th of the following month. Deductions for donations are paid on the 21st of the following month.

The balance of Pacific Inc.'s accrued managerial payroll account at 1 June 2016 is $609 000, being the deductions from managers' salaries for income tax, health insurance premiums and donations for May 2016. These amounts are paid during June 2016.

During June 2016, Pacific Inc.'s managers earned gross salaries of $2.5 million. The managers actually received $1 820 500, being the net wages and salaries after deductions for income tax, health insurance premiums and donations to charities. In total, $679 500 was deducted from managers' salaries for June 2016. This amount is a liability at the end of June 2016. The amounts deducted from employees' salaries during June 2016 are remitted during July 2016.

The journal entries to record Pacific Inc.'s payroll and remittances for June 2016 are as follows:

June 3	Accrued Payroll Bank (Payment of May payroll deductions for Total Health Care Fund)	Dr Cr	40 000	40 000
	Accrued Payroll Bank (Payment of May payroll deductions for National Health Fund)	Dr Cr	32 000	32 000
June 13	Salaries Expense Accrued Payroll (Managerial payroll for June)	Dr Cr	2 500 000	2 500 000
June 14	Accrued Payroll Bank (Payment of net salaries for June)	Dr Cr	1 820 500	1 820 500
June 20	Accrued Payroll Bank (Payment of May payroll deductions for withheld income tax)	Dr Cr	530 000	530 000
June 21	Accrued Payroll Bank (Payment of May payroll deductions for UNICEF)	Dr Cr	7000	7000

10.4.3 Accrual of wages and salaries

The end of the payroll period often differs from the end of the reporting period because payrolls are usually determined on a weekly or fortnightly basis. Accordingly, it is usually necessary to recognise an expense and a liability for employee benefits for the business days between the last payroll period and the end of the reporting period. This is demonstrated in illustrative example 10.2.

Canterbury plc pays its employees on a fortnightly basis. The last payroll in the year ended 30 November 2016 was for the fortnight (10 working days) ended Friday 25 November 2016. There were three business days between the end of the final payroll period and the end of the reporting period. Assuming the cost of employee benefits for the remaining three days was £720 000, Canterbury plc would record the following accrual:

Wages and Salaries Expense	Dr	720 000	
Accrued Wages and Salaries	Cr		720 000
(Accrual of wages and salaries)			

The accrued wages and salaries is a liability for short-term employee benefits. Paragraph 16 of IAS 19 requires accrued short-term employee benefits to be measured at nominal value; that is, the amount expected to be paid to settle the obligation.

10.4.4 Short-term paid absences

Employees may be entitled to be paid during certain absences, such as annual recreational leave or short periods of illness. Some entities also offer other forms of paid leave, including maternity leave, parental leave, carers' leave and bereavement leave. Entitlements to short-term paid absences are those entitlements that are expected to be settled within 12 months after the end of the reporting period.

Short-term paid absences may be either accumulating or non-accumulating. Non-accumulating paid absences are leave entitlements that the employee may not carry forward to a future period. For example, an employment contract may provide for 5 days of paid, non-cumulative sick leave. If the employee does not take sick leave during the year, the unused leave lapses; that is, it does not carry forward to an increased entitlement in the following year.

Accumulating paid absences are leave entitlements that the employee may carry forward to a future period if unused in the current period. For example, an employment contract may provide for 20 days of paid annual leave. If the employee takes only 15 days of annual leave during the year, the remaining 5 days may be carried forward and taken in the following year.

Accumulating paid absences may be vesting or non-vesting. If accumulating paid absences are vesting, the employee is entitled, upon termination of employment, to cash settlement of unused leave. If accumulating paid absences are non-vesting, the employee has no entitlement to cash settlement of unused leave. For example, an employment contract may provide for cumulative annual leave of 20 days, vesting to a maximum of 30 days, and non-vesting cumulative sick leave of 10 days per annum. After 2 years of service, the employee would have been entitled to take 40 days of annual leave and 20 days of sick leave, but if the employee resigned after 2 years of employment, during which no annual leave or sick leave had been taken, the termination settlement would include payment for 30 days' unused annual leave (the maximum allowed by the employment contract). There would be no cash settlement of the unused sick leave because it was non-vesting.

Paragraph 13(a) of IAS 19 requires expected short-term accumulating paid absences to be recognised when the employee renders services that increase the entitlement. For example, if its employees are entitled to 2 weeks of cumulative sick leave for every year of service, the entity is required to accrue the sick leave throughout the year. The employee benefit — that is, the accumulated leave — is measured as the amount that the entity expects to pay to settle the obligation that has accumulated at the end of the reporting period. If the leave is cumulative but non-vesting, it is possible that there will not be a future settlement for some employees. The sick leave might remain unused when the employment contract is terminated. However, the sick leave must still be accrued throughout the period of employment because an obligation arises when the employee provides services that give rise to the leave entitlement. If the leave is non-vesting, it is necessary to estimate the amount of accumulated paid absence that the entity expects to pay.

For non-accumulating short-term paid absences, paragraph 13(b) requires the entity to recognise the employee benefit when the paid absence occurs. A liability is not recognised for unused non-accumulating leave entitlements because the employee is not entitled to carry them forward to a future period. Hence there is no obligation.

The alternative forms of short-term paid absences and the corresponding recognition and measurement requirements are depicted in figure 10.2.

Accumulation	Vesting/non-vesting	Recognition	Liability measurement
Accumulating — employee may carry forward unused entitlement	Vesting — employee is entitled to cash settlement of unused leave	Recognised as employee provides services giving rise to entitlement	Nominal, amount expected to be paid, i.e. total vested accumulated leave
	Non-vesting — no cash settlement of unused leave	Recognised as employee provides services giving rise to entitlement	Nominal, amount expected to be paid, requires estimation of amount that will be used
Non-accumulating — unused entitlement lapses each period		Recognised when paid absences occur	No liability is recognised

FIGURE 10.2 Short-term paid absences

The following illustrative examples demonstrate accounting for short-term paid absences. First, illustrative example 10.3 demonstrates accounting for annual leave.

ILLUSTRATIVE EXAMPLE 10.3 Accounting for annual leave

Schnee AG has four employees in its Alpine branch. Each employee is entitled to 20 days of paid recreational leave per annum, referred to as annual leave (AL). At 1 January 2016, the balance of the provision for annual leave was €4360. During the year employees took a total of 70 days of annual leave, which cost Schnee AG €9160. After annual leave taken during the year had been recorded, the provision for annual leave account had a debit balance of €4800 in the trial balance at 31 December 2016 before end-of-period adjustments. All annual leave accumulated at 31 December 2016 is expected to be paid by 31 December 2017. The following information is obtained from the payroll records for the year ended 31 December 2016:

Employee	Wage per day	AL 1 January 2016 in days	Increase in entitlement in days	AL taken in days
Bauer	€120	9	20	16
Fiedler	€160	7	20	16
Goetz	€180	8	20	14
Wagner	€ 90	8	20	24

A liability must be recognised for accumulated annual leave at 31 December 2016. This is measured as the amount that is expected to be paid. As annual leave is vesting, all accumulated leave is expected to be paid. The first step in measuring the liability is to calculate the number of days of accumulated annual leave for each employee at 31 December 2016. Although this calculation would normally be performed by payroll software, we will manually calculate the number of days to enhance your understanding of the process. The next step is to multiply the number of days of accumulated annual leave by each employee's daily wage.

Employee	AL 1 January in days	Increase in entitlement in days	AL taken in days	Accumulated AL 31 December 2016 in days	Liability for AL 31 December 2016 €
Bauer	9	20	16	13	1 560
Fiedler	7	20	16	11	1 760
Goetz	8	20	14	14	2 520
Wagner	8	20	24	4	360
					6 200

The calculation of accumulated annual leave in days and the resultant liability are as follows:

Bauer: 9 + 20 − 16 = 13 days × €120 per day = €1560
Fiedler: 7 + 20 − 16 = 11 days × €160 per day = €1760
Goetz: 8 + 20 − 14 = 14 days × €180 per day = €2520
Wagner: 8 + 20 − 24 = 4 days × €90 per day = €360

Thus Schnee AG should recognise a liability of €6200 for annual leave at 31 December 2016. After recording annual leave taken during the year, the unadjusted trial balance shows a debit balance of €4800 for the provision for annual leave. Thus, a journal entry is required to record an increase of €11 000.

Wages and Salaries Expense	Dr	11 000	
Provision for Annual Leave	Cr		11 000
(Accrual of liability for annual leave)			

In illustrative example 10.3, an annual adjustment was made to the provision for annual leave. Some entities make accruals for annual leave more frequently to facilitate more comprehensive internal reporting to management. This is easily achieved with electronic accounting systems or payroll software.

Accounting for accumulating sick leave is demonstrated in illustrative example 10.4. In this illustration, the accumulating sick leave is non-vesting.

ILLUSTRATIVE EXAMPLE 10.4 Accounting for accumulating sick leave

Atlantic Inc. has 10 employees who are each paid $500 per week for a 5-day working week (i.e. $100 per day). Employees are entitled to 5 days of accumulating non-vesting sick leave each year. At 1 January 2016 the accumulated sick leave brought forward from the previous year was 10 days in total. During the year ended 31 December 2016 employees took 35 days of paid sick leave and 10 days of unpaid sick leave. One employee resigned at the beginning of the year. At the time of her resignation she had accumulated 5 days of sick leave. It is estimated that 60% of the unused sick leave will be taken during the following year and that the remaining 40% will not be taken at all.

After recording sick leave taken during the year, the unadjusted trial balance shows that the provision for sick leave had a debit balance of $3000 at 31 December 2016.

The following table presents information used to calculate the amount of the provision for sick leave that Atlantic Inc. should recognise at 31 December 2016:

			Sick leave		Leave expected to be taken	
No. of employees	Base pay/day $	Balance b/d 1 January 2016 Days	Accumulated in 2016 Days	Taken or lapsed Days	Within 12 months %	After 1 year %
10	100	10	50	40	60	0

The 10 employees who were employed for all of the year ended 31 December 2016 each became entitled to 5 days of sick leave during the year. Thus the total increase in entitlement during the year is 50 days. During the year, 35 days of paid sick leave were taken and 5 days of sick leave entitlement lapsed because an employee with 5 days' accumulated sick leave resigned without having used her entitlement. Thus, the aggregate sick leave entitlement reduced by 40 days during the year.

The first step in measuring the amount of the liability is to calculate the number of days of accumulated sick leave entitlement at 31 December 2016.

	Days
Brought forward 1 January 2016	10
Increase in entitlement for services provided in the current year	50
Sick leave entitlement taken or lapsed during the year	(40)
Sick leave carried forward 31 December 2016	20

The number of days of accumulated sick leave at the end of the reporting period is multiplied by the proportion of days expected to be taken, in this case, 60%. This amount, 12 days, is then multiplied by the current rate of pay per day:

$$20 \text{ days} \times 60\% \times \$100 \text{ per day} = \$1200$$

Thus the provision for sick leave should be $1200 Cr at 31 December 2016. The unadjusted balance of the provision for sick leave is $3000 Dr. Accordingly, the provision must be increased by $4200 as follows:

Wages and Salaries Expense	Dr	4 200	
Provision for Sick Leave	Cr		4 200
(Accrual of liability for sick leave)			

For simplicity, the accrual adjustment to recognise sick leave is made at the end of the year in this example. Many companies make such adjustments throughout the year to provide more complete internal reporting to management. This is facilitated by payroll software that automates the calculation of accumulated entitlements.

10.4.5 Profit-sharing and bonus plans

Employers may offer profit-sharing arrangements and bonuses to their employees. Bonuses may be determined as a lump-sum amount or based on accounting or market-based measures of performance. Many large companies use bonuses in management incentive schemes. For example, the remuneration received by the senior executives of BHP Billiton includes base salary, both cash-based and share-based bonuses linked to performance (incentive-based remuneration) and pension benefits. The components of remuneration for the chief executive officer (CEO) for 2014 are shown in figure 10.3. As can be seen, the majority of a senior executive's remuneration can be in forms other than base salary.

Name: Andrew Mackenzie Position: Chief executive officer (CEO)	2015 U$'000	2014 U$'000
Base salary	1 700	1 700
Benefits: tax return preparation in required countries; private family health insurance; and spouse business-related travel	145	92
Short-term incentive awarded for 2014:50% in cash; and 50% in deferred share-based awards, subject to shareholder approval	2 312	3 136
Long-term incentive: vesting of LTI awards on 20 August 2014 for performance for the five years ended 30 June 2014	0	2 635
Pension: BHP Billiton's contribution to defined contribution pension plans	425	425
Total	4 582	7 988

FIGURE 10.3 BHP Billiton CEO Remuneration
Source: BHP Billiton (2015, p. 176).

Paragraph 19 of IAS 19 requires an entity to recognise a liability for profit-sharing and bonus payments if it has a present obligation to make such payments and the amount can be estimated reliably. A present obligation exists if the entity has no realistic opportunity to avoid making the payments. The employee's performance under an employment contract may give rise to a legal obligation to pay a bonus. Alternatively, a constructive obligation may arise if the entity has a well-established practice of paying the bonus and has no realistic alternative but to pay the bonus because non-payment may be harmful to the entity's relations with its employees.

Liabilities for short-term profit-sharing arrangements and bonuses are measured at the nominal (i.e. undiscounted) amount that the entity expects to pay. Thus, if payment under a profit-sharing arrangement is subject to the employee still being employed when the payment is due, the amount recognised as a liability is reduced by the amount that is expected to go unpaid due to staff turnover. For example, assume an entity has a profit-sharing arrangement in which it is obligated to pay 1% of profit for the period to employees and the amount becomes payable 3 months after the end of the reporting period. Based on staff turnover in prior years, the entity estimates that only 95% of employees will be eligible to receive a share of profit 3 months after the end of the reporting period. Accordingly, the amount of the liability that should be recognised for the profit-sharing scheme is equal to 0.95% of the entity's profit for the period. In this simple example it is assumed the bonus is distributed equally among employees.

10.5 POST-EMPLOYMENT BENEFITS

Post-employment benefits are benefits, other than termination benefits *(which are considered in section 10.9)*, that are payable after completion of employment, typically after the employee retires. Where post-employment benefits involve significant obligations, it is common (and in some countries compulsory) for employers to contribute to a post-employment benefit plan for employees.

Post-employment benefit plans are defined in paragraph 8 of IAS 19 as arrangements through which an entity provides post-employment benefits. They are also referred to as pension plans, employee retirement plans and pension plans. The employer makes payments to a fund. The fund, which is a separate entity, typically a trust, invests the contributions and provides post-employment benefits to the employees, who are the members of the fund. Figure 10.4 shows the relations between the employer, the pension fund (plan) and the employees (members of the fund).

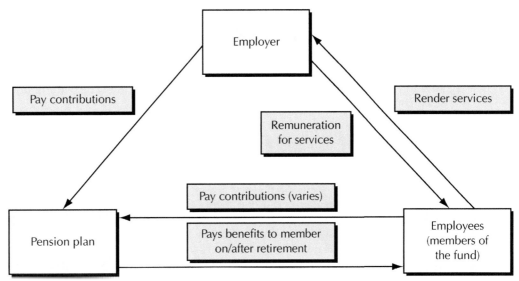

FIGURE 10.4 Relationships between the employer, pension plan and employees

The two types of post-employment benefit plans are:
- defined benefit plans and
- defined contribution plans, including multi-employer plans.

Paragraph 8 of IAS 19 refers to defined contribution plans as post-employment plans for which an entity pays fixed contributions into a separate entity. The contributions are normally based on the wages and salaries paid to employees. The contributing entity has no legal or constructive obligation to pay further contributions if the fund does not hold sufficient assets to pay all employee benefits relating to employees' services in the current and prior periods. The amount received by employees on retirement is dependent upon the level of contributions and the return earned by the fund on its investments.

In paragraph 8 of IAS 19, defined benefit plans are defined as post-employment plans other than defined contribution plans. If a post-employment plan is not classified as a defined contribution plan, by default, it is a defined benefit plan. Critical to the definition of a defined contribution post-employment benefit plan is the absence of an obligation for the employer to make further payments if the plan is unable to pay all the benefits accruing to members for their past service. Thus, defined benefit post-employment plans are those in which the employer has some obligation to pay further contributions to enable the plan to pay members' benefits. In a defined benefit post-employment plan, the benefit received by members on retirement is determined by a formula reflecting their years of service and level of remuneration. It is not dependent upon the performance of the plan. If the plan has insufficient funds to pay members' post-employment benefits, the trustee of the plan will require the employer, who is the sponsor of the plan, to make additional payments. Similarly, if the plan achieves higher returns than are required to pay members' post-employment benefits, the employer may be able to take a 'contribution holiday'. Employers often prefer defined contribution plans because there is no risk of liability for further contributions if the plan fails to earn an adequate return.

IAS 19 prescribes accounting treatment for contributions to post-employment benefit plans and assets and liabilities arising from post-employment benefit plans from the perspective of the employer. It does not prescribe accounting requirements for the post-employment benefit plan.

10.6 ACCOUNTING FOR DEFINED CONTRIBUTION POST-EMPLOYMENT PLANS

As described above, entities that participate in defined contribution post-employment plans make payments to a post-employment benefit plan. The amount is determined as a percentage of remuneration paid to employees who are members of the plan. Contributions payable to defined contribution funds are recognised in the period the employee renders services. The contributions payable during the period are recognised as expenses unless another standard permits the cost of employment benefits to be allocated to the carrying amount of an asset, such as internally constructed plant in accordance with IAS 16 *Property, Plant and Equipment.*

If the amount paid to the defined contribution plan by the entity during the year is less than the amount payable in relation to services rendered by employees, a liability for unpaid contributions must be recognised at the end of the period. The liability is measured at the undiscounted amount payable to the extent that contributions are due within 12 months after the reporting period. Paragraph 52 of IAS 19 requires discounting of liabilities for contributions to defined contribution plans that are due more than 12 months after the reporting period in which the employee provides the related services. The discount rate used to discount a post-employment benefit obligation is determined by reference to market yields on high-quality corporate bonds in accordance with IAS 19 paragraph 83. If the obligation is to be settled in a country that does not have a deep market in high-quality corporate bonds, the market yield on government bonds must be used.

If the amount paid to the defined contribution plan by the entity during the year is greater than the amount of contributions payable in relation to services rendered by employees, the entity recognises an asset to the extent that it is entitled to a refund or reduction in future contributions. In this situation, the asset would be a prepayment, or prepaid expenses.

ILLUSTRATIVE EXAMPLE 10.5 Accounting for defined contribution post-employment plans

Arctic Ltd provides a defined contribution pension plan for its employees. Arctic Ltd is required to contribute 9% of gross wages, salaries and commissions payable for services rendered by employees. It makes quarterly payments of $80 000 to the pension plan. If the amount paid to the pension plan during the financial year is less than 9% of gross wages, salaries and commissions for that year, Arctic Ltd must pay the outstanding contributions by 31 March of the following financial year. If the amount paid during the financial year is more than 9% of the gross wages, salaries and bonuses for the year, the excess contributions are deducted from amounts payable in the following year.

Arctic Ltd's annual reporting period ends on 31 December.

Arctic Ltd's employee benefits for the year ended 31 December 2016 comprise:

	$
Gross wages and salaries	3 900 000
Gross commissions	100 000
	4 000 000

The deficit in Arctic Ltd's pension plan contributions for 2016 is determined as follows:

	$
Contributions payable:	
9% × gross wages, salaries and commissions	360 000
Contributions paid during 2014: $80 000 × 4	320 000
Pension contribution payable	40 000

Arctic Ltd must recognise a liability for the unpaid pension plan contributions. The liability is not discounted because it is a short-term employee benefits liability. Arctic Ltd would record the following entry for 31 December 2016:

Wages and Salaries Expense	Dr	40 000	
Pension contributions payable	Cr		40 000
(Accrual of liability for unpaid pension plan contributions)			

10.7 ACCOUNTING FOR DEFINED BENEFIT POST-EMPLOYMENT PLANS

As described in section 10.5, the employer pays contributions to a plan, which is a separate entity from the employer. The plan accumulates assets through contributions and returns on investments. The accumulated assets are used to pay post-employment benefits to members (retired employees). The return on investments held by the pension plan comprises dividend and interest income and changes in the fair value of investments. The benefits paid to members are a function of their remuneration levels while employed and the number of years of service. The trustee of the plan may require the employer to make additional contributions if there is a shortfall. Thus, the employer effectively underwrites the actuarial and investment risks of the plan. In other words, the entity bears the risk of the plan being unable to pay benefits.

The assets of the pension plan, which are mostly investments, do not always equal its obligation to pay post-employment benefits to members. The pension plan has a deficit to the extent that the present value of the defined benefit obligation (i.e. post-employment benefits that are expected to be paid to employees for their services up to the end of the reporting period) exceeds the fair value of the plan assets. Conversely, a surplus arises when the fair value of the plan assets exceeds the present value of the defined benefit obligation.

Whether the deficit (surplus) of the defined benefit pension plan is a liability (asset) of the sponsoring employer is debatable. Some argue that the surplus in the pension plan does not satisfy all of the characteristics of an asset. Arguably, the assets of the plan are not controlled by the employer because they cannot be used for its benefit. For example, the employer may not use the surplus of the defined benefit pension plan to pay its debts; the assets of the plan are only used to generate cash flows to pay post-employment benefits to the members of the plan. Although the surplus is expected to result in future cash savings, such as lower contributions in future, it could be argued that the employer has not obtained control over those benefits through a past event where the reduction in contributions is at the discretion of the trustee of the pension plan.

Similarly, it has been argued that a deficit in the defined benefit pension plan is not a liability of the sponsoring employer because it does not have a present obligation to make good the shortfall. For instance, the employer may modify the post-employment benefits payable so as to avoid some of the obligation.

The perspective adopted in IAS 19 is that the surplus or deficit of the defined benefit pension plan is an asset, or liability, respectively, of the sponsoring employer. In some cases, the entity might not have a legal obligation to make good any shortfall in the pension plan. For example, the terms of the trust deed may allow the employer to change or terminate its obligation under the plan. Although the employer might not have a legal obligation to make up any shortfall, it typically has a constructive obligation because terminating its obligations under the plan may make it difficult to retain and recruit staff. Accordingly, the accounting treatment prescribed by IAS 19 for an entity's obligations arising from sponsorship of a defined benefit plan assumes that the entity will continue to promise the post-employment benefits over the remaining working lives of its employees. Similarly, the standard reflects the view that any surplus of the fund represents expected future inflows, in the form of reduced contributions, arising from having contributed more than is needed in the past. The standard and Basis for Conclusions focus on how to measure the resulting asset rather than justifying whether it meets the definition and recognition criteria.

If adopting the view that a deficit or surplus of the defined benefit pension plan is a liability or asset of the sponsoring employer, the next conceptual issue is whether it should be recognised and, if so, how it should be measured. Before looking at how the standard setters resolved these issues, we will consider the possibilities, which are shown in figure 10.5. At one extreme, the deficit or surplus is not recognised in the financial statements of the entity that sponsors the defined benefit pension plan. In other words, the deficit or surplus is 'off balance sheet'. At the other extreme, referred to as 'net capitalisation', the deficit (surplus) of the fund is recognised as a liability (asset) on the statement of financial position of the entity that sponsors the defined benefit pension plan. Under net capitalisation, the net pension liability or asset is usually measured as the difference between the present value of post-employment benefits earned by employees for services in the current and prior periods and the fair value of plan assets. Between these two extremes are various partial capitalisation methods in which some amount of the surplus or deficit of the fund remains off balance sheet. For example, an earlier version of IAS 19 permitted increments in the defined benefit obligation resulting from prior periods (referred to as past service costs) to be recognised progressively over the average remaining period until they became vested.

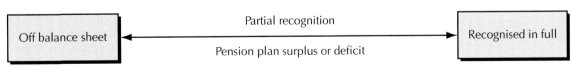

FIGURE 10.5 Alternative approaches to accounting for defined benefit pension plans

In the absence of accounting regulation, preparers were able to select different approaches to accounting for defined benefit post-employment benefits, ranging from off balance sheet to net capitalisation. For instance, many companies in the United States kept their obligations for defined benefit pension plans off balance sheet prior to the introduction of FAS 158: Defined Benefit Pension and other Post-retirement Pension Plans in 2006.

Obviously, the use of different methods of accounting for post-employment benefits reduces the comparability of financial statements. Concerns were also raised about delays in recognition of liabilities perpetuated by partial capitalisation methods. Untimely recognition of assets or liabilities arising under post-employment benefit plans results in misleading information in the statement of financial position which is not adequately resolved by additional disclosures in the notes. The International Accounting Standards Board (IASB®) and the US Financial Accounting Standards Board (FASB) jointly undertook a project to enhance the comparability and transparency of accounting for post-employment benefits (IASB 2008), resulting in a revised version of IAS 19 *Employee Benefits*. We will now turn to the requirements of IAS 19 for accounting for defined benefit post-employment benefits.

The net capitalisation approach is adopted by IAS 19. Thus, the sponsoring employer recognises a net defined benefit liability or asset, representing its exposure to the defined benefit pension plan at the end of the reporting period. Contributions paid into the plan by the employer increase the assets of the plan, and thus increase a surplus or reduce any deficit of the plan. The employer accounts for its contributions to the plan as a decrease in the net defined benefit liability, or an increase in the net defined benefit asset. The employer recognises expenses in relation to its sponsorship of the defined benefit pension plan when service costs and interest costs are incurred, rather than when contributions are paid. This will become clear as we work through the revised requirements of IAS 19 for accounting for defined benefit pension plans.

The key steps involved in accounting by the employer for a defined benefit post-employment plan in accordance with IAS 19 (paragraph 57) are:
1. determining the deficit or surplus of the plan
2. determining the amount of the net defined benefit liability (asset), which is the amount of the deficit or the surplus, adjusted for any effect of limiting a net-defined benefit asset to the asset ceiling, which is explained below
3. determining the amounts to be recognised in profit or loss for current service cost, any past service cost and net interest expense (income) on the net defined benefit liability (asset)
4. determining the remeasurement of the net defined benefit liability (asset) to be recognised in other comprehensive income, which comprises actuarial gains and losses, return on plan assets (other than amounts included in net interest), and any change in the effect of the asset ceiling (other than amounts included in net interest).

We will now take a closer look at each step.

10.7.1 Step 1: Determining the deficit or surplus of the plan

There are two elements to determining the deficit or surplus of the plan — the obligation to pay benefits and any plan assets. Paragraph 67 of IAS 19 requires an entity to use the projected unit credit method to determine the present value of post-employment benefits earned by employees for services in the current and prior periods. Other names for the projected unit credit method include the *accrued benefit method pro-rated on service* and the *benefits/years of service method*. The projected unit credit method, which attributes a proportionate amount of additional benefit to each period of service, is shown in illustrative example 10.6.

ILLUSTRATIVE EXAMPLE 10.6 Determining the present value of the defined benefit obligation using the projected unit credit method

Dickens plc provides a defined benefit pension plan in which employees receive post-employment benefits determined as 1% of their final year salary, for every year of service. Salaries are expected to increase by 5% (compound) each year. The accountant has determined that the appropriate discount rate is 10% p.a. Charles commenced working for Dickens plc on 2 January 2016 with an annual salary of £40 000 and is expected to retire on 31 December 2018. For simplicity, this example ignores the additional adjustment that would be necessary to reflect the probability that Charles will resign or retire at a different date.

To understand the table below, you will need to read the following explanation which commences with the figure in the bottom right cell. At 31 December 2018 Charles will be entitled to 3% of his final year salary for three years of service. If his salary increases by 5% p.a., his salary for the year ended 31 December 2018 will be £44 100. At 3% of final year salary, Charles' post-employment benefit will be £1323 (£44 100 × 3%). Note that this is the amount in the 'Total current and prior years' of the column labelled 'Year ended 31/12/18'. The benefit attributed to each year is 1/n of the total benefit payable after n years. In this example, the amount attributed to each year is £441, being 1/3 of £1323. The amount of £441 is the amount in the row labelled 'Current year' in the column for each year. The total current and prior year amount for each year is carried forward in the table as the prior year amount in the next year.

Schedule of changes in the defined benefit obligation			
	Year ended 31/12/16 £	Year ended 31/12/17 £	Year ended 31/12/18 £
Prior year	0	441	882
Current year	441	441	441
Total current and prior years	441	882	1 323

The obligation is measured as the present value of the accumulated post-employment benefit at the end of each period. In this example a discount rate of 10% is used. Each period the present value increases partly as a result of current year benefits relating to service, and partly because the discounting period is reduced as the time to settlement decreases. The present value of the accrued benefits increases as the expected settlement time approaches because the expected settlement is discounted over a shorter period of time. The difference in the present value attributable to discounting over a shorter period is accounted for as interest expense. The interest component is calculated for each period by multiplying the opening balance of the liability by the interest rate.

The following table illustrates the increase in the defined benefit obligation over the 3-year period, differentiating between the service cost and interest elements. The opening obligation is the present value of the benefit attributed to Charles' prior years. The interest cost for the year ended 31 December 2016 is nil because the opening balance of the obligation is nil for that year. The current service cost is the present value of the defined benefit attributed to the current year. For example, the benefit attributed to current service is £441 for 2016, as per the table above. This is the increase in Charles' defined benefit entitlements attributable to his services during 2016. This amount is expected to be settled 2 years later, on 31 December 2018. Accordingly, the current service cost for 2016 is measured as the present value of the benefit attributed to that year, which is calculated as $£441/(1 + 0.1)^2 = £365$. The closing obligation is the present value of the benefit attributed to current and prior years. The closing balance of one year forms the opening balance of the next year. Thus the opening balance for 2017 is £365 and the interest cost for that year is £36, being £365 × 10%.

Schedule of current service cost, interest and present value of the defined benefit obligation			
	Year ended 31/12/16 £	Year ended 31/12/17 £	Year ended 31/12/18 £
Opening obligation	0	365	802
Interest at 10%	0	36	80
Current service cost	365	401	441
Closing obligation	365	802	1 323

To complete the first step, it is necessary to determine the difference between the fair value of plan assets and the present value of the defined benefit obligation. The excess of the defined benefit obligation over the fair value of the plan assets is the deficit of the plan. Conversely, any excess of the fair value of plan assets over the present value of the defined benefit obligation is a surplus of the plan. The previous example is based on an individual to simplify the calculations of accrued benefits. However, the plan would typically provide multiple members and the plan assets would generate cash inflows to be used to settle obligations to all members.

ILLUSTRATIVE EXAMPLE 10.7 Determining the deficit or surplus of the defined benefit pension plan

To illustrate the calculation of the deficit or surplus of the defined benefit pension plan, we will assume the following information about the assets and obligations for post-employment benefits of Dickens Employee Pension Plan:

	31/12/16 £	31/12/17 £	31/12/18 £
Closing obligation	4 900	5 700	6 550
Fair value of plan assets	4 500	5 400	6 600
Deficit (surplus) of the plan	400	300	(50)

The closing obligation is the present value of the defined benefit obligation at the end of each reporting period. The plan has a deficit of £400 at 31 December 2016. This amount is calculated as '£4900 – £4500', which is the amount by which the present value of the defined benefit obligation exceeds the fair value of plan assets. At 31 December 2017, the plan has a deficit of £300, being the excess of the obligation of £5700 over the fair value of plan assets, £5400. At 31 December 2018, the fair value of plan assets exceeds the defined benefit obligation. Accordingly, the defined benefit pension plan has a surplus of £50, being the fair value of plan assets, £6600, less the defined benefit obligation, £6550.

Obligations to pay pensions during employees' lives or that of their eligible dependants can further complicate the measurement of accrued benefits because the total payment is dependent upon the mortality rate of the employees and their eligible beneficiaries. Companies often rely on actuarial assessments to estimate the defined benefit obligation and the level of investment required to enable the plan to pay accumulated benefits as and when they fall due. Actuaries apply mathematical, statistical, economic and financial analysis to assess risks associated with contracts, such as insurance policies and pension plans. Actuarial estimates rely on assumptions, such as the employee retention rates and the rate at which salaries are expected to increase. Actuaries also provide financial planning advice, on matters such as the level of investment needed to generate sufficient future cash flows to meet the expected obligations as and when they fall due.

10.7.2 Step 2: Determining the amount of the net defined benefit liability (asset)

A net defined benefit liability arises when the defined benefit pension plan has a deficit. The net defined benefit liability is measured as the amount of the deficit of the defined benefit pension plan, which is calculated following the procedure described in step 1. For example, in illustrative example 10.7 the amount of the net defined benefit liability for the year ended 31 December 2017 is £300.

A net defined benefit asset arises when the defined benefit pension plan has a surplus. The net defined benefit asset is measured as the amount of the surplus, adjusted for any effect of limiting a net defined benefit asset to the asset ceiling. The asset ceiling is defined in paragraph 8 of IAS 19 as 'the present value of any economic benefits available in the form of refunds from the plan or reductions in future contributions to the plan'. The net defined benefit asset is the lower of the surplus of the defined benefit pension plan and the asset ceiling. For example, if we assume that the present value of reductions in Dickens plc's future contributions to the plan at 31 December 2018 were £60, the net defined benefit asset of Dickens plc would be measured as £50, being the lower of the surplus of the defined benefit plan and the asset ceiling. However, if the present value of reductions in Dickens plc's future contributions to the plan at 31 December 2018 were only £40, its net defined benefit asset would be measured as £40.

10.7.3 Step 3: Determining the amounts to be recognised in profit or loss

The amount of the net defined benefit liability (asset) is affected by the present value of the defined benefit obligation and the fair value of plan assets. The present value of the defined benefit obligation is affected by the service cost, which comprises current service cost, past service cost and any gain or loss on settlement of the defined benefit.

Current service cost is 'the increase in the present value of defined benefit obligation resulting from employee service in the current period' (IAS 19 paragraph 8). The service cost for each year in illustrative example 10.6 is a current service cost to Dickens plc because it is the increase in the present value of the defined benefit obligation attributed to employment services rendered by Charles during each year.

Past service cost is defined in paragraph 8 of IAS 19 as the change in the present value of the defined benefit obligation for employee service in prior periods. This occurs if the plan is amended or curtailed.

Illustrative example 10.8 draws on the same information as used in illustrative example 10.6, with the addition of an amendment to the terms of the pension plan.

Paragraph 8 of IAS 19 defines the *net interest on the net defined benefit liability (asset)* as the change in the net defined benefit liability (asset) that arises from the passage of time. The net interest on net defined benefit liability (asset) is measured by multiplying the discount rate that is used to measure the defined benefit obligation at the beginning of the period by the net defined benefit liability (asset) (IAS 19 paragraph 123). Paragraph 83 requires the discount rate to be determined with reference to market yields on high-quality corporate bonds. In the absence of a deep market in such bonds, the market yield on government bonds should be used. The standard requires contributions received and benefits paid by the plan to be taken into account when calculating interest. This involves recalculating interest for part of the year each time the plan assets are increased by a contribution or where payment of benefits resulted in settlement gains or losses, giving rise to change in the net defined benefit liability or asset. Throughout this text, this process is simplified by applying the discount rate to the opening balance of the net defined benefit liability (asset), effectively assuming contributions and benefits are paid at the end of each year.

When the pension plan pays benefits to a member, both the plan assets and the defined benefit obligation are reduced. If, at the time of settlement, the carrying amount of the obligation to the member is equal to the amount actually payable, the settlement will have no effect on the surplus or deficit of the plan. However, the carrying amount of the defined benefit obligation results from numerous actuarial estimates which may differ from amounts actually due at settlement. Differences between the carrying amount of the defined benefit obligation of the plan and the amount actually paid to a member give rise to a gain or loss on settlement, which is a service cost recognised in profit or loss.

ILLUSTRATIVE EXAMPLE 10.8 Modifications to a defined benefit pension plan

At the beginning of 2018 Dickens plc modified the terms of the defined benefit pension plan from 1% of final year salary per year of service to 0.9% of final year salary per year of service. The modification applied retrospectively to services rendered before 2018. Accordingly, after the modification the defined benefit payable at 31 December 2018 is expected to be 2.7% of final year salary instead of 3% of final salary, which had been used in the measurement of the defined benefit obligation at 31 December 2017.

The revised defined benefit payable to Charles at 31 December 2018 is expected to be £1191. This is calculated as 2.7% of Charles' final year salary (2.7% × £44 100 = £1191). Applying the projected credit method, the annual service cost is £397.

Schedule of changes in the defined benefit obligation			
Benefit attributed to:	Year ended 31/12/16 £	Year ended 31/12/17 £	Year ended 31/12/18 £
Prior year	0	397	794
Current year	397	397	397
Total current and prior years	397	794	1 191

The following schedule shows the current service cost, interest cost and present value of the defined benefit obligation on the basis of the revised terms of the plan, under which the benefit payable is 0.9% of salary for each year of service. The present value of the increase in the defined benefit obligation attributed to current service cost is £328 and £361 in 2016 and 2017, respectively. These present values are determined using the discount rate of 10%.

Schedule of current service cost, interest and present value of the defined benefit obligation			
	Year ended 31/12/16 £	Year ended 31/12/17 £	Year ended 31/12/18 £
Opening obligation	0	328	722
Interest at 10%	0	33	72
Current service cost	328	361	397
Closing obligation	328	722	1 191

Workings:

2016 Current service cost = £397/(1 + 0.1)^2 = £328
2017 Current service cost = £397/(1 + 0.1)^1 = £361; Interest cost = £328 × 10% = £33
2018 Interest cost = £722 × 10% = £72

Recall that the terms of the defined benefit pension plan were modified at the beginning of 2018. Until 31 December 2017, the measurement of the present value of the defined benefit obligation had been based on a benefit of 1% of final salary for each year of service. This yielded a present value of £802 at 31 December 2017 as shown in illustrative example 10.6. From the beginning of 2018, the amount of the present value of the defined benefit obligation should be remeasured based on a benefit of only 0.9% of final year salary for each year of service. This yields a present value of £722 as shown in the immediately preceding schedule. Accordingly, the opening obligation for the year ended 31 December 2018 should be adjusted for a past service cost of (£80) as follows:

	Year ended 31/12/17 £	Year ended 31/12/18 £
Opening obligation	365	802
Past service costs arising from modifications to the plan	—	(80)
Adjusted obligation		722
Interest at 10%	36	72
Current service cost	401	397
Closing obligation	802	1 191

Current and past service cost, interest income or expense and settlement gains or losses are recognised in profit or loss.

10.7.4 Step 4: Determining the remeasurements of the net defined benefit liability (asset) to be recognised in other comprehensive income

Changes in the net defined benefit liability (asset) that result from remeasurements comprise actuarial gains and losses, return on plan assets (other than amounts included in net interest), and any change in the effect of the asset ceiling (excluding amounts included in net interest).

Actuarial gains and losses occur when changes in actuarial assumptions or experience adjustments affect the present value of the defined benefit obligation. The measurement of the defined benefit obligation is sensitive to assumptions such as employee turnover and the rate of increase in salaries. For example, an increase in the rate of salary increase used in measuring the defined benefit obligation would increase the expected future settlement and, hence, the present value of the defined benefit obligation. An increase in the rate of salary increase results in an actuarial loss because it increases the present value of the defined benefit obligation. Another example of a change in an actuarial assumption is a change in the discount rate used to determine the present value of the obligation. An increase in the discount rate results in an actuarial gain because it reduces the present value of the defined benefit obligation.

Experience adjustments refer to differences between the actual results and previous actuarial estimates used to measure the defined benefit obligation. An example is the difference between the estimated employee turnover for the year and the actual employee turnover during the year. Experience adjustments may also relate to early retirement, mortality rates and the rate of increase in salaries.

The return on plan assets is determined after deducting the costs of managing the plan assets and tax payable by the pension plan on its income derived from plan assets. Other administration costs are not deducted from the return on plan assets (IAS 19 paragraph 130).

The effects of remeasurements of the net defined benefit liability (asset) are recognised in other comprehensive income. Amounts recognised in other comprehensive income as a result of remeasurments of the net defined benefit liability are not able to be reclassified to profit or loss. *(The reclassification of items of other comprehensive income to profit or loss is considered in chapter 16.)* The recognition of actuarial gains and losses as items of other comprehensive income shields reported profit from the volatility that these items can cause.

ILLUSTRATIVE EXAMPLE 10.9 Accounting for a defined benefit pension plan

Gesundheit GmbH has a defined benefit pension plan for its senior managers. Members of the plan had been entitled to 10% of their average salary for every year of service.

The following information is available about the Gesundheit Pension Plan:

		€'000
31 December 2016		
Present value of defined benefit obligation at 31 December 2016		26 000
Fair value of plan assets at 31 December 2016		30 000
Asset ceiling at 31 December 2016		4 200
Interest rate used to measure the defined benefit obligation 31 December 2016	7%	
1 January 2017		
Past service costs		5 000
Year ended 31 December 2017		
Current service cost		4 000
Contributions received by the plan		4 500
Benefits paid by the plan		Nil
Return on plan assets		800
Actuarial gain resulting from change in the discount rate, 31 December 2017		1 470
Present value of defined benefit obligation at 31 December 2017		35 700
Fair value of plan assets at 31 December 2017		37 400
Asset ceiling at 31 December 2017		2 500
Interest rate used to measure the defined benefit obligation 31 December 2017	8%	

Additional information

(a) The current service cost is given as €4 million. This estimation is based on actuarial advice provided by the manager of the pension plan.

(b) Actuarial advice has been obtained for the present value of the defined benefit obligation at 31 December 2016 and 2017.

(c) On 1 January 2017 Gesundheit GmbH revised its defined benefits and increased the entitlement to 11% of average salary. The revision to the defined benefit plan resulted in an increase in the defined benefit obligation of €5 million on 1 January 2017.

(d) During 2017, Gesundheit GmbH contributed €4 500 000 to the plan. All of the contributions to the Gesundheit Pension Plan are paid by Gesundheit GmbH. The senior managers of Gesundheit GmbH, who are the members of the plan, do not pay any contributions.

(e) The discount rate used to measure the defined benefit obligation was increased from 7% to 8% on 31 December 2017, resulting in a decrease of €1 470 000 in the present value of the defined benefit obligation.

(f) The fair value of plan assets is derived from valuations performed by Helf & Gott Valuers each year.

The information shown above is used to prepare the journal entries to account for Gesundheit GmbH's pension liability (asset) for 2017 in accordance with IAS 19. But first we will determine the amount of the net defined benefit liability (asset) at 31 December 2016.

Gesundheit Pension Plan had a surplus of €4 000 000, being the excess of the fair value of plan assets over the present value of the defined benefit obligation, at 31 December 2016. Gesundheit GmbH recognised a net defined benefit asset of €4 000 000, being the lesser of the surplus and the asset ceiling of €4 200 000.

Next we will consider the four steps involved in accounting by the employer for a defined benefit post-employment plan identified by IAS 19 (paragraph 57). The defined benefit worksheet, which is shown below for the Gesundheit Pension Plan, incorporates the four steps and provides workings for the summary journal entries to account for the defined benefit post-employment plan in the books of the employer and provides a basis for the disclosure requirements required by IAS 19.

Gesundheit Defined Benefit Pension Plan Worksheet for the year ended 31 December 2017						
	Gesundheit GmbH				Gesundheit Pension Plan	
	Profit/loss €'000	OCI €'000	Bank €'000	Net DBL(A) €'000	DBO €'000	Plan Assets €'000
Balance 31/12/16				4 000 Dr	26 000 Cr	30 000 Dr
Past service cost	5 000 Dr				5 000 Cr	
Revised balance 1/1/17				1 000 Cr	31 000 Cr	30 000 Dr
Net interest at 7%	70 Dr				2 170 Cr	2 100 Dr
Current service cost	4 000 Dr				4 000 Cr	
Contributions to the plan			4 500 Cr			4 500 Dr
Benefits paid by the plan					0	0
Return on plan assets		800 Cr				800 Dr
Actuarial gain: DBO		1 470 Cr			1 470 Dr	
Journal entry	9 070 Dr	2 270 Cr	4 500 Cr	2 300 Cr		
Balance 31/12/17				1 700 Dr	35 700 Cr	37 400 Dr
Adjustment for asset ceiling if < deficit				Not applicable		
Balance 31/12/17				1 700 Dr	35 700 Cr	37 400 Dr

Step 1: Determining the deficit or surplus of the fund

The pension plan has a surplus of €1 700 000 at 31 December 2017. This is shown in the last row of the defined benefit worksheet, and can be calculated as the excess of the fair value of plan assets (€37 400 000) over the present value of the defined benefit obligation (DBO) (€35 700 000).

Step 2: Determining the amount of the net defined benefit liability (asset) — DBL(A)

The net defined benefit asset (DBA) is €1 700 000, being the lesser of the surplus of €1 700 000 and the asset ceiling of €2 500 000 at 31 December 2017.

Step 3: Determining the amounts to be recognised in profit or loss

The increase in the DBO of €5 000 000 resulting from the past service cost is recognised as an expense in profit or loss. The revised balance of the net defined benefit liability is €1 000 000, calculated as the deficit of the plan, being the excess of the DBO over the fair value of plan assets after accounting for the past service cost. The revised balance of the DBL(A) is used in the calculation of the interest cost.

The net interest is €70 000 determined as 7% of the net DBL after taking into account the past service cost, as shown in the defined benefit worksheet. The net interest is recognised in profit or loss. The interest component of the increase in the DBO and the fair value of plan assets is €2 170 000 and €2 100 000, respectively.

The current service cost of €4 000 000 increases the DBO. The current service cost is recognised in profit or loss.

Thus the three items recognised in profit or loss, the past service cost, the net interest and the current service cost, amount to €9 070 000 as shown in the journal entry line of the defined benefit worksheet.

Step 4: Determining the amount of remeasurements to be recognised in other comprehensive income

There are two remeasurements of the net defined benefit asset during 2017. One remeasurement results from the return on plan assets exceeding the interest income included in net interest recognised in profit or loss. The return on plan assets affects the fair value of plan assets as shown in the defined benefit worksheet. The other remeasurement results from the increase in the discount rate used to measure the present value of the DBO, which reduces the DBO by €1 470 000, as shown in the defined benefit worksheet. The effects of the remeasurements are recognised in other comprehensive income (OCI) as shown in the defined benefit worksheet.

The payment of contributions during 2017 increases the net defined benefit asset and increases the plan assets.

Any benefits paid to members during the period would reduce both the plan assets and the DBO. It appears in the pension plan columns only because it is a transaction of the plan, and not a transaction of the sponsoring employer.

The worksheet provides working papers for the journal entries to account for the defined benefit pension plan in the books of Gesundheit GmbH. The summary journal entries are shown below.

Summary entry				
	Pension Expense (P/L)	Dr	9 070 000	
	Pension Plan Gain (OCI)	Cr		2 270 000
	Bank	Cr		4 500 000
	Net Defined Benefit Pension Asset	Cr		2 300 000
	(Payment of pension contributions and recognition of changes in net pension asset)			

The defined benefit worksheet also provides a basis for preparation of notes to the financial statements for some of the disclosures required by IAS 19 in respect of defined benefit post-employment plans. Paragraph 140 includes a requirement for a reconciliation of the opening balance to the closing balance of the net defined benefit liability (asset), showing separate reconciliations for plan assets, the present value of the defined benefit obligation and the effect of the asset ceiling. Each reconciliation is required to show the effect, if applicable, of past service cost and gains and losses arising on settlement, current service cost, interest income or expense, and remeasurement of the net defined liability (asset), showing separately return on plan assets excluding amounts included in interest, actuarial gains arising from changes in demographic assumptions, actuarial gains and losses arising from changes in financial assumptions and changes in the effect, if any, of the asset ceiling (IAS 19 paragraph 141). Paragraph 141 also requires disclosure of contributions, distinguishing between those paid by the employer and those paid by the members of the plan, and benefits paid. Other reconciliation items include the effects of changes in foreign exchange rates and the effects of business combinations and disposals.

The net capitalisation method can result in large gains and losses being recognised in profit or loss, or other comprehensive income, due to changes in the surplus or deficit of the fair value of plan assets over the present value of the defined benefit obligation. For instance, the present value of the defined benefit obligation increases if employee retention is greater than the amount assumed in the previous actuarial estimate. Similarly, an unexpected decline in the return on investment of plan assets may cause the plan assets to grow at a slower rate than the present value of the defined benefit obligation, giving rise to an increase in the pension liability recognised by the employer. The net capitalisation method is unpopular with some preparers of financial statements who would prefer less volatility of earnings.

10.8 OTHER LONG-TERM EMPLOYEE BENEFITS

Long-term employee benefits are benefits for services provided in the current or prior periods that will not be paid until more than 12 months after the end of the period. *Post-employment benefits were considered in section 10.5.* This section considers long-term employee benefits that are provided to employees during the period of their employment. A common form of long-term employee benefit is long service leave, which is a paid absence after the employee has provided a long period of service, such as 3 months of paid leave after 10 years of continuous employment.

Long service leave accrues to employees as they provide service to the entity. The principle adopted by IAS 19 is that an obligation arises for long service leave when the employees provide services to the employer, even though the employees may have no legal entitlement to the leave. Thus, a liability is recognised for long service leave as it accrues. Long service leave payments reduce the long service leave liability.

Accounting for other long-term employee benefits is similar to accounting for defined benefit post-employment plans except that the effects of remeasurements are not recognised in other comprehensive income (IAS 19 paragraphs 154–55). Thus the net liability (asset) for long-term employee benefits is measured as the net of the present value of the defined benefit obligation at the reporting date minus the fair value at the reporting date of plan assets (if any) out of which the obligations are to be settled directly, subject to adjustment of a net asset for the effects of an asset ceiling, if applicable.

In some countries it is extremely unusual to establish plan assets to provide for the payment of long service leave benefits to employees. Thus, the accounting treatment for long service leave benefits is usually confined to the recognition of the present value of the obligation measured in accordance with the projected unit credit method.

The projected unit credit method measures the obligation for long-term employee benefits by calculating the present value of the expected future payments that will result from employee services provided to date. The measurement of the present value of the obligation for long service leave payments is complicated by the need to make several estimates. These include estimation of when the leave will be taken, projected salary levels, and the proportion of employees who will continue in the entity's employment long enough to become entitled to long service leave. Actuarial advice is often used in the measurement of long service leave obligations.

The steps involved in the measurement of a liability for long service leave are as follows:

1. *Estimate the number of employees who are expected to become eligible for long service leave.* The probability that employees will become eligible for long service leave generally increases with the period of employment. For example, if an entity provides long service leave after 10 years of employment, the probability that employees who have already been working for the entity for 7 years will continue in employment for another 3 years is very high, as the closer proximity to long service leave entitlement provides an incentive to employees to stay with their current employer.

2. *Estimate the projected wages and salaries at the time that long service leave is expected to be paid.* This step involves the application of expected inflation rates or other cost adjustment rates over the remaining period before long service leave is paid. Applying an estimated inflation rate:

$$\text{Projected salaries} = \text{current salaries} \times (1 + \text{inflation rate})^n$$
$$\text{where } n = \text{number of years until long service leave is expected to be paid.}$$

   For example, for employees who have 3 years remaining before long service leave is expected to be paid, current salaries are projected over a period of 3 years.

3. *Determine the accumulated benefit.* The projected unit credit is determined as the proportion of projected long service leave attributable to services that have already been provided by the employee. The accumulated benefit is calculated as:

$$\frac{\text{Years of employment}}{\text{Years required for LSL}} \times \frac{\text{weeks of paid leave}}{52} \times \text{projected salaries}$$

4. *Measure the present value of the accumulated benefit.* The accumulated benefit is discounted at a rate determined by reference to market yields on high-quality corporate bonds, in accordance with paragraph 83. If the country in which the long service leave entitlement will be paid does not have a deep market in high-quality corporate bonds, the government bond rate is used.

$$\text{Present value} = \frac{\text{accumulated benefit}}{(1 + i)^n}$$
$$\text{where } i \text{ is the interest rate on high-quality corporate bonds maturing } n \text{ years later.}$$

The liability for long service leave is a provision. After determining the amount of the obligation for long service leave at the end of the period, following steps 1 to 4 above, the provision is increased or decreased as required.

Illustrative example 10.10 demonstrates the measurement of the obligation for long service leave, applying the projected unit credit method in accordance with IAS 19, and the entries to account for changes in the provision for long service leave.

ILLUSTRATIVE EXAMPLE 10.10 Accounting for long service leave

Green Ltd commenced operations on 2 January 2016 and had 150 employees. Average salaries were $60 000 per annum for the year. Green Ltd accounts for all recognised employee costs as expenses. Employees are entitled to 13 weeks of long service leave after 10 years of employment. The following information is based on advice received from actuarial consultants at 31 December 2016:

Number of years unit credit	1 year
Number of years until long service leave is expected to be paid	9 years
Probability that long service leave will be taken (proportion of employees expected to stay long enough to become entitled to long service leave)	50%
Expected increase in salaries (based on inflation)	2% p.a.
Yield on 9-year high-quality corporate bonds at 31/12/16	10%

The discount rate is determined using 9-year bonds because the long service leave is expected to be paid 9 years after the end of the reporting period.

Step 1: Estimate the number of employees who are expected to become eligible for long service leave.

$$50\% \times 150 \text{ employees} = 75 \text{ employees}$$

Step 2: Estimate the projected salaries.

$$= \text{Salary} \times (1 + \text{inflation rate})^n$$
$$= \$60\,000 \times 75 \text{ employees} \times (1 + 0.02)^9 = \$5\,377\,917$$

The current salary is inflated over 9 years because employees are expected to take long service leave 9 years after the end of the reporting period.

Step 3: Determine the accumulated benefit.

$$= \frac{\text{Years of employment}}{\text{Years required for LSL}} \times \frac{\text{weeks of paid leave}}{52} \times \text{projected salaries}$$

$$= \frac{1}{10} \times \frac{13}{52} \times \$5\,377\,917 = \$134\,448$$

Step 4: Measure the present value of the accumulated benefit.

$$= \frac{\text{Accumulated benefit}}{(1 + i)^n}$$
$$= \$134\,448 / (1 + 0.1)^9 \text{ [or } \$134\,448 \times 0.4241 \text{ from present value tables]}$$
$$= \$57\,019$$

The change in the provision for long service leave is recorded by the following journal entry:

2016				
31 December	Long Service Leave Expense	Dr	57 019	
	Provision for Long Service Leave	Cr		57 019
	(Increase in provision for long service leave)			

Note there was no beginning of period provision for long service leave as this is the first year.

During the following year, Green Ltd's 150 employees continued to work for the company. Average salaries increased to $68 000 per annum for the year. The following information is based on advice received from actuarial consultants at 31 December 2017:

Number of years unit credit	2 years
Number of years until long service leave is expected to be paid	8 years
Probability that LSL will be taken (proportion of employees expected to stay long enough to be entitled)	55%
Expected increase in salaries (based on inflation)	2% p.a.
Yield on 8-year high-quality corporate bonds 31/12/17	9%

The discount rate is determined using 8-year bonds because the long service leave is expected to be paid 8 years after the end of the reporting period.

Step 1: Estimate the number of employees who are expected to become eligible for long service leave.

$$55\% \times 150 \text{ employees} = 82.5 \text{ employees}$$

Step 2: Estimate the projected salaries.

$$= \text{Salary} \times (1 + \text{inflation rate})^n$$
$$= \$68\,000 \times 82.5 \text{ employees} \times (1 + 0.02)^8 = \$6\,573\,009$$

The current salary is inflated over 8 years because employees are expected to take long service leave 8 years after the end of the reporting period.

Step 3: Determine the accumulated benefit.

$$= \frac{\text{Years of employment}}{\text{Years required for LSL}} \times \frac{\text{weeks of paid leave}}{52} \times \text{projected salaries}$$

$$= \frac{2}{10} \times \frac{13}{52} \times \$6\,573\,009 = \$328\,650$$

Step 4: Measure the present value of the accumulated benefit.

$$= \frac{\text{Accumulated benefit}}{(1 + i)^n}$$
$$= \$328\,650/(1 + 0.09)^8 \text{ [or } \$328\,650 \times 0.50187 \text{ from present value tables]}$$
$$= \$164\,939$$

The increase in the long service leave is $107 920 (calculated as $164 939 less $57 019) because there have been no long service leave payments during the year to reduce the provision from the amount recognised at the end of the previous year. The change in the provision for long service leave is recorded by the following journal entry:

2017				
31 December	Long Service Leave Expense	Dr	107 920	
	Provision for Long Service Leave	Cr		107 920
	(Increase in provision for long service leave)			

The increase in the provision for long service leave during 2017 can be attributed to several factors:
• an increase in unit credit accumulated by employees. In the first year, the employees' accumulation was 10% of the leave, but, by the end of the second year, 20% had been accumulated because the employees had completed a second year of service.
• the interest cost, being the increase in the present value arising from discounting the future cash flows over a shorter period.
• an increase in projected salaries resulting from an increase in remuneration. That is, salaries increased beyond the projected 2% during 2017.
• a reduction in the interest rate used from 10% at 31 December 2016 to 9% at 31 December 2017.

10.9 TERMINATION BENEFITS

When an employee is retrenched or made redundant, the employer may be obliged to pay termination benefits. For example, a downturn in the economy may cause a manufacturer to reduce the scale of its operations, resulting in some portion of the entity's workforce being made redundant. Termination benefits are typically lump sum payments. Paragraph 8 of IAS 19 refers to termination benefits as employee benefits that are payable as a result of either the employer deciding to terminate an employment contract, other than through normal retirement, or an employee accepting an offer of benefits in return for termination of employment.

Thus, the obligation to pay termination benefits arises from the termination of an employment contract, rather than from past services provided by the employee. Although the obligation arises from a decision to terminate employment, the extent of past services provided by each employee is usually a factor in determining the amount of the payment.

The decision to undertake a redundancy program is not sufficient for the recognition of a liability for termination benefits. Merely deciding to undertake a redundancy programme does not create an obligation to a third party and thus does not meet the definition of a liability in accordance with the *Conceptual Framework*.

As stated above, an obligation to pay termination benefits can result from a decision of the employee to accept an offer, such as a redundancy arrangement, or a decision by the employer to terminate the employment contract. These alternative decisions are reflected in the requirement to recognise a liability and expense for termination benefits at the earlier of the following dates in accordance with paragraph 165 of IAS 19:

(a) when the entity can no longer withdraw the offer of the benefits; and
(b) when the entity recognises costs for a restructuring that is within the scope of IAS 37 and that involves the payment of termination benefits.

Paragraph 166 elaborates on when the entity can no longer withdraw an offer for termination benefits that become payable as a result of the employee's acceptance of an offer. The entity is unable to withdraw an offer after the employee accepts it. Further, the entity may be prevented from withdrawing an offer by existing regulations, contracts or laws. The entity can no longer withdraw an offer once such restrictions take effect.

Paragraph 167 is concerned with termination benefits that become payable as a result of the entity's decision to terminate employment. In this case, the offer can no longer be withdrawn when the entity has communicated to affected employees a plan of termination that meets all the following criteria (IAS 19 paragraph 167):

(a) steps taken to complete the plan indicate that it is unlikely to change significantly;

(b) the plan identifies the location, function or job classification, the number of employees whose services are to be terminated, and the expected completion date; and

(c) the plan is sufficiently detailed to enable employees to determine the type and amount of benefits they will receive.

If at the time of initial recognition, termination benefits are expected to be settled wholly within 12 months after the end of the annual reporting period, they are measured at the nominal (undiscounted) amount that the entity expects to pay. However, if the termination benefits are not expected to be settled wholly within 12 months after the end of the reporting period, they must be measured at present value. The expected payments required to settle the obligation are discounted at a rate determined by reference to market yields on high-quality corporate bonds, in accordance with paragraph 83. This is consistent with the measurement of other long-term employee benefits.

ILLUSTRATIVE EXAMPLE 10.11 Termination benefits

During December 2016, the board of directors of Universal plc approved a plan to outsource its data processing operations. The closure of the data processing operations is expected to result in the retrenchment of 180 employees in England and Wales. The chief financial officer provided an estimate of redundancy costs of £1.2 million. The board expected that it would take at least 6 months to select a contractor for outsourcing the data processing and a further 3 months for training before internal data processing operations could be discontinued.

During November 2017, redundancy packages were negotiated with trade union representatives and communicated to employees. Data processing operations were to be transferred to an external service provider in India on 1 March 2018.

When should Universal plc recognise an expense and liability for the redundancy payments?

2016

The termination benefits become payable as a result of Universal plc's decision to terminate employment, rather than as a result of an offer being accepted by employees. Accordingly, Universal plc must recognise a liability for termination benefits when it can no longer withdraw from a plan of termination communicated to affected employees, and that plan meets the criteria specified in paragraph 167 of IAS 19.

At 31 December 2016, the termination plan meets some of the criteria. Management had specified the location (England and Wales) and function (data processing) of the employees becoming redundant, and estimated their number at 180. The termination benefit payable for each job specification is likely to have formed the basis of the estimated redundancy costs of £1.2 million. However, until Universal plc has identified an alternative source of data processing, it will not be able to decide on a time at which the redundancy plan should be implemented. Further, although the decision to discontinue the internal data processing operation had been made by Universal plc's board of directors, it has not been communicated to the employees. Therefore, Universal plc should not recognise an expense and liability for termination benefits in association with the planned closure of its data processing operations at 31 December 2016 in accordance with IAS 19.

2017

By November 2017, the company had completed the formal detailed termination plan by specifying when it is to be implemented. The negotiations with unions over the amount of redundancy payments and entering into a contract with an external provider demonstrate that it is unlikely that significant changes will be made to the amount or timing of the redundancy plan. The termination plan has been communicated to affected employees. Accordingly, Universal plc should recognise an expense and a liability for termination benefits in association with the planned closure of its data processing operations in its financial statements for the period ended 31 December 2017 in accordance with IAS 19.

SUMMARY

Employee benefits are a significant expense for most reporting entities. Accounting for employee benefits is complicated by the diversity of arrangements for remuneration for services provided by employees. This area of accounting is further complicated by the different methods prescribed by IAS 19 to account for various forms and categories of employee benefits. Liabilities for short-term employee benefits, such as salaries, wages, sick leave, annual leave and bonuses payable within 12 months after the reporting period, are measured at the undiscounted amount that the entity expects to pay. Long-term liabilities for defined benefits, such as long service leave, are measured at the present value of the defined benefit obligations less the fair value of plan assets, if any, out of which the obligation is to be settled. The obligation for long service leave is measured using the projected unit credit method. IAS 19 also prescribes accounting treatment for post-employment benefit plans. Accounting for defined contribution post-employment plans is relatively straightforward: a liability is recognised by the entity for contributions payable for the period in excess of contributions paid. Conversely, an asset is recognised if contributions paid exceed the contributions payable to the extent that the entity expects the excess contributions to be refunded or deducted from future contributions. An entity's net exposure to a defined benefit post-employment plan is measured at the present value of the defined benefit obligations less the fair value of plan assets. If the defined benefit plan has a surplus, the net defined benefit asset recognised by the entity is subject to an asset ceiling. In this chapter, we have also considered termination benefits. The measurement of a liability for termination benefits depends on whether they are expected to be settled wholly within 12 months of the annual reporting period in which they were first recognised. The principles for the measurement of the termination benefits liability are consistent with those for short-term employee benefits and other long-term employee benefits.

Discussion questions

1. What is a paid absence? Provide an example.
2. What is the difference between accumulating and non-accumulating sick leave? How does the recognition of accumulating sick leave differ from the recognition of non-accumulating sick leave?
3. What is the difference between vesting and non-vesting sick leave? How does the recognition and measurement of vesting sick leave differ from the recognition and measurement of non-vesting sick leave?
4. Explain how a defined contribution pension plan differs from a defined benefit pension plan.
5. During October 2008, there was a sudden global decline in the price of equity securities and credit securities. Many pension funds made negative returns on investments during this period. How would this event affect the wealth of employees and employers? Consider both defined benefit and defined contribution pension funds in your answer to this question.
6. Explain how an entity should account for its contribution to a defined contribution pension plan in accordance with IAS 19.
7. Compare the off-balance-sheet approach to accounting for a defined benefit post-employment plan with the net capitalisation approach adopted by IAS 19. Can these approaches be explained by different underlying views as to whether a deficit or surplus in the plan meets the definition of a liability or asset of the sponsoring employer?
8. In relation to defined benefit post-employment plans, paragraph 56 of IAS 19 states, 'the entity is, in substance, underwriting the actuarial and investment risks associated with the plan'. Evaluate whether the requirements for the recognition and measurement of the net defined benefit liability reflect the underlying assumptions about the entity's risks.
9. Identify and discuss the assumptions involved in the measurement of a provision for long service leave. Assess the consistency of these requirements with the fundamental qualitative characteristics of financial information prescribed by the *Conceptual Framework*.
10. Explain the projected unit credit method of measuring and recognising an obligation for long-term employee benefits. Illustrate your answer with an example.
11. The board of directors of City Scooters GmbH met in December 2016 and decided to close down a branch of the company's operations when the lease expired in the following August. The chief financial officer advised that termination benefits of €2.0 million are likely to be paid. Should the company recognise a liability for termination benefits in its financial statements for the year ended 31 December 2016? Justify your judgement with reference to the requirements of IAS 19.

References

BHP Billiton 2015, *Annual Report*, BHP Billiton, www.bhpbilliton.com.
HSBC Holdings plc 2014, *Annual Report 2014*, HSBC Holdings plc, London, www.hsbc.com.
IASB 2008, *Discussion paper: Preliminary views on amendments to IAS 19 Employee Benefits*, www.ifrs.org.

Exercises

STAR RATING ★ BASIC ★★ MODERATE ★★★ DIFFICULT

Exercise 10.1 ACCOUNTING FOR SICK LEAVE

★ Ontario Ltd has 200 employees who each earn a gross wage of $140 per day. Ontario Ltd provides 5 days of paid non-accumulating sick leave for each employee per annum. During the year, 150 days of paid sick leave and 20 days of unpaid sick leave were taken. Staff turnover is negligible.

Required

Calculate the employee benefits expense for sick leave during the year and the amount that should be recognised as a liability, if any, for sick leave at the end of the year.

Exercise 10.2 ACCOUNTING FOR ANNUAL LEAVE

★ Newcastle plc provides employees with 4 weeks (20 days) of annual leave for each year of service. The annual leave is accumulating and vesting up to a maximum of 6 weeks. Thus, all employees take their annual leave (AL) within 6 months after the end of each reporting period so that it does not lapse. Refer to the following extract from Newcastle plc's payroll records for the year ended 31 December 2016:

Employee	Wage/day	AL 1 January 2016 Days	Increase in entitlement Days	AL taken Days
Chand	£160	6	20	15
Kim	£125	3	20	16
Smith	£150	2	20	13
Zhou	£100	4	20	17

Required

Calculate the amount of annual leave that should be accrued for each employee.

Exercise 10.3 ACCOUNTING FOR PROFIT-SHARING ARRANGEMENTS

★ Schwarzwald GmbH has a profit-sharing arrangement in which 1% of profit for the period is payable to employees, paid 3 months after the end of the reporting period. Employees' entitlements under the profit-sharing arrangement are subject to their continued employment at the time the payment is made. Based on past staff turnover levels, it is expected that 95% of the share of profit will be paid. Schwarzwald GmbH's profit for the period was €70 million.

Required

Prepare a journal entry to record Schwarzwald GmbH's liability for employee benefits arising from the profit-sharing arrangement at the end of the reporting period.

Exercise 10.4 ACCOUNTING FOR DEFINED CONTRIBUTION PENSION PLANS

★ Southern Inc. provides a defined contribution pension fund for its employees. The company pays contributions equivalent to 10% of annual wages and salaries. Contributions of $50 000 per month were paid for the year ended 31 December 2016. Actual wages and salaries were $7 million. Three months after the reporting period, there is a settlement of the difference between the amount paid and the annual amount payable determined with reference to Southern Inc.'s audited payroll information. The settlement at 31 March involves either an additional contribution payment by Southern Inc. or a refund of excess contributions paid.

Required

Prepare all journal entries required during 2016 for Southern Inc.'s payment of, and liability for, pension plan contributions.

ACCOUNTING FOR THE PAYROLL AND ACCRUAL OF WAGES AND SALARIES

★ Lavender plc pays its employees on a fortnightly basis. All employee benefits are recognised as expenses. The following information is provided for its July and August payrolls:

	July		August	
	£	£	£	£
Fortnightly payroll		580 000		700 000
		720 000		600 000
Gross payroll for the month		1 300 000		1 300 000
Deductions payable to:				
Taxation authority	250 000		245 000	
Health fund	20 000		20 000	
Community charity	4 000		4 000	
Union fees	6 500		6 500	
Total deductions for the month		280 500		275 500
Net wages and salaries paid				
14 July, 11 August	458 775		553 230	
28 July, 25 August	560 725	1 019 500	471 270	1 024 500
		1 300 000		1 300 000

The two fortnightly payrolls in August were for the fortnight ended Friday 7 August and Friday 21 August. The payrolls were processed and paid on the following Monday and Tuesday respectively. Payroll deductions are remitted as follows:

Health fund deductions	3rd day of the following month
Union fees	3rd day of the following month
Taxation authority	15th day of the following month
Community charity	21st day of the following month

Required

1. Prepare all journal entries to account for the August payroll and all payments relating to employee benefits during August.
2. Prepare a journal entry to accrue wages for the remaining days in August not included in the final August payroll. Use the same level of remuneration as per the final payroll for August.

ACCOUNTING FOR SICK LEAVE

★ Nagaland Ltd opened a call centre on 1 January 2016. The company provides 1 week (5 days) of sick leave entitlement for the employees working at the call centre. The following information has been obtained from Nagaland Ltd's payroll records and actuarial assessments for the year ended 31 December 2016. The column headed 'Term. in 2016' indicates the leave entitlement pertaining to service of employees whose employment was terminated during the year. The actuary has estimated the percentage of unused leave that would be taken within 12 months if Nagaland Ltd allowed leave to accumulate. Due to high staff turnover, the remaining leave would lapse (or be settled in cash, if vesting) within 1 year after the end of the reporting period.

Employee category	Base pay/day £	Current service Days	Leave taken in 2016 Days	Term. in 2016 Days	Estimated leave used 2016 %	Estimated termination 2016 %
Supervisors	100	30	20	3	90	10
Operators	80	500	400	60	70	30

Required

Calculate the employee benefits expense for sick leave for the year and the amount that should be recognised as a liability for sick leave at 31 December 2016, assuming that sick leave entitlements are:
(a) non-accumulating
(b) accumulating and non-vesting
(c) accumulating and vesting.

Exercise 10.7	ACCOUNTING FOR DEFINED BENEFIT PENSION PLANS

★★ Washington Inc. provides a defined benefit pension plan for its managers. The assistant accountant has completed some sections of the defined benefit worksheet based on information provided in an actuary's report on the Washington DB Pension Plan for the year ended 31 December 2016:

WASHINGTON DB PENSION PLAN
Defined Benefit Worksheet for the year ended 31 December 2016

	Washington Inc.				Washington DB Pension Plan	
	Profit/loss $'000	OCI $'000	Bank $'000	Net DBL(A) $'000	DBO $'000	Plan Assets $'000
Balance 31/12/15				1 000 Cr	6 000 Cr	5 000 Dr
Net interest at 10%						
Current service cost					400 Cr	
Contributions to the plan			600 Cr			600 Dr
Benefits paid by the plan					100 Cr	100 Dr
Actuarial loss: DBO					300 Cr	
Journal Entry						
Balance 31/12/16					7 200 Cr	6 000 Dr
Adjustment for asset ceiling if < deficit						
Balance 31/12/16						

Additional information
The asset ceiling was $600 000 at 31 December 2016.

Required

1. Determine the surplus or deficit of the plan at 31 December 2016.
2. Determine the net defined benefit asset or liability at 31 December 2016.
3. Calculate the net interest and distinguish between the interest expense component of the defined benefit obligation and the interest income component of the change in the fair value of plan assets for 2016.
4. Determine the amount to be recognised in profit or loss in relation to the defined benefit pension plan for 2016.
5. Determine the amount to be recognised in other comprehensive income in relation to the defined benefit pension plan for the year ended 31 December 2016.

Exercise 10.8	ACCOUNTING FOR DEFINED BENEFIT PENSION PLANS

★★ For each of the following scenarios, determine (i) the surplus or deficit in the defined benefit pension plan and (ii) the net defined benefit liability or asset that should be recognised by the sponsoring employer in accordance with IAS 19:

	Present value of DBO $'000	Fair value of plan assets $'000	Asset ceiling $'000
(a)	1 300	1 000	$Nil
(b)	1 550	1 200	$Nil
(c)	2 000	2 200	100
(d)	2 400	2 500	250

ACCOUNTING FOR LONG SERVICE LEAVE

★★ Geranium Ltd provides long service leave for its retail staff. Long service leave entitlement is determined as 13 weeks of paid leave for 10 years of continued service. The following information is obtained from Geranium Ltd's payroll records and actuarial reports for its retail staff at 31 December 2016:

Unit credit (years)	No. of employees	% expected to become entitled	Annual salary per employee	No. of years until vesting	Yield on HQ corporate bonds
1	60	20%	€27 000	9	10%
2	50	30%	€27 000	8	9%
3	30	50%	€27 000	7	9%
4	10	60%	€27 000	6	9%

Additional information
(a) The estimated annual increase in retail wages is 1% p.a. for the next 10 years, reflecting expected inflation.
(b) The provision for long service leave for retail staff at 31 December 2015 was €22 000.
(c) No employees were eligible to take long service leave during 2016.

Required

Prepare the journal entry to account for Geranium Ltd's provision for long service leave at 31 December 2016.

ACCOUNTING FOR DEFINED BENEFIT PENSION PLANS

★★★ Lily Ltd provides a defined benefit pension plan for its managers. The following information is available in relation to the plan.

	2016 $
Present value of the defined benefit obligation 31 December 2015	10 000 000
Fair value of plan assets 31 December 2015	9 500 000
Current service cost	1 150 000
Contributions paid by Lily Ltd to the plan during the year	1 000 000
Benefits paid by the plan during the year	1 200 000
Present value of the defined benefit obligation 31 December 2016	10 750 000
Fair value of plan assets at 31 December 2016	10 047 500

Additional information
(a) No past service costs were incurred during 2016.
(b) The interest rate used to measure the present value of defined benefits at 31 December 2015 was 9%.
(c) The interest rate used to measure the present value of defined benefits at 31 December 2016 was 10%.
(d) There was an actuarial gain pertaining to the present value of the defined benefit obligation as a result of an increase in the interest rate.
(e) The only remeasurement affecting the fair value of plan assets is the return on plan assets.
(f) The asset ceiling was nil at 31 December 2015 and 31 December 2016.
(g) All contributions received by the plan were paid by Lily Ltd. Employees make no contributions.

Required

1. Determine the surplus or deficit of Lily Ltd's defined benefit plan at 31 December 2016.
2. Determine the net defined benefit asset or liability that should be recognised by Lily Ltd at 31 December 2016.
3. Calculate the net interest for 2016.
4. Calculate the actuarial gain or loss for the defined benefit obligation for 2016.
5. Calculate the return on plan assets, excluding any amount recognised in net interest, for 2016.
6. Present a reconciliation of the opening balance to the closing balance of the net defined benefit liability (asset), showing separate reconciliations for plan assets and the present value of the defined benefit obligation.
7. Prepare a summary journal entry to account for the defined benefit pension plan in the books of Lily Ltd for the year ended 31 December 2016.

As discussed in the chapter a fundamental question arises whether the pension asset or liability should be included in the sponsoring firm's balance sheet. While recognising a liability is consistent with future funding needs, it is not clear that plan assets that are owned by the employees (through a trust) should appear on the sponsoring firm's balance sheet.

IAS 19 changed disclosure and recognition rules relative to what was domestically required in many countries that adopted IFRS® Standards. One issue that has been of interest to accounting researchers is whether the new rules have influenced the trend observed in many countries to curtail defined benefit (DB) plans and replace them with defined contribution (DC) plans. A possible explanation for this trend is that many employers find it hard to manage the various uncertainties embedded in DB plans (e.g., increasing life expectancy, inflation, interest rates). It is also possible that employers have found DC to be cheaper to run in that contribution rates are lower than funding pension plan assets under DB programmes. Kiosse and Peasnell (2009) review comment letters sent to the UK's Accounting Standard Board (ASB) when it deliberated FRS 17 (which is very similar to IAS 19). They observe that many commentators were concerned that rules to fully recognise the pension liability may lead sponsors to shut down DB plans. The prime concern was the added volatility that new rules will introduce to the income statement and balance sheet.

Short of termination of the DB plans, the effect of IAS 19 adoption may be seen in the effect on the strategy of investment in plan assets. Amir et al. (2010) provide evidence that pertains to this effect. They find that UK companies shifted to investment in bonds in and after 2005 — when IFRS Standards and IAS 19 were adopted. Moreover, they find that this shift was more pronounced in firms with larger pension plans. They argue that such firms were more exposed to higher volatility in the financial statements post-adoption and consequently had a greater incentive to reduce this volatility through the less-risky strategy of investment in bonds as opposed to investment in equities.

Prior to SFAS 158 (FASB, 2006) in the US and the 2011 revision to IAS 19, sponsoring firms calculated pension expense on a different basis. In particular, the income from plan assets was based on the notional expected rate of return (ERR) on plan assets. Importantly the selection of ERR was to a large extent subject to managerial discretion. Researchers have therefore been interested in understanding the degree to which this discretion was employed. Amir and Benartzi (1998) examine a sample of US firms that reported under these previous rules. They take advantage of a proprietary dataset that provides details of the composition of plan assets and examine how ERR varies with this composition. Amir and Benartzi (1998) argue that firms that invest a greater proportion of pension plan assets in equity investments should employ a higher ERR to reflect the higher level of risk associated with equity investments. Thus, a high correlation between the percentage of equities in plan assets and ERR should be observed. However, Amir and Benartzi (1998) find that this correlation is weak in that ERR changed only slightly as the percentage of equities increased. This suggests that managers were quite conservative in selecting ERR. This is further supported by the additional finding that

ERR is a poorer predictor of future return on plan assets than the percentage of investment in equities.

More broadly, assumptions underlying the calculation of pension expense and liability could be used opportunistically by managers. Amir and Gordon (1996) find evidence consistent with this hypothesis. Specifically, they find that the assumptions employed by managers worked to reduce reported pension liability. Their evidence further suggests that this is more pronounced in highly leveraged firms. Bergstresser et al. (2006) show that firms whose plan assets are large relative to operating income tend to select higher ERR than other firms. Higher ERR is also observed in firms that meet certain earnings thresholds. Interestingly, in some circumstances, managers may prefer to increase reported pension expense and liability. Comprix and Muller (2011) examine cases where companies froze the pension plans (i.e., stopped accruing pension obligations for existing and new members) to be able to make future savings. Since this decision could lead to labour disputes, managers may be motivated to exaggerate the pension problem to reduce disagreement with employees. They find that the number of employees affected and presence of labour union is negatively related to the likelihood of the freezing decision. This is consistent with concerns about employee reaction influencing managers against freezing. Furthermore, Comprix and Muller (2011) find that the ERR and discount rate selected by freezing sponsor firms are lower than non-freezing firms in the years preceding the freezing year. Because such lower estimates work to increase pension expense and pension liability, the evidence in Comprix and Muller (2011) is consistent with managerial discretion to reduce the likelihood of labour disputes by worsening reported performance and financial position.

References

Amir, E., and Benartzi, S., 1998. The expected rate of return on pension funds and asset allocation as predictors of portfolio performance. *The Accounting Review*, 73, 335–352.

Amir, E., and Gordon, E. A., 1996. Firms' choice of estimation parameters: Empirical evidence from SFAS No. 106. *Journal of Accounting, Auditing and Finance*, 11, 427–448.

Amir, E., Guan, Y., and Oswald, D., 2010. The effect of pension accounting on corporate pension asset allocation. *Review of Accounting Studies*, 15, 345–366.

Bergstresser, D., Desai, M., and Rauh, J., 2006. Earnings manipulations, pension assumptions and managerial investment decisions. *The Quarterly Journal of Economics*, 121, 157–194.

Comprix, J., and Muller, K. A., 2011. Pension plan accounting estimates and the freezing of defined benefit pension plans. *Journal of Accounting and Economics*, 51(1), 115–133.

Financial Accounting Standards Board (FASB), 2006. Statement of financial accounting standards (SFAS) No. 158, employers' accounting for defined benefit pension and other postretirement plans — an amendment of FASB statements No. 87, 88, 106 and 132(R). Norwalk, CT: FASB

Kiosse, P. V., and Peasnell, K., 2009. Have changes in pension accounting changed pension provision? A review of the evidence. *Accounting and Business Research*, 39(3), 255–267.

11

Property, plant and equipment

ACCOUNTING STANDARDS IN FOCUS

IAS 16 *Property, Plant and Equipment*

LEARNING OBJECTIVES

After studying this chapter, you should be able to:

1. describe the nature of property, plant and equipment
2. recall the recognition criteria for initial recognition of property, plant and equipment
3. demonstrate how to measure property, plant and equipment on initial recognition
4. explain the alternative ways in which property, plant and equipment can be measured subsequent to initial recognition
5. explain the cost model of measurement and understand the nature and calculation of depreciation
6. explain the revaluation model of measurement
7. discuss the factors to consider when choosing which measurement model to apply
8. account for derecognition
9. implement the disclosure requirements of IAS 16
10. explain the accounting issues relating to investment properties.

11.1 THE NATURE OF PROPERTY, PLANT AND EQUIPMENT

The accounting standard analysed in this chapter is IAS 16 *Property, Plant and Equipment*. The standard was first issued by the International Accounting Standards Board (IASB®) in March 1982, amended on numerous occasions, exposed in May 2002 as part of the IASB project on improvements to IASs, and issued in its present form in 2004. As a result of this process, the IASB has clarified selected matters and provided additional guidance. It has not reconsidered the fundamental approach to the accounting for property, plant and equipment contained in IAS 16.

According to paragraph 2 of IAS 16, the standard applies in accounting for property, plant and equipment except where another standard requires or permits a different accounting treatment. IAS 16 does not apply to property, plant and equipment classified as held for sale in accordance with IFRS 5 *Non current Assets Held for Sale and Discontinued Operations*; biological assets related to agricultural activity as these are accounted for under IAS 41 *Agriculture*; or mineral rights and mineral reserves such as oil, gas and similar non-regenerative resources. However, IAS 16 does apply to property, plant and equipment used to develop or maintain biological assets and mineral rights and reserves.

Paragraph 6 of IAS 16 defines property, plant and equipment as follows:

Property, plant and equipment are tangible items that:
(a) are held for use in the production or supply of goods or services, for rental to others, or for administrative purposes; and
(b) are expected to be used during more than one period.

Note the following:
- The assets are 'tangible' assets. *The distinction between tangible and intangible assets is discussed in depth in chapter 13.* However, a key feature of tangible assets is that they are physical assets, such as land, rather than non-physical, such as patents and trademarks.
- The assets have specific uses within an entity; namely, for use in production/supply, rental or administration. Assets that are held for sale, including land, or held for investment are not included under property, plant and equipment. Instead, assets held for sale are accounted for in accordance with IFRS 5.
- The assets are non-current assets, the expectation being that they will be used for more than one accounting period.

Property, plant and equipment may be divided into classes for disclosure purposes, a class of assets being a grouping of assets of a similar nature and use in an entity's operations. Examples of classes of property, plant and equipment are land, machinery, motor vehicles and office equipment. The notes to the statement of financial position of Marks & Spencer plc, at 29 March 2014, as shown in figure 11.1, provide an indication of what is contained in that category as well as the reasons for the movements in this category of assets.

In this chapter, accounting for property, plant and equipment is considered as follows:
- recognition of the asset — the point at which the asset is brought into the accounting records
- initial measurement of the asset — determining the initial amount at which the asset is recorded in the accounts
- measurement subsequent to initial recognition — determining the amount at which the asset is reported subsequent to acquisition, including the recording of any depreciation of the asset
- derecognition of the asset.

FIGURE 11.1 Property, plant and equipment

	Land and buildings £m	Fixtures, fittings and equipment £m	Assets in the course of construction £m	Total £m
At 31 March 2012				
Cost	2 759.4	5 612.9	330.1	8 702.4
Accumulated depreciation and asset write-offs	(270.6)	(3 641.9)	–	(3 912.5)
Net book value	2 488.8	1 971.0	330.1	4 789.9
Year ended 30 March 2013				
Opening net book value	2 488.8	1 971.0	330.1	4 789.9
Additions	17.3	430.3	186.6	634.2
Transfers	16.1	189.8	(205.9)	–

FIGURE 11.1 *(continued)*

	Land and buildings £m	Fixtures, fittings and equipment £m	Assets in the course of construction £m	Total £m
Disposals	(0.4)	(4.6)	–	(5.0)
Asset write-offs	(0.6)	(16.2)	–	(16.8)
Depreciation charge	(11.7)	(362.4)	–	(374.1)
Exchange difference	2.1	1.8	1.6	5.5
Closing net book value	2 511.6	2 209.7	312.4	5 033.7
At 30 March 2013				
Cost	2 817.1	6 198.1	312.4	9 327.6
Accumulated depreciation and asset write-offs	(305.5)	(3 988.4)	–	(4 293.9)
Net book value	2 511.6	2 209.7	312.4	5 033.7
Year ended 29 March 2014				
Opening net book value	2 511.6	2 209.7	312.4	5 033.7
Additions	34.6	362.7	155.8	553.1
Transfers	41.7	169.1	(210.8)	–
Disposals	(15.2)	(5.3)	–	(20.5)
Asset write-offs	(14.3)	(14.9)	(6.0)	(35.2)
Depreciation charge	(15.0)	(364.7)	–	(379.7)
Exchange difference	(3.7)	(6.6)	(1.2)	(11.5)
Closing net book value	2 539.7	2 350.0	250.2	5 139.9
At 29 March 2014				
Cost	2 871.7	6 686.8	256.2	9 814.7
Accumulated depreciation and asset write-offs	(332.0)	(4 336.8)	(6.0)	(4 674.8)
Net book value	2 539.7	2 350.0	250.2	5 139.9

The net book value above includes land and buildings of £43.7m (last year £43.9m) and equipment of £4.2m (last year £11.1m) where the Group is a lessee under a finance lease.

Additions to property, plant and equipment during the year amounting to £nil (last year £nil) were financed by new finance leases.

Source: Marks & Spencer plc (*Annual Report* 2014, p. 110).

11.2 INITIAL RECOGNITION OF PROPERTY, PLANT AND EQUIPMENT

Paragraph 7 of IAS 16 contains the principles for recognition of property, plant and equipment:

> The cost of an item of property, plant and equipment shall be recognised as an asset if, and only if:
> (a) it is probable that future economic benefits associated with the item will flow to the entity; and
> (b) the cost of the item can be measured reliably.

This is a *general* recognition principle for property, plant and equipment. It applies to the initial recognition of an asset, when parts of that asset are replaced, and when costs are incurred in relation to that asset during its useful life. To recognise a cost as an asset, the outlay must give rise to the expectation of future economic benefits.

The criteria for recognition in paragraph 7 differ from the recognition criteria for the elements of financial statements in paragraph 4.38 of the *Conceptual Framework*. Under the *Conceptual Framework*, an asset can be recognised when the *cost or value* can be measured with reliability; under IAS 16, recognition can occur only if the *cost* can be measured reliably. Assets for which the cost cannot be reliably measured but whose initial *fair value* can be measured reliably cannot be recognised in the entity's records.

11.2.1 Asset versus expense

For most items of property, plant and equipment, the entity will incur some initial expenditure. One of the key problems for the entity is determining whether the outlay should be expensed or capitalised as an asset. As paragraph 7 of IAS 16 states, the elements of that decision relate to whether the entity expects there to be future economic benefits, whether the receipt of those benefits is probable, and whether the benefits will flow specifically to the entity. As noted in paragraph 4.45 of the *Conceptual Framework*, the expensing of outlays:

> does not imply either that the intention of management in incurring expenditure was other than to generate future economic benefits for the entity or that management was misguided. The only implication is that the degree of certainty that economic benefits will flow to the entity beyond the current accounting period is insufficient to warrant the recognition of an asset.

As property, plant and equipment consists of physical assets such as land and machinery, such assets are normally traded in a market. One test of the existence of future benefits is then to determine whether there exists a market for the item in question. A problem with some assets is that once items have been acquired and installed, there is no normal market for them. However, in many cases, the expected economic benefits arise because of the use of that asset in conjunction with other assets held by the entity. At a minimum, the future benefits would be the scrap value of the item. Where the assets are intangible, such as costs associated with the generation of software, the absence of a physical asset causes more problems in terms of asset recognition. *Chapter 13 discusses in detail the problems associated with the recognition of intangible assets.*

11.2.2 Separate assets — significant parts

The total property, plant and equipment of an entity may be broken down into separate assets. This is sometimes referred to as a 'significant parts' approach to asset recognition. An entity allocates the amount initially recognised in respect of an asset to its significant parts and accounts for each part separately. Paragraph 9 of IAS 16 notes that the identification of what constitutes a separate item of plant and equipment requires the exercise of judgement, because the standard does not prescribe the unit of measure for recognition. The key element in determining whether an asset should be further subdivided into its significant parts is an analysis of what is going to happen in the future to that asset. Having identified an asset, the entity wants to recognise the expected benefits as they are consumed by the entity, with the recognition being in the period in which the benefits are received. Hence, if an asset has a number of significant parts that have different useful lives then, in order for there to be an appropriate recognition of benefits consumed, significant parts with different useful lives need to be identified and accounted for separately.

For example, consider an aircraft as an item of property, plant and equipment. Is it sufficient to recognise the aircraft as a single asset? An analysis of the aircraft may reveal that there are various parts of the aircraft that have different useful lives. Parts of the aircraft include the engines, the frame of the aircraft and the fittings (seats, floor coverings and so on). It may be necessary to refit the aircraft every 5 years, whereas the engines may last twice as long. Similarly, an entity that deals with the refining of metals may have a blast furnace, the lining of which needs to be changed periodically. The lining of the blast furnace therefore needs to be separated from the external structure in terms of asset recognition and subsequent accounting for the asset. Further, as noted in paragraph 9 of IAS 16, it may be appropriate to aggregate individually insignificant items (such as moulds, tools and dies) and apply the criteria to the aggregate value.

11.2.3 Generation of future benefits

Paragraph 11 of IAS 16 notes that certain assets may not of themselves generate future benefits, but instead it may be necessary for the entity itself to generate future benefits. For example, some items of property, plant and equipment may be acquired for safety or environmental reasons, such as equipment associated with the safe storage of dangerous chemicals. The entity's generation of the benefits from use of the chemicals can occur only if the safety equipment exists. Hence, even if the safety equipment does not of itself generate cash flows, its existence is necessary for the entity to be able to use chemicals within the business.

11.3 INITIAL MEASUREMENT OF PROPERTY, PLANT AND EQUIPMENT

Having established that an asset can be recognised, the entity must then assign to it a monetary amount. Paragraph 15 of IAS 16 contains the principles for initial measurement of property, plant and equipment: 'An item of property, plant and equipment that qualifies for recognition as an asset shall be measured at its cost.' Paragraph 16 specifies three elements of cost, namely:
- purchase price
- directly attributable costs

- initial estimate of the costs of dismantling and removing the item or restoring the site on which it is located.

These elements are considered separately in the following sections.

11.3.1 Purchase price

'Purchase price' is not defined in IAS 16, but paragraph 16(a) states that the purchase price includes import duties and non-refundable purchase taxes, and is calculated after deducting any trade discounts and rebates. The essence of what constitutes purchase price is found in the definition of cost in paragraph 6 of the standard, which states: 'Cost is the amount of cash or cash equivalents paid or the fair value of the other consideration given to acquire an asset at the time of its acquisition or construction.'

Where an item of property, plant and equipment is acquired for cash, determination of the purchase price is relatively straightforward. One variation that may arise is that some or all of the cash payment is deferred. In this case, as noted in paragraph 23 of IAS 16, the cost is the cash price equivalent at the recognition date, determined by measuring the cash payments on a present value basis (done by discounting the cash flows). Interest is then recognised as the payments are made.

More difficulties arise where the exchange involves assets other than cash. In a non-cash exchange, the acquiring entity receives a non-cash asset and in return provides a non-cash asset to the seller. In measuring the cost of the asset acquired, the question is whether the measurement should be based on the value of the asset given up by the acquirer, or by reference to the value of the asset acquired from the seller. In relation to the application of the cost principle of measurement, note the following:

1. Cost is determined by reference to the fair value of what is given up by the acquirer rather than by the fair value of the item acquired. The cost represents the sacrifice made by the acquirer. This principle is inherent in the definition of cost in paragraph 6 of IAS 16. Further, paragraph 26 states that where both the fair value of what is given up by the acquirer and the asset received are reliably measurable, then the fair value of the asset given up is used to measure the cost of the asset received, unless the fair value of the asset received is more clearly evident. 'More clearly evident' presumably relates to the cost and difficulty of determining the fair value as, in the paragraph 26 example, the fair values of both the asset received and the asset given up can be measured reliably.

2. Cost is measured by reference to fair value (paragraph 24). The term fair value is defined in paragraph 6 of IAS 16 as 'the price that would be received to sell an asset or paid to transfer a liability in an orderly transaction between market participants at the measurement date'.

   Fair value is an exit price. The process of determining fair value necessarily involves judgement and estimation. The acquiring company is not actually trading the items given up in the marketplace for cash, but is trying to estimate what it would get for those items if it did so. Hence, the determination of fair value is only an estimation. A further practical problem in determining fair value is that the nature of the market in which the goods given up are normally traded may make estimation difficult. The market may be highly volatile with prices changing daily, or the market may be relatively inactive. *Chapter 3 contains detailed information on the measurement of fair value.*

   If the acquirer gives up an asset at fair value, and the carrying amount of the asset is different from the fair value, then the entity will recognise a gain or a loss. According to paragraph 34 of IAS 1 *Presentation of Financial Statements*, gains and losses on the disposal of non-current assets are reported by deducting from the proceeds on disposal the carrying amount of the asset and related selling expenses.

   Assume then that an entity acquires a piece of machinery and gives in exchange a block of land. The land is carried by the entity at original cost of £100 000 and has a fair value of £150 000. The journal entry to record the acquisition of the machinery is:

Machinery	Dr	150 000	
Gain on Sale of Land	Cr		50 000
Land	Cr		100 000

The entity then reports a gain on sale of land of £50 000.

If, instead of giving land in exchange, the entity issued shares having a fair value of £150 000, the journal entry is:

Machinery	Dr	150 000	
Share Capital	Cr		150 000
(Acquisition of machinery by issue of shares)			

Further discussion on the measurement of the fair value of equity instruments issued by the acquirer in exchange for assets is found in chapter 14.

3. Paragraph 24 of IAS 16 requires the use of fair value to measure the cost of an asset received unless the exchange transaction lacks commercial substance. Commercial substance is concerned with whether the

transaction has a discernible effect on the economics of an entity. Paragraph 25 states that an exchange transaction has commercial substance if:

(a) *the configuration (risk, timing and amount) of the cash flows of the asset received differs from the configuration of the cash flows of the asset transferred.* This would not occur if similar assets (e.g. an exchange of commodities such as oil or milk) were exchanged as would occur where, for example, suppliers exchanged inventories in various locations to fulfil demand on a timely basis in a particular location; or

(b) *the entity-specific value of the portion of the entity's operations affected by the transaction changes as a result of the exchange.* Paragraph 6 defines entity-specific value as 'the present value of the cash flows an entity expects to arise from the continuing use of an asset and from its disposal at the end of its useful life or expects to incur when settling a liability'. If there is no change in the expected cash flows to the entity as a result of the exchange, as in the case of the exchange of similar items, then the transaction lacks commercial substance; and

(c) *the difference in (a) or (b) is significant relative to the fair value of the assets exchanged.* In both (a) and (b), the change in cash flows or configuration must be material, with materiality being measured in relation to the fair value of the assets exchanged.

Where the transaction lacks commercial substance, the asset acquired is measured at the carrying amount of the asset given up.

4. Paragraph 24 of IAS 16 also covers the situation where, in an exchange of assets, neither the fair value of the assets given up nor the fair value of the assets acquired can be measured reliably. Such situations could occur where the assets exchanged are both traded in weak markets where market transactions are infrequent. In this situation, the acquirer measures the cost of the asset acquired at the carrying amount of the asset given up.

Acquisition date

One of the problems in recording the acquisition of an item of property, plant and equipment relates to the determination of the fair values of the assets involved in the exchange. As noted above, accounting for the asset exchange requires that potentially both the fair values of the assets acquired and assets given up must be determined. However, where the markets for these assets are volatile, choosing the appropriate fair value may be difficult. This can be seen where an entity issues shares in exchange for an asset. The fair value of the shares issued may change on a daily basis. At what point in time should the fair values be measured?

Some likely dates that may be considered are:

* the date the contract to exchange the assets is signed
* the date the consideration is paid
* the date on which the assets acquired are received by the acquirer
* the date on which an offer becomes unconditional.

The advantage of these dates is that they relate to a point of time that can be determined objectively, such as the date the item of property, plant and equipment arrives at the acquirer's premises. A problem is that there may be a number of dates involved if, for example, an item of equipment arrives in stages or payment for the equipment is to be made in instalments over time.

The date on which the fair values should be measured is the date on which the acquirer *obtains control of the asset or assets acquired* — hereafter referred to as the 'acquisition date'. The definition of cost in paragraph 6 of IAS 16 refers to the 'time of its [the asset's] acquisition'. There is no specific date defined in the standard. In IFRS 3 *Business Combinations*, acquisition date is defined as 'the date on which the acquirer obtains control of the acquiree'.

The measurement of the fair value relates to the date the assets acquired are recognised in the records of the acquirer. At this date, the acquirer must be able to reliably measure the cost of the asset. Recognition of an asset requires the acquirer to have control of expected future benefits. Hence, when the item acquired becomes the asset of the acquirer (i.e. when the expected benefits come under the control of the acquirer), this is the point in time when the measurements of the fair values of assets acquired and given up are made. Paragraph 23 of IAS 16 states that the cost of an item of property, plant and equipment is the cash price equivalent at the 'recognition date'. Recognition date is normally the same as acquisition date.

Acquisition of multiple assets

The above principles as stated in IAS 16 apply to the acquisition of individual items of property, plant and equipment. However, an acquisition may consist of more than one asset, such as a block of land and a number of items of machinery. The acquirer may acquire the assets as a group, paying one total amount for the bundle of assets. The cost of acquiring the bundle of assets is determined as per IAS 16, namely by measuring the fair value of what is given up by the acquirer to determine the purchase price, and adding to this any directly attributable costs. However, even if the total cost of the bundle of assets can be determined, for accounting purposes it is necessary to determine the cost of each of the separate assets as they may be in different classes, or some may be depreciable and others not. No guidance is given in this standard for determining the costs of each of the assets. However, IFRS 3 *Business Combinations* paragraph 2(b) states:

The cost of the group shall be allocated to the individual identifiable assets and liabilities on the basis of their relative *fair values* at the date of purchase. Such a transaction or event does not give rise to goodwill.

In this situation, the cost of each asset to be recorded separately is calculated by allocating the cost of the bundle of assets over the assets acquired in proportion to the fair values of the assets acquired. To illustrate this allocation procedure, assume an entity acquired land, buildings and furniture at a total cost of £300 000 cash. In order to separately record each asset acquired at cost, the entity determines the fair value of each asset, for example:

Land	£ 40 000
Buildings	200 000
Furniture	80 000
	£320 000

The total cost of £300 000 is then allocated to each asset on the basis of these fair values as follows:

Land	£40 000/£320 000 × £300 000	=	£ 37 500
Buildings	£200 000/£320 000 × £300 000	=	187 500
Furniture	£80 000/£320 000 × £300 000	=	75 000
			£300 000

The acquisition of the three assets is recorded by the entity as follows:

Land	Dr	37 500	
Buildings	Dr	187 500	
Furniture	Dr	75 000	
Cash	Cr		300 000
(Acquisition of assets for cash)			

Under IAS 16, the basic principle of recording assets acquired is to record at cost. Where a bundle of assets is acquired, the cost of the separate assets must be estimated, and the fair values of the assets acquired can be used in this process. Where the cost of the assets in total is less than the sum of the fair values of the assets acquired, a bargain purchase has been made. However, as the assets are to be recognised initially at cost, no gain is recognised on acquisition.

11.3.2 Directly attributable costs

The key feature of those costs included in the cost of acquisition is that they are directly attributable *to bringing the asset to the location and condition necessary for it to be capable of operating in the manner intended by management* (IAS 16 paragraph 16(b)).

Costs to be included

Paragraph 17 of IAS 16 provides examples of directly attributable costs:
- costs of employee benefits arising directly from the construction or acquisition of the item of property, plant and equipment
- costs of site preparation
- initial delivery and handling costs
- installation and assembly costs — where buildings are acquired, associated costs could be the costs of renovation
- costs of testing whether the asset is functioning properly
- professional fees.

It can be seen that all these costs are incurred before the asset is used, and are necessary in order for the asset to be usable by the entity. Note, however, the use of the word 'necessary'. There may be costs incurred that were not necessary; for example, the entity may have incurred fines, or a concrete platform may have been placed in the wrong position and had to be destroyed and a new one put in the right place. These costs should be written off to an expense rather than being capitalised as part of the cost of the acquired asset.

A further cost that may be capitalised into the cost of an item of property, plant and equipment is that of borrowing costs. Borrowing costs (i.e. interest and other costs associated with the borrowing of funds) are accounted for under IAS 23 *Borrowing Costs*. Paragraph 8 of IAS 23 states that borrowing costs that are directly attributable to the acquisition, construction or production of a qualifying asset must be capitalised as part of the cost of the asset. (A qualifying asset is one that necessarily takes a substantial period of time to get ready for its intended use or sale, such as a building.)

Costs not to be included

Paragraphs 19 and 20 of IAS 16 contain examples of costs that should not be included in directly attributable costs:

- *costs of opening a new facility.* These costs are incurred after the item of property, plant and equipment is capable of being used; the opening ceremony, for example, does not enhance the operating ability of the asset.
- *costs of introducing a new product or service, including costs of advertising and promotional activities.* These costs do not change the location or working condition of the asset.
- *costs of conducting business in a new location or with a new class of customer (including costs of staff training).* Unless the asset is relocated, there is no change in the asset's ability to operate.
- *administration and other general overhead costs.* These costs are not directly attributable to the asset, but are associated generally with the operations of the entity.
- *costs incurred while an item capable of operating in the manner intended by management has yet to be brought into use or is operated at less than full capacity.* These costs are incurred because of management's decisions regarding the timing of operations rather than being attributable to getting the asset in a position for operation.
- *initial operating losses, such as those incurred while demand for the item's output builds up.* These are not incurred before the asset is ready for use.
- *costs of relocating or reorganising part or all of the entity's operations.* If a number of currently operating assets are relocated to another site, then the costs of relocation are general, and not directly attributable to the item of property, plant and equipment.

Income earned

Paragraph 17(e) of IAS 16 notes that the cost of the asset should be determined after deducting the net proceeds from selling any items produced when bringing the asset to that location and condition, such as proceeds from the sale of samples produced during the testing process. The principle here is that any flows, whether in or out, that occur before the asset is in a position to operate as management intends must be taken into account in determining the cost of the asset. The testing process is a necessary part of readying the asset for its ultimate use. Paragraph 21 provides an example of where income may be earned before the asset is ready for use but should not be included in the calculation of the cost of the asset. The example given is of income earned from the use of the construction site as a car park while there is a delay before the construction of a building. These revenues have nothing to do with the creation of the asset. They are incidental to the development activity, and should be separately recognised.

Acquisition for zero or nominal cost

An entity may acquire an asset for zero cost, or be required to pay an amount substantially different from the fair value of the asset. For example, an entity may be given a computer for no charge, or be required to pay only half price for a block of land or a building. Applying IAS 16, where there is zero cost, the entity receiving the asset would not record the asset. In the case of a heavily discounted asset, the asset would be recorded at the cost, namely the purchase price paid plus the directly attributable costs.

11.3.3 Costs of dismantling, removal or restoration

At the date an asset is initially recognised, an entity is required to estimate any costs necessary to eventually dismantle and remove the asset and restore its site. For example, when an asset such as an offshore oil platform is constructed, an entity knows that in the future it is required by law to dismantle and remove the platform in such a manner that the environment is cared for. The construction of the platform gives rise to a liability for restoration under IAS 37 *Provisions, Contingent Liabilities and Contingent Assets*. The expected costs, measured on a present value basis, are capitalised into the cost of the platform as the construction of the platform brings with it the responsibility of disposing of it. Acceptance of the liability for dismantling and removal is an essential part of bringing the asset to a position of intended use. As with directly attributable costs, the dismantling and removal costs are depreciated over the life of the asset. There may be restoration costs associated with the use of land, such as where the land is used for mining or farming. These costs are capitalised into the cost of the land at the acquisition date and, although the land is not depreciated, the restoration costs are depreciated over the period in which the benefits from use of the land are received.

As explained in paragraphs BC14–BC15 of the Basis for Conclusions on IAS 16, because of the limited scope of the revisions undertaken during the Improvements project, the IASB concentrated on the initial estimate of the costs of dismantling, removal and restoration. Issues relating to changes in that estimate, changes in interest rates, and the emergence of obligations subsequent to the asset's acquisition are not covered in IAS 16. However, the IASB did note that, regardless of whether the obligation is incurred when the item is acquired or when it is being used, the obligation's underlying nature and its association with the asset are the same. Hence, where obligations arise because of the use of an asset, these should be included in the cost of the asset.

11.4 MEASUREMENT SUBSEQUENT TO INITIAL RECOGNITION

As previously mentioned, at the point of initial recognition of an item of property, plant and equipment, the asset is measured at *cost*. After this initial recognition, an entity has a choice on the measurement basis to be adopted. IAS 16 paragraph 29 recognises two possible measurement models:
- the cost model
- the revaluation model.

The choice of model is an accounting policy decision. That policy is not applied to individual assets but to an entire *class* of property, plant and equipment. Hence, for each class of assets, an entity must decide the measurement model to be used. Having chosen a particular measurement model for a specific class of assets, the entity may later change to the alternative basis. For example, an entity that initially chose the revaluation model may at a later date change to the cost model. In order to change from one basis to another, the principles of IAS 8 *Accounting Policies, Changes in Accounting Estimates and Errors* must be applied. Paragraph 14 of IAS 8 states:

> An entity shall change an accounting policy only if the change:
> (a) is required by an IFRS; or
> (b) results in the financial statements providing reliable and more relevant information about the effects of transactions, other events or conditions on the entity's financial position, financial performance or cash flows.

It is part (b) that establishes the principle for change. The key is whether the change in measurement basis will make the financial statements more useful to users; in particular, will the information be more relevant and/or more reliable? In general, a change from the cost model to the revaluation model would be expected to increase the relevance of information provided because more current information is being made available. However, the change may make the information less reliable, as the determination of fair value requires estimation to occur. The entity would need to assess the overall benefit of the change in order to justify the change. In contrast, changing from the revaluation model would generally lead to a decrease in the relevance of the information. However, it may be that the determination of fair value has become so unreliable that the fair values determined have little meaning. Again, a judgement of the relative trade-offs between relevance and reliability needs to be made.

Paragraph 17 of IAS 8 notes that the accounting for a change from the cost model to the revaluation model constitutes a change in accounting policy, but the accounting for such a change is done in accordance with the principles in IAS 16 rather than those in IAS 8, namely by applying the principles of the revaluation model. No such statement is made about a change from fair value back to cost. It would appear that the accounting for this is based on IAS 8, paragraph 22 in particular. This paragraph requires the change to be applied retrospectively, and the information disclosed as if the new accounting policy had always been applied. Hence, a change from the revaluation model to the cost model would require adjustments to the accounting records to show the information as if the cost model had always been applied. Adjustments can be taken through the opening balance of retained earnings. Comparative information would also need to be restated.

11.5 THE COST MODEL

Paragraph 30 of IAS 16 states:

> After recognition as an asset, an item of property, plant and equipment shall be carried at its cost less any accumulated depreciation and any accumulated impairment losses.

The cost is as described in *section 11.3*, and includes outlays incurred up to the point where the asset is at the location and in the working condition to be capable of operating in the manner intended by management. Note that this entails management determining a level of operations, a capacity of production or a use for the item of property, plant and equipment. In getting a machine to an appropriate working condition, management may need to undertake certain outlays to keep the machine running efficiently at that level. In relation to a vehicle that is needed to take a driver from point A to point B, the car needs to run efficiently and at a required safety level, without breaking down. In order for this to occur, the car needs to be regularly serviced, have tune-ups and incur any other routine checks. Costs associated with keeping the item of property, plant and equipment at the required working condition are expensed, and not added to the depreciable cost of the asset. These costs are generally referred to as repairs and maintenance.

Similar examples can be seen with other assets, such as escalators that need to be regularly maintained to ensure they achieve the basic task of moving passengers from one level to another. Most items of plant with moving parts require some form of regular maintenance. Paragraph 12 of IAS 16 notes the existence of these 'repairs and maintenance' costs, stating that these costs should not be capitalised into the cost of the asset. These costs relate to the day-to-day servicing of the asset and consist mainly of labour and consumables, but may also include the cost of small parts. Costs of repairs and maintenance are expensed as incurred.

After acquisition, management may also outlay funds refining the ability of the asset to operate. These are not outlays associated with repairs, maintenance or replacement. Examples of such expenditures relate to outlays designed to increase the remaining useful life of the asset, increase its capacity, improve the quality of the output, and adjust the asset to reduce operating costs.

A decision to capitalise these outlays requires the application of the recognition principle in paragraph 7 of IAS 16. Capitalisation requires there to be an increase in probable future economic benefits associated with the asset; that is, it should be probable that the expenditure increases the future economic benefits embodied in the asset in excess of its standard of performance assessed at the time the expenditure is made. Note the timing of the assessment process: at the time the expenditure is *incurred*. The comparison is not with the original capacity to operate or the expected future benefits at acquisition, but with the capacity existing at the time the subsequent expenditure is incurred. Hence, if the capacity of the asset had reduced over time, expenditure to revive the asset to its original capacity would be capitalised. The assessment of capacity requires judgement, and needs to take into account matters such as the level of maintenance performed before the incurrence of the subsequent expenditure. The latter could not include the costs of any as yet unperformed maintenance work.

11.5.1 Depreciation

Under the cost model, after initial recognition, an asset continues to be recorded at its original cost. The subsequent carrying amount is determined after adjustments are made only for depreciation and impairment losses. *(Impairment losses are discussed in chapter 15.)* The main point of the following discussion is to determine the depreciation in relation to an item of property, plant and equipment.

In order to understand the accounting principles for depreciation, it is necessary to consider the definitions of depreciation, depreciable amount, useful life and residual value contained in paragraph 6 of IAS 16:

Depreciation is the systematic allocation of the depreciable amount of an asset over its useful life.

Depreciable amount is the cost of an asset, or other amount substituted for cost, less its residual value.

The *residual value* of an asset is the estimated amount that an entity would currently obtain from disposal of the asset, after deducting the estimated costs of disposal, if the asset were already of the age and in the condition expected at the end of its useful life.

Useful life is:
(a) the period over which an asset is expected to be available for use by an entity; or
(b) the number of production or similar units expected to be obtained from the asset by an entity.

Process of allocation

Depreciation is a process of allocation. Assets by definition are expected future benefits and, *as noted in section 11.2*, the initial recognition of an item of property, plant and equipment requires that it is probable that the future benefits will flow to the entity. On acquiring these benefits, an entity will have expectations as to the period over which these benefits are to be received and the pattern of these benefits (e.g. they could be received evenly over the life of the asset). The purpose of determining the depreciation charge for the period is to measure the consumption of benefits allocable to the current period, ensuring that, over the useful life of the asset, each period will be allocated its fair share of the cost of the asset acquired. This principle is found in paragraphs 50 and 60 of IAS 16:

50 The depreciable amount of an asset shall be allocated on a systematic basis over its useful life.
60 The depreciation method used shall reflect the pattern in which the asset's future economic benefits are expected to be consumed by the entity.

By describing depreciation as a process of allocation, the IASB is effectively arguing that an increase in value is not sufficient justification for not depreciating an asset. The IASB wants to consider separately the consumption of benefits and the changes in value over a period. In its 1996 discussion paper, 'Measurement of tangible fixed assets', the Accounting Standards Board in the United Kingdom provided the following example (paragraph 5.15) to illustrate the difference between consumption and changes in value:

Even where there are no general price changes, a change in the value of a tangible asset might still not reflect the consumption of economic benefits of the asset. For example, the drop in value of a new car during its first year would be unlikely to equate to the consumption of economic benefits of the car during the same period resulting from the use of the car. This difference occurs because the price change reflects the market's evaluation of the decline in economic benefits, which may differ from that made by a business. In this example the price change reflects the market's evaluation of the additional economic benefits a new car has over a second-hand car (e.g. the purchaser of a new car can specify exactly what features he wants while the purchaser of a second-hand car cannot, a new car has a known history etc.), but does not reflect the business's evaluation of the remaining economic benefits.

Under IAS 16, the depreciation charge for the period reflects the consumption of the economic benefits over the period and ignores the fall in the asset's fair value. As paragraph 52 of the standard states, depreciation is recognised even if the fair value of an asset is greater than its carrying amount (which is the amount at which an asset is recognised after deducting any accumulated depreciation and accumulated impairment losses). However, depreciation is not recognised if the asset's residual value exceeds the carrying amount.

As noted later in this chapter, where a revalued amount is used rather than cost, the depreciation charge affects current period income, and an increase in the value of the asset affects revaluation surplus. If both amounts affected income, then it would be important to determine whether it is useful to try to measure separately the two components of the change in value of the asset. If depreciation is capitalised into the cost of production, it may be argued that only the amount relating to the consumption of benefits should affect the cost of inventory produced.

Methods of depreciation

The accounting policy that an entity must adopt for depreciation is specified in paragraphs 50 and 60 of IAS 16, namely the systematic allocation of the cost or other revalued amount of an asset over its useful life in a manner that reflects the pattern in which the asset's future economic benefits are expected to be consumed. There are many methods of allocation, depending on the pattern of benefits. Paragraph 62 of the standard notes three methods:

- *Straight-line method.* This is used where the benefits are expected to be received evenly over the useful life of the asset. The depreciation charge for the period is calculated as:

$$\frac{\text{Depreciable amount}}{\text{Useful life}} = \frac{\text{Cost less residual value}}{\text{Useful life}}$$

If an item of plant had an original cost of £100 000, a residual value of £10 000, and a useful life of 4 years, the depreciation charge each year is:

$$\text{Depreciation expense p.a.} = \tfrac{1}{4}(\text{£}100\,000 - \text{£}10\,000)$$
$$= \text{£}22\,500$$

- The journal entry is:

Depreciation Expense – Plant	Dr	22 500
Accumulated Depreciation – Plant	Cr	22 500
(Depreciation on plant per annum)		

Note that both the residual value and the useful life may change during the life of the asset as expectations change.

- *Diminishing-balance method.* This method is used where the pattern of benefits is such that more benefits are received in the earlier years in the life of the asset. As the asset increases in age, the benefits each year are expected to reduce.

    It is possible to calculate a rate of depreciation that would result in the depreciable amount being written off over the useful life, with the depreciation charge each year being calculated by multiplying the rate by the carrying amount at the beginning of the year. The formula is:

$$\text{Depreciation rate} = 1 - \sqrt[n]{\frac{r}{c}}$$

where n = useful life
           r = residual value
           c = cost or other revalued amount

Using the same information as in the example for the straight-line method, the depreciation rate under the diminishing-balance method is:

$$\text{Depreciation rate} = 1 - \sqrt[4]{\frac{10\,000}{100\,000}}$$

$$= 44\% \text{ approximately}$$

The depreciation expense each year following acquisition of the item of plant at the beginning of the first year is:

$$
\begin{aligned}
\text{Year 1 depreciation expense} &= 44\% \times £100\,000 &&= £44\,000 \\
\text{Year 2 depreciation expense} &= 44\% \times £56\,000 &&= £24\,640 \\
\text{Year 3 depreciation expense} &= 44\% \times £31\,360 &&= £13\,798 \\
\text{Year 4 depreciation expense} &= £13\,798 - £10\,000 &&= £\;\;3\,798
\end{aligned}
$$

The depreciation charge then reflects a decreasing pattern of benefits over the asset's useful life.

• *Units-of-production method.* This method is based on the expected use or output of the asset. Variables used could be production hours or production output.

Using the above example again, assume that over the 4-year life of the asset the expected output of the asset is as follows:

Year 1	17 000 units
Year 2	15 000 units
Year 3	12 000 units
Year 4	6 000 units
	50 000 units

The depreciation expense in each of the 4 years is:

$$
\begin{aligned}
\text{Year 1 depreciation expense} &= 17/50 \times £90\,000 = £30\,600 \\
\text{Year 2 depreciation expense} &= 15/50 \times £90\,000 = £27\,000 \\
\text{Year 3 depreciation expense} &= 12/50 \times £90\,000 = £21\,600 \\
\text{Year 4 depreciation expense} &= \;\;6/50 \times £90\,000 = £10\,800 \\
&\hspace{4.5cm} £90\,000
\end{aligned}
$$

IAS 16 does not specify the use of any specific method of depreciation. The method chosen by an entity should be based on which method most closely reflects the expected pattern of consumption of the future economic benefits embodied in the asset.

Paragraph 61 of IAS 16 requires an entity to review the depreciation method chosen to ensure that it is providing the appropriate systematic allocation of benefits. The review process should occur at least at the end of each financial year. If there has been a change in the pattern of benefits such that the current method is inappropriate, the method should be changed to one that reflects the changed pattern of benefits. This change is not a change in an accounting policy, simply a change in accounting method. As such it is accounted for as a change in an accounting estimate, with the application of IAS 8. Under paragraph 36 of IAS 8, the change is recognised prospectively with adjustments being made to the amounts recognised in the current period and future periods as appropriate.

The depreciation method is applied from the date the asset is available for use; that is, when it is in the location and condition necessary for it to perform as intended by management. As noted in paragraph 55 of IAS 16, depreciation continues even if the asset is temporarily idle, dependent on movements in residual value and expected useful life. However, under methods such as the units-of-production method, no depreciation is recognised where production ceases.

Useful life

Determination of useful life requires estimation on the part of management, because the way in which an item of property, plant and equipment is used and the potential for changes in the market for that item affect estimates of useful life. Paragraph 56 of IAS 16 provides the following list of factors to consider in determining useful life:

(a) the *expected usage* of the asset by the entity; this is assessed by reference to the asset's expected capacity or physical output

(b) the expected *physical wear and tear*, which depends on operational factors such as the number of work shifts for which the asset will be used and the repair and maintenance programme of the entity, and the care and the maintenance of the asset while it is idle

(c) *technical or commercial obsolescence* arising from changes or improvements in production, or from a change in the market demand for the product or service output of the asset. For example, computers may be regarded as having a relatively short useful life. The actual period over which they may be expected to work is probably considerably longer than the period over which they may be considered to be technologically efficient. The useful life for depreciation purposes is related to the period over which the entity intends to use them, which is probably closer to their technological life than the period over which they would be capable of being used

(d) *legal or similar limits* on the use of the asset, such as expiry dates of related leases.

There is no necessary relationship between useful life to the entity and the economic life of the asset. Management may want to hold only relatively new assets, and a policy of replacement after specified periods of time may mean that assets are held for only a proportion of their economic lives. In other words, useful life for the purpose of calculating depreciation is defined in terms of the asset's expected usefulness to the entity. As noted earlier, the useful life of an asset covers the entire time the asset is available for use, including the time the asset is idle but available for use.

As noted in paragraph 58 of IAS 16, land is a special type of asset. Unless the land is being used for a purpose where there is a limited life imposed on the land, such as a quarry, it is assumed to have an unlimited life. Such land is not subject to depreciation. Hence, when accounting for land and buildings, these assets are dealt with separately so that buildings are subject to depreciation. If, however, the cost of land includes the expected costs of dismantling, removal or restoration, then these costs are depreciated over the period in which the benefits from use of the land are received.

Just as the depreciation method requires a periodic review, so the useful life of an asset is subject to review. According to paragraph 51 of IAS 16, the review should occur at least at each financial year-end. A change in the assessment of the useful life will result in a change in the depreciation rate used. As this is a change in accounting estimate, changes are made prospectively in accordance with IAS 8 paragraph 36.

ILLUSTRATIVE EXAMPLE 11.1 Assessment of useful life

Future View is in the business of making camera lenses. The machine used in this process is very well made, and could be expected to provide a service in making the lenses currently demanded for another 20 years. As the machine is computer-driven, the efficiency of making lenses is affected by the sophistication of the computer program to define what is required in a lens. Technological advances are being made all the time, and it is thought that a new machine with advanced technology will be available within the next 5 years. The type of lens required is also a function of what cameras are considered to be in demand by consumers. Even if there is a change in technology, it is thought that cameras with the old style lens could still be marketable for another 7 years.

Required

What useful life should management use in calculating depreciation on the machine?

Solution

Three specific time periods are mentioned:
- physical life: 20 years
- technical life: 5 years
- commercial life: 7 years.

A key element in determining the appropriate life is assessing the strategy used by management in marketing its products. If management believes that to retain market share and reputation it needs to be at the cutting edge of technology, 5 years will be appropriate. If, however, the marketing strategy is aimed at the general consumer, 7 years will be appropriate. In essence, management needs to consider at what point it expects to replace the machine.

Residual value

Note again the definition of residual value in paragraph 6 of IAS 16:

> The *residual value* of an asset is the estimated amount that the entity would currently obtain from disposal of the asset, after deducting the estimated costs of disposal, if the asset were already of the age and in the condition expected at the end of its useful life.

Residual value is an estimate based on what the entity would *currently* obtain from the asset's disposal; that is, what could be obtained at the time of the estimate — not at the expected date of disposal at the end of the useful life. The estimate is based on what could be obtained from disposal of *similar* assets that are currently, at the date of the estimate, at the end of their useful lives, and which have been used in a similar fashion to the asset being investigated. Where assets are unique, this estimation process is much more difficult than for assets that are constantly being replaced. For an asset such as a vehicle, which may have a useful life of 10 years, the residual value of a new vehicle is the net amount that could be obtained now for a 10-year-old vehicle of the same type as the one being depreciated. In many cases, the residual value will be negligible or scrap value.

This form of assessment means that the residual value will not be adjusted for expected changes in prices. Basing the residual value calculation on current prices relates to the adoption in IAS 16 of depreciation as a process of allocating economic benefits. If the residual value were adjusted for future prices, then there may be no measure of benefits consumed during the period as the residual value may exceed the carrying amount at the beginning of the period. It is also debatable whether the residual value should take into account possible technological developments. In relation to computers it may reasonably be expected that there will be such changes within a relatively short period of time, whereas with motor vehicles, trying to predict cars being powered with something other than oil is more difficult. Management is not required to be a predictor of future inventions. Expectations of technological change are already built into current second-hand asset prices. Management should then take into account reasonable changes in technological development and the effect on prices. Where assets are expected to be used for the whole or the majority of their useful lives, the residual values are zero or immaterial in amount.

In paragraphs BC28–BC29 of the Basis for Conclusions on IAS 16, the IASB raises the issue of why an entity deducts an asset's residual value from the cost of the asset for measurement of depreciation. Two reasons are proposed. First, the objective is one of precision; that is, reducing the amount of depreciation so that it reflects the item's net cost. The second is one of economics; that is, stopping depreciation if the entity expects the asset to increase in value by an amount greater than that by which it will diminish. The IASB did not adopt either the net cost or the economic objective completely. Expected increases in value do not override the need to depreciate an asset. An increase in the expected residual value of an asset because of past events affects the depreciable amount; expectations of future changes in residual value other than the effects of expected wear and tear will not.

Where residual values are material, an entity must, under paragraph 51 of IAS 16, review the residual value at each financial year-end. If a change is required, again the change is a change in estimate and is accounted for prospectively as an adjustment to future depreciation.

Significant parts depreciation

It has been mentioned previously in this chapter that a significant parts approach requires an entity to allocate the cost of an asset to its significant parts and account for each part separately; for example, the cost of an aeroplane is allocated to such parts as the frame, the engines and the fittings. According to paragraph 43 of IAS 16, *each part* of an item of property, plant and equipment with a *cost that is significant* in relation to the total cost of the item must be depreciated *separately*. In other words, an entity is required to separate each item of property, plant and equipment into its significant parts, with each part being separately depreciated. Any remainder is also depreciated separately.

Paragraph 13 of the standard discusses the replacement or renewal of the parts of an asset:

> Under the recognition principle in paragraph 7, an entity recognises in the carrying amount of an item of property, plant and equipment the cost of replacing part of such an item when that cost is incurred if the recognition criteria are met. The carrying amount of those parts that are replaced is derecognised in accordance with the derecognition provisions of this Standard (see paragraphs 67–72).

As is consistent with accounting for all separate items of property, plant and equipment, once an acquired asset is separated into the relevant significant parts, if one of those parts needs regular replacing or renewing, the part is generally accounted for as a separate asset. The replaced asset is depreciated over its useful life, and derecognised on replacement.

To illustrate the accounting for parts, consider the case of a building with a roof that periodically needs replacing. If the roof is accounted for as a separate part, then the roof is accounted for as a separate asset and is depreciated separately. On replacement, paragraph 13 of IAS 16 is applied, and the carrying amount (if any) of the old roof is written off. In order for this derecognition to occur, it is necessary to know the original cost of the roof and the depreciation charged to date. The new roof is accounted for as the acquisition of a new asset, assessed under paragraph 7 and, if capitalised as an asset, subsequently depreciated. If, however, the roof is not treated as a separate part from the acquisition date of the building, then on replacement of the roof, calculation of the amount to be derecognised is more difficult. An estimation may need to be made of the cost of the roof at acquisition date in order to derecognise the roof.

Another example of dealing with a part of an asset arises where assets are subject to regular major inspections to ensure that they reach the requisite safety and quality requirements. Under paragraph 14 of IAS 16, such major inspections may be capitalised as a replacement part. In order for the cost of the inspection to be capitalised, the recognition criteria in paragraph 7 of the standard must be met. In particular, it must be probable that future economic benefits associated with the outlay will flow to the entity. For example, if there is a 5-year inspection of aircraft by a specific party, and this is required every 5 years in order for the plane not to be grounded, then the cost of the inspection provides benefits to the owner of the aircraft for that period of time by effectively providing a licence to continue flying. The capitalised amount is then depreciated over the relevant useful life, most probably the time until the next inspection.

11.6 THE REVALUATION MODEL

Use of the revaluation model of measurement is the alternative treatment to the cost model. Paragraph 31 of IAS 16 states:

> After recognition as an asset, an item of property, plant and equipment whose fair value can be measured reliably shall be carried at a revalued amount, being its fair value at the date of the revaluation less any subsequent accumulated depreciation and subsequent accumulated impairment losses. Revaluations shall be made with sufficient regularity to ensure that the carrying amount does not differ materially from that which would be determined using fair value at the end of the reporting period.

In relation to this paragraph, note the following points:
1. The measurement basis is fair value, defined in Appendix A of IFRS 13 *Fair Value Measurement* as 'the price that would be received to sell an asset or paid to transfer a liability in an orderly transaction between market participants at the measurement date'. Fair value is an exit price and is measured in accordance with IFRS 13. Under this standard, there are a number of methods that may be used to measure fair value such as the market approach, the cost approach and the income approach. There are also a variety of inputs to these valuation techniques which are prioritised into three levels — Level 1, Level 2 and Level 3. This fair value hierarchy gives highest priority to observable inputs rather than unobservable inputs. *See chapter 3 for more information on fair value measurement.*
2. IAS 16 does not specify how often revaluations must take place. The principle established is that the revaluations must be of sufficient regularity such that the carrying amount of the asset does not materially differ from fair value. The frequency of revaluations depends on the nature of the assets themselves. For some assets, frequent revaluations are necessary because of continual change in the fair values owing to a volatile market. For other assets, revaluation every 3 or 5 years may be appropriate (paragraph 34). Paragraph 38 notes that assets may be revalued on a rolling basis provided that the total revaluation is completed within a short period of time, and that at no time is the total carrying amount of the class of assets materially different from fair value.
3. To understand the type of information that might be observed in determining whether there is a need to revalue an asset, it is useful to note the inputs into the valuation techniques. For example, in paragraph B35(g) of IFRS 13, in relation to buildings held and used, it is noted that a Level 2 input would be the price per square metre for the building derived from observable market data; for example, multiples derived from process in observed transactions involving comparable or similar buildings in similar locations.

Paragraph 36 of IAS 16 notes that the revaluation model is not applied to individual items of property, plant and equipment; instead, the accounting policy is applied to a class of assets. Hence, for each class of assets, management must choose whether to apply the cost model or the revaluation model.

A class of property, plant and equipment 'is a grouping of assets of a similar nature and use in an entity's operations' (IAS 16 paragraph 37). Examples of separate classes are:
• land
• land and buildings
• machinery
• ships
• aircraft
• motor vehicles
• furniture and fixtures
• office equipment.

There are two purposes for requiring revaluation to be done on a class rather than on an individual asset basis. First, this limits the ability of management to selectively choose which assets to revalue. Thus in order to be able to adopt the revaluation model, the fair values need to be capable of being reliably measured for all assets within the class. Second, the requirement to have all assets within the class measured on a fair value basis means that there is consistent measurement for the same type of assets in the entity.

According to paragraph 31 of IAS 16, where an asset is carried at a revalued amount, recognition of the asset should occur only when the fair value can be measured reliably. One question arising here is that, if a class of assets is being carried at fair value but there are assets within that class for which the fair value cannot be reliably measured, should those assets be written off because the recognition criteria cannot be met? The problem is that writing off these assets provides less relevant information than including the assets at cost.

11.6.1 Applying the revaluation model: revaluation increases

Paragraphs 39 and 40 of IAS 16 contain the principles for applying the fair value method to revaluation increases. These paragraphs apply to individual items of property, plant and equipment. In other words, even though revaluations are done on a class-by-class basis, the accounting is done on an asset-by-asset basis.

The first part of paragraph 39 states:

> If an asset's carrying amount is increased as a result of a revaluation, the increase shall be recognised in other comprehensive income and accumulated in equity under the heading of revaluation surplus.

Note two points here:

1. *The increase is recognised in comprehensive income.* In the statement of profit or loss and other comprehensive income, the comprehensive income for a period is divided into profit or loss (P/L) for the period and other comprehensive income (OCI). Revaluation increases are recognised in other comprehensive income, not profit or loss. An example of a statement of profit or loss and other comprehensive income showing the disclosure of profit for the year separately from the other comprehensive income items is given in figure 11.2.

XYZ GROUP
Statement of Profit or Loss and Other Comprehensive Income
for the year ended 31 December 20X7

(illustrating the presentation of profit or loss and other comprehensive income in one statement and the classification of expenses within profit by function)
(in thousands of currency units)

	20X7	20X6
Revenue	390 000	355 000
Cost of sales	(245 000)	(230 000)
Gross profit	145 000	125 000
Other income	20 667	11 300
Distribution costs	(9 000)	(8 700)
Administrative expenses	(20 000)	(21 000)
Other expenses	(2 100)	(1 200)
Finance costs	(8 000)	(7 500)
Share of profit of associates	35 100	30 100
Profit before tax	161 667	128 000
Income tax expense	(40 417)	(32 000)
Profit for the year from continuing operations	121 250	96 000
Loss for the year from discontinued operations		(30 500)
Profit for the year	121 250	65 500
Other comprehensive income		
Items that will not be reclassified to profit or loss		
Gains on property revaluation	933	3 367
Actuarial gains (losses) on defined benefit pension plans	(667)	1 333
Share of gain (loss) on property revaluation of associates	400	(700)
Income tax relating to items that will not be reclassified	(166)	(1 000)
	500	3 000
	20X7	20X6
Items that may be reclassified subsequently to profit or loss		
Exchange differences on translating foreign operations	5 334	10 667
Available-for-sale financial assets	(24 000)	26 667
Cash flow hedges	(667)	(4 000)
Income tax relating to items that may be reclassified	4 833	(8 334)
	(14 500)	25 000
Other comprehensive income for the year, net of tax	(14 000)	28 000
TOTAL COMPREHENSIVE INCOME FOR THE YEAR	107 250	93 500

FIGURE 11.2 Statement of profit or loss and other comprehensive income
Source: International Accounting Standards Board (2011, p. B1026).

Hence the initial journal entry for a revaluation increase is:

Asset	Dr	xxx	
Gain on Revaluation of Non-Current Asset (OCI)	Cr		xxx
(Revaluation of asset)			

In accordance with paragraph 42 of IAS 16, the effects of any taxes on income need to be accounted for in accordance with IAS 12 *Income Taxes*. A revaluation of an asset causes a change between the tax base and the carrying amount of the asset, giving rise to a temporary difference, and a deferred tax liability needs to be raised (see paragraph 20 of IAS 1). Paragraph 90 of IAS 1 *Presentation of Financial Statements* requires the disclosure of 'the amount of income tax relating to each item of other comprehensive income'. To reflect the tax effect of the gain, the required entry is:

Gain on Revaluation of Asset (OCI)	Dr	xxx	
Deferred Tax Liability	Cr		xxx
(Recognition of tax effect of revaluation increase)			

The reason for the immediate recognition of the deferred tax effect is because, as explained below, the gain on revaluation of non-current assets is accumulated in equity.
2. Having recognised the gain in other comprehensive income, the gain, net of tax, is transferred to equity under the heading of revaluation surplus. The required entry is:

Gain on Revaluation of Non-Current Asset (OCI)	Dr	xxx	
Asset Revaluation Surplus	Cr		xxx
(Accumulation of net revaluation gain in equity)			

The asset revaluation surplus is disclosed in the reserve section of the statement of financial position.

ILLUSTRATIVE EXAMPLE 11.2 Revaluation increases and tax effect

On 1 January 2014, XYZ Group carries an item of land at a cost of £100 000, this amount also being the tax base of the asset. The land is revalued to £120 000. The tax rate is 30%.

The tax base of the asset is £100 000 and the new carrying amount is £120 000, giving rise to a taxable temporary difference of £20 000. A deferred tax liability of £6000 must be raised to account for the expected tax to be paid in relation to the increase in expected benefits from the asset. The asset revaluation surplus raised will be the net after-tax increase in the asset (£20 000 − £6000 = £14 000). The appropriate accounting entries on revaluation of the asset are shown in figure 11.3.

Land	Dr	20 000	
Gain on Revaluation of Land (OCI)	Cr		20 000
(Recognition of revaluation increase: £120 000 − £100 000)			
Gain on Revaluation of Land (OCI)	Dr	6 000	
Deferred Tax Liability	Cr		6 000
Gain on Revaluation of Land (OCI)	Dr	14 000	
Asset Revaluation Surplus	Cr		14 000
(Accumulation of net revaluation gain in equity)			

FIGURE 11.3 Journal entries for revaluation with associated tax effect

---

Where the item of property, plant and equipment is depreciable, there are two possible accounting treatments under paragraph 35 of IAS 16:
1. restate proportionately with the change in the gross carrying amount of the asset so that the carrying amount of the asset after revaluation equals its revalued amount; or
2. eliminate the accumulated depreciation balance against the gross carrying amount of the asset and then restate the net amount to the fair value of the asset. This method is applied in this chapter.

ILLUSTRATIVE EXAMPLE 11.3 Revaluation increases and depreciable assets

On 30 June 2014, an item of plant has a carrying amount of £42 000, being the original cost of £70 000 less accumulated depreciation of £28 000. The fair value of the asset is £50 000. The tax rate is 30%. The entries are shown in figure 11.4.

The revaluation is done in two steps:

The first step is to write off the accumulated depreciation of the plant, reducing the asset to its carrying amount of £42 000.

Accumulated Depreciation Plant	Dr	28 000	
Plant	Cr		28 000
(Write down asset to its carrying amount)			

The second step is to adjust the carrying amount of £42 000 to the fair value of the asset, £50 000, being an increase of £8000. This increase is tax-effected, and the net gain accumulated to equity

Plant	Dr	8 000	
Gain on Revaluation of Plant (OCI)	Cr		8 000
(Revaluation of asset to fair value)			
Gain on Revaluation of Plant (OCI)	Dr	2 400	
Deferred Tax Liability	Cr		2 400
(Tax effect of revaluation increase)			
Gain on Revaluation of Plant (OCI)	Dr	5 600	
Asset Revaluation Surplus	Cr		5 600
(Accumulation of net revaluation gain in equity)			

FIGURE 11.4 Revaluation increase and depreciable assets

ILLUSTRATIVE EXAMPLE 11.4 Revaluation increase and the tax-effect worksheet

Assume that the depreciable asset in illustrative example 11.3 was acquired for £70 000 on 1 July 2012. Depreciation rates are on a straight-line basis at 20% p.a. for accounting and 35% for tax. The tax rate is 30%. On 30 June 2013, the carrying amount and the tax base of the asset are as follows:

	Accounting	Tax
Original cost	£ 70 000	£ 70 000
Accumulated depreciation	(14 000)	(24 500)
Net amount	56 000	45 500

Hence, the taxable temporary difference at 30 June 2013 is £10 500 (£56 000 − £45 500), with a deferred tax liability of £3150 being recognised.

On 30 June 2014, the asset has a carrying amount and tax base as follows:

	Accounting	Tax
Original cost	£ 70 000	£ 70 000
Accumulated depreciation	(28 000)	(49 000)
Net amount	42 000	21 000

Assume that on this date the asset is revalued to £50 000. The appropriate entries are:

2014				
June 30	Accumulated Depreciation	Dr	28 000	
	Plant	Cr		28 000
	(Write down asset to its carrying amount)			
	Plant	Dr	8 000	
	Gain on Revaluation of Plant (OCI)	Cr		8 000
	(Revaluation of asset to fair value)			
	Gain on Revaluation of Plant (OCI)	Dr	2 400	
	Deferred Tax Liability	Cr		2 400
	(Tax effect of revaluation increase)			

				Dr	5 600	
Gain on Revaluation of Plant (OCI)						
Asset Revaluation Surplus				Cr		5 600
(Accumulation of net revaluation gain in equity)						

For the purpose of determining required entries for tax-effect accounting at the end of the year, the carrying amount of the asset on 30 June 2014 in the accounting records is now £50 000, but its tax base is unchanged at £21 000. This gives a taxable temporary difference of £29 000, and a total deferred tax liability of £8700 at a 30% tax rate. As the beginning deferred tax liability for the year is £3150 and £2400 of the deferred tax liability is already recognised in the revaluation entry above, the adjustment required in the current year ending 30 June 2014 is £3150 (8700 − 3150 − 2400) or (£6300 − £3150). In order to recognise the adjustment to the deferred tax liability, the appropriate entry is as follows:

2014			Dr	3 150	
June 30	Income Tax Expense				
	Deferred Tax Liability		Cr		3 150
	(Recognition of deferred tax liability)				

The tax-effect worksheet is shown in figure 11.5.

	Carrying amount	Taxable amount	Deductible amount	Tax base	Taxable temporary differences	Deductible temporary differences
Plant	£50 000	£(50 000)	£21 000	£21 000	£29 000	
Temporary difference					29 000	
Deferred tax liability — closing balance					8 700 Cr	
Beginning balance					3 150 Cr	
					5 550	
Movement during the year					2 400 Cr	
Adjustment					3 150 Cr	

FIGURE 11.5 Tax-effect worksheet on revaluation of assets

Revaluation increase reversing previous revaluation decrease

The full text of paragraph 39 of IAS 16 is as follows:

> If an asset's carrying amount is increased as a result of a revaluation, the increase shall be recognised in other comprehensive income and accumulated in equity under the heading of revaluation surplus. However, the increase shall be recognised in profit or loss to the extent that it reverses a revaluation decrease of the same asset previously recognised in profit or loss.

Hence, a revaluation increase is credited to an asset revaluation surplus unless the increase reverses a revaluation decrease previously recognised as an expense in which case it is recognised as income. The accounting treatment for revaluation decreases is discussed in the next section.

11.6.2 Applying the revaluation model: revaluation decreases

Paragraph 40 of IAS 16 states:

> If an asset's carrying amount is decreased as a result of a revaluation, the decrease shall be recognised in profit or loss. However, the decrease shall be recognised in other comprehensive income to the extent of any credit balance existing in the revaluation surplus in respect of that asset.

As with revaluation increases, this paragraph covers two situations: a revaluation decrease, and a revaluation decrease following a previous revaluation increase.

The accounting for a revaluation decrease involves an immediate recognition of a loss in the period of the revaluation. As the change in the carrying amount of the asset directly affects income, the tax effect is dealt with in the normal workings of tax-effect accounting. Hence, no extra tax-effect entries outside those generated via the tax-effect worksheet are necessary in accounting for revaluation decrease.

Assume an item of plant has a carrying amount of £50 000, being original cost of £60 000 less accumulated depreciation of £10 000. If the asset is revalued downwards to £24 000, the appropriate journal entries are:

Accumulated Depreciation	Dr	10 000	
Plant	Cr		10 000
(Write down asset to its carrying amount of £50 000)			
Loss – Downward Revaluation of Plant (P/L)	Dr	26 000	
Plant	Cr		26 000
(Revaluation of asset from carrying amount of £50 000 to fair value of £24 000)			

In relation to the tax-effect worksheet, if the carrying amount and the tax base in this example were the same immediately before the revaluation, then there would be a deductible temporary difference of £26 000. A deferred tax asset of £7800 would be raised via the tax-effect worksheet analysis at the end of the reporting period.

Decrease reversing previous revaluation increase

Where an asset revaluation surplus has been raised via a previous revaluation increase, in accounting for a subsequent revaluation decrease for the same asset, the surplus must be eliminated before any expense is recognised. In adjusting for the previous revaluation increase, both the asset revaluation surplus and the related deferred tax liability must be reversed.

Assume XYZ Group has a block of land with a carrying amount of £200 000. When the land was revalued upwards from £100 000, the following entries were passed:

Land	Dr	100 000	
Gain on Revaluation of Land (OCI)	Cr		100 000
(Revaluation of asset to fair value)			
Gain on revaluation of land (OCI)	Dr	30 000	
Deferred Tax Liability	Cr		30 000
(Tax effect of revaluation increase)			
Gain on Revaluation of Land (OCI)	Dr	70 000	
Asset Revaluation Surplus	Cr		70 000
(Accumulation of net revaluation gain in equity)			

If the asset is *revalued downwards* to £160 000, the £40 000 write-down is a partial reversal of the previous upward revaluation. The accounting entries then reflect:
- a recognition of the decrease on other comprehensive income, and
- a decrease in accumulated equity, namely, asset revaluation surplus.

Loss on Revaluation of Land (OCI)	Dr	40 000	
Land	Cr		40 000
(Revaluation downwards of land)			
Deferred Tax Liability	Dr	12 000	
Loss on Revaluation of Land (OCI)	Cr		12 000
(Tax effect of revaluation decrease)			
Asset Revaluation Surplus	Dr	28 000	
Loss on Revaluation of Land (OCI)	Cr		28 000
(Reduction in accumulated equity due to revaluation decrease on land)			

If the asset is *revalued downwards* to £80 000, which is a reduction of £120 000, the asset is written down to an amount £20 000 less than the original cost of the asset.

In accordance with paragraph 40, the downward revaluation requires a loss to be recognised in profit or loss, as well as a decrease to be recognised in other comprehensive income. Effectively this will result in the elimination of the deferred tax liability and the asset revaluation surplus previously raised. The appropriate entries are:

Loss on Revaluation of Land (P/L)	Dr	20 000	
Loss on Revaluation of Land (OCI)	Dr	100 000	
Land	Cr		120 000
(Revaluation downwards of land)			
Deferred Tax Liability	Dr	30 000	
Loss on Revaluation of Land (OCI)	Cr		30 000
(Tax effect of loss on revaluation of land)			
Asset Revaluation Surplus	Dr	70 000	
Loss on Revaluation of Land (OCI)	Cr		70 000
(Reduction in accumulated equity due to revaluation decrease on land)			

The tax-effect worksheet, assuming the original revaluation increase occurred in a previous period, is shown in figure 11.6.

	Carrying amount	Taxable amount	Deductible amount	Tax base	Taxable temporary differences	Deductible temporary differences
Land	£80 000	£(80 000)	£100 000	£100 000		£20 000
Temporary difference						20 000
Deferred tax liability — closing balance					—	
Deferred tax asset — closing balance						6 000 Cr
Beginning balance					£30 000 Cr	
Movement during the year					30 000 Dr	
Adjustment						6 000 Dr

FIGURE 11.6 Tax-effect worksheet on revaluation of assets

The tax-effect worksheet shows that XYZ Group would recognise a deferred tax asset of £6000, reflecting the fact that the carrying amount of the asset is £20 000 less than the tax base.

Net revaluation increase reversing previous revaluation decrease

Where an asset is revalued upwards, an asset revaluation surplus is credited except where the increase reverses a revaluation decrease previously recognised as a loss. In this case, the revaluation increase must be recognised as a gain.

ILLUSTRATIVE EXAMPLE 11.7 Revaluation increase reversing previous decrease

Assume XYZ Group has an item of plant whose current carrying amount is £200 000 (accumulated depreciation being £20 000). The asset had cost £300 000. It was revalued downwards from a carrying amount of £270 000 to £220 000, with the following accounting entries being passed:

Accumulated Depreciation	Dr	30 000	
Plant	Cr		30 000
(Write down asset to its carrying amount of £270 000)			

Loss – Downward Revaluation of Plant (P/L) Plant (Revaluation of asset from carrying amount of £270 000 to fair value of £220 000)	Dr Cr	50 000	50 000

If the asset is assessed as having a fair value of £230 000, there is a revaluation increase of £30 000. However as there was a previous decrease of £50 000, the appropriate revaluation entry must reverse part of this previously recognised revaluation loss. The entries are:

Accumulated Depreciation Plant (Write down asset to its carrying amount of £200 000)	Dr Cr	20 000	20 000
Plant Gain on Revaluation of Plant (P/L) (Revaluation of asset from carrying amount of £200 000 to fair value of £230 000, subsequent to prior write-down of the asset)	Dr Cr	30 000	30 000

If the asset is assessed as having a fair value of £280 000, the accounting entries recognise the increase of £80 000 as consisting of two parts:
1. the reversal of the previously recognised write-down loss of £50 000; the reversal is recognised as a gain, and disclosed in profit or loss
2. the £30 000 increase recognised in other comprehensive income and accumulated in asset revaluation surplus.
The entries are:

Accumulated Depreciation Plant (Write down asset to its carrying amount of £200 000)	Dr Cr	20 000	20 000

Plant
    Gain on Revaluation of Plant (P/L)
    Gain on Revaluation of Plant (OCI)
(Revaluation of plant from carrying amount of £200 000 to
fair value of £280 000)
	Dr
	Cr
	Cr
		80 000	50 000
			30 000

Gain on Revaluation of Plant (OCI) Deferred Tax Liability (Tax effect of revaluation gain)	Dr Cr	9 000	9 000
Gain on Revaluation of Plant (OCI) Asset Revaluation Surplus (Accumulation of revaluation gain in equity)	Dr Cr	21 000	21 000

11.6.3 Effects of accounting on an asset-by-asset basis

If the fair value basis of measurement is chosen, IAS 16 requires it to be applied to items of property, plant and equipment on a class-by-class basis. However, in accounting for revaluation increases and decreases, the accounting is done on an individual asset basis within the class. Practising accountants and standard setters have often argued that a better accounting treatment would be to account for revaluation increases and decreases on a class-by-class basis. The rationale for this is that under IAS 16 revaluation increases (gains) are recognised in other comprehensive income and accumulated in equity while revaluation decreases (losses) are recognised in profit or loss in the period the revaluation occurs. If revaluation was done on a class-by-class basis, then it would be the net increase that would be accounted for, providing a netting of the gains and losses. Figure 11.7 illustrates this.

Assets	Carrying amount £	Fair value £	Increase/(decrease) £
Plant A	1 500 000	2 000 000	500 000
Plant B	1 500 000	1 200 000	(300 000)
Total	3 000 000	3 200 000	200 000

FIGURE 11.7 Revaluation by asset or class of asset?

Applying IAS 16, both Plant A and Plant B, being in the one class of assets, have to be revalued to fair value if the revaluation model is applied to plant. However, in accounting for the movements in fair value, each asset is dealt with separately. With Plant A, as there is a revaluation increase of £500 000, the increase results in a £500 000 gain being recognised in other comprehensive income and £350 000 (assuming a tax rate of 30%) being accumulated in equity affecting an asset revaluation surplus. With Plant B, the revaluation decrease of £300 000 is recognised as an expense affecting current period profit or loss. For those who argue that revaluations should be accounted for on a class-by-class basis, the net revaluation increase on plant is £200 000. Accounting on a class basis would result in recognising a £200 000 gain in other comprehensive income and then accumulating £140 000 in an asset revaluation surplus with no effect on current period profit or loss. The argument for the class method of accounting is that it reduces the biased effect that the IAS 16 method has on current period profit or loss. However the two methods produce the same total comprehensive income for the period.

11.6.4 Applying the revaluation model: transfers from asset revaluation surplus

Paragraph 41 of IAS 16 covers the accounting for the asset revaluation surplus subsequent to its creation. There are two circumstances where the asset revaluation surplus may be transferred to retained earnings. Note that there is no requirement that the asset revaluation surplus must be transferred, only a specification of situations where it may be transferred. The *first* situation is where the asset is derecognised (i.e. removed from the statement of financial position, for example, by sale of the asset). In this case, the whole or part of the surplus may be transferred. The *second* situation is where an asset is being used up over its useful life, a proportion of the revaluation surplus may be transferred to retained earnings, the proportion being in relation to the depreciation on the asset. In this case, the amount of the surplus transferred would be equal to the difference between depreciation based on the original cost, and depreciation based on the revalued amount, adjusted for the tax effect relating to the surplus. This second situation is shown in illustrative example 11.8.

ILLUSTRATIVE EXAMPLE 11.8 Transferring revaluation surplus to retained earning

Assume an item of plant is acquired for £100 000. The plant is immediately revalued to £120 000. The asset has a useful life of 10 years and the tax rate is 30%.

The revaluation entries are:

Plant	Dr	20 000	
Gain on Revaluation of Plant (OCI)	Cr		20 000
(Revaluation of plant from £100 000 to £120 000)			
Gain on Revaluation of Plant (OCI)	Dr	6 000	
Deferred Tax Liability	Cr		6 000
(Tax effect of revaluation of plant)			
Gain on Revaluation of Plant (OCI)	Dr	14 000	
Asset Revaluation Surplus	Cr		14 000
(Accumulation of revaluation gain in equity)			

At the end of the year, depreciation expense of £12 000 is recorded. As the remaining useful life of the asset is 10 years (revaluation took place at acquisition), XYZ Group may transfer 10% of the asset revaluation surplus to retained earnings. The entry is:

Asset Revaluation Surplus	Dr	1 400	
Retained earnings	Cr		1 400
(Transfer from asset revaluation surplus to retained earnings)			

11.6.5 Applying the revaluation model: depreciation of revalued assets

Section 11.5.1 discusses the accounting treatment for depreciation under IAS 16. As noted, the term 'depreciable amount' includes 'other amount substituted for cost'. This includes fair value. Paragraph 50 of IAS 16 notes that depreciation is a process of allocation. Hence, even though an asset is measured at fair value, depreciation is not determined simply as the change in fair value of the asset over a period. As with the cost method, depreciation for a period is calculated after considering the pattern of economic benefits relating to the asset and the residual value of the asset.

ILLUSTRATIVE EXAMPLE 11.9 Depreciation of revalued assets

Assume XYZ Group has an item of plant that was revalued to £1000 at 30 June 2014. The asset is expected to have a remaining useful life of 5 years, with benefits being received evenly over that period. The residual value is calculated to be £100. Consider two situations.

Situation 1

At 30 June 2015, no formal revaluation occurs and the management of XYZ Group assess that the carrying amount of the plant is not materially different from fair value.

The appropriate journal entry for the 2014–15 period is:

2015				
June 30	Depreciation Expense	Dr	180	
	Accumulated Depreciation	Cr		180
	(Depreciation on plant 1/5[£1000 − £100])			

The asset is reported in the statement of financial position at a carrying amount of £820, equal to a gross amount of £1000 less accumulated depreciation of £180, the carrying amount being equal to fair value.

Situation 2

At 30 June 2015, a formal revaluation occurs and the external valuers assess the fair value of the plant to be £890. Tax rate is 30%.

The appropriate journal entries for the 2014–15 period are:

2015				
June 30	Depreciation Expense	Dr	180	
	Accumulated Depreciation	Cr		180
	(Depreciation on plant 1/5[£1000 − £100])			
	Accumulated Depreciation	Dr	180	
	Plant	Cr		180
	(Write down asset to its carrying amount)			
	Plant	Dr	70	
	Gain on Revaluation of Plant (OCI)	Cr		70
	(Revaluation of plant from £820 to £890)			
	Gain on Revaluation of Plant (OCI)	Dr	21	
	Deferred Tax Liability	Cr		21
	(Tax effect of revaluation of plant)			
	Gain on Revaluation of Plant (OCI)	Dr	49	
	Asset Revaluation Surplus	Cr		49
	(Accumulation of net revaluation gain in equity)			

In other words, there is a two-step process. Depreciation is allocated in accordance with normal depreciation principles. Then, as a formal revaluation occurs, the accumulated depreciation is written off and the asset revalued to fair value. The asset is reported in the statement of financial position at fair value of £890 with no associated accumulated depreciation.

It may be argued that the accounting in situation 2 is inappropriate. Whereas the depreciation charge affects profit or loss, the gain on the revaluation of the asset affects other comprehensive income. The economic benefits in relation to the asset for the period are not only those achieved by consumption

---

of the asset, but also those obtained by changes in the market value of the asset. However, these are accounted for differently under IAS 16. It could then be argued that the appropriate depreciation in situation 2 should be the change in fair value over the period, namely £110 (£1000 − £890), with the journal entry being:

Depreciation Expense	Dr	110	
Accumulated Depreciation	Cr		110
(Depreciation on plant)			

No revaluation entry is then necessary. Note, however, that this entry is not allowed under IAS 16.

Subsequent to revaluation, XYZ Group should reassess the useful life and residual value of the revalued asset because these may change as a result of economic changes affecting XYZ Group and its use of assets. Using the example in scenario 2, following the revaluation at 30 June 2015, assume XYZ Group determines that the residual value is £110 and the remaining useful life is 4 years. In the 2015–16 period, the depreciation entry is:

Depreciation Expense	Dr	195	
Accumulated Depreciation	Cr		195
(Depreciation on plant 1/4[£890 − £110])			

11.7 CHOOSING BETWEEN THE COST MODEL AND THE REVALUATION MODEL

Given that IAS 16 allows entities a choice between the cost model and the revaluation model, it is of interest to consider what motivates entities to choose between the two measurement models.

Arguments relating to the choice of models generally claim that a current price (a fair value) will provide more relevant information than a past price (the original cost). However, the requirement under IAS 16 to continuously adjust the carrying amounts of assets measured at fair value so that they are not materially different from current fair values provides a cost disincentive to management to adopt the revaluation model. Costs associated with adopting the revaluation model include the cost of employing valuers, annual costs associated with reviewing the carrying amounts to assess whether a revaluation is necessary, extra record-keeping costs associated with the revaluations, including accounting for the associated revaluation increases and decreases, and increased audit costs relating to the review of changing revalued amounts.

A further factor that influences some entities' measurement choice in favour of the cost model is harmonisation with US GAAP, which does not allow the revaluation of non-current assets.

Another factor that entities have to consider when choosing their measurement bases for classes of property, plant and equipment is the effect of the model on the statement of profit or loss and other comprehensive income. Where assets are measured on a fair value basis, the depreciation per annum is expected to be higher as the depreciable amount is higher.

Besides the effect of lower depreciation, there will be the effect on the disposal of the asset. Where an asset is measured at fair value, there is expected to be an immaterial amount of profit or loss on sale as, at the time of sale, the recorded amount of the asset should be close to that of the market price. For an asset measured at cost, any gain or loss on sale will be reported in the statement of profit or loss and other comprehensive income.

What, apart from increased relevance and reliability arguments, are the incentives for management to use the revaluation model? The effect of adopting the revaluation model is to increase the entity's assets and equities (via the revaluation surplus). Hence, entities that need to report higher amounts in these areas would consider adoption of the revaluation model. The incentives for entities to adopt fair value measures then tend to be entity-specific because the entities face pressures relating to external circumstances. Examples of such pressures are:

- Entities with debt covenants generally have constraints relating to their debt–asset ratios, such as the requirement that the debt–asset ratio must not exceed 50%. Hence, for an entity with increasing debt, adoption of the revaluation model for a class of assets that is increasing in value will ease pressures on the debt–asset ratio by increasing the asset base of the entity. This assumes that the debt covenant allows revaluations to be taken into account in measuring assets.
- An entity's reported profit figure may be under scrutiny from a specific source, such as a trade union seeking reasons to support claims for higher pay, or regulators looking at monopoly control within an industry.

Where there are pressures to report lower profits, adoption of the revaluation model provides scope for higher depreciation charges. These are reflected in the profit or loss for the period. The increases in the values of the non-current assets do not affect profit or loss but are reported in other comprehensive income. If ratios such as rates of return on assets or equity are based on profit rather than comprehensive income, lower reported profits and higher asset/equity bases will result in an entity being seen in a less favourable light.

However, as noted above, the incentives relating to playing with profit and asset numbers tend to rely on users of the information having no knowledge of accounting rules or movements in prices within industries or sectors, or being unable to make comparisons across entities within an industry segment. One of the key elements of analysing entities within an industry is comparability of information. If all entities in the sector are applying the cost model, analysts can make their judgements by comparing the information between the entities and applying information from sources other than accounting reports, such as movements in price indexes. The entity then has less reason to incur the costs of adopting the revaluation model of measurement.

11.8 DERECOGNITION

As noted in paragraph 3 of IAS 16, the standard does not apply to non-current assets classified as held for sale and accounted for under IFRS 5. IAS 16 then deals with the disposal of non-current assets that have not previously been classified as held for sale.

Paragraph 67 of IAS 16 identifies two occasions where derecognition of an item of property, plant and equipment should occur:
- on disposal, such as the sale of the asset
- when no future economic benefits are expected, either from future use or from disposal.

When items of property, plant and equipment are sold, regardless of whether there are many or few remaining economic benefits, the selling entity will recognise a gain or loss on the asset, this being determined as the difference between the net proceeds from sale and the carrying amount of the asset at the time of sale (IAS 16 paragraph 71). In calculating the net proceeds from sale, any deferred consideration must be discounted, and the proceeds calculated at the cash price equivalent (IAS 16 paragraph 72). As the carrying amount is net of depreciation and impairment losses, it is necessary to calculate the depreciation from the beginning of the reporting period to the point of sale. Failing to do this, whether under the cost model or the revaluation model, would be out of step with the key principle established in IAS 16 that depreciation is a process of allocation and each period must bear its fair share of the cost or revalued amount of the asset.

The gain or loss on sale is included in the profit or loss for the period. Note paragraph 34 of IAS 1 *Presentation of Financial Statements*:

> IFRS 15 *Revenue from Contracts with Customers* requires an entity to measure revenue from contracts with customers at the amount of consideration to which the entity expects to be entitled in exchange for transferring promised goods or services. For example, the amount of revenue recognised reflects the amount of any trade discounts and volume rebates the entity allows. An entity undertakes, in the course of its ordinary activities, other transactions that do not generate revenue but are incidental to the main revenue-generating activities. An entity presents the results of such transactions, when this presentation reflects the substance of the transaction or other event, by netting any income with related expenses arising on the same transaction. For example:
> (a) an entity presents gains and losses on the disposal of non-current assets, including investments and operating assets, by deducting from the proceeds on disposal the carrying amount of the asset and related selling expenses; ...

Paragraph 34 requires only the disclosure of the gain or loss on sale, as opposed to separate disclosure of the income and the carrying amount of the asset (see also paragraph 98(c) of IAS 1). The argument for the netting of the income and expense is that gains/losses on the disposal of property, plant and equipment result from activities that are not considered to be the main revenue-generating activities of an entity.

In paragraph BC35 of the Basis of Conclusions on IAS 16, the IASB argued:

> users of financial statements would consider these gains and the proceeds from an entity's sale of goods in the course of its ordinary activities differently in their evaluation of an entity's past results and their projections of future cash flows. This is because revenue from the sale of goods is typically more likely to recur in comparable amounts than are gains from sales of items of property, plant and equipment. Accordingly, the Board concluded that an entity should not classify as revenue gains on disposals of items of property, plant and equipment.

However, in preparing a cash flow statement, proceeds from the sale of property, plant and equipment are normally shown as a cash flow from investing activities.

XYZ Group acquired an item of plant on 1 July 2013 for £100 000. The asset had an expected useful life of 10 years and a residual value of £20 000. On 1 January 2016, XYZ Group sold the asset for £81 000.

Required

Prepare the journal entries relating to this asset in the year of sale.

Solution

At the point of sale, the depreciation on the asset must be calculated for that part of the year for which the asset was held before the sale. Hence, for the half-year before the sale, under the straight-line method, depreciation of £4000 (i.e. $0.5 \times 1/10[£100\,000 - £20\,000]$) must be charged as an expense. The entry is:

Depreciation Expense	Dr	4 000	
Accumulated Depreciation	Cr		4 000
(Depreciation charge up to point of sale)			

The gain or loss on sale is the difference between the proceeds on sale of £81 000 and the carrying amount at time of sale of £80 000 (i.e. $£100\,000 - 2.5[1/10 \times £80\,000]$), which is £1000. The required journal entry is:

Cash	Dr	81 000	
Accumulated Depreciation	Dr	20 000	
Plant	Cr		100 000
Gain on Sale of Plant	Cr		1 000
(Gain on sale of asset)			

In this example, the asset was sold for £81 000. Assume that the asset, now referred to as Plant A, was traded in for another asset, Plant B. Plant B had a fair value of £280 000, with XYZ Group making a cash payment of £202 000 as well as giving up Plant A. The trade-in amount is then £78 000. The journal entries to record this transaction are:

Plant B	Dr	280 000	
Loss on Sale of Plant A (P/L)	Dr	2 000	
Accumulated Depreciation – Plant A	Dr	20 000	
Plant A	Cr		100 000
Cash	Cr		202 000
(Acquisition of Plant B and trade-in of Plant A)			

11.9 DISCLOSURE

Paragraphs 73–79 of IAS 16 contain the required disclosures relating to property, plant and equipment. Information in paragraph 73 is required on a class-by-class basis, and paragraph 77 relates only to assets stated at revalued amounts. Paragraph 79 contains information that entities are encouraged to disclose, but are not required to do so. Figure 11.8 provides an illustration of the disclosures required by IAS 16.

FIGURE 11.8 Illustrative disclosures required by IAS 16

	IAS 16 paragraph
Note 1: Summary of accounting policies (extract) **Property, plant and equipment** Freehold land and buildings on freehold land are measured on a fair value basis. At the end of each reporting period, the value of each asset in these classes is reviewed to ensure that it does not differ materially from the asset's fair value at that date. Where necessary, the asset is revalued to reflect its fair value. In June 2014, revaluations were carried out by an independent	*73(a)* *77(a)*

(continued)

FIGURE 11.8 *(continued)*

valuer; since then valuations have been made internally. The basis for the assessment of fair value has been by reference to observable transactions in the property market, including an analysis of prices paid in recent market transactions for similar properties. No other valuation techniques were used.

77(b)

77(a)

All other classes of property, plant and equipment are measured at cost.

73(a)

Depreciation

Depreciation is provided on a straight-line basis for all property, plant and equipment, other than freehold land.

73(b)

The useful lives of the assets are:

73(c)

	2016	2015
Freehold buildings	40 years	40 years
Plant and equipment	5 to 15 years	5 to 15 years

Note 10: Property, plant and equipment

	Land and buildings		Plant and equipment		
	2016	2015	2016	2015	
	£'000	£'000	£'000	£'000	
Balance at beginning of year	1 861	1 765	2 840	2 640	*73(d)*
Accumulated depreciation	(400)	(364)	(732)	(520)	
Carrying amount	1 461	1 401	2 108	2 120	
Additions	—	123	755	372	*73(e)(i)*
Disposals	(466)	(18)	(181)	(158)	*73(e)(ii)*
Acquisitions via business combinations	739	—	412	—	*73(e)(iii)*
Impairment losses	—	—	(100)	—	*73(e)(v)*
Depreciation	(20)	(36)	(161)	(212)	*73(e)(vii)*
Transfer to assets held for sale	(438)	—	(890)	—	*73(e)(ix)*
Net exchange differences	11	(9)	8	(14)	*73(e)(viii)*
Carrying amount at end of year	1 287	1 461	1 951	2 108	*73(d)*
Property, plant and equipment:					
At cost	1 707	1 861	2 944	2 840	
Accumulated depreciation and impairment losses	(420)	(400)	(993)	(732)	
Carrying amount at end of year	1 287	1 461	1 951	2 108	*73(d)*

For the freehold land and buildings measured at fair value, the carrying amount that would have been recognised if they had been carried at cost is:

77(e)

	2016	2015
	£'000	£'000
Carrying amount at end of year	942	824

Plant and equipment of £420 000 have been pledged as security for loans to the company.

74(a)

The company has entered into a contract to acquire £640 000 of plant equipment over the next 2 years.

74(c)

Activity in the revaluation surplus for land and buildings is as follows:

77(f)

	2016	2015
	£'000	£'000
Balance at beginning of year	309	303
Revaluation of gains on land and buildings	42	9
Deferred tax liability	(13)	(3)
Balance at end of year	338	309

There are no restrictions on the distribution of the balance of the surplus to shareholders.

11.10 INVESTMENT PROPERTIES

IAS 40 *Investment Properties* requires that an entity differentiate between investment properties and other properties, such as owner-occupied property.

For an item to be classified as investment property, it must meet the definition of investment property. Investment property is essentially property from which the entity intends to earn capital appreciation or rental income or both.

11.10.1 Definition and classification

Investment property is defined in paragraph 5 of IAS 40 as land or buildings (or both, or part of a building), held by an owner or leased by a lessee under a finance lease:
- to earn rentals or for capital appreciation or both;
- rather than for use in the production or supply of goods or services or for administrative purposes or sale in the ordinary course of business.

In addition, a property held under an operating lease may be classified as an investment property (see below).

The following are examples of properties that *are* classified as investment property:
- property held for long-term capital appreciation;
- a building that is leased out to a third party under an operating lease; or a vacant building that is held with the intention to lease it out under an operating lease;
- a property being constructed or developed for future use as an investment property; and
- land whose use is undecided (the standard assumes that the land is held for capital appreciation).

The following are examples of properties that *are not* classified as investment property:
- property that is owner-occupied (it is classified as property, plant and equipment in terms of IAS 16 *Property, Plant and Equipment*);
- property that is leased out to a third party under a finance lease (it is treated in terms of IAS 17 *Leases*); and
- property held for sale in the ordinary course of business (it is classified as inventory in terms of IAS 2 *Inventory*).

11.10.2 Transfers in and out of investment property

Transfers in and out of investment property take place when and only when there is a change in use. Examples of such a change in use where a property that was classified as investment property would cease to be classified as an investment property include:
- when the investment property becomes owner-occupied — in which case it must be transferred to property, plant and equipment;
- when there is commencement of development of the investment property with the view to resale — in which case it must be transferred to inventory.

Conversely, examples of such a change in use where a property that *was not* classified as investment property would become classified as an investment property would include:
- when a property that was owner-occupied ceases to be occupied by the owners — in which case it is immediately transferred from property, plant and equipment to investment property; and
- when a property that was held for sale in the ordinary course of business is rented out under an operating lease — in which case it is immediately transferred from inventories to investment property.

Note that if the rental agreement is structured as a finance lease instead of an operating lease, the property would not become classified as investment property but would instead be classified as a finance lease, in terms of IAS 17 *Leases*.

11.10.3 Joint use properties

It is common for land and buildings to be used for a variety of purposes, for example, a portion of the property is used to earn rental income and a portion of the property is used in the production or supply of goods or services.

The result is that a portion of the property meets the definition of investment property (the part used to earn rental income) and a portion of the property meets the definition of property, plant and equipment (the part used in the production or supply of goods or services). These properties are referred to as joint use properties.

Paragraph 10 of IAS 40 provides guidance on how to classify joint use properties. If each portion can be sold or leased out separately (under a finance lease), then each portion is classified separately (one as an investment property and the other as an owner-occupied property). On the other hand, if each portion cannot be sold or leased out separately, then the entire property is classified as property, plant and equipment, unless the owner-occupied portion is an insignificant portion, in which case the entire property is classified as investment property.

Professional judgement is required to determine whether the owner-occupied portion is insignificant and the resultant classification of the property.

11.10.4 Ancillary services

An entity may provide ancillary services to the occupants of its property, for example, maintenance of the building or security. In such circumstances, the property may only be classified as an investment property if these services are insignificant or incidental.

If the ancillary services provided are considered to be significant, then the entity can no longer be considered to be an inactive investor and classification as investment property may not be appropriate.

11.10.5 Measurement of investment properties

On acquisition, an investment property is initially measured at cost. Subsequent measurement permits a choice between the cost model and the fair value model, which must then be applied to all investment property, although the fair value model is encouraged by the standard.

Note, however, that the cost model is compulsory if the fair value is not reliably measurable on a continuing basis. This scenario then forces the property to be measured under the cost model and it may not be measured under the fair value model at a later stage, but this does not prevent the entity from using the fair value model for its other investment properties. In addition, the fair value model is compulsory for a property held by a lessee under an operating lease, where the lessee has chosen to classify it as investment property.

It is important to note that if the fair value model is chosen, it is almost impossible to subsequently change to the cost model. Paragraph 55 of IAS 40 does not permit a change from the fair value model to the cost model if the fair value becomes difficult to measure. Rather, the property is then measured at the last known fair value until such time that a revised fair value becomes available.

Further, IAS 8 *Accounting Policies, Changes in Accounting Estimates and Errors*, only allows a change in policy if the new accounting policy results in reliable and more relevant information, which is unlikely to be the case when considering a change in policy from the fair value model to the cost model.

Use of the cost model

The cost model used for investment properties is the same as the cost model used for property, plant and equipment.

An investment property held under the cost model is measured at cost and depreciated annually (in terms of IAS 16 *Property, Plant and Equipment*); it is also tested for impairments (in terms of IAS 36 *Impairment of Assets*).

Use of the fair value model

The fair value model requires that the investment property be initially measured at cost and at the end of the reporting period it is remeasured to its fair value. Any subsequent gains or losses resulting from a change in the fair value of the investment property are recognised in profit or loss for the period in which they arise in terms of paragraph 35 of IAS 40.

It is important to note that the fair value model used to measure investment properties differs from the revaluation model used for property, plant and equipment. Revalued property, plant and equipment is depreciated and tested for impairment; revaluations are recognised in other comprehensive income. However, investment property measured at fair value is not depreciated or tested for impairment; and fair value changes are recognised in profit or loss.

Fair value is a market-based value measured in terms of IFRS 13, which must reflect, inter alia, rental incomes from current leases, and other assumptions that market participants would use when pricing investment property under current market conditions.

11.10.6 Disclosure

Paragraph 75(a)–(c) of IAS 40 requires that the accounting policy note should disclose:
- whether the fair value model or cost model is used;
- the criteria used to classify property leased by the entity under an operating lease as investment property;
- where it was difficult to decide, the criteria that the entity used to determine whether a property is classified as investment property, owner-occupied property or inventory.

Paragraphs 75(d), (e) and (g) of IAS 40 requires that the investment property note should disclose:
- whether the fair value was measured by an independent, suitably qualified valuer with relevant experience in the location and type of property;
- any restrictions on the property;
- a reconciliation of the opening balance to the closing balance.

Paragraph 75(f) of IAS 40 requires the profit before tax note to disclose:
- rental income earned from investment property;
- direct operating expenses related to all investment property, split into:
  - those that earned rental income, and
  - those that did not earn rental income (IAS 40 paragraph 75(f)).

There are additional disclosure requirements specific to the fair value model or cost model. Paragraphs 76–78 of IAS 40 require the following disclosure if the fair value model was used:
- a reconciliation between the opening balance and closing balance of investment property;
- if a specific property is measured using the cost model because the fair value could not be reliably measured then the following must be disclosed in relation to that property:
  - a description of the property;
  - a separate reconciliation from opening balance to closing balance;
  - an explanation as to why the fair value could not be measured reliably;
  - the range of estimates within which the fair value is highly likely to lie;
  - if such a property is disposed of, a statement to this effect including the carrying amount at the time of sale and the resulting gain or loss on disposal.

Paragraph 79(c)–(d) of IAS 40 requires the following disclosure if the cost model had been used:
- a reconciliation between the opening balance and closing balance of investment property must show all:
  - the gross carrying amount and accumulated depreciation (at the beginning and end of the year);
  - depreciation for the current year (and in the profit before tax note);
  - impairments (and reversals) for the current year (and in the profit before tax note);
  - additions (either through acquisition or a business combination);
  - subsequent expenditure that was capitalised;
  - transfers to and from inventories and property, plant and equipment;
  - exchange differences;
  - other changes.

SUMMARY

'Property, plant and equipment' covers a wide range of assets such as vehicles, aircraft, all types of buildings, and specific structures such as oil and gas offshore platforms. These assets have a variety of useful lives, expected benefits, risk of receipt of benefits, movements in value over time, and expected value at point of derecognition. In some cases at derecognition, assets such as oil platforms require entities to incur costs rather than receive a residual value on sale. IAS 16, although recognising this variety, provides common principles to be applied to all items of property, plant and equipment.

Initial recognition occurs when the recognition criteria are met and assets are then recorded at cost. Subsequent to initial recognition, entities have a choice of measurement model, namely the cost model and the revaluation model. Under both measurement models, assets are subject to depreciation, this being a process of allocation and not a process of change in value. The measurement of depreciation requires judgements to be made by the accountant, including useful lives, residual values and pattern of receipt of benefits. Use of the revaluation model has additional accounting complications with revaluation increases and decreases potentially affecting asset revaluation surplus accounts, and having tax-effect consequences. Because of the judgements having to be made, IAS 16 requires extensive disclosures to be made.

DEMONSTRATION PROBLEM 11.1 Movements in assets, depreciation

Munich Manufacturing Ltd's post-closing trial balance at 30 June 2015 included the following balances:

Machinery Control (at cost)	£244 480
Accumulated Depreciation – Machinery Control	113 800
Fixtures (at cost; purchased 2 December 2012)	308 600
Accumulated Depreciation – Fixtures	134 138

The Machinery Control and Accumulated Depreciation — Machinery Control accounts are supported by subsidiary ledgers. Details of machines owned at 30 June 2015 are as follows:

Machine	Acquisition date	Cost	Estimated useful life	Estimated residual value
1	28 April 2011	£74 600	5 years	£3800
2	4 February 2013	82 400	5 years	4400
3	26 March 2014	87 480	6 years	5400

Additional information

(a) Munich Manufacturing Ltd uses the general journal for all journal entries, records depreciation to the nearest month, balances its books every 6 months, and records amounts to the nearest pound.

(b) The company uses straight-line depreciation for machinery and diminishing-balance depreciation at 20% per annum for fixtures.

The following transactions and events occurred from 1 July 2015 onwards:

2015	
July 3	Exchanged items of fixtures (having a cost of £100 600; a carrying amount at exchange date of £56 872; and a fair value at exchange date of £57 140) for a used machine (Machine 4). Machine 4's fair value at exchange date was £58 000. Machine 4 originally cost £92 660 and had been depreciated by £31 790 to exchange date in the previous owner's accounts. Munich Manufacturing Ltd estimated Machine 4's useful life and residual value to be 3 years and £4580 respectively.
Oct. 10	Traded in Machine 2 for a new machine (Machine 5) that cost £90 740. A trade-in allowance of £40 200 was received and the balance was paid in cash. Freight charges of £280 and installation costs of £1600 were also paid in cash. Munich Manufacturing Ltd estimated Machine 5's useful life and residual value to be 6 years and £5500 respectively.
2016	
April 24	Overhauled Machine 3 at a cash cost of £16 910, after which Munich Manufacturing Ltd revised its residual value to £5600 and extended its useful life by 2 years.
May 16	Paid for scheduled repairs and maintenance on the machines of £2370.
June 30	Recorded depreciation and scrapped Machine 1.

Required

1. Prepare journal entries to record the above transactions and events.
2. Prepare the Accumulated Depreciation — Machinery Control and Accumulated Depreciation — Fixtures ledger accounts for the period 30 June 2015 to 30 June 2016.

Solution

1. *Journal entries*

Calculate the depreciation on each of the depreciable assets so that when events such as a sale occur, depreciation up to the date of the transaction can be calculated. Depreciation is calculated as:

$$\text{(Cost – residual value)/expected useful life}$$

For the three items of machinery, the depreciation per month is calculated as follows:

> Machine 1 depreciation = (£74 600 – £3800)/60 months = £1180 per month
> Machine 2 depreciation = (£82 400 – £4400)/60 months = £1300 per month
> Machine 3 depreciation = (£87 480 – £5400)/72 months = £1140 per month

On 3 July, the company exchanges items of fixtures for a machine. After assessing that the transaction has commercial substance, the fixtures are derecognised by eliminating both the asset account and the accumulated depreciation.

The acquired machine (Machine 4) is recognised at cost. Cost is measured using the fair value of the consideration given by the acquirer. As cost is the measurement used, the fair value of the machine is not relevant. Similarly, the carrying amount of the asset in the seller's records is also not relevant. The entry also records the profit on sale.

2015				
July 3	Machinery (M4)	Dr	57 140	
	Accumulated Depreciation – Fixtures*	Dr	43 728	
	Fixtures	Cr		100 600
	Profit on sale of fixtures (P/L)	Cr		268
	*£100 600 – £56 872			

The depreciation per month for M4 is then calculated:

> Machine 4 depreciation = (£57 140 – £4580)/36 months = £1460 per month

On 10 October, Machine 2 is traded in for Machine 5. Depreciation up to point of sale on Machine 2 is determined, being £1300 per month for the 3 months from July to September.

Oct. 10	Depreciation – Machinery (M2)*	Dr	3 900	
	Accumulated Depreciation – Machinery (M2)	Cr		3 900
	*£1300 × 3 months			

Machine 2 is derecognised with the machine and related accumulated depreciation being written out of the records. Machine 5 is recorded at cost. Cost is determined as the sum of the purchase price and directly attributable costs. Purchase price is the fair value of consideration given up by the acquirer. In the absence of a fair value for Machine 2, the consideration is based on the fair value of Machine 5, namely £90 740. The directly attributable costs are the freight charges of £280 and installation costs of £1600, both being necessarily incurred to get the asset into the condition for management's intended use. The cash outlay is then the sum of the balance paid to the seller of Machine 5 and the directly attributable costs.

	Machinery (M5)*	Dr	92 620	
	Accumulated Depreciation – Machinery (M2)**	Dr	41 600	
	Loss on sale of Machinery (P/L)	Dr	600	
	Machinery (M2)	Cr		82 400
	Cash	Cr		52 420
	*£90 740 + £280 + £1 600			
	**£1300 × 32 months			

The depreciation per month for Machine 5 is then calculated:

Machine 5 depreciation = (£92 620 − £5500)/72 months = £1210 per month

On 24 April 2016, Machine 3 received an overhaul. This resulted in a change in the capacity of the machine, which increased the residual value and extended its useful life. Because this results in a change in the depreciation per month, depreciation based on the rate before the overhaul for the period up to the date of the overhaul is recorded.

2016				
April 24	Depreciation – Machinery (M3)*	Dr	11 400	
	Accumulated Depreciation – Machinery (M3).	Cr		11 400
	*£1140 × 10 months			

Because the overhaul increases the expected benefits from the asset — that is, the outlay for the overhaul results in probable future benefits, the cost of the overhaul is capitalised, increasing the overall cost of the asset.

| | Machinery (M3) | Dr | 16 910 | |
| | Cash | Cr | | 16 910 |

The overhaul results in a change in expectations, so it is necessary to calculate a revised depreciation per month:

M3:	New depreciable amount	= £87 480 + £16 910 – £5600	= £98 790
	Accumulated depreciation balance	= £1140 × 25 months	= £28 500
	Carrying amount to be depreciated	= £98 790 – £28 500	= £70 290
	New useful life	= 72 months – 25 months + 24 months = 71 months	
	Revised depreciation	= £70 290/71 months	= £990 per month

Because outlays on repairs and maintenance do not lead to increased future benefits, these outlays are expensed.

May 16	Repairs and Maintenance Expense	Dr	2 370	
	Cash	Cr		2 370

At the end of the reporting period, depreciation is accrued on all depreciable assets:

Machinery:	M1	1180 × 10 months		£ 11 800
	M3	£990 × 2 months		1 980
	M4	£1460 × 12 months		17 520
	M5	£1210 × 9 months		10 890
				£ 42 190*
Fixtures:	£308 600 – £100 600			£208 000
	Less: £134 138 – £43 728			(90 410)
				£117 590
	20% × £117 590			£ 23 518**

June 30	Depreciation – Machinery*	Dr	42 190	
	Depreciation – Fixtures**	Dr	23 518	
	Accumulated Depreciation – Machinery	Cr		42 190
	Accumulated Depreciation – Fixtures	Cr		23 518

Machine 1 is scrapped, so the asset is derecognised by writing off the asset and related accumulated depreciation. The undepreciated amount is recognised as an expense. A residual value of £3800 was expected but not received, so the company incurs a loss of £3800.

	Accumulated Depreciation – Machinery (M1)*	Dr	70 800	
	Loss on scrapping (P/L) (M1)**	Dr	3 800	
	Machinery (M1)	Cr		74 600
	*£1180 × 60 months			
	**£74 600 – $70 800			

2. *Ledger accounts*

Accumulated Depreciation – Machinery Control

10/10/15	Machinery	41 600	30/6/15	Balance b/d	113 800
31/12/15	Balance c/d	76 100	10/10/15	Depreciation	3 900
		117 700			117 700
30/6/16	Machinery	70 800	31/12/15	Balance b/d	76 100
	Balance c/d	58 890	24/4/16	Depreciation	11 400
			30/6/16	Depreciation	42 190
		129 690			129 690
			30/6/16	Balance b/d	58 890

Accumulated Depreciation – Fixtures

3/7/15	Fixtures	43 728	30/6/15	Balance b/d	134 138
31/12/15	Balance c/d	90 410			
		134 138			134 138
			31/12/15	Balance b/d	90 410
30/6/16	Balance c/d	113 928	30/6/16	Depreciation	23 518
		113 928			113 928
			30/6/16	Balance b/d	113 928

On 1 July 2014, Weinheim Ltd acquired a number of assets from Berlin Ltd. The assets had the following fair values at that date:

Plant A	£300 000
Plant B	180 000
Furniture A	60 000
Furniture B	50 000

In exchange for these assets, Weinheim Ltd issued 200 000 shares with a fair value of £2.95 per share. The directors of Weinheim Ltd decided to measure plant at fair value under the revaluation model and furniture at cost. The plant was considered to have a further 10-year life with benefits being received evenly over that period, whereas furniture is depreciated evenly over a 5-year period.

At 31 December 2014, Weinheim Ltd assessed the carrying amounts of its assets as follows:
- Plant A was valued at £296 000, with an expected remaining useful life of 8 years.
- Plant B was valued at £168 000, with an expected remaining useful life of 8 years.
- Furniture A's carrying amount was considered to be less than its recoverable amount.
- Furniture B's recoverable amount was assessed to be £40 000, with an expected remaining useful life of 4 years.

Appropriate entries were made at 31 December 2014 for the half-yearly accounts.

At 30 June 2015, Weinheim Ltd assessed the carrying amounts of its assets as follows:
- Plant A was valued at £274 000.
- Plant B was valued at £161 500.
- The carrying amounts of furniture were less than their recoverable amounts.

The tax rate is 30%.

Required

Prepare the journal entries passed during the 2014–15 period in relation to the non-current assets in accordance with IAS 16 *Property, Plant and Equipment*.

Solution

The assets acquired are recorded at cost. The total cost of the assets is the fair value of the shares issued, namely £590 000 (i.e. 200 000 shares at £2.95 per share). This exactly equals the sum of the fair values of the assets acquired, hence the cost of each of the assets acquired is assumed to be equal to its fair value. If the amount were different from £590 000, say £550 000, then the cost of each asset would be determined based on the proportion of fair value to total fair value.

2014				
July 1	Plant A	Dr	300 000	
	Plant B	Dr	180 000	
	Furniture A	Dr	60 000	
	Furniture B	Dr	50 000	
	Share Capital	Cr		590 000
	(Acquisition of assets)			

At the end of each reporting period, depreciation is calculated and recorded. The next two entries record the depreciation on Plant A and Plant B after 6 months, at 31 December 2014.

Dec. 31	Depreciation Expense – Plant A	Dr	15 000	
	Accumulated Depreciation	Cr		15 000
	(Depreciation, 10% × ½ × £300 000)			
	Depreciation Expense – Plant B	Dr	9 000	
	Accumulated Depreciation	Cr		9 000
	(Depreciation, 10% × ½ × £180 000)			

Plant is measured using the revaluation model. At 31 December, the fair values of plant are assessed. In relation to Plant A, the carrying amount of the asset is £285 000 (i.e. £300 000 − £15 000). The fair value is assessed to be £296 000. There is then a revaluation increase of £11 000. The first journal entry is to write off any accumulated depreciation at the point of revaluation:

Accumulated Depreciation – Plant A Plant A (Write down Plant A to its carrying amount)	Dr Cr	15 000	 15 000

The second journal entry recognises the increase in other comprehensive income:

Plant A Gain on Revaluation of Plant (OCI) (Revaluation of Plant A from carrying amount of £285 000 to fair value of £296 000)	Dr Cr	11 000	 11 000

The third entry recognises the tax effect of the gain:

Gain on Revaluation of Plant (OCI) Deferred Tax Liability (Tax effect of gain on revaluation of plant)	Dr Cr	3 300	 3 300

The fourth entry accumulates the after-tax gain in equity, in the asset revaluation surplus account:

Gain on Revaluation of Plant (OCI) Asset Revaluation Surplus – Plant A (Accumulation of net revaluation gain in equity)	Dr Cr	7 700	 7 700

Assets are revalued by class. However, accounting for revaluations is on an asset-by-asset basis. It is therefore important to associate any revaluation surplus with the asset that created that surplus. Accordingly, in the above entry the surplus is associated with Plant A.

With Plant B, the carrying amount at 31 December is £171 000 (i.e. £180 000 − £9000). The fair value is assessed to be £168 000. The revaluation decrease is £3000. This amount is recognised as a loss in current period profit or loss.

Accumulated Depreciation – Plant B Plant B (Write down Plant B to its carrying amount)	Dr Cr	9 000	 9 000
Loss on Revaluation of Plant (P/L) Plant B (Revaluation of Plant B from carrying amount of £171 000 to fair value of £168 000)	Dr Cr	3 000	 3 000

Furniture is measured under the cost model. Depreciation for the 6-month period is calculated based on an allocation of the cost over a 5-year period:

Depreciation Expense – Furniture A Accumulated Depreciation (Depreciation, $\frac{1}{5} \times \frac{1}{2} \times £60\,000$)	Dr Cr	6 000	 6 000
Depreciation Expense – Furniture B Accumulated Depreciation (Depreciation, $\frac{1}{5} \times \frac{1}{2} \times £50\,000$)	Dr Cr	5 000	 5 000

The carrying amount of Furniture B at 31 December is £45 000 (i.e. £50 000 − £5000). The recoverable amount is £40 000. The asset is written down to recoverable amount, with the write-down being added to the accumulated depreciation account, and reported as an impairment loss.

Impairment Loss – Furniture B	Dr	5 000	
Accumulated Depreciation and Impairment Losses – Furniture B	Cr		5 000
(Write-down of asset to recoverable amount)			

At 30 June, depreciation is recorded for plant assets based on an allocation of the fair values at 31 December 2014.

June 30	Depreciation Expense – Plant A	Dr	18 500	
	Accumulated Depreciation	Cr		18 500
	(Depreciation, $1/8 \times 1/2 \times £296\,000$)			
	Depreciation Expense – Plant B	Dr	10 500	
	Accumulated Depreciation	Cr		10 500
	(Depreciation, $1/8 \times 1/2 \times £168\,000$)			

The fair value of Plant A is assessed to be £274 000. Since the carrying amount is £277 500 (i.e. £296 000 – £18 500), there is a revaluation decrease of £3500. Before recognising any expense on the revaluation decrease, there needs to be a reversal of the effects of any previous revaluation increase. For Plant A, at 31 December 2014, there was a revaluation increase of £11 000 which resulted in the recording of a £3300 deferred tax liability and a £7700 asset revaluation surplus. Hence, with the revaluation decrease of £3500, the normal adjustment would be to debit the deferred tax liability with £1050 (being 30% × £3500) and debit the asset revaluation surplus with £2450 (being 70% × £3500). However, because of the bonus dividend, the balance in the asset revaluation surplus for Plant A is only £2100 (i.e. £7700 – £5600). There is a deficiency of £350 in relation to the surplus.

The required journal entries at 30 June 2015 for Plant A are:
- *the elimination of the accumulated depreciation account:*

Accumulated Depreciation – Plant A	Dr	18 500	
Plant A	Cr		18 500
(Write down Plant A to its carrying amount)			

- *the recognition of the revaluation decrease in other comprehensive income:*

Loss on Revaluation of Plant (OCI)	Dr	3 500	
Plant A	Cr		3 500
(Revaluation of Plant A from carrying £277 500 to fair value of £274 000)			

- *the tax effect of the revaluation write-down:*

Deferred Tax Liability	Dr	1 050	
Loss on Revaluation of Plant (OCI)	Cr		1 050
(Tax effect of loss on revaluation of plant)			

- *the accumulation of the loss on revaluation to equity:*

Asset Revaluation Surplus – Plant A	Dr	2 450	
Loss on Revaluation of Plant (OCI)	Cr		2 450
(Accumulation of revaluation loss to equity)			

For Plant B, the carrying amount is £157 500 (i.e. £168 000 – £10 500). The fair value is £161 500. There is a revaluation increase of £4000. The accounting for this increase requires a reversal of any prior decrease. With Plant B at 31 December 2014, an expense of £3000 was recognised as a result of a revaluation decrease. The reversal of the previous decrease requires the recognition of income of £3000. The £1000 balance of the current increase (i.e. £4000 – £3000) is accounted for as other comprehensive income with a deferred tax liability and asset revaluation surplus being recognised.

The required journal entries for Plant B are:
- *the elimination of the accumulated depreciation account:*

Accumulated Depreciation – Plant B	Dr	10 500
Plant B	Cr	10 500
(Write down Plant B to its carrying amount)		

- *the recognition of both a gain in profit or loss (for the reversal of the prior decrease) and a gain in other comprehensive income on the revaluation of Plant B:*

Plant B	Dr	4 000
Gain on Revaluation of Plant (OCI)	Cr	1 000
Gain on Revaluation of Plant (P/L)	Cr	3 000
(Recognition of revaluation increase in profit or loss and other comprehensive income)		

- *Tax effect of revaluation gain:*

Gain on Revaluation of Plant (OCI)	Dr	300
Deferred Tax Liability	Cr	300
(Tax effect of gain on revaluation of plant)		

- *accumulation of the revaluation gain in equity:*

Gain on Revaluation of Plant (OCI)	Dr	700
Asset Revaluation Surplus – Plant B	Cr	700
(Accumulation of net revaluation gain in equity)		

Furniture at cost is depreciated for the final 6 months of the year.

Depreciation Expense – Furniture A	Dr	6 000
Accumulated Depreciation	Cr	6 000
(Depreciation, $\frac{1}{5} \times \frac{1}{2} \times £60\,000$)		
Depreciation Expense – Furniture B	Dr	5 000
Accumulated Depreciation	Cr	5 000
(Depreciation, $\frac{1}{5} \times \frac{1}{2} \times £40\,000$)		

Discussion questions

1. How should items of property, plant and equipment be measured at point of initial recognition, and would gifts be treated differently from acquisitions?
2. How is cost determined?
3. What choices of measurement model exist subsequent to assets being initially recognised?
4. What factors should entities consider in choosing alternative measurement models?
5. What is meant by 'depreciation expense'?
6. How is useful life determined?
7. What is meant by 'residual value' of an asset?
8. Should accounting for revaluation increases and decreases be done on an asset-by-asset basis or on a class-of-assets basis?
9. What differences occur between asset-by-asset or class-of-asset bases in accounting for revaluation increases and decreases?
10. When should property, plant and equipment be derecognised?

References

Accounting Standards Board 1996, 'Measurement of tangible fixed assets', discussion paper, www.frc.org.uk.

Marks & Spencer plc 2014, *Annual Report*, http://corporate.marksandspencer.com/investors/reports-results-and-presentations.

International Accounting Standards Board 2011, IASB documents published to accompany International Accounting Standard 1 *Presentation of Financial Statements*, IASB, www.ifrs.org.

International Accounting Standards Board 2014, IAS 16 *Property, plant & equipment*, www.ifrs.org.

Exercises   STAR RATING ★ BASIC ★★ MODERATE ★★★ DIFFICULT

Exercise 11.1 | FAIR VALUE BASIS FOR MEASUREMENT

★ The management of an entity has decided to use the fair value basis for the measurement of its equipment. Some of this equipment is very hard to obtain and has in fact increased in value over the current period. Management is arguing that, as there has been no decline in fair value, no depreciation should be charged on these pieces of equipment. Discuss.

Exercise 11.2 | ANNUAL DEPRECIATION CHARGE

★ A company is in the movie rental business. Movies are generally kept for 2 years and then either sold or destroyed. However, management wants to show increased profits, and believes that the annual depreciation charge can be lowered by keeping the movies for 3 years. Discuss.

Exercise 11.3 | REVALUATION OF ASSETS

★ In the 30 June 2014 annual report of Sonner Ltd, the equipment was reported as follows:

Equipment (at cost)	£ 500 000
Accumulated Depreciation	(150 000)
	350 000

The equipment consisted of two machines, Machine A and Machine B. Machine A had cost £300 000 and had a carrying amount of £180 000 at 30 June 2014, and Machine B had cost £200 000 and was carried at £170 000. Both machines are measured using the cost model, and depreciated on a straight-line basis over a 10-year period.

On 31 December 2014, the directors of Sonner Ltd decided to change the basis of measuring the equipment from the cost model to the revaluation model. Machine A was revalued to £180 000 with an expected useful life of 6 years, and Machine B was revalued to £155 000 with an expected useful life of 5 years.

At 30 June 2015, Machine A was assessed to have a fair value of £163 000 with an expected useful life of 5 years, and Machine B's fair value was £136 500 with an expected useful life of 4 years.

The tax rate is 30%.

Required

1. Prepare the journal entries during the period 1 July 2014 to 30 June 2015 in relation to the equipment.
2. According to accounting standards, on what basis may management change the method of asset measurement, for example from cost to fair value?

Exercise 11.4 | STRAIGHT-LINE DEPRECIATION VS DIMINISHING-BALANCE DEPRECIATION

★★ Asia Ltd uses tractors as a part of its operating equipment, and it applies the straight-line depreciation method to depreciate these assets. Asia Ltd has just taken over Pacific Ltd, which uses similar tractors in its operations. However, Pacific Ltd has been using a diminishing-balance method of depreciation for these tractors. The accountant in Asia Ltd is arguing that for both entities the same depreciation method should be used for tractors. Provide arguments for and against this proposal.

| Exercise 11.5 | **DEPRECIATION CHARGES** |

★★ A new accountant has been appointed to Dettum Ltd and has implemented major changes in the calculation of depreciation. As a result, some parts of the factory have much larger depreciation charges. This has incensed some operations managers who believe that, as they take particular care with the maintenance of their machines, their machines should not attract large depreciation charges that reduce the profitability of their operations and reflect badly on their management skills. The operations managers plan to meet the accountant and ask for change. How should the new accountant respond?

| Exercise 11.6 | **EXPENSING OF COSTS** |

★★ Mehna Ltd has acquired a new building for £500 000. It has incurred incidental costs of £10 000 in the acquisition process for legal fees, real estate agent's fees and stamp duties. Management believes that these costs should be expensed because they have not increased the value of the building and, if the building was immediately resold, these amounts would not be recouped. In other words, the fair value of the building is considered to still be £500 000. Discuss how these costs should be accounted for.

| Exercise 11.7 | **DEPRECIATION** |

★★ Plaaz Ltd was formed on 1 July 2012 to provide delivery services for packages to be taken between the city and the airport. On this date, the company acquired a delivery truck from Frensdorf Trucks. The company paid cash of £50 000 to Frensdorf Trucks, which included government charges of £600 and registration of £400. Insurance costs for the first year amounted to £1200. The truck is expected to have a useful life of 5 years. At the end of the useful life, the asset is expected to be sold for £24 000, with costs relating to the sale amounting to £400.

The company went extremely well in its first year, and the management of Plaaz Ltd decided at 1 July 2013 to add another vehicle, a flat-top, to the fleet. This vehicle was acquired from a liquidation auction at a cash price of £30 000. The vehicle needed some repairs for the elimination of rust (cost £2300), major servicing to the engine (cost £480) and the replacement of all tyres (cost £620). The company believed it would use the flat-top for another 2 years and then sell it. Expected selling price was £15 000, with selling costs estimated to be £400. On 1 July 2013, both vehicles were fitted out with a radio communication system at a cost per vehicle of £300. This was not expected to have any material effect on the future selling price of either vehicle. Insurance costs for the 2013–14 period were £1200 for the first vehicle and £900 for the newly acquired vehicle.

All went well for the company except that, on 1 August 2014, the flat-top that had been acquired at auction broke down. Plaaz Ltd thought about acquiring a new vehicle to replace this one but, after considering the costs, decided to repair the flat-top instead. The vehicle was given a major overhaul at a cost of £6500. Although this was a major expense, management believed that the company would keep the vehicle for another 2 years. The estimated selling price in 3 years' time is £12 000, with selling costs estimated at £300. Insurance costs for the 2014–15 period were the same as for the previous year.

Required

Prepare the journal entries for the recording of the vehicles and the depreciation of the vehicles for each of the 3 years. The financial year ends on 30 June.

| Exercise 11.8 | **DEPRECIATION** |

★★ Red Sun Ltd constructed a building for use by the administration section of the company. The completion date was 1 July 2007, and the construction cost was £840 000. The company expected to remain in the building for the next 20 years, at which time the building would probably have no real salvage value and have to be demolished. It is expected that demolition costs will amount to £15 000. In December 2013, following some severe weather in the city, the roof of the administration building was considered to be in poor shape so the company decided to replace it. On 1 July 2014, a new roof was installed at a cost of £220 000. The new roof was of a different material to the old roof, which was estimated to have cost only £140 000 in the original construction, although at the time of construction it was thought that the roof would last for the 20 years that the company expected to use the building. Because the company had spent the money replacing the roof, it thought that it would delay construction of a new building, thereby extending the original life of the building from 20 years to 25 years.

Required

Discuss how you would account for the depreciation of the building and how the replacement of the roof would affect the depreciation calculations.

REVALUATION OF ASSETS AND TAX-EFFECT ACCOUNTING

★★ Farida Ltd acquired a machine on 1 July 2012 at a cost of £100 000. The machine has an expected useful life of 5 years, and the company adopts the straight-line basis of depreciation. The tax depreciation rate for this type of machine is 12.5% p.a. The company tax rate is 30%.

Farida Ltd measures this asset at fair value. Movements in fair values are as follows:

30 June 2013	$85 000	Remaining useful life: 4 years
30 June 2014	60 000	Remaining useful life: 3 years
30 June 2015	45 000	

Owing to a change in economic conditions, Farida Ltd sold the machine for £45000 on 30 June 2015. The asset was revalued to fair value immediately before the sale.

Required

1. Provide the journal entries used to account for this machine over the period 2012 to 2015.
2. For each of the 3 years ended 30 June 2013, 2014 and 2015, calculate the carrying amount and the tax base of the asset, and determine the appropriate tax-effect entry in relation to the machine. Explain your answer.

ACQUISITION AND SALE OF ASSETS, DEPRECIATION

★★ Thader Turf Farm owned the following items of property, plant and equipment as at 30 June 2014:

Land (at cost)		£120 000
Office building (at cost)	150 000	
Accumulated depreciation	(23 375)	126 625
Turf cutter (at cost)	65 000	
Accumulated depreciation	(42 367)	22 633
Water desalinator (at fair value)		189 000

Additional information (at 30 June 2014)

(a) The straight-line method of depreciation is used for all depreciable items of property, plant and equipment. Depreciation is charged to the nearest month and all figures are rounded to the nearest pound.
(b) The office building was constructed on 1 April 2010. Its estimated useful life is 20 years and it has an estimated residual value of £40 000.
(c) The turf cutter was purchased on 21 January 2011, at which date it had an estimated useful life of 5 years and an estimated residual value of £3200.
(d) The water desalinator was purchased and installed on 2 July 2013 at a cost of £200 000. On 30 June 2014, the plant was revalued upwards by £7000 to its fair value on that day. Additionally, its useful life and residual value were re-estimated to 9 years and £18000 respectively.

The following transactions occurred during the year ended 30 June 2015:

(*Note:* All payments are made in cash.)

(e) On 10 August 2014, new irrigation equipment was purchased from Pond Supplies for £37 000. On 16 August 2014, the business paid £500 to have the equipment delivered to the turf farm. Thomas Schwazer was contracted to install and test the new system. In the course of installation, pipes worth £800 were damaged and subsequently replaced on 3 September. The irrigation system was fully operational by 19 September and Thomas Schwazer was paid £9600 for his services. The system has an estimated useful life of 4 years and a residual value of £0.
(f) On 1 December 2014, the turf cutter was traded in on a new model worth £80 000. A trade-in allowance of £19 000 was received and the balance paid in cash. The new machine's useful life and residual value were estimated at 6 years and £5000 respectively.
(g) On 1 January 2015, the turf farm's owner Helmut Dorf decided to extend the office building by adding three new offices and a meeting room. The extension work started on 2 February and was completed by 28 March at a cost of £49 000. The extension is expected to increase the useful life of the building by 4 years and increase its residual value by £5000.
(h) On 30 June 2015, depreciation expense for the year was recorded. The fair value of the water desalination plant was £165 000.

Required

(Show all workings and round amounts to the nearest pound.)

Prepare general journal entries to record the transactions and events for the reporting period ended 30 June 2015 (narrations are not required).

REVALUATION OF ASSETS

★★ On 1 July 2012, Themar Ltd acquired two assets within the same class of plant and equipment. Information on these assets is as follows:

	Cost	Expected useful life
Machine A	£100 000	5 years
Machine B	60 000	3 years

The machines are expected to generate benefits evenly over their useful lives. The class of plant and equipment is measured using fair value.

At 30 June 2013, information about the assets is as follows:

	Fair value	Expected useful life
Machine A	£84 000	4 years
Machine B	38 000	2 years

On 1 January 2014, Machine B was sold for £29 000 cash. On the same day, Themar Ltd acquired Machine C for £80 000 cash. Machine C has an expected useful life of 4 years. Themar Ltd also made a bonus issue of 10 000 shares at £1 per share, using £8000 from the general reserve and £2000 from the asset revaluation surplus created as a result of measuring Machine A at fair value.

At 30 June 2014, information on the machines is as follows:

	Fair value	Expected useful life
Machine A	£61 000	3 years
Machine C	68 500	3.5 years

The income tax rate is 30%.

Required

Prepare the journal entries in the records of Themar Ltd to record the described events over the period 1 July 2012 to 30 June 2014, assuming the ends of the reporting periods are 30 June 2013 and 30 June 2014.

ACQUISITIONS, DISPOSALS, TRADE-INS, OVERHAULS, DEPRECIATION

★★ Axel Schulz is the owner of Wremen Fishing Charters. The business's final trial balance on 30 June 2012 (end of the reporting period) included the following balances:

Processing Plant (at cost, purchased 4 April 2010)	$148 650
Accumulated Depreciation — Processing plant	(81 274)
Charter Boats	291 200
Accumulated Depreciation — Boats	188 330

The following boats were owned at 30 June 2012:

Boat	Purchase date	Cost	Estimated useful life	Estimated residual value
1	23 February 2008	$62 000	5 years	$3 000
2	9 September 2008	$66 400	5 years	$3 400
3	6 February 2009	$78 600	4 years	$3 600
4	20 April 2010	$84 200	6 years	$3 800

Additional information

Wremen Fishing Charters calculates depreciation to the nearest month using straight-line depreciation for all assets except the processing plant, which is depreciated at 30% on the diminishing-balance method. Amounts are recorded to the nearest pound.

Part A

The following transactions and events occurred during the year ended 30 June 2013:

2012 July 26	Traded in Boat 1 for a new boat (Boat 5) which cost £84 100. A trade-in allowance of £8900 was received and the balance was paid in cash. Registration and stamp duty costs of £1500 were also paid in cash. Axel Schulz estimated Boat 5's useful life and residual value at 6 years and £4120 respectively.
Dec. 4	Overhauled the processing plant at a cash cost of £62 660. As the modernisation significantly expanded the plant's operating capacity and efficiency, Axel Schulz decided to revise the depreciation rate to 25%.
2013 Feb. 6	Boat 3 reached the end of its useful life but no buyer could be found, so the boat was scrapped.
June 30	Recorded depreciation.

Required

Prepare general journal entries (narrations are required) to record the transactions and events for the year ended 30 June 2013.

Part B

On 26 March, Axel Schulz was offered fish-finding equipment with a fair value of £9500 in exchange for Boat 2. The fish-finder originally cost its owner £26600 and had a carrying value of £9350 at the date of offer. The fair value of Boat 2 was £9100.

Required

If Axel Schulz accepts the exchange offer, what amount would the business use to record the acquisition of the fish-finding equipment? Why? Justify your answer by reference to the requirements of IAS 16 relating to the initial recognition of a property, plant and equipment item.

Exercise 11.13 REVALUATION OF ASSETS AND TAX-EFFECT ACCOUNTING

★★★ For Chartres Ltd, profit before income tax for the year ended 30 June 2013 amounted to £375 000, including the following expenses:

Depreciation of plant	£50 000
Goodwill impairment*	13 000
Long-service leave	40 000
Holiday pay	30 000
Doubtful debts	55 000
Entertainment*	12 000
Depreciation of furniture	5 000
*Non-deductible for taxation	

The statement of financial position of Chartres Ltd at 30 June 2012 and 2013 showed the assets and liabilities of the company as follows:

Assets	2012	2013
Cash	£ 73 000	£ 82 000
Inventory	127 000	158 000
Receivables	430 000	585 000
Allowance for doubtful debts	(20 000)	(40 000)
Plant (net)	350 000	320 000
Furniture (net)	75 000	65 000
Goodwill	63 000	50 000
Deferred tax asset	21 000	?
Liabilities		
Payables	247 000	265 000
Provision for long-service leave	30 000	50 000
Provision for holiday pay	20 000	30 000
Deferred tax liability	11 250	?

Additional information

(a) Plant and furniture are different classes of assets. Both are measured at fair value. The furniture was revalued downward to £65 000 at 30 June 2013. Furniture had not previously been revalued upwards. Tax depreciation for the year ended 30 June 2013 was £7500, giving a carrying amount for tax purposes at 30 June 2013 of £55 000. The plant was revalued upwards at 30 June 2013 to £320 000. Tax depreciation on plant was £75 000, giving a carrying amount for tax purposes at 30 June 2013 of £250 000.

(b) Total bad debts written off for the 2012–13 year were £35 000.

(c) The tax rate is 30%.

Required

1. Calculate, by using worksheets, the amounts of income tax expense and current and deferred income tax assets/liabilities for the reporting period ended 30 June 2013.
2. Prepare the deferred tax asset and deferred tax liability accounts.

Exercise 11.14   **COST OF ACQUISITION**

★★★ Borod Ltd started business early in 2013. During its first 9 months, Borod Ltd acquired real estate for the construction of a building and other facilities. Operating equipment was purchased and installed, and the company began operating activities in October 2013. The company's accountant, who was not sure how to record some of the transactions, opened a Property ledger account and recorded debits and (credits) to this account as follows.

(a)	Cost of real estate purchased as a building site	£ 170 000
(b)	Paid architect's fee for design of new building	23 000
(c)	Paid for demolition of old building on building site purchased in (a)	28 000
(d)	Paid land tax on the real estate purchased as a building site in (a)	1 700
(e)	Paid excavation costs for the new building	15 000
(f)	Made the first payment to the building contractor	250 000
(g)	Paid for equipment to be installed in the new building	148 000
(h)	Received from sale of salvaged materials from demolishing the old building	(6 800)
(i)	Made final payment to the building contractor	350 000
(j)	Paid interest on building loan during construction	22 000
(k)	Paid freight on equipment purchased	1 900
(l)	Paid installation costs of equipment	4 200
(m)	Paid for repair of equipment damaged during installation	2 700
	Property ledger account balance	£1 009 700

Required

1. Prepare a schedule with the following column headings. Analyse each transaction, enter the payment or receipt in the appropriate column, and total each column.

Item no.	Land	Land Improvements	Building	Manufacturing equipment	Other

2. Prepare the journal entry to close the £1 009 700 balance of the Property ledger account.

Depreciation is an inter-period allocation method that is subject to considerable managerial discretion. It is therefore interesting to learn whether it could be relevant to users of financial statements. Barth et al. (2001) argue that if investments in depreciable assets generate total cash flows in excess of cost, the annual depreciation should be positively associated with future operating cash flows. Their findings are broadly consistent with this prediction, although this does not hold in several industries analysed in this paper. In a more direct test of how investors perceive depreciation, Kang and Zhao (2010) find that annual changes in depreciation expense are not associated with stock returns. They also fail to find that accumulated depreciation is associated with stock prices. Therefore, taken together from these two papers, the evidence on the usefulness to investors of depreciation and accumulated depreciation is mixed.

IAS 16 permits companies to adopt the revaluation model for property, plant and equipment (PPE). Casual observation nevertheless suggests that fewer companies have revalued their PPE in recent years and that the method was more common prior to the adoption of IFRS® Standards. The research on revaluations therefore goes several years back. Easton et al. (1993) examine a sample of Australian companies that revalued their PPE in the 1980s. Based on interviews with the chief financial officers, the authors conjecture that revaluations are reported with the view to lower the debt-to-equity ratio in order to be seen as less leveraged. This opportunistic behaviour possibly contrasts with a motivation to give a 'true and fair view' of the financial statements, which was also highlighted as another reason for revaluations given by company officers. Consistent with information usefulness perspective, this paper documents a positive association between revaluation reserve (and changes in the reserve) and the market-to-book ratio. The documented association, however, is stronger for higher debt-to-equity firms. A potential explanation of this is that revaluing firms avoid violation of debt covenants and that the market perceives this as a beneficial outcome. However, stock returns are unrelated to the change in the revaluation reserve in almost all years examined. The latter may be explained by poor timeliness of revaluation disclosure.

Aboody et al. (1999) examine 347 UK firms that revalued their PPE upward during 1983–1995. They find that these have predictive ability with respect to 1–3-year ahead changes in operating income and changes in operating cash flows. Similar to Easton et al. (1993) they examine the association of revaluation information with stock prices and stock returns and find it is positive and significant. In additional analysis the authors find that their results are weaker for high debt-to-equity firms. This is suggestive of opportunistic revaluations. Notwithstanding the statistical significance of these results, they are somewhat hard to interpret. First, the authors do not outline the theoretical link between revaluations and future performance. Second, the exclusion of negative revaluations does not permit a more comprehensive view of the information role of revaluations. More recent analysis of revaluations of fixed assets is presented by Lopes and Walker (2012). They analyse 177 Brazilian firms that revalued their fixed assets during 1998–2004. Employing research design similar to Aboody et al. (1999) they find that future performance

is *negatively* related to revaluations. Furthermore they find that the revaluation balance is negatively related to share price and that the revaluation increment is negatively related to stock returns. An interpretation of these results is that Brazilian firms that anticipate deterioration in performance take a pre-emptive action to fortify their balance sheets.

The above-mentioned conflicting results may be explained, at least in part, by whether the revaluations are based on managers' estimates or external assessors' valuations. The latter may be perceived as more reliable estimates by investors. Barth and Clinch (1998) find in an Australian sample that revaluations of PPE by both internal directors and external appraisers are positively associated with stock prices. However, their evidence seems to suggest that this association is stronger for internal valuations. This is inconsistent with the notion that internal valuations are more prone to manipulations and is indicative of superior information held by insiders. Cotter and Richardson (2002) extend this analysis to model the choice of the appraiser, again using an Australian sample. Their analysis suggests that the likelihood of selecting an independent appraiser is negatively related to measures of a CEO's control of the board of directors. Cotter and Richardson (2002) then further examine if upward revaluations are followed by reversals, and whether this is dependent on appraiser type. They argue that reversals can be used as a measure of the reliability of the initial upward revaluation. For plant and equipment they find that independent revaluations are more reliable than internal revaluations. However, this result is not robust to an alternative measure of reliability.

Prior to the adoption of IFRS Standards it was required in the UK that fair values are recognised for investment property companies. Dietrich et al. (2001) argue that the reliability of fair values reported can be examined by reference to gains or losses booked when the properties are sold. If revaluations are good estimates of sale prices, one should not observe large losses or gains upon disposal of the properties. They examine a sample of 76 firms for the period 1988–1996 and find that, on average, disposals of investment properties entail a gain that is equivalent to 6% of the selling price. This is consistent with conservative fair value estimates used for revaluations. An alternative explanation is that managers select to sell assets that increased in value after the last revaluation. Dietrich et al. (2001) further find that annual revaluations are positively related to future debt issues, which is broadly consistent with the debt-related motivation identified by Easton et al. (1993). Muller and Riedl (2002) also employ a sample of UK investment property companies to investigate if the choice of internal vs. external appraiser is capable of reducing information asymmetry. They provide evidence from an analysis of bid–ask spreads that suggests valuations carried out by external appraisers reduce information asymmetry more than internal appraisers. This is indicative of higher accuracy of externally generated estimates.

There are only a few studies that directly examine reporting requirements set in IAS 16 and IAS 40. Muller et al. (2011) provide direct evidence as to the effect of mandating IAS 40 following the adoption of IFRS Standards on information asymmetry. In a sample of European investment property companies they find that companies that disclosed fair values of their investment properties prior to IFRS Standards did not benefit from a decline in information asymmetry. However, such a decline was observed for firms that disclosed the required information only following the adoption. This speaks as to the benefits to investors of disclosing fair value estimates of certain long-lived assets. Christensen and Nikolaev (2013) postulate that market forces are a factor in firms' choice whether to revalue their PPE when IFRS Standards offer this option. Specifically, they argue that the demand for revaluations is stronger in the UK than in Germany. They also conjecture that revaluations are more common for investment properties than PPE. They find that UK (German) firms are more likely to use fair value model (historical cost basis), but that in both countries investment property companies tend to use the fair value model more than companies from other industries.

References

Aboody, D., Barth, M. E., and Kasznik, R. 1999. Revaluations of fixed assets and future firm performance, evidence from the UK. *Journal of Accounting and Economics*, 26(1–3), 149–178.

Barth, M., and Clinch, G. 1998. Revalued financial, tangible, and intangible Assets: Associations with share prices and non-market based value estimates. *Journal of Accounting Research*, 36 (Supplement), 199–233.

Barth, M., Cram, D. P., and Nelson K. K. 2001. Accruals and the prediction of future cash flows. *The Accounting Review*, 76(1), 27–58.

Christensen, H. B., and Nikolaev, V. V. 2013. Does fair value accounting for non-financial assets pass the market test? *Review of Accounting Studies*, 18(3), 734–775.

Cotter, J., and Richardson, S. 2002. Reliability of asset revaluations: The impact of appraiser independence. *Review of Accounting Studies*, 7(4), 435–457.

Dietrich, D., Harris, M., and Muller, K. 2001. The reliability of investment property fair value estimates. *Journal of Accounting and Economics*, 30(2), 125–158.

Easton, P., Eddey, P., and Harris, T. 1993. An investigation of revaluations of tangible long-lived assets. *Journal of Accounting Research*, 31 (Supplement), 1–38.

Kang, S. H., and Zhao, Y. 2010. Information content and value relevance of depreciation: A cross-industry analysis. *The Accounting Review*, 85(1), 227–260.

Lopes, A. B., and Walker, M. 2012. Asset revaluations, future firm performance and firm-level corporate governance arrangements: New evidence from Brazil. *The British Accounting Review*, 44(2), 53–67.

Muller, K., and Riedl. E. 2002. External monitoring of property appraisal estimates and information asymmetry. *Journal of Accounting Research*, 40(3), 865–881.

Muller, K., Riedl, E., and Sellhorn, T. 2011. Mandatory fair value accounting and information asymmetry: Evidence from the European real estate industry. *Management Science*, 57(6), 1138–1153.

12 Leases

ACCOUNTING STANDARDS IN FOCUS

IAS 17 *Leases*

LEARNING OBJECTIVES

After studying this chapter, you should be able to:

1. discuss the characteristics of a lease
2. explain the difference between a finance lease and an operating lease
3. understand and apply the guidance necessary to classify leases
4. account for finance leases from the perspective of a lessee
5. account for finance leases from the perspective of a lessor
6. account for finance leases by manufacturer or dealer lessors
7. account for operating leases from the perspective of both lessors and lessees
8. recognise and account for sale and leaseback transactions
9. discuss the 2016 changes to lease accounting.

INTRODUCTION

The rapid growth of leasing as a means of gaining access to the economic benefits embodied in assets during the 1970s led to a concern among standard setters worldwide that the credibility of financial reports was compromised by extensive use of such 'off-balance-sheet' arrangements. Accordingly, the 1980s saw the issue of leasing standards by both international and national standard-setting bodies. These standards adopted similar accounting treatments based on the premise that, when a lease transfers substantially all of the risks and rewards incidental to ownership to the lessee, that lease is in substance equivalent to the acquisition of an asset on credit by the lessee, and to a sale or financing by the lessor (i.e. a 'finance lease'). The mandatory recognition of the asset/liability relating to a finance lease is justified by two arguments put forth in IAS 17 *Leases*.

First:

> Although the legal form of a lease agreement is that the lessee may acquire no legal title to the leased asset, in the case of finance leases the substance and financial reality are that the lessee acquires the economic benefits of the use of the leased asset for the major part of its economic life in return for entering into an obligation to pay for that right an amount approximating, at the inception of the lease, the fair value of the asset and the related finance charge (paragraph 21).

Second:

> If such lease transactions are not reflected in the lessee's statement of financial position, the economic resources and the level of obligations of an entity are understated, thereby distorting financial ratios (paragraph 22).

Interestingly, these justifications for the recognition of lease assets and liabilities make no reference to the *Conceptual Framework* definitions and recognition criteria, but concentrate on the substance of the exchange of benefits and the reliability of financial information. This rationale seems to view a finance lease transaction as the quasi-purchase of an asset, in the sense that an entity records the acquisition of an asset even though no transfer of legal title takes place.

The leasing standards have remained essentially unchanged over time even though there were many calls for major change. In 2006, the International Accounting Standards Board (IASB®) and the Financial Accounting Standards Board in the United States each decided to add a leasing project to its respective agenda, but those projects would be undertaken jointly. In March 2009, the IASB and the FASB issued a discussion paper entitled *Leases — Preliminary Views*. In August 2010, the IASB and FASB issued nearly identical exposure drafts (EDs) of a proposed, converged new standard on leases. As a result of comments received on the ED and after redeliberations, the IASB and the FASB issued a second ED in May 2013. Rede-liberations on the second ED took place in 2014 and 2015 with the IASB and the FASB reaching different decisions relating to lease classification and the recognition, measurement and presentation of leases for lessees and lessors. The IASB issued its new standard, IFRS 16 *Leases*, in 2016. IFRS 16 is effective from 1 January 2019, with limited early application permitted. The FASB also issued its new leases standard in 2016.

 ## 12.1 WHAT IS A LEASE?

IAS 17 paragraph 4 defines a lease as:

> an agreement whereby the lessor conveys to the lessee in return for a payment or series of payments the right to use an asset for an agreed period of time.

Thus, under a lease agreement the lessee acquires, not the asset itself, but the *right* to use the asset for a set time. Lease agreements may also result in the eventual transfer of ownership from lessor to lessee. For example, under a hire purchase agreement, the lessee will use the asset while paying for its acquisition. The agreed period of time may vary from a short period, such as the daily hire of a motor vehicle, to a longer period, such as the rental of office space by a company. The key feature of a lease is the existence of an asset owned by one party (the lessor) but used, for some or all of its economic life, by another party (the lessee).

IFRIC® Interpretation 4 *Determining whether an Arrangement contains a Lease* (IFRIC 4 paragraph 1) was issued to assist account preparers in determining whether arrangements that are not in the legal form of a lease may in fact convey the right to use an item for an agreed period of time in return for a series of payments, and should, therefore, be treated as a lease for accounting purposes. Such arrangements may include:

- outsourcing arrangements . . .
- arrangements in the telecommunications industry, in which suppliers of network capacity enter into contracts to provide purchasers with rights to capacity
- take-or-pay contracts, in which purchasers must make specified payments regardless of whether they take delivery of the contracted products or services.

The assessment of whether an arrangement contains a lease must be done at the inception of the arrangement using the information available at that time. If the provisions of the arrangement are subsequently changed, a reassessment will be made. Under IFRIC 4 paragraph 6, an arrangement contains a lease if:

(a) fulfilment of the arrangement is dependent on the use of a specific asset or assets (the asset); and
(b) the arrangement conveys a right to use the asset.

IFRIC 4 uses an illustrative example of a purchaser who enters into a take-or-pay arrangement with an industrial gas supplier. If that supplier provides the gas from a plant that is built on the purchaser's premises, to the purchaser's specifications and is used solely to provide gas under the arrangement then, applying the above criteria, the arrangement contains a lease of the gas plant.

If an arrangement contains a lease component, then that part of the arrangement must be segregated and accounted for in accordance with IAS 17. This would require classification as an operating or finance lease at the inception of the arrangement. Payments made under the arrangement would need to be separated into lease payments and payments for other services based on their relative fair values, as specified in IFRIC 4.

Service agreements relating to the provision of services, such as cleaning or maintenance, between two parties are not regarded as leases because the contract does not involve the use of an asset. These agreements are regarded as executory contracts (addressed in sections 12.3.2 and 12.5.2) — that is, both parties are still to perform to an equal degree the actions required by the contract. Thus, each party is regarded as having a right and obligation to participate in a future exchange or, alternatively, to compensate or be compensated for the consequences of not doing so. A cleaning contract entitles an entity to receive cleaning services on a regular basis and creates an obligation to pay for those services after they have been received. The key issue is the performance of the service. Until the cleaning services are delivered, the contract is merely an exchange of promises, not of future economic benefits. The existence of a non-cancellable service agreement or one that includes significant penalties for non-performance may, however, result in the service recipient acquiring control over future economic benefits (the right to receive cleaning services) that are likely to be delivered and can be reliably measured — in other words, an asset.

12.1.1 Scope of application of IAS 17

IAS 17 excludes the following types of arrangements from its scope:
- lease agreements to explore for or use minerals, oil, natural gas and similar non-regenerative resources
- licensing agreements for such items as motion picture films, video recordings, plays, manuscripts, patents and copyrights.

No explanation is given for the exclusion of resource exploitation rights and licensing agreements, which means that the standard is generally applied only to leases for assets with physical substance. An agreement allowing a licensee to use a patented process provides future economic benefits to that licensee and meets the *Conceptual Framework's* definition of an asset in just the same way as a motor vehicle lease. The exclusion of these agreements from the scope of IAS 17 is difficult to justify other than by citing the fact that the standard 'applies to agreements that transfer the right to use assets' (IAS 17 paragraph 3), not the right of access, which is generally the right that is conveyed in non-exclusive license agreements. Presumably, the expectation when IAS 17 was issued was that accounting standards on extractive industries, self-generating and renewable assets and intangibles would deal with leases of this type.

Additionally, the standard must not be applied as the basis of measurement for leased investment properties or leased biological assets, because the measurement requirements for such assets are contained in IAS 40 *Investment Property* and IAS 41 *Agriculture*, respectively.

12.2 CLASSIFICATION OF LEASES

IAS 17 requires both lessees and lessors to classify each lease arrangement as either an *operating lease* or a *finance lease* and to make this classification at the inception of the lease. 'Inception' is defined as 'the earlier of the date of the lease agreement and the date of commitment by the parties to the principal provisions of the lease' (IAS 17 paragraph 4). This classification process is vitally important because the accounting treatment and disclosures prescribed by the standard for each type of lease differ significantly.

A finance lease is defined as 'a lease that transfers substantially all the risks and rewards incidental to ownership of an asset. Title may or may not eventually be transferred' (IAS 17 paragraph 4). An operating lease is simply defined as 'a lease other than a finance lease' (IAS 17 paragraph 4).

The key criterion of a finance lease is the transfer of substantially all the risks and rewards without a transfer of ownership. The classification process, therefore, consists of two steps. First, the potential rewards and potential risks associated with the asset must be identified. Second, the lease agreement must be analysed to determine the nature and extent of the rewards and risks transferred from the lessor to the lessee.

The *risks* of ownership include:
- unsatisfactory performance, with the asset unable to provide benefits or service at the expected level or quality
- obsolescence, particularly with regard to the development of more technically advanced items
- idle capacity
- decline in residual value or losses on eventual sale of the asset
- uninsured damage and condemnation of the asset.

The *rewards* include:
- any benefits obtained from using the asset to provide benefit or service to the entity
- appreciation in residual value or gains on the eventual sale of the asset.

The risks and rewards relating to movements in realisable value are the most difficult to transfer without transferring the title. If the leased asset is to be returned to the lessor, then the risk of an adverse movement in realisable value has not been transferred unless the lessee guarantees some or all of the value of the asset at the end of the lease term.

 ## 12.3 CLASSIFICATION GUIDANCE

IAS 17 (paragraph 10) provides examples of situations that individually or in combination would normally lead to a lease transaction being classified as a finance lease:

(a) the lease transfers ownership of the asset by the end of the lease term;
(b) the lessee has the option to purchase the asset at a price that is expected to be sufficiently lower than the fair value at the date the option becomes exercisable for it to be reasonably certain that the option will be exercised;
(c) the lease term is for the major part of the economic life of the asset even if title is not transferred;
(d) at the inception of the lease, the present value of the minimum lease payments amounts to substantially all of the fair value of the leased asset; and
(e) the leased assets are of such a specialised nature that only the lessee can use them without major modification.

IAS 17 paragraph 11 also provides indicators of situations that individually or in combination also could lead to a lease being classified as a finance lease:

(a) if the lessee can cancel the lease, the lessor's losses associated with the cancellation are borne by the lessee;
(b) gains or losses from the fluctuation in the fair value of the residual accrue to the lessee; and
(c) the lessee has the ability to continue the lease for a secondary period at a rental that is substantially less than market rent.

Note that these examples and indicators are guidelines in assessing whether substantially all the risks and rewards are transferred. Each example or indicator then relates to some measure of risk or reward. Although not described in IAS 17 as such, the examples and indicators are often referred to as lease classification 'tests'. Unlike the application of similar tests in US GAAP, the existence of only one of the examples or indicators would not necessarily result in a lease being classified as a finance lease except when:

- the ownership of the leased asset transfers to the lessee (example (a) above); or
- the lessee is reasonably certain to exercise an option to purchase the underlying asset (example (b) above).

Throughout this chapter, the examples and indicators (hereinafter referred to as 'guidelines') have been restated as eight questions, as represented in figure 12.1, to aid in classifying lease arrangements as either operating leases or finance leases.

Therefore when classifying leases, account preparers will need to examine three main conditions of the lease agreement:

- whether the lease transfers ownership of the underlying asset to the lessee by the end of the lease term;
- whether the lessee is reasonably certain to exercise an option to purchase the underlying asset; and
- whether the lease otherwise transfers substantially all the risks and rewards incidental to ownership of the underlying asset.

IAS 17 does not define the terms 'major part' (example (c) above) or 'substantially all' (example (d) above) or prescribe classification criteria. This is left as a judgement call. By omitting quantitative examples, the IASB has placed the classification decision back in the hands of account preparers, who must decide what is 'major' and 'substantially all' for their entity and particular circumstances. The disadvantage of this approach is that similar or even identical lease agreements may be classified differently because of varying interpretations of what the terms 'major part' and 'substantially all' mean.

12.3.1 Lease term

An important element in the classification process is to determine the term of the lease. The lease term is defined in IAS 17 paragraph 4 as:

> the non-cancellable period for which the lessee has contracted to lease the asset together with any further terms for which the lessee has the option to continue to lease the asset, with or without further payment, when at the inception of the lease it is reasonably certain that the lessee will exercise the option.

A non-cancellable lease locks both parties into the agreement and ensures that the exchange of risks and rewards will occur. The definition of a non-cancellable lease provided in IAS 17 deems cancellable leases with the following characteristics to be 'non-cancellable':

- leases that can be cancelled only upon the occurrence of some remote contingency
- leases that can be cancelled only with the permission of the lessor

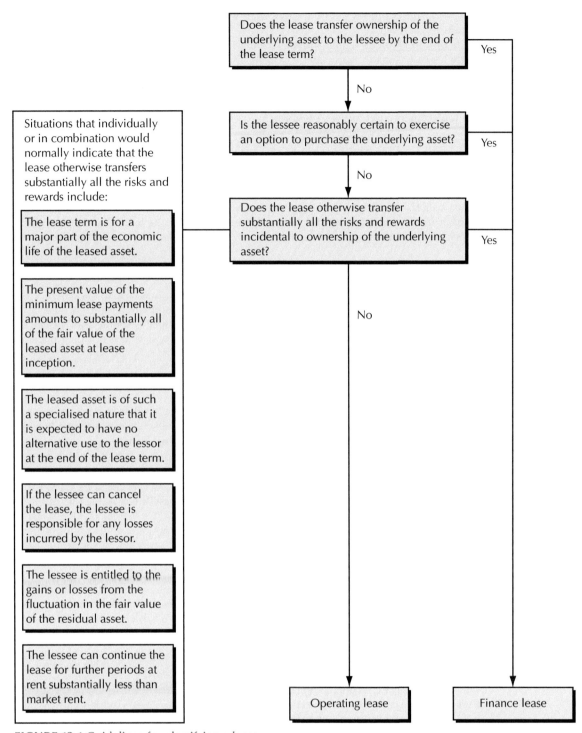

FIGURE 12.1 Guidelines for classifying a lease

- leases in which the lessee, upon cancellation, is committed to enter into a further lease for the same or equivalent asset with the same lessor
- leases that provide that the lessee, upon cancellation, incurs a penalty large enough to discourage cancellation in normal circumstances.

A careful examination of the lease agreement is necessary to ensure that cancellable leases are correctly designated.

IAS 17 does not define 'reasonably certain'. The assessment of whether the lessee is reasonably certain to exercise an option to extend a lease beyond the initial non-cancellable period of the lease is not based on the lessee's intentions or past practice. Instead, it is based on facts and circumstances at lease inception relevant to the decision the lessee will make to exercise or not to exercise the option.

Following are examples of circumstances in which an option to extend a lease is considered reasonably certain of exercise:

- the option is priced significantly below market
- the lessee has made significant leasehold improvements to the asset that are expected to have significant economic value when the option to extend becomes exercisable
- the design of the asset and/or the location of the asset is specialised for the lessee such that the costs associated with identifying another asset or location and costs associated with negotiating and securing a replacement asset are not economic.

12.3.2 Lease classification guidelines

Does the lease transfer ownership of the underlying asset to the lessee by the end of the lease term?

When ownership of the underlying asset transfers to the lessee at the end of the lease term, the arrangement is, in effect, a purchase and sale of the asset. As such, the lessor has transferred the risks and rewards of ownership to the lessee and such a lease is normally classified as a finance lease.

Is the lessee reasonably certain to exercise an option to purchase the underlying asset?

Lease arrangements often contain an option for the lessee to purchase the underlying asset at the end of the lease term. As previously stated, IAS 17 does not define 'reasonably certain'. In practice, a purchase option is considered reasonably certain of exercise when the option price is significantly below market (i.e. a bargain purchase option). When a lease contains a bargain purchase option, it is normally classified as a finance lease.

Is the lease term for a major part of the economic life of the leased asset?

This classification guideline requires measurement of the lease term against the asset's economic life. IAS 17 paragraph 4 defines an asset's economic life as either:

(a) the period over which an asset is expected to be economically usable by one or more users; or
(b) the number of production or similar units expected to be obtained from the asset by one or more users.

This guideline represents an attempt to measure the extent of the transfer of rewards to the lessee. What percentage of the asset's economic life represents a 'major' part — 60%? 70%? 80%? The lack of clear guidance in the accounting standard could result in differing classifications of similar lease arrangements. For example, a 6-year lease of an asset with an economic life of 8 years could be classified as a finance lease by entity A on the grounds that the lease term is 74% of the asset's economic life, but treated as an operating lease by entity B, which applies an 85% 'cut off'.

This classification guideline assumes that the consumption pattern of economic benefits across the economic life of the asset will be straight-line (equal in each year). However, some assets, such as vehicles, may provide more of their benefits in the early years of their economic lives, so a time-based classification criterion may not be appropriate.

When a lease is for the major part of the economic life of an asset, it is unlikely that the lessor expects to earn its return on the asset from another party. However, this guideline is not necessarily conclusive as there may be other factors that suggest the lessor retains the risks and rewards associated with the asset, such as obsolescence risks. Therefore, judgement is required when evaluating this guideline.

Does the present value of minimum lease payments amount to substantially all of the fair value of the lease asset at lease inception?

The minimum lease payments represent payments for benefits transferred to the lessee. At lease inception date, the relationship of the present value of the minimum lease payments to the fair value of the asset indicates the proportion of benefits being paid for by the lessee.

To apply this guideline, the following information must be gathered or determined at the inception of the lease:

- fair value of the leased asset;
- minimum lease payments for each period; and
- discount rate.

Fair value of the leased asset

Fair value is defined in IAS 17 paragraph 4 as 'the amount for which an asset could be exchanged, or a liability settled, between knowledgeable, willing parties in an arm's length transaction.'

This definition of fair value is different from the definition in IFRS 13 *Fair Value Measurement (see chapter 3 for a discussion of fair value measurement)*. Under IAS 17, fair value is normally a market price. However, if the lease relates to specialised equipment constructed or obtained for the lease contract, a fair value may be difficult to obtain. The fair value is regarded as representing the future rewards available to the user of the asset, discounted by the market to allow for the risk that the rewards will not eventuate and for changes in the purchasing power of money over time.

Minimum lease payments

The definition of minimum lease payments in IAS 17 can be expressed as follows:

> Minimum lease payments =   (i) Payments over the lease term
>   + (ii) Guaranteed residual value
>   + (iii) Bargain purchase option
>   − (iv) Contingent rent
>   − (v) Reimbursement of costs paid by the lessor

(i) Payments over the lease term are simply the total of all amounts payable under the lease agreement.

(ii) The guaranteed residual value is that part of the residual value of the leased asset guaranteed by the lessee or a third party.

The lessor will estimate the residual value of the leased asset at the end of the lease term based on market conditions at the inception of the lease, and the lessee will guarantee that, when the asset is returned to the lessor, it will realise at least that amount. The guarantee may range from 1% to 100% of the residual value, and is a matter for negotiation between the lessor and lessee. If the guarantee is provided by a party related to the lessor rather than the lessee, that part of the residual value is regarded, for the purposes of IAS 17, as unguaranteed. When a lessee guarantees some or all of the residual value of the asset, the lessor has transferred risks associated with movements in the residual value to the lessee.

Lessees include in minimum lease payments amounts the lessee guarantees or amounts guaranteed by a party related to the lessee. Lessors include in minimum lease payments residual value guarantees by the lessee, a related party of the lessee or a third-party financially able to settle the guarantee.

(iii) A bargain purchase option is a clause in the lease agreement allowing the lessee to purchase the asset at the end of the lease for a pre-set amount significantly less than the expected residual value at the end of the lease term.

Together, amounts (i), (ii) and (iii) above represent the maximum possible payment the lessee is legally obliged to make under the lease agreement, assuming that the guaranteed amount must be paid in full or the purchase option will be exercised.

(iv) Payments may be increased during the lease term by the occurrence of events specified in the lease agreement. Additional payments arising from such changes are called contingent rent. For example, an agreement to lease a photocopier may specify an additional charge when the number of copies made in a month exceeds 100 000. These charges relate to the use of the leased asset but, as the occurrence of the contingent event is uncertain at lease inception date, they are ignored when calculating the minimum lease payments.

(v) Payments under a lease may include two components: a charge for using the asset, and a charge to reimburse the lessor for operating expenses paid on behalf of the lessee. Operating expenses generally include insurance, maintenance, consumable supplies, replacement parts and rates. These expenses are referred to as 'executory costs' in this chapter. Amounts paid to reimburse such costs are excluded from minimum lease payments because they do not relate to the value of the asset transferred between lessor and lessee. Payments for executory costs are recognised in the financial statements in the period they are incurred, separate from 'lease payments'.

Discount rate

The minimum lease payments are discounted to present value by applying an appropriate discount rate. Discounting is not necessary if the lease contains a bargain purchase option or a 100% guaranteed residual value because, in both cases, the present value of the minimum lease payments will equal the fair value of the leased asset. Hence, a complete transfer of risks and rewards is deemed to have taken place.

To discount the minimum lease payments, the lessee/lessor will need to determine the interest rate implicit in the lease. This is defined in IAS 17 paragraph 4 as:

> the discount rate that, at the inception of the lease, causes the aggregate present value of
> (a) the minimum lease payments; and
> (b) the unguaranteed residual value
> to be equal to the sum of
> (i) the fair value of the leased asset, and
> (ii) any initial direct costs of the lessor.

Initial direct costs of the lessor are incremental costs that are directly attributable to negotiating and arranging a lease, except for such costs incurred by manufacturer or dealer lessors. Examples include commissions, legal fees and internal costs, but exclude general overheads such as those incurred by a sales and marketing team. Such costs incurred by a manufacturer/dealer lessor are excluded from the definition of initial direct costs in IAS 17 paragraph 46 because the costs of negotiating and arranging a finance lease are 'mainly related to earning the manufacturer's or dealer's selling profit'. Thus, for the purposes of determining the interest rate implicit in the lease, any initial direct costs incurred by a lessee or a manufacturer/dealer lessor are ignored.

The interest rate implicit in the lease is determined at the inception date of the lease, and this may differ from the commencement date of the lease term, which is a date set by the agreement. This may lead to the use of a distorted discount rate if the inception date of the lease differs significantly from the commencement of the lease term, the latter being the date from which the lessee is entitled to exercise its right to use the leased asset and presumably the date from which the lessor is entitled to receive the lease payments. As minimum lease payments and the unguaranteed residual value equal the future economic rewards obtainable from the asset, the interest rate is that used by the market to determine the fair value. From this comes the notion that the rate is implicit in the terms of the agreement.

If it is not possible for the lessee to determine the residual value at the end of the lease term, initial direct costs of the lessor, or, in the unusual case of a highly specialised asset, the fair value of the asset at the inception of the lease, then the interest rate implicit in the lease cannot be calculated. In this situation, the lessee uses its incremental borrowing rate to discount the minimum lease payments. The incremental borrowing rate is the rate of interest the lessee would have to pay on a similar lease or, if this is not determinable, the rate that (at the inception of the lease) the lessee would incur to borrow over a similar term, and with a similar security, the funds necessary to purchase the asset.

Substantial transfer?

As previously discussed, IAS 17 does not define 'substantially all'. Some national GAAPs contain a threshold of 90% and in practice IFRS reporters often use this as a guideline. However, because of a lack of quantitative guidelines in the standard, a judgement must be made as to whether the present value of the minimum lease payments represents the transfer of 'substantially all' of the fair value of the asset from the lessor to the lessee. This exercise of judgement may result in the inconsistent classification of similar lease arrangements.

Is the leased asset of such a specialised nature that it is expected to have no alternative use to the lessor at the end of the lease term?

In some arrangements, the lessor manufactures an asset for the specific needs of the lessee and the asset is not able to be used by another lessee without the lessor incurring significant costs to modify it. In this situation, it is likely that other guidelines above also have been met as the arrangement would be designed for the lessor to generate all of its returns from the one lessee, and such a lease normally would be a finance lease.

If the lessee can cancel the lease, is the lessee responsible for any losses incurred by the lessor?

This guideline suggests that the residual value risk is essentially borne by the lessee. Suppose a lessee leases a car for 5 years and is required to compensate the lessor for any decreases in the residual value if the lessee decides to cancel the lease after 3 years. If the residual value is lower than anticipated, the lessee bears more of the risks and rewards associated with the asset, which may indicate a finance lease.

Is the lessee entitled to the gains or exposed to the losses from the fluctuation in the fair value of the residual asset?

If, for example, a lessee is required to reimburse the lessor for declines in the fair value of the asset at the end of the lease, the lessee would be exposed to the risks of the residual value in the asset. This would indicate that the lessor was compensated for the asset from the payments received from the lessee and suggests a finance lease.

Can the lessee continue the lease for futher periods at a rent substantially less than market rent?

- An option to renew a lease at substantially less than market rent, i.e a 'bargain renewal option', is considered reasonably certain of exercise. Therefore, the periods covered by such an option are included in the lease term when assessing whether the lease term is for a major part of the economic life of the leased asset, as discussed above. Depending on the number of renewal terms and the renewal period in relation to the economic life of the asset, such options could result in a finance lease.

ILLUSTRATIVE EXAMPLE 12.1 Classification of a lease agreement

On 31 December 2015, Gisborne Ltd leased a vehicle to Phillip Ltd. Gisborne Ltd had purchased the vehicle on that day at an amount equal to its fair value of £89 721. The lease agreement, which cost Gisborne Ltd £1457 to have drawn up, contained the following terms:

Lease term	4 years
Annual payment, payable in advance on 31 December each year	£23 900
Economic life of vehicle	6 years
Estimated residual value at end of lease term	£15 000
Residual value guaranteed by lessee	£7 500

If Phillip Ltd terminates the lease before the end of the 4-year lease term, Phillip Ltd will incur a monetary penalty equivalent to 2 years rental payments.

Included in the annual payment is an amount of £1900 to cover reimbursement for the costs of insurance and maintenance paid by Gisborne Ltd.

IAS 17 requires the lease to be classified as either a finance lease or an operating lease, based on the extent to which the risks and rewards associated with the vehicle have been transferred from Gisborne Ltd to Phillip Ltd.

Does the lease transfer ownership of the vehicle by the end of the lease term?
The lease terms do not transfer ownership of the vehicle to Phillip Ltd.

Is Phillip Ltd reasonably certain to exercise an option to purchase the vehicle?
The lease terms do not contain an option to purchase the underlying asset.

Is the lease term for a major part of the economic life of the vehicle?
Because Phillip Ltd is required to pay a termination payment equivalent to the present value of the remaining lease payments, the lease is essentially non-cancellable as it is reasonably certain that Phillip Ltd will continue the lease for the term specified in the lease agreement. Such term is included when assessing whether the lease term is for a major part of the economic life of the vehicle.

The lease term is 4 years, which is 66% of the vehicle's economic life of 6 years. If expected benefits were receivable evenly over the vehicle's useful life, it would be doubtful that the lease arrangement is for the major part of its life.

Is the present value of the minimum lease payments substantially all of the fair value of the vehicle?
Minimum lease payments
The minimum lease payments consist of:
- lease payments net of cost reimbursement — there is an immediate payment of £22 000 (being £23 900 – $1900) and four subsequent payments of £22 000
- guaranteed residual value — an amount of £7500 is guaranteed at the end of the fourth year.
The unguaranteed residual value is £7500.

Interest rate implicit in the lease
The discount rate is the rate that discounts the rental payments and the residual value to £91 178, which is the sum of the vehicle's fair value at 1 January 2014 of £89 721 and the initial direct costs (IDC) of £1457 incurred by Gisborne Ltd. This rate is found by trial and error using present value tables or a financial calculator.

The implicit interest rate in this example is 7%, that is:

$$\text{Present value} = £22\,000 + (£22\,000 \times 2.6243\ [T2\ 7\%\ 3y]) + (£15\,000 \times 0.7629\ [T1\ 7\%\ 4y])$$
$$= £22\,000 + £57\,735 + £11\,443$$
$$= £91\,178$$

when T = present value table
y = years

Note the following:
- As the first payment is made at the inception of the lease, it is not discounted.
- The discount factor used is an annuity factor based on three equal payments of £22 000 for the next 3 years at 7%.
- The discount factor used is based on a single payment of £15 000 (the residual value) at the end of the lease term in 4 years at a rate of 7%. The £15 000 comprises £7500 guaranteed by the lessee plus the unguaranteed balance of £7500.
The present value is equal to the fair value (FV) plus IDC, so the interest rate implicit in the lease is 7%.

Present value of minimum lease payments (PV of MLP)

$$\text{PV of MLP} = £22\,000 + (£22\,000 \times 2.6243\ [T2\ 7\%\ 3y]) + (£7500 \times 0.7629\ [T1\ 7\%\ 4y])$$
$$= £22\,000 + £57\,735 + £5722$$
$$= £85\,457$$

$$\text{FV} + \text{IDC} = £91\,178$$

$$\text{PV}/(\text{FV} + \text{IDC}) = (£85\,457/£91\,178) \times 100\%$$
$$= 93.7\%$$

At a 93.7% level, Phillip Ltd considers the present value of the minimum lease payments to be substantially all of the fair value of the vehicle.

Other considerations required by IAS 17
- Is the leased asset of such a specialised nature that it is expected to have no alternative use to Gisborne Ltd at the end of the lease term? No.
- Is Phillip Ltd responsible for any losses incurred by Gisborne Ltd if Phillip Ltd decides to cancel the lease before the end of the lease term? No.
- Is Phillip Ltd entitled to the gains or losses from the fluctuation in the fair value of the residual asset? No.
- Can Phillip Ltd continue to use the leased asset for further periods at rent substantially less than market rent? No. The terms of the lease agreement do not contain any renewal options. If Phillip Ltd decides to continue to lease the vehicle, this would be subject to new negotiations with Gisborne Ltd and a new agreement, which would require a new analysis of classification under IAS 17.

Classification of the lease
Application of the lease classification guidelines provides mixed signals. The key criterion in classifying leases is whether substantially all the risks and rewards incidental to ownership have been transferred. This requires an overall analysis of the arrangement. The different signals coming from the lease term guideline and the present value guideline may be due to the fact that the majority of the rewards will be transferred in the early stages of the life of the asset, which is the case with motor vehicles. This is reflected in the relatively low residual value at the end of the lease term. These mixed signals demonstrate that the classification guidelines must be used for guidance only and not treated as specific criteria that must be met.

Based on the nature of the asset and the assessment that the lessee will pay substantially all of the fair value of the asset over the lease term, it is concluded that the lease agreement should be classified as a finance lease because substantially all the risks and rewards incident to ownership have been passed to the lessee.

12.4 ACCOUNTING FOR FINANCE LEASES BY LESSEES

Once an arrangement has been classified as a finance lease, the asset and liability arising from it must be determined and recognised in the accounts.

12.4.1 Initial recognition

When a lease has been classified as a finance lease, IAS 17 requires the lessee to recognise, at the commencement of the lease term, an asset and a liability, each determined at the inception of the lease, equal in amount to the fair value of the leased property or, if lower, the present value of the minimum lease payments. The form of the entry is:

| Lease Asset | Dr | PV of MLP | |
| Lease Liability | Cr | | PV of MLP |

The commencement of the lease term is the date from which the lessee is entitled to exercise its right to use the leased asset, and may be the same date as the inception of the lease or a later date. If the lessee incurs initial direct costs associated with negotiating and securing the lease arrangement, these costs are added to the amount recognised as an asset. The journal entry is:

Lease Asset	Dr	PV of MLP + IDC	
Lease Liability	Cr		PV of MLP
Cash	Cr		IDC

12.4.2 Subsequent measurement

After initial recognition, IAS 17 prescribes differing accounting treatments for the lease asset and the lease liability.

Leased assets

Leased assets under finance leases are depreciated in a manner consistent with owned assets, as prescribed by IAS 16 *Property, Plant and Equipment* and IAS 38 *Intangible Assets.*

Depreciable assets are those whose future benefits are expected to expire over time or by use. The asset is depreciated over its useful life in a pattern reflecting the consumption or loss of the rewards embodied in the asset. The length of a leased asset's useful life depends on whether or not ownership of the asset will transfer at the end of the lease term. If the asset is to be returned to the lessor, then its useful life is the lease term. If ownership is reasonably certain to transfer to the lessee, then its useful life is its economic life or remainder thereof. Additionally, to determine whether a leased asset has become impaired, the lessee must apply IAS 36 *Impairment of Assets.*

Lease liability

Because lease payments are made over the lease term, the lease liability is increased by interest expense incurred and decreased by the minimum lease payments made. The lease liability recognised at the commencement of the lease term represents the present value of future lease payments relating to the use of the asset. This present value is determined, *as described in section 12.3.2,* by applying the interest rate implicit in the lease. In practice, lessees may not be able to determine the rate implicit in the lease and, therefore, will use their incremental borrowing rate. The interest expense is calculated by applying the same rate to the outstanding lease liability at the beginning of the payment period. A payments schedule can be used to determine the interest expense and the reduction in the liability over the lease period.

Accounting for the reimbursement of lessor costs and contingent rent

The standard is silent about the component of lease payments that represents a reimbursement of costs incurred by the lessor other than stating that these costs are not minimum lease payments and, therefore, are not reflected in the lease liability or the lease asset. *As discussed in 12.3.2,* these 'executory costs' are effectively borne by the lessee, and the payments are recognised as an expense. Consideration must be given to the pattern of consumption relating to those expenses and normal prepayment and accrual requirements apply.

Contingent rent must be recognised as an expense of the period in which it is incurred.

ILLUSTRATIVE EXAMPLE 12.2 Accounting for finance leases by lessees

Using the facts from illustrative example 12.1, the lease payments schedule prepared by Phillip Ltd, based on annual lease payments of £22 000 for the vehicle and an interest rate of 7%, would be:

PHILLIP LTD
Lease Payments schedule

	Minimum lease payments[a]	Interest expense[b]	Reduction in liability[c]	Balance of liability[d]
31 December 2015[e]				£85 457[f]
31 December 2015	£22 000	£ —	£22 000	63 457
31 December 2016	22 000	4 442	17 558	45 899
31 December 2017	22 000	3 213	18 787	27 112
31 December 2018	22 000	1 898	20 102	7 010
31 December 2019	7 500	490	7 010	—
	£95 500	£10 043	£85 457	

(a) Four annual payments of £22 000 payable in advance on 31 December of each year, plus a guaranteed residual value of £7500 on the last day of the lease.

(b) Interest expense = balance of liability each prior year-end multiplied by 7%. No interest expense is incurred in the year ended 31 December 2015 because payment is made at 31 December 2015, the commencement of the lease.

(c) Reduction in liability = minimum lease payments less interest expense. The total of this column must equal the initial liability, which may require rounding the final interest expense figure.

(d) The balance is reduced each year by the amount in column 3.

(e) At lease inception.

(f) Initial liability = present value of minimum lease payments. As the present value of minimum lease payments is less than the fair value of the asset, paragraph 20 of IAS 17 requires the lower amount to be recognised.

The payment schedule is used to prepare lease journal entries and financial statement disclosures each year. The journal entries recorded by Phillip Ltd for the 4 years of the lease in accordance with IAS 17 are:

PHILLIP LTD
General Journal

Year ended 31 December 2015
31 December 2015:

Leased Vehicle	Dr	85 457	
Lease Liability	Cr		85 457
(Initial recording of lease asset/liability)			
Lease Liability	Dr	22 000	
Prepaid Executory Costs*	Dr	1 900	
Cash	Cr		23 900
(First lease payment)			

*Executory costs have been recognised as an asset because the insurance and maintenance benefits will not be received until the next reporting period.

Year ended 31 December 2016
1 January 2016:

Executory Costs	Dr	1 900	
Prepaid Executory Costs	Cr		1 900
(Reversal of prepayment)**			

31 December 2016:

Lease Liability	Dr	17 558	
Interest Expense	Dr	4 442	
Prepaid Executory Costs	Dr	1 900	
Cash	Cr		23 900
(Second lease payment)			
Depreciation Expense	Dr	19 489	
Accumulated Depreciation	Cr		19 489
(Depreciation charge for the period [£85 457 − £7 500]/4)***			

***Because the asset will be returned at the end of the lease term, the useful life is the lease term of 4 years and the depreciable amount is the net present value of the minimum lease payments less the guaranteed residual value.

Year ended 31 December 2017
1 January 2017:

Executory Costs	Dr	1 900	
Prepaid Executory Costs	Cr		1 900
(Reversal of prepayment)**			

31 December 2017:

Lease Liability	Dr	18 787	
Interest Expense	Dr	3 213	
Prepaid Executory Costs	Dr	1 900	
Cash	Cr		23 900
(Third lease payment)			
Depreciation Expense	Dr	19 489	
Accumulated Depreciation	Cr		19 489
(Depreciation charge for the period [£85 457 − £7 500]/4)			

Year ended 31 December 2018
1 January 2018:

Executory Costs	Dr	1 900	
Prepaid Executory Costs	Cr		1 900
(Reversal of prepayment)**			

31 December 2018:

Lease Liability	Dr	20 102	
Interest Expense	Dr	1 898	
Prepaid Executory Costs	Dr	1 900	
Cash	Cr		23 900
(Fourth lease payment)			

Depreciation Expense	Dr	19 489	
Accumulated Depreciation	Cr		19 489
(Depreciation charge for the period [£85 457 − £7 500]/4)			

Year ended 31 December 2019
1 January 2019:

Executory Costs	Dr	1 900	
Prepaid Executory Costs	Cr		1 900
(Reversal of prepayment)**			

31 December 2019:

Lease Liability	Dr	7 010	
Interest Expense	Dr	490	
Leased Vehicle	Cr		7 500
(Return of leased vehicle)****			

****The final 'payment' is the return of the asset at its guaranteed residual value. If the asset is being purchased, this entry will record a cash payment. Another entry will then be required to reclassify the undepreciated balance of the asset from a 'leased' asset to an 'owned' asset.

Depreciation Expense	Dr	19 490	
Accumulated Depreciation	Cr		19 490
(Depreciation charge for the period [£85 457 − £7 500]/4)			

Accumulated Depreciation	Dr	77 957	
Leased Vehicle	Cr		77 957
(Fully depreciated asset written off)			

**For simplicity, reversal of executory costs is shown on 1 January. However, executory costs are recognised as incurred, which in this example would be over the entire year.

If the fair value of the leased asset is lower than the guaranteed residual value of £7500, Phillip Ltd would recognise additional expense.

12.4.3 Disclosures required

Figure 12.2 shows the lease accounting policy disclosures and extracts from the expenses; property, plant and equipment; long-term borrowings; and commitments notes to the financial statements of International Airlines Group for the year ended 31 December 2014.

FIGURE 12.2 Note extracts from International Airlines Group annual report 31 December 2014

2 Summary of significant accounting policies
Foreign currency translation

. . .

d Leased assets

Where assets are financed through finance leases, under which substantially all the risks and rewards of ownership are transferred to the Group, the assets are treated as if they had been purchased outright. The amount included in the cost of property, plant and equipment represents the aggregate of the capital elements payable during the lease term. The corresponding obligation, reduced by the appropriate proportion of lease payments made, is included in borrowings.

The amount included in the cost of property, plant and equipment is depreciated on the basis described in the preceding paragraphs on fleet and the interest element of lease payments made is included as an interest expense in the income statement.

Total minimum payments measured at inception, under all other lease arrangements, known as operating leases, are charged to the income statement in equal annual amounts over the period of the lease. In respect of aircraft, certain operating lease arrangements allow the Group to terminate the leases after a limited initial period, without further material financial obligations. In certain cases the Group is entitled to extend the initial lease period on predetermined terms; such leases are described as extendable operating leases.

. . .

(continued)

FIGURE 12.2 *(continued)*

g Lease classification

A lease is classified as a finance lease when substantially all the risks and rewards of ownership are transferred to the Group. In determining the appropriate classification, the substance of the transaction rather than the form is considered. Factors considered include but are not limited to the following: whether the lease transfers ownership of the asset to the lessee by the end of the lease term; the lessee has the option to purchase the asset at the price that is sufficiently lower than the fair value exercise date; the lease term is for the major part of the economic life of the asset; and the present value of the minimum lease payments amounts to at least substantially all the fair value of the leased asset.

6 Expenses by nature

Operating profit is after charging/(crediting)

Operating lease costs:

€ million		2014	2013
Minimum lease rentals	— aircraft	551	499
	— property and equipment	187	186
Sub-lease rentals received		(54)	(38)
		684	647

13 Property, plant and equipment

€ million Net book values				
31 December 2014	**9 974**	**1 260**	**550**	**11 784**
31 December 2013	8 515	1 218	495	10 228
Analysis at 31 December 2014				
Owned	4 290	1 173	411	**5 874**
Finance leased	5 398	5	32	**5 435**
Progress payments	286	82	107	**475**
Property, plant and equipment	**9 974**	**1 260**	**550**	**11 784**
Analysis at 31 December 2013				
Owned	4 274	1 153	422	5 849
Finance leased	3 789	5	48	3 842
Progress payments	452	60	25	537
Property, plant and equipment	8 515	1 218	495	10 228

23 Long-term borrowings continued

d Total loans and finance leases

Finance leases		
US dollar	**$3 772**	$2 935
Euro	**€1 084**	€456
Japanese yen	**¥37 105**	¥18 557
Pound sterling	£771	£874
	€5 384	€3 770
	€6 617	€5 122

e Obligations under finance leases

The Group uses finance leases principally to acquire aircraft. These leases have both renewal options and purchase options at the option of the Group. Future minimum lease payments under finance leases are as follows:

FIGURE 12.2 *(continued)*

€ million	2014	2013
Future minimum payments due:		
Within 1 year	**676**	492
After more than 1 year but within 5 years	**2 463**	1 893
In 5 years or more	**3 100**	1 858
	6 239	4 243
Less: Finance charges	**(855)**	(473)
Present value of minimum lease payments	**5 384**	3 770
The present value of minimum lease payments is analysed as follows:		
Within 1 year	**549**	404
After more than 1 year but within 5 years	**2 079**	1 650
In 5 years or more	**2 756**	1 716
	5 384	3 770

The Group's finance lease for one Airbus A340-600 is subject to financial covenants which are tested annually. The lease is part of a syndicate family. The Group has informed the syndicate that it had failed to meet the covenants for the year to 31 December 2014. As a result of these covenant breaches, the finance lease has technically become repayable on demand and $79 million (€65 million) has been classified as current. The institutions formally waived the breach on 25 February 2015.

24 Operating lease commitments

The Group has entered into commercial leases on certain properties, equipment and aircraft. These leases have durations ranging from less than 1 year for aircraft to 132 years for ground leases. Certain leases contain options for renewal.

The aggregate payments, for which there are commitments under operating leases, fall due as follows:

€ million	2014			2013		
	Fleet	Property, plant and equipment	Total	Fleet	Property, plant and equipment	Total
Within 1 year	**712**	**171**	**883**	543	156	699
Between 1 and 5 years	**1 580**	**325**	**1 905**	1 537	383	1 920
Over 5 years	**934**	**2 027**	**2 961**	1 009	1 958	2 967
	3 226	**2 523**	**5 749**	3 089	2 497	5 586

Sub-leasing

Sub-leases entered into by the Group relate to surplus rental properties and aircraft assets held under non-cancellable leases to the third parties. These leases have remaining terms of 1 to 23 years and the assets are surplus to the Group's requirements. Future minimum rentals receivable under non-cancellable operating leases are as follows:

€ million	2014			2013		
	Fleet	Property, plant and equipment	Total	Fleet	Property, plant and equipment	Total
Within 1 year	**2**	**12**	**14**	-	9	9
Between 1 and 5 years	**-**	**6**	**6**	-	14	14
Over 5 years	**-**	**2**	**2**	-	3	3
	2	**20**	**22**	-	26	26

Three of the Group's Airbus A340-600 operating leases are also subject to financial covenants which are tested annually. The Group has informed the syndicate that it had failed to meet the covenants for the year to 31 December 2014. The remaining operating lease payments of $156 million (€128 million) will technically fall due within 1 year. The institutions have provided positive feedback and are expected to formally waive the breach in March 2015.

Source: International Airlines Group, *Annual Report 2014* (pp. 102–103, 109, 113, 120, 130–131).

Figure 12.3 provides an illustration of the disclosures required by IAS 17, and is based on the figures used in illustrative example 12.2 for the year ended 31 December 2017.

	IAS 17 paragraph
Note 1: Summary of accounting policies (extract) **Leasing** The Entity leases vehicles under finance leases with terms of 4 years. Leases are classified as finance leases whenever the terms of the lease transfer substantially all the risks and rewards of ownership to the Entity. All other leases are classified as operating leases *The Entity as a lessee* Assets held under finance leases are recognised as assets of the Entity at their fair value at the date of acquisition or, if lower, at the present value of the minimum lease payments. The corresponding liability to the lessor is included in the statement of financial position as a finance lease liability. Lease payments are apportioned between finance charges and reduction of the lease liability to achieve a constant rate of interest on the remaining balance of the liability. Finance charges are charged directly against income unless they are directly attributable to qualifying assets, in which case they are capitalised in accordance with the Entity's general policy on borrowing costs.	*31(e)*
Note 16: Property, plant and equipment (extract) The carrying amount of the Entity's plant and equipment includes an amount of £46 479 (2016: £65 968) relating to leased assets.	*31(a)*

Note 36: Finance lease liabilities
The following is a summary of future minimum lease payments for finance leases:

	Minimum lease payments 2017	PV of payments 2017	Minimum lease payments 2016	PV of payments 2016	IAS 17 paragraph
Amounts payable under finance leases:					
Within 1 year	22 000	20 102	22 000	18 787	*31(b)*
After 1 year but not more than 5 years[(1)]	7 500	7 010	29 500	27 112	
Total minimum lease payments	29 500	27 112	51 500	45 899	
Less: Finance charges	(2 388)		(5 601)		
Present value of minimum lease payments	27 112		45 899		

(1) If the lease term in illustrative example 12.2 was for more than 5 years, Phillip Ltd would also disclose the total amounts payable more than 5 years.

FIGURE 12.3 Illustrative disclosures required by IAS 17 for lessees of finance leases

If Phillip Ltd's lease contained contingent rentals, renewal or purchase options, escalation clauses or any restrictions (such as those limiting the payment of dividends), those terms would be required to be disclosed (IAS 17 paragraphs 31(c) and (e)). In addition, if Phillip Ltd sublet the vehicle, the future minimum lease payments under that sub-lease arrangement (if it were non-cancellable) also would be required to be disclosed (IAS 17 paragraph 31(d)).

12.5 ACCOUNTING FOR FINANCE LEASES BY LESSORS

When a lease is classified as a finance lease, the lessor will need to derecognise the leased asset and record a lease receivable.

12.5.1 Initial recognition

In theory, the classification process required by IAS 17 should result in identical classifications by both lessors and lessees. In reality, differing circumstances may result in the same lease being classified differently; for example, when the lessor benefits from a residual value guarantee provided by a party unrelated to the lessee.

Paragraph 36 of IAS 17 requires the lessor to recognise an asset held under a finance lease in its statement of financial position and present it as a receivable at an amount equal to the net investment in the lease. In paragraph 4 the net investment in the lease is defined as 'the gross investment in the lease discounted at the interest rate implicit in the lease' and the gross investment is the total of:

(a) the minimum lease payments receivable by the lessor . . . and
(b) any unguaranteed residual value accruing to the lessor.

This value would normally equate to the fair value of the asset at the inception of the lease. Initial direct costs (except those incurred by manufacturer or dealer lessors) are included in the initial measurement of the finance lease receivable and in the calculation of the implicit interest rate, thereby reducing the amount of interest revenue recognised over the lease term. Lessees are required to recognise assets and liabilities associated with finance leases at the commencement of the lease term but no date for recognition is specified for lessors; presumably, it would be the same date.

The recognition of the fair value of the leased asset as a receivable raises a conceptual issue in that the 'receivable', for leases with no purchase option, has both a monetary component (the rent payments) and non-monetary component (the return of the asset). *As discussed in section 12.9*, lessor accounting is substantially unchanged under the IASB's new leases standard and, therefore, this conceptual flaw will continue to exist.

12.5.2 Subsequent measurement

Because the lease payments are received from the lessee over the lease term, the lease receivable is increased by interest revenue earned and decreased by minimum lease payments received (i.e. lease payments excluding payments for services and contingent rent). The lease receivable recognised at the commencement of the lease term represents the present value of future lease payments relating to the use of the asset. This present value is determined by applying the interest rate implicit in the lease. The interest revenue can be obtained by applying the same rate to the outstanding lease receivable at the beginning of the payment period. A receipts schedule can be used to determine the interest revenue and the reduction in the receivable over the lease period.

Accounting for executory costs and contingent rentals

Payments for services, such as insurance or maintenance (i.e. executory costs), are not included in the lease receivable. Receipts for executory costs are recorded as revenue in the same period in which the related expenses are incurred, when the lessor is acting as principal *(see discussion of the principal/agent distinction in section 4.9.3)*.

IAS 17 is silent on lessor treatment of contingent rent. However, as these receipts meet the definition of income in the *Conceptual Framework*, contingent rent is recognised as revenue in the period it is earned.

ILLUSTRATIVE EXAMPLE 12.3 Accounting for finance leases by lessors

On 31 December 2015, Gisborne Ltd leased a vehicle to Phillip Ltd. Gisborne Ltd had purchased the vehicle on that day at an amount equal to its fair value of £89 721. The lease agreement, which cost Gisborne Ltd £1457 to have drawn up, contained the following terms:

Lease term	4 years
Annual payment, payable in advance on 31 December each year	£23 900
Economic life of vehicle	6 years
Estimated residual value at end of economic life	£2 000
Estimated residual value at end of lease term	£15 000
Residual value guaranteed by lessee	£7 500

If Phillip Ltd terminates the lease before the end of the 4-year lease term, Phillip Ltd will incur a monetary penalty equivalent to 2 years' rental payments.

Included in the annual payments is an amount of £1900 to cover reimbursement for the costs of insurance and maintenance paid by the lessor.

IAS 17 requires the lease to be classified as either a finance lease or an operating lease, based on the extent to which the risks and rewards associated with the vehicle have been transferred from Gisborne Ltd to Phillip Ltd.

Classification of the lease by the lessor
Gisborne Ltd applies the IAS 17 guidelines and classifies the lease as a finance lease. See illustrative example 12.1 for workings.

The lease receipts schedule based on annual payments of £22 000 for the vehicle and an interest rate implicit in the lease of 7% shows:

GISBORNE LTD Lease Receipts Schedule			
	Minimum lease receipts[(a)]	Interest revenue[(b)]	Reduction in receivable[(c)]	Balance of receivable[(d)]
31 December 2015[(e)]				£91 178[(f)]
31 December 2015	£ 22 000	£ —	£22 000	69 178
31 December 2016	22 000	4 842	17 158	52 020
31 December 2017	22 000	3 641	18 359	33 661
31 December 2018	22 000	2 356	19 644	14 017
31 December 2019	15 000	983	14 017	—
	£103 000	£11 822	£91 178	

(a) Four annual receipts of £22 000 payable in advance on 31 December of each year, plus a residual value of £15 000 (of which £7 500 is guaranteed by the lessee) on the last day of the lease.

(b) Interest revenue = balance of receivable each prior year-end multiplied by 7%. No interest revenue is earned in the year ended 31 December 2015 because the payment is received at 31 December 2015, the commencement of the lease.

(c) Reduction in receivable = minimum lease payments received less interest revenue. The total of this column must equal the initial receivable, which may require rounding the final interest revenue figure.

(d) The balance is reduced each year by the amount in column 3.

(e) At lease inception.

(f) Initial receivable = vehicle's fair value of £89 721 plus IDC of £1 457. This figure equals the present value of minimum lease payments receivable and the present value of the unguaranteed residual value.

The lease receipts schedule is used to prepare lease journal entries and financial statement disclosures each year. The journal entries recorded by Gisborne Ltd for the 4 years of the lease in accordance with IAS 17 are:

GISBORNE LTD General Journal			
Year ended 31 December 2015			
31 December 2015:			
Vehicle	Dr	89 721	
Cash	Cr		89 721
(Purchase of motor vehicle)			
Lease Receivable	Dr	89 721	
Vehicle	Cr		89 721
(Lease of vehicle to Phillip Ltd)			
Lease Receivable	Dr	1 457	
Cash	Cr		1 457
(Payment of IDC)			
Cash	Dr	23 900	
Lease Receivable	Cr		22 000
Reimbursement in Advance*	Cr		1 900
(Receipt of first lease payment)			

* The reimbursement of executory cost has been carried forward to 2015, when Gisborne Ltd will pay the costs.

Year ended 31 December 2016			
1 January 2016:			
Reimbursement in Advance	Dr	1 900	
Reimbursement Revenue	Cr		1 900
(Reversal of accrual)**			
31 December 2016:			
Insurance and Maintenance**	Dr	1 900	
Cash	Cr		1 900
(Payment of costs on behalf of lessee)			

Cash	Dr	23 900	
Lease Receivable	Cr		17 158
Interest Revenue	Cr		4 842
Reimbursement in Advance	Cr		1 900
(Receipt of second lease payment)			

Year ended 31 December 2017
1 January 2017:

Reimbursement in Advance	Dr	1 900	
Reimbursement Revenue	Cr		1 900
(Reversal of accrual)**			

31 December 2017:

Insurance and Maintenance**	Dr	1 900	
Cash	Cr		1 900
(Payment of costs on behalf of lessee)			
Cash	Dr	23 900	
Lease Receivable	Cr		18 359
Interest Revenue	Cr		3 641
Reimbursement in Advance	Cr		1 900
(Receipt of third lease payment)			

Year ended 31 December 2018
1 January 2018:

Reimbursement in Advance	Dr	1 900	
Reimbursement Revenue	Cr		1 900
(Reversal of accrual)**			

31 December 2018:

Insurance and Maintenance**	Dr	1 900	
Cash	Cr		1 900
(Payment of costs on behalf of lessee)			
Cash	Dr	23 900	
Lease Receivable	Cr		19 644
Interest Revenue	Cr		2 356
Reimbursement in Advance	Cr		1 900
(Receipt of fourth lease payment)			

Year ended 31 December 2019
1 January 2019:

Reimbursement in Advance	Dr	1 900	
Reimbursement Revenue	Cr		1 900
(Reversal of accrual)**			

31 December 2019:

Insurance and Maintenance**	Dr	1 900	
Cash	Cr		1 900
(Payment of costs on behalf of lessee)			
Vehicle	Dr	15 000	
Interest Revenue	Cr		983
Lease Receivable	Cr		14 017
(Return of vehicle at end of lease)			

**For simplicity, recognition of executory costs and associated revenue are recognised on 1 January 2015 and 31 December 2015, respectively. However, the costs would be incurred and associated revenue generally would be earned over the entire year.

12.5.3 The initial direct costs anomaly

The inclusion (by the standard setters) of initial direct costs incurred by lessors in the definition of the interest rate implicit in the lease creates an interest rate differential between the lessee and lessor when a lease agreement transfers all of the risks and rewards related to an asset.

To illustrate: consider the same situation as described in illustrative example 12.3 but increasing the guaranteed residual value to £15 000 (100% of the residual), which effectively transfers all of the benefits of the vehicle from Gisborne Ltd to Phillip Ltd. The present value of the minimum lease payments would then be:

$$\begin{aligned}
\text{PV of MLP} &= £22\,000 + (£22\,000 \times 2.6243\ [T_2\ 7\%\ 3y]) + (£15\,000 \times 0.7629\ [T_1\ 7\%\ 4y]) \\
&= £22\,000 + £57\,735 + £11\,443 \\
&= £91\,178
\end{aligned}$$

Generally, the rate of return the lessor expects to earn will be different depending on whether the residual value is guaranteed or not, and the lease payments would be adjusted accordingly. For simplicity, the lease payments are not changed in this example.

This figure equals the fair value of the asset, £89 721, plus the IDC incurred by the lessor of £1457.

However, paragraph 20 of IAS 17 requires lessees to recognise, at the commencement of the lease, an asset and a liability equal to the inception date fair value of the leased asset or, if lower, the present value of the minimum lease payments. As the present value of the minimum lease payments using the 7% interest rate implicit in the lease is higher than the asset's fair value, it cannot be recognised by the lessee even though it would be recognised by the lessor. The lessee, Phillip Ltd, can only recognise a lease asset and liability of £89 721, and must recalculate the interest rate implicit in the lease in order to determine interest expense charges over the lease term.

The interest rate that discounts the lease payments to £89 721 is 8%, so Phillip Ltd will calculate its interest expense at 8% and Gisborne Ltd will calculate its interest revenue at 7%. The difference represents the recovery of the IDC by Gisborne Ltd via the lease payments received.

12.5.4 Disclosures required

Figure 12.4 provides an illustration of the disclosures required by IAS 17. The information used in this figure is derived from the Gisborne Ltd lease shown in illustrative example 12.3 for the year ended 31 December 2017.

FIGURE 12.4 Illustrative disclosures required by IAS 17 for lessors of finance leases

					IAS 17 paragraph
Note 1: Summary of accounting policies (extract) **Leasing** The Entity leases vehicles under finance leases with terms of 4 years. Leases are classified as finance leases whenever the terms of the lease transfer substantially all the risks and rewards of ownership to the lessee. All other leases are classified as operating leases.					*47(f)*
The Entity as a lessor Amounts due from lessees under finance leases are recorded as a receivable at the amount of the Entity's net investment in the leases. Finance lease income is allocated to accounting periods, so as to reflect a constant periodic rate of return on the Entity's net investment outstanding in respect of the leases.					
Note 36: Finance lease receivables Future minimum lease payments receivable under finance leases are as follows:					
	Investment in lease 2017	PV of receivables 2017	Investment in lease 2016	PV of receivables 2016	
Amounts receivable under finance leases:					*47(a)*
Within 1 year	22 000	19 644	22 000	18 359	
After 1 year but not more than 5 years[(1)]	15 000	14 017	37 000	33 661	
Total minimum lease payments receivable	37 000	33 661	59 000	52 020	
Less: Unearned finance income	(3 339)		(6 980)		*47(b)*
Present value of minimum lease payments	33 661		52 020		

FIGURE 12.4 *(continued)*

Unguaranteed residual values of assets leased under finance leases at the end of the reporting period are estimated at 7500 (2015: 7500)	*47(c)*

(1) If the lease term in illustrative example 12.3 was for more than 5 years, Gisborne Ltd would also disclose the total amounts receivable more than 5 years.

If Gisborne Ltd's lease contained contingent rentals or if Gisborne Ltd recognised an allowance for uncollectible minimum lease payments receivable, those amounts would be required to be disclosed (IAS 17 paragraphs 47(e) and (d), respectively).

12.6 ACCOUNTING FOR FINANCE LEASES BY MANUFACTURER OR DEALER LESSORS

When manufacturers or dealers offer customers the choice of either buying or leasing an asset, a lease arrangement gives rise to two types of income:
- profit or loss equivalent to the outright sale of the asset being leased
- finance income over the lease term.

Accounting for the lease is identical to that required by non-manufacturer/dealer lessors except for an initial entry to recognise profit or loss and the treatment of initial direct costs, which is described below.

IAS 17 requires manufacturer and dealer lessors to recognise selling profit or loss at the commencement of the lease, in accordance with their policy for sales. When artificially low interest rates have been offered to entice the customer to enter the lease, the selling profit recorded must be limited to the selling profit that would be realised if the manufacturer/dealer charged a market rate of interest.

The sales revenue recognised is equal to the fair value of the asset or, if lower, the minimum lease payments calculated at a market rate of interest. The cost of sales expense is the cost or carrying amount of the leased property less the present value of any unguaranteed residual value. Sales revenue less cost of sales expense equals selling profit or loss. Additionally, the initial direct costs incurred by the manufacturer or dealer in negotiating and arranging the lease are recognised as an expense when the profit is recognised. Such costs are regarded as part of earning the profit on sale rather than a cost of leasing.

ILLUSTRATIVE EXAMPLE 12.4 Calculating and recognising profit on sale with initial direct costs

Napier S.A. manufactures specialised moulding machinery for both sale and lease. On 1 January 2016, Napier S.A. leased a machine to Bliss S.A., incurring €1500 in costs to negotiate, prepare and execute the lease document. The machine cost Napier S.A. €195 000 to manufacture, and its fair value at the inception of the lease was €212 515. The interest rate implicit in the lease is 10%, which is in line with current market rates. Under the terms of the lease, Bliss S.A. has guaranteed €25 000 of the asset's expected residual value of €37 000 at the end of the 5-year lease term.

After classifying the lease as a finance lease, Napier S.A. records the following entries on 1 January 2016:

Lease Receivable[(a)]	Dr	212 515	
Cost of Sales[(b)]	Dr	187 548	
Inventory[(c)]	Cr		195 000
Sales Revenue[(d)]	Cr		205 063
(Initial recognition of lease receivable and recording sale of machinery)			
Lease Costs	Dr	1 500	
Cash	Cr		1 500
Payment of IDC			

Notes:
(a) The lease receivable represents the net investment in the lease and is equal to the fair value of the leased machine.
(b) Cost of sales represents the cost of the leased machine (€195 000) less the present value of the unguaranteed residual value (€12 000 × 0.620921 = €7452).
(c) Inventory is reduced by the cost of the leased machine.
(d) Sales revenue represents the present value of the minimum lease payments, which in this situation is less than the fair value of the asset due to the existence of an unguaranteed residual value.

12.7 ACCOUNTING FOR OPERATING LEASES

Operating leases are all leases other than those in which substantially all the risks and rewards incidental to ownership are transferred to the lessee. Operating leases are treated like executory arrangements, with lessees recognising no asset or liability on their statement of financial position and lessors continuing to carry the asset on their statement of financial position.

12.7.1 Accounting treatment

Lessees

IAS 17 paragraph 33 requires the lessee to recognise lease payments 'as an expense on a straight-line basis over the lease term unless another systematic basis is more representative of the time pattern of the user's benefit.'

Lessors

Lease receipts

IAS 17 paragraph 50 requires lessors to account for receipts from operating leases as 'income on a straight-line basis over the lease term, unless another systematic basis is more representative of the time pattern in which the benefit derived from the leased asset is diminished.'

Initial direct costs

As discussed previously, the IAS 17 definition of initial direct costs excludes costs incurred by manufacturers and dealers in negotiating and executing a lease. Any initial direct costs incurred by non-dealer/manufacturer lessors in negotiating operating leases are 'added to the carrying amount of the leased asset and recognised as an expense over the lease term on the same basis as the lease income' (paragraph 52). This is illustrated as follows:

Asset	€ xxx
Less: Accumulated depreciation	(xxx)
	xxx
Plus: Initial direct costs	xxx
	xxx

Depreciation of leased assets

Leased assets are required to be presented in the statement of financial position according to the nature of the asset. Depreciation of assets under operating leases must be consistent with the lessor's normal depreciation policy for similar assets, and calculated in accordance with IAS 16 and IAS 38.

ILLUSTRATIVE EXAMPLE 12.5 Accounting for operating leases

On 1 January 2015, Matheson Corporation leased a bobcat from West Inc. The bobcat cost West Inc. €35 966 on that same day. The lease agreement, which cost West Inc. €381 to have drawn up, contained the following terms:

Lease term	3 years
Estimated economic life of the bobcat	10 years
Annual rental payment, in arrears (commencing 31 December 2015)	€3 900
Residual value at end of the lease term	€31 000
Residual guaranteed by Matheson Corporation	€0
Interest rate implicit in lease	6%

IAS 17 requires the lease to be classified as either a finance lease or an operating lease based on the extent to which the risks and rewards associated with the vehicle have been effectively transferred between Matheson Corporation and West Inc.

Does the lease transfer ownership of the bobcat by the end of the lease term?
The lease terms do not transfer ownership of the bobcat to Matheson Corporation.

Is Matheson Corporation reasonably certain to exercise an option to purchase the bobcat?
The lease terms do not contain an option for Matheson Corporation to purchase the bobcat.

Is the lease term for the major part of the economic life of the bobcat?
The lease term is 3 years, which is only 30% of the bobcat's economic life of 10 years. Therefore, it would appear that the lease arrangement is not for the major part of the asset's life.

Is the present value of the minimum lease payments substantially all of the fair value of the bobcat?
Minimum lease payments
The minimum lease payments consist of three payments, in arrears, of €3900. There are no residual value guarantees by any party.

Present value of minimum lease payments

$$PV\ of\ MLP \quad = €3\,900 \times 2.6730\ [3\ years\ T_2\ 6\%] = €10\,425$$
$$PV/FV \quad = €10\,425/€35\,966$$
$$= 29\%$$

At 29%, the present value of the minimum lease payments is not substantially all of the fair value of the bobcat.

Other considerations required by IAS 17
- Is the bobcat of such a specialised nature that it is expected to have no alternative use to West Inc. at the end of the lease term? No.
- Is Matheson Corporation responsible for any losses incurred by West Inc. if Matheson Corporation decides to cancel the lease before the end of the lease term? No.
- Is Matheson Corporation entitled to the gains or losses from the fluctuation in the fair value of the residual asset? No.
- Can Matheson Corporation continue to use the bobcat for further periods at rent substantially less than market rent? No. The terms of the lease agreement do not contain any renewal options. If Matheson Corporation decides to continue to lease the bobcat, this would be subject to new negotiations with West Inc. and a new agreement, which would require a new analysis of classification under IAS 17.

Classification of the lease
On the basis of the facts presented, there has not been a transfer of substantially all the risks and rewards associated with the bobcat to Matheson Corporation. Hence, the lease would be classified and accounted for as an operating lease.

Journal entries
The following journal entries would be recorded in the books of both Matheson Corporation and West Inc.

MATHESON CORPORATION General Journal			
31 December 2015:			
Lease Expense	Dr	3 900	
Cash	Cr		3 900
(Payment of first year's rental in arrears)			

Note: Expense would accrue throughout the period; it is illustrated at 31 December for simplicity.

WEST INC. General Journal			
1 January 2015:			
Plant and Equipment	Dr	35 966	
Cash	Cr		35 966
(Purchase of bobcat)			
Deferred IDC— Plant and Equipment	Dr	381	
Cash	Cr		381
(IDC incurred for lease)			
31 December 2015:			
Cash	Dr	3 900	
Lease Income	Cr		3 900
(Receipt of first year's rental in arrears)			
Depreciation Expense	Dr	127	
Deferred IDC— Plant and Equipment	Cr		127
(Recognition of initial direct cost: €381/3 years)			
Depreciation Expense	Dr	3 597	
Accumulated Depreciation	Cr		3 597
(Depreciation charge for the period: €35,966/10)			

12.7.2 Disclosures required

Lessees

Figure 12.5 provides an illustration of the disclosures required by IAS 17. The information used in this figure is derived from the Matheson Corporation lease shown in illustrative example 12.5 for the fiscal year ended 31 December 2016.

	IAS 17 paragraph
Note 1: Summary of accounting policies (extract) **Leasing** The Entity leases equipment under operating leases with terms of three years. Leases are classified as finance leases whenever the terms of the lease transfer substantially all the risks and rewards of ownership to the Entity. All other leases are classified as operating leases.	*35(d)*
The entity as a lessee Rentals payable under operating leases are charged to income on a straight-line basis over the term of the relevant lease.	
Note 43: Operating lease arrangements Minimum lease payments recorded as expense amounted to €3 900 (2015: €3 900) for the period.	*35(c)*

Future minimum lease payments under non-cancellable operating leases are as follows:

	2016	2015	
Within 1 year	3 900	3 900	*35(a)*
After 1 year but not more than 5 years[(1)]		3 900	
	3 900	7 800	

(1) If the lease term in illustrative example 12.5 was for more than 5 years, the entity would also disclose the total amounts payable more than 5 years.

FIGURE 12.5 Illustrative disclosures required by IAS 17 for lessees of operating leases

If Matheson Corporation's lease contained contingent rentals, renewal or purchase options, escalation clauses or any restrictions (such as those limiting the payment of dividends), those terms would be required to be disclosed (IAS 17 paragraph 35(d)). In addition, if Matheson Corporation sublet the bobcat, the future minimum lease payments under that sub-lease arrangement (if it were non-cancellable) also would be required to be disclosed (IAS 17 paragraph 35 (c)).

The key feature of these disclosures is the identification of future commitments with respect to those operating leases which are non-cancellable. This information allows users of financial statements to factor in lease expenses against expected future profits, and alerts potential creditors to the fact that some future cash flows are not available to service new liabilities.

Lessors

Figure 12.6 provides an illustration of the disclosures required by IAS 17 for lessors of operating leases. It is not based on illustrative examples from elsewhere in this chapter.

FIGURE 12.6 Illustrative disclosures required by IAS 17 for lessors of operating leases

	IAS 17 paragraph
Note 1: Summary of accounting policies (extract) **Leasing** The Entity is the lessor in lease agreements for machinery and equipment. These leases have remaining terms of 12 years as at 31 December 2016. Some of the Entity's leases provide for contingent rentals based upon usage. The terms of the Entity's leases generally contain renewal options.	*56(c)*
Leases are classified as finance leases whenever the terms of the lease transfer substantially all the risks and rewards of ownership to the lessee. All other leases are classified as operating leases.	
The Entity as a lessor Rental income from operating leases is recognised on a straight-line basis over the term of the relevant lease.	

FIGURE 12.6 *(continued)*

Note 43: Operating lease arrangements

Future minimum lease payments receivable under non-cancellable operating leases are as follows:

	2016	2015	
Within 1 year	81 000	60 200	*56(a)*
After 1 year but not more than 5 years	317 900	324 000	
More than 5 years	153 900	228 800	
	552 800	613 000	

Contingent rent income amounting to €15 600 (2015: nil) was recognised during the period.   *56(b)*

12.7.3 Accounting for lease incentives

In order to induce prospective lessees to enter into non-cancellable operating leases, lessors may offer lease incentives such as rent-free periods, upfront cash payments or contributions towards lessee expenses such as fit-out or removal costs. However attractive these incentives appear, it is unlikely that they are truly free because the lessor will structure the rental payments so as to recover the costs of the incentives over the lease term. Thus, rental payments will be higher than for leases that do not offer incentives.

IAS 17 is silent about incentives, and deals only with accounting for the rental payments made under the operating lease agreement. As a result, SIC (Standing Interpretations Committee) Interpretation 15 *Operating Leases — Incentives* (SIC 15) provides guidance on accounting for incentives by both lessors and lessees. SIC 15 requires that all incentives associated with an operating lease be regarded as part of the net consideration agreed for the use of the leased asset, irrespective of the nature or form of the incentive or the timing of the lease payments.

* For lessors — the aggregate cost of the incentives is treated as a reduction in rental income over the lease term on a straight-line basis.
* For lessees — the aggregate benefit of incentives is treated as a reduction in rental expense over the lease term on a straight-line basis.

In both cases, another systematic basis can be used if it better represents the diminishment of the leased asset.

ILLUSTRATIVE EXAMPLE 12.6 Accounting for lease incentives

As an incentive to enter a 4-year operating lease for a warehouse, Nelson Ltd receives an upfront cash payment of €600 upon signing an agreement to pay Hutt Ltd an annual rental of €11 150.

Nelson Ltd will make the following journal entries with respect to the lease incentive:

At inception of the lease			
Cash	Dr	600	
Incentive from Lessor	Cr		600
(Recognition of liability to lessor)			
Payment entry (year 1)			
Lease Expense	Dr	11 000	
Incentive from Lessor*	Dr	150	
Cash	Cr		11 150
(Record payment of rent and reduction in liability)			
*Being 600/4.			

Hutt Ltd will make the following journal entries with respect to the lease incentive:

At inception of the lease			
Incentive to Lessee	Dr	600	
Cash	Cr		600
(Recognition of receivable)			
Receipt entry (year 1)			
Cash	Dr	11 150	
Incentive to Lessee*	Cr		150
Rent income	Cr		11 000
(Record receipt of rent and reduction in receivable)			
*Being 600/4.			

This broad-brush approach assumes that all incentives are the same, but a number of issues are not addressed in SIC 15 or elsewhere in the standards, including:

- distinguishing between capital incentives such as property fit-outs, particularly in the retail industry, and cash incentives such as rent-free periods;
- distinguishing between property fit-outs that became part of the structure of a leased property and owned by the lessor, and fit-outs that are owned by the lessee; and
- determining whether market rentals are being paid by tenants who received incentives to lease space.

12.8 ACCOUNTING FOR SALE AND LEASEBACK TRANSACTIONS

A 'sale and leaseback' is a type of arrangement that involves the sale of an asset that is then leased back from the purchaser for all or part of its remaining economic life. Hence, the original owner becomes the lessee. In substance, the lessee gives up legal ownership but still retains control over some or all of the asset's future economic benefits via the lease agreement. Generally, the asset is sold at a price equal to, lesser or greater than its fair value, and is leased back for lease payments sufficient to repay the purchaser for the cash invested plus a reasonable return. Therefore, the lease payment and the sale price are usually interdependent because they are negotiated as a package.

Entities normally enter into sale and leaseback arrangements to generate immediate cash flows while still retaining the use of the asset. Such arrangements are particularly attractive when the fair value of an asset is considerably higher than its carrying amount, or when a large amount of capital is tied up in property and plant.

The major accounting issue revolves around the sale rather than the lease component of the transaction. The lease is classified and accounted for in exactly the same fashion as normal lease transactions, but accounting for the sale transaction differs according to whether the lease is classified as a finance lease or an operating lease.

12.8.1 Finance leasebacks

If a sale and leaseback transaction results in a finance lease, the excess of proceeds over the carrying amount is deferred and amortised over the lease term rather than recognised immediately. This accounting treatment is justified on the basis that the leaseback of the asset negates the sale transaction. In other words, there is a finance agreement between the lessor and the lessee — not a sale — with the asset used as security. For this reason any excess of sales proceeds over the carrying amount is not reflected as income.

The standard provides no guidance on how the deferred income is to be classified in the statement of financial position. In this chapter, any deferred income is recognised separately and classified as 'other' liabilities on the statement of financial position. Amortisation is on a straight-line basis over the lease term.

ILLUSTRATIVE EXAMPLE 12.7 Sale and leaseback

In an attempt to alleviate its liquidity problems, Napier S.A. entered into an agreement on 1 January 2016 to sell its processing plant to Whale Company for €3.5 million (which is the fair value of the plant). At the date of sale, the plant had a carrying amount of €2.75 million. Whale Company immediately leased the processing plant back to Napier S.A. The terms of the lease agreement were:

Lease term	6 years
Economic life of plant	8 years
Annual rental payment, in arrears (commencing 31 December 2016)	€765 000
Residual value of plant at end of lease term (fully guaranteed)	€560 000
Interest rate implicit in the lease	10%

The lease is non-cancellable. The annual rental payment includes €35 000 to reimburse the lessor for maintenance costs incurred on behalf of the lessee.

Accounting for the sale of the processing plant

Step 1 — Classify the leaseback

Napier S.A. must determine whether the leaseback has resulted in the company retaining substantially all of the risks and rewards associated with the processing plant, even though legal title has passed to Whale Company, before classifying the lease as a finance lease in accordance with IAS 17 requirements.

Based on the following, both Napier S.A. and Whale Company conclude that the lease should be classified as a finance lease:

- the lease term is a major part of the economic life of the processing plant
- the present value of the minimum lease payments is substantially all of the fair value of the processing plant. It was calculated as follows:

$$PV \text{ of } MLP = (€730\,000 \times 4.3553) + (€560\,000 \times 0.5645)$$
$$= €3\,179\,369 + €316\,120 = €3\,495\,489$$
$$PV/FV \quad = €3\,495\,489/€3\,500\,000$$
$$= 99.9\%$$

Step 2 — Record the 'sale' transaction

This illustrative example shows only those journal entries relating to the sale of the processing plant to Whale Company. The lease is recorded as shown in illustrative example 12.2.

NAPIER S.A. GENERAL JOURNAL			
Year ended 31 December 2016			
1 January 2016:			
Cash	Dr	3 500 000	
Deferred Gain on Sale	Cr		750 000
Processing Plant	Cr		2 750 000
(Sale of plant under sale and leaseback agreement)			
31 December 2016:			
Deferred Gain on Sale	Dr	125 000	
Gain on Sale of Leased Plant	Cr		125 000
(Amortisation of deferred gain: €750 000/6)			

The deferred gain is recognised as income on a straight-line basis over the lease term.

In addition, the leaseback would lead to the recognition of property, plant and equipment of €3 495 489 and a corresponding lease liability.

12.8.2 Operating leasebacks

All operating leases are accounted for in the same way regardless of whether a sale and leaseback transaction is involved. The only accounting issue involves the initial recognition of the sale transaction.

The accounting treatment of the gain or loss on sale is determined by the relationship between the sale price of the asset and the asset's fair value on the date of sale. Essentially, a gain or loss on sale can be recognised immediately only when it equates to the gain or loss that would have been earned on a sale at fair value. Excess or reduced gains or losses that are not recognised immediately are deferred and amortised over the lease term. Table 12.1 is part of the implementation guidance to IAS 17, and sets out the alternative treatments as required by paragraphs 61–63 of the standard.

Table 12.1 Alternative treatments of gain or loss on sale			
	Carrying amount equal to fair value	**Carrying amount less than fair value**	**Carrying amount above fair value**
Sale price at fair value (paragraph 61)			
Profit	No profit	Recognise profit immediately	Not applicable
Loss	No loss	Not applicable	Recognise loss immediately
Sale price below fair value (paragraph 61)			
Profit	No profit	Recognise profit immediately	No profit (note 1)
Loss not compensated for by future lease payments at below market price	Recognise loss immediately	Recognise loss immediately	(note 1)
Loss compensated for by future lease payments at below market price	Defer and amortise loss	Defer and amortise loss	(note 1)

(continued)

Table 12.1 (continued)			
	Carrying amount equal to fair value	Carrying amount less than fair value	Carrying amount above fair value
Sale price above fair value (paragraph 61)			
Profit	Defer and amortise profit	Defer and amortise excess of profit (note 3)	Defer and amortise profit (note 2)
Loss	No loss	No loss	(note 1)

Notes:
1. These parts of the table represent circumstances dealt with in paragraph 63 of the standard. Paragraph 63 requires the carrying amount of an asset to be written down to fair value where it is subject to a sale and leaseback.
2. Profit is the difference between the fair value and sale price because the carrying amount would have been written down to fair value in accordance with paragraph 63.
3. The excess profit (the excess of selling price over fair value) is deferred and amortised over the period for which the asset is expected to be used. Any excess of fair value over the carrying amount is recognised immediately.

Source: IAS 17, *Guidance on Implementing IAS 17 Leases.*

12.8.3 Disclosures required

Sale and leaseback transactions are subject to the same disclosure requirements for lessees and lessors under both operating and finance leases. Unique or unusual provisions of the agreement are disclosed as part of the required description of material leasing arrangements. Additionally, sale and leaseback transactions may fall under the separate disclosure criteria in IAS 1 *Presentation of Financial Statements* with respect to gains or losses on the sale of assets.

12.9 CHANGES TO THE LEASING STANDARDS

Accounting for leases in most countries is very comparable, in that most countries require the application of principles similar to those in IAS 17. However, it is also recognised that those accounting principles have flaws.

In July 2006, as a result of the agreement between the IASB and the FASB to converge accounting standards, a joint working party was formed between the two bodies to develop a new accounting standard on leases. The aims of the project were:
- to produce an improved accounting standard that faithfully reports the economics of leasing transactions
- to develop a principles-based standard
- to produce a converged standard that can be applied internationally.

The main concerns about IAS 17 are:
- the dividing line between finance and operating leases is hard to define in a principled way
- any dividing line means that similar transactions are accounted for differently
- obligations under non-cancellable leases are little different from borrowings, but for operating leases they are not recognised as liabilities
- assets used in a lessee's business that are held under operating leases are not shown on the statement of financial position, thereby overstating return on assets
- leases are scoped out of the financial instruments standards, leading to inconsistencies between leases and similar transactions.

Since 2006, the IASB and the FASB issued one discussion paper and two exposure drafts of a proposed new leasing standard. The Boards issued their respective new standards in 2016. In many respects the IASB and the FASB standards are converged, but they do contain some differences relating to lease classification and the recognition, measurement and presentation of leases for lessees and lessors.

Under IFRS 16, a lease is defined as 'a contract, or part of a contract, that conveys the right to use an asset (the underlying asset) for a period of time in exchange for consideration' (IFRS 16 *Leases*, Appendix A, Defined terms).

Lessees will be required to recognise right-of-use assets and lease liabilities for most leases. That is, most leases will be on the statement of financial position. Lessees applying IFRS will have a single accounting model for all leases, with exemptions for leases of 'low-value assets' and short-term leases. Lessor accounting for IFRS reporters is substantially unchanged from IAS 17. Lessees and lessors applying US GAAP will have a dual model for all recognised leases, similar to the two lease classifications for lessees today, with lessees having a recognition exemption for short-term leases.

Lessees will recognise a liability to pay rentals with a corresponding asset. Under the IASB's standard, lessees will recognise separate amounts for interest and depreciation resulting in an accelerated expense recognition pattern (for lessees that use straight-line depreciation) as compared to today's operating leases. Lessees will be required to reassess certain key considerations (e.g. lease term, variable rents based on an index or rate, discount rate) upon certain events.

The IASB decided to include an overall disclosure objective to enable users of the financial statements to assess the effect that leases have on the financial position, financial performance and cash flows of lessees and lessors. IFRS 16 requires lessees and lessors to make more extensive disclosures than under IAS 17.

IFRS 16 will have a major effect on lessees that have a large number of operating leases as these will be accounted for in essentially the same way as finance leases today. There is little change for lessors.

Some have questioned the conceptual merit of differentiating lease arrangements and non-lease executory contracts due to the very different accounting that would result under the new standard. The IASB concluded that lease arrangements create rights and obligations for the lessee that meet the definitions of an asset and a liability under the *Conceptual Framework*. The IASB believes that at the commencement of a lease, the lessor fulfils its obligation under the contract by delivering the asset to the lessee and, therefore, the lessee has an unconditional obligation to pay for the right to use the asset. In a non-lease executory contract, at the commencement of the arrangement the customer does not receive an asset it controls and the vendor has remaining obligations; consequently, the customer 'typically has an unconditional obligation to pay only for services provided to date. In addition, although fulfilment of a service contract will often require the use of assets, 'fulfilment typically does not require making those assets available for use by the customer throughout the contractual term.' (Basis for Conclusions, IFRS 16, *Leases*, paragraph BC34).

The new standard is effective for annual periods beginning on or after 1 January 2019.

SUMMARY

Leases are arrangements whereby the right to use an asset is transferred to a lessee but ownership is retained by the lessor. By definition, finance leases transfer substantially all of the risks and rewards incidental to ownership from the lessor to the lessee. Operating leases do not. All leases must be classified as either operating leases or finance leases at the inception of the lease.

For finance leases, lessees must record a lease asset and a lease liability measured at the lower of the fair value of the leased property and the present value of the minimum lease payments. The asset is subsequently depreciated over the lease term or its economic life if ownership is to be transferred at the end of the lease. The liability is reduced as lease payments are made.

For finance leases, lessors must transfer their net investment in the lease to a receivable account, which is subsequently reduced by lease receipts and the eventual return of the asset at the end of the lease. Manufacturer and dealer lessors also record a profit or loss on sale of the asset at the beginning of the lease term.

Operating leases are treated as a rental arrangement with lessors recording rental revenue and lessees recording rental expense over the term of the lease.

IAS 17 has been subject to criticism for many years for, among other reasons, enabling economically similar transactions to be accounted for very differently and, thus, reducing comparability. The IASB issued a new lease accounting standard in 2016 that will address many of the criticisms of accounting for leases by lessees.

Discussion questions

1. What are 'minimum lease payments'?
2. If a lease agreement states that 'the lessee guarantees a residual value, at the end of the lease term, of $20 000', what does this mean?
3. What is meant by 'the interest rate implicit in a lease'?
4. Identify three possible adverse effects on a lessee entity's financial statements arising from the classification of a lease arrangement as a finance lease.
5. How, according to IAS 17 requirements, are operating leases accounted for by lessees?
6. Explain how a profit made by a lessee on a sale and leaseback transaction is to be accounted for.

Exercises   STAR RATING ★ BASIC ★★ MODERATE ★★★ DIFFICULT

Exercise 12.1	IDENTIFICATION OF LEASES

★ For the following arrangements, discuss whether they are 'in substance' lease transactions, and thus fall under the ambit of IAS 17.

(a) Entity A leases an asset to Entity B, and obtains a non-recourse loan from a financial institution using the lease rentals and asset as collateral. Entity A sells the asset subject to the lease and the loan to a trustee, and leases the same asset back.

(b) Entity A enters into an arrangement to buy petroleum products from Entity B. The products are produced in a refinery built and operated by Entity B on a site owned by Entity A. Although Entity B could provide the products from other refineries which it owns, it is not practical to do so. Entity B retains the right to sell products produced by the refinery to other customers but there is only a remote possibility that it will do so. The arrangement requires Entity A to make both fixed unavoidable payments and variable payments based on input costs at a target level of efficiency to Entity B.

(c) Entity A leases an asset to Entity B for its entire economic life and leases the same asset back under the same terms and conditions as the original lease. The two entities have a legally enforceable right to set off the amounts owing to one another, and an intention to settle these amounts on a net basis.

(d) Entity A enters into a non-cancellable 4-year lease with Entity B for an asset with an expected economic life of 10 years. Entity A has an option to renew the lease for a further 4 years at the end of the lease term. At the conclusion of the lease arrangement, the asset will revert back to Entity B. In a separate agreement, Entity B is granted a put option to sell the asset to Entity A should its market value at the end of the lease be less than the residual value.

Exercise 12.2	LEASE CLASSIFICATION AND DETERMINATION OF INTEREST RATES

★ *This exercise contains three multiple-choice questions. Select the correct answer and show any workings required.*

1. Pukekohe Ltd sells land that originally cost $150 000 to Taupo Ltd for $230 000 when the land's fair value is $215 000, and then enters into a cancellable lease agreement to use the land for 2 years at an annual rental of $2000. In the current year, how much profit would Pukekohe Ltd record on the sale of the land?
   (a) $15 000
   (b) $80 000
   (c) $65 000
   (d) Nil

2. Using the information from part 1 above, how would Taupo Ltd record the annual cash received from Pukekohe Ltd?
   (a) As rental revenue
   (b) As a reduction of the lease receivable
   (c) As rental expense
   (d) As interest revenue and a reduction of the lease receivable

3. On 1 July 2016, Masterton Ltd leases a machine with a fair value of $109 445 to Tokoroa Ltd for 5 years at an annual rental (in advance) of $25 000, and Tokoroa Ltd guarantees in full the estimated residual value of $15 000 on return of the asset. What would be the interest rate implicit in the lease?
   (a) 10%   (c) 9%
   (b) 12%   (d) 14%

Exercise 12.3	FINANCE LEASE

★ If a lease has been capitalised as a finance lease, identify two circumstances in which the lease receivable raised by the lessor will differ from the lease asset raised by the lessee.

Exercise 12.4	LEASE CLASSIFICATION; ACCOUNTING BY LESSEE

★★ On 1 July 2016, Otago Ltd leased a plastic-moulding machine from Nelson Ltd. The machine cost Nelson $130 000 to manufacture and had a fair value of $154 109 on 1 July 2016. The lease agreement contained the following provisions:

Lease term	4 years
Annual rental payment, in advance on 1 July each year	$41 500
Residual value at end of the lease term	$15 000
Residual guaranteed by lessee	nil
Interest rate implicit in lease	8%
The lease is cancellable only with the permission of the lessor.	

The expected useful life of the machine is 6 years. Otago Ltd intends to return the machine to the lessor at the end of the lease term. Included in the annual rental payment is an amount of $1500 to cover the costs of maintenance and insurance paid for by the lessor.

Required

1. Classify the lease for both lessee and lessor based on the guidance provided in IAS 17. Justify your answer.
2. Prepare (a) the lease schedules for the lessee (show all workings), and (b) the journal entries in the books of the lessee for the year ended 30 June 2017.

Exercise 12.5   **ACCOUNTING BY LESSEE AND LESSOR**

★★   On 1 July 2016, Christchurch Ltd leased a processing plant to Wellington Ltd. The plant was purchased by Christchurch Ltd on 1 July 2016 for its fair value of $467 112. The lease agreement contained the following provisions:

Lease term	3 years
Economic life of plant	5 years
Annual rental payment, in arrears (commencing 30/6/2017)	$150 000
Residual value at end of the lease term	$90 000
Residual guaranteed by lessee	$60 000
Interest rate implicit in lease	7%
The lease is cancellable only with the permission of the lessor.	

Wellington Ltd intends to return the processing plant to the lessor at the end of the lease term. The lease has been classified as a finance lease by both the lessee and the lessor.

Required

1. Prepare:
   (a) the lease payment schedule for the lessee (show all workings)
   (b) the journal entries in the records of the lessee for the year ended 30 June 2018.
2. Prepare:
   (a) the lease receipt schedule for the lessor (show all workings)
   (b) the journal entries in the records of the lessor for the year ended 30 June 2018.

Exercise 12.6   **LEASE SCHEDULES AND JOURNAL ENTRIES (YEAR 1)**

★★   On 1 July 2016, Island Ltd leased a crane from Pacific Ltd. The crane cost Pacific Ltd $120 307, considered to be its fair value on that same day. The finance lease agreement contained the following provisions:

The lease term is for 3 years, starting on The lease is non-cancellable	1 July 2016
Annual lease payment, payable on 30 June each year	$39 000
Estimated useful life of crane	4 years
Estimated residual value of crane at end of lease term	$22 000
Residual value guaranteed by Island Ltd	$16 000
Interest rate implicit in the lease	7%
The lease was classified as a finance lease by both Island Ltd and Pacific Ltd at 1 July 2016.	

Required

1. Prepare the lease schedules for both the lessee and the lessor.
2. Prepare the journal entries in the records of the lessee only for the year ended 30 June 2017.

Exercise 12.7   **FINANCE LEASE — LESSEE (INCLUDING DISCLOSURES)**

★★   Dunedin Ltd decided to lease from Rotorua Ltd a motor vehicle that had a fair value at 30 June 2014 of $38 960. The lease agreement contained the following provisions:

Lease term (non-cancellable)	3 years
Annual rental payments (commencing 30/6/14)	$11 200
Guaranteed residual value (expected fair value at end of lease term)	$12 000
Extra rental per annum if the car is used outside the metropolitan area	$1 000

The expected useful life of the vehicle is 5 years. At the end of the 3-year lease term, the car was returned to the lessor, which sold it for $10 000. The annual rental payments include an amount of $1200 to cover the cost of maintenance and insurance arranged and paid for by the lessor. The car was used outside the metropolitan area in the 2015–16 year. The lease is considered to be a finance lease.

Required
1. Prepare the journal entries for Dunedin Ltd from 30 June 2014 to 30 June 2017.
2. Prepare the relevant disclosures required under IAS 17 for the years ending 30 June 2016 and 30 June 2017.
3. How would your answer to requirement 1 change if the guaranteed residual value was only $10 000, and the expected fair value at the end of the lease term was $12 000?

Exercise 12.8   **LEASE CLASSIFICATION; ACCOUNTING AND DISCLOSURES**

★★★   Birkenhead Ltd has entered into an agreement to lease a D9 bulldozer to Albert Ltd. The lease agreement details are as follows:

Length of lease	5 years
Commencement date	1 July 2015
Annual lease payment, payable 30 June each year commencing 30 June 2016	$8 000
Fair value of the bulldozer at 1 July 2015	$34 797
Estimated economic life of the bulldozer	8 years
Estimated residual value of the plant at the end of its economic life	$2000
Residual value at the end of the lease term, of which 50% is guaranteed by Albert Ltd	$7200
Interest rate implicit in the lease	9%

The lease is cancellable, but a penalty equal to 50% of the total lease payments is payable on cancellation. Albert Ltd does not intend to buy the bulldozer at the end of the lease term. Birkenhead Ltd incurred $1000 to negotiate and execute the lease agreement. Birkenhead Ltd purchased the bulldozer for $34 797 just before the inception of the lease.

Required
1. State how both companies should classify the lease. Give reasons for your answer.
2. Prepare a schedule of lease payments for Albert Ltd.
3. Prepare a schedule of lease receipts for Birkenhead Ltd.
4. Prepare journal entries to record the lease transactions for the year ended 30 June 2016 in the records of both companies.
5. Prepare an appropriate note to the financial statements of both companies as at 30 June 2016.

Exercise 12.9   **FINANCE LEASE — LESSEE AND LESSOR**

★★★   On 1 July 2014, Wellington Ltd acquired a new car. The manager of Wellington Ltd, Jack Wellington, went to the local car yard, Hamilton Autos, and discussed the price of a new Racer Special with John Hamilton. Jack and John agreed on a price of $37 876. As Hamilton Autos had acquired the vehicle from the manufacturer for $32 000, John was pleased with the deal. On discussing the financial arrangements in relation to the car, Jack decided that a lease arrangement was the most suitable. John agreed to arrange for Dunedin Ltd, a local finance company, to set up the lease agreement. Hamilton Autos then sold the car to Dunedin Ltd for $37 876.

Dunedin Ltd wrote a lease agreement, incurring initial direct costs of $534 in the process.

The lease agreement contained the following clauses:

Initial payment on 1 July 2014	$13 000
Payments on 1 July 2015 and 1 July 2016	$13 000
Interest rate implicit in the lease	6%

The lease agreement also specified for Dunedin Ltd to pay for the insurance and maintenance of the vehicle, the latter to be carried out by Hamilton Autos at regular intervals. A cost of $3000 per annum was included in the lease payments to cover these services.

Jack wanted the lease to be considered an operating lease for accounting purposes. To achieve this, the lease agreement was worded as follows:

- The lease is cancellable by Wellington Ltd at any stage. However, if the lease is cancelled, Wellington Ltd agrees to lease, on similar terms, another car from Dunedin Ltd.
- Wellington Ltd is not required to guarantee the payment of any residual value. At the end of the lease term, 30 June 2017, or if cancelled earlier, the car automatically reverts to the lessor with no payments being required from Wellington Ltd.

The vehicle had an expected economic life of 6 years. The expected fair value of the vehicle at 30 June 2017 was $12 000. Because of concern over the residual value, Dunedin Ltd required Jack to sign another contractual arrangement separate from the lease agreement which gave Dunedin Ltd the right to sell the car to Wellington Ltd if the fair value of the car at the end of the lease term was less than $10 000.

Costs of maintenance and insurance paid by Dunedin Ltd to Hamilton Autos over the years ended 30 June 2015 to 30 June 2017 were $2810, $3020 and $2750.

At 30 June 2017, Jack returned the vehicle to Dunedin Ltd. The fair value of the car was determined by to be $9000. Dunedin Ltd invoked the second agreement. With the consent of Wellington, Dunedin Ltd sold the car to Hamilton Autos for a price of $9000 on 5 July 2017, and invoiced Wellington Ltd for $1000. Wellington Ltd subsequently paid this amount on 13 July 2017.

Required

Assuming the lease is classified as a finance lease, prepare:
1. a schedule of lease payments for Wellington Ltd
2. journal entries in the records of Wellington Ltd for the years ending 30 June 2015, 30 June 2017 and 30 June 2018
3. a schedule of lease receipts for Dunedin Ltd
4. journal entries in the records of Dunedin Ltd for the years ending 30 June 2015, 30 June 2017 and 30 June 2018.

Early research into the accounting for leases was concerned with measuring the magnitude of the off-balance-sheet financing that operating leases represent. In particular, the concern has been that leaving assets and debt off the balance sheet distorts commonly used ratios. Imhoff et al. (1991) posit that it is quite plausible that managers "game" the accounting rules to avoid classifying lease contracts as finance leases. They propose a method for capitalisation of operating leases and assess its impact for a small sample of firms chosen from several industries. Their calculations suggest that the effect of capitalising operating leases on ratios such as return on assets (ROA) and debt-to-equity can be very large. For example, they calculate that ROA can decrease by 55% while debt-to-equity can increase by more than 300%. Beattie et al. (1998) employ the method suggested by Imhoff et al. (1991) to a large UK sample comprising 300 firms that reported operating leases during 1981 to 1994. They examine a wide range of ratios for this sample and demonstrate that the effect of capitalisation on many of the ratios can be very large. Cornaggia et al. (2013) provide recent analysis that also looks at the trend over time in the use of operating leases. They document an increasing tendency by US firms to use off-balance-sheet financing through operating leases in the past three decades. Over the same time, on-balance-sheet financing through finance leases has fallen. This suggests that for analytical purposes it is increasingly important to capitalise operating leases.

Researchers have also been interested in the degree to which leases are used as a substitute, or perhaps as a complement, to ordinary debt financing. Ang and Petersen (1984) expect to find a substitutive effect whereby more (less) debt is associated with less (more) lease financing. However, in a study spanning the 1976 to 1981 period that includes only finance leases they fail to find consistent relation. Adedeji and Stapleton (1996) rectify several methodological problems in the approach taken by Ang and Petersen (1984) using a UK sample and find that there is a substitution effect whereby a reduction of £1 in debt is associated with an increase in leases of roughly £2. Further evidence supporting a substitutive effect is provided by Schallheim et al. (2013) who examine a sample of sale-and-leaseback transactions. The advantage of this sample vis-à-vis other studies is that the underlying asset base is kept the same because the leased-back asset is retained by the lessee. Beattie et al. (2000) take this research further by incorporating measures of capitalised operating leases. They examine a sample of over 560 UK firms during 1990 to 1994 and find that, once operating leases are capitalised, debt and leases are substitutes. Moreover, since most of lease-borrowing stems from operating leases, this result suggests that the substitutive effect is largely due to operating lease financing.

All the above mentioned studies, however, do not address the question of whether users of financial statements regard operating leases as debt financing. Altamuro et al. (2014) provide helpful and rare input into this question. They examine whether banks regard operating leases as debt (that is, as finance leases) or periodic expense. They argue that if operating leases are in-substance debt, then banks should adjust the interest charge accordingly. In other words, the interest banks charge on their loans is expected to be a function of leverage and other ratios that are adjusted for the capitalisation of operating leasees. They first report that the interest charge is higher the larger the amount of outstanding payments on operating leases. They then show that models that feature adjusted ratios explain the variations in interest charges. However, this is not the case for operating leases in the retail business. They conclude that leases of store space are regarded as periodic expense by lending banks.

Ely (1995) adopts a shareholders' perspective rather than creditors' perspective as in Altamuro et al. (2014). She argues that the distinguishing factor between operating and finance leases is the degree to which the lessee is exposed to risk from employing the leased assets. She therefore relates equity risk to two key ratios: ROA (capturing asset risk) and debt-to-equity (capturing financial risk). Her sample is based on 212 US firms that provide disclosures about minimum lease payments (MLPs) that are classified as operating lease in 1987 and 102 firms that disclosed no information about operating leases. As with other studies, Ely (1995) capitalises these MLPs to examine, in her case, the association with a measure of equity risk. She finds that debt-to-equity ratios adjusted for the capitalised amounts are positively related to equity risk. This result suggests that investors perceive operating lease obligations as similar to debt. Nevertheless, the results regarding ROA are mixed and it is not clear if investors perceive operating leases as increased asset risk.

References

Adedeji, A., and Stapleton, R. C. 1996. Leases debt and taxable capacity. *Applied Financial Economics*, 6, 71–83.

Altamuro, J., Johnston, R., Pandit, S. S., and Zhang, H. H. 2014. Operating leases and credit assessments. *Contemporary Accounting Research*, 31(2), 551–580.

Ang, J., and Peterson, P. P. 1984. The leasing puzzle. *Journal of Finance*, 39, 1055–1065.

Beattie, V. A., Edwards, K., and Goodacre, A. 1998. The impact of constructive operating lease capitalisation on key accounting ratios. *Accounting and Business Research*, 28, 233–254.

Beattie, V., Goodacre, A., and Thomson, S. 2000. Operating leases and the assessment of lease–debt substitutability. *Journal of Banking & Finance*, 24(3), 427–470.

Cornaggia, K. J., Franzen, L. A., and Simin, T. T. 2013. Bringing leased assets onto the balance sheet. *Journal of Corporate Finance*, 22, 345–360.

Ely, K. M. 1995. Operating lease accounting and the market's assessment of equity risk. *Journal of Accounting Research*, 33(2), 397–415.

Imhoff, E. A., Lipe, R. C., and Wright, D. A. 1991. Operating leases: Impact of constructive capitalization. *Accounting Horizons*, 5, 51–63.

Schallheim, J., Wells, K., and Whitby, R. J. 2013. Do leases expand debt capacity? *Journal of Corporate Finance, 23*, 368–381.

13 Intangible assets

ACCOUNTING STANDARDS IN FOCUS

IAS 38 *Intangible Assets*

LEARNING OBJECTIVES

After studying this chapter, you should be able to:

1. understand the key characteristics of an intangible asset

2. explain the criteria relating to the initial recognition of intangible assets and their measurement at point of initial recognition, distinguishing between acquired and internally generated intangibles

3. explain how to measure intangibles subsequent to initial recognition, including the principles relating to the amortisation of intangibles

4. explain the accounting for retirement and disposal of intangible assets

5. apply the disclosure requirements of IAS 38.

INTRODUCTION

Chapter 11 discusses the accounting standards for the tangible assets of property, plant and equipment. This chapter examines the standards for intangible assets. The International Accounting Standards Board (IASB®) believes it is necessary to distinguish between tangible assets (such as property, plant and equipment) and intangible assets (such as patents and brand names). In analysing the accounting for intangible assets, the question that must always be kept in mind is whether there should be any difference in the accounting treatment for tangible and intangible assets. What is it that is different about intangible assets that makes a separate accounting standard, and presumably different accounting rules, for intangible and tangible assets necessary?

Historically, it is common for entities to report all their tangible assets on the statement of financial position but be less consistent in the reporting of intangible assets. As a result, there are sometimes large differences between the market value of an entity and its recorded net assets. As Jenkins and Upton (2001, p. 4) noted:

> The problem that confronts businesses, users of business and financial reporting, standard-setters and regulators is how best to understand and communicate the difference between the value of a company (usually expressed as the market capitalisation) and the accounting book value of that company.

To assist in understanding the difference between these two numbers, Jenkins and Upton (2001, p. 5) provided the analysis shown in figure 13.1. Item 6 in this figure is not an area that accounting can directly address, although the quality of the accounting may affect the degree to which it exists. At 31 December 2000, the market-to-book gap of Enron was approximately $64 billion. However, Lev (2002, pp. 133–4) argued that this was not related to intangibles:

> The best evidence that Enron lacked substantial intangibles is that its demise made hardly a ripple in the energy trading market, and had practically no effect on electricity prices. Intangibles, by definition, are unique factors of production that cannot be quickly imitated by competitors. The fact that Enron's competitors quickly stepped in to fill the gap is inconsistent with the existence of intangibles conferring on their owners sustained competitive advantages.
>
> So the answer to the question posed at the opening of this note — where have Enron's intangibles gone? — is a simple one. Nowhere. Enron did not have substantial intangibles, that is, if hype, glib, and earnings manipulation do not count as intangibles.

1. Accounting book value	£xxx
2. + Market assessments of differences between accounting measurement and underlying value of recognised assets and liabilities	xxx
3. + Market assessments of the underlying value of items that meet the definition of assets and liabilities but are not recognised in financial statements (e.g. patents developed through internal research and development)	xxx
4. + Market assessments of intangible value drivers or value impairers that do not meet the definition of assets and liabilities (e.g. employee morale)	xxx
5. + Market assessments of the entity's future plans, opportunities and business risks	xxx
6. + Other factors, including puffery, pessimism and market psychology	xxx
7. Market capitalisation	£xxx

FIGURE 13.1 Differences between market capitalisation and accounting book value
Source: Jenkins and Upton (2001, p. 5). © 2001. Reproduced with the permission of CPA Australia Ltd.

How can accounting assist in providing more information about what causes the gap between accounting book value and market capitalisation numbers? How much information should be provided about all the assets and liabilities of an entity? What should be in the financial statements and what should be in the notes to those statements? These are questions for accounting standard setters to solve.

The standards on accounting for intangibles are contained in IAS 38 *Intangible Assets*. In its 2004 revision, the IASB did not attempt to revisit all areas of accounting for intangibles. Its emphasis in this revision was to reflect changes as a result of decisions made in the Business Combinations project, particularly relating to accounting for intangibles acquired as part of a business combination. Hence, there still may be areas of inconsistency between accounting for intangibles obtained outside a business combination and those acquired as part of a business combination.

IAS 38 covers the accounting for all intangible assets except, as detailed in paragraphs 2 and 3, those specifically covered by another accounting standard: financial assets; and mineral rights and expenditure on exploration for, or development and extraction of, minerals, oil, natural gas and similar non-regenerative resources. Other intangible assets specifically covered by standards other than IAS 38 are:
- intangible assets held by an entity for sale in the ordinary course of business (see IAS 2 *Inventories*)
- intangible assets arising from insurance contracts with policyholders (IFRS 4 *Insurance Contracts*)
- deferred tax assets (IAS 12 *Income Taxes*)

- leases within the scope of IAS 17 *Leases*
- assets arising from employee benefits (IAS 19 *Employee Benefits*)
- goodwill acquired in a business combination (IFRS 3 *Business Combinations*)
- non-current intangible assets held for sale (IFRS 5 *Non-current Assets Held for Sale and Discontinued Operations*).

An example of the assets that are being considered in this chapter is shown in figure 13.2, which contains the intangible assets disclosed by Christian Dior in its 2014 annual report. Note that brands and trade names comprise the majority of the intangible assets but other intangibles include licences and computer software.

FIGURE 13.2 Examples of intangible assets

NOTE 3 — BRANDS, TRADE NAMES AND OTHER INTANGIBLE ASSETS

(EUR millions)	Gross	June 30, 2014 (12 months) Amortization and impairment	Net	June 30, 2013 (2 months) Net	April 30, 2013 (12 months) Net
Brands	13 261	(543)	12 718	11 420	11 444
Trade names	3 285	(1 337)	1 948	2 024	2 025
License rights	24	(23)	1	—	—
Leasehold rights	723	(331)	392	306	310
Software, websites	981	(739)	242	199	203
Other	567	(318)	249	225	228
TOTAL	18 841	(3 291)	15 550	14 174	14 210
Of which:					
Assets held under finance leases	14	(14)	—	—	—

3.3 Brands and trade names
The breakdown of brands and trade names by business group is as follows:

(EUR millions)	Gross	June 30, 2014 (12 months) Amortization and impairment	Net	June 30, 2013 (2 months) Net	April 30, 2013 (12 months) Net
Christian Dior Couture	34	(10)	24	32	32
Wines and Spirits	2 990	(77)	2 913	2 914	2 922
Fashion and Leather Goods	5 189	(369)	4 820	3 527	3 530
Perfumes and Cosmetics	1 284	(23)	1 261	1 264	1 264
Watches and Jewelry	3 524	(6)	3 518	3 498	3 509
Selective Retailing	3 243	(1 290)	1 953	2 029	2 030
Other activities	282	(105)	177	180	182
BRANDS AND TRADE NAMES	16 546	(1 880)	14 666	13 444	13 469

The brands and trade names recognized are those that the Group has acquired. The principal acquired brands and trade names as of June 30, 2014 are:
- Wines and Spirits: Hennessy, Moët & Chandon, Veuve Clicquot, Krug, Château d'Yquem, Château Cheval Blanc, Belvedere, Glenmorangie, Newton Vineyards and Numanthia Termes;
- Fashion and Leather Goods: Louis Vuitton, Loro Piana, Fendi, Donna Karan New York, Céline, Loewe, Givenchy, Kenzo, Thomas Pink, Berluti and Pucci;
- Perfumes and Cosmetics: Parfums Christian Dior, Guerlain, Parfums Givenchy, Make Up for Ever, Benefit Cosmetics, Fresh and Acqua di Parma;
- Watches and Jewelry: Bulgari, TAG Heuer, Zenith, Hublot, Chaumet and Fred;
- Selective Retailing: DFS Galleria, Sephora, Le Bon Marché, Ile de Beauté and Ole Henriksen;
- Other activities: the publications of the media group Les Echos-Investir, the Royal Van Lent-Feadship brand and the patisserie brand Cova.

(continued)

FIGURE 13.2 (*continued*)

These brands and trade names are recognized in the balance sheet at their value determined as of the date of their acquisition by the Group, which may be much less than their value in use or their net selling price as of the closing date for the consolidated financial statements of the Group. This is notably the case for the brands Louis Vuitton, Christian Dior Couture, Veuve Clicquot, and Parfums Christian Dior, or the trade name Sephora, with the understanding that this list must not be considered as exhaustive.

Brands developed by the Group, notably Dom Pérignon, as well as the De Beers Diamond Jewellers brand developed as a joint venture with the De Beers group, are not capitalized in the balance sheet.

Brands and trade names developed by the Group, in addition to Louis Vuitton, Moët & Chandon, Ruinart, Hennessy, Veuve Clicquot, Parfums Christian Dior and Sephora, represented 34% of total brands and trade names capitalized in the balance sheet and 59% of the Group's consolidated revenue.

Please refer also to Note 5 for the impairment testing of brands, trade names and other intangible assets with indefinite useful lives.

Source: Christian Dior (2014, pp. 131, 133, 134).

13.1 THE NATURE OF INTANGIBLE ASSETS

Paragraph 8 of IAS 38 defines an intangible asset as follows:

> an identifiable non-monetary asset without physical substance.

According to the IAS 38 definition, there are three key characteristics of an intangible asset: identifiable, non-monetary in nature and without physical substance. Each characteristic is there for a reason, generally to exclude certain assets from being classified as intangible assets.

13.1.1 Non-monetary in nature

Monetary assets are defined in IAS 38 as 'money held and assets to be received in fixed or determinable amounts of money'. The reason for including 'non-monetary' in the definition of intangible assets is to exclude financial assets such as loans and receivables from being classified as intangible assets. The accounting for financial assets is covered in IFRS 9 *Financial Instruments* and IAS 39 *Financial Instruments: Recognition and Measurement*.

13.1.2 Identifiable

IAS 38 does not contain a definition of 'identifiable'. However, paragraph 12 of this standard sets down two criteria, either of which must be met for an asset to be classified as an intangible asset. Paragraph 12 states:

> An asset is identifiable if it either:
> (a) is separable, i.e. is capable of being separated or divided from the entity and sold, transferred, licensed, rented or exchanged, either individually or together with a related contract, identifiable asset or liability, regardless of whether the entity intends to do so; or
> (b) arises from contractual or other legal rights, regardless of whether those rights are transferable or separable from the entity or from other rights and obligations.

There are thus two parts to the concept of identifiability.

First, consider the criterion of separability. Separability tests whether an entity can divide an asset from other assets and transfer it to another party.

Consider the cost of the advertising campaign. It is not separable as it cannot be separated from the entity and sold, transferred, rented or exchanged. Furthermore, the advertising campaign does not arise from contractual or legal rights. Thus the cost of the advertising campaign is not identifiable.

Although many intangible assets are both separable and arise from contractual or legal rights, under the laws of some jurisdictions, for example, some licences granted to an entity are not transferable except by sale of the entity as a whole.

IAS 38's requirement that an intangible asset must be 'identifiable' was introduced to try to distinguish it from internally generated goodwill (which, outside a business combination, should not be recognised as an asset), but also to emphasise that, especially in the context of a business combination, there will be previously unrecorded items that should be recognised in the financial statements as intangible assets separately from goodwill.

Examples include assets such as high staff morale and customer relationships, which may be capable of being named and discussed, and actions may be taken to adjust the levels of them within an entity, but such assets cannot be transferred to another entity.

Why was the criterion of separability included in the definition of an intangible asset? The answer is reliability of measurement. If an asset can be transferred to another entity, then probably a market exists for that asset. If no transfer can occur, then there will be no market. If there is no market, there is no market price. It would seem that the standard setters are afraid that preparers of financial statements will include assets such as staff morale on their balance sheet at some form of non-market valuation, and they are concerned about the reliability of such measurements. By including separability in the definition of intangible assets, there is a limit placed on the assets that could potentially appear on a balance sheet.

The second criterion to the concept of identifiability is if it 'arises from contractual or other legal rights'. As noted earlier, this criterion is an alternative to separability. Hence there are some intangible assets that are not separable but meet the definition of an intangible asset because of part (b) in paragraph 12 of IAS 38. In paragraph BC10 of the Basis for Conclusions on IAS 38, the IASB stated:

> Some contractual-legal rights establish property interests that are not readily separable from the entity as a whole. For example, under the laws of some jurisdictions some licences granted to an entity are not transferable except by sale of the entity as a whole.

Examples of assets fitting into this category generally relate to situations where a government gives or sells a right to an entity, such as:
- an entity has a right to use 2 million litres of water per annum in its production process
- an entity has a right to emit a specified quantity of greenhouse gases into the atmosphere per annum.

A condition of receiving this right is that the right cannot be transferred between entities; hence, if an entity used only 1 million litres of water, it could not sell/transfer the remaining right to 1 million litres of water to another entity. The right is then not separable. However the IASB believed that these assets could be distinguished from other assets held by an entity and should be disclosed as intangible assets. Separability was then not seen as the only criterion for identifiability.

As noted earlier, one of the problems with non-separable assets is the ability to measure them. Some assets, such as an excellent workforce and a high level of customer satisfaction, are interrelated in that very good employees will lead to high customer satisfaction. To recognise these as separate assets would raise difficulties in determining the value of one separately from the other. With the measurement of tangible assets, the emphasis is generally not on measuring the benefits from the asset, but on recording the cost of the asset. Benefits from assets are often measured at the level of a cash-generating unit rather than at the individual asset level, as is the case when determining impairment of assets *(see chapter 15)*.

13.1.3 Lack of physical substance

Lack of physical substance is the third characteristic in the definition of an intangible asset. It is the characteristic that separates assets such as property, plant and equipment from intangible assets, in that property, plant and equipment would generally meet both the other criteria of an intangible asset; that is, IAS 16 *Property, Plant and Equipment* provides accounting policies for identifiable, non-monetary assets.

Note at the outset that some intangible assets may be associated with a physical item, such as software contained on a computer disk. However, the asset is really the software and not the disk itself. As noted in paragraph 4 of IAS 38, judgement in some cases is required to determine which element, tangible or intangible, is most important to the classification of the asset. Use of the physical substance characteristic is interesting in that paragraph 4.11 of the *Conceptual Framework* states:

> physical form is not essential to the existence of an asset; hence patents and copyrights, for example, are assets if future economic benefits are expected to flow from them to the entity and if they are controlled by the entity.

If physical substance is not intrinsic to the determination of assets, why then is it necessary to distinguish between physical and non-physical assets?

Lev (2001, p. 47) answers this question as follows:

> Intangibles are inherently difficult to trade. Legal property rights are often hazy, contingent contracts are difficult to draw, and the cost structure of many intangibles (large sunk costs, negligible marginal costs) is not conducive to stable pricing. Accordingly, at present there are no active, organized markets in intangibles. This could soon change with the advent of Internet-based exchanges, but it will require specific enabling mechanisms, such as valuation and insurance schemes. Private trades in intangibles in the form of licensing and alliances proliferate, but they do not provide information essential for the measurement and valuation of intangibles.

Because non-physical assets have the above characteristics, they cause particular problems for accountants. The two key activities for accountants in relation to assets are the recognition and measurement of the assets. With non-physical assets, the determination of when they should be recognised (Should one wait for a point of discovery? Does an asset exist when the investment is made? Is there an asset at the point employee training occurs?), and how they should be measured (Where is the market? Can the specific benefits be isolated? Are the property rights over the expected benefits fuzzy?) is in general more difficult. Hence, the need for a specific standard on non-physical assets arises from the need for extra guidance on the recognition and measurement of those assets — not because such assets are of any greater or lesser value than physical assets. With physical assets, where there are thin markets or where the assets are of a specialised nature, the guidance in IAS 38 could be considered to be equally applicable to tangible assets.

13.1.4 The definition of an asset and identifying intangible assets

Paragraph 4.4 of the *Conceptual Framework* describes an asset as 'a resource controlled by the entity'. Paragraphs 13–16 of IAS 38 discuss the application of the characteristic of 'control' and the classification of certain items as intangible assets.

The crux of the debate is whether items that probably do not meet the identifiability criterion — such as effective advertising programmes, trained staff, favourable government relations and fundraising capabilities — qualify as assets. According to paragraphs 13–16 of IAS 38, items such as market and technical knowledge (paragraph 14), staff skills, specific management or technical talent (paragraph 15) and a portfolio of customers, market share, customer relationships and customer loyalty (paragraph 16) do not meet the definition of intangible assets. The key reason for excluding such items as assets is the interpretation of the term 'control' as used in the definition of an asset. According to paragraph 13 of IAS 38, control normally stems from 'legal rights that are enforceable in a court of law'. In the absence of legal rights, it is more difficult to demonstrate control.

Consider an entity that invests in its future staff by outlaying funds on training programmes. The entity has invested in its staff, but it has no control over whether staff remain employed by it. Nevertheless, it has an expectation that it will receive most if not all of the benefits from the training programmes. If the staff stay, the entity has control over the benefits from the increased sales that arise from the training programmes. Access to the future benefits that arise from the well-trained staff who stay with the entity can be denied to other entities. Not all the expected benefits may eventuate but, if they do, they belong to the entity. In fact, if past experience indicates that the entity has a fine record of retaining staff, it can be inferred or construed from the facts in the particular situation that the benefits will flow to the entity. So, if custom and usual business practice are a guide, the benefits will flow to the entity. Although the staff could decide to go to another entity and provide it with the benefits of their training, that entity cannot argue that there are any grounds, such as normal business practice, for suggesting that this will occur. The second entity may form an expectation that the other entity's staff will change employment but there are no legal, equitable or constructive reasons for suggesting that its expectation is any more than a hope.

The difficulties in determining whether certain intangibles meet the definition of an asset caused the standard setters to introduce the further test of identifiability. By requiring identifiability for recognition of intangibles, they diffused the debate as to whether an item such as good staff relations is an asset. Regardless of whether it is an asset, it is not an intangible asset because it does not meet the identifiability criterion, and so can only be recognised, if at all, as part of goodwill. However, reducing the number of assets recognised in the financial statements because of measurement problems may also reduce the relevance of the information provided in those financial statements.

13.2 RECOGNITION AND INITIAL MEASUREMENT

IAS 38 sets out the principles in relation to the recognition and initial measurement of intangible assets.

13.2.1 Criteria for recognition and initial measurement

After determining that an asset exists and that it meets the definition of an intangible asset, the asset must meet the two criteria in paragraph 21 of IAS 38 before it can be recognised. The criteria are:
- it is *probable* that the future economic benefits attributable to the asset will flow to the entity
- the *cost* of the asset can be measured *reliably*.

These criteria are the same as those for the recognition of property, plant and equipment in IAS 16 *Property, Plant and Equipment*. If the cost of the asset cannot be reliably measured, but the fair value is determinable, an asset cannot be recognised under either IAS 16 or IAS 38 because both standards require initial measurement at cost. As noted later, this has consequences for the recognition of intangible assets that are internally generated rather than acquired, as well as causing differences in the statements of financial position of entities that internally generate assets and those that acquire assets.

In relation to the initial measurement of an intangible asset, paragraph 24 of IAS 38 states:

An intangible asset shall be measured initially at cost.

With the reliable measurement of cost as one of the recognition criteria, this cost forms the basis for initial measurement.

These recognition criteria and the requirement for initial measurement should be viewed as general principles only. Having established these criteria, IAS 38 then proceeds to examine the accounting for intangibles based upon how these assets were generated. The standard analyses intangibles in terms of four ways in which an entity could have obtained the assets:
- separate acquisition
- acquisition as part of a business acquisition
- acquisition by way of a government grant
- internally generated assets.

For each of these situations, IAS 38 provides specific recognition criteria and measurement rules. It is these that are applied in accounting for intangibles rather than the general criteria noted in paragraphs 21 and 24. Presumably the standard setters considered that there were particular measurement issues that arose under each of these situations requiring different principles to be established for each situation.

13.2.2 Separate acquisition

In recognising assets acquired separately, paragraph 25 of IAS 38 notes that:

> the probability recognition criterion in paragraph 21(a) is always considered to be satisfied for separately acquired intangible assets.

The standard setters argue that the price paid for the asset automatically takes into account the probability of the expected benefits being received; hence, it is unnecessary to apply a further probability test. For example, if an asset had expected cash inflows of £1000, and the probability of these inflows being received was 40%, then an acquirer would pay £400 for the asset. The standard setters argue that these benefits are now automatically probable. Further, paragraph 26 of IAS 38 states:

> In addition, the cost of a separately acquired intangible asset can usually be measured reliably. This is particularly so when the purchase consideration is in the form of cash or other monetary assets.

The measurement of cost may, however, be more difficult if the exchange involves the acquirer giving up non-monetary assets rather than cash.

An intangible asset acquired separately is initially measured at cost. As with property, plant and equipment, the cost of an asset is the sum of the purchase price and the directly attributable costs (IAS 38 paragraph 27). The purchase price is measured as the fair value of what is given up by the acquirer in order to acquire the asset, and the directly attributable costs are those necessarily incurred to get the asset into the condition where it is capable of operating in the manner intended by management. *(These concepts are discussed further in sections 11.3.1 and 11.3.2 in relation to property, plant and equipment.)* The principles of accounting for separately acquired intangibles and property, plant and equipment are the same.

In summary, where a for-profit entity acquires an intangible asset as a separate asset, there is only one recognition criterion to be applied, namely reliable measurement of the cost of the asset.

13.2.3 Acquisition as part of a business combination

Where assets are acquired as part of a business combination, IFRS 3 *Business Combinations* is applied. Appendix A of this standard contains a definition of a 'business combination' and a 'business'. *This standard is discussed in detail in chapter 14.* In this section, a reference to a business combination indicates that the acquiring entity has acquired a group of assets rather than a single asset and one of the assets in that group is an intangible asset. The group of assets could be an operating division or a segment of another entity. The key issue is then how to account for the acquisition of an intangible asset when it is acquired as part of a group of assets rather than as a single asset. Note, however, that IFRS 3 prescribes different accounting for the acquisition of a group of assets that constitutes a business and for a group that does not constitute a business. In applying the principles in IAS 38 relating to acquisition of assets as part of a business combination, it is first necessary to ensure that the group of assets being acquired is a business.

With respect to recognition criteria to apply when intangible assets are acquired in a business combination, IAS 38 states that *no* recognition criteria need be applied. Provided the assets meet the definition of an intangible asset, they must be recognised as separate assets. As with separately acquired intangible assets, paragraph 33 of IAS 38 provides that, where intangible assets are acquired as part of a business combination, the effect of probability is reflected in the measurement of the asset. Hence, the probability recognition criterion is automatically met. Further, it is argued in paragraph 33 of IAS 38 that the requirement for reliability of measurement is always met as sufficient information always exists to measure reliably the fair value of the asset. This non-application of recognition criteria in accounting for intangibles acquired in a business combination is also seen in IFRS 3 where paragraphs 11 and 12 note that the recognition conditions for the identifiable assets must meet the definition of an asset in the *Conceptual Framework*, as well as be a part of what the acquirer and the acquiree exchanged in the business combination transaction.

In dissenting from the issue of IAS 38, Professor Whittington (a former IASB member) argued that the probability test in paragraph 21(a) should be applied in testing the recognition of all intangibles, stating that issues relating to the recognition criteria in the *Conceptual Framework* should be resolved before having different recognition criteria for intangible assets acquired in a business combination. The justification for different criteria is presumably that there is an increased relevance of information in reporting the separate intangible assets rather than subsuming them into goodwill.

The application of these recognition requirements means that an acquirer must, in recognising separately the acquiree's intangible assets, recognise intangible assets that the acquiree has not recognised in its records, such as in-process research and development that cannot be recognised under IAS 38 as internally generated assets (discussed later in this section). As noted in paragraph 34, recognition by an acquirer of an acquiree's in-process research and development project only depends on whether the project meets the definition of an intangible asset. It can be seen that entities that acquire intangible assets in a business combination will be able, and in fact are required, to recognise intangible assets that are not separately recognisable when acquired by other means.

The measurement of intangible assets acquired in a business combination is established in paragraph 33 of IAS 38:

> In accordance with IFRS 3 *Business Combinations*, if an intangible asset is acquired in a business combination, the cost of that intangible asset is its fair value at the acquisition date.

Note firstly that it is IFRS 3 that determines the measurement of assets acquired in a business combination. Under IFRS 3 acquired assets are measured at fair value. Hence, intangible assets acquired in a business combination must be measured at initial recognition at fair value. This is then a departure from the general measurement rule in paragraph 24. Paragraph 33 of IAS 38 does say that 'the cost ... is its fair value'; however, the acquiring entity does not attempt to measure the cost, rather it measures the fair value.

The measurement of fair value is determined in accordance with IFRS 13 *Fair Value Measurement*. IFRS 13 defines fair value in Appendix A as:

> The price that would be received to sell an asset or paid to transfer a liability in an orderly transaction between market participants at the measurement date.

Chapter 3 provides information on the measurement of fair value under IFRS 13.

13.2.4 Acquisition by way of a government grant

According to paragraph 44 of IAS 38, some intangible assets, such as licences to operate radio or television stations, are allocated to entities via government grants. These intangibles are accounted for in accordance with IAS 20 *Accounting for Government Grants and Disclosure of Government Assistance*, whereby an entity may choose to initially recognise both the intangible asset and the grant at fair value. If an entity does not choose to use the fair value measurement option, it will recognise the asset initially at a nominal amount plus directly attributable costs.

13.2.5 Internally generated intangible assets

The recognition criteria and measurement rules are different for intangible assets acquired as a separate asset or acquired in a business combination. The approach taken in accounting for internally generated assets is different again. The recognition criteria in paragraph 21 are not applied at all. The measurement approach used is one of capitalisation of outlays incurred by the entity.

This continuous change in accounting for intangible assets leaves the standard setters open to criticism for lack of consistency in the accounting for acquired intangibles versus internally generated intangibles. The problem from an accounting point of view with internally generated intangibles is determining at what point in time an asset should be recognised. An entity may outlay funds in an exploratory project, such as developing software to overcome a specific problem, or designing a tool for a special purpose. There is no guarantee of success at the start of the project. The program may not work or the tool may be unsatisfactory for the purpose. Should the accountant capitalise the costs from the beginning of the project, or wait until there is some indication of success? A further problem with some intangible assets such as brand names is whether the costs outlaid relate solely to increasing the worth of the brand name or simply to enhancing the overall reputation of the entity.

The standard setters' solution to the problem of when to begin capitalising costs is to classify the generation of the asset into two phases: the research phase and the development phase. These terms are defined in paragraph 8 of IAS 38 as follows:

> *Research* is original and planned investigation undertaken with the prospect of gaining new scientific or technical knowledge and understanding.

> *Development* is the application of research findings or other knowledge to a plan or design for the production of new or substantially improved materials, devices, products, processes, systems or services before the start of commercial production or use.

It can be seen from these definitions that the earlier stages of a project are defined as research and, at some point in time, the project moves from a research phase to a development phase. Examples of research activities are given in paragraph 56 of IAS 38, such as the search for new knowledge or for alternatives for materials, devices, products, processes, systems or services. Examples of development activities are found in paragraph 59, such as the design, construction and operation of a non-commercial pilot plant, and the design of pre-production prototypes and models. From an accounting perspective, expenditure on research is expensed when incurred (paragraph 54), and expenditure on development is capitalised as an intangible asset. It is obviously important to be able to distinguish one phase from the other.

Paragraph 57 of IAS 38 is the key paragraph in this regard. It contains a list of criteria, all of which must be met in order for a development outlay to be capitalised. In order to capitalise development outlays, an entity must be able to demonstrate all of the following:

(a) the technical feasibility of completing the intangible asset so that it will be available for use or sale;
(b) its intention to complete the intangible asset and use or sell it;
(c) its ability to use or sell the intangible asset;

(d) how the intangible asset will generate probable future economic benefits. Among other things, the entity can demonstrate the existence of a market for the output of the intangible asset or the intangible asset itself or, if it is to be used internally, the usefulness of the intangible asset;

(e) the availability of adequate technical, financial and other resources to complete the development and to use or sell the intangible asset; and

(f) its ability to measure reliably the expenditure attributable to the intangible asset during its development.

Given the degree of difficulty in distinguishing research activities from development activities, it seems simpler to disregard any attempt to distinguish between the two activities and just allow capitalisation when the criteria in paragraph 57 are met. In other words, for an entity to decide whether to capitalise an outlay, the decision will not be based on an application of the definitions of research and development, but rather on whether the criteria in paragraph 57 are met. If the criteria are met, it will then be decided that the project is in the development stage. The definitions of research and development are then superfluous. The recognition criteria for an internally generated intangible asset are then those contained in paragraphs 18, 21 and 57 of IAS 38.

The criteria in paragraph 57 are designed to help determine whether, in relation to a project, it is probable that there will be future benefits flowing to the entity. If there are markets for the output, the project is feasible, and the resources are available to complete the project, then it becomes probable that there will be future cash inflows. The criteria in paragraph 57 are then an elaboration — the provision of more detailed requirements — on the criteria in paragraph 18. This approach in IAS 38 provides more certainty in obtaining comparable accounting across entities than simply relying on an accounting principle that states that, if there are probable expected future benefits, an entity should capitalise the outlay.

If the criteria in paragraph 57 are all met, IAS 38 requires the intangible asset to be measured at cost. This cost is not, however, the total cost relating to the project. The amount to be capitalised is the 'sum of expenditure incurred from the date when the intangible asset first meets the recognition criteria in paragraphs 21, 22 and 57' (paragraph 65). Paragraph 71 explicitly prohibits the reinstatement of amounts previously expensed. Recognition of an asset that is not yet available for use requires an entity to subject that asset to an annual impairment test as per IAS 36 *Impairment of Assets*. Paragraphs 66–67 of IAS 38 note that the cost comprises all directly attributable costs necessary to create, produce and prepare the asset to be capable of operating in a manner intended by management, and provide examples of such costs as well as items that are not components of the cost.

It may seem that the use of the terms 'research' and 'development', which may be associated with such assets as patents and software development, are not applicable to all internally generated intangibles, such as brand names. However, it needs to be remembered that all intangible assets must meet the identifiability criterion, one part of which is separability, which is the capability of being separated and sold or transferred. In relation to certain assets, paragraph 63 of IAS 38 provides a major exclusion in an entity's ability to capitalise internally generated intangibles:

> Internally generated brands, mastheads, publishing titles, customer lists and items similar in substance shall not be recognised as intangible assets.

The standard setters concluded that, even though the criteria in paragraph 57(a)–(f) are met, the listed items in paragraph 63 cannot be recognised. As paragraph 64 states, the standard setters do not believe that the costs associated with developing the listed assets can be distinguished from the cost of developing the business as a whole. For example, it may be argued that funds spent on developing a brand name also enhance the overall image of the entity, and therefore the outlays cannot be solely attributable to the brand name.

13.2.6 Explaining the non-recognition of internally generated assets

There are a number of problems associated with the treatment of internally generated assets versus that required for acquired intangibles. In particular, there are inconsistencies in the accounting for internally generated intangibles and intangibles acquired in a business combination. Note, in this regard:

(a) *The initial recognition of intangible assets.* IAS 38 requires intangible assets to be initially recognised at cost. However, for assets acquired in a business combination, an intangible asset can be recognised at fair value. Internally generated intangibles cannot be recognised, even if the fair value can be reliably measured. For example, outlays on research cannot be recognised as an asset. However, if an entity acquires another entity that has in-process research, an intangible asset can be recognised if the fair value can be measured reliably. Further, the research so recognised can be revalued if this class of asset is measured at fair value.

(b) *The measurement of fair value.* One of the reasons given in paragraph BCZ38(c) of the Basis for Conclusions on IAS 38 for disallowing the recognition of internally generated intangible assets is the impossibility of determining the fair value of an intangible asset reliably if no active market exists for the asset, and active markets are unlikely to exist for internally generated intangible assets. However, for intangible assets recognised in a business combination, it is assumed that fair value can be measured (reliably, it is hoped) without the existence of active markets. IAS 38 allows the use of other measurement techniques or even what an entity would have paid based on the best information available. Hence, in a business combination, the fair values of intangibles can be measured reliably using measures determined outside an active market, but these same measures cannot be used to measure the fair values of internally generated assets for asset recognition purposes. As a protection, the requirements of IAS 36 *Impairment of Assets* can be applied to both acquired and internally generated intangible assets.

(c) *Brands, mastheads, publishing titles and customer lists.* Paragraph 63 of IAS 38 prohibits the recognition of internally generated brands and items similar in substance. However, such assets can be recognised when acquired in a business combination (as well as if acquired as a separate asset). As far as the measurement of the fair value of these assets goes, the argument presented in point (b) applies — if the fair value of a brand can be determined in a business combination then it can be determined if internally generated. Further, it has been noted previously that the reason given in paragraph 64 of IAS 38 for non-recognition of internally generated brands is that the cost of these items 'cannot be distinguished from the cost of developing the business as a whole'. If this argument is true for internally generated brands, the same argument could be applied to acquired brands.

13.2.7 Recognition of an expense

Paragraphs 68–71 of IAS 38 cover the issue of when expenditure on an intangible asset should be expensed. However, if the previous rules in IAS 38 are followed, then the appropriate outlays are expensed when the criteria are not met. These paragraphs add nothing particularly new to the accounting for intangible assets. However, paragraph 69 provides a list of other examples of outlays that should always be recognised as an expense when incurred, these being expenditures on:

- start-up activities
- training activities
- advertising and promotional activities
- relocating or reorganising part or all of an entity.

Provision of this list ensures no asset will be recognised in relation to these activities, taking the judgement away from preparers of the financial statements.

Paragraph 46 of the Basis for Conclusions on IAS 38 clarifies and makes an important distinction between expenditure incurred on future advertising and promotional activities and prepayments for advertising and promotional activities.

Where an entity has received goods or services that it would use to develop or communicate an advertisement or promotion (for example, brochures), the entity should not recognise as an asset goods or services in respect of its future advertising or promotional activities. This expenditure should be expensed on receipt of the goods or services and not when they are used (for example, when the brochures are distributed). However, if an entity pays for advertising goods or services in advance and the other party has not yet provided those goods or services, the entity has a different asset. That asset is the right to receive those goods and services.

Paragraph 71 is important. This paragraph prohibits the recognition at a later date of past expenditure as assets. In other words, if amounts relating to research have been expensed, these amounts cannot then be capitalised, nor can appropriate adjustments to equity be made, when an intangible asset is created at the development stage.

13.2.8 Internally generated goodwill

Paragraph 49 of IAS 38 states categorically that internally generated goodwill is not recognised as an asset. Hence, goodwill can be recognised only when it is acquired as part of a business combination and measured in accordance with IFRS 3 *Business Combinations*.

The reason given in paragraph 49 of IAS 38 for non-recognition is that goodwill is not identifiable; that is, it is not separable, nor does it arise from contractual or other legal rights. A second reason given for non-recognition, as stated in paragraph 49, is that the cost of internally generated goodwill cannot be reliably determined. The fair value of goodwill could be determined by comparing the fair value of the entity as a whole and subtracting the sum of the fair values of the identifiable assets and liabilities of the entity. However, under IAS 38, the principle for recognition is that identifiable intangible assets as well as goodwill must initially be measured at cost, not at fair value. As is discussed in more detail in the next section, this principle makes the recognition of internally generated intangibles harder than the recognition of acquired intangibles.

13.3 MEASUREMENT SUBSEQUENT TO INITIAL RECOGNITION

13.3.1 Measurement basis

Consistent with IAS 16, after the initial recognition of an intangible asset at cost, an entity must choose for each class of intangible asset whether to measure the assets using the *cost model* or the *revaluation model* — see paragraph 72. *(These models are discussed in greater detail in chapter 11.)*

Cost model

Under the cost model, the asset is recorded at the initial cost of acquisition and is then subject to amortisation *(see section 13.3.3)* and impairment testing *(see chapter 15)*.

Revaluation model

Under the revaluation model, the asset is carried at fair value, and is subject to amortisation and impairment charges. As with property, plant and equipment, if this model is chosen, revaluations are made with sufficient regularity so that the carrying amount of the asset does not materially differ from the current fair value at the end of the reporting period.

One specification that applies to intangible assets but is not required for property, plant and equipment is how the fair value is to be measured. Under paragraph 75 of IAS 38, the fair value must be measured by reference to an active market. An active market is defined in IFRS 13 as a market in which transactions for the asset or liability take place with sufficient frequency and volume to provide pricing information on an ongoing basis. This means that an intangible asset acquired in a business combination and measured at fair value using some measurement technique cannot subsequently use that same measurement technique if it adopts the revaluation model. In the absence of an active market, the intangible asset would be kept at the fair value determined at the date of the business combination and accounted for by the cost basis. As paragraph 76 notes, the choice of revaluation model does not allow the recognition of intangible assets that cannot be recognised initially at cost. However, paragraph 77 allows an asset for which only part of the cost was recognised to be fully revalued to fair value.

Paragraph 78 of IAS 38 states that intangibles such as brands, newspaper mastheads, patents and trademarks cannot be measured at fair value, as there is no active market for these assets because they are unique. As with the recognition of these types of intangible assets, the standard setters have stated specifically that they can be measured only at cost.

Selection of the revaluation model requires all assets in the one class to be measured at fair value. Because of the insistence on using active markets for the measurement of fair value, the standard recognises that there will be cases where fair values cannot be determined for all assets within one class. Hence, under paragraph 81 of IAS 38, where there is no active market for an asset, the asset can be measured at cost even if the class is measured using the revaluation model. Further, if the ability to measure the asset at fair value disappears because the market for the asset no longer meets the criteria to be classified as active, the asset is carried at the latest revalued amount and effectively accounted for under the cost model. If the market again becomes active, the revaluation model can be resumed.

Accounting for intangible assets measured using the revaluation model is exactly the same as for property, plant and equipment *(see chapter 11)*. Where there is a revaluation increase, the asset is increased and the increase is credited directly to a revaluation surplus. However, if the revaluation increase reverses a previous revaluation decrease relating to the same asset, the revaluation increase is recognised as income (IAS 38 paragraph 85). Any accumulated amortisation is eliminated at the time of revaluation.

Where there is a revaluation decrease, the decrease is recognised as an expense unless there has been a previous revaluation increase. In the latter case, the adjustment must first be made against any existing revaluation surplus before recognising an expense (IAS 38 paragraph 86). Any accumulated amortisation is eliminated at the time of the revaluation.

As with a revaluation surplus on property, plant and equipment, paragraph 87 of IAS 38 states that the revaluation surplus may be transferred to retained earnings when the surplus is realised on the retirement or disposal of the asset. Alternatively, the revaluation surplus may progressively be taken to retained earnings in proportion to the amortisation of the asset.

13.3.2 Subsequent expenditures

Paragraph 20 of IAS 38 discusses subsequent expenditures in general. It is argued in this paragraph that the unique nature of intangibles means that subsequent expenditures should be expensed rather than capitalised. Subsequent expenditures maintain expected benefits rather than increase them. Further, with many subsequent expenditures, it may be difficult to attribute them to specific intangible assets rather than to the entity as a whole. Paragraph 20 notes that with the paragraph 63 intangibles, whether acquired or internally generated, subsequent expenditures are always expensed.

Paragraph 42 provides specific guidance on subsequent expenditures relating to acquired in-process research and development projects. Effectively, the same criteria for initially recognising an asset and expensing are applied to account for subsequent expenditures. The results of this application are:
- to expense research outlays
- to expense development outlays not meeting the criteria in paragraph 57
- to add to the acquired in-process research or development project if the development expenditure satisfies the paragraph 57 criteria.

13.3.3 Amortisation of intangible assets

Useful life

A key determinant in the amortisation process for intangible assets is whether the useful life is finite or indefinite. If finite, then the asset has to be amortised over that life. If the asset has an indefinite life, then there is no annual amortisation charge. Paragraph 88 of IAS 38 states:

> An entity shall assess whether the useful life of an intangible asset is finite or indefinite and, if finite, the length of, or number of production or similar units constituting, that useful life. An intangible asset shall be regarded by the entity as having an indefinite useful life when, based on an analysis of all the relevant factors, there is no foreseeable limit to the period over which the asset is expected to generate net cash inflows for the entity.

The term 'indefinite' does not mean that the asset has an infinite life; that is, that it is going to last forever. As paragraph 91 notes, an indefinite life means that, with the proper maintenance, there is no foreseeable end to the life of the asset. Paragraph 90 provides a list of factors that should be considered in determining the useful life of the asset:

- the expected use of the asset by the entity and whether the asset could be managed efficiently by another management team
- typical product life cycles for the asset, and public information on estimates of useful lives of similar assets that are used in a similar way
- technical, technological, commercial or other types of obsolescence
- the stability of the industry, and changes in market demand
- expected actions by competitors
- the level of maintenance expenditure required and the entity's ability and intent to reach such a level
- the period of control over the asset and legal or similar limits on the use of the asset
- whether the useful life of the asset depends on the useful lives of other assets of the entity.

Paragraph 94 of IAS 38 notes that, as a general rule, assets whose lives depend on contractual or legal lives will be amortised over those lives or shorter periods in some cases. If renewal is possible, then the useful life applied can include the renewal period providing there is evidence to support renewal by the entity without significant cost.

Figure 13.3 contains two examples from those in the illustrative examples accompanying IAS 38 in relation to the assessment of useful lives.

Example: An acquired broadcasting licence that expires in 5 years

The broadcasting licence is renewable every 10 years if the entity provides at least an average level of service to its customers and complies with the relevant legislative requirements. The licence may be renewed indefinitely at little cost and has been renewed twice before the most recent acquisition. The acquiring entity intends to renew the licence indefinitely and evidence supports its ability to do so. Historically, there has been no compelling challenge to the licence renewal. The technology used in broadcasting is not expected to be replaced by another technology at any time in the foreseeable future. Therefore, the licence is expected to contribute to the entity's net cash inflows indefinitely.

The broadcasting licence would be treated as having an indefinite useful life because it is expected to contribute to the entity's net cash inflows indefinitely. Therefore, the licence would not be amortised until its useful life is determined to be finite. The licence would be tested for impairment under IAS 36 annually and whenever there is an indication that it may be impaired.

Example: An acquired trademark used to identify and distinguish a leading consumer product that has been a market-share leader for the past 8 years

The trademark has a remaining legal life of 5 years but is renewable every 10 years at little cost. The acquiring entity intends to renew the trademark continuously and evidence supports its ability to do so.

An analysis of (1) product life cycles, (2) market, competitive and environmental trends, and (3) brand extension opportunities provides evidence that the trademarked product will generate net cash inflows for the acquiring entity for an indefinite period.

The trademark would be treated as having an indefinite useful life because it is expected to contribute to net cash inflows indefinitely. Therefore, the trademark would not be amortised until its useful life is determined to be finite. It would be tested for impairment under IAS 36 annually and whenever there is an indication that it may be impaired.

FIGURE 13.3 Examples of indefinite lives for intangible assets

---

Rather than considering the existence of an indefinite life for intangible assets, the standard setters could have set a maximum useful life such as 40 years. However, as noted in paragraph BC63 of the Basis for Conclusions on IAS 38, the IASB considers that writing standards in such a fashion would not accord with the principle that the accounting numbers should be representationally faithful. The principles in IAS 38 provide management with more discretion but allow for the provision of more relevant information. In order for an intangible asset (such as a trademark) to have an indefinite life, an entity is required to outlay funds on an annual basis to maintain the trademark. Consider in this regard the annual expenditure by soft-drink companies to maintain the value of their trademarks. The annual profit figure is then affected by these outlays. To require amortisation charges to be levied as well, when the asset is being maintained, would be to affect the statement of profit or loss and other comprehensive income twice.

Intangible assets with finite useful lives

Paragraph 97 of IAS 38 states the principles relating to the amortisation period and choice of amortisation method. In general, the principles of amortisation are the same as those for depreciating property, plant and equipment under IAS 16. In both cases, the process involves the allocation of the depreciable amount on a systematic basis over the useful life, with the method chosen reflecting the pattern in which the expected benefits are expected to be consumed by the entity. Paragraph 98 notes that an amortisation method will rarely result in an amortisation charge that is lower than if a straight-line method had been used. Further, in accordance with paragraph 104, the amortisation period and amortisation method should be reviewed at least at the end of each annual reporting period, which is the same for property, plant and equipment.

However, IAS 38 contains a number of rules that are specific to intangible assets, presumably because of the relative uncertainty associated with intangible assets:
- Where the pattern of benefits cannot be determined reliably, the straight-line method is to be used (paragraph 97). This is, presumably, to bring some consistency and comparability into the calculations.
- The residual value is assumed to be zero unless there is a commitment by a third party to purchase the asset at the end of its useful life, *or* there is an active market for the asset, and:
  – residual value can be determined by reference to that market and
  – it is probable that such a market will exist at the end of the asset's useful life (paragraph 100).

Any changes in residual value, amortisation method or useful life are changes in accounting estimates, and accounted for prospectively with an effect on the current and future amortisation charges.

Intangible assets with indefinite useful lives

As noted earlier, where an intangible asset has an indefinite useful life, there is no amortisation charge (IAS 38 paragraph 107). As with finite useful lives, the useful life of an intangible that is not being amortised must be reviewed each period (paragraph 109). Any change from indefinite to finite useful life for an asset is treated as a change in estimate and affects the amortisation charge in current and future periods. Intangible assets with indefinite useful lives are subject to annual impairment tests *(see chapter 15)*.

13.4 RETIREMENTS AND DISPOSALS

Accounting for the retirements and disposals of intangible assets is identical to that for property, plant and equipment under IAS 16. In particular, under IAS 38:
- intangible assets are to be derecognised on disposal or when there are no expected future benefits from the asset (paragraph 112)
- gains or losses on disposal are calculated as the difference between the proceeds on disposal and the carrying amount at point of sale, with amortisation calculated up to the point of sale (paragraph 113)
- amortisation of an intangible with a finite useful life does not cease when the asset becomes temporarily idle or is retired from active use (paragraph 117).

13.5 DISCLOSURE

Paragraph 118 of IAS 38 requires disclosures for each class of intangibles, and for internally generated intangibles to be distinguished from other intangibles. Examples of separate classes are given in paragraph 119:
- brand names
- mastheads and publishing titles
- computer software
- licences and franchises
- copyrights, patents and other industrial property rights, service and operating rights
- recipes, formulas, models, designs and prototypes
- intangible assets under development.

Disclosures required by paragraph 118(a) and (b) would be contained in the summary of significant accounting policies, as illustrated in figure 13.4. Disclosures required by paragraphs 118 and 122 of IAS 38 are illustrated in figure 13.5.

Note 1: Summary of significant accounting policies (extract)	IAS 38 paragraph 118
Intangible assets Intangible assets are initially recognised at cost. Intangible assets that have indefinite useful lives are tested for impairment on an annual basis. Intangible assets that have finite useful lives are amortised over those lives on a straight-line basis.	*(b)*
Patents and copyrights These have all been acquired by the company. Costs relating to these assets are capitalised and amortised on a straight-line basis over the following periods: 　Patent — packaging 5 years 　Patent — tools 10 years 　Copyright 10 years	*(b)*
Licence The licence relating to television broadcasting rights is determined to be indefinite.	*(a)*
Research and development Research costs are expensed as incurred. Development costs are expensed except those that it is probable will generate future economic benefits, this being determined by an analysis of factors such as technical feasibility and the existence of markets. Such costs are currently being amortised on a straight-line basis over the following periods: 　Tool design project 5 years 　Water cooling project 10 years	*(a)* *(b)*

FIGURE 13.4 Illustrative disclosures required by paragraph 118(a) and (b) of IAS 38

Other disclosures required, where relevant, by paragraph 118 of IAS 38 are:
- the line item in the statement of profit or loss and other comprehensive income in which any amortisation of intangible assets is included (paragraph 118(d))
- increases or decreases during the period resulting from revaluations under paragraphs 75, 85 and 86 and from impairment losses recognised or reversed directly in equity (paragraph 118(e)(iii))
- impairment losses reversed in profit or loss during the period (paragraph 118(e)(v)).

FIGURE 13.5 Illustrative disclosures required by paragraphs 118 and 122 of IAS 38

Note 11: Intangible assets				IAS 38 paragraph 122
Details about the Company's intangible assets are provided below. All intangibles are considered to have finite useful lives except for a patent held for a tool used in the manufacture of steel windmills. As this tool is able to substantially lessen the cost of manufacturing windmills, and all entities manufacturing windmills acquire the special tool from the company for use in their production process, the continued use of the tool in the manufacturing process is considered to be infinite. Hence, the patent is considered to have an indefinite life. The tool has a carrying amount of £155 000 [2013: £155 000].				*(a)*
Apart from the above, the main items constituting the intangible assets of the Company are:				

	Carrying amount		Remaining amortisation period		
	2014 £'000	2013 £'000	2014 years	2013 years	*(b)*
Patents and copyrights					
Patent — packaging	31	45	7	8	
Patent — tools	52	66	5	6	
Copyright — manuals	15	24	3	4	
Deferred development expenditure					
Tool design	322	312	5	6	
Packaging design	95	110	3	4	

FIGURE 13.5 *(continued)*

Note 11: Intangible assets					IAS 38 paragraph 122
	Patents and copyrights		Deferred development expenditure		paragraph 118
	2014 £'000	2013 £'000	2014 £'000	2013 £'000	
Balance at beginning of year, at cost	576	545	592	361	*(c)*
Accumulated amortisation	276	234	166	110	
Carrying amount at beginning of year	300	311	426	251	
Additions:					*(e)(i)*
Acquisition of subsidiary	—	22	—	54	
Internal development	—	—	72	182	
Acquired separately	10	15	—	—	
Disposals	(15)	—	—	—	*(e)(ii)*
Amortisation	(38)	(32)	(52)	(44)	*(e)(vi)*
Impairment	—	(10)	—	(12)	*(e)(iv)*
Exchange differences	5	(6)	5	(5)	*(e)(vii)*
Carrying amount at end of year	262	300	451	426	
Intangible assets:					
At cost	557	576	669	592	*(c)*
Accumulated amortisation	295	276	218	166	
Carrying amount at end of year	262	300	451	426	

Paragraph 122 of IAS 38 also requires the following disclosures, if relevant:
- for intangible assets acquired by way of a *government grant* and initially recognised at fair value (paragraph 122(c)):
  – the fair value initially recognised for these assets
  – their carrying amount
  – whether they are measured after recognition under the cost model or the revaluation model.
- the existence and carrying amounts of intangible assets whose *title is restricted* and the carrying amounts of intangible assets *pledged as security* for liabilities (paragraph 122(d)).
- the amount of *contractual commitments* for the acquisition of intangible assets (paragraph 122(e)).

Paragraph 124 details further disclosures where intangible assets are carried at revalued amounts. An example of this disclosure is contained in figure 13.6.

			IAS 38 paragraph 124
Intangibles carried at revalued amounts			
The company has recognised its Internet domain name as an intangible asset. The asset was recognised			*(a)(i)*
initially at cost in 2012. The revaluation model was used to measure this asset from 1 January 2013. At the			*(a)(ii)*
end of the reporting period, 31 December 2014, the carrying amount of this asset is £52 500. If the cost			*(a)(iii)*
method had continued to be applied, the carrying amount would have been £33 600.			
The revaluation surplus in relation to this asset is as follows:			
	2014	2013	*(b)*
Balance at beginning of year	£48 000	£45 000	
Increase	4 500	3 000	
Balance at end of year	£52 500	£48 000	
There are no restrictions on the distribution of this balance to shareholders.			

FIGURE 13.6 Disclosures required by paragraph 124 of IAS 38

Paragraph 126 requires disclosure of the aggregate amount of research and development expenditure recognised as an expense during the period. Disclosures in paragraph 128 that are encouraged but not required include a description of any fully amortised intangible asset that is still in use, and a brief description of significant intangible assets controlled by the entity but not recognised as assets because they did not meet the recognition criteria in IAS 38.

An example of disclosure of intangible assets is in figure 13.7, which shows the intangible assets disclosed by GSK in its 2014 annual report.

19 Other intangible assets

	Computer software £m	Licences, patents, etc. £m	Amortised brands £m	Indefinite life brands £m	Total £m
Cost at 1 January 2013	1 501	10 604	412	2 184	14 701
Exchange adjustments	(27)	(143)	—	(37)	(207)
Capitalised development costs	79	246	—	—	325
Additions through business combinations	—	191	7	—	198
Capitalised borrowing costs	5	1	—	—	6
Other additions	99	141	—	—	240
Disposals and asset write-offs	(26)	(346)	—	—	(372)
Transfer (to)/from assets held for sale	—	(222)	—	44	(178)
Cost at 31 December 2013	1 631	10 472	419	2 191	14 713
Exchange adjustments	11	52	3	(6)	60
Capitalised development costs	—	242	—	—	242
Capitalsed borrowing costs	6	3	—	—	9
Other additions	179	108	—	—	287
Reclassifications	12	—	—	—	12
Disposals and asset write-offs	(21)	(9)	—	—	(30)
Transfer to assets held for sale	—	(587)	—	(30)	(617)
Cost at 31 December 2014	1 818	10 281	422	2 155	14 676
Amortisation at 1 January 2013	(1 012)	(2 473)	(106)	—	(3 591)
Exchange adjustments	17	65	1	—	83
Charge for the year	(128)	(536)	(18)	—	(682)
Disposals and asset write-offs	21	2	—	—	23
Transfer to assets held for sale	—	85	—	—	85
Amortisation at 31 December 2013	(1 102)	(2 857)	(123)	—	(4 082)
Exchange adjustments	(13)	(63)	—	—	(76)
Charge for the year	(115)	(578)	(11)	—	(704)
Disposals and asset write-offs	17	6	—	—	23
Amortisation at 31 December 2014	(1 213)	(3 492)	(134)	—	(4 839)
Impairment at 1 January 2013	(39)	(729)	(129)	(52)	(949)
Exchange adjustments	—	9	—	1	10
Impairment losses	(6)	(702)	(11)	(26)	(745)
Disposals and asset write-offs	4	332	—	—	336
Impairment at 31 December 2013	(41)	(1 090)	(140)	(77)	(1 348)
Exchange adjustments	2	(18)	—	—	(16)
Impairment losses	(7)	(131)	(14)	(5)	(157)
Disposals and asset write-offs	4	—	—	—	4
Impairment at 31 December 2014	(42)	(1 239)	(154)	(82)	(1 517)
Total amortisation and impairment at 31 December 2013	(1 143)	(3 947)	(263)	(77)	(5 430)
Total amortisation and impairment at 31 December 2014	(1 255)	(4 731)	(288)	(82)	(6 356)
Net book value at 1 January 2013	450	7 402	177	2 132	10 161
Net book value at 31 December 2013	488	6 525	156	2 114	9 283
Net book value at 31 December 2014	563	5 550	134	2 073	8 320

FIGURE 13.7 Example of disclosure of intangible assets
Source: GSK (2014, p. 162).

SUMMARY

Intangible assets are considered to be sufficiently different from other assets such as property, plant and equipment for the standard setters to provide a separate standard. The reason for having such a standard is that the nature of intangibles is such that there are particular measurement problems associated with these assets that require specific accounting principles to be established. IAS 38 *Intangible Assets* is concerned with the definition, recognition, measurement and disclosure of intangibles.

The characteristic of 'identifiability' is critical to the identification of intangibles, and is the same concept that arises in IFRS 3 *Business Combinations* in relation to identifiable assets, liabilities and contingent liabilities recognised by the acquirer. In considering the accounting for intangibles, it is important to consider the differences in accounting depending on the source of the intangibles. Intangible assets acquired within a business combination are easier to recognise than those internally generated by the entity. This is because within a business combination the measurement issues are limited by the amount of the cost of the combination.

Amortisation of intangibles raises particular issues in terms of the useful lives of assets. The potential to assess some intangible assets as having indefinite useful lives and hence not subject to amortisation makes the decision on what is the useful life of an asset very significant. It is important to understand how to make such a decision. Aspects of that decision process are required to be specifically disclosed.

DEMONSTRATION PROBLEM 13.1 Development outlays

This demonstration problem illustrates the application of the criteria in paragraph 57 of IAS 38, determining when development outlays are capitalised or expensed.

Pretoria Ltd is a highly successful engineering company that manufactures filters for air conditioning systems. Due to its dissatisfaction with the quality of the filters currently available, on 1 January 2014 it commenced a project to design a more efficient filter. The following notes record the events relating to that project:

2014	
January	Paid £145 000 in salaries of company engineers and consultants who conducted basic tests on available filters with varying modifications.
February	Spent £165 000 on developing a new filter system, including the production of a basic model. It became obvious that the model in its current form was not successful because the material in the filter was not as effective as required.
March	Acquired the fibres division of Durban Ltd for £330 000. The fair values of the tangible assets of this division were: property, plant and equipment, £180 000; inventories, £60 000.
	This business was acquired because one of the products it produced was a fibrous compound, sold under the brand name Springbok, that Pretoria Ltd considered would be excellent for including in the filtration process.
	By buying the fibres division, Pretoria Ltd acquired the patent for this fibrous compound.
	Pretoria Ltd valued the patent at £50 000 and the brand name at £40 000, using a number of valuation techniques. The patent had a further 10-year life but was renewable on application.
	Further costs of £54 000 were incurred on the new filter system during March.
April	Spent a further £135 000 on revising the filtration process to incorporate the fibrous compound. By the end of April, Pretoria Ltd was convinced that it now had a viable product because preliminary tests showed that the filtration process was significantly better than any other available on the market.
May	Developed a prototype of the filtration component and proceeded to test it within a variety of models of air conditioners. The company preferred to sell the filtration process to current manufacturers of air conditioners if the process worked with currently available models. If this proved not possible, the company would then consider developing its own brand of air conditioners using the new filtration system. By the end of May, the filtration system had proved successful on all but one of the currently available commercial models. Costs incurred were £65 000.
June	Various air conditioner manufacturers were invited to demonstrations of the filtration system. Costs incurred were £25 000, including £12 000 for food and beverages for the prospective clients. The feedback from a number of the companies was that they were prepared to enter negotiations for acquiring the filters from Pretoria Ltd. The company now believed it had a successful model and commenced planning the production of the filters. Ongoing costs of £45 000 to refine the filtration system, particularly in the light of comments by the manufacturers, were incurred in the latter part of June.

Required

Explain the accounting for the various outlays incurred by Pretoria Ltd.

Solution

The main problem in accounting for the costs is determining at what point of time costs can be capitalised. This is resolved by applying the criteria in paragraph 57 of IAS 38:

- *Technical feasibility*. At the end of April, the company believed that the filtration process was technically feasible.
- *Intention to complete and sell*. At the end of April, the company was not yet sure that the system was adaptable to currently available models of air conditioners. If it wasn't adaptable, the company would have to test whether development of its own brand of air conditioners would be a commercial proposition. Hence, it was not until the end of May that the company was convinced it could complete the project and had a product that it could sell.
- *Ability to use or sell*. By the end of May, the company had a product that it believed it had the ability to sell. Being a filter manufacturer, it knew the current costs of competing products and so could make an informed decision about the potential for the commercial sale of its own filter.
- *Existence of a market*. The market comprised the air conditioning manufacturers. By selling to the manufacturers, the company had the potential to generate probable future cash flows. This criterion was met by the end of May.
- *Availability of resources*. From the beginning of the project, the company was not short of resources, being a highly successful company in its own right.
- *Ability to measure costs reliably*. Costs are readily attributable to the project throughout its development.

On the basis of the above analysis, the criteria in paragraph 57 of IAS 38 were all met at the end of May. Therefore, costs incurred before this point are expensed, and those incurred after this point are capitalised. Hence, the following costs would be written off as incurred:

January	£145 000
February	165 000
March	54 000
April	135 000
May	65 000

In acquiring the fibres division from Durban Ltd, Pretoria Ltd would pass the following entry:

Property, plant and equipment	Dr	180 000	
Inventories	Dr	60 000	
Brand	Dr	40 000	
Patent	Dr	50 000	
Cash	Cr		330 000
(Acquisition of assets)			

The patent would initially be depreciated over a 10-year useful life. However, this would need to be reassessed upon application of the fibrous compound to the air conditioning filtration system. This alternative use may extend the expected useful life of the product, and hence of the patent. The brand name would be depreciated over the same useful life of the patent, because it is expected that the brand has no real value unless backed by the patent.

The company would then capitalise development costs of £45000 in June.

The marketing costs incurred in June of £25000 would be expensed because they are not part of the development process.

Discussion questions

1. What are the key characteristics of an intangible asset?
2. Explain what is meant by 'identifiability'.
3. How do the principles for amortisation of intangible assets differ from those for depreciation of property, plant and equipment?

4. Explain what is meant by an 'active market'.
5. How is the useful life of an intangible asset determined?
6. What intangibles can never be recognised if internally generated? Why?
7. Explain the difference between 'research' and 'development'.
8. Explain when development outlays can be capitalised.

References

Christian Dior 2014, *Annual Report*, www.dior-finance.com.

GSK 2014, *Annual Report*, https://www.gsk.com/en-gb/investors/corporate-reporting/.

Jenkins, E., and Upton, W. 2001, 'Internally generated intangible assets: Framing the discussion', *Australian Accounting Review*, vol. 11, no. 2, pp. 4–11.

Lev, B. 2001, *Intangibles: management, measurement, and reporting*, Brookings Institution Press, Washington, DC.

Lev, B. 2002, 'Where have all of Enron's intangibles gone?' *Journal of Accounting and Public Policy*, vol. 21, no. 2, pp. 131–135.

Upton, W. S. 2001, *Business and financial reporting, challenges from the new economy*, Financial Accounting Series No. 219-A, Financial Accounting Standards Board, Norwalk, CT, USA.

Exercises

STAR RATING ★ BASIC ★★ MODERATE ★★★ DIFFICULT

Exercise 13.1 | USEFUL TRADEMARK LIFE

★ X Ltd holds a trademark that is well known within consumer circles and has enabled the company to be a market leader in its area. The trademark has been held by the company for 9 years. The legal life of the trademark is 5 years, but is renewable by the company at little cost to it.

Required

Discuss how the company should determine the useful life of the trademark, noting in particular what form of evidence it should collect to justify its selection of useful life.

Exercise 13.2 | BRANDS AND FORMULAS

★ Wayne Upton (2001, p. 71) in his discussion of the lives of intangible assets noted that the formula for Coca-Cola has grown more valuable over time, not less, and that Sir David Tweedie, former chairman of the IASB, joked that the brand name of his favourite Scotch whisky is older than the United States of America — and, in Sir David's view, the formula for Scotch whisky has contributed more to the sum of human happiness.

Required

Outline the accounting for brands under IAS 38, and discuss the difficulties for standard setters in allowing the recognition of all brands and formulas on the statement of financial position.

Exercise 13.3 | RESEARCH AND DEVELOPMENT

★★ Because of the low level of rainfall in Simonstown, householders find it difficult to keep their gardens and lawns sufficiently watered. As a result, many householders have installed bores that allow them to access underground water suitable for using on the garden. This is a cheaper option than incurring excess water bills by using the government-provided water system. One of the problems with much of the bore water is that its heavy iron content leaves a brown stain on paths and garden edges. This can make homes look unsightly and lower their value.

Noting this problem, Strand Laboratories believed that it should research the problem with the goal of developing a filter system that could be attached to a bore and remove the effects of the iron content in the water. This process, if developed, could be patented and filters sold through local reticulation shops.

In 2011, Strand commenced its work on the problem, resulting in August 2015 in a patent for the NoMoreIron filter process. Costs incurred in this process were as shown below.

2011–12	Research conducted to develop filter	£125 000
2012–13	Research conducted to develop filter	132 000
2013–14	Design and construction of prototype	152 000
2014–15	Testing of models	51 000
2015–16	Fees for preparing patent application	12 000
2016–17	Research to modify design	34 000
2017–18	Legal fees to protect patent against cheap copies	15 000

Required

Discuss how the company should account for each of these outlays.

Exercise 13.4

RECOGNITION OF INTANGIBLES

★★ Soweto Ltd is unsure of how to obtain computer software. Four possibilities are:
1. Purchase computer software externally, including packages for payroll and general ledger.
2. Contract to independent programmers to develop specific software for the company's own use.
3. Buy computer software to incorporate into a product that the company will develop.
4. Employ its own programmers to write software that the company will use.

Required

Discuss whether the accounting will differ depending on which method is chosen.

Exercise 13.5

RESEARCH AND DEVELOPMENT

★★ Stellenbosch Laboratories Ltd manufactures and distributes a wide range of general pharmaceutical products. Selected audited data for the reporting period ended 31 December 2014 are as follows:

Gross profit	£17 600 000
Profit before income tax	1 700 000
Income tax expense	(500 000)
Profit for the period	1 200 000
Total assets:	
Current	7 300 000
Non-current	11 500 000

The company uses a standard mark-up on cost.

From your audit files, you ascertain that total research and development expenditure for the year amounted to £4 700 000. This amount is substantially higher than in previous years and has eroded the profitability of the company. Mr Bosch, the company's finance director, has asked for your firm's advice on whether it is acceptable accounting practice for the company to carry forward any of this expenditure to a future accounting period.

Your audit files disclose that the main reason for the significant increase in research and development costs was the introduction of a planned 5-year laboratory programme to attempt to find an antidote for the common cold. Salaries and identifiable equipment costs associated with this programme amounted to £2 350 000 for the current year.

The following additional items were included in research and development costs for the year:
(a) Costs to test a new tamper-proof dispenser pack for the company's major selling line (20% of sales) of antibiotic capsules — £760 000. The new packs are to be introduced in the 2013 financial year.
(b) Experimental costs to convert a line of headache powders to liquid form — £59 000. The company hopes to phase out the powder form if the tests to convert to the stronger and better handling liquid form prove successful.
(c) Quality control required by stringent company policy and by law on all items of production for the year — £750 000.
(d) Costs of a time and motion study aimed at improving production efficiency by redesigning plant layout of existing equipment — £50 000.
(e) Construction and testing of a new prototype machine for producing hypodermic needles — £200 000. Testing has been successful to date and is nearing completion. Hypodermic needles accounted for 1% of the company's sales in the current year, but it is expected that the company's market share will increase following introduction of this new machine.

Required

Respond to Mr Bosch's question for each of these items.

RESEARCH AND DEVELOPMENT

★★ Capetown Ltd has been involved in a project to develop an engine that runs on extracts from sugar cane. It started the project in February 2014. Between the starting date and 30 June 2014, the end of the reporting period for the company, Capetown Ltd spent £254 000 on the project. At 30 June 2014, there was no indication that the project would be commercially feasible, although the company had made significant progress and was sufficiently sure of future success that it was prepared to outlay more funds on the project.

After spending a further £120 000 during July and August, the company had built a prototype that appeared to be successful. The prototype was demonstrated to a number of engineering companies during September, and several of these companies expressed interest in the further development of the engine. Convinced that it now had a product that it would be able to sell, Capetown Ltd spent a further £65 000 during October adjusting for the problems that the engineering firms had pointed out. On 1 November, Capetown Ltd applied for a patent on the engine, incurring legal and administrative costs of £35 000. The patent had an expected useful life of 5 years, but was renewable for a further 5 years upon application.

Between November and December 2014, Capetown Ltd spent an additional amount of £82 000 on engineering and consulting costs to develop the project such that the engine was at manufacturing stage. This resulted in changes in the overall design of the engine, and costs of £5000 were incurred to add minor changes to the patent authority.

On 1 January 2015, Capetown Ltd invited tenders for the manufacture of the engine for commercial sale.

Required

Discuss how Capetown Ltd should account for these costs. Provide journal entries with an explanation of why these are the appropriate entries.

ACCOUNTING FOR BRANDS

★★★ Jon West Ltd is a leading company in the sale of frozen and canned fish produce. These products are sold under two brand names. Fish caught in southern Australian waters are sold under the brand 'Arctic Fresh', which is the brand the company developed when it commenced operations and which is still used today. Fish caught in the northern oceans are sold under the brand name 'Tropical Taste', the brand developed by Fishy Tales Ltd. Jon West Ltd acquired all the assets and liabilities of Fishy Tales Ltd a number of years ago when it took over that company's operations.

Jon West Ltd has always marketed itself as operating in an environmentally responsible manner, and is an advocate of sustainable fishing. The public regards it as a dolphin-friendly company as a result of its previous campaigns to ensure dolphins are not affected by tuna fishing. The marketing manager of Jon West Ltd has noted the efforts of a ship, the *Steve Irwin*, to disrupt and hopefully stop the efforts of Japanese whalers in the southern oceans and the publicity that this has received. He has recommended to the board of directors that Jon West Ltd strengthen its environmentally responsible image by guaranteeing to repair any damage caused to the *Steve Irwin* as a result of attempts to disrupt the Japanese whalers. He believes that this action will increase Jon West Ltd's environmental reputation, adding to the company's goodwill. He has told the board that such a guarantee will have no effect on Jon West Ltd's reported profitability. He has explained that, if any damage to the *Steve Irwin* occurs, Jon West Ltd can capitalise the resulting repair costs to the carrying amounts of its brands, as such costs will have been incurred basically for marketing purposes. Accordingly, as the company's net asset position will increase, and there will be no effect on the statement of profit or loss and other comprehensive income, this will be a win–win situation for everyone.

Required

The chairman of the board knows that the marketing manager is very effective at selling ideas but knows very little about accounting. The chairman has, therefore, asked you to provide him with a report advising the board on how the proposal should be accounted for under International Financial Reporting Standards and how such a proposal would affect Jon West Ltd's financial statements.

There is an extant accounting literature on intangibles, only a small fraction of which can be reviewed here. Wyatt (2008) offers a comprehensive review of the literature for the interested reader. Broadly, the literature can be split into two strands. The first is with respect to intangible assets that are recognised on the balance sheet (other than goodwill — see chapter 14). The second strand is with respect to assessing the adequacy of the expensing requirements that apply to most internally generated intangibles.

Starting with recognised intangibles, Aboody and Lev (1998) examine the value relevance of capitalised software development costs in a sample of 163 software companies between 1987 and 1995. They argue that software firms reporting under US GAAP (SFAS 86 (FASB, 1985) and now ASC 985-20) face considerable flexibility with the capitalisation decision. As a result, about one fifth of sample firms expensed the development cost in full in every year examined. They find that the annual amount capitalised is smaller in bigger and more profitable firms, and is larger when the development costs (before capitalisation) are larger. They further find that stock returns are positively related to changes in annual amounts of capitalisation, but unrelated to the change in development expense recognised in the income statement. Because capitalising firms amortise the intangible asset, the amortisation figures may be informative, for example with respect to managers' estimate of the useful life. Consistent with that, the authors find that changes in amortisation expense are negatively related to stock returns. Levels analysis also confirms that stock prices are positively related to the amount of software development cost recognised on the balance sheet. Collectively, this evidence suggests that investors regard capitalised amounts as assets. Mohd (2005) extends this analysis by looking at differences in information asymmetry between capitalising and expensing firms. He employs bid–ask spreads and trading volume as measures of information asymmetry. Consistent with the view that investors better understand the financials of capitalising firms, he finds evidence of lower information asymmetry for capitalising firms. Hence, both Aboody and Lev (1998) and Mohn (2005) are supportive of capitalisation of software development cost because they provide more useful information to investors.

Markarian et al. (2008) provide evidence from Italy about capitalisation of R&D expenses prior to the adoption of IFRS® Standards in 2005. Domestic Italian rules were quite similar to the capitalisation rules set in IAS 38 for development cost. Therefore this study is helpful in understanding how discretion is used under IAS 38. This paper employs 130 firm-year observations during 2001–2003. The degree of capitalisation is on average 10% of total R&D costs. The paper fails to find consistent evidence as to the determinants of the amount capitalised, although some evidence suggests that more profitable firms capitalise less. Cazavan-Jeny and Jeanjean (2006) focus on a French sample, also pre IFRS Standards. During 1993–2002 domestic French rules allowed considerable flexibility to managers with respect to the capitalisation decision. Their sample consists of 197 firms and 770 firm-year observations, with 250 observations under capitalisation. Unlike Aboody and Lev (1998) they find that (1) capitalised amounts are negatively related to stock prices, and (2) changes in capitalised amounts are negatively related to stock returns. This evidence is consistent with usefulness of reported numbers under capitalisation. Nevertheless, the negative relation could be indicative of investor perception that the decision to capitalise is opportunistic in nature and is adopted by weaker firms.

Wyatt (2005) employs an Australian sample during 1993–1997. During this period Australian GAAP allowed considerable flexibility for companies as to whether to capitalise internally generated intangibles. Wyatt (2005) examines several hypotheses as to what drives the capitalisation decision. In particular she predicts that the degree to which a firm can capture future benefits positively influences the capitalisation decision. Wyatt (2005) provides evidence that is consistent with this prediction using several proxies. This suggests that Australian firms used the discretion to capitalise in line with underlying economic fundamentals rather than in an opportunistic fashion.

IAS 38 axiomatically assumes that acquired intangibles always satisfy asset-recognition criteria. Nevertheless, to the extent that uncertainty about future benefits is an inherent feature of intangibles, it is questionable if acquired intangibles should be initially capitalised. Amir and Livne (2005) raise this point when they examine human-capital intangibles. Specifically, they take advantage of a unique industry arrangement — the football industry — whereby clubs that sign up new players often pay a transfer fee to the player's former club. This fee normally corresponds to the talent and stature of the player. Nevertheless, as the form of the player and his fit with the new team and coach are far from being certain, it is not clear that they should be capitalised. Amir and Livne (2005) examine the relation between measures of future benefits and transfer fees paid, employing financials of 58 UK football clubs between 1990 and 2003. While they find a positive association between current sales, operating profit and operating cash flows on one hand and past transfer fees on the other hand, it seems that the investments are not fully recoverable. In addition, the useful life of transfer fees is found to be shorter than the amortisation period used by the clubs. Amir and Livne (2005) also examine the relation between transfer fees paid and stock prices and establish it is positive. They therefore conclude that market participants do regard fees paid as an asset. While the setting examined in Amir and Livne (2005) is industry-specific, it nevertheless raises some doubt about the requirement to show purchased intangibles as assets.

Turning to unrecognised intangibles, a number of studies have criticised the immediate expensing rule that applies to internally generated intangibles, mostly advertising and R&D. Hirschey and Weygandt (1985) is one of the earlier studies to suggest advertising and R&D should be capitalised. Specifically, they examine the association between the ratio of market value of equity to replacement cost of equity (a measure of the premium of market price over book value of equity) and advertising and R&D expenses. Inconsistent with standard-setters' view, the results indicate a positive relation, which is expected if investors regard these expenditures as assets.

Lev and Sougiannis (1996) advance a method for estimating the amortised cost of intangible R&D assets. They employ more than 11,600 observations to estimate economic amortisation rates that subsequently were used to estimate the hypothetical amount to be recognised as an R&D asset in balance sheet. They also calculate the difference between reported earnings (and equity) and capitalisation-with-amortisation adjusted earnings (and equity). Lev and Sougiannis (1996) find that these differences are positively associated with stock prices, especially for high R&D-intensity firms. A stock returns analysis modestly supports the levels analysis. This evidence collectively suggests that investors pay attention to these differences, which in turn indicates that for R&D-intensive firms investors adjust reported numbers as if R&D expense is capitalised.

Lev and Zarowin (1999) take the charge against expensing of R&D a step further. They look at the ability of earnings and changes in earnings to explain stock returns over a period of 20 years. In addition to the changes analysis they look at the ability of earnings and book value of equity to explain stock prices (levels analysis) over the same period. They provide evidence that suggests that (1) the usefulness of accounting numbers has declined over the period examined and (2) at the same time there has been an increase in the rate of change businesses have faced. The central claim of the Lev and Zarowin's (1999) paper is that the changes in business environment are attributable to the role of R&D and technology. To support this assertion they show that firms that increase (decrease) their R&D intensity over time exhibit lower (higher) usefulness of their financial reports. They then argue that the expensing rule may have contributed to the decline in usefulness, although in this paper they do not furnish direct evidence pertaining to this claim.

Not all studies agree that R&D should be capitalised. Kothari et al. (2002) show that the variability of future profits is increasing with R&D expense, and more so than capital expenditure (CAPEX). This is consistent with standard setters' view that the uncertainty surrounding future benefits is high in the case of R&D. Amir et al. (2007) nevertheless argue, and provide evidence to that effect, that the risk in CAPEX can exceed that of R&D in several industries. The evidence provided in Amir et al. (2007) is intriguing because it challenges the view that CAPEX should always be capitalised.

Further research has been conducted also with respect to other intangibles that existing accounting rules disallow their capitalisation. For example, Barth et al. (2008) employ brand estimates reported by Financial World that, in turn, are based on valuation methodology developed by Interbrand Ltd. The authors find evidence supporting the view that unrecognised brands are regarded as assets by market participants. Livne et al. (2011) examine the valuation role of customer acquisition cost, a major expense in several service-based firms. They provide evidence from the wireless industry that these expenses are positively related to customer retention and future operating profit. This suggests that such expenses meet asset recognition criteria. Bonacchi et al. (2014) extend this research by looking at subscription-based enterprises. They develop a valuation model for customer equity using 576 firm-year observations and find that it is positively related to stock prices. Since internally generated customer relationships cannot be capitalised, the evidence in Livne et al. (2011) and Bonacchi et al. (2014) calls for a change in existing rules regarding customer relationships.

References

Aboody, D., and Lev, B. 1998. The value relevance of intangibles: The case of software capitalization. *Journal of Accounting Research*, 161–191.

Amir, E., Guan, Y., and Livne, G. 2007. The association of R&D and capital expenditures with subsequent earnings variability. *Journal of Business Finance & Accounting*, 34 (1 and 2), 222–246.

Amir, E., and Livne, G. 2005. Accounting, valuation and duration of football player contracts. *Journal of Business Finance & Accounting*, 32(3–4), 549–586.

Barth, M. E., Clement, M. B., Foster, G., and. Kasznik, R. 1998. Brand values and capital market valuation. *Review of Accounting Studies*, 3(1), 41–68.

Bonacchi, M., Kolev, K., and Lev, B. 2014. Customer franchise—A hidden, yet crucial asset. *Contemporary Accounting Research*, 32(3), 1024–1049.

Cazavan-Jeny, A., and Jeanjean, T. 2006. The negative impact of R&D capitalization: A value relevance approach. *European Accounting Review*, 15(1), 37–61.

Financial Accounting Standards Board. 1985. Accounting for the Costs of Computer Software to Be Sold, Leased, or Otherwise Marketed. SFAS 86. Stamford, CT.

Hirschey, M., and Weygandt, J. J. 1985. Amortization policy for advertising and research and development expenditures. *Journal of Accounting Research*, 326–335.

Kothari, S. P., Laguerre, T. E., and Leone, A. J. 2002. Capitalization versus expensing: Evidence on the uncertainty of future earnings from capital expenditures versus R&D outlays. *Review of Accounting Studies*, 7(4), 355–382.

Lev, B., and Sougiannis, T. 1996. The capitalization, amortization, and value-relevance of R&D. *Journal of Accounting and Economics*, 21(1), 107–138.

Lev, B., and Zarowin, P. 1999. The Boundaries of financial reporting and how to extend them. *Journal of Accounting Research*, 37(2), 353–385.

Livne, G., Simpson, A., and Talmor, E. 2011. Do customer acquisition cost, retention and usage matter to firm performance and valuation? *Journal of Business Finance & Accounting*, 38(3), 334–63.

Markarian, G., Pozza, L., and Prencipe, A. 2008. Capitalization of R&D costs and earnings management: Evidence from Italian listed companies. *The International Journal of Accounting*, 43(3), 246–267.

Mohd, E. 2005. Accounting for software development costs and information asymmetry. *The Accounting Review*, 80(4), 1211–1231.

Wyatt, A. 2005. Accounting recognition of intangible assets: Theory and evidence on economic determinants. *The Accounting Review*, 80(3), 967–1003.

Wyatt, A. 2008. What financial and non-financial information on intangibles is value-relevant? A review of the evidence. *Accounting and Business Research*, 38(3), 217–256.

14 Business combinations

ACCOUNTING STANDARDS IN FOCUS

IFRS 3 *Business Combinations*

LEARNING OBJECTIVES

After studying this chapter, you should be able to:

1. understand the nature of a business combination and its various forms
2. explain the basic steps in the acquisition method of accounting for a business combination
3. account for a business combination in the records of the acquirer
4. recognise and measure the assets acquired and liabilities assumed in the business combination
5. understand the nature of and the accounting for goodwill and gain from bargain purchase
6. account for shares acquired in the acquiree
7. prepare the accounting records of the acquiree
8. account for subsequent adjustments to the initial accounting for a business combination
9. provide the disclosures required under IFRS 3.

14.1 THE NATURE OF A BUSINESS COMBINATION

The accounting standard relevant for accounting for business combinations is IFRS 3 *Business Combinations* issued by the International Accounting Standards Board (IASB®) in January 2008.

A business combination is defined in Appendix A to IFRS 3 as:

A transaction or other event in which an acquirer obtains control of one or more businesses.

The meaning of control is the same as in IFRS 10 *Consolidated Financial Statements*. Control exists when an investor is exposed, or has rights, to variable returns from its involvement with the investee and has the ability to affect those returns through its power over the investee.

The term business is defined in Appendix A as:

An integrated set of activities and assets that is capable of being conducted and managed for the purpose of providing a return in the form of dividends, lower costs or other economic benefits directly to investors or other owners, members or participants.

The purpose of defining a business is to distinguish between the acquisition of a group of assets that does not constitute a business and the acquisition of a business.

Combining two or more separate businesses requires the combination of the assets and liabilities of the acquirer with those acquired from the acquiree(s). This can occur in a number of ways. For example, if A Ltd is to be combined with B Ltd, the following possibilities might arise:

1. A Ltd acquires all the assets and liabilities of B Ltd.
   B Ltd continues as a company, holding shares in A Ltd.
2. A Ltd acquires all the assets and liabilities of B Ltd.
   B Ltd liquidates.
3. C Ltd is formed to acquire all the assets and liabilities of A Ltd and B Ltd.
   A Ltd and B Ltd liquidate.
4. A Ltd acquires a group of net assets of B Ltd, the group of net assets constituting a business, such as a division, branch or segment, of B Ltd.
   B Ltd continues to operate as a company.

These possibilities are covered in this chapter.

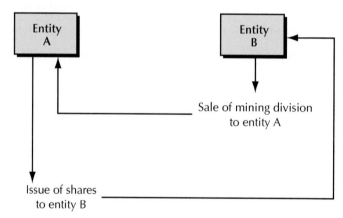

FIGURE 14.1 Identification of a business combination

The most obvious way in which control can be achieved is through one entity acquiring sufficient shares of another entity on the open market to have a controlling interest. Accounting for that form of business combination requires the application of the principles discussed in this chapter, but the application further involves the preparation of consolidated financial statements. *Accounting for these forms of business combinations is discussed in chapters 20 to 24.*

A business combination could also occur without any exchange of assets or equity between the entities involved in the exchange. For example, a business combination could occur where two entities merged under a contract. The shareholders of the two entities could agree to adjust the rights of each of their shareholdings so that they receive a specified share of the profits of both the combined entities. As a result of the contract, both entities would be under the control of a single management group.

There are many other forms of business combinations that can occur, such as A Ltd acquiring the assets only of B Ltd, and B Ltd paying off its liabilities and then liquidating. Alternatively, A Ltd may acquire all of B Ltd's assets and some of its liabilities, followed by B Ltd settling its remaining liabilities before liquidating. The three approaches identified in figure 14.2 cover most of the arrangements that are likely to occur in practice.

IFRS 3 applies to all business combinations except those listed in paragraph 2 of the standard, namely:

* *Where the business combination results in the formation of a joint venture.* Such a business combination is accounted for under IFRS 11 *Joint Arrangements*.

- *Where the business combination involves entities or businesses under common control.* This occurs where all of the combining entities are controlled by the same party or parties both before and after the combination, and where control is not transitory. For example, P Ltd owns 100% of S Ltd's issued share capital. If P Ltd formed a new wholly owned entity, X Ltd, that acquired all of S Ltd's equity, then this would simply constitute an internal reconstruction. All of the combining entities would be controlled by P Ltd both before and after the reconstruction.

FIGURE 14.2 General forms of business combinations

Alternative 1

A Ltd acquires net assets of B Ltd	*B Ltd continues, holding shares in A Ltd*
A Ltd:	B Ltd:
• Receipt of assets and liabilities of B Ltd	• Sale of assets and liabilities to A Ltd
• Consideration transferred, e.g. shares, cash or other consideration	• Gain or loss on sale
	• Receipt of consideration transferred, e.g. shares, cash or other consideration

Alternative 2

A Ltd acquires net assets of B Ltd	*B Ltd liquidates*
A Ltd:	B Ltd:
• As for alternative 1 above, A Ltd	• Liquidation account, including gain/loss on liquidation
	• Receipt of purchase consideration
	• Distribution of consideration to appropriate parties, including shareholders via the Shareholders' Distribution account

Alternative 3

C Ltd formed	*A Ltd and B Ltd liquidate*
C Ltd:	A Ltd and B Ltd:
• Formation of C Ltd with issue of shares	• As for alternative 2 above, B Ltd
• Acquisition of assets and liabilities of A Ltd and B Ltd	
• Payment for net assets of A Ltd and B Ltd via cash outlays or issue of shares in C Ltd	

14.2 ACCOUNTING FOR A BUSINESS COMBINATION — BASIC PRINCIPLES

The required method of accounting for a business combination under paragraph 4 of IFRS 3 is the *acquisition method*. The four key steps in this method are noted in paragraph 5 of the standard:
1. Identify the acquirer.
2. Determine the acquisition date.
3. Recognise and measure the identifiable assets acquired, the liabilities assumed, and any non-controlling interest in the acquiree.
4. Recognise and measure goodwill or a gain from a bargain purchase.

The acquisition date is the date that the acquirer obtains control of the acquiree. IFRS 3 deals with the acquisition itself and also with the subsequent measurement and accounting for assets and liabilities recognised initially at acquisition date.

14.2.1 Identifying the acquirer [step 1]

Paragraph 7 of IFRS 3 states that the acquirer is 'the entity that obtains *control* of another entity, i.e. the acquiree'.

The key criterion, then, in identifying an acquirer is that of control. This term is the same as that used in IFRS 10 *Consolidated Financial Statements* for identifying a parent–subsidiary relationship (see chapter 20). It is often straightforward to identify the acquirer. For example, entity A might acquire shares in entity B.

In other situations, identification of an acquirer requires judgement. Consider the situation where entity A combines with entity B. To effect the combination, a new company (entity C) is formed, which issues shares to acquire all the shares of both entities A and B. The subsequent organisational structure is as shown in figure 14.3.

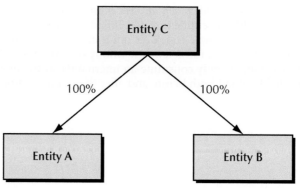

FIGURE 14.3 Example of entity combination and subsequent organisational structure

As entity C is created solely to formalise the organisation structure, it is not the acquirer, even though it is the legal parent of both of the other entities. Paragraph B18 of Appendix B to IFRS 3 states that one of the entities that existed before the combination must be identified as the acquirer. Entity C is not a party to the decisions associated with creating the business combination, it is just a vehicle used to facilitate the combination. If entity A is identified as the acquirer, then entity B's assets and liabilities are measured at fair value at acquisition date.

Paragraphs B14–B18 of Appendix B to IFRS 3 provide some indicators to assist in assessing which entity is the acquirer:

- *What are the relative voting rights in the combined entity after the business combination?* The acquirer is usually the entity whose owners have the largest portion of the voting rights in the combined entity. As noted in paragraph B19, in a reverse acquisition, entity X may issue its shares to acquire the shares of entity Y. However, because of the greater number of X shares given to the former Y shareholders relative to those held by the shareholders in entity X before the combination, the former shareholders in entity Y may have the majority of shares in entity X and be able to determine the operating and financial policies of the combined entities.
- *Is there a large minority voting interest in the combined entity?* The acquirer is usually the entity that has the largest minority voting interest in an entity that has a widely dispersed ownership.
- *What is the composition of the governing body of the combined entity?* The acquirer is usually the combining entity whose owners have the ability to elect or appoint or to remove a majority of the members of the governing body of the combined entity.
- *What is the composition of the senior management that governs the combined entity subsequent to the combination?* This is an important indicator given that the criterion for identification of an acquirer is that of control. If X and Y combine, is the senior management group of the combined entity dominated by former senior managers of X or Y?
- *What are the terms of the exchange of equity interests?* Has one of the combining entities paid a premium over the pre-combination fair value of one of the combining entities, an amount paid in order to gain control?
- *Which entity is the larger?* This could be measured by reference to the fair value of each of the combining entities, or relative revenues or profits. In a takeover, it is normally the larger company that takes over the smaller company (that is, the larger company is the acquirer).
- *Which entity initiated the exchange?* Normally the entity that is the acquirer is the one that undertakes action to take over the acquiree.

Determining the controlling entity is the key to identification of the acquirer. However, doing so may not be straightforward in many business combinations, and the accountant might be required to make a reasoned judgement based on the circumstances.

Paragraph 6 requires an acquirer to be identified in every business combination, even though it may be argued that it is not always possible to do so. In the case of a 'true' merger, neither party would claim to be dominant.

It can also prove difficult to identify an acquirer under a combination achieved by contract alone. Such a combination may not involve the exchange of readily measurable consideration.

The need to identify the acquirer stems from the need to measure the acquiree's assets at fair value, but not those of the acquirer.

14.2.2 Determining the acquisition date [step 2]

The acquisition date is defined in Appendix A to IFRS 3 as:

> [t]he date on which the **acquirer** obtains control of the **acquiree**.

Other dates, such as the date that the contract is signed or the date on which the assets are delivered may be important issues for management, but they do not necessarily reflect the acquisition date. As noted in paragraph 9 of IFRS 3, on the closing date of the combination, the acquirer legally transfers the consideration — cash or shares — and acquires the assets and assumes the liabilities of the acquiree. However, in some cases this may not be the acquisition date.

The definition of acquisition date then relates to the point in time when the net assets of the acquiree become the net assets of the acquirer — in essence, the date on which the acquirer can recognise the net assets acquired in its own records.

Identifying the acquisition date is important because:
- The identifiable assets acquired and liabilities assumed by the acquirer are measured at their fair values on the acquisition date. If markets are volatile then the date could affect the fair value.
- The consideration paid by the acquirer is determined as the sum of the fair values of assets given, equity issued and/or liabilities undertaken in exchange for the net assets or shares of another entity. Share prices can fluctuate daily, so the choice of date can affect the measure of fair value.
- The acquirer may acquire only some of the shares of the acquiree. The owners of the balance of the shares of the acquiree are called the non-controlling interest. This non-controlling interest is measured at fair value at acquisition date.
- The acquirer may have previously held an equity interest in the acquiree prior to obtaining control of the acquiree. For example, entity X may have previously acquired 20% of the shares of entity Y, and now acquires the remaining 80% giving it control of entity Y. The acquisition date is the date when entity X acquired the 80% interest. The 20% share holding will be recorded as an asset in the records of entity X. At acquisition date, the fair value of this investment is measured.

The effect of determining the acquisition date is that the financial position of the combined entity at acquisition date should report the assets and liabilities of the acquiree at that date, and any profits reported as a result of the acquiree's operations within the business combination should reflect profits earned after the acquisition date.

14.3 ACCOUNTING IN THE RECORDS OF THE ACQUIRER

Where the acquirer purchases assets and assumes liabilities of another entity, it has to consider:
(a) the recognition and measurement of the identifiable assets acquired and the liabilities assumed (step 3 of the acquisition method)
(b) the recognition and measurement of goodwill or a gain from a bargain purchase (step 4 of the acquisition method).

Chapters 20 to 24 deal with the preparation of consolidated financial statements for business combinations where the acquirer purchases the shares of the acquiree. The only aspect of such business combinations that will be covered in this chapter is the recognition and measurement of the investment by the acquirer *(see section 14.6)*.

14.4 RECOGNITION AND MEASUREMENT OF ASSETS ACQUIRED AND LIABILITIES ASSUMED [STEP 3]

14.4.1 Recognition

Paragraph 10 of IFRS 3 states:

> As of the acquisition date, the acquirer shall recognise, separately from goodwill, the identifiable assets acquired, the liabilities assumed and any non-controlling interest in the acquiree. Recognition of identifiable assets acquired and liabilities assumed is subject to the conditions specified in paragraphs 11 and 12.

Paragraph 4.38 of the *Conceptual Framework* specifies two recognition criteria for assets and liabilities, stating that recognition occurs if:
- it is probable that any future economic benefit will flow to or from the entity
- the item has a cost or value that can be reliably measured.

The probability criterion does not really apply in the context of a business combination because the use of fair values automatically incorporates the probabilities of future economic benefits into the valuation. For example, an asset whose future expected cash flows were regarded as risky would have a lower fair value.

Paragraph 10 requires the recognition of any non-controlling interest in the acquiree. Non-controlling interests are discussed in chapter 23.

In paragraphs 11 and 12 of IFRS 3, there are two conditions that have to be met prior to the recognition of assets and liabilities acquired in the business combination:

Firstly, at the acquisition date, the assets and liabilities recognised by the acquirer must meet the definitions of assets and liabilities in the *Conceptual Framework*. Any expected future costs cannot be included in the calculation of assets acquired and liabilities assumed.

Secondly, the item acquired or assumed must be part of the business acquired rather than the result of a separate transaction.

The first of these conditions can have implications for the treatment of contingent liabilities. If the liability is contingent upon a future event, such as the outcome of legal action against the acquiree, then nothing needs to be done. If the liability has been treated as contingent because the future outflows are not regarded as 'probable' or because the amounts cannot be measured with sufficient reliability, then it is necessary to attach a fair value, even though it would have been a breach of IAS 37 *Provisions, Contingent Liabilities and Contingent Assets* for the acquiree to have recognised the liability in its financial statements before the combination.

The second condition applies substance over form. For example, suppose the acquiree had a claim outstanding against the acquirer before the acquisition date. If the acquirer agrees to settle the claim as part of the combination and part of the consideration includes a sum in settlement of the claim then it would be necessary to account for the acquisition as two transactions and the sum paid in settlement would have to be separated out from the consideration.

Paragraph 13 of IFRS 3 notes that a possible result of applying the principles of IFRS 3 may be the recognition of assets and liabilities as a result of the business combination that were not previously recognised by the acquiree. For example, internally generated intangibles that were not recognised by the acquiree because of the requirements of IAS 38 *Intangible Assets* may have to be recognised by the acquirer at fair value.

Paragraph 15 of IFRS 3 requires that the acquirer classifies or designates assets and liabilities on the basis of the contractual terms, economic conditions, its operating or accounting policies and other pertinent conditions that exist at acquisition date. This could, for example, affect the classification of financial assets at fair value or at amortised cost.

As a part of the illustrative examples accompanying IFRS 3, the IASB provided examples of items acquired in a business combination that would meet the definition of an intangible asset (see figure 14.4).

CLASS	BASIS
Marketing-related intangible assets	
Trademarks, trade names, service marks, collective marks and certification marks	Contractual
Trade dress (unique colour, shape or package design)	Contractual
Newspaper mastheads	Contractual
Internet domain names	Contractual
Non-competition agreements	Contractual
Customer-related intangible assets	
Customer lists	Non-contractual
Order or production backlog	Contractual
Customer contracts and related customer relationships	Contractual
Non-contractual customer relationships	Non-contractual
Artistic-related intangible assets	
Plays, operas and ballets	Contractual
Books, magazines, newspapers and other literary works	Contractual
Musical works such as compositions, song lyrics and advertising jingles	Contractual
Pictures and photographs	Contractual
Video and audiovisual material, including motion pictures or films, music videos and television programs	Contractual
Contract-based intangible assets	
Licensing, royalty and standstill agreements	Contractual
Advertising, construction, management, service or supply contracts	Contractual
Lease agreements (whether the acquiree is the lessee or lessor)	Contractual
Construction permits	Contractual
Franchise agreements	Contractual
Operating and broadcasting rights	Contractual
Servicing contracts such as mortgage servicing contracts	Contractual
Employment contracts	Contractual
Use rights, such as drilling, water, air, timber cutting and route authorities	Contractual
Technology-based intangible assets	
Patented technology	Contractual
Computer software and mask works	Contractual
Unpatented technology	Non-contractual
Databases including title plants	Non-contractual
Trade secrets such as secret formulas, processes and recipes	Contractual

FIGURE 14.4 Intangible assets, IFRS 3 Illustrative Examples

14.4.2 Measurement

Paragraph 18 requires an acquirer to measure the identifiable assets acquired and the liabilities assumed at their fair values on acquisition date.

Fair value is defined in Appendix A to IFRS 3 as follows:

the price that would be received to sell an asset or paid to transfer a liability in an orderly transaction between market participants at the measurement date.

Fair value is discussed in detail in chapter 3.

Paragraph BC198 of the Basis for Conclusions on IFRS 3 argues that fair values are relevant, comparable and understandable.

14.5 GOODWILL AND GAIN ON BARGAIN PURCHASE [STEP 4]

Paragraph 32 of IFRS 3 states:

The acquirer shall recognise goodwill as of the acquisition date measured as the excess of (a) over (b) below:

(a) the aggregate of:
  (i) the consideration transferred measured in accordance with this IFRS, which generally requires acquisition-date fair value (see paragraph 37);
  (ii) the amount of any non-controlling interest in the acquiree measured in accordance with this IFRS; and
  (iii) in a business combination achieved in stages (see paragraphs 41 and 42), the acquisition-date fair value of the acquirer's previously held equity interest in the acquiree.
(b) the net of the acquisition-date amounts of the identifiable assets acquired and the liabilities assumed measured in accordance with this IFRS.

In relation to parts (a)(ii) and (iii) in paragraph 32, these will affect calculations only where the acquirer obtains control by acquiring shares in the acquiree. *This is discussed in chapters 20 to 24.* This means that for business combinations discussed in this chapter, goodwill is determined by comparing the consideration transferred by the acquirer with the net fair value of the identifiable assets and liabilities acquired.

The net fair value of the identifiable assets and liabilities acquired is determined as step 3. The first part of step 4 is then the measurement of consideration transferred.

14.5.1 Consideration transferred

According to paragraph 37, the consideration transferred:
- is measured at fair value at acquisition date
- is calculated as the sum of the acquisition-date fair values of the assets transferred by the acquirer, the liabilities incurred by the acquirer to former owners of the acquiree, and the equity interest issued by the acquirer.

In a specific exchange, the consideration transferred to the acquiree could include just one form of consideration, such as cash, but could equally well consist of a number of forms such as cash, other assets, shares and contingent consideration. These are considered in the following pages.

Cash or other monetary assets

The fair value is the amount of cash or cash equivalent dispersed. The amount is usually readily determinable. One problem that may occur arises when the settlement is deferred to a time after the acquisition date. For a deferred payment, the fair value to the acquirer is the amount the entity would have to borrow to settle the debt immediately. The discount rate used is the entity's incremental borrowing rate.

Use of cash, including a deferred payment, to acquire net assets results in the acquirer recording the following form of entry at the acquisition date:

Net assets	Dr	xxx	
Cash	Cr		xxx
Payable to Acquiree	Cr		xxx
(Acquisition of net assets with partially deferred payment)			

When the deferred payment is made to the acquiree, the interest component needs to be recognised:

Payable to Acquiree	Dr	xxx	
Interest Expense	Dr	xxx	
Cash	Cr		xxx
(Payment of deferred amount)			

Non-monetary assets

Non-monetary assets are assets such as property, plant and equipment, investments, licences and patents. *Chapter 3 discusses how fair values are determined.*

The acquirer is effectively selling the non-monetary asset to the acquiree. Hence, it is earning income equal to the fair value on the sale of the asset. Where the carrying amount of the asset in the records of the acquirer is different from fair value, a gain or loss on the asset is recognised at acquisition date. This principle is explained in paragraph 38 of IFRS 3: 'the acquirer shall remeasure the transferred assets or liabilities to their fair values as of the acquisition date and recognise the resulting gains or losses, if any, in profit or loss'.

Use of a non-monetary asset such as plant as part of the consideration to acquire net assets results in the acquirer recording the following entries (assume a cost of plant of $180, a carrying amount of $150 and fair value of $155):

Accumulated Depreciation	Dr	30	
Plant	Cr		25
Gain	Cr		5
(Remeasurement as part of consideration transferred in a business combination)			
Net Assets Acquired	Dr	xxx	
Plant	Cr		155
Other Consideration Payable	Cr		xxx
(Acquisition of net assets)			

The acquirer recognises a gain on the non-current asset and the asset is then included in the consideration transferred at fair value.

Equity instruments

If an acquirer issues its own shares as consideration, it needs to determine the fair value of those shares at the acquisition date. For listed entities, reference is made to the quoted prices of the shares. As noted in paragraph BC342 of the Basis for Conclusions on IFRS 3, 'equity instruments issued as consideration in a business combination should be measured at their fair values on the acquisition date'.

Liabilities assumed

The fair values of liabilities assumed are best measured by the present values of expected future cash outflows. Future losses or other costs expected to be incurred as a result of the combination are not liabilities of the acquirer and are therefore not included in the calculation of the fair value of consideration paid.

Costs of issuing debt and equity instruments

Paragraph 53 of IFRS 3 indicates costs to issue debt and equity instruments are accounted for in accordance with IAS 32 *Financial Instruments: Presentation* and IFRS 9 *Financial Instruments*. In issuing equity instruments such as shares as part of the consideration paid, transaction costs such as stamp duties, professional advisers' fees, underwriting costs and brokerage fees may be incurred. Paragraph 35 of IAS 32 states that these outlays should be treated as a reduction in the share capital of the entity as such costs reduce the proceeds from the equity issue, net of any related income tax benefit. Hence, if costs of $1000 are incurred in issuing shares as part of the consideration paid, the journal entry in the records of the acquirer is:

Share Capital	Dr	1 000	
Cash	Cr		1 000
(Costs of issuing equity instruments)			

Similarly, the costs of arranging and issuing financial liabilities are an integral part of the liability issue transaction. These costs are included in the initial measurement of the liability. *Financial liabilities are discussed further in chapter 7.*

Contingent consideration

Appendix A to IFRS 3 provides the following definition of contingent consideration:

> Usually, an obligation of the **acquirer** to transfer additional assets or **equity interests** to the former owners of an **acquiree** as part of the exchange for **control** of the **acquiree** if specified future events occur or conditions are met. However, contingent consideration also may give the **acquirer** the right to the return of previously transferred consideration if specified conditions are met.

Consider two examples of contingencies. The first is where, because the future income of the acquirer is regarded as uncertain, the agreement contains a clause that requires the acquirer to provide additional consideration to the acquiree if the income of the acquirer is not equal to or exceeds a specified amount over some specified period. The second situation is where the acquirer issues shares to the acquiree and the acquiree is concerned that the issue of these shares may make the market price of the acquirer's shares decline over time. Therefore, the acquirer may offer additional cash or shares if the market price falls below a specified amount over a specified period of time.

According to paragraph 39 of IFRS 3, consistent with other measurements in transferred consideration, the acquirer shall recognise the acquisition-date fair values of contingent consideration as part of the consideration transferred.

14.5.2 Acquisition-related costs

In addition to the consideration transferred by the acquirer to the acquiree, a further item to be considered in determining the cost of the business combination is the costs directly attributable to the combination, which includes costs such as 'finder's fees; advisory, legal, accounting, valuation and other professional or consulting fees; [and] general administrative costs, including the costs of maintaining an internal acquisitions department' (IFRS 3 paragraph 53).

In IAS 16 *Property, Plant and Equipment* and IAS 38 *Intangible Assets*, directly attributable costs are considered as a part of the cost of acquisition and capitalised into the cost of the asset acquired. In contrast, the acquisition-related costs associated with a business combination are accounted for as expenses in the periods in which they are incurred and the services are received. The key reasons given for this approach are provided in paragraph BC366 of the Basis for Conclusions on IFRS 3:

- Acquisition-related costs are not part of the fair value exchange between the buyer and seller.
- They are separate transactions for which the buyer pays the fair value for the services received.
- These amounts do not generally represent assets of the acquirer at acquisition date because the benefits obtained are consumed as the services are received.

The IFRS 3 accounting for these outlays is a result of the decision to record the identifiable assets acquired and liabilities assumed at fair value. In contrast, under IAS 16 and IAS 38, the assets acquired are initially recorded at cost.

ILLUSTRATIVE EXAMPLE 14.1 Consideration transferred in a business combination

The trial balance below represents the financial position of Whiting Ltd at 1 January 2016.

WHITING LTD Trial Balance as at 1 January 2016		
	Debit	Credit
Share capital		
Preference — 6000 fully paid shares		$ 6 000
Ordinary — 30 000 fully paid shares		30 000
Retained earnings		21 500
Equipment	$42 000	
Accumulated depreciation – equipment		10 000
Inventory	18 000	
Accounts receivable	16 000	
Patents	3 500	
Debentures		4 000
Accounts payable		8 000
	$79 500	$79 500

At this date, the business of Whiting Ltd is acquired by Salmon Ltd, with Whiting Ltd going into liquidation. The terms of acquisition are as follows:

1. Salmon Ltd is to take over all the assets of Whiting Ltd as well as the accounts payable of Whiting Ltd.
2. Costs of liquidation of $350 are to be paid by Whiting Ltd with funds supplied by Salmon Ltd.
3. Preference shareholders of Whiting Ltd are to receive two fully paid preference shares in Salmon Ltd for every three shares held or, alternatively, $1 per share in cash payable at acquisition date.
4. Ordinary shareholders of Whiting Ltd are to receive two fully paid ordinary shares in Salmon Ltd for every share held or, alternatively, $2.50 in cash, payable half at the acquisition date and half on 31 December 2016.
5. Debenture holders of Whiting Ltd are to be paid in cash out of funds provided by Salmon Ltd. These debentures have a fair value of $102 per $100 debenture.
6. All shares being issued by Salmon Ltd have a fair value of $1.10 per share. Holders of 3000 preference shares and 5000 ordinary shares elect to receive the cash.

7. Costs of issuing and registering the shares issued by Salmon Ltd amount to $40 for the preference shares and $100 for the ordinary shares.
8. Costs associated with the business combination and incurred by Salmon Ltd were $1000.

The calculation of the consideration transferred in the business combination to Salmon Ltd is shown in figure 14.5. The incremental borrowing rate for Salmon Ltd is 10% p.a.

Consideration transferred:			Fair value
Cash:	Costs of liquidation	$ 350	
	Preference shareholders (3000 × $1.00)	3 000	
	Ordinary shareholders		
	– payable immediately (1/2 × 5000 × $2.50)	6 250	
	– payable later (1/2 × 5000 × $2.50 × 0.909091)*	5 682	
	Debentures, including premium ($4000 × 1.02)	4 080	$19 362
Shares:	Preference shareholders (2000 × $1.10)	2 200	
	Ordinary shareholders (50 000 × $1.10)	55 000	57 200
Consideration transferred			**$76 562**

$5682 is the cash payable in 1 year's time discounted at 10% p.a.

FIGURE 14.5 Consideration transferred in the business combination

In acquiring the net assets of Whiting Ltd, Salmon Ltd passes the journal entries shown in figure 14.6.

2016				
Jan. 1	Net Assets Acquired	Dr	76 562	
	Consideration Payable	Cr		19 362
	Share Capital – Preference	Cr		2 200
	Share Capital – Ordinary	Cr		55 000
	(Acquisition of the net assets of Whiting Ltd)			
	Consideration Payable	Dr	13 680	
	Cash	Cr		13 680
	(Payment of cash consideration to Whiting Ltd: $19 362 less $5682 payable later)			
	Share Capital – Ordinary	Dr	100	
	Share Capital – Preference	Dr	40	
	Cash	Cr		140
	(Share issue costs)			
	Acquisition-Related Expenses	Dr	1 000	
	Cash	Cr		1 000
	(Acquisition-related expenses)			
Dec. 31	Consideration Payable	Dr	5 682	
	Interest Expense	Dr	568	
	Cash	Cr		6 250
	(Balance of consideration paid)			

FIGURE 14.6 Journal entries in the acquirer's records

14.5.3 Goodwill

As noted at the beginning of section 14.5, goodwill is the excess of the consideration transferred over the net fair value of the identifiable assets acquired and liabilities assumed.

> Goodwill = Consideration transferred
> less
> Acquirer's interest in the net fair value of the acquiree's identifiable assets and liabilities

Goodwill is accounted for as an asset and is defined in Appendix A to IFRS 3 as:

An asset representing the future economic benefits arising from other assets acquired in a **business combination** that are not individually identified and separately recognised.

The criterion of 'being individually identified' relates to the characteristic of 'identifiability' as used in IAS 38 *Intangible Assets* to distinguish intangible assets from goodwill. Note paragraph 11 of IAS 38 in this regard:

> The definition of an intangible asset requires an intangible asset to be identifiable to distinguish it from goodwill. Goodwill recognised in a business combination is an asset representing future economic benefits arising from other assets acquired in a business combination that are not individually identified and separately recognised. The future economic benefits may result from synergy between the identifiable assets acquired or from assets that, individually, do not qualify for recognition in the financial statements.

In order to be identifiable, an asset must be capable of being separated or divided from the entity, or arise from contractual or other legal rights. The notion of being 'separately recognised' is also then a part of the criterion of 'identifiability'. *This criterion is discussed further in chapter 13.*

Goodwill is then a residual, after the acquirer's interest in the identifiable tangible assets, intangible assets, and liabilities of the acquiree is recognised.

The components of goodwill

Johnson and Petrone (1998, p. 295) identified six components of goodwill:

1. *Excess of the fair values over the book values of the acquiree's recognised assets.* In a business acquisition, as assets acquired are measured at fair value, these excesses should not exist. Subsequent to the acquisition, the acquiree's goodwill could include such excesses where assets are measured at cost.
2. *Fair values of other net assets not recognised by the acquiree.* The assets of concern here are those tangible assets which are incapable of reliable measurement by the acquiree, and non-physical assets that do not meet the identifiability criteria for intangible assets.
3. *Fair value of the 'going concern' element of the acquiree's existing business.* This represents the ability of the acquiree to earn a higher return on an assembled collection of net assets than would be expected from those net assets operating separately. This reflects synergies of the assets, as well as factors relating to market imperfections such as an ability of an entity to earn a monopoly profit, or where there are barriers to competitors entering a particular market.
4. *Fair value from combining the acquirer's and acquiree's businesses and net assets.* This stems from the synergies that result from the combination, the value of which is unique to each combination.
5. *Overvaluation of the consideration paid by the acquirer.* This relates to errors in valuing the consideration paid by the acquirer, and may arise particularly where shares are issued as consideration with differences in prices for small parcels of shares as opposed to controlling parcels of shares. There could also be overvaluation of the fair values of the assets acquired. This component could then relate to all errors in measuring the fair values in the business combination.
6. *Overpayment (or underpayment) by the acquirer.* This may occur if the price is driven up in the course of bidding; conversely, goodwill could be understated if the acquiree's net assets were obtained through a distress or fire sale.

In paragraph BC130 of the Basis for Conclusions on IFRS 3, the IASB recognised that components 1 and 2 are not conceptually part of goodwill. Johnson and Petrone (1998, p. 295) and the IASB (paragraph BC131) recognised that components 5 and 6 in the above list also are not conceptually part of goodwill, but rather relate to measurement errors. The two components that are seen as part of goodwill are components 3 and 4, described by Johnson and Petrone (p. 296) as 'going-concern goodwill' and 'combination goodwill' respectively, with the combination of the components being referred to as 'core goodwill'. This is represented diagrammatically in figure 14.7.

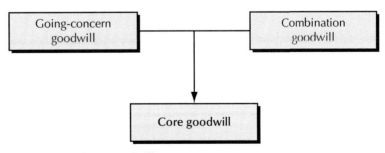

FIGURE 14.7 Core goodwill
Source: Data derived from Johnson and Petrone (1998).

It is this 'core goodwill' that the IASB is concerned with in determining how to account for goodwill. The IASB in paragraph BC137 of the Basis for Conclusions on IFRS 3 notes how IFRS 3 tries to avoid subsuming the first, second and fifth components into the amount calculated as goodwill by requiring an acquirer to make every effort to:

- measure the consideration accurately (eliminating or reducing component 5)
- recognise the identifiable net assets acquired at their fair values rather than their carrying amounts (eliminating or reducing component 1)
- recognise all acquired intangible assets (reducing component 2).

Is goodwill an asset?

IFRS 3 accounts for goodwill as an asset, although it is debatable whether it meets the definition of an asset as set out in the *Conceptual Framework*.

The problem with goodwill is that it is a unique asset. It arises as a residual. As Leo, Hoggett and Radford (1995, pp. 44–7) noted, the key difference between identifiable net assets and goodwill is measurement:

> The difference between the measurement method used for goodwill and that for measurement of all other assets of the business is whether the method involves determining the value of the business as a whole or part thereof.

The authors defined unidentifiable assets (p. 46) as those assets that meet the recognition criteria and cannot be measured without measuring the total net assets of a business entity. The existence of goodwill depends on the measurement of the entity as a whole. In recognising this, the IASB argued in paragraph BC323 of the Basis for Conclusions on IFRS 3:

> control of core goodwill is provided by means of the acquirer's power to direct the policies and management of the acquiree. Therefore, both the IASB and the FASB concluded that core goodwill meets the conceptual definition of an asset.

Accounting for goodwill

As noted earlier, goodwill is calculated as the excess of the consideration transferred in the business combination over the acquirer's interest in the net fair value of the identifiable assets acquired and liabilities assumed from the acquiree. Hence, to calculate goodwill as a part of the acquisition analysis it is necessary to calculate the consideration transferred and the net fair value of the identifiable assets acquired and liabilities assumed. A comparison of these two amounts determines the existence of goodwill. The acquirer then recognises goodwill as an asset in the same way as for all other identifiable assets acquired.

ILLUSTRATIVE EXAMPLE 14.2 Acquisition analysis

Using the figures from illustrative example 14.1, assume that Salmon Ltd assesses the fair values of the identifiable assets and liabilities of Whiting Ltd to be as follows:

Equipment	$36 000
Inventory	20 000
Accounts receivable	9 000
Patents	10 000
Accounts payable	8 000

To determine the entries to be passed by the acquirer, prepare an acquisition analysis that compares the consideration transferred with the net fair value of the identifiable assets, liabilities and contingent liabilities acquired. The analysis for this example is shown in figure 14.8.

Acquisition analysis

Net fair value of identifiable assets acquired and liabilities assumed:

Equipment	$36 000
Inventory	20 000
Accounts receivable	9 000
Patents	10 000
	75 000
Accounts payable	8 000
Net fair value	$67 000

Consideration transferred:
This was calculated in figure 14.5 as $76 562.

Goodwill acquired:

Net fair value acquired	= $67 000
Consideration transferred	= $76 562
Goodwill	= $76 562 − $67 000
	= $9 562

FIGURE 14.8 Acquisition analysis by the acquirer

The journal entries for Salmon Ltd at acquisition date are as shown in figure 14.9.

Equipment	Dr	36 000	
Inventory	Dr	20 000	
Accounts Receivable	Dr	9 000	
Patents	Dr	10 000	
Goodwill	Dr	9 562	
Accounts Payable	Cr		8 000
Consideration Payable	Cr		19 362
Share Capital – Preference	Cr		2 200
Share Capital – Ordinary	Cr		55 000
(Acquisition of the assets and liabilities of Whiting Ltd)			
Consideration Payable	Dr	13 680	
Cash	Cr		13 680
(Payment of cash consideration)			
Acquisition-Related Expenses	Dr	1 000	
Cash	Cr		1 000
(Acquisition-related costs)			
Share Capital – Ordinary	Dr	100	
Share Capital – Preference	Dr	40	
Cash	Cr		140
(Share issue costs)			

FIGURE 14.9 Journal entries of the acquirer, including recognition of goodwill, at acquisition date

14.5.4 Accounting for a gain on a bargain purchase

Where the acquirer's interest in the net fair value of the acquiree's identifiable assets and liabilities is greater than the consideration transferred, the difference is called a gain on a bargain purchase. In equation format, it can be represented as follows:

> Gain on bargain purchase = Acquirer's interest in the net fair value of the acquiree's identifiable assets and liabilities
> *less*
> Consideration transferred

The existence of a bargain purchase is considered by the standard setters (paragraph BC371) as an anomalous transaction as parties to the business combination do not knowingly sell assets at amounts lower than their fair value. However, because the acquirer has excellent negotiation skills, or because the acquiree has made a sale for other than economic reasons or is forced to sell owing to specific circumstances such as cash flow problems, such situations do arise.

The standard setters adopt the view that most business combinations are an exchange of equal amounts, given markets in which the parties to the business combinations are informed and willing participants in the transaction. Therefore, the existence of a bargain purchase is expected to be an unusual or rare event.

Paragraph 36 of IFRS 3 requires that before a gain is recognised, the acquirer must reassess whether it has correctly:

- identified all the assets acquired and liabilities assumed
- measured at fair value all the assets acquired and liabilities assumed
- measured the consideration transferred.

The objective here is to ensure that all the measurements at acquisition date reflect all the information that is available at that date.

Note that one effect of recognising a bargain purchase is that there is no recognition of goodwill. A gain on bargain purchase and goodwill cannot be recognised in the same business combination.

Using the information regarding the consideration transferred in a business combination from illustrative examples 14.1 and 14.2, assume the fair values of the identifiable assets and liabilities of Whiting Ltd are assessed to be:

Equipment	$45 000
Inventory	25 000
Accounts receivable	9 000
Patents	11 000
	90 000
Accounts payable	8 000
	$82 000

The acquisition analysis now shows:

Net fair value of assets and liabilities acquired	= $82 000
Consideration transferred	= $76 562
Gain on bargain purchase	= $82 000 − $76 562
	= $5438

Assuming that the reassessment process did not result in any changes to the fair values calculated, the first journal entry in Salmon Ltd to record the acquisition of the net assets of Whiting Ltd is:

Equipment	Dr	45 000	
Inventory	Dr	25 000	
Accounts Receivable	Dr	9 000	
Patents	Dr	11 000	
Accounts Payable	Cr		8 000
Consideration Payable	Cr		19 362
Share Capital – Preference	Cr		2 200
Share Capital – Ordinary	Cr		55 000
Gain (Profit or Loss)	Cr		5 438
(Acquisition of assets and liabilities acquired from Whiting Ltd, and the gain on bargain purchase)			

14.6 SHARES ACQUIRED IN THE ACQUIREE

Where an entity acquires shares in another entity, rather than the net assets of that entity, the measurement of the initial investment in these financial assets is in accordance with IFRS 9 *Financial Instruments* at fair value plus transaction costs.

Accounting for financial assets is covered in chapter 7.

14.7 ACCOUNTING IN THE RECORDS OF THE ACQUIREE

Where the acquirer purchases the acquiree's assets and liabilities, the acquiree may continue in existence or may liquidate. The acquiree accounts affected by the business combination will differ according to the actions of the acquiree.

14.7.1 Acquiree does not liquidate

In the situation where the acquiree disposes of a business, the journal entries required in the records of the acquiree are shown in figure 14.10. Under IAS 16 *Property, Plant and Equipment*, when an item of property, plant and equipment is sold, gains or losses are recognised in the statement of profit or loss and other comprehensive income. Similarly, on the sale of a business, the acquiree recognises a gain or loss.

Receivable from Acquirer	Dr	xxx	
Liability A	Dr	xxx	
Liability B	Dr	xxx	
Liability C	Dr	xxx	
Asset A	Cr		xxx
Asset B	Cr		xxx
Asset C	Cr		xxx
Gain on Sale of Operation	Cr		xxx
(Sale of operation)			
Shares in Acquirer	Dr	xxx	
Cash	Dr	xxx	
Receivable from Acquirer	Cr		xxx
(Receipt of consideration from acquirer)			

FIGURE 14.10 Journal entries of acquiree on sale of business

14.7.2 Acquiree liquidates

The entries required in the records of the acquiree when it sells *all* its net assets to the acquirer are shown in figure 14.11. The accounts of the acquiree are transferred to two accounts, the Liquidation account and the Shareholders' Distribution account.

To the *Liquidation account* are transferred:
- all assets taken over by the acquirer, including cash if relevant, as well as any assets not taken over and which have a zero value, including goodwill
- all liabilities taken over
- the expenses of liquidation if paid by the acquiree
- additional expenses to be paid by the acquiree but not previously recognised by the acquiree
- consideration from the acquirer as proceeds on sale of net assets
- all reserves, including retained earnings.

The balance of the Liquidation account is then transferred to the Shareholders' Distribution account.

FIGURE 14.11 Journal entries of acquiree on liquidation after sale of net assets

Liquidation	Dr	xxx	
Asset A	Cr		xxx
Asset B	Cr		xxx
Asset C	Cr		xxx
(Transfer of all assets acquired by acquirer, at their carrying amounts)			
Liability A	Dr	xxx	
Liability B	Dr	xxx	
Liability C	Dr	xxx	
Liquidation	Cr		xxx
(Transfer of all liabilities assumed by the acquirer)			
Liquidation	Dr	xxx	
Cash	Cr		xxx
(Liquidation and other expenses not recognised previously, if paid by the acquiree)			
Receivable from Acquirer	Dr	xxx	
Liquidation	Cr		xxx
(Consideration for net assets sold)			
Cash	Dr	xxx	
Shares in Acquirer	Dr	xxx	
Receivable from Acquirer	Cr		xxx
(Receipt of consideration)			
Other Reserves	Dr	xxx	
Retained Earnings	Dr	xxx	
Liquidation	Cr		xxx
(Transfer of reserves)			

(continued)

FIGURE 14.11 (continued)

Liquidation	Dr	xxx	
Shareholders' Distribution	Cr		xxx
(Transfer of balance of liquidation)			
Share Capital	Dr	xxx	
Shareholders' Distribution	Cr		xxx
(Transfer of share capital)			
Shareholders' Distribution	Dr	xxx	
Cash	Cr		xxx
Shares in Acquirer	Cr		xxx
(Distribution of consideration to shareholders)			

To the *Shareholders' Distribution* account are transferred:
- the balance of share capital
- the balance of the Liquidation account
- the portion of the consideration received from the acquirer that is distributed to the shareholders. Some of the consideration received by the acquiree may be used to pay for liabilities not assumed by the acquirer, and for liquidation expenses.

ILLUSTRATIVE EXAMPLE 14.4 Entries in the acquiree's records

Using the information from illustrative example 14.1, the entries in the records of Whiting Ltd are shown in figure 14.12.

FIGURE 14.12 Liquidation of acquiree

Liquidation	Dr	69 500	
Accumulated Depreciation – Equipment	Dr	10 000	
Equipment	Cr		42 000
Inventory	Cr		18 000
Accounts Receivable	Cr		16 000
Patents	Cr		3 500
(Assets taken over)			
Accounts Payable	Dr	8 000	
Liquidation	Cr		8 000
(Liabilities taken over)			
Liquidation	Dr	350	
Liquidation Expenses Payable	Cr		350
(Liquidation expenses payable by acquiree)			
Liquidation	Dr	80	
Debenture Holders Payable	Cr		80
(Premium expense on debentures to be paid on redemption)			
Receivable from Salmon Ltd	Dr	76 562	
Liquidation	Cr		76 562
(Consideration receivable)			
Cash	Dr	13 680	
Shares in Salmon Ltd	Dr	57 200	
Receivable from Salmon Ltd	Cr		70 880
(Receipt of consideration from acquirer)			
Retained Earnings	Dr	21 500	
Liquidation	Cr		21 500
(Transfer of retained earnings)			
Liquidation	Dr	36 132	
Shareholders' Distribution	Cr		36 132
(Balance of Liquidation account transferred to Shareholders' Distribution)			

FIGURE 14.12 (continued)

Share Capital – Ordinary	Dr	30 000	
Share Capital – Preference	Dr	6 000	
Shareholders' Distribution	Cr		36 000
(Transfer of share capital)			
Debentures	Dr	4 000	
Debenture Holders Payable	Cr		4 000
(Transfer of debentures to payable account)			
Liquidation Expenses Payable	Dr	350	
Debenture Holders Payable	Dr	4 080	
Cash	Cr		4 430
(Payment of liabilities)			
Shareholders' Distribution	Dr	72 132	
Cash	Cr		9 250
Shares in Salmon Ltd	Cr		57 200
Receivable from Salmon Ltd	Cr		5 682
(Payment to shareholders)			

14.7.3 Acquirer buys only shares in the acquiree

When the acquirer buys only shares in the acquiree, there are no entries in the records of the acquiree because the transaction is between the acquirer and the shareholders of the acquiree entity. The acquiree itself is not involved.

14.8 SUBSEQUENT ADJUSTMENTS TO THE INITIAL ACCOUNTING FOR A BUSINESS COMBINATION

Three areas where adjustments may need to be made subsequent to the initial accounting after acquisition date are:
- goodwill
- contingent liabilities
- contingent consideration.

Goodwill

Having recognised goodwill arising in the business combination, the subsequent accounting is directed from other accounting standards:
- goodwill is not subject to amortisation but is subject to an annual impairment test as detailed in IAS 36 *Impairment of Assets (see chapter 15)*.
- goodwill cannot be revalued because IAS 38 *Intangible Assets* does not allow the recognition of internally generated goodwill.

Contingent liabilities

Having recognised any contingent liabilities of the acquiree as liabilities, the acquirer must then determine a subsequent measurement for the liability. The liability is initially recognised at fair value. Subsequent to acquisition date, according to paragraph 56 of IFRS 3, the liability is measured as the higher of:
- (a) the amount that would be recognised in accordance with IAS 37; and
- (b) the amount initially recognised less, if appropriate, cumulative amortisation recognised in accordance with IAS 18 *Revenue*.

Under IAS 37 paragraph 36, the liability would be measured at the best estimate of the expenditure required to settle the present obligation at the end of the reporting period. This would be used, for example, where a liability was recognised in relation to a court case. However, the IASB was also concerned about contingent liabilities such as guarantees or other financial liabilities. Under IAS 39 paragraph 47, the subsequent measurement of financial liabilities requires preparers to use the higher of the IAS 37 measurements and the amount initially recognised subject to amortisation in line with IAS 18. In order for IFRS 3 to be consistent with IAS 39, the measurement method to be used in subsequent accounting for contingent liabilities was made the same as that in IAS 39.

Contingent consideration

At acquisition date, the contingent consideration is measured at fair value, and is classified either as equity (e.g. the requirement for the acquirer to issue more shares subject to subsequent events) or as a liability (e.g. the requirement to provide more cash subject to subsequent events). Subsequent to the business combination, paragraph 54 of IFRS 3 requires the accounting for contingent consideration to be in accordance with the accounting standard that would normally apply to these accounts. However, IFRS 3 provides guidance on the measures to be used.

Where the contingent consideration is classified as equity, no remeasurement is required, and the subsequent settlement is accounted for within equity (IFRS 3 paragraph 58(a)). This means that if extra equity instruments are issued they are effectively issued for no consideration and there is no change to share capital.

Where the contingent consideration is a financial liability, it will be accounted for under IAS 39 and measured at fair value with movements being accounted for in accordance with that standard. If it is a liability not within the scope of IAS 39, it is accounted for in accordance with IAS 37. So, if there were changes in the amount of an expected cash outflow, the liability would be adjusted and an amount recognised in profit or loss.

It should be noted that the subsequent accounting for contingent consideration is to treat it as a post-acquisition event; that is, not affecting the measurements made at acquisition date. Hence, any subsequent adjustments do not affect the goodwill calculated at acquisition date.

ILLUSTRATIVE EXAMPLE 14.5 Comprehensive example

Labrador Ltd's major business is in the pet food industry. It makes a number of canned pet foods, mainly for cats and dogs, as well as having a very promising line in dry dog food. It has been interested for some time in the operations of Pelican Ltd, an entity that deals with the processing of grain products for a number of other industries including flour-processing, health foods and, in more recent times, the production of grain products for feeding birds. Given its interest in the pet food industry and its desire to stay as one of the leaders in this area, Labrador Ltd began negotiations with Pelican Ltd to acquire its birdseed product division.

Negotiations began in July 2015. After months of discussion between the relevant parties of both companies, an agreement was reached on 15 February 2016 for Labrador Ltd to acquire the birdseed division. The agreement document was taken to the board of directors of Pelican Ltd who ratified the agreement on 1 March 2016. The net assets were exchanged on this date.

The net assets of the birdseed division at 1 March 2016, showing the carrying amounts at that date and the fair values as estimated by Labrador Ltd from documentation supplied by Pelican Ltd, were as shown below:

	Carrying amount	Fair value
Plant and equipment	$160 000	$167 000
Land	70 000	75 000
Motor vehicles	30 000	32 000
Inventory	24 000	28 000
Accounts receivable	18 000	16 000
Total assets	302 000	318 000
Accounts payable	35 000	35 000
Bank overdraft	55 000	55 000
Total liabilities	90 000	90 000
Net assets	$212 000	$228 000

Details of the consideration Labrador Ltd agreed to provide in exchange for the net assets of the division are described below:
- 100 000 shares in Labrador Ltd — movements in the share price were as follows:

1 July 2015	$1.00
1 October 2015	1.10
1 January 2016	1.15
1 February 2016	1.30
15 February 2016	1.32
16 February 2016	1.45
1 March 2016	1.50

- Because of doubts as to whether it could sustain a share price of at least $1.50, Labrador Ltd agreed to supply cash to the value of any decrease in the share price below $1.50 for the 100 000 shares issued, this guarantee of the share price lasting until 31 July. Labrador Ltd believed that there was a 90% chance that the share price would remain at $1.50 or higher and a 10% chance that it would fall to $1.48.
- Cash of $40 000, half to be paid on the date of acquisition and half in 1 year's time.

- Supply of a patent relating to the manufacture of packing material. This has a fair value of $60 000 but has not been recognised in the records of Labrador Ltd because it resulted from an internally generated research project.
- Pelican Ltd was currently being sued for damages relating to a claim by a bird breeder who had bought some seed from the company, and claimed that this resulted in the death of some prime breeding pigeons. Labrador Ltd agreed to pay any resulting damages in relation to the court case. The expected damages were $40 000. Lawyers estimated that there was only a 20% chance of losing the case.

Labrador Ltd supplied the cash on the acquisition date as well as surrendering the patent. The shares were issued on 5 March, and the costs of issuing the shares amounted to $1000. The incremental borrowing rate for Labrador Ltd is 10% p.a. Acquisition-related costs paid by Labrador Ltd in relation to the acquisition amounted to $5000.

On 31 July the share price of Labrador Ltd's shares was $1.52.

Required

Prepare the journal entries in the records of the acquirer.

Solution

Acquisition analysis

Net fair value of assets acquired and liabilities assumed	
Plant and equipment	$167 000
Land	75 000
Motor vehicles	32 000
Inventory	28 000
Accounts receivable	16 000
	318 000
Accounts payable	35 000
Bank overdraft	55 000
Provision for damages (20% × $40 000)	8 000
	98 000
	$220 000
Consideration transferred	
Purchase consideration:	
Shares: 100 000 × $1.50	$150 000
Guarantee: 10% ($1.50 − $1.48) × 100 000	200
Cash: Payable now	20 000
Deferred ($20 000 × 0.909 091)	18 182
Patent	60 000
	$248 382
Goodwill ($248 382 − $220 000)	$ 28 382

The journal entries of the acquirer, Labrador Ltd, are shown in figure 14.13.

FIGURE 14.13 Journal entries of the acquirer

2016				
March 1	Plant and Equipment	Dr	167 000	
	Land	Dr	75 000	
	Motor Vehicles	Dr	32 000	
	Inventory	Dr	28 000	
	Accounts Receivable	Dr	16 000	
	Goodwill	Dr	28 382	
	Accounts Payable	Cr		35 000
	Bank Overdraft	Cr		55 000
	Provision for Damages	Cr		8 000
	Share Capital	Cr		150 000
	Provision for Loss in Value of Shares	Cr		200
	Cash	Cr		20 000
	Consideration Payable	Cr		18 182
	Gain on Sale of Patent	Cr		60 000
	(Acquisition of birdseed division from Pelican Ltd)			

(continued)

FIGURE 14.13 (continued)

	Acquisition-Related Expenses	Dr	5 000	
	Cash	Cr		5 000
	(Acquisition-related costs)			
March 5	Share Capital	Dr	1 000	
	Cash	Cr		1 000
	(Costs of issuing shares)			
July 31	Provision for Loss in Value of Shares	Dr	200	
	Gain	Cr		200
	(Contingency not having to be paid)			

14.9 DISCLOSURE — BUSINESS COMBINATIONS

LO9

Paragraphs 59–63 of IFRS 3 contain information on disclosures required in relation to business combinations. To meet these disclosure requirements it is necessary to apply Appendix B of IFRS 3, which is an integral part of IFRS 3 containing application guidance.

Paragraph 59 requires entities to disclose information about the nature and financial effect of business combinations occurring during the current reporting period, or after the end of the reporting period but before the financial statements are authorised for issue. Paragraphs B64–B66 contain information to assist preparers to meet the disclosure objective in paragraph 59.

Note the qualitative information required to be disclosed under paragraph B64. In particular, note B64(d) which requires disclosure of the primary reasons for the business combination as well as a description of how the acquirer obtained control of the acquiree. This information should assist users to evaluate the success of the business combination and judge the ability of management to make investment decisions.

Also note that paragraph B64(e) requires disclosure of 'a qualitative description of the factors that make up goodwill recognised, such as expected synergies from combining operations of the acquiree and the acquirer, intangible assets that do not qualify for separate recognition or other factors'. Goodwill is not to be considered just a residual calculation. *As explained in section 14.5.3*, core goodwill can consist of elements such as combination goodwill and going-concern goodwill. An understanding of where the synergies exist will assist management in managing the earnings from goodwill as well as in any later impairment tests of goodwill *(see chapter 15 for more details concerning impairment testing)*. Unrecognised intangible assets may also be included in goodwill *(see chapter 13 for information on accounting for intangible assets in a business combination)*.

Paragraph 61 of IFRS 3 requires the disclosure of information to assist in the evaluation of the financial effects of adjustments recognised in the current period that relate to business combinations occurring in previous periods. Paragraph B67 details disclosures required in meet the information objective in paragraph 61.

An example of the required disclosures is provided in figure 14.14.

FIGURE 14.14 Disclosures required by Labrador Ltd under IFRS 3

26. Business combinations	IFRS 3 paragraph
Acquisition of division from Pelican Ltd During the current reporting period, the company acquired the birdseed division of Pelican Ltd. The acquisition date was 1 March 2016. The company has not had to dispose of any operations as a result of this combination. The primary reason for the business combination was to gain synergies in terms of the sales outlets for products sold by both entities.	B64(a) B64(b) B64(d)

The consideration transferred to Pelican Ltd was $248 382. The components of the cost were:
    Shares in the company $150 000
    Cash paid and payable   38 182
    Patent for packaging   60 000
    Guarantee relating to the maintenance of the company's share price   200
	B64(f)
	
	B64(g)(i)

The contingent consideration — the guarantee — was measured at acquisition date at $200 being based on an analysis of probable movements in share prices and budgeted information on future sales. The company issued 100 000 shares, determining a fair value of $1.50 based on the current market price of the company at 1 March 2016 as reported by the stock exchange.	B64(g)(ii) B64(f)(iv)

FIGURE 14.14 *(continued)*

The assets acquired and liabilities assumed from Pelican Ltd were, as at 1 March 2016:   *B64(i)*

	Carrying amount	Fair value
Plant and equipment	$160 000	$167 000
Land	70 000	75 000
Motor vehicles	30 000	32 000
Inventory	24 000	28 000
Accounts receivable	18 000	16 000
	302 000	318 000
Accounts payable	35 000	35 000
Bank overdraft	55 000	55 000
	90 000	90 000
Contingent liability acquired	8 000	8 000
		98 000
Net assets acquired		$220 000

Goodwill of $28 382 was recognised in the acquisition, the extra consideration being paid due to the excellent reputation and customer following relating to the quality of the birdseed products.   *B64(e)*

An adjustment of $2000 was made to the fair value of the plant and equipment and goodwill subsequent to the acquisition due to the provisional nature of the fair value of some of the specialised equipment determined at acquisition date.   *B67(a)*

The contingent liability acquired related to a court case involving a claim from a customer that certain bird food was of poor quality. If the court case were lost, which is not expected, the damages could be $40 000. A present obligation is regarded as existing at the end of the reporting period.   *B64(j)*

Subsequent to the end of the reporting period, the provision in relation to the company's guarantee in relation to maintenance of the share price expired. No extra payment was required, as the share price had been maintained.   *B64(g)(iii)*

Acquisition-related costs amounted to $5 000, all of which was recognised as an expense against the line item 'operating expenses'. Share issue costs of $1000 were treated as a reduction in share capital.   *B64(m)*

Acquisition of shares in Cages Ltd

On 1 August 2015, the company acquired 100% of the shares in Cages Ltd, a company involved mainly in manufacturing bird cages, for $100 000. The primary reason for acquiring the company was to expand the variety of products sold to customers in the same industry. The consideration paid was cash.   *B64(a),(b),(c)*
B64(d)
B64(f)

The assets and liabilities of Cages Ltd at acquisition date were: *B64(i)*

	Carrying amount	Fair value
Plant and equipment	$ 82 000	$ 88 000
Vehicles	22 000	20 000
Cash	12 000	12 000
Accounts receivable	8 000	7 000
	124 000	127 000
Accounts payable	32 000	32 000
Net assets	$ 92 000	$ 95 000

Goodwill of $5000 was acquired, attributable to a quality, well-trained workforce. The consolidated revenue for the consolidated group is $952 000. If the business combinations occurring during the year had occurred on 1 July 2015 instead of during the year, it is estimated that consolidated revenue would have been $985 000. The consolidated profit under the same assumption would have been $322 000 instead of $299 000.   *B64(e)*
B64(q)

(continued)

FIGURE 14.14 *(continued)*

27. Goodwill

	2016	2015	
Gross amount at beginning of period	$20 600	$19 600	*B67(d)(i)*
Accumulated impairment losses	500	300	
	20 100	19 300	
Goodwill acquired	35 380	3 000	*B67(d)(ii)*
	55 480	22 300	
Adjustments — tax assets recognised	—	2 000	*B67(d)(iii)*
		20 300	
Impairment losses for current period	—	200	*B67(d)(iv)*
Carrying amount at end of period	$55 480	$20 100	
Consisting of:			*B67(d)(viii)*
Gross amount at end of period	$55 980	$20 600	
Accumulated impairment losses	500	500	
	$55 480	$20 100	

SUMMARY

IFRS 3 was issued in January 2008 on completion of a major project on business combinations undertaken by the IASB. IFRS 3 specifies accounting standards that have implications not only for the exchanges of assets between entities but also for the accounting for subsidiaries and associated entities. The standard specifies how an acquirer accounts for the assets and liabilities acquired as well as the measurement of the consideration transferred. In making these calculations, the acquirer must determine the acquisition date as all fair value measurements are made at acquisition date. The standard interacts with other standards such as IAS 38 *Intangible Assets* and IAS 37 *Provisions, Contingent Liabilities and Contingent Assets* because the acquirer has to recognise intangible assets and liabilities acquired in a business combination. The nature and calculation of goodwill is also covered in this accounting standard, as is the treatment of a gain on a bargain purchase.

Entities commonly trade with each other, exchanging one set of assets for another. When a grouping of assets constitutes a business, the accounting for the exchange transaction is determined by IFRS 3. IFRS 3 requires the application of the acquisition method under which the accountant must be able to identify which of the entities involved in the combination is the acquirer. The identifiable assets and liabilities acquired are measured at fair value at the acquisition date.

Goodwill or the gain on a bargain purchase is determined as a residual which, for the business combinations considered in this chapter, is generally determined by comparing the consideration transferred and the net fair value of the identifiable assets and liabilities acquired. Where the acquirer acquires the shares in the acquiree and where the acquirer already holds some shares in the acquiree at the acquisition date, the determination of goodwill is more involved. Understanding the nature of goodwill is essential to understanding how to account for it. With the existence of the accounting standard on impairment of assets, goodwill is not required to be amortised. Where a bargain purchase arises, the gain is recognised in current period income.

DEMONSTRATION PROBLEM 14.1 Acquisition analyses

On 1 January 2016, Trevally Ltd concluded agreements to take over the operations of Mackerel Ltd and to acquire the rest of the shares of Perch Ltd. The statements of financial position of the three companies as at that date were:

	Trevally Ltd	Mackerel Ltd	Perch Ltd
Cash	$ 20 000	$ 1 000	$ 12 500
Accounts receivable	35 000	19 000	30 000
Inventory	52 000	26 500	40 000
Property, plant and equipment (net)	280 500	149 500	107 500
Shares in Perch Ltd (15 000 shares)	19 000	—	—
Debentures in Hangi Ltd	45 000	18 000	—
	$451 500	$214 000	$190 000

	Trevally Ltd	Mackerel Ltd	Perch Ltd
Accounts payable	$ 78 000	$ 76 000	$ 27 500
Loan payable	—	40 000	
$10 debentures — nominal value	—	—	50 000
Share capital — issued at $1	300 000	80 000	70 000
Retained earnings	73 500	18 000	42 500
	$451 500	$214 000	$190 000

Mackerel Ltd included in the notes to its accounts a contingent liability relating to a guarantee for a loan. Although a present obligation existed, a liability was not recognised by Mackerel Ltd because of the difficulty of measuring the ultimate amount to be paid.

The details of the acquisition agreements are as follows.

Mackerel Ltd

Trevally Ltd is to acquire all the assets (except cash) and all the liabilities of Mackerel Ltd. In exchange for every four shares in Mackerel Ltd, shareholders are to receive three shares in Trevally Ltd and $1.00 in cash. Each share in Trevally Ltd has a fair value of $1.80. Trevally Ltd is to pay additional cash to Mackerel Ltd to cover the total liquidation expenses of Mackerel Ltd which are expected to amount to $6000. The cash already held by Mackerel Ltd is to go towards the liquidation costs. The assets of Mackerel Ltd are all recorded in Mackerel Ltd's records at cost (depreciated if applicable). The fair values of Mackerel Ltd's assets are:

Receivables	$ 17 500
Inventory	32 000
Property, plant and equipment	165 500
Debentures in Hangi Ltd	19 000

Mackerel Ltd had been undertaking research into new manufacturing machinery, and had expensed a total of $10 000 research costs. Trevally Ltd determined that the fair value of this in-process research was $2000 at acquisition date. The contingent liability relating to the guarantee was considered to have a fair value of $1500.

External accounting advice and valuers' fees amounted to $3000.

Perch Ltd

Trevally Ltd is to acquire the remaining issued capital of Perch Ltd. In exchange, the shareholders in Perch Ltd are to receive four shares in Trevally Ltd for every five shares held in Perch Ltd. The shares already held in Perch Ltd are valued at $21 600. They have been measured at fair value with movements in fair value being recognised in profit or loss.

The legal costs incurred by Trevally Ltd in issuing its shares to Mackerel Ltd and Perch Ltd amounted to $1300 and $800 respectively.

Required

Prepare the acquisition analyses and journal entries necessary to record the acquisition of both Mackerel Ltd and Perch Ltd in the records of Trevally Ltd.

Solution

Prepare acquisition analyses and journal entries

The first step is to analyse the nature of the business combination, in particular what happens to each entity involved in the transactions. In this example, Trevally Ltd is the acquirer. It acquires assets and liabilities of Mackerel Ltd, probably with the latter entity going into liquidation. With Perch Ltd, Trevally Ltd acquires only shares in that entity; hence, the transaction is between Trevally Ltd and the shareholders of Perch Ltd and not with Perch Ltd.

Considering the combination between Trevally Ltd and Mackerel Ltd, the first step is to prepare an acquisition analysis. This involves looking at the two sides of the transaction, determining the fair value of the identifiable assets acquired and liabilities assumed and calculating the consideration transferred. The difference between these two amounts will be goodwill or gain on bargain purchase.

1. Acquisition analysis — Trevally Ltd and Mackerel Ltd

Trevally Ltd acquired all the assets except cash, and assumed all the liabilities of Mackerel Ltd. These assets and liabilities are now measured at fair value.

Accounts receivable	$ 17 500
Inventory	32 000
Property, plant and equipment	165 500
Debentures in Hangi Ltd	19 000
In-process research	2 000
	236 000
Provision for guarantee	1 500
Loan payable	40 000
Accounts payable	76 000
	117 500
Net fair value	$ 118 500

Consideration transferred

The consideration transferred is the purchase consideration payable to Mackerel Ltd and is measured as the sum of the fair values of shares issued, liabilities undertaken and assets given up by the acquirer. In this example, Trevally Ltd issues shares and gives up cash. The share price is the fair value of the shares at the acquisition date.

Consideration transferred		
Shares: Share capital of Mackerel Ltd	$80 000	
Shares issued by Trevally Ltd (3/4)	60 000 × $1.80	$108 000
Cash: 80 000/4 × $1.00	20 000	
Liquidation costs	6 000	
Less: Held by Mackerel Ltd	(1 000)	25 000
Consideration transferred		$133 000

The consideration transferred is then compared with the net fair value of the identifiable assets and liabilities acquired to determine whether goodwill or a gain arises. In this case the consideration transferred is greater; hence, goodwill has been acquired.

$$\text{Goodwill} = \$133\,000 - \$118\,500 = \$14\,500$$

2. Acquisition analysis — Trevally Ltd and Perch Ltd

In this situation, Trevally Ltd acquires the shares in the acquiree rather than the actual assets and liabilities. Note that Trevally Ltd can gain control over the net assets of another entity by either buying the actual net assets or by acquiring a controlling interest in the entity that holds those net assets. The acquisition of the shares as an asset is not a business combination. However, by acquiring the shares, a business combination may have occurred, and a set of consolidated financial statements is prepared for the combined businesses using the principles of IFRS 3.

Cost of shares acquired	
Share capital of Perch Ltd	$70 000
Already held by Trevally Ltd	15 000
To acquire	$55 000
Trevally Ltd to issue 55 000 × 4/5 × $1.80 =	$79 200

The shares already held by Trevally Ltd in Perch Ltd are recorded at $19 000 at acquisition date. The fair value is $21 600. The investment is revalued at acquisition date to fair value, and the difference between these two amounts, $2600, is recorded as a gain.

The general journal entries in Trevally Ltd can then be read from the acquisition analysis. Note that when shares are issued the relevant account is 'Share Capital'.

Accounts Receivable	Dr	17 500	
Inventory	Dr	32 000	
Property, Plant and Equipment	Dr	165 500	
Debentures in Hangi Ltd	Dr	19 000	
In-process Research	Dr	2 000	
Goodwill	Dr	14 500	
Accounts Payable	Cr		76 000
Loan Payable	Cr		40 000
Provision for Guarantee	Cr		1 500
Share Capital	Cr		108 000
Payable to Mackerel Ltd	Cr		25 000
(Acquisition of net assets of Mackerel Ltd)			
Payable to Mackerel Ltd	Dr	25 000	
Cash	Cr		25 000
(Payment of consideration transferred)			
Acquisition-Related Expenses	Dr	3000	
Cash	Cr		3000
(Acquisition-related costs)			
Shares in Perch Ltd	Dr	2 600	
Gain on Revaluation of Investment	Cr		2 600
(Revaluation of investment to fair value)			
Shares in Perch Ltd	Dr	79 200	
Share Capital	Cr		79 200
(Purchase of remaining shares in Perch Ltd)			
Share Capital	Dr	2 100	
Cash	Cr		2 100
(Share issue costs incurred)			

Note that the costs of share issue reduce the Share Capital account which shows the net proceeds from share issues.

DEMONSTRATION PROBLEM 14.2 Acquisition and liquidation

On 1 July 2016, Smetana Ltd and Bay Ltd sign an agreement whereby the operations of Bay Ltd are to be taken over by Smetana Ltd. Bay Ltd will liquidate after the transfer is complete. The statements of financial position of the two companies on that day were as shown below.

	Smetana Ltd	Bay Ltd
Cash	$ 50 000	$ 20 000
Accounts receivable	75 000	56 000
Inventory	46 000	29 000
Land	65 000	—
Plant and equipment	180 000	167 000
Accumulated depreciation — plant and equipment	(60 000)	(40 000)
Patents	10 000	—
Shares in Cape Ltd	—	26 000
Debentures in Brett Ltd (nominal value)	10 000	—
	$376 000	$258 000
Accounts payable	$ 62 000	$ 31 000
Mortgage loan	75 000	21 500
10% debentures (face value)	100 000	30 000
Contributed equity:		
Ordinary shares of $1, fully paid	100 000	
A class shares of $2, fully paid	—	40 000
B class shares of $1, fully paid		60 000
Retained earnings	39 000	75 500
	$376 000	$258 000

Smetana Ltd is to acquire all the assets of Bay Ltd (except for cash). The assets of Bay Ltd are recorded at their fair values except for:

	Carrying amount	Fair value
Inventory	$ 29 000	$ 39 200
Plant and equipment	127 000	155 000
Shares in Cape Ltd	26 000	22 500

In exchange, the A class shareholders of Bay Ltd are to receive one 7% debenture in Smetana Ltd, redeemable on 1 July 2016, for every share held in Bay Ltd. The fair value of each debenture is $3.50. Smetana Ltd will also provide one of its patents to be held jointly by the A class shareholders of Bay Ltd and for which they will receive future royalties. The patent is carried at $4000 in the records of Smetana Ltd, but is considered to have a fair value of $5000.

The B class shareholders of Bay Ltd are to receive two shares in Smetana Ltd for every three shares held in Bay Ltd. The fair value of each Smetana Ltd share is $2.70. Costs to issue these shares amount to $900. Additionally, Smetana Ltd is to provide Bay Ltd with sufficient cash, additional to that already held, to enable Bay Ltd to pay its liabilities. The outstanding debentures are to be redeemed at a 10% premium. Annual leave entitlements of $16 200 outstanding at 1 July 2016 and expected liquidation costs of $5000 have not been recognised by Bay Ltd. Costs incurred in arranging the business combination amounted to $1600.

Required

(a) Prepare the journal entries in the records of Smetana Ltd to record the acquisition of Bay Ltd.
(b) Prepare the Liquidation, Liquidator's Cash and Shareholders' Distribution ledger accounts in the records of Bay Ltd.

Solution

1. *Prepare the journal entries of Smetana Ltd*

The nature of the transaction in this question is that the acquirer, Smetana Ltd, is acquiring the operations (assets and liabilities) of Bay Ltd with the acquiree going into liquidation.

The first step is to prepare the acquisition analysis, which is a comparison of the fair value of the identifiable assets acquired and liabilities assumed with the consideration transferred.

Acquisition analysis — Smetana Ltd and Bay Ltd

Note that all the assets acquired and the liabilities assumed by the acquirer are measured at fair value.

Accounts receivable	$ 56 000
Inventory	39 200
Plant and equipment	155 000
Shares in Cape Ltd	22 500
	$272 700

Consideration transferred

The consideration transferred is measured by calculating the fair value of the assets given up, liabilities undertaken and shares issued by the acquirer. In this example, the acquirer issues shares and debentures in itself, gives up a patent and provides cash.

Purchase consideration			
Shareholders			
Debentures:	A shares of Bay Ltd	20 000	
	Debentures in Smetana (1/1)	20 000 × $3.50	$ 70 000
Shares:	B shares of Bay Ltd	60 000	
	Shares in Smetana (2/3)	40 000 × $2.70	108 000
Patent			5 000
Creditors		30 000	
Cash:	Debentures issued	3 000	
	Plus premium (10%)	33 000	
	Accounts payable	31 000	

Mortgage loan	21 500	
Liquidation costs	5 000	
Annual leave	16 200	
Total cash required	106 700	
Less: Already held	(20 000)	$ 86 700
Total consideration transferred		269 700

Because the total consideration transferred is less than the net fair value of the identifiable assets and liabilities acquired, the acquirer has to assess the measurements undertaken in the acquisition analysis. Having been assured that all relevant assets and liabilities have been included and that the fair values are reliable, the difference is then accounted for as a bargain purchase, and is included in current period income.

Gain on bargain purchase [$272 700 − $269 700]	$3 000

The general journal entries can then be read from the acquisition analysis. Note that when shares are issued the relevant account is 'Share Capital'.

In relation to the patent, prior to accounting for the business combination, the acquirer remeasures the asset to fair value.

Patent	Dr	1000	
Gain	Cr		1000
(Remeasurement to fair value as part of consideration transferred on business combination)			
Accounts Receivable	Dr	56 000	
Inventory	Dr	39 200	
Property, Plant and Equipment	Dr	155 000	
Shares in Cape Ltd	Dr	22 500	
Payable to Bay Ltd	Cr		156 700
Share Capital	Cr		108 000
Patent	Cr		5 000
Gain on Bargain Purchase	Cr		3 000
(Acquisition of Bay Ltd)			
Payable to Bay Ltd	Dr	156 700	
7% Debentures	Cr		70 000
Cash	Cr		86 700
(Payment of consideration)			
Acquisition-Related Expenses	Dr	1 600	
Cash	Cr		1600
(Acquisition-related costs)			
Share Capital	Dr	900	
Cash	Cr		900
(Payment of share issue costs)			

Note that the costs of share issue reduce the share capital issued with the Share Capital account then showing the net proceeds from share issues.

2. *Prepare the ledger accounts of Bay Ltd*

The Liquidation account effectively records the sale of the assets and the receipt of the purchase consideration.

- All items being sold by the acquiree — whether assets or a package of assets and liabilities — are taken at their carrying amount to the Liquidation account.
- Any amounts arising during the liquidation process and not previously recorded by the acquiree are also taken to the Liquidation account. In this example, there are three such items: premium on debentures, annual leave payable and liquidation costs. The relevant amounts are debited to the Liquidation account and liabilities are raised in relation to these items.
- Any reserves recognised by the acquiree — in this example it is retained earnings — are taken to the Liquidation account.
- The consideration transferred is credited to the Liquidation account, with the recognition of assets received, namely cash, patent, shares in Smetana Ltd and debentures in Smetana Ltd.

The balance of the Liquidation account is transferred to the Shareholders' Distribution account.

Liquidation

Receivables	56 000	Retained Earnings	75 500
Inventory	29 000	Accumulated Depreciation	40 000
Plant and Equipment	167 000	Receivable from Smetana Ltd	269 700
Shares in Cape Ltd	26 000		
Debentures – Premium	3 000		
Annual Leave Payable	16 200		
Liquidation Costs Payable	5 000		
Shareholders' Distribution	83 000		
	385 200		385 200

The cash received via the consideration transferred and the balance originally held by the acquiree is used to pay the liabilities of the acquiree, including liabilities such as liquidation costs payable raised during the liquidation process.

Liquidator's Cash

Opening balance	20 000	Accounts Payable	31 000
Receivable from Smetana Ltd	86 700	Debentures	33 000
		Mortgage Loan	21 500
		Liquidation Costs Payable	5 000
		Annual Leave Payable	16 200
	106 700		106 700

The capital balances of the acquiree, in this example the capital relating to both A and B shares issued by the acquiree, are taken to the credit side of the Shareholders' Distribution account. The assets to be distributed to the former shareholders of the acquiree are transferred to the debit side of the account. In this case they consist of the debentures and shares in Smetana Ltd and the patent, all these having been received as part of the consideration transferred from the acquirer. The account balances when the balance transferred from the Liquidation account is included. At this stage, all accounts of the acquiree are closed.

Shareholders' Distribution

Debentures in Smetana Ltd	70 000	Share Capital – A Shares	40 000
Shares in Smetana Ltd	108 000	Share Capital – B Shares	60 000
Patent	5 000	Liquidation	83 000
	183 000		183 000

Discussion questions

1. What is meant by a 'business combination'?
2. Discuss the importance of identifying the acquisition date.
3. What is meant by 'contingent consideration' and how is it accounted for?
4. Explain the key components of 'core' goodwill.
5. What recognition criteria are applied to assets acquired and liabilities assumed in a business combination?
6. How is an acquirer identified?
7. Explain the key steps in the acquisition method.
8. How is the consideration transferred calculated?
9. If an acquiree liquidates, what are the key accounts raised by the acquiree and which accounts are transferred to these accounts?
10. How is a gain on bargain purchase accounted for?
11. Why is it important to identify an acquirer in a business combination?

References

Johnson, L. T., & Petrone, K. R. 1998, 'Is goodwill an asset?', *Accounting Horizons*, vol. 12, no. 3, pp. 293–303.
Leo, K. J., Hoggett, J. R., and Radford, J. 1995, *Accounting for identifiable intangibles and goodwill*, Australian Society of Certified Practising Accountants, Melbourne.

Exercises

STAR RATING ★ BASIC ★★ MODERATE ★★★ DIFFICULT

Exercise 14.1 ACCOUNTING BY THE ACQUIRER

★ On 1 July 2016, New Ltd acquired the following assets and liabilities from Day Ltd:

	Carrying amount	Fair value
Land	$300 000	$350 000
Plant (cost $400 000)	280 000	290 000
Inventory	80 000	85 000
Cash	15 000	15 000
Accounts payable	(20 000)	(20 000)
Loans	(80 000)	(80 000)

In exchange for these assets and liabilities, New Ltd issued 100 000 shares that had been issued for $1.20 per share but at 1 July 2016 had a fair value of $6.50 per share.

Required

1. Prepare the journal entries in the records of New Ltd to account for the acquisition of the assets and liabilities of Day Ltd.
2. Prepare the journal entries assuming that the fair value of New Ltd shares was $6 per share.

Exercise 14.2 ACQUISITION OF SHARES IN ACQUIREE

★ On 1 January 2016, Desert Ltd acquired all the issued shares of Island Ltd. At this date the equity of Island Ltd consisted of:

Share capital — 100 000 shares issued at $5 per share	$500 000
General reserve	200 000
Asset revaluation surplus	100 000
Retained earnings	50 000

In exchange for these shares, Desert Ltd agreed to pay the former shareholders of Island Ltd two shares in Desert Ltd, these having a fair value of $4 per share, plus $1.50 cash for each share held in Island Ltd. The costs of issuing the shares were $800.

Required

Prepare the journal entries in the records of Desert Ltd to record these events.

Exercise 14.3 DETERMINING THE FAIR VALUE OF EQUITY ISSUED BY THE ACQUIRER

★ On 1 December 2016, Trout Ltd acquired all the assets and liabilities of Dory Ltd, with Trout Ltd issuing 100 000 shares to acquire them. The fair values of Dory Ltd's assets and liabilities at this date were:

Cash	$ 50 000
Furniture and fittings	20 000
Accounts receivable	5 000
Plant	125 000
Accounts payable	15 000
Current tax liability	8 000
Annual leave payable	2 000

The financial year for Trout Ltd is January to December.

Required

1. Prepare the journal entries for Trout Ltd to record the business combination at 1 December 2016, assuming the fair value of each Trout Ltd share at acquisition date is $1.90. Prepare any note disclosures for Trout Ltd at 31 December 2016 in relation to the business combination.
2. Assume the fair value of each Trout Ltd share at acquisition date is $1.90. At acquisition date, the acquirer could only determine a provisional fair value for the plant. On 1 March 2017, Trout Ltd received the final value from the independent appraisal, the fair value at acquisition date being $131 000. Assuming the plant had a further 5-year life from the acquisition date, explain how Trout Ltd will account for the business combination both at acquisition date and in the financial statements for 2017.
3. Prepare the journal entries for Trout Ltd to record the business combination at 1 December 2016, assuming the fair value of each Trout Ltd share at acquisition date is $1.70.

CHAPTER 14 Business combinations   **407**

IDENTIFYING THE ACQUIRER

★★ White Ltd has been negotiating with Cloud Ltd for several months, and agreements have finally been reached for the two companies to combine. In considering the accounting for the combined entities, management realises that, in applying IFRS 3, an acquirer must be identified. However, there is debate among the accounting staff as to which entity is the acquirer.

Required

1. What factors/indicators should management consider in determining which entity is the acquirer?
2. Why is it necessary to identify an acquirer? In particular, what differences in accounting would arise if White Ltd or Cloud Ltd were identified as the acquirer?

CONSIDERATION TRANSFERRED

★★ On 1 September 2016, the directors of Monkfish Ltd approached the directors of Cod Ltd with the following proposal for the acquisition of the issued shares of Cod Ltd, conditional on acceptance by 90% of the shareholders of Cod Ltd by 30 November 2016:

- Two fully paid ordinary shares in Monkfish Ltd plus $3.10 cash for every preference share in Cod Ltd, payable at acquisition date.
- Three fully paid ordinary shares in Monkfish Ltd plus $1.20 cash for every ordinary share in Cod Ltd. Half the cash is payable at acquisition, and the other half in 1 year's time.

By 30 November, 90% of the ordinary shareholders and all of the preference shareholders of Cod Ltd had accepted the offer. The directors of Monkfish Ltd decided *not* to acquire the remaining ordinary shares. Share transfer forms covering the transfer were dated 30 November 2016, and showed a price per Monkfish Ltd ordinary share of $4.20. Monkfish Ltd's incremental borrowing rate is 8% p.a.

The statement of financial position of Cod Ltd at 30 November 2016 was as follows:

COD LTD Statement of Financial Position as at 30 November 2016		
Current assets		$120 000
Non-current assets		
Land and buildings	$203 000	
Plant and equipment	168 000	
Less: Accumulated depreciation	(45 000)	
Shares in other companies listed on stock exchange at cost (market $190 000)	30 000	
Government bonds, at cost	50 000	
Total non-current assets		406 000
Total assets		526 000
Current liabilities		30 000
Net assets		$496 000
Equity		
Share capital		
80 000 ordinary shares fully paid	$160 000	
50 000 6% preference shares fully paid	100 000	$260 000
Retained earnings		236 000
Total equity		$496 000

Monkfish Ltd then appointed a new board of directors of Cod Ltd. This board took office on 1 December 2016 and immediately:

- revalued the asset Shares in Other Companies to its market value (assume no tax effect)
- used the surplus so created to make a bonus issue of $32 000 to ordinary shareholders, each shareholder being allocated two ordinary shares for every ten ordinary shares held.

Required

Prepare all journal entries (in general form) to record the transactions in the records of (a) Monkfish Ltd and (b) Cod Ltd.

ACCOUNTING FOR BUSINESS COMBINATION BY ACQUIRER, LIQUIDATION ACCOUNTS OF ACQUIREE

On 1 July 2016, two companies — New Starfish Ltd and Tuna Ltd — sign an agreement whereby the operations of Tuna Ltd are to be taken over by New Starfish Ltd. Tuna Ltd is to liquidate after the transfer is complete. The statements of financial position of the two companies on that day were as follows:

	New Starfish Ltd	Tuna Ltd
Cash	$ 50 000	$ 20 000
Accounts receivable	75 000	56 000
Inventory	56 000	29 000
Land	65 000	—
Plant and equipment	180 000	167 000
Accumulated depreciation — plant and equipment	(60 000)	(40 000)
Shares in Sefton Ltd	—	26 000
Debentures in Akaroa Ltd (face value)	10 000	—
	$376 000	$258 000
Accounts payable	$ 62 000	$ 31 000
Mortgage loan	75 000	21 500
10% debentures (face value)	100 000	30 000
Share capital:		
Ordinary shares of $1, fully paid	100 000	—
A class shares of $2, fully paid	—	40 000
B class shares of $1, fully paid		60 000
Retained earnings	39 000	75 500
	$376 000	$258 000

Acquisition of Tuna Ltd

New Starfish Ltd is to acquire all of the assets of Tuna Ltd (except for cash). The assets of Tuna Ltd are recorded at their fair values except for the following:

	Carrying amount	Fair value
Inventory	$ 29 000	$ 39 200
Plant and equipment	127 000	140 000
Shares in Sefton Ltd	26 000	22 500

In exchange, the A class shareholders of Tuna Ltd are to receive one 7% debenture in New Starfish Ltd, redeemable on 1 July 2018, for every share held in Tuna Ltd. The fair value of each debenture is $3.50. The B class shareholders of Tuna Ltd are to receive two shares in New Starfish Ltd for every three shares held in Tuna Ltd. The fair value of each New Starfish Ltd share is $2.70. Costs to issue these shares will amount to $900.

Additionally, New Starfish Ltd is to provide Tuna Ltd with sufficient cash, additional to that already held, to enable Tuna Ltd to pay its liabilities. The outstanding debentures are to be redeemed at a 10% premium. Annual leave entitlements of $16 200 outstanding at 1 July 2016 and expected liquidation costs of $5000 have not been recognised by Tuna Ltd. Costs associated with undertaking the acquisition amounted to $1600.

Required

1. Prepare the acquisition analysis and journal entries in the books of New Starfish Ltd to record the acquisition of Tuna Ltd.
2. Prepare the Liquidation, Liquidator's Cash, and Shareholders' Distribution ledger accounts in the records of Tuna Ltd.

ACCOUNTING FOR BUSINESS COMBINATION BY ACQUIRER, JOURNAL ENTRIES FOR LIQUIDATION OF ACQUIREE

Ling Ltd and Steenbras Ltd are small family-owned companies engaged in vegetable growing and distribution. The Spencer family owns the shares in Steenbras Ltd and the Rokocoko family owns the shares in Ling Ltd. The head of the Spencer family wishes to retire but his two sons are not interested in carrying on the family business. Accordingly, on 1 July 2016, Ling Ltd is to take over the operations of Steenbras Ltd, which will then liquidate. Ling Ltd is asset-rich but has limited overdraft facilities so the following arrangement has been made.

Ling Ltd is to acquire all of the assets, except cash, delivery trucks and motor vehicles, of Steenbras Ltd and will assume all of the liabilities except accounts payable. In return, Ling Ltd is to give the shareholders of Steenbras Ltd a block of vacant land, two delivery vehicles and sufficient additional cash to enable the company to pay off the accounts payable and the liquidation costs of $1500. The land and vehicles had the following values at 30 June 2016:

	Carrying amount	Fair value
Freehold land	$50 000	$120 000
Delivery trucks	30 000	28 000

On the liquidation of Steenbras Ltd, Mr Spencer is to receive the land and the motor vehicles and his two sons are to receive the delivery trucks.

The statements of financial position of the two companies as at 30 June 2016 were as follows:

	Ling Ltd	Steenbras Ltd
Cash	$ 3 500	$ 2 000
Accounts receivable	25 000	15 000
Freehold land	250 000	100 000
Buildings (net)	25 000	30 000
Cultivation equipment (net)	65 000	46 000
Irrigation equipment	16 000	22 000
Delivery trucks	45 000	36 000
Motor vehicles	25 000	32 000
	$454 500	$283 000
Accounts payable	$ 26 000	$ 23 500
Loan — Bank of NZ	150 000	80 000
Loan — Trevally Bros	35 000	35 000
Loan — Long Cloud	70 000	52 500
Share capital — 100 000 shares	100 000	—
— 60 000 shares	—	60 000
Reserves	28 500	—
Retained earnings	45 000	32 000
	$454 500	$283 000

All the assets of Steenbras Ltd are recorded at fair value, with the exception of:

	Fair value
Freehold land	$120 000
Buildings	40 000
Cultivation equipment	40 000
Motor vehicle	34 000

Required

1. Prepare the acquisition analysis and the journal entries to record the acquisition of Steenbras Ltd's operations in the records of Ling Ltd.
2. Prepare the journal entries to record the liquidation of Steenbras Ltd.
3. Prepare the statement of financial position of Ling Ltd after the business combination, including any notes relating to the business combination.

Exercise 14.8 **ACCOUNTING FOR BUSINESS COMBINATION BY ACQUIRER**

★★   Sweetlip Ltd and Warehou Ltd are two family-owned flax-producing companies in New Zealand. Sweetlip Ltd is owned by the Wood family and the Bradbury family owns Warehou Ltd. The Wood family has only one son and he is engaged to be married to the daughter of the Bradbury family. Because the son is currently managing Warehou Ltd, it is proposed that, after the wedding, he should manage both companies. As a result, it is agreed by the two families that Sweetlip Ltd should take over the net assets of Warehou Ltd.

The statement of financial position of Warehou Ltd immediately before the takeover is as follows:

	Carrying amount	Fair value
Cash	$ 20 000	$ 20 000
Accounts receivable	140 000	125 000
Land	620 000	840 000
Buildings (net)	530 000	550 000
Farm equipment (net)	$ 360 000	$ 364 000
Irrigation equipment (net)	220 000	225 000
Vehicles (net)	160 000	172 000
	$2 050 000	
Accounts payable	$ 80 000	80 000
Loan — Trevally Bank	480 000	480 000
Share capital	670 000	
Retained earnings	820 000	
	$2 050 000	

The takeover agreement specified the following details:
- Sweetlip Ltd is to acquire all the assets of Warehou Ltd except for cash, and one of the vehicles (having a carrying amount of $45 000 and a fair value of $48 000), and assume all the liabilities except for the loan from the Trevally Bank. Warehou Ltd is then to go into liquidation. The vehicle is to be transferred to Mr and Mrs Bradbury.
- Sweetlip Ltd is to supply sufficient cash to enable the debt to the Trevally Bank to be paid off and to cover the liquidation costs of $5500. It will also give $150 000 to be distributed to Mr and Mrs Bradbury to help pay the costs of the wedding.
- Sweetlip Ltd is also to give a piece of its own prime land to Warehou Ltd to be distributed to Mr and Mrs Bradbury, this eventually being available to be given to any offspring of the forthcoming marriage. The piece of land in question has a carrying amount of $80 000 and a fair value of $220 000.
- Sweetlip Ltd is to issue 100 000 shares, these having a fair value of $14 per share, to be distributed via Warehou Ltd to the soon-to-be-married-daughter of Mr and Mrs Bradbury, who is currently a shareholder in Warehou Ltd.

The takeover proceeded as per the agreement, with Sweetlip Ltd incurring incidental acquisition costs of $25 000 and $18 000 share issue costs.

Required

Prepare the acquisition analysis and the journal entries to record the acquisition of Warehou Ltd in the records of Sweetlip Ltd.

Exercise 14.9	ACCOUNTING FOR ACQUISITIONS OF A BUSINESS AND SHARES IN ANOTHER ENTITY

★★★ Tailor Ltd is seeking to expand its share of the pet care market and has negotiated to acquire the operations of Flathead Ltd and the shares of Octopus Ltd.

At 1 July 2016, the trial balances of the three companies were:

	Tailor Ltd	Flathead Ltd	Octopus Ltd
Cash	$ 145 000	$ 5 200	$ 84 000
Accounts receivable	34 000	21 300	12 000
Inventory	56 000	30 000	25 400
Shares in listed companies	16 000	22 000	7 000
Land and buildings (net)	70 000	40 000	36 000
Plant and equipment (net)	130 000	105 000	25 000
Goodwill (net)	6 000	5 000	5 600
	$ 457 000	$ 228 500	$ 195 000

	Tailor Ltd	Flathead Ltd	Octopus Ltd
Accounts payable	$ 65 000	$ 40 000	$ 29 000
Bank overdraft	0	0	1 500
Debentures	50 000	0	100 000
Mortgage loan	100 000	30 000	0
Contributed equity:			
Ordinary shares of $1, fully paid	200 000	150 000	60 000
Other reserves	15 000	6 500	2 500
Retained earnings (30/6/16)	27 000	2 000	2 000
	$ 457 000	$ 228 500	$ 195 000

Flathead Ltd

Tailor Ltd is to acquire all assets (except cash and shares in listed companies) of Flathead Ltd. Acquisition-related costs are expected to be $7600. The net assets of Flathead Ltd are recorded at fair value except for the following:

	Carrying amount	Fair value
Inventory	$ 30 000	$ 26 000
Land and buildings	40 000	80 000
Shares in listed companies	22 000	18 000
Accounts payable	(40 000)	(49 100)
Accrued leave	0	(29 700)

In exchange, the shareholders of Flathead Ltd are to receive, for every three Flathead Ltd shares held, one Tailor Ltd share worth $2.50 each. Costs to issue these shares are $950. Additionally, Tailor Ltd will transfer to Flathead Ltd its 'Shares in listed companies' asset, which has a fair value of $15 000. These shares, together with those already owned by Flathead Ltd, will be sold and the proceeds distributed to the Flathead Ltd shareholders. Assume that the shares were sold for their fair values.

Tailor Ltd will also give Flathead Ltd sufficient additional cash to enable Flathead Ltd to pay all its creditors. Flathead Ltd will then liquidate. Liquidation costs are estimated to be $8700.

Octopus Ltd

Tailor Ltd is to acquire all the issued shares of Octopus Ltd. In exchange, the shareholders of Octopus Ltd are to receive one Tailor Ltd share, worth $2.50, and $1.50 cash for every two Octopus Ltd shares held.

Required

1. Prepare the acquisition analysis and journal entries to record the acquisitions in the records of Tailor Ltd.
2. Prepare the Liquidation account and Shareholders' Distribution account for Flathead Ltd.
3. Explain in detail why, if Flathead Ltd has recorded a goodwill asset of $5000, Tailor Ltd calculates the goodwill acquired via an acquisition analysis. Why does Tailor Ltd not determine a fair value for the goodwill asset and record that figure as it has done for other assets acquired from Flathead Ltd?
4. If Tailor Ltd subsequently receives a dividend cheque for $1500 from Octopus Ltd, paid from retained earnings earned before its acquisition of the shares in Octopus Ltd, how should Tailor Ltd account for that cheque? Why?
5. Shortly after the business combination, the liquidator of Flathead Ltd receives a valid claim of $25 000 from a creditor. As Tailor Ltd has agreed to provide sufficient cash to pay all the liabilities of Flathead Ltd at acquisition date, the liquidator requests and receives a cheque for $25 000 from Tailor Ltd. How should Tailor Ltd record this payment? Why?

Exercise 14.10 **ACQUISITION OF TWO BUSINESSES**

★★★ Queenfish Ltd is a manufacturer of specialised industrial machinery seeking to diversify its operations. After protracted negotiations, the directors decided to purchase the assets and liabilities of Blackfish Ltd and the spare parts retail division of Hoklo Ltd.

At 30 June 2016 the statements of financial position of the three entities were as follows:

	Queenfish Ltd	Blackfish Ltd	Hoklo Ltd
Land and buildings (net)	$ 60 000	$ 25 000	$ 40 000
Plant and machinery (net)	100 000	36 000	76 000
Office equipment (net)	16 000	4 000	6 000
Shares in listed companies	24 000	15 000	20 800
Debentures in listed companies	20 000	—	—
Accounts receivable	35 000	26 000	42 000
Inventory	150 000	54 000	30 200

	Queenfish Ltd	Blackfish Ltd	Hoklo Ltd
Cash	$ 59 000	$ 11 000	$ 9 000
Goodwill	—	7 000	—
	$ 464 000	$ 178 000	$ 224 000
Accounts payable	26 000	14 000	27 000
Current tax liability	21 000	6 000	7 000
Provision for leave	36 000	10 000	17 500
Bank loan	83 000	16 000	43 500
Debentures	60 000	50 000	—
Share capital (issued at $1, fully paid)	200 000	60 000	90 000
Retained earnings	38 000	22 000	39 000
	$ 464 000	$ 178 000	$ 224 000

The acquisition agreement details are as follows:

Blackfish Ltd

Queenfish Ltd is to acquire all the assets (other than cash) and liabilities (other than debentures, provisions and tax liabilities) of Blackfish Ltd for the following purchase consideration:

- Shareholders in Blackfish Ltd are to receive three shares in Queenfish Ltd, credited as fully paid, in exchange for every four shares held. The shares in Queenfish Ltd are to be issued at their fair value of $3 per share. Costs of share issue amounted to $2000.
- Queenfish Ltd is to provide sufficient cash which, when added to the cash already held, will enable Blackfish Ltd to pay out the current tax liability and provision for leave, to redeem the debentures at a premium of 5%, and to pay its liquidation expenses of $2500.

The fair values of the assets and liabilities of Blackfish Ltd are equal to their carrying amounts with the exception of the following:

	Fair value
Land and buildings	$60 000
Plant and machinery	50 000

Incidental costs associated with the acquisition amount to $2500.

Hoklo Ltd

Queenfish Ltd is to acquire the spare parts retail business of Hoklo Ltd. The following information is available concerning that business, relative to the whole of Hoklo Ltd:

	Total amount	Spare parts division	
	Carrying amount	Carrying amount	Fair value
Land and buildings (net)	$40 000	$20 000	$30 000
Plant and machinery (net)	76 000	32 000	34 500
Office equipment (net)	6 000	2 000	2 500
Accounts receivable	42 000	21 000	20 000
Inventory	30 200	12 000	12 000
Accounts payable	27 000	14 000	14 000
Provision for leave	17 500	7 000	7 000

The divisional net assets are to be acquired for $10 000 cash, plus 11 000 ordinary shares in Queenfish Ltd issued at their fair value of $3, plus the land and buildings that have been purchased from Blackfish Ltd.

Incidental costs associated with the acquisition are $1000.

Required

1. Prepare the acquisition analysis for the acquisition transactions of Queenfish Ltd.
2. Prepare the liquidation account for Blackfish Ltd.
3. Prepare the journal entries for the acquisition transactions in the records of Queenfish Ltd and Hoklo Ltd.

One of the interesting questions about business combinations is whether earnings management plays a role in the acquisition price. One context where earnings may play a role is when the acquisition is funded by stock-for-stock swap. Here managers of the acquiring firm may attempt to inflate earnings to increase the price of their stock. This, in turn, can produce a more favourable exchange ratio for the acquiring firm's shareholders. Erickson and Wang (1999) examine this question for 55 stock-for-stock mergers that took place between 1985 and 1990. Earnings management is captured by abnormal accruals and is shown to increase in the quarters preceding the merger announcement, but decrease following the announcement. To enhance the strength of the conclusion that earnings management is present mostly in stock-for stock acquisitions, the authors also analyse 64 cash deals, but do not find similar results. Louis (2004) extends this line of inquiry to mergers between 1992 and 2000 comprising 236 stock swaps and 137 cash deals. He finds that stock-swap acquirers experienced negative abnormal returns in the 2 years prior to the merger announcement. This poor performance may have exerted pressure on managers to manipulate earnings. Consistent with this, Louis (2004) finds strong evidence of greater earnings management in the quarter preceding the merger announcement in stock acquirers than cash acquirers. Additionally, he finds that abnormal stock returns in the 3 years following the merger are negatively related to the measure of abnormal accruals in the quarter preceding the announcement. This is consistent with successful earnings management by managers of stock swap-acquirers. Moreover, the evidence suggests that market participants do not fully understand the effect of pre-merger announcement earnings management.

As business combinations represent a major corporate event, investors would benefit from additional disclosures that could help them form expectations about future performance. Shalev (2009) assembles a sample of 297 acquiring firms involved in 1019 acquisitions between 1 July 2001 to 31 December 2004 to examine what determines the level of disclosure. He posits that acquirers that are more confident about the acquisition outcome would tend to be more forthcoming in their disclosures. He finds that disclosure levels are negatively related to the amount of goodwill recognised. This is consistent with goodwill capturing overpayment and hence bad news that acquirers would like to withhold. Acquirers that provide more disclosure also tend to report higher ROA in the year of acquisition and the following year. Consistent with Shalev's (2009) hypothesis, these acquirers also experience positive abnormal stock returns in the year following the filing of the annual report for the acquisition year.

Another question is whether earnings management plays a role in the allocation of the purchase consideration to net assets and goodwill. Under IFRS® Standards, the purchase consideration is allocated to goodwill after the fair value of net assets acquired is determined. This implies a one-to-one substitution effect between fair value adjustments and goodwill. For example, allocating purchase consideration to higher fair value of depreciable assets would reduce goodwill as well

as future profits owing to higher depreciation. The opposite is also true since goodwill is not amortised. Shalev et al. (2013) explore how managerial compensation affects this price allocation. They examine 320 acquisitions between 2001 and 2008 and test for the association between a CEO's cash bonus (which is typically based on accounting numbers) and the percentage of the purchase price that is allocated to goodwill and intangibles with indefinite life. Shalev et al. (2013) provide evidence that suggests that greater bonus intensity is positively associated with the percentage of purchase price that is allocated to goodwill and intangibles with indefinite life. This is consistent with managers of acquiring firms using discretion to allocate a greater fraction of the purchase price to assets that are not subject to depreciation and amortisation which, in turn, boosts future profits.

Since goodwill is the difference between price paid and fair value of net assets acquired it is not clear what its economic meaning is. Furthermore, insofar as goodwill is manipulated, it is interesting to see if it has any predictive value and whether its power to predict future performance is moderated by managerial discretion. These questions are addressed by Lee (2011). Lee (2011) first establishes that goodwill is positively related to 1 year ahead operating cash flows. This provides support to the view that goodwill is an asset. Importantly, this relation is not found to be sensitive to the degree of managerial discretion.

The above-mentioned studies are based on US samples; not much academic research has been conducted into IFRS 3. One of the few studies to do so is Glaum et al. (2013) who examine the degree of compliance with the disclosure requirements of IFRS 3 and IAS 36, the latter governing goodwill impairment rules. They examine compliance in a sample of 357 European firms involved in acquisitions in 2005 — the year when IFRS became mandatory in the EU. Glaum et al. (2013) develop a 100-item disclosure checklist that is based on the requirements of the two standards. Compliance is found to vary across countries, industries and auditor type. For example, Switzerland shows the highest level of compliance and Austria the lowest. Companies audited by big audit firms tend to comply more than companies audited by smaller auditors. Glaum et al. (2013) further find from a multivariate analysis that compliance increases with the size of recorded goodwill. A second study of IFRS 3 is Hamberg et al. (2011) who examine IFRS 3 adoption in a sample of Swedish firms. They find that goodwill-intensive firms experience higher stock returns than no-goodwill firms upon adoption of IFRS 3. It is not clear, however, if investors correctly interpret goodwill as a signal of better performance.

References

Erickson, M., and Wang, S. W. 1999. Earnings management by acquiring firms in stock for stock mergers. *Journal of Accounting and Economics*, 27(2), 149–176.

Glaum, M., Schmidt, P., Street, D. L., and Vogel, S. 2013. Compliance with IFRS 3- and IAS 36-required disclosures across 17 European countries: Company- and country-level determinants. *Accounting and Business Research*, 43(3), 163–204.

Hamberg, M., Paananen, M., and Novak, J. 2011. The adoption of IFRS 3: The effects of managerial discretion and stock market reactions. *European Accounting Review*, 20(2), 263–288.

Lee, C. 2011. The effect of SFAS 142 on the ability of goodwill to predict future cash flows. *Journal of Accounting and Public Policy*, 30(3), 236–255.

Louis, H. 2004. Earnings management and the market performance of acquiring firms. *Journal of Financial Economics*, 74(1), 121–148.

Shalev, R. 2009. The information content of business combination disclosure level. *The Accounting Review*, 84(1), 239–270.

Shalev, R., Zhang, I. X., and Zhang, Y. 2013. CEO compensation and fair value accounting: Evidence from purchase price allocation. *Journal of Accounting Research*, 51(4), 819–854.

15

Impairment of assets

ACCOUNTING STANDARDS IN FOCUS	IAS 36 *Impairment of Assets*

LEARNING OBJECTIVES	*After studying this chapter, you should be able to:*

 understand the purpose of the impairment test for assets

 understand when to undertake an impairment test

 explain how to undertake an impairment test for an individual asset

 identify a cash-generating unit, and account for an impairment loss for a cash-generating unit — not including goodwill

 account for the impairment of goodwill

 account for reversals of impairment losses

apply the disclosure requirements of IAS 36.

15.1 INTRODUCTION TO IAS 36

Chapters 11 and 13 discuss the measurement and recognition criteria for property, plant and equipment, and intangibles. These assets are measured at cost or revalued amount and, for each asset, the cost or revalued amount is allocated over its useful life. The exception is where intangible assets have indefinite useful lives, in which case no amortisation is charged. In the statement of financial position at the end of a reporting period, the assets are reported at cost or revalued amount less the accumulated depreciation/ amortisation. Because there are many judgements in the depreciation/amortisation process — estimates of useful life, residual values and the pattern of benefits — the question to be asked at the end of the reporting period is whether the carrying amounts of the assets in the statement of financial position over-state the worth of the assets. In other words, can an entity expect to recover in future periods the carrying amounts of an entity's assets? Recovery can be from future use of the asset and/or from the eventual disposal of the asset. The entity has an impairment loss in relation to an asset if the expected recovery is less than the carrying amount of that asset. Paragraph 6 of IAS 36 *Impairment of Assets* defines an impairment loss as follows:

> An impairment loss is the amount by which the carrying amount of an asset or a cash-generating unit exceeds its recoverable amount.

This chapter examines the impairment test for assets. The accounting standard covering impairment is IAS 36 *Impairment of Assets*. The standard was issued initially by the International Accounting Standards Board (IASB®) in July 1998 and amended on numerous occasions, including an amendment in 2013.

Under IAS 36, an entity is required to conduct impairment tests for its assets to see whether it has incurred any impairment losses. The purpose of the impairment test is to ensure that assets are not carried at amounts that exceed their recoverable amounts or, more simply, that assets are not overstated.

Key questions in relation to the impairment test are:
- How does the test work?
- Is the test the same for all assets?
- Should the test apply to individual assets or to groups of assets? If to groups, which groups?
- Is the accounting treatment the same for assets measured at cost and for those measured at revalued amount?
- When should the test be carried out? Should it be done annually, every 3 years or some other time?
- Can the results of the impairment test be reversed; that is, if an asset is written down because it is impaired, can later events lead to the reversal of that write-down?

15.1.1 Scope of IAS 36

Paragraph 2 of IAS 36 notes that the standard does not apply to all assets; that is, not all assets are subject to impairment testing. Assets to which IAS 36 does not apply are:
- inventories — IAS 2 *Inventories*
- assets arising from construction contracts — IAS 11 *Construction Contracts*
- deferred tax assets — IAS 12 *Income Taxes*
- assets arising from employee benefits — IAS 19 *Employee Benefits*
- financial assets — IAS 39 *Financial Instruments: Recognition and Measurement*
- investment properties measured at fair value — IAS 40 *Investment Property*
- biological assets measured at fair value less costs to sell — IAS 41 *Agriculture*
- deferred acquisition costs and intangible assets relating to insurance contracts — IFRS 4 *Insurance Contracts*
- non-current assets or disposal groups classified as held for sale — IFRS 5 *Non-current Assets Held for Sale and Discontinued Operations*.

The accounting standards listed contain the principles for recognition and measurement of the particular assets covered by those standards. Note that in some of these standards the assets are required to be recorded at fair value, or fair value less costs of disposal. *Fair value is discussed in detail in chapter 3.* Where assets are recorded at fair value, there is no need to test for recoverability of the carrying amount of the asset. Under IAS 2, inventory is recorded at the lower of cost and net realisable value. As net realisable value is defined in terms of estimated selling price, IAS 2 has an inbuilt impairment test requiring inventory to be written down when the cost is effectively greater than the recoverable amount.

15.2 WHEN TO UNDERTAKE AN IMPAIRMENT TEST

As noted earlier, the purpose of the impairment test is to ensure that disclosed assets do not have carrying amounts in excess of their recoverable amounts. However, under IAS 36 it is not necessary at the end of each reporting period to test each asset in order to determine whether it is impaired. The only assets that need to be tested at the end of the reporting period are those where there is any *indication* that an asset may be impaired (see paragraph 9 of IAS 36). An entity therefore must determine by looking at various sources of information whether there is sufficient evidence to suspect that an asset may be impaired. If there is no such evidence, then an entity can assume that impairment has not occurred.

For most assets, the need for an impairment test can be assessed by analysing sources of evidence. However, there are some assets for which an impairment test *must* be undertaken every year. Paragraph 10 identifies these assets:
- intangible assets with indefinite useful lives
- intangible assets not yet available for use
- goodwill acquired in a business combination.

The reason for singling out these assets for automatic impairment testing is that the carrying amounts of these assets are considered to be more uncertain than those of other assets. None of these assets are subject to an annual amortisation charge, and so there is no ongoing reduction in the carrying amounts of the assets. As the assets are not being reduced via amortisation, it is considered essential that the carrying amounts be tested against the recoverable amounts.

Another important reason for remeasuring assets and testing for impairment relates to the concept of depreciation adopted by the IASB. *As noted in chapter 11*, depreciation is viewed as a process of allocation rather than as a valuation process, even when an asset is measured at a revalued amount. Therefore, the carrying amount of an asset reflects the unallocated measure of the asset rather than the benefits to be derived from the asset in the future. The impairment test relates to the assessment of recoverability of the asset, which is not a feature of the depreciation allocation process.

15.2.1 Collecting evidence of impairment

The purpose of the impairment test is to determine whether the carrying amount of an asset exceeds its recoverable amount. The recoverable amount will be discussed in more detail below, but it is essentially the higher of the asset's fair value and the net present value of the cash flows that will be generated by that asset. Time and effort can be saved by establishing whichever of the two figures is the easier to determine. If that figure exceeds the carrying value then the asset cannot be impaired and the other figure is unnecessary. For example, an entity owns property with a carrying value of $10 million. Management believes that the fair value is 'at least' $12 million. The value of the cash flows associated with the property is irrelevant and so there is no need to establish it.

IAS 36 requires management to consider sources of evidence that might indicate the possibility of impairment. Evidence can come from internal and external sources.

External sources of information

Paragraph 12 of IAS 36 lists four sources of information relating to the external environment in which the entity operates:
1. *Asset's value.* Might the asset's value have declined more than would normally be expected during the period? For example, are revenues from the products made using the asset declining? Are observable market prices for similar assets declining on the open market?
2. *Entity's environment/market.* Have significant adverse changes occurred or will they occur in the technological, market, economic or legal environment in which the entity operates, or in the market to which the asset is dedicated? For example, a competitor may have developed a product or technology that is likely to cause or has caused a significant and permanent reduction in the entity's market share.
3. *Interest rates.* Have market interest rates or market rates of return increased during the period? If so, then discounting future cash flows at this higher rate will reduce their net present value.
4. *Market capitalisation.* Is the carrying amount of the net assets of the entity greater than the market capitalisation of the entity?

Internal sources of information

Paragraph 12 of IAS 36 lists three sources of information based on events within the entity itself:
1. *Obsolescence or physical damage.* Does an analysis of the asset reveal physical damage or obsolescence?
2. *Changed use within the entity.* Is the asset expected to be used differently within the entity? For example, the asset may become idle; there may be a restructure in the entity that changes the use of the asset; there may be plans to sell the asset; or the useful life of an intangible may be changed from indefinite to finite.
3. *Economic performance of the asset.* Do internal reports indicate that the economic performance of the asset is worse than expected? Evidence of this consists of:
   - actual cash flows for maintenance or operating the asset may be significantly higher than expected
   - actual cash inflows or profits may be lower than expected
   - expected cash flows for maintenance of operations may have increased, or expected profits may be lower.

In analysing the information from the above sources, paragraph 15 of IAS 36 notes that materiality must be taken into account. For example, an increase in short-term interest rates that is not expected to persist would have very little impact on net present values.

In its notes to the 2014 consolidated financial statements, Nokia provided details of the factors that trigger an impairment review for the entity (see figure 15.1).

Assessment of the recoverability of long-lived assets, intangible assets and goodwill
The Group assesses the carrying value of goodwill annually or more frequently if events or changes in circumstances indicate that such carrying value may not be recoverable. The carrying value of identifiable intangible assets and long-lived assets is assessed if events or changes in circumstances indicate that such carrying value may not be recoverable. Factors that trigger an impairment review include, but are not limited to, underperformance relative to historical or projected future results, significant changes in the manner of the use of the acquired assets or the strategy for the overall business, and significant negative industry or economic trends.

FIGURE 15.1 Indicators of impairment for Nokia Corporation
Source: Nokia Corporation (2014, p. 133).

15.3 IMPAIRMENT TEST FOR AN INDIVIDUAL ASSET

The impairment test involves comparing the carrying amount of an asset with its recoverable amount. To understand the nature of this test, it is necessary to understand a number of definitions given in paragraph 6 of IAS 36:

> The recoverable amount of an asset or a cash-generating unit is the higher of its fair value less costs of disposal and its value in use.
>
> Fair value is the price that would be received to sell an asset or paid to transfer a liability in an orderly transaction between market participants at the measurement date. *(See IFRS 13 Fair Value Measurement.)*
>
> Costs of disposal are incremental costs directly attributable to the disposal of an asset or cash-generating unit, excluding finance costs and income tax expense.
>
> Value in use is the present value of the future cash flows expected to be derived from an asset or cash-generating unit.

Note the phrase 'an asset or cash-generating unit' in the above definitions. The discussion in this section focuses on an individual asset, and it is assumed that, for the asset being tested for impairment, there are specific cash flows that can be associated with the asset. *Cash-generating units are discussed in section 15.4.*

From the definition of recoverable amount, there are two possible amounts against which the carrying amount can be tested for impairment: (1) fair value less costs of disposal and (2) value in use. Although the definition of recoverable amount refers to the 'higher' of these two amounts, an impairment occurs if the carrying amount exceeds recoverable amount (paragraph 8). However, it is not always necessary to measure both amounts when testing for impairment. If either one of these amounts is greater than carrying amount, the asset is not impaired (paragraph 19). Where there are active markets, determining fair value less costs of disposal is probably easier than calculating value in use. However, where the carrying amount exceeds the fair value less costs of disposal, it is necessary to calculate the value in use. Figure 15.2 is a diagrammatic representation of the impairment test.

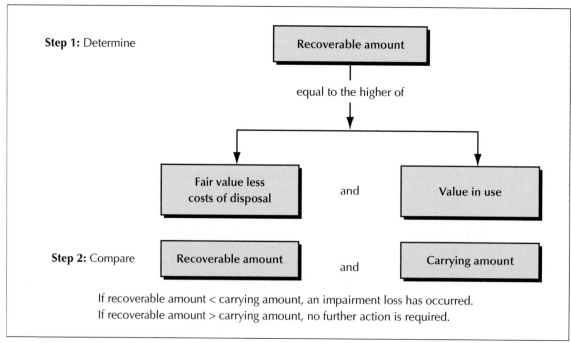

FIGURE 15.2 The impairment test

In calculating either fair value less costs of disposal or value in use, paragraph 23 of IAS 36 notes that in 'some cases, estimates, averages and computational shortcuts may provide reasonable approximations', rather than an entity having to perform in-depth calculations annually. It is also possible to use the most recent detailed calculation of recoverable amount made in a preceding year (paragraph 24) in the case of an intangible asset with an indefinite useful life. The latter is possible if *all* the following criteria are met:

- for the intangible asset, if tested as part of a cash-generating unit *(see section 15.4)*, the other assets and liabilities in the unit have not changed significantly
- in the preceding year's calculation, the difference between the carrying amount and recoverable amount was substantial
- an analysis of all evidence relating to events affecting the asset suggests that the likelihood of the recoverable amount being less than carrying amount is remote.

15.3.1 Calculating fair value less costs of disposal

There are two parts to the determination of fair value less costs of disposal, namely *fair value* and *costs of disposal*. Fair value is measured in accordance with IFRS 13 *Fair Value Measurement and is discussed in detail in chapter 3*. Fair value is defined as an exit price and can be measured using a number of valuation techniques using various observable or unobservable inputs.

Paragraph 28 of IAS 36 provides the following examples of costs of disposal: legal costs, stamp duty and similar transaction taxes, costs of removing the asset, and direct incremental costs to bring the asset into condition for sale. The costs must be directly associated with either the sale of the asset or getting the asset ready for sale. Any costs arising after the sale of the asset, even if arising as a result of the sale, are not regarded as costs of disposal.

Paragraph 5 of IAS 36 provides guidance where an asset is measured at a revalued amount (i.e. fair value). Fair value as a measure does not include a consideration of disposal costs. Hence, if an asset's fair value is equal to its market value, the difference between fair value and fair value less costs of disposal is the disposal costs of the asset. If the disposal costs are immaterial, then there is no significant difference between fair value and fair value less costs of disposal. If the fair value is up to date then the asset could only be impaired if the disposal costs were material. When that is the case, the entity will have to determine the asset's value in use because the asset will not be impaired if its value in use exceeds its carrying value.

Figure 15.3 describes how Nokia calculated the fair value less costs of disposal of one of its cash-generating units. Note that the purpose of the calculation was to determine a disposal price.

Carrying value of the HERE cash-generating unit

The recoverable amount of the HERE CGU is determined using the fair value less costs of disposal method. Estimation and judgment are required in determining the components of the recoverable amount calculation, including the discount rate, the terminal growth rate, estimated revenue growth rates, profit margins, costs of disposal and the cost level of operational and capital investment. The discount rate reflects current assessments of the time value of money, relevant market risk premiums, and industry comparisons. Risk premiums reflect risks and uncertainties for which the future cash flow estimates have not been adjusted. Terminal values are based on the expected life of products and forecasted life cycle, and forecasted cash flows over that period. In 2014, the Group recorded an impairment loss of EUR 1209 million to reduce the carrying amount of the HERE CGU to its recoverable amount. The remaining carrying amount of the HERE goodwill is EUR 2273 million. As the carrying amount of the HERE CGU has been written down to its recoverable amount, any increase in the discount rate, any decrease in the terminal growth rate, or any material change in other valuation assumptions could result in further impairment.

FIGURE 15.3 Calculation of fair value less costs of disposal
Source: Nokia Corporation (2014, p. 138).

15.3.2 Calculating value in use

Value in use is the present value of future cash flows relating to the asset being measured. These should be discounted at an appropriate rate that takes account of the risks inherent in future cash flows from the asset. Paragraph 53A of IAS 36 *Impairment of Assets* notes that fair value differs from value in use because of factors that are likely to be specific to the entity:

(a) additional value derived from the grouping of assets (such as the creation of a portfolio of investment properties in different locations);
(b) synergies between the asset being measured and other assets;

(c) legal rights or legal restrictions that are specific only to the current owner of the asset; and

(d) tax benefits or tax burdens that are specific to the current owner of the asset.

Determining future cash flows

Paragraphs 33–54 of IAS 36 provide guidance in measuring future cash flows. Some important guidelines are:

- Cash flow projections should be based on *management's best estimate* of the range of economic conditions that will exist over the remaining useful life of the asset. These should be modified by an analysis of past cash flows and management's success in the past in predicting future cash flows accurately. Where external evidence is available, this should be given greater weight than simple reliance on management's expectations.
- Cash flow projections should be based on the most recent *financial budgets and forecasts*. These projections should cover a maximum period of 5 years unless a longer period can be justified. For most entities, a detailed analysis of future operations rarely extends beyond 5 years.
- Expectations concerning *growth rate* should be realistic and in line with observable rates. The cash inflows should include those from *continuing use* of the asset over its expected useful life as well as those expected to be received on *disposal* of the asset. Further, any cash *outflows* necessary to achieve the projected inflows must be taken into account.
- Projected cash flows must be estimated for the asset in its *current* condition (paragraph 44). Where there is an expected restructuring of the entity in future periods, or where there are possibilities for improving or enhancing the performance of the asset by subsequent expenditure, projections of cash flows will not take these possible events into consideration. Such enhancements can only be taken into consideration once the entity is committed to the restructure. Day-to-day servicing costs are included in the outflows used to measure value in use, as are the costs of major inspections.
- Cash flows relating to *financing activities* or *income tax* are not included in the calculations of future cash flows. As the discount rate is based on a pre-tax basis, the future cash flows must also be on a pre-tax basis.
- In assessing cash flows from *disposal*, the expected disposal price will take into account specific future price increases/decreases, and be based on an analysis of prices prevailing at the date of the estimate for similar assets in conditions similar to those expected for the asset under consideration at the end of its useful life.
- Appendix A to IAS 36, described as an 'integral part of the standard', contains guidance on the use of present value techniques in measuring value in use. Essentially, expected values may be used when probabilities can be estimated.

Determining the discount rate

Paragraph 55 of IAS 36 notes that the discount rate should:

- reflect the time value of money
- reflect the risks specific to the asset for which the future cash flow estimates have not been adjusted.

The rate may be determined by viewing rates used for similar assets in the market, or from the weighted average cost of capital of a listed entity that has a single asset, or portfolio of assets, similar to the asset under review (paragraph 56).

Figure 15.4 contains information provided in Note 19 to the financial statements in the 2014 annual report of Amcor Ltd. Note in particular the information provided about the calculation of the recoverable amount using value-in-use calculations.

FIGURE 15.4 Calculation of value in use

(b) Impairment tests for goodwill

For the purpose of impairment testing, goodwill acquired in a business combination is allocated to cash generating units or groups of cash generating units (CGUs) according to the level at which management monitors goodwill. The goodwill amounts allocated below are tested annually or semi-annually if there are indicators of impairment, by comparison with the recoverable amount of each CGU or group of CGU's assets. Recoverable amounts for CGUs are measured at the higher of fair value less costs of disposal and value in use. Value in use is calculated from cash flow projections for five years using data from the consolidated entity's latest internal forecasts. The key assumptions for the value in use calculations are those regarding discount rates, growth rates and expected changes in margins. The forecasts used in the value in use calculations are management's estimates in determining income, expenses, capital expenditure and cash flows for each asset and CGU. Changes in selling prices and direct costs are based on past experience and management's expectation of future changes in the markets in which the consolidated entity operates. Cash flows beyond the five year period are extrapolated using estimated growth rates. The following table presents a summary of the goodwill allocation and the key assumptions used in determining the recoverable amount of each CGU:

FIGURE 15.4 *(continued)*

CGU	Goodwill Allocation		Pre-Tax Discount Rate		Growth Rate	
	2014 $ million	2013 $ million	2014 %	2013 %	2014 %	2013 %
Continuing Operations						
Rigid Plastics						
Rigid Plastics	712.7	725.2	11.8	12.2	11	—
Flexibles						
Flexibles Europe & Americas	515.3	500.1	7.6	7.6	—	—
Tobacco Packaging	321.0	303.7	7.6	7.6	—	—
Flexibles Asia Pacific	246.2	192.4	9.6	9.9	3.0	3.0
Discontinued Operations						
Australasia and Packaging Distribution						
Australasia	—	85.6	—	9.1	—	—
Packaging Distribution	—	116.6	—	8.9	—	3.0
	1 795.2	1 923.6				

The discount rate used in performing the value in use calculations reflects the consolidated entity's weighted average cost of capital, as adjusted for specific risks relating to each geographical region in which the CGUs operate. The pre-tax discount rates are disclosed above. The growth rate represents the average rate applied to extrapolate CGU cash flows beyond the five year forecast period. These growth rates are determined with regard to the long-term performance of each CGU in their respective market and are not expected to exceed the long-term average growth rates in the applicable market.

Source: Amcor Ltd (2014, p. 115).

15.3.3 Recognition and measurement of an impairment loss for an individual asset

Paragraphs 58–64 of IAS 36 provide the principles for recognition and measurement of an impairment loss for an individual asset. If the recoverable amount of an asset is less than its carrying amount, an impairment loss occurs, and the asset must be written down from its carrying amount to the recoverable amount.

Where an asset is measured using the *cost model*, according to paragraph 60 of IAS 36 an impairment loss is recognised immediately in profit or loss. In relation to the other side of the accounting entry to the loss, reference should be made to paragraph 73(d) of IAS 16 *Property, Plant and Equipment*. According to this paragraph, for items of property, plant and equipment 'the gross carrying amount and the accumulated depreciation (aggregated with accumulated impairment losses) at the beginning and end of the period' should be disclosed. When impairment occurs, there is no need to write off any existing accumulated depreciation or create a separate accumulated impairment account. The impairment write-down can be included in accumulated depreciation, preferably referred to as 'Accumulated Depreciation and Impairment Losses'.

Hence, if an asset having a carrying amount of $100 (original cost $160) has a recoverable amount of $90, the appropriate journal entry to account for the impairment loss is:

Impairment Loss	Dr	10	
Accumulated Depreciation and Impairment Losses	Cr		10
(Impairment loss on asset)			

Where an asset is measured using the *revaluation model* (i.e. at fair value), according to paragraph 60 of IAS 36 any impairment loss is treated as a revaluation increase and accounted for as set out in IAS 16. If an asset at the end of an accounting period has a carrying amount of $100, being previously calculated as fair value of $120 less accumulated depreciation of $20, and the asset's recoverable amount (and possibly its fair value) at the end of the period is determined to be $90, the accounting entry is:

Accumulated Depreciation	Dr	20	
Asset	Cr		20
(Write-down of asset)			

Loss – Downward Revaluation of Asset (P/L)	Dr	10	
Asset	Cr		10
(Revaluation of asset)			

If the revalued asset had a previous revaluation increase of $20, giving rise to a revaluation surplus of $14 and a deferred tax liability (using a tax rate of 30%) of $6, then the entry to write the asset down to a recoverable amount of $90 requires an adjustment directly against the revaluation surplus:

Accumulated Depreciation	Dr	20	
Asset Revaluation Surplus	Dr	7	
Deferred Tax Liability	Dr	3	
Asset	Cr		30
(Write-down of asset to recoverable amount)			

Regardless of whether the cost model or the revaluation model is used, once the impairment loss is recognised, any subsequent depreciation/amortisation is based on the new recoverable amount. In accordance with paragraph 63 of IAS 36, the depreciation charge is that necessary to allocate the asset's revised carrying amount (the recoverable amount) less its residual value (if any) on a systematic basis over its remaining useful life, which may have to be reviewed in light of the circumstances leading to the impairment.

It is possible that the recoverable amount is negative owing to large expected future cash outflows relating to the asset, so the impairment loss could be greater than the carrying amount of the asset. According to paragraph 62 of IAS 16, a liability for the excess should be raised only if another standard requires it.

Figure 15.5 contains information disclosed in Note 10 to the 2014 financial statements of Nokia Corporation relating to its impairment of specific assets.

FIGURE 15.5 Impairment of assets

10. Impairment
Impairment charges by asset category are:

EURm	2014	2013	2012
Continuing operations			
Goodwill	1 209	—	—
Other intangible assets	—	—	8
Property, plant and equipment	—	12	23
Investments in associated companies	—	—	8
Available-for-sale investments	15	8	31
Total	1 224	20	70

Goodwill
Goodwill impairment assessment for the HERE CGU was carried out at September 30, 2014. The previous assessment date was October 1, 2013. The assessment date was brought forward to September 30, 2014 due to an adjustment to the HERE strategy and the related new long-range plan, which incorporates the slower than expected increase in net sales directly to consumers, and the Group's plans to curtail its investment in certain higher-risk and longer-term growth opportunities. This represented a triggering event resulting in an interim impairment test to assess if events or changes in circumstances indicate that the carrying amount of HERE goodwill may not be recoverable. The goodwill impairment assessment for the HERE CGU was rolled forward to October 1, 2014 to align with the annual assessment date. The goodwill impairment assessment for the Nokia Networks Radio Access Networks group of CGUs in Mobile Broadband and Global Services group of CGUs was carried out at November 30, 2014 (November 30 in 2013).

The carrying value of goodwill allocated to each of the Group's CGUs at each of the respective years' impairment testing dates is:

EURm	2014	2013
HERE [(1)]	2 273	3 219
Global Services	106	91
Radio Access Networks in Mobile Broadband	96	88
Devices & Services (Discontinued operations)	—	1 417

[(1)]The carrying value of goodwill after the 2014 impairment charge.

FIGURE 15.5 *(continued)*

The recoverable amounts of the Group's CGUs were determined using the fair value less costs of disposal method. In the absence of observable market prices, the recoverable amounts were estimated based on an income approach, specifically a discounted cash flow model. The valuation method is in line with previous years, with the exception that the cash flow forecast period is five years in comparison with ten years previously. The cash flow projections used in calculating the recoverable amounts are based on financial plans approved by management covering an explicit forecast period of five years and reflect the price that would be received to sell the CGU in an orderly transaction between market participants at the measurement date. The level of fair value hierarchy within which the fair value measurement is categorized is level 3. Refer to Note 19, Fair value of financial instruments for the fair value hierarchy.

The recoverable amount of the HERE CGU at September 30, 2014 was EUR 2,031 million, which resulted in an impairment charge of EUR 1,209 million. The impairment charge is the result of an evaluation of the projected financial performance and net cash flows of the HERE CGU and was allocated entirely against the carrying value of HERE goodwill. The evaluation incorporates the slower than expected increase in net sales directly to consumers, and the Group's plans to curtail its investment in certain higher-risk and longer-term growth opportunities. It also reflects the current assessment of risks related to the growth opportunities that management plans to continue pursuing, as well as the related terminal value growth assumptions. After consideration of all relevant factors, management reduced the net sales projections for the HERE CGU, particularly in the latter years of the valuation. The HERE CGU corresponds to the HERE operating and reportable segment. Refer to Note 2, Segment information.

The key assumptions applied in the impairment testing analysis for each CGU are:

Key assumption %	2014	2013	2014	2013	2014	2013
	HERE	**CGU**	**Radio Access Networks group of CGUs in Mobile Broadband**		**Global Services group of CGUs**	
Terminal growth rate [1]	1.2	1.7	2.6	1.5	1.6	0.5
Post-tax discount rate	11.0	10.6	9.4	10.8	9.1	10.1

[1]Based on a five-year forecast period (ten-year forecast period in 2013).

Terminal growth rates reflect long-term average growth rates for the industry and economies in which the CGUs operate. The discount rates reflect current assessments of the time value of money and relevant market risk premiums. Risk premiums reflect risks and uncertainties for which the future cash flow estimates have not been adjusted. Other key variables in future cash flow projections include assumptions on estimated sales growth, gross margin and operating margin. All cash flow projections are consistent with external sources of information, wherever possible.

Management has determined the recoverable amount of the HERE CGU to be most sensitive to changes in both the discount rate and the terminal growth rate. As the carrying value of the HERE CGU has been written down to its recoverable amount, any increase in the discount rate or any decrease in the terminal growth rate would result in further impairment. Management's estimates of the overall automotive volumes and market share, customer adoption of the new location-based platform and related service offerings, and assumptions regarding industry pricing are the main drivers for the HERE net cash flow projections. The Group's cash flow forecasts reflect the current strategic views that license fee-based models will remain important in both the near and long term. Management expects that when license fee-based models are augmented with software and services, transactions fees will grow in the future as more customers demand complete, end-to-end location solutions and as cloud computing and cloud-based services gain greater market acceptance. Actual short- and long-term performance could vary from management's forecasts and impact future estimates of recoverable amount.

Management has determined the discount rate and the terminal growth rate to be the key assumptions for the Nokia Networks Radio Access Networks group of CGUs and the Global Services group of CGUs. The recoverable amounts calculated based on the sensitized assumptions do not indicate impairment in 2014 or 2013. Further, no reasonably possible changes in other key assumptions on which the Group has based its determination of the recoverable amounts would result in impairment in 2014 or 2013.

In 2013, the recoverable amount of the Devices & Services CGU was determined using the fair value less costs of disposal method, based on the agreed purchase price, excluding any consideration attributable to patents or patent applications.

(continued)

FIGURE 15.5 *(continued)*

Other intangible assets

In 2012, Nokia Networks recognized an impairment charge of EUR 8 million on intangible assets attributable to the decision to transition certain operations into maintenance mode. These charges were recorded in Other operating expenses.

Property, plant and equipment

In 2013, Nokia Networks recognized an impairment charge of EUR 6 million (EUR 23 million in 2012) following the remeasurement of the Optical Networks disposal group at fair value less cost of disposal. In 2013, the Group recognized impairment losses of EUR 6 million relating to certain properties attributable to Group Common Functions.

Investments in associated companies

In 2012, the Group recognized an impairment charge of EUR 8 million to adjust the Group's investment in associated companies to the recoverable amount. These charges were recorded in Other operating expenses and included in Group Common Functions.

Available-for-sale investments

The Group recognized an impairment charge of EUR 15 million (EUR 8 million in 2013 and EUR 31 million in 2012) as certain equity and interest-bearing securities held as available-for-sale suffered a significant or prolonged decline in fair value. These charges are recorded in Other expenses and Financial income and expenses.

Source: Nokia Corporation (2014, p. 149).

15.4 CASH-GENERATING UNITS — EXCLUDING GOODWILL

The discussion above *(section 15.3)* focuses on individual assets and whether they have been impaired. The impairment test in such cases involves the determination of recoverable amount, and this requires the measurement of fair value less costs of disposal and value in use of the asset being tested for impairment. However, for some assets, fair value less costs of disposal may be determinable, because the asset is separable and a market for that asset exists, but it may be impossible to determine the value in use. Value in use requires determining the expected cash flows to be received from an asset.

Some assets do not individually generate cash flows because the cash flows generated are the result of a combination of several assets. For example, a machine in a factory works in conjunction with the rest of the assets in the factory to produce sellable goods. For such assets, if the carrying amount exceeds the fair value less costs of disposal, some other measure relating to value in use must be used.

Paragraph 66 of IAS 36 requires that, where there is any indication an asset may be impaired, if possible the recoverable amount should be estimated for the individual asset.

However, if this is not possible, the entity should 'determine the recoverable amount of the cash-generating unit to which the asset belongs'. In other words, the impairment test is applied to a cash-generating unit rather than to an individual asset. Paragraph 6 contains the following definition of a cash-generating unit:

> A cash-generating unit is the smallest identifiable group of assets that generates cash inflows that are largely independent of the cash inflows from other assets or groups of assets.

15.4.1 Identifying a cash-generating unit

The identification of a cash-generating unit requires judgement. As is stated in the definition, the key is to determine the 'smallest identifiable group of assets', and this group must create 'independent' cash flows from continuing use. Guidelines given in paragraphs 67–73 of IAS 36 include the following:

- Consider how management monitors the entity's operations, such as by product lines, businesses, individual locations, districts or regional areas.
- Consider how management makes decisions about continuing or disposing of the entity's assets and operations.
- If an active market exists for the output of a group of assets, this group constitutes a cash-generating unit.
- Even if some of the output of a group is used internally, if the output could be sold externally, then these prices can be used to measure the value in use of the group of assets.
- Cash-generating units should be identified consistently from period to period for the same group of assets.

For example, an entity owns eight shops, spread across the same city. Head office sets selling prices and designs shop layout. All inventory is purchased centrally. Factors that would indicate that each store is a cash generating unit include the following:

- Does management monitor the profitability of each store separately?
- Does the location of the store suggest that each will have its own unique customer base?

426 PART 2 Elements

Or consider a steel mill that manufactures a particular grade of steel that is transferred to another factory owned by the entity. If the steel could be sold on the open market (even if all output is transferred internally) then the mill is likely to be a separate cash-generating unit. If there is no external market then the mill and the factory may have to be combined into a single cash-generating unit.

The identification of cash-generating units can be a little arbitrary. That leaves scope for the identification of cash-generating units in such a way that assets that are likely to decrease in value are combined with others that are likely to increase, so that impairment losses are unlikely to be recognised.

One alternative to the cash-generating unit is the segment concept as in IFRS 8 *Operating Segments*. Although determination of segments is also arbitrary, an accounting standard covers the identification of segments, which should improve the comparability across entities, and the identified segments are reported to the public. Note, however, that IAS 36 allows a segment to be used as the cash-generating unit only if the segment equates to the smallest identifiable group of assets that generate independent cash flows. Figure 15.6 shows how in Lafarge Malaysia Berhad Note 15 to its 2014 financial statements reported the company's allocation of goodwill to its cash-generating units.

Goodwill acquired in a business combination is allocated, at acquisition, to the cash-generating unit ("CGU") that is expected to benefit from that business combination. Before recognition of any impairment losses, the carrying amount of goodwill has been allocated to the following business segments as independent CGUs:

	Group	
	2014 RM'000	2013 RM'000
Cement	1 149 458	1 151 285
Aggregates and concrete	54 219	54 219
	1 203 677	1 205 504

FIGURE 15.6 Allocation of goodwill to cash-generating units
Source: Lafarge Malaysia Berhad (2014, p. 98).

15.4.2 Impairment loss for a cash-generating unit — excluding goodwill

An impairment loss occurs when the carrying amount of the assets of a cash-generating unit exceeds their recoverable amount.

Determining the impairment loss

In determining the carrying amount of the assets, all those assets that are directly attributable to the cash-generating unit and that contribute to generating the cash flows used in measuring recoverable amount must be included. There must be consistency between what is being measured for recoverable amount — namely cash flows relating to a group of assets — and the measurement of the carrying amount of those assets.

The principles for determining the recoverable amount of a cash-generating unit are the same as those previously described for an individual asset *(section 15.3)*. However, note that paragraph 76(b) of IAS 36 requires that the carrying amount of a cash-generating unit does not include the carrying amount of any recognised liability. This is because, as stated in paragraph 43(b), the calculation of the future cash flows of the cash-generating unit does not include cash outflows that relate to obligations that have been recognised as liabilities, such as payables and provisions.

Accounting for an impairment loss in a cash-generating unit

If an impairment loss is recognised in a cash-generating unit that has not recorded any goodwill, paragraph 104 of IAS 36 states that the impairment loss should be allocated to reduce the carrying amount of the assets of the unit by allocating the impairment loss pro rata based on the carrying amount of each asset in the unit. The reduction in each carrying amount relates to each specific asset, and should be treated as an impairment of each asset, even though the impairment loss was based on an analysis of a cash-generating unit. The loss is accounted for in the same way as that for an individual asset *as described in section 15.3*, with losses relating to an asset measured at cost being recognised immediately in profit or loss.

Paragraph 105 of IAS 36 places some restrictions on an entity's ability to write down assets as a result of the allocation of the impairment loss across the carrying amounts of the assets of the cash-generating unit. For each asset, the carrying amount should not be reduced below the highest of:
(a) its fair value less costs of disposal (if measurable);
(b) its value in use (if determinable); and
(c) zero.

If there is an amount of impairment loss allocated to an asset, but a part of it would reduce the asset below, say, its fair value less costs of disposal, then that part is allocated across the other assets in the cash-generating unit on a pro rata basis (see illustrative example 15.1). However, as paragraph 106 notes, if the recoverable amount of each of the assets cannot be estimated without undue costs or effort, then an arbitrary allocation of the impairment loss between the assets of the unit will suffice because all the assets of a cash-generating unit work together.

ILLUSTRATIVE EXAMPLE 15.1 Impairment of a cash-generating unit

A cash-generating unit has been assessed for impairment and it has been determined that the unit has incurred an impairment loss of $12 000. The carrying amounts of the assets and the allocation of the impairment loss on a proportional basis are as shown below.

	Carrying amount	Proportion	Allocation of impairment loss	Net carrying amount
Buildings	$ 500 000	5/12	$ 5 000	$495 000
Equipment	300 000	3/12	3 000	297 000
Land	250 000	2.5/12	2 500	247 500
Fittings	150 000	1.5/12	1 500	148 500
	$1 200 000		$12 000	

However, if the fair value less costs of disposal of the buildings was $497 000, then this is the maximum to which these assets could be reduced. Hence, the balance of the allocated impairment loss to buildings of $2000 (i.e. $5000 − [$500 000 − $497 000]) has to be allocated across the other assets:

	Carrying amount	Proportion	Allocation of impairment loss	Net carrying amount
Buildings				$497 000
Equipment	$297 000	297/693	$ 857	296 143
Land	247 500	247.5/693	714	246 786
Fittings	148 500	148.5/693	429	148 071
	$693 000		$2 000	

The journal entry to reflect the recognition of the impairment loss is:

Impairment Loss	Dr	12 000	
Accumulated Depreciation and Impairment Losses – Buildings	Cr		3 000
Accumulated Depreciation and Impairment Losses – Equipment	Cr		3 857
Land	Cr		3 214
Accumulated Depreciation and Impairment Losses – Fittings	Cr		1 929

Corporate assets

One problem that arises when dividing an entity into separate cash-generating units is dealing with corporate assets. Corporate assets, such as the headquarters building or the information technology support centre, are integral to all cash-generating units generating cash flows but do not by themselves independently generate cash flows. Paragraph 102 of IAS 36 sets out how corporate assets should be dealt with in determining impairment losses for an entity:

Step 1: If any corporate assets can be allocated on a reasonable and consistent basis to cash-generating units, then this should be done. Each unit is then, where appropriate, tested for an impairment loss. Where a loss occurs in a cash-generating unit, the loss is allocated pro rata across the assets including the portion of the corporate asset allocated to the unit.

Step 2: If some corporate assets cannot be allocated across the cash-generating units, the entity:
- compares the carrying amount of each unit being tested (excluding the unallocated corporate asset) with its recoverable amount and recognises any impairment loss by allocating the loss across the assets of the unit

- identifies the smallest cash-generating unit that includes the unit under review and to which a portion of the unallocated corporate asset can be allocated on a reasonable and consistent basis
- compares the carrying amount of the larger cash-generating unit, including the portion of the corporate asset, with its allocated amount. Any impairment loss is then allocated across the assets of the larger cash-generating unit.

Illustrative example 15.2 provides the accounting for corporate assets.

ILLUSTRATIVE EXAMPLE 15.2 Accounting for corporate assets

Singapore Engineering has two cash generating units, A and B. The assets of the two units are as follows:

	Unit A	Unit B
Plant	$500	$400
Land	300	220

Singapore Engineering has two corporate assets: the headquarters building and a research centre. The headquarters is assumed to be used equally by both units. The carrying amount of the research centre cannot be allocated on a reasonable basis to the two units. The headquarters building has a carrying amount of $160. The research centre's assets consist of furniture of $40 and equipment of $30. Neither of the corporate assets produces cash flows for Singapore Engineering.

The recoverable amounts of the two cash-generating units are:

Unit A	$900
Unit B	$665

The *first* step is to calculate the impairment losses for each of the cash generating units. To do this, the carrying amount of the headquarters building is allocated equally between the two units as it is used equally by those units. Impairment losses are then as follows:

	Unit A	Unit B
Plant	$ 500	$400
Land	300	220
Headquarters building	80	80
	880	700
Recoverable amount	900	665
Impairment loss	$ 0	$ 35

The impairment loss of $35 for Unit B is then allocated across all non-excluded assets in that unit:

	Carrying amount	Proportion of loss	Loss	Adjusted carrying amount
Plant	$400	400/700	$20	$380
Land	220	220/700	11	209
Headquarters building	80	80/700	4	76
			$35	

The second step is to deal with the research centre. This requires the determination of any impairment loss for the smallest cash-generating unit that includes the research centre. In this case, the smallest cash-generating unit is the entity as a whole. The impairment loss is calculated as follows:

Unit A	
Plant	$ 500
Land	300
Headquarters building [$80 + $76]	156
Unit B	
Plant	380
Land	209
Research Centre	
Furniture	40
Equipment	30
	1 615
Recoverable amount [$900 + $665]	1 565
Impairment loss	$ 50

This impairment loss is then allocated across these assets on a pro rata basis:

	Carrying amount	Proportion of loss	Loss	Adjusted carrying amount
Unit A				
Plant	$ 500	500/1 615	$15	$485
Land	300	300/1 615	9	291
Headquarters building [$80 + $76]	156	156/1 615	5	151
Unit B				
Plant	380	380/1 615	12	368
Land	209	209/1 615	7	202
Research Centre				
Furniture	40	40/1 615	1	39
Equipment	30	30/1 615	1	29
	$1 615		$50	

15.5 CASH-GENERATING UNITS AND GOODWILL

In accounting for impairment losses for cash-generating units, one of the assets that may be recorded by an entity is goodwill. IAS 36 contains specific requirements for accounting for goodwill and how its existence affects the allocation of impairment losses across the assets of a cash-generating unit.

Goodwill is recognised only when it is acquired in a business combination. It is not possible to determine a fair value less costs of disposal for goodwill, or to identify a set of cash flows that relates specifically to goodwill.

Accounting for goodwill acquired in a business combination is specified in paragraph 32 of IFRS 3 *Business Combinations*. The acquirer measures goodwill acquired in a business combination at cost less any accumulated impairment losses. Goodwill is not subject to amortisation. Instead, the acquirer tests the carrying amount of goodwill annually in accordance with IAS 36.

When a business combination occurs, and goodwill is calculated as part of accounting for that combination, the goodwill acquired is allocated to one or more cash-generating units (IAS 36 paragraph 80). Even though goodwill was acquired in relation to the entity as a whole, the cash flow earning capacity of goodwill must be allocated across the cash-generating units. The aim is to allocate all assets, whether corporate assets or goodwill, to the cash-generating units so they can be associated with the cash flows received by those units.

When deciding which units should have goodwill allocated to them, consideration should be given to how internal management monitors the goodwill. According to paragraph 80, the goodwill should be allocated to the *lowest level* at which management monitors the goodwill. When the business combination occurred, the acquirer would have analysed the earning capacity of the entity it proposed to acquire, and would have equated aspects of goodwill to various cash-generating units. It is possible that the allocation of goodwill would be made to each of the segments identified by management under the application of IFRS 8 *Operating Segments*. Paragraph 80 of IAS 36 states that the units to which goodwill is allocated should not be larger than a segment based on either the entity's primary or secondary reporting format. This is due to the fact that IFRS 8 requires the determination of business and geographical segments based on areas that are subject to different risks and return, and the internal financial reporting system within the entity is used as a basis for identifying these segments.

Under IFRS 3, there is an allowance for a provisional initial accounting for the business combination. Paragraph 84 of IAS 36 therefore provides, consistent with IFRS 3, that where the allocation of goodwill cannot be completed before the end of the annual period in which the business combination occurred, the initial allocation is to be completed before the end of the first annual period beginning after the acquisition date.

15.5.1 Impairment testing of goodwill

A cash-generating unit that has goodwill allocated to it must be tested for impairment *annually* or more frequently if there is an indication the unit may be impaired (IAS 36 paragraph 90). As with other impairment tests, this involves comparing the carrying amount of the unit's assets, including goodwill, with the recoverable amount of the unit's assets.

Recoverable amount exceeds carrying amount

If the recoverable amount exceeds the carrying amount, there is no impairment loss. In particular, there is no impairment of goodwill. The goodwill balance remains unadjusted; that is, it is not reduced due to impairment loss.

In practice, it is impossible to distinguish purchased goodwill from other assets that might increase the recoverable amount:

- *internally generated goodwill* — possibly created since the business combination.
- *unrecognised identifiable net assets* — intangibles may exist which do not meet the recognition criteria under IAS 38 *Intangible Assets*.
- *excess value over carrying amount of recognised assets* — the impairment test uses the carrying amount of the unit's recognised assets. If the fair values of these assets are greater than their carrying amounts, the extra benefits relating to these assets increase the recoverable amount of the unit.

The IASB acknowledges that these factors could reduce the likelihood of recognising impairment losses for goodwill. The impairment test for goodwill is, at best, ensuring that the carrying amount of goodwill is recoverable from cash flows generated by both acquired and internally generated goodwill. While this may be inconsistent with the requirement that purchased goodwill should be reviewed annually for impairment, it simplifies that annual review.

Users of the financial statements can take appropriate care when interpreting financial statements that show a significant goodwill balance.

Carrying amount exceeds recoverable amount

If the carrying amount exceeds the recoverable amount, there is an impairment loss, and this loss is recognised in accordance with paragraph 104 of IAS 36. This paragraph states that the impairment loss must be allocated to reduce the carrying amount of the assets of the unit, or group of units, in the following order:

- firstly, to reduce the carrying amount of any goodwill allocated to the cash-generating unit
- then, to the other assets of the unit pro rata on the basis of the carrying amount of each asset in the unit.

These reductions in carrying amounts are treated as impairment losses on the individual assets of the unit and recognised as any other impairment losses on assets.

However, paragraph 105 of IAS 36 provides some restrictions on the write-downs to individual assets:

> In allocating an impairment loss in accordance with paragraph 104, an entity shall not reduce the carrying amount of an asset below the highest of:
> (a) its fair value less costs of disposal (if measurable);
> (b) its value in use (if determinable); and
> (c) zero.
> The amount of the impairment loss that would otherwise have been allocated to the asset shall be allocated pro rata to the other assets of the unit (group of units).

Timing of impairment tests

As noted earlier, goodwill has to be tested for impairment annually. However, the test does not have to occur at the end of the reporting period. As paragraph 96 of IAS 36 notes, the test may be performed at any time during the year, provided it is performed at the same time every year. According to paragraph BC171 of the Basis for Conclusions on IAS 36, this measure was allowed as a means of reducing the costs of applying the test. However, if a business combination has occurred in the current period, and an allocation has been made to one or more cash-generating units, all units to which goodwill has been allocated must be tested for impairment before the end of that year — *see paragraph 96 of IAS 36*.

It is not necessary for all cash-generating units to be tested for impairment at the same time. If there are two units being tested for impairment, one being a smaller cash-generating unit within a larger unit and the larger unit contains an allocation of goodwill, it is necessary to test the smaller unit for impairment first. This ensures that, if necessary, the assets of the smaller unit are adjusted before the testing of the larger unit. Similarly, if the assets of a cash-generating unit containing goodwill are being tested at the same time as the unit, then the assets must be tested first.

Other impairment issues relating to goodwill

IAS 36 raises a number of other issues that need to be considered in accounting for the impairment of goodwill within a cash-generating unit:

- *Disposal of an operation within a cash-generating unit.* Where the cash-generating unit has a number of distinct operations and goodwill has been allocated to the unit, if one of the operations is disposed of, it is necessary to consider whether any of the goodwill relates to the operation disposed of. If it does, the amount of goodwill is measured on the basis of the relative values of the operation disposed of and the portion of the cash-generating unit retained, unless the entity can demonstrate that some other method better reflects the goodwill associated with the operation disposed of. In calculating the gain or loss on disposal of the operation, the allocated portion of the goodwill is included in the carrying amount of the assets sold (paragraph 86).

For example, if part of a cash-generating unit was sold for $200 and the recoverable amount of the remaining part of the unit is $600, then it is assumed that 25% ($200/[$200 + 600]) of the goodwill has been sold and is included in the carrying amount of the operation disposed of.

- *Reorganisation of the entity.* Where an entity containing a number of cash-generating units restructures, changing the composition of the cash-generating units, and where goodwill has been allocated to the original units, paragraph 87 requires the reallocation of the goodwill to the new units. The allocation is done on a relative value basis similar to that used where a cash-generating unit is disposed of, again unless the entity can demonstrate that some other method better reflects the goodwill associated with the operation disposed of.

15.6 REVERSAL OF AN IMPAIRMENT LOSS

An impairment loss is recognised after an entity analyses the future prospects of an individual asset or a cash-generating unit. Subsequent to an impairment loss occurring because of doubts about the performance of assets, it is possible for circumstances to change such that, when the recoverable amount of the assets increases, consideration can be given to a reversal of a past impairment loss. Paragraph 110 of IAS 36 requires an entity to assess *at the end of each reporting period* whether there are indications that an impairment loss recognised in previous periods may not exist or may have decreased. If such indications exist, the entity should estimate the recoverable amount of the asset or unit.

If there is evidence of a favourable change in the estimates in relation to an asset (and only if there has been a change in the estimates), a reversal of impairment loss can be recognised. The reversal process requires the recognition of an increase in the carrying amount of the asset to its recoverable amount.

The ability to recognise a reversal of an impairment loss and the accounting for that reversal depend on whether the reversal relates to an individual asset, a cash-generating unit or goodwill.

15.6.1 Reversal of an impairment loss — individual asset

Where the recoverable amount is greater than the carrying amount of an individual asset (other than goodwill), the reversal of a previous impairment loss requires adjusting the carrying amount of the asset to recoverable amount. In determining the amount by which the carrying amount is to be adjusted, one limitation, as outlined in paragraph 117 of IAS 36, is that the carrying amount cannot be increased to an amount in excess of the carrying amount that would have been determined had no impairment loss been recognised.

15.6.2 Reversal of an impairment loss — cash-generating unit

If the reversal of the impairment loss relates to a cash-generating unit, in accordance with paragraph 122 of IAS 36 the reversal of the impairment loss is allocated pro rata to the assets of the unit, except for goodwill, with the carrying amounts of those assets. These reversals will then relate to the specific assets of the cash-generating unit and will be accounted for as detailed above for individual assets. In relation to those individual assets, the carrying amount of an asset cannot, as per paragraph 123 of IAS 36, be increased above the lower of its recoverable amount (if determinable) and the carrying amount that would have been determined had no impairment loss been recognised for the asset in previous periods.

If the situation envisaged in paragraph 123 occurs, then the amount of impairment loss reversal that cannot be allocated to an individual asset is then allocated on a pro rata basis to the other assets of the cash-generating unit, except for goodwill.

15.6.3 Reversal of an impairment loss — goodwill

Paragraph 124 of IAS 36 states that an impairment loss recognised for goodwill shall *not* be reversed in a later period.

ILLUSTRATIVE EXAMPLE 15.3 Reversal of impairment loss

At 30 June 2015, Jimena SL incurred an impairment loss of $5000, of which $3000 was used to write off the goodwill and $2000 to write down the assets. The allocation of the impairment loss to the assets was as follows:

	Carrying amount	Proportion of loss	Loss	Adjusted carrying amount
Land	$10 000	1/5	$ 400	$ 9 600
Plant	40 000	4/5	1 600	38 400
	$50 000		$2 000	

The plant had previously cost $100 000 and was being depreciated at 10% per annum, requiring a depreciation charge of $10 000 per annum. Subsequent to the impairment, the asset was depreciated on a straight-line basis over 3 years, at $12 800 per annum.

At 30 June 2016, the business situation had improved and Jimena SL believed that it should reverse past impairment losses. A comparison of the carrying amounts of the assets at 30 June 2016 and their recoverable amounts revealed:

Land	$ 9 600
Plant [$38 400 − $12 800]	25 600
Furniture	800
	36 000
Recoverable amount	38 800
Excess of recoverable amount over carrying amount	$ 2 800

The excess cannot be allocated to the goodwill as impairment losses on goodwill can never be reversed. If the excess were allocated to the assets it can only be allocated to the assets existing at the previous impairment write-down as assets cannot be written up above their original cost. The excess of recoverable amount is then allocated to the relevant assets on a pro rata basis:

	Carrying amount	Share of loss	Adjusted carrying amount
Land	$ 9 600	$ 764	$10 364
Plant	25 600	2 036	27 636
	$35 200	$ 2 800	

These assets cannot be written up above the amounts that they would have been recorded at if there had been no previous impairment. These amounts would be:

Land	$10 000
Plant	$30 000 [$40 000 less $10 000 depreciation for the 2015–16 financial year]

As the land cannot be written up above $10 000, $364 of the $764 that was allocated to it must be reallocated to the plant. This would increase the carrying amount of the plant to $28 000 (being $27 636 + $364). This is still less than the maximum of $30 000. The journal entry to record the reversal of the impairment loss is:

Land	Dr	400	
Accumulated Depreciation and Impairment Loss – Plant	Dr	2 400	
Income – Reversal of Impairment Loss	Cr		2 800
(Reversal of impairment loss)			

15.7 DISCLOSURE

Paragraph 126 of IAS 36 requires the following disclosures for each class of assets:

(a) the amount of impairment losses recognised in profit or loss during the period and the line item(s) of the statement of comprehensive income in which those impairment losses are included;

(b) the amount of reversals of impairment losses recognised in profit or loss during the period and the line item(s) of the statement of comprehensive income in which those impairment losses are reversed;

(c) the amount of impairment losses on revalued assets recognised in other comprehensive income during the period; and

(d) the amount of reversals of impairment losses on revalued assets recognised in other comprehensive income during the period.

As noted in chapter 11, paragraph 73(e) of IAS 16 *Property, Plant and Equipment* requires, in relation to the reconciliation of the carrying amount at the beginning and end of the period for each class of property, plant and equipment, disclosure of:

• increases or decreases during the period resulting from impairment losses recognised or reversed in other comprehensive income

• impairment losses recognised in profit or loss during the period

• impairment losses reversed in profit or loss during the period.

Similar disclosures are required for intangibles under paragraph 118 of IAS 38 *Intangible Assets* for each class of intangible asset.

As paragraph 128 of IAS 36 states, the disclosures required by paragraph 126 may be presented or included in a reconciliation of the carrying amount of assets at the beginning and end of the period. *(Such disclosures were illustrated in chapter 11.)* For parts (a) and (b) of paragraph 126, disclosure is required of the relevant line item(s) used. If these were included in other expenses or other income then information relating to impairment losses or reversals would be required in the note to the statement of profit or loss and other comprehensive income relating to these line items in the statement of profit or loss and other comprehensive income.

Paragraph 129 of IAS 36 details information to be disclosed for each reportable segment where an entity applies IFRS 8 *Operating Segments*.

Paragraph 133 of IAS 36 requires disclosures in relation to any goodwill that has not been allocated to a cash-generating unit at the end of the reporting period. In particular, an entity must disclose the amount of the unallocated goodwill and the reasons that amount has not been allocated to the cash-generating units in the entity.

Because the calculation of recoverable amount requires assumptions and estimates relating to future cash flows, IAS 36 requires disclosures relating to the calculation of recoverable amount. Paragraph 132 encourages, but does not require, disclosure of *key assumptions* used to determine the recoverable amounts of assets or cash-generating units.

Paragraph 134 of IAS 36 requires disclosures about the *estimates* used to measure the recoverable amount of a cash-generating unit when goodwill or an intangible asset with an indefinite life is included in the carrying amount of the unit, and the carrying amount of goodwill or intangible assets with indefinite useful lives allocated to that unit is *significant* in comparison with the entity's total carrying amount of goodwill or intangible assets with indefinite useful lives. Where the carrying amount of goodwill or intangible assets is not significant for a unit, paragraph 135 requires that fact to be disclosed. If, for a number of such units, the recoverable amounts are based on the same key assumptions and the aggregate carrying amount of goodwill or intangible assets with indefinite lives is significant in comparison to the total for the entity, paragraph 135 requires similar, but not as extensive, disclosures to those in paragraph 134.

SUMMARY

It is important that users of financial statements can rely on the information provided. In particular they need to be assured that the assets in the statement of financial position are not stated at amounts greater than an entity could expect to recover from those assets. It needs to be recognised that an entity can obtain cash flows from two sources in relation to any asset: (1) by using the asset or (2) by selling the asset. One of these involves an ongoing use of the asset whereas the other relates to an immediate sale of the asset. Any test of the carrying amounts of assets against their recoverable amounts must take both sources of cash flows into account.

For an entity to conduct an impairment test, there must be indications of impairment. Entities then need to continuously obtain information about factors that may indicate that assets are impaired. These sources of information may consist of an analysis of economic factors external to the organisation, such as actions of competitors, or economic factors within the entity itself, such as the performance of the entity's property, plant and equipment over time. When there are indications of impairment, an entity conducts an impairment test, comparing the carrying amounts of relevant assets and their recoverable amounts. The latter involves measurement of value in use and fair value less costs of disposal.

In many cases, single assets do not produce cash flows for the entity. Instead, the assets of the entity are allocated to units, called cash-generating units, as each unit produces independent cash flows for an entity. In such cases, impairment tests are conducted on the cash-generating units, rather than on individual assets. Where an impairment loss occurs, the loss must be allocated across the assets of the unit, with goodwill being the first asset affected. Where corporate assets such as research facilities exist, it may be necessary to combine a number of cash-generating units together in order to test for impairment of the corporate asset.

Having written down assets as a result of impairment tests, entities may see potential improvement in the recoverable amounts of assets by observing the same indicators used for detecting impairment losses. In such cases, where the recoverable amounts of assets have increased, impairment losses may be reversed, subject to constraints. Impairment losses relating to goodwill, however, can never be reversed.

DEMONSTRATION PROBLEM 15.1 Impairment losses, no corporate assets

Eastern Ltd has two divisions, Kamal and Katherine, each of which is a separate cash-generating unit (CGU). Eastern Ltd adopts a decentralised management approach whereby unit managers are expected to operate their units. However, there is one corporate asset, the information technology network, which is centrally controlled and provides a computer network to the company as a whole. The information technology network is not a depreciable asset.

At 31 December 2016 the net assets of each division, including its allocated share of the information technology network, were as follows:

	Kamal	Katherine
Information technology (IT) network	$ 284 000	$ 116 000
Land	450 000	290 000
Plant (20% p.a. straight-line depreciation)	1 310 000	960 000
Accumulated depreciation (plant)	(917 000)	(384 000)
Goodwill	46 000	32 000
Patent (10% straight-line amortisation)	210 000	255 000
Accumulated amortisation (patent)	(21 000)	(102 000)
Cash	20 000	12 000
Inventory	120 000	80 000
Receivables	34 000	40 000
	1 536 000	1 299 000
Liabilities	(276 000)	(189 000)
Net assets	$1 260 000	$1 110 000

Additional information as at 31 December 2016:
- Kamal's land had a fair value less costs of disposal of $437 000.
- Katherine's patent had a carrying amount below fair value less costs of disposal.
- Katherine's plant had a fair value less costs of disposal of $540 000.
- Receivables were considered to be collectable.
- The IT network is not depreciated, as it is assumed to have an indefinite life.

Eastern Ltd's management undertook impairment testing at 31 December 2016 and determined the recoverable amount of each cash-generating unit to be: $1 430 000 for Kamal and $1 215 000 for Katherine.

Required

Prepare any journal entries necessary to record the results of the impairment testing for each of the CGUs.

Solution

The first step is to determine whether either CGU has an impairment loss. This is done by comparing the carrying amount of the assets of each CGU with the recoverable amount of these assets. Note that it is the carrying amount of the assets not the net assets that is used — the test is for the impairment of assets, not net assets.

	Kamal	Katherine
Carrying amount of assets	$1 536 000	$1 299 000
Recoverable amount	1 430 000	1 215 000
Impairment loss	$ (106 000)	$ (84 000)

As a result of the comparison, both CGUs have suffered impairment losses.

For each CGU, the impairment loss is used to write off any goodwill and then to allocate any balance across the other assets in proportion to their carrying amounts.

Kamal CGU

Kamal has goodwill of $46 000. Therefore, the first step is to write off goodwill of $46 000.

The second step is to allocate the remaining impairment loss of $60 000 (i.e. $106 000 − $46 000). Note that although all the assets are included in the calculation to determine whether the CGU has incurred an impairment loss, the allocation of that loss is only to those assets that will be written down as a result of the allocation process. Cash and receivables are not written down as they are recorded at amounts equal to fair value. The inventory is recorded under IAS 2 at the lower of cost and net realisable value, and as such is excluded from the impairment test write-down under IAS 36. The allocation of the balance of the impairment loss is done on a pro rata basis, in proportion to the assets' carrying amounts.

	Carrying amount	Proportion	Allocation of loss	Adjusted carrying amount
IT network	$ 284 000	284/1 316	$12 948	$271 052
Land	450 000	450/1 316	20 517	429 483
Plant	393 000	393/1 316	17 918	375 082
Patent	189 000	189/1 316	8 617	180 383
	$1 316 000		$60 000	

After the initial allocation across the assets, a check has to be made on the amount of each write-down as IAS 36 places limitations on the amount to which assets can be written down. Paragraph 105 of IAS 36 states that for each asset the carrying amount should not be reduced below the highest of the following:

- its fair value less costs of disposal
- its value in use
- zero.

In this example, the land has a fair value less costs of disposal of $437 000. Hence it cannot be written down to $429 483 as per the above allocation table. Only $13 000 (to write the asset down from $450 000 to $437 000) of the impairment loss can be allocated to it. Therefore, the remaining $7517 allocated loss (i.e. $20 517 − $13 000) must be allocated to the other assets. This allocation is based on the adjusted carrying amounts, the right-hand column of the table above.

	Carrying amount	Proportion	Allocation of loss	Adjusted carrying amount
IT Network	$271 052	271 052/826 517	$2 465	$268 587
Plant	375 082	375 082/826 517	3 411	371 671
Patent	180 383	180 383/826 517	1 641	178 742
	$826 517		$7 517	

The impairment loss for each asset is then based, where relevant, on the accumulation of both allocations. With non-depreciable assets such as land, the asset is simply written down, whereas with depreciable assets such as plant, the account increased is the Accumulated Depreciation and Impairment losses account.

The journal entry for Kamal is:

Impairment Loss	Dr	106 000	
Goodwill	Cr		46 000
Land	Cr		13 000
IT Network [$12 948 + $2 465]	Cr		15 413
Accumulated Depreciation and Impairment Losses – Plant [$17 918 + $3 411]	Cr		21 329
Accumulated Depreciation and Impairment Losses – Patent [$8 617 + $1 641]	Cr		10 258

Katherine CGU

As with the Kamal CGU, the impairment loss is used to write off the goodwill balance, $32 000, and then the balance of the impairment loss, $52 000 (i.e. $84 000 − $32 000), is allocated across the remaining assets, except for cash, receivables and inventory. Further, as the patent's carrying amount is below fair value less costs of disposal, no impairment loss can be allocated to it.

	Carrying amount	Proportion	Allocation of loss	Adjusted carrying amount
IT network	$116 000	116/982	$ 6 143	$109 857
Land	290 000	290/982	15 356	274 644
Plant	576 000	576/982	30 501	545 499
	$982 000		$52 000	

Because the plant has a fair value less costs of disposal of $540 000 and this is below the adjusted carrying amount of $545 499, the full impairment loss of $30 501 can be allocated to it.

The journal entry for Katherine is:

Impairment Loss	Dr	84 000	
Goodwill	Cr		32 000
IT Network	Cr		6 143
Land	Cr		15 356
Accumulated Depreciation and Impairment Losses – Plant	Cr		30 501

Parkes Ltd has three CGUs, a head office and a research facility. The carrying amounts of the assets and their recoverable amounts are as follows:

	Unit A	Unit B	Unit C	Head office	Research facility	Parkes Ltd
Carrying amount	$100	$150	$200	$150	$50	$650
Recoverable amount	129	164	271			584

The assets of the head office are allocable to the three units as follows:
• Unit A: $19
• Unit B: $56
• Unit C: $75
The assets of the research facility cannot be reasonably allocated to the CGUs.

Required

Assuming all assets can be adjusted for impairment, prepare the journal entry relating to any impairment of the assets of Parkes Ltd.

Solution

For each unit there needs to be a comparison between the carrying amounts of the assets of the units and their recoverable amounts to determine which, if any, of the CGUs is impaired. As the asset of the head office can be allocated to each of the units, the carrying amounts of each of the units must then include the allocated part of the head office.

Calculation of impairment losses for units

	Unit A	Unit B	Unit C
Carrying amount	$119	$206	$275
Recoverable amount	129	164	271
Impairment loss	$ —	$ 42	$ 4

Because the assets of Unit A are not impaired, no write-down is necessary. For Units B and C, the impairment losses must be allocated to the assets of the units. The allocation is in proportion to the carrying amounts of the assets.

Allocation of impairment loss

	Unit B		Unit C	
To head office	$11	[42 × 56/206]	$1	[4 × 75/275]
To other assets	31	[42 × 150/206]	3	[4 × 200/275]
	$42		$4	

In relation to the research centre, the assets of the centre cannot be allocated to the units, so the impairment test is based on the smallest CGU that contains the research centre, which in this case is the entity as a whole, Parkes Ltd. For this calculation, the carrying amounts of the assets of the units as well as the head office are reduced by the impairment losses already allocated. The total assets of Parkes Ltd consist of all the assets of the entity.

Impairment testing for CGU as a whole

	Unit A	Unit B	Unit C	Head office	Research centre	Parkes Ltd
Carrying amount	100	150	200	150	50	650
Impairment loss	–	31	3	12	—	46
Net	100	119	197	138	50	604
Recoverable amount						584
Impairment loss						20

Because the carrying amount of the assets of Parkes Ltd is greater than the recoverable amount of the entity, the entity has incurred an impairment loss. This loss is allocated across all the assets of the entity in proportion to their carrying amounts.

Allocation of impairment loss

	Carrying amount	Proportion	Allocation of loss	Adjusted carrying amount
Unit A	$100	100/604 × 20	$ 3	$ 97
Unit B	119	119/604 × 20	4	116
Unit C	197	197/604 × 20	6	191
Head office	138	138/604 × 20	5	132
Research centre	50	50/604 × 20	2	48
	$604		$20	

Journal entry for impairment loss

The journal entry for the impairment loss recognises the reduction in each of the assets. As the composition of the assets is not detailed in this question, the credit adjustments are made against the asset accounts. They could also have been made against an Accumulated Depreciation and Impairment losses account. Obviously if the composition of each of the assets of each unit had been given, the impairment loss would have been allocated to specific assets rather than assets as a total category as in the solution here.

Impairment Loss	Dr	66	
Assets – Unit A	Cr		3
Assets – Unit B	Cr		34
Assets – Unit C	Cr		9
Assets – Head Office	Cr		18
Assets – Research Facility	Cr		2

Discussion questions

1. What is an impairment test?
2. Why is an impairment test considered necessary?
3. When should an entity conduct an impairment test?
4. What are some external indicators of impairment?
5. What are some internal indicators of impairment?
6. What is meant by recoverable amount?
7. How is an impairment loss calculated in relation to a single asset accounted for?
8. What are the limits to which an asset can be written down in relation to impairment losses?
9. What is a cash-generating unit?
10. How are impairment losses accounted for in relation to cash-generating units?
11. Are there limits in adjusting assets within a cash-generating unit when impairment losses occur?
12. How is goodwill tested for impairment?
13. What is a corporate asset?
14. How are corporate assets tested for impairment?
15. When can an entity reverse past impairment losses?
16. What are the steps involved in reversing an impairment loss?

References

Amcor Ltd 2014, *Annual Report 2014*, Amcor Limited, Australia, www.amcor.com.au.
European Financial Reporting Advisory Group 2003, *Comments of EFRAG on Exposure Draft 3 Business Combinations*, 4 April, p. 10, www.iasplus.com.
Lafarge Malaysia Berhad 2014, *Annual Report 2014*, www.lafarge.com.my.
Nokia Corporation 2014, *Nokia in 2014*, Nokia Corporation, Finland, www.nokia.com.

Exercises

Exercise 15.1
CASH-GENERATING UNITS

★ Fresh Milk Ltd owns a large number of dairy farms. It has a number of factories that are used to produce milk products that are then sent to other factories to be converted into milk-based products such as yoghurt and custard. In applying IAS 36 *Impairment of Assets*, the accountant for Fresh Milk Ltd is concerned about correctly identifying the cash-generating units (CGUs) for the company, and has sought your advice on such questions as to whether the milk production section is a separate CGU even though the company does not sell milk directly to other parties, or whether it should be included in the milk-based products CGU.

Required

Write a report to the accountant of Fresh Milk Ltd, including the following:
1. Define a CGU.
2. Explain why impairment testing requires the use of CGUs, rather than being based on single assets.
3. Explain the factors that the accountant should consider in determining the CGUs for Fresh Milk Ltd.

Exercise 15.2
IMPAIRMENT TESTING AND GOODWILL

★ At 30 June 2016, Longreach Ltd is considering undertaking an impairment test. Having only recently adopted the international accounting standards, the management of Longreach Ltd seeks your advice in relation to this test under IAS 36 *Impairment of Assets*.

Required

Write a report to management, specifically explaining:
1. the purpose of the impairment test
2. how the existence of goodwill will affect the impairment test
3. the basic steps to be followed in applying the impairment test.

Exercise 15.3
FREQUENCY OF IMPAIRMENT TEST

★ In setting up its systems to apply IAS 36 *Impairment of Assets*, management of Durban Ltd wants to know how often the company needs to apply an impairment test on its assets, and what information it needs to generate to determine whether a test is needed.

Required

Prepare a response to management.

Exercise 15.4
IMPAIRMENT LOSS

★ Tambo Ltd has determined that its fine china division is a cash-generating unit. The carrying amounts of the assets at 30 June 2016 are as follows:

Factory	$ 210 000
Land	150 000
Equipment	120 000
Inventory	60 000

Tambo Ltd calculated the recoverable amount of the division to be $510 000.

Required

Provide the journal entry(ies) for the impairment loss, assuming that the fair value less costs of disposal of the land are (a) $140 000 and (b) $145 000.

Exercise 15.5
IDENTIFICATION OF CGUS

★★ Burger Queen is a chain of fast-food restaurants — most reasonably sized towns in the country have a Burger Queen outlet. The key claim to fame of the Burger Queen restaurants is that their fried chips are extra crunchy. Also, to ensure that there is a consistent standard of food and service across the country, the management of the chain of restaurants conducts spot checks on restaurants. Failure to provide the high standard expected by Burger Queen management can mean that the franchise to a particular location can be taken away from the franchisee. Burger Queen management is responsible for the television advertising across the country as well as the marketing program, including the special deals that may be available at any particular time.

Each restaurant is responsible for its own sales, cooking of food, training of staff, and general matters such as cleanliness of the store. However, all material used in the making of the burgers and other items sold are provided at a given cost from the central management, which can thereby control the quality and the price.

Required

Identify the cash-generating unit(s) in this scenario. Give reasons for your conclusions.

Exercise 15.6	**IDENTIFICATION OF CGUS**

★★ Marla Macalister is in the business of making rubber tubing that comes in all sorts of sizes and shapes. Marla has established three factories in the north, south and east parts of the city. Each factory has a large machine that can be adjusted to produce all the varieties of tubing that Marla sells. Each machine is capable of producing around 100 000 metres of tubing a week, depending on diameter and shape. Marla's current sales amount to about 250 000 metres a week. Each factory is never worked to full capacity. However, sales are sufficiently high that Marla cannot afford to shut one of the factories.

In order to satisfy customer demand as quickly as possible, all orders are directed to Marla, who allocates the jobs to the various factories depending on the current workload of each factory. This also ensures that efficient runs of particular types of tubing can be done at the same time. Each factory is managed individually in terms of maintenance of the machines, the hiring of labour and the packaging and delivery of the finished product.

Required

Identify the cash-generating unit(s) in this scenario. Give reasons for your conclusions.

Exercise 15.7	**VALUE IN USE**

★★ Management is assessing the future cash flows in relation to an entity's assets, and considers that there are two possible scenarios for future cash flows. The first, for which there is a 70% probability of occurrence, would provide future cash flows of $5 million. The second, which has a probability of occurrence of 30%, would provide future cash flows of $8 million. Management has decided that the calculation of value in use should be based on the most likely scenario, namely the one that will produce cash flows of $5 million.

Required

Evaluate management's decision.

Exercise 15.8	**15.8 WRITE-DOWN**

★★ Joburg Enterprises Ltd acquired a building in which to conduct its operations at a cost of $10 million. The building generates no cash flows on its own and is considered a part of the cash-generating unit, which is the firm as a whole. Since the building was acquired, the value of inner-city properties has declined owing to an overabundance of office space and the downturn in the economy. The company would receive only $8 million dollars if it decided to sell the building now. However, the company believes the building is serving its purpose and the profits are high, so there is no current intention of selling the building.

Required

Discuss whether the building should be written down to $8 million. Provide any journal entries necessary.

Exercise 15.9	**ASSET IMPAIRMENT**

★★ Parkes Ltd acquired a network facility for its administration section on 1 July 2014. The network facility cost $550 000 and was depreciated using a straight-line method over a 5-year period, with a residual value of $50 000. On 30 June 2016, the company assessed the current market value of the facility given that there was an active market for such facilities as many companies used a similar network. The value was determined to be $300 000.

Required

Discuss whether the network facility asset is impaired and whether it should be written down to $300 000. Provide any journal entries necessary.

Exercise 15.10	**ALLOCATION OF CORPORATE ASSETS AND GOODWILL**

★★ Cheng Ltd acquired all the assets and liabilities of Roma Ltd on 1 January 2017. Roma Ltd's activities were run through three separate businesses, namely the Sandstone Unit, the Sapphire Unit and the Silverton Unit. These units are separate cash-generating units. Cheng Ltd allowed unit managers to effectively operate each of the units, but certain central activities were run through the corporate office. Each unit was allocated a share of the goodwill acquired, as well as a share of the corporate office.

At 31 December 2017, the assets allocated to each unit were as follows:

	Sandstone	Sapphire	Silverton
Factory	$ 820	$ 750	$ 460
Accumulated depreciation	(420)	(380)	(340)
Land	200*	300**	150*
Equipment	300	410	560
Accumulated depreciation	(60)	(320)	(310)
Inventory	120	80	100*
Goodwill	40	50	30
Corporate property	200	150	120

* These assets have carrying amounts less than fair value less costs of disposal.
** This asset has a fair value less costs of disposal of $293.

Cheng Ltd determined the recoverable amount of each of the business units at 31 December 2017:

Sandstone	$1 170
Sapphire	900
Silverton	800

Required

Determine how Cheng Ltd should allocate any impairment loss at 31 December 2017.

Exercise 15.11

ALLOCATION OF CORPORATE ASSETS AND GOODWILL

★★★ Liao Ltd has two cash-generating units, Division One and Division Two. At 30 June 2017, the net assets of the two divisions were as follows:

	Division One	Division Two
Cash	$ 12 000	$ 8 000
Inventory	30 000	40 000
Receivables	20 000	8 000
Plant	320 000	0
Accumulated depreciation (Plant)	(120 000)	0
Land	90 000	150 000
Buildings	110 000	140 000
Accumulated depreciation (Buildings)	(40 000)	(60 000)
Furniture & fittings	0	30 000
Accumulated depreciation (Furniture & fittings)	0	(10 000)
Total assets	422 000	306 000
Provisions	20 000	40 000
Borrowings	30 000	66 000
Total liabilities	50 000	106 000
Net assets	$ 372 000	$ 200 000

Additional information regarding the divisions' assets is as follows:
- the receivables of both divisions were considered to be collectable
- Division Two's land had a fair value less costs of disposal of $135 000 at 30 June 2017.

At 30 June 2017 Liao Ltd also had the following corporate assets, which Liao's management decided to allocate equally to the two divisions:
- goodwill of $14 000
- a head office building with a carrying amount of $160 000 (net of $50 000 accumulated depreciation).

Liao Ltd's management conducted impairment testing on the company's assets at 30 June 2017 and determined that Division One's recoverable amount was $415 000 and Division Two's recoverable amount was $310 000.

Required

Prepare the journal entries required at 30 June 2017 to account for any impairment losses.

CORPORATE ASSETS, ALLOCATED AND UNALLOCATED

★★★   Ararat Ltd has three divisions, Aramac, Alpha and Amby, which operate independently of each other to produce milk products. The company has a headquarters and a research centre located in Albury, with the divisions located throughout South Africa. The research centre interacts with all the divisions to assist in the improvement of the manufacturing process and the quality of the products manufactured by the entity.

There is not as yet any basis on which to determine how the work of the research centre will be allocated to each of the three divisions, as this will depend on priorities of the company overall and issues that arise in each division. The company headquarters provides approximately equal services to each of the divisions, but an immaterial amount to the research centre.

Neither the headquarters nor the research centre generates cash inflows.

On 30 June 2017, the net assets of Ararat Ltd were as follows:

	Aramac	Alpha	Amby	Head office	Research centre
Land	$ 440 000	$ 280 000	$ 160 000	$110 000	$ 67 000
Plant & equipment	840 000	620 000	540 000	80 000	45 000
Accumulated depreciation	(240 000)	(200 000)	(160 000)	(10 000)	(12 000)
Inventories	240 000	180 000	140 000	0	0
Accounts receivable	120 000	100 000	60 000	0	0
	$1 400 000	$ 980 000	$ 740 000	$180 000	$100 000
Liabilities	120 000	100 000	100 000	0	0
Net assets	$1 280 000	$ 880 000	$ 640 000	$180 000	$100 000

Management of Ararat Ltd believes there are economic indicators to suggest that the company's assets may have been impaired. Accordingly, they have had recoverable amount assessed for each of the divisions:

Aramac	$ 1 550 000
Alpha	1 000 000
Amby	750 000

The land held by Aramac Ltd was measured at fair value using the revaluation model because of the specialised nature of the land. At 30 June 2017, the fair value was $440 000. The land held by Alpha Ltd was measured at cost, and had a fair value less costs of disposal of $270 264 at 30 June 2017.

Required

Determine how Ararat Ltd should account for any impairment of the entity. Justify your decisions and complete any required journal entries.

IMPAIRMENT LOSS

★★★   Casey Ltd prepared the following draft statement of financial position at 30 June 2017:

Cash	$ 5 000	Share capital	$1 000 000
Receivables	15 000	Retained earnings	280 000
Land (at fair value 1/7/16)	160 000	General reserve	120 000
Company headquarters	1 000 000		1 400 000
Accumulated depreciation	(180 000)	Long-term loans	400 000
Factories	1 790 000	Provisions	40 000
Accumulated depreciation	(910 000)	Other liabilities	160 000
Goodwill	60 000		600 000
Accumulated impairment losses	(40 000)		
Intangibles	150 000		
Accumulated amortisation	(50 000)		
Total assets	2 000 000	Equity and liabilities	2 000 000

At the end of the reporting period, after undertaking an analysis, management determined that it was probable that the assets of the entity were impaired. Management conducted an impairment test, determining that the recoverable amount for the entity's assets was $1 820 000. The whole entity was regarded as a cash-generating unit.

Land is measured by Casey Ltd at fair value, while all other assets are accounted for by the cost model. At 30 June 2017, the fair value of the land was determined to be $150 000. The land had previously been revalued upwards by $20 000. The tax rate is 30%.

Required

(Show all workings.)

1. Prepare the journal entries required on 30 June 2017 in relation to the measurement of the assets of Casey Ltd.
2. Assume that, as the result of the allocation of the impairment loss, the factories were to be written down to $800 000. If the fair value less costs of disposal of the factories was determined to be $750 000, outline the adjustments, if any, that would need to be made to the journal entries you prepared in requirement 1, and explain why adjustments are or are not required.

The two main types of impairment examined in accounting research are of long-term tangible assets and goodwill. We start with long-term tangible assets. Bartov et al. (1998) examine the market reaction to announcements of these impairments. Like research findings before them they observe that the stock market reaction seems to be small relative to the magnitude of recorded impairments. One possible explanation for this is that the recording of the impairment is delayed relative to the underlying economic loss event. If this is the case, then the market might have reacted beforehand and so the accounting impairment conveys no new information. Another explanation may be that markets do not initially fully comprehend the significance of the impairment. To explore these explanations Bartov et al. (1998) examine 373 impairments during the 1981–1985 period. For impairments recorded in the context of business changes (e.g., restructuring) they do not find significant market reactions, but for other impairments they document negative stock return during a 4-day window around the impairment announcement. Nevertheless, all impairment-announcing firms experience a decline in stock prices in the 2 years leading up to the announcement. This evidence therefore suggests that markets reacted to the underlying economic events before the recording of the loss in the books. Interestingly, the trend in falling prices continues for an additional year following the impairment announcement. Hence the evidence suggests both that the loss recognition is delayed relative to the underlying economic event and that it is not fully assessed by market participants.

Alciatore et al. (2000) examine write-downs in a specific industry — the oil and gas industry — and provide interesting evidence that pertains to the delay in loss recognition. Companies in this industry who trade on a US exchange are required to compare the cost of wells recorded on the balance sheet to the present value of future cash flows, which in this industry are closely tied to oil prices. Thus the economic loss event is clearly identifiable. Focusing on the period of 1984 to mid-1988 when oil and gas prices declined, the authors provide evidence that the recording of the write-downs takes place after the decline in oil and gas prices. This is broadly consistent with managerial incentive to delay recognition of bad news (Kothari et al., 2009).

Riedl (2004) further explores the link between impairments and underlying economic factors. He postulates that the quality of recorded impairments should be judged with respect to whether they capture the effect of underlying economic factors. He employs several proxies for economic factors, including changes in GDP, change in industry ROA, and change in sales. His sample is based on over 2750 firm-year observations including 455 firm-year observations with impairment charges (including impairments of goodwill). Some of these impairments were recorded following the implementation of SFAS 121 (FASB, 1995) in the US, which is similar to IAS 36 in many respects. In his sample, impairment firms generally perform worse than non-impairment firms. His most intriguing result, however, is that whereas impairments are related to economic factors pre-SFAS 121, they are not in the post-standard period. As Riedl (2004) points out, the aim of the standard was to reduce the level of discretion that was available to managers before SFAS 121. His evidence therefore suggests that the standard did not succeed in curtailing managerial discretion.

Turning to studies of goodwill, Henning et al. (2000) provide evidence consistent with the view that goodwill is an asset (see also the Academic Perspective to chapter 14). Specifically, they regress market value of equity on goodwill and other assets and liabilities and find that goodwill is positively related to the firm's market value. This positive association indicates that capital markets perceive goodwill as an asset. Hayn and Hughes (2006) turn attention to impairments by attempting to quantify the delay in such impairments. They identify 58 companies who had impaired goodwill 6 or more years after the acquisition. Hayn and Hughes (2006) then provide evidence of unusual poor performance by the acquirers of up to 5 years before the impairment is recognised. This evidence therefore suggests that impairments of goodwill are recorded with considerable delay.

One possible underlying reason for goodwill impairments is that the acquiring firms overpay for target firms in the first place. This is more likely in cases where the acquisition is financed by the acquirer's own shares. Gu and Lev (2011) argue that the overpayment problem is more pronounced when the acquirer's stock is overpriced itself. They develop an index that captures the overpricing of the acquirer's stock. The index is based on three underlying measures, including industry-adjusted price-to-earnings ratio, discretionary accruals, and net equity issues. They then employ a large sample for 1990–2006 including 7055 acquisitions and show that stock-funded acquisitions are associated with larger increases in recorded goodwill than cash-funded acquisitions. The difference in recorded goodwill between stock- and cash-bidders becomes larger with the measure of overpricing of the acquirers' own stock. Gu and Lev (2011) then examine goodwill impairments recorded in 2001–2006 for firms that were involved in acquisition activity in 1990–2000. They find that the magnitude of the impairment is positively related to the overpricing of the acquirers' own stock.

Impairment of goodwill is based on managers' estimates of the underlying cash flows that the cash-generating unit is expected to produce in the future. This estimate is largely subject to managerial discretion. Ramanna and Watts (2012) examine a sample of firms for which the book-to-market (BM) ratio is greater than 1 for 2 consecutive years. The authors argue that goodwill impairment is more likely in such firms as the market-based value of goodwill is negative. Hence, firms that exhibit BM > 1 for 2 consecutive years may be avoiding recognising impairments. One reason for this could be because managers of these firms expect improvement in future performance that would negate the need to impair goodwill. That is, these managers possess good news not known to investors. Ramanna and Watts (2012) proxy for insider good news is insider purchase of own stock. However, they do not find that insider purchase of own stock is at a different level than of insiders of firms that do recognise goodwill impairments. The authors therefore conclude that delayed impairments of goodwill are not owed to impending good news.

Taken together, the literature reviewed here suggests that impairments are prone to significant managerial discretion. This is manifested in delayed recording of impairments, impairments that are divorced from underlying economic events, and in the case of goodwill, these impairments are predictable insofar as they are more likely to take place in stock-for-stock acquisitions where the acquirer's stock is overpriced.

References

Alciatore, M., Easton, P., and Spear, N. 2000. Accounting for the impairment of long-lived assets: Evidence from the petroleum industry. *Journal of Accounting and Economics*, 29(2), 151–172.

Bartov, E., Lindahl, F. W., and Ricks, W. E. 1998. Stock price behavior around announcements of write-offs. *Review of Accounting Studies*, 3(4), 327–346.

Financial Accounting Standards Board (FASB). 1995. Accounting for the impairment of long-lived assets and for long-lived assets to be disposed of. SFAS No. 121. Norwalk, CT: FASB.

Gu, F., and Lev, B. 2011. Overpriced shares, ill-advised acquisitions, and goodwill impairment. *The Accounting Review*, 86(6), 1995–2022.

Hayn, C., and Hughes, P. J. 2006. Leading indicators of goodwill impairment. *Journal of Accounting, Auditing & Finance*, 21(3), 223–265.

Henning, S. L., Lewis, B. L., and Shaw, W. H. 2000. Valuation of the components of purchased goodwill. *Journal of Accounting Research*, 38(2), 375–386.

Kothari, S., Shu, S., and Wysocki, P. 2009. Do managers withhold bad news? *Journal of Accounting Research* 47(1), 241–276.

Ramanna, K., and Watts, R. L. 2012. Evidence on the use of unverifiable estimates in required goodwill impairment. *Review of Accounting Studies*, 17(4), 749–780.

Riedl, E. J. 2004. An examination of long-lived asset impairments. *The Accounting Review*, 79(3), 823–852.

Part 3

Presentation and disclosures

16 Financial statement presentation   449
17 Statement of cash flows   485
18 Operating segments   517
19 Other key notes disclosures   537

16 Financial statement presentation

ACCOUNTING STANDARDS IN FOCUS

IAS 1 *Presentation of Financial Statements*

IAS 8 *Accounting Policies, Changes in Accounting Estimates and Errors*

IAS 10 *Events after the Reporting Period*

LEARNING OBJECTIVES

After studying this chapter, you should be able to:

1. describe the main components of financial statements

2. explain the general principles underlying the preparation and presentation of financial statements

3. apply the requirements for the classification of items reported in the statement of financial position, and apply the requirements for the presentation of information in the statement of financial position and/or in the notes

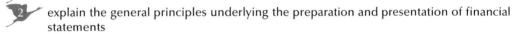

4. apply the requirements for the presentation of information in the statement of profit or loss and other comprehensive income and/or in the notes

5. apply the requirements for the presentation of information in the statement of changes in equity and/or in the notes

6. discuss other disclosures required by IAS 1 in the notes to the financial statements

7. apply the requirements of IAS 8 regarding the selection and application of accounting policies, and in respect of accounting for changes in accounting policies, changes in accounting estimates and errors

8. distinguish between adjusting and non-adjusting events after the reporting period in accordance with IAS 10.

INTRODUCTION

You are probably already familiar with financial statements. In this chapter we will build on your existing knowledge as we take a closer look at the requirements of IFRS® Standards for dealing with some complex and technical issues in the presentation of financial statements. You have probably noticed that current and non-current assets and liabilities are usually separately identified in the statement of financial position. Do they have to be classified this way? How do preparers decide whether an asset should be classified as current or non-current? Why is there so much variation in the way that companies report on profit and comprehensive income? What should preparers do if they realise there has been an error in the financial statements of previous periods? How should entities account for changes of accounting policies and accounting estimates? If events occur after the end of the reporting period, can they be reflected in the financial statements? IFRS Standards are principles-based accounting standards. In this chapter we will consider the principles that underlie the preparation of general purpose financial statements in order to provide information that is useful for creditors and investors and other users in making decisions about providing resources to the entity.

 ## 16.1 COMPONENTS OF FINANCIAL STATEMENTS

The principles and other considerations relating to the presentation of financial statements are contained in IAS 1 *Presentation of Financial Statements*. A complete set of financial statements is defined in paragraph 10 and comprises:
- a statement of financial position
- a statement of profit or loss and other comprehensive income
- a statement of changes in equity
- a statement of cash flows
- notes, comprising significant accounting policies and other explanatory information
- comparative information, such as financial statements and notes for the preceding period, are also a component of a complete set of financial statements: when an entity retrospectively applies an accounting policy or makes retrospective adjustments to the amount or classification of items in financial statements, the complete set of financial statements includes a statement of financial position as at the beginning of the preceding period *(we will return to this requirement in section 16.7)*.

Each component of the financial statements must be clearly identified in the financial statements and distinguished from other information reported in the same document (IAS 1 paragraphs 49–51). While IAS 1 refers to the statements as a 'statement of financial position', a 'statement of profit or loss and other comprehensive income', a 'statement of changes in equity' and a 'statement of cash flows', reporting entities may use other labels when presenting these financial statements in accordance with IAS 1. For example, BHP Billiton labels its statement of financial position a 'balance sheet'.

Paragraph 51 requires identification of the following:
- name of the reporting entity and any change in that name since the preceding reporting period
- whether the financial statement covers an individual entity or a group of entities
- the date of the end of the reporting period (e.g. for a statement of financial position) or the reporting period covered by the financial statement (for reports on flows, such as the statement of profit or loss and other comprehensive income)
- the presentation currency, as defined in IAS 21 *The Effects of Changes in Foreign Exchange Rates*
- the level of rounding used in presenting amounts in the financial statements, usually thousands or millions.

Entities often present other information, such as certain financial ratios or a narrative review of operations by management or the directors. These reports are sometimes referred to as 'management discussion and analysis'. In addition, some entities voluntarily prepare sustainability reports or corporate social responsibility reports. This other information is reported outside the financial statements and is not within the scope of pronouncements issued by the International Accounting Standards Board (IASB®).

IAS 1 applies to all general purpose financial statements, except that its requirements relating to the structure and content of financial statements do not apply to condensed interim financial statements prepared in accordance with IAS 34 *Interim Financial Reporting*. This chapter deals with the requirements of IAS 1 for the presentation of the statement of financial position, the statement of profit or loss and other comprehensive income, the statement of changes in equity and notes. *(The statement of cash flows is considered in chapter 17.)* The requirements of IAS 8 *Accounting Policies, Changes in Accounting Estimates and Errors* and IAS 10 *Events after the Reporting Period* are also considered *(see sections 16.7 and 16.8, respectively)*.

In addition to the disclosure requirements covered in this chapter, IFRS Standards prescribe disclosures relating to specific financial statement elements and transactions and events. Specific disclosures relevant to the topics of the various chapters of this book are outlined in those chapters.

16.2 GENERAL PRINCIPLES OF FINANCIAL STATEMENTS

IAS 1 describes eight general principles that need to be applied in the presentation of financial statements. These requirements are intended to ensure that the financial statements of an entity are a faithful presentation of its financial position, financial performance and cash flows in accordance with the *Conceptual Framework (see chapter 1)*.

16.2.1 Fair presentation and compliance with IFRS Standards

Paragraph 15 of IAS 1 states that 'financial statements shall present fairly the financial position, financial performance and cash flows of an entity'. This means that the *Conceptual Framework*'s definitions and recognition criteria for assets, liabilities, equity, income and expenses should be applied in faithfully representing the effects of transactions, other events and conditions.

Does compliance with IFRS Standards result in financial statements that 'present fairly'? Paragraph 10 makes the explicit assumption that it does, subject to additional disclosures, when necessary. This is reiterated in paragraph 17, which states that compliance with IFRS Standards achieves fair presentation in virtually all circumstances. Fair presentation requires (paragraph 17):

- selecting and applying accounting policies in accordance with IAS 8 *(see section 16.7.1)*;
- presenting information in a way that provides relevant, reliable, comparable and understandable information; and
- providing additional disclosures, where necessary.

However, paragraph 19 of IAS 1 notes that, in extremely rare circumstances, management may conclude that compliance with the requirements of an IFRS Standard would be so misleading that it would conflict with the objective of financial statements specified in the *Conceptual Framework*. The reporting requirements that arise in this situation are considered later *(see section 16.6.1)*.

16.2.2 Going concern

Paragraph 25 of IAS 1 states that financial statements shall be prepared on a going concern basis unless management intends to either liquidate the entity or cease trading, or has no realistic alternative but to do so. The *Conceptual Framework* makes a similar underlying assumption. When management is aware of any material uncertainties that cast doubt upon the entity's ability to continue as a going concern, those uncertainties must be disclosed (IAS 1 paragraph 25). When financial statements are not prepared on a going concern basis, that fact must be disclosed, together with the basis on which the financial statements are prepared and the reason why the entity is not regarded as a going concern.

If, for example, an entity has been placed in receivership and it is anticipated that liquidation will follow, the going concern assumption would be inappropriate. In such circumstances, the financial statements would typically be prepared on a 'liquidation' basis, which means that assets and liabilities are measured at the amounts expected to be received or settled on liquidation. In the case of assets, this will often be a 'fire-sale' value rather than a fair value *(for discussion of fair value measurement, see chapter 3)*.

16.2.3 Accrual basis of accounting

Financial statements, except for the statement of cash flows, must be prepared using the accrual basis of accounting. This is discussed further in the *Conceptual Framework (see chapter 1)*.

16.2.4 Materiality and aggregation

Paragraph 7 of IAS 1 states:

> Omissions or misstatements of items are material if they could, individually or collectively, influence the economic decisions that users make on the basis of the financial statements.

Paragraph 7 goes on to explain that judgements about materiality should be made in the context of surrounding circumstances, taking into consideration the size and nature of the item.

Financial statements result from processing large volumes of transactions that are then aggregated into classes according to their nature or function. These classes form the line items on the statement of financial position, statement of profit or loss and other comprehensive income, statement of changes in equity, and statement of cash flows. Paragraph 29 requires separate presentation of each material class of similar items in the financial statements. As explained in paragraph 30A, an entity should not obscure material information by aggregating it with immaterial items because this practice would reduce the understandability of financial statements. Items of a dissimilar nature or function must be presented separately unless they are immaterial.

The minimum line items specified by IAS 1 are discussed later in the chapter *(see sections 16.3, 16.4 and 16.5)*. Paragraph 31 confirms that these minimum requirements and requirements for disclosures in the notes prescribed by IAS 1 and other IFRS Standards are subject to materiality.

16.2.5 Offsetting

- If certain assets and liabilities are offset in the statement of financial position, it means they are represented on a net basis. For example, if a receivable of $10 000 were offset against a payable of $25 000, a net liability of $15 000 would be reported. Paragraph 32 of IAS 1 states that an entity shall not offset assets and liabilities, or income and expenses, unless required or permitted by an IFRS Standard. For example, IAS 32 *Financial Instruments: Presentation* permits financial assets and liabilities to be offset if there is a legal right of set-off and the entities intend to settle amounts owed to/by each other on a net basis.
- Offsetting detracts from the understandability of financial statements unless it reflects the substance of transactions or events (paragraph 33). For example, in reporting on the disposal of a non-current asset, it is usually appropriate to offset the carrying amount of the asset against the proceeds to report a net gain or loss. The application of offsetting is an area of considerable judgement and subjectivity.

16.2.6 Frequency of reporting

Financial statements must be prepared at least annually. If an entity's reporting period changes, the length of the reporting period will be greater or less than a year in the period of the change. For example, if an entity with a reporting period ending on 31 March changed its reporting period to end on 31 December, the first financial statements it prepares for the period ending 31 December would only cover a 9-month period. When this occurs, paragraph 36 of IAS 1 requires the entity to disclose why the reporting period is longer or shorter and the fact that the amounts presented in the financial statements are not entirely comparable.

16.2.7 Comparative information

IAS 1 paragraph 38 requires the disclosure of comparative information for the preceding period for all amounts reported in the financial statements, unless otherwise permitted by an IFRS Standard. This includes narrative information where it is relevant to understanding the current period financial statements. For example, comparative narrative details of a contingent liability that has developed over time may be relevant to users.

Presentation of additional comparative information beyond the minimum required is permitted provided that the additional information complies with IFRS Standards. For example, an entity may choose to provide a third statement of cash flows as an additional comparative statement.

Due to changed circumstances, or in order to provide a fair representation, an entity may change the classification of items reported in financial statements. For example, an entity may change the classification of a real estate asset from investment property to property, plant and equipment. If the presentation or classification of an item in the financial statements is changed, the entity must reclassify comparative amounts, to the extent practicable (IAS 1 paragraph 41). Further, the entity must present a statement of financial position for the end of the current period, the end of the preceding period, and the beginning of the previous period (IAS 1 paragraphs 40A and 40B). Thus in the event of a change in the presentation or classification of items presented in financial statements, at least three statements of financial position must be presented.

Additional comparative information must also be disclosed in the event of changes in accounting policies or corrections of errors. The accounting treatment of changes in accounting policies and correction of errors, including additional disclosure requirements for retrospective adjustments, are dealt with in IAS 8 (and addressed later in this chapter).

16.2.8 Consistency of presentation

Paragraph 45 of IAS 1 requires the presentation and classification of items in the financial statements to be consistent from one period to the next. However, this requirement does not apply where an IFRS Standard requires a change in presentation. A change in presentation is also permitted if there has been a significant change in the nature of the entity's operations and a change in presentation is considered appropriate using the criteria specified in IAS 8 for the selection of accounting policies.

When such a change is made, the comparative information must also be reclassified. For example, if, after a major change in operations, an entity elects to change the way it classifies expenses, the comparative financial information must also be reclassified.

16.3 STATEMENT OF FINANCIAL POSITION

As discussed in chapter 1, a major purpose of financial statements is to provide information about an entity's financial position. Accordingly, the statement of financial position summarises the elements directly related to the measurement of financial position: an entity's assets, liabilities and equity. It thus provides the basic information for evaluating an entity's capital structure and analysing its liquidity, solvency and financial flexibility. It also provides a basis for computing summary indicators, such as return on total assets and the ratio of liabilities to equity.

However, the view of an entity's financial position presented by the statement of financial position has some limitations arising from:

- the requirement or flexibility to measure certain assets at historical cost or depreciated historical cost instead of a current value, such as fair value *(see chapter 3 for further details)*
- the mandatory omission of certain internally generated intangible assets, such as internally generated brand names, from the statement of financial position in accordance with IAS 38 *Intangible Assets (see chapter 13 for further details)*
- off-balance-sheet rights and obligations — for example, the rights and obligations pertaining to non-cancellable operating leases are not recognised on the statement of financial position *(see chapter 12 for further details)*.

The notes to the financial statements are an important source of information that can mitigate the effects of these limitations.

16.3.1 Statement of financial position classifications

The statement of financial position presents a structured summary of the assets, liabilities and equity of an entity. To help users of financial statements to evaluate an entity's financial structure and its liquidity, solvency and financial flexibility, assets and liabilities are classified according to their function in the operations of the entity, and their liquidity and financial flexibility characteristics.

Paragraph 60 of IAS 1 requires an entity to classify assets and liabilities as current or non-current in its statement of financial position, unless a presentation based on liquidity is considered to provide more relevant and reliable information. When that exception arises, all assets and liabilities are required to be presented broadly in order of liquidity.

IAS 1 specifies criteria for classification of assets and liabilities as current. When an entity applies the current/non-current classification, assets and liabilities that do not meet the criteria for classification as current are classified as non-current.

Current assets are described in paragraph 66 of IAS 1 as those that:

(a) are expected to be realised, sold or consumed within the entity's normal operating cycle;

(b) are held for trading;

(c) are expected to be realised within 12 months after the reporting period; or

(d) are cash or cash equivalents.

For example, inventory is classified as current because it is expected to be sold within the entity's normal operating cycle.

Current liabilities are described in paragraph 69 of IAS 1 as those that:

(a) are expected to be settled within the entity's normal operating cycle;

(b) are held for trading;

(c) are due to be settled within 12 months after the reporting period; or

(d) the entity does not have an unconditional right to defer for at least 12 months after the reporting period.

Paragraph 73 of IAS 1 explains that if an entity has the discretion to refinance or roll over an obligation for at least 12 months after the reporting period under the terms of an existing loan facility, and expects to do so, the obligation is classified as non-current, even if it would otherwise be due within 12 months of the end of the reporting period. This would be an unconditional right referred to in paragraph 69(d). The criterion of an unconditional right to defer settlement has been a source of ambiguity in paragraph 69(d) resulting in uncertainty in the classification of liabilities that are subject to an annual review. At the time of writing the IASB has issued an exposure draft with proposed changes to the wording of this paragraph to reduce ambiguity.

The criteria for classifying liabilities as current or non-current are based solely on the conditions existing at the end of the reporting period. For example, if an entity had a long-term loan that fell due in August 2016 and entered into an agreement after 30 June 2016 to refinance or to reschedule payments on the loan, the liability would be classified as current in the statement of financial position at 30 June 2016. Similarly, paragraph 74 explains that if an entity breaches an undertaking under a long-term loan agreement during the reporting period with the effect that the loan is repayable on demand, the loan is classified as current. However, the loan should be classified as non-current if the lender agrees by the end of the reporting period to waive the right to demand immediate repayment for at least 12 months after the reporting period.

Figure 16.1 shows the classification of assets in the consolidated statement of financial position of BHP Billiton at 30 June 2015, while figure 16.2 shows the classification of liabilities. Note that some of BHP Billiton's interest bearing liabilities and other financial liabilities are classified as current liabilities and some as non-current liabilities.

	Notes	2015 US$M	2014 US$M
ASSETS			
Current assets			
Cash and cash equivalents	7	6 753	8 803
Trade and other receivables	8	4 321	6 741
Other financial assets	21	83	87
Inventories	10	4 292	6 013
Current tax assets		658	318
Other		262	334
Total current assets		16 369	22 296
Non-current assets			
Trade and other receivables	8	1 499	1 867
Other financial assets	21	1 159	2 349
Inventories	10	466	463
Property, plant and equipment	11	94 072	108 787
Intangible assets	12	4 292	5 439
Investments accounted for using the equity method	31	3 712	3 664
Deferred tax assets	13	2 861	6 396
Other		150	152
Total non-current assets		108 211	129 117
Total assets		124 580	151 413

FIGURE 16.1 Consolidated current and non-current assets of BHP Billiton at 30 June 2015
Source: BHP Billiton (2015, p. 208).

	Notes	2015 US$M	2014 US$M
LIABILITIES			
Current liabilities			
Trade and other payables	9	7 389	10 145
Interest bearing liabilities	15	3 201	4 262
Other financial liabilities	22	251	16
Current tax payable		207	919
Provisions	14, 20, 26	1 676	2 504
Deferred income		129	218
Total current liabilities		12 853	18 064
Non-current liabilities			
Trade and other payables	9	29	113
Interest bearing liabilities	15	27 969	30 327
Other financial liabilities	22	1 031	303
Deferred tax liabilities	13	4 542	7 066
Provisions	14, 20, 26	7 306	9 891
Deferred income		305	267
Total non-current liabilities		41 182	47 967
Total liabilities		54 035	66 031

FIGURE 16.2 Consolidated current and non-current liabilities of BHP Billiton at 30 June 2015
Source: BHP Billiton (2015, p. 208).

The current/non-current classification is ordinarily considered to be more relevant when an entity has a clearly identifiable operating cycle. This is because it distinguishes between those assets and liabilities that are expected to circulate within the entity's operating cycle and those used in the entity's operations over the long term. The typical cycle operates from cash, purchase of inventory (in the case of a manufacturer, production) and then receivables through sales of inventory and finally back to cash through collection of the receivables. The average time of the operating cycle varies with the nature of the operations and may extend beyond 12 months. Long operating cycles are common in real estate development, construction and forestry.

Current assets may include inventories and receivables that are expected to be sold, consumed or realised as part of the normal operating cycle beyond 12 months after the reporting period. Similarly, current liabilities may include payables that are expected to be settled more than 12 months after the reporting period if the operating cycle exceeds 12 months. Because of these possibilities paragraph 61 of IAS 1 requires disclosure that distinguishes between the amount that is expected to be recovered or settled within 12 months after the reporting period and more than 12 months after the reporting period for each line item of assets and liabilities. This requirement is irrespective of whether assets and liabilities are classified on the current/non-current basis or in order of liquidity.

A presentation based broadly on order of liquidity is usually considered to be more relevant than a current/non-current presentation for the assets and liabilities of financial institutions. This is because financial institutions do not supply goods or services within a clearly identifiable operating cycle. For example, HSBC Holdings plc presents the assets and liabilities of the group in order of liquidity. Figure 16.3 shows an extract from HSBC Holdings plc's statement of financial position.

	Notes	2014 US$M	2013 US$M
Assests			
Cash and balances at central banks		129 957	166 599
Items in the course of collection from other banks		4 927	6 021
Hong Kong Government certificates of indebtedness		27 674	25 220
Trading assets	12	304 193	303 192
Financial assets designated at fair value	15	29 037	38 430
Derivatives	16	345 008	282 265
Loans and advances to banks		112 149	120 046
Loans and advances to customers		974 660	992 089
Reverse repurchase agreements – non-trading	17	161 713	179 690
Financial investments	18	415 467	425 925
Prepayments, accrued income and other assets	23	75 176	76 842
Current tax assets		1 309	985
Interests in associates and joint ventures	20	18 181	16 640
Goodwill and intangible assets	21	27 577	29 918
Deferred tax assets	8	7 111	7 456
Total assets at 31 December		2 634 139	2 671 318

FIGURE 16.3 Consolidated assets of HSBC Holdings plc as at 31 December 2014
Source: Reproduced with permission from HSBC Holdings plc Annual Report and Accounts 2014 (p. 337).

The classification of assets and liabilities as current or non-current is a particularly important issue for calculating summary indicators for assessing an entity's liquidity and solvency. For example, an entity's current ratio (current assets to current liabilities) is often used as an indicator of liquidity and solvency. Lenders may also include terms in debt contracts requiring the borrower to maintain a minimum ratio of current assets to current liabilities. If the entity falls below that ratio then the financier has the right to demand repayment of the borrowing, which may, in turn, affect the assessment of whether the entity is a going concern.

16.3.2 Information required to be presented in the statement of financial position

IAS 1 does not prescribe a standard format that must be adopted for the statement of financial position. Rather, it prescribes a list of items that are considered to be sufficiently different in nature or function to warrant presentation in the statement of financial position as separate line items. These items are listed in paragraph 54:
(a) property, plant and equipment;
(b) investment property;
(c) intangible assets;
(d) financial assets (excluding amounts under (e), (h) and (i));
(e) investments accounted for using the equity method;
(f) biological assets;
(g) inventories;
(h) trade and other receivables;
(i) cash and cash equivalents;

(j) the total of assets classified as held for sale and assets included in disposal groups classified as held for sale in accordance with IFRS 5 *Non-current Assets Held for Sale and Discontinued Operations*;

(k) trade and other payables;

(l) provisions;

(m) financial liabilities (excluding amounts shown under (k) and (l));

(n) liabilities and assets for current tax, as defined in IAS 12 *Income Taxes*;

(o) deferred tax liabilities and deferred tax assets, as defined in IAS 12;

(p) liabilities included in disposal groups classified as held for sale in accordance with IFRS 5;

(q) non-controlling interests, presented within equity; and

(r) issued capital and reserves attributable to owners of the parent.

Most entities would not present all of the items shown above because they may not have any amounts to report for particular items, or the item may be considered to be immaterial. As an example, compare the list from paragraph 54 with the line items reported by BHP Billiton in its statement of financial position, *as shown in figures 16.1 and 16.2*.

Paragraph 55 of IAS 1 requires additional line items, headings and subtotals to be included in the statement of financial position when they are relevant to an understanding of the entity's financial position. In accordance with paragraph 58 of IAS 1, judgement about the presentation of additional items should be based on an assessment of the nature and liquidity of assets, the function of assets, and the amounts, nature and timing of liabilities.

For example, HSBC Holdings plc presents 'Prepayments, accrued income and other assets' as a separate line item, in addition to several separate line items for different types of financial assets in its consolidated balance sheet (statement of financial position) *as shown in figure 16.3*.

Figure 16.4 presents the equity section of BHP Billiton's consolidated balance sheet (statement of financial position) at 30 June 2015. Does BHP Billiton present any additional line items of equity beyond the minimum listed in paragraph 54 of IAS 1?

	Notes	2015 US$M	2014 US$M
EQUITY			
Share capital – BHP Billiton Limited	17	1 186	1 186
Share capital – BHP Billiton plc	17	1 057	1 069
Treasury shares	17	(76)	(587)
Reserves	18	2 557	2 927
Retained earnings	18	60 044	74 548
Total equity attributable to members of BHP Billiton Group		64 768	79 143
Non-controlling interests	18	5 777	6 239
Total equity		70 545	85 382

FIGURE 16.4 Consolidated equity of BHP Billiton at 30 June 2015
Source: BHP Billiton (2015, p. 208).

16.3.3 Information required to be presented in the statement of financial position or in the notes

To provide greater transparency and enhance the understandability of the statement of financial position, paragraph 77 of IAS 1 requires the subclassification of line items to be reported either in the statement or in the notes. For example, an entity might provide subclassification of intangible assets as brand names, licences and patents. Paragraph 78 of IAS 1 explains that subclassifications of line items in the statement of financial position are also dependent on the size, nature and function of the amounts involved. Judgement about the need for subclassifications should be made with regard to the same factors previously outlined when judging whether additional line items should be presented in the statement of financial position *(see section 16.2.4)*. Some subclassifications are governed by specific IFRS Standards. For example, IAS 16 requires items of property, plant and equipment to be disaggregated into classes *(see chapter 11)*. Entities typically report land and buildings as a separate class from machinery and equipment.

Figure 16.5 shows the subclassifications of inventories reported in note 12 to the 2015 consolidated financial statements of BHP Billiton. The Group subclassifies its inventory as raw materials, work in progress and finished goods. Amounts measured at cost and net realisable value are separately identified. Note 10 also provides information about inventory write-downs recognised during the period with comparative information.

	2015 US$M	2014 US$M
Current		
Raw materials and consumables – at net realisable value[a]	–	39
– at cost	1 453	2 161
	1 453	2 200
Work in progress – at net realisable value[a]	260	185
– at cost	1 913	2 269
	2 173	2 454
Finished goods – at net realisable value[a]	29	239
– at cost	637	1 120
	666	1 359
Total current inventories	4 292	6 013
Non-current		
Raw materials and consumables – at net realisable value[a]	–	–
– at cost	230	225
	230	225
Work in progress – at net realisable value[a]	6	4
– at cost	118	130
	124	134
Finished goods – at net realisable value[a]	33	–
– at cost	79	104
	112	104
Total non-current inventories	466	463

(a) US$182 million of inventory write-downs were recognised during the year (2014: US$95 million; 2013: US$62 million). Inventory write-downs of US$42 million made in previous periods were reversed during the year (2014: US$69 million; 2013: US$18 million).

FIGURE 16.5 Consolidated inventories of BHP Billiton at 30 June 2015
Source: BHP Billiton (2015, p. 220).

Paragraph 79(a) of IAS 1 requires additional disclosures about the entity's shares such as units in a trust, in the statement of financial position, the statement of changes in equity, or in the notes. The most commonly applicable of these disclosures include, for each class of capital:
- the number of authorised shares, issued and fully paid shares, and issued but not fully paid shares
- par value, or that there is no par value
- a reconciliation of the number of outstanding (issued) shares at the beginning and end of the period.

Other required disclosures about equity pertain to: rights, preferences and restrictions on dividends and repayment of capital; shares held by the entity, its subsidiaries or its associates; and shares subject to options and contracts. Paragraph 79(b) requires disclosure of the nature and purpose of each reserve within equity.

Entities that have no share capital must disclose equivalent information to that required by paragraph 79(a) for each category of equity interests. For example, a unit trust would report on the number of units authorised by the trust deed, details about units issued, par value, a reconciliation of the number of units at the beginning and end of the period, rights to and restrictions on distributions, equity held in subsidiaries and units reserved under options and contracts.

16.4 STATEMENT OF PROFIT OR LOSS AND OTHER COMPREHENSIVE INCOME

The statement of profit or loss and other comprehensive income is the prime source of information about an entity's financial performance. It can also be used to assist users to predict an entity's future performance and future cash flows.

However, limitations of the statement of profit or loss and other comprehensive income can arise from:
- the mandatory expensing of expenditure relating to certain self-generated intangible assets as required by IAS 38 *(see chapter 13)*; and
- earnings management through selective judgements relating to the recognition and measurement of items of income or expense, such as an impairment loss, with the objective of achieving a reported profit outcome, such as smoothing earnings, meeting earnings targets or projecting an image of earnings growth.

16.4.1 Items of comprehensive income

The statement of profit or loss and other comprehensive income reports on all non-owner transactions and valuation adjustments affecting net assets during the period. Profit or loss is the most common measure of an entity's performance. It is used in the determination of other summary indicators, such as earnings per share and the return on equity. Profitability ratios may be used in contracts, such as executive remuneration plans.

While the statement of profit or loss and other comprehensive income incorporates all income and expenses, a distinction is made between profit or loss for the period and other comprehensive income. However, the distinction between items recognised in profit or loss and those recognised in other comprehensive income is dependent upon prescriptions of accounting standards and accounting policy choices, rather than being driven by conceptual differences. For example, IAS 16 requires asset revaluation losses to be recognised in profit or loss, unless reversing a previous revaluation gain. However, IAS 16 also requires asset revaluation gains to be recognised in other comprehensive income, unless reversing a previous revaluation loss *(see chapter 11)*. Accordingly, a revaluation loss would be reported in profit or loss while a revaluation gain would be reported below the profit line in other comprehensive income.

16.4.2 Information required to be presented in the statement of profit or loss and other comprehensive income

IAS 1 does not prescribe a standard format for the statement of profit or loss and other comprehensive income. It does, however, require that the statement of profit or loss and other comprehensive income be presented either as:
- a single statement with a profit or loss section and another section for comprehensive income or a statement of profit or loss and a separate statement presenting comprehensive income.
The single statement format is illustrated in figure 16.6.
Paragraph 81A requires disclosure of:
- profit or loss
- total other comprehensive income
- total comprehensive income.

Can you can find each of these items in figure 16.6?
(Check: profit for 2016 = $121 250 000; other comprehensive income for 2016 = a loss of $14 000 000; and total comprehensive income for 2016 = $107 250 000.)
Paragraph 81B of IAS 1 requires the following items to be presented in the statement of profit or loss and other comprehensive income:

(a) profit or loss for the period attributable to:
    (i) non-controlling interests; and
    (ii) owners of the parent; and
(b) comprehensive income for the period attributable to:
    (i) non-controlling interests; and
    (ii) owners of the parent.

These items may arise when preparing consolidated financial statements for groups *(see chapter 23)*. Can you can find each of these items in figure 16.6?
(Check: profit attributable to non-controlling interests for 2016 = $24 250 000; and total comprehensive income attributable to non-controlling interests for 2016 = $21 450 000.)
The following sections will consider the items that are considered to be of sufficient importance to the reporting of the performance of an entity to warrant their presentation in the statement of profit or loss and other comprehensive income. The profit or loss section and the other comprehensive income section are considered separately.

Profit or loss section

Profit or loss is the total of income less expenses, excluding the items of other comprehensive income (IAS 1 paragraph 7). Paragraph 82 of IAS 1 identifies the items that must be presented in the profit or loss section:

(a) revenue;
(b) finance costs;
(c) share of profit or loss of associates and joint ventures accounted for using the equity method *(see online chapter C)*;
(d) tax expense;
(e) [deleted]
(ea) a single amount for the total of discontinued operations (see IFRS 5).

Other comprehensive income section

Income and expenses are recognised in other comprehensive income if that treatment is required or permitted by another IFRS Standard. Paragraph 82A of IAS 1 requires the presentation of items of other comprehensive income classified by nature and grouped on the basis of whether, in accordance with another IFRS Standard:
(a) they will not be reclassified subsequently to profit or loss; and
(b) they will be reclassified subsequently to profit or loss when specific conditions are met.

Reclassification of items to profit or loss is discussed further in section 16.4.3. If an entity recognises the share of other comprehensive income of associates and joint ventures accounted for using the equity method, these amounts must be presented as separate items. *(See online chapter C.)* Similar to other items presented in this section, items that may be reclassified subsequent to profit or loss are distinguished from those that will not be reclassified to profit or loss.

Examples of the items of other comprehensive income include:
- asset revaluation gains *(see chapter 11)*
- foreign currency gains and losses on translation of the financial statements of net investments in foreign operations *(see chapter 24)*
- remeasurement of the net defined benefit liability (asset) *(see chapter 10).*

Items classified as other comprehensive income may be reported net of tax in the statement of profit or loss and other comprehensive income. Alternatively, each item of other comprehensive income may be shown on a before-tax basis, along with aggregate amounts of income tax relating to other comprehensive income, distinguishing between income tax applicable to the group of items that might be subsequently reclassified to profit or loss, and the group of items that will not be subsequently reclassified to profit or loss. Further, an entity must disclose the amount of income tax relating to each item of other comprehensive income, in accordance with paragraph 90 of IAS 1. This may be presented either in the statement of profit or loss and other comprehensive income or in the notes.

Additional line items and labelling

Paragraph 85 of IAS 1 requires additional line items, headings and subtotals to be presented in the statement of profit or loss and other comprehensive income when they are relevant to understanding the entity's financial performance. Disclosure of additional line items may help users to understand the entity's performance and to make predictions about future earnings and cash flow because items may vary in frequency and the extent to which they recur. Paragraph 86 further explains that the nature, function and materiality of the items of income and expense should be considered in making judgements concerning the inclusion of additional line items.

An entity may also amend the descriptions used and the ordering of items when this is necessary to explain the elements of financial performance. However, paragraph 87 of IAS 1 specifically prohibits the presentation of any items of income and expense as 'extraordinary items' either in the statement of profit or loss and other comprehensive income or in the notes. This prohibition was introduced in an earlier accounting standard. 'Extraordinary items' had previously been defined as income or expenses that were non-recurring and did not arise from the ordinary activities of the entity. The IASB concluded at the time that items previously reported as extraordinary items, such as a loss on the disposal of part of the business, resulted from the normal business activities. However, entities may indicate that some items are unusual and less likely to recur through their description or the use of other labels. For example, the BHP Billiton financial statements report on 'exceptional items', including the gain on sale of the Pinto Valley mining operations, in the notes.

Figure 16.6 illustrates a statement of profit or loss and other comprehensive income as a single statement, with expenses classified according to function. *The classification of expenses is discussed in section 16.4.3.* Figure 16.6 is based on an illustrative example in the IASB *Implementation Guidance* that accompanies, but is not part of, IAS 1.

FIGURE 16.6 Statement of profit or loss and other comprehensive income in one statement with expenses classified according to function

XYZ GROUP Statement of Profit or Loss and Other Comprehensive Income for the year ended		
	2016 $'000	2015 $'000
Revenue	390 000	355 000
Cost of sales	(245 000)	(230 000)
Gross profit	145 000	125 000

(continued)

FIGURE 16.6 *(continued)*

	2016 $'000	2015 $'000
Other income	20 667	11 300
Distribution costs	(9 000)	(8 700)
Administrative expenses	(20 000)	(21 000)
Other expenses	(2 100)	(1 200)
Finance costs	(8 000)	(7 500)
Share of profit of associates	35 100	30 100
Profit before tax	161 667	128 000
Income tax expense	(40 417)	(32 000)
Profit for the year from continuing operations	121 250	96 000
Loss for the year from discontinued operations	—	(30 500)
PROFIT FOR THE YEAR	121 250	65 500
Other comprehensive income:		
Items that will not be reclassified to profit or loss:		
Gains on property revaluations	933	3 367
Remeasurements of defined benefit pension plans	(667)	1 333
Share of gain (loss) on property revaluation of associates	400	(700)
Income tax relating to items that will not be reclassified	(166)	(1 000)
	500	3 000
Items that may be reclassified subsequently to profit or loss:		
Exchange differences on translating foreign operations	5 334	10 667
Available-for-sale financial assets	(24 000)	26 667
Cash flow hedges	(667)	(4 000)
Income tax relating to items that may be reclassified	4 833	(8 334)
	(14 500)	25 000
Other comprehensive income for the year, net of tax	(14 000)	28 000
TOTAL COMPREHENSIVE INCOME FOR THE YEAR	107 250	93 500
Profit attributable to:		
Owners of the parent	97 000	52 400
Non-controlling interests	24 250	13 100
	121 250	65 500
Total comprehensive income attributable to:		
Owners of the parent	85 800	74 800
Non-controlling interests	21 450	18 700
	107 250	93 500
Earnings per share:	$	$
Basic and diluted	0.46	0.30

Source: Adapted from IASB 2012, pp. B1030–31.

16.4.3 Information required to be presented in the statement of profit or loss and other comprehensive income or in the notes

To enhance the understandability of the statement of profit or loss and other comprehensive income, paragraph 97 of IAS 1 requires the separate disclosure of the nature and amount of material items of income and expense. Paragraph 98 identifies circumstances that would give rise to the separate disclosure of items of income and expense as including:

(a) write-downs of inventories to net realisable value or of property, plant and equipment to recoverable amount, as well as reversals of such write-downs;
(b) restructurings of the activities of an entity and reversals of any provisions for the costs of restructuring;
(c) disposals of items of property, plant and equipment;
(d) disposals of investments;
(e) discontinued operations;

(f) litigation settlements; and

(g) other reversals of provisions.

Disclosure of material items is important to users of financial statements wishing to predict the likely future profit and cash flows. For example, a gain or loss on disposal of operations is typically non-recurring and the disposal may have implications for the generation of future cash flows.

Paragraph 99 of IAS 1 requires an entity to present an analysis of expenses classified either by their function or nature. Classification by function (e.g. cost of sales, distribution expenses) is illustrated in figure 16.6. Classification by nature (e.g. raw materials and consumables used, employee benefits expense, depreciation expense) is illustrated in figure 16.7. An entity should adopt the presentation that provides more relevant and reliable information. Disclosure of the subclassification of expenses helps users of financial statements to identify relationships between expenses and various measures of the volume of activity, such as the ratio of cost of sales to sales revenue. If the classification of expenses is by function, the entity must disclose additional information about the nature of expenses, including depreciation and amortisation expense and employee benefits expense, because it is useful for predicting future cash flows (IAS 1 paragraph 105).

ALPHA LTD Statement of Profit or Loss and Other Comprehensive Income (EXTRACT) for the year ended		
	2016 $'000	2015 $'000
Revenue	330 000	300 000
Other income	16 700	13 500
Changes in inventories of finished goods and work in progress	(85 000)	(78 000)
Raw materials and consumables used	(80 500)	(73 000)
Employee benefits expense	(92 000)	(90 000)
Depreciation and amortisation expense	(18 000)	(18 000)
Impairment of property, plant and equipment	(2 200)	—
Other expenses	(5 000)	(4 500)
Finance costs	(9 000)	(10 000)
Profit before tax	55 000	40 000
Income tax expense	(16 500)	(12 000)
Profit for the year from continuing operations	38 500	28 000
Loss for the year from discontinued operations	(3 500)	—
PROFIT FOR THE YEAR	35 000	28 000
Profit attributable to:		
Owners of the parent	30 000	25 000
Non-controlling interests	5 000	3 000
	35 000	28 000
Earnings per share:	$	$
Basic and diluted	0.60	0.50

FIGURE 16.7 Profit or loss section with expenses classified according to nature

Some income and expense items are required to be initially recognised in other comprehensive income and subsequently reclassified to profit or loss. For example, *as discussed in chapter 7*, gains and losses on a financial asset measured at fair value through other comprehensive income are recognised in other comprehensive income and accumulated in equity, and when the financial asset is derecognised, the accumulated gain or loss is reclassified from equity to profit or loss. The subsequent recognition in profit or loss of an item previously recognised in other comprehensive income is referred to as a reclassification adjustment in IAS 1. While the standard uses the term 'reclassification', in practice, it is also commonly referred to as recycling of gains and losses through profit or loss.

Not all items recognised in other comprehensive income are subject to potential reclassification. For example, revaluation gains recognised in accordance with IAS 16 *Property, Plant and Equipment* are not reclassified to profit or loss.

Paragraph 92 of IAS 1 requires the disclosure of reclassification adjustments relating to items of other comprehensive income. A reclassification adjustment is included with the related item of other comprehensive income in the period that the adjustment is reclassified to profit or loss. These amounts may have been recognised in other comprehensive income in a previous period. They could also have been recognised in other comprehensive income in the same period. For example, some of the gains and losses accumulated in equity pertaining to a financial instrument may have been recognised in other comprehensive income in both the current reporting period and previous periods.

In accounting for a reclassification adjustment, gains previously recognised in other comprehensive income are deducted from other comprehensive income in the period in which they are recognised in profit or loss. This is to avoid double counting of the gain. Conversely, losses previously recognised in other comprehensive income are added back to other comprehensive income in the period in which they are recognised in profit or loss. Illustrative example 16.1 demonstrates how to present a reclassification adjustment in the statement of profit or loss and other comprehensive income.

ILLUSTRATIVE EXAMPLE 16.1 Reclassification adjustment

During March 2016 Investor Ltd purchased a small parcel of shares in other companies for $120 000, which was their fair value at that time. The shares were measured at fair value and Investor Ltd elected to present in other comprehensive income any gains and losses arising from changes in fair value of the shares, as permitted by IFRS 9 *Financial Instruments*, taking into consideration the business model under which the shares are held *(see chapter 7)*.

On 31 December 2016 Investor Ltd revalued the shares to their fair value of $146 000. The gain was $20 000, net of income tax of $6000.

On 31 December 2017 Investor Ltd revalued the shares to their fair value of $170 000. The gain was $18 000, net of income tax of $6000.

The gains and losses on revaluation of the shares are recognised in other comprehensive income and accumulated in the 'Investment in equity instruments reserve' in equity.

On 31 December 2017, Investor Ltd sold the shares for $170 000. At that time the accumulated credit in the 'Investment in equity instruments' in relation to the shares was $38 000 (net of tax of $12 000). There were no other items of other comprehensive income for the year ended 31 December 2016 or 31 December 2017.

INVESTOR LTD Statements of Profit or Loss and Other Comprehensive Income for the year ended 31 December			
	Notes	2017 $'000	2016 $'000
Revenue	2	980	740
Cost of sales	3	(400)	(300)
Selling and administrative expenses	4	(240)	(200)
Finance costs	4	(100)	(100)
Reclassification of gain on financial instruments	5	50	—
Profit before taxation		290	140
Income tax expense	6	(100)	(40)
PROFIT FOR THE YEAR		190	100
Other comprehensive income:			
Items that may be reclassified subsequently to profit or loss:			
Gain on revaluation of financial instruments	7	18	20
Reclassification adjustment for gains on revaluation of financial instruments	7	(38)	—
Other comprehensive income for the year, net of tax		(20)	20
TOTAL COMPREHENSIVE INCOME FOR THE YEAR		170	120
Profit attributable to:			
Owners of Investor Ltd		180	95
Non-controlling interests		10	5
		190	100
Total comprehensive income attributable to:			
Owners of Investor Ltd		(20)	20
Non-controlling interests		0	0
		(20)	120

Prior to the disposal of the shares, Investor Ltd had recognised gains in other comprehensive income over two periods, comprising $20 000 in 2016 and $18 000 in 2017. On the disposal and derecognition of the shares the accumulated gain of $38 000 must be reclassified to profit. The gain is presented as $50 000, being the amount before tax. The related tax effect of $12 000 is included in the income tax expense line item. To avoid double counting, the gain is deducted from other comprehensive income and added to profit. Thus, the reclassification adjustment of $38 000 has no net effect on total comprehensive income in 2017 because it increases profit by $38 000 and decreases other comprehensive income by the same amount.

16.5 STATEMENT OF CHANGES IN EQUITY

The statement of changes in equity provides a reconciliation of the opening and closing amounts of each component of equity for the period. The purpose of the statement of changes in equity is to report transactions with owners, such as the issue of new shares and the payment of dividends, and the effects of any retrospective adjustments to beginning-of-period components of equity *(see section 16.7)*.

16.5.1 Presentation of the statement of changes in equity

The statement of changes in equity presents information about movements in the components of equity, which include share capital, retained earnings and amounts accumulated in equity for each class of items recognised in other comprehensive income, such as the asset revaluation surplus and the foreign currency translation reserve. The statement is often presented as a table with the components of equity listed in separate columns. The opening balance, current period movements and closing balance are shown in different rows. As for the other financial statements, comparative amounts are required to be reported in the statement of changes in equity. The comparative figures are often presented in a separate table from the current period figures.

16.5.2 Information required to be reported in the statement of changes in equity

Paragraph 106 of IAS 1 requires the following information to be presented in the statement of changes in equity:
- total comprehensive income for the period, distinguishing between amounts attributable to owners of the parent entity and to non-controlling interests;
- the effects of retrospective application or retrospective restatement recognised in accordance with IAS 8 for each component of equity; and
- a reconciliation between the carrying amount at the beginning and the end of the period for each item of equity.

The reconciliation of the carrying amount must include, as a minimum, the changes resulting from profit or loss, other comprehensive income; and transactions with owners in their capacity as owners, showing separately contributions by and distributions to owners and changes in ownership interests in subsidiaries.

Profit (loss) for the period increases (decreases) retained earnings. Other items of comprehensive income affect other components of equity. For example, a gain on revaluing assets, net of its tax effect, increases the asset revaluation surplus.

Figure 16.8 shows the consolidated statement of changes in equity of the BHP Billiton for the year ended 30 June 2015. The complete statement also presents comparative information, following the same tabular format.

16.5.3 Information to be presented in the statement of changes in equity or in the notes

An analysis of other comprehensive income by item must be included in the statement of changes in equity or in the notes. Similarly, the amount of dividends recognised as distributions to owners during the period and the amount of dividends per share for the period must be disclosed either in the statement of changes in equity or in the notes.

FIGURE 16.8 Consolidated statement of changes in equity of BHP Billiton for the year ended 30 June 2015

US$M	Share capital BHP Billiton Limited	Share capital BHP Billiton plc	Treasury shares	Reserves	Retained earnings	Total equity attributable to members of BHP Billiton Group	Non-controlling interests	Total equity
Balance as at 1 July 2014	1 186	1 069	(587)	2 927	74 548	79 143	6 239	85 382
Total comprehensive income	—	—	—	(96)	1 865	1 769	973	2 742
Transactions with owners:								
Shares cancelled	—	(12)	501	12	(501)	—	—	—
Purchase of shares by ESOP Trusts	—	—	(355)	—	—	(355)	—	(355)
Employee share awards exercised net of employee contributions and other adjustments	—	—	363	(461)	101	3	—	3
Employee share awards forfeited	—	—	—	(13)	13	—	—	—
Accrued employee entitlement for unexercised awards	—	—	—	247	—	247	—	247
Distribution to option holders	—	—	—	(1)	—	(1)	(1)	(2)
Dividends	—	—	—	—	(6 596)	(6 596)	(639)	(7 235)
In-specie dividend on demerger – refer to note 29 'Discontinued operations'	—	—	—	—	(9 445)	(9 445)	—	(9 445)
Equity contributed	—	—	—	1	—	1	52	53
Transfers within equity on demerger	—	—	—	(59)	59	—	—	—
Conversion of controlled entities to equity accounted investments	—	—	2	—	—	2	(847)	(845)

Balance as at 30 June 2015	1 186	1 057	(76)	2 557	60 044	64 768	5 777	70 545
Balance as at 1 July 2013	1 186	1 069	(540)	1 970	66 982	70 667	4 624	75 291
Total comprehensive income	—	—	—	(24)	13 901	13 877	1 392	15 269
Transactions with owners:								
Purchase of shares by ESOP Trusts	—	—	(368)	—	—	(368)	—	(368)
Employee share awards exercised net of employee contributions	—	—	321	(221)	(91)	9	—	9
Employee share awards forfeited	—	—	—	(32)	32	—	—	—
Accrued employee entitlement for unexercised awards	—	—	—	247	—	247	—	247
Distribution to option holders	—	—	—	(2)	—	(2)	(2)	(4)
Dividends	—	—	—	—	(6 276)	(6 276)	(252)	(6 528)
Equity contributed	—	—	—	989	—	989	477	1 466
Balance as at 30 June 2014	1 186	1 069	(587)	2 927	74 548	79 143	6 239	85 382
Balance as at 1 July 2012	1 186	1 069	(533)	1 912	61 892	65 526	3 789	69 315
Total comprehensive income	—	—	—	77	11 309	11 386	1 599	12 985
Transactions with owners:								
Purchase of shares by ESOP Trusts	—	—	(445)	—	—	(445)	—	(445)
Employee share awards exercised net of employee contributions	—	—	438	(243)	(178)	17	—	17
Employee share awards forfeited	—	—	—	(17)	17	—	—	—
Accrued employee entitlement for unexercised awards	—	—	—	210	—	210	—	210
Issue of share options to non-controlling interests	—	—	—	49	—	49	—	49
Dividends	—	—	—	—	(6 076)	(6 076)	(837)	(6 913)
Equity contributed	—	—	—	—	—	—	73	73
Divestment of equity accounted investment	—	—	—	(18)	18	—	—	—
Balance as at 30 June 2013	1 186	1 069	(540)	1 970	66 982	70 667	4 624	75 291

Source: BHP Billiton (2015, p. 210).

16.6 NOTES

Notes are an integral part of the financial statements. Their purpose is to enhance the understandability of the statement of financial position, statement of profit or loss and other comprehensive income, statement of cash flows and statement of changes in equity. An entity should present the notes in a systematic order and cross-reference each item in the financial statement, such as the statement of financial position, in accordance with paragraph 113 of IAS 1. An earlier version of IAS 1 suggested a particular order for notes but the standard was amended, effective from 1 January 2016, to emphasise the need to consider understandability and comparability in determining an appropriate systematic order for the presentation of notes.

The following information must be disclosed in the notes in accordance with paragraph 112 of IAS 1:

- information about the basis of preparation of the financial statements and the specific accounting policies used, in accordance with paragraphs 117–24
- information required by other IFRS Standards unless presented in the financial statements
- other information that is relevant to understanding the financial statements, unless presented elsewhere.

We will first consider the statements about compliance with IFRS Standards followed by the summary of significant accounting policies used and sources of estimation uncertainty, information about capital, and other disclosures.

16.6.1 Compliance with IFRS Standards

An explicit and unreserved statement of compliance with IFRS Standards should be made if, and only if, the financial statements comply with the requirements of IFRS Standards (IAS 1 paragraph 16). If applicable, the statement is often included in the note about the basis of preparation of the financial statements.

In extremely rare circumstances, management may conclude that compliance with a requirement in an IFRS Standard would be so misleading that it would conflict with the objective of financial statements. Does this mean that management should depart from compliance with IFRS Standards in order to present financial statements that serve the decision-making needs of present and potential investors, lenders and other creditors? The answer to this question depends on domestic reporting requirements. In some countries the law may require compliance with IFRS Standards. In some jurisdictions departure from the requirements of an IFRS Standard may be permitted in the extremely rare circumstances referred to in IAS 1, where management believe it would be misleading.

When assessing whether compliance would be misleading, management must consider why the objectives of financial statements would not be achieved in the current circumstances and how the entity's circumstances differ from other entities that do comply with the requirement.

What should managers do if they conclude that compliance with IFRS Standards would be so misleading as to defeat the objectives of financial reporting? The answer to this depends on whether departure from IFRS Standards is permitted in the domestic reporting regime, as shown in figure 16.9.

Disclosures required by IAS 1 when management concludes compliance with an IFRS Standard would be misleading		
Domestic reporting regime	**Domestic reporting regime permits departure from an IFRS Standard**	**Domestic reporting regime prohibits departure from an IFRS Standards**
Action	**Depart from the IFRS Standard**	**Do not depart from the IFRS Standards**

Disclosure	• that management has concluded that the financial statements present fairly the entity's financial position, financial performance and cash flows
	• that the financial statements are in compliance with IFRS Standards except for the specific departure to achieve a fair presentation
	• the title of the IFRS Standard from which the entity has departed
	  – the treatment required by the IFRS Standard
	  – the nature of the departure
	  – why the treatment would be so misleading in the circumstances that it would be in conflict with the objectives of financial statements specified in the *Conceptual Framework*
	  – the financial effect of the departure on each item in the financial statements for each period presented.
		• the title of the relevant IFRS Standard
		• the nature of the requirement
		• the reason for management's conclusion that compliance is misleading and
		• the adjustments necessary to each item for each period presented that are required to achieve a fair presentation.

Relevant paragraphs	IAS 1, paragraphs 19–22	IAS 1, paragraphs 23–24

FIGURE 16.9 Reporting requirements when management concludes compliance with an IFRS Standard would be misleading

16.6.2 Statement of significant accounting policies and sources of estimation uncertainty

In deciding whether to disclose particulars of an accounting policy, managers must consider its relevance in assisting users to understand how transactions and events have been reported in the financial statements. In some cases, disclosure is prescribed by other IFRS Standards. For example, IAS 16 requires disclosure of the depreciation methods used for each class of property, plant and equipment (paragraph 73(b)) *(see chapter 11)*.

Paragraph 117 of IAS 1 explains that the summary of significant accounting policies should include the measurement bases used. For example, an entity should disclose whether cost or fair value has been used in measuring property, plant and equipment subsequent to initial recognition. Paragraph 73(a) of IAS 16 also requires disclosure of this information.

The measurement of some assets and liabilities can involve assumptions, such as the rate of growth used in the measurement of the recoverable amount. An entity must disclose information about the assumptions concerning the future, and other major sources of estimation uncertainty at the end of the reporting period, where there is a significant risk that they may result in material adjustments to the carrying amounts of assets and liabilities within the next financial year (IAS 1 paragraph 125). It is not uncommon for entities to include the disclosures about measurement uncertainty in that section of the notes.

The application of IFRS Standards often requires the exercise of judgement. For example, the application of IAS 17 *Leases* often involves judgement about whether substantially all the risks and rewards of ownership have been transferred by a lease *(see chapter 12)*. Paragraph 122 of IAS 1 requires disclosure of the judgements that have the most significant effect on the amounts recognised in financial statements in the summary of accounting policies.

16.6.3 Information about capital

Paragraph 134 of IAS 1 requires disclosure of information that enables users of financial statements to evaluate the entity's management of capital. This requirement encompasses qualitative information about objectives, policies and processes, including a description of what is managed as capital, the nature of any externally imposed capital requirements, whether the entity has complied with externally imposed requirements, and, if the entity has not complied with external requirements, the implications of non-compliance.

Quantitative disclosures are also required, including summary data of what is managed as capital. This may differ from reported equity because an entity may exclude some components of equity, such as foreign currency translation reserves, from what is managed as capital, while including some items that are classified as liabilities, such as subordinated debt.

The standard adopts a management perspective by focusing on how capital is viewed by management, rather than prescribing specific definitions of capital for the purposes of the disclosures. The entity is required to base its capital disclosures on the information provided internally to key management personnel (paragraph 135).

16.6.4 Other disclosures

It is not uncommon for dividends to be proposed or declared (i.e. approved by the appropriate authorising body, such as the board of directors) after the reporting date but before the financial statements are issued. Unless the dividends are declared before the end of the reporting period they cannot be recognised in the financial statements. IAS 10 *Events after the Reporting Period* requires disclosure in the notes of any dividends that have been proposed or declared before the release of the financial statements but not recognised in the financial statements. Paragraph 137(a) of IAS 1 requires the disclosure to include the amount of the dividends that have been proposed or declared but not recognised, and the related amount per share. The amount of any cumulative preference dividends that have not been recognised as liabilities must also be disclosed (paragraph 137(b)).

Paragraph 138 of IAS 1 requires disclosure of certain non-financial information including:
- the legal form of the entity, such as whether it is a company or a trust
- the country of incorporation
- the address of the registered office or the principal place of business (if different from the registered office)
- a description of the nature of the entity's operations and its principal activities
- the name of the parent and the ultimate parent of the group
- if a limited-life company, the length of its life.

16.7 ACCOUNTING POLICIES, CHANGES IN ACCOUNTING ESTIMATES AND ERRORS

We will now consider how to:
- select and account for changes in accounting policies
- account for changes in accounting estimates
- correct prior period errors.

The requirements are specified in IAS 8 *Accounting Policies, Changes in Accounting Estimates and Errors*.

The term *accounting policy* refers to principles or conventions applied in preparing the financial statements, such as using the straight-line method of depreciation for property, plant and equipment. An accounting *estimate* is a judgement applied in determining the carrying amount of an item in the financial statements such as an estimate of the useful life of a depreciable asset. The use of reasonable estimates is an essential part of the process of preparing financial statements because many items reported in the financial statements — such as provisions for warranties — cannot be calculated with precision. For example, an entity's accounting *policy* may be to measure its provision for warranty claims based on history, the volume of sales and the length of outstanding warranty periods. The *calculation* of the amount of the warranty provision is an accounting *estimate* that applies this accounting policy.

A *prior period error* is an omission or misstatement in the financial statements of a prior period resulting from the misuse or failure to use reliable information. Errors may arise from mathematical miscalculations, mistakes in applying accounting policies, oversights or misinterpretations of facts, and fraud (IAS 8 paragraph 5). For example, assume Company C owns a building from which it derives rental income. In testing for impairment, Company C measures the value in use of the building by discounting future rental income. The amount of rental income should be reduced by any waivers of rent allowed to tenants, such as rent-free periods offered to new tenants. Assume that in measuring the value in use in a prior period, the cash inflows forgone from rent-free periods were added to annual rentals, instead of being deducted, and that this resulted in an overstated carrying amount of the building. The misstatement would be classified as an error in the prior-period financial statements because it results from a mistake in the application of information that was available at the time. In contrast, if, in hindsight, the building was found to have been overstated because the estimated rental growth rates used in a prior period were too high, the subsequent restatement of the carrying amount of the building would be treated as a change of accounting estimate.

16.7.1 Selecting and changing accounting policies

Accounting standards prescribe accounting policies for certain topics, transactions or events. IAS 8 deals with situations where there are no applicable accounting standards, and sets out the principles that entities must apply in selecting appropriate accounting policies. Paragraph 10 of IAS 8 specifies that where there is no IFRS Standard dealing with a particular transaction, preparers should use judgement in developing and applying accounting policies so that the resulting information is relevant and reliable. The concept of reliability encompasses:
- faithful representation
- reflecting economic substance over legal form
- neutrality, freedom from bias
- prudence and
- completeness in all material respects.

The concept of substance over form is particularly important. This is an area revealed as a weakness in the rules-based approach to standard setting used by the US and implicated in some of the corporate collapses in that country in 2001 and 2002. Transactions that were, in substance, financing transactions were accounted for as sales, applying very literal interpretations of the US rules. Applying the principle of substance over form should result in transactions being accounted for in accordance with their underlying economic implications. The accounting treatment of certain preference shares provides an example of applying the principle of substance over form. While the form of the preference shares is equity, their economic substance is a liability if the terms allow for redemption at the option of the holder. Accordingly, in applying the principle of substance over form, IAS 32 requires such preference shares to be classified as liabilities.

IAS 8 provides what is commonly termed the 'hierarchy' of relevant sources of information to be used by management in selecting and applying accounting policies. Paragraph 11 states that management must firstly consider the requirements and guidance of any IFRS Standard dealing with similar or related issues. Secondly, management must consider the *Framework*'s definitions, recognition criteria and measurement concepts of assets, liabilities, income and expenses. Provided they do not conflict with the sources in paragraph 11, management may also consider the most recent pronouncements of other standard setters that use a similar conceptual framework, other accounting literature and accepted industry practices.

Paragraph 13 of IAS 8 requires an entity to apply accounting policies consistently for similar transactions, events or conditions unless otherwise required by an accounting standard. Accordingly, IAS 8 paragraph 14 specifies only two circumstances in which an entity is permitted to change an accounting policy. These are:

- if the change is *required* by an IFRS Standard; or
- if the change, *made voluntarily*, results in the financial statements providing reliable and more relevant information about the effects of transactions, other events or conditions on the entity's financial position, financial performance or cash flows.

However, the initial application of a policy to revalue assets in accordance with IAS 16 *Property, Plant and Equipment* or IAS 38 *Intangible Assets* must be accounted for as a revaluation in accordance with those standards and not as a change in accounting policy under IAS 8. Note that this applies to the *initial* application of a revaluation policy only. IAS 8 would apply if an entity initially chooses the revaluation method under IAS 16 or IAS 38, and then changes to the cost method at a later date.

Where an entity changes an accounting policy because it is required to do so, it must account for that change in accordance with the transitional provisions of the accounting standard requiring the change. If the accounting standard does not specify how to account for the change, then the change must be applied *retrospectively*. Retrospective application is also required for all voluntary changes in accounting policy (IAS 8 paragraph 19). Retrospective application means applying a new accounting policy to transactions, other events and conditions as if that policy had always been applied (paragraph 5). When an entity retrospectively applies a change of accounting policy, the *opening* balance of each affected component of equity for the earliest prior period presented must be adjusted, and the other comparative amounts must be disclosed for each prior period presented as if the new accounting policy had always been applied (IAS 8 paragraph 22). Further, when an entity applies an accounting policy retrospectively (or other retrospective restatement or reclassification), paragraph 40A of IAS 1 requires presentation of a statement of financial position as at the beginning of the preceding period if it has a material effect on the information presented. As clarified in paragraph 40B, the entity would be required to present three statements of financial position as at:
- the end of the current period;
- the end of the preceding period; and
- the beginning of the preceding period.

IAS 8 requires extensive disclosures when an entity changes its accounting policy. These include:
- the nature of the change in accounting policy
- for the current period and each prior period presented, to the extent practicable, the amount of the adjustment for:
  - each financial statement line item affected and
  - basic and diluted earnings per share, if IAS 33 *Earnings per Share* applies to the entity
- the amount of the adjustment relating to periods before those presented, to the extent practicable
- if retrospective application is impracticable, the reason for that condition and a description of how and from when the change in accounting policy has been applied.

Additional disclosures are required for changes required by an IFRS Standard and for voluntary changes, as follows:
- Change of accounting policy required by an IFRS Standard
  - the title of the IFRS Standard
  - that the change in accounting policy is made in accordance with its transitional provisions, if applicable
  - a description of the transitional provisions, if applicable
  - the transitional provisions that might have an effect on future periods, if applicable.
- Voluntary change of accounting policy
  - the reasons why the new accounting policy provides reliable and more relevant information.

As noted in section 16.5.2, paragraph 106(b) of IAS 1 requires disclosure of the effects of retrospective adjustments for each component of equity in the statement of changes in equity.

Illustrative example 16.2 shows how to apply retrospectively a change in accounting policy.

ILLUSTRATIVE EXAMPLE 16.2 Applying a change in accounting policy retrospectively

Ace Ltd operates in the agricultural industry and has many large orchards of fruit trees. Effective from 1 January 2016, Ace Ltd changed its accounting policy for fruit trees as a result of changes to IAS 41 *Agriculture* and IAS 16 *Property, Plant and Equipment*. Until the end of 2015 Ace Ltd had measured its fruit trees at fair value with changes in fair value recognised in profit or loss.

The changes in accounting standards resulted in fruit trees being classified as property, plant and equipment and accounted for in accordance with IAS 16. Thus the fruit trees are accounted for at cost until they reach maturity. Then, the entity has a choice of retaining the cost model or choosing the revaluation model, with revaluation gains recognised in other comprehensive income and accumulated in equity, unless reversing a previous downward revaluation.

The orchards had been acquired at the beginning of 2013 at a cost of $2 400 000. By the end of 2014 (and therefore at the beginning of 2015) the fair value of the fruit trees was $3 000 000. The gains on revaluation of the fruit trees recognised through profit or loss by 31 December 2014 had increased retained earnings by $420 000. The deferred tax liability arising from the temporary difference between the carrying amount and the tax base of the fruit trees was $180 000.

On 31 December 2015 Ace Ltd revalued the fruit trees by $400 000 to their fair value of $3 400 000 in accordance with IAS 41. The gain on revaluation was recognised in profit. The following information was obtained from Ace Ltd's 2015 financial statements:

	2015 $'000	2014 $'000
Revenue	5 200	
Gain on revaluation of fruit trees	400	
Depreciation expense	(200)	
Profit before tax	1 050	
Income tax expense	(315)	
Profit for the period	735	
Agricultural assets – fruit trees	3 400	3 000
Deferred tax liability	365	245
Retained earnings at the end of the year	1 385	650

Ace Ltd chose the cost model to account for the fruit trees in accordance with IAS 16. The useful life of the fruit trees was estimated as 16 years with no residual value. The annual depreciation expense for the fruit trees is $150 000, being $2 400 000/16 years.

Retrospective application of the changes to IAS 16 means that Ace Ltd's financial statements should be presented as if the cost model under IAS 16 had always been applied.

The tax rate is 30%.

In applying IAS 16, Ace Ltd would make the following adjustments to the comparative financial statements for the year ended 31 December 2015:
(a) Profit before tax is decreased by $550 000 comprising:
   i. the gain on revaluation, $400 000, which would not have been recognised under the cost model; and
   ii. the depreciation of the fruit trees, $150 000.
(b) Income tax expense is decreased by $165 000, comprising:
   i. decrease of $120 000 pertaining to the reversal of the temporary difference arising from the decrease in the carrying amount of the fruit trees [($3 400 000 − $3 000 000) × 30%]; and
   ii. decrease of $45 000 pertaining to the temporary difference arising from the depreciation of the fruit trees [($2 400 000 − $2 250 000) × 30%].
(c) The fruit trees are measured at cost of $2 400 000 less accumulated depreciation.
(d) Accumulated depreciation of the fruit trees is recognised and measured as $450 000 at 31 December 2015 ($150 000 × 3).
(e) Retained earnings at the beginning of 2015 is reduced by $630 000, comprising:
   i. $420 000, being the accumulated revaluation gains, net of tax, that would not have been recognised under the cost model.
   ii. $210 000, being the depreciation expense, net of tax, for the 2 years ended 31 December 2014 [$150 000 × (1 − 30%) × 2 years].
(f) Deferred tax liability is decreased by $435 000 comprising:
   i. $180 000, reversal of the temporary difference at the end beginning of 2015;
   ii. $120 000, reversal of temporary difference (refer item (b)(i) above);
   iii. $135 000, temporary difference arising from retrospective depreciation of fruit trees which does not affect the tax base (refer item (d) above).

The following extracts from the financial statements of Ace Ltd for the year ended 31 December 2016 illustrate the retrospective application of the change in accounting policy.

ACE LTD Statements of Profit or Loss and Other Comprehensive Income for the year ended 31 December		
	2016 $'000	Restated 2015 $'000
Revenue	5 850	5 200
Cost of goods sold	(2 900)	(2 500)
Wages and salaries expenses	(1 200)	(1 100)
Depreciation expense	(350)	(350)
Other expenses	(850)	(750)

Profit before tax	550	500
Income tax expense	(165)	(150)
Profit for the period	385	350
Other comprehensive income for the year	—	—
TOTAL COMPREHENSIVE INCOME FOR THE YEAR	385	350

ACE LTD
Statements of Changes in Equity
for the year ended 31 December 2016

	Share capital $'000	Retained earnings $'000	Total $'000
Balance at 31 December 2015 as restated	1 200	370	1 570
Comprehensive income for the year ended 31 December 2016	—	385	385
Balance at 31 December 2016	1 200	755	1 955

ACE LTD
Statements of Changes in Equity
for the year ended 31 December 2015

	Share capital $'000	Retained earnings $'000	Total $'000
Balance at 31 December 2014 as previously reported	1 200	650	1 850
Change in accounting policy for fruit trees	—	(630)	(630)
Balance at 31 December 2014 as restated	1 200	20	1 220
Comprehensive income for the year ended 31 December 2015	—	350	350
Balance at 31 December 2015	1 200	370	1 570

ACE LTD
Statements of Financial Position
at 31 December

	2016 $'000	Restated 2015 $'000	Restated 2014 $'000
Assets			
Current assets			
Cash and cash equivalents	50	50	50
Accounts receivable	850	800	650
Total current assets	900	850	700
Non-current assets			
Fruit trees	1 800	1 950	2 100
Other property, plant and equipment	1 200	1 400	1 600
Total non-current assets	3 000	3 350	3 700
Total assets	3 900	4 200	4 400

Liabilities and equity			
Current liabilities			
Accounts payable	440	400	550
Current tax payable	210	190	200
Provisions	150	250	290
Total current liabilities	800	840	1 040
Non-current liabilities			
Provisions	50	150	195
Deferred tax liability	15	60	105
Financial liabilities	1 080	1 580	1 840
Total non-current liabilities	1 145	1 790	2 140
Total liabilities	1 945	2 630	3 180
Equity			
Share capital	1 200	1 200	1 200
Retained earnings	755	370	20
Total equity	1 955	1 570	1 220
Total liabilities and equity	3 900	4 200	4 400

Additional disclosures in the notes for the change in accounting policy

The company has adopted IAS 16 *Property, Plant and Equipment*, as amended in 2014. As a result, fruit trees are accounted for under the cost model. In accordance with the transitional provisions of IAS 16, the change in accounting policy was applied retrospectively. The comparative financial statements for 2015 have been restated. The effect of the change for each line item affected is tabulated below:

	Effect on 2015 $'000
Decrease in gain on revaluation of fruit trees	(400)
Increase in depreciation expense	(150)
Decrease in profit before tax	(550)
Decrease in income tax expense	(165)
Decrease in profit for the period	(385)
Decrease in fruit trees	(1 450)
Decrease in deferred tax liability	(435)
Decrease in retained earnings	(1 015)

	Effect on 2014 $'000
Decrease in fruit trees	(900)
Decrease in deferred tax liability	(270)
Decrease in retained earnings	(630)

Paragraphs 23–25 of IAS 8 deal with circumstances where retrospective application of a change in accounting policy is impracticable and thus cannot be applied. In the context of IAS 8 'impracticable' means 'the entity cannot apply it after making every reasonable effort to do so' (paragraph 5). For example, the retrospective application of an accounting policy would be impracticable if it required assumptions about what management's intent might have been at a prior point in time. Hindsight is not used when applying a new accounting policy retrospectively. For example, an asset measured on the fair value basis retrospectively should be measured at the fair value as at the date of the retrospective adjustment and should not take into account subsequent events. When it is impracticable for an entity to apply a new accounting policy retrospectively because it cannot determine the cumulative effect of applying the policy

to all prior periods, the entity should apply the new policy prospectively from the start of the earliest period practicable. This may be the current period.

16.7.2 Changes in accounting estimates

Recall that an accounting estimate is a judgement applied in determining the carrying amount of an item in the financial statements. An estimate may need to be revised if changes occur in the circumstances on which it was based, or as a result of new information or more experience. Paragraph 36 of IAS 8 requires changes in accounting estimates to be accounted for *prospectively*. Prospective application is defined in paragraph 5. When a new accounting estimate is applied prospectively the effect of the change is recognised in the current period and any future periods affected by the change but no adjustment is made to prior periods.

Paragraph 37 of IAS 8 states that if the change in estimate affects assets, liabilities or equity, then the carrying amounts of those items shall be adjusted in the period of the change. Paragraphs 39 and 40 prescribe disclosures for changes in accounting estimates that have an effect in the current or future periods. The entity must disclose the nature and amount of the change. However, if it is impracticable to estimate the effect on future periods the entity must disclose that fact.

Illustrative example 16.3 demonstrates accounting for a change in an accounting estimate, including the required disclosures.

ILLUSTRATIVE EXAMPLE 16.3 Accounting for a change in an accounting estimate

Company Z installed factory plant in January 2012. The company had been depreciating its factory plant on a straight-line basis, with an estimated useful life of 15 years and nil residual value. Four years later, in January 2016, the directors of Company Z determined that, due to technological developments, the factory plant's useful life was 10 years in total — that is, it had a remaining useful life of 6 years. Company Z's reporting period ends on 31 December. As at 1 January 2016, the balance of factory plant was as follows:

Cost	$ 150 000
Accumulated depreciation	(40 000)
Carrying amount	110 000

For the year ended 31 December 2016, Company Z's depreciation expense will be $18 333. This is calculated as $110 000/6 (being the carrying amount of the asset at 1 July 2016 divided by the remaining useful life).

Extract from Company Z's financial statements for the year ended 31 December 2016:

Company Z has historically depreciated its factory plant over 15 years. The company's directors determined that, effective from 1 January 2016, the factory plant should be depreciated over 10 years. The effect of the change in the estimated useful life of the factory plant in the current period is to increase the depreciation expense from $10 000 to $18 333 and to increase accumulated depreciation by $8333. In future periods, annual depreciation expense for the factory plant will be $18 333 over the remaining useful life of the plant.

16.7.3 Correction of errors

An 'error' is an omission or misstatement in the financial statements. If a material error is discovered in a subsequent period, paragraph 42 of IAS 8 requires retrospective correction by restating comparative amounts for each prior period presented in which the error occurred. Where the error occurred before the first prior period presented, the entity must restate opening balances of assets, liabilities and equity of the earliest period presented.

Retrospective restatement is required unless it is impracticable to do so (IAS 8 paragraphs 43–45). Similar disclosures are required for correction of errors as for changes in accounting policy (paragraph 49). However, as the correction of errors requires the retrospective restatement of items in the financial statements, a statement of financial position as at the beginning of the earliest comparative period must also be presented (IAS 1 paragraph 40A).

16.8 EVENTS AFTER THE REPORTING PERIOD

The objective of IAS 10 is to prescribe when an entity should adjust its financial statements for events after the reporting period, and what disclosures the entity should make about events after the reporting period. IAS 10 paragraph 3 defines an *event after the reporting period* as occurring after the end of the reporting period but before the financial statements are authorised for issue. Events after the reporting period are classified as being:

- adjusting events, which provide further evidence of conditions that existed at the end of the reporting period, and can include an event that indicates that the going concern assumption may be inappropriate; and
- non-adjusting events, which indicate conditions that arose after the end of the reporting period, such as the unintended destruction of property that existed at the end of the reporting period.

Usually the date at which financial statements are authorised for issue is when the directors or other governing body formally approve the financial statements for issue to shareholders and/or other users. Although subsequent ratification by the shareholders at an annual meeting may be required, that is not usually the date of authorisation for issue.

16.8.1 Adjusting events after the reporting period

Paragraph 8 of IAS 10 requires an entity to adjust the amounts recognised in its financial statements to reflect adjusting events after the reporting period. Examples of adjusting events after the reporting period include the following:

- the receipt of information after the reporting period that indicates an asset was impaired as at the end of the reporting period — this may occur, for example, if a trade receivable recorded at the end of the reporting period is shown to be irrecoverable because of the insolvency of the customer that occurs after the reporting period
- the sale of inventories after the reporting period that provides evidence of their net realisable value at the end of the reporting period
- the judge's decision on a court case, after the reporting period, confirming that the entity had a present obligation at the end of the reporting period.

Illustrative example 16.4 demonstrates accounting for an adjusting event after the reporting period.

ILLUSTRATIVE EXAMPLE 16.4 Accounting for an adjusting event after the reporting period

Blue Ltd's financial statements for the year ended 31 December 2016 included a receivable of $35 000 in respect of a major customer, Red Ltd. On 31 January 2017 the liquidator of Red Ltd advised that the company was insolvent and would be unable to repay the full amount owed. The liquidator advised Blue Ltd in writing that Red Ltd's creditors would receive 10 cents in the dollar (i.e. 10 cents for every dollar owed). The liquidator estimated that the amount would be paid in November 2017. Blue Ltd's financial statements were authorised for issue by the directors on 25 February 2017.

In accordance with IAS 10, the insolvency of Red Ltd is an adjusting event after the reporting period because it provides further evidence of the collectability of the receivable at 31 December 2016. Blue Ltd will adjust the receivable from $35 000 to $3500 as follows:

Impairment Loss	Dr	31 500	
Receivables	Cr		31 500
(Impairment of receivable)			

16.8.2 Non-adjusting events after the reporting period

Paragraph 10 of IAS 10 states that an entity shall not adjust the amounts recognised in its financial statements to reflect non-adjusting events after the reporting period. Examples of non-adjusting events include:

- a major business combination after the reporting period
- the destruction of property by fire after the reporting period
- the issuance of new share capital after the reporting period
- commencing major litigation arising solely out of events that occurred after the reporting period.

Although these events are not adjusted for, paragraph 21 of IAS 10 requires the following disclosure for each material category of non-adjusting event after the reporting period:

- the nature of the event; and
- an estimate of its financial effect, or a statement that such an estimate cannot be made.

Paragraph 11 of IAS 10 refers to a controversial area of accounting for events after the reporting period. It states that a decline in the market value of investments between the end of the reporting period and the date when the financial statements are authorised for issue is a non-adjusting event, because the decline in market value does not normally relate to the condition of the investments at the end of the reporting period but instead reflects circumstances that have arisen subsequently. This appears to be inconsistent with the treatment of the receivables referred to in paragraph 9(b)(i) of IAS 10, regarding the insolvency of a debtor after the reporting period. IAS 10 paragraph 9(b)(i) states that this would constitute an adjusting event because the insolvency confirms that a loss existed at the end of the reporting period. The critical issue here is the amount and uncertainty of the future cash flows arising from the receivable, not whether the debtor was insolvent at the end of the reporting period. There may have been some concerns about collectability at the end of the reporting period.

A view that reconciles the differing treatment is that the additional information about the debtor's insolvency provides further evidence that the receivable was impaired and enables a better assessment of the extent of impairment. However, for assets, such as investments in securities that are traded in an active market, the market value at the reporting date would have been observable. Thus, the position taken in paragraph 11 is that the change in market value of the securities observed after the reporting period is indicative of conditions that arose after the reporting period, and, as such, is a non-adjusting event after the reporting period.

SUMMARY

IAS 1 *Presentation of Financial Statements*, IAS 8 *Accounting Policies, Changes in Accounting Estimates and Errors* and IAS 10 *Events after the Reporting Period* deal with fundamental disclosures and considerations that underpin financial statement presentation.

IAS 1 prescribes overall considerations to be applied in the preparation of financial statements, and the structure and content of financial statements, which comprise a statement of financial position, statement of profit or loss and other comprehensive income, statement of cash flows, statement of changes in equity and notes. The prescribed disclosures are designed to enhance the understandability of the financial statements for the users of general purpose financial statements in their economic decision making.

IAS 8 prescribes the accounting treatment for changes in accounting policies, changes in accounting estimates and correction of prior period errors. Changes in accounting policies and corrections of errors are applied retrospectively, while changes in accounting estimates are recognised prospectively.

IAS 10 distinguishes between two types of events after the reporting period — adjusting and non-adjusting. Adjusting events must be recognised in the financial statements, whereas non-adjusting events must be disclosed only.

Discussion questions

1. Describe the eight general principles to be applied in the presentation of financial statements. Which principles are more subjective? Explain your answer.
2. Why is it important for entities to disclose the measurement bases used in preparing the financial statements?
3. How do the presentation and disclosure requirements of IFRS Standards reflect the objectives of financial statements? Illustrate your argument with examples from IAS 1, IAS 8 and IAS 10.
4. What is the purpose of a statement of financial position? What comprises a complete set of financial statements in accordance with IAS 1?
5. What are the major limitations of a statement of financial position as a source of information for users of general purpose financial statements?
6. Under what circumstances are assets and liabilities ordinarily classified broadly in order of liquidity rather than on a current/non-current classification?
7. Can an asset that is not realisable within 12 months be classified as a current asset? If so, under what circumstances?
8. Explain the difference between classification of expenses by nature and by function.
9. Does the separate identification of profit and items of other comprehensive income provide a meaningful distinction between the effects of different types of non-owner transactions and events?
10. What is the objective of a statement of changes in equity?
11. Why is a summary of accounting policies important to ensuring the understandability of financial statements to users of general purpose financial statements?
12. Provide an example of a judgement made in preparing the financial statements that can lead to estimation uncertainty at the end of the reporting period. Describe the disclosures that would be required in the notes.
13. What disclosures are required in the notes in regard to accounting policy judgements?
14. What is the difference between an accounting policy and an accounting estimate? Provide an example of each.

15. Explain the difference between retrospective application of a change in accounting policy and prospective application of a change in accounting estimate. Why do you think the standard setters require prospective application of a change in accounting estimate?

16. Explain the difference between adjusting and non-adjusting events after the reporting period. Provide examples to illustrate your answer.

References

BHP Billiton 2015, *Annual Report 2015*, BHP Billiton, www.bhpbilliton.com.

HSBC Holdings plc 2014, *Annual Report 2014*, HSBC Holdings plc, London, www.hsbc.com.

International Accounting Standards Board (IASB) 2012, *IASB documents published to accompany International Accounting Standard 1 Presentation of Financial Statements*, IASB, London, www.ifrs.org.

Exercises

STAR RATING ★ BASIC ★★ MODERATE ★★★ DIFFICULT

Exercise 16.1	CURRENT ASSET AND LIABILITY CLASSIFICATIONS

★ The general ledger trial balance of Joshua Limited at 31 December 2016 includes the following asset and liability accounts:

(a) Interest payable	£ 2 000
(b) Trade receivables	100 000
(c) Accounts payable	85 000
(d) Prepayments	12 000
(e) Inventory of finished goods	120 000
(f) Allowance for doubtful debts	8 000
(g) Cash	10 000
(h) Accrued wages and salaries	20 000
(i) Inventory of raw materials	60 000
(j) Loan (due 31 October 2017)	100 000
(k) Lease liability	75 000
(l) Current tax payable	30 000

Additional information
- The lease liability includes an amount of £13 000 for lease payments due before 31 December 2017.
- The company classifies assets and liabilities using a current/non-current basis.

Required

Prepare the current assets and current liabilities sections of the statement of financial position of Joshua Limited as at 31 December 2016, using the minimum line items permitted under IAS 1.

Exercise 16.2	STATEMENT OF PROFIT OR LOSS AND OTHER COMPREHENSIVE INCOME

★ The general ledger trial balance of Lachlan Ltd includes the following accounts at 31 December 2016:

(a) Sales revenue	$1 200 000
(b) Interest income	24 000
(c) Gain on sale of plant	5 000
(d) Valuation gain on trading securities	20 000
(e) Dividend revenue	5 000
(f) Cost of sales	840 000
(g) Finance expenses	18 000
(h) Selling and distribution expenses	76 000
(i) Administrative expenses	35 000
(j) Income tax expense	85 000

Additional information
- Lachlan Ltd also recognised a loss of $1000 net of tax on valuation of investment securities. Valuation gains and losses on the investment securities are recognised in other comprehensive income.
- A gain of $4000 net of tax was recognised on the revaluation of land.
- Lachlan Ltd uses the single statement format for the statement of profit or loss and other comprehensive income.
- Lachlan Ltd classifies expenses by function.

Required

Prepare the statement of profit or loss and other comprehensive income of Lachlan Ltd for the year ended 31 December 2016, showing the analysis of expenses in the statement.

STATEMENT OF CHANGES IN EQUITY

★ The shareholders' equity section of the statement of financial position of Riley Ltd at 31 December 2016 is shown below.

	2016	2015
Share capital	£200 000	£160 000
General reserve	50 000	40 000
Foreign currency translation reserve	74 000	60 000
Retained earnings	170 000	160 000
	£494 000	£420 000

Additional information
- Riley Ltd issued 16 000 shares at £2.50 each on 31 May 2016 for cash.
- A transfer of £10 000 was made from retained earnings to the general reserve.
- Comprehensive income for the year was £144 000, including a foreign currency translation gain of £14 000 recognised in other comprehensive income.
- Dividends paid during 2016 comprised: final dividend for 2015, £50 000; interim dividend, £60 000.

Required

Prepare the statement of changes in equity of Riley Ltd for the year ended 31 December 2016 in accordance with IAS 1.

MATERIALITY, OFFSETTING

★ Company A is a retailer that imports about 30% of its goods. The following foreign exchange gains and losses were recognised in profit during the year:

	Loss €m	Gain €m
Foreign currency borrowings with Bank L	50	
Forward exchange contracts used as hedging instruments		1
Forward exchange contracts not used as hedges	3	
Foreign currency borrowings with Bank S		10

Additional information
Materiality has been determined as €5 million for items recognised in profit or loss.

Required

Identify which of the above gains and losses are permitted to be offset in Company A's financial statements.

ACCOUNTING POLICIES, ACCOUNTING ESTIMATES

★ State whether each of the following is an accounting policy or an accounting estimate for Company A:
(a) The useful life of depreciable plant is determined as being 6 years.
(b) Company A recognises income arising from service contracts on the basis of the stage of completion.
(c) Company A determines that it will calculate its warranty provision using past experience of defective products.
(d) The current year's warranty provision is calculated by providing for 1% of current year sales, based on last year's warranty claims amounting to 1% of sales.

PREPARATION OF A STATEMENT OF FINANCIAL POSITION

★ The summarised general ledger trial balance of Noah Ltd includes the following accounts at 31 December 2016:

	Dr	Cr
Cash deposits	$ 117 000	
Trade debtors	1 163 000	
Allowance for doubtful debts		$ 50 000

	Dr	Cr
Sundry receivables	270 000	
Prepayments	94 000	
Sundry loans (current)	20 000	
Raw materials on hand	493 000	
Finished goods	695 000	
Investments in corporate bonds	30 000	
Land (at cost)	234 000	
Buildings (at cost)	687 000	
Accumulated depreciation – buildings		80 000
Plant and equipment (at cost)	6 329 000	
Accumulated depreciation – plant and equipment		3 036 000
Goodwill	2 425 000	
Brand names	40 000	
Patents	25 000	
Deferred tax asset	189 000	
Trade payables		1 078 000
Sundry payables		568 000
Bank overdraft		115 000
Bank loans		1 848 000
Other loans		646 000
Current tax payable		74 000
Provision for employee benefits		222 000
Dividends payable		100 000
Provision for warranty		20 000
Share capital		3 459 000
Retained earnings		1 515 000
	$12 811 000	$12 811 000

Additional information
- The bank overdraft is payable within 12 months. It does not form part of cash equivalents.
- Bank loans include $620 000 repayable within 1 year.
- Other loans outstanding are repayable within 1 year.
- Provision for employee benefits includes $143 000 payable within 1 year.
- Provision for warranty is in respect of a 6-month warranty given over certain goods sold.
- The investments in corporate bonds are long-term investments.

Required

Prepare the statement of financial position of Noah Ltd at 31 December 2016 in accordance with IAS 1, using the captions that a listed company is likely to use.

Exercise 16.7   **STATEMENT OF PROFIT OR LOSS AND OTHER COMPREHENSIVE INCOME**

★★ The general ledger trial balance of James Ltd includes the following accounts at 31 December 2016:

(a) Sales revenue	$975 000
(b) Interest income	20 000
(c) Share of profit of associates accounted for using the equity method	15 000
(d) Gain on sale of securities investments	10 000
(e) Decrease in inventories of finished goods	25 000
(f) Raw materials and consumables used	350 000
(g) Employee benefit expenses	150 000
(h) Loss on translation of foreign operations (nil tax effect)	25 000
(i) Depreciation of property, plant and equipment	45 000
(j) Impairment loss on property	80 000
(k) Finance costs	35 000
(l) Other expenses	45 000
(m) Income tax expense (current)	75 000

Additional information
- Securities investments are revalued regularly, with changes in fair value recognised in other comprehensive income and accumulated in equity in the investments revaluation reserve. When securities are sold, the accumulated amount recognised in equity for the asset is reclassified to profit

or loss. Movements in the investments revaluation reserve during the year ended 31 December 2016 comprised:
- gross revaluation increases recognised $44 000 (related deferred income tax $14 000)
- gross reclassifications on sale of securities investments $10 000 gain (related income tax $3000).
- James Ltd uses the single statement format for the statement of profit or loss and other comprehensive income.
- James Ltd presents an analysis of expenses by nature in the statement of profit or loss and other comprehensive income.

Required

Prepare the statement of profit or loss and other comprehensive income of James Ltd for the year ended 31 December 2016.

Exercise 16.8 | PRESENTATION OF ITEMS IN THE FINANCIAL STATEMENTS

★★ Consider the following items for Cooper Ltd at 31 December 2016:
(a) contingent liabilities
(b) the effect on retained earnings of the correction of a prior period error
(c) cash and cash equivalents
(d) capital contributed during the year
(e) revaluation gain on land (not reversing any previous revaluation)
(f) judgements that management has made in classifying financial assets
(g) income tax expense
(h) provisions.

Required

State whether each item is reported:
1. in the statement of financial position
2. in profit or loss in the statement of profit or loss and other comprehensive income
3. in other comprehensive income in the statement of profit or loss and other comprehensive income
4. in the statement of changes in equity
5. in the notes to the financial statements.

Exercise 16.9 | ACCOUNTING POLICIES, ACCOUNTING ESTIMATES, ERRORS

★★ State whether the following changes should be accounted for and, if so, whether retrospectively or prospectively, in accordance with IAS 8:
(a) A change in accounting policy made voluntarily.
(b) A change in accounting policy required by an accounting standard.
(c) A change in an accounting estimate.
(d) An immaterial error discovered in the current year, relating to a transaction recorded 2 years ago.
(e) A material error discovered in the current year, relating to a transaction recorded 2 years ago. Management determines that retrospective application would cause undue cost and effort.
(f) A change in accounting policy required by an accounting standard. Retrospective application of that standard would require assumptions about what management's intent would have been in the relevant period(s).

Exercise 16.10 | CHANGE IN ACCOUNTING ESTIMATE

★★ On 1 January 2011 Company H acquired a building. The company depreciated the building on a straight-line basis, with an estimated useful life of 15 years and nil residual value. In 2016, Company H's directors reviewed the depreciation rates for similar buildings used in its industry and decided that the buildings should be depreciated over a total period of 20 years. Company H's reporting period ends on 31 December.

As at 1 January 2016, the balance of administration buildings was as follows:

Cost	$ 5 000 000
Accumulated depreciation	(1 666 667)
Carrying amount	3 333 333

Required

Prepare the note describing Company H's change in accounting estimate for the year ended 31 December 2016, including comparative figures, in accordance with IAS 8. Show all workings.

Exercise 16.11 ADJUSTING/NON-ADJUSTING EVENTS AFTER THE REPORTING PERIOD

★★★ The financial statements of Company N are authorised for issue on 12 February 2017 and the end of the reporting period is 31 December 2016. State whether each of the following material items would be an adjusting or non-adjusting event after the reporting period in the financial statements of Company N. Give reasons for your answer.

(a) At 31 December Company N had recorded an overdue receivable from Company P at $25 000 because collection of the full amount of $40 000 was in doubt. On 16 January, a receiver was appointed to Company P. The receiver informed Company N that the $40 000 would be paid in full by 30 April 2017.

(b) On 24 January Company N issued corporate bonds for $1 000 000, with interest of 5% payable semi-annually in arrears.

(c) Company N's investments in listed shares are held-for-trading and measured at fair value, with gains and losses recognised in profit or loss. As at 31 December, these investments were recorded at the market value at that date, which was $500 000. During January and February 2017, there was a steady decline in the market values of all the shares in the portfolio. By 12 February 2017 the market value of the investments had fallen to $400 000.

(d) Company N had reported a contingent liability at 31 December in respect of a lawsuit against the company by an employee who was injured during 2016. The case was not heard until the first week of February 2017. On 11 February, the judge handed down her decision, against Company N. The judge determined that Company N was liable to pay damages and costs totalling $3 000 000.

(e) As in part (d), except that the damages and costs awarded against Company N were $50 million, leading Company N to place itself into voluntary liquidation.

Exercise 16.12 PREPARATION OF A STATEMENT OF FINANCIAL POSITION, STATEMENT OF PROFIT OR LOSS AND OTHER COMPREHENSIVE INCOME AND STATEMENT OF CHANGES IN EQUITY

★★★ The summarised general ledger trial balance of Matthew Ltd, a manufacturing company, for the year ended 31 December 2016 is detailed below:

	Dr	Cr
Sales revenue		$5 000 000
Interest income		22 000
Sundry income		25 000
Change in inventory of work in progress	$ 125 000	
Change in inventory of finished goods		60 000
Raw materials used	2 200 000	
Employee benefit expense	950 000	
Depreciation expense	226 000	
Amortisation – patent	25 000	
Rental expense	70 000	
Advertising expense	142 000	
Insurance expense	45 000	
Freight out expense	133 000	
Doubtful debts expense	10 000	
Interest expense	30 000	
Other expenses	8 000	
Income tax expense	320 000	
Cash	4 000	
Cash on deposit, at call	80 000	
Trade receivables	495 000	
Allowance for doubtful debts		18 000
Other receivables	27 000	
Raw materials inventory, 31 December 2016	320 000	
Finished goods inventory, 31 December 2016	385 000	
Land	94 000	
Buildings	220 000	
Accumulated depreciation – land and buildings		52 000
Plant and equipment	1 380 000	
Accumulated depreciation – plant and equipment		320 000
Patents	140 000	

	Dr	Cr
Accumulated amortisation – patent		50 000
Goodwill	620 000	
Bank loans		92 000
Other loans		450 000
Trade payables		452 000
Provision for employee benefits		120 000
Income tax payable		35 000
Deferred tax liability		140 000
Retained earnings, 31 December 2015		310 000
Dividends paid	210 000	
Share capital		1 137 000
Dividends reinvested		41 000
Deferred cash flow hedge (equity)	65 000	
	$8 324 000	$8 324 000

Additional information
- All of the deferred cash flow hedge arose in the current period. This item was recognised in other comprehensive income. The related tax was nil.
- $20 000 of bank loans is repayable within 1 year.
- $90 000 of other loans is repayable within 1 year.
- Matthew Ltd uses the single statement format for the statement of profit or loss and other comprehensive income and presents an analysis of expenses by nature in the statement.

Required

Prepare the statement of financial position, statement of profit or loss and other comprehensive income and statement of changes in equity of Matthew Ltd for the year ended 31 December 2016 in accordance with the requirements of IAS 1, using statement captions that a listed company is likely to use.

Under IAS 1 certain changes in net assets are reported as other comprehensive income (OCI) rather than in the income statement (IS). One concern that academics have raised is whether items reported in OCI are interpreted differently than items reported in the IS. Dhaliwal et al. (1999) examine a sample of over 11,000 firm-year observations between 1994 and 1995 and find that most companies report non-zero OCI. They then examine the association between stock returns and the sum of net income and OCI — or, adjusted income — and establish that it is positive. The explanatory power of adjusted income for stock return is larger than that of net income alone. This is consistent with decision usefulness of OCI. However, further investigation reveals that the additional usefulness primarily stems from fair-value adjustments of available-for-sale securities that are reported in OCI and not from other sources of OCI. The authors also explore the association between net income and adjusted income with stock prices. They find that the association is stronger for net income. Moreover, net income is more closely related to future cash flows and future net income than adjusted income. The conclusion the authors draw from this evidence is that OCI is a noisy measure of performance and hence is not as useful as net income. However, this finding may be due to the fact that Dhaliwal et al. (1999) do not separate between net income and OCI to see how each component individually and incrementally is used by investors. This task is performed by Barton et al. (2010) employing a very large international sample (46 countries) between 1996 and 2005. They examine an alternative specification whereby net income and total comprehensive income are tested separately and incrementally to each other. This alternative specification, however, does not change the insight that OCI is measured with considerable noise and is not value relevant. However, conflicting evidence is provided by Chambers et al. (2007). Specifically, they find from a US sample of 2705 firm-year observations in the 1998–2003 period that OCI is positively related to stock returns. The contrast with Dhaliwal et al. (1999) is explained by the fact that Dhaliwal et al. (1999) do not actually use OCI numbers as prescribed by SFAS 130 (now ASC 220) (FASB, 1997), but proxy for these numbers. Similarly, Barton et al. (2010) largely employ reports prepared under older versions of IAS 1.

While IFRS Standards now require the reporting of OCI either immediately following the income statement or in the statement of comprehensive income, this has not always been the case. In the US, for example, certain items of OCI could be reported in the statement of changes in equity. Adopting this approach therefore shifts the location of OCI from a performance-focused statement — the statement of comprehensive income — to the balance sheet. But, does the location of OCI reporting matter? One may argue that the most important issue is that the relevant figures are clearly reported, regardless of their location. However, if investors have limited attention, as is argued by Hirshleifer and Teoh (2003), they may focus on performance measures at the expense of information disclosed elsewhere in the financials (e.g., the statement of changes in equity). Experimental evidence indeed suggests that location may matter. Maines and McDaniel (2000) provide evidence that non-professional investors ignore the volatility of OCI if it is reported in the statement of changes in equity. Hirst and Hopkins (1998) run an experiment based on professional subjects who examine a case where a fictitious firm sells available-for-sale (AFS) instruments to realise a holding gain. The sale of the AFS instruments is not expected to affect the firms' value because they were already carried at fair value. However, Hirst and Hopkins (1998) find that the location of information about this gain matters for valuation. Specifically, reporting the resulting changes in comprehensive income attracts lower valuations than reporting in the statement of changes in equity. The implication is that professional investors focus on performance measures such as comprehensive income and analyse related disclosures more diligently.

Bamber et al. (2010) build on the above-mentioned research to argue that managers believe that reporting OCI in a performance statement will increase investors' perception of performance volatility. This acts as an incentive to report OCI in the statement of changes in equity. Bamber et al. (2010) further hypothesise that this incentive is stronger for managers whose compensation is more equity-based (because higher volatility reduces stock prices) and who face the threat of dismissal. To test their hypotheses Bamber et al. (2010) assemble a sample of 440 S&P 500 firms between 1998 and 2001. They find that 81% of sample firms report OCI in the statement of changes in equity. They also find evidence that the likelihood of reporting OCI in the statement of changes in equity is greater for managers that receive more equity compensation but decreases with measures of CEO power (which is inversely related to dismissal risk).

Older versions of IAS 1 required that financial statements give a 'true and fair view' (TFV) of the financial affairs of the reporting entity. Older versions of IAS 1 further required that a reporting entity departs from promulgated standards if by following them the reporting will be misleading, and hence inconsistent with TFV. Such a departure is called TFV override. In preparation for the 2005 adoption of IFRS Standards in Europe IAS 1 was revised to require fair presentation, and, furthermore, to discourage TFV overrides (the language of the standard now speaks about *rare* circumstances in which an override can be invoked). An important question in this context is whether companies use TFV overrides to improve the quality of financial reports, or do so only when it is convenient for them. There is unfortunately scarce empirical research on this topic, in part because following the adoption of IFRS Standards most firms have been discouraged from overrides. An exception is the study by Livne and McNichols (2009) who examine TFV overrides in the UK prior to the 2005 adoption of IFRS Standards. The authors first develop a classification system to assess the severity of an override. A more costly override is expected to be invoked to the extent that it delivers better outcomes to managers. Livne and McNichols (2009) find that more costly overrides (overrides of UK GAAP) are associated with poor performance. This evidence therefore suggests that overrides were invoked opportunistically in an effort to improve reported performance and financial position. Further, firms that invoked TFV overrides are associated with poorer quality of financial statements. This evidence suggests that allowing more flexibility to invoke an override may lead to unintended consequences.

References

Bamber, L.S., Jiang, J., Petroni, K.R., and Wang, I.Y., 2010. Comprehensive income: Who's afraid of performance reporting? *The Accounting Review*, 85(1), 97–126.

Barton, J., Hansen, T.B., and Pownall, G., 2010. Which performance measures do investors around the world value the most—and why? *The Accounting Review*, 85(3), 753–789.

Chambers, D., Linsmeier, T.J., Shakespeare, C., and Sougiannis, T., 2007. An evaluation of SFAS No. 130 comprehensive income disclosures. *Review of Accounting Studies*, 12(4), 557–593.

Dhaliwal, D., Subramanyam, K.R., and Trezevant, R., 1999. Is comprehensive income superior to net income as a measure of firm performance? *Journal of Accounting and Economics*, 26(1), 43–67.

Financial Accounting Standards Board (FASB). 1997. Reporting comprehensive income. SFAS No. 130. Stamford, CT: FASB

Hirshleifer, D., and Teoh, S.H., 2003. Limited attention, information disclosure, and financial reporting. *Journal of Accounting and Economics*, 36(1), 337–386.

Hirst, D.E., and Hopkins, P.E., 1998. Comprehensive income reporting and analysts' valuation judgments. *Journal of Accounting Research*, 36, 47–75.

Livne, G., and McNichols, M., 2009. An empirical investigation of the true and fair override in the United Kingdom. *Journal of Business Finance & Accounting*, 36(1–2), 1–30.

Maines, L.A., and McDaniel, L.S., 2000. Effects of comprehensive-income characteristics on nonprofessional investors' judgments: The role of financial-statement presentation format. *The Accounting Review*, 75(2), 179–207.

17
Statement of cash flows

ACCOUNTING STANDARDS IN FOCUS

IAS 7 *Statement of Cash Flows*

LEARNING OBJECTIVES

After studying this chapter, you should be able to:

 1   explain the purpose of a statement of cash flows and its usefulness

 2   explain the definition of cash and cash equivalents

 3   explain the classification of cash flow activities and classify cash inflows and outflows into operating, investing and financing activities

 4   contrast the direct and indirect methods of presenting net cash flows from operating activities

 5   prepare a statement of cash flows and use a worksheet to prepare a statement of cash flows with more complex transactions

 6   prepare other disclosures required or encouraged by IAS 7.

INTRODUCTION AND SCOPE

Ultimately, all existing and potential investors, lenders and other creditors would like to receive cash from their investment. Consequently, information about an entity's receipts and payments is important to such users of financial statements. The statement of cash flows provides this information by reporting cash inflows and outflows classified into operating, investing and financing activities, and the net movement in cash and cash equivalents during the period.

This chapter explains how to present a statement of cash flows in accordance with IAS 7 *Statement of Cash Flows*.

17.1 PURPOSE OF A STATEMENT OF CASH FLOWS

The overall purpose of a statement of cash flows is to present information about the historical changes in cash and cash equivalents of an entity during the period classified by operating, investing and financing activities. The statement of cash flows can help users of financial statements to:

• evaluate the entity's ability to generate cash and cash equivalents
• predict future cash flows
• evaluate the accuracy of past cash flow predictions and forecasts.

When used in combination with other financial statements, the statement of cash flows can help users to:

• evaluate an entity's financial structure (including liquidity and solvency) and its ability to meet its obligations and to pay dividends
• evaluate the entity's ability to affect the amount and timing of future cash flows, to enable it to adapt to changing business opportunities and circumstances
• understand the reasons for the difference between profit or loss for a period and the net cash flow from operating activities (the reasons for the differences are often helpful in evaluating the quality of earnings of an entity)
• compare the operating performance of different entities because cash flows are not directly affected by different accounting choices and judgements under accrual accounting.

17.2 DEFINING CASH AND CASH EQUIVALENTS

Paragraph 6 of IAS 7 defines cash and cash equivalents as follows:

> *Cash* comprises cash on hand and demand deposits.
>
> *Cash equivalents* are short-term, highly liquid investments that are readily convertible to known amounts of cash and which are subject to an insignificant risk of changes in value.

Paragraph 7 of IAS 7 explains that cash equivalents are held for the purpose of meeting short-term cash commitments, and not for investment or other purposes. Cash equivalents must be able to be converted into a known amount of cash. This means that the amount of cash that will be received must be known at the time of the initial investment in the cash equivalent. It must also have no more than an insignificant risk of changing in value. Therefore, an investment will qualify as a cash equivalent only if it has a short maturity (usually 3 months or less). Examples of cash and cash equivalents include cash on hand, cash at bank, short-term money market securities and 90-day term deposits. Equity investments typically do not qualify as cash equivalents, but it is necessary to consider their substance; equity instruments such as preferred shares acquired shortly before their specified maturity date may fall within the definition of cash equivalents.

Bank borrowings are ordinarily classified as a financing activity. A bank overdraft is a special case. It can arise where a customer has a facility with the bank that allows the customer's account to be overdrawn (i.e. to go below nil). The amount of the bank overdraft can vary on a daily basis up to an agreed limit. This would not usually be considered as part of cash and cash equivalents. However, if the bank overdraft is repayable on demand and forms an integral part of an entity's cash management, it is included in cash and cash equivalents. Such overdrafts may fluctuate from being overdrawn to being positive (i.e. cash at bank).

The statement of cash flows reports on changes in aggregate cash and cash equivalents. Therefore, movements between items classified as cash and cash equivalents, such as a transfer from cash at bank to a 90-day term deposit, are not reported in the statement of cash flows. The concept of cash and cash equivalents used in IAS 7 is summarised and illustrated in figure 17.1.

	Form	Conditions	Examples
Cash	Cash on hand		Notes and coins
	Demand deposits		Call deposits held at financial institutions
Cash equivalents	Short-term, highly liquid investments	Readily convertible into known amounts of cash and subject to an insignificant risk of change in value	Bank bills
			Non-bank bills
			Deposits on short-term money market, such as 7-day deposits
	Bank overdraft	Repayable on demand and form an integral part of an entity's cash management	Cheque account that is in overdraft and which is repayable on demand

FIGURE 17.1 Concept of cash and cash equivalents used in IAS 7
Source: Loftus et al. 2015.

17.3 CLASSIFYING CASH FLOW ACTIVITIES

As stated earlier, cash flow activities reported in the statement of cash flows are classified into operating, investing and financing activities. Paragraph 6 of IAS 7 defines these activities as follows:

Operating activities are the principal revenue-producing activities of the entity and other activities that are not investing or financing activities.

Investing activities are the acquisition and disposal of long-term assets and other investments not included in cash equivalents.

Financing activities are activities that result in changes in the size and composition of the contributed equity and borrowings of the entity.

Only expenditures that result in a recognised asset in the statement of financial position are eligible for classification as investing activities. For example, Green GmbH incurs expenditure of €50 000 on research for a carbon-neutral air conditioner. Expenditure incurred in the research phase must be recognised as an expense in accordance with IAS 38 *Intangible Assets*. Accordingly, the cash paid in relation to the research project is not classified as an investing cash flow because it has not resulted in the recognition of an asset in the statement of financial position of Green GmbH.

Note that the operating activities category is a default category; it includes all activities that are not classified as either investing activities or financing activities. Figure 17.2 summarises typical cash receipts and payments of an entity, classified by activity.

Operating activities

Cash inflows from:
 Sale of goods
 Rendering of services
 Royalties, fees, commissions
 Interest received (or investing activity)
 Dividends received (or investing activity)

Cash outflows for:
 Payments to suppliers of goods and services
 Payments to employees for services
 Payments to the government for income
  tax and other taxes
 Payments to lenders for interest or other
  borrowing cost (or finance activity)

Investing activities

Cash inflows from:
 Sale of property, plant and equipment
 Sale of intangibles
 Sale of shares and debt instruments of
  other entities
 Repayment of loans by other parties

Cash outflows for:
 Purchases of property, plant and equipment
 Purchases of intangibles
 Purchases of shares and debt instruments
  of other entities
 Loans to other entities

Financing activities

Cash inflows from:
 Issuing shares and other equity instruments
 Issuing debentures, unsecured notes
 Borrowings, such as loans

Cash outflows for:
 Buying back own shares (reduction in capital)
 Repayment of debentures, unsecured notes
 Repayment of borrowings, such as loans
 Payment of dividends to shareholders (or operating)

FIGURE 17.2 Typical cash receipts and payments classified by activity

17.3.1 Classifying interest and dividends received and paid

IAS 7 does not prescribe how interest and dividends received and paid should be classified. Rather, paragraph 31 of IAS 7 requires cash flows from interest and dividends received and paid to be disclosed separately and classified consistently from period to period as operating, investing or financing activities. Although most financial institutions classify interest paid and interest and dividends received as operating cash flows there is no consensus on how to classify these cash flows for other entities. Some entities classify interest paid and interest and dividends received as operating cash flows because they may relate to items that determine profit or loss, while other entities classify interest paid as financing cash flows and interest and dividends received as investing cash flows, viewing them as the costs of financing or the returns on investments respectively. Paragraph 34 notes that dividends paid may be classified as financing cash flows because they are a cost of obtaining equity finance or as cash from operating activities, to assist users to determine the ability of the entity to pay dividends from operating cash flows.

BHP Billiton classifies interest received and interest paid as cash flows from operating activities as shown in figure 17.3.

	2015 US$M	2014 US$M Restated	2013 US$M Restated
Operating activities			
Profit before taxation from Continuing operations	**8 056**	21 735	20 828
Adjustments for:			
Non-cash or non-operating exceptional items	**3 196**	(551)	(331)
Depreciation and amortisation expense	**9 158**	7 716	6 067
Net gain on sale of non-current assets	**(9)**	(73)	(17)
Impairments of property, plant and equipment, financial assets and intangibles	**828**	478	344
Employee share awards expense	**247**	247	210
Net finance costs	**614**	914	1 149
Share of operating profit of equity accounted investments	**(548)**	(1 185)	(1 142)
Other	**265**	(79)	5
Changes in assets and liabilities:			
Trade and other receivables	**1 431**	(349)	904
Inventories	**151**	(158)	(276)
Trade and other payables	**(990)**	238	(239)
Net other financial assets and liabilities	**(8)**	(90)	89
Provisions and other liabilities	**(771)**	475	(565)
Cash generated from operations	**21 620**	29 318	27 026
Dividends received	**17**	14	6
Dividends received from equity accounted investments	**723**	1 250	710
Interest received	**86**	120	112
Interest paid	**(627)**	(915)	(960)
Income tax refunded	**348**	848	—
Income tax paid	**(3 225)**	(6 123)	(6 921)
Royalty-related taxation refunded	**—**	216	—
Royalty-related taxation paid	**(1 148)**	(1 088)	(956)
Net operating cash flows from Continuing operations	**17 794**	23 640	19 017
Net operating cash flows from Discontinued operations	**1 502**	1 724	1 137
Net operating cash flows	**19 296**	25 364	20 154

FIGURE 17.3 BHP Billiton cash flows from operating activities for the year ended 30 June 2015
Source: BHP Billiton (2015, p. 209).

17.3.2 Classifying taxes on income

Paragraph 35 of IAS 7 requires income tax paid to be separately disclosed in the statement of cash flows and classified as cash flows from operating activities, unless it can be specifically identified with financing or investing activities. As noted in paragraph 36 of IAS 7, while the tax expense may often be readily identifiable with investing or financing activities, the associated cash flows may arise in different periods, making it very difficult to classify tax payments as cash paid for investing or financing activities. Accordingly, taxes paid are usually classified as cash flows from operating activities. Refer to figure 17.3 to identify the income tax paid reported by BHP Billiton in the operating activities section of the statement of cash flows.

17.4 FORMAT OF THE STATEMENT OF CASH FLOWS

The general format of a statement of cash flows follows the three cash flow activities. Cash flows from operating activities are presented first, followed by cash flows from investing activities and then those from financing activities. The resultant net increase or decrease in cash and cash equivalents during the period is then used to report the movement in cash and cash equivalents from the balance at the beginning of the period to the balance at the end of the period.

17.4.1 Reporting cash flows from operating activities

Paragraph 18 of IAS 7 provides that cash flows from operating activities may be reported using one of two methods:
- the *direct method* — which presents major classes of gross cash receipts and gross cash payments in the statement of cash flows
- the *indirect method* — which adjusts profit or loss for the effects of transactions of a non-cash nature, any deferrals or accruals of past or future operating cash receipts or payments, and items of income or expense associated with investing or financing cash flows. Alternatively, the cash flows from operations may be presented under the indirect method by adjusting revenues for changes in receivables and adjusting expenses for changes in inventories, payables and other accruals (IAS 7 paragraph 20). Although both methods are permitted, IAS 7 explicitly encourages the use of the direct method.

Figure 17.4 illustrates the typical format of a statement of cash flows that uses the direct method.

Statement of Cash Flows for the year ended 31 December . . .		
Cash flows from operating activities		
Cash receipts from customers	$ xxx	
Cash paid to suppliers and employees	(xxx)	
Cash generated from operations	xxx	
Interest received	xxx	
Interest paid	(xxx)	
Income taxes paid	(xxx)	
Net cash from operating activities		xxx
Cash flows from investing activities		
Acquisition of subsidiary, net of cash acquired	(xxx)	
Purchase of property and plant	(xxx)	
Proceeds from sale of plant	xxx	
Net cash used in investing activities		(xxx)
Cash flows from financing activities		
Proceeds from share issue	xxx	
Proceeds from borrowings	xxx	
Payment of borrowings	(xxx)	
Dividends paid	(xxx)	
Net cash from financing activities		xxx
Net increase in cash and cash equivalents		xxx
Cash and cash equivalents at beginning of year		xxx
Cash and cash equivalents at end of year		xxx

FIGURE 17.4 Typical format of a statement of cash flows using the direct method of reporting cash flows from operating activities

Figure 17.5 illustrates the typical format of the indirect method of reporting cash flows from operating activities.

As can be seen in figure 17.5, depreciation expense is added back to profit in calculating cash flows from operating activities. This is because depreciation expense reduces profit but has no effect on cash flows. The loss on the sale of investment is added back to profit because it reduces profit but does not affect cash flows from operating activities. Conversely, a gain on the disposal of equipment would be deducted from profit in calculating cash flows from operations. The related cash flow (i.e. the cash proceeds on the sale of the equipment) is included in cash flows from investing activities.

Profit before tax is adjusted for the difference between an amount recognised in profit and the corresponding operating cash flows, such as the change in receivables, which reflects the difference between sales revenue and cash collected from customers. This process is explained in more detail later (*see section 17.5*). In applying the indirect method, the total amount of interest income is deducted, rather than the difference between interest income measured on an accrual basis and the amount of interest received. This is because paragraph 31 of IAS 7 requires disclosure of interest received in the statement of cash flows, irrespective of whether cash flows from operating activities are presented using the direct method or the indirect method.

Statement of Cash Flows for the year ended 31 December . . .	
Profit before tax	$ xxx
Adjustments for:	
Depreciation	xxx
Foreign exchange loss	xxx
Loss on sale of equipment	xxx
Interest income	(xxx)
Interest expense	xxx
Increase in trade and other receivables	(xxx)
Decrease in inventories	xxx
Increase in accounts payable	xxx
Decrease in accrued liabilities	(xxx)
Cash generated from operations	xxx
Interest received	xxx
Interest paid	(xxx)
Income taxes paid	(xxx)
Net cash from operating activities	xxx

FIGURE 17.5 Typical format for the indirect method of reporting cash flows from operating activities

Can you tell the difference between the two methods of presenting the operating activities section of the statement of cash flows? Test yourself. Which method is used by BHP Billiton in figure 17.3?

17.4.2 Reporting cash flows from investing and financing activities

Paragraph 21 of IAS 7 requires separate reporting of the major classes of gross cash receipts and gross cash payments arising from investing and financing activities, except for certain cash flows (outlined in the following section) that may be reported on a net basis.

17.4.3 Reporting cash flows on a net basis

Paragraph 22 of IAS 7 allows the following cash flows to be reported on a net basis:

(a) cash receipts and payments on behalf of customers when the cash flows reflect the activities of the customer rather than those of the entity, such as the acceptance and repayment of a bank's demand deposits, and rents collected from tenants by an agent and paid to the property owners; and

(b) cash receipts and payments for items in which the turnover is quick, the amounts are large, and the maturities are short. For example, assume an entity finances some of its operations with a 90-day bill acceptance facility with its bank. This means that the entity writes commercial bills, giving rise to a contractual obligation to pay the face value of the bill. The bank accepts the bill and pays the entity a discounted amount, with the difference being interest effectively paid by the entity. Thus, the entity is borrowing the discounted amount of the bill and repaying the face value, which is the sum of the amount borrowed and interest. The entity will have cash inflows from financing activities each time a commercial bill is accepted by the bank and cash outflows from financing activities each time one of its commercial bills matures. The entity may offset the cash received for the 90-day bills against the repayment on maturity, such that only the net movement in the level of borrowing is reported.

Paragraph 24 of IAS 7 permits the following cash flows to be reported on a net basis by financial institutions:

(a) cash receipts and payments for the acceptance and repayment of deposits with a fixed maturity date;
(b) the placement of deposits with and withdrawal of deposits from other financial institutions; and
(c) cash advances and loans made to customers and the repayment of those advances and loans.

17.5 PREPARING A STATEMENT OF CASH FLOWS

Unlike the statement of financial position and statement of profit or loss and other comprehensive income, the statement of cash flows is not prepared from an entity's general ledger trial balance. Preparation requires information to be compiled about the cash inflows and cash outflows of the entity for the reporting period. It is possible to compile the required information through a detailed analysis and summary of the entity's records of cash receipts and cash payments, such as cash receipts and cash payments journals. However, a statement of cash flows is usually prepared from comparative statements of financial position to determine the net amount of changes in assets, liabilities and equities over the period. This method can also be used to prepare the consolidated statement of cash flows for a group of entities. The comparative statements of financial position are supplemented by various items of information from the statement of profit or loss and other comprehensive income and additional information extracted from the accounting records of the entity to enable certain cash receipts and payments to be fully identified. There are two main approaches to calculations and workings for the statement of cash flows: one approach uses a formula based on the reconstruction of ledger accounts; and the other approach uses a worksheet to analyse movements in items reported in the comparative statements of financial position. We will commence with the first approach using the information presented in figure 17.6.

FIGURE 17.6 Financial statements and additional accounting information of Violet Inc.

VIOLET INC. Statement of Profit or Loss and Other Comprehensive Income for the year ended 31 December 2017		
Income		
Sales revenue		$800 000
Interest income		5 000
Gain on sale of plant		4 000
		809 000
Expenses		
Cost of sales	$480 000	
Wages and salaries expense	120 000	
Depreciation — plant and equipment	25 000	
Interest expense	4 000	
Other expenses	76 000	705 000
Profit before tax		104 000
Income tax expense		30 000
Profit for the year		74 000
Other comprehensive income		
Gain on revaluation of land	2 000	
Income tax	(600)	
Other comprehensive income net of tax		1 400
Total comprehensive income for the year		$ 75 400

VIOLET INC. Comparative Statements of Financial Position as at:			
	31 December 2016	31 December 2017	Increase (decrease)
Cash at bank	$ 60 000	$ 56 550	$ (3 450)
Accounts receivable	70 000	79 000	9 000
Inventory	65 000	70 000	5 000
Prepayments	8 000	9 500	1 500
Interest receivable	150	100	(50)
Plant and equipment[a]	150 000	165 000	15 000
Land	12 000	14 000	2 000
Intangible assets[b]	—	15 000	15 000
	$365 150	$409 150	

(continued)

FIGURE 17.6 (continued)

	VIOLET INC. Comparative Statements of Financial Position as at:		
	31 December 2016	31 December 2017	Increase (decrease)
Accounts payable	42 000	45 000	3 000
Wages and salaries payable	4 000	5 000	1 000
Accrued interest		200	200
Other expenses payable	3 000	1 800	(1 200)
Current tax payable	14 000	16 000	2 000
Deferred tax liability	5 000	8 600	3 600
Long-term borrowings^c	60 000	70 000	10 000
Share capital	200 000	200 000	—
Retained earnings^d	37 150	61 150	24 000
Revaluation surplus	—	1 400	1 400
	$365 150	$409 150	

Additional information extracted from the company's records:

(a) Plant that had a carrying amount of $10 000 was sold for $14 000 cash. New equipment purchased for cash amounted to $50 000.

(b) All intangibles were acquired for cash.

(c) An additional borrowing of $10 000 in cash was made during the year.

(d) Dividends paid in cash were $50 000.

17.5.1 Cash flows from operating activities

The first step in preparing a statement of cash flows is to determine the cash flows from operating activities. The process used varies according to whether the direct or the indirect method of presentation is used. First we will work the approach for the direct method using a series of equations to calculate the gross cash inflows and gross cash outflows that are presented in the operating activities section of the statement of cash flows.

Determining cash receipts from customers

The starting point for determining how much cash was received from customers is the sales revenue reported in the statement of profit or loss and other comprehensive income. This figure reflects sales made by the entity during the period irrespective of whether the customers have paid for their purchases. Credit sales are recorded by a debit to accounts receivable and a credit to sales revenue. However, cash received from customers includes sales made in the previous period if cash is not collected until the current period, and excludes sales made in the current period if customers have not paid by the end of the current period. Hence, cash received from customers (assuming there have been no bad debts written off or settlement discounts given) equals:

Sales revenue + Beginning accounts receivable – Ending accounts receivable

Using the Violet Inc. information from figure 17.6, receipts from customers is determined as follows:

Sales revenue	$800 000
+ Beginning accounts receivable	70 000
Cash collectable from customers	870 000
– Ending accounts receivable	(79 000)
Receipts from customers	$791 000

The entity may offer settlement discounts to customers for prompt or early payment of their accounts. For example, if a customer who owes $100 takes advantage of an offer of a 5% discount for prompt payment, the customer would pay only $95 to settle the receivable, and the entity would record an expense of $5 for discount allowed for the non-cash reduction in receivables. Settlement discounts are accounted for as a non-cash expense (discount allowed) in profit or loss and a reduction in accounts receivable. Thus, settlement discounts allowed reduce the amount of cash that can be collected from customers. Accordingly, discount allowed must be adjusted for in calculating cash receipts from customers. Similarly, adjustment would be necessary for bad debts written off if the entity used the direct write-off method of accounting for uncollectable debts. Calculation of cash receipts from customers under the allowance method of accounting for uncollectable debts is considered later in this chapter.

The logic of this calculation is apparent from the following summarised Accounts Receivable account in the general ledger for the year:

Accounts Receivable			
Opening balance	70 000	Bad Debts Expense	—
Sales Revenue	800 000	Discount Allowed	—
		Cash receipts	791 000
		Closing balance	79 000
	870 000		870 000

The above summarised general ledger account can be reconstructed from the statement of financial position including comparative amounts (the opening and closing balances) and statement of profit or loss and other comprehensive income (bad debts expense, discount allowed and sales revenue). The cash receipts amount is then determined as the 'plug' figure (balancing item) in the Accounts Receivable account.

The above approach may be simplified by working with the change in receivables over the period. Under this approach, cash received from customers (assuming there are no bad debts written off or discounts allowed) equals:

$$\text{Sales revenue} \quad \begin{array}{l} - \text{ Increase in accounts receivable} \\ \text{or} \\ + \text{ Decrease in accounts receivable} \end{array}$$

Thus, cash received from customers for Violet Inc. can alternatively be determined as:

$$\$800\,000 - \$9000 = \$791\,000$$

Determining interest received

A similar approach is used to determine interest received, which equals:

$$\text{Interest revenue} \quad \begin{array}{l} - \text{ Increase in interest receivable} \\ \text{or} \\ + \text{ Decrease in interest receivable} \end{array}$$

Thus, Violet Inc.'s interest received is:

$$\$5000 + \$50 = \$5050$$

Determining cash paid to suppliers and employees

Payments to suppliers may comprise purchases of inventory and payments for services. However, not all inventory purchased during the year is reflected in profit or loss as cost of sales because cost of sales includes beginning inventory and excludes ending inventory. The cost of purchases of inventory made during the period equals:

$$\text{Cost of sales} - \text{Beginning inventory} + \text{Ending inventory}$$

Alternatively, this could be expressed as:

$$\text{Cost of sales} \quad \begin{array}{l} + \text{ Increase in inventory} \\ \text{or} \\ - \text{ Decrease in inventory} \end{array}$$

Using a similar approach to that outlined for cash receipts from customers, it is then necessary to adjust for accounts payable at the beginning and end of the period to calculate cash paid to suppliers for purchases of inventory. Thus, cash paid to suppliers of inventories is calculated as:

$$\text{Purchases of inventories} + \text{Beginning accounts payable} - \text{Ending accounts payable}$$

Alternatively, this could be expressed as:

Purchases of inventory + Decrease in accounts payable
or
− Increase in accounts payable

As shown in figure 17.6, Violet Inc.'s comparative statements of financial position report an increase in inventory of $5000 and in accounts payable of $3000. Hence, cash paid to suppliers for purchases is calculated as follows:

Cost of sales	$480 000
+ Increase in inventory	5 000
Purchases for year	485 000
− Increase in accounts payable	(3 000)
Payments to suppliers for purchases of inventory	$482 000

If the entity receives a discount from its suppliers for prompt or early payment of accounts payable the settlement discount received is accounted for as discount revenue and a reduction in accounts payable. Thus, settlement discounts reduce the amount of cash paid to suppliers and must be deducted in calculating cash paid to suppliers.

The logic of the previous calculations incorporating the adjustment for discount received is apparent from the following summarised inventory and accounts payable (for inventory) accounts in the general ledger for the year:

Inventory				Accounts Payable			
Opening balance	65 000	Cost of Sales	480 000	Discount Received	—	Opening balance	42 000
Purchases	485 000	Closing balance	70 000	Cash payments	482 000	Purchases	485 000
				Closing balance	45 000		
	550 000		550 000		527 000		527 000

The above summarised general ledger accounts can be reconstructed from the information contained in the comparative statements of financial position (the opening and closing balances) and the statement of profit or loss and other comprehensive income (cost of sales). The purchases amount is then determined in the Inventory account and inserted on the credit side of the Accounts Payable account. The amount of cash payments can then be determined as the 'plug' figure in reconciling the Accounts Payable account.

A similar approach is taken to determine the amount of payments made to suppliers for services and to employees. Adjustments must be made to the relevant expenses recognised in profit or loss for changes in the beginning and ending amounts of prepayments and relevant accounts payable and accrued liabilities. Thus, the amount of cash paid to suppliers for services is calculated as follows:

Expenses charged to profit or loss − Beginning prepayments
+ Ending prepayments
+ Beginning accounts payable/accruals
− Ending accounts payable/accruals

Alternatively, this could be expressed as:

Expenses charged to profit or loss + Increase in prepayments
or
− Decrease in prepayments
+ Decrease in accounts payable/accruals
or
− Increase in accounts payable/accruals

Violet Inc.'s comparative statements of financial position show:

Increase in prepayments	$ 1 500
Increase in wages and salaries payable	1 000
Decrease in other expenses payable	(1 200)

Thus cash paid to suppliers of services is calculated as follows:

Other expenses	$76 000
+ Increase in prepayments	1 500
+ Decrease in other expenses payable	1 200
Payments to suppliers of services	$78 700

Similarly, cash paid to employees is calculated as follows:

Wages and salaries expense	$120 000
– Increase in wages and salaries payable	1 000
Payments to employees	$119 000

Using the previous calculations, total payments to suppliers and employees to be reported in the statement of cash flows comprise:

Payments to suppliers for purchases	$482 000
Payments to suppliers for services	78 700
Payments to employees	119 000
Total payments to suppliers and employees	$679 700

Determining interest paid

Using the same approach as for other expenses, Violet Inc.'s interest paid is determined as follows:

Interest expense	$4 000
– Increase in accrued interest	200
Interest paid	$3 800

Determining income tax paid

The determination of income tax paid can be complicated because in addition to current tax payable, the application of tax effect accounting can give rise to deferred tax assets and deferred tax liabilities. Further, some of the movements in the current and deferred tax accounts might not be reflected in the income tax expense recognised in profit or loss. Certain gains and losses and associated tax effects are recognised in OCI and accumulated in equity accounts. For example, *as explained in chapter 6,* deferred tax may arise from a revaluation of property, plant and equipment that causes a difference between the book value and tax base of those assets, thereby resulting in a charge for income tax being made to the Revaluation Surplus account. As a result, it is often simpler to reconstruct the Deferred Tax Liability account to determine the allocation of income tax expense. We can use this reconstruction to determine the deferred component of income tax expense recognised in profit or loss, if this is not already identified in the statement of profit or loss and other comprehensive income.

Deferred Tax Liability			
		Opening balance	5 000
		Tax effect recognised in OCI	600
Closing balance	8 600	Income Tax Expense	3 000
	8 600		8 600

The above summarised general ledger account can be reconstructed from the comparative statements of financial position (opening and closing balances) and the statement of profit or loss and other comprehensive income. The income tax expense shown in the reconstruction of the Deferred Tax Liability account is the deferred component of income tax expense — that is, the amount of income tax expense pertaining to the movement in deferred tax balances.

• The movement in the Deferred Tax Liability account for Violet Inc. can be summarised as follows:

Opening balance	$5 000
+ Tax recognised directly in OCI	600
+ Income tax expense (deferred component)	3 000
Closing balance	$8 600

The current component of income tax expense can then be calculated by deducting the deferred component of income tax expense from the total income tax expense recognised in profit or loss. The current component of income tax expense for Violet Inc. can be calculated as follows:

Income tax expense	$30 000
– Deferred component of income tax expense	(3 000)
Current component of income tax expense	$27 000

The opening balance of Current Tax Payable of $14 000 is increased by the current component of income tax expense, $27 000. If no payments were made, the closing balance would be $41 000. However, as the closing balance is only $16 000, we can conclude that the amount of income tax paid must have been $25 000. To illustrate, the movement in Violet Inc.'s Current Tax Payable account may be summarised as follows:

Opening balance	$14 000
+ Income tax expense	27 000
– Income tax paid	25 000
Closing balance	$16 000

For Violet Inc., the amount of income tax paid consists of the final balance in respect of the previous year's current tax payable, and instalments paid in respect of the current year.

Summarising cash flows from operating activities

The operating activities section of Violet Inc.'s statement of cash flows for the year are presented using the direct method in figure 17.7.

VIOLET INC. **Statement of Cash Flows (extract)** **for the year ended 31 December 2017**	
Cash flows from operating activities	
Cash receipts from customers	$ 791 000
Cash paid to suppliers and employees	(679 700)
Cash generated from operations	111 300
Interest received*	5 050
Interest paid**	(3 800)
Income taxes paid	(25 000)
Net cash from operating activities	$ 87 550
* May be classified as investing ** May be classified as financing	

FIGURE 17.7 Cash flows from operating activities (direct method)

The presentation of Violet Inc.'s cash flows from operating activities under the indirect method is shown in figure 17.8. The statement commences with profit before tax and shows the gross amount of tax paid as a separate item. Similarly, it is necessary to adjust for the full amount of the interest income and interest expense so that amount of cash received or paid for these items is disclosed in full in the statement of cash flows. In this illustration, the increase in wages and salaries payable of $1000 and the decrease in other expenses payable of $1200 are combined as one line item and shown as a net reduction of $200.

17.5.2 Cash flows from investing activities

Determining cash flows from investing activities requires identifying cash inflows and outflows relating to the acquisition and disposal of long-term assets and other investments not included in cash equivalents.

The comparative statements of financial position of Violet Inc. in figure 17.6 show that plant has increased by $15 000, land by $2000 and intangibles by $15 000. To determine the cash flows relating to these increases, it is necessary to analyse the underlying transactions.

VIOLET INC.
Statement of Cash Flows (extract)
for the year ended 31 December 2017

Cash flows from operating activities	
Profit before tax	$104 000
Adjustment for:	
Depreciation	25 000
Interest income	(5 000)
Gain on sale of plant	(4 000)
Interest expense	4 000
Increase in accounts receivable	(9 000)
Increase in inventory	(5 000)
Increase in prepayments	(1 500)
Increase in accounts payable	3 000
Decrease in other payables	(200)
Cash generated from operations	111 300
Interest received*	5 050
Interest paid**	(3 800)
Income taxes paid	(25 000)
Net cash from operating activities	$ 87 550

* May be classified as investing   ** May be classified as financing

FIGURE 17.8 Cash flows from operating activities (indirect method)

The plant and equipment reported in the statement of financial position is net of accumulated depreciation. The net increase reflects the recording of purchases, disposals and depreciation of plant and equipment. Using the data provided, the analysis of the movement in plant and equipment (net of accumulated depreciation) is as follows:

Opening balance	$150 000
Purchases	50 000
Disposals	(10 000)
Depreciation for year	(25 000)
Closing balance	$165 000

The additional information provided in figure 17.6 states that the acquisitions were made for cash during the period, so no adjustment is necessary for year-end payables. The cash paid for equipment purchases for the year is $50 000 (note (a) in figure 17.6). Any payables for plant and equipment purchases outstanding at the beginning of the period would need to be added to purchases and any payables for plant and equipment outstanding at the end of the period would need to be deducted to calculate the amount of cash paid for plant and equipment during the period.

Plant with a carrying amount of $10 000 was sold, as stated in additional information (a) of figure 17.6. This amount is shown as a deduction from the net carrying amount plant and equipment.

The gain or loss on disposal of plant is the difference between the carrying amount and the proceeds on the sale of plant. Thus, the proceeds on sale of plant can be calculated as:

Carrying amount of plant sold   +   Gain on disposal of plant
or
−   Loss on disposal of plant

For Violet Inc., the calculation is as follows:

$$\$10\,000 + 4000 = \$14\,000$$

However, the proceeds from the sale of plant equals the cash inflow for the year only if there are no receivables outstanding arising from the sale of plant at either the beginning or end of the year. If receivables for the sale of plant exist, the cash inflow is determined using the approach that was previously outlined for sales revenue and interest receivable. For simplicity, it is assumed that Violet Inc. had no receivables outstanding, at the beginning or end of the year, arising from the sale of plant.

Land increased by $2000 during the year, as shown in the comparative statements of financial position. This increase relates to the gain on revaluation of land reported in the statement of profit or loss and other comprehensive income. Thus the movement in land does not affect cash flows from investing activities.

The comparative statements of financial position for Violet Inc. show that the movement in intangibles equals the additional cash acquisitions made during the period, as detailed in the additional information presented in figure 17.6. Note, however, that the movement in intangibles equals the cash outflows for the year because there were no related accounts payable at the beginning or end of the year. If payables exist, the cash outflow is determined using the approach that was previously outlined for cash paid to suppliers and employees.

Using the above information, the cash flows from investing activities reported in Violet Inc.'s statement of cash flows for 2017 are presented in figure 17.9.

VIOLET INC. Statement of Cash Flows (extract) for the year ended 31 December 2017	
Cash flows from investing activities	
Purchase of intangibles	$(15 000)
Purchase of equipment	(50 000)
Proceeds from sale of plant	14 000
Net cash used in investing activities	$(51 000)

FIGURE 17.9 Cash flows from investing activities

17.5.3 Cash flows from financing activities

Determining cash flows from financing activities requires identification of cash flows that resulted in changes in the size and composition of contributed equity and borrowings.

Violet Inc.'s comparative statements of financial position report an increase in borrowings of $10 000. The additional information (c) in figure 17.6 confirms that the increase arose from an additional borrowing received in cash. It would normally be necessary to analyse the net movement in borrowings in order to identify whether the movement reflects repayments and additional borrowings, and whether any new borrowings arose from non-cash transactions, such as entering into a finance lease *(see chapter 12)*.

If the entity had issued shares during the period this would be reflected in a change in share capital. An alternative source of information about capital contributions is the statement of changes in equity. Any share issues for non-cash consideration, such as shares issued as part of a dividend reinvestment scheme, should be deducted from the movement in share capital to determine cash proceeds from share issues. Violet Inc.'s share capital is unchanged at $200 000, as shown in figure 17.6.

Dividends distributed by the entity can be identified by analysing the change in retained earnings. Profit increases retained earnings and losses decrease retained earnings. Dividends decrease retained earnings. Any non-cash dividends should be deducted from total dividends to determine cash dividends paid. Information about dividends is also reported in the statement of changes in equity. The movement in Violet Inc.'s retained earnings of $24 000 reflects:

Profit for the period	$ 74 000	
Dividends (paid in cash)	(50 000)	((d) in figure 17.6)
Net movement	$ 24 000	

Using the previous information, the financing cash flow section of Violet Inc.'s statement of cash flows for 2017 is presented in figure 17.10.

VIOLET INC. Statement of Cash Flows (extract) for the year ended 31 December 2017	
Cash flows from financing activities	
Proceeds from borrowings	$ 10 000
Dividends paid*	(50 000)
Net cash used in financing activities	$ (40 000)

*Dividends paid may be classified as an operating cash flow.

FIGURE 17.10 Cash flows from financing activities

All that remains to complete the statement of cash flows for Violet Inc. is the determination of the net increase or decrease in cash held, and to use this net change to reconcile cash at the beginning and end of the year.

The complete statement of cash flows for Violet Inc. (using the direct method for reporting cash flows from operating activities) is shown in figure 17.11. The balance of cash at year-end of $56 550 shown in figure 17.11 agrees with the cash at bank balance shown in the statement of financial position at 31 December 2017 in figure 17.6. There are no cash equivalents such as short-term deposits.

VIOLET INC. Statement of Cash Flows for the year ended 31 December 2017		
Cash flows from operating activities		
Cash receipts from customers	$ 791 000	
Cash paid to suppliers and employees	(679 700)	
Cash generated from operations	111 300	
Interest received	5 050	
Interest paid	(3 800)	
Income taxes paid	(25 000)	
Net cash from operating activities		$ 87 550
Cash flows from investing activities		
Purchase of intangibles	$ (15 000)	
Purchase of plant	(50 000)	
Proceeds from sale of plant	14 000	
Net cash used in investing activities		(51 000)
Cash flows from financing activities		
Proceeds from borrowings	$ 10 000	
Dividends paid	(50 000)	
Net cash used in financing activities		(40 000)
Net decrease in cash and cash equivalents		(3 450)
Cash and cash equivalents at beginning of year		60 000
Cash and cash equivalents at end of year		$ 56 550

FIGURE 17.11 Complete statement of cash flows of Violet Inc.

17.5.4 The worksheet approach

This section introduces the use of a worksheet to prepare a statement of cash flows and applies it to more complex financial statements. Figure 17.12 presents the financial statements and additional information for Silber GmbH. The worksheet is presented in figure 17.13, followed by an explanation of each reconciling adjustment. Finally, figure 17.14 illustrates the statement of cash flows using the indirect method of presenting cash flows from operating activities.

FIGURE 17.12 Financial statements and additional information of Silber GmbH

SILBER GMBH Comparative Statements of Financial Position as at:			
	31 December 2016	31 December 2017	Increase (decrease)
Cash	€ 60 000	€ 69 800	€ 9 800
Short-term deposits	120 000	140 000	20 000
Accounts receivable, net	140 000	190 000	50 000
Inventory	130 000	155 000	25 000
Prepayments	16 000	19 000	3 000
Interest receivable	300	200	(100)
Investment in associate	40 000	45 000	5 000
Land	80 000	120 000	40 000
Plant	300 000	420 000	120 000
Accumulated depreciation	(50 000)	(65 000)	(15 000)
Intangibles	90 000	60 000	(30 000)
	€926 300	€1 154 000	€227 700

(continued)

FIGURE 17.12 *(continued)*

SILBER GMBH Comparative Statements of Financial Position as at:	31 December 2016	31 December 2017	Increase (decrease)
Accounts payable	84 000	90 000	6 000
Accrued liabilities	14 000	12 000	(2 000)
Current tax payable	28 000	32 000	4 000
Deferred tax liability	20 000	25 000	5 000
Borrowings	120 000	180 000	60 000
Share capital	600 000	680 000	80 000
Retained earnings	60 300	135 000	74 700
	€926 300	€1 154 000	€227 700

SILBER GMBH
Statement of Profit or Loss and Other Comprehensive Income
for the year ended 31 December 2017

Revenue		
Sales revenue		€1 600 000
Interest income		10 000
Share of profits of associate		10 000
Gain on sale of plant		8 000
		€1 628 000
Expenses		
Cost of sales	€960 000	
Wages and salaries	240 000	
Depreciation — plant	40 000	
Impairment — intangibles	30 000	
Interest expense	12 000	
Doubtful debts	8 000	
Other expenses	132 000	1 422 000
Profit before tax		206 000
Income tax expense		(65 000)
Profit for the year		141 000
Other comprehensive income		—
Total comprehensive income		€ 141 000

Other information used in worksheet:

(a) Changes in equity:

	Share capital	Retained earnings
Balance at 31 December 2016	€ 600 000	€ 60 300
Profit for the year	—	141 000
Dividends — cash	—	(36 300)
— reinvested under dividend scheme	30 000	(30 000)
Cash share issue	50 000	—
Balance at 31 December 2017	€ 680 000	€ 135 000

(b) Investment in associate (equity method)

Balance at 31 December 2016	€ 40 000
Share of profit of associate	10 000
Dividend received	(5 000)
Balance at 31 December 2017	€ 45 000

(c) Land

Additional land acquired	€ 40 000
Finance provided by vendor	(35 000)
Cash paid	€ 5 000

(d) Plant

Acquisitions	€180 000
Cash paid	171 000
Accounts payable outstanding at year-end	9 000
	€180 000
Disposals — cost	60 000
Accumulated depreciation	(25 000)
Proceeds received in cash	43 000

(e) Intangibles

There were no acquisitions or disposals.

Impairment write-down	€ 30 000

	2016	2017
(f) Accounts payable comprises:		
Purchase of inventory	€ 49 000	€ 56 000
Purchase of plant	15 000	9 000
Other purchases	20 000	25 000
Balance at 31 December	€ 84 000	€ 90 000
(g) Accrued liabilities comprises accruals for:		
Wages, salaries and other expenses	$ 12 800	€ 9 900
Interest expense	1 200	2 100
Balance at 31 December	€ 14 000	€ 12 000

(h) Increase in borrowings of €60 000 reflects:

Land vendor finance	€ 35 000
Additional cash borrowing	25 000
	€ 60 000

(i) Income tax expense comprises:

Currently payable	€ 60 000
Movement in deferred tax	5 000
	€ 65 000

(j) Movement in current tax payable:

Balance at 31 December 2016	€ 28 000
Income tax expense	60 000
Payments made	(56 000)
Balance at 31 December 2017	€ 32 000

FIGURE 17.13 Worksheet for statement of cash flows

SILBER GMBH
Statement of Cash Flows Worksheet
for year ended 31 December 2017

	Balance 31.12.16	Reconciling items Debits		Reconciling items Credits		Balance 31.12.17
Cash	€ 60 000	(28) €	9 800			€ 69 800
Short-term deposits	120 000	(29)	20 000			140 000
Accounts receivable, net	140 000	(2)	50 000			190 000
Interest receivable	300			(13)	100	200
Inventory	130 000	(3)	25 000			155 000
Prepayments	16 000	(4)	3 000			19 000
Investment in associate	40 000	(7)	5 000			45 000
Land	80 000	(18)	5 000			120 000
		(19)	35 000			
Plant	300 000	(9)	8 000	(21)	43 000	420 000
		(20)	180 000	(22)	25 000	
Accumulated depreciation	(50 000)	(22)	25 000	(10)	40 000	(65 000)
Intangibles	90 000			(11)	30 000	60 000
	€926 300					€1 154 000

(continued)

FIGURE 17.13 (continued)

	Balance 31.12.16	Reconciling items				Balance 31.12.17
		Debits		**Credits**		
Accounts payable	€ 84 000	(27) € 6 000		(5) € 12 000		€ 90 000
Accrued liabilities	14 000	(6) 2 900		(14) 900		12 000
Current tax payable	28 000			(16) 4 000		32 000
Deferred tax liability	20 000			(17) 5 000		25 000
Borrowings	120 000			(19) 35 000		180 000
				(23) 25 000		
Share capital	600 000			(24) 50 000		680 000
				(25) 30 000		
Retained earnings	60 300	(15) 65 000		(1) 206 000		135 000
		(25) 30 000				
		(26) 36 300				
	€926 300					€1 154 000

Statement of cash flows data						
Operating activities						
Profit before tax		(1) €206 000				€ 206 000
Increase in accounts receivable				(2) € 50 000		(50 000)
Increase in inventory				(3) 25 000		(25 000)
Increase in prepayments				(4) 3 000		(3 000)
Increase in accounts payable		(5) 12 000				12 000
Decrease in accrued liabilities				(6) 2 900		(2 900)
Share of profits of associate				(7) 10 000		(10 000)
Interest income				(8) 10 000		(10 000)
Gain on sale of plant				(9) 8 000		(8 000)
Depreciation — plant		(10) 40 000				40 000
Impairment — intangibles		(11) 30 000				30 000
Interest expense		(12) 12 000				12 000
Cash generated from operations		300 000		108 900		191 100
Interest received		(8) 10 000				10 100
		(13) 100				
Dividend received from associate		(7) 5 000				5 000
Interest paid		(14) 900		(12) 12 000		(11 100)
Income tax paid		(16) 4 000		(15) 65 000		(56 000)
		(17) 5 000				
Net cash from operating activities		325 000		185 900		139 100
Investing activities						
Purchase of land				(18) 5 000		(5 000)
Purchase of plant				(20) 180 000		(186 000)
				(27) 6 000		
Proceeds from sale of plant		(21) 43 000				43 000
Net cash used in investing activities		43 000		191 000		(148 000)
Financing activities						
Proceeds from borrowings		(23) 25 000				25 000
Proceeds from share issue		(24) 50 000				50 000
Payment of cash dividends				(26) 36 300		(36 300)
Net cash flows from financing activities		75 000		36 300		38 700
Net increase in cash and cash equivalents		443 000		413 200		€ 29 800
Increase in cash				(28) 9 800		
Increase in short-term deposits				(29) 20 000		
		€443 000		€443 000		

Explanations of the reconciling adjustments made in compiling the statement of cash flows worksheet in figure 17.13 are presented below.

A — Profit before tax

When using the indirect method of presenting cash flows from operating activities, the starting point is profit before tax. Accordingly, adjustment (1) for €206 000 is made between retained earnings and the cash flow (operating activities) section of the worksheet to reflect the profit before tax for the year; and a separate adjustment (15) is made for income tax expense.

B — Increase in net accounts receivable

The net increase in accounts receivable of €50 000 reflects the excess of sales revenue over the cash collected from receivables. It must therefore be deducted from profit before tax (adjustment (2)). Because the indirect method is being used, there is no need to include separate adjustments for bad debts written off, changes in any allowance for doubtful debts or discounts allowed. Such adjustments are only necessary to determine cash flows from customers under the direct method.

C — Increase in inventory

The increase in inventory of €25 000 represents the amount by which purchases of inventory exceed the amount included in profit or loss as cost of sales. It is deducted from profit before tax in calculating cash from operating activities (adjustment (3)).

D — Increase in prepayments

The increase in prepayments of €3000 is an operating cash outflow during the period that is not reflected in profit before tax (adjustment (4)).

E — Movement in accounts payable

As per additional information item (f) in figure 17.12, accounts payable comprises:

	2016	2017	Increase (decrease)	
Amount arising from the:				
Purchase of inventory and services	€ 69 000	€ 81 000	€12 000	(Adjustment (5))
Purchase of plant	15 000	9 000	(6 000)	(Adjustment (27))
	€ 84 000	€ 90 000	€ 6 000	

The increase in accounts payable arising from the purchase of inventory and services reflects the amount by which the purchases exceed the payments. The increase in accounts payable is added to operating profit before tax because it does not involve an operating cash outflow for the period (adjustment (5)). In this example, the increase in accounts payable partly offsets the increase in inventory reflected in adjustment (3).

The reduction in accounts payable arising from the purchase of plant of €6000 increases the cash outflow for the purchase of plant as shown in the investing cash activities section of the cash flow worksheet (adjustment (27)).

F — Movement in accrued liabilities

As per additional information item (g) in figure 17.12, accrued liabilities comprise:

	2016	2017	Increase (decrease)	
Amount arising from:				
Wages, salaries and other expenses	€12 800	€ 9 900	€ (2 900)	(Adjustment (6))
Accrued interest	1 200	2 100	900	(Adjustment (14))
	€14 000	€12 000	€ (2 000)	

The reduction in accrued liabilities for wages, salaries and other expenses increases operating cash outflows for the year and is reflected in adjustment (6). The increase in accrued interest payable is the amount by which interest expense exceeds the amount of interest paid and is reflected in adjustment (14), as part of the calculation of interest paid.

G — Share of profits of associate

As per additional information item (b) in figure 17.12, the investment in associate (accounted for under the equity method) increased by €5000, comprising the share of profits of the associate of €10 000, net of a dividend received of €5000. Adjustment (7) includes the €5000 dividend received in net cash from operating activities but excludes the share of profits from cash generated from operations because it does not represent a cash flow.

H — Interest income

When completing the worksheet, interest income is initially transferred out of profit before tax in order to arrive at cash generated from operations (adjustment (8)) and shown as a separate item (interest received). The reduction in interest receivable of €100 (adjustment (13)) is added to the interest income to calculate interest received, as shown in the operating activities section of the worksheet. Alternatively, the interest received could be classified as an investing activity.

I — Gain on sale of plant

Note that the accumulated depreciation for the plant that has been sold is transferred to the plant account (adjustment (22)). This transfer reflects the following journal entries:

Accumulated Depreciation	Dr	25 000	
Plant	Cr		25 000
(Closing accumulated depreciation against the plant account on disposal of the plant)			

The carrying amount of the plant that was sold is €35 000 (being the difference between its cost and accumulated depreciation, per additional information item (d) in figure 17.12). The gain on disposal is the amount by which the proceeds on disposal exceed the carrying amount of the plant. Silber GmbH would have made the following combined journal entry to record the sale of the plant:

Cash	Dr	43 000	
Plant	Cr		35 000
Gain on Disposal	Cr		8 000
(Disposal of plant)			

Plant is reduced by the net amount of €35 000, which is represented in the worksheet as a credit adjustment to plant for the cash proceeds from the sale, €43 000 (Cr), and the debit adjustment against plant for the gain on disposal of €8000 (Dr). Gain on disposal of plant of €8000 is not a cash inflow, so it is deducted from profit before tax in arriving at net cash from operating activities (adjustment (9)). A separate adjustment is made for the proceeds from sale of plant of €43 000 as an investing cash flow. The reduction in plant for plant sold of €60 000 comprises the following adjustments:

Proceeds on sale of plant	€43 000	Cr	(Adjustment (21))
Accumulated depreciation	€25 000	Cr	(Adjustment (22))
Gain on sale	€ 8 000	Dr	(Adjustment (9))
Cost of plant sold	€60 000	Cr	Net effect on Plant

J — Depreciation of plant and impairment of intangibles

Depreciation charged in the current period reduces profit before tax and increases the accumulated depreciation in the statement of financial position. The recognition of an impairment loss for intangibles reduces profit before tax and reduces the net carrying amount of intangibles in the statement of financial position. Depreciation expenses and impairment losses are not cash flows. Accordingly, they are added back to profit before tax to calculate cash from operating activities (depreciation expense of €40 000, adjustment (10); and impairment loss of €30 000, adjustment (11)).

K — Interest expense

Interest expense is initially transferred from profit before tax to a separate item for interest paid (adjustment (12)). It is then reduced by the increase in accrued interest €900 (adjustment (14)) to calculate interest paid (see explanation F). Alternatively, the interest cash outflow could be classified as a financing activity.

L — Income tax paid

Income tax expense of €65 000 (adjustment (15)) is reduced by the increase in current tax payable of €4000 (adjustment (16)) and the increase in deferred tax liability of €5000 (adjustment (17)) to determine the income tax paid (€56 000). In this example, there are no tax charges — such as on revaluation surplus — accumulated in equity accounts. This is evident because there are no items of other comprehensive income (see figure 17.12).

M — Purchase of land and plant

Additional land was acquired at a cost of €40 000, of which €35 000 was financed by the vendor. Adjustment (18) records the cash outflow of €5000. The vendor-financed purchases are reflected in adjustment (19) between land and borrowings.

Plant acquisitions for the year are €180 000 (adjustment (20)). This amount is increased by the reduction in plant accounts payable of €6000 (adjustment (27)) *as discussed in explanation E.*

N — Proceeds from borrowings

The cash proceeds from borrowings of €25 000 (adjustment (23)) is calculated as the increase in borrowings of €60 000 (€180 000 − €120 000) reduced by €35 000, being the vendor-financed purchase of land (adjustment (19)); *see explanation M.*

O — Proceeds from share issue and payment of cash dividends

To determine the proceeds from share issue (adjustment (24)), the increase in share capital of €80 000 (€680 000 − €600 000) is reduced by the €30 000 reinvested dividends (adjustment (25)), which did not involve a cash flow. Similarly, cash flows from financing activities include only the €36 300 of dividends paid in cash (adjustment (26)).

P — Increase in cash and short-term deposits

Short-term deposits held by Silber GmbH are cash equivalents. The increase of €9 800 and €20 000 in cash and short term deposits, respectively, are shown in the worksheet as the increase in cash and cash equivalents for the period (adjustments (28) and (29), respectively).

Figure 17.14 illustrates the statement of cash flows for Silber GmbH for the year ended 31 December 2017 (without comparatives).

FIGURE 17.14 Statement of cash flows of Silber GMBH

SILBER GMBH Statement of Cash Flows for year ended 31 December 2017		
Cash flows from operating activities		
Profit before tax	€ 206 000	
Adjustments for:		
Depreciation	40 000	
Impairment of intangibles	30 000	
Gain on sale of plant	(8 000)	
Share of profits of associate	(10 000)	
Interest income	(10 000)	
Interest expense	12 000	
Increase in receivables	(50 000)	
Increase in inventory	(25 000)	
Increase in prepayments	(3 000)	
Increase in accounts payables	12 000	
Decrease in accrued liabilities	(2 900)	
Cash generated from operations	191 100	
Interest received	10 100	
Dividend received from associate	5 000	
Interest paid	(11 100)	
Income taxes paid	(56 000)	
Net cash from operating activities		€ 139 100
Cash flows from investing activities		
Purchase of land (Note A)	(5 000)	
Purchase of plant	(186 000)	
Proceeds from sale of plant	43 000	
Net cash used in investing activities		(148 000)
Cash flow from financing activities		
Proceeds from borrowings	25 000	
Proceeds from share issue (Note B)	50 000	
Dividends paid (Note B)	(36 300)	
Net cash from financing activities		38 700

(continued)

FIGURE 17.14 *(continued)*

Net increase in cash and cash equivalents	29 800
Cash and cash equivalents at beginning of year (Note C)	180 000
Cash and cash equivalents at end of year (Note C)	**€ 209 800**

Notes:

A Land

During the year, land was acquired at a cost of €40 000, of which €5000 was paid in cash and €35 000 was financed by the vendor.

B Dividends

During the year, shareholders elected to reinvest dividends of €30 000 under the company's dividend reinvestment scheme. (This information will be reported in the company's statement of changes in equity. A cross-reference to that statement may be used instead of this note.)

C Cash and cash equivalents

Cash and cash equivalents included in the statement of cash flows comprise the following amounts reported in the statement of financial position:

	2017	2016
Cash	€ 69 800	€ 60 000
Short-term deposits	140 000	120 000
	€209 800	€180 000

The note shows both the current and prior period comparative figures. It is customary to show the current period first, followed by the comparative figures, reading from left to right. However, comparative data were presented in the worksheets to facilitate working from left to right in calculating movements in line items used to determine cash flows.

17.6 OTHER DISCLOSURES

IAS 7 prescribes additional disclosures in the notes to the financial statements, including information about the components of cash and cash equivalents, changes in ownership interests of subsidiaries and other businesses, and non-cash investing and financing transactions. Additional information is often necessary to obtain a complete understanding of the change in an entity's financial position because not all transactions are simple cash transactions. Significant changes can result from the acquisition or disposal of subsidiaries or other business units, or from financing and investing transactions that do not involve cash flows in the current period.

17.6.1 Components of cash and cash equivalents

The components of cash and cash equivalents must be disclosed and reconciled to amounts reported in the statement of financial position. The reconciliation provides better transparency of how items are reported in the financial statements. In some cases, cash and cash equivalents may include a bank overdraft. The end-of-period amount of cash and cash equivalents reported in the statement of cash flows may differ from that reported in the statement of financial position because the cash and short-term deposits are reported as current assets while the overdraft is a liability. Figure 17.15 illustrates the reconciliation between cash and cash equivalents in the statement of cash flows with the corresponding items reported in the statement of financial position for BHP Billiton.

Paragraph 48 requires disclosure of the amount of significant cash and cash-equivalent balances held that are not available for general use. This may include cash held by a foreign subsidiary that is subject to foreign exchange controls. Figure 17.15 illustrates disclosures made by BHP Billiton in accordance with paragraph 48.

17.6.2 Changes in ownership interests of subsidiaries and other businesses

Part 4 of this book deals with the financial reporting of consolidated groups of entities. When a parent entity obtains control of another entity, or loses control of an existing subsidiary, the comparative consolidated statement of financial position of the group before and after the acquisition or disposal will frequently reflect significant changes in the assets and liabilities arising from the acquisition or disposal. Financial statement users need to be aware of the effects of changes in ownership and control in order to understand the change in financial position of the consolidated group.

IAS 7 specifies additional reporting requirements relating to changes in control of subsidiaries and other businesses.

Note 7 Cash and cash equivalents

For the purpose of the consolidated cash flow statement, cash equivalents include highly liquid investments that are readily convertible to cash and with a maturity date of less than 90 days, bank overdrafts and interest bearing liabilities at call.

	2015 US$M	2014 US$M	2013 US$M
Cash and cash equivalents comprise:			
Cash	931	1 726	2 521
Short term deposits	5 822	7 077	3 156
Total cash and cash equivalents[a][b][c]	6 753	8 803	5 677
Bank overdraft and short-term borrowings	(140)	(51)	(10)
Total cash and cash equivalents, net of overdrafts	6 613	8 752	5 667

[a] Cash and cash equivalents include US$493 million (2014: US$738 million; 2013: US$674 million), which is restricted by legal or contractual arrangements.

[b] Cash and cash equivalents include US$50 million (2014: US$600 million; 2013: US$794 million), which is subject to restrictions imposed by governments where approval is required to repatriate cash out of a country.

[c] Cash and cash equivalents include US$6 553 million denominated in USD, US$58 million denominated in CAD, US$33 million denominated in GBP, US$17 million denominated in AUD and US$92 million denominated in other currencies (2014: US$8 360 million denominated in USD, US$48 million denominated in CAD, US$26 million denominated in GBP, US$100 million denominated in AUD and US$269 million denominated in other currencies; 2013: US$5 205 million denominated in USD, US$71 million denominated in CAD, US$18 million denominated in GBP, US$125 million denominated in AUD and US$258 million denominated in other currencies).

FIGURE 17.15 Disclosures about cash and cash equivalents for BHP Billiton at 30 June 2015
Source: BHP Billiton (2015, p. 219).

Paragraph 39 requires the aggregate cash flow effects of obtaining control of subsidiaries or other businesses to be reported as one item in the investing activities section of the statement of cash flows. When an entity obtains control of a subsidiary or other business, any cash and cash equivalents acquired are deducted from the cash consideration paid in determining the cash flow effects of obtaining control. For example, Major plc obtained control over Minor plc by acquiring all of the ordinary shares of Minor plc. Major plc paid consideration of £1 500 000 in cash. Minor plc held cash and cash equivalents of £100 000 at the time of the acquisition. Thus, the net cash flow effect of Major plc obtaining control of Minor plc is a cash outflow of £1 400 000 (i.e. £1 500 000 − £100 000). This would be reported in the investing activities section of Major plc's consolidated statement of cash flows.

Similarly, paragraph 39 of IAS 7 requires the aggregate cash flow effects of losing control of subsidiaries or other businesses to be reported as one item in the investing activities section of the statement of cash flows. If an entity loses control of a subsidiary or other business, any cash and cash equivalents held by that subsidiary or other business at the time of the disposal are deducted from the cash consideration received in reporting the cash flow effects of losing control. For example, if Major plc sold its interest in several subsidiaries for a total cash consideration of £8 000 000, and those subsidiaries held cash and cash equivalents of £100 000, Major plc would report a net cash inflow of £7 900 000 for the proceeds from the sale of subsidiaries in the investing activities section of its statement of cash flows. Figure 17.16 illustrates the application of paragraph 39 of IAS 7 in the investing activities section of Major plc's statement of cash flows.

	2017 £'000	2016 £'000
Cash flows from investing activities		
Payments for property, plant and equipment	(5 500)	(4 800)
Proceeds from sale of subsidiaries (net of cash held)	7 900	
Payment for purchase of subsidiary (net of cash acquired)	(1 400)	—
Proceeds from the sale of property, plant and equipment	1 100	1 300
Net cash from (used in) investing activities	2 100	(3 500)

FIGURE 17.16 Investing activities section of statement of cash flows of Major plc for the year ended 31 December 2017

Separate presentation of the cash flow effects of transactions to obtain or to surrender control of subsidiaries or other businesses is required. The cash flow effects of transactions resulting in the loss of control, such as the sale of a subsidiary, are not deducted from the cash flows of transactions that obtain control, such as the acquisitions of a subsidiary. Both the aggregate cash flow effects of obtaining control of subsidiaries and other businesses and the aggregate cash flow effects of losing control of subsidiaries and other businesses are reported separately in the investing activities section of the statement of cash flows as shown in figure 17.16.

Paragraph 40 of IAS 7 prescribes disclosure of the aggregate amounts of each of the following items:
(a) the total consideration;
(b) how much of the consideration comprises cash and cash equivalents;
(c) the amount of cash and cash equivalents held by the subsidiaries or other businesses; and
(d) the amount of other assets and liabilities held by the subsidiaries or other businesses, summarised by each major category.

Separate disclosures must be made for subsidiaries and other businesses over which control has been obtained, and those over which control has been lost. Disclosures provided by Major plc in accordance with paragraph 40(a)–(c) are shown in figure 17.17.

During the year Major plc obtained control of Minor plc by acquiring all of the ordinary shares of Minor plc. All of the consideration was paid in cash. Details of the consideration and analysis of the cash flows are summarised below:

Total consideration (included in cash flows from investing activities)	£1 500 000
Cash acquired in subsidiary (included in cash flows from investing activities)	(100 000)
Net cash flows on acquisition	£1 400 000

During the year Major plc sold its retail business for total consideration of £9 000 000. Details of the consideration and analysis of the cash flows are summarised below:

Total consideration, comprising cash and equity investments	£9 000 000
Cash consideration (included in cash flows from investing activities)	£8 000 000
Cash acquired in subsidiary (included in cash flows from investing activities)	(100 000)
Net cash flows on disposal of the business	£7 900 000

FIGURE 17.17 Selected disclosures about transactions resulting in the acquisition or loss of control over other entities by Major plc for the year ended 31 December 2017

17.6.3 Non-cash transactions

Not all investing or financing transactions involve current cash flows. However, non-cash investing and financing activities need to be understood because they can significantly affect the financial position of an entity. Examples include:
• acquisition of assets by means of a finance lease or by assuming other liabilities
• acquisition of assets or an entity by means of an equity issue
• conversion of debt to equity
• conversion of preference shares to ordinary shares
• refinancing of long-term debt
• payment of dividends through a dividend reinvestment scheme.

Investing and financing transactions that do not involve the payment or receipt of cash and cash equivalents are not reported in the statement of cash flows. However, paragraph 43 of IAS 7 requires disclosure 'elsewhere in the financial statements in a way that provides all the relevant information about these investing and financing activities'.

Figure 17.18 illustrates BHP Billiton's disclosure on non-cash investing and financing activities in the notes to its financial statements. The acquisition of plant and equipment by a finance lease is a non-cash

Note 37 Notes to the consolidated cash flow statement			
Significant non-cash investing and financing transactions	2015 U$M	2014 U$M	2013 U$M
Property, plant and equipment acquired under finance leases	10	501	Nil
Property, plant and equipment acquired under vendor financing arrangements	Nil	Nil	49

FIGURE 17.18 Non-cash investing and financing activities of BHP Billiton for the year ended 30 June 2015
Source: BHP Billiton (2015, p. 264).

transaction that increases plant and equipment (leased plant and equipment) and borrowings (lease liabilities). The other non-cash transactions, reported in aggregate, are vendor-financed purchases of property, plant and equipment.

17.6.4 Disclosures that are encouraged but not required

The following disclosures are specifically encouraged by paragraph 50 of IAS 7:
- the amount of undrawn borrowing facilities that may be available to pay for future operating activities or to settle commitments, and any restrictions on their use;
- the distinction between aggregate cash flows for increases in operating capacity and aggregate cash flows that are required to maintain operating capacity; and
- cash flows arising from the operating, investing and financing activities of each reportable segment.

SUMMARY

IAS 7 *Statement of Cash Flows* is a disclosure standard requiring the presentation of a statement of cash flows as an integral part of an entity's financial statements. The statement of cash flows is particularly useful to investors, lenders and others when evaluating an entity's ability to generate cash and cash equivalents, and to meet its obligations and pay dividends. The statement is required to report cash flows classified into operating, investing and financing activities, as well as the net movement in cash and cash equivalents during the period. Net cash flows from operating activities may be presented using either the direct or the indirect method. IAS 7 requires additional information to be disclosed about investing and financing activities that do not involve cash flows and are therefore excluded from a statement of cash flows. The standard also requires additional disclosures relating to the cash flow effects of obtaining or losing control of subsidiaries and other businesses.

Discussion questions

1. What is the purpose of a statement of cash flows?
2. How might a statement of cash flows be used?
3. What is the meaning of 'cash equivalent'?
4. Explain the required classifications of cash flows under IAS 7.
5. What sources of information are usually required to prepare a statement of cash flows?
6. Explain the differences between the presentation of cash flows from operating activities under the direct method and their presentation under the indirect method. Do you consider one method to be more useful than the other? Why?
7. The statement of cash flows is said to be of assistance in evaluating the financial strength of an entity, yet the statement can exclude significant non-cash transactions that can materially affect the financial strength of an entity. How does IAS 7 seek to overcome this issue?
8. An entity may report profits over a number of successive years and still experience negative net cash flows from its operating activities. How can this happen?
9. An entity may report losses over a number of successive years and still report positive net cash flows from operating activities over the same period. How can this happen?
10. What supplementary disclosures are required when a consolidated statement of cash flows is being prepared for a group that has obtained or lost control of a subsidiary?

References

BHP Billiton 2015, *Annual Report 2015*, www.bhpbilliton.com.
Loftus, J., Leo, K., Boys, N., Daniliuc, S., Luke, B., Hong, A., and Byrnes, K. 2015, *Financial Reporting*, John Wiley & Sons Australia.

Exercises

STAR RATING ★ BASIC ★★ MODERATE ★★★ DIFFICULT

Exercise 17.1 CASH RECEIVED FROM CUSTOMERS

★ At 31 December 2016, Ruby Inc. had net accounts receivable of $180 000. At 31 December 2017, accounts receivable were $220 000 and sales for the year amounted to $1 800 000. Doubtful debts expense was $55 000 for the year. Discount allowed was $35 000 for the year.

Required

Calculate cash received from customers by Ruby Inc. for the year ended 31 December 2017.

CASH PAYMENTS TO SUPPLIERS

★ Purple Ltd had the following balances:

	31 Dec 2016	31 Dec 2017
Inventory	£170 000	£210 000
Accounts payable for inventory purchases	50 000	65 000

Cost of sales was £1 700 000 for the year ended 31 December 2017.

Required

Calculate cash payments to suppliers for the year ended 31 December 2017.

INVESTING CASH FLOWS

★ The following information has been compiled from the accounting records of Navy Inc. for the year ended 31 December 2017:

Purchase of land, with the vendor financing $150 000 for 2 years	$350 000
Purchase of plant	250 000
Sale of plant:	
Carrying amount	50 000
Cash proceeds	42 000

Required

Determine the amount of investing net cash outflows Navy Inc. would report in its statement of cash flows for the year ended 31 December 2017.

FINANCING CASH FLOWS

★ The following information has been compiled from the accounting records of Mustard Ltd for the year ended 31 December 2017:

Dividends — paid	$200 000
Dividend reinvested under a reinvestment scheme	120 000
Additional cash borrowing	250 000
Issue of shares — cash	300 000
— dividend reinvestment	120 000

Required

Determine the amount of net cash from financing activities Mustard Ltd would report in its statement of cash flows for the year ended 31 December 2017.

PREPARATION OF A STATEMENT OF CASH FLOWS

★ A summarised comparative statement of financial position of Black Inc. is presented below:

	31 Dec 2016	31 Dec 2017
Cash	$ 25 000	$ 45 000
Trade receivables	50 000	65 000
Investments in financial assets	40 000	50 000
Plant	130 000	180 000
Accumulated depreciation	(45 000)	(60 000)
	$200 000	$280 000
Trade accounts payable	$ 6 000	$ 4 000
Interest payable	7 000	
Current tax payable	20 000	28 000
Deferred tax liability		3 000
Borrowings	40 000	10 000
Share capital	100 000	130 000
Retained earnings	27 000	105 000
	$200 000	$280 000

Additional information

(a) There were no disposals of plant during the year.

(b) There were no purchases or sales of investments in financial assets during the year. Gains and losses on changes in the fair value of investments in financial assets are recognised in profit or loss.

(c) Black Inc. settled a loan (borrowings) of $30 000 by issuing ordinary shares. There were no other repayments of borrowings.

(d) Profit for the year was $101 000, interest expense was $14 000, and income tax expense was $31 000. There were no items of other comprehensive income.

(e) A $23 000 dividend was paid during the year.

(f) Service revenue for the year was $300 000. There was no other revenue.

(g) Black Inc. classifies interest as an operating activity.

Required

1. Using the indirect method of presenting cash flows from operating activities, prepare a statement of cash flows in accordance with IAS 7 for the year ended 31 December 2017.

2. Prepare the operating section of the statement of cash flows using the direct method.

Exercise 17.6

PRESENTATION OF A STATEMENT OF CASH FLOWS

★ A summarised comparative statement of financial position of Denim Ltd is presented below, together with the statement of profit or loss and other comprehensive income for the year ended 31 December 2017:

	31 Dec 2016	31 Dec 2017
Cash	£ 30 000	£ 68 000
Trade receivables	46 000	70 000
Inventory	30 000	32 000
Investments in shares	35 000	40 000
Plant	125 000	150 000
Accumulated depreciation	(23 000)	(35 000)
	£243 000	£325 000
Accounts payable	£ 39 000	£ 43 000
Accrued interest	3 000	5 000
Current tax payable	10 000	12 000
Deferred tax liability	—	1 500
Borrowings	60 000	100 000
Share capital	100 000	100 000
Retained earnings	31 000	60 000
Investment revaluation reserve	—	3 500
	£243 000	£325 000

Statement of Profit or Loss and Other Comprehensive Income for the year ended 31 December 2017	
Sales	£ 700 000
Cost of sales	(483 000)
Gross profit	217 000
Distribution costs	(62 000)
Administration expenses	(74 000)
Interest expense	(6 000)
Profit before tax	75 000
Income tax expense	(23 000)
Profit for the year	52 000
Other comprehensive income	
Gain on revaluation of investments (net of tax)	3 500
Total comprehensive income	£ 55 500

Additional information

(a) There were no disposals of investments or plant during the year.

(b) A dividend of £23 000 was paid during the year.

(c) Revaluations gains and losses on Denim Ltd's investments are recognised in other comprehensive income and accumulated in equity. The deferred tax liability is in relation to investments.

(d) Accounts payable is for purchases of inventory.

(e) Borrowings of £35 000 were repaid during the year.

(f) Denim Ltd classifies interest as an operating activity.

Required

Using the direct method of presenting cash flows from operating activities, prepare a statement of cash flows in accordance with IAS 7 for the year ended 31 December 2017.

Exercise 17.7 | **PREPARATION OF A STATEMENT OF CASH FLOWS**

★★ A comparative statement of financial position of Aqua Ltd is presented below:

	31 Dec 2016	31 Dec 2017
Cash	£ 20 000	£ 18 000
Trade receivables	184 000	204 000
Inventory	100 000	160 000
Land (at valuation)	150 000	162 000
Plant (at cost)	460 000	520 000
Accumulated depreciation	(90 000)	(120 000)
	£824 000	£ 944 000
Accounts payable	£ 50 000	£ 55 000
Accrued interest	12 000	16 000
Other accrued liabilities	45 000	43 000
Current tax payable	30 000	34 000
Provision for employee benefits	38 000	42 000
Dividend payable	—	60 000
Borrowings	195 000	105 000
Deferred tax liability	58 000	39 000
Share capital	350 000	380 000
Revaluation surplus	12 000	20 000
Retained earnings	34 000	150 000
	£824 000	£ 944 000

Statement of Profit or Loss and Other Comprehensive Income **for the year ended 31 December 2017**	
Sales	£ 3 580 000
Cost of sales	(2 864 000)
Gross profit	716 000
Gain on sale of plant	16 000
Dividend income	4 000
Distribution expenses	(185 000)
Administrative expenses	(160 000)
Interest expense	(8 000)
Other expenses	(40 000)
Profit before tax	343 000
Income tax expense	(103 000)
Profit for the year	240 000
Other comprehensive income	
Gain on asset revaluation (net of tax)	8 000
Total comprehensive income	£ 248 000

Additional information

(a) The increase in land is the result of a revaluation. The increase to the revaluation surplus is net of deferred tax of £4000.

(b) Plant with a carrying amount of £60 000 (cost £85 000, accumulated depreciation £25 000) was sold for £76 000.

(c) Accounts payable at 31 December 2017 include £22 000 for plant acquisitions.

(d) There were no additional borrowings during the year.

(e) The increase in share capital of £30 000 arose from the company's dividend reinvestment scheme.

(f) Dividends declared out of profits for the year were: interim dividend £64 000, final dividend £60 000. Dividends are classified as financing cash flows.

(g) Aqua Ltd classifies interest as an operating activity.

Required

1. Using the direct method of presenting cash flows from operating activities, prepare a statement of cash flows in accordance with IAS 7 for the year ended 31 December 2017.
2. Using the indirect method, prepare the operating activities section of the statement of cash flows in accordance with IAS 7.

Exercise 17.8 PREPARING A STATEMENT OF CASH FLOWS WITH NOTES

★★ The statement of profit or loss and other comprehensive income and comparative statements of financial position of Blue Inc. were as follows:

BLUE INC.
Statement of Financial Position
as at 31 December

	2016	2017
Current assets		
Cash at bank	$ 16 000	$ 22 000
Cash deposits (30-day)	40 000	70 000
Accounts receivable	110 000	117 000
Allowance for doubtful debts	(12 000)	(16 000)
Interest receivable	2 000	3 000
Inventory	194 000	200 000
Prepayments	13 000	9 000
	363 000	405 000
Non-current assets		
Land	230 000	290 000
Plant	600 000	700 000
Accumulated depreciation	(140 000)	(180 000)
Investments in associate	80 000	92 000
Brand names	120 000	90 000
	890 000	992 000
Total assets	$1 253 000	$1 397 000
Current liabilities		
Accounts payable	$ 180 000	$ 196 000
Accrued liabilities	85 000	92 000
Current tax payable	40 000	43 000
Current portion of long-term borrowings	20 000	20 000
	325 000	351 000
Non-current liabilities		
Borrowings	98 000	138 000
Deferred tax liability	35 000	40 000
Provision for employee benefits	40 000	43 000
	173 000	221 000
Total liabilities	498 000	572 000
Equity		
Share capital	500 000	530 000
Retained earnings	255 000	295 000
	755 000	825 000
Total liabilities and equity	$1 253 000	$1 397 000

BLUE INC.
Statement of Profit or Loss and Other Comprehensive Income
for the year ended 31 December 2017

Sales	$ 1 780 000
Cost of sales	(1 030 000)
Gross profit	750 000
Interest income	2 000
Share of profits of associate	20 000
Gain on sale of plant	8 000
Total income	780 000

(continued)

Expenses	
Salaries and wages	(352 000)
Depreciation	(50 000)
Discount allowed	(8 000)
Doubtful debts	(6 000)
Interest expense	(21 000)
Other (includes loss on impairment of brand names $30 000)	(186 000)
Profit before tax	157 000
Income tax expense	(47 000)
Profit for the period	110 000
Other comprehensive income	—
Total comprehensive income	$ 110 000

The following additional information has been extracted from the accounting records of Blue Inc.:

1. 30-day cash deposits are used in the course of the daily cash management of the company.

2. Movement in allowance for doubtful debts:

Balance 31 December 2016	$ 12 000
Charge for year	6 000
Bad debts written off	(2 000)
Balance 31 December 2017	$ 16 000

3. Land

Additional cash purchase	$ 60 000

4. Plant

Purchases for year (including $50 000 financed by the vendor)	$150 000

5. Disposals

Cost of disposals	$ 50 000
Accumulated depreciation	(10 000)

6. Investments in associate accounted for under the equity method

Share of profit	$ 20 000
Dividends received	8 000

7. Accounts payable

Includes amounts owing in respect of plant purchases:

31 December 2016	$ 12 000
31 December 2017	18 000

8. Accrued liabilities

Includes accrued interest payable:

31 December 2016	$ 4 000
31 December 2017	5 000

Interest is classified as an operating activity.

9. Income tax expense comprises:

Current tax payable	$ 42 000
Deferred tax	5 000
Income tax expense	$ 47 000

10. Dividends paid

Under a dividend reinvestment scheme, shareholders have the right to receive additional shares instead of dividends.

Dividends paid comprise:	
Dividends paid in cash during the year	$ 40 000
Dividends reinvested	30 000
Total dividends	$ 70 000

Required

1. Using the direct method of presenting cash flows from operating activities, prepare a statement of cash flows in accordance with IAS 7 for the year ended 31 December 2017.
2. Prepare any notes to the statement of cash flows that you consider are required by IAS 7.
3. Prepare the operating activities section of the statement of cash flows using the indirect method of presentation in accordance with IAS 7 for the year ended 31 December 2017.

Accounting researchers have been looking into the information content — that is, decision usefulness — of the statement of cash flows. In addition, accounting research has attempted to assess whether cash flows are as useful as earnings and accruals. For the purpose of understanding the various research findings described below, it will be constructive first to establish the link between earnings (E), accruals (ACCR) and operating cash flows (CFO). E = CFO + ACCR. Note that ACCR includes items such as changes in inventory, receivables and payables, as well as other items that appear under the indirect method.

In one of the earlier studies of cash flows, Wilson (1986) develops a model for the link between surprises in E, CFO and ACCR and abnormal stock returns. Specifically, abnormal stock returns are measured as the sum of returns in the 2 days around the earnings announcement and 9 days around the filing day of the quarterly report. Employing a sample of 322 observations in 1981 and 1982 Wilson (1986) finds that abnormal stock returns are positively associated with surprises in earnings and CFO, but negatively related to the surprise in the current portion of ACCR. This is consistent with CFO and ACCR being useful to investors.

While the findings in Wilson (1986) suggest that this is the case, Bernard and Stober (1989) re-examine the evidence. In contrast to Wilson (1986), Bernard and Stober (1989) look at a longer period, 1977–1984, and assemble a much larger sample. Looking at the 9-days window centred at the filing date of the financials, they find no evidence of association between abnormal stock returns and cash flows. Because earnings announcements take place prior to the filing day, Bernard and Stober (1989) conclude that, conditional on knowing earnings, investors ignore cash flow information.

The above-mentioned studies were conducted before the introduction of the cash flow standard, SFAS, in the US. SFAS 95 (now ASC 230) (FASB, 1987) was the first to set formal requirements for a cash flow statement with its three parts (operating cash flows (CFO), investing cash flows (CFI) and financing cash flows (CFF)). Livnat and Zarowin (1990) were among the first to examine the value relevance of the three parts although they also employ pre-standard data. Their main findings are as follows. First, they show that cumulative abnormal annual stock returns (CAR) are positively associated with their estimates of CFO and ACCR. Second, when CFF and CFI are added as explanatory variables, they show that CAR is positively (negatively) related to CFF (CFI) although with a low magnitude. Third, they show that within CFO cash collections from customers are positively related to CAR, but cash payments to suppliers, employees and interest are negatively related to CAR. Overall, therefore, Livnat and Zarowin (1990) demonstrate the usefulness of the components of the cash flow statement.

Clinch et al. (2002) examine the usefulness of the direct and indirect methods for CFO. They take advantage of Australian rules from the time before the adoption of IFRS® Standards, which required the preparation of the statement of cash flows that is accompanied by disclosures of both methods. Their sample consists of 648 firm-year observations between 1992 and 1997. They provide evidence that some components of both direct CFO and indirect CFO are associated with annual stock returns. Clinch et al. (2002) interpret the association of various components of the direct and indirect method with annual returns as evidence in their usefulness in predicting future CFO. Consistent with this view they find that the usefulness of these components for investors is increasing with their predictive ability.

Barth et al. (2001) expand the analysis of the predictability of future cash flows using a large US sample during 1987–1996. They find that 1-year-ahead CFO is positively related to current and lagged earnings (up to 6 years). The magnitude of the relation, however, diminishes over time. They further show that components of current ACCR (e.g., changes in inventory and receivables) have predictive ability with respect to next year's CFO incrementally to that of current CFO. Interestingly, they find that depreciation and amortisation — non-cash expenses — also have predictive ability for future cash flows. Barth et al. (2001) then further explore the finding that current and prior earnings can predict future CFO. Specifically, they break current and two lags of earnings into their CFO and ACCR aggregate components. Here they find that while current and lagged CFO predict future CFO, past aggregate ACCR do not, only present ACCR. Nevertheless, when past aggregate ACCR are broken into the various components Barth et al. (2001) show that these provide incremental predictive ability over current and past CFO. The overall conclusion is that the structure of the indirect method for CFO is quite useful for predicting future cash flows. Consistent with this, the various components of ACCR are found to be associated with market value of equity and stock returns.

In a more recent study, Clacher et al. (2013) investigate the value relevance of core direct cash flows, which they define as cash receipts from customers and cash paid to suppliers and employees. Using a sample of 459 Australian listed firms, they compare the value relevance of core cash flows before and after the adoption of IFRS Standards. They find that core cash flows are correlated with the value of the firm (i.e, value relevant) before the adoption of IFRS Standards. After adoption of IFRS Standards, core cash flows remain value relevant for firms in all industries and increase significantly in value relevance for industrial firms.

Although earnings and accruals are useful in that they are associated with stock returns, Cheng et al. (1996) argue that the relative information role of earnings is lower if earnings are more transitory. Using a large dataset from 1988 to 1992, the authors regress abnormal annual stock returns on earnings, change in earnings, CFO and change in CFO. They find that these variables are positively related to abnormal stock returns. This is consistent with both earnings and cash flows being useful to investors. However, the association between the earnings variables and abnormal stock returns are weaker when earnings take large extreme values (a proxy for transitory earnings). The explanation for this is that large earning changes are not seen as credible or sustainable and so investors rely more heavily on cash flows.

All the papers mentioned so far examine the usefulness of cash flows with respect to stock prices and returns. However, cash flow information may also be used by credit analysts and investors in debt markets. Using data reported under SFAS 95, Billings and Morton (2002) examine the link between cash-based interest coverage ratio and credit ratings while controlling for other common risk measures (e.g. CAPM's Beta). The authors find that the cash-based interest coverage ratio has incremental explanatory power for ratings. This suggests that rating agencies employ cash flow information in forming their rating assessments.

References

Barth, M.E., Cram, D.P. and Nelson, K.K., 2001. Accruals and the prediction of future cash flows. *The Accounting Review*, 76(1), 27–58.

Bernard, V.L. and Stober, T.L., 1989. The nature and amount of information in cash flows and accruals. *The Accounting Review*, 64(4), 624–652.

Billings, B.K. and Morton, R.M., 2002. The relation between SFAS No. 95 cash flows from operations and credit risk. *Journal of Business Finance & Accounting*, 29(5–6), 787–805.

Cheng, C.A., Liu, C.S. and Schaefer, T.F., 1996. Earnings permanence and the incremental information content of cash flows from operations. *Journal of Accounting Research*, 173–181.

Clacher, I., De Ricquebourg, A.D. and Hodgson, A., 2013. The value relevance of direct cash flows under International Financial Reporting Standards. *ABACUS*, 49(3), 367–395.

Clinch, G., Sidhu, B. and Sin, S., 2002. The usefulness of direct and indirect cash flow disclosures. *Review of Accounting Studies*, 7(4), 383–404.

Financial Accounting Standards Board (FASB), 1987. Statement of Financial Accounting Standards No. 95. Norwalk, CT: FASB.

Livnat, J. and Zarowin, P., 1990. The incremental information content of cash-flow components. *Journal of Accounting and Economics*, 13(1), 25–46.

Wilson, G.P., 1986. The relative information content of accruals and cash flows: Combined evidence at the earnings announcement and annual report release date. *Journal of Accounting Research*, 24(3), 165–200.

18 Operating segments

ACCOUNTING STANDARDS IN FOCUS

IFRS 8 *Operating Segments*

LEARNING OBJECTIVES

After studying this chapter, you should be able to:

1. discuss the objectives of financial reporting by segments
2. identify the types of entities that are within the scope of IFRS 8
3. explain and evaluate the controversy surrounding the issuance of IFRS 8
4. identify operating segments in accordance with IFRS 8
5. distinguish between operating segments and reportable segments
6. apply the definition of reportable segments
7. explain the disclosure requirements of IFRS 8
8. analyse the disclosures made by companies applying IFRS 8 in practice
9. discuss the outcome of the post-implementation review of IFRS 8.

18.1 OBJECTIVES OF FINANCIAL REPORTING BY SEGMENTS

In Europe, the introduction of IFRS 8 *Operating Segments* was controversial, as a result of which the process to endorse IFRS 8 in the European Union was not completed until November 2007, a year after the standard had been published *(see section 18.3)*.

IFRS 8 is primarily a disclosure standard and is particularly relevant for large organisations that operate in different geographic locations and/or in diverse businesses.

Paragraph 1 of IFRS 8 sets out the standard's core principle:

> An entity shall disclose information to enable users of its financial statements to evaluate the nature and financial effects of the business activities in which it engages and the economic environments in which it operates.

Many entities operate in different geographical areas or provide products or services that are subject to differing rates of profitability, opportunities for growth, future prospects and risks. Information about an entity's operating segments is relevant to assessing the risks and returns of a diversified or multinational entity where often that information cannot be determined from aggregated data. Therefore, segment information is regarded as necessary to help users of financial statements:

- better understand the entity's past performance
- better assess the entity's risks and returns
- make more informed judgements about the entity as a whole.

Many securities analysts rely on the segment disclosures to help them assess not only an entity's past performance but also to help them predict future performance. Analysts use these assessments to determine an entity's share price. Segment disclosures are widely regarded as some of the most useful disclosures in financial statements because of the extent to which they disaggregate financial information into meaningful and often revealing groupings. For example, an entity may appear profitable on a consolidated basis, but segment disclosures may reveal that one part of the business is performing poorly while another part is performing well. The part that is performing poorly may be significant to the entity as a whole and over time continued poor performance by that part (or segment) may cause the entire entity's performance to suffer. This is the kind of information that has an impact on an entity's share price because analysts frequently focus on predicting future cash flows in making their share price determinations.

On the other hand, preparers of financial statements may not wish to reveal too much information on a disaggregated basis to their competitors. Some may consider the disclosure requirements of IFRS 8 to be too revealing. For example, a user may be able to determine an entity's profit margin by segment when reading the segment disclosures. This is a key reason why it is unlikely that entities would volunteer to disclose segment information *(see section 18.2)*. Another reason is that it is often a time-consuming exercise to prepare the segment disclosures.

IFRS 8 was the first standard subject to a post-implementation review, which was completed in 2013 and is discussed later in the chapter *(see section 18.9)*

18.2 SCOPE

IFRS 8 applies to the financial statements of an entity 'whose debt or equity instruments are traded in a public market' or 'that files, or is in the process of filing, its financial statements with a securities commission or other regulatory organisation for the purpose of issuing any class of instruments in a public market' (IFRS 8 paragraph 2). Most commonly, 'traded in a public market' would mean a public stock exchange such as the London Stock Exchange or the Hong Kong Stock Exchange.

Where financial statements contain both consolidated financial statements and the parent's separate financial statements, segment information is required only for the consolidated financial statements (IFRS 8 paragraph 4). However, if consolidated financial statements are *not* prepared, and the entity is within the scope of the standard, it must apply the standard in its separate or individual financial statements (IFRS 8 paragraph 2(a)).

If an entity voluntarily chooses to disclose segment information then it must fully comply with IFRS 8; otherwise it must not describe the disclosed information as segment information (IFRS 8 paragraph 3). Voluntary disclosure may occur, for example, where a large company that is not listed, but has a large number of dependent users such as a number of minority shareholders, employees and creditors, elects to provide segment information.

18.3 A CONTROVERSIAL STANDARD
18.3.1 Overview

In January 2006, the International Accounting Standards Board (IASB®) issued Exposure Draft (ED) 8 *Operating Segments*, which it proposed as a replacement to IAS 14 *Segment Reporting*. The ED was part of the IASB's programme for achieving convergence with standards issued by the US Financial Accounting Standards Board (FASB) and essentially adopted the requirements of the FASB Statement of Financial Accounting Standards No. 131 (SFAS 131) *Disclosures about Segments of an Enterprise and Related Information*. The major change from IAS 14 was adoption of the management approach to identifying segments as the only acceptable approach. ED 8 was finally issued as a new standard, IFRS 8 *Operating Segments*, in November 2006. IFRS 8 was applicable for annual reporting periods beginning on or after 1 January 2009, with early adoption permitted.

18.3.2 Reasons for the controversy

In Europe, the replacement of IAS 14 with IFRS 8 was highly controversial, mainly because of the management approach allowed by IFRS 8 compared with the more prescriptive approach previously required by IAS 14. The management approach in IFRS 8 requires segment information to be reported externally based on how information is reported internally to the company's management *(see section 18.4)*. In contrast, IAS 14 contained very prescriptive requirements as to what should be reported and how. The European Parliament is required to endorse all IASB standards and IFRIC® Interpretations in order for the standards and interpretations to come into effect. The European Financial Reporting Advisory Group (EFRAG) reviews the proposed standards and makes its recommendations to the European Commission as to whether or not the parliament should endorse the standards and interpretations. When ED 8 was issued, concern was expressed about the management approach by many commentators to both the IASB and EFRAG. After the IASB issued IFRS 8, the European Commission sought further feedback, by means of a questionnaire, on whether or not the European Parliament should endorse IFRS 8. The questions focused on the management approach, the lack of mandatory disclosure requirements and whether these were perceived as positive or negative by commentators.

A paper prepared and presented by Nicolas Véron, Research Fellow at Bruegel (a European think-tank created to contribute to the quality of economic policy making in Europe), argued that IFRS 8 should not be endorsed. The paper (Véron, 2007) argued that the success of IFRS® Standards thus far can be attributed both to market (investor) demand and to European Union (EU) leadership and that convergence with US GAAP 'is far from universally accepted as an appropriate framework for setting the current standard-setting agenda'. The paper contended that 'segment information is one of the most vital aspects of financial reporting for investors and other users' and is also inherently divisive between preparers of financial statements on the one hand, who want to control the information, and users on the other, who want it to be specifically objective. The risks and rewards approach to identifying segments (previously contained in IAS 14) arguably meets the needs of users while the management approach arguably meets the needs of preparers, although both approaches may be consistent (as envisaged by IAS 14). The paper argues that the discretion permitted by IFRS 8 in determining the content of segment profit or loss and segment assets and in making or not making certain disclosures (e.g. disclosure of liabilities, statement of profit or loss and other comprehensive income line items and geographical information) contrasts with the prescribed measurement and disclosure requirements of IAS 14, favouring preparers over users. The paper quotes from various respondents' letters to the IASB, particularly those of analysts, who did not support changing IAS 14 and moving to a standard based on SFAS 131, because they regarded SFAS 131 as inferior to IAS 14.

It is also notable that two IASB board members dissented from the issuance of IFRS 8 (refer to the dissenting opinion in IFRS 8) because of the lack of definition of segment profit or loss and because IFRS 8 does not require consistent attribution of assets and profit or loss to segments. In addition, these board members also believed that the changes from IAS 14 were not justified by the need for convergence with US GAAP because IAS 14 is a disclosure standard and therefore does not affect the reconciliation of IFRS amounts to US GAAP.

The preparer's viewpoint is argued, for example, in the submission by the Association of German Banks to the European Commission's questionnaire referred to above (Bundesverband Deutscher Banken 2007). This letter argues that IFRS 8 should be endorsed and that the information provided under the management approach will be more relevant and reliable because it will, inter alia, enable investors to evaluate the entity on the same basis as that used by management in its decision making and that any concerns about understandability are addressed by the reconciliation requirements of IFRS 8.

Despite the objections, IFRS 8 was finally endorsed by the European Parliament in November 2007. In its endorsement resolution, the European Parliament stated that the IASB should carry out a review of the new standard 2 years after its implementation. Further, the Parliament's requirement that the European Commission 'follow closely the application of IFRS 8 and (to) report back to Parliament no later than 2011,[1] inter alia regarding reporting of geographical segments, segment profit or loss, and use of non-IFRS measures, underlines that if the Commission discovers deficiencies in the application of IFRS 8 it has a duty to rectify such deficiencies'.

The message from the European Parliament to European companies is therefore that entities will be watched closely to determine whether they are taking advantage of the discretionary approach of IFRS 8 in order to control reported information. *Refer to section 18.9 for a discussion of the IASB's post-implementation review of IFRS 8.*

---

[1] At the time of writing (October 2015), no report had yet been issued

18.4 IDENTIFYING OPERATING SEGMENTS

An operating segment is defined in paragraph 5 of IFRS 8 as a component of an entity:

(a) that engages in business activities from which it may earn revenues and incur expenses (including revenues and expenses relating to transactions with other components of the same entity);

(b) whose operating results are regularly reviewed by the entity's chief operating decision maker to make decisions about resources to be allocated to the segment and assess its performance; and

(c) for which discrete financial information is available.

The chief operating decision maker (CODM) refers to the function of allocating resources and assessing performance of the operating segments, and not necessarily to a manager with a specific title. That function may be carried out by a group of people, for example, an executive committee. Generally, an operating segment has a segment manager who is directly accountable to the CODM. As with the CODM, the term 'segment manager' identifies a function, not necessarily a manager with a specific title. A single manager may be the segment manager for more than one operating segment and the CODM may also be the segment manager for one or more operating segments. When an entity has a matrix structure, for example, with some managers responsible for different product and service lines and other managers responsible for specific geographic areas, and the CODM regularly reviews the operating results for both sets of components, the entity uses the core principle *(see section 18.1 and Illustrative Example 18.2)* to determine its operating segments (IFRS 8 paragraph 10).

Figure 18.1 summarises the key decision points in identifying operating segments.

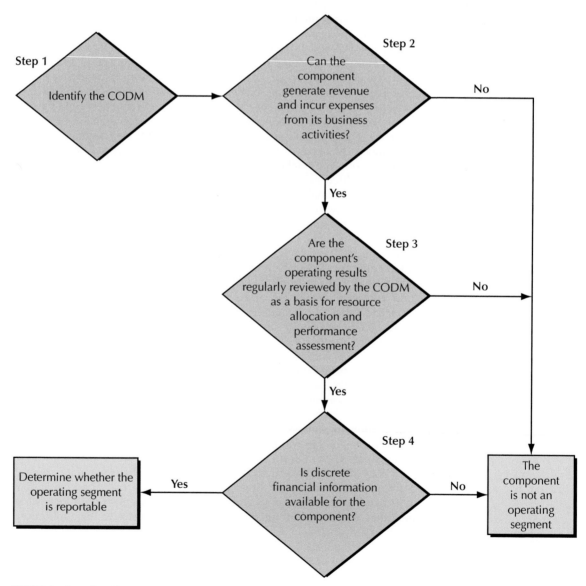

FIGURE 18.1 Identifying operating segments under IFRS 8
Source: Ernst & Young (2009, p. 9). © 2009 EYGM Limited. All rights reserved.

The following examples illustrate the steps in identifying operating segments.

ILLUSTRATIVE EXAMPLE 18.1 Identifying operating segments under IFRS 8 — the four steps

Sargsyan has a chief executive officer (CEO), a chief operating officer (COO) and an executive committee comprising the CEO, COO and the heads (general managers) of three business units — units X, Y and Z. Every month, financial information is presented to the executive committee for each of business units X, Y and Z and for Sargsyan as a whole in order to assess the performance of each business unit and of the company as a whole. Units X, Y and Z each generate revenue and incur expenses from their business activities. Unit Y derives the majority of its revenue from Unit Z. Corporate headquarter costs that are not allocated to units X, Y or Z are also reported separately each month to the executive committee in order to determine the results for Sargsyan as a whole.

Step 1: Identify the CODM
In this case, the CODM is likely to be the executive committee, since it is this group that regularly reviews the operating results of all business units and the company as a whole. However, if the business unit heads only join the committee meetings to report on their specific business unit and then leave the meeting, and the CEO and COO are the only people who review all the business units and the company as a whole, and are the ones who make resource allocation decisions, for example, about changing the structure of the business units, then the CODM would be the CEO and COO. In practice, this would not likely make any difference to the identification of the operating segments since the operating results information regularly reviewed by the entire committee is likely to be identical to that reviewed by the CEO and COO (see step 2).

Step 2: Can the component generate revenue and incur expenses from its business activities?
For units X and Z, the answer is clearly yes. For Unit Y, the answer is also yes — even though its revenue is derived internally this does not prevent it from being identified as an operating segment (IFRS 8 paragraph 5(a)). For the corporate headquarters, the answer is no as it does not derive revenues; it only incurs costs. Therefore, the corporate headquarters would not be identified as an operating segment and would not require further assessment.

Step 3: Are the component's operating results regularly reviewed by the CODM as a basis for resource allocation and performance assessment?
Yes, the operating results for units X, Y and Z are regularly reviewed by the CODM.

Step 4: Is discrete financial information available for the component?
Yes, discrete financial information is available for units X, Y and Z.

Conclusion
Units X, Y and Z are identified as Sargsyan's operating segments.

ILLUSTRATIVE EXAMPLE 18.2 Identifying operating segments under IFRS 8 — matrix structure

Lothian has a chief executive officer (CEO), a chief operating officer (COO) and an executive committee comprising the CEO, COO and the heads (general managers) of three business units organised according to the company's main products — units X, Y and Z. The company also operates in two distinct geographic regions — the United Kingdom and North America. The heads of these geographic regions attend executive committee meetings, have input into decisions about the distribution of the company's products into their geographic regions and give their views on the performance of the company's products in their regions. However, the CEO can override any decisions made by the committee. Every month, financial information is presented to the executive committee for each of business units X, Y and Z, geographic regions UK and North America and for Lothian as a whole in order to assess the performance of each business unit, each geographic region and of the company as a whole. Corporate headquarter costs that are not allocated to units X, Y or Z or to the geographic regions are also reported separately each month to the executive committee in order to determine the results for Lothian as a whole. There is necessarily an overlap between the financial information presented for each of units X, Y and Z and UK and North American geographic regions because the product performance reported for each unit is reported again, with that of the other two product units, by geographic region.

Step 1: Identify the CODM
In this case, the CODM is likely to be the CEO, since he or she has overriding decision making authority.

Step 2: Can the component generate revenue and incur expenses from its business activities?
For units X, Y and Z, the answer is clearly yes. For the geographic regions, the answer is also yes, even though the revenues are generated from deployment of the products from units X, Y and Z in the

regions. For the corporate headquarters, the answer is no as it does not derive revenues; it only incurs costs. Therefore, the corporate headquarters would not be identified as an operating segment and would not require further assessment.

Step 3: Are the component's operating results regularly reviewed by the CODM as a basis for resource allocation and performance assessment?
For units X, Y, Z, and the geographic regions, the answer is yes.

Step 4: Is discrete financial information available for the component?
For units X, Y, Z, and the geographic regions, the answer is yes.

Conclusion
This leaves the entity potentially having two sets of operating segments — units X, Y and Z, and geographic regions UK and North America. It is in this situation that paragraph 10 of IFRS 8 directs the entity to the core principle of the standard. This means management must exercise judgement consistent with the management approach founded on what is important to the CODM. For example, if the CEO uses the information and advice provided by the three business unit general managers in order to make decisions about the allocation of resources to those business units, such as whether to invest in new production technologies, but only looks to the geographical region heads for insight into regional product performance, then perhaps the CODM focuses more on the information provided by the three product line business units than the geographical information when allocating resources and assessing performance.

18.5 IDENTIFYING REPORTABLE SEGMENTS

18.5.1 The basic criteria

Paragraph 11 of IFRS 8 requires that an entity report separately information about each operating segment that:
(a) has been identified as an operating segment in accordance with the four steps discussed above, or results from aggregating two or more of those segments in accordance with specific aggregation criteria; and
(b) exceeds the specified quantitative thresholds.

An entity must report separately information about an operating segment that meets *any* of the following quantitative thresholds:
(a) its reported revenue is 10% or more of the combined revenue of all operating segments (revenue includes both external and internal revenue)
(b) its reported profit or loss is, in absolute terms, 10% or more of the greater of (1) the combined reported profit of all operating segments that reported a profit, and (2) the combined reported loss of all operating segments that reported a loss
(c) its assets are 10% or more of the combined assets of all operating segments.

If management believes that information about an operating segment would be useful to users, it may treat that segment as a reportable segment even if the quantitative thresholds are not met (IFRS 8 paragraph 13).

18.5.2 The aggregation criteria

The aggregation criteria in paragraph 12 provide that two or more operating segments may be aggregated into a single operating segment if aggregation is consistent with the core principle of the standard, the segments have similar economic characteristics and the segments are similar in *each* of the following respects:
(a) the nature of the products and services
(b) the nature of the production processes
(c) the type or class of customer for their products and services
(d) the methods used to distribute their products or provide their services
(e) if applicable, the nature of the regulatory environment, for example, banking, insurance or public utilities.

An entity may combine operating segments that do not meet the quantitative thresholds to produce a reportable segment only if the segments have similar economic characteristics and meet the above aggregation criteria (IFRS 8 paragraph 14).

Paragraph 15 of IFRS 8 requires that an entity must identify operating segments until at least 75% of the entity's consolidated *external* revenue is included in reportable segments.

Paragraph 16 of IFRS 8 states that business activities and operating segments that are not reportable must be combined and disclosed as 'all other segments' separately from the reconciling items required by paragraph 28 *(see section 18.7.5)*.

Note that IFRS 8 does not distinguish between revenues and expenses from transactions with third parties and those from transactions *within the group* for the purposes of identifying operating segments (IFRS 8 paragraph 5). Therefore, in an entity with internal vertically integrated businesses, it is possible that such internal businesses might be identified as operating segments under IFRS 8.

IFRS 8 provides additional guidance to entities regarding the maximum number of reportable segments — indicating that ten is a reasonable maximum (IFRS 8 paragraph 19).

Figure 18.2 summarises the key decision points in identifying reportable segments, and follows on from figure 18.1

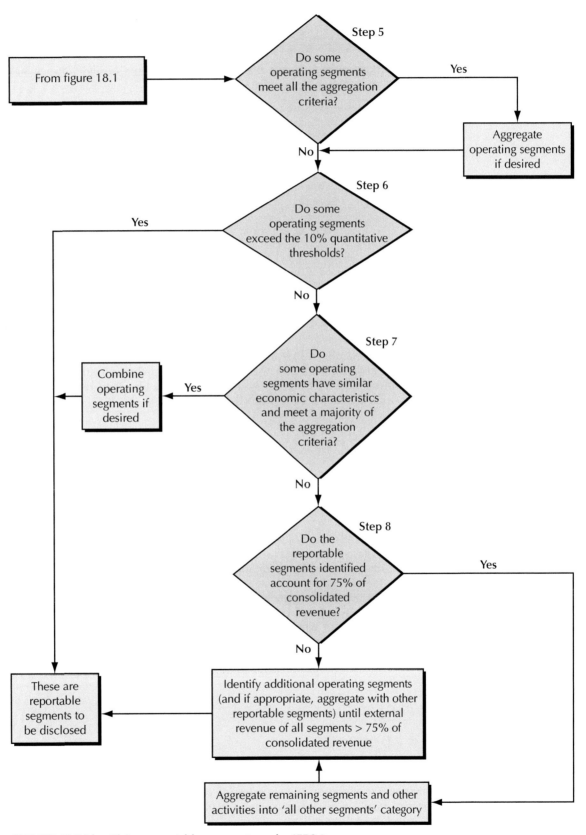

FIGURE 18.2 Identifying reportable segments under IFRS 8
Source: Ernst & Young (2009, p. 12). © 2009 EYGM Limited. All rights reserved.

18.6 APPLYING THE DEFINITION OF REPORTABLE SEGMENTS

Building on illustrative example 18.1, the following example illustrates how Sargsyan identifies its reportable segments under IFRS 8.

ILLUSTRATIVE EXAMPLE 18.3 Identifying reportable segments under IFRS 8

Sargsyan has identified units X, Y and Z as operating segments (see illustrative example 18.1). The following additional information is provided:

	Unit X $'000	Unit Y $'000	Unit Z $'000	Total operating segments $'000	Corporate headquarters $'000	Other businesses $'000	Total Sargsyan (consolidated) $'000
Revenue	200	100 (80 earned from Unit Z)	400	700	—	230	850
Profit/(loss)	50	30 (10 earned from Unit Z)	100	180	(25)	20	165
Assets	800	300	950	2 050	250	200	2 500

Management has determined that units X, Y and Z do not meet the aggregation criteria of IFRS 8. Unit Z has no inventory on hand at year-end in respect of purchases from unit Y.

Quantitative thresholds: note that the quantitative thresholds are in respect of the *totals for the operating segments* — not the total for Sargsyan (IFRS 8 paragraph 13):

	Revenue % of total	Profit % of total	Assets % of total
Unit X	29%	28%	39%
Unit Y	14%	17%	15%
Unit Z	57%	55%	46%

Therefore, all three units meet all three of the quantitative thresholds. (Note that only one threshold needs to be met.) Thus, all three units are reportable segments.

The next question is whether the reportable segments account for 75% of consolidated revenue. This test is applied to the *external* revenues of the segments (IFRS 8 paragraph 15). Total consolidated revenue (after inter-segment eliminations) is $850 000. Total external operating segment revenue is: Unit X: $200 000; Unit Y: $20 000 and Unit Z: $400 000, giving a total of $620 000. This constitutes 73% of total consolidated revenue, which is below the 75% requirement. Therefore, additional operating segments need to be identified. Management will need to further analyse the 'other businesses' and identify another reportable segment from that component.

18.7 DISCLOSURE

18.7.1 Overall approach

IFRS 8 sets out a general approach to disclosure and largely allows management to determine what is disclosed and how the amounts disclosed are measured based on those measures used by the CODM for determining resource allocation and for assessing performance.

The general principle of disclosure is set out in paragraph 20 of IFRS 8, which is, in effect, a restatement of the core principle of the standard:

> An entity shall disclose information to enable users of its financial statements to evaluate the nature and financial effects of the business activities in which it engages and the economic environments in which it operates.

To give effect to this principle, paragraph 21 of IFRS 8 requires an entity to disclose:

(a) general information on segments identified for reporting;
(b) reported segment profit or loss, including information about specified revenues and expenses included in reported profit or loss, segment assets and segment liabilities (if reported to the CODM) and the basis of measurement; and
(c) reconciliations of the totals of segment revenues, reported segment profit or loss, segment assets, segment liabilities and other material segment items to the corresponding entity amounts in the financial statements.

18.7.2 General information

An entity is required to disclose:

(a) the factors used to identify the entity's reportable segments, including the basis of organisation, for example, whether management has chosen to organise the entity by different products and services, geographical areas, regulatory environments, or a combination of factors, and whether segments have been aggregated;
(b) the judgements made by management in applying the aggregation criteria *(discussed in section 18.5.2)*, including a brief description of the operating segments that have been aggregated and the economic indicators that were considered in determining that the aggregated operating segments share similar characteristics; and
(c) the types of products or services from which each reportable segment derives its revenues.

18.7.3 Information about profit or loss, assets and liabilities

Paragraph 23 of IFRS 8 states that an entity shall report 'a measure' of profit or loss for each reportable segment. An entity is also required to disclose a measure of total assets and total liabilities for each reportable segment, but *only* if such amounts are regularly reported to the CODM.

These measures are those used by the CODM for the purposes of making decisions about allocating resources to the segment and assessing its performance (IFRS 8 paragraph 25). In other words, whatever the CODM uses to measure and assess the operating segment is what is disclosed under IFRS 8. This extends to the allocation of amounts of profit or loss and assets and liabilities to segments. If the CODM uses information based on amounts that are allocated to segments, then those amounts should be allocated for the purposes of disclosing 'a measure'. If the CODM does not use that information, the amounts should not be allocated.

In respect of segment profit or loss, certain line items are also required to be disclosed *only* if these items are included in the measure of segment profit or loss reported to the CODM, or are otherwise regularly provided to the CODM:

(a) revenues from external customers
(b) inter-segment revenues
(c) interest revenue
(d) interest expense
(e) depreciation and amortisation
(f) material items of income and expense disclosed in accordance with paragraph 97 of IAS 1
(g) the entity's interest in the profit or loss of associates and joint ventures accounted for by the equity method
(h) income tax expense or income
(i) material non-cash items other than depreciation and amortisation (IFRS 8 paragraph 23).

Interest revenue and interest expense may be reported on a net basis only if a majority of the segment's revenues are from interest and the CODM relies primarily on net interest revenue to assess the performance of the segment. This may be the case, for example, in the banking industry.

In respect of segment assets, certain line items are also required to be disclosed if these items are included in the measure of segment assets reported to the CODM, or are otherwise regularly provided to the CODM:

(a) the amount of investment in associates and joint ventures accounted for by the equity method
(b) the amounts of additions to non-current assets (with certain exceptions) (IFRS 8 paragraph 24).

The notable feature of these disclosure requirements is the lack of prescription. If the items listed (with the exception of a measure of segment profit or loss, which must always be disclosed) are reported to the CODM, then they must be disclosed. This means that what is not reported internally is not disclosed externally. Furthermore, *how* the amount is measured internally is used for external measurement purposes, even if the measurement basis is not in accordance with IFRS.

18.7.4 Measurement

Because management has discretion about measurement, IFRS 8 requires disclosure of *how* the entity has determined the measures of profit or loss, and, if applicable, assets and liabilities, for each reportable segment (IFRS 8 paragraph 27). This includes:

(a) the basis of accounting for any transactions between reportable segments;
(b) if not apparent from the required reconciliations *(see section 18.7.5)*, the nature of any differences between the measurements of total reported segment profit or loss and the entity's profit or loss before

income taxes and discontinued operations (i.e. the profit or loss reported in the statement of profit or loss and other comprehensive income in accordance with IFRSs). For example, if the CODM uses concepts such as 'cash profit' for measuring the segment profit or loss, the entity would need to disclose how 'cash profit' is determined and how it differs from the IFRS measure of profit before income taxes and discontinued operations. This could include, for example, the fact that the CODM determines 'cash profit' to be profit or loss before fair value movements, depreciation and amortisation, and impairment charges;

(c) if not apparent from the required reconciliations, the nature of any differences between the measurements of total reported segment assets and the entity's assets. For example, this could include accounting policies and policies for allocation of jointly used assets in determining segment assets;

(d) if not apparent from the required reconciliations, the nature of any differences between the measurements of total reported segment liabilities and the entity's liabilities. For example, this could include accounting policies and policies for allocation of jointly used liabilities in determining segment liabilities;

(e) the nature of any changes from prior periods in the measurement methods used to determine segment profit or loss, including the financial effect, if any, of those changes. For example, if the CODM decides to change the measure of segment profit or loss used from one that excludes fair value movements to one that includes fair value movements, this fact would need to be disclosed together with the impact on reported segment profit or loss; and

(f) the nature and effect of any asymmetrical allocations to reportable segments. For example, an entity might allocate depreciation expense to a segment without allocating the related depreciable assets to that segment.

18.7.5 Reconciliations

An entity is required to provide reconciliations of all of the following:

(a) the total of the reportable segments' revenues to the entity's revenue. In illustrative example 18.3, ignoring the identification of additional segments to meet the 75% threshold, this would be a reconciliation of total segment revenues of $700 000 to Sargsyan's revenue of $850 000;

(b) the total of the reportable segments' measures of profit or loss to the entity's profit or loss before income tax and discontinued operations (or, if items such as income tax are allocated to segments, to profit or loss after income tax). In illustrative example 18.3, ignoring the identification of additional segments to meet the 75% threshold, this would be a reconciliation of total segment profits of $180 000 to Sargsyan's profit of $165 000;

(c) the total of the reportable segments' assets (if reported) to the entity's assets. In illustrative example 18.3, ignoring the identification of additional segments to meet the 75% threshold, this would be a reconciliation of total segment assets of $2.05 million to Sargsyan's assets of $2.5 million;

(d) the total of segment liabilities (if reported) to the entity's liabilities; and

(e) the total of segment amounts for every other material item of information disclosed to the corresponding amount for the entity.

All material reconciling items must be separately identified and described. For example, in illustrative example 18.3, assuming the amounts are material, the entity would need to disclose its reconciliation of total segment profits to Sargsyan's profit as follows:

	$'000
Total segment profits:	180
Less: Inter-segment profit	(10)
Less: Corporate headquarters costs not allocated to reportable segments	(25)
Add: Profit from other businesses not identified as reportable segments	20
Total Sargsyan profit	165

18.7.6 Entity-wide disclosures

The following disclosures apply to all entities subject to IFRS 8, including those that have only one reportable segment (unless the information is already provided as part of the reportable segment information).

• Information about products and services: revenues from external customers for *each product and service* or for each group of similar products and services. In this case, the amount of revenues must be based on the financial information used to produce the entity's financial statements, *not* based on amounts reported to the CODM. If the information is not available and the cost to develop it would be excessive, the entity need not disclose the information but it must state this fact (IFRS 8 paragraph 32). This requirement is potentially onerous in that it is possible that one reportable segment includes numerous products and/or services.

- Information about geographical areas: revenues from external customers and non-current assets (i) attributed to/located in the entity's country of domicile and (ii) attributed to/located in foreign countries. If revenues or non-current assets attributed to/located in an individual foreign country are material, those revenues/assets shall be disclosed separately. The entity must also disclose the basis for attributing revenues from external customers to individual countries. In this case, as in paragraph 32, the amount of revenues and assets must be based on the financial information used to produce the entity's financial statements. If the information is not available and the cost to develop it would be excessive then the entity need not disclose the information but it must state this fact (IFRS 8 paragraph 33).
- Information about major customers: if revenues from transactions with a single external customer account for 10% or more of an entity's total revenues, disclose that fact, the total amount of revenues from each such customer, and the reportable segment or segments reporting the revenues. The identity of the customer or customers does not have to be disclosed.

18.7.7 Comparative information

There are a few circumstances in which comparative information must be restated or otherwise taken into account.

(a) If an operating segment was a reportable segment for the immediately preceding prior period but is not for the current period, and management decides that the segment is of continuing significance, information about that segment must continue to be reported in the current period (IFRS 8 paragraph 17).

(b) If an operating segment becomes a reportable segment for the current period, comparative information must be restated to reflect the newly reportable segment, even if that segment did not meet the criteria for reportability in the prior period. This is required unless the information is not available and the cost to develop it would be excessive (IFRS 8 paragraph 18).

(c) If an entity changes any of its segment measures, including how segment profit or loss is determined, or changes the allocation of income, expenses, assets or liabilities to segments, without a change to the composition of its reportable segments, the general principles of IAS 1 for changes in presentation or classification apply *(see chapter 16)*. Therefore, comparative information would be restated, unless this is impracticable (IAS 1 paragraph 41).

(d) If an entity changes the structure of its internal organisation in a manner that causes the composition of its reportable segments to change, the corresponding information for prior periods, including interim periods, must be restated. This applies unless the information is not available and the cost to develop it would be excessive (IFRS 8 paragraph 29). Note that in this case the exemption from restatement applies to each individual item of disclosure. This could result in restatement of some items and not of others.

(e) If an entity changes the structure of its internal organisation in a manner that causes the composition of its reportable segments to change and the corresponding information for prior periods is *not* restated, the entity must disclose the segment information for the current period on both the old and the new basis. This applies unless the information is not available and the cost to develop it would be excessive (IFRS 8 paragraph 30).

18.8 APPLYING THE DISCLOSURES IN PRACTICE

Figure 18.3 contains extracts from the 2014 annual report of Daimler AG, a company listed on the Frankfurt and Stuttgart stock exchanges.

Firstly, note how the company describes the segmentation of its activities into its principal business activities and specific product lines. The company then goes on to describe how its segment measures are determined, the impact of various restructuring initiatives and significant transactions, followed by the required quantitative information, including reconciliations.

FIGURE 18.3 Extracts from Daimler AG's annual report — Segment Reporting Note

1. Segment reporting
Reportable segments. The reportable segments of the Group are Mercedes-Benz Cars, Daimler Trucks, Mercedes-Benz Vans, Daimler Buses and Daimler Financial Services. The segments are largely organized and managed separately according to nature of products and services provided, brands, distribution channels and profile of customers.

The vehicle segments develop and manufacture passenger cars and off-road vehicles, trucks, vans and buses. Mercedes-Benz Cars sells passenger cars and off-road vehicles under the Mercedes-Benz brand and small cars under the smart brand. Daimler Trucks distributes its trucks under the brand names Mercedes-Benz, Freightliner, FUSO, Western Star, Thomas Built Buses and BharatBenz. The vans of the Mercedes-Benz Vans segment are primarily sold under the brand name Mercedes-Benz and also under the Freightliner brand. Daimler Buses sells completely built-up buses under the brand names Mercedes-Benz and Setra. In addition, Daimler Buses produces and sells bus chassis. The vehicle segments also sell related spare parts and accessories.

(continued)

FIGURE 18.3 *(continued)*

The Daimler Financial Services segment supports the sales of the Group's vehicle segments worldwide. Its product portfolio mainly comprises tailored financing and leasing packages for customers and dealers. The segment also provides services such as insurance, fleet management, investment products and credit cards, as well as various mobility services.

Management and reporting systems. The Group's management reporting and controlling systems principally use accounting policies that are the same as those described in Note 1 in the summary of significant accounting policies according to IFRS.

The Group measures the performance of its operating segments through a measure of segment profit or loss which is referred to as "EBIT" in our management and reporting system.

EBIT comprises gross profit, selling and general administrative expenses, research and non-capitalized development costs, other operating income and expense, and our share of profit/loss from equity-method investments, net, as well as other financial income/expense, net. Although amortization of capitalized borrowing costs is included in cost of sales, it is not included in EBIT.

Intersegment revenue is generally recorded at values that approximate third-party selling prices.

Segment assets principally comprise all assets. The industrial business segments' assets exclude income tax assets, assets from defined benefit pension plans and other post-employment benefit plans, and certain financial assets (including liquidity).

Segment liabilities principally comprise all liabilities. The industrial business segments' liabilities exclude income tax liabilities, liabilities from defined benefit pension plans and other post-employment benefit plans, and certain financial liabilities (including financing liabilities).

Daimler Financial Services' performance is measured on the basis of return on equity, which is the usual procedure in the banking business.

The residual value risks associated with the Group's operating leases and finance lease receivables are generally borne by the vehicle segments that manufactured the leased equipment. Risk sharing is based on agreements between the respective vehicle segments and Daimler Financial Services; the terms vary by vehicle segment and geographic region.

Non-current assets consist of intangible assets, property, plant and equipment and equipment on operating leases.

Capital expenditures for property, plant and equipment and intangible assets reflect the cash effective additions to these property, plant and equipment and intangible assets as far as they do not relate to capitalized borrowing costs, goodwill and finance leases.

Depreciation and amortization may also include impairments as far as they do not relate to goodwill.

Amortization of capitalized borrowing costs is not included in the amortization of intangible assets or depreciation of property, plant and equipment since it is not considered as part of EBIT.

Reconciliation. Reconciliation includes corporate items for which headquarters are responsible. Transactions between the segments are eliminated in the context of consolidation and the eliminated amounts are included in the reconciliation.

The effects of certain legal proceedings are excluded from the operative results and liabilities of the segments if such items are not indicative of the segments' performance, since their related results of operations may be distorted by the amount and the irregular nature of such events. This may also be the case for items that refer to more than one reportable segment.

Reconciliation also includes corporate projects and equity interests not allocated to the segments. If the Group hedges investments in associated companies for strategic reasons, the related financial assets and earnings effects are generally not allocated to the segments.

Information related to geographic areas. With respect to information about geographical regions, revenue is allocated to countries based on the location of the customer; non-current assets are presented according to the physical location of these assets.

Mercedes-Benz Cars. In 2014, in the segment Mercedes-Benz Cars the restructuring of the Group's sales organization had an effect of €81 million (see also Note 5). Furthermore, the segment profit of Mercedes-Benz Cars includes in profit/loss from equity-method investments an impairment of €30 million (2013: €174 million) on an investment in the area of alternative drive systems.

Daimler Trucks. In January 2013, Daimler Trucks decided on workforce adjustments in Germany and Brazil, which were continued in 2014. Expenses recorded in this regard and for the restructuring of the Group's sales organization amounted to €165 million in 2014 (2013: €116 million). In 2014, the optimization programs led to a cash outflow of €170 million (2013: €50 million) (see also Note 5).

Mercedes-Benz Vans. In 2014, profit/loss from equity method investments for the segment Mercedes-Benz Vans includes the reversal of an impairment on the investment in FBAC of €61 million (2013: €0 million). In addition, the restructuring of the Group's sales organization affected Mercedes-Benz Vans by an amount of €17 million.

Daimler Buses. Expenses from the measures described under Daimler Trucks and from the restructuring of the Group's sales organization impacted Daimler Buses in 2014 with a total amount of €14 million. In the previous year, the expenses of €39 million included effects from the optimization programs in Western Europe and North America (see also Note 5).

Daimler Financial Services. The interest income and interest expenses of Daimler Financial Services are included in revenue and cost of sales, and are presented in Notes 4 and 5.

Table ⤢ E.87 presents segment information as of and for the years ended December 31, 2014 and 2013.

E.87

Segment information

	Mercedes-Benz Cars	Daimler Trucks	Mercedes-Benz Vans	Daimler Buses	Daimler Financial Services	Total Segments	Reconciliation	Consolidated Group
In millions of euros								
2014								
External revenue	70 899	30 302	9 601	4 155	14 915	129 872	—	129 872
Intersegment revenue	2 685	2 087	367	63	1 076	6 278	–6 278	—
Total revenue	73 584	32 389	9 968	4 218	15 991	136 150	–6 278	129 872
Segment profit (EBIT)	5 853	1 878	682	197	1 387	9 997	755	10 752
thereof profit/loss from equity-method investments	103	–1	63	1	–15	151	746	897
thereof expenses from compounding of provisions and changes in discount rates	–247	–70	–20	–11	–4	–352	–1	–353
Segment assets	51 950	20 181	5 895	3 562	105 454	187 042	2 593	189 635
thereof equity-method investments	936	545	97	8	30	1 616	678	2 294
Segment liabilities	34 811	12 131	4 349	2 622	97 837	151 750	–6 699	145 051
Additions to non-current assets	10 949	1 896	1 004	507	9 899	24 255	10	24 265
thereof investments in intangible assets	1 238	77	115	13	20	1 463	—	1 463
thereof investments in property, plant and equipment	3 621	788	304	105	23	4 841	3	4 844
Depreciation and amortization of non-current assets[1]	4 562	1 435	452	225	3 368	10 042	15	10 057
thereof amortization of intangible assets	1 086	284	93	15	20	1 498	—	1 498
thereof depreciation of property, plant and equipment[1]	2 446	766	197	75	14	3 498	3	3 501

[1] Includes impairments of property, plant and equipment of €93 million from the planned sale of selected sites of the Group's sales network, of which €64 million relates to Mercedes-Benz Cars, €13 million to Daimler Trucks, €14 million to Mercedes-Benz Vans and €2 million to Daimler Buses.

	Mercedes-Benz Cars	Daimler Trucks	Mercedes-Benz Vans	Daimler Buses	Daimler Financial Services	Total Segments	Reconciliation	Consolidated Group
In millions of euros								
2013								
External revenue	61 883	29 431	9 021	4 044	13 603	117 982	—	117 982
Intersegment revenue	2 424	2 042	348	61	919	5 794	–5 794	—
Total revenue	64 307	31 473	9 369	4 105	14 522	123 776	–5 794	117 982
Segment profit (EBIT)	4 006	1 637	631	124	1 268	7 666	3 149	10 815
thereof profit/loss from equity-method investments	–127	69	3	1	1	–53	3 398	3 345
thereof expenses from compounding of provisions and changes in discount rates	–57	–20	–8	–3	–5	–93	–2	–95

(continued)

FIGURE 18.3 (continued)

Segment assets	46 752	21 105	5 578	3 256	89 370	166 061	2 457	168 518
thereof equity-method investments	706	2 109	2	6	13	2 836	596	3 432
Segment liabilities	28 917	11 005	3 987	2 403	82 774	129 086	–3 931	125 155
Additions to non-current assets	11 110	1 960	1 196	384	8 301	22 951	70	23 021
thereof investments in intangible assets	1 533	166	189	6	38	1 932	—	1 932
thereof investments in property, plant and equipment	3 710	839	288	76	19	4 932	43	4 975
Depreciation and amortization of non-current assets	3 857	1 457	375	200	2 824	8 713	35	8 748
thereof amortization of intangible assets	961	316	65	23	11	1 376	—	1 376
thereof depreciation of property, plant and equipment	1 972	784	151	72	14	2 993	–1	2 992

E.88
Reconciliation to Group figures

In millions of euros	2014	2013
Total of segments' profit (EBIT)	9 997	7 666
Result from the disposal of the investment in RRPSH	1 006	—
Equity-method investments		
Remeasurement of the investment in Tesla	718	—
Remeasurement and sale of the investment in EADS	—	3 397
Other income from equity-method investments[1]	28	1
Other corporate items	–1 039	–331
Eliminations	42	82
Group EBIT	10 752	10 815
Amortization of capitalized borrowing costs[2]	–9	–4
Interest income	145	212
Interest expense	–715	–884
Profit before income taxes	10 173	10 139
Total of segments' assets	187 042	166 061
Carrying amount of equity-method investments[3]	678	596
Income tax assets[4]	4 028	1 939
Unallocated financial assets (including liquidity) and assets from pensions and similar obligations[4]	13 886	14 560
Other corporate items and eliminations	–15 999	–14 638
Group assets	189 635	168 518
Total of segments' liabilities	151 750	129 086
Income tax liabilities[4]	47	61
Unallocated financial liabilities and liabilities from pensions and similar obligations[4]	9 661	11 551
Other corporate items and eliminations	–16 407	–15 543
Group liabilities	145 051	125 155

[1] Mainly comprises the Group's proportionate share of profits and losses of BAIC Motor.
[2] Amortization of capitalized borrowing costs is not considered in the internal performance measure "EBIT" but is included in cost of sales.
[3] Mainly comprises the carrying amount of the investment in BAIC Motor.
[4] Industrial business.

Reconciliations. Reconciliations of the total segment amounts to the respective items included in the consolidated financial statements are shown in table ↗ E.88.

530   PART 3 Presentation and disclosures

Other corporate items in the reconciliation of the total segments' profit to Group EBIT. In 2014, the line item other corporate items comprises expenses of €600 million in connection with the ongoing EU Commission antitrust proceedings concerning European commercial vehicle manufacturers as well as further expenses in connection with legal proceedings. This line item also includes expenses of €212 million from the hedging of the Tesla share price (2013: €0 million) and income of €88 million from the sale of the Tesla shares (2013: €0 million), as well as expenses of €118 million from the measurement of the RRPSH put option (2013: €60 million). In the prior year, a loss of €140 million was disclosed in connection with the disposal of the remaining shares in EADS, which was reported within other financial income/expense, net.

Revenue and non-current assets by region. Revenue from external customers and non-current assets by region are shown in table ⬈ E.89.

E.89
Revenue and non-current assets by region

	Revenue		Non-current assets	
	2014	2013	2014	2013
In millions of euros				
Western Europe	43 722	41 123	40 519	38 371
thereof Germany	20 449	20 227	32 882	32 070
United States	33 310	28 597	18 161	14 839
Other American countries	9 550	10 168	2 778	2 496
Asia	29 446	24 481	1 859	1 667
thereof China	13 294	10 705	79	41
Other countries	13 844	13 613	2 282	1 954
	129 872	117 982	65 599	59 327

Source: Daimler AG (2014, pp. 264–268).

Points to note about figure 18.3:
1. The 'measure' of segment result that is reported to the CODM is referred to as 'EBIT' and comprises gross profit, selling and general administrative expenses, research and non-capitalised development costs, other operating income and expense, share of profit/loss from equity-method investments, net, as well as other financial income/expense, net. This means that this is the measure considered relevant to and therefore reported to the CODM for the segments. The segment result is reconciled to the IFRS profit before income taxes as required by paragraph 28 of IFRS 8.
2. There is disclosure of segment assets and liabilities. This means that these are reported internally to the CODM.
3. The disclosures required by paragraph 23 of IFRS 8 are provided, other than segment interest expense/income and segment income tax expense/income, which are presumably not reported internally to the CODM.
4. The company has reported revenue from external customers by geographic area in accordance with paragraph 33(a) of IFRS 8. This information shows that the company's revenue base is highly geographically diversified (based on the location of the customer).
5. The other entity-wide disclosures required by paragraphs 32 and 33 are also given. However, there is no disclosure of the information about major customers as required by paragraph 34. Presumably this is because there is no single external customer whose revenues amount to 10% or more of the company's total revenues.

18.9 RESULTS OF THE POST-IMPLEMENTATION REVIEW OF IFRS 8

As noted *in section 18.1*, IFRS 8 was the first standard to have been subject to a post-implementation review (PIR) by the IASB. The first phase of the PIR consisted of an initial assessment of the issues related to IFRS 8 and consultation with interested parties about these issues. That initial phase identified the areas of focus to be considered. As a second step of the PIR, the IASB issued in July 2012 its first due process document, *Request for Information – Post-implementation Review: IFRS 8 Operating Segments*, which was intended to formally gather information from the IASB's constituents about their experience with implementing IFRS 8.

In July 2013, the IASB issued its *Report and Feedback Statement – Post-implementation Review: IFRS 8 Operating Segments*, which summarised the PIR process, the feedback received and conclusions reached by the

IASB. The IASB found that preparers, auditors, accounting firms, standard setters and regulators were generally supportive of the standard, although some improvements were suggested for its application. However, feedback from investor groups was mixed, with investors being more positive about the benefits of the standard when segment information is aligned to the measures used by management elsewhere in the financial statements and other information accompanying them.

Based on all of the feedback, the IASB concluded that the benefits of applying the standard were largely as expected and that overall the standard achieved its objectives and has improved financial reporting.

However, the IASB acknowledged that some issues could be considered for improvement and warrant further investigation. The areas identified for potential improvement and amendment comprise requests for implementation guidance and requests for improved disclosures.

The IASB confirmed that any proposed changes to IFRS 8 would be assessed within the context of its more general review of disclosure requirements and would also take into account concerns about disclosure overload.

SUMMARY

IFRS 8 *Operating Segments* is primarily a disclosure standard and is particularly relevant for large organisations that operate in different geographical locations and/or in diverse businesses. Information about an entity's segments is relevant to assessing the risks and returns of a diversified or multinational entity where often that information cannot be determined from aggregated data.

Discussion questions

1. Segment disclosures are widely regarded as some of the most useful disclosures in financial statements because of the extent to which they disaggregate financial information into meaningful and often revealing groupings. Discuss this assertion by reference to the objectives of financial reporting by segments.
2. Explain what the 'management approach' used in IFRS 8 means.
3. Evaluate whether the reconciliations required by paragraph 28 of IFRS 8 address a concern about lack of comparability between entities caused by management's ability to select any measurement basis it chooses in reporting segment information.

References

Bundesverband Deutscher Banken 2007, *Endorsement of IFRS 8 Operating Segments — analysis of potential impacts, response from the Association of German Banks,* 28 June.
Daimler AG 2014, *Annual Report,* Daimler AG, www.daimler.com.
Ernst & Young 2009, *IFRS 8 Operating Segments: implementation guidance,* www.ey.com.
Véron, N. 2007, *EU adoption of the IFRS 8 standard on operating segments,* presented to the Economic Monetary Affairs Committee of the European Parliament, 19 September.

Exercises

STAR RATING ★ BASIC ★★ MODERATE ★★★ DIFFICULT

| Exercise 18.1 | DEFINING OPERATING SEGMENTS |

★ IFRS 8 sets out four key steps that need to be followed in order to identify an operating segment.

Required

List the four key steps.

| Exercise 18.2 | AGGREGATING OPERATING SEGMENTS |

★★ Company B is a listed manufacturing company. It produces most of its products in Australia but exports 90% of these products to the United States, Canada and Germany. It has only one main product line: scientific equipment. Company B is organised internally into two main business units: local and export. The export business unit is in turn divided into two sub-units: North America and Germany (North America includes Canada). Each business unit reports separate financial and operational information to the chief executive officer (CEO) and chief financial officer (CFO) who are identified as the CODM. The results of the two business units are then aggregated to form the consolidated financial information. Details of the identified operating segments are as follows:

	United States	Canada	Germany	Australia
Economic and political conditions	Stable	Stable. Closely related to US environment	Stable	Stable
Relationships between operations	Closely linked to Canadian operations	Closely linked to US Operations	Self-sustaining	Self-sustaining
Proximity of operations	Closely linked to Canadian operations	Closely linked to US operations	Not close to other operations	Not close to other operations
Special risks	None	None	Stricter regulations	Small market
Exchange control regulations	None	None	None	None
Currency risks	None	Low	Low	Low to medium

Required

Identify which operating segments, if any, meet the aggregation criteria of IFRS 8 paragraph 12. Give reasons for your answer.

Exercise 18.3 | **IDENTIFYING REPORTABLE SEGMENTS**

★ Using the information from exercise 18.2, identify Company B's operating segments.

Exercise 18.4 | **DISCLOSURES**

★★ Company X has three reportable segments, A, B and C, which represent distinct geographical areas. The CODM receives financial information about the geographical areas. Segment A produces Product P and Product Y. Segment B produces Product P only. Segment C produces Product Y and sells Service Z. The following financial information about each segment is reported to the CODM:
- revenues from external customers
- earnings before interest, depreciation and amortisation and tax (EBITDA)
- depreciation and amortisation.

Required

State whether each of the following statements is true or false, by reference to the relevant requirements of IFRS 8:
1. Company X must disclose EBITDA for each reportable segment.
2. Company X must disclose total assets for each reportable segment.
3. Company X must reconcile the total EBITDA of Segments A, B and C to its reported IFRS profit before income tax and discontinued operations.
4. Company X must disclose total liabilities for each reportable segment.
5. Company X must disclose depreciation and amortisation for each reportable segment.
6. Company X must disclose revenue from external customers for each of Product P, Product Y and Service Z.

Exercise 18.5 | **REPORTABLE SEGMENTS, ALLOCATING AMOUNTS TO SEGMENTS**

★★ Company A is a listed diversified retail company. Its stores are located mainly in Australia. It has three main types of stores: general department stores, liquor stores and specialist toy stores. Each of these stores has different products, customer types and distribution processes. Company A has three business units: general department stores, liquor stores and specialist toy stores.

For the year ended 30 June 2013 each business unit reported the following financial information to Company A's CODM:

	General department stores $m	Liquor stores $m	Toy stores $m	All segments $m
Revenue	400	100	50	550
Segment result (profit)	15	7	4	26
Assets	900	200	100	1 200

All three business units earn their revenue from external customers. Total consolidated revenue of Company A for the year ended 30 June 2013 is $800 million. Included in general department stores' revenue is $50 million of revenue from toy stores. As at the end of the reporting period toy stores owed general department stores $45 million. This amount is included in general department stores' assets. Within the general department stores business unit there are five different legal entities including legal entities Y and Z. As at 30 June 2013 legal entity Z owed $23 million to legal entity Y. These amounts have not been eliminated in determining the assets of the general department stores segment. Inter-segment asset balances are reported to the CODM but are not used by the CODM as the basis for determining reportable segments. Intra-segment assets are reported to the CODM and are eliminated in determining reportable segments.

Required

State whether the following statements are true or false. Give reasons for your answers.
1. Company A has three reportable segments.
2. The revenue figure that should be used by the general department stores segment for the purposes of determining whether or not it is a reportable segment is $350 million.
3. Company A must disclose the toy stores segment liabilities after deducting the $45 million owed to general department stores.
4. The assets figure that should be used by the general department stores segment for the purposes of determining whether or not it is a reportable segment is $900 million.
5. The assets figure that should be used by the general department stores segment for the purposes of determining whether or not it is a reportable segment is $855 million.
6. The assets figure that should be used by the general department stores segment for the purposes of determining whether or not it is a reportable segment is $877 million.
7. Company A must disclose a reconciliation of total segment assets to its consolidated assets of $1132 million.

Exercise 18.6   **ANALYSING THE SEGMENT INFORMATION**

★★★ Company A is a listed diversified manufacturing company. It is listed on the London Stock Exchange and produces most of its products in China and India. Its markets are in the European Union and the Asia–Pacific region. It produces three types of products and services: home furniture; office furniture and soft furnishings.

The CODM has determined that Company A's operating segments should be based on geographical markets and has identified the reportable segments as listed below. The following information is reported to the CODM for each of the markets:
1. earnings before interest, depreciation and amortisation and taxation (EBITDA)
2. revenues from external customers.

The following table sets out the financial information provided to the CODM for the year ended 31 December 2014. Each operating segment has been identified as a reportable segment. All amounts are in pounds.

	France £	Germany £	United Kingdom £	India £	China £	Australia and New Zealand £
Revenue from external customers	22 300 000	35 654 000	21 587 600	5 325 000	7 324 800	8 763 400
Inter-segment revenue	—	—	—	10 000 000	7 324 800	—
EBITDA	6 400 000	7 325 000	5 325 000	5 324 000	7 625 000	2 325 000

Other information disclosed in the company's 31 December 2014 financial statements:
(a) Total consolidated revenue: £125 000 000.
(b) Inter-segment revenues represent wholesale sales from China and India to the other operating segments.
(c) Net profit before taxation: £25 625 000.
(d) Total consolidated assets: £1 041 670 000.
(e) Revenue from external customers for each type of product is:
    (i) Home furniture: £78 525 000.
    (ii) Office furniture: £17 700 000.
    (iii) Soft furnishings: £28 775 000.

Required

Analyse Company A's business with reference to its reported segment information. Show all workings to support your analysis.

The academic literature on segment reporting has focused on how managers select reportable segments and which to aggregate with other segments (i.e., conceal). Another point of interest has been the effect of the changes in the rules governing segment reporting on reportable segments and resultant information environment. As discussed earlier in this chapter, the change from IAS 14 to IFRS 8 was hotly debated. The main concern was with respect to the management approach adopted by IFRS 8, which may be more prone to managerial discretion than IAS 14. The change in IFRS followed a similar change in 1998 in the US from SFAS 14 (FASB, 1976) to SFAS 131 (now ASC 280) (FASB, 1997); hence many US studies are quite relevant to assessing the change in rules. (For a comparison between the various standards, see Nichols et al., 2013; this is also a good review paper on segment reporting.)

The analytical paper of Hayes and Lundholm (1996) provides some initial guidance on the issue of managers' discretion regarding which segments to report separately and which to conceal. In their model a disclosing manager is aware that segment information is used by a competitor. In the face of this competition, the disclosing manager prefers to aggregate segments so the competitor cannot infer which line of business is the more profitable one. However, if segment profitability is similar, there is little loss to the manager in disclosing the segments separately because (s)he is indifferent as to the competitor's action.

The proprietary cost argument identified by Hayes and Lundholm (1996) explains why profitable segments may be concealed. The reaction of a competitor to a disclosure of segment information is expected to be more harmful when a segment generates abnormal profit. The latter, in turn, is more likely in less competitive industries (e.g., in a duopoly). Harris (1998) examines this prediction employing several proxies for the degree of competition within an industry. Her sample consists of 929 multi-segment firms between 1987 and 1991. She first shows that the number of reported segments (under old US rules) is lower than the actual number of industries a sample firm operates in. This suggests that many segments are not separately reported by sample firms. More importantly, the degree to which segments are unreported increases as competition weakens.

Managers may also have an incentive to conceal poorly performing lines of business, owing to agency costs. Berger and Hann (2007) posit that managers wishing to avoid scrutiny and criticism by boards and investors could do so by aggregating poor- with well-performing segments. Their results are based on a comparison of segment reporting in the US before and after SFAS 131 and are consistent with the presence of agency cost, but are mixed with respect to proprietary costs. Bens et al. (2011) employ a unique data review to further explore the aggregation issue and find that agency and proprietary costs drive aggregation when a firm discloses several segments, but not when it reports a single segment. Hope and Thomas (2008) also report results that are consistent with agency costs. Under SFAS 131 companies can reduce the number of foreign segments they report relative to SFAS 14. Hope and Thomas (2008) conjecture that firms that stopped reporting geographical segments are poor-performing firms.

They identify firms that under SFAS 14 disclosed foreign segments in the 5 years before the change in the rule and followed these firms over the first 5 years under SFAS 131. This results in a large sample of 4773 firm-year observations. They find evidence that suggests that foreign operations in non-disclosing firms (firms that did not disclose at least two foreign segments in the first 2 years of SFAS 131) are less profitable and that the valuation of these firms is lower than that of firms that are identified as disclosers. While this is consistent with the presence of agency cost to disclosure, the evidence also suggests that SFAS 131 avails more latitude for managers to conceal poor performance.

Has the move to the management approach been successful? In the US several studies have documented an increase in the number of reported segments under SFAS 131 (e.g., Herrmann and Thomas, 2000; Berger and Hann, 2003; Botosan and Stanford, 2005). A similar trend is observed following the adoption of IFRS 8. Nichols et al. (2012) look at a sample of 326 large EU companies and find that in 62% there has been no change in the number of reported segments under IFRS 8 than under IAS 14. However, 27% (11%) of sample firms increased (decreased) the number of reported segments. The average increase is 0.35 segments. Leung and Verriest (2015) find that the effect of IFRS 8 on the number of reported segments, controlling for other confounding forces, is positive for both geographical and business segments. Their sample includes 1178 European firms in 2008 and 2009, of which 737 (632) report geographical (business) segments.

Even if the number of reported segments has increased under new rules, it is not clear that the overall informativeness of financial statements has consequently improved. Both Nichols et al. (2012) and Leung and Verriest (2015) document a decline in overall items disclosed under IFRS 8, suggesting there may be less information available to users of segment reporting. Interestingly, Leung and Verriest (2015) find that the decline in the amount of information provided under IFRS 8 is more pronounced in firms that provided little disclosure under IAS 14.

Botosan and Stanford (2005) further examine this issue by looking at the effect of SFAS 131 on analysts. Specifically, they collect data on 615 firms in 1998 that reported a single segment under old US rules but multi-segment under new rules. They compare this sample to two other samples. The first is of 1945 firms that remained single-segment and the second including 592 firms that matched the main sample industry membership based on three-digit SIC code numbers. Botosan and Stanford (2005) present evidence that suggests that disclosure under new rules increased the amount of information common to all analysts. However, they do not find conclusive evidence on reduction in overall uncertainty and forecast error that financial analysts face following the new disclosure rules.

Ettredge et al. (2005) investigate a similar question using a different approach. They argue that if the new disclosure rules are more informative, this should be reflected in a stronger association between current stock returns and future earnings. That is predicated on the notion that stock returns are based on investors' expectation of future performance. Their sample is large, containing 6827 firms and 21698 firm-year observations between 1995 and 2001. They find that the association between stock returns and future earnings is larger following the adoption of SFAS 131. This suggests the management approach provides more useful information.

References

Bens, D.A., Berger, P.G., and Monahan, S.J., 2011. Discretionary disclosure in financial reporting: An examination comparing internal firm data to externally reported segment data. *The Accounting Review*, 86(2), 417–449.

Berger, P.G., and Hann, R., 2003. The impact of SFAS no. 131 on information and monitoring. *Journal of Accounting Research*, 41(2), 163–223.

Berger, P.G., and Hann, R., 2007. Segment profitability and the proprietary and agency Costs of disclosure. *The Accounting Review*, 82(4), 869–906.

Botosan, C.A., and Stanford, M., 2005. Managers' motives to withhold segment disclosures and the effect of SFAS No. 131 on analysts' information environment. *The Accounting Review*, 80(3), 751–772.

Ettredge, M.L., Kwon, S.Y., Smith, D.B., and Zarowin, P.A., 2005. The impact of SFAS No. 131 business segment data on the market's ability to anticipate future earnings. *The Accounting Review*, 80(3), 773–804.

Financial Accounting Standards Board (FASB), 1976. *Financial reporting for segments of a business enterprise*. Statement of Financial Accounting Standards No. 14. Norwalk, CT: FASB.

Financial Accounting Standards Board (FASB), 1997. *Disclosures about segments of an enterprise and related Information*. Statement of Financial Accounting Standards No. 131. Norwalk, CT: FASB.

Harris, M., 1998. The association between competition and managers' business segment reporting decisions. *Journal of Accounting Research*, 36(1), 111–28.

Hayes, R.M., and Lundholm, R., 1996. Segment reporting to the capital market in the presence of a competitor. *Journal of Accounting Research*, 34(2), 261–79.

Herrmann, D., and Thomas W.B., 2000. An analysis of segment disclosures under SFAS No.131 and SFAS No. 14. *Accounting Horizons*, 14(3), 287–302.

Hope, O.K., and Thomas, W.B., 2008. Managerial empire building and firm disclosure. *Journal of Accounting Research*, 46(3), 591–626.

Leung, E., and Verriest, A., 2015. The impact of IFRS 8 on geographical segment information. *Journal of Business Finance & Accounting*, 42(3–4), 273–309.

Nichols, N., Street D., and Cereola, S., 2012. An analysis of the impact of applying IFRS 8 on the segment disclosures of European blue chip companies. *Journal of International Accounting Auditing and Taxation*, 21(2), 79–105.

Nichols, N.B., Street, D.L., and Tarca, A., 2013. The impact of segment reporting under the IFRS 8 and SFAS 131 management approach: A research review. *Journal of International Financial Management & Accounting*, 24(3), 261–312.

19

Other key notes disclosures

ACCOUNTING STANDARDS IN FOCUS

IAS 24 *Related Party Disclosures*

IAS 33 *Earnings per Share*

LEARNING OBJECTIVES

After studying this chapter, you should be able to:

1. explain the potential effect of related party relationships

2. explain the objective and scope of IAS 24

3. identify an entity's related parties

4. identify relationships that do not give rise to a related party relationship as envisaged under IAS 24

5. describe and apply the disclosures required by IAS 24

6. explain why a government-related entity has a partial exemption from related party disclosures

7. explain the objective of IAS 33

8. discuss the application and scope of IAS 33

9. discuss the components of basic earnings per share and examine how it is measured

10. explain the concept of diluted earnings per share and how it is measured

11. explain the need for retrospective adjustment of earnings per share

12. describe and apply the disclosure requirements of IAS 33.

INTRODUCTION

Regardless of the industry or geographical location of an entity, there are two key aspects of disclosures that are commonly found in an entity's financial statements in accordance with IFRS® Standards — related party disclosures under IAS 24 *Related Party Disclosures* and earnings per share disclosures under IAS 33 *Earnings per Share*. Given the widespread application and importance to a user of an entity's financial statements, we will discuss the main requirements of both these standards in this chapter.

19.1 RELATED PARTY DISCLOSURES

It is not uncommon in business for entities to establish relationships with other entities and individuals, to interact with those parties, and to have outstanding balances and commitments with them. For example, groups of entities may conduct their business activities through subsidiary organisations, associated entities or joint venture operations. If an entity engages in transactions with other closely connected entities there is a danger that the economics of the transaction may not be the same had the transaction been negotiated by independent parties in an arm's length arrangement. For example, an entity might have an incentive to shift risks and returns in the form of profits or losses, income or expense flows, or assets or liabilities to a party that it is able to influence or control. Paragraph 6 of IAS 24 explains that related parties may enter into transactions on terms and conditions that would not apply to unrelated parties. For example an entity might transact with an associate on more or less favourable terms than it would use with another, unrelated individual or entity. Thus, a related party association has the potential to have an impact on the profit or loss and financial position of an entity that might not otherwise occur.

Paragraph 9 of IAS 24 provides a definition of when one party is considered to be related to another party which includes close family members of a reporting entity, situations where control, joint control, or significant influence exists, and where a person or entity is a member of the key management personnel of a reporting entity.

The simple existence of a related party relationship has the potential to affect transactions with other parties. As an example, a subsidiary entity might operate on the instructions of its parent entity. Accordingly, knowledge of business relationships, related party transactions, outstanding balances and commitments with related parties may affect assessments of the business risks faced by entities. For these reasons, IAS 24 requires identification and disclosure of related parties, including related party transactions and any outstanding balances and commitments.

19.1.1 Objective and scope

As mentioned, IAS 24 applies to the identification of related party relationships and transactions and outstanding balances and commitments with related parties. It is used to identify the circumstances in which the disclosure of these items should occur, and the relevant disclosures to make.

The objective of IAS 24 as outlined in paragraph 1 is to ensure that an organisation's financial statements contain the disclosures necessary to an understanding of the potential effect of transactions and outstanding balances and commitments with related parties.

An alternative to the disclosure of related parties, transactions, balances and commitments could be to restate the events as though they had occurred between independent parties in arm's length transactions. However, in many instances valuation of the events and their impacts would be very difficult, if not impossible, to determine as comparable transactions simply may not exist. Thus the objective of disclosing related party information is to ensure that the users of financial statements are provided with sufficient knowledge to enable them to undertake an independent assessment of the risks and opportunities facing entities which engage in related party transactions.

The major issues that must be considered, when determining the disclosures necessary to provide sufficient knowledge to financial statement users, include identifying related parties and related party arrangements, and deciding on the type and extent of the disclosure to be made. So, in summary, IAS 24 is applied in identifying related party relationships and transactions, identifying outstanding balances and commitments between related parties, and determining when and what related party disclosures must be made.

Paragraphs 3 and 4 of IAS 24 note that related party relationships, transactions, outstanding balances and commitments are disclosed in the consolidated and separate financial statements of a parent, venturer or investor presented in accordance with IFRS 10 *Consolidated Financial Statements* or IAS 27 *Separate Financial Statements*. However, intragroup transactions and balances are eliminated from consolidated financial statements.

19.1.2 Identifying related parties

IAS 24 considers close family who are able to control or significantly influence the activities of the other 'related' entity to be related parties. This relationship is detailed in paragraph 9 of IAS 24. If any of the conditions in paragraph 9 apply to an entity then it is regarded as a related party.

Definition of a related party

The conditions indicating whether one party is considered to be related to another are summarised in table 19.1.

TABLE 19.1 Definition of a related party — IAS 24 (paragraph 9a, b)

	Part a — A person or a close member of the person's family is related to a reporting entity if that person:
(i)	has control or joint control of the reporting entity
(ii)	has significant influence over the reporting entity
(iii)	is a member of the key management personnel of the reporting entity or of a parent of the reporting entity

	Part b — An entity is related to a reporting entity if any of the following conditions apply:
(i)	The entity and the reporting entity are members of the same group
(ii)	The entity is an associate or joint venture of the entity (or an associate or joint venture of a member of a group of which the other entity is a member)
(iii)	Both entities are joint ventures of the same third party
(iv)	An entity is a joint venture of a third entity and the other entity is an associate of the third entity
(v)	The entity is a post-employment benefit plan for the benefit of employees of either the reporting entity or an entity related to the reporting entity. If the reporting entity is such a plan, the sponsoring employers are also related to the reporting entity
(vi)	The entity is controlled or jointly controlled by a person identified in part (a)
(vii)	A person identified in (a)(i) has significant influence over the entity or is a member of the key management personnel of the entity or of a parent of the entity

Source: IAS 24, paragraph 9.

A close member of the family of a person

Under paragraph 9, close family members are those who may be expected to influence or be influenced by that person in their dealings with the entity. Thus, in determining who to consider close family members, judgement is required. However, a person's children, spouse or domestic partner, children of the spouse or domestic partner, and dependants of the person or of their spouse or domestic partner, are always to be considered close family members of a person, regardless of whether they are expected to influence or be influenced by that person. Therefore, the close family members definition is an example of IFRS Standards combining an underlying principle with a rule-based approach in determining relevant disclosures.

Control, joint control, significant influence

Control is deemed to be when an investor is exposed, or has rights to variable returns from its involvement in the investee and has the ability to affect those returns through its power over the investee. Joint control is the contractually agreed sharing of control of an arrangement. Significant influence is the power to participate in the financial and operating policy decisions of an entity, and may be gained by share ownership, statute or agreement.

Determining whether a close family relationship has related party disclosure consequences is demonstrated in illustrative example 19.1.

Xavier is married to Yvonne and he has a controlling investment in Alpha Ltd. Yvonne holds an investment in Bracken Ltd that gives her significant influence over that company. In this relationship:

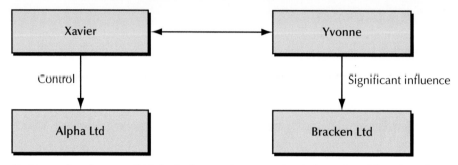

- Bracken Ltd is a related party of Alpha Ltd as Xavier controls Alpha Ltd and his close family member (his wife, Yvonne) has significant influence over Bracken Ltd.
- Alpha Ltd is a related party of Bracken Ltd as Yvonne has significant influence over Bracken Ltd and her close family member (her husband, Xavier) controls Alpha Ltd.
- If Xavier only has significant influence over Alpha Ltd, then Alpha Ltd and Bracken Ltd are not regarded as related entities under IAS 24.

Note: Several of the illustrative examples included in this chapter are derived from similar examples of the Illustrative Examples appendices of IAS 24 and IAS 33.

Key management personnel

Under paragraph 9, key management personnel of the entity or the entity's parent are related parties. Key management personnel are people who have authority and responsibility for planning, directing and controlling an entity's activities either directly or indirectly. This includes directors whether they are executive or otherwise.

An example of key management personnel identified by Billabong International Ltd, and disclosed in its 2014 annual report, is shown in figure 19.1.

FIGURE 19.1 Billabong International Ltd's key management personnel

(a) Directors
The following persons were Directors of Billabong International Limited during the financial year:
 (i) Non-Executive Chairman

Non-Executive Chairman
Ian Pollard

(ii) Executive Directors

Executive Directors	
Neil Fiske	Managing Director and Chief Executive Officer (CEO) from 21 September 2013
Launa Inman	Managing Director and CEO until 2 August 2013
Paul Naude	President of the Americas (President Americas) until 5 August 2013

(iii) Non-Executive Directors

Non-Executive Directors	
Tony Froggatt	Director until 4 November 2013
Gordon Merchant AM	Director
Howard Mowlem	Director
Jason Mozingo	Director from 4 November 2013
Colette Paull	Director until 30 January 2014

FIGURE 19.1 *(continued)*

Sally Pitkin	Director
Jesse Rogers	Director from 23 July 2013 until 4 November 2013
Keoni Schwartz	Director from 23 July 2013 until 4 November 2013
Matthew Wilson	Director from 4 November 2013

(b) Other key management personnel

The following persons also had authority and responsibility for planning, directing and controlling the activities of the Group, directly or indirectly, during the financial year:

Other Key Management Personnel (KMP)		Employer
Paul Burdekin	Acting General Manager, Billabong Group Asia Pacific (GM Asia Pacific) from 3 March 2014. Role confirmed 17 July 2014.	GSM (Operations) Pty Ltd
Franco Fogliato	General Manager, Billabong Group Europe (GM Europe) until 2 November 2013.	GSM Europe Pty Ltd
Colin Haggerty	Group Executive - Global Retail from 5 July 2012 until 19 November 2013. During the year also performed the role of Acting President Americas from 19 November 2012 to 4 October 2013.	GSM (Operations) Pty Ltd
Ed Leasure	Acting President Americas (President Americas) from 8 October 2013. Role confirmed 10 December 2013.	Burleigh Point, Ltd
Peter Myers	Chief Financial Officer (CFO) from 14 January 2013. During the year also performed the role of Acting Chief Executive Officer from 5 August 2013 to 21 September 2013.	GSM (Operations) Pty Ltd
Shannan North	General Manager, Billabong Group Asia Pacific (GM Asia Pacific) until 3 March 2014, then Global President, Brand Billabong from 3 March 2014.	GSM (Operations) Pty Ltd
Jean-Louis Rodrigues	Acting General Manager, Billabong Group Europe (GM Europe) from 25 September 2013. Role confirmed 10 December 2013.	GSM Europe Pty Ltd
Jeffrey Streader	Global Chief Operating Officer (COO) from 4 May 2014.	Burleigh Point, Ltd

Source: Billabong International Ltd (2014).

Determining whether a party is related to a member of key management personnel is demonstrated in illustrative example 19.2.

ILLUSTRATIVE EXAMPLE 19.2 Key management personnel

Jack has a 100% interest in Henty Ltd and he is also a member of the key management personnel of Courier Ltd. Persimmon Ltd has a controlling interest in Courier Ltd.

In this set of circumstances:

- For Courier Ltd's financial statements, Henty Ltd is a related entity because Jack controls Henty Ltd and he is also a member of the key management personnel of Courier Ltd
- For Henty Ltd's financial statements, Courier Ltd is a related entity because Jack controls Henty Ltd and he is also a member of Courier Ltd's key management personnel.

An associate of the entity

Under paragraph 9, any party that is determined to be an associate of the reporting entity is also considered to be a related party. An associated entity is one that is subject to the significant influence of another party as described in IAS 28 *Investments in Associates and Joint Ventures*. An associate includes subsidiaries of the associate (paragraph 12).

A joint venture

Any relationship that is determined to be a joint venture as defined in IAS 28 is regarded as a related party. A joint venture includes subsidiaries of the joint venture. For example, an investor that jointly controls a joint venture is related to the joint venture's subsidiary (paragraph 12).

Post-employment benefit plan

A post-employment benefit plan includes pensions and other retirement benefits and post-employment life insurance and medical care. IAS 24 does not provide an indication of why post-employment benefit plans are defined as related parties. However, it is likely that an entity sponsoring a post-employment benefit plan is likely to have either control or significant influence over the plan. There may also be obligations or commitments outstanding at the end of a reporting period.

19.1.3 Relationships that are not related parties

Although the existence of related parties relationships are not uncommon in normal business life, there are many transactions and events between parties that do not necessarily give rise to a related party relationship as envisaged under IAS 24. For example, an employee of a large retailer such as Billabong International Ltd might purchase goods on normal trading terms in a Billabong store. It would be exceedingly difficult for all such transactions to be identified and recorded, and the benefit of reporting them to users is likely to be trivial. Further, in deciding whether a relationship exists that is subject to the disclosure requirements of IAS 24, paragraph 10 makes it clear that it is the substance, and not merely the legal form of a relationship or transaction, that is important. In this context, paragraph 11 identifies relationships that are not regarded as related parties. For instance, entities are not related parties simply because they have a director or a member of key management personnel in common, or because they share joint control in a joint venture. Similarly, parties an entity engages with for a significant volume of its business are not related parties to the entity simply as a result of the economic dependence that may arise.

19.1.4 Disclosures

In order for users of financial statements to form a view about the effects of the related party relationships of an entity, paragraph 13 of IAS 24 requires the disclosure of the relationship where control exists, irrespective of whether there have been transactions between the parties. If there have been transactions, then the nature of the relationship together with sufficient information to enable an understanding of the potential effect of the transactions on the financial statements must be disclosed.

Related party transactions and related party relationships

If the relationship is between parent and subsidiary entities, the identification of the parties is in addition to the disclosure requirements of IFRS 12 *Disclosure of Interests in Other Entities*, IAS 27 *Separate Financial Statements* and IAS 28. If the parent entity or the ultimate controlling entity does not make financial statements publicly available, then under paragraph 13 of IAS 24 the name of the closest parent that does so must be disclosed.

All entities

To assist users of financial statements to form their view about the effects of related party relationships on an entity, a range of information is required to be disclosed separately for each parent, entity with joint control or significant influence, subsidiary, associate, joint venture in which the entity is a venturer, key management personnel, and other related parties. The minimum disclosures are detailed under paragraph 18 and are summarised below.
(a) the amount of the transactions
(b) the amount of the outstanding balances and commitments including:
   (i) their terms and conditions and whether they are secured, and the nature of the settlement consideration to be provided
   (ii) details of any guarantees provided or received
(c) provisions for doubtful debts related to outstanding balances
(d) the expense recognised during the period in respect of bad or doubtful debts due from related parties.
  A major focus of the disclosure requirements of IAS 24 is directed towards revealing the remuneration arrangements made for key management personnel. These requirements are intended to improve the transparency of related party relationships with directors and influential senior executives. These disclosures, contained in paragraph 17, are required in total and for each of a range of categories and are shown below:
(a) short-term employee benefits
(b) post-employment benefits
(c) other long-term benefits
(d) termination benefits
(e) share-based payment.
  The key management personnel compensation disclosures provided by Billabong International Ltd in its 2014 annual report are shown in figure 19.2.

(c) Key management personnel compensation

	2014 $	2013 $
Short-term employee benefits	7 017 192	7 671 090
Long-term employee benefits — long service leave	48 899	44 390
Termination benefits	3 087 799	735 374
Post-employment benefits	134 440	148 593
Share-based payments	(1 231 383)	(130 286)
	9 056 947	8 469 161

Detailed remuneration disclosures are provided in the Remuneration Report.

FIGURE 19.2 Billabong International Ltd — key management personnel compensation
Source: Billabong International Ltd (2014, p. 137–138).

Examples of related party transactions that must be disclosed include the purchases or sales of goods or services whether incomplete or finished, and the acquisition or disposal of assets including property. Lease arrangements, transfers of research and development, transfers under licence agreements or finance arrangements including loans and equity contributions require disclosure. Provisions of guarantees, commitments including executory contracts, and the settlement of liabilities on behalf of the entity or by the entity on behalf of a related party must also be disclosed.

An example of transactions with related parties and key management personnel is shown in the notes accompanying Billabong's 2014 annual report and is summarised in figure 19.3.

(e) Other transactions with Directors and other key management personnel
Directors of Billabong International Limited
During 2013 a subsidiary of the Company leased a retail store in South Africa from the wife of Director P. Naude. The rental agreement was based on normal commercial terms and conditions.

FIGURE 19.3 Billabong International Ltd — transactions with directors and other key management personnel
Source: Billabong International Ltd (2014, Note 33, p. 140).

19.1.5 Government-related entities

Numerous countries, for example, China, Germany, France, Russia and Eastern European nations, have a sizeable number of entities that are controlled by the government. Often the practical difficulties and costs for government-controlled entities of complying with the extensive disclosure requirements of IAS 24 are likely to outweigh the benefits to financial statement users. Accordingly, paragraph 25 provides an exemption from some of the disclosure requirements for transactions between entities that are controlled, jointly controlled or significantly influenced by a government and with other entities that are related because they are controlled by the same government.

If an entity chooses to apply the exemption, it is still required to identify the government to which it is related and to provide a range of other relevant disclosures. These include: the nature of the relationship; the nature and amount of each individually significant transaction; and either a qualitative or a quantitative indication of the extent of other transactions that are, in aggregate, significant.

19.2 EARNINGS PER SHARE

Earnings per share, commonly known as *EPS*, is a ratio that is calculated by comparing an entity's profit with the number of ordinary shares it has on issue. The earnings per share ratio is used to compare the after-tax profit available to ordinary shareholders of an entity on a per share basis, with that of other entities.

The purpose of this section is to examine and understand the earnings per share information that is presented in a reporting entity's financial statements. In an effort to improve the information provided by reporting entities, and with the objective of improving the consistency of comparisons between entities and across different time periods, IAS 33 prescribes the principles for the computation and the presentation of earnings per share.

Under paragraph 10 of IAS 33, the approach taken to the calculation of the earnings per share ratio is to divide profit or loss (earnings) attributable to ordinary shareholders of a parent entity, by the weighted average number of ordinary shares the entity has on issue (outstanding) during the reporting period. 'Profit' is the numerator (top line) in the calculation and 'outstanding shares' is the denominator (bottom line). The resultant ratio is known as 'basic earnings per share', and the objective of providing this information is to show a measure of the interests of an ordinary shareholder in the performance (profit) of an entity across a reporting period.

The earnings per share ratio has other important uses including as an indicator of future performance and growth. Earnings revisions which impact earnings per share, whether they indicate improvements or downgrades, provide information to the market and are usually reflected in a changing share price. Earnings per share is also often used as a key performance indicator when determining the remuneration entitlements of directors and executives. For example, Billabong International Ltd uses earnings per share targets as performance hurdles when determining entitlements to long-term incentive bonuses. Billabong International Ltd's remuneration approach is presented in figure 19.4.

Awards under the ELTIP vest only if the performance hurdles are satisfied in the relevant performance period. The performance periods are summarised in the table below:

Grant	Performance hurdle		% of award that vests	Performance Period
2013–14	EPS performance	2.0 cents per share	50%	Financial year ended 30 June 2016
		4.0 cents per share	100%	
	TSR performance relative to comparator group	50th percentile or above	50%	1 January 2014 until 30 September 2016
		75th percentile or above	100%	

50% of awards are based on Executives meeting the Group's 3-year EPS performance targets. EPS is a financial indicator of the Group's earnings in the final year of the performance period. In previous periods the EPS performance hurdle was determined based upon 3-year compound growth rates in EPS from a base year. However, due to the significant changes to the capital structure of the Group, the Board has selected EPS (rather than the growth rate of EPS) as the appropriate internal performance metric.

FIGURE 19.4 Billabong International Ltd's remuneration report
Source: Billabong International Ltd (2014, p. 37).

The utility of earnings per share has been criticised because of the flexibility that entities have in choosing accounting methods when determining their profit. While accounting policy *choice* enables entities to select the accounting methods that are the most appropriate to reflect their actual business operations, it results in inconsistencies between entities in the determination of their profit. For example, entities may select the depreciation method that best reflects the pattern of usage of their physical assets (see IAS 16 *Property, Plant and Equipment,* paragraph 60). If one entity chooses the straight-line method then a constant charge is made against its profit across the useful life of its assets. However, if another entity selects the diminishing balance method, then the expense charged against its profit will decrease over its assets' useful lives. Therefore, it must be recognised that earnings per share data disclosed by reporting entities have limitations because of the different accounting methods that can be used in the determination of profit. Furthermore, it is not uncommon for entities to disclose so-called 'adjusted earnings' measures, accompanied by adjusted earnings per share. Comparing such non-GAAP measures across companies requires insight into the adjustments made. Entities disclosing adjusted earnings per share measures should therefore reconcile the adjusted earnings to the profit or loss measure applied under IAS 33 (paragraphs 73 and 73A).

Another limitation to the utility of the earnings per share ratio for comparison purposes is that it can be altered simply by changing the number of shares used in the denominator. The focus taken in IAS 33 is that a consistently determined denominator in the earnings per share calculation enhances financial reporting (paragraph 1). Despite the limitations of earnings per share as an indicator of the performance of an entity, it is widely used in share analysis.

19.2.1 Scope

IAS 33 applies to the computation and presentation of earnings per share by reporting entities whose shares are publicly traded, or of entities that are in the process of issuing ordinary shares that will be traded in public markets (paragraph 1).

Under paragraph 4, if an entity presents both consolidated and separate financial statements, the IAS 33 disclosures need only be determined on the basis of consolidated information. As the parent entity earnings per share information may be helpful to some users, entities have the option of also disclosing earnings per share figures for the parent entity. However this information can only be presented in the parent's separate financial statements and not in the consolidated financial statements (IAS 33 BC paragraphs 5, 6). The earnings per share information presented by Nestlé Group in its 2014 income statement is presented in figure 19.5.

Earnings per share (in CHF)			
Basic earnings per share	16	4.54	3.14
Diluted earnings per share	16	4.52	3.13

FIGURE 19.5 Earnings per share disclosed in income statement of Nestlé Group
Source: Nestlé Group (2014, p. 58) [only the EPS disclosures].

19.2.2 Basic earnings per share

As mentioned, earnings per share is measured by dividing profit (or loss) attributable to ordinary shareholders by the weighted average number of ordinary shares outstanding during the period. This measurement approach, which results in a ratio known as 'basic' earnings per share (paragraph 9), is demonstrated in figure 19.6.

$$\frac{\text{Profit attributable to ordinary shareholders of the parent entity}}{\text{Weighted average number of ordinary shares outstanding during the reporting period}}$$

FIGURE 19.6 Basic earnings per share ratio

Earnings

The profit or loss (profit) that is used in the calculation of basic earnings per share must be from continuing operations. It must also include any income or expense attributable to ordinary shareholders that has been recognised in the reporting period. This will mean that any tax expense and any dividends on preference shares that have been classified as liabilities will be deducted as part of the determination of profit. Tax expense is a normal component of the profit of an entity, and therefore it is a normal part of the calculation of profit. Preference dividends do not belong to the ordinary shareholders and therefore they must be included in the profit calculation as a deduction. This approach to the determination of the profit to be used in the calculation of earnings per share is outlined in paragraphs 12 and 13, and is demonstrated in figure 19.7.

Profit before tax expense	100 000
Less: Tax expense	(30 000)
Profit after tax	70 000
Less: Preference dividends	(10 000)
Profit attributable to ordinary equity holders (earnings)	60 000 (numerator)

FIGURE 19.7 Earnings calculation to include tax expense and preference dividends

The preference dividends are to be on an after-tax basis, and for non-cumulative preference dividends they are to include any amounts declared during the period. In respect of cumulative dividends, paragraph 14 requires the after-tax amount to be deducted whether or not a dividend is declared during the period. Any cumulative dividends paid during the period but which relate to prior periods are not part of the calculation.

If an entity presents discontinued operations under IFRS 5 *Non-current Assets Held for Sale and Discontinued Operations*, the entity shall also disclose the earnings per share for the discontinued operations. An entity may choose to disclose earnings per share from discontinued operations in the notes, instead of on the face of the statement of comprehensive income.

Repurchases and conversion of preference shares

If an entity chooses to repurchase preference shares it has on issue, then the excess of the fair value of the consideration paid over the carrying amount of the shares represents a return to preference shareholders and a charge against retained earnings. Paragraph 16 requires this amount to be included in the calculation of earnings per share, as a deduction when determining the profit attributable to ordinary shareholders.

Similarly, any excess of the fair value of the ordinary shares issued on conversion of preference shares over the fair value of the ordinary shares issuable under the original conversion terms must be deducted in calculating the profit attributable to ordinary shareholders (paragraph 17).

The treatment of cumulative and non-cumulative dividends is demonstrated in illustrative example 19.3.

ILLUSTRATIVE EXAMPLE 19.3 Non-cumulative and cumulative preference dividends

Poulos Ltd has 100 000 Class A preference shares on issue, each carrying a non-cumulative dividend right of 3% of the $1 par value of the share. A non-cumulative dividend was declared during the reporting period. The company also has 200 000 Class B preference shares outstanding which carry a cumulative dividend right of 2% per share based on the par value of $1 per share. The company has a profit for the period from continuing operations amounting to $1.5 million, and tax is payable at the rate of 30%.

The earnings (profit attributable to ordinary shareholders) to be used in the calculation of basic earnings per share for Poulos Ltd is calculated as shown below.

Determination of earnings to include tax expense and preference dividends

Calculation	$
Profit before tax	1 500 000
Tax expense	(450 000)
Profit after tax	1 050 000
Preference dividends	(7 000)*
Profit attributable to ordinary equity holders	1 043 000

*([100 000 × 3%] + [200 000 × 2%])

Shares

As the earnings per share calculation is focused on the ordinary equity of an entity, the denominator in the calculation contains only ordinary share capital. Because entities are able to make new share issues during a reporting period, the number of shares on issue can increase. They are also able to repurchase or cancel shares, which will decrease the number of shares on issue, and to split or to consolidate shares, which will vary the number of shares on issue. Other actions, including the conversion of convertible preference shares or other convertible securities into ordinary shares, can also vary the amount of shares outstanding. Accordingly, the number of ordinary shares that is used in the calculation of basic earnings per share is adjusted by a time-weighting factor, which is the number of days in the reporting period that the shares are outstanding as a proportion of the total number of days in the period (paragraph 20).

Shares are included in the calculation from the date that the consideration for shares is receivable (paragraph 21). For example, shares issued for cash is included when cash is receivable; ordinary shares issued on the reinvestment of dividends are included when the dividends are reinvested; shares issued when debt is converted or when the shares replace interest or principal on other financial instruments are included from the date interest ceases to accrue. If ordinary shares are issued in exchange for the settlement of a liability, then they are included from the settlement date or, if they are issued in exchange for services rendered, they are included from the date of rendering the services. Any ordinary shares issued as consideration for the acquisition of a non-cash asset are included in the calculation from the date on which the acquisition is recognised; and if shares are issued as part of the consideration in a business combination, they are included from the acquisition date as this reflects the date from which the acquiree's profits are included in the acquirer's income.

Share consolidation and share repurchase

While a consolidation of shares will decrease the number of shares on issue, there is no corresponding reduction in the entity's resources. However, when a repurchase occurs, the entity's resources (e.g. cash) will also be reduced. Shares that are repurchased and held by the issuing entity are termed 'Treasury' shares. If a purchase of Treasury shares (share repurchase) occurs, then the weighted average number of shares outstanding for the period in which the transaction takes place must be adjusted for the reduction in the number of shares from the date of the event (paragraph 29).

The calculation of the weighted average number of ordinary shares where a new share issue and a share repurchase have occurred during the period is demonstrated in illustrative example 19.4.

Singapore Ltd has 11 000 ordinary shares on issue at 1 January 2015, which is the beginning of its reporting period, of which 500 have been repurchased in previous reporting periods. On 30 June 2015, it issued a further 1000 ordinary shares for cash. On 1 November 2015, Singapore Ltd repurchased 300 shares at fair value in a market transaction.

		Issued shares	Treasury shares	Shares outstanding
1 January 2015	Balance at the beginning of the year	11 000	500	10 500
30 June 2015	Issue of new ordinary shares for cash	1 000		11 500
1 November 2015	Repurchase of issued shares		300	11 200
31 December 2015	Balance at the end of the year	12 000	800	11 200

The weighted average number of shares for use in the earnings per share calculation is determined as follows:

$$= (10\,500 \times 6/12) + (11\,500 \times 4/12) + (11\,200 \times 2/12)$$
$$= 5250 + 3833 + 1867$$
$$= 10\,950 \text{ shares}$$

Contingently issuable shares

An entity may have contingently issuable shares outstanding. These are ordinary shares that the entity can issue for little or no cash or other consideration once a specified condition has been satisfied (paragraph 5). If an entity has contingently issuable shares, then these must be treated as outstanding and they are included in the calculation of basic earnings per share from the date when all necessary conditions have been satisfied (paragraph 24). The impact of contingently issuable shares on diluted earnings per share is discussed later (see section 19.2.3).

Bonus issues and share splits

If an entity announces a bonus issue of shares, or if it splits issued shares thereby increasing the number of shares outstanding, there is usually no consideration involved and therefore no corresponding increase in the entity's resources. The number of ordinary shares outstanding before the event must be adjusted for the proportionate change in the number of ordinary shares outstanding as if it had occurred at the beginning of the earliest period presented in the financial statements (paragraph 28). For example, under a two-for-one bonus issue, multiplying the number of ordinary shares outstanding before the bonus issue determines the number of additional ordinary shares. The effect of a bonus issue of shares on the basic earnings per share calculation is demonstrated in illustrative example 19.5.

Jackson Ltd determined its profit attributable to ordinary shareholders for the reporting period ended 31 December 2015 as $360 000 (2014: $320 000). The number of ordinary shares on issue up to 30 April 2015 was 50 000. Jackson Ltd announced a two-for-one bonus issue of shares effective for each ordinary share outstanding at 30 April 2015 on 1 May 2015.

Basic earnings per share is calculated as follows:

Bonus issue on 1 May 2015	$50\,000 \times 2$	$= 100\,000$
Basic earnings per share 31 December 2015	$\dfrac{360\,000}{50\,000 + 100\,000}$	$= \$2.40$
Basic earnings per share 31 December 2014	$\dfrac{320\,000}{50\,000 + 100\,000}$	$= \$2.13$

Because the bonus shares were issued for no consideration, the event is treated as if it had occurred before the beginning of the 2014 reporting period, the earliest period presented in the financial statements (paragraph 28).

Rights issues

In a bonus issue as the shares are usually issued for no consideration there is an increase in the number of shares outstanding, which is not accompanied by a corresponding increase in the resources of the issuing entity. However, in a rights issue the exercise price is usually lower than the fair value of the shares issued. This means that the rights issue includes a bonus element. In this case, the application guidance in IAS 33 (paragraph A2) requires that the number of ordinary shares used in the calculation of earnings per share, for all periods before the rights issue, is to be the number of ordinary shares outstanding before the rights issue multiplied by an adjustment factor. The components of the adjustment factor are shown in figure 19.8.

$$\frac{\text{Fair value per share immediately before the exercise of rights}}{\text{Theoretical ex-rights fair value per share}}$$

FIGURE 19.8 Adjustment factor for rights issues containing a bonus element

The 'theoretical ex-rights fair value per share' is calculated by adding the aggregate market value of the shares immediately before the exercise of the rights to the proceeds from the exercise of the rights, and then dividing by the number of shares outstanding after the exercise of the rights, as shown in figure 19.9.

$$\frac{\text{Fair value of all outstanding shares immediately before the exercise of rights} + \text{total proceeds from the exercise of the rights}}{\text{Number of shares outstanding after the exercise of the rights}}$$

FIGURE 19.9 Theoretical ex-rights value per share

Fair value is the share price at the close of the last day on which the shares were traded together with the rights. The calculation of basic earnings per share where there is a rights issue during the period is demonstrated in illustrative example 19.6.

ILLUSTRATIVE EXAMPLE 19.6 Rights issue

Georgiou Ltd determined its profit attributable to ordinary shareholders for the reporting period ended 31 December 2015 as $5000. At the beginning of the reporting period the company had 1000 ordinary shares on issue. It announced a rights issue with the following details:
- date of rights issue, 1 January 2015
- last date to exercise rights, 1 March 2015
- one new share for each four outstanding (250 total)
- exercise price, $10
- market price of one share immediately before exercise on 1 March 2015, $12.

Determine the theoretical ex-rights value per share

$$\frac{\text{Fair value of all outstanding shares immediately before the exercise of rights} + \text{total proceeds from the exercise of the rights}}{\text{Number of shares outstanding after the exercise of the rights}}$$

$$\frac{(\$12 \times 1000 \text{ shares}) + (\$10 \times 250 \text{ shares})}{1000 \text{ shares} + 250 \text{ shares}} = \$11.60$$

Determine the adjustment factor

$$\frac{\text{Fair value per share immediately before the exercise of rights}}{\text{Theoretical ex-rights fair value per share}} \quad \frac{\$12}{\$11.60} = 1.03$$

Basic earnings per share is calculated as follows:

$$\text{Profit attributable to ordinary shareholders 30 June 2014} \quad \frac{5000}{(1000 \times 1.03 \times 2/12) + (1250 \times 10/12)} = \$4.12$$

LO10 19.2.3 Diluted earnings per share

In addition to calculating the basic earnings per share ratio, if an entity has options, warrants, contingently issuable shares or convertible securities, then it must also recognise the effect of potential dilution to its earnings per share ratio. The potential dilution effect stems from assumptions that the entity's convertible securities are converted, its warrants or options are exercised or that its contingently issuable shares are issued on the satisfaction of their specified conditions. Adjustments must be made to the profit (or loss) attributable to the ordinary shareholders. The adjustments are for the after-tax amount of dividends, interest or other income or expenses recognised in the reporting period in respect of the dilutive securities that would no longer arise if they were indeed converted into ordinary shares. Adjustments must also be made to increase the weighted average number of ordinary shares outstanding to reflect what the weighted average would have been, assuming that all potential ordinary shares (dilutive securities) had been converted.

The information regarding potential (dilutive) ordinary shares appearing in the financial statements of Billabong International Ltd is presented in figure 19.10.

(e) Information concerning the classification of securities

Performance shares and conditional rights
Performance shares and conditional rights granted to employees under the Billabong Executive Performance Share Plan are considered to be potential ordinary shares and have not been included in the determination of diluted earnings per share because they are anti-dilutive for the year ended 30 June 2014. The performance shares and conditional rights have also been excluded in the determination of basic earnings per share. Details relating to the rights are set out in note 45.

Options
The 314 503 options granted on 31 October 2008 in relation to the Billabong Performance and Retention Plan are not included in the calculation of diluted earnings per share because they are anti-dilutive for the year ended 30 June 2014. These options could potentially dilute basic earnings per share in the future.

The 42 259 790 options granted on 16 July 2013 to the Altamont Consortium are not included in the calculation of diluted earnings per share because they are anti-dilutive for the year ended 30 June 2014. These options could potentially dilute basic earnings per share in the future.

The 29 581 852 options granted on 3 December 2013 to the C/O Consortium are not included because they are anti-dilutive for the year ended 30 June 2014. These options could potentially dilute basic earnings per share in the future.

The 1 200 000 options granted on 31 January 2014 to Pat Tenore, the founder of RVCA, are not included in the calculation of diluted earnings per share because they are anti-dilutive for the year ended 30 June 2014. These options could potentially dilute basic earnings per share in the future.

Deferred shares
Rights to deferred shares granted to executives under the Group's short-term incentive scheme are included in the calculation of diluted earnings per share assuming all outstanding rights will vest. The rights are not included in the determination of basic earnings per share. Further information about the rights is provided in note 45.

FIGURE 19.10 Billabong International Ltd — potential (dilutive) ordinary shares
Source: Billabong International Ltd (2014, Note 44, p. 154).

IAS 33 regards potential ordinary shares as dilutive only if their conversion to ordinary shares would decrease earnings per share (or increase loss per share) from the continuing operations of an entity (paragraph 41). Potential ordinary shares can be anti-dilutive. An anti-dilutive effect would occur if the conversion of potential ordinary shares would increase earnings per share (paragraph 5).

In Figure 19.11 the disclosure of potential ordinary shares not being dilutive in UBS Group AG's 2014 financial statements is presented.

If potential ordinary shares were to be converted, any dividends or interest payable in relation to those dilutive securities would no longer arise. Instead the new ordinary shares would be entitled to participate in profit. Therefore the profit must be increased to remove the impact of the dividends or interest that would otherwise have been payable. Similarly any other income or charges such as transaction costs, that are related to the potential ordinary shares and that have been included in profit, must be removed (paragraph 33).

Any consequential changes in income or expenses arising as a result of the potential conversion of dilutive securities must also be adjusted in determining the earnings amount used in the diluted earnings per share ratio. Consequential changes may include a reduction in interest expense related to potential ordinary shares resulting in an increase in profit (paragraph 35).

The table below outlines the potential shares which could dilute basic earnings per share in the future, but were not dilutive for the periods presented.

Number of shares	31.12.14	31.12.13	31.12.12	% change from 31.12.13
Potentially dilutive instruments				
Employee share-basad compensation awards	94 335 120	117 623 624	233 256 208	(20)
Other equity derivative contracts	6 728 173	16 517 384	15 386 605	(59)
SNB warrants[2]	0	0	100 000 000	
Total	101 063 293	134 141 008	348 642 813	(25)

[2]These warrants related to the SNB transaction. The SNB provided a loan to a fund owned and controlled by the SNB (the SNB StabFund), to which UBS transferred certain illiquid securities and other positions in 2008 and 2009. As part of this arrangement, UBS granted warrants on shares to the SNB, which would have been exercisable if the SNB incurred a loss on its loan to the SNB StabFund. In 2013, These warrants were terminated following the full repayment of the loan.

FIGURE 19.11 UBS Group AG — potential (non-dilutive) ordinary shares
Source: UBS Group AG (2014, Note 9, p. 438). Earnings.

Shares

The diluted earnings per share ratio must include an adjustment to increase the weighted average number of ordinary shares that would be outstanding if all of the dilutive securities were converted into ordinary shares. Paragraph 36 deems that the potential ordinary shares are to be regarded as having been converted into ordinary shares at the beginning of the period or, if later, the date of the issue of the potential ordinary shares.

The potential ordinary shares shall be weighted for the period that they are outstanding. If any of the dilutive securities lapse or are cancelled, they are included in the calculation only for the portion of time during which they are outstanding. Any dilutive securities that are converted into ordinary shares during the period are included in the calculation of diluted earnings per share from the beginning of the period to the date of conversion (paragraph 38). If the terms of dilutive securities include more than one basis for conversion into ordinary shares, then under paragraph 39, the most favourable conversion rate or price from the perspective of the security holder is used.

Dilutive potential ordinary shares

As mentioned, potential ordinary shares are regarded by IAS 33 as dilutive only if their conversion to ordinary shares would decrease earnings per share or increase loss per share (paragraph 41). In deciding whether potential ordinary shares are dilutive (or anti-dilutive) each issue or series of potential dilutive securities is considered separately. The conversion, exercise or other issue of potential ordinary shares that would have an anti-dilutive effect on earnings per share is not assumed in the calculation of diluted earnings per share (paragraph 43).

When determining the dilutive effect of potential ordinary shares, each issue or series of dilutive securities is considered in sequence from most dilutive to least dilutive (paragraph 44). This means that the securities with the lowest earnings impact, per incremental share, are included in the calculation before those securities with the highest earnings impact per incremental share. This generally means that options and warrants are included first, because they do not usually affect the numerator (earnings) in the ratio.

Options and warrants

The proceeds from options and warrants are regarded as received from the issue of ordinary shares at the average market price during the period. Paragraphs 45–46 require that the difference between the number of ordinary shares issued and the number that would have been issued at the average market price be treated as an issue of ordinary shares for no consideration. The application guidance to IAS 33 indicates that a simple average of the weekly or monthly closing prices of ordinary shares is usually adequate for determining the average market price (paragraphs A4–A5). However, this approach will need to be adjusted when shares prices fluctuate widely.

Options and warrants are regarded as dilutive if they would result in the issue of ordinary shares for less than the average market price during the period (i.e. when they are 'in the money'). The amount of the dilution is determined as the average market price of ordinary shares during the period minus the issue price. Employee share options and non-vested ordinary shares are regarded as options in the calculation of diluted earnings per share (paragraph 48).

The effect of share options on basic and diluted earnings per share is demonstrated in illustrative example 19.7.

ILLUSTRATIVE EXAMPLE 19.7 Effect of share options on earnings per share

Harlem Ltd determined its profit attributable to ordinary shareholders for the reporting period ended 30 June 2015 as $480 000. The average market price of the entity's shares during the period is $4.00 per share. The weighted average number of ordinary shares on issue during the period is 1 000 000. The weighted average number of shares under share options arrangements during the year is 200 000 and the exercise price of shares under option is $3.50.

	Earnings $	Shares	Per share $
Basic earnings per share is calculated as follows:			
Profit attributable to ordinary shareholders for the reporting period ended 30 June 2015	480 000		
Weighted average shares on issue during the period		1 000 000	
Basic earnings per share			0.48
Diluted earnings per share is calculated as follows:			
Weighted average number of shares under option		200 000	
Weighted average number of shares that would have been issued at average market price is (200 000 x $3.50) / $4.00		(175 000)	
Diluted earnings per share	480 000	1 025 000	0.47

Convertible securities

If convertible preference shares are dilutive they are included in the diluted earnings per share calculation. They are regarded as anti-dilutive if the amount of the dividend declared or accumulated in the current period per ordinary share, obtainable on the conversion, exceeds basic earnings per share. Similarly, convertible debt is regarded as anti-dilutive whenever its interest (net of tax and other changes in income or expenses) per ordinary share obtainable on conversion, exceeds basic earnings per share.

Contingently issuable shares

Contingently issuable shares such as performance-based employee share options are regarded as outstanding, and if their conditions are satisfied they are included in the calculation of diluted earnings per share from the beginning of the period (or the date of the contingent share agreement, if later). If the conditions are not satisfied, the number of contingently issuable shares that is included in the diluted earnings per share calculation is based on the number of shares that would be issuable if the end of the period were the end of the contingency period (paragraph 52).

If the number of contingently issuable ordinary shares is dependent on both future earnings and future prices of ordinary shares, then the number of ordinary shares included in the diluted earnings per share calculation is based on both conditions. That is, it is based on both earnings to date and on the current market price of the ordinary shares at the end of the reporting period (paragraph 55). Unless both conditions are met, contingently issuable shares are not included in the diluted earnings per share calculation.

Contracts that may be settled in ordinary shares or cash

If an entity has issued a contract that may be settled in cash or ordinary shares at the entity's option, then under paragraph 58 it is assumed that the settlement will be in ordinary shares. As a result the potential ordinary shares are included in the diluted earnings per share calculation if the effect is dilutive.

For contracts that can be settled in cash or in ordinary shares at the holder's option, then the more dilutive of either the cash settlement or the share settlement is used in the diluted earnings per share calculation (paragraph 60). Such contracts could include an option that provides the holder with settlement choice of cash or ordinary shares.

As mentioned, when determining the dilutive effect of potential ordinary shares, each issue or series of dilutive securities is considered in sequence from most dilutive to least dilutive (paragraph 44). Securities with the lowest earnings impact per additional share are included in the calculation first. Determining the order in which to include dilutive securities is demonstrated in illustrative example 19.8.

Bruin Ltd extracted the following information from its financial records in order to determine its basic earnings per share and diluted earnings per share for its reporting period ended 31 December 2015.

Profit from continuing operations	$16 400
Less: Dividends on preference shares	(6 400)
Profit from continuing operations attributable to ordinary shareholders	10 000
Loss from discontinued operations	(4 000)
Profit attributable to ordinary shareholders	6 000

Ordinary shares on issue	2 000
Average market price of one ordinary share during the period	$ 7.50

Potential ordinary shares (potentially dilutive securities):

1. Options	10 000 with an exercise price of $6.00
2. Convertible preference shares	800 shares with an issue value of $100 entitled to a cumulative dividend of $8 per share. Each preference share is convertible to two ordinary shares.

Determine the increase in earnings attributable to ordinary shareholders on conversion of potential ordinary shares

Options	
Increase in earnings	$0
Additional shares issued for no consideration 10 000 × (7.50 − 6.00) / 7.50	2 000
Earnings per additional share	$0
Convertible preference shares	
Increase in earnings ($80 000 × 0.08)	$6 400
Additional shares (2 × 800)	1 600
Earnings per additional share	$4.00

The dilutive securities are included in the earnings per share calculation in the following order:
1. Options
2. Convertible preference shares

Determine dilutive effect of convertible securities

	$	Shares	$ per share	
Profit from continuing operations attributable to ordinary shareholders	10 000	2 000	5.00	
Increase in earnings from options	0	2 000		
	10 000	4 000	2.50	Dilutive
Increase in earnings from convertible preference shares*	6 400	1 600		
	16 400	5 600	2.93	Anti-dilutive

* *As the convertible preference shares increased diluted earnings per share they would be considered anti-dilutive and ignored in the calculation of diluted earnings per share.*

Calculate basic EPS and diluted EPS

	Basic EPS $	Diluted EPS $
Profit from continuing operations attributable to ordinary shareholders	5.00	2.50
Loss from discontinued operations attributable to ordinary shareholders ($4 000/2 000) ($4 000/4 000)	(2.00)	(1.00)
Profit attributable to ordinary shareholders ($6 000/2 000) ($6 000/4 000)	3.00	1.50

19.2.4 Retrospective adjustments

Retrospective adjustments are made to restate the values of relevant items so that valid comparisons across time can be made. If, for example, the number of issued shares increases during a reporting period as a result of a bonus issue for no consideration, then the operating profit for the whole period in which the bonus issue occurred will be attributable to the increased number of shares and not to the lesser number of shares outstanding at the beginning of the reporting period.

IAS 33 paragraph 64 requires that if the number of ordinary shares or of potential ordinary shares outstanding increases as a result of a:
- capitalisation
- bonus issue
- share split;
  or if the number decreases as a result of a:
- consolidation (reverse share split); then,

the calculation of both basic earnings per share and diluted earnings per share must be adjusted retrospectively for all periods that are presented in the financial statements. The retrospective adjustment to the number of shares also applies to the period from the end of the reporting period but before the financial statements are authorised for issue. Further, basic and diluted earnings per share are both subject to retrospective adjustment for the effects of any errors or adjustments resulting from changes in accounting policies that are accounted for retrospectively.

19.2.5 Disclosures

The basic earnings per share and diluted earnings per share ratios must be presented in an entity's statement of profit or loss and other comprehensive income (paragraph 66) even if the amounts are negative (paragraph 69). If the items of profit or loss are presented in a separate statement then the basic and diluted earnings per share ratios are required to be presented in that separate statement. The two ratios must be displayed with equal prominence, and they must be calculated for each class of ordinary shares that have different rights to share in the profit of the period. If diluted earnings per share is presented for one period, then it must be shown for all periods that are presented in the financial statements, even if it is the same as the basic earnings per share. And, if the entity has a discontinued operation, then it must also calculate and disclose the basic and diluted earnings per share ratios for the discontinued operation in the statement of profit or loss and other comprehensive income.

Paragraphs 70–73 of IAS 33 prescribe various disclosures relating to earnings per share. The objective of these disclosures is to provide sufficient additional information to assist financial statement users to understand the composition of the earnings per share ratios.

For instance, Nestlé Group includes a reconciliation of the weighted average number of shares used in its basic and diluted earnings per share calculation in Note 16 in its 2014 financial statements. The reconciliations are presented in figure 19.12.

Reconciliation of weighted average number of shares outstanding (in millions of units)		
Weighted average number of shares outstanding used to calculate basic earnings par share	3 188	3 191
Adjustment for share-based payment schemes, where dilutive	8	9
Weighted average number of shares outstanding used to calculate diluted earnings per share	3 196	3 200

FIGURE 19.12 Reconciliation of weighted average number of shares — Nestlé Group
Source: Nestlé Group (2014, p. 117).

As discussed earlier *(see sections 19.2.2 and 19.2.3)*, if, in addition to calculating basic and diluted earnings per share, an entity uses a numerator other than the one required by IAS 33, then it must still use the denominator as prescribed under IAS 33 (paragraph 73). These additional ratios must be displayed with equal prominence as the prescribed basic EPS and diluted EPS ratios and presented in the notes to the financial statements. The basis on which the numerator is determined, including whether the amounts per share are before or after tax, must also be disclosed.

IAS 33 also encourages the voluntary disclosure of the terms and conditions of financial instruments and contracts that incorporate terms and conditions affecting the measurement of basic and diluted earnings per share.

SUMMARY

This chapter covers two common key disclosures in an entity's IFRS Standards financial statements — related party disclosures and earnings per share disclosures.

IAS 24 is a disclosure standard that defines related party relationships and prescribes the events, transactions, balances and commitments that must be revealed in the financial statements and reports of disclosing entities. As related party relationships can be expected to affect the profit or loss or the financial position of an entity, disclosures about them are particularly helpful to investors, lenders and other users when they evaluate and assess the risks and opportunities facing entities. The main features of IAS 24 are that it:

- considers key management personnel and their close family members to be related parties
- considers compensation benefits for key management personnel to be related party transactions.

Determining when related party relationships exist and identifying the circumstances in which disclosures about such relationships must be disclosed involves a certain amount of judgement. In making that judgement, entities must take into account the definitions of related parties provided in IAS 24. The definition of related parties includes:

- relationships affected by control or significant influence or joint venture arrangements
- key management personnel and close family members.

IAS 33 provides principles for the calculation and presentation of basic and diluted earnings per share. Earnings per share is a ratio which is used to compare the after-tax profit available to ordinary shareholders of an entity on a per share basis, with that of other entities. It is calculated by dividing profit or loss (earnings) attributable to ordinary shareholders, by the weighted average number of ordinary shares outstanding during a reporting period.

The objective of IAS 33 is to improve the information provided by reporting entities, and the consistency of comparisons between entities and across different time periods.

The main features of the standard are that it requires:

- the profit (or loss) used in the calculation of basic earnings per share to be from continuing operations. This means that any tax expense and dividends on preference shares that have been classified as liabilities will be deducted as part of the determination of profit.
- the denominator in the calculation to contain only ordinary shares
- the number of ordinary shares used in the calculation of basic earnings per share to be adjusted by a time-weighting factor which is the number of days in the reporting period that the shares are outstanding as a proportion of the total number of days in the period.

In addition to calculating the basic earnings per share ratio, if an entity has options, warrants, contingently issuable shares or securities that are convertible to ordinary shares, IAS 33 requires that the effect of dilution must be recognised in the entity's earnings per share. Adjustments to calculate diluted earnings per share must be made to:

- the profit (or loss) attributable to the ordinary shareholders for the after-tax amount of dividends, interest or other income or expenses that would no longer arise if the dilutive securities were converted into ordinary shares
- increase the weighted average number of ordinary shares outstanding to reflect what the weighted average would have been assuming that all potential ordinary shares (dilutive securities) had been converted.

Discussion questions

Related party disclosures

1. Why do standard setters formulate rules for the disclosure of related party relationships?
2. Explain why key management personnel are regarded as related parties.
3. Explain why a parent company and its subsidiary entities are regarded as related parties.
4. Distinguish between control, joint control and significant influence.
5. Explain how an entity determines whether a family member is a related party.

Earnings per share

1. What is the earnings per share ratio used for?
2. Why is a time-weighting factor used to determine the number of shares that is used in the calculation of basic earnings per share?
3. What is the treatment applied to treasury shares when calculating the weighted average number of shares used in the earnings per share calculation?
4. Distinguish between basic earnings per share and diluted earnings per share.
5. Explain the effect of potential ordinary shares on the calculation of diluted earnings per share.
6. Why are retrospective adjustments made to earnings per share ratios?

References

Billabong International Ltd 2014, *2014 Full Financial Report*, Billabong International Limited, Australia, www.billabongbiz.com.

Durkin, P. 2009, 'Board forced to rethink exec pay', *Australian Financial Review*, 9 November.

International Accounting Standards Board 2009, *IAS 24 Related Party Disclosures*, www.ifrs.org.

International Accounting Standards Board 2010, *IAS 33 Earnings per Share*, International Accounting Standards Committee Foundation, London.

Nestlé Group, *Annual Report* 2014, http://www.nestle.com/asset-library/documents/library/documents/financial_statements/2014-financial-statements-en.pdf.

UBS Group AG 2014, *Annual Report 2014*, www.ubs.com.

Williams, F. 2009, 'Hegarty moving again', *Herald Sun*, 20 March, p. 63.

Exercises

STAR RATING ★ BASIC ★★ MODERATE ★★★ DIFFICULT

Exercise 19.1

SCOPE OF IAS 24

★ Which of the following is the related party of an entity within the scope of IAS 24? Give reasons for your answer.

(a) A person who has the authority to plan, direct and control the activities of the entity.

(b) The domestic partner and children of a director of the entity.

(c) The non-dependant sister of a director of the entity.

(d) A subsidiary company that is directly controlled by the entity.

(e) Dividend payment to employees who are holders of an entity's shares.

Exercise 19.2

RECOGNITION PRINCIPLES

★ Jay Wendt is a newly appointed director of Armstrong Ltd, a listed company that organises major sporting events. Jay has provided consultancy services to Armstrong Ltd for the past 10 years. In the most recent financial year these services amounted to $500 000.

Required

Determine whether the consultancy service provided by Jay is a related party transaction that should be disclosed in the financial statements of Armstrong Ltd. Explain your answer.

Exercise 19.3

DETERMINING WHETHER PARTIES ARE RELATED

★★ Jacques holds 100% of the shares in Cannes Ltd and he is also a director of Revoir Ltd. All of the shares in Revoir Ltd are held by Baroque Ltd.

Required

Determine the related party relationships for Cannes Ltd.

Exercise 19.4

EFFECT OF RELATED PARTY DISCLOSURES

★★ The following is an extract illustrating the potential impact of disclosing information about the remuneration arrangements of key management personnel.

> **Board forced to rethink exec pay**
>
> Large sharemarket-listed companies are being forced to review their remuneration practices after almost a quarter of those in the top 200 that have already held their annual general meetings suffered protest votes of 25 per cent or more from investors.
>
> Nearly half the top 200 companies that have held their AGMs reported a protest vote of more than 10 per cent against their pay plans, despite a big drop in bonus payments this year as boards promised to rein in executive pay after the global financial crisis.

Source: Durkin (2009, p. 1).

Required

Identify the disclosures that IAS 24 requires to be provided regarding key management personnel. Do you think the costs of making such disclosures outweigh the benefits? Explain your answer.

COMPONENTS OF BASIC EARNINGS PER SHARE

★ Which of the following is a component of earnings used in the calculation of basic earnings per share? Give reasons for your answer.
(a) Profit before tax expense
(b) Preference dividends declared during the period
(c) Income tax expense
(d) Profit from discontinued operations
(e) Prior year dividend paid to holders of cumulative preference shares

BONUS ISSUE OF SHARES

★★ On 1 January 2013, Regis Ltd has 200 000 ordinary shares outstanding. On 1 March 2013, the company announces a bonus issue of two shares for every share held on that date. By the end of the year Regis Ltd's profit attributable to ordinary shareholders amounts to $900 000 (2012: $600 000).

Required

Calculate the 2013 and 2012 basic earnings per share amounts that Regis Ltd must disclose in its financial statements for the year ended 31 December 2013.

THEORETICAL EX-RIGHTS VALUE

★★ Kenny Ltd has 30 000 ordinary shares on issue. The company announced a one-for-three rights issue with an exercise price of $4 for each right. The market price of one ordinary share immediately before the exercise of the rights was $6.

Required

Determine the theoretical ex-rights value per share.

RIGHTS ADJUSTMENT FACTOR AND ADJUSTED BASIC EARNINGS PER SHARE

★★ Assume that in exercise 19.7 Kenny Ltd announced the rights issue at the beginning of its reporting period (1 July 2014) and the last date for exercising the rights was 1 October 2014. Kenny Ltd announced profit attributable to ordinary shareholders of $109 725 for the full reporting period.

Required

Use the theoretical ex-rights value per share determined in exercise 19.7 to calculate the adjustment factor, and calculate adjusted basic earnings per share.

EFFECT OF SHARE OPTIONS ON DILUTED EARNINGS PER SHARE

★★ Xenia Ltd determines its profit attributable to ordinary shareholders for the reporting period ended 30 June 2014 as $96 000. The company has calculated its weighted average number of ordinary shares on issue during the period as 480 000. The weighted average number of shares under share options arrangements during the period is 24 000.
    The average market price of the entity's shares during the period is $2.40 per share, and the exercise price of shares under option is $1.50.

Required

Prepare a schedule setting out the calculation of basic earnings per share and diluted earnings per share.

ACADEMIC PERSPECTIVE — CHAPTER 19

IFRS® Standards prescribe, for each standard, a minimum set of additional information that should be disclosed in the notes. A basic question that academics have pondered in this context is whether managers would like to provide disclosure even without regulation (or in the case of regulated disclosure, to provide disclosure above the required level). From a theoretical point of view, the answer seems to be yes. If investors maintain that lack of disclosure implies that managers withhold bad news, then managers will furnish disclosure to avoid being seen as bad performers (Grossman, 1981). However, in practice it seems that voluntary disclosure is not uniformly observed. One potential explanation of this phenomenon is that managers who do not disclose may be concerned that providing too much disclosure may benefit other parties, such as competitors, trade unions or litigants suing the corporation. Verrecchia (1983) argues that good news may be withheld owing to such disclosure costs. Hence, investors will not be certain if lack of disclosure is due to bad news or withholding of potentially costly good news. In equilibrium firms release good news only if the benefit from the good news exceeds the cost of its disclosure. Other firms will withhold information and will be assessed at the expected average value of non-disclosing firms.

One possible benefit of disclosures is a reduction in cost of equity capital. In the case of a single company, better disclosure reduces information asymmetry and hence cost of capital. This is less clear when investors can diversify and invest in a large number of firms and so individual risk becomes less of an issue. The theoretical model of Lambert et al. (2007) provides the necessary link between disclosure and cost of capital in a multi-security market. This is based on the argument that better disclosure helps investors to assess the covariance between a firm's future cash flows and that of the market as a whole. Because this covariance is a risk factor for investors, more disclosure therefore reduces this risk, increases current prices and reduces expected return. These disclosure effects are consistent with lower cost of capital.

Botosan (1997) empirically examines the link between voluntary disclosures in annual reports and cost of capital. She compiles a dataset of detailed disclosures made by 122 manufacturing firms in 1990. Based on a long list of 46 potential disclosure elements Botosan (1997) calculates a disclosure score for each company. Each firm is then ranked according to its disclosure score. Botosan (1997) then computes a measure of cost of equity capital by employing well-known valuation models. The main finding is that for firms with low level of analyst following, higher disclosure rank is negatively related to cost of equity capital. This suggests that the information environment is rich for firms that are followed by many analysts; hence the incremental effect of voluntary disclosure is small. In contrast, when the information environment is poor, voluntary disclosures work to reduce cost of capital.

Kothari et al. (2009) extend this line of research by looking at the link between three measures for the cost of equity capital and the *content* of corporate disclosures. Using special software that analyses the content of these disclosures for 889 firms between 1996 and 2001, Kothari et al. (2009) classify these disclosures as either favourable or unfavourable in nature. They find that favourable corporate disclosures reduce cost of capital while unfavourable disclosures increase cost of capital. However, the effect of favourable disclosures is quite small (and much smaller than the effect of unfavourable disclosures), suggesting that investors largely disregard positive corporate disclosures. The rather modest and mixed results may be due to the fact that theory suggests a link between the precision of disclosure and cost of capital, rather than a link between the favourableness of disclosures and cost of capital.

Another interesting question that has attracted academic scrutiny is whether recognition of a number in the main statements is assessed differently than if, instead, the same number is disclosed only in the accompanying notes. This has been termed as the "recognition versus disclosure" concept. It should be nevertheless noted that disclosure in the notes can serve several purposes (Schipper, 2009), not just as an alternative to recognition in the main statements.

One reason a disclosed amount could be assessed differently than a recognised amount is that the reliability of the two numbers differ. This can be the case if, for example, auditors scrutinise less carefully disclosed amounts than recognised ones. Barth et al. (2003) advance another reason for possible differences in valuation effects of disclosed versus recognised amounts. They argue that disclosed-only amounts may not be looked at by all investor types. Specifically, sophisticated investors would look at disclosed information while incurring some cost for exerting this effort. In contrast, unsophisticated investors prefer to look at recognised amounts only. In such a case the degree to which disclosed information is impounded in price is a function of the number of sophisticated investors in the market. Limited attention to disclosed amounts may also be relevant in this context (Hirshleifer and Teoh, 2003).

One of the more persuasive studies of recognition vs. disclosure is conducted by Ahmed et al. (2006). The authors examine accounting regulation of derivatives in the US. Under old US standards information about fair value of derivatives was comprehensively provided. However, while a subset of derivatives was recognised on the balance sheet at fair value, other derivatives were either recognised at historical cost or zero cost. For these derivatives disclosure in the notes provided the relevant fair values. Under the new rules, all derivatives have to be recognised at fair value on the balance sheet. Crucially for this research, fair values were consistently estimated under both old and new rules. Ahmed et al. (2006) analyse the link between fair values of derivatives in 146 bank holding companies and the banks' market value of equity (MVE). They find that disclosed fair values (under old rules) are not associated with MVE, while recognised fair values (under old rules) exhibit positive relation with MVE. The authors then look at 82 banks that only disclosed fair values of derivatives under old rules but then had to recognise them under new rules. They find that recognised fair values (under new rules) are more closely related to MVE than disclosed amounts under old rules. This suggests that the value relevance of recognised fair values is greater than that of disclosed ones. Müller et al. (2015) provide corroborating results by taking advantage of the fact that under IFRS Standards fair values of investment properties may be either recognised or disclosed. Another interesting study on this issue is Aboody (1999). He examines a sample of 71 firms in the oil and gas industry, some of which had to recognise impairments of their wells in the income statement and some that only needed to disclose these impairments. He finds evidence suggesting that while recognised impairments affect stock prices, disclosed impairments do not.

Taken together, the evidence on disclosure versus recognition suggests that recognised amounts are more value relevant than disclosed amounts.

References

Aboody, D., 1996. Recognition versus disclosure in the oil and gas industry, *Journal of Accounting Research*, 21–32.

Ahmed, A.S., Kilic, E. and Lobo, G.J., 2006. Does recognition versus disclosure matter? Evidence from value-relevance of banks' recognized and disclosed derivative financial instruments, *The Accounting Review*, 81(3), 567–588.

Barth, M.E., Clinch, G. and Shibano, T., 2003. Market effects of recognition and disclosure, *Journal of Accounting Research*, 41(4), 581–609.

Botosan, C.A., 1997. Disclosure level and the cost of equity capital, *The Accounting Review*, 72(3), 323–349.

Grossman, S. J. 1981. The informational role of warranties and private disclosure about product quality, *The Journal of Law & Economics*, 24(3), 461–483.

Hirshleifer, D. and Teoh, S.H., 2003. Limited attention, information disclosure, and financial reporting, *Journal of Accounting and Economics*, 36(1), 337–386.

Kothari, S.P., Li, X. and Short, J.E., 2009. The effect of disclosures by management, analysts, and business press on cost of capital, return volatility, and analyst forecasts: A study using content analysis, *The Accounting Review*, 84(5), 1639–1670.

Lambert, R., Leuz, C. and Verrecchia, R. E. 2007, accounting information, disclosure, and the cost of capital, *Journal of Accounting Research*, 45: 385–420.

Müller, M., Riedl, E.J. and Sellhorn, T., 2015. Recognition versus disclosure of fair values, *The Accounting Review*, 90(6), 2411–2447.

Schipper, K., 2007. Required disclosures in financial reports, *The Accounting Review*, 82(2), 301–326.

Verrecchia, R. 1983. Discretionary disclosure. *Journal of Accounting and Economics*, 5, 365–380.

Part 4

Economic entities

20 Consolidation: controlled entities   561
21 Consolidation: wholly owned subsidiaries   577
22 Consolidation: intragroup transactions   605
23 Consolidation: non-controlling interest   635
24 Translation of the financial statements of foreign entities   679

Visit the companion website to access additional chapters
online at: www.wiley.com/college/picker

Online chapter C Associates and joint ventures

Online chapter D Joint arrangements

20 Consolidation: controlled entities

ACCOUNTING STANDARDS IN FOCUS

IFRS 10 *Consolidated Financial Statements*

IFRS 12 *Disclosure of Interests on Other Entities*

LEARNING OBJECTIVES

After studying this chapter, you should be able to:

 explain the meaning of consolidated financial statements

 discuss the meaning and application of the criterion of control

 discuss which entities should prepare consolidated financial statements

 understand the relationship between a parent and an acquirer in a business combination

 explain the differences in disclosure requirements between single entities and consolidated entities.

INTRODUCTION

The purpose of this chapter is to discuss the preparation of a single set of financial statements, referred to as the consolidated financial statements. The preparation of consolidated financial statements views the group as the economic entity that is of interest to users of financial statements. It involves combining the financial statements of the individual entities so that they show the financial position and financial performance of the group of entities, presented as if they were a single economic entity.

The first issue covered in this chapter is the determination of which entities are required to prepare consolidated financial statements. This involves a discussion of the criterion for consolidation and its application to economic situations. The second issue in this chapter is the accounting procedures for preparing the consolidated financial statements. The application in this chapter is to a very simple group structure involving two entities, one of which owns all the issued shares in the other. Further issues associated with the preparation of consolidated financial statements are discussed in the chapters that follow (*see chapters 21–23*).

The accounting standards governing the preparation of consolidated financial statements are IFRS 3 *Business Combinations* issued in 2008 and IFRS 10 *Consolidated Financial Statements* issued in 2011.

The objective of IFRS 3, as stated in paragraph 1:

is to establish principles and requirements for how the acquirer:

(a) recognises and measures in its financial statements the identifiable assets acquired, the liabilities assumed and any non-controlling interest in the acquiree;

(b) recognises and measures the goodwill acquired in the business combination or a gain from a bargain purchase; and

(c) determines what information to disclose to enable users of the financial statements to evaluate the nature and financial effects of the business combination.

The objective of IFRS 10 is stated in paragraph 1:

to establish principles for the presentation and preparation of consolidated financial statements when an entity controls one or more other entities.

To achieve this, IFRS 10 then:

- requires a parent to present consolidated financial statements
- establishes control as the criterion for consolidation
- defines the criterion of control
- provides guidance on identifying when one entity controls another
- sets out the accounting requirements for the preparation of consolidated financial statements.

20.1 CONSOLIDATED FINANCIAL STATEMENTS

Consolidated financial statements are defined in Appendix A of IFRS 10 as follows:

The financial statements of a **group** in which the assets, liabilities, equity, income, expenses and cash flows of the **parent** and its **subsidiaries** are presented as those of a single economic entity.

Consider figure 20.1. P Ltd has investments in a number of other companies. A shareholder's wealth in P Ltd is dependent not only on how well P Ltd performs, but also on the performance of the other entities in which P Ltd has an investment. Rather than require a shareholder in P Ltd to analyse each of the companies in the economic group, if P Ltd prepared a set of financial statements by adding together the financial statements of all entities in the group, this would assist investors in P Ltd to analyse their investment. Assuming that one share equals one voting right, P Ltd owns 70% of S1 Ltd and effectively owns 42% (70% × 60%) of S2 Ltd. However, P Ltd controls both S1 Ltd and S2 Ltd (through S1 Ltd's control of S2 Ltd). P Ltd also owns and controls 100% of S3 Ltd.

Consolidated financial statements perform this function as they are a consolidation, or an adding together, of the financial statements of all entities within an economic entity. As stated in paragraph B86 of IFRS 10, consolidated financial statements 'combine like items of assets, liabilities, equity, income, expenses and cash flows' of the entities in the group.

This process of adding the financial statements together can be seen in its simplest form in figure 20.2. In this example there are two entities in the group, P Ltd and S Ltd. The consolidated financial statements are prepared by adding together the assets and liabilities of both entities. In chapter 21 a consolidation worksheet is used to perform this addition process.

This aggregation process is subject to a number of adjustments, and these are covered in detail in later chapters. However, in this chapter, the process of consolidation should be seen simply as a process of aggregation of the financial statements of all entities within the group. Note that the consolidation process does *not* involve making adjustments to the individual financial statements or the accounts of the entities in the group. This is because the individual companies within the group remain separate legal entities. The consolidated financial statements are an additional set of financial statements and are prepared using a worksheet to facilitate the addition and adjustment process.

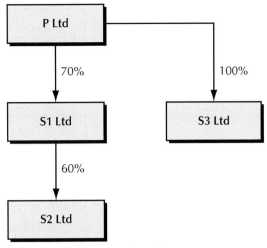

FIGURE 20.1 A group of entities

	P Ltd		S Ltd		Consolidation of P Ltd and S Ltd
Non-current assets*	150 000	+	120 000	=	270 000
Current assets	50 000	+	20 000	=	70 000
Total assets	200 000		140 000		340 000
Total liabilities	(80 000)	+	(30 000)	=	(110 000)
Net assets	$120 000		$110 000		$ 230 000

*Excluding P Ltd's investment in S Ltd (*explained in chapter 21*)

FIGURE 20.2 The consolidation process

The consolidated financial statements consist of a consolidated statement of financial position, consolidated statement of profit or loss and other comprehensive income, a consolidated statement of changes in equity, and a consolidated statement of cash flows.

The following definitions are contained in Appendix A of IFRS 10:

Group   A **parent** and its **subsidiaries**.
Parent   An entity that **controls** one or more entities.
Subsidiary An entity that is controlled by another entity.

The consolidated financial statements combine the financial statements of all the entities within a group. The entities in the group consist of two types; namely, parent and subsidiary. There is only one parent in a group, which is the controlling entity; that is, the entity that controls all other entities in the group. *Section 20.2* discusses the meaning of control. All other entities in the group — the controlled entities — are called subsidiaries. Hence, in figure 20.1, assuming that P Ltd controls all other companies in the figure, P Ltd is the parent entity, and all other entities in the group are subsidiaries.

Note that for a number of entities that are interconnected there may be a number of groups. Consider figure 20.3. If B Ltd controls C Ltd, then B Ltd is a parent and C Ltd is its subsidiary, and together they form a group. If A Ltd controls both B Ltd and C Ltd, then A Ltd is a parent and both B Ltd and C Ltd are its subsidiaries, and all together they form a group.

20.1.1 Reasons for consolidation

There are several reasons why consolidated financial statements are prepared:

1. *Supply of relevant information.* The information obtained from the consolidated financial statements is relevant to investors in the parent entity. These investors have an interest in the group as a whole, not just in the parent entity. To require these investors to source their information from the financial statements of each of the entities comprising the group would place a large cost burden on the investors.
2. *Comparable information.* Some entities are organised into a group structure such that different activities are undertaken by separate members of the group. Other entities are organised differently, with some having all activities conducted within the one entity. For an investor to make useful comparisons between entities, access to consolidated financial statements makes the comparative analysis an easier task.

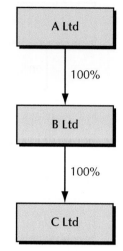

FIGURE 20.3 Multiple groups

3. *Accountability.* A key purpose for all financial reporting is the discharge of accountability by management. Entities that are responsible or accountable for managing a pool of resources, being the recipients of economic benefits and responsible for payment of obligations, are generally required to report on their activities, and are held accountable for the management of those activities. The management of the parent entity is not just responsible for the management of the assets and liabilities of the parent itself. As the parent controls the assets of all subsidiaries, the assets under the control of the parent entity's management are the assets of the group. The consolidated financial statements report the assets under the control of the group management as well as the claims on those assets.

4. *Reporting of risks and benefits.* There are risks associated with managing an entity, and an entity rarely obtains control of another without obtaining significant opportunities to benefit from that control. The consolidated financial statements allow an assessment of these risks and benefits at a group level.

Notwithstanding these advantages, it should be noted that the aggregation process of the consolidation results in little information being available for the individual subsidiaries. Hence, users of consolidated financial statements would not normally be able to identify individual subsidiaries that exhibit better or worse financial position and performance.

 20.2 CONTROL AS THE CRITERION FOR CONSOLIDATION

In Appendix A of IFRS 10, a parent is defined as an entity that *controls* one or more entities while a subsidiary is a controlled entity. The entity that is responsible for preparing the consolidated financial statements is the parent. An entity must then determine when it is a parent and which entities it controls. The determination of whether one entity controls another is crucial to the determination of which entities need to prepare consolidated financial statements. Paragraph 5 of IFRS 10 notes that 'an investor' must determine whether it is a parent by assessing whether it controls an 'investee'.

Under IFRS 10, the criterion for consolidation is control. It should first be noted that determination of whether control exists is a matter of judgement. In many situations it will not be clear cut that one entity controls another, and determination will have to be made by considering all available facts and circumstances (paragraph 8 of IFRS 10). As noted later in this section, IFRS 10 provides numerous factors to be considered in making the decision concerning the existence of control. Hence, it is important to understand the meaning of the term 'control' and what evidence may be accumulated to determine its existence or non-existence in specific circumstances. Further, if those circumstances change, there may be a need to assess whether control still exists.

Second, note that control is an exclusionary power. In a group there can be only one parent. If two or more investors join together to direct the activities of the investees, neither investor controls the investee — decision-making ability cannot be shared.

Control of an investee is defined in Appendix A of IFRS 10 as follows:

An investor controls an investee when the investor is exposed, or has rights, to variable returns from its involvement with the investee and has the ability to affect those returns through its power over the investee.

Paragraph 7 of IFRS 10 identifies three elements, all of which must be held by an investor in order for it to have control, namely:

1. power over the investee
2. exposure, or rights, to variable returns from its involvement with the investee
3. the ability to use its power over the investee to affect the amount of the investor's returns.

These three elements are discussed in detail in the following sections.

20.2.1 Power

Power is defined in Appendix A of IFRS 10 as follows:

> Existing rights that give the current ability to direct the *relevant activities*.

Note the key features of this definition.

Power arises from rights

These rights generally arise from some form of legal contract. For example, the rights that are held by the owner of an ordinary share in a company may include voting rights, rights to dividends or rights on liquidation of the company. Rights could also exist because of a contract between one entity and another entity. For example, an entity might engage another entity to manage its activities — the latter entity then has management rights but potentially no rights to dividends. The rights that are of importance in determining whether power exists are those relating to the ability to direct the relevant activities of an investee. Rights in relation to purely administration tasks are not rights that affect power. Examples of rights that affect who has power are listed in paragraph B15 of IFRS 10, namely:

- voting rights
- rights to appoint, reassign or remove members of an investee's key management personnel
- rights to appoint or remove another entity that participates in management decisions
- rights to direct the investee to enter into, or veto any changes to, transactions that affect the investee's returns.

Some questions that could be asked to assist in determining whether certain rights give rise to power are as follows (based on paragraph B18 of IFRS 10):

- Can the investor appoint or approve the investee's key management personnel who direct the relevant activities?
- Can the investor direct the investee to enter into or veto any changes to significant transactions that affect the investor's returns?
- Can the investor dominate either the nominations process of electing members of the investee's governing body or the obtaining of proxies from other holders of voting rights?

The rights must also be *substantive* rights. According to paragraph B22 of IFRS 10, for rights to be substantive the holders must have the practical ability to exercise the rights; that is, there are no barriers to the holders exercising the rights. The rights need to give the holder the current ability to direct the relevant activities when decisions about those activities need to be made.

As judgement is required in assessing whether rights are substantive, paragraph B23 of IFRS 10 provides some factors to consider in making that determination:

- whether the party or parties that hold the rights would benefit from the exercise of those rights, for example, potential voting rights.
- whether there are any barriers — economic or otherwise — that prevent a holder from the exercising of rights. Examples of such barriers are financial penalties, terms and conditions that make it unlikely that rights will be exercised, and the absence of specialised services necessary for exercising the rights. Paragraph B23(a) of IFRS 10 provides a detailed list of possible barriers.
- where more than one party is involved, whether there is a mechanism in place to enable those parties to practically exercise the rights.

If the rights are purely protective rights, the holder does not have power (paragraph 14). Protective rights are defined in Appendix A of IFRS 10 as follows:

> Rights designed to protect the interest of the party holding those rights without giving that party power over the entity to which those rights relate.

Paragraph B28 of IFRS 10 provides examples of protective rights, which include:

(a) a lender's right to restrict a borrower from undertaking activities that could significantly change the credit risk of the borrower to the detriment of the lender.

(b) the right of a party holding a non-controlling interest in an investee to approve capital expenditure greater than that required in the ordinary course of business, or to approve the issue of equity or debt instruments.

(c) the right of a lender to seize the assets of a borrower if the borrower fails to meet specified loan repayment conditions.

A non-controlling interest is equity in a subsidiary not attributable to a parent. For example, if a parent owns 80% of the shares of a subsidiary, then the non-controlling interest in the subsidiary is 20%.

Power is the ability to direct

There is a distinction between ability to direct and actually directing. An entity that has the ability to direct may decide not to exercise that ability and so allow another entity to actually direct. For example, Entity C may have two owners — Entity A that owns 55% of the shares in Entity C and Entity B that holds the remaining 45% of issued shares. Entity A may have the ability to direct the activities of Entity C but, as it is an investment company and holds shares purely for cash flow via dividends, may have no interest in management of other entities. Entity B may then actually undertake the management of Entity C. In such a circumstance, Entity B is the parent as it has the ability to direct the activities of Entity C.

The ability to direct must be current

The investor must be able to exercise its rights to direct at the time decisions are made concerning the activities of an investee. However, there are circumstances where power is still held by an investor even though there may be a time period to pass, or an activity that needs to be undertaken, before the right to direct can be currently exercisable. Paragraph B24 of IFRS 10 provides examples of these circumstances. One example is:

> An investor holds an option to acquire the majority of shares in an investee that is exercisable in 25 days and that would generate a profit for the investor upon exercising the option; that is, the value of the share exceeds the exercise price. A special meeting to change existing policies requires 30 days' notice. The existing shareholders cannot change existing policies before the exercise of the option. The investor has a substantive right that gives them the current ability to direct the relevant activities even before the option is exercised.

In contrast, assume the investor held a forward contract to acquire the majority of shares at a settlement date in 6 months' time. The existing shareholders would have the current ability to direct the activities of the investee as they can change the existing policies before the forward contract is settled.

It is relevant activities that are directed

Relevant activities are defined in Appendix A of IFRS 10 as:

> activities of the investee that significantly affect the investee's returns.

The determination of relevant activities may change over time and differ between entities; hence it may be necessary to analyse the purpose and design of an investee. For many investees, the relevant decisions are those that govern the financial and operating policies of the investee. Paragraph B11 of IFRS 10 provides examples of some possible relevant activities, including:
- selling and purchasing goods and services
- managing financial assets
- selecting, acquiring and disposing of assets
- researching and developing new products
- determining a funding structure or obtaining funding.

To have power, an investor need not be able to make any decision it likes in relation to an investee, as the investor is constrained by corporate and contract laws under which the interests of non-controlling investors, creditors and others are protected.

Level of share ownership

Ownership of ordinary shares in a company normally provides voting rights that enable the holder of the majority of shares to dominate the appointment of directors or an entity's governing board. As paragraph B35 of IFRS 10 states, where an investor holds more than half of the voting rights of an investee, the investor has power providing:

(a) the relevant activities are directed by a vote of the holder of the majority of voting rights, or
(b) a majority of the members of the governing body that directs the relevant activities are appointed by a vote of the holder of the majority of the voting rights.

Hence, in the absence of other evidence, where an investor holds a majority of voting shares that investor would be considered to have power over the investee.

Where an investor holds less than 50% of the shares of an investee, the determination of whether the investor has power over the investee is more difficult. In determining the existence of power, it is necessary to examine the potential actions of the holders of the other shares in the investee. Some factors to assist in this process are:
- *Size of the voting interest.* The more voting shares an investor has, the more likely it is that it will have power. A further consideration is the number of shareholders who hold the remaining voting shares and the extent of their holdings. Where the remaining voting shares are held by a large number of shareholders, each holding a small number of shares, the probability of these other shareholders getting together to outvote the shareholder who holds a substantial proportion, but not a majority, of the shares must be considered. Note that, where the remaining shares are held by a small number of shareholders, the probability that they could get together and outvote the holder of the large parcel of shares is higher. Paragraphs B44–B45 of IFRS 10 provide examples of these circumstances.

  In the first example, investor A holds 45% of the voting rights of an investee. Two other investors each hold 26% of the voting rights of the investee. The remaining voting rights are held by investors who hold less than 1% each. There are no other arrangements that affect decision making. In this case, consideration of the size of investor A's voting interest and its relative size to the other shareholdings is sufficient to conclude that investor A does not have power. The two investors who hold 26% each would need to cooperate to be able to prevent investor A from controlling the investee.

  In the second example, an investor holds 40% of the voting rights of an investee, with the next two largest holdings of voting rights being 10% and 4%. The remaining voting rights are held by thousands of shareholders, none holding more than 1% of the voting rights. None of the shareholders has any arrangements to consult each other or make collective decisions. In this case, on the basis of the absolute size of its holding and the relative size of the other shareholdings, the investor has a sufficiently dominant voting interest to meet the power criterion without the need to consider any other evidence of power.

- *Attendance at annual general meetings.* Although all shareholders may attend general meetings and vote in matters relating to governance of the entity, it is rare for this to occur. If, therefore, only 60% of the eligible votes are cast at a general meeting and an entity has more than a 30% interest in that entity, it can cast the majority of votes at that meeting. It then has power over that entity.
- *The existence of contracts.* As noted in paragraph B39 of IFRS 10, the contractual arrangement between an investor and other holders of shares may give the investor sufficient voting rights to give the investor power. An example of such a contract is provided in application example 5 of paragraph B43 of IFRS 10:

  Investor A holds 40% of voting rights of an investee and twelve other investors each hold 5% of voting rights of the investee. A shareholder agreement grants investor A the right to appoint, remove and set the remuneration of management responsible for directing the relevant activities.

  In this case, consideration of the absolute size of the investor's holding and the relative size of the other shareholdings alone is not conclusive to determine the investor has rights sufficient to give it power. However, the fact that investor A has the contractual right to appoint, remove and set the compensation of key management is sufficient to conclude that investor A has power over the investee. The fact that investor A might not have exercised this right yet or the likelihood of investor A exercising their right to select, appoint or remove key management should not be considered when assessing whether investor A has power.

- *Level of disorganisation or apathy of the remaining shareholders.* This factor is affected by the dispersion of the shareholders, and reflected in their attendance at general meetings. Holders of small parcels of shares are often not organised into forming voting blocks. Shareholders with environmental or ethical concerns may be less apathetic about the actions of an entity and its management policies, and may form voting blocks.

The assessment of the existence of power where the investor holds less than a majority of voting shares is difficult and requires judgement. In many cases that assessment relies on an analysis of the non-action of other shareholders. Do the non-voting shareholders at an annual general meeting not vote because they are happy with the management ability of the investor, as opposed to being apathetic? Would they be willing to combine to outvote the investor if the latter's decisions were considered untenable? The success of the investee under the control of the investor is a further measure of the potential for generally passive shareholders to be sufficiently concerned to cast a vote at the next annual general meeting. When an investee is performing poorly, the interest of shareholders as well as their willingness to become involved generally increases. Poor performance with resultant lowering of share prices may also result in a current or new shareholder acquiring a large block of shares and changing the voting mix at general meetings.

Numerous problems arise in applying the concept of power under IFRS 10. First, there is the question of temporary control. Where the investor holds more than 50% of the voting shares of the investee, there is no danger of a change in the identity of the parent. However, if the identification of the parent is based on factors that may change over time, the process becomes more difficult. For example, the percentage of votes cast at general meetings may historically be 70%, but in a particular year it may be 50%. A shareholder with 30% of the voting shares has control in the latter circumstance but not in the former. Similarly, consider the situation where there are two substantial block holdings of voting shares, meaning that neither has power over the investee. One of the holders of a substantial block of shares may then sell its shares to a large number of buyers. The other holder of a substantial block may suddenly find that it has the power to control, regardless of whether this investor wants to exercise control or not.

Second, the ability of an entity to control another may be affected by relationships with other entities. For example, a holder of 40% of the voting shares may be 'friendly' with the holder of another 11% of shares. The 11% shareholder might be a financial institution that has invested in the holder of the 40% of votes and plans to vote with that entity to increase its potential for repayment of loans. However, business relationships and loyalties are not always permanent.

These two examples illustrate some of the practical issues in applying the concept of power in IFRS 10.

Potential voting rights

Paragraphs B47–B50 of IFRS 10 discuss the issue of whether potential voting rights should be considered in assessing the existence of power. Potential voting rights are rights to obtain voting rights of an investee, such as those within an option or convertible instrument (paragraph B47).

As noted earlier in this section:
- the rights must be substantive
- the investor must have a current ability to exercise those rights.

Where this occurs, potential voting rights must be taken into consideration when assessing the existence of power. Illustrative examples 20.1 and 20.2 provide some examples of potential voting rights adapted from paragraph B50 of IFRS 10.

ILLUSTRATIVE EXAMPLE 20.1 Potential voting rights — exercisable options

Arctic holds 70% of the voting rights of an investee. Baltic holds the other 30% but also holds an option to acquire half of Arctic's voting rights, with the option being exercisable at a fixed price over the next 2 years.

If the option is deeply 'out of the money' (that is, the fixed price is too high relative to the current share price of the investee) then Arctic would be considered to hold power as the current economic conditions are such that the rights associated with the option are not substantive, in that it is not practicable for Baltic to exercise the option.

If the option was 'in the money' (that is, where the underlying share price is well above the exercise price) then Baltic would be considered to have power as it could exercise the option and direct the activities of the investee.

Source: Adapted from IASB 2011, IFRS 10 *Consolidated Financial Statements*, Example 9, p. 33.

ILLUSTRATIVE EXAMPLE 20.2 Potential voting rights — convertible debt instruments

An investee has three shareholders — Ant and two other investors. Each investor holds one-third of the voting rights. Ant also holds debt instruments that are convertible into voting shares of the investee at a fixed price that is 'out of the money', but not by a large amount. If the debt was converted, Ant would hold 60% of the shares of the investee. Because of the advantages of controlling the investee, it may be considered that Ant has power over the investee given Ant's ability to convert the debt instrument into shares. Additional information would need to be considered, including the current influence that Ant has on directing the activities of the investee.

Source: Adapted from IASB 2011, IFRS 10 *Consolidated Financial Statements*, Example 10, p. 33.

20.2.2 Exposure or rights to variable returns

Besides having power to direct the activities of an investee, an investor must also have the rights to variable returns from that investee. IFRS 10 does refer to this explicitly, but it appears that the standard equates control with exposure to risk.

Where an investor holds ordinary shares in an investee, it expects returns in relation to dividends, changes in the value of the investment, and residual interests on liquidation. These returns can be positive or negative; hence, the use of the term 'returns' rather than 'benefits'. The returns are not exclusive to the parent, but may also be received by other non-controlling shareholders. Other returns include (see paragraph B57 of IFRS 10 for examples of returns):

- returns from structuring activities with the investee; for example, obtaining a secure supply or raw material, access to a port facility, or a distribution network
- returns from denying or regulating access to a subsidiary's assets; for example, obtaining control of a patent for a competing product and stopping production
- returns from economies of scale
- remuneration from provision of services such as servicing of assets, and management.

The returns must have the potential to vary based on the performance of the investee. Examples of such variability are:

- dividends from ordinary shares that will change based on the profit performance of the investee
- fixed interest payments from a bond, as they expose the investor to the credit risk of the issuer of the bond, namely the investee
- fixed performance fees for management of the investee's assets, as they expose the investor to the performance risk of the investee.

20.2.3 Ability to use power to affect returns

Besides having power to direct the activities of the investee and rights to variable returns from the investee, a parent must have the ability to use its power over the investee to affect the returns received from the investee. This requires that the parent be able to use its power to increase its benefits and limit its losses from the subsidiary's activities. There is then a link between the holding of the power and the returns receivable. However, there is no specification of the level of returns to be received. IFRS 10 only requires that some variable returns be receivable and that the investor by its actions can affect the amount of those returns.

20.2.4 Agents

In determining whether control exists over an investee, an investor with decision-making rights needs to assess whether it is a principal or an agent.

Paragraph B58 of IFRS 10 explains that an agent is a party primarily engaged to act on behalf and for the benefit of another party or parties, being the the principal and therefore does not control the investee when it exercises its decision-making authority. The agent has a fiduciary relationship to the principal.

Paragraph B60 of IFRS 10 provides a number of factors to consider in determining whether a decision maker is a principal or an agent:

- the scope of its decision-making authority over the investee — this relates to the range of activities that the decision maker is permitted to direct
- the rights held by other parties; for example, whether another entity has substantive removal rights over the decision maker
- the remuneration to which it is entitled in accordance with the remuneration agreement — the remuneration of an agent would be expected to be commensurate with the level of skills needed to provide the management service while the remuneration agreement would contain terms and conditions normally included in arrangements for similar services
- the decision maker's exposure to variability of returns from other interest that it holds in the investee — the greater the decision maker's exposure to variable returns from its involvement in the investee, the more likely it is that the decision maker is not an agent.

An agent cannot be a parent. Where a controlling decision maker is determined to be an agent, it is the principal that would be considered to be the parent.

20.3 PREPARATION OF CONSOLIDATED FINANCIAL STATEMENTS

Paragraph 4(a) of IFRS 10 requires *all* parents to prepare consolidated financial statements, except in those circumstances where it meets *all* the following conditions:

(i) it is a wholly owned subsidiary or is a partially owned subsidiary of another entity and all its other owners, including those not otherwise entitled to vote, have been informed about, and do not object to, the parent not presenting consolidated financial statements;

(ii) its debt or equity instruments are not traded in a public market (a domestic or foreign stock exchange or an over-the-counter market, including local and regional markets);

(iii) it did not file, nor is it in the process of filing, its financial statements with a securities commission or other regulatory organisation for the purpose of issuing any class of instruments in a public market; and

(iv) its ultimate or any intermediate parent produces consolidated financial statements that are available for public use and comply with IFRSs.

The essence of these conditions is to ensure that only companies with no public accountability are exempted from the requirement to prepare consolidated financial statements.

Consider the group structure in figure 20.4. A Ltd is a parent entity with two subsidiaries. According to paragraph 4 of IFRS 10, A Ltd is required to prepare consolidated financial statements, combining the financial statements of A Ltd, B Ltd and C Ltd. B Ltd is also a parent with C Ltd being its subsidiary. Is B Ltd also required to prepare consolidated financial statements?

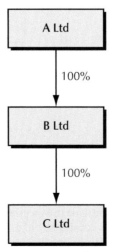

FIGURE 20.4 A parent and its subsidiaries

If B Ltd meets all the conditions in paragraph 4(a), it does not have to prepare consolidated financial statements. To determine this the following questions are asked:

- *Is B Ltd itself a wholly owned subsidiary?* In figure 20.4, B Ltd is itself a wholly owned subsidiary of A Ltd, hence this meets the first condition in paragraph 4(a)(i). Note also in paragraph 4(a)(i), that even if A Ltd owned only, say, 80% of B Ltd, making B Ltd a partially owned subsidiary, B Ltd may still be exempted from preparing consolidated financial statements if the 20% non-controlling interest in B Ltd has been informed about and do not object to the parent not presenting consolidated financial statements.
- *Has B Ltd filed its financial statements with a regulatory agency for the purpose of issuing any debt or equity instruments in a public market or are the debt and equity instruments of B Ltd traded in a public market?* If B Ltd intends to issue such instruments of if they are traded in a public market, then there are potential users for a set of consolidated financial statements from B Ltd. Where B Ltd is a wholly owned subsidiary, it is unlikely that its equity instruments would be traded in a public market.
- *Has A Ltd produced consolidated financial statements complying with IFRS® Standards?*

20.4 BUSINESS COMBINATIONS AND CONSOLIDATION

As noted in chapter 14, accounting for a business combination under the acquisition method requires the identification of an acquirer. The acquirer is the combining entity that obtains *control* of the other combining entities or businesses. Hence, as the criterion for identification of a parent–subsidiary relationship is control, it is expected that when a business combination is formed by the creation of a parent–subsidiary relationship, the parent will be identified as the acquirer. As noted in paragraph 3 of IFRS 10, the accounting requirements for business combinations and their effect on consolidation, including goodwill arising on a business combination, are set out in IFRS 3 *Business Combinations*.

However, there are situations where the parent entity is not the acquiring entity. In paragraph B19 of Appendix B to IFRS 3, a distinction is made between the legal acquirer/acquiree and the accounting acquirer/acquiree. The parent entity is usually the legal acquirer as it issues its equity interests as consideration in the combination transaction, with the subsidiary being the legal acquiree. This parent has control of the group subsequent to the business combination occurring. However, the accounting acquirer in a business combination is determined based on which entity participating in the business combination is the entity that obtains control of the other entities.

20.4.1 Formation of a new entity

Consider the situation in figure 20.5 in which A Ltd and B Ltd combine by the formation of a new entity, C Ltd, which acquires all the shares of both of these entities with the issue of shares in C Ltd. C Ltd controls both A Ltd and B Ltd.

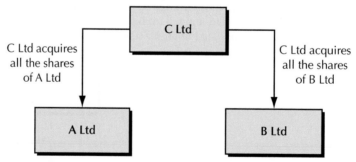

FIGURE 20.5 Identification of an acquirer where a new entity is formed

Paragraph B18 of IFRS 3 states: '[I]f a new entity is formed to issue equity interests to effect a business combination, one of the combining entities that existed before the business combination shall be identified as the acquirer by applying the guidance in paragraphs B13–B17.' In other words, even though C Ltd is acquiring the shares of both A Ltd and B Ltd, it is not to be considered the accounting acquirer; either A Ltd or B Ltd must be considered to be the accounting acquirer.

Deciding which entity is the acquirer involves a consideration of factors such as which of the combining entities initiated the combination, and whether the assets and revenues of one of the combining entities significantly exceed those of the others. The reasons for this decision by the International Accounting Standards Board (IASB®) are given in paragraphs BC98–BC101 of the Basis for Conclusions on IFRS 3

Business Combinations. The key reason for the standard setter's decision is in paragraph BC100. The argument is that the new entity, C Ltd, may have no economic substance, and the accounting result for the combination of the three entities should be the same if A Ltd simply combined with B Ltd without the formation of C Ltd. It is argued in paragraph BC100 that to account otherwise would 'impair both the comparability and the reliability of the information'.

However, the problem that then arises in the scenario in figure 20.5 is that a choice has to be made: is A Ltd or B Ltd the acquirer? In deciding on which entity is the acquirer, paragraphs B14–B18 of Appendix B to IFRS 3 provide some indicators to consider in situations where it may be difficult to identify an acquirer. The entity likely to be the acquirer is the one:

- that has a significantly greater fair value
- that gives up the cash or other assets, in the case where equity instruments are exchanged for cash or other assets
- whose management is able to dominate the business combination.

In this circumstance, although C Ltd is the legal parent of the subsidiaries A Ltd and B Ltd, it is not the acquirer in the business combination.

20.4.2 Reverse acquisitions

A further situation considered in paragraphs B19–B27 of IFRS 3 is the 'reverse acquisition' form of business combination. Consider the situation in figure 20.6.

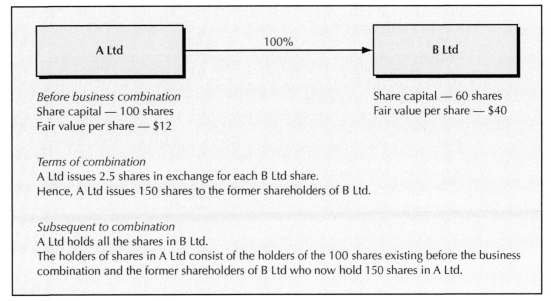

FIGURE 20.6 Reverse acquisition

A Ltd acquired all the shares in B Ltd, and A Ltd can therefore legally control the financial and operating policies of B Ltd. However, an analysis of the shareholding in A Ltd shows that the former shareholders of B Ltd hold 60% (i.e. 150/250) of the shares of A Ltd. Some people argue that the substance of the business combination is that B Ltd has really taken over A Ltd because the former shareholders of B Ltd are in control. Paragraph BC96 of the Basis for Conclusions on IFRS 3 provides a further example of a reverse acquisition:

> The IASB also observed that in some reverse acquisitions, the acquirer may be the entity whose equity interests have been acquired and the acquiree is the issuing entity. For example, a private entity might arrange to have itself 'acquired' by a smaller public entity through an exchange of equity interests as a means of obtaining a stock exchange listing. As part of the agreement, the directors of the public entity resign and are replaced by directors appointed by the private entity and its former owners. The IASB observed that in such circumstances, the private entity, which is the legal subsidiary, has the power to govern the financial and operating policies of the combined entity so as to obtain benefits from its activities. Treating the legal subsidiary as the acquirer in such circumstances is thus consistent with applying the control concept for identifying the acquirer.

The problem with the reverse acquisitions argument is that it relies on an analysis of which shareholders control the decision making — that is, the acquiring entity is the one whose owners control the combined entity and who have the power to govern the financial and operating policies of the entity so as to obtain benefits from its activities.

20.5 DISCLOSURE

There are no disclosures specified in IFRS 10. IFRS 12 *Disclosure of Interests in Other Entities*, issued in 2011 at the same time as IFRS 10, outlines the disclosures required in the consolidated financial statements for subsidiaries. IAS 27 *Separate Financial Statements*, also issued in 2011, sets out disclosures required in the separate financial statements of the parent.

20.5.1 Disclosures required by IFRS 12

The key objective of IFRS 12 is stated in paragraph 1:

> The objective of this IFRS is to require an entity to disclose information that enables users of its financial statements to evaluate:
>
> (a) the nature of, and risks associated with, its *interests in other entities*, and
> (b) the effects of those interests on its financial position, financial performance and cash flows.

Notice the emphasis on the ability of users of financial statements to be able to evaluate risks. In the introduction to IFRS 12 *Disclosure of Interests in Other Entities*, in paragraph IN5, the IASB noted that 'the global financial crisis that started in 2007 highlighted a lack of transparency about the risks to which a reporting entity was exposed from its involvement with structured entities'. As a result, IFRS 12 requires an entity to disclose the significant judgements and assumptions it has made in determining the nature of its interest in another entity (paragraph 2(a)), and in particular judgements, assumptions and changes in these in relation to subsidiaries (paragraph 7). Paragraph 9 of IFRS 12 provides the following examples of situations where it is necessary to disclose significant judgements and assumptions:

- where an entity does not control another entity but it holds more than half of the voting rights in the other entity
- where an entity controls another entity but it holds less than half of the voting rights of the other entity
- where an entity is an agent or a principal.

To assist users in understanding the nature of the group, paragraph 10 of IFRS 12 states:

> An entity shall disclose information that enables users of its consolidated financial statements
>
> (a) to understand:
> (i) the composition of the group; and
> (ii) the interest that non-controlling interests have in the group's activities and cash flows (paragraph 12); and
> (b) to evaluate:
> (i) the nature and extent of significant restrictions on its ability to access or use assets, and settle liabilities, of the group (paragraph 13);
> (ii) the nature of, and changes in, the risks associated with its interests in consolidated structured entities (paragraphs 14–17);
> (iii) the consequences of changes in its ownership interest in a subsidiary that do not result in a loss of control (paragraph 18); and
> (iv) the consequences of losing control of a subsidiary during the reporting period (paragraph 19).

Where the financial statements of a subsidiary are as of a date that differs from that of the parent, the entity must disclose both the date used by the subsidiary as well as the reason for using a different date (paragraph 11). As the parent controls the subsidiary, the choice of a different date must be one made by the parent and not the subsidiary.

Where a non-controlling interest exists in a subsidiary, paragraph 12 of IFRS 12 requires that an entity disclose for each such subsidiary:

- (a) the name of the subsidiary.
- (b) the principal place of business (and country of incorporation if different from the principal place of business) of the subsidiary.
- (c) the proportion of ownership interests held by non-controlling interests.
- (d) the proportion of voting rights held by non-controlling interests, if different from the proportion of ownership interests held.
- (e) the profit or loss allocated to non-controlling interests of the subsidiary during the reporting period.
- (f) accumulated non-controlling interests of the subsidiary at the end of the reporting period.
- (g) summarised financial information about the subsidiary (see paragraph B10).

Paragraph B10 of IFRS 12 states:

For each subsidiary that has non-controlling interests that are material to the reporting entity, an entity shall disclose:

(a) dividends paid to non-controlling interests.
(b) summarised financial information about the assets, liabilities, profit or loss and cash flows of the subsidiary that enables users to understand the interest that non-controlling interests have in the group's activities and cash flows. That information might include but is not limited to, for example, current assets, non-current assets, current liabilities, non-current liabilities, revenue, profit or loss and total comprehensive income.

Paragraph B11 notes that the summarised financial information is required *before* adjusting for intragroup transactions. Paragraph 13 of IFRS 12 provides disclosures required where an entity has significant restrictions on its ability to access or use the assets or settle the liabilities of the group. Paragraph 14 of IFRS 12 deals with consolidated structured entities. In Appendix A, a structured entity is defined as:

An entity that has been designed so that voting or similar rights are not the dominant factor in deciding who controls the entity, such as when any voting rights relate to administrative tasks only and the relevant activities are directed by means of contractual arrangements.
    Paragraphs B22–B24 provide further information about structured entities.

According to paragraph B22, a structured entity may have the following features:

(a) restricted activities.
(b) a narrow and well-defined objective, such as to effect a tax-efficient lease, carry out research and development activities, provide a source of capital or funding to an entity or provide investment opportunities for investors by passing on risks and rewards associated with the assets of the structured entity to investors.
(c) insufficient equity to permit the structured entity to finance its activities without subordinated financial support.
(d) financing in the form of multiple contractually linked instruments to investors that create concentrations of credit or other risks (tranches).

The following examples of entities that are regarded as structured entities are noted in paragraph B23:

(a) securitisation vehicles.
(b) asset-backed financings.
(c) some investment funds.

Disclosures in relation to consolidated structured entities required by IFRS 12 include:
- the terms of any contractual arrangement that could require a parent or its subsidiaries to supply financial support to a consolidated structured entity
- information about the provision of financial support supplied without the parent or its subsidiaries having a contractual obligation to do so
- current intentions to provide financial or other support to a consolidated structured entity.

Where the structured entity is *not* consolidated, paragraphs 24–31 of IFRS 12 provide information on the disclosures required. As these structured entities are not consolidated, it is important that users are aware of any risks associated with involvement with these entities. In particular paragraph 26 requires disclosure about:

its interests in unconsolidated structured entities, including, but not limited to, the nature, purpose, size and activities of the structured entity and how the structured entity is financed.

To assist in the evaluation of risks associated with unconsolidated structured entities, paragraph 29 requires an entity to disclose in tabular format, unless another format is more appropriate, a summary of:

(a) the carrying amounts of the assets and liabilities recognised in its financial statements relating to its interests in unconsolidated structured entities.
(b) the line items in the statement of financial position in which those assets and liabilities are recognised.
(c) the amount that best represents the entity's maximum exposure to loss from its interests in unconsolidated structured entities, including how the maximum exposure to loss is determined. If an entity cannot quantify its maximum exposure to loss from its interests in unconsolidated structured entities it shall disclose that fact and the reasons.
(d) a comparison of the carrying amounts of the assets and liabilities of the entity that relate to its interests in unconsolidated structured entities and the entity's maximum exposure to loss from those entities.

Paragraphs 18 and 19 set out disclosures required where there are changes in the parent's ownership interest in a subsidiary as well as when a parent loses control of a subsidiary.

20.5.2 Disclosures required by IAS 27

Paragraph 4 of IAS 27 contains the following definition of separate financial statements:

Separate financial statements are those presented by a parent (ie an investor with control of a subsidiary) or an investor with joint control of, or significant influence over, an investee, in which the investments are accounted for at cost or in accordance with IFRS 9 *Financial Instruments*.

There are two situations where separate financial statements are prepared:

1. *Where a parent is exempted from preparing consolidated financial statements in accordance with paragraph 4(a) of IFRS 10.*

   In this case, paragraph 16 of IAS 27 requires the parent to supply the following information in the separate financial statements prepared by the parent:

   (a) the fact that the financial statements are separate financial statements; that the exemption from consolidation has been used; the name and principal place of business (and country of incorporation, if different) of the entity whose consolidated financial statements that comply with International Financial Reporting Standards have been produced for public use; and the address where those consolidated financial statements are obtainable;

   (b) a list of significant investments in subsidiaries, jointly controlled entities and associates, including the name, country of incorporation or residence, proportion of ownership interest and, if different, proportion of voting power held; and

   (c) a description of the method used to account for the investments listed under (b).

2. *Where a parent prepares separate financial statements in addition to consolidated financial statements.*

   Paragraph 17 of IAS 27 requires the following information to be disclosed in the separate financial statements:

   (a) the fact that the statements are separate financial statements and the reasons why those statements are prepared if not required by law;

   (b) a list of significant investments in subsidiaries, joint ventures and associates, including:

      (i) the name of those investees.

      (ii) the principal place of business (and country of incorporation, if different) of those investees.

      (iii) its proportion of the ownership interest (and its proportion of the voting rights, if different) held in those investees.

   (c) a description of the method used to account for the investments listed under (b).

The parent or investor shall also identify the financial statements prepared in accordance with IFRS 10, IFRS 11 or IAS 28 (as amended in 2011) to which they relate.

SUMMARY

Where entities form relationships with other entities, accounting standards often require additional disclosure so that users of financial statements can understand the economic substance of the entities involved. Where an entity is classified as a subsidiary of another, the parent, IFRS Standards establish principles for the preparation of consolidated financial statements. These statements are in addition to those prepared for either the parent or a subsidiary as separate legal entities. The consolidated financial statements are prepared by adding the financial statements of a parent and each of its subsidiaries, with adjustments being made during this process.

An important decision is the determination of whether the relationship between two entities is such as to be classified as a parent–subsidiary relationship. The existence of this relationship is determined by whether one entity has control over another. The existence of control requires the assessment of the power an entity has over another entity, whether the investor is exposed or has rights to variable returns from its involvement in the investee, and the ability of the investor to use its power over the investee to affect the amount of those returns. This analysis requires the accountant to exercise judgement in analysing the specific relationships between entities, since the existence of control is not simply a matter of determining whether an entity owns a majority of shares in another.

In general, parent entities are responsible for the preparation of the consolidated financial statements. However, IFRS 10 exempts parent entities that meet specified criteria from the preparation of these statements. For those parents preparing consolidated financial statements, IFRS 3 will need to be applied as the formation of a parent–subsidiary relationship is normally also a business combination.

IFRS 10 does not contain disclosure requirements for consolidated financial statements. The disclosure requirements are found in IFRS 12 and IAS 27.

Discussion questions

1. What is a subsidiary?
2. What is meant by the term 'control'?
3. When are potential voting rights considered when deciding if one entity controls another?
4. Are only those entities in which another entity owns more than 50% of the issued shares classified as subsidiaries?
5. What benefits could be sought by an entity that obtains control over another entity?

Exercises

Exercise 20.1 CONVERTIBLE DEBENTURES

★

Pea Ltd establishes Soup Ltd for the sole purpose of developing a new product to be manufactured and marketed by Pea Ltd. Pea Ltd engages Mr Smith to lead the team to develop the new product. Mr Smith is named Managing Director of Soup Ltd at an annual salary of £100 000, £10 000 of which is advanced to Mr Smith by Soup Ltd at the time Soup Ltd is established. Mr Smith invests £10 000 in the project and receives all of Soup Ltd's initial issue of 10 voting ordinary shares.

Pea Ltd transfers £500 000 to Soup Ltd in exchange for 7%, 10-year debentures convertible at any time into 500 voting ordinary shares of Soup Ltd. Soup Ltd has enough shares authorised to fulfil its obligation if Pea Ltd converts its debentures into voting ordinary shares.

The constitution of Soup Ltd provides certain powers for the holders of voting common shares and the holders of securities convertible into voting ordinary shares that require a majority of each class voting separately. These include:
(a) the power to amend the corporate purpose of Soup Ltd
(b) the power to authorise and issue voting shares of securities convertible into voting shares.

At the time Soup Ltd is established, there are no known economic legal impediments to Pea Ltd converting the debt.

Required

Discuss whether Soup Ltd is a subsidiary of Pea Ltd.

Exercise 20.2 OPTIONS

★

Palau Ltd and India Ltd own 80% and 20% respectively of the ordinary shares that carry voting rights at a general meeting of shareholders of Cook Islands Ltd. Palau Ltd sells half of its interest in Cook Islands Ltd to Kobe Ltd and buys call options from Kobe Ltd that are exercisable at any time at a premium to the market price when issued and, if exercised, would give Palau Ltd its original 80% ownership interest and voting rights. At 30 June 2014, the options are out of the money.

Required

Discuss whether Palau Ltd is the parent of Cook Islands Ltd.

Exercise 20.3 CONTROL

★★

Pluto Ltd has acquired, during the current year, the following investments:

Sun Ltd	€120 000 (40% of issued capital)
Saturn Ltd	€117 000 (35% of issued capital)

Pluto Ltd is unsure how to account for these investments and has asked you, as the auditor, for some professional advice.

Specifically, Pluto Ltd is concerned that it may need to prepare consolidated financial statements under IFRS 10. To help you, the company has provided the following information about the two investee companies:

Sun Ltd
- The remaining shares in Sun Ltd are owned by a diverse group of investors who each hold a small parcel of shares.
- Historically, only a small number of the shareholders attend the general meetings or question the actions of the directors.
- Pluto Ltd has nominated three new directors and expects that they will be appointed at the next annual general meeting. The current board of directors has five members.

Saturn Ltd
- The remaining shares in Saturn Ltd are owned by a small group of investors who each own approximately 15% of the issued shares. One of these shareholders is Sun Ltd, which owns 17%.
- The shareholders take a keen interest in the running of the company and attend all meetings.
- Two of the shareholders, including Sun Ltd, already have representatives on the board of directors who have indicated their intention of nominating for re-election.

Required

1. Advise Pluto Ltd as to whether, under IFRS 10, it controls Sun Ltd and/or Saturn Ltd. Support your conclusion.
2. Would your conclusion be different if the remaining shares in Sun Ltd were owned by three institutional investors each holding 20%? If so, why?

Exercise 20.4	SUBSIDIARY STATUS

★★ Pumpkin Ltd owns 40% of the shares of Soup Ltd, and holds the only substantial block of shares in that entity; no other party owns more than 3% of the shares. The annual general meeting of Soup Ltd is to be held in 1 month's time. Two situations that may arise are:

- Pumpkin Ltd will be able to elect a majority of Soup Ltd's board of directors as a result of exercising its votes as the largest holder of shares. As only 75% of shareholders voted in the previous year's annual meeting, Pumpkin Ltd may have the majority of the votes that are cast at the meeting.
- By obtaining the proxies of other shareholders and, after meeting with other shareholders who normally attend general meetings of Soup Ltd and convincing these shareholders to vote with it, Pumpkin Ltd may obtain the necessary votes to have its nominees elected as directors of the board of Soup Ltd, regardless of the attendance at the general meeting.

Required

Discuss the potential for Soup Ltd being classified as a subsidiary of Pumpkin Ltd.

Exercise 20.5	DETERMINING SUBSIDIARY STATUS

★★ **Required**

In the following independent situations, determine whether a parent–subsidiary relationship exists, and which entity, if any, is a parent required to prepare consolidated financial statements under IFRS 10.

1. Perth Ltd is a company that was hurt by a recent global financial crisis. As a result, it experienced major trading difficulties. It previously obtained a significant loan from Fremantle Bank, and when Perth Ltd was unable to make its loan repayments, the bank made an agreement with Perth Ltd to become involved in the management of that company. Under the agreement between the two entities, the bank had authority for spending within Perth Ltd. Perth Ltd's managers had to obtain authority from the bank for acquisitions over $10 000, and was required to have bank approval for its budgets.
2. Broome Ltd owns 80% of the equity shares of Shark Bay Ltd, which owns 100% of the shares of Geraldton Ltd. All companies prepare reports under IFRS Standards. Although the shares of Shark Bay Ltd are not traded on any stock exchange, its debt instruments are publicly traded.
3. Denmark Ltd is a major financing company whose interest in investing is return on the investment. Denmark Ltd does not get involved in the management of its investments. If the investees are not managed properly, Denmark Ltd sells its shares in that investee and selects a more profitable investee to invest in. It previously held a 35% interest in Esperance Ltd as well as providing substantial convertible debt finance to that entity. Recently, Esperance Ltd was having cash flow difficulties and persuaded Denmark Ltd to convert some of the convertible debt into equity so as to ease the effects of interest payments on cash flow. As a result, Denmark Ltd's equity interest in Esperance Ltd increased to 52%. Denmark Ltd still wanted to remain as a passive investor, with no changes in the directors on the board of Esperance Ltd. These directors were appointed by the holders of the 48% of shares not held by Denmark Ltd.

Exercise 20.6	LESS THAN MAJORITY OWNERSHIP

★★ On 1 March 2015, Pink Ltd acquired 40% of the voting shares of Scarlet Ltd. Under the company's constitution, each share is entitled to one vote. On the basis of past experience, only 65% of the eligible votes are typically cast at the annual general meetings of Scarlet Ltd. No other shareholder holds a major block of shares in Scarlet Ltd.

The financial year of Scarlet Ltd ends on 31 December each year. The directors of Pink Ltd argue that they are not required under IFRS 10 to include Scarlet Ltd as a subsidiary in Pink Ltd's consolidated financial statements at 31 December 2015 as there is no conclusive evidence that Pink Ltd can control the financial and operating policies of Scarlet Ltd. The auditors of Pink Ltd disagree, referring specifically to past years' voting figures.

Required

Provide a report to Pink Ltd on whether it should regard Scarlet Ltd as a subsidiary in its preparation of consolidated financial statements at 31 December 2015.

21

Consolidation: wholly owned subsidiaries

ACCOUNTING STANDARDS IN FOCUS

IFRS 3 *Business Combinations*

IFRS 10 *Consolidated Financial Statements*

IFRS 12 *Disclosure of Interests in Other Entities*

LEARNING OBJECTIVES

After studying this chapter, you should be able to:

1 understand the nature of the group covered in this chapter, and the initial adjustments required in the consolidation worksheet

2 explain how a consolidation worksheet is used

3 prepare an acquisition analysis for the parent's acquisition in a subsidiary

4 prepare the worksheet entries at the acquisition date, being the business combination valuation entries and the pre-acquisition entries

5 prepare the worksheet entries in periods subsequent to the acquisition date, adjusting for movements in assets and liabilities since acquisition date and dividends from pre-acquisition equity

6 prepare the worksheet entries where the subsidiary revalues its assets at acquisition date

7 prepare the disclosures required by IFRS 3 and IFRS 12.

21.1 THE CONSOLIDATION PROCESS

This chapter discusses the preparation of consolidated financial statements. As discussed in chapter 20, under IFRS 10 *Consolidated Financial Statements* consolidated financial statements are the result of combining the financial statements of a parent and all its subsidiaries. *(The determination of whether an entity is a parent or a subsidiary is discussed in chapter 20.)* The two accounting standards mainly used in this chapter are IFRS 10 and IFRS 3 *Business Combinations*. The accounting principles relevant for business combinations have been discussed earlier *(see chapter 14)* and an in-depth understanding of that chapter is essential to the preparation of consolidated financial statements because the parent's acquisition of shares in a subsidiary is simply one form of a business combination.

In IFRS 3 Appendix A, 'acquisition date' is defined as the date on which the acquirer obtains control of the acquiree. As discussed in chapter 14, both the fair values of the identifiable assets and liabilities of the subsidiary and the consideration transferred are measured at the acquisition date. In this chapter, the only combinations considered are those where the parent acquires its controlling interest in a subsidiary and, as a result, owns all the issued shares of the subsidiary — the subsidiary is then a wholly owned subsidiary. This may occur by the parent buying all the shares in a subsidiary in one transaction, or by the parent acquiring the controlling interest after having previously acquired shares in the subsidiary.

Note, however, as discussed in chapter 20, control of a subsidiary does not necessarily involve the parent acquiring shares in a subsidiary. The consolidated financial statements of a parent and its subsidiaries include information about a subsidiary from the date the parent obtains control of the subsidiary; that is, from the acquisition date. A subsidiary continues to be included in the parent's consolidated financial statements until the parent no longer controls that entity; that is, until the date of disposal of the subsidiary.

Before undertaking the consolidation process, it may be necessary to make adjustments in relation to the content of the financial statements of the subsidiary:

- If the end of a subsidiary's reporting period does not coincide with the end of the parent's reporting period, adjustments must be made for the effects of significant transactions and events that occur between those dates, with additional financial statements being prepared where it is practicable to do so (IFRS 10 paragraphs B92–B93). In most cases where there are different dates, the subsidiary will prepare adjusted financial statements as at the end of the parent's reporting period, so that adjustments are not necessary on consolidation. Where the preparation of adjusted financial statements is unduly costly, the financial statements of the subsidiary, prepared at a different date from the parent, may be used subject to adjustments for significant transactions. However, as paragraph B93 states, for this to be a viable option, the difference between the ends of the reporting periods can be no longer than 3 months. Further, the length of the reporting periods, as well as any difference between the ends of the reporting periods, must be the same from period to period.
- The consolidated financial statements are to be prepared using uniform accounting policies for like transactions and other events in similar circumstances (IFRS 10 paragraph 19). Where different policies are used, adjustments are made so that like transactions are accounted for under a uniform policy in the consolidated financial statements.

The preparation of the consolidated financial statements involves adding together the financial statements of the parent and its subsidiaries as well as processing a number of adjustments, these being expressed in the form of consolidating journal entries:

- As required by IFRS 3, at the acquisition date the acquirer must recognise the identifiable assets acquired and liabilities assumed of the subsidiary at fair value. Adjusting the carrying amounts of the subsidiary's assets and liabilities to fair value and recognising any identifiable assets acquired and liabilities assumed as a part of the business combination but not recorded by the subsidiary is a part of the consolidation process. The entries used to make these adjustments are referred to in this chapter as the *business combination valuation entries*. As noted later *(see section 21.2)* these adjusting entries are generally not made in the records of the parent or of the subsidiary, but in a consolidation worksheet.
- Where the parent has an ownership interest (i.e. owns shares) in a subsidiary, adjusting entries are made, referred to in this chapter as the *pre-acquisition entries*. As noted in paragraph B86(b) of IFRS 10, this involves eliminating the carrying amount of the parent's investment in each subsidiary and the parent's portion of pre-acquisition equity in each subsidiary. The name of these entries is derived from the fact that the equity of the subsidiary at the acquisition date is referred to as pre-acquisition equity, and it is this equity that is being eliminated. These entries are also made in the consolidation worksheet and not in the records of the parent or subsidiary.
- The third set of adjustments to be made is for transactions between the entities within the group subsequent to the acquisition date, including events such as sales of inventory or non-current assets. These *intragroup* transactions are referred to in IFRS 10 paragraph B86(c) *(adjustments for these transactions are discussed in detail in chapter 22)*.

In this chapter, the group under discussion is one where:

- there are only two entities within the group: one parent and one subsidiary (see figure 21.1)
- both entities have share capital

FIGURE 21.1 A wholly owned group

- the parent owns all the issued shares of the subsidiary; that is, the subsidiary is wholly owned (partially owned subsidiaries, where it is necessary to account for the non-controlling interest, are covered later *(see chapter 23)*)
- there are no intragroup transactions between the parent and its subsidiary after the acquisition date.

21.2 CONSOLIDATION WORKSHEETS

The consolidated financial statements are prepared by adding together the financial statements of the parent and the subsidiary. It is the *financial statements* of the parent and the subsidiary, rather than the underlying accounts, which are added together. There are no consolidated ledger accounts. The financial statements that are added together are the statements of financial position, statements of profit or loss and other comprehensive income and statements of changes in equity prepared by the management of the parent and the subsidiary. Consolidated statements of cash flows must also be prepared, but these are beyond the scope of this book.

To facilitate the addition process, particularly where there are several subsidiaries, as well as to make the necessary valuation and pre-acquisition entry adjustments, a worksheet or computer spreadsheet is often used. From the worksheet, the external statements are prepared — the consolidated statement of financial position, statement of profit or loss and other comprehensive income and statement of changes in equity.

The format for the worksheet is presented in figure 21.2, which contains the information used for the consolidation of the parent, P Ltd, and the subsidiary, S Ltd. Assume that P has paid £20 000 for all of the shares of S. At the time of acquisition S reported £15 000 in share capital and £5000 in retained earnings. Note that this simple example does not deal with goodwill or fair value adjustments, which are discussed later.

Financial statements	Parent P Ltd	Subsidiary S Ltd	Adjustments			Consolidation
			Dr	Cr		
Investment in S Ltd	20 000	—		20 000	1	—
Other assets	35 000	27 000				62 000
	55 000	27 000		20 000		£62 000
Share capital	30 000	15 000	1	15 000		30 000
Retained earnings	25 000	12 000	1	5 000		32 000
	55 000	27 000		20 000		£62 000

FIGURE 21.2 Consolidation worksheet — basic format

Note the following points about the worksheet:
- The first column contains the names of the accounts, as the financial statements are combined on a line-by-line basis.
- The second and third columns contain the internal financial statements of the parent, P Ltd, and its subsidiary, S Ltd. These statements are obtained from the separate legal entities. The number of columns is expanded if there are more subsidiaries within the group.
- The next set of columns, headed 'Adjustments', are used to make the adjustments required in the consolidation process. These include adjustments for valuations at acquisition date, pre-acquisition equity, and intragroup transactions such as sales of inventory between the parent and subsidiary. The adjustments, written in the form of journal entries, are recorded on the worksheet. Where there are many adjustments, each journal entry should be numbered so that it is clear which items are being affected by a particular adjustment entry. In figure 21.2 there is only one

worksheet entry, hence the number '1' is entered against each adjustment item. The worksheet adjustment entry is:

(1) Share Capital of S	Dr	15 000
(1) Retained Earnings of S (balance at acquisition)	Dr	5 000
Investment in S Ltd	Cr	20 000

- As noted earlier, the process of consolidation is one of adding together the financial statements of the members of the group and making various adjustments. Hence, figures for each line item in the right-hand column, headed 'Consolidation', arise through addition and subtraction as you proceed horizontally across the worksheet.
- The share capital and the retained earnings at acquisition date (on S Ltd's financial statements) are eliminated against the Investment in S Ltd (on P Ltd's financial statements).
- For example, for share capital, retained earnings and the shares in S Ltd, the effect of the adjustments are:

Share capital: £30 000 + £15 000 − £15 000 = £30 000
Retained earnings: £25 000 + £12 000 − £5 000 = £32 000
Investment in S Ltd: £20 000 − £20 000 = £0

The figures in the right-hand column provide the information for the preparation of the consolidated financial statements of the group, P Ltd and S Ltd. Note that the retained earnings reported by the group include only £7 000 of the £15 000 reported by S. This is because S Ltd generated this amount in undistributed profit *since* acquisition. The subsidiary's retained earnings at acquisition amounted to £5 000 whereas at the date of consolidation this amount had increased to £12 000. Only the earnings of the subsidiary post acquisition are attributable to the group's performance and hence only £7 000 is absorbed into the consolidated retained earnings.

In preparing the consolidated financial statements, *no* adjustments are made in the accounting records of the individual entities that constitute the group. The adjusting entries recorded in the columns of the worksheet do not affect the accounts of the individual entities. They are recorded in a separate consolidation journal, not in the journals of any of the entities within the group, and are then recorded on the consolidation worksheet. Hence, where consolidated financial statements are prepared over a number of years, a particular entry (such as a pre-acquisition entry) needs to be made *every time* a consolidation worksheet is prepared, because the entry never affects the actual financial statements of the individual entities.

21.3 THE ACQUISITION ANALYSIS: DETERMINING GOODWILL OR BARGAIN PURCHASE

On acquisition involving 100% of the shares in the acquired entity, there are three main measurement tasks that should be performed at acquisition date. First, the value of consideration paid to the previous shareholders of the acquired entity must be determined. In a simple case, this is the cash amount paid. Often, however, the acquirer uses other payment methods. Under one popular method, the acquirer issues its own shares in return for the shares in the target company (or a combination of cash and shares). In this case, the fair value of the shares issued should be determined. Occasionally, the fair value of the target's shares, rather than the acquirer's, may be measured more reliably and hence used instead (paragraph 33 of IFRS 10). The fair value of the consideration given should also take into account contingent payments (payments that are made in the future to the previous shareholders of the target company if certain conditions are met). These should also be fair-valued (paragraph 37). A slight complication arises when the acquisition is done in steps (step acquisition). For example, in the first step 30% of the target's shares are acquired and in the second step an additional 70% stake is purchased. In such a case the acquirer has to combine the value of consideration transferred in the last stage with the acquisition-date fair value of the initial 30% (paragraphs 41–42). The total of these two components is then regarded as the overall value of the 100% stake assumed *(see section 21.3.2)*.

The second measurement task requires the determination of the fair value of net assets (assets less liabilities) in the target's acquisition-date balance sheet. This typically involves fair-valuing of all on-balance-sheet assets and liabilities, as well as some off-balance-sheet items (e.g. intangible assets and contingent liabilities) *(see chapter 14)*.

The third measurement task is to assess the value of goodwill to show in the consolidated balance sheet. As discussed in chapter 14, this is done by comparing the value of considerations transferred (plus, possibly, the value of a previously held stake) to the fair value of net assets acquired. If the fair value of consideration transferred (plus, possibly, the value of a previously held stake) exceeds that of fair value of net assets acquired, then goodwill arises. If there is no excess whereby the fair value of net assets is higher, then negative goodwill arises. This is regarded as a bargain purchase. In such a case IFRS 10 (paragraph 36) requires the acquirer to conduct a review of its calculations. If the calculations hold, the negative goodwill is recorded in income (paragraph 35).

It should be noted that any acquisition-related costs, such as finders' fees; advisory, legal, accounting, valuation and other professional or consulting fees do not enter the above calculations and they need to be expensed (paragraph 53).

We discuss next several scenarios that may arise on acquisition date.

21.3.1 Parent has no previously held equity interest in the subsidiary

In this case, the parent acquires all the shares of the subsidiary at acquisition date in one transaction. In terms of paragraph 32 of IFRS 3 and as mentioned above, goodwill arises when the consideration transferred (32(a)(i)) is greater than the net fair value of the identifiable assets and liabilities acquired (32(b)). Where the reverse occurs, a gain on bargain purchase is recognised.

An acquisition analysis is conducted at acquisition date because it is necessary to recognise the identifiable assets and liabilities of the subsidiary at fair value, and to determine whether there has been an acquisition of goodwill or a bargain purchase gain.

The first step in the consolidation process is to undertake the above acquisition analysis in order to obtain the information necessary for making both the business combination valuation and pre-acquisition entry adjustments for the consolidation worksheet. Consider the example in figure 21.3.

On 1 July 2013, Parent Ltd acquired all the issued share capital of Sub Ltd (300 000 shares), giving in exchange 100 000 shares in Parent Ltd, these having a fair value of £5 per share. At acquisition date, the statements of financial position of Parent Ltd and Sub Ltd, and the fair values of Sub Ltd's assets and liabilities, were as follows:

	Parent Ltd	Sub Ltd	
	Carrying amount	Carrying amount	Fair value
ASSETS			
Land	£120 000	£150 000	£170 000
Equipment	620 000	480 000	330 000
Accumulated depreciation	(380 000)	(170 000)	
Investment in Sub Ltd	500 000		
Inventory	92 000	75 000	80 000
Cash	15 000	5 000	5 000
Total assets	£967 000	£540 000	£585 000
LIABILITIES AND EQUITY			
Liabilities			
Provisions	30 000	60 000	60 000
Trade and other payables	27 000	34 000	34 000
Tax payable	10 000	6 000	6 000
Total liabilities	£ 67 000	£100 000	£100 000
Equity			
Share capital	550 000	300 000	
Retained earnings	350 000	140 000	
Total equity	900 000	440 000	
Total liabilities and equity	£967 000	£540 000	

At acquisition date, Sub Ltd has an unrecorded patent with a fair value of £20 000, and a contingent liability with a fair value of £15 000. This contingent liability relates to a loan guarantee made by Sub Ltd which did not recognise a liability in its records because it did not consider it could reliably measure the liability. The tax rate is 30%.

FIGURE 21.3 Information at acquisition date

The analysis at acquisition date consists of comparing the fair value of the consideration transferred and the net fair value of the identifiable assets and liabilities of the subsidiary at acquisition date. The net fair value of the subsidiary could be calculated by revaluing the assets and liabilities of the subsidiary from the carrying amounts to fair values, remembering that under IAS 12 *Income Taxes* where there is a difference between the carrying amount and the tax base caused by the revaluation, the tax effect of such a difference has to be recognised. However, in calculating the net fair value of the subsidiary, because particular information is required to prepare the valuation and pre-acquisition entries, the calculation is done by adding the recorded equity of the subsidiary (which represents the recorded net assets of the subsidiary) and the differences between the carrying amounts of the assets and liabilities and their fair values, adjusted for tax. The book equity of the subsidiary in figure 21.3 consists of:

£300 000 capital + £140 000 retained earnings

These fair value adjustments, are recorded initially against the *business combination valuation reserve* (BCVR). This reserve is not an account recognised in the subsidiary's records, but it is recognised in the consolidation process as part of the business combination. For example, for land there is a difference of £20 000 in the fair value carrying amount and, on revaluation of the land to fair value, a business combination valuation reserve of £14 000 (i.e. £20 000 (1 − 30%)) is raised. The total of pre-tax fair value adjustments is £50 000, giving rise to deferred tax liability of £15 000.

The acquisition analysis, including the determination of the goodwill of the subsidiary, is as shown in figure 21.4.

	Sub Ltd		
	Carrying amount	Fair value adjustment	Fair value
ASSETS			
Land	£150 000	£20 000	£170 000
Equipment	310 000	20 000	330 000
Patent		20 000	20 000
Inventory	75 000	5 000	80 000
Cash	5 000		5 000
Total assets	£540 000	£65 000	£605 000
LIABILITIES			
Provisions	60 000		60 000
Trade and other payables	34 000		34 000
Contingent liability — loan guarantee		15 000	15 000
Deferred tax liability		15 000	15 000
Tax payable	6 000		6 000
Total liabilities	100 000	30 000	130 000
Net Assets	£440 000	£35 000	£475 000
Determination of goodwill:			
1 July 2013			
Consideration paid	500 000		
Less: Fair value of net assets acquired	475 000		
Goodwill	£ 25 000		

FIGURE 21.4 Acquisition analysis — no previously held equity interests

The information from the completed acquisition analysis is used to prepare the adjustment entries for the consolidation worksheet. These entries are illustrated below (*see section 21.4*).

In this book, it is assumed that the tax base of the subsidiary's assets and liabilities is unchanged as a result of the parent's acquisition of the subsidiary. In some jurisdictions, where the group becomes the taxable entity, there is a change in the tax base to the fair value amounts. In this case, no tax effect would be recognised in relation to the assets and liabilities acquired.

21.3.2 Parent has previously held equity interest in the subsidiary

The situation used in figure 21.3 will be used here with the only difference being that on 1 July 2013 Parent Ltd acquires 80% of the shares in Sub Ltd, giving in exchange 80 000 shares in Parent Ltd, these having a fair value of £5 per share. Parent Ltd had previously acquired the other 20% stake in Sub Ltd for £75 000. At 30 June 2013, this investment in Sub Ltd was recorded at £92 000. The appreciation in value was recorded in income since the investment was classified as an equity instrument and measured at fair value through income. At 1 July 2013, these shares had been reassessed to have a fair value of £100 000.

In accordance with IFRS 3 paragraph 42, Parent Ltd revalues the previously held investment to fair value, recognising the increase in profit or loss. If previously changes in fair value are recognized in other comprehensive income, then these amounts are then taken into profit or loss as a reclassification adjustment. The journal entries in Parent Ltd at acquisition date, both for the previously held investment as well as the acquisition of the remaining shares in Sub Ltd, are as follows:

Investment in Sub Ltd	Dr	8 000	
Profit or Loss	Cr		8 000
(Revaluation to fair value)			
Investment in Sub Ltd	Dr	400 000	
Share Capital	Cr		400 000
(Acquisition of shares in Sub Ltd: 80 000 at £5 per share)			

The determination of goodwill is shown in figure 21.5.

Determination of goodwill:	
1 July 2013	
Value of previously acquired 20% stake	£100 000
Consideration paid	400 000
	500 000
Less: Fair value of net assets acquired	475 000
Goodwill	£ 25 000

FIGURE 21.5 Determination of goodwill — previously held equity interests

As a result of the numbers used in this example, the goodwill number is the same as that shown in figure 21.4. There are no subsequent effects on the consolidation process because the parent had previously held an investment in the subsidiary.

21.4 WORKSHEET ENTRIES AT THE ACQUISITION DATE

As noted earlier, the consolidation process does not result in any entries being made in the actual records of either the parent or the subsidiary. The adjustment entries are made in the consolidation worksheet. Hence, adjustment entries need to be passed each time a worksheet is prepared, and these entries change over time. In this section, the adjustment entries that would be passed in a consolidation worksheet prepared *immediately after the acquisition date* are analysed.

21.4.1 Business combination valuation entries

In figure 21.3, there are three identifiable assets recognised by the subsidiary whose fair values differ from their carrying amounts at acquisition date, as well as an intangible asset and a contingent liability recognised as part of the business combination. The entries for the business combination valuations are done in the consolidation worksheet rather than in the records of the subsidiary *(see section 21.6 for a discussion on making these adjustments in the records of the subsidiary itself).*

The identifiable assets and liabilities that require adjustment to fair value can be easily identified by reference to the acquisition analyses in figures 21.4 and 21.5, namely land, equipment, inventory, patent and the unrecorded guarantee. Goodwill also has to be recognised on consolidation. These differences are all recognised using business combination valuation entries. Consolidation worksheet adjustment entries for each of these assets and the unrecorded liability are given in figure 21.6.

Business combination valuation entries			
(1) Land	Dr	20 000	
Deferred Tax Liability	Cr		6 000
Business Combination Valuation Reserve	Cr		14 000
(2) Accumulated Depreciation – Equipment	Dr	170 000	
Equipment	Cr		150 000
Deferred Tax Liability	Cr		6 000
Business Combination Valuation Reserve	Cr		14 000
(3) Inventory	Dr	5 000	
Deferred Tax Liability	Cr		1 500
Business Combination Valuation Reserve	Cr		3 500
(4) Patent	Dr	20 000	
Deferred Tax Liability	Cr		6 000
Business Combination Valuation Reserve	Cr		14 000
(5) Business Combination Valuation Reserve	Dr	10 500	
Deferred Tax Asset	Dr	4 500	
Provision for Loan Guarantee	Cr		15 000
(6) Goodwill	Dr	25 000	
Business Combination Valuation Reserve	Cr		25 000

FIGURE 21.6 Business combination valuation entries at acquisition date

The total balance of the business combination valuation reserve at this stage is £60 000. It will be cancelled to zero when the pre-acquisition entries are processed. The adjustments to assets and liabilities at acquisition date could be achieved by one adjusting entry, giving a net balance to the business combination valuation reserve. However, in order to keep track of movements in that reserve as assets are depreciated or sold, liabilities paid or goodwill impaired, it is practical to prepare a valuation entry for each component of the valuation process. The valuation entries are passed in the adjustment columns of the worksheet, *which is illustrated in section 21.4.3*. Note that, in relation to entry (6) for goodwill, there is no deferred tax liability. This is because paragraph 21 of IAS 12 states that no such deferred tax liability is recognised, as goodwill is measured as a residual, and the recognition of a deferred tax liability would increase its carrying amount. Further, note that the goodwill is recognised on the consolidated balance sheet and not on the balance sheet of the acquiring company.

21.4.2 Pre-acquisition entries

As noted in paragraph B86(b) of IFRS 10, an entry is required to eliminate the carrying amount of the parent's investment in the subsidiary against the parent's stake in the subsidiary's equity.

The investment in subsidiary on the parent's balance sheet represents the underlying assets and liabilities. As the consolidation process adds the net assets of the parent and subsidiary together to form the consolidated balance sheet, the investment in the subsidiary on the parent's balance sheet is eliminated to avoid double counting.

When the parent holds 100% of outstanding shares, this implies a full elimination of the subsidiary's equity as at the acquisition date. However, when the parent holds less than 100%, then the investment account is eliminated against the relevant portion of the subsidiary's equity on acquisition date *(see chapter 23)*. The pre-acquisition entries, then, involve two areas:

• the Investment in Subsidiary, as shown in the financial statements of the parent
• the equity of the subsidiary at the acquisition date (i.e. the pre-acquisition equity). The pre-acquisition equity is not just the equity recorded by the subsidiary but includes the business combination valuation reserve recognised on consolidation via the valuation entries.

Using the example in figure 21.3, and reading the information from the acquisition analysis in figure 21.4 (including the business combination valuation reserve for the revalued assets including goodwill and the contingent liability), the pre-acquisition entry at acquisition date is as shown in figure 21.7. The pre-acquisition entry in this figure is numbered (7) because there were six previous valuation entries.

			Dr		
Pre-acquisition entry					
(7) Retained Earnings (1 July 2013)			Dr	140 000	
Share Capital			Dr	300 000	
Business Combination Valuation Reserve			Dr	60 000	
Investment in Sub Ltd			Cr		500 000

FIGURE 21.7 Pre-acquisition entry at acquisition date

The pre-acquisition entry is necessary to avoid overstating the equity and net assets of the group. To illustrate, consider the information in figure 21.3 relating to Parent Ltd's acquisition of the shares of Sub Ltd. Having acquired the shares in Sub Ltd, Parent Ltd records the asset 'Investment in Sub Ltd' at £500 000. This asset represents the actual net assets of Sub Ltd; that is, the ownership of the shares gives Parent Ltd the right to the net assets of Sub Ltd. To include both the asset 'Investment in Sub Ltd' and the net assets of Sub Ltd in the consolidated statement of financial position would double count the assets of the group, because the investment account is simply the right to the other assets. On consolidation, the investment account is therefore eliminated and, in its place, the net assets of the subsidiary are included in the consolidated statement of financial position.

Similarly, to include both the equity of the parent and the equity of the subsidiary in the consolidated statement of financial position would double-count the equity of the group. In the example, Parent Ltd has equity of £900 000, which is represented by its net assets including the investment in the subsidiary. Because the investment in the subsidiary is the same as the net assets of the subsidiary, the equity of the parent effectively relates to the net assets of the subsidiary. To include in the consolidated statement of financial position the equity of the subsidiary at acquisition date as well as the equity of the parent would double-count equity in relation to the net assets of the subsidiary.

The credit balance on the business combination valuation reserve is also eliminated as it represents a valuation adjustment to the net assets of Sub Ltd and is also included in the £500 000 acquisition price.

21.4.3 Consolidation worksheet

Figure 21.8 contains the consolidation worksheet prepared at acquisition date, with adjustments being made for business combination valuation and pre-acquisition entries. The right-hand column reflects the consolidated statement of financial position, showing the position of the group. In relation to the figures in this column, note the following:

- In relation to the two equity accounts — share capital and retained earnings — only the parent's balances are carried into the consolidated statement of financial position. At acquisition date, all the equity of the subsidiary is pre-acquisition and eliminated as well as the business combination reserve. With the business combination valuation reserve, the valuation entry establishes the reserve, and the pre-acquisition entry eliminates it because it is by nature pre-acquisition equity.
- The assets of the subsidiary are carried forward into the consolidated statement of financial position at fair value.
- The adjusting journal entries have equal debits and credits (as shown in the line 'Total adjustments'), which is essential if the statement of financial position is to balance.

FIGURE 21.8 Consolidation worksheet at acquisition date

Financial statements	Parent Ltd	Sub Ltd	Adjustments					Consolidation
				Dr		Cr		
ASSETS								
Land	£ 120 000	£ 150 000	1	£ 20 000				£ 290 000
Equipment	620 000	480 000			150 000		2	950 000
Accumulated depreciation	(380 000)	(170 000)	2	170 000				(380 000)
Investment in Sub Ltd	500 000	—			500 000		7	—
Inventory	92 000	75 000	3	5 000				172 000
Cash	15 000	5 000						20 000
Patent	—	—	4	20 000				20 000
Goodwill	—	—	6	25 000				25 000
Total assets	£ 967 000	£ 540 000						£1 097 000

(continued)

FIGURE 21.8 *(continued)*

Provisions	£ 30 000	£ 60 000			£ 15 000		5	£ 105 000
Trade and other payables	27 000	34 000						61 000
Tax payables	10 000	6 000						16 000
Deferred tax liability			5	4 500	6 000		1	
					6 000		2	
					1 500		3	
					6 000		4	15 000
Total Liabilities	£ 67 000	£ 100 000						£ 197 000
EQUITY								
Share capital	550 000	300 000	7	300 000				550 000
Retained earnings								
(1 July 2013)	350 000	140 000	7	140 000				350 000
	900 000	440 000						900 000
Total liabilities and equity	£ 967 000	£ 540 000						£1 097 000
Business combination valuation reserve			5	10 500	14 000		1	
			7	60 000	14 000		2	
					3 500		3	
					14 000		4	
					25 000		6	
Total adjustment				£ 75 500	£ 75 500			

21.4.4 Subsidiary has recorded dividends at acquisition date

Using the information in figure 21.3, assume that one of the trade and other payables at acquisition date is a dividend payable of £10 000. The parent can acquire the shares in the subsidiary on a *cum div.* or an *ex div.* basis.

If the shares are acquired on a *cum div. basis*, then the parent acquires the right to the dividend declared at acquisition date. In this case, if Parent Ltd pays £500 000 for the shares in Sub Ltd, then the right to receive dividend effectively reduces the consideration given by £10 000 to £490 000. The entry it passes to record the business combination is:

Investment in Sub Ltd	Dr	490 000	
Dividend Receivable	Dr	10 000	
Share Capital	Cr		500 000

In other words, the parent acquires two assets — the investment in the subsidiary and the dividend receivable. In calculating the goodwill in the subsidiary therefore, the consideration given is £490 000. Deducting the fair value of net assets received of £475 000 then results in goodwill of £15 000. The pre-acquisition entry is:

(7) Retained Earnings (1 July 13)	Dr	140 000	
Share Capital	Dr	300 000	
Business Combination Valuation Reserve	Dr	50 000	
Investment in Shares in Sub Ltd	Cr		490 000

A further consolidation worksheet entry is also required:

Dividend Payable	Dr	10 000	
Dividend Receivable	Cr		10 000

This entry is necessary so that the consolidated statement of financial position shows only the assets and liabilities of the group; that is, only those benefits receivable from and obligations payable to entities external to the group. In relation to the dividend receivable recorded by Parent Ltd, this is not an asset of the group, because that entity does not expect to receive dividends from a party external to it. Similarly, the dividend payable recorded by the subsidiary is not a liability of the group. That dividend will be paid within the group, not to entities outside the group.

If the shares are acquired on an *ex div. basis*, then the parent only acquires the shares, as the dividend will be paid to previous shareholders and not the parent company. The dividend has no effect on the acquisition analysis. If Parent Ltd had paid £500 000 for the shares in Sub Ltd on an *ex div. basis*, then the acquisition analysis is:

Net fair value of identifiable assets and liabilities of Sub Ltd	= £475 000 (see the *cum div.* basis)
Consideration transferred	= 100 000 shares × £5 = £500 000
Goodwill	= 500 000 − 475 000
	= 25 000

The pre-acquisition entry is:

Retained Earnings (1/7/13)	Dr	140 000	
Share Capital	Dr	300 000	
Business Combination Valuation Reserve	Dr	60 000	
Investment in in Sub Ltd	Cr		500 000

21.4.5 Gain on bargain purchase

In figure 21.3, Parent Ltd paid £500 000 for the shares in Sub Ltd. Consider the situation where Parent Ltd paid £470 000 for these shares. The gain on bargain purchase analysis is as shown in figure 21.9.

Determination of gain on bargain purchase:	
1 July 2013	
Consideration paid	£470 000
Less: Fair value of net assets acquired	475 000
Gain on bargain purchase	5 000

FIGURE 21.9 Gain on bargain purchase

As the net fair value of the identifiable assets and liabilities of the subsidiary is greater than the consideration transferred, in accordance with paragraph 36 of IFRS 3 the acquirer must firstly reassess the identification and measurement of the subsidiary's identifiable assets and liabilities as well as the measurement of the consideration transferred. The expectation under IFRS 3 is that the excess of the net fair value over the consideration transferred is usually the result of measurement errors rather than being a real gain to the acquirer. However, having confirmed the identification and measurement of both amounts paid and net assets acquired, if an excess still exists, under paragraph 34 it is recognised immediately in the consolidated (rather than the acquirer's) profit as a gain on bargain purchase. This may happen, for example, when the subsidiary is in poor financial health and the subsidiary's shareholders are forced to offer a discount to a potential buyer.

Existence of a gain on bargain purchase implies that the entry (6) in Figure 21.6 cannot be passed. However, if the subsidiary has previously recorded goodwill a business combination revaluation a business combination revaluation entry crediting goodwill and debiting business combination valuation reserve for the amount of goodwill recorded by the subsidiary would be required. The reason for this is that if the acquisition price paid by the parent is less than the subsidiary's identifiable net assets, this implies that no goodwill can exist in the subsidiary.

With a bargain purchase we replace entry (6) in Figure 21.6, as follows:

(6) Business Combination Valuation Reserve	Dr	5 000	
Gain on Bargain Purchase	Cr		5 000

The pre-acquisition entry for the situation in figure 21.9 is as shown in figure 21.10.

Pre-acquisition entry			
(7) Retained Earnings (1 July 2013)	Dr	140 000	
Share Capital	Dr	300 000	
Business Combination Valuation Reserve	Dr	30 000	
Investment in Sub Ltd	Cr		470 000

FIGURE 21.10 Pre-acquisition entry at acquisition date — gain on bargain purchase

21.5 WORKSHEET ENTRIES SUBSEQUENT TO THE ACQUISITION DATE

At acquisition date, the business combination valuation entries result in the economic entity recognising assets and liabilities not recorded by the subsidiary. Subsequently, changes in these assets and liabilities occur as assets are depreciated or sold, liabilities paid and goodwill impaired. Movements in the subsidiary's equity also occur as dividends are paid or declared and transfers are made within equity.

21.5.1 Business combination valuation entries

In the example used in figure 21.3, there were five items for which valuation entries were made — land, equipment, inventory, patent and the guarantee (a contingent liability). In this section, a 3-year time period subsequent to the acquisition date, 1 July 2013, is analysed (giving an end of reporting period of 30 June 2016) with the following events occurring:

- the land is sold in the 2015/16 period, for net proceeds of £199 000
- the equipment is depreciated on a straight-line basis over a 5-year period
- the inventory on hand at 1 July 2013 is all sold by 30 June 2014, the end of the first year
- the patent has an indefinite life, and is tested for impairment annually, with an impairment loss of £5000 recognised in the 2014/15 period
- the liability for the guarantee results in a payment of £10 000 in June 2014, with no further liability existing
- goodwill is written down by £5000 in the 2014/15 period as a result of an impairment test (*see chapter 15 for impairment of goodwill*).

The statements of financial position of Parent Ltd and Sub Ltd, and the fair values of Sub Ltd's assets and liabilities, as of 30 June 2016 are shown in figure 21.11.

	Parent Ltd	Sub Ltd	
	Carrying amount	Carrying amount	Fair value of net assets acquired on 1 July 2013 that are still included in Sub Ltd's balance sheet
Assets			
Land	£170 000	£50 000	
Equipment	750 000	680 000	£530 000
Accumulated depreciation	(448 000)	(456 000)	(298 000)
Patent			15 000
Investment in shares in Sub Ltd	500 000		
Inventory	52 000	75 000	
Cash	65 000	95 000	
Total assets	**£1 089 000**	**£444 000**	
Equity and Liabilities			
Provisions	40 000	40 000	
Trade and other payables	32 000	24 000	
Tax payable	12 000	16 000	
Total liabilities	**£84 000**	**£80 000**	
Equity			
Share capital	550 000	300 000	
Retained earnings	455 000	64 000	
Total equity	**£1 005 000**	**£364 000**	
Total liabilities and equity	**£1 089 000**	**£444 000**	

FIGURE 21.11 Statements of financial position at 30 June 2016

The income statements for Parent Ltd and Sub Ltd for the year ended 30 June 2016 are shown in figure 21.12.

Income statements	Parent Ltd	Sub Ltd
Revenue	120 000	95 000
Expenses	85 000	72 000
	35 000	23 000
Gain on sale of non-current assets	15 000	31 000
Profit before tax	50 000	54 000
Income tax expense	15 000	21 000
Profit for the period	35 000	33 000
Retained earnings (1 July 2015)	420 000	220 000
Retained earnings (30 June 2016)	455 000	253 000

FIGURE 21.12 Income statements at 30 June 2016

We next analyse the effect of each of these items on the consolidation process.

Equipment

Of net assets acquired on 1 July 2013, the subsidiary's statement of financial position features only the equipment and the patent. The equipment had a remaining useful life of 5 years on acquisition date. Hence, Sub Ltd recorded an annual depreciation expense of ((£480 000 − £170 000)/5 = £62 000) bringing total accumulated depreciation for acquisition date's equipment to £356 000 and net book value of £124 000.

However, from the group's perspective the initial fair value adjustment was £20 000. Hence the equipment was restated to £330 000 with zero accumulated depreciation. For the purpose of consolidated statements, therefore, subsequent annual depreciation expense is £66 000, or £4000 higher than what was booked by Sub Ltd. After 3 years the net book value of this equipment is £132 000 (£330 000 − £198 000). Note that the carrying value of the equipment at Sub Ltd's stand-alone balance sheet (£124 000) is lower than the carrying value in the consolidated balance sheet (£132 000). The difference of £8 000 reflects 40% of the fair value adjustment recorded on acquisition date, because the remaining useful life of this adjustment is 2 (out of 5) years.

Note also the effect on the group's earning. The consolidation process effectively absorbs 100% of the profit reported by the subsidiary *since* acquisition. However, the calculation of this profit, which is reflected in Sub Ltd's equity, is *not* based on acquisition date's fair values. Hence, relative to the group, over the 3-year period, Sub Ltd's pre-tax profits are higher by £12 000 owing to lower annual depreciation expense (£32 000 vs. £36 000). After tax, Sub Ltd's retained earnings are higher by £8 400. The £8 400 reduction in retained earnings is split between a reduction of £5 600 to opening retained earnings, and a reduction to the 2014/15 after-tax profit of £2 800 (£4000 depreciation less £1200 tax saving).

Valuation entry for 2015/16 is shown in figure 21.13.

(1) Accumulated Depreciation — Equipment	Dr	158 000	
Depreciation Expense	Dr	4 000	
Retained Earnings — 30 June 2015	Dr	5 600	
Equipment — Cost	Cr		150 000
Deferred Tax Liability	Cr		2 400
Tax Expense	Cr		1 200
Business Combination Valuation Reserve	Cr		14 000

FIGURE 21.13 Business combination valuation entries at 30 June 2016

Note that the total effect on consolidated retained earnings as at 30 June 2016 is a reduction of £8400 (£5600 + £4000 − £1200).

Patent

The patent was impaired in 2014/15 to £15 000. Since the patent is not recorded in Sub Ltd's stand-alone balance sheet, the impairment was recorded only in consolidated income in the previous year. Hence, Sub Ltd's retained earnings as of 30 June should be reduced by £3 500 (£5000 × 70%). Deferred tax liability should also be reduced by £1 500 and stand at £400 in the 30 June 2016 consolidated statement of financial position.

Valuation entry for 2015/16:

(2) Patent	Dr	15 000	
Retained Earnings — 30 June 2015	Dr	3 500	
Deferred Tax Liability	Cr		4 500
Business Combination Valuation Reserve	Cr		14 000

Land

The land was sold in 2015/16. Because Sub Ltd recorded a gain that is based on lower carrying value than what was recorded in the 30 June 2015 consolidated balance sheet, its 2015/16 profit is higher by £14 000 (£20 000 × 70%). Therefore, this should be deducted from Sub Ltd's income for the year.
Valuation entry for 2015/16:

(3) Gain on Sale of Land	Dr	20 000	
Tax Expense	Cr		6 000
Business Combination Valuation Reserve	Cr		14 000

Inventory

The inventory was sold in 2013/14. Because Sub Ltd recorded gross profit that is based on lower carrying value than what was recorded in the 1 July 2013 consolidated balance sheet, its 2013/14 profit is higher by £3500 (£5000 × 70%).
Valuation entry for 2015/16:

(4) Retained Earnings — 30 June 2015	Dr	3 500	
Business Combination Valuation Reserve	Cr		3 500

Contingent liability

The guarantee liability was originally stated at £15 000 on the acquisition date consolidated balance sheet. Since in 2013/14 the settlement involved a payment of only £10 000, the group needs to record a pre-tax gain of £5 000. Sub Ltd's income statement in 2013/14 recorded a pre-tax loss of £10 000, because in its stand-alone balance sheet on 1 July 2013 no liability was recognised for the guarantee. Hence there is a difference of £15 000 between Sub Ltd's income and the group's income. Sub Ltd's retained earnings need to be increased by £10 500 (£15 000 × 70%) in the consolidation process.
Valuation entry for 2015/16:

(5) Business Combination Valuation Reserve	Dr	10 500	
Retained Earnings — 30 June 2015	Cr		10 500

The above analysis is summarised in the tables below:

	Analysis of effect of acquisition-date adjustments on subsequent balance sheet				
			Effect on		
	(1)	(2)	(3)	(4)	(5)
	Balance sheet 30 June 2016	Balance sheet 1 July 2013	Deferred tax liability 30 June 2016	Deferred tax liability 1 July 2013	Retained earnings 30 June 2016
Equipment	−150 000	−150 000			
Accumulated Depreciation	158 000	170 000			
	8 000	20 000	2 400	6 000	(8 400)
Land	0	20 000	0	6 000	(14 000)
Patent	15 000	20 000	4 500	6 000	(3 500)
Inventory	0	5 000		1 500	(3 500)
Contingent Liability — Guarantee	0	(15 000)	0	(4 500)	10 500
Total	**£23 000**	**£50 000**	**£6 900**	**£15 000**	**£(18 900)**

			Effect on		
	(1)	(2)	(3)	(4)	(5)
	Balance sheet 30 June 2016	Balance sheet 30 June 2015	Deferred tax liability 30 June 2016	Deferred tax liability 1 July 2013	After-tax profit 2015/16
Equipment	−150 000	−150 000			
Accumulated Depreciation	158 000	162 000			
	8 000	12 000	2 400	3 600	(2 800)
Land	0	20 000	0	6 000	(14 000)
Patent	15 000	15 000	4 500	4 500	0
Inventory	0	0	0	0	0
Contingent Liability — Guarantee	0	0	0	0	0
Total	£23 000	£47 000	£6 900	£14 100	£(16 800)

Analysis of effect of acquisition-date adjustments on 2015/16 profit

Note:
Column (3) = 30% of column (1)
Column (4) = 30% of column (2)
Column (5) = [column (1) − column (2)] − [column (3) − column (4)]

Goodwill

Impairment tests for goodwill are undertaken annually. Goodwill is written down by £5000 in the 2014/15 period as a result of an impairment test. In the consolidation worksheet prepared at 30 June 2015, the business combination valuation entry will recognise the loss and reduction in goodwill. Because goodwill impairment is not tax deductible (i.e. it is a permanent difference) there is no effect on deferred tax liability or tax expense.

Valuation entry for 2015/16:

(6) Retained Earnings — 30 June 2015	Dr	5 000	
Goodwill	Dr	20 000	
Business Combination Valuation Reserve	Cr		25 000

21.5.2 Pre-acquisition entry

With the above entries (1)–(6) recorded, the final entry is to eliminate the investment in Sub Ltd account against the equity of the subsidiary as it was on acquisition date:

(7) Retained Earnings	Dr	140 000	
Share Capital	Dr	300 000	
Business Combination Valuation Reserve	Dr	60 000	
Investment in Sub Ltd	Cr		500 000

We are now ready to prepare the consolidated statement of financial position and income statement (see figure 21.14).

21.5.3 Dividends paid/payable from subsidiary equity

Prior to July 2008, IAS 27 *Consolidated and Separate Financial Statements* described a cost method in relation to accounting for a parent's investment in a subsidiary. The equity of the subsidiary was then classified into pre-acquisition and post-acquisition components based upon whether the equity existed before or after the acquisition date. Dividends from pre-acquisition equity were accounted for as a recovery of a parent's investment in a subsidiary and recognised as a reduction in the cost of the investment. Dividends from post-acquisition equity were accounted for by a parent as revenue.

In 2008, the IASB made amendments to IAS 27. These amendments deleted the definition of the cost method from IAS 27 and required that all dividends paid or payable by a subsidiary were to be accounted for as revenue by the parent.

	Parent Ltd	Sub Ltd	Adjustments			Consolidation
			Dr	Cr		
Assets						
Land	£ 170 000	£ 50 000				£ 220 000
Equipment	750 000	680 000		150 000	1	1 280 000
Accumulated depreciation	(448 000)	(456 000)	1 158 000			(746 000)
Patent			2 15 000			15 000
Investment in Sub Ltd	500 000			500 000	7	
Inventory	52 000	75 000				127 000
Cash	65 000	95 000				160 000
Goodwill			6 20 000			20 000
Total assets	£1 089 000	£ 444 000				£1 076 000
Liabilities						
Provisions	40 000	40 000				80 000
Trade and other payables	32 000	24 000				56 000
Tax payable	12 000	16 000				28 000
Deferred tax liability				2 400	1	6 900
				4 500	2	
Total liabilities	£ 84 000	£ 80 000				£ 170 900
Equity						
Share capital	550 000	300 000	7 300 000			550 000
Retained earnings:						
Revenues	120 000	95 000				215 000
Expenses	85 000	72 000	1 4 000			161 000
	35 000	23 000				54 000
Gain on sale of non-current assets	15 000	31 000	3 20 000			26 000
Profit before tax	50 000	54 000		1 200	1	80 000
Income tax expense	15 000	21 000		6 000	3	28 800
Profit for the period	35 000	33 000	24 000	7 200		51 200
Retained earnings (30 June 2015)			1 5 600	10 500	5	
			2 3 500			
			4 3 500			
			6 5 000			
	420 000	31 000	7 140 000			303 900
Retained earnings (30 June 2016)	455 000	64 000				355 100
Total equity	£1 005 000	£ 364 000	£481 600	£ 17 700		£ 905 100
Total liabilities and equity	£1 089 000	£ 444 000	£481 600	£ 24 600		£1 076 000
Business combination valuation reserve			5 10 500	14 000	1	
			7 60 000	14 000	2	
				14 000	3	
				3 500	4	
				25 000	6	
Total adjustments			£745 100	£745 100		

FIGURE 21.14 Consolidation worksheet at 30 June 2016

In 2011, the International Accounting Standards Board (IASB®) issued a new IAS 27 *Separate Financial Statements*. Paragraph 12 of this standard states:

> An entity shall recognise a dividend from a subsidiary, a joint venture or an associate in profit or loss in its separate financial statements when its right to receive the dividend is established.

Under IAS 27, all dividends paid or payable by the subsidiary to a parent are recognised as revenue in the profit or loss of the parent. In relation to dividends, there is no need to classify the equity of the subsidiary into pre-acquisition and post-acquisition equity. Effectively, all dividends are accounted for as if they are paid from post-acquisition equity.

Paragraphs BC14 to BC20 of IAS 27, as issued in 2011, discuss the reasons for the accounting for dividends received from a subsidiary, a joint venture or an associate. BC14 notes that one of the driving forces for the current accounting for dividends was the problem of classifying equity into pre- and post-acquisition components on first-time adoption of IFRS® Standards by entities. To reduce any risk from removing the cost method and any possible overstatement of income by a parent, the IASB looked at the impairment testing of the investment account recorded by the parent. As a result, as part of the internal sources of information used to determine whether there is any indication of impairment of an asset, paragraph 12(h) of IAS 36 *Impairment of Assets* states:

> for an investment in a subsidiary, joint venture or associate, the investor recognises a dividend from the investment and evidence is available that:
>
> (i) the carrying amount of the investment in the separate financial statements exceeds the carrying amounts in the consolidated financial statements of the investee's net assets, including associated goodwill; or
> (ii) the dividend exceeds the total comprehensive income of the subsidiary, joint venture or associate in the period the dividend is declared.

Bonus share dividends

Bonus share dividends involve a subsidiary issuing shares instead of a cash dividend to shareholders. There are no entries in the records of the parent as a result of this transaction. Hence, the IASB's amendments to IAS 27 do not apply to this transaction. The effect to be adjusted for in the pre-acquisition entry is that this transaction results in moving pre-acquisition equity from one account to another, with no change in total pre-acquisition equity.

Assume that in the 2013/14 period the subsidiary pays a dividend of £3000 by the issue of bonus shares. The entries passed in the parent and the subsidiary as a result of the dividend are:

Parent	Subsidiary			
No entry required	Bonus Dividend Paid	Dr	3 000	
	Share Capital	Cr		3 000

No entry is required by the parent because its share of wealth in the subsidiary is unchanged by the bonus share issue. The pre-acquisition entries for the 2013/14 period are shown in figure 21.15.

Retained Earnings (1 July 2013)	Dr	140 000	
Share Capital	Dr	300 000	
Business Combination Valuation Reserve	Dr	60 000	
Investment in Subsidiary	Cr		500 000
Share Capital	Dr	3 000	
Bonus Dividend Paid	Cr		3 000

FIGURE 21.15 Dividend provided for in the current period.

The effect of the bonus dividend is to increase the share capital of the subsidiary by £3000 and to reduce the retained earnings by the same amount. There is no overall change in the pre-acquisition equity of the subsidiary, just a transfer from one equity account to another. Accordingly, there is no change in the balance of the investment account in the records of the parent.

The pre-acquisition entry in subsequent periods is:

Retained Earnings (opening balance) [£140 000 − £3000]	Dr	137 000	
Share Capital	Dr	303 000	
Business Combination Valuation Reserve	Dr	60 000	
Investment in Subsidiary	Cr		500 000

21.5.4 Pre-acquisition reserve transfers

From time to time the subsidiary may transfer retained earnings to reserves, or make transfers from reserves to retained earnings. These do not cause any change in the total pre-acquisition equity but simply change the composition of that equity. Therefore, there is no change in the investment account recorded by the parent entity. In fact, the parent is unaffected by these transfers. However, the parent needs to decide if for consolidation purposes such transfers should be reflected in consolidated equity. With such approval, there is not anything to account for in the consolidation purpose. For example, if the subsidiary makes a transfer out from retained earnings to a restricted reserve, and this is approved, or even instructed, by the parent, the restricted reserve should appear in the consolidated balance sheet. In what follows, however, we would assume this is not the case.

Assume for the cases illustrated below that the pre-acquisition entry for the year ending 30 June 2014, apart from the effect of reserve transfers, is as follows:

Retained Earnings (1/7/13)	Dr	140 000	
Share Capital	Dr	300 000	
Business Combination Valuation Reserve	Dr	60 000	
Investment in Subsidiary	Cr		500 000

Case 1: Transfers from retained earnings to other reserves

Assume that in the 2013/14 period the subsidiary transfers £4 000 to general reserve from retained earnings. The entry passed in the subsidiary as a result of the transfer is:

Retained Earnings	Dr	4 000	
General Reserve	Cr		4 000

The pre-acquisition entries for the 2013/14 period are shown in figure 21.16.

Retained Earnings (1 July 2013)	Dr	140 000	
Share Capital	Dr	300 000	
Business Combination Valuation Reserve	Dr	60 000	
Investment in Subsidiary	Cr		500 000
General Reserve	Dr	4 000	
Retained Earnings	Cr		4 000

FIGURE 21.16 Transfer to general reserve in the current period

As both the transfer to general reserve and the general reserve accounts are pre-acquisition in nature, they are eliminated as part of the pre-acquisition entry. The pre-acquisition entry in subsequent periods is:

Retained Earnings (opening balance) [£140 000 − £4000]	Dr	136 000	
Share Capital	Dr	300 000	
Business Combination Valuation Reserve	Dr	60 000	
General Reserve	Dr	4 000	
Investment in Subsidiary	Cr		500 000

In this case and in the following cases, the only equity account in which movements (transfers to and from) are specifically identified is retained earnings. Movements within the general reserve account are not specifically noted. This is because, as illustrated in figure 21.13, the retained earnings account and changes therein are used to connect the statement of profit or loss and other comprehensive income accounts and the statement of financial position accounts. In preparing the consolidated statement of changes in equity, where movements in all equity accounts are disclosed, adjustments for pre-acquisition transfers must be taken into account. Whether such adjustments are necessary can be seen from viewing the consolidation worksheet and the adjustments made to individual equity accounts. A similar issue arises in preparing other notes to the consolidated financial statements, such as for property, plant and equipment, where movements such as additions and disposals must be disclosed.

Case 2: Transfers to retained earnings from other reserves

This case uses the information in case 1, in which a £4 000 general reserve was created. Assume that in the 2014/15 period the subsidiary transfers £1 000 to retained earnings from general reserve. The entry passed in the subsidiary as a result of the transfer is:

General Reserve	Dr	1 000	
Retained Earnings	Cr		1 000

The pre-acquisition entries for the 2014/15 period are shown in figure 21.17.

Retained Earnings (1 July 2014)	Dr	136 000	
Share Capital	Dr	300 000	
Business Combination Valuation Reserve	Dr	60 000	
General Reserve	Dr	4 000	
Investment in Subsidiary	Cr		500 000
Retained Earnings	Dr	1 000	
General Reserve	Cr		1 000

FIGURE 21.17 Transfer from general reserve in the current period

Since both the transfer from general reserve and general reserve accounts are pre-acquisition in nature, they are eliminated as part of the pre-acquisition entry. The pre-acquisition entry in subsequent periods is:

Retained Earnings (opening balance) [£140 000 − £4000 + £1000]	Dr	137 000	
Share Capital	Dr	300 000	
Business Combination Valuation Reserve	Dr	60 000	
General Reserve	Dr	3 000	
Investment in Subsidiary	Cr		500 000

21.6 REVALUATIONS IN THE RECORDS OF THE SUBSIDIARY AT ACQUISITION DATE

IFRS 3 does not discuss whether the valuation of the assets of the subsidiary at acquisition date should be done in the consolidation worksheet or in the records of the subsidiary. It is expected that most entities will make their adjustments in the consolidation worksheet, for two reasons:
• Adjustments for assets such as goodwill and inventory are not allowed in the actual records of the subsidiary. Goodwill is not allowed to be revalued because it would amount to the recognition of internally generated goodwill, and inventory cannot be written to an amount greater than cost.
• The revaluation of non-current assets in the records of the subsidiary means that the subsidiary has effectively adopted the revaluation model of accounting for those assets. *As discussed in chapter 11*, IAS 16 *Property, Plant and Equipment* requires the assets to be recorded at amounts not materially different from fair value. For entities wanting to measure assets using the cost model, the revaluation of subsidiary assets would be undertaken in the consolidation worksheet.

Note that the business combination valuation entries applied in the consolidation worksheet for property, plant and equipment assets in this chapter are of the same form as those applied for property, plant and equipment in chapter 11. The revaluation surplus created in the financial statements of the subsidiary will be eliminated as part of the pre-acquisition entries and the underlying asset will be shown on the consolidated statement of financial position at fair value. Hence, the consolidated financial statements at acquisition date are the same regardless of whether revaluation occurs on consolidation or in the records of the subsidiary. In future periods, differences will arise because there is no requirement for valuations done in the consolidation worksheet to be updated for subsequent changes in the fair values of the assets.

21.7 DISCLOSURE

Paragraphs B64–B67 of Appendix B to IFRS 3 cover the disclosure of information about business combinations. These paragraphs require an acquirer to disclose information that enables users of its financial statements to evaluate the nature and financial effect of business combinations that occurred during the reporting period, as well as those that occur between the end of the reporting period and when the financial statements are authorised for issue. Examples of disclosures required by these paragraphs are given in figure 21.18.

FIGURE 21.18 Disclosure of business combinations

Note 4. Business combinations	IFRS 3 paragraph
On 20 October 2013, Libra Ltd acquired 100% of the voting shares of Pisces Ltd, a listed company specialising in the manufacture of electronic parts for sound equipment. The primary reason for the acquisition was to gain access to specialist knowledge relating to electronic systems. Control was obtained by acquisition of all the shares of Pisces Ltd.	B64(a), (b), (c) B64(d)

To acquire this ownership interest, Libra Ltd issued 600 000 ordinary shares, valued at £2.50 per share, which rank equally for dividends after the acquisition date. The fair value is based on the published market price at acquisition date. *B64(f)(iv)*

The total consideration transferred was £1 800 000 and consisted of: *B64(f)*

	£'000
Shares issued, at fair value	1 500
Cash paid	240
Cash payable in 2 years' time	60
Total consideration transferred	1 800

The fair values and the carrying amounts of the assets acquired and liabilities assumed in Pisces Ltd as at 20 October 2013 were *B64(f)*

	Fair value £'000	Carrying amount £'000
Property, plant and equipment	1 240	1 020
Receivables	340	340
Inventory	160	130
Intangibles	302	22
Goodwill	54	0
	2 096	1 512
Payables	152	152
Provisions	103	103
Tax liabilities	41	41
	296	296
Fair value of net assets of Pisces Ltd	1 800	

Goodwill in Pisces Ltd can be attributed to the synergies existing within the company, and relate to the high level of training given to the staff as well as the professional expertise of the employees. Further, there exist in-process research activities in Pisces Ltd for which it was impossible to determine reliable fair values for the separate recognition of intangible assets. *B64(e)*

Pisces Ltd earned a profit for the period from 20 October 2013 to 30 June 2014 of £520 000. This has been included in the consolidated statement of profit or loss and other comprehensive income for the year ended 30 June 2014. *B64(q)(i)*

None of the above information has been prepared on a provisional basis. *B67*

The consolidated profit is shown in the consolidated statement of profit or loss and other comprehensive income at £5 652 000, which includes the £520 000 contributed by Pisces Ltd from 20 October 2013 to the end of the period. If Pisces Ltd had been acquired at 1 July 2013, it is estimated that the consolidated entity would have reported: *B64(q)(ii)*

	£'000
Consolidated revenue	36 654
Consolidated profit	6 341

In relation to the business combination in the 2012/13 period when Libra Ltd acquired all the shares in Orion Ltd, an adjustment was made in the current period relating to the provisional measurement of specialised equipment held by Orion Ltd. A loss of £250 000 was recognised in the current reporting period because of the write-down of this equipment. *B67(a)(iii)*

FIGURE 21.18 *(continued)*

Included in the current period profit are gains on the sale of land acquired as a part of the business combination with Pisces Ltd. The gain amounted to £100 000 and arose due to an upsurge in demand for inner-city properties.	*B67(e)*

Goodwill		*B67(d)*
	£'000	
Gross amount at 1 July 2013	120	
Accumulated impairment losses	(15)	
Carrying amount at 1 July 2013	105	
Goodwill recognised in current period	54	
Carrying amount at 30 June 2014	159	
Gross amount at 30 June 2014	174	
Accumulated impairment losses	(15)	
Carrying amount at 30 June 2014	159	

IFRS 12 *Disclosure of Interests in Other Entities* also requires disclosures in relation to a parent's interest in its subsidiaries. Figure 21.19 illustrates some of these disclosures.

Note 5. Subsidiaries	IFRS 12 paragraph
Aries Ltd has a 40% interest in Virgo Ltd. Although it has less than half the voting power, Aries Ltd believes it has control of the financial and operating policies of Virgo Ltd. Aries Ltd is able to exercise this control because the remaining ownership in Virgo Ltd is diverse and widely spread, with the next single largest ownership block being 11%.	*9(b)*
Aries Ltd has invested in a special purpose entity established by Pictor Ltd. Pictor Ltd established Cetus Ltd as a vehicle for distributing the sailing boats it makes. Aries Ltd currently owns 60% of the shares issued by Cetus Ltd. However, because of the limited decisions that the board of Cetus Ltd can make owing to the constitution of that entity, Aries Ltd believes that it does not have any real control over the operations of Cetus Ltd, so it sees its role in Cetus Ltd as that of an investor.	*9(a)*
Aries Ltd has a wholly owned subsidiary, Gemini Ltd, which operates within the electricity generating industry. The end of its reporting period is 31 May. Gemini Ltd continues to use this date because the government regulating authority requires all entities within the industry to provide financial information to it based on financial position at that date.	*11*
Aries Ltd has a wholly owned subsidiary, Hercules Ltd, in the country of Mambo. Because of constraints on assets leaving the country recently imposed by the new military government, there are major restrictions on the subsidiary being able to transfer funds to Aries Ltd.	*10(b)(i)*

FIGURE 21.19 Disclosures concerning subsidiaries

Disclosures in relation to subsidiaries are set out in IFRS 12 *Disclosure of Interests in Other Entities*, issued in 2011. *These are discussed in chapter 20.* Note, however, the following extract from paragraph 10.
An entity shall disclose information that enables users of its consolidated financial statements
(a) to understand:
   (i) the composition of the group; and
   (ii) the interest that non-controlling interests have in the group's activities and cash flows (paragraph 12); and
(b) to evaluate:
   (i) the nature and extent of significant restrictions on its ability to access or use assets, and settle liabilities, of the group (paragraph 13);
   (ii) the nature of, and changes in, the risks associated with its interests in consolidated structured entities (paragraphs 14–17) . . .

SUMMARY

This chapter covers the preparation of the consolidated financial statements for a group consisting of a parent and a wholly owned subsidiary. Because of the requirements of IFRS 3 to recognise the identifiable assets acquired and liabilities assumed of an acquired entity at fair value, an initial adjustment to be made on consolidation concerns any assets or liabilities for which there are differences between fair value and carrying amount at the acquisition date. Further, although some intangible assets and liabilities of the subsidiary may not have been recognised in the subsidiary's records, they are recognised as part of the business combination.

The preparation of the consolidated financial statements is done using a consolidation worksheet, the left-hand columns of which contain the financial statements of the members of the group. The adjustment columns contain the consolidation worksheet entries that adjust the right-hand columns to form the consolidated financial statements. The adjustment entries have no effect on the actual financial records of the parent and its subsidiaries.

At acquisition date, an acquisition analysis is undertaken. The key purposes of this analysis are to determine the fair values of the identifiable assets and liabilities of the subsidiary, and to calculate any goodwill or gain on bargain purchase arising from the business combination. From this analysis, the main consolidation worksheet adjustment entries at acquisition date are the business combination valuation entries (to adjust carrying amounts of the subsidiaries' assets and liabilities to fair value) and the pre-acquisition entries.

In preparing consolidated financial statements in periods after acquisition date, the consolidation worksheet will contain valuation entries and pre-acquisition entries. However, these entries are not necessarily the same as those used at acquisition date. If there are changes to the assets and liabilities of the subsidiaries since acquisition date, or there have been movements in pre-acquisition equity, changes must be made to these entries.

Discussion questions

1. Explain the purpose of the pre-acquisition entries in the preparation of consolidated financial statements.
2. When there is a dividend payable by the subsidiary at acquisition date, under what conditions should the existence of this dividend be taken into consideration in preparing the pre-acquisition entries?
3. Is it necessary to distinguish pre-acquisition dividends from post-acquisition dividends? Why?
4. If the subsidiary has recorded goodwill in its records at acquisition date, how does this affect the preparation of the pre-acquisition entries?
5. Explain how the existence of a bargain purchase affects the pre-acquisition entries, both in the year of acquisition and in subsequent years.

Exercises

STAR RATING   ★ BASIC   ★★ MODERATE   ★★★ DIFFICULT

| Exercise 21.1 | ACCOUNTING FOR ASSETS AND LIABILITIES |

★ Mensa Ltd has acquired all the shares of Cancer Ltd. The accountant for Mensa Ltd, having studied the requirements of IFRS 3 *Business Combinations*, realises that all the identifiable assets and liabilities of Cancer Ltd must be recognised in the consolidated financial statements at fair value. Although he is happy about the valuation of these items, he is unsure of a number of other matters associated with accounting for these assets and liabilities. He has approached you and asked for your advice.

Required

Write a report for the accountant at Mensa Ltd advising on the following issues:
1. Should the adjustments to fair value be made in the consolidation worksheet or in the accounts of Cancer Ltd?
2. What equity accounts should be used when revaluing the assets, and should different equity accounts such as income (similar to recognition of an excess) be used in relation to recognition of liabilities?
3. Do these equity accounts remain in existence indefinitely, since they do not seem to be related to the equity accounts recognised by Cancer Ltd itself?

CONSOLIDATION WORKSHEET ENTRIES 1 YEAR AFTER ACQUISITION DATE

★ At 1 July 2013, Pisces Ltd acquired all the shares of Ursa Ltd for £283 000. At this date the equity of Ursa Ltd consisted of:

Share capital — 100 000 shares	£200 000
General reserve	50 000
Retained earnings	20 000

All the identifiable assets and liabilities of Ursa Ltd were recorded at amounts equal to fair value except for the following assets:

	Carrying amount	Fair value
Inventory	£ 60 000	£ 65 000
Plant (cost £280 000)	200 000	210 000

The inventory was all sold by 30 June 2014. The plant has a further 5-year life, and depreciation is calculated on a straight-line basis. When revalued assets are sold or fully consumed, any related revaluation surplus is transferred to retained earnings.

The tax rate is 30%.

Required

Prepare the consolidation worksheet entries at 30 June 2014 for the preparation of the consolidated financial statements of Pisces Ltd.

ACQUISITION ANALYSIS, PARENT HOLDS PREVIOUSLY ACQUIRED SHARES IN SUBSIDIARY, WORKSHEET ENTRIES AT ACQUISITION DATE

★ At 1 July 2014, Pavo Ltd acquired 60% of the shares of Octans Ltd for £153 000 on a cum div. basis. Pavo Ltd had acquired 40% of the shares of Octans Ltd 2 years earlier for £80 000. This investment, classified as a financial asset, was recorded using the equity method on 1 July 2014 of £102 000. At 1 July 2014, the equity of Octans Ltd consisted of:

Share capital	£160 000
Retained earnings	40 000

At this date, the identifiable assets and liabilities of Octans Ltd were recorded at fair value except for:

	Carrying amount	Fair value
Inventory	£ 40 000	£ 44 000
Plant (cost £120 000)	100 000	105 000

At 1 July 2014, Octans Ltd's assets and liabilities included a dividend payable of £5 000. An analysis of the unrecorded intangibles of Octans Ltd revealed that the company had unrecorded internally generated brands, considered to have a fair value of £50 000. Further, Octans Ltd had expensed research outlays of £80 000 that were considered to have a fair value of £20 000. In its financial statements at 30 June 2014, Octans Ltd had reported a contingent liability relating to a potential claim by customers for unsatisfactory products, the fair value of the claim being £10 000.

The tax rate is 30%.

Required

Prepare the acquisition analysis at 1 July 2014, and the consolidation worksheet entries for preparation of consolidated financial statements of Pavo Ltd at that date.

BUSINESS COMBINATION VALUATION AND PRE-ACQUISITION ENTRIES

★ On 1 July 2013, Pyxis Ltd acquired all the share capital of Gemini Ltd for £218 500. At this date, Gemini Ltd's equity comprised:

Share capital — 100 000 shares	£100 000
General reserve	50 000
Retained earnings	36 000

All identifiable assets and liabilities of Gemini Ltd were recorded at fair value as at 1 July 2013 except for the following:

	Carrying amount	Fair value
Inventory	£27 000	£35 000
Land	75 000	90 000
Equipment (cost £100 000)	50 000	60 000

The equipment is expected to have a further 10-year life. All the inventory was sold by June 2014. The tax rate is 30%.

On 30 June 2014, the directors of Gemini Ltd decided to transfer £25 000 from the general reserve to retained earnings.

Required

Prepare the consolidation worksheet entries for the preparation of consolidated financial statements for Pyxis Ltd and its subsidiary Gemini Ltd as at:
1. 1 July 2013
2. 30 June 2014.

BARGAIN PURCHASE

★★ The accountant for Carina Ltd, Ms Finn, has sought your advice on an accounting issue that has been puzzling her. When preparing the acquisition analysis relating to Carina Ltd's acquisition of Lyra Ltd, she calculated that there was a gain on bargain purchase of £10 000. Being unsure of how to account for this, she was informed by accounting acquaintances that this should be recognised as income. However, she reasoned that this would have an effect on the consolidated profit in the first year after acquisition date. For example, if Lyra Ltd reported a profit of £50 000, then consolidated profit would be £60 000. She is unsure of whether this profit is all post-acquisition profit or a mixture of pre-acquisition profit and post-acquisition profit.

Required

Compile a detailed report on the nature of an excess, how it should be accounted for and the effects of its recognition on subsequent consolidated financial statements.

PARENT HOLDS PREVIOUSLY ACQUIRED INVESTMENT, CONSOLIDATION WORKSHEET

★★ On 1 December 2009, Reticulum Ltd acquired 20% of the shares of Dorado Ltd for £10 000. These were classified as a financial investment by Reticulum Ltd with changes in fair value being recognised in other comprehensive income. At 30 June 2013, these were recorded at a fair value of £20 400. Reticulum Ltd acquired the remaining 80% of the share capital of Dorado Ltd for £81 600 on 1 July 2013 when the equity of Dorado Ltd consisted of:

Share capital — 50 000 shares	£50 000
Retained earnings	30 000

All identifiable assets and liabilities of Dorado Ltd were recorded at amounts equal to fair value, except as follows:

	Carrying amount	Fair value
Inventory	£20 000	£25 000
Plant (cost £80 000)	60 000	70 000

The plant is expected to have a further useful life of 5 years. All the inventory on hand at 1 July 2013 was sold by 31 December 2013.

The income tax rate is 30%.
At 30 June 2015, the information below was obtained from both entities.

Required

1. Prepare the consolidation worksheet entries for the preparation of consolidated financial statements for Reticulum Ltd and its subsidiary, Dorado Ltd, as at 1 July 2013.
2. Prepare the consolidation worksheet entries and the consolidation worksheet for the preparation of consolidated financial statements for Reticulum Ltd and its subsidiary, Dorado Ltd, as at 30 June 2015.

For the year ending 30 June 2015	Reticulum Ltd	Dorado Ltd
Profit before tax	£ 50 000	£ 40 000
Income tax expense	(20 000)	(15 000)
Profit	30 000	25 000
Retained earnings (1/7/14)	50 000	35 000
	80 000	60 000
Transfer to general reserve (approved by parent)	(20 000)	(5 000)
Retained earnings (30/6/15)	£ 60 000	£ 55 000

Statement of Financial Position 30 June 2015		
Cash	£ 13 000	£ 14 000
Accounts receivable	30 000	25 000
Inventory	70 000	50 000
Investment in Dorado Ltd	102 000	—
Plant	200 000	80 000
Accumulated depreciation	(85 000)	(44 000)
Total assets	£330 000	£125 000
Provisions	65 000	10 000
Payables	20 000	5 000
Total liabilities	£ 85 000	£ 15 000
Share capital	150 000	50 000
General reserve	35 000	5 000
Retained earnings	60 000	55 000
Total equity	245 000	110 000
Total liabilities and equity	£330 000	£125 000

Exercise 21.7 **CONSOLIDATION WORKSHEET**

★★ Cepheus Ltd gained control of Aquarius Ltd by acquiring its share capital on 1 January 2013. The statement of financial position of Aquarius Ltd at that date showed:

Land	£ 20 000	Liabilities	£ 15 000
Plant and machinery	120 000	Share capital	60 000
Accumulated depreciation	(20 000)	Retained earnings	40 000
Inventory	15 000	Asset revaluation surplus	20 000
	£135 000		£135 000

At 1 January 2013, the recorded amounts of Aquarius Ltd's assets and liabilities were equal to their fair values except as follows:

	Carrying amount	Fair value
Plant and machinery	£100 000	£102 000
Inventory	15 000	18 000

Half of this inventory was sold by Aquarius Ltd in the following 12 months. The depreciable assets have a further 5-year life, benefits being received evenly over this period. Any business combination valuation adjustments are made on consolidation. The tax rate is 30%.

At 31 December 2013, the following information was obtained from both entities:

	Cepheus Ltd	Aquarius Ltd
Land	—	£ 20 000
Plant and machinery	£575 000	120 000
Accumulated depreciation	(20 000)	(25 000)
Inventory	15 000	23 000
Investment in Aquarius Ltd	130 000	—
Total assets	£700 000	£138 000
Total liabilities	£ 42 000	£ 4 000
Profit before tax	100 000	15 000
Income tax expense	(20 000)	(5 000)
Profit for the year	80 000	10 000
Retained earnings (1/1/13)	103 000	40 000
	183 000	50 000
Retained earnings (31/12/13)	183 000	50 000
Share capital	445 000	60 000
Retained earnings	173 000	46 000
Asset revaluation surplus*	30 000	24 000
	£700 000	£138 000

*This reserve relates to certain items of plant. At 1/1/13, the balances of the account were £15 000 for Cepheus Ltd and £20 000 for Aquarius Ltd.

Required

1. Prepare the consolidated financial statements for Cepheus Ltd at 31 December 2013.
2. Prepare the valuation and pre-acquisition entries at 31 December 2017, assuming that, on consolidation, business combination valuation reserves are transferred to retained earnings when the related asset is sold or fully consumed.

Exercise 21.8 **REVALUATION IN SUBSIDIARY'S RECORDS**

★★   On 1 July 2013, Cancer Ltd acquired all the shares of Grus Ltd (totalling £40 000) for a cash outlay of £100 000. At that date the other reserves and retained earnings of Grus Ltd were as follows:

General reserve	£30 000
Retained earnings	20 000

All identifiable assets and liabilities of Grus Ltd were recorded at fair value at 1 July 2013 except as follows:

	Carrying amount	Fair value
Land	£30 000	£34 000
Plant (cost £28 000)	20 000	22 000
Inventory	40 000	44 000

The plant has a further 5-year life. Of the inventory on hand at 1 July 2013, 90% was sold by 30 June 2014. The tax rate is 30%.

Required

1. Prepare the consolidation worksheet entries at 30 June 2014 assuming Grus Ltd revalued the land and plant to their fair values in its records just before it was acquired at 1 July 2013.
2. Prepare the consolidation worksheet entries at 30 June 2014 assuming all business combination valuations are made in the consolidation worksheet.
3. If the balance of inventory was sold, what would be the business combination valuation and the pre-acquisition entries at 30 June 2015, assuming requirement 2 above?

CONSOLIDATION WORKSHEET AND RESERVE TRANSFER

★★★

Financial statements	Triangulum Ltd	Cygnus Ltd	Adjustments Dr	Cr	Consolidation
Profit	£ 6 000	£ 4 000			
Retained earnings (1/7/15)	22 000	18 000			
	28 000	22 000			
Transfer from general reserve	5 000	3 000			
Retained earnings (30/6/16)	£33 000	£25 000			

An extract from the consolidation worksheet of Triangulum Ltd and its subsidiary, Cygnus Ltd, as at 30 June 2016, is shown above. Triangulum Ltd acquired all the share capital (cum div.) of Cygnus Ltd on 1 July 2012 for £127 000 when the equity of Cygnus Ltd consisted of:

Share capital	£85 000
General reserve	18 000
Retained earnings	12 000

All the identifiable assets and liabilities of Cygnus Ltd at 1 July 2012 were recorded at fair value except for:

	Carrying amount	Fair value
Plant (cost £100 000)	£80 000	£82 000
Inventory	6 000	7 000

The plant had a further 5-year life. All the inventory was sold by Cygnus Ltd by 22 September 2012. The tax rate is 30%. The liabilities of Cygnus Ltd included a dividend payable of £6000. Cygnus Ltd had not recorded any goodwill. At 1 July 2012, Cygnus Ltd had incurred research and development outlays of £5000, which it had expensed. Triangulum Ltd placed a fair value of £2000 on this item. The project was still in progress at 30 June 2016, with Cygnus Ltd capitalising £3000 in the 2015/16 period. Valuation adjustments are made on consolidation.

The transfer from general reserve during the current period ending 30 June 2016 is from pre-acquisition reserves, and is the only such transfer since the acquisition date.

Required

1. Prepare the consolidation worksheet entries at 30 June 2016.
2. Complete the worksheet extract above.

BARGAIN PURCHASE, CONSOLIDATION WORKSHEET

★★★ The financial statements of Equuleus Ltd and its subsidiary, Fornax Ltd, at 30 June 2015 contained the following information:

	Equuleus Ltd	Fornax Ltd
Land	£ 8 600	£ 5 100
Plant	17 000	8 000
Accumulated depreciation	(5 000)	(1 000)
Financial assets	3 000	2 000
Inventory	3 000	4 000
Cash	300	360
Investment in Fornax Ltd	15 000	—
Total assets	£41 900	£18 460
Liabilities	£ 5 000	£ 1 300

	Equuleus Ltd	Fornax Ltd
Profit before tax	£ 3 200	£ 1 800
Income tax expense	(1 300)	(240)
Profit for the year	1 900	1 560
Retained earnings (1/7/14)	1 500	2 100
	3 400	3 660
Dividend paid	(500)	(0)
Retained earnings (30/6/15)	2 900	3 660
Share capital	25 000	10 000
General reserve	8 000	3 000
Other components of equity*	1 000	500
Total equity	£36 900	£17 160
Total liabilities and equity	£41 900	£18 460

*This relates to the financial assets. The balances of the accounts at 1/7/14 were £1500 (Equuleus Ltd) and £300 (Fornax Ltd).

Equuleus Ltd had acquired all the share capital of Fornax Ltd on 1 July 2013 for £15 000 when the equity of Fornax Ltd consisted of:

Share capital — 10 000 shares	£10 000
General reserve	2 000
Retained earnings	1 500

At the acquisition date by Equuleus Ltd, Fornax Ltd's non-monetary assets consisted of:

	Carrying amount	Fair value
Land	£ 4 000	£6 000
Plant (cost £6000)	5 500	6 500
Inventory	3 000	4 000

The plant had a further 5-year life. All the inventory was sold by 30 June 2014. All valuation adjustments to non-current assets are made on consolidation. The land was sold in January 2015 for £6000. The relevant business combination valuation reserves are transferred, on consolidation, to retained earnings.

The tax rate is 30%.

In September 2013, Fornax Ltd transferred £500 from its general reserve, earned before 1 July 2013, to retained earnings.

Required

Prepare the consolidated financial statements for the year ended 30 June 2015.

22

Consolidation: intragroup transactions

ACCOUNTING STANDARDS IN FOCUS

IFRS 10 *Consolidated Financial Statements*

LEARNING OBJECTIVES

After studying this chapter, you should be able to:

1. explain the need for making adjustments for intragroup transactions
2. prepare worksheet entries for intragroup transactions involving profits and losses in beginning and ending inventory
3. prepare worksheet entries for intragroup services such as management fees
4. prepare worksheet entries for intragroup dividends
5. prepare worksheet entries for intragroup borrowings.

INTRODUCTION

In this chapter, the group under discussion is restricted to one where:
- there are only two entities within the group (i.e. one parent and one subsidiary)
- the parent owns all the shares of the subsidiary.
  Diagrammatically, then, the group is as shown in figure 22.1.

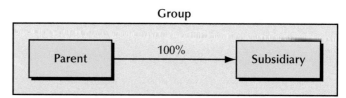

FIGURE 22.1 Group

In chapter 20, it is explained that the process of consolidation involves adding together the financial statements of a parent and its subsidiaries to reflect an overall view of the financial affairs of the group of entities as a single economic entity. It is also pointed out that two major adjustments are necessary to effect the process of consolidation:

(a) adjustments involving equity at the acquisition date, namely the business combination valuation entries (if any) and the elimination of investment in subsidiary, eliminating the investment account in the parent's financial statements against the pre-acquisition equity of the subsidiary *(see chapter 21)*

(b) elimination of intragroup balances and the effects of transactions whereby profits or losses are made by different members of the group through trading with each other.

This chapter focuses on (b), adjustments for intragroup balances and transactions. The chapter analyses transactions involving inventory, depreciable assets, services, dividends and borrowings.

22.1 RATIONALE FOR ADJUSTING FOR INTRAGROUP TRANSACTIONS

Whenever related entities trade with each other, or borrow and lend money to each other, the separate legal entities disclose the effects of these transactions in the assets and liabilities recorded and the profits and losses reported. For example, if a subsidiary sells inventory to its parent, the subsidiary records a sale of inventory, including the profit on sale and reduction in inventory assets, and the parent records the purchase of inventory at the amount paid to the subsidiary. If, then, in preparing the consolidated financial statements, the separate financial statements of the legal entities are simply added together without any adjustments for the effects of the intragroup transactions, the consolidated financial statements include not only the results of the group transacting with external entities (i.e. entities outside the group) but also the results of transactions within the group. This conflicts with the purpose of the consolidated financial statements to provide information about the financial performance and financial position of the group as a result of its dealings with external entities. Hence, the effects of transactions within the group must be adjusted for in the preparation of the consolidated financial statements.

The requirement for the full adjustment for the effects of intragroup transactions is stated in paragraph B86(c) of IFRS 10 *Consolidated Financial Statements*:

> eliminate in full intragroup assets and liabilities, equity, income, expenses and cash flows relating to transactions between entities of the group (profits or losses resulting from intragroup transactions that are recognised in assets, such as inventory and fixed assets, are eliminated in full). Intragroup losses may indicate an impairment that requires recognition in the consolidated financial statements. IAS 12 *Income Taxes* applies to temporary differences that arise from the elimination of profits and losses resulting from intragroup transactions.

Besides adjusting for the effects of transactions occurring in the current period, it is also necessary to adjust the current period's consolidated financial statements for the ongoing effects of transactions in previous periods. Because the consolidation adjustment entries are applied in a worksheet only, and not in the accounts of either the parent or the subsidiary, any continuing effects of previous periods' transactions must be considered. This affects transactions such as loans between, say, a parent and a subsidiary where a balance owing at the end of a number of periods is reduced over time as repayments are made. Similarly, where assets such as inventory are transferred at the end of one period and then are still on hand at the beginning of the next period, consolidation adjustments are required to be made in both periods.

Some intragroup transactions do not affect the carrying amounts of assets and liabilities (e.g. where there is a management fee paid by one entity to another within the group). In that case, the items affected are fee revenue and fee expense. However, in other circumstances, there are assets and liabilities recognised by the group at amounts different from the amounts recognised by the individual legal entities. For example, consider the situation where a subsidiary sold an item of inventory to the parent for $1000 and the inventory had cost the subsidiary $800. The parent recognises the inventory at cost of $1000, whereas the cost of the inventory to the group is only $800. As is explained in more detail later in this chapter, consolidation adjustment entries are necessary to adjust for both the profit on the intragroup transaction and the carrying amount of the inventory.

Under IAS 12 *Income Taxes*, deferred tax accounts must be raised where there are temporary differences between the carrying amount of an asset or liability and its tax base. Any difference between the carrying amount of an asset or a liability and its tax base in a legal entity within the group is accounted for by the legal entity. However, on consolidation, in relation to intragroup transactions, adjustments may be made to the carrying amounts of assets and liabilities. Hence, in adjusting for intragroup transactions wherever there are changes to the carrying amounts of assets and liabilities, any associated tax effect must be considered. Paragraph B86(c) of IFRS 10 recognises the need to apply tax-effect accounting for temporary differences arising from the elimination of profits and losses from intragroup transactions.

For example, assume an asset is recorded by a subsidiary at a carrying amount of $1000, and that the tax base is $800. In the records of the subsidiary, the application of tax-effect accounting will account for the temporary difference of $200, raising a deferred tax liability of $60, assuming a tax rate of 30%. If, on consolidation, an adjustment is made to reduce the carrying amount of the asset, say to $950, the consolidation adjustment entries must include an adjustment for the tax effect of the change in the carrying amount of the asset, namely a reduction in the deferred tax liability of $15 (i.e. 30% × $50). The consolidated financial statements then show a deferred tax liability of $45 (i.e. $60 − $15). The combination of the tax-effect entries in the subsidiaries and the tax-effect adjustments on consolidation will account for the temporary difference caused by the group showing the asset at $950 and the tax base being $800, namely a deferred tax liability of $45 (i.e. 30% × ($950 − $800)).

As can be seen in this example, in preparing the consolidation adjustments it is unnecessary to consider the tax-effect entries made in the individual entities in the group. If the appropriate tax-effect adjustments are made for changes in the carrying amounts of the assets, then the combination of those adjustments and the tax-effect entries made in the entities themselves will produce the correct answer.

In this book, it is assumed that each subsidiary is a tax-paying entity. Under the tax consolidation system in some countries, groups comprising a parent and its wholly owned subsidiaries can elect to consolidate and be treated as a single entity for tax purposes. Such entities prepare a consolidated tax return, and the effects of intragroup transactions are eliminated. Under such a scheme, the tax-effect adjustments demonstrated in this chapter would not apply.

Just as the elimination of investment in subsidiary is used in a consolidation worksheet to eliminate the investment and to adjust for pre-acquisition equity, adjustment journal entries are prepared for intragroup transactions and are recorded in the consolidation worksheet. The same two adjustment columns are used to effect these adjustments. For example, if it were necessary to adjust downwards by $10 000 the sales revenue recorded by the legal entities, the consolidation worksheet would show the following line:

			Adjustments		
	Parent	Subsidiary	Dr	Cr	Group
Sales revenue	100 000	80 000	10 000		170 000

In the following sections of this chapter, two types of intragroup transactions are discussed — transfers of inventory and intragroup services. In each of the specific sections covering these transactions, the process of determining when profits are realised for the different types of transactions is discussed.

22.2 TRANSFERS OF INVENTORY

In the following examples, assume that Jessica Ltd owns all the share capital of Amelie Ltd, and that the consolidation process is being carried out on 30 June 2016, for the year ending on that date. Assume also a tax rate of 30%. All entries shown as being for the individual entities assume the use of a perpetual inventory system, and adjustments will be made, where necessary, to cost of sales.

22.2.1 Sales of inventory

Example: Intragroup sales of inventory

On 1 January 2016, Jessica Ltd acquired $10 000 worth of inventory for cash from Amelie Ltd. The inventory had previously cost Amelie Ltd $8000.

In the accounting records of Amelie Ltd, the following journal entries are made on 1 January 2016:

Cash	Dr	10 000	
Sales Revenue	Cr		10 000
Cost of Sales	Dr	8 000	
Inventory	Cr		8 000

In Jessica Ltd, the journal entry is:

| Inventory | Dr | 10 000 | |
| Cash | Cr | | 10 000 |

From the viewpoint of the group in relation to this transaction, no sales of inventory were made to any party outside the group, nor has the group acquired any inventory from external entities. Hence, if the financial statements of Jessica Ltd and Amelie Ltd are simply added together for consolidation purposes, 'sales', 'cost of sales' and 'inventory' will need to be adjusted on consolidation as the consolidated financial statements must show only the results of transactions with entities external to the group.

22.2.2 Realisation of profits or losses

Paragraph B86(c) of IFRS 10 states that the profits and losses resulting from intragroup transactions that require consolidation adjustments to be made are those 'recognised in assets'. These profits can be described as 'unrealised profits'. The test for realisation is the involvement of an external party in relation to the item involved in the intragroup transaction. If an item of inventory is transferred from a subsidiary to the parent entity (or vice versa), no external party is involved in that transaction. The profit made by the subsidiary is unrealised to the group. If the parent then sells that inventory item to a party external to the group, the intragroup profit becomes realised to the group. For example, assume a subsidiary, Amelie Ltd, sells inventory to its parent, Jessica Ltd, for $100, and that inventory cost Amelie Ltd $90. The profit on this transaction is unrealised. If Jessica Ltd sells the inventory to an external party for $100, the intragroup profit is realised. The group sold inventory that cost the group $90 to an external party for $100. The group has made $10 profit. Hence, the consolidation adjustments for profits on intragroup transfers of inventory depend on whether the acquiring entity has sold the inventory to entities outside the group. In other words, the adjustments depend on whether the acquiring entity still carries some or all of the transferred inventory as ending inventory at the end of the financial period.

22.2.3 Profits in ending inventory

The following example uses the information in the example in section 22.2.1 and provides information about whether the inventory transferred is still on hand at the end of the financial period.

Example: Transferred inventory still on hand

On 30 June 2016, all the inventory sold by Amelie Ltd to Jessica Ltd is still on hand. The adjustment entries in the consolidation worksheet at 30 June 2016 are:

Sales Revenue	Dr	10 000	
Cost of Sales	Cr		8 000
Inventory	Cr		2 000

The sales adjustment is necessary to eliminate the effects of the original sale in the current period. Amelie Ltd recorded sales of $10 000. From the group's viewpoint, as no external party was involved in the transaction, no sales should be shown in the consolidated financial statements. To adjust sales revenue downwards, a debit adjustment is necessary. The effect of this adjustment on the consolidation process is seen in figure 22.2. Hence, an adjustment is necessary to eliminate the sales recorded by Amelie Ltd.

Using similar reasoning as with the adjustment for sales revenue, the subsidiary has recorded cost of sales of $8000, but the group has made no sales to entities external to the group. Hence, the consolidation worksheet needs to have a reduction in cost of sales of $8000 in order to show a zero amount in the consolidation column. Note also that adjusting sales by $10 000 and cost of sales by $8000 effectively reduces consolidated profit by $2000. In other words, the $2000 profit recorded by Amelie Ltd on selling inventory to Jessica Ltd is eliminated and a zero profit is shown on consolidation. As no external party was involved in the transfer of inventory, the whole of the profit on the intragroup transaction is unrealised. This is illustrated in figure 22.2.

			Adjustments			
	Parent	Subsidiary		Dr	Cr	Group
Sales revenue	0	10 000	1	10 000		—
Cost of sales	0	8 000			8 000	1	—
		2 000				
Tax expense	0	600			600	2	—
Profit		1 400				—
Inventory	10 000	—			2 000	1	8 000
Deferred tax asset	—	—	2	600		600

FIGURE 22.2 Extract from consolidation worksheet — profit in closing inventory

The previous explanation dealing with the effect on profit covers only the statement of profit or loss and other comprehensive income part of the adjustment. Under the historical cost system, assets in the consolidated statement of financial position must be shown at cost to the group. Inventory is recorded in Jessica Ltd at $10 000, the cost to Jessica Ltd. The cost to the group is, however, $8000, the amount that was paid for the inventory by Amelie Ltd to entities external to the group. Hence, if inventory is to be reported at $8000 in the consolidated financial statements, and it is recorded in Jessica Ltd's records at $10 000, a credit adjustment of $2000 is needed to reduce the inventory to $8000, the cost to the group. This effect is seen in figure 22.2.

Jessica Ltd has recorded the inventory in its records at $10 000. This amount is probably also its tax base. However, *as explained in section 22.1*, any difference between the tax base and the carrying amount in Jessica Ltd is accounted for in the tax-effect entries in Jessica Ltd. On consolidation, a tax-effect entry is necessary where an adjustment entry causes a difference between the carrying amount of an asset or a liability in the records of the legal entity and the carrying amount shown in the consolidated financial statements. In the adjustment entry relating to profit in ending inventory in the above example, the carrying amount of inventory is reduced downwards by $2000. The carrying amount and tax base of the inventory in Jessica Ltd is $10 000, but the carrying amount in the group is $8000. This $2000 difference is a deductible temporary difference giving rise to a deferred tax asset of $600 (i.e. 30% × $2000), as well as a corresponding decrease in income tax expense. The appropriate consolidation worksheet adjustment entry is:

Deferred Tax Asset	Dr	600	
Income Tax Expense	Cr		600

The effects of this entry are shown in figure 22.2.

The deferred tax asset recognises that the group is expected to earn profits in the future that will not require the payment of tax to the Taxation Office. When the inventory is sold by Jessica Ltd in a future period, this temporary difference is reversed. To illustrate this effect, assume that in the following period Jessica Ltd sells this inventory to an external entity for $11 000. Jessica Ltd will record a before-tax profit of $1000 (i.e. $11 000 – $10 000) and an associated tax expense of $300. From the consolidated group position, the profit on sale is $3000 (i.e. $11 000 – $8000). The group will show current tax payable of $300, reverse the $600 deferred tax asset, and recognise an income tax expense of $900. These effects are further illustrated below.

Example: Transferred inventories partly sold

On 1 January 2016, Jessica Ltd acquired $10 000 worth of inventory for cash from Amelie Ltd. The inventory had previously cost Amelie Ltd $8000. By the end of the year, 30 June 2016, Jessica Ltd had sold $7500 of the transferred inventory for $14 000 to external entities. Thus, $2500 of the inventory is on hand in Jessica Ltd at 30 June 2016.

The adjustment entry for the preparation of consolidated financial statements at 30 June 2016 is:

Sales	Dr	10 000	
Cost of Sales	Cr		9 500
Inventory	Cr		500

The total sales recorded by the *legal entities* are $24 000; that is, $10 000 by Amelie Ltd and $14 000 by Jessica Ltd. The sales by the *group*, being those sold to entities external to the group, are $14 000. The consolidation adjustment to sales revenue is then $10 000, being the amount necessary to eliminate the sales within the group.

The total cost of sales recorded by the *legal entities* is $15 500; that is, $8000 by Amelie Ltd and $7500 by Jessica Ltd (i.e. 75% × $10 000). The cost of sales to the *group*, being those to entities external to the group, is $6000 (i.e. 75% × $8000). Hence, the consolidation adjustment is $9500; that is, $15 500 (sum of recorded sales) less $6000 (group). The adjustment is that necessary to adjust the sum of the amounts recorded by the legal entities to that to be recognised by the group.

Note that the combined adjustments to sales and cost of sales result in a $500 reduction in before-tax profit. Of the $2000 intragroup profit on the transfer of inventory from Amelie Ltd to Jessica Ltd, since three-quarters of the inventory has been sold by Jessica Ltd to an external party, $1500 of the profit is realised to the group and only $500, the profit remaining in ending inventory, is unrealised. It is the unrealised profit that is adjusted for in the worksheet entry.

The group profit is then $500 less than that recorded by the legal entities. The sum of profits recorded by the legal entities is $8500, consisting of $2000 recorded by Amelie Ltd and $6500 (being sales of $14 000 less cost of sales of $7500) recorded by Jessica Ltd. From the group's viewpoint, profit on sale of inventory to external entities is only $8000, consisting of sales of $14 000 less cost of sales of $6000 (being 75% of original cost of $8000). Hence, an adjustment of $500 is necessary to reduce recorded profit of $8500 to group profit of $8000.

The $500 adjustment to inventory reflects the proportion of the total profit on sale of the transferred inventory that remains in the inventory on hand at the end of the period. Since 25% of the transferred inventory is still on hand at the end of the period, then 25% of the total profit on transfer of inventory (i.e. 25% × $2000) needs to be adjusted at the end of the period. The adjustment entry reduces the inventory on hand at 30 June 2016 from the recorded cost to Jessica Ltd of $2500 to the group cost of $2000 (being 25% of the original cost of $8000).

The adjustments above have been determined by comparing the combined amounts recorded by the parent and the subsidiary with the amounts that the group wants to report in the consolidated financial statements. This process could be shown in the form of a table, as follows:

	Parent	Subsidiary	Total Recorded	Group	Adjustment
Sales	14 000	10 000	24 000	14 000	Dr 10 000
Cost of sales	(7 500)	(8 000)	(15 500)	(6 000)	Cr 9 500
Profit	6 500	2 000	8 500	8 000	
Inventory	2 500	0	2 500	2 000	Cr $500

Consider the *tax effect* of this adjustment. The carrying amount of the inventory is reduced by $500, reflecting the fact that the carrying amount to the group is $500 less than the carrying amount in Jessica Ltd. This gives rise to a deductible temporary difference of $500. Hence, a deferred tax asset of $150 (i.e. 30% × $500) must be raised on consolidation with a corresponding effect on income tax expense. The expectation of the group is that, in some future period, it will recognise the remaining $500 profit in transferred inventory when it sells the inventory to an external party, but will not have to pay tax on the $500 as Amelie Ltd has already paid the relevant tax. This expected tax saving to the group will be shown in the consolidated financial statements by a debit adjustment of $150 to the Deferred Tax Asset account.

The tax-effect adjustment entry is then:

Deferred Tax Asset	Dr	150	
Income Tax Expense	Cr		150

Example: Transferred inventory completely sold

On 1 January 2016, Jessica Ltd acquired $10 000 worth of inventory for cash from Amelie Ltd. The inventory had previously cost Amelie Ltd $8000. By the end of the year, 30 June 2016, Jessica Ltd had sold all the transferred inventory to an external party for $18 000.

Amelie Ltd records a profit of $ 2 000 (i.e. $10 000 − $8000)
Jessica Ltd records a profit of $ 8 000 (i.e. $18 000 − $10 000)
Total recorded profit is $10 000

Profit to the group = Selling price to external entities less cost to the group
= $18 000 − $8000
= $10 000

Since the recorded profit equals the profit to the group, there is no need for a profit adjustment on consolidation. Further, as there is no transferred inventory still on hand, there is no need for an adjustment to inventory. Because all the inventory has been sold to an external entity, the whole of the intragroup profit is realised to the group. Note, however, that an adjustment for the sales and cost of sales is still necessary. As noted previously, the sales within the group amount to $18 000 whereas the sales recorded by the legal entities total $28 000 (i.e. $10 000 + $18 000). Hence, sales must be reduced by $10 000. The total recorded cost of sales is $18 000, being $8000 by Amelie Ltd and $10 000 by Jessica Ltd. The group's cost of sales is the original cost of the transferred inventory, $8000. Hence, cost of sales is reduced by $10 000 on consolidation. The adjustment entry is then:

| Sales | Dr | 10 000 | |
| Cost of Sales | Cr | | 10 000 |

Since there is no adjustment to the carrying amounts of assets or liabilities, there is no need for any *tax-effect* adjustment.

Where inventory is transferred in the current period and some or all of that inventory is still on hand at the end of the period, the general form of the worksheet entries is:

Sales Revenue	Dr	xxx	
Cost of Sales	Cr		xxx
Inventory	Cr		xxx
(The adjustment to inventory is based on the profit remaining in inventory on hand at the end of the period)			
Deferred Tax Asset	Dr	xxx	
Income Tax Expense	Cr		xxx
(The tax rate times the adjustment to ending inventory)			

22.2.4 Profits in opening inventory

Any transferred inventory remaining unsold at the end of one period is still on hand at the beginning of the next period. Because the consolidation adjustments are made only in a worksheet and not in the records of any of the legal entities, any differences in balances between the legal entities and the consolidated group at the end of one period must still exist at the beginning of the next period.

Example: Transferred inventory on hand at the beginning of the period

On 1 July 2015, the first day of the current period, Amelie Ltd has on hand inventory worth $7000, transferred from Jessica Ltd in June 2015. The inventory had previously cost Jessica Ltd $4500. The tax rate is 30%.

In this example, in the preparation of the consolidated financial statements at *30 June 2015* the following adjustment entries for the $2500 profit in ending inventory would have been made in the consolidation worksheet:

Sales	Dr	7 000	
Cost of Sales	Cr		4 500
Inventory	Cr		2 500
Deferred Tax Asset	Dr	750	
Income Tax Expense	Cr		750
(30% × $2500)			

Since the ending inventory at 30 June 2015 becomes the beginning inventory for the next year, an adjustment is necessary in the consolidated financial statements prepared at 30 June 2015. The required adjustment is:

| Retained Earnings (1/7/15) | Dr | 2 500 | |
| Cost of Sales | Cr | | 2 500 |

In making this consolidation worksheet adjustment, it is assumed that the inventory is sold to external entities in the current period. If this is not the case, then the adjustment to inventory as made at 30 June 2015 will need to be made again in preparing the consolidated financial statements at 30 June 2016.

In making a *credit adjustment* of $2500, cost of sales is reduced. The cost of sales recorded by Amelie Ltd in the 2015–16 period is $2500 greater than that which the group wants to show, because the cost of sales recorded by Jessica Ltd is $7000, whereas the cost of sales to the group is only $4500. A reduction in cost of sales means an increase in profit. Hence, in the 2015–16 period, the group's profit is greater than the sum of the legal entities' profit.

The *debit adjustment* to the opening balance of retained earnings reduces that balance; that is, the group made less profit in previous years than the sum of the retained earnings recorded by the legal entities. This is because, in June 2015, Jessica Ltd recorded a $2500 profit on the sale of inventory to Amelie Ltd, this profit not being recognised by the group until the 2015–16 period.

Consider the *tax effect* of these entries. If the previous period's tax-effect adjustment were carried forward into this year's worksheet it would be:

Deferred Tax Asset	Dr	750	
Retained Earnings (1/7/15)	Cr		750

On sale of the inventory in the 2015–16 period, the deferred tax asset is reversed, with a resultant effect on income tax expense:

Income Tax Expense	Dr	750	
Deferred Tax Asset	Cr		750

On combining these two entries, the worksheet entry required is:

Income Tax Expense	Dr	750	
Retained Earnings (1/7/15)	Cr		750

In summary, the adjustment to cost of sales, retained earnings and income tax expense can be combined into one entry as follows:

Retained Earnings (1/7/15)	Dr	1 750	
Income Tax Expense	Dr	750	
Cost of Sales	Cr		2 500

Note that this entry has no effect on the closing balance of retained earnings at 30 June 2016. As the inventory has been sold outside the group, the whole of the profit on the intragroup transaction is realised to the group. There is no unrealised profit to be adjusted for at the end of the period.

Where inventory was transferred in a previous period and some or all of that inventory is still on hand at the beginning of the current period, the general form of the entries is:

Retained Earnings (opening balance)	Dr	xxx	
Cost of Sales	Cr		xxx
Income Tax Expense	Dr	xxx	
Retained Earnings (opening balance)	Cr		xxx

It can be seen that the consolidation worksheet entries for inventory transferred within the current period are different from those where the inventory was transferred in a previous period. *Before preparing the adjustment entries, it is essential to determine the timing of the transaction.*

ILLUSTRATIVE EXAMPLE 22.1 Intragroup transactions involving transfers of inventory

Leah Ltd acquired all the issued shares of Sophia Ltd on 1 January 2015. The following transactions occurred between the two entities:

1. On 1 June 2016, Leah Ltd sold inventory to Sophia Ltd for $12 000, this inventory previously costing Leah Ltd $10 000. By 30 June 2016, Sophia Ltd had onsold 20% of this inventory to other entities for $3000. The other 80% was all sold to external entities by 30 June 2017 for $13 000.
2. During the 2016–17 period, Sophia Ltd sold inventory to Leah Ltd for $6000, this being at cost plus 20% mark-up. Of this inventory, $1200 remained on hand in Leah Ltd at 30 June 2017.

The tax rate is 30%.

Required

Prepare the consolidation worksheet entries for Leah Ltd at 30 June 2017 in relation to the intragroup transfers of inventory.

Solution

(1) Sale of inventory in previous period

Retained Earnings (1/7/16)	Dr	1 120	
Income Tax Expense	Dr	480	
Cost of Sales	Cr		1 600

Working:
- this is a prior period transaction
- profit after tax remaining in inventory at 1/7/16 is $1120 (= 80% × $2000 (1 – 30%))
- cost of sales recorded by Sophia Ltd is $9600 (= 80% × $12 000); cost of sales to the group is $8000 (= 80% × $10 000). The adjustment is then $1600.

(2) Sale of inventory in current period

Sales	Dr	6 000	
Cost of Sales	Cr		5 800
Inventory	Cr		200
Deferred Tax Asset	Dr	60	
Income Tax Expense	Cr		60

Working:
- this is a current period transaction
- sales within the group are $6000
- cost of sales recorded by the members of the group are $5000 for Sophia Ltd and $4800 (= 4/5 × $6000) for Leah Ltd; a total of $9800. Cost of sales for the group is $4000 (= 4/5 × $5000). The adjustment is then $5800
- the inventory remaining at 30 June 2017 is recorded by Leah Ltd at $1200. The cost to the group is $1000 (= 1/5 × $5000). The adjustment to inventory is then $200
- as the inventory is adjusted by $200, the tax effect is $60 (= 30% × $200).

22.3 INTRAGROUP SERVICES

LO3

Many different examples of services between related entities exist. For instance:
- Jessica Ltd may lend to Amelie Ltd some specialist personnel for a limited period of time for the performance of a particular task by Amelie Ltd. For this service, Jessica Ltd may charge Amelie Ltd a certain fee, or expect Amelie Ltd to perform other services in return.
- One entity may lease or rent an item of plant or a warehouse from the other.
- A subsidiary may exist solely for the purpose of carrying out some specific task, such as research activities for the parent, and a fee for such research is charged. In this situation, all service revenue earned by the subsidiary is paid for by the parent, and must be adjusted in the consolidation process.

Example: Intragroup services

During 2015–16, Jessica Ltd offered the services of a specialist employee to Amelie Ltd for 2 months in return for which Amelie Ltd paid $30 000 to Jessica Ltd. The employee's annual salary is $155 000, paid for by Jessica Ltd.

The journal entries in the records of Jessica Ltd and Amelie Ltd in relation to this transaction are:

Jessica Ltd			
Cash	Dr	30 000	
Service Revenue	Cr		30 000
Amelie Ltd			
Service Expense	Dr	30 000	
Cash	Cr		30 000

From the group's perspective there has been no service revenue received or service expense made to entities external to the group. Hence, to adjust from what has been recorded by the legal entities to the group's perspective, the consolidation adjustment entry is:

Service Revenue	Dr	30 000
Service Expense	Cr	30 000

No adjustment is made in relation to the employee's salary since, from the group's view, the salary paid to the employee is a payment to an external party.

Since there is no effect on the carrying amounts of assets or liabilities, there is no temporary difference and no need for any income tax adjustment.

Example: Intragroup rent

Jessica Ltd rents office space from Amelie Ltd for $150 000 p.a.

In accounting for this transaction, Jessica Ltd records rent expense of $150 000 and Amelie Ltd records rent revenue of $150 000. From the group's view, the intragroup rental scheme is purely an internal arrangement, and no revenue or expense is incurred. The recorded revenue and expense therefore need to be eliminated. The appropriate consolidation adjustment entry is:

Rent Revenue	Dr	150 000
Rent Expense	Cr	150 000

There is no tax-effect entry necessary as assets and liabilities are unaffected by the adjustment entry.

22.3.1 Realisation of profits or losses

With the transfer of services within the group, the consolidation adjustments do not affect the profit of the group. In a transaction involving a payment by a parent to a subsidiary for services rendered, the parent shows an expense and the subsidiary shows revenue. The net effect on the group's profit is zero. Hence, from the group's view, with intragroup services there are no realisation difficulties.

22.4 INTRAGROUP DIVIDENDS

In this section, consideration is given to dividends declared and paid after Jessica Ltd's acquisition of Amelie Ltd. As explained earlier *(see section 21.5.3)*, all dividends received by the parent from the subsidiary are accounted for as revenue by the parent, regardless of whether the dividends are paid from pre- or post-acquisition equity.

Two situations are considered in this section:
- dividends declared in the current period but not paid
- dividends declared and paid in the current period.

It is assumed that the company expecting to receive the dividend recognises revenue when the dividend is declared.

22.4.1 Dividends declared in the current period but not paid

Assume that, on 25 June 2016, Amelie Ltd declares a dividend of $4000. At the end of the period, the dividend is unpaid. The entries passed by the legal entities are:

Amelie Ltd		
Dividend Declared (In retained earnings)	Dr	4 000
Dividend Payable	Cr	4 000
Jessica Ltd		
Dividend Receivable	Dr	4 000
Dividend Revenue	Cr	4 000

The entry made by Amelie Ltd both reduces retained earnings and raises a liability account. From the group's perspective, there is no reduction in equity and the group has no obligation to pay dividends outside the group. Similarly, the group expects no dividends to be received from entities outside the group. Hence, the appropriate consolidation adjustment entries are:

Dividend Payable	Dr	4 000	
Dividend Declared	Cr		4 000
(To adjust for the effects of the entry made by Amelie Ltd)			
Dividend Revenue	Dr	4 000	
Dividend Receivable	Cr		4 000
(To adjust for the effects of the entry made by Jessica Ltd)			

In the following period when the dividend is paid, no adjustments are required in the consolidation worksheet. As there are no dividend revenue, dividend declared, or receivable items left open at the end of the period, then the position of the group is the same as the sum of the legal entities' financial statements.

22.4.2 Dividends declared and paid in the current period

Assume Amelie Ltd declares and pays an interim dividend of $4000 in the current period. Entries by the *legal entities* are:

Jessica Ltd

Cash	Dr	4 000	
Dividend Revenue	Cr		4 000

Amelie Ltd

Interim Dividend Paid (In retained earnings)	Dr	4 000	
Cash	Cr		4 000

From the outlook of the *group*, no dividends have been paid and no dividend revenue has been received. Hence, the adjustment necessary for the consolidated financial statements to show the affairs of the group is:

Dividend Revenue	Dr	4 000	
Interim Dividend Paid	Cr		4 000

Tax effect of dividends

Generally, dividends are tax-free. There are, therefore, no tax-effect adjustment entries required in relation to dividend-related consolidation adjustment entries.

ILLUSTRATIVE EXAMPLE 22.2 Intragroup dividends

Alice Ltd owns all the issued shares of Abigail Ltd, having acquired them for $250 000 on 1 January 2015. In preparing the consolidated financial statements at 30 June 2017, the accountant documented the following transactions:

2016

Jan. 15	Abigail Ltd paid an interim dividend of $10 000.
June 25	Abigail Ltd declared a dividend of $15 000, this being recognised in the records of both entities.
Aug. 1	The $15 000 dividend declared on 25 June was paid by Abigail Ltd.

2017

Jan. 18	Abigail Ltd paid an interim dividend of $12 000.
June 23	Abigail Ltd declared a dividend of $18 000, this being recognised in the records of both entities.

The tax rate is 30%.

Required

Prepare the consolidation worksheet adjustment entries for the preparation of consolidated financial statements at 30 June 2017.

Solution

The required entries are:

(1) *Interim dividend paid*

Dividend Revenue	Dr	12 000	
Dividend Paid	Cr		12 000

(2) *Final dividend declared*

Dividend Payable	Dr	18 000	
Dividend Declared	Cr		18 000
Dividend Revenue	Dr	18 000	
Dividend Receivable	Cr		18 000

 22.5 INTRAGROUP BORROWINGS

Members of a group often borrow and lend money among themselves, and charge interest on the money borrowed. In some cases, an entity may be set up within the group solely for the purpose of handling group finances and for borrowing money on international money markets. Consolidation adjustments are necessary in relation to these intragroup borrowings and interest thereon because, from the stance of the group, these transactions create assets and liabilities and revenues and expenses that do not exist in terms of the group's relationship with external entities.

Example: Advances

Jessica Ltd lends $100 000 to Amelie Ltd, the latter paying $15 000 interest to Jessica Ltd. The relevant journal entries in each of the legal entities are:

Jessica Ltd			
Advance to Amelie Ltd	Dr	100 000	
Cash	Cr		100 000
Cash	Dr	15 000	
Interest Revenue	Cr		15 000
Amelie Ltd			
Cash	Dr	100 000	
Advance from Jessica Ltd	Cr		100 000
Interest Expense	Dr	15 000	
Cash	Cr		15 000

The consolidation adjustments involve eliminating the monetary asset created by Jessica Ltd, the monetary liability raised by Amelie Ltd, the interest revenue recorded by Jessica Ltd and the interest expense paid by Amelie Ltd:

Advance from Jessica Ltd	Dr	100 000	
Advance to Amelie Ltd	Cr		100 000
Interest Revenue	Dr	15 000	
Interest Expense	Cr		15 000

The adjustment to the asset and liability is necessary as long as the intragroup loan exists. In relation to any past period's payments and receipt of interest, no ongoing adjustment to accumulated profits (opening balance) is necessary as the net effect of the consolidation adjustment is zero on that item.

Because the effect on net assets of the consolidation adjustment is zero, no tax-effect entry is necessary.

SUMMARY

Intragroup transactions can take many forms and may involve transfers of inventory or property, plant and equipment, or they may relate to the provision of services by one member of the group to another member. To prepare the relevant worksheet entries for a transaction, it is necessary to consider the accounts affected in the entities involved in the transaction.

Intragroup transfers of inventory, services, dividends and debentures and their adjustment in the consolidation process are associated with a need to consider the implications of applying tax-effect accounting in the consolidation process.

The basic approach to determining the consolidation adjustment entries for intragroup transfers is:
(a) Analyse the events within the records of the legal entities involved in the intragroup transfer. Determine whether the transaction is a prior period or current period event.
(b) Analyse the position from the group's viewpoint.
(c) Create adjusting entries to change from the legal entities' position to that of the group.
(d) Consider the tax effect of the adjusting entries.

Note again that there are no actual adjusting entries made in the records of the individual legal entities which constitute the group. However, if required, a special journal could be set up by the parent entity to keep a record of the adjustments made in the process of preparing the consolidated financial statements. Alternatively, the consolidation process may be performed by the use of special consolidation worksheets.

Why a particular adjustment is the correct one involves an explanation of each line in the adjustment entry including why an account was adjusted, why it was increased or decreased, and why a particular adjustment amount is appropriate. This generally involves a comparison of what accounts were affected in the records of the legal entities with the financial picture the group wants to present in the consolidated financial statements.

DEMONSTRATION PROBLEM 22.1 Intragroup transfers of assets

The following example illustrates procedures for the preparation of a consolidated statement of profit or loss and other comprehensive income, a consolidated statement of changes in equity and a consolidated statement of financial position where the subsidiary is 100% owned. The consolidation worksheet adjustments for intragroup transactions including inventory are also demonstrated.

Details
On 1 July 2014, Eliza Ltd acquired all the share capital of Ebony Ltd for $472 000. At that date, Ebony Ltd's equity consisted of the following.

Share capital	$ 300 000
General reserve	96 000
Retained earnings	56 000

At 1 July 2014, all the identifiable assets and liabilities of Ebony Ltd were recorded at fair value.

Financial information for Eliza Ltd and Ebony Ltd for the year ended 30 June 2016 is presented in the left-hand columns of the worksheet illustrated in figure 22.3 overleaf. It is assumed that both companies use the perpetual inventory system.

Additional information
(a) On 1 January 2016, Ebony Ltd sold merchandise costing $30 000 to Eliza Ltd for $50 000. Half this merchandise was sold to external entities for $28 000 before 30 June 2016.
(b) At 1 July 2015, there was a profit in the inventory of Eliza Ltd of $6000 on goods acquired from Ebony Ltd in the previous period.
(c) The tax rate is 30%.

Required

Prepare the consolidated financial statements for the year ended 30 June 2016.

Solution

The first step is to determine the pre-acquisition entries at 30 June 2016. These entries are prepared after undertaking an acquisition analysis.
At 1 July 2014:

Net fair value of the identifiable assets and liabilities of Ebony Ltd	= $300 000 + $96 000 + $56 000
	= $452 000
Consideration transferred	= $472 000
Goodwill	= $20 000

Consolidation worksheet entries

(1) *Business combination valuation entry*

As all the identifiable assets and liabilities of Ebony Ltd are recorded at amounts equal to their fair values, the only business combination valuation entry required is that for goodwill.

| Goodwill | Dr | 20 000 | |
| Business Combination Valuation Reserve | Cr | | 20 000 |

(2) *Elimination of investment in subsidiary*

The entry at 30 June 2016 is the same as that at acquisition date as there have not been any events affecting that entry since acquisition date:

Retained Earnings (1/7/15)	Dr	56 000	
Share Capital	Dr	300 000	
General Reserve	Dr	96 000	
Business Combination Valuation Reserve	Dr	20 000	
Shares in Ebony Ltd	Cr		472 000

The next step is to prepare the adjustment entries arising because of the existence of intragroup transactions. It is important that students classify the intragroup transactions into 'current period' and 'previous period' transactions. The resultant adjustment entries should reflect those decisions since previous period transactions would be expected to affect accounts such as retained earnings rather than accounts such as sales and cost of sales.

(3) *Profit in ending inventory*

The transaction occurred in the current period. The adjustment entries are:

Sales	Dr	50 000	
Cost of Sales	Cr		40 000
Inventory	Cr		10 000
($10 000 = ½ × [$50 000 − $30 000])			
Deferred Tax Asset	Dr	3 000	
Income Tax Expense	Cr		3 000
(30% × $10 000)			

Sales: The members of the group have recorded total sales of $78 000, being $50 000 by Ebony Ltd and $28 000 by Eliza Ltd. The group recognises only sales to entities outside the group, namely the sales by Eliza Ltd of $28 000. Hence, in preparing the consolidated financial statements, sales must be reduced by $50 000.

Cost of sales: Ebony Ltd recorded cost of sales of $30 000, and Eliza Ltd recorded cost of sales of $25 000 (being half of $50 000). Recorded cost of sales then totals $55 000. The cost of the sales to entities external to the group is $15 000 (being half of $30 000). Cost of sales must then be reduced by $40 000.

Inventory: At 30 June 2016, Eliza Ltd has inventory on hand from intragroup transactions, and records them at cost of $25 000 (being half of $50 000). The cost of this inventory to the group is $15 000 (being half of $30 000). Inventory is then reduced by $10 000.

Deferred tax asset/income tax expense: Under tax-effect accounting, temporary differences arise where the carrying amount of an asset differs from its tax base. In the first adjustment entry above, inventory is reduced by $10 000; that is, the carrying amount of inventory is reduced by $10 000. This then gives rise to a temporary difference, and because the carrying amount has been reduced, tax benefits are expected in the future when the asset is sold. Hence a deferred tax asset, equal to the tax rate times the change to the carrying amount of inventory (30% × $10 000), of $3000 is raised. Given there is no Deferred Tax Asset in the worksheet in figure 22.3, the adjustment is made against the Deferred Tax Liability line item.

(4) *Profit in beginning inventory*

This is a previous period transaction. The required consolidation worksheet entry is:

Retained Earnings (1/7/14)	Dr	6 000	
Cost of Sales	Cr		6 000
Income Tax Expense	Dr	1 800	
Retained Earnings (1/7/14)	Cr		1 800
(30% × $6000)			

Retained earnings: In the previous period, Ebony Ltd recorded a $6000 before-tax profit, or a $4200 after-tax profit on sale of inventory within the group. Because the sale did not involve external entities, the profit must be eliminated on consolidation.

Cost of sales: In the current period, the transferred inventory is onsold to external entities. Eliza Ltd records cost of sales at $6000 greater than to the group. Hence, cost of sales is reduced by $6000. Note that this increases group profit by $6000, reflecting the realisation of the profit to the group in the current period, when it was recognised by the legal entity in the previous period.

Income tax expense: At the end of the previous period, in the consolidated statement of financial position a deferred tax asset of $1800 was raised because of the difference in cost of the inventory recorded by the legal entity and that recognised by the group. This deferred tax asset is reversed when the asset is sold. The adjustment to income tax expense reflects the reversal of the deferred tax asset raised at the end of the previous period.

Figure 22.3 shows the completed worksheet for preparation of the consolidated financial statements of Eliza Ltd and its subsidiary Ebony Ltd at 30 June 2016. Once the effects of all adjustments are added or subtracted horizontally in the worksheet to calculate figures in the right-hand 'consolidation' column, the consolidated financial statements can be prepared, as shown in figure 22.4(a), (b) and (c).

Financial Statements	Eliza Ltd	Ebony Ltd		Adjustments Dr		Cr		Consolidation
Sales revenue	1 196 000	928 000	3	50 000				2 074 000
Cost of sales	(888 000)	(670 000)				40 000	3	(1 512 000)
Wages and salaries	(57 500)	(32 000)						(89 500)
Depreciation	(5 200)	(4 800)						(10 000)
Other expenses	(4 000)	—						(4 000)
Total expenses	(954 700)	(706 800)						(1 615 500)
Profit before income tax	241 300	221 200						458 500
Income tax expense	(96 120)	(118 480)	4	1 800		3 000	3	(213 400)
Profit for the year	145 180	102 720						245 100
Retained earnings (1/7/15)	100 820	70 280	2	56 000		1 800	4	110 900
			4	6 000				
	246 000	173 000						356 000
Dividend paid	(80 000)	—						(80 000)
Retained earnings (30/6/16)	166 000	173 000						276 000
Share capital	500 000	300 000	2	300 000				500 000
Business combination valuation reserve			2	20 000		20 000	1	—
General reserve	135 000	96 000	2	96 000				135 000
	801 000	569 000						911 000
Other components of equity (1/7/15)	4 000	10 000						14 000
Gains on financial assets	1 000	3 000						4 000
Other components of equity (30/6/16)	5 000	13 000						18 000
Total equity	806 000	582 000						929 000
Deferred tax liability	52 000	30 000	3	3 000				79 000
Total equity and liabilities	858 000	612 000						1 008 000
Shares in Ebony Ltd	472 000	—				472 000	2	—
Cash	80 000	73 000						153 000
Inventory	169 000	36 000				10 000	3	195 000
Other current assets	10 000	300 000						310 000
Financial assets	15 000	68 000						83 000
Land	70 000	120 000						190 000
Plant and equipment	52 000	28 000						80 000
Accumulated depreciation	(10 000)	(13 000)						(23 000)
Goodwill	—	—	1	20 000				20 000
	857 000	612 000		588 928		588 928		1 008 000

FIGURE 22.3 Consolidation worksheet — intragroup transfers of assets

ELIZA LTD
Consolidated Statement of Profit or Loss and Other Comprehensive Income
for the year ended 30 June 2016

Revenues	$2 074 000
Expenses	1 615 425
Profit before income tax	458 500
Income tax expense	213 400
Profit for the year	$ 245 100
Other comprehensive income	
Gains on financial assets	4 000
TOTAL COMPREHENSIVE INCOME FOR THE YEAR	$ 249 100

FIGURE 22.4(a) Consolidated statement of profit or loss and other comprehensive income

ELIZA LTD
Consolidated Statement of Changes in Equity
for the year ended 30 June 2016

TOTAL COMPREHENSIVE INCOME FOR THE YEAR	$249 100
Retained earnings at 1 July 2015	$110 900
Profit for the year	$245 100
Dividend paid	$ (80 000)
Retained earnings at 30 June 2016	$276 000
General reserve at 1 July 2015	$140 000
General reserve at 30 June 2016	$140 000
Other components of equity at 1 July 2015	$ 14 000
Gains on financial assets	$ 4 000
Other components of equity at 30 June 2016	$ 18 000
Share capital at 1 July 2015	$500 000
Share capital at 30 June 2016	$500 000

FIGURE 22.4(b) Consolidated statement of changes in equity

FIGURE 22.4(c) Consolidated statement of financial position

ELIZA LTD
Consolidated Statement of Financial Position
as at 30 June 2016

Current assets			
Cash assets			$ 153 000
Inventories			195 000
Financial assets			83 000
Other			310 000
Total current assets			741 000
Non-current assets			
Property, plant and equipment:			
Plant and equipment	$ 80 000		
Accumulated depreciation	$(23 000)	$ 57 000	
Land		190 000	247 000
Goodwill			20 000
Total non-current assets			267 000
Total assets			1 008 000
Non-current liabilities			
Deferred tax liabilities			(79 000)
Net assets			$ 929 000

FIGURE 22.4(c) *(continued)*

Equity	
Share capital	$ 500 000
General reserve	135 000
Retained earnings	276 000
Other components of equity	18 000
Total equity	**$ 929 000**

DEMONSTRATION PROBLEM 22.2 Dividends and borrowings

On 1 July 2015, Lilly Ltd acquired all the share capital of Tahlia Ltd and Eva Ltd for $187 500 and $150 000 respectively. At that date, equity of the three companies was:

	Lilly Ltd	Tahlia Ltd	Eva Ltd
Share capital	$150 000	$100 000	$100 000
General reserve	90 000	60 000	40 000
Retained earnings	20 000	17 500	10 000

At 1 July 2015, the identifiable net assets of all companies were recorded at fair values.

For the year ended 30 June 2016, the summarised financial information for the three companies show the following details:

	Lilly Ltd	Tahlia Ltd	Eva Ltd
Sales revenue	$ 388 500	$ 200 000	$ 150 000
Dividend revenue	9 000	—	—
Other revenue	10 000	—	—
Total revenues	407 500	200 000	150 000
Total expenses	(360 000)	(176 000)	(138 000)
Profit before income tax	47 500	24 000	12 000
Income tax expense	(15 000)	(10 000)	(5 000)
Profit	32 500	14 000	7 000
Retained earnings (1/7/15)	20 000	17 500	10 000
Total available for appropriation	52 500	31 500	17 000
Interim dividend paid	(7 500)	(2 500)	—
Final dividend declared	(15 000)	(5 000)	(5 500)
Transfer to general reserve	(2 000)	(5 000)	—
	(24 500)	(12 500)	(5 500)
Retained earnings (30/6/16)	$ 28 000	$ 19 000	$ 11 500
Shares in Tahlia Ltd	$ 187 500	—	—
Shares in Eva Ltd	150 000	—	—
Dividend receivable	6 500	—	—
Loan receivable	5 000	—	—
Property, plant and equipment	18 500	$ 205 000	$ 167 000
Total assets	367 500	205 000	167 000
Final dividend payable	15 000	5 000	1 500
Loan payable	—	5 000	—
Other non-current liabilities	82 500	11 000	10 000
Total liabilities	97 500	21 000	11 500
Net assets	$ 270 000	$ 184 000	$ 155 500
Share capital	$ 150 000	$ 100 000	$ 104 000
General reserve	92 000	65 000	40 000
Retained earnings	28 000	19 000	11 500
Total equity	$ 270 000	$ 184 000	$ 155 500

Additional information
(a) Lilly Ltd has lent $5000 to Tahlia Ltd, the loan having 10% interest rate attached.
(b) Lilly Ltd has recognised both the interim and final dividends from Tahlia Ltd and Eva Ltd as revenue.

Required

Prepare the consolidated financial statements as at 30 June 2016 for Lilly Ltd and its two subsidiaries, Tahlia Ltd and Eva Ltd. Assume all reserve transfers are from post-acquisition profits.

Solution

The relationship between the parent and subsidiaries may be expressed as shown in figure 22.5.

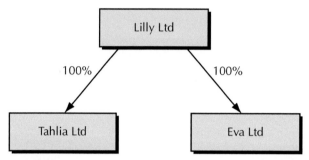

FIGURE 22.5 Relationship between parent and subsidiaries

Figure 22.6 overleaf illustrates the consolidation worksheet necessary to consolidate the financial statements of Lilly Ltd and its two subsidiaries. Detailed discussion of each adjustment is provided below. Note that:
- no adjustment entries are made for transfers to and from reserves if post-acquisition equity only is affected
- the dividends paid and declared by the parent to its shareholders are not adjusted for in the consolidated financial statements, because these dividends are paid by the group to external entities.

Acquisition analysis: Lilly Ltd and Tahlia Ltd
At 1 July 2015:

Net fair value of identifiable assets and liabilities of Tahlia Ltd	= $100 000 + $60 000 + $17 500
	= $177 500
Consideration transferred	= $187 500
Goodwill	= $10 000

Consolidation worksheet adjustment entries
(1) *Business combination valuation entry: Lilly Ltd and Tahlia Ltd*

Goodwill	Dr	10 000	
Business Combination Valuation Reserve	Cr		10 000

(2) *Elimination of investment in subsidiary: Lilly Ltd and Tahlia Ltd*
The elimination of investment in subsidiary at 30 June 2016 is then:

Retained Earnings (1/7/15)	Dr	17 500	
Share Capital	Dr	100 000	
General Reserve	Dr	60 000	
Business Combination Valuation Reserve	Dr	10 000	
Shares in Tahlia Ltd	Cr		187 500

Acquisition analysis: Lilly Ltd and Eva Ltd
At 1 July 2015:

Net fair value of identifiable assets and liabilities of Eva Ltd	= $100 000 + $40 000 + $10 000
	= $150 000
Consideration transferred	= $150 000
Goodwill	= zero

No business combination valuation entry is required.

(3) *Elimination of investment in subsidiary: Lilly Ltd and Eva Ltd*

The elimination of investment in subsidiary at 30 June 2016 is then:

Retained Earnings (1/7/15)	Dr	10 000	
Share Capital	Dr	100 000	
General Reserve	Dr	40 000	
Shares in Eva Ltd	Cr		150 000

(4) *Interim dividend: Tahlia Ltd*

This is a current period transaction. The consolidation worksheet entry is:

Dividend Revenue	Dr	2 500	
Dividend Paid	Cr		2 500

Tahlia Ltd paid a dividend in cash to Lilly Ltd. Lilly Ltd recognised dividend revenue and Tahlia Ltd recognised dividends paid. From the group's perspective, there were no dividends paid to entities external to the group. Hence, on consolidation it is necessary to eliminate both the Dividend Paid and Dividend Revenue accounts raised by the parent and the subsidiary.

(5) *Final dividend declared: Tahlia Ltd*

This is a current period transaction. The consolidation worksheet entry is:

Final Dividend Payable	Dr	5 000	
Final Dividend Declared	Cr		5 000
Dividend Revenue	Dr	5 000	
Dividend Receivable	Cr		5 000

The subsidiary declares a dividend, recognising a liability to pay the dividend and reducing retained earnings. The parent, which expects to receive the dividend, raises a receivable asset and recognises dividend revenue. From the group's point of view, because the dividend is not receivable or payable to entities external to the group, it does not want to recognise any of these accounts. Hence, on consolidation, all the accounts affected by this transaction in the records of the parent and the subsidiary are eliminated.

(6) *Final dividend declared: Eva Ltd*

This is a current period transaction. The consolidation worksheet entry is:

Final Dividend Payable	Dr	5 500	
Final Dividend Declared	Cr		5 500
Dividend Revenue	Dr	5 500	
Dividend Receivable	Cr		5 500

The explanation for this entry is the same as that for the dividend declared by Tahlia Ltd.

(7) *Loan: Lilly Ltd to Tahlia Ltd*

The loan may have been made in a previous period or the current period. The consolidation worksheet entry is the same:

Loan Payable	Dr	5 000	
Loan Receivable	Cr		5 000

This entry eliminates the receivable raised by the parent and the payable raised by the subsidiary. From the group's point of view, there are no loans payable or receivable to entities external to the group.

(8) *Interest on loan*

The interest paid/received is a current period transaction. In some situations where interest is accrued, interest may relate to previous or future periods. The consolidation worksheet entry is:

Interest Revenue	Dr	500	
Interest Expense	Cr		500
(10% × $5000)			

The parent records interest revenue of $500 and the subsidiary records interest expense of $500. No interest was paid or received by the group from entities external to the group, so these accounts must be eliminated on consolidation.

Financial statements	Lilly Ltd	Tahlia Ltd	Eva. Ltd		Adjustments Dr	Cr		Group
Sales revenue	388 500	200 000	150 000					738 500
Dividend revenue	9 000	—	—	4	2 500			—
				6	5 000			
				7	1 500			
Other revenue	10 000	—	—	9	500			9 500
	407 500	200 000	150 000					748 000
Expenses	(360 000)	(176 000)	(138 000)			500	9	(673 500)
Profit before income tax	47 500	24 000	12 000					74 500
Income tax expense	(15 000)	(10 000)	(5 000)					(30 000)
Profit	32 500	14 000	7 000					44 500
Retained earnings (1/7/15)	20 000	17 500	10 000	2	17 500			20 000
				3	10 000			
	52 500	31 500	17 000					64 500
Interim dividend paid	(7 500)	(2 500)	—			2 500	4	(7 500)
Final dividend declared	(15 000)	(5 000)	(1 500)			5 000	5	(15 000)
						1 500	6	
Transfer to general reserve	(2 000)	(5 000)	0					(7 000)
	24 500	12 500	5 500					29 500
Retained earnings (30/6/16)	28 000	19 000	11 500					35 000
Share capital	150 000	100 000	100 000	2	100 000			150 000
				3	100 000			
General reserve	92 000	65 000	40 000	2	60 000			97 000
				3	40 000			
Business combination valuation reserve				2	10 000	10 000	1	—
Final dividend payable	15 000	5 000	1 500	5	5 000			15 000
				6	1 500			
Loan payable	—	5 000	—	7	5 000			—
Other non-current liabilities	82 500	11 000	10 000					103 500
Total equity and liabilities	367 500	205 000	167 000					400 500
Shares in Tahlia Ltd	187 500	—	—			187 500	2	—
Shares in Eva Ltd	150 000	—	—			150 000	3	—
Dividend receivable	6 500	—	—			5 000	5	—
						1 500	6	
Loan receivable	5 000	—	—			5 000	7	—
Property, plant and equipment	18 500	205 000	167 000					390 500
Goodwill	—	—	—	1	10 000			10 000
	367 500	205 000	167 000		372 500	372 500		400 500

FIGURE 22.6 Consolidation worksheet — dividends

From figure 22.6, after all adjustments have been entered in the worksheet and amounts totalled across to the consolidation column, the consolidated financial statements can be prepared in suitable format as shown in figure 22.7(a), (b) and (c).

LILLY LTD **Consolidated Statement of Profit or Loss and Other Comprehensive Income** **for the year ended 30 June 2016**	
Revenues	$748 000
Expenses	673 500
Profit before income tax	74 500
Income tax expense	(30 000)
Profit for the year	$ 44 500
Other comprehensive income	—
TOTAL COMPREHENSIVE INCOME FOR THE YEAR	$ 44 500

FIGURE 22.7(a) Consolidated statement of profit or loss and other comprehensive income

LILLY LTD Consolidated Statement of Changes in Equity for the year ended 30 June 2016	
TOTAL COMPREHENSIVE INCOME FOR THE YEAR	$ 44 500
Retained earnings at 1 July 2015	$ 20 000
Profit for the year	44 500
Interim dividend paid	(7 500)
Final dividend declared	(15 000)
Transfer of general reserve	(7 000)
Retained earnings at 30 June 2016	$ 31 000
General reserve at 1 July 2015	$ 90 000
Transfer from retained earnings	7 000
General reserve at 30 June 2016	$ 97 000
Share capital as at 1 July 2015	$150 000
Share capital at 30 June 2016	$150 000

FIGURE 22.7(b) Consolidated statement of changes in equity

LILLY LTD Consolidated Statement of Financial Position as at 30 June 2016	
Non-current assets	
Property, plant and equipment	$390 500
Goodwill	10 000
Total non-current assets	400 500
Total assets	400 500
Current liabilities	
Final dividend payable	15 000
Non-current liabilities	103 500
Total liabilities	118 500
Net assets	$282 000
Equity	
Share capital	$150 000
Other reserves:	
General reserve	$ 97 000
Retained earnings	35 000
Total equity	$282 000

FIGURE 22.7(c) Consolidated statement of financial position

Discussion questions

1. Why is it necessary to make adjustments for intragroup transactions?
2. In making consolidation worksheet adjustments, sometimes tax-effect entries are made. Why?
3. Why is it important to identify transactions as current or previous period transactions?
4. Where an intragroup transaction involves a depreciable asset, why is depreciation expense adjusted?
5. Are adjustments for post-acquisition dividends different from those for pre-acquisition dividends? Explain.
6. What is meant by 'realisation of profits'?
7. When are profits realised in relation to inventory transfers within the group?

Exercises

STAR RATING ★ BASIC ★★ MODERATE ★★★ DIFFICULT

Exercise 22.1 — CONSOLIDATION ADJUSTMENTS

★ Jessica Ltd sold inventory during the current period to its wholly owned subsidiary, Amelie Ltd, for $15 000. These items previously cost Jessica Ltd $12 000. Amelie Ltd subsequently sold half the items to Ningbo Ltd for $8000. The tax rate is 30%.

The group accountant for Jessica Ltd, Li Chen, maintains that the appropriate consolidation adjustment entries are as follows:

Sales	Dr	15 000	
Cost of Sales	Cr		13 000
Inventory	Cr		2 000
Deferred Tax Asset	Dr	300	
Income Tax Expense	Cr		300

Required

1. Discuss whether the entries suggested by Li Chen are correct, explaining on a line-by-line basis the correct adjustment entries.
2. Determine the consolidation worksheet entries in the following year, assuming the inventory is onsold, and explain the adjustments on a line-by-line basis.

Exercise 22.2 — ELIMINATION OF INVESTMENT IN SUBSIDIARY AND INTRAGROUP TRANSACTIONS, NO FAIR VALUE — CARRYING AMOUNT DIFFERENCES AT ACQUISITION DATE

★★ On 1 January 2013, Molly Ltd acquired all the share capital of Mia Ltd for $300 000. The equity of Mia Ltd at 1 January 2013 was:

Share capital	$200 000
Retained earnings	50 000
General reserve	20 000
	$270 000

At this date, all identifiable assets and liabilities of Mia Ltd were recorded at fair value. Goodwill is tested annually for impairment. By 31 December 2016, no impairment has occurred. At 1 January 2013, no goodwill had been recorded by Mia Ltd.

On 1 May 2016, Mia Ltd transferred $15 000 from the general reserve (pre-acquisition) to retained earnings. The current tax rate is 30%. Assuming consolidated financial statements are required for the period 1 January 2015 to 31 December 2016, provide journal entries (including the elimination of investment in subsidiary) to show the adjustments that would be made in the consolidation worksheets. Use the following information:

(a) At 31 December 2016, Mia Ltd holds $100 000 of 7% debentures issued by Molly Ltd on 1 January 2015. All necessary interest payments have been made.
(b) At the end of the reporting period, Mia Ltd owes Molly Ltd $1000 for items sold on credit.
(c) Mia Ltd undertook an advertising campaign for Molly Ltd during the year. Molly Ltd paid $8000 to Mia Ltd for this service.
(d) The beginning and ending inventories of Molly Ltd and Mia Ltd in relation to the current period included the following unsold intragroup inventory:

	Molly Ltd	Mia Ltd
Beginning inventory:		
Transfer price	$2 000	$1 200
Original cost	1 400	800
Ending inventory:		
Transfer price	500	900
Original cost	300	700

Molly Ltd sold inventory to Mia Ltd during the current period for $3000. This was $500 above the cost of the inventory to Molly Ltd. Mia Ltd sold inventory to Molly Ltd in the current period for $2500, recording a pre-tax profit of $800.

(e) Molly Ltd received dividends totalling $63 000 during the current period from Mia Ltd. All of this related to dividends paid in the current period.

Exercise 22.3 — INTRAGROUP TRANSACTIONS, EXPLANATION OF RATIONALE

★★ Alexis Ltd owns 100% of the shares of Ruby Ltd. During the 2015–16 period, Alexis Ltd sold inventory for $10 000 which had been sold to it by Ruby Ltd in June 2016. The inventory originally cost Ruby Ltd $6000 and was sold to Alexis Ltd for $9000.

Required

1. Prepare the adjustments required in the consolidation worksheet at 30 June 2016, assuming an income tax rate of 30%.
2. Explain the rationale behind the entries you have prepared.

Exercise 22.4 — CONSOLIDATION WORKSHEET, CONSOLIDATED FINANCIAL STATEMENTS

★★ On 1 July 2015, Sienna Ltd acquired all the shares of Amber Ltd for $160 000. The financial statements of the two entities at 30 June 2016 contained the following information:

	Sienna Ltd	Amber Ltd
Sales revenue	$ 234 800	$ 200 000
Dividend revenue	17 000	—
Other income	6 600	—
	258 400	200 000
Cost of sales	(123 000)	(120 000)
Other expenses	(34 600)	(20 000)
	(157 600)	(140 000)
Profit before income tax	100 800	60 000
Income tax expense	(32 000)	(20 000)
Profit for the year	68 800	40 000
Retained earnings (1/7/15)	24 000	12 000
Total available for appropriation	92 800	52 000
Dividend paid from 2014–15 profit	(18 000)	(5 000)
Interim dividend paid from 2015–16 profit	(16 000)	(4 800)
Dividend declared from 2015–16 profit	(16 000)	(7 200)
Transfer to general reserve	(8 000)	—
	(58 000)	(17 000)
Retained earnings (30/6/16)	$ 34 800	$ 35 000
Current assets		
Cash	$ 1 000	$ 40
Receivables	27 000	12 100
Allowance for doubtful debts	(500)	(300)
Financial assets	20 000	10 000
Inventory	48 000	47 000
Total current assets	95 500	68 840
Non-current assets		
Plant and machinery	100 000	70 000
Accumulated depreciation	(40 000)	26 000
Land	102 300	190 000
Debentures in Amber Ltd	57 000	—
Shares in Amber Ltd	160 000	
Total non-current assets	379 300	234 000
Total assets	474 800	302 840
Current liabilities		
Dividend payable	16 000	7 200
Provisions	12 000	8 800
Bank overdraft	—	14 840
Current tax liabilities	11 000	10 000
Total current liabilities	39 000	40 840
Non-current liabilities		
12% mortgage debentures	—	80 000
Deferred tax liabilities	13 000	5 000
Total non-current liabilities	13 000	85 000
Total liabilities	52 000	125 840
Net assets	$ 422 800	$ 177 000

(continued)

	Sienna Ltd	Amber Ltd
Equity		
Share capital	$ 320 000	$ 120 000
General reserve	60 000	20 000
Retained earnings	34 800	35 000
Other components of equity	8 000	2 000
Total equity	$ 422 800	$ 177 000

Additional information

(a) At 1 July 2015, all identifiable assets and liabilities of Amber Ltd were recorded at fair values except for inventory, for which the fair value was $1000 greater than the carrying amount. This inventory was all sold by 30 June 2016. At 1 July 2015, Amber Ltd had research and development outlays that it had expensed as incurred. Sienna Ltd measured the fair value of the in-process research and development at $8000. By 30 June 2016, it was assessed that $2000 of this was not recoverable. At 1 July 2015, Amber Ltd had reported a contingent liability relating to a guarantee that was considered to have a fair value of $7000. This liability still existed at 30 June 2016. At 1 July 2015, Amber Ltd had not recorded any goodwill.

(b) The debentures were issued by Amber Ltd at nominal value on 1 July 2014, and are redeemable on 30 June 2020. Sienna Ltd acquired its holding ($60 000) of these debentures on the open market on 1 January 2016, immediately after the half-yearly interest payment had been made. All interest has been paid and brought to account in the records of both entities.

(c) During the 2015–16 period, Sienna Ltd sold inventory to Amber Ltd for $40 000, at a mark-up of cost plus 25%. At 30 June 2016, $10 000 worth of inventory was still held by Amber Ltd.

(d) The Other Components of Equity account relates to the financial assets. For the 2015–16 period, Sienna Ltd recorded an increase in these assets of $3000, and Amber Ltd recorded a decrease of $2000.

(e) The income tax rate is 30%.

Required

Prepare the consolidated financial statements for Sienna Ltd and its subsidiary for the year ended 30 June 2016.

Exercise 22.5   **CONSOLIDATION WORKSHEET, IMPAIRMENT OF GOODWILL**

★★   Financial information for Amy Ltd and its 100% owned subsidiary, Zara Ltd, for the year ended 31 December 2016 is provided below:

	Amy Ltd	Zara Ltd
Sales revenue	$25 000	$23 600
Dividend revenue	1 000	—
Other income	1 000	2 000
Proceeds from sale of property, plant and equipment	5 000	22 000
Total	32 000	47 600
Cost of sales	21 000	18 000
Other expenses	3 000	1 000
Carrying amount of property, plant and equipment sold	4 000	20 000
Total expenses	28 000	39 000
Profit before income tax	4 000	8 600
Income tax expense	(1 350)	(1 950)
Profit for the period	2 650	6 650
Retained earnings (1/1/16)	6 000	3 000
	8 650	9 650
Interim dividend paid	(2 500)	(1 000)
Retained earnings (31/12/16)	$ 6 150	$ 8 650

Amy Ltd acquired its shares in Zara Ltd at 1 January 2016, buying the 10 000 shares in Zara Ltd for $20 000 — Zara Ltd recorded share capital of $10 000. The shares were bought on a cum div. basis as Zara Ltd had declared a dividend of $3000 that was not paid until March 2016.

At 1 January 2016, all identifiable assets and liabilities of Zara Ltd were recorded at fair value except for inventory, for which the carrying amount of $2000 was $400 less than fair value. Some of this inventory has been a little slow to sell, and 10% of it is still on hand at 31 December 2016. Inventory on hand in Zara Ltd at 31 December 2016 also includes some items acquired from Amy Ltd during the year. These were sold by Amy Ltd for $5000, at a profit before tax of $1000. Half the goodwill was written off as the result of an impairment test on 31 December 2016.

During March 2016, Amy Ltd provided some management services to Zara Ltd at a fee of $500.

By 31 December 2016, the financial assets acquired by Amy Ltd and Zara Ltd increased by $1000 and $650 respectively, with gains being recognised in other comprehensive income.

The tax rate is 30%.

Required

1. Prepare the consolidated statement of profit or loss and other comprehensive income for Amy Ltd and its subsidiary, Zara Ltd, at 31 December 2016.
2. Discuss the concept of 'realisation' using the intragroup transactions in this question to illustrate the concept.

Exercise 22.6 ★★ **CONSOLIDATION WORKSHEET, CONSOLIDATED STATEMENT OF PROFIT OR LOSS AND OTHER COMPREHENSIVE INCOME**

Financial information for Jasmine Ltd and Poppy Ltd for the year ended 30 June 2016 is shown below:

	Jasmine Ltd	Poppy Ltd
Sales revenue	$78 000	$40 000
Proceeds from sale of office furniture	—	3 000
Dividend revenue	4 400	1 600
Total income	82 400	44 600
Cost of sales	60 000	30 000
Other expenses	10 800	7 500
Total expenses	70 800	37 500
Profit before income tax	11 600	7 100
Income tax expense	(3 000)	(2 200)
Profit for the year	8 600	4 900
Retained earnings (1/7/15)	14 500	2 800
	23 100	7 700
Interim dividend paid	4 000	2 000
Final dividend declared	8 000	2 400
	12 000	4 400
Retained earnings (30/6/16)	$11 100	$ 3 300

Additional information

(a) On 1 July 2014, Jasmine Ltd purchased 100% of the shares of Poppy Ltd for $50 000. At that date the equity of the two entities was as follows:

	Jasmine Ltd	Poppy Ltd
Asset revaluation surplus	$25 000	$ 4 000
Retained earnings	14 500	2 800
Share capital	50 000	40 000

At 1 July 2014, all the identifiable assets and liabilities of Poppy Ltd were recorded at fair value except for the following:

	Carrying amount	Fair value
Plant and equipment (cost $80 000)	$60 000	$61 000
Inventory	3 000	3 500

All of this inventory was sold by December 2014. The plant and equipment had a further 5-year life. Any valuation adjustments are made on consolidation.

(b) Jasmine Ltd records dividend receivable as revenue when dividends are declared.

(c) The opening inventory of Poppy Ltd included goods which cost Poppy Ltd $2000. Poppy Ltd purchased this inventory from Jasmine Ltd at cost plus 33$^1/_3$%.

(d) Intragroup sales totalled $10 000 for the year. Sales from Jasmine Ltd to Poppy Ltd, at cost plus 10%, amounted to $5600. The closing inventory of Jasmine Ltd included goods which cost Jasmine Ltd $4400. Jasmine Ltd purchased this inventory from Poppy Ltd at cost plus 10%.

(e) On 31 December 2015, Poppy Ltd sold Jasmine Ltd office furniture for $3000. This furniture originally cost Poppy Ltd $3000 and was written down to $2500 when sold. Jasmine Ltd depreciates furniture at the rate of 10% p.a. on cost.

(f) The asset revaluation surplus relates to the use of the revaluation model for land. The following movements occurred in this account:

	Jasmine Ltd	Poppy Ltd
1 July 2014 to 30 June 2015	$3 000	$(500)
1 July 2015 to 30 June 2016	$2 000	$ 500

(g) The tax rate is 30%.

Required

Prepare the consolidated statement of profit or loss and other comprehensive income for the year ended 30 June 2016.

Exercise 22.7

★★★

CONSOLIDATED WORKSHEET, CONSOLIDATED STATEMENT OF PROFIT OR LOSS AND OTHER COMPREHENSIVE INCOME

On 1 April 2015, Abby Ltd acquired all the issued ordinary shares (cum div.) of Ella Ltd for $100 000. At that date, relevant balances in the records of Ella Ltd were:

Share capital	$80 000
Asset revaluation surplus	5 000
Retained earnings	5 000
Dividend payable	4 000

All the identifiable assets and liabilities of Ella Ltd were recorded at fair values except for the following:

	Carrying amount	Fair value
Inventory	$10 000	$12 000
Plant (cost $80 000)	50 000	53 000

Immediately after the acquisition of its shares by Abby Ltd, Ella Ltd revalued its plant to fair value. The plant was expected to have a further 5-year life. All the inventory on hand at 1 April 2015 was sold by the end of the financial year.

At 1 April 2015, Ella Ltd had recorded goodwill of $2000. As a result of an impairment test on 31 March 2016, Ella Ltd wrote goodwill down by $1500 in the consolidation worksheet.

The dividend payable was subsequently paid in June 2015.

During the period ending 31 March 2016, intragroup sales consisted of $40 000 from Abby Ltd to Ella Ltd at a profit to Abby Ltd of $10 000. These were all sold to external entities by Ella Ltd for $42 000 before 31 March 2016. Ella Ltd also sold some inventory to Abby Ltd for $10 000. This had cost Ella Ltd $6000. Abby Ltd since has sold all the items to external entities for $8000, except one batch on which Ella Ltd recorded a $500 profit before tax (original cost to Ella Ltd was $1000).

Both entities use the revaluation model in accounting for land. During the 2015–16 period, Abby Ltd and Ella Ltd both recorded revaluation increments, these being $2200 and $1100 respectively.

The following information was obtained from the companies for the year ended 31 March 2016:

	Abby Ltd	Ella Ltd
Sales	$146 000	$120 000
Dividend revenue	4 000	—
Proceeds on sale of non-current asset	30 000	—
	180 000	120 000
Cost of sales	88 000	68 000
Other expenses	44 000	19 000
	132 000	87 000
Profit before income tax	48 000	33 000
Income tax expense	(12 000)	(14 000)
Profit for the year	36 000	19 000
Retained earnings (1/4/15)	10 000	5 000
Total available for appropriation	46 000	24 000
Dividend paid	(8 000)	(4 000)
Retained earnings (31/3/16)	$ 38 000	$ 20 000

Required

Prepare the consolidated statement of profit or loss and other comprehensive income as at 31 March 2016. Assume a tax rate of 30%.

Exercise 22.8 **CONSOLIDATION WORKSHEET, CONSOLIDATED FINANCIAL STATEMENTS**

★★★ On 31 December 2011, Lara Ltd acquired all the issued shares of Jade Ltd. On this date, the share capital of Jade Ltd consisted of 200 000 shares paid to 50c per share. Other reserves and retained earnings at this date consisted of:

General reserve	$25 000
Retained earnings	20 000

At 31 December 2011, all the identifiable assets and liabilities of Jade Ltd were recorded at fair value except for some plant and machinery. This plant and machinery, which cost $100 000, had a carrying amount of $85 000 and a fair value of $90 000. The estimated remaining useful life was 10 years. Adjustments for fair values are made on consolidation.

Immediately after acquisition, a dividend of $10 000 was declared and paid out of retained earnings. Also, 1 year after acquisition, Jade Ltd used $20 000 from the general reserve on hand at acquisition date to partly pay the balance unpaid on the issued shares.

The trial balances of Lara Ltd and Jade Ltd at 31 December 2016 were as shown below:

Trial Balances as at 31 December 2016	Lara Ltd	Jade Ltd
Credits		
Share capital	$ 500 000	$ 120 000
General reserve	25 000	5 000
Asset revaluation surplus	10 000	6 000
Retained earnings (1/1/16)	40 000	65 000
Other components of equity	15 000	10 000
Current tax liabilities	22 000	18 000
Deferred tax liabilities	6 240	5 200
Payables	22 000	14 000
Sales revenue	250 000	120 000
Other income	20 000	5 000
Proceeds from sale of property, plant and equipment	14 000	50 000
	$ 924 240	$ 418 200
Debits		
Income tax expense	$ 20 000	$ 10 000
Dividend declared	10 000	8 000
Plant and machinery	425 000	337 000
Accumulated depreciation	(300 000)	(261 000)
Motor vehicles	284 200	152 600
Accumulated depreciation	(160 000)	(100 000)
Receivables	25 000	7 310
Financial assets	60 000	40 000
Inventory	106 440	72 000
Bank	46 900	5 990
Deferred tax assets	12 700	6 300
Shares in Jade Ltd	160 000	—
Cost of sales	188 000	80 000
Other expenses	28 000	5 000
Carrying amount of property, plant and equipment sold	18 000	55 000
	$ 924 240	$ 418 200

Additional information
(a) During the current period, Lara Ltd sold inventory to Jade Ltd for $20 000. This had originally cost Lara Ltd $18 200. Jade Ltd has, by 31 December 2016, sold half this inventory for $12 310.
(b) The tax rate is 30%.
(c) Certain specialised items of plant, considered a separate class of assets, are measured using the revaluation model. At 1 January 2015, the balances of the asset revaluation surplus were $8000 (Lara Ltd) and $7000 (Jade Ltd).

(d) The Other Components of Equity account reflects movements in the financial assets. The balances of this account at 1 January 2015 were $12 000 (Lara Ltd) and $8000 (Jade Ltd).

Required

Prepare the consolidated financial statements as at 31 December 2016.

CONSOLIDATION WORKSHEET

★★★ On 1 July 2014, Monique Ltd acquired all the shares of Madeleine Ltd for $137 200. At acquisition date, the equity of Madeleine Ltd consisted of:

Share capital	$80 000
General reserve	16 000
Retained earnings	21 000

On this date, all the identifiable assets and liabilities of Madeleine Ltd were recorded at fair value except for the following assets:

	Carrying amount	Fair value
Inventory	$50 000	$56 000
Motor vehicles (cost $18 000)	15 000	16 000
Furniture and fittings (cost $30 000)	24 000	32 000
Land	18 480	24 480

The inventory and land on hand in Madeleine Ltd at 1 July 2014 were sold during the following 12 months. The motor vehicles, which at acquisition date were estimated to have a 4-year life, were sold on 1 January 2016. Except for land, valuation adjustments are made on consolidation and, on realisation of a business combination valuation reserve, a transfer is made to retained earnings on consolidation. The furniture and fittings were estimated to have a further 8-year life. At 1 July 2014, Madeleine Ltd had not recorded any goodwill.

The following trial balances were prepared for the companies at 30 June 2016:

Credits	Monique Ltd	Madeleine Ltd
Share capital	$170 000	$ 80 000
General reserve	41 000	22 000
Retained earnings (1/7/15)	16 000	29 500
Debentures	120 000	—
Final dividend payable	10 000	3 000
Current tax liabilities	8 000	2 500
Other payables	34 800	10 100
Advance from Monique Ltd	—	10 000
Sales revenue	85 000	65 000
Other income	23 000	22 000
Accumulated depreciation		
— Motor vehicles	4 000	2 000
— Furniture and fittings	2 000	6 000
	$513 800	$252 100
Debits		
Cost of sales	$ 65 000	$ 53 500
Other expenses	22 000	27 000
Shares in Madeleine Ltd	137 200	—
Land	—	24 480
Motor vehicles	28 000	22 000
Furniture and fittings	34 000	37 300
Inventory	171 580	70 320
Other assets	8 620	3 100
Income tax expense	7 200	2 000
Interim dividend paid	4 000	2 000
Final dividend declared	10 000	3 000
Deferred tax assets	16 200	7 400
Advance to Madeleine Ltd	10 000	—
	$513 800	$252 100

Additional information

(a) Intragroup transfers of inventory consisted of:

1/7/14 to 30/6/15:	
Sales from Monique Ltd to Madeleine Ltd	$12 000
Profit in inventory on hand 30/6/15	200
1/7/15 to 30/6/16:	
Sales from Monique Ltd to Madeleine Ltd	15 000
Profit in inventory on hand 30/6/16	
(incl. $50 from previous period sales)	1 000

(b) The tax rate is 30%.

Required

Prepare the consolidation worksheet for the preparation of the consolidated financial statements for the period ended 30 June 2016.

23

Consolidation: non-controlling interest

ACCOUNTING STANDARDS IN FOCUS

IFRS 10 *Consolidated Financial Statements*

IFRS 3 *Business Combinations*

IAS 1 *Presentation of Financial Statements*

IFRS 12 *Disclosure of Interests in Other Entities*

LEARNING OBJECTIVES

After studying this chapter, you should be able to:

1. discuss the nature of the non-controlling interest (NCI)

2. explain the effects of the NCI on the consolidation process

3. explain how to calculate the NCI share of equity

4. explain how the calculation of the NCI is affected by the existence of intragroup transactions

5. explain how the NCI is affected by the existence of a gain on bargain purchase.

23.1 NON-CONTROLLING INTEREST EXPLAINED

In chapters 21 and 22, the group under consideration consisted of two entities where the parent owned *all* the share capital of the subsidiary. In this chapter, the group under discussion consists of a parent that has only a *partial* interest in the subsidiary; that is, the subsidiary is less than wholly owned by the parent.

23.1.1 Nature of the non-controlling interest (NCI)

Ownership interests in a subsidiary other than the parent are referred to as the non-controlling interest, or NCI. Appendix A of IFRS 10 *Consolidated Financial Statements* contains the following definition of NCI:

> Equity in a **subsidiary** not attributable, directly or indirectly, to a **parent**.

In figure 23.1, the group shown is illustrative of those discussed in this chapter. In this case, the parent entity owns 75% of the shares of a subsidiary. There are two owners in this group — the parent shareholders and the NCI. The NCI is a contributor of equity to the group.

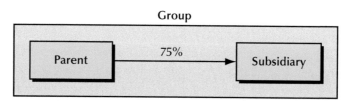

FIGURE 23.1 The group

According to paragraph 22 of IFRS 10, the NCI is to be identified and presented within equity, separately from the parent shareholders' equity; that is, it is regarded as an equity contributor to the group, rather than a liability of the group. This is because the NCI does not meet the definition of a liability as contained in the *Conceptual Framework*, because the group has no present obligation to provide economic outflows to the NCI. The NCI receives a share of consolidated equity, and is therefore a participant in the residual equity of the group.

Classification of the NCI as equity affects both the calculation of the NCI as well as how it is disclosed in the consolidated financial statements.

23.1.2 Calculation of the NCI share of equity

The NCI is entitled to a share of consolidated equity, because it is a contributor of equity to the consolidated group. Because consolidated equity is affected by profits and losses made in relation to transactions within the group, the calculation of the NCI is affected by the existence of intragroup transactions. In other words, the NCI is entitled to a share of the equity of the subsidiary adjusted for the effects of profits and losses made on intragroup transactions. *This is discussed in more detail in section 22.4.*

23.1.3 Disclosure of the NCI

According to paragraph 22 of IFRS 10:

> A parent shall present non-controlling interests in the consolidated statement of financial position within equity, separately from the equity of the owners of the parent.

IAS 1 *Presentation of Financial Statements* confirms these disclosures. Paragraph 81B of IAS 1 requires the profit or loss and other comprehensive income for the period to be disclosed in the statement of profit or loss and other comprehensive income, showing separately the comprehensive income attributable to non-controlling interests, and that attributable to owners of the parent. Figure 22.2 shows how the statement of profit or loss and other comprehensive income may be shown. Note that in terms of the various line items in the statement, such as revenues and expenses, it is the total consolidated amount that is disclosed. It is only the consolidated profit and comprehensive income that is divided into parent share and NCI share.

According to paragraph 106(a) of IAS 1, the total comprehensive income for the period must be disclosed in the statement of changes in equity, showing separately the total amounts attributable to owners of the parent and to non-controlling interests. Figure 23.3 provides an example of disclosures in the statement of changes of equity. Note that the only line item for which the NCI must be shown is the total comprehensive income for the period. There is no requirement to show the NCI share of each equity account.

IRIS LTD
Consolidated Statement of Profit or Loss and Other Comprehensive Income
for the year ended 30 June 2016

	2016 $m	2015 $m
Revenue	500	450
Expenses	280	260
Gross profit	220	190
Finance costs	40	35
	180	155
Share of after-tax profit of associates	30	25
Profit before tax	210	180
Income tax expense	(28)	(22)
PROFIT FOR THE YEAR	182	158
Other comprehensive income	31	24
TOTAL COMPREHENSIVE INCOME FOR THE YEAR	213	182
Profit attributable to:		
Owners of the parent	151	140
Non-controlling interests	31	18
	182	158
Total comprehensive income attributable to:		
Owners of the parent	179	160
Non-controlling interests	34	22
	213	182

FIGURE 23.2 Disclosure of NCI in the statement of profit or loss and other comprehensive income

IRIS LTD
Consolidated Statement of Changes in Equity (extract)
for the year ended 30 June 2016

	Total equity					Non-controlling interest	Owners of the parent
	Share capital $m	Revaluation surplus $m	Translation reserve $m	Retained earnings $m	Total $m	$m	$m
Balance at 1 July 2015	400	120	100	250	870	130	740
Changes in accounting policy	—	—	—	—	—	—	—
Total comprehensive income for the period	—	21	10	182	213	34	179
Dividends	—	—	—	(150)	(150)	(10)	(140)
Issue of share capital	—	—	—	—	—	—	—
Balance at 30 June 2016	400	141	110	282	933	154	779

FIGURE 23.3 Disclosure of NCI in the statement of changes in equity

Similarly, paragraph 54(q) of IAS 1 requires disclosure in the statement of financial position of the total NCI share of equity while paragraph 54(r) requires disclosure of the issued capital and reserves attributable to owners of the parent. The equity section of the statement of financial position could then appear as in figure 23.4. In the statement of financial position, only the total NCI share of equity is disclosed, rather than the NCI share of the different categories of equity. The NCI share of the various categories of equity and the changes in those balances can be seen in the statement of changes in equity. Note that the consolidated assets and liabilities are those for the whole of the group; it is only equity that is divided into parent and NCI shares.

IRIS LTD Statement of Financial Position (extract) as at 30 June 2016		
	2014 $m	2015 $m
EQUITY		
Share capital	400	400
Other reserves	251	220
Retained earnings	282	250
	933	870
Non-controlling interests	154	130
Equity attributable to owners of the parent	779	740

FIGURE 23.4 Disclosure of NCI in the statement of financial position

IFRS 12 *Disclosure of Interests in Other Entities* also contains disclosures required for subsidiaries in which there are non-controlling interests. Paragraph 12 of IFRS 12 states:

An entity shall disclose for each of its subsidiaries that have non-controlling interests that are material to the reporting entity:
(a) the name of the subsidiary.
(b) the principal place of business (and country of incorporation if different from the principal place of business) of the subsidiary.
(c) the proportion of ownership interests held by non-controlling interests.
(d) the proportion of voting rights held by non-controlling interests, if different from the proportion of ownership interests held.
(e) the profit or loss allocated to non-controlling interests of the subsidiary during the reporting period.
(f) accumulated non-controlling interests of the subsidiary at the end of the reporting period.
(g) summarised financial information about the subsidiary (see paragraph B10).

23.2 EFFECTS OF AN NCI ON THE CONSOLIDATION PROCESS

Paragraph 32 of IFRS 3 states:

The acquirer shall recognise goodwill as of the acquisition date measured as the excess of (a) over (b) below:
(a) the aggregate of:
   (i) the consideration transferred measured in accordance with this IFRS, which generally requires acquisition-date fair value (see paragraph 37);
   (ii) the amount of any non-controlling interest in the acquiree measured in accordance with this IFRS; and
   (iii) in a business combination achieved in stages (see paragraphs 41 and 42), the acquisition date fair value of the acquirer's previously held equity interests in the acquiree.
(b) the net of the acquisition-date amounts of the identifiable assets acquired and the liabilities assumed measured in accordance with this IFRS.

Note that this choice is not an accounting policy choice, but is made for each business combination.

Consider a situation where A Ltd acquires 50% of the shares of B Ltd, having previously acquired 20% of the shares of B Ltd. Holding 70% of the shares of B Ltd gives A Ltd control of that entity. At acquisition date, there is an NCI of 30%. Note:

• Where the parent acquires less than all the shares of a subsidiary, it acquires only a portion of the total equity or total net assets of the subsidiary. Hence, the consideration transferred is for only a portion of the net assets of the subsidiary; in this example, 50%.

• In essence, the 20% investment held prior to the parent obtaining control must be revalued at acquisition date to fair value.

The next step is to measure the amount of the 30% non-controlling interest in the subsidiary. The problem with this step is that IFRS 3 allows alternative treatments. Paragraph 19 of IFRS 3 states:

For each business combination, the acquirer shall measure at the acquisition date components of non-controlling interests in the acquiree that are present ownership interests and entitle their holders to a proportionate share of the entity's net assets in the event of liquidation at either:
(a) fair value; or
(b) the present ownership instruments' proportionate share in the recognised amounts of the acquiree's identifiable net assets.
All other components of non-controlling interests shall be measured at their acquisition-date fair values, unless another measurement basis is required by IFRSs.

Which alternative is chosen affects the determination of goodwill and the subsequent consolidation adjustments. Where the first alternative is used, the goodwill attributable to both the NCI and the parent is measured. Under the second alternative, only the goodwill attributable to the parent is measured. The methods are sometimes referred to as the 'full goodwill' and the 'partial goodwill' methods — see paragraph BC205 of the Basis for Conclusions on IFRS 3 for further elaboration. These terms are used in this chapter to distinguish between the two methods. *The methods are demonstrated in sections 23.2.1 and 23.2.2 and the reasons for the standard setters allowing optional measurements, as well as factors to consider in choosing between the methods, is discussed in section 23.2.3.*

23.2.1 Full goodwill method

Under this method, at acquisition date, the NCI in the subsidiary is measured at fair value. The fair value is determined on the basis of the market prices for shares not acquired by the parent, or, if these are not available, a valuation technique is used.

It is not sufficient to use the consideration paid by the acquirer to measure the fair value of the NCI. For example, if a parent paid $80 000 for 80% of the shares of a subsidiary, then the fair value of the NCI cannot be assumed to be $20 000 (i.e. 20/80 × $80 000). It may be that the acquirer paid a control premium in order to acquire a controlling interest in the subsidiary. Relating this to the nature of goodwill in chapter 13, core goodwill includes the component of combination goodwill, relating to synergies arising because of the combination of the parent and the subsidiary. The parent would increase the consideration it was prepared to pay due to these synergies. However, these synergies may result in increased earnings in the parent and not the subsidiary. In this case, the NCI does not receive any share of those synergies. Hence, the consideration paid by the parent could not be used to measure the fair value of the NCI in the subsidiary.

To illustrate the method, assume that P Ltd paid $169 600 for 80% of the shares of S Ltd on 1 July 2013. All identifiable assets and liabilities of the subsidiary were recorded at fair value, except for land for which the fair value was $10 000 greater than cost. The tax rate is 30%. The NCI in S Ltd was considered to have a fair value of $42 000. At acquisition date, the equity of S Ltd consisted of:

Share capital	$100 000
General reserve	60 000
Retained earnings	40 000

The acquisition analysis is as follows:

Net fair value of identifiable assets and liabilities of S Ltd	= $100 000 + $60 000 + $40 000 + $10 000(1 − 30%) (BCVR — land) = $207 000
(a) Consideration transferred	= $169 600
(b) Non-controlling interest in S Ltd	= $42 000
Aggregate of (a) and (b)	= $211 600
Goodwill	= $211 600 − $207 000 = $4600
Goodwill of S Ltd	
Fair value of S Ltd	= $42 000/20% = $210 000
Net fair value of identifiable assets and liabilities of S Ltd	= $207 000
Goodwill of S Ltd	= $210 000 − $207 000 = $3000
Goodwill of P Ltd	
Goodwill acquired	= $4600
Goodwill of S Ltd	= $3000
Goodwill of P Ltd – control premium	= $1600

Note the following:
• The acquired goodwill of $4600 calculated in the acquisition analysis consists of both the goodwill of the subsidiary and the premium paid by the parent to acquire control over the subsidiary.

- As the fair value of the NCI (20%) is determined to be $42 000, if P Ltd were to acquire 80% of S Ltd, it would expect to pay $168 000 (i.e. 80/20 × $42 000). As P Ltd paid $169 600, it paid a control premium of $1600. This is recognised as goodwill attributable to P Ltd. Effectively the goodwill of $4600 is broken down into:

Control premium paid by P Ltd	$1600
Parent's share of S Ltd's goodwill	$2400 [$4000 − $1600 or 80% × $3000]
NCI share of S Ltd's goodwill	$600 [20% × $3000]

- The goodwill attributable to P Ltd — both share of S Ltd's goodwill and the control premium — could be calculated as follows:

Net fair value acquired by P Ltd	= 80% × $207 000
	= $165 600
Consideration transferred	= $169 600
Goodwill attributable to P Ltd	= $169 600 − $165 600
	= $4000

- The control premium is recognised as part of goodwill on consolidation, but is not attributable to the NCI.

In accounting for the goodwill, a business combination valuation reserve is raised for the goodwill of the subsidiary, namely $3000. This reserve is then attributed on a proportional basis to the parent and the NCI, being $2400 to the parent and $600 to the NCI. The control premium goodwill is recognised in the adjustment to eliminate the investment in the subsidiary only as the earnings from this combination goodwill flow into the parent's earnings and not that of the subsidiary — otherwise it would be included in the valuation of the NCI interest in the subsidiary.

The consolidation worksheet entries are as follows:

1. Business combination valuation entries			
Land	Dr	10 000	
Deferred Tax Liability	Cr		3 000
Business Combination Valuation Reserve	Cr		7 000
(Revaluation of land)			
Goodwill	Dr	3 000	
Business Combination Valuation Reserve	Cr		3 000
(Recognition of subsidiary goodwill)			
2. Elimination of investment in subsidiary			
Retained Earnings [80% × $40 000]	Dr	32 000	
Share Capital [80% × $100 000]	Dr	80 000	
General Reserve [80% × $60 000]	Dr	48 000	
Business Combination Valuation Reserve [80% ($7000 + $3000)]	Dr	8 000	
Goodwill	Dr	1 600	
Shares in S Ltd	Cr		169 600

Two *business combination valuation entries* are required: one for the revaluation of the land to fair value, and the second to recognise the goodwill of the subsidiary.

In relation to the equity on hand at acquisition date, 80% is attributable to the parent, and 20% is attributable to the NCI. The *elimination of investment in subsidiary* relates to the investment by the parent in the subsidiary, and thus relates to 80% of the amounts shown in the acquisition analysis. The adjustments to equity in the elimination of investment in subsidiary are then determined by taking 80% of the recorded equity of the subsidiary and 80% of the business combination valuation reserves recognised as a result of differences between fair values and carrying amounts of the subsidiary's identifiable assets and liabilities at acquisition date and the goodwill of the subsidiary. The goodwill relating to the control premium is recognised in the elimination of investment in subsidiary.

23.2.2 Partial goodwill method

Under the second option, at acquisition date, the NCI is measured as the NCI's proportionate share of the acquiree's identifiable net assets. The NCI therefore does not get a share of any equity relating to goodwill as goodwill is defined in Appendix A of IFRS 3 as the future economic benefits arising from assets not individually identified. The only goodwill recognised is that acquired by the parent in the business combination — hence the term 'partial' goodwill. According to paragraph 32 of IFRS 3, using the measurement of the NCI share of equity based on the NCI's proportionate share of the acquiree's identifiable net assets:

> Goodwill = consideration transferred *plus* previously acquired investment by parent *plus* NCI share of identifiable assets and liabilities of subsidiary *less* net fair value of identifiable assets and liabilities of subsidiary.

To illustrate, using the same example as in section 23.2.1, assume that P Ltd paid $169 600 for 80% of the shares of S Ltd on 1 July 2013. All identifiable assets and liabilities of the subsidiary were recorded at fair value, except for land for which the fair value was $10 000 greater than cost. The tax rate is 30%. At acquisition date, the equity of S Ltd consisted of:

Share capital	$100 000
General reserve	60 000
Retained earnings	40 000

The acquisition analysis is as follows:

Net fair value of identifiable assets and liabilities of S Ltd	= $100 000 + $60 000 + $40 000
	+ $10 000(1 − 30%) (BCVR — land)
	= $207 000
(a) Consideration transferred	= $169 600
(b) Non-controlling interest in S Ltd	= 20% × $207 000
	= $41 400
Aggregate of (a) and (b)	= $211 000
Goodwill	= $211 000 − $207 000
	= $4000

Note that the $4000 goodwill is the same as the parent's share calculated in section 23.2.1, consisting of the parent's share of the subsidiary's goodwill (80% × $3000 = $2400) and any control premium ($1600).

The consolidation worksheet entries are:

Business combination valuation entry			
Land	Dr	10 000	
Deferred Tax Liability	Cr		3 000
Business Combination Valuation Reserve	Cr		7 000
Elimination of investment in subsidiary			
Retained Earnings [80% × $40 000]	Dr	32 000	
Share Capital [80% × $100 000]	Dr	80 000	
General Reserve [80% × $60 000]	Dr	48 000	
Business Combination Valuation Reserve [80% × $7000]	Dr	5 600	
Goodwill	Dr	4 000	
Shares in S Ltd	Cr		169 600

Note firstly that there is no business combination valuation entry for goodwill. This is because only the parent's share of the goodwill is recognised. A business combination valuation adjustment to recognise goodwill is only used under the full goodwill method where both the parent's and the NCI's share of goodwill is recognised.

In relation to the equity on hand at acquisition date, only 80% is attributable to the parent, and 20% is attributable to the NCI. The elimination of investment in subsidiary relates to the investment by the parent in the subsidiary, and thus relates to 80% of the amounts shown in the acquisition analysis. The adjustments to equity in the elimination of investment in subsidiary are then determined by taking 80% of the recorded equity of the subsidiary and 80% of the business combination valuation reserves recognised as a result of differences between fair value and carrying amounts of the subsidiary's identifiable assets and liabilities at acquisition date. Because only the parent's share of goodwill is recognised, this is accounted for in the elimination of investment in subsidiary which also relates to the investment by the parent in the subsidiary.

23.2.3 Reasons for, and choosing between, the options

The International Accounting Standards Board (IASB®) supports the principle of measuring all components of a business combination at fair value (paragraph BC212); however, paragraph BC213 notes some arguments against applying this to the NCI in the acquiree:

- It is more costly to measure the NCI at fair value than at the proportionate share of the net fair value of the identifiable net assets of the acquiree.
- There is not sufficient evidence to assess the marginal benefits of reporting the acquisition-date fair value of NCIs.
- Respondents to the exposure draft saw little information of value in the reported NCI, regardless of how it is measured.

One of the options considered by the IASB in writing the standard was to require the use of the fair value method for measuring the NCI but allowing entities to use the proportionate method where there exists 'undue cost or effort' in measuring the fair value. However, the IASB rejected this option as it did not think the term undue cost or effort would be applied consistently (paragraph BC215).

The IASB noted three main differences in outcome that occur where the partial goodwill method is used instead of the full goodwill method:

1. The amounts recognised for the NCI share of equity and goodwill would be lower.
2. Where IAS 36 *Impairment of Assets* is applied to a cash-generating unit containing goodwill, as the goodwill recognised by the CGU is lower, this affects the impairment loss relating to goodwill.
3. There is also an effect where an acquirer subsequently obtains further shares in the subsidiary at a later date. An explanation of this effect is beyond the scope of this book.

In choosing which method to use — full or partial goodwill — it is these three effects on the financial statements, both current and in the future, that must be taken into consideration. For example, if management has future intentions of acquiring more shares in the subsidiary (i.e. by acquiring some of the shares held by the NCI), then the potential impact on equity when that acquisition occurs will need to be considered.

23.2.4 Intragroup transactions

As already noted *(see chapter 22)*, because the transactions occur within the economic entity, the full effects of transactions within the group are adjusted on consolidation. In essence, the worksheet adjustment entries used in chapter 22 are the same regardless of whether the subsidiary is wholly or partly owned by its parent. The only exception to the entries used in chapter 22 is for dividends.

Where an NCI exists, any dividends declared or paid by a subsidiary are paid proportionately (to the extent of the ownership interest in the subsidiary) to the parent and proportionately to the NCI. In adjusting for dividends paid by a subsidiary, only the dividend paid or payable to the parent is eliminated on consolidation. In other words, there is a proportional adjustment of the dividend paid or declared. As with other intragroup transactions, the adjustment relates to the flow within the group. A payment or a declaration of dividends by a subsidiary reduces the NCI share of subsidiary equity because the equity of the subsidiary is reduced by the payment or declaration of dividends. In calculating the NCI share of subsidiary equity, the existence of dividends must be taken into consideration *(see section 23.3.3)*. Where a dividend is declared, the NCI share of equity is reduced, and a liability to pay dividends to the NCI is shown in the consolidated statement of financial position.

To illustrate, assume a parent owns 80% of the share capital of a subsidiary. In the current period, the subsidiary pays a $1000 dividend and declares a further $1500 dividend. The adjustment entries in the consolidation worksheet in the current period are:

Dividend Revenue	Dr	800	
Dividend Paid	Cr		800
(80% × $1000)			
Dividend Payable	Dr	1 200	
Dividend Declared	Cr		1 200
(80% × $1500)			
Dividend Revenue	Dr	1 200	
Dividend Receivable	Cr		1 200
(80% × $1500)			

23.2.5 Consolidation worksheet

Because the disclosure requirements for the NCI require the extraction of the NCI share of various equity items, the consolidation worksheet is changed to enable this information to be produced. Figure 23.5 contains an example of the changed worksheet. In particular, note that two new columns are added, a *debit column* and a *credit column* for the calculation of the NCI share of equity. These two columns are not adjustment or elimination columns. Instead, they are used to divide consolidated equity into NCI share and parent entity share. The worksheet shown in figure 23.5 also contains a column showing the figures for the consolidated group. This column is shown between the adjustment columns and the NCI columns, and it is the summation of the financial statements of the group members and the consolidation adjustments. The parent figures are then determined by subtracting the NCI share of equity from the total consolidated equity of the group.

			Adjustments			Non-controlling interest		
Financial statements	P Ltd	S Ltd	Dr	Cr	Group	Dr	Cr	Parent
Profit/(loss)	5 000	4 000			9 000	400		8 600
Retained earnings (opening balance)	10 000	8 000			18 000	800		17 200
Transfer from reserves	4 000	2 000			6 000	200		5 800
Total available for appropriation	19 000	14 000			33 000			31 600
Interim dividend paid	2 000	1 500			3 500		150	3 350
Final dividend declared	4 000	2 500			6 500		250	6 250
Transfer to reserves	3 000	1 000			4 000		100	3 900
	9 000	5 000			14 000			13 500
Retained earnings (closing balance)	10 000	9 000			19 000			18 100
Share capital	50 000	40 000			90 000	4 000		86 000
Other reserves	30 000	20 000			50 000	2 000		48 000
	90 000	69 000			159 000			152 100
Asset revaluation surplus (opening balance)	4 000	5 000			9 000	500		8 500
Revaluation increases	2 000	2 000			4 000	200		3 800
Asset revaluation surplus (closing balance)	6 000	7 000			13 000			12 300
Total equity: parent								164 400
Total equity: NCI							7 600	7 600
Total equity	96 000	76 000			172 000	8 100	8 100	172 000
Current liabilities	3 000	2 000			5 000			
Non-current liabilities	8 000	6 000			14 000			
Total liabilities	11 000	8 000			19 000			
Total equity and liabilities	107 000	84 000			191 000			

FIGURE 23.5 Consolidation worksheet containing NCI columns

In figure 23.5, the amounts in the debit NCI column record the NCI share of the relevant equity item. This amount is subtracted in the consolidation process so that the consolidation column contains the parent's share of consolidated equity.

The first line in figure 23.5 is the consolidated profit/(loss) for the period. This amount is then attributed to the parent and the NCI. In all subsequent equity lines, the NCI share is recorded in the debit NCI column, and the parent's share of each equity account is calculated. The total NCI share of equity is then added to the parent column to give total consolidated equity.

The NCI share of retained earnings is increased by subsidiary profits and transfers from reserves, and decreased by transfers to reserves and payments and declarations of dividends. The total NCI share of equity is then the sum of the NCI share of capital, other reserves and retained earnings. The assets and liabilities of the group are shown in total and not allocated to the equity interests in the group — see, for example, the liabilities section in figure 23.5.

23.3 CALCULATING THE NCI SHARE OF EQUITY

Non-controlling interests in the net assets consist of the amount of those non-controlling interests at the date of the original combination calculated in accordance with IFRS 3 and the non-controlling interests' share of changes in equity since the date of the combination.

Changes in equity since the acquisition date must be taken into account. Note that these changes not only are in the recorded equity of the subsidiary, but also relate to other changes in consolidated equity. As noted earlier in this chapter, the NCI is entitled to a share of *consolidated* equity. This requires taking into account adjustments for profits or losses made as a result of intragroup transactions because these profits or losses are not recognised by the group.

The calculation of the NCI is done in two stages: (1) the NCI share of recorded equity is measured *(see section 23.3.1)*, and (2) this share is adjusted for the effects of intragroup transactions *(see section 23.4)*.

23.3.1 NCI share of recorded equity of the subsidiary

The equity of the subsidiary consists of the equity contained in the actual records of the subsidiary as well as any business combination valuation reserves created on consolidation at the acquisition date, where the identifiable assets and liabilities of the subsidiary are recorded at amounts different from their fair values. The NCI is entitled to a share of subsidiary equity at the end of the reporting period, which consists of the equity on hand at acquisition date plus any changes in that equity between acquisition date and the end of the reporting period. The calculation of the NCI share of equity at a point in time is done in three steps:

1. Determine the NCI share of equity of the subsidiary at acquisition date.
2. Determine the NCI share of the change in subsidiary equity between the acquisition date and the beginning of the current period for which the consolidated financial statements are being prepared.
3. Determine the NCI share of the changes in subsidiary equity in the current period.

The calculation could be represented diagrammatically, as shown in figure 23.6.

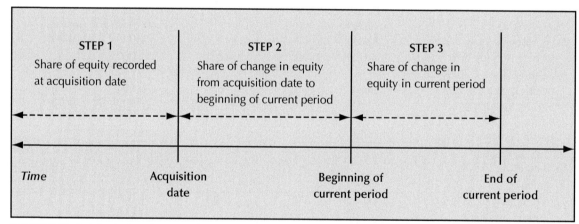

FIGURE 23.6 Calculating the NCI share of equity
Source: Based on a diagram by Peter Gerhardy, Ernst & Young, Adelaide.

Note that, in calculating the NCI share of equity at the end of the current period, the information relating to the NCI share of equity from steps 1 and 2 should be available from the previous period's consolidation worksheet.

To illustrate the above procedure, consider the calculation of the NCI share of retained earnings over a 5-year period. Assume the following information in relation to Cormorant Ltd:

Retained earnings as at 1 July 2011	$10 000
Retained earnings as at 30 June 2015	50 000
Profit for the 2015–16 period	15 000
Retained earnings as at 30 June 2016	65 000

Assume that Pelican Ltd had acquired 80% of the share capital of Cormorant Ltd at 1 July 2011, and the consolidated financial statements were being prepared at 30 June 2016. The 20% NCI in Cormorant Ltd is therefore entitled to a share of the retained earnings balance of $65 000, a share equal to $13 000. This share is calculated in three steps:

Step 1. A share of the balance at 1 July 2011 (20% × $10 000)	= $ 2 000
Step 2. A share of the change in retained earnings from the acquisition date to the beginning of the current period (20% × [$50 000 − $10 000])	= 8 000
Step 3. A share of the current period increase in retained earnings (20% × $15 000) =	3 000
	$13 000

The increase in retained earnings is broken into these three steps because accounting is based on time periods. The NCI is entitled to a share of the profits of past periods as well as a share of the profits of the current period. Note that, in calculating the NCI share of retained earnings for Cormorant Ltd at 30 June 2017 (1 year after the above calculation), the total of steps 1 and 2 for the 2017 calculation would be $13 000, as calculated above. The only additional calculation would be the share of changes in retained earnings in the 2016–17 period.

The separate calculations are not based on a division of equity into pre-acquisition and post-acquisition equity. The division of equity is based on *time* — changes in equity are calculated on a period-by-period basis for accounting purposes.

The NCI columns in the consolidation worksheet contain the amounts relating to the three steps noted above. The journal entries used in the NCI columns of the consolidation worksheet to reflect the NCI share of equity are based on the three-step approach. The form of these entries is:

Step 1: NCI at acquisition date

Share Capital	Dr	xxx	
Business Combination Valuation Reserve	Dr	xxx	
Retained Earnings (opening balance)	Dr	xxx	
NCI	Cr		xxx

Step 2: NCI share of changes in equity between acquisition date and beginning of the current period

Retained Earnings (opening balance)	Dr	xxx	
NCI	Cr		xxx

Step 3: NCI share of changes in equity in the current period

NCI Share of Profit/(Loss)	Dr	xxx	
NCI	Cr		xxx
Asset Revaluation Increases	Dr	xxx	
NCI	Cr		xxx
NCI	Dr	xxx	
Dividend Paid	Cr		xxx
NCI	Dr	xxx	
Dividend Declared	Cr		xxx

The effects of these journal entries can be seen in the consolidation worksheet in figure 23.5. The above entries are illustrative only, and there may be others where there are transfers to or from reserves that affect the balances of equity in the subsidiary. The effects of these transactions are illustrated in the next section.

23.3.2 Accounting at acquisition date

This section illustrates the effects that the existence of an NCI has on the valuation entries, the acquisition analysis and the elimination of investment in subsidiary, as well as the step 1 calculation of the NCI share of equity at acquisition date. *As noted in section 23.2*, the acquisition analysis and subsequent consolidation worksheet entries are affected by whether the full goodwill or partial goodwill option is used in the measurement of the NCI's share of the subsidiary at acquisition date. The choice of method affects the accounting at acquisition date but has an effect on accounting subsequent to acquisition date only if there is an impairment of goodwill or the parent changes its equity interest in the subsidiary. Neither of these events is covered in this book.

Full goodwill method

On 1 July 2013, Heron Ltd acquired 60% of the shares (cum div.) of Petrel Ltd for $45 600 when the equity of Petrel Ltd consisted of:

Share capital	$40 000
General reserve	2 000
Retained earnings	2 000

At acquisition date, the liabilities of Petrel Ltd included a dividend payable of $1000. All the identifiable assets and liabilities of Petrel Ltd were recorded at fair value except for equipment and inventory:

	Carrying amount	Fair value
Equipment (cost $250 000)	$180 000	$200 000
Inventory	40 000	50 000

The tax rate is 30%. The fair value of the NCI in Petrel Ltd at 1 July 2013 was $28 000.

Acquisition analysis

Net fair value of identifiable assets and liabilities of Petrel Ltd	= $40 000 (capital) + $2000 (general reserve) + $2000 (retained earnings) + $20 000(1 − 30%) (BCVR — equipment) + $10 000(1 − 30%) (BCVR — inventory) = $65 000
(a) Consideration transferred	= $45 600 − (60% × $1000) (dividend receivable) = $45 000
(b) Non-controlling interest in Petrel Ltd	= $28 000
Aggregate of (a) and (b)	= $73 000
Goodwill	= $73 000 − $65 000 = $8000
Goodwill of Petrel Ltd	
Fair value of Petrel Ltd	= $28 000/40% = $70 000
Net fair value of identifiable assets and liabilities of Petrel Ltd	= $65 000
Goodwill of Petrel Ltd	= $70 000 − $65 000 = $5000
Goodwill of Heron Ltd	
Goodwill acquired	= $8000
Goodwill of Petrel Ltd	= $5000
Goodwill of Heron Ltd — control premium	= $3000

Where an NCI exists, because the parent acquires only a part of the ownership interest of the subsidiary, the parent acquires only a proportionate share of each of the equity amounts in the subsidiary.

(1) *Business combination valuation entries*

The valuation entries are unaffected by the existence of an NCI. The purpose of these entries, in accordance with IFRS 3, is to show the assets and liabilities of the subsidiary at fair value at acquisition date. The entries for a consolidation worksheet (see figure 23.7 overleaf) prepared at acquisition date are:

		Dr	70 000	
Accumulated Depreciation – Equipment		Dr	70 000	
Equipment		Cr		50 000
Deferred Tax Liability		Cr		6 000
Business Combination Valuation Reserve		Cr		14 000
Inventory		Dr	10 000	
Deferred Tax Liability		Cr		3 000
Business Combination Valuation Reserve		Cr		7 000
Goodwill		Dr	5 000	
Business Combination Valuation Reserve		Cr		5 000

The business combination valuation reserve is pre-acquisition equity because it is recognised on consolidation at acquisition date. The NCI is entitled to a proportionate share of this reserve.

(2) *Elimination of investment and recognition of goodwill*

The first journal entry is read from the pre-acquisition analysis. The parent's proportional share of the various recorded equity accounts of the subsidiary, as well as the parent's share of the business combination valuation reserves, are eliminated against the investment account in the pre-acquisition entry. The goodwill relating to the control premium is also recognised. In this illustrative example, the elimination of investment in subsidiary is:

	Dr	1 200	
Retained Earnings (1/7/13)	Dr	1 200	
[60% × $2000]			
Share Capital	Dr	24 000	
[60% × $40 000]			
Business Combination Valuation Reserve	Dr	15 600	
[60% × ($14 000 + $7000 + $5000)]			
General Reserve	Dr	1 200	
[60% × $2000]			
Goodwill	Dr	3 000	
Shares in Petrel Ltd	Cr		45 000

At acquisition date, the subsidiary has recorded a dividend payable and the parent entity a dividend receivable. An adjustment entry is required because these are not dividends receivable or payable to parties external to the group. The adjustment is a proportional one as it relates only to the amount payable within the group:

	Dr	600	
Dividend Payable	Dr	600	
Dividend Receivable	Cr		600
[60% × $1000]			

No further adjustment is required once the dividend has been paid.

(3) *NCI share of equity at acquisition date*

The NCI at acquisition date (the step 1 calculation) is determined as the proportional share of the equity recorded by the subsidiary at that date and the valuation reserves recorded on consolidation:

Share capital	40% × $40 000	= $16 000
General reserve	40% × $2000	= 800
Business combination valuation reserve	40% × ($14 000 + $7000 + $5000)	= 10 400
Retained earnings	40% × $2000	= 800
		$28 000

The following entry is then passed in the NCI columns of the consolidation worksheet:

		Dr	800	
Retained Earnings (1/7/13)		Dr	800	
Share Capital		Dr	16 000	
Business Combination Valuation Reserve		Dr	10 400	
General Reserve		Dr	800	
NCI		Cr		28 000

This entry is passed as the step 1 NCI entry in all subsequent consolidation worksheets. It is never changed. Any subsequent changes in pre-acquisition equity are dealt with in the step 2 NCI calculation.

Figure 23.7 shows an extract from a consolidation worksheet for Heron Ltd and its subsidiary, Petrel Ltd, at acquisition date. Only the equity section of the worksheet is shown. The worksheet entries are (1) the business combination valuation entries, (2) the elimination of the investment and the recognition of goodwill (the dividend adjustment is not shown in figure 23.7 because only an extract from the worksheet is reproduced), and (3) the NCI step 1 entry.

Financial statements	Heron Ltd	Petrel Ltd	Adjustments				Group	Non-controlling interest				Parent
				Dr	Cr				Dr	Cr		
Retained earnings (1/7/13)	50 000	2 000	2	1 200			50 800	3	800			50 000
Share capital	100 000	40 000	2	24 000			116 000	3	16 000			100 000
General reserve	20 000	2 000	2	1 200			20 800	3	800			20 000
Business combination valuation reserve			2	15 600	14 000	1	10 400	3	10 400			0
					7 000	1						
					5 000	1						
Total equity: parent												170 000
Total equity: NCI										28 000	3	28 000
Total equity	170 000	44 000					198 000		28 000	28 000		198 000

FIGURE 23.7 Consolidation worksheet (extract) at acquisition date

Note that, in figure 23.7, the adjustment columns eliminate the parent's share of the pre-acquisition equity accounts and the NCI columns extract the NCI share of total equity. The parent column contains only the parent's share of post-acquisition equity, which in this case, being at acquisition date, is zero.

Partial goodwill method

ILLUSTRATIVE EXAMPLE 23.2 Consolidation worksheet entries at acquisition date

On 1 July 2013, Heron Ltd acquired 60% of the shares (cum div.) of Petrel Ltd for $45 600 when the equity of Petrel Ltd consisted of:

Share capital	$40 000
General reserve	2 000
Retained earnings	2 000

At acquisition date, the liabilities of Petrel Ltd included a dividend payable of $1000. All the identifiable assets and liabilities of Petrel Ltd were recorded at fair value except for equipment and inventory:

	Carrying amount	Fair value
Equipment (cost $250 000)	$180 000	$200 000
Inventory	40 000	50 000

The tax rate is 30%.

Acquisition analysis

Net fair value of identifiable assets and liabilities of Petrel Ltd	= $40 000 (capital) + $2000 (general reserve)
	+ $2000 (retained earnings)
	+ $20 000(1 – 30%) (BCVR — equipment)
	+ $10 000(1 – 30%) (BCVR — inventory)
	= $65 000
(a) Consideration transferred	= $45 600 – (60% × $1000) (dividend receivable)
	= $45 000
(b) Non-controlling interest in Petrel Ltd	= 40% × $65 000
	= $26 000
Aggregate of (a) and (b)	= $71 000
Goodwill	= $71 000 – $65 000
	= $6000

Where an NCI exists, because the parent acquires only a part of the ownership interest of the subsidiary, the parent acquires only a proportionate share of each of the equity amounts in the subsidiary.

(1) *Business combination valuation entries*

The valuation entries are unaffected by the existence of an NCI. The purpose of these entries, in accordance with IFRS 3, is to show the assets and liabilities of the subsidiary at fair value at acquisition date. The entries for a consolidation worksheet (see figure 23.8 overleaf) prepared at acquisition date are:

Accumulated Depreciation – Equipment	Dr	70 000	
Equipment	Cr		50 000
Deferred Tax Liability	Cr		6 000
Business Combination Valuation Reserve	Cr		14 000
Inventory	Dr	10 000	
Deferred Tax Liability	Cr		3 000
Business Combination Valuation Reserve	Cr		7 000

Note that there is no business combination valuation entry for goodwill as under the partial goodwill method only the parent's share of goodwill is recognised, and this is done in the pre-acquisition entry. The business combination valuation reserve is pre-acquisition equity because it is recognised on consolidation at acquisition date. The NCI is entitled to a proportionate share of this reserve. Because the reserve is recognised by the group, but not in the records of the subsidiary, this affects later calculations for the NCI share of equity.

(2) *Elimination of investment and recognition of goodwill*

The first elimination of investment in subsidiary is read from the pre-acquisition analysis. The parent's proportional share of the various recorded equity accounts of the subsidiary, as well as the parent's share of the business combination valuation reserves, are eliminated against the investment account in the pre-acquisition entry, and the parent's share of goodwill is recognised. In this illustrative example, the elimination of investment in subsidiary is:

Retained Earnings (1/7/13)	Dr	1 200	
[60% × $2000]			
Share Capital	Dr	24 000	
[60% × $40 000]			
Business Combination Valuation Reserve	Dr	12 600	
[60% × ($14 000 + $7000)]			
General Reserve	Dr	1 200	
[60% × $2000]			
Goodwill	Dr	6 000	
Shares in Petrel Ltd	Cr		45 000

At acquisition date, the subsidiary has recorded a dividend payable and the parent entity a dividend receivable. An adjustment entry is required because these are not dividends receivable or payable to parties external to the group. The adjustment is a proportional one as it relates only to the amount payable within the group:

Dividend Payable	Dr	600
Dividend Receivable	Cr		600
[60% × $1000]		

No further adjustment is required once the dividend has been paid.

(3) *NCI share of equity at acquisition date*

The NCI at acquisition date (the step 1 calculation) is determined as the proportional share of the equity recorded by the subsidiary at that date and the valuation reserves recorded on consolidation:

Share capital	40% × $40 000	= $16 000
General reserve	40% × $2000	= 800
Business combination valuation reserve	40% × ($14 000 + $7000)	= 8 400
Retained earnings	40% × $2000	= 800
		$26 000

The following entry is then passed in the NCI columns of the consolidation worksheet:

Retained Earnings (1/7/13)	Dr	800
Share Capital	Dr	16 000
Business Combination Valuation Reserve	Dr	8 400
General Reserve	Dr	800
NCI	Cr	26 000

This entry is passed as the step 1 NCI entry in all subsequent consolidation worksheets. It is never changed. Any subsequent changes in pre-acquisition equity are dealt with in the step 2 NCI calculation.

Figure 23.8 shows an extract from a consolidation worksheet for Heron Ltd and its subsidiary, Petrel Ltd, at acquisition date. Only the equity section of the worksheet is shown. The worksheet entries are (1) the business combination valuation entries, (2) the elimination of investment and recognition of goodwill (the dividend adjustment is not shown in figure 23.8 because only an extract from the worksheet is reproduced), and (3) the NCI step 1 entry.

Note that, in figure 23.8, the adjustment columns eliminate the parent's share of the pre-acquisition equity accounts and the NCI columns extract the NCI share of total equity. The parent column contains only the parent's share of post-acquisition equity, which in this case, being at acquisition date, is zero.

Financial statements	Heron Ltd	Petrel Ltd	Adjustments					Non-controlling interest				Parent
				Dr		Cr	Group		Dr		Cr	
Retained earnings (1/7/13)	50 000	2 000	2	1 200			50 800	3	800			50 000
Share capital	100 000	40 000	2	24 000			116 000	3	16 000			100 000
General reserve	20 000	2 000	2	1 200			20 800	3	800			20 000
Business combination valuation reserve			2	12 600	14 000	1	8 400	3	8 400			0
					7 000	1						
Total equity: parent												170 000
Total equity: NCI										26 000	3	26 000
Total equity	170 000	44 000					196 000		26 000	26 000		196 000

FIGURE 23.8 Consolidation worksheet (extract) at acquisition date

23.3.3 Accounting subsequent to acquisition date

Using illustrative example 23.2, the consolidation worksheet entries at the end of the period 3 years after the acquisition date are now considered. These entries are based on the *partial goodwill* method. However, the effects of the events occurring subsequent to acquisition date on the elimination of investment and recognition of goodwill and business combination valuation entries are the same for the full goodwill method. Assume that:

- all inventory on hand at 1 July 2013 is sold by 30 June 2014
- the dividend payable at acquisition date is paid in August 2013
- the equipment has an expected useful life of 5 years
- goodwill has not been impaired
- in the 3 years after the acquisition date, Petrel Ltd recorded the changes in equity shown in figure 23.9.

In preparing the consolidated financial statements at 30 June 2016, the consolidation worksheet contains the valuation entries, the elimination of investment and recognition of goodwill entries, the NCI entries and the adjustments for the dividend transactions.

	2013–14	2014–15	2015–16
Profit for the period	$ 8 000	$12 000	$15 000
Retained earnings (opening balance)	2 000	7 800	16 000
	10 000	19 800	31 000
Transfer from general reserve	—	—	500
	10 000	19 800	31 500
Transfer to general reserve	—	1 000	—
Dividend paid	1 000	1 200	1 500
Dividend declared	1 200	1 600	2 000
	2 200	3 800	3 500
Retained earnings (closing balance)	7 800	16 000	28 000
Share capital	40 000	40 000	40 000
General reserve	2 000	3 000	2 500
Other components of equity*	2 000	2 500	2 400

* Resulted from movement in fair value of financial assets.

FIGURE 23.9 Changes in equity over a 3-year period

(1) *Business combination valuation entries*

The valuation entries for the 2015–16 period differ from those prepared at acquisition date in that the equipment is depreciated, and the inventory has been sold. The entries at 30 June 2016 are:

Accumulated Depreciation – Equipment	Dr	70 000	
Equipment	Cr		50 000
Deferred Tax Liability	Cr		6 000
Business Combination Valuation Reserve	Cr		14 000
Depreciation Expense	Dr	4 000	
Retained Earnings (1/7/15)	Dr	8 000	
Accumulated Depreciation	Cr		12 000
(20% × $20 000 p.a.)			
Deferred Tax Liability	Dr	3 600	
Income Tax Expense	Cr		1 200
Retained Earnings (1/7/15)	Cr		2 400
(30% × $4000 p.a.)			

(If the full goodwill method had been used, the business combination entry relating to goodwill would be included at 30 June 2016 and would be the same as that used at acquisition date.)

(2) *Elimination of investment and recognition of goodwill*

The elimination of investment and recognition of goodwill entries have to take into consideration the following events occurring since acquisition date:

- The dividend of $1000 on hand at acquisition date has been paid.
- The inventory on hand at acquisition date has been sold.

The entry at 30 June 2016 is:

Retained Earnings (1/7/15)*	Dr	5 400	
Share Capital	Dr	24 000	
Business Combination Valuation Reserve**	Dr	8 400	
General Reserve	Dr	1 200	
Goodwill	Dr	6 000	
Shares in Petrel Ltd	Cr		45 000

    * $1200 + (60% × $7000) (BCVR transfer — inventory)
    ** 60% × $14 000

(3) *NCI share of equity at acquisition date (step 1)*

The NCI share of equity at acquisition date is as calculated previously. This entry is never changed from that calculated at that date — this applies whether the full goodwill or partial goodwill method is used.

Retained Earnings (1/7/15)	Dr	800	
Share Capital	Dr	16 000	
Business Combination Valuation Reserve	Dr	8 400	
General Reserve	Dr	800	
NCI	Cr		26 000

(4) *NCI share of changes in equity between acquisition date and beginning of the current period* (i.e. from 1 July 2013 to 30 June 2015) *(step 2)*

To calculate this entry, it is necessary to note any changes in subsidiary equity between the two dates. The changes will generally relate to movements in retained earnings and reserves, but changes in share capital, such as when a bonus dividend is paid, could occur.

In this example, there are four changes in subsidiary equity, as shown in figure 23.9:

- Retained earnings increased from $2000 to $16 000 — this will increase the NCI share of retained earnings.
- In the 2014–15 period, $1000 was transferred to the general reserve. Because the transfer has reduced retained earnings, the NCI share of retained earnings as calculated above has been reduced by this transfer; an increase in the NCI share of general reserve needs to be recognised as well as an increase in NCI in total.
- The sale of inventory in the 2013–14 period resulted in a transfer of $7000 from the business combination valuation reserve to retained earnings. Because the profits from the sale of inventory are recorded in the profits of the subsidiary, the NCI receives a share of the increased wealth relating to inventory. The NCI share of the business combination valuation reserve as recognised in step 1 must be reduced, with a reduction in NCI in total.
- Other components of equity increased by $2500, increasing the NCI share of equity by $1000.

Before noting the effects of these events in journal entry format, adjustments relating to the equipment on hand at acquisition date need to be considered. In the business combination valuation entry, the equipment on hand at acquisition date was revalued to fair value and the increase taken to the valuation reserve. By recognising the asset at fair value at acquisition date, the group recognises the extra benefits over and above the asset's carrying amount to be earned by the subsidiary. As expressed in the depreciation of the equipment (see the valuation entries above), the group expects the subsidiary to realise extra after-tax benefits of $2800 (i.e. $4000 depreciation expense less the credit of $1200 to income tax expense) in each of the 5 years after acquisition. Whereas the group recognises these extra benefits at acquisition date via the valuation reserve, the subsidiary recognises these benefits as profit in its records only as the equipment is used. Hence, the profit after tax recorded by the subsidiary in each of the 5 years after acquisition date will contain $2800 benefits from the equipment that the group recognised in the valuation reserve at acquisition date.

In calculating the NCI share of equity from acquisition date to the beginning of the current period, the NCI calculation will double-count the benefits from the equipment if there is no adjustment for the depreciation of the equipment. This occurs because the share of the NCI in equity calculated at acquisition date includes a share of the business combination valuation reserve created at that date in the consolidation worksheet. Therefore, giving the NCI a full share of the recorded profits of the subsidiary in the 5 years after acquisition date double-counts the benefits relating to the equipment. The NCI has already received a share of the valuation reserve in the step 1 calculation. Hence, in calculating the NCI share of changes in equity between acquisition date and the beginning of the current period (the step 2 calculation), there needs to be an adjustment for the extra depreciation of the equipment in relation to each of the years since acquisition date.

The adjustment for depreciation can be read directly from the valuation entry that records the depreciation on the equipment since acquisition date. In the valuation entry required for the 2015–16 consolidated financial statements (see (1) *Business combination valuation entries above*), there is a net debit adjustment to retained earnings (1/7/15) of $5600 (i.e. the $8000 adjustment for previous periods' depreciation less the $2400 adjustment for previous periods' tax effect) in relation to the after-tax effects of depreciating the equipment. This reflects the extra benefits received by the subsidiary as a result of using the equipment and recorded by the subsidiary in its retained earnings account.

In this example, the only adjustment to retained earnings in the business combination valuation entry is that relating to the equipment. In other examples, there may be a number of adjustments to retained earnings depending on the number of assets being revalued. All such adjustments must be taken into account in order not to double-count the NCI share of equity. In other words, to determine the adjustments needed to avoid double-counting, all adjustments to retained earnings in the valuation entries must be taken into consideration.

In illustrative example 23.2, the NCI share of changes in *retained earnings* is determined by calculating the change in retained earnings over the period, less the adjustment against retained earnings in the valuation entry relating to depreciation of the equipment. The amount is calculated as follows:

$$40\% \times (\$16\,000 - \$2000 - [\$8000 - \$2400]) = \$3360$$

The NCI is also entitled to a share of the change in *general reserve* between acquisition date and the beginning of the current period, the change being the transfer to general reserve in the 2014–15 period. As the general reserve is increased, the NCI share of that account is also increased. The calculation is:

$$40\% \times \$1000 = \$400$$

The NCI is also entitled to a share of the movement in *other components of equity*. There was no balance in this account at acquisition date, and balance at 30 June 2015 is $2500, so the NCI's share is:

$$40\% \times \$2500 = \$1000$$

The NCI is also affected by the transfer on consolidation from the *business combination valuation reserve* to retained earnings as a result of the sale of inventory. The NCI share of the valuation reserve is decreased, with a reduction in NCI in total. The calculation is:

$$40\% \times \$7000 = \$2800$$

The consolidation worksheet entries in the NCI columns for the step 2 NCI calculation are:

Retained Earnings (1/7/15)	Dr	3 360	
NCI	Cr		3 360
(40% × [$16 000 − $2000 − ($8000 − $2400)])			
General Reserve	Dr	400	
NCI	Cr		400
(40% × $1000)			
Other Components of Equity	Dr	1 000	
NCI	Cr		1 000
(40% × $2500)			
NCI	Dr	2 800	
Business Combination Valuation Reserve	Cr		2 800
(40% × $7000)			

These entries may be combined as:

Retained Earnings (1/7/15)	Dr	3 360	
General Reserve	Dr	400	
Other Components of Equity	Dr	1 000	
Business Combination Valuation Reserve	Cr		2 800
NCI	Cr		1 960

(5) *NCI share of current period changes in equity (step 3)*

From figure 23.9 it can be seen that there are four changes in equity in the 2015–16 period:

- Petrel Ltd has reported a profit of $15 000.
- There has been a transfer from general reserve of $500.
- The subsidiary has paid a dividend of $1500 and declared a dividend of $2000.
- Other components of equity has decreased by $100.

In relation to both dividends and transfer to/from reserves, from an NCI perspective note that it is irrelevant whether the amounts are from pre- or post-acquisition equity. The NCI receives a share of all equity accounts regardless of whether it existed before acquisition date or was created after that date.

The NCI share of *current period profit* is based on a 40% share of the recorded profit of $15 000. However, just as in step 2, there must be an adjustment made to avoid the double counting caused by the subsidiary recognising profits from the use of the equipment, these benefits having been recognised on consolidation in the business combination valuation reserve. Again, reference needs to be made to the valuation entries, and in particular to the amounts in these entries affecting current period profit. In the valuation entries, there is a debit adjustment to depreciation expense of $4000 and a credit adjustment to income tax expense of $1200. In other words, in the current period, Petrel Ltd recognised in its profit an amount of $2800 from the use of the equipment that was recognised by the group in the business combination valuation reserve. Since the NCI has been given a share of the valuation reserve in step 1, to give the NCI a share of the recorded profit without adjusting for the current period's depreciation would double-count the NCI share of equity. The NCI share of current period profit is, therefore, 40% of the net of recorded profit of $15 000 less the after-tax depreciation adjustment of $2800.

The consolidation worksheet entry in the NCI columns is:

NCI Share of Profit/(Loss)	Dr	4 880	
NCI	Cr		4 880
(40% × [$15 000 − ($4000 − $1200)])			

In the current period, a change in equity is caused by the $500 *transfer from general reserve* to retained earnings. This transaction does not change the amount of equity in total because it is a transfer between equity accounts, so there is no change to the NCI in total. However, the NCI share of general reserve has decreased and the NCI share of retained earnings has increased. For the latter account, the appropriate line item is 'Transfer from General Reserve'. The consolidation worksheet entry in the NCI columns is:

Transfer from General Reserve	Dr	200	
General Reserve	Cr		200
(40% × $500)			

The third change in equity in the current period relates to *dividends paid and declared*. Dividends are a reduction in retained earnings. The NCI share of equity is reduced as a result of the payment or declaration of dividends. Where dividends are paid, the NCI receives a cash distribution as compensation for the reduction in equity. Where dividends are declared, the group recognises a liability to make a future cash payment to the NCI as compensation for the reduction in equity. The consolidation worksheet entries in the NCI column are:

NCI	Dr	600	
Dividend Paid	Cr		600
(40% × $1500)			
NCI	Dr	800	
Dividend Declared	Cr		800
(40% × $2000)			

The fourth change in equity is the $100 reduction in *other components of equity*. This results in a reduction in the NCI share of this account that relates to financial assets as well as a reduction in NCI in total. The entry in the NCI columns is:

NCI	Dr	40	
Other Components of Equity	Cr		40
(40% × $100)			

(6) *Adjustments for intragroup transactions: dividends*

The entries below and shown in the adjustment columns of the worksheet are necessary to adjust for the dividend transactions in the current period — note that the amounts are based on the proportion of dividends paid within the group.

Dividend Revenue	Dr	900	
Dividend Paid	Cr		900
(60% × $1500)			
Dividend Payable	Dr	1 200	
Dividend Declared	Cr		1 200
(60% × $2000)			
Dividend Revenue	Dr	1 200	
Dividend Receivable	Cr		1 200
(60% × $2000)			

Using the figures for the subsidiary for the year ended 30 June 2016, as given in figure 23.9, and assuming information for the parent, a consolidation worksheet showing the effects of the entries developed in illustrative example 23.2 is given in figure 23.10.

Financial statements	Heron Ltd	Petrel Ltd		Adjustments Dr	Cr		Group		Non-controlling interest Dr	Cr		Parent
Profit/(loss) for the period	20 000	15 000	1 6 6	4 000 900 1 200	1 200	1	30 100	5	4 880			25 220
Retained earnings (1/7/17)	25 000	16 000	1 2	8 000 5 400	2 400	1	30 000	3	800			25 840
Transfer from general reserve	—	500					500	5	200			300
	45 000	31 500					60 600					51 360
Dividend paid	10 000	1 500			900 300	2 6	10 600			600	5	10 000
Dividend declared	5 000	2 000				6	5 800			800	5	5 000
	15 000	3 500					16 400					15 000
Retained earnings (30/6/18)	30 000	28 000					44 200					36 660
Share capital	100 000	40 000	2	24 000			116 000	3	16 000			
General reserve	20 000	2 500	2	1 200			21 300	3 4	800 400	200	5	20 300
Business combination valuation reserve	—	—	2	8 400	14 000	1	5 600	3	8 400	2 800	4	—
	150 000	70 500					187 100					156 660
Other components of equity (1/7/17)	10 000	2 500					12 500	4	1 000			11 500
Increases/(decreases)	2 000	(100)					1 900			40	5	1 940
Other components of equity (30/6/18)	12 000	2 400					14 400					13 440
Total equity: parent												170 100
Total equity: NCI								5 5 5	600 800 40	26 000 1 960 4 880	3 4 5	31 400
Total equity	162 000	72 900					201 500		37 280	37 280		201 500

FIGURE 23.10 Consolidation worksheet with NCI columns

23.4 ADJUSTING FOR THE EFFECTS OF INTRAGROUP TRANSACTIONS

The justification for considering adjustments for intragroup transactions in the calculation of the NCI share of equity is that the NCI is classified as a contributor of capital to the group. Thus, the calculation of the NCI is based on a share of *consolidated equity* and not equity as recorded by the subsidiary. Consolidated equity is determined as the sum of the equity of the parent and the subsidiaries after making adjustments for the effects of intragroup transactions. The NCI share of that equity must, therefore, be based on subsidiary equity after adjusting for intragroup transactions that affect the subsidiary's equity.

To illustrate, assume that during the current period a subsidiary in which there is an NCI of 20% has recorded a profit of $20 000 which includes a before-tax profit of $2000 on sale of $18 000 inventory to the parent. The inventory is still on hand at the end of the current period. In the adjustment columns of the consolidation worksheet, the adjustment entries for the sale of inventory, assuming a tax rate of 30%, are:

Sales	Dr	18 000	
Cost of Sales	Cr		16 000
Inventory	Cr		2 000
Deferred Tax Asset	Dr	600	
Income Tax Expense	Cr		600

The group does not regard the after-tax profit of $1400 as being a part of consolidated profit. Hence, in calculating the NCI share of consolidated profit, the NCI is entitled to $3720; that is, 20% × ($20 000 recorded profit − $1400 intragroup profit).

The NCI share of equity is therefore adjusted for the effects of intragroup transactions. However, note that the NCI share of consolidated equity is essentially based on a share of *subsidiary* equity. Therefore, only intragroup transactions that affect the subsidiary's equity need to be taken into consideration. Profits made on inventory sold by the parent to the subsidiary do not affect the calculation of the NCI because the profit is recorded by the parent, not the subsidiary — the subsidiary equity is unaffected by the transaction.

In section 23.3, it is explained that the NCI share of the equity recorded by the subsidiary is calculated in three steps:

Step 1. share of equity at acquisition date
Step 2. share of changes in equity between acquisition date and the beginning of the current period
Step 3. share of changes in equity in the current period.

These calculations are based on the *recorded* subsidiary equity; that is, equity that will include the effects of the intragroup transactions. Having calculated the NCI as a result of the three-step process, the subsidiary needs to make further adjustments for the effects of intragroup transactions. Rather than adjust for these transactions in the NCI entries relating to the three-step process, the adjustments to the NCI are determined when the adjustments are made for the effects of the specific intragroup transactions.

For example, consider the case above where a subsidiary in which the NCI is 20% records a profit of $20 000, which includes a $2000 before-tax profit on the sale of inventory to the parent (cost $4000, selling price $6000). In the step 3 NCI calculation, the worksheet entry passed in the NCI columns is:

NCI Share of Profit/(Loss)	Dr	4 000	
NCI	Cr		4 000
[20% × $20 000 recorded profit]			

In making the adjustment for the effects of intragroup transactions to be passed in the adjustment columns of the worksheet, the following entries are made:

Profit in closing inventory: subsidiary to parent			
Sales	Dr	6 000	
Cost of Sales	Cr		4 000
Inventory	Cr		2 000
Deferred Tax Asset	Dr	600	
Income Tax Expense	Cr		600
[30% × $2000]			

As this adjustment affects the profit of the subsidiary by an amount of $1400 after tax (i.e. $2000 − $600), this triggers the need to make an adjustment to the NCI, and the following entry is passed in the NCI columns of the worksheet:

NCI	Dr	280	
NCI Share of Profit/(Loss)	Cr		280
[20% × $1400]			

[This entry is explained in more detail in illustrative example 23.3 later in this chapter.]

The combined effect of the step 3 NCI entry and this last entry is that the NCI totals $3720 — that is, $4000 less $280. Thus the NCI is given a share of recorded profit adjusted for the effects of intragroup transactions.

23.4.1 The concept of 'realisation' of profits or losses

Not all transactions require an adjustment entry for the NCI. For a transaction to require an adjustment to the calculation of the NCI share of equity, it must have the following characteristics:
- The transaction must result in the subsidiary recording a profit or a loss.
- After the transaction, the other party to the transaction (for two-company structures this is the parent) must have on hand an asset (e.g. inventory) on which the unrealised profit is accrued.
- The initial consolidation adjustment for the transaction should affect both the statement of financial position and the statement of profit or loss and other comprehensive income (including appropriations of retained earnings), unlike payments of debenture interest, which affect only the statement of profit or loss and other comprehensive income.

In determining the transactions requiring an adjusting entry for the NCI, it is important to work out which transactions involve unrealised profit. *The concept of 'realisation' is discussed in chapter 22.* The test for realisation is the involvement of a party external to the group, based on the concept that the consolidated financial statements report the affairs of the group in terms of its dealings with entities external to the group. Consolidated profits are therefore realised profits as they result from dealing with entities external to the group. Profits made by transacting within the group are unrealised because no external entity is involved. Once the profits or losses on an intragroup transaction become realised, the NCI share of equity no longer needs to be adjusted for the effects of an intragroup transaction because the profits or losses recorded by the subsidiary are all realised profits.

In this section, the key point to note is when, for different types of transactions, unrealised profits on intragroup transactions become realised.

Inventory

With inventory, realisation occurs when the acquiring entity sells the inventory to an entity outside the group. Consolidation adjustments for inventory are based on the profit or loss remaining in inventory on hand at the end of a financial period. If inventory is sold in the current period by the subsidiary to the parent at a profit, giving the NCI a share of the recorded profit will overstate the NCI share of consolidated equity, because the group does not recognise the profit until the inventory is sold outside the group. Hence, whenever consolidated adjustments are made for profit remaining in inventory on hand at the end of the period, an NCI adjustment is necessary to reduce the NCI share of current period profit and the NCI total. Following the consolidation adjustment for the unrealised profit in inventory, an NCI adjustment entry is made in the NCI columns of the worksheet. The general form of the entry is:

NCI	Dr	xxx	
NCI Share of Profit/(Loss)	Cr		xxx

If there is inventory on hand at *the beginning of the current period*, the NCI share of the previous period's profit must be reduced as the subsidiary's previous year's recorded profit contains unrealised profit. As the group realises the profit in the current period when the inventory is sold to external parties, the NCI share of the current period profit must be increased. Following the worksheet adjustment for the profit remaining in beginning inventory, an NCI adjustment entry is made in the NCI columns of the worksheet. The general form of the NCI entry is:

NCI Share of Profit/(Loss)	Dr	xxx	
Retained Earnings (opening balance)	Cr		xxx

Intragroup transfers for services and interest

For transactions involving services and interest, the group's profit is unaffected because the general consolidation adjustment reduces both expense and revenue equally. However, from the NCI's perspective, there has been a change in the equity of the subsidiary; for example, the subsidiary may have recorded interest revenue as a result of a payment to the parent entity relating to an intragroup loan. The revenue is unrealised in that no external entity has been involved in the transaction. Theoretically, the NCI should be adjusted for such transactions. However, as noted in paragraph B86(c) of IFRS 10, it is profits or losses 'recognised in assets' that are of concern. In other words, where there are transfers between entities that do not result in the retention within the group of assets on which the profit has been accrued, it is *assumed* that the profit is realised by the group immediately on payment within the group. For transactions such as payments for intragroup services, interest and dividends, there are no assets recorded with accrued profits attached, since the transactions are cash transactions. Hence, the profit is assumed to be immediately realised. The reason for the assumption of immediate realisation of profits on these types of transactions is a pragmatic one based on the cost benefit of determining a point of realisation.

 ## 23.5 GAIN ON BARGAIN PURCHASE

This chapter has used examples of business combinations where goodwill has been acquired. In the rare case that a gain on bargain purchase may arise, such a gain has no effect on the calculation of the NCI share of equity. Further, whereas the goodwill of the subsidiary may be determined by calculating the goodwill acquired by the parent entity and then grossing this up to determine the goodwill for the subsidiary, this process is not applicable for the gain on bargain purchase. The gain is made by the parent paying less than the net fair value of the acquirer's share of the identifiable assets, liabilities and contingent liabilities of the subsidiary. The NCI receives a share of the fair value of the subsidiary, and has no involvement with the gain on bargain purchase.

To illustrate, assume a subsidiary has the following statement of financial position:

Equity	$80 000
Identifiable assets and liabilities	$80 000

Assume all identifiable assets and liabilities of the subsidiary are recorded at amounts equal to fair value. If a parent acquires 80% of the shares of the subsidiary for $63 000, then the acquisition analysis, assuming the use of the partial goodwill method, is:

Net fair value of subsidiary	= $80 000
(a) Consideration transferred	= $63 000
(b) Non-controlling interest in subsidiary	= 20% × $80 000
	= $16 000
Aggregate of (a) and (b)	= $79 000
Gain on bargain purchase	$80 000 – $79 000
	= $1000

Assuming all fair values have been measured accurately, the consolidation worksheet entries at acquisition date are:

Business combination valuation entry
No entry required in this simple example.

Elimination of investment in subsidiary

Equity	Dr	64 000
Gain on Bargain Purchase	Cr	1 000
Shares in Subsidiary	Cr	63 000

Non-controlling interest (step 1)

Equity	Dr	16 000
NCI	Cr	16 000
(20% × $80 000)		

Note that the NCI does not receive any share of the gain on bargain purchase.

An example of the process of calculating NCI when intragroup transactions exist is given in illustrative example 23.3.

Bat Ltd owns 80% of the issued shares of Snake Ltd. In the year ending 30 June 2014, the following transactions occurred:

(a) In July 2013, Bat Ltd sold $2000 worth of inventory that had been sold to it by Snake Ltd in May 2013 at a profit to Snake Ltd of $500.

(b) In February 2014, Bat Ltd sold $10 000 worth of inventory to Snake Ltd, recording a profit before tax of $2000. At 30 June 2014, 20% of this inventory remained unsold by Snake Ltd.

(c) In March 2014, Snake Ltd sold $12 000 worth of inventory to Bat Ltd at a mark-up of 20%. At 30 June 2014, $1200 of this inventory remained unsold by Bat Ltd.

(d) At 30 June 2014, Bat Ltd recorded depreciation of $10 000 in relation to plant sold to it by Snake Ltd on 1 July 2011. Bat Ltd uses a 10% p.a. straight-line depreciation method for plant. At date of sale to Bat Ltd, this plant had a carrying amount of $90 000 in the accounts of Snake Ltd.

Required

Given a tax rate of 30%, prepare the consolidation worksheet entries for these transactions as at 30 June 2014.

Solution

(a) *Sale of inventory in previous period: Snake Ltd to Bat Ltd*
The entry in the adjustment columns of the worksheet is:

Retained Earnings (1/7/13)	Dr	350	
Income Tax Expense	Dr	150	
Cost of Sales	Cr		500

Since the inventory was originally sold by the subsidiary to the parent, the entry in the NCI columns of the worksheet is:

NCI Share of Profit/(Loss)	Dr	70	
Retained Earnings (1/7/13)	Cr		70
(20% × $350)			

(b) *Sale of inventory in current period: Bat Ltd to Snake Ltd*

Sales	Dr	10 000	
Cost of Sales	Cr		9 600
Inventory	Cr		400
Deferred Tax Asset	Dr	120	
Income Tax Expense	Cr		120

Because the sale was from parent to subsidiary, there is no NCI adjustment required.

(c) *Sale of inventory in current period: Snake Ltd to Bat Ltd*
The entries in the adjustment columns of the worksheet are:

Sales	Dr	12 000	
Cost of Sales	Cr		11 800
Inventory	Cr		200
Deferred Tax Asset	Dr	60	
Income Tax Expense	Cr		60

Because the sale was from subsidiary to parent, the following entry is required in the NCI columns of the worksheet:

NCI	Dr	28	
NCI Share of Profit/(Loss)	Cr		28
(20% × $140)			

(d) *Sale of plant in prior period: Snake Ltd to Bat Ltd*
The entry in the adjustment columns of the worksheet is:

Retained Earnings (1/7/13)	Dr	7 000	
Deferred Tax Asset	Dr	3 000	
Plant	Cr		10 000

Since the plant was sold by the subsidiary to the parent, the entry in the NCI columns of the worksheet is:

NCI	Dr	1 400	
Retained Earnings (1/7/13)	Cr		1 400
(20% × $7000)			

Depreciation on plant
The entries in the adjustment columns of the worksheet are:

Accumulated Depreciation	Dr	2 000	
Depreciation Expense	Cr		1 000
Retained Earnings (1/7/13)	Cr		1 000
Retained Earnings (1/7/13)	Dr	300	
Income Tax Expense	Dr	300	
Deferred Tax Asset	Cr		600

The entry in the NCI column of the worksheet is:

NCI Share of Profit/(Loss)	Dr	140	
Retained Earnings (1/7/13)	Dr	140	
NCI	Cr		280
(20% × $700 p.a.)			

SUMMARY

Where a subsidiary is not wholly owned, the equity of the subsidiary is divided into two parts, namely the parent's share and the non-controlling interest (NCI) share. IAS 1 *Presentation of Financial Statements* requires that, with the disclosure of specific equity amounts, the parent's share and the NCI share should be separately disclosed. This affects the consolidation process. The NCI is classified as equity with the result that in statements of profit or loss and other comprehensive income and statements of financial position where equity amounts are disclosed the parent's share and the NCI share are separately disclosed.

The existence of an NCI will have different effects on the consolidation worksheet entries used, depending on whether the full goodwill or partial goodwill method is used. Under the full goodwill method, goodwill is recognised in the business combination valuation entries, and shared between the parent and the NCI. Where the partial goodwill method is used, the existence of an NCI has no effect on the business combination valuation entries. However, as a result of these entries, business combination valuation reserves are created of which the NCI has a share. With the elimination of investment in subsidiary, the existence of an NCI has an effect as this entry is based on the parent's share of pre-acquisition equity only. Hence, a proportionate adjustment is required. The adjustments for intragroup transactions also affect the calculation of the NCI share of equity. There is no effect on the adjustment for an intragroup transaction itself — this is the same regardless of the ownership interest of the parent in the subsidiary. However, the adjustment for an intragroup transaction affects the calculation of the NCI share of equity. Since the NCI is entitled to a share of consolidated equity rather than the recorded equity of the subsidiary, where an intragroup transaction affects the equity of the subsidiary, entries in the NCI columns of the worksheet are required, affecting the calculation of the NCI. It is then necessary to observe the flow of the transaction — upstream or downstream — to determine whether an NCI adjustment is necessary. One area where the NCI is unaffected is where a gain on bargain purchase arises, because the elimination of investment in subsidiary adjusts for the parent's share only. The gain calculated relates only to the parent and not the NCI.

Seal Ltd acquired 80% of the shares of Swan Ltd on 1 July 2012 for $540 000, when the equity of Swan Ltd consisted of:

Share capital	$500 000
General reserve	80 000
Retained earnings	50 000
Asset revaluation surplus	20 000

All identifiable assets and liabilities of Swan Ltd are recorded at fair value at this date except for inventory for which the fair value was $10 000 greater than carrying amount, and plant which had a carrying amount of $150 000 (net of $40 000 accumulated depreciation) and a fair value of $170 000. The inventory was all sold by 30 June 2013, and the plant had a further 5-year life with depreciation based on the straight-line method.

Financial information for both companies at 30 June 2016 is as follows:

	Seal Ltd	Swan Ltd
Sales revenue	$ 720 000	$ 530 000
Other revenue	240 000	120 000
	960 000	650 000
Cost of sales	(610 000)	(410 000)
Other expenses	(230 000)	(160 000)
	(840 000)	(570 000)
Profit before tax	120 000	80 000
Tax expense	(40 000)	(25 000)
Profit for the period	80 000	55 000
Retained earnings at 1/7/15	200 000	112 000
	280 000	167 000
Dividend paid	(20 000)	(10 000)
Dividend declared	(25 000)	(15 000)
	(45 000)	(25 000)
Retained earnings at 30/6/16	235 000	142 000
Share capital	600 000	500 000
Asset revaluation surplus*	20 000	60 000
General reserve	80 000	100 000
Total equity	935 000	802 000
Dividend payable	25 000	15 000
Other liabilities	25 000	25 000
Total liabilities	50 000	40 000
Total equity and liabilities	$ 985 000	$ 842 000
Receivables	$ 80 000	$ 30 000
Inventory	100 000	170 000
Plant and equipment	200 000	500 000
Accumulated depreciation	(115 000)	(88 000)
Land at fair value	100 000	80 000
Shares in Swan Ltd	540 000	—
Deferred tax assets	50 000	40 000
Other assets	30 000	110 000
Total assets	$ 985 000	$ 842 000

*The balances of the surplus at 1 July 2015 were $35 000 (Seal Ltd) and $50 000 (Swan Ltd).

The following transactions took place between Seal Ltd and Swan Ltd:
(a) During the 2015–16 period, Swan Ltd sold inventory to Seal Ltd for $23 000, recording a profit before tax of $3000. Seal Ltd has since resold half of these items.
(b) During the 2015–16 period, Seal Ltd sold inventory to Swan Ltd for $18 000, recording a profit before tax of $2000. Swan Ltd has not resold any of these items.
(c) On 1 June 2016, Swan Ltd paid $1000 to Seal Ltd for services rendered.
(d) During the 2014–15 period, Swan Ltd sold inventory to Seal Ltd. At 30 June 2015, Seal Ltd still had inventory on hand on which Swan Ltd had recorded a before-tax profit of $4000.
(e) On 1 July 2014, Swan Ltd sold plant to Seal Ltd for $150 000, recording a profit of $20 000 before tax. Seal Ltd applies a 10% p.a. straight-line method of depreciation in relation to these assets.

Required

1. Given an income tax rate of 30%, prepare the consolidated financial statements for Seal Ltd for the year ended 30 June 2016 using the *partial goodwill method* to measure the non-controlling interest at acquisition date.
2. What differences would occur in the consolidation worksheet entries at 30 June 2016 if the *full goodwill method* was used to calculate the non-controlling interest at acquisition date? Assume the value of the non-controlling interest in the subsidiary at acquisition date is $134 500.

Solution

1. Consolidated financial statements using partial goodwill method

The first step is to prepare the acquisition analysis. Determining the net fair value is the same as for wholly owned subsidiaries. Where an NCI exists, it is necessary to determine the net fair value acquired by the parent.

In this problem, the parent acquired 80% of the shares of the subsidiary. The net fair value of what was acquired is then compared with the consideration transferred, and a goodwill or gain is determined. Note that the goodwill or gain is only that attributable to the parent, since the residual relates to what was paid by the parent and the proportion of net fair value of the subsidiary acquired by the parent.

Acquisition analysis

Net fair value of the identifiable assets and liabilities of Swan Ltd	= $500 000 + $80 000 + $50 000 + $20 000 + $10 000(1 − 30%) (BCVR — inventory) + $20 000(1 − 30%) (BCVR — plant)
	= $671 000
(a) Consideration transferred	= $540 000
(b) Non-controlling interest in Swan Ltd	= 20% × $671 000
	= $134 200
Aggregate of (a) and (b)	= $674 200
Goodwill	= $674 200 − $671 000
	= $3200

Consolidation worksheet entries at 30 June 2016
(1) *Business combination valuation reserve entries*

The business combination entries are unaffected by the existence of an NCI. Under IFRS 3, all identifiable assets and liabilities acquired in the acquiree/subsidiary must be measured at fair value. This principle is unaffected by the existence of an NCI.

Accumulated Depreciation	Dr	40 000	
Plant	Cr		20 000
Deferred Tax Liability	Cr		6 000
Business Combination Valuation Reserve	Cr		14 000
Depreciation Expense	Dr	4 000	
Retained Earnings (1/7/15)	Dr	12 000	
Accumulated Depreciation	Cr		16 000
Deferred Tax Liability	Dr	4 800	
Income Tax Expense	Cr		1 200
Retained Earnings (1/7/15)	Cr		3 600

(2) Elimination of investment in subsidiary

Retained Earnings (1/7/15)	Dr	45 600
Share Capital	Dr	400 000
General Reserve	Dr	64 000
Asset Revaluation Surplus (1/7/15)	Dr	16 000
Business Combination Valuation Reserve	Dr	11 200
Goodwill	Dr	3 200
Shares in Swan Ltd	Cr	540 000

These elimination of investment and recognition of goodwill entries differ from the entries prepared for a wholly owned subsidiary in that the adjustment to equity accounts is measured as the parent's share of the equity accounts. This can be seen in the acquisition analysis where the parent's share of equity (80%) is applied to the net fair value before making a comparison with the cost of the combination. Hence the adjustment to share capital is $400 000; that is, 80% of the recorded $500 000. With retained earnings (1/7/15), the adjustment is calculated as:

$$(80\% \times \$50\,000)\ (\text{opening balance}) + (80\% \times \$7000)\ (\text{BCVR inventory})$$

The adjustment to the BCVR is:

$$80\% \times \$14\,000\ (\text{BCVR plant})$$

Non-controlling interest

The next three adjustment entries relate to the calculation of the NCI. These entries are passed in the NCI columns of the worksheet, not the adjustment columns. The three entries cover the three steps used in the calculation of the NCI share of total equity.

(3) NCI share of equity at acquisition date, 1 July 2012 (step 1)

Step 1 is to calculate the NCI share of the equity of the subsidiary at acquisition date. This consists of the recorded equity of the subsidiary plus any reserves raised on consolidation at acquisition date, namely the business combination valuation reserve.

Pre-acquisition equity of Swan Ltd		**20%**
Retained earnings (1/7/12)	$ 50 000	$ 10 000
Share capital	500 000	100 000
General reserve	80 000	16 000
Asset revaluation surplus (1/7/12)	20 000	4 000
Business combination valuation reserve	21 000	4 200
		$134 200

The worksheet entry in the NCI columns is:

Retained Earnings (1/7/15)	Dr	10 000
Share Capital	Dr	100 000
General Reserve	Dr	16 000
Asset Revaluation Surplus (1/7/15)	Dr	4 000
Business Combination Valuation Reserve	Dr	4 200
NCI	Cr	134 200

Note that the adjustments to the equity accounts are debits, because these amounts will be subtracted from the balances in the group column in order to determine the parent's share of equity. On the other hand, the NCI account has a credit adjustment because the NCI is classified as equity, and the balance of pre-acquisition equity is a positive amount.

(4) NCI share of equity from 1 July 2012 to 30 June 2015 (step 2)

In step 2, the calculation is of the NCI share of equity between the acquisition date and the beginning of the current period; that is, between 1 July 2012 and 30 June 2015. This requires the calculation of movements in the subsidiary's equity accounts between these two dates.

General reserve: The balance at 30 June 2015, read from the financial information at 30 June 2016 and noting no transfers occurred in the current period, is $100 000. The difference between this and the balance at 1 July 2012 of $80 000 is $20 000. The NCI is entitled to 20% of this increase in equity. The combination of step 1 and step 2 effectively gives the NCI a 20% share of the total $100 000 balance.

Retained earnings: The balance at 30 June 2015 is the same as the opening balance in the current period, which is read from the financial information provided, namely $112 000. The difference between this amount and the balance recorded by the subsidiary at acquisition reflects movements in the amounts recorded by the subsidiary, such as reserve transfers and dividends. What is not reflected in the difference calculated are amounts affecting retained earnings not recorded by the subsidiary but recognised on consolidation. In this problem, the transaction that needs to be taken into account is the depreciation of the plant on hand at acquisition date, as shown in the business combination valuation reserve entries. As the plant is used, the recorded profit of the subsidiary recognises the extra benefits received. The NCI in relation to retained earnings (1/7/15) is therefore:

$$20\% \times [\$112\,000 \text{ (balance at 1/7/15)} - \$50\,000 \text{ (balance at acquisition)} - (\$12\,000 - \$3600)]$$

Asset revaluation surplus: The balance at acquisition date is $20 000 and the balance at 30 June 2015 is $50 000. The NCI is entitled to a 20% share of the difference between these two amounts.

Business combination valuation reserve: The balance at acquisition date was $21 000. As a result of the sale of the inventory, this has been reduced at 30 June 2015 to $14 000, a reduction of $7000, because there has been a transfer from this reserve to retained earnings. Since the reserve has decreased in amount, this results in a decrease in the NCI share of this account. The total NCI in equity has not changed because the recorded retained earnings has increased by $7000 as a result of the sale of inventory by the subsidiary.

A summary of these movements is then:

	Change in equity	20%
General reserve ($100 000 − $80 000)	$ 20 000	$ 4 000
Retained earnings ($112 000 − $50 000 − ($12 000 − $3600))	53 600	10 720
Asset revaluation surplus ($50 000 − $20 000)	30 000	6 000
Business combination valuation reserve ($14 000 − $21 000)	(7 000)	(1 400)

The worksheet entry in the NCI columns is:

Retained Earnings (1/7/15)	Dr	10 720	
General Reserve	Dr	4 000	
Asset Revaluation Surplus	Dr	6 000	
Business Combination Valuation Reserve	Cr		1 400
NCI	Cr		19 320

(5) *NCI in equity from 1 July 2015 to 30 June 2016 (step 3)*
Steps 1 and 2 determine the NCI share of equity recorded up to the beginning of the current year. Step 3 calculates the NCI share of changes in equity in the current year — 1 July 2015 to 30 June 2016.

The combination of all three steps determines the NCI share of equity at the end of the reporting period.
   There are a number of changes in equity in the current period, with each change attracting its own adjustment entry in the NCI columns of the worksheet.

Profit for the period:
The NCI receives a share of recorded profit of the subsidiary. As with step 2, this is adjusted by the depreciation on the plant on hand at acquisition date. The recorded profit of the subsidiary includes benefits gained by use of the plant. The NCI share is then:

$$20\% \, [\$55\,000 - (\$4000 - \$1200)]$$

The worksheet entry in the NCI columns is:

NCI Share of Profit/(Loss)	Dr	10 440	
NCI	Cr		10 440

The first line in the entry is a debit because in the consolidation worksheet this is deducted from group profit in order to calculate the parent share of profit. Note that, in later calculations, increases in the NCI share of profit require a debit adjustment to this account and decreases in the NCI share of profit require a credit adjustment.

Dividend paid:
The dividend paid by the subsidiary reduces the equity of the subsidiary. The adjustment to the NCI share of equity as a result of the dividend paid must take into consideration the full dividend paid with the effect of reducing the NCI share of total equity. The entry in the NCI columns of the worksheet is:

NCI	Dr	2 000
Dividend Paid	Cr	2 000
(20% × $10 000)		

Dividend declared:
As with the dividend paid, the NCI has been given a full share of equity before the declaration of dividends. Because the dividend declared reduces the equity of the subsidiary, the NCI share of equity is also reduced. The entry in the NCI columns of the worksheet is:

NCI	Dr	3 000
Dividend Declared	Cr	3 000
(20% × $15 000)		

Asset revaluation surplus:
The balance of the subsidiary's asset revaluation surplus at 1 July 2015 was $50 000. The balance at 30 June 2016 is $60 000. The NCI share of equity is increased by 20% of the change during the period. The debit adjustment is recognised in the worksheet against the Gains/Losses on Asset Revaluation account as this account reflects the increase in the reserve balance. The adjustment is a debit because it reduces the group gain so that the left-hand column of the worksheet shows the parent share of the gain. The entry in the NCI columns of the worksheet is:

Gains/Losses on Asset Revaluation	Dr	2 000
NCI	Cr	2 000
(20% × [$60 000 − $50 000])		

Intragroup transactions

(6) *Dividend paid*
The entry in the adjustment columns of the consolidation worksheet to adjust for the $10 000 dividend paid is:

Dividend Revenue	Dr	8 000
Dividend Paid	Cr	8 000
(80% × $10 000)		

(7) *Dividend declared*
The subsidiary declared a dividend of $15 000 of which $12 000 is payable within the group.
The entries in the adjustment columns of the worksheet are:

Dividend Payable	Dr	12 000
Dividend Declared	Cr	12 000
Dividend Revenue	Dr	12 000
Dividend Receivable	Cr	12 000

(8) *Sale of inventory: Swan Ltd to Seal Ltd*
The worksheet entries in the adjustment columns are:

Sales	Dr	23 000	
Cost of Sales	Cr		21 500
Inventory	Cr		1 500
(Unrealised profit on sale of inventory 50% × $3000)			
Deferred Tax Asset	Dr	450	
Income Tax Expense	Cr		450
(Tax effect, 30% × $1500)			

(9) *Adjustment to NCI: unrealised profit in ending inventory*
The profit on sale was made by the subsidiary. The NCI is therefore affected. The total after-tax profit on the intragroup sale of inventory was $2100 (i.e. $3000 – $900 tax). However, since half the inventory is sold to an external entity, this portion is realised. The adjustment to the NCI relates only to the unrealised profits remaining in the inventory still on hand (half of $2100, or $1050). This is the same after-tax figure used to adjust profits in entry (8) above.

The transaction occurs in the current period. Therefore, it is the NCI share of current period profit that is affected. In adjustment entry (5), the NCI is given a share of the total recorded subsidiary profit for the current period. Because the realised profit is less than the recorded profit, the NCI share of equity must be reduced, specifically the NCI share of current period profit.

The worksheet entry in the NCI columns of the worksheet is:

NCI	Dr	210	
NCI Share of Profit/(Loss)	Cr		210
(20% × $1050)			

The debit adjustment shows a reduction in total equity attributable to the NCI, and the credit adjustment shows a reduction in the NCI share of current period profits.

(10) *Sale of inventory: Seal Ltd to Swan Ltd*
The entries in the adjustment columns of the worksheet are:

Sales	Dr	18 000	
Cost of Sales	Cr		16 000
Inventory	Cr		2 000
Deferred Tax Asset	Dr	600	
Income Tax Expense	Cr		600

Because the profit on the transaction is made by the parent entity and does not affect the equity of the subsidiary, there is no need to make any adjustment to the NCI.

(11) *Payment for services: Swan Ltd to Seal Ltd*
The entry in the adjustment columns of the worksheet is:

Other Revenues	Dr	1 000	
Other Expenses	Cr		1 000

The profit of the subsidiary is affected by the transaction even though the payment may, in effect, be from the parent to the subsidiary. However, if it is assumed that realisation occurs on payment for the services for this type of transaction, then no unrealised profit or loss exists in the subsidiary. Hence, there is no need to make any adjustment to the NCI share of equity.

(12) *Sale of inventory in previous period: Swan Ltd to Seal Ltd*
The entries in the adjustment columns of the worksheet are:

Retained Earnings (1/7/13)	Dr	2 800	
Income Tax Expense	Dr	1 200	
Cost of Sales	Cr		4 000

(13) *Adjustment to NCI: unrealised profit in beginning inventory*

The profit on this transaction was made by the subsidiary, so an adjustment to the NCI share of equity is required. There are two effects on the NCI because the transaction affects both last year's and the current period's figures.

First, the profit made by the subsidiary in the previous period was unrealised last year. Hence, the subsidiary's retained earnings (1/7/15) account contains $2800 unrealised profit. An adjustment is necessary to reduce the NCI share of the previous period's profit:

NCI	Dr	560
Retained Earnings (1/7/15)	Cr	560
(20% × $2800)		

Second, in relation to the current period, because the inventory transferred last period is sold in the current period to an external entity, the profit previously recorded by the subsidiary becomes realised in the current period. Since the profit is realised to the NCI in the current period but was recorded by the subsidiary last period, the NCI share of current period profit needs to be increased. The adjustment is:

NCI Share of Profit/(Loss)	Dr	560
NCI	Cr	560
(20% × $2800)		

These two entries can be combined and passed in the NCI columns of the worksheet:

NCI Share of Profit/(Loss)	Dr	560
Retained Earnings (1/7/15)	Cr	560

This entry has no effect on the total NCI share of equity. It simply reduces the NCI share of equity recorded last period and increases the NCI share of current period profit. This reflects the fact that the subsidiary recorded the profit in the previous period whereas the group recognised the profit in the current period.

The consolidation worksheet for Seal Ltd at 30 June 2016 is shown in figure 23.11.

FIGURE 23.11 Consolidation worksheet showing NCI and the effects of intragroup transactions

Financial statements	Seal Ltd	Swan Ltd		Adjustments Dr	Cr		Group	Non-controlling interest Dr	Cr		Parent
Sales revenue	720 000	530 000	8	23 000			1 209 000				
			10	18 000							
Other revenues	240 000	120 000	6	8 000							
			7	12 000							
			11	1 000							
	960 000	650 000					1 548 000				
Cost of sales	(610 000)	(410 000)			21 500	8	(978 500)				
					16 000	10					
					4 000	12					
Other expenses	(230 000)	(160 000)	1	4 000	1 000	11	(391 000)				
	(840 000)	(570 000)					(1 369 500)				
Profit before tax	120 000	80 000					178 500				
Tax expense	(40 000)	(25 000)	12	1 200	1 200	1	(63 950)				
					600	10					
					450	8					
Profit	80 000	55 000					112 550	5	10 440	210	9	
								13	560			101 760

(continued)

FIGURE 23.11 (continued)

Financial statements	Seal Ltd	Swan Ltd		Dr	Cr		Group		Dr	Cr		Parent
			Adjustments					Non-controlling interest				
Retained earnings (1/7/15)	200 000	112 000	1	12 000	3 600	1		3	10 000	560	13	235 040
			2	45 600				4	10 720			
			12	2 800			242 600					
	280 000	167 000					355 150					336 800
Dividend paid	(20 000)	(10 000)			8 000	6	(22 000)			2 000	5	(20 000)
Dividend declared	(25 000)	(15 000)			12 000	7	(28 000)			3 000	5	(25 000)
	(45 000)	(25 000)					(50 000)					(45 000)
Retained earnings (30/6/16)	235 000	142 000					306 550					291 800
Share capital	600 000	500 000	2	400 000			700 000	3	100 000			600 000
General reserve	80 000	100 000	2	64 000			116 000	3	16 000			96 000
								4	4 000			
Business combination valuation reserve	0	0	2	11 200	14 000	1	2 800	3	4 200	1 400	4	0
	915 000	742 000	1	16 000			1 125 350					987 800
Asset revaluation surplus (1/7/15)	35 000	50 000					69 000	3	4 000			59 000
								4	6 000			
Gains/losses on asset revaluation	(15 000)	10 000					(5 000)	5	2 000			(7 000)
Asset revaluation surplus (30/6/16)	20 000	60 000					64 000					52 000
Total equity: parent												1 039 800
Total equity: NCI								5	2 000	134 200	3	160 750
								5	3 000	19 320	4	
								9	210	10 440	5	
										2 000	5	
Total equity	935 000	802 000					1 189 350		182 370	182 370		1 200 550
Dividend payable	25 000	15 000	7	12 000			28 000					
Other liabilities	25 000	25 000	1	4 800	6 000	1	51 200					
Total liabilities	50 000	40 000					79 200					
Total equity and liabilities	985 000	842 000					1 279 750					
Receivables	80 000	30 000			12 000	6	98 000					
Inventory	100 000	170 000			1 500	8	266 500					
					2 000	10						
Plant and equipment	200 000	500 000			20 000	1	680 000					
Accumulated depreciation	(115 000)	(88 000)	1	40 000	16 000	1	(179 000)					
Land	100 000	80 000					180 000					
Shares in Swan Ltd	540 000	0			540 000	2	0					
Deferred tax asset	50 000	40 000	8	450			91 050					
			10	600								
Goodwill	0	0	2	3 200			3 200					
Other assets	30 000	110 000					140 000					
Total assets	985 000	842 000		705 050	705 050		1 279 750					

The consolidated financial statements for Seal Ltd and its subsidiary, Swan Ltd, for the year ended 30 June 2016 are as shown in figure 23.12(a), (b) and (c).

SEAL LTD
Consolidated Statement of Profit or Loss and Other Comprehensive Income
for the year ended 30 June 2016

Revenue:	
Sales	$ 1 209 000
Other	339 000
Total revenue	1 548 000
Expenses:	
Cost of sales	(978 500)
Other	(391 000)
Total expenses	(1 371 500)
Profit before tax	176 500
Income tax expense	(63 950)
PROFIT FOR THE PERIOD	$ 112 550
Other comprehensive income	
Revaluation decreases	$ (5 000)
TOTAL COMPREHENSIVE INCOME	$ 107 550
Profit attributable to:	
Owners of the parent	$ 101 760
Non-controlling interest	10 790
	$ 112 550
Comprehensive income attributable to:	
Owners of the parent	$ 94 760
Non-controlling interest	12 790
	$ 107 550

FIGURE 23.12(a) Consolidated statement of profit or loss and other comprehensive income

SEAL LTD
Consolidated Statement of Changes in Equity
for the year ended 30 June 2016

	Share capital	Retained earnings	General reserve	Asset revaluation surplus	Business combination valuation reserve	Total: Owners of the parent	Non-controlling interest	Total equity
Balance at 1 July 2015	$600 000	$235 040	$96 000	$59 000	0	$ 990 040	$154 960	$1 145 000
Total comprehensive income		101 760		(7 000)		94 760	10 790	105 550
Dividends paid		(20 000)				(20 000)	(2 000)	(22 000)
Dividends declared		(25 000)				(25 000)	(3 000)	(28 000)
Balance at 30 June 2016	$600 000	$291 800	$96 000	$52 000		$1 039 800	$160 750	$1 200 550

FIGURE 23.12(b) Consolidated statement of changes in equity

SEAL LTD	
Consolidated Statement of Financial Position	
as at 30 June 2016	
ASSETS	
Current assets	
Receivables	$ 98 000
Inventory	266 500
Total current assets	364 500
Non-current assets	
Plant and equipment	$ 680 000
Accumulated depreciation	(179 000)
Land	180 000
Deferred tax asset	91 050
Goodwill	3 200
Other	140 000
Total non-current assets	915 250
Total assets	$1 279 750
LIABILITIES	
Current liabilities: Dividend payable	$ 28 000
Non-current liabilities	51 200
Total liabilities	$ 79 200
Net assets	$1 200 550
EQUITY	
Share capital	$ 600 000
General reserve	96 000
Asset revaluation surplus	52 000
Retained earnings	291 800
Parent interest	$1 039 800
Non-controlling interest	$ 160 750
Total equity	$1 200 550

FIGURE 23.12(c) Consolidated statement of financial position

2. Consolidation worksheet changes under full goodwill method

Under the full goodwill method, the acquisition analysis would change as goodwill is calculated by taking into consideration the fair value of the NCI in the subsidiary.

Acquisition analysis

Net fair value of the identifiable assets and liabilities of Swan Ltd	= $500 000 + $80 000 + $50 000 + $20 000
	+ $10 000(1 − 30%) (BCVR — inventory)
	+ $20 000(1 − 30%) (BCVR — plant)
	= $671 000
(a) Consideration transferred	= $540 000
(b) Non-controlling interest in subsidiary	= $134 500
Aggregate of (a) and (b)	= $674 500
Goodwill	= $674 500 − $671 000
	= $3500
Goodwill of Swan Ltd	
Fair value of Swan Ltd	= $134 500/20%
	= $672 500
Net fair value of identifiable assets and liabilities of Swan Ltd	= $671 000
Goodwill of Swan Ltd	= $672 500 − $671 000
	= $1500

Goodwill of Seal Ltd
Goodwill acquired	=	$3500
Goodwill of Swan Ltd	=	$1500
Goodwill of Seal Ltd — control premium	=	$2000

Consolidation worksheet entries at 30 June 2016

(1) *Business combination valuation reserve entries*

Because the full goodwill method is used, there will need to an extra business combination valuation entry in relation to the goodwill of the subsidiary:

Goodwill	Dr	1 500	
Business Combination Valuation Reserve	Cr		1 500

(2) *Elimination of investment and recognition of goodwill entries*

Retained Earnings (1/7/15)	Dr	45 600	
Share Capital	Dr	400 000	
General Reserve	Dr	64 000	
Asset Revaluation Surplus (1/7/15)	Dr	16 000	
Business Combination Valuation Reserve [80% × ($14 000 + $1 500)]	Dr	12 400	
Goodwill	Dr	2 000	
Shares in Swan Ltd	Cr		540 000

(3) *NCI share of equity at acquisition date, 1 July 2012 (step 1)*

Under the full goodwill method this will change as the business combination valuation reserve in relation to goodwill has been recognised. The NCI share is calculated to be:

Pre-acquisition equity of Swan Ltd

Retained earnings (1/7/12): 20% × $50 000	=	$ 10 000
Share capital: 20% × $500 000	=	100 000
General reserve: 20% × $80 000	=	16 000
Asset revaluation surplus (1/7/12):		
20% × $20 000	=	4 000
Business combination valuation reserve:		
20% × ($14 000 + $7 000 + $1 500)	=	$ 4 500
		$134 500

The worksheet entry in the NCI columns is:

Retained Earnings (1/7/15)	Dr	10 000	
Share Capital	Dr	100 000	
General Reserve	Dr	16 000	
Asset Revaluation Surplus (1/7/15)	Dr	4 000	
Business Combination Valuation Reserve	Dr	4 500	
NCI	Cr		134 500

No other changes are required.

Discussion questions

1. What is meant by the term 'non-controlling interest' (NCI)?
2. How does the existence of an NCI affect the business combination valuation entries?
3. How does the existence of an NCI affect the elimination of investment and recognition of goodwill entries?
4. Why is it necessary to change the format of the worksheet where an NCI exists in the group?
5. Explain how the adjustment for intragroup transactions affects the calculation of the NCI share of equity.
6. Explain whether an NCI adjustment needs to be made for all intragroup transactions.
7 What is meant by 'realisation of profit'?

Exercises

STAR RATING ★ BASIC ★★ MODERATE ★★★ DIFFICULT

Exercise 23.1

★

EQUITY CLASSIFICATION

Len Inn is the accountant for Falcon Trucks Ltd. This entity has an 80% holding in the entity Tyres-R-Us Ltd. Len is concerned that the consolidated financial statements prepared under IFRS 10 may be misleading. He believes that the main users of the consolidated financial statements are the shareholders of Falcon Trucks Ltd. The key performance indicators are then the profit numbers relating to the interests of those shareholders. He therefore wants to prepare the consolidated financial statements showing the non-controlling interest in Tyres-R-Us Ltd in a category other than equity in the statement of financial performance, and for the statement of changes in equity to show the profit numbers relating to the parent shareholders only.

Required

Discuss the differences that would arise in the consolidated financial statements if the non-controlling interests were classified as debt rather than equity, and the reasons the standard setters have chosen the equity classification in IFRS 10.

Exercise 23.2

★

CONSOLIDATION WORKSHEET, CONSOLIDATED FINANCIAL STATEMENTS, PARTIAL GOODWILL METHOD

Jellyfish Ltd purchased 75% of the capital of Mouse Ltd for $250 000 on 1 July 2010. At this date the equity of Mouse Ltd was:

Share capital	$100 000
General reserve	60 000
Retained earnings	40 000

At this date, Mouse Ltd had not recorded any goodwill, and all identifiable assets and liabilities were recorded at fair value except for the following assets:

	Carrying amount	Fair value
Inventory	$ 70 000	$100 000
Plant (cost $170 000)	150 000	190 000
Land	50 000	100 000

The plant has a remaining useful life of 10 years. As a result of an impairment test, all goodwill was written off in 2013. All the inventory on hand at 1 July 2010 was sold by 30 June 2011. Differences beween carrying amounts and fair values are recognised on consolidation. The tax rate is 30%. Jellyfish Ltd uses the partial goodwill method.

The trial balances of Jellyfish Ltd and Mouse Ltd at 30 June 2016 are:

	Jellyfish Ltd	Mouse Ltd
Shares in Mouse Ltd	$ 250 000	—
Plant	425 500	$190 000
Land	110 000	50 000
Current assets	162 000	84 000
Cost of sales	225 000	35 000
Other expenses	65 000	7 000
Income tax expense	50 000	5 000
	$1 287 500	$371 000

Share capital	$400 000	$100 000
General reserve	60 000	80 000
Retained earnings (1/7/15)	120 000	75 000
Sales revenue	510 600	80 000
Payables	72 900	12 000
Accumulated depreciation (plant)	124 000	24 000
	$1 287 500	$371 000

Required

1. Prepare the consolidation worksheet entries immediately after acquisition date.
2. Prepare the consolidation worksheet entries for Jellyfish Ltd at 30 June 2011. Assume a profit for Mouse Ltd for the 2010–11 period of $40 000.
3. Prepare the consolidated financial statements as at 30 June 2016.

Exercise 23.3 CONSOLIDATION WORKSHEET ENTRIES INCLUDING NCI

★ On 1 July 2016, Norilsk Ltd acquired 90% of the capital of Rudny Ltd for $290 160. The equity of Rudny Ltd at this date consisted of:

Share capital	$ 200 000
Retained earnings	80 000

The carrying amounts and fair values of the assets and liabilities recorded by Rudny Ltd at 1 July 2016 were as follows:

	Carrying amount	Fair value
Fittings	$ 20 000	$ 20 000
Land	90 000	100 000
Inventory	10 000	12 000
Machinery (net)	200 000	220 000
Liabilities	40 000	40 000

The machinery and fittings have a further 10-year life, benefits to be received evenly over this period. Differences between carrying amounts and fair values are recognised on consolidation. Norilsk Ltd uses the partial goodwill method.

The tax rate is 30%. All inventory on hand at 1 July 2016 is sold by 30 June 2017.

Required

1. What are the entries for the consolidation worksheet if prepared immediately after 1 July 2016?
2. What are the entries for the consolidation worksheet if prepared at 30 June 2017? Assume a profit for Rudny Ltd for the 2016–17 period of $20 000.
3. If the non-controlling interest had a fair value of $31 800 on 1 July 2016, and the full goodwill method had been used, what entries in parts 1 and 2 above would change? Prepare the changed entries.

Exercise 23.4 CONSOLIDATION WORKSHEET ENTRIES, MULTIPLE YEARS, PARTIAL GOODWILL METHOD

★ On 1 July 2012, Eagle Ltd acquired 75% of the issued shares of Heron Ltd for $125 750. At this date, the accounts of Heron Ltd included the following balances:

Share capital	$80 000
General reserve	20 000
Retained earnings	40 000

All the identifiable assets and liabilities of Heron Ltd were recorded at fair value except for the following:

	Carrying amount	Fair value
Plant (cost $50 000)	$35 000	$41 000
Land	50 000	70 000
Inventory	20 000	24 000

Adjustments for the differences between carrying amounts and fair values are to be made on consolidation except for land which is to be measured in Heron Ltd's accounts at fair value. The plant has a further 3-year life. All the inventory was sold by 30 June 2013. Eagle Ltd uses the partial goodwill method.

During the 4 years since acquisition, Heron Ltd has recorded the following annual results:

Year ended	Profit/(loss)	Total comprehensive income
30 June 2013	$10 000	$12 000
30 June 2014	23 000	28 000
30 June 2015	(6 000)	1 000
30 June 2016	22 000	22 000

The other comprehensive income relates to gains/losses on revaluation of land.

There have been no transfers to or from the general reserve or any dividends paid or declared by Heron Ltd since the acquisition date.

The land owned by Heron Ltd on 1 July 2012 was sold on 1 March 2014 for $75 000. The group transfers the valuation reserves to retained earnings when an asset is sold or fully consumed. The tax rate is 30%.

Required

1. Prepare the consolidation worksheet entries as at 1 July 2012.
2. Prepare the consolidation worksheet entries for the year ended 30 June 2013.
3. Prepare the consolidation worksheet entries for the year ended 30 June 2014.
4. Prepare the consolidation worksheet entries for the year ended 30 June 2015.
5. Prepare the consolidation worksheet entries for the year ended 30 June 2016.

Exercise 23.5   **CONSOLIDATION WORKSHEET, CONSOLIDATED FINANCIAL STATEMENTS, FULL GOODWILL METHOD**

★ In June 2014, Osprey Ltd made an offer to the shareholders of Kite Ltd to acquire a controlling interest in the company. Osprey Ltd was prepared to pay $1.50 cash per share, provided that 70% of the shares could be acquired (enough shares to gain control).

The directors of Kite Ltd recommended that the offer be accepted. By 1 July 2014, when the offer expired, 75% of the shares had changed hands and were now in the possession of Osprey Ltd. The statement of financial position of Kite Ltd on that date is shown below.

KITE LTD Statement of financial position as at 1 July 2014	
Current assets	$368 000
Non-current assets	244 000
	$612 000
Share capital — 400 000 shares	$400 000
General reserve	50 000
Asset revaluation surplus	40 000
Other components of equity	30 000
Retained earnings	40 000
Current liabilities	52 000
	$612 000

At 1 July 2014, all the identifiable assets and liabilities of Kite Ltd were recorded at amounts equal to fair value. Osprey Ltd uses the full goodwill method. The fair value of the non-controlling interest at 1 July 2014 was $147 000.

The draft financial statements of the two companies on 30 June 2015 revealed the following details:

	Osprey Ltd	Kite Ltd
Sales revenue	$ 878 900	$ 388 900
Cost of sales	374 400	112 400
Gross profit	504 500	276 500
Other income	282 100	102 500
	786 600	379 000
Other expenses	216 200	115 800
Profit from trading	570 400	263 200
Gain on sale of non-current assets	20 000	10 000
Profit before tax	590 400	273 200
Income tax expense	112 400	50 000
Profit	478 000	223 200
Retained earnings (1/7/14)	112 000	40 000
	590 000	263 200
Dividend paid	40 000	30 000
Dividend declared	50 000	10 000
	90 000	40 000
Retained earnings (30/6/15)	500 000	223 200
Share capital	1 200 000	400 000
General reserve	24 000	50 000
Asset revaluation surplus	70 000	60 000
Other components of equity	30 000	40 000
Current liabilities	177 000	124 400
	$2 001 000	$ 897 600
Financial assets	$ 280 000	$ 204 000
Receivables	320 000	175 000
Inventory	287 500	210 600
Investments — Shares in Kite Ltd	450 000	—
— Other investments	47 000	—
Equipment	650 000	360 000
Accumulated depreciation	(250 000)	(160 000)
Land	216 500	108 000
	$2 001 000	$ 897 600

Additional information
(a) Osprey Ltd had made an advance of $80 000 to Kite Ltd. This advance was repayable in June 2016.
(b) The directors of Osprey Ltd and Kite Ltd had declared final dividends of $50 000 and $10 000 respectively, from current period's profits.
(c) Kite Ltd holds at the end of the reporting period inventory purchased from Osprey Ltd during the year for $55 000. Osprey Ltd invoices goods to its subsidiary at cost plus 10%.

(d) On 1 July 2014, Kite Ltd sold to Osprey Ltd some display equipment for $60 000. At that date, the carrying amount of the equipment was $52 000 and the equipment was estimated to have a useful life of 10 years if used constantly over that period.
(e) Assume a tax rate of 30%.
(f) For Osprey Ltd, balances of Asset Revaluation Surplus and Other Components of Equity at 1 July 2014 were $40 000 and $25 000 respectively.

Required

Prepare the consolidated financial statements for Osprey Ltd and its subsidiary as at 30 June 2015.

Exercise 23.6   ADJUSTMENT FOR THE NCI SHARE OF EQUITY

★★   The consolidated financial statements of Whale Submarine Works Ltd are being prepared by the group accountant, Raz Putin. He is currently in dispute with the auditors over the need to adjust for the NCI share of equity in relation to intragroup transactions. He understands the need to adjust for the effects of the intragroup transactions, but believes that it is unnecessary to adjust for the NCI share of equity. He argues that the NCI group of shareholders has its interest in the subsidiary and as a result is entitled to a share of what the subsidiary records as equity. He also disputes with the auditors about the notion of 'realisation' of profit in relation to the NCI. If realisation requires the involvement of an external entity in a transaction, then in relation to transactions such as intragroup transfers of vehicles and services such as interest payments, there is never any external party involved. Those transactions are totally within the group and never involve external entities. As a result, the more appropriate accounting is to give the NCI a share of subsidiary equity and not be concerned with the fictitious involvement of external entities.

Required

Write a report to Raz convincing him that his argument is fallacious.

Exercise 23.7   THE STEP APPROACH

★★   In December 2013, Frog Ltd acquired 60% of the shares of Kovrov Ltd. The accountant for Frog Ltd, Nikki Romanov, is concerned about the approach she should take in preparing the consolidated financial statements for the newly established group. In particular, she is concerned about the calculation of the NCI share of equity, particularly in the years after acquisition date. She has heard accountants in other companies talking about a 'step' approach, and in particular how this makes accounting in periods after the acquisition date very easy as it is then necessary to prepare only one step.

Required

Prepare a report for Nikki, explaining the step approach to the calculation of NCI and the effects of this approach in the years after acquisition date.

Exercise 23.8   EFFECTS OF INTRAGROUP TRANSACTIONS

★★   Because the Moth Cement Works Ltd has a number of subsidiaries, Star Lin is required to prepare a set of consolidated financial statements for the group. She is concerned about the calculation of the NCI share of equity particularly where there are intragroup transactions. The auditors require that when adjustments are made for intragroup transactions the effects of these transactions on the NCI should also be adjusted for. Star has two concerns. First, why is it necessary to adjust the NCI share of equity for the effects of intragroup transactions? Second, is it necessary to make NCI adjustments in relation to *all* intragroup transactions?

Required

Prepare a report for Star, explaining these two areas of concern.

Exercise 23.9   CONSOLIDATION WORKSHEET ENTRIES, DIVIDENDS, EQUITY TRANSFERS

★★   On 1 July 2012, Crocodile Ltd acquired 80% of the shares (cum div.) of Turtle Ltd for $202 000. At this date, the equity of Turtle Ltd consisted of:

Share capital — 100 000 shares	$100 000
General reserve	40 000
Retained earnings	50 000

The carrying amounts and fair values of the assets of Turtle Ltd were as follows:

	Carrying amount	Fair value
Land	$70 000	$90 000
Plant (cost $100 000)	80 000	85 000
Fittings (cost 40 000)	20 000	20 000
Goodwill	5 000	10 000

Any adjustment for the differences in carrying amounts and fair values is recognised on consolidation. Crocodile Ltd uses the partial goodwill method.

Both plant and fittings were expected to have a further 5-year life, with benefits being received evenly over those periods. The plant was sold on 1 January 2015. In the year of the sale of plant, on consolidation the valuation reserve relating to the plant was transferred to retained earnings. At 1 July 2012, Turtle Ltd had not recorded an internally generated trademark that Crocodile Ltd considered to have a fair value of $50 000. This intangible asset was considered to have an indefinite useful life.

Additional information

(a) The following profits were recorded by Turtle Ltd:

For the 2012–13 period	$ 20 000
For the 2013–14 period	25 000
For the 2014–15 period	30 000

(b) In June 2014, Turtle Ltd transferred $5000 to general reserve, and in June 2015, a further $6000 was transferred.

(c) In August 2012, the dividend payable of $5000 on hand at 1 July 2012 was paid by Turtle Ltd.

(d) Other dividends declared or paid since 1 July 2012 are:
  - $8000 dividend declared in June 2013, paid in August 2013
  - $6000 dividend declared in June 2014, paid in August 2014
  - $5000 dividend paid in December 2014
  - $8000 dividend declared in June 2015, expected to be paid in August 2015.

Required

1. Prepare the worksheet entries for the preparation of the consolidated financial statements of Crocodile Ltd and its subsidiary, Turtle Ltd, at 30 June 2015.
2. Assume Crocodile Ltd uses the full goodwill method and the value of the non-controlling interest at 1 July 2012 was $49 250. Prepare the entries that would differ from those in requirement 1.

24

Translation of the financial statements of foreign entities

ACCOUNTING STANDARDS IN FOCUS

IAS 21 *The Effects of Changes in Foreign Exchange Rates*

LEARNING OBJECTIVES

After studying this chapter, you should be able to:

1. identify the reason for translation of financial statements and the applicable accounting standard
2. explain the difference between functional and presentation currencies
3. discuss the rationale underlying the choice of a functional currency
4. apply the indicators in choosing a functional currency
5. translate a set of financial statements from local currency into the functional currency
6. account for changes in the functional currency
7. translate financial statements into the presentation currency
8. prepare consolidated financial statements including foreign subsidiaries when the local currency is the functional currency
9. prepare consolidated financial statements including foreign subsidiaries when the functional currency is that of the parent entity
10. explain what constitutes the net investment in a foreign operation
11. prepare the disclosures required by IAS 21.

24.1 TRANSLATION OF A FOREIGN SUBSIDIARY'S STATEMENTS

A parent entity may have subsidiaries that are domiciled in a foreign country. In most cases, the financial statements of the foreign subsidiary are prepared in the currency of the foreign country. In order for the financial statements of the foreign operation to be included in the consolidated financial statements of the parent, it is necessary to translate the foreign operation's financial statements to the currency used by the parent entity for reporting purposes. The purpose of this chapter is to discuss the process for translating and presenting the consolidated financial statements of a parent entity where at least one of its subsidiaries is a foreign subsidiary.

The accounting standard that deals with this process is IAS 21 *The Effects of Changes in Foreign Exchange Rates*. IAS 21 was first issued by the IASC in July 1983, revised in 1993, and further revised as a part of the Improvements project in 2003. This latter revision provided convergence with GAAP in the United States, in particular Statement of Financial Accounting Standards No. 52 (SFAS 52) *Foreign Currency Translation*. Other minor revisions have been made up to January 2016.

24.2 FUNCTIONAL AND PRESENTATION CURRENCIES

Paragraph 3 of IAS 21 notes that its two areas of application are:
- translating the results and financial position of foreign operations that are included in the financial statements of the entity by consolidation or the equity method
- translating an entity's results and financial position into a presentation currency.

Note that there are two different translation processes here. In order to understand this, it is necessary to distinguish between three different types of currency: local currency, functional currency and presentation currency. Not all foreign subsidiaries experience all three currencies.
- *Local currency*. This is the currency of the country in which the foreign operation is based.
- *Functional currency*. This is defined in paragraph 8 of IAS 21 as 'the currency of the primary economic environment in which the entity operates'. As is explained in more detail later, this is the currency of the country in which the foreign operation is based. This term is not defined in IAS 21.
- *Presentation currency*. Paragraph 8 defines this as 'the currency in which the financial statements are presented'.

To illustrate, Foreign Ltd is a subsidiary of Parent Ltd. Parent Ltd is an Australian company and Foreign Ltd is based in Singapore. The operations in Singapore are to sell goods manufactured in France. In this case, Foreign Ltd would most likely maintain its accounts in Singaporean dollars, the local currency, while the functional currency could be the euro, reflecting the major economic operations in France. However, for presentation in the consolidated financial statements of Parent Ltd, the presentation currency could be the Australian dollar. As the accounts are maintained in Singaporean dollars, they may firstly have to be translated into the functional currency, the euro, and then translated again into the Australian dollar for presentation purposes. It is these two translation processes that are referred to in paragraph 3 of IAS 21.

24.3 THE RATIONALE UNDERLYING THE FUNCTIONAL CURRENCY CHOICE

This section relies heavily on the discussion in the seminal paper by Lawrence Revsine, published in 1983, in which he emphasised the need to understand the rationale underlying the choice of an exchange rate as an entity's functional currency.

As noted by Revsine (1984, p. 514):

> A much more real danger is that firms, their auditors, and outside analysts may not understand the subtle philosophy that underlies the functional currency choice. As a consequence, innocent but incorrect choices and assessments may be made, and compatibility may not be achieved.

According to paragraphs 4(a) and 4(b) of SFAS 52, the objectives of the translation process are:
1. to provide information that is generally compatible with the expected economic effects of an exchange rate change on an entity's cash flows and equity
2. to reflect in consolidated statements the financial results and relationships of the individual consolidated entities as measured in their functional currencies in conformity with US generally accepted accounting principles.

Note in particular the first objective. As the foreign subsidiary operates in another country, it is important that the financial effects on the parent entity of a change in the exchange rate are apparent from the translation process. The parent entity has an investment in a foreign operation and so has assets that are exposed to a change in the exchange rate. Capturing the extent of this exposure should be reflected in the choice of translation method. The economic relationship between the parent and the subsidiary affects the extent to which a change in exchange rate affects the parent entity. This can be seen by noting the differences in the following three cases adapted from Revsine (1984).

24.3.1 Case 1

Protea Ltd is an Australian company that wants to sell its product in Hong Kong. On 1 January 2013, when the exchange rate is A$1 = HK$5, Protea Ltd acquires a building in Hong Kong to be used to distribute the Australian product. The building cost HK$1 million, equal to A$200 000. It also deposited A$55 000 (equal to HK$275 000) in a Hong Kong bank. By 31 January 2013, the company had made credit sales in Hong Kong of HK$550 000. The exchange rate at this time was still A$1 = HK$5. The goods sold had cost A$90 000 to manufacture. The receivables were collected in February 2013 when the exchange rate was A$1 = HK$5.5. This cash receipt is transferred back to Australia immediately.

Note, in this case the company has no subsidiary but acquired an overseas asset, deposited money in an overseas bank and sold goods overseas. The company would record these transactions as follows, in Australian dollars:

Building	Dr	200 000	
Cash	Cr		200 000
Cash — HK Bank	Dr	50 000	
Cash	Cr		50 000
Receivables	Dr	110 000	
Sales	Cr		110 000
Cost of Sales	Dr	90 000	
Inventory	Cr		90 000
Foreign Exchange Loss	Dr	10 000	
Receivables	Cr		10 000
(Loss on receivables when exchange rate changed from 1:5 to 1:5.5)			
Cash	Dr	100 000	
Receivables	Cr		100 000
Foreign Exchange Loss	Dr	5 000	
Cash in HK Bank	Cr		5 000
(Loss on holding HK$55 000 when exchange rate changed from 1:5.0 to 1:5.5)			

Note two effects of this accounting procedure:
- Foreign currency transactions, whether completed (the sale) or uncompleted (the deposit), have an immediate or potentially immediate effect on the future cash flows of the parent. As a result, foreign currency gains/losses are recorded as they occur and immediately affect income.
- Non-monetary assets held in the foreign country are recorded at historical cost and are unaffected by exchange rate changes.

24.3.2 Case 2

Assume that, instead of transacting directly with customers in Hong Kong, Protea Ltd formed a subsidiary, Banksia Ltd, to handle the Hong Kong operation. As with case 1, all goods are transferred from the Australian parent to the Hong Kong subsidiary, which sells them in Hong Kong and remits profits back to the Australian parent.

Hence, Banksia Ltd is established with a capital structure of HK$1 250 000 (equal to A$250 000), an amount necessary to acquire the Hong Kong building and establish the bank account. On selling the inventory to Banksia Ltd, Protea Ltd passes the following entries:

Receivable — Banksia Ltd	Dr	110 000	
Sales Revenue	Cr		110 000
Cost of Sales	Dr	90 000	
Inventory	Cr		90 000

Assuming that the parent bills the subsidiary in Hong Kong dollars, namely HK$110 000, on receipt of the cash, the parent would pass the entry:

Foreign Exchange Loss	Dr	10 000	
Cash	Dr	100 000	
Receivable	Cr		110 000

The subsidiary will show:

Sales	HK$ 110 000
Cost of sales	110 000
Profit	—
Equity	HK$ 1 250 000
Building	HK$ 1 000 000
Cash	250 000
	HK$ 1 250 000

Note that the underlying transactions are the same in case 1 and case 2. The organisational form does not change the underlying economic effects of the transactions. The translation of the HK subsidiary must therefore show the position as if the parent had undertaken the transactions itself. This is the purpose behind the choice of the functional currency approach.

Where the subsidiary is simply a conduit for transforming foreign currency transactions into dollar cash flows, the consolidation approach treats the foreign currency statements of the subsidiary as artefacts that must be translated into the currency of the parent.

In case 2, the translation of the subsidiary's statements must show:
- the assets of the subsidiary at cost to the parent; that is, what the parent would have paid in its currency at acquisition date
- the revenues and expenses of the subsidiary at what it would have cost the parent in its currency at the date those transactions occurred
- monetary gains and losses being recognised immediately in income as they affect the parent directly.

Note, in case 2, that the functional currency of the subsidiary is the Australian dollar. It is the currency of the primary economic environment in which the entity operates. The inventories are sourced in Australian dollars, the dollars financing the subsidiary are Australian dollars, and the cash flows that influence the actions of the parent in continuing to operate in Hong Kong are Australian dollars.

The key to determining the functional currency in case 2 is the recognition of the subsidiary as an *intermediary for the parent's activities*. The alternative is for the subsidiary to act as a *free-standing unit*. Consider case 3 in this regard.

24.3.3 Case 3

Assume that Protea Ltd establishes a subsidiary in Hong Kong for HK$1 250 000, the money again being used to acquire a building and set up a bank account. However, in this case the Hong Kong operation is established to manufacture products in Hong Kong for sale in Hong Kong.

Chinese labour is used in the manufacturing process and profits are used to reinvest in the business for expansion purposes. Remittances of cash to the parent are in the form of dividends.

The economics of case 3 are different from those in case 2. The subsidiary is not just acting as a conduit for the parent. Apart from the initial investment, the cash flows, both inflows and outflows, for the subsidiary are dependent on the economic environment of Hong Kong rather than Australia. The effect of a change in the exchange rate between Australia and Hong Kong has no immediate effect on the operations of the Hong Kong subsidiary. It certainly affects the worth of the parent's investment in the subsidiary, but it has no immediate cash flow effect on the parent. In this circumstance, the functional currency is the Hong Kong dollar rather than the Australian dollar.

In analysing the success of the overseas subsidiary, the interrelationships between variables such as sales, profits, assets and equity should be the same whether they are expressed in Hong Kong or Australian dollars. In other words, the translation process should adjust all items by the same exchange rate to retain these interrelationships.

The key point of Revsine's article is that the choice of translation method should be such as to reflect the underlying economics of the situation. In particular, it is necessary to select the appropriate functional currency to reflect these underlying economic events.

24.4 IDENTIFYING THE FUNCTIONAL CURRENCY

LO4

Paragraphs 9–14 of IAS 21 provide information on determining the functional currency. As the assessment of the functional currency requires judgement, in accordance with paragraph 12 of IAS 21, management gives priority to the primary indicators in paragraph 9 before considering the indicators in paragraphs 10 and 11, which supply supporting evidence to that determined from assessment using the paragraph 9 indicators. The indicators are:

Paragraph 9: normally the one in which it primarily *generates and expends cash*
Consider the currency:
- in which *sales prices* are denominated or which influences sales prices
- of the country whose competitive forces and regulations influence *sales prices*
- in which *input costs* — labour, materials — are denominated and settled, or which influences such costs.

Paragraph 10: consider two factors:
- the currency in which funds from *financing activities* are generated
- the currency in which *receipts from operating activities* are retained.

Paragraph 11: consider:
- whether the activities of the foreign operation are carried out as an *extension* of the reporting entity
- whether *transactions with the reporting entity* are a high or low proportion of the foreign operation's activities
- whether *cash flows* from the activities of the foreign operation *directly affect* the cash flows of the reporting entity and are readily available for remittance to it
- whether *cash flows* from the foreign operation are sufficient to *service existing and expected debt* obligations without funds being made available by the reporting entity.

Paragraph 12: management should use judgement to determine which currency most faithfully reflects the economic effects of the underlying transactions and events.

These factors are not significantly different from those stated in paragraph 42 of the US FASB's SFAS 52. Jeter and Chaney (2003) provided the basis for the information provided in figure 24.1, which illustrates the functional currency indicators as set down by the FASB.

Economic indicators	Indicators pointing to local overseas currency as functional currency	Indicators pointing to parent entity's currency as functional currency
Cash flows	Primarily in the local currency and do not affect the parent's cash flows.	Directly affect the parent's cash flows on a current basis and are readily available for remittance to the parent.
Sales prices	Are not primarily responsive in the short term to exchange rate changes. They are determined primarily by local conditions.	Are primarily responsive to exchange rate changes in the short term and are determined primarily by worldwide competition.
Sales market	Active local market, although there may be significant amounts of exports.	Sales are mostly in the country of the parent entity, or denominated in the parent entity's currency.
Expenses	Production costs and operating expenses are determined primarily by local conditions.	Production costs and operating expenses are obtained primarily from parent entity sources.
Financing	Primarily denominated in the local currency, and the foreign entity's cash flow from operations is sufficient to service existing and normally expected obligations.	Primarily from parent or other parent country-denominated obligations, or the parent entity is expected to service the debt.
Intragroup transactions	Low volume of intragroup transactions and there is not an extensive interrelationship between the operations of the foreign entity and those of the parent. However, the foreign entity may rely on the parent's or affiliates' competitive advantages, such as patents and trademarks.	High volume of intragroup transactions; there is an extensive interrelationship between the operations of the parent and those of the foreign entity, or the foreign entity is an investment or financing device for the parent.

FIGURE 24.1 Functional currency indicators — FASB
Source: Jeter and Chaney (2003, p. 618).

In applying the criteria shown in figure 24.1 for a parent and a single subsidiary, such as an Australian parent and a subsidiary in Hong Kong, there are three scenarios:
1. the functional currency of the subsidiary is the Australian dollar
2. the functional currency is the Hong Kong dollar
3. the functional currency is another currency, say, the Malaysian ringgit.

In relation to the choice between the first two alternatives, the extreme situations are those alluded to in the analysis of the Revsine cases. For the *Australian dollar* to be the functional currency, the expectation is that the subsidiary is a conduit for the parent entity. In the easy case, the product being sold is made in Australia, and the selling price is determined by worldwide competition. Further, because the entire product sold by the subsidiary emanates from the parent, there is significant traffic between the two entities, including cash being transferred from the subsidiary to the parent. For the *Hong Kong dollar* to be the functional currency, it is expected that the Hong Kong operation is independent of the parent entity. The products are sourced in Hong Kong and the sales prices depend on the local currency. The only regular transactions between the two entities are the annual dividends.

However, between these two scenarios there are many others where the determination of the functional currency is blurred. For example, the product being sold may require some Australian raw materials but be assembled in Hong Kong using some local raw materials. There are then material transactions between the two entities, but the subsidiary may be self-sufficient in terms of finance. In these cases, cash is generated in Hong Kong but expended in both Australia and Hong Kong. In determining the functional currency, management will need to apply judgement. The key to making a correct decision is, in accordance with Revsine, understanding what the translation process is trying to achieve in terms of reporting the underlying economic substance of the events and transactions.

In relation to the situation where another currency, such as the Malaysian ringgit, is the functional currency, this could occur where the Australian parent establishes a subsidiary in Hong Kong that imports raw materials from Malaysia and elsewhere, assembles them in Hong Kong and sells the finished product in Malaysia.

It is possible therefore for a parent entity that has a large number of foreign subsidiaries to have a number of functional currencies, particularly if the foreign subsidiaries are all relatively independent.

24.5 TRANSLATION INTO THE FUNCTIONAL CURRENCY

In the situation where it is determined that the Hong Kong dollar is the functional currency for the Hong Kong subsidiary, the financial statements of the subsidiary prepared in Hong Kong dollars are automatically in the functional currency. Where the Hong Kong subsidiary uses the Australian dollar as its functional currency, it is necessary to translate the Hong Kong accounts from Hong Kong dollars into Australian dollars.

The process of translating one currency into another is given in paragraphs 21 and 23 of IAS 21. Paragraph 21 deals with items reflected in the statement of profit or loss and other comprehensive income that concern transactions occurring in the current period:

> A foreign currency transaction shall be recorded, on initial recognition in the functional currency, by applying to the foreign currency amount the spot exchange rate between the functional currency and the foreign currency at the date of the transaction.

Hence, in translating the revenues and expenses in the statement of profit or loss and other comprehensive income, theoretically each item of revenue and expense should be translated at the spot exchange rate between the functional currency and the foreign currency on the date that the transaction occurred. However, given the large number of transactions being reported on in the statement of profit or loss and other comprehensive income, paragraph 22 of IAS 21 provides for an averaging system to be used. A rate that approximates the actual rate at the date of the transaction can be used; for example, an average rate for a week or month might be used for all transactions within those periods. The extent to which averaging can be used depends on the extent to which there is a fluctuation in the exchange rate over a period and the evenness with which transactions occur throughout the period. For example, where the transactions are made evenly throughout a financial year — no seasonal effect, for example — and there is an even movement of the exchange rate over that year, a yearly average exchange rate could be used.

In relation to statement of financial position accounts, paragraph 23 of IAS 21 states:

> At the end of each reporting period:
> (a) foreign currency monetary items shall be translated using the closing rate;
> (b) non-monetary items that are measured in terms of historical cost in a foreign currency shall be translated using the exchange rate at the date of the transaction; and
> (c) non-monetary items that are measured at fair value in a foreign currency shall be translated using the exchange rates at the date when the value was measured.

Monetary items are defined in paragraph 8 as 'units of currency held and assets and liabilities to be received or paid in a fixed or determinable number of units of currency'. As noted in paragraph 16, examples of monetary liabilities include pensions and other employee benefits to be paid in cash and provisions to be settled in cash, including cash dividends that are recognised as a liability. Examples of monetary assets include cash and accounts receivable. All of these items are translated using the spot exchange rate at the end of the reporting period — the closing rate. As noted in case 1 previously, this reflects the amounts available in the functional currency.

For non-monetary items such as plant and equipment, IAS 16 *Property, Plant and Equipment (see chapter 11)* allows the use of the cost basis or the revaluation model of measurement. Where the cost basis is used, the appropriate translation rate is the spot rate at the date the asset was initially recorded by the subsidiary. Where the revaluation model is used, the appropriate rate is the spot rate at the date of the valuation to fair value. Paragraph 25 of IAS 21 notes that certain non-monetary assets such as inventory are to be reported at the lower of cost and net realisable value in accordance with IAS 2 *Inventories*. In such a case, it is necessary to calculate the cost, translated using the spot rate at acquisition date, and the net realisable value translated at the spot rate at the date of valuation. The lower amount is then used — this may require a write-down in the functional currency statements that would not occur in the local currency statements.

The basic principles of the translation method follow.

24.5.1 Statement of financial position items

- *Assets*. Assets should first be classified as monetary or non-monetary. Monetary assets are translated at the current rate existing at the end of the reporting period. With a non-monetary asset, the exchange rate used is that current at the date at which the recorded amount for the asset has been entered into the accounts. Hence, for non-monetary assets recorded at historical cost, the rates used are those existing when the historical cost was recorded. For non-monetary assets that have been revalued, whether upwards or downwards, the exchange rates used will relate to the dates of revaluation.
- *Liabilities*. The principles enunciated for assets apply also for liabilities. The liabilities are classified as monetary and non-monetary and, for the latter, it is the date of valuation that is important.
- *Equity*. In selecting the appropriate exchange rate two factors are important. First, equity existing at the date of acquisition or investment is distinguished from post-acquisition equity. Second, movements in other reserves and retained earnings constituting transfers within or internal to equity are treated differently from other reserves.
- *Share capital*. If on hand at acquisition or created by investment, the capital is translated at the rate existing at acquisition or investment. If the capital arises as the result of a transfer from another equity account, such as a bonus dividend, the rate is that current at the date the amounts transferred were originally recognised in equity.
- *Other reserves*. If on hand at acquisition, the reserves are translated at the rate existing at acquisition. If the reserves are post-acquisition and result from internal transfers, the rate used is that at the date the amounts transferred were originally recognised in equity. If the reserves are post-acquisition and not created from internal transfers, the rate used is that current at the date the reserves are first recognised in the accounts.
- *Retained earnings*. If on hand at acquisition, the retained earnings are translated at the rate of exchange current at the acquisition date. Any dividends paid from pre-acquisition profits are also translated at this rate. Post-acquisition profits are carried forward balances from translation of previous periods' statements of profit or loss and other comprehensive income.

24.5.2 Statement of profit or loss and other comprehensive income items

- *Income and expenses*. In general, these are translated at the rates current at the dates the applicable transactions occur. For items that relate to non-monetary items, such as depreciation and amortisation, the rates used are those used to translate the related non-monetary items.
- *Dividends paid*. These are translated at the rate current at the date of payment.
- *Dividends declared*. These are translated at the rate current at the date of declaration.
- *Transfers to/from reserves*. As noted earlier, if internal transfers are made, the rates applicable are those existing when the amounts transferred were originally recognised in equity.

The application of these rules will result in exchange differences. Exchange differences arise mainly from translating the foreign operation's monetary items at current rates in the same way as for the foreign currency monetary items of the entity. Because the non-monetary items are translated using a historical rate that is the same from year to year, no exchange differences arise in relation to the non-monetary items. Further, items in the statement of profit or loss and other comprehensive income such as sales, purchases and expenses give rise to monetary items such as cash, receivables and payables. Hence, the exchange difference over the period can be explained by examining the movements in the monetary items over the period. The accounting for the exchange difference is explained in paragraph 28 of IAS 21:

> Exchange differences arising on the settlement of monetary items or on translating monetary items at rates different from those at which they were translated on initial recognition during the period or in previous financial statements shall be recognised in profit or loss in the period in which they arise, except as described in paragraph 32.

The exchange differences are then taken to the current period's statement of profit or loss and other comprehensive income in the same way as movements in the exchange rates on an entity's own foreign currency monetary items. *See section 24.10 for a discussion of the paragraph 32 exception.*

As stated in paragraph 34 of IAS 21, the application of the basic principles of the translation method means that when an entity keeps its records in a currency other than its functional currency all amounts are remeasured in the functional currency. This produces the same amounts in that currency as would have occurred had the items been recorded initially in the functional currency.

Sentosa Ltd, a company operating in Singapore, is a wholly owned subsidiary of Taupo Ltd, a company listed in New Zealand. Taupo Ltd formed Sentosa Ltd on 1 July 2015 with an investment of NZ$310 000. Sentosa Ltd's records and financial statements are prepared in Singaporean dollars (S$). Sentosa Ltd has prepared the financial information at 30 June 2016, as shown in figure 24.2.

SENTOSA LTD
Statement of Financial Position
as at 30 June 2016

	2016 S$
Current assets:	
Inventory	210 000
Monetary assets	190 000
Total current assets	400 000
Non-current assets:	
Land — acquired 1/7/15	100 000
Buildings — acquired 1/10/15	120 000
Plant and equipment — acquired 1/11/15	110 000
Accumulated depreciation	(10 000)
Deferred tax asset	10 000
Total non-current assets	330 000
Total assets	730 000
Current liabilities:	
Current tax liability	70 000
Borrowings	50 000
Payables	100 000
Total current liabilities	220 000
Non-current liabilities:	
Borrowings	150 000
Total liabilities	370 000
Net assets	360 000
Equity:	
Share capital	310 000
Retained earnings	50 000
Total equity	360 000

SENTOSA LTD
Statement of Profit or Loss and Other Comprehensive Income
for the year ended 30 June 2016

	S$	S$
Sales revenue		1 200 000
Cost of sales:		
Purchases	1 020 000	
Ending inventory	210 000	810 000
Gross profit		390 000
Expenses:		
Selling	120 000	
Depreciation	10 000	
Interest	20 000	
Other	90 000	240 000
Profit before income tax		150 000
Income tax expense		60 000
Profit for the period		90 000

The only movement in equity, other than in profit, was a dividend paid during the period of S$40 000.

Additional information
(a) Exchange rates over the period 1 July 2015 to 30 June 2016 were:

	S$1.00 = NZ$
1 July 2015	1
1 October 2015	0.95
1 November 2015	0.9
1 January 2016	0.85
1 April 2016	0.75
30 June 2016	0.75
Average rate for year	0.85
Average rate for final quarter	0.77

(b) Proceeds of long-term borrowings were received on 1 July 2015 and are payable in four annual instalments commencing 1 July 2016. Interest expense relates to this loan.
(c) The inventory on hand at balance date represents approximately the final 3 months' purchases.
(d) Revenues and expenses are spread evenly throughout the year.
(e) Deferred tax asset relates to depreciation of the plant and equipment.
(f) The dividends were paid on 1 April 2016.

Required

The functional currency is determined to be the New Zealand dollar. Translate the financial statements of Sentosa Ltd into the functional currency.

Solution

The translation process is as shown in figure 24.2.

FIGURE 24.2 Translation into functional currency

	S$	Rate	NZ$
Sales	1 200 000	0.85	1 020 000
Cost of sales:			
Purchases	1 020 000	0.85	867 000
Ending inventory	210 000	0.77	161 700
	810 000		705 300
Gross profit	390 000		314 700
Expenses:			
Selling	120 000	0.85	102 000
Depreciation	10 000	0.90	9 000
Interest	20 000	0.85	17 000
Other	90 000	0.85	76 500
	240 000		204 500
			110 200
Foreign exchange translation loss	0		1 000
Profit before tax	150 000		109 200
Income tax expense	60 000	0.85	51 000
Profit for the period	90 000		58 200
Retained earnings at 1/7/15	0		0
	90 000		58 200
Dividends paid	40 000	0.75	30 000
Retained earnings at 30/6/16	50 000		28 200
Share capital	310 000	1.00	310 000
Non-current borrowings	150 000	0.75	112 500
Current tax liability	70 000	0.75	52 500
Current borrowings	50 000	0.75	37 500
Payables	100 000	0.75	75 000
	730 000		615 700

(continued)

FIGURE 24.2 *(continued)*

Inventory	210 000	0.77	161 700
Monetary assets	190 000	0.75	142 500
Land	100 000	1.00	100 000
Buildings	120 000	0.95	114 000
Plant and equipment	110 000	0.90	99 000
Accumulated depreciation	(10 000)	0.90	(9 000)
Deferred tax asset	10 000	0.75	7 500
	730 000		615 700

Exchange differences arise mainly from translating the foreign operation's monetary items at current rates in the same way as for the foreign currency monetary items of the entity. Because the non-monetary items are translated using a historical rate that is the same from year to year, exchange differences in relation to non-monetary items arise only in the periods in which they are acquired or sold. Items in the statement of profit or loss and other comprehensive income such as sales, purchases and expenses give rise to monetary items such as cash, receivables and payables. Hence, exchange differences are going to arise by examining the movements in the monetary items over the period.

From figure 24.2, the net monetary assets of Sentosa Ltd at 30 June 2016 consist of:

	S$
Monetary assets	190 000
Deferred tax asset	10 000
Borrowings: non-current	(150 000)
Borrowings: current	(50 000)
Current tax liability	(70 000)
Payables	(100 000)
Net monetary assets at 1/7/15	(170 000)

The changes in the net monetary assets are determined from the statement of profit or loss and other comprehensive income. The exchange differences are calculated by comparing the difference between the exchange rate used in the translation process and the current rate at the reporting date:

	S$	Current rate less rate applied	NZ$ gain (loss)
Net monetary assets at 1 July 2015	310 000	(0.75–1.00)	(77 500)
Increases in monetary assets:			
Sales	1 200 000	(0.75–0.85)	(120 000)
	1 510 000		(197 500)
Decreases in monetary assets:			
Land	100 000	(0.75–1.00)	25 000
Buildings	120 000	(0.75–0.95)	24 000
Plant	110 000	(0.75–0.90)	16 500
Purchases	1 020 000	(0.75–0.85)	102 000
Selling expenses	120 000	(0.75–0.85)	12 000
Interest	20 000	(0.75–0.85)	2 000
Other expenses	90 000	(0.75–0.85)	9 000
Dividend paid	40 000	(0.75–0.75)	—
Income tax expense*	60 000	(0.75–0.85)	6 000
	1 680 000		196 500
Net monetary assets at 30 June 2016	(170 000)		(1 000)

*The entry for the period is:			
		S$	S$
Income tax expense	Dr	60 000	
Deferred tax asset	Dr	10 000	
Current tax liability	Cr		70 000

In preparing the translated financial statements for the following period, it should be noted that the balance of retained earnings at 30 June 2016, as translated in figure 24.2, is carried forward into the next period. In other words, there is no direct translation of the retained earnings (opening balance) within the translation process.

24.6 CHANGING THE FUNCTIONAL CURRENCY

LO6

In the example used in the previous section, the foreign operation in Singapore used the New Zealand dollar as its functional currency. Because of changes in the foreign operation's circumstances, such as the source of raw materials or the variables that determine the selling price of the entity's products, it may be that the functional currency changes into, for example, Japanese yen. According to paragraph 33 of IAS 21, where there is a change in the functional currency the translation procedures apply from the date of the change. Further, paragraph 35 notes that the effect of a change is accounted for prospectively.

Assume, therefore that the Singaporean operation used New Zealand dollars as the functional currency until 1 June 2017, and then decided that the Japanese yen was the appropriate functional currency. The financial statements of the Singaporean entity at the date of change, 1 June 2017, would then be translated at the rate of exchange between the Japanese yen and the Singaporean dollar. This rate would be the historical rate for all non-monetary assets held at the date of change. Any exchange differences recognised in the statements translated into New Zealand dollars would not be recognised in the new translation. These gains/losses would resurface until the parent disposed of the foreign operation, and all exchange gains/losses would be taken into account at that point.

24.7 TRANSLATION INTO THE PRESENTATION CURRENCY

LO7

Consider an Australian entity that has two subsidiaries, one in Malaysia and one in Hong Kong, and the functional currency for each of these subsidiaries is the Hong Kong dollar. The Australian parent will have to prepare a set of consolidated financial statements for the group. In which currency should the consolidated financial statements be prepared?

Theoretically, any currency could be the presentation currency. It may be the Australian dollar if management perceives it as the currency in which users prefer to read the financial statements. In that case, the two subsidiaries' financial statements would be prepared in Hong Kong dollars, which is the functional currency for them both. These would then be translated into Australian dollars and consolidated with the parent entity's statements.

It is possible that the presentation currency could be the Hong Kong dollar, for example if the majority of shareholders in the parent entity were Hong Kong residents. In that case, the parent entity's statements would be translated from the Australian dollar into the Hong Kong dollar and consolidated with those of the subsidiaries as presented in their functional currency.

Hence, having prepared the parent's and the subsidiaries' financial statements in the relevant functional currencies, a presentation currency is chosen and all statements not already in that currency are translated into the presentation currency. Obviously, a number of presentation currencies could be chosen, and multiple translations undertaken.

Paragraph 39 of IAS 21 states the principles for translating from the functional currency into the presentation currency:

> The results and financial position of an entity whose functional currency is not the currency of a hyperinflationary economy shall be translated into a different presentation currency using the following procedures:
> (a) assets and liabilities for each statement of financial position presented (i.e. including comparatives) shall be translated at the closing rate at the date of that statement of financial position;
> (b) income and expenses for each statement presenting profit or loss and other comprehensive income (i.e. including comparatives) shall be translated at exchange rates at the dates of the transactions; and
> (c) all resulting exchange differences shall be recognised in other comprehensive income.

Paragraph 40 notes that average rates over a period for statement of profit or loss and other comprehensive income items may be used unless exchange rates fluctuate significantly over the period.

An elaboration of these procedures for a foreign subsidiary is as follows.

24.7.1 Statement of financial position items

- *Assets.* All assets, whether current or non-current, monetary or non-monetary, are translated at the exchange rate current at the reporting date. This includes all contra-asset accounts such as accumulated depreciation and allowance for doubtful debts.
- *Liabilities.* All liabilities are translated at the same rate as assets, namely the exchange rate current at the reporting date.
- *Equity.* In selecting the appropriate rate, two factors need to be kept in mind. First, equity existing at the acquisition date or investment is distinguished from post-acquisition equity. Second, movements in other reserves and retained earnings constituting transfers within or internal to shareholders' equity are treated differently from other reserves.
- *Share capital.* If on hand at acquisition date or created by investment, this is translated at the rate current at acquisition date or investment. If created by transfer from a reserve, such as general reserve via a bonus issue, this is translated at the rate current at the date the amounts transferred were originally recognised in equity.

- *Other reserves*. If on hand at acquisition date, these are translated at the current exchange rate existing at acquisition date. If reserves are post-acquisition and created by an internal transfer within equity, they are translated at the rate existing at the date the reserve from which the transfer was made was originally recognised in the accounts. If post-acquisition and not the result of an internal transfer (e.g. an asset revaluation surplus), the rate used is that current at the date the reserve is recognised in the accounts.
- *Retained earnings*. If on hand at acquisition date, they are translated at the current exchange rate existing at acquisition. Any dividends from pre-acquisition profits are also translated at this rate. Post-acquisition profits are carried forward balances from translation of previous periods' statements of profit or loss and other comprehensive income.

24.7.2 Statement of profit or loss and other comprehensive income items

- *Income and expenses*. These are translated at the rates current at the applicable transaction dates. For items, such as purchases of inventory and sales, that occur regularly throughout the period, for practical reasons average or standard rates that approximate the relevant rates may be employed. This will involve considerations of materiality. In relation to items such as depreciation, which are allocations for a period, even though they may be recognised in the accounts only at year-end (because they reflect events occurring throughout the period) an average-for-the-period exchange rate may be used.
- *Dividends paid*. These are translated at the rates current when the dividends were paid.
- *Dividends declared*. These are translated at the rates current when the dividends are declared, generally at end-of-year rates.
- *Transfers to/from reserves*. As noted earlier, if these are transfers internal to equity, the rate used for the transfer and the reserve created is that existing when the amounts transferred were originally recognised in equity.

Using the example in figure 24.2 and, assuming that the functional currency of Sentosa Ltd is Singaporean dollars, the translation into New Zealand dollars as a presentation currency is shown in figure 24.3.

FIGURE 24.3 Translation into presentation currency

	S$	Rate	NZ$
Sales	1 200 000	0.85	1 020 000
Cost of sales:			
Purchases	1 020 000	0.85	867 000
Ending inventory	210 000	0.77	161 700
	810 000		705 300
Gross profit	390 000		314 700
Expenses:			
Selling	120 000	0.85	102 000
Depreciation	10 000	0.85	8 500
Interest	20 000	0.85	17 000
Other	90 000	0.85	76 500
	240 000		204 000
Profit before tax			110 700
Income tax expense	60 000	0.85	51 000
Profit for the period	90 000		59 700
Retained earnings at 1/7/15	0		0
	90 000		59 700
Dividends paid	40 000	0.75	30 000
Retained earnings at 30/6/16	50 000		29 700
Share capital	310 000	1.00	310 000
Non-current borrowings	150 000	0.75	112 500
Current tax liability	70 000	0.75	52 500
Current borrowings	50 000	0.75	37 500
Payables	100 000	0.75	75 000
Foreign currency translation reserve			(69 700)
	730 000		547 500

FIGURE 24.3 *(continued)*

Inventory	210 000	0.75	157 500
Monetary assets	190 000	0.75	142 500
Land	100 000	0.75	75 000
Buildings	120 000	0.75	90 000
Plant and equipment	110 000	0.75	82 500
Accumulated depreciation	(10 000)	0.75	(7 500)
Deferred tax asset	10 000	0.75	7 500
	730 000		547 500

The exchange difference arising as a result of the translation is NZ$(86 500) — there has been an exchange loss over the period. This loss arises for two reasons, as explained in paragraph 41 of IAS 21:
* *The income and expense items are translated at dates of the transactions and not the closing rate:* The profit represents the net movements in income and expenses:

Profit	= S$90 000
Profit as translated	= NZ$59 700
Profit × closing rate	= S$90 000 × 0.75
	= NZ$67 500
Translation gain	= NZ$7 800

* *In the case of a net investment in a foreign operation, translating the opening net assets at an exchange rate different from the closing rate:*

Net investment at 1 July 2015	= S$310 000
Net investment × opening rate	= S$310 000 × 1.00
	= NZ$310 000
Net investment × closing rate	= S$310 000 × 0.75
	= NZ$232 500
Translation loss	= NZ$(77 500)

* The total translation loss is NZ$(69 700) equal to (NZ$7800 + NZ$(77 500)).
Note the following in relation to the translation into presentation currency:
* The exchange differences are not taken into current period income or expense. As explained in paragraph 41 of IAS 21, these exchange differences have little or no direct effect on the present and future cash flows from operations. The translation is for presentation only. It is the functional currency statements that recognise exchange differences in current period income and expense.
* In the Basis for Conclusions to IAS 21, in paragraphs BC10–BC14, the International Accounting Standards Board (IASB®) discusses whether the entity should (a) be permitted to present its financial statements in a currency other than the functional currency, (b) be allowed a limited choice of presentation currencies or (c) be permitted to present their financial statements in any currency. The IASB concluded that entities should be permitted to present in any currency or currencies. The IASB noted that some jurisdictions require the use of a specific presentation which will put constraints on some entities anyway. Further, many large groups have a large number of functional currencies and it is not clear which currency should be the presentation currency. In fact, in such circumstances management may prefer to use a number of presentation currencies.

24.8 CONSOLIDATING FOREIGN SUBSIDIARIES — WHERE LOCAL CURRENCY IS THE FUNCTIONAL CURRENCY

Paragraphs 44–47 of IAS 21 deal with matters relating to the consolidation of foreign subsidiaries. As noted in paragraph 45, normal consolidation procedures as set down in IFRS 10 apply to foreign subsidiaries. Where a parent establishes or sets up a subsidiary in a foreign country, the determination of what exists at acquisition date is relatively simple. This is because generally the investment recorded by the parent is equal to the initial share capital of the subsidiary. Where a parent entity obtains an overseas subsidiary by acquiring an already existing operation, the date of control determines the point of time at which historical rates for translation are determined.

For example, assume on 1 July 2015 Canberra Ltd acquires all the shares of Tokyo Ltd, a Japanese entity that has been in existence for many years. The group commences on the date of control, namely 1 July 2015. Tokyo Ltd may have some land that it acquired in 2006 for 1000 yen. The historical cost in the records of the company is 1000 yen. In other words, even though the overseas entity has held the land prior to the date that Canberra Ltd obtained control over the foreign entity, the date for measurement of the historical rate is the date of control. This is because, under IFRS 3 *Business Combinations*, all assets and liabilities of the subsidiary are measured at fair value at acquisition date.

24.8.1 Acquisition analysis

Assume that Canberra Ltd acquired all the shares of Tokyo Ltd at 1 July 2015 for A$30 000, when the exchange rate between the Australian dollar and the Japanese yen was 1:5. At acquisition date, the equity of that company consisted of:

	¥	A$
Share capital	100 000	20 000
Retained earnings	40 000	8 000

All the identifiable assets and liabilities of Tokyo Ltd were recorded at fair value except for plant, for which the fair value was ¥5000 (equal to A$1000) greater than the carrying amount. The plant has a further 5-year life. The Japanese tax rate is 20%. The Australian tax rate is 30%. At 30 June 2016, the exchange rate is A$1 = ¥6. The average rate for the year is A$1 = ¥5.5.

> At acquisition date:
> Net fair value of identifiable assets
>   and liabilities of Tokyo Ltd   = A$20 000 + 8 000 + 1 000(1 − 20%) (BCVR — plant)
>   = A$28 800
> Consideration transferred   = A$30 000
> Goodwill   = A$1 200
>   = ¥(1 200 × 5)
>   = ¥6 000

As noted in paragraph 47 of IAS 21, the goodwill is regarded as an asset of the subsidiary.

24.8.2 Business combination valuation entries

Goodwill

At acquisition date, the entry in Japanese yen is:

		¥	¥
Goodwill	Dr	6 000	
Business Combination Valuation Reserve	Cr		6 000

The valuation reserve continues to be translated at the rate at acquisition date as it is pre-acquisition equity. Assuming the functional currency is the yen, the financial statements of Tokyo Ltd would be translated into Australian dollars for presentation purposes. The goodwill is translated at the closing rate of 1:5, giving rise to a foreign currency translation loss, recognised in equity. Hence, on consolidation, the worksheet entry at 30 June 2016 is:

		A$	A$
Goodwill	Dr	1 000	
Foreign Currency Translation Reserve	Dr	200	
Business Combination Valuation Reserve	Cr		1 200

Plant

Similarly to goodwill, as noted in paragraph 47 of IAS 21, any fair value adjustments to the carrying amounts of assets and liabilities at acquisition date are treated as assets and liabilities of the foreign operation.

At acquisition date, the valuation entry is:

		A$	A$
Plant (¥5000/5)	Dr	1 000	
Deferred Tax Liability	Cr		200
Business Combination Valuation Reserve	Cr		800

At 30 June 2016, the valuation reserve is translated at the exchange rate at acquisition date and, as with goodwill, a foreign exchange loss is recognised — in this case on both the plant and the deferred tax liability:

		A$	A$
Plant (¥5000/6)	Dr	833	
Foreign Currency Translation Reserve	Dr	134	
Deferred Tax Liability (20% × 833)	Cr		167
Business Combination Valuation Reserve	Cr		800

The plant is depreciated at 20% per annum. This is based on the ¥5000 adjustment, giving a depreciation of ¥1000 per annum. The plant is translated at closing rates while the depreciation is translated at average rates.

Depreciation Expense [¥1000/5.5]	Dr	182	
Accumulated Depreciation [¥1000/6.0]	Cr		167
Foreign Currency Translation Reserve	Cr		15
Deferred Tax Liability [¥200/6.0 or 20% × 167]	Dr	33	
Foreign Currency Translation Reserve	Dr	3	
Income Tax Expense [¥200/5.5]	Cr		36

24.8.3 Elimination of investment

The entry at acquisition date and at 30 June 2016 is:

Retained Earnings (1/7/15)	Dr	8 000	
Share Capital	Dr	20 000	
Business Combination Valuation Reserve [800 + 1200]	Dr	2 000	
Shares in Tokyo Ltd	Cr		30 000

24.8.4 Non-controlling interest (NCI)

The NCI receives a share of the recorded equity of the subsidiary as well as the valuation reserves raised on consolidation. The NCI also receives a share of the foreign currency translation reserve raised on the translation into the presentation currency. This share will need to be adjusted for any movements in that reserve as a result of movements raised via the revaluation process.

24.8.5 Intragroup transactions

As with any transactions within the group, the effects of transactions between a parent and its foreign subsidiaries, or between foreign subsidiaries, must be eliminated in full. Neither IAS 21 nor IFRS 10 provide specific guidance in relation to transactions with foreign entities. A key matter of concern is whether the adjustment should be affected by changes in the exchange rate. In this regard, note paragraphs 136 and 137 of the Basis for Conclusions relating to the US Statement of Financial Accounting Standards (SFAS) No. 52 *Foreign Currency Translation*:

> 136. An intercompany sale or transfer of inventory, machinery, etc., frequently produces an intercompany profit for the selling entity and, likewise, the acquiring entity's cost of the inventory, machinery, etc., includes a component of intercompany profit. The Board considered whether computation of the amount of intercompany profit to be eliminated should be based on exchange rates in effect on the date of the intercompany sale or transfer, or whether that computation should be based on exchange rates as of the date the asset (inventory, machinery, etc.) or the related expense (cost of sales, depreciation, etc.) is translated.
>
> 137. The Board decided that any intercompany profit occurs on the date of sale or transfer and that exchange rates in effect on that date or reasonable approximations thereof should be used to compute the amount of any intercompany profit to be eliminated. The effect of subsequent changes in exchange rates on the transferred asset or the related expense is viewed as being the result of changes in exchange rates rather than being attributable to intercompany profit.

It needs to be emphasised that the process of making the consolidation adjustments is to eliminate the *effects* of intragroup transactions. The exchange rate change is not an effect of the transaction but an economic effect on the group resulting from having assets in foreign entities.

Example 1: Parent sells inventory to foreign subsidiary
Assume Aust Ltd, an Australian company, owns 100% of the shares of a foreign operation, F Ltd. During the current period, when the exchange rate is F1 = $2, Aust Ltd sells $10 000 worth of inventory to F Ltd, at a before-tax profit of $2000. At the end of the period, F Ltd still has all inventory on hand. At the year-end reporting date, the exchange rate is F1 = $2.50. The Australian tax rate is 30%, while the tax rate in the foreign country is 20%.

Assuming the financial statements of F Ltd have been translated from the functional currency (F) to the presentation currency (Australian dollars), the consolidation worksheet adjustment entries for the intragroup transaction are:

Sales	Dr	10 000
Cost of Sales	Cr	8 000
Inventory	Cr	2 000

Deferred Tax Asset	Dr	400
Income Tax Expense	Cr	400
(20% × 2000)		

The above entries eliminate the sales and cost of sales as recorded by the parent. The inventory would have been recorded by F Ltd at F5000. The translation process at balance date would mean the F5000 of inventory would be translated using the closing rate of F1 = $2.50, giving a translated figure for inventory of $12 500. After passing the consolidation adjustment entry, inventory in the consolidated statement of financial position would be reported at $10 500 (i.e. $12 500 – $2000). This figure is greater than the original cost of $8000 due to the exchange rate change between the transaction date and the balance date. The US FASB would argue that no further entry is necessary as the effect of changes in the exchange rates on the transferred asset is viewed as the result of changes in exchange rates rather than intragroup profit.

Note that the tax rate used is that of the country holding the asset — in this case, the foreign country. This is because the adjustment for the tax effect is required because of the adjustment to the carrying amount of the inventory in the first journal entry. As the inventory is held by the foreign entity, it is the foreign country's tax rate that is applicable.

Example 2: Foreign subsidiary sells inventory to parent
Assume F Ltd, the foreign subsidiary, sells an item of inventory to Aust Ltd, the Australian parent, during the current period. The inventory had cost F Ltd F5000 and was sold to Aust Ltd for F7500. At the date of sale, the exchange rate was F1 = $2. The tax rate in Australia is 30%. All inventory was still on hand at the end of the period when the closing exchange rate was F1 = $2.50.

The consolidation worksheet entry is:

Sales	Dr	15 000
Cost of Sales	Cr	10 000
Inventory	Cr	5 000
Deferred Tax Asset	Dr	1 500
Income Tax Expense	Cr	1 500

Both sales and cost of sales as recorded by F Ltd are translated at the exchange rate existing at the date of the transaction, namely F1 = $2. The inventory sold to the parent is recorded by that entity at $15 000. The profit on sale is adjusted against inventory at the exchange rate existing at date of sale, giving an adjustment of $5000. Hence, in the consolidated statement of financial position at the end of the period, the inventory is reported at $10 000, equal to the original cost to F Ltd.

ILLUSTRATIVE EXAMPLE 24.2 Consolidation — functional currency is the subsidiary's local currency

On 1 January 2016, Kangaroos Ltd, an Australian company, acquired 80% of the shares of All Blacks Ltd, a New Zealand company, for A$2 498 000. The 2016 trial balance of All Blacks Ltd prepared in New Zealand dollars, which is also the functional currency, showed the following information:

	1 January 2016 NZ$'000	1 December 2016 NZ$'000
Revenue		6 450
Cost of sales		4 400
Gross profit		2 050
Expenses:		
Depreciation		280
Other		960
		1 240
Profit before income tax		810
Income tax expense		120

	1 January 2016 NZ$'000	1 December 2016 NZ$'000
Profit		690
Retained earnings at beginning of year		1 440
		2 130
Dividend paid		100
Dividend declared		100
		200
Retained earnings at end of year		1 930
Cash and receivables	1 000	1 760
Inventories	1 200	1 000
Land	800	800
Buildings	2 200	2 200
Accumulated depreciation	(900)	(990)
Equipment	1 130	1 330
Accumulated depreciation	(200)	(390)
Total assets	5 230	5 710
Current liabilities	590	420
Non-current liabilities	1 200	1 360
Total liabilities	1 790	1 780
Net assets	3 440	3 930
Share capital	2 000	2 000
Retained earnings	1 440	1 930
Total equity	3 440	3 930

Additional information

1. Direct exchange rates for the New Zealand dollar are as follows:

1 January 2016	1.20
1 July 2016	1.25
1 November 2016	1.35
31 December 2016	1.40
Average for the year	1.30

2. At 1 January 2016, all the assets and liabilities of All Blacks Ltd were recorded at fair value except for the land, for which the fair value was NZ$1 000 000, and the equipment, for which the fair value was $1 010 000. The undervalued equipment had a further 4-year life. The tax rate in New Zealand is 25%.
3. Additional equipment was acquired on 1 July 2016 for NZ$200 000 by issuing a note for NZ$160 000 and paying the balance in cash.
4. Sales and expenses were incurred evenly throughout the year.
5. Dividends of NZ$100 000 were paid on 1 July 2016.
6. On 1 November 2016, All Blacks Ltd sold inventory to Kangaroos Ltd for NZ$25 000. The inventory had cost All Blacks Ltd $20 000. Half of the inventory is still on hand at 31 December 2016. The Australian tax rate is 30%.

Required

1. Translate the New Zealand financial statements into the Australian dollar, which is the presentation currency.
2. Prepare the consolidation worksheet entries for consolidating the New Zealand subsidiary into the consolidated financial statements of Kangaroos Ltd. The partial goodwill method is used.

Solution

1. Translation into presentation currency

	NZ$	Rate	A$
Revenue	6 450	1/1.30	4 962
Cost of sales	4 400	1/1.30	3 385
Gross profit	2 050		1 577
Depreciation	280	1/1.30	215
Other	960	1/1.30	739
	1 240		954

	NZ$	Rate	A$
Profit before tax	810		623
Income tax expense	120	1/1.30	92
Profit	690		531
Retained earnings as at 1/1/16	1 440	1/1.20	1 200
	2 130		1 731
Dividend paid	100	1/1.25	80
Dividend declared	100	1/1.40	71
	200		151
Retained earnings as at 31/12/16	1 930		1 580
Share capital	2 000	1/1.20	1 667
Non-current liabilities	1 360	1/1.40	971
Current liabilities	420	1/1.40	300
Foreign currency translation reserve			(439)
	5 710		4 079
Cash and receivables	1 760	1/1.40	1 257
Inventories	1 000	1/1.40	714
Land	800	1/1.40	572
Buildings	2 200	1/1.40	1 572
Accumulated depreciation	(990)	1/1.40	(707)
Equipment	1 330	1/1.40	950
Accumulated depreciation	(390)	1/1.40	(279)
	5 710		4 079

In relation to the foreign currency translation reserve:
• *The income and expense items are translated at dates of the transactions and not the closing rate:*
The profit represents the net movements in income and expenses:

Profit	= NZ$690 000
Profit as translated	= A$530 800
Profit × closing rate	= NZ$690 000 × 1/1.40
	= A$492 857
Translation loss	= A$(37 943)
Dividend paid as translated	= A$80 000
Dividend paid at closing rate	= NZ$100 000 × 1/1.40
	= A$71 429
Translation gain	= A$8 571

• *In the case of a net investment in a foreign operation, translating the opening net assets at an exchange rate different from the closing rate:*

Net investment at 1 January 2016	= NZ$3 440 000
Net investment × opening rate	= NZ$3 440 000 × 1/1.20
	= A$2 866 667
Net investment × closing rate	= NZ$3 440 000 × 1/1.40
	= A$2 457 143
Translation loss	= A$(409 524)

• Total translation loss is A$(438 896) = (A$(37 943) + A$(409 524)) + A$8 571
2. **Consolidation worksheet entries: (in $000)**

Net fair value of identifiable assets and liabilities of All Blacks Ltd	= A$[2 000 + 1 440 + 200(1 × 25%) (land) + 80(1 − 25%) (equipment)] 1/1.20
	= A$[1 667 + 1 200 + 125 + 50]
Net fair value acquired	= 80% × A$[1 667 + 1 200 + 125 + 50]
	= A$[1 334 + 960 + 100 + 40]
Consideration transferred	= A$2 434
Goodwill acquired	= A$2 498
	= NZ$77 (i.e. 64 × 1.20)

(i) Business combination valuation entries

Land (200/1.40)	Dr	143	
Foreign Currency Translation Reserve	Dr	18	
Business Combination Valuation Reserve (150/1.20)	Cr		125
Deferred Tax Liability (50/1.40)	Cr		36
Accumulated Depreciation (200/1.40)	Dr	143	
Equipment (120/1.40)	Cr		86
Foreign Currency Translation Reserve	Dr	7	
Deferred Tax Liability (25% × (80/1.40))	Cr		14
Business Combination Valuation Reserve (60/1.20)	Cr		50
Depreciation Expense ([1/4 × 80]/1.30)	Dr	15	
Accumulated Depreciation ([1/4 × 80]/1.40)	Cr		14
Foreign Currency Translation Reserve	Cr		1
Deferred Tax Liability ([25% × 20]/1.30)	Dr	3.5	
Foreign Currency Translation Reserve	Dr	0.3	
Income Tax Expense ([25% × 20]/1.30)	Cr		3.8

(At acquisition the deferred tax liability was NZ$20 = 25% × NZ$80)

(ii) Elimination of investment

Retained Earnings (1/1/16)	Dr	960	
Share Capital	Dr	1 334	
Business Combination Valuation Reserve	Dr	140	
Goodwill	Dr	64	
Shares in All Blacks Ltd	Cr		2 498
Foreign Currency Translation Reserve	Dr	9	
Goodwill ((77/1.40) − 64)	Cr		9

(iii) Non-controlling interest
Share at acquisition date

Retained Earnings (1/1/16) (20% × 1200)	Dr	240	
Share Capital (20% × 1667)	Dr	333	
Business Combination Valuation Reserve (20% [125 + 50])	Dr	35	
NCI	Cr		608

Share from 1/1/16–31/12/16
(i) Current period profit — the share is based on the translated profit of the subsidiary

NCI Share of Profit	Dr	104	
NCI	Cr		104
(20% × A$[531 − (15 − 3.8)])			

(ii) The share of the foreign currency translation reserve is based on the amount of the reserve calculated as a result of the translation process adjusted by any changes in that reserve recognised in the valuation entries

NCI	Dr	93	
Foreign Currency Translation Reserve	Cr		93
(20% [439 + 18 + 7 + 1 + 0.3])			

(iii) Dividend paid

NCI	Dr	16	
Dividend Paid	Cr		16
(20% × A$80)			

(iv) Dividend declared

NCI	Dr	14	
Dividend Declared	Cr		14
(20% × A$71)			

Intragroup transactions:
(i) Dividends

Dividend Revenue	Dr	64	
Dividend Paid	Cr		64
(80% × (100/1.25))			
Dividend Revenue	Dr	57	
Dividend Receivable	Cr		57
(80% × (100/1.40))			
Dividend Payable	Dr	57	
Dividend Declared	Cr		57

(ii) Sale of inventory: subsidiary to parent

Sales Revenue (25/1.35)	Dr	19	
Cost of Sales	Cr		17
Inventory (1/2 × 5 × 1/1.35)	Cr		2
Deferred Tax Asset (30% × 2)	Dr	0.6	
Income Tax Expense	Cr		0.6

(iii) Adjustment to NCI

NCI	Dr	0.28	
NCI Share of Profit	Cr		0.28
(20% × (2 − 0.6))			

24.9 CONSOLIDATING FOREIGN SUBSIDIARIES — WHERE FUNCTIONAL CURRENCY IS THAT OF THE PARENT ENTITY

In this circumstance, the subsidiary's financial statements are prepared in the local currency, and, as the parent's currency is the functional currency, they are translated into the parent's currency. The main difference in preparing the consolidated financial statements in this case is in the valuation entries. This is because the translation of non-monetary assets differs when the translation is for presentation purposes rather than for functional currency purposes.

Under the method described in paragraph 23 of IAS 21, the non-monetary assets of the subsidiary are translated using exchange rates at the date of the transaction (i.e. historical rates). In contrast, in illustrative example 24.2, where the translation is based on paragraph 39 of IAS 21, the non-monetary assets are translated at the closing rate.

Using the information in illustrative example 24.2:

- at acquisition date, 1 January 2016, goodwill of the subsidiary was measured to be NZ$96
- the land had a fair value-carrying amount difference of NZ$200
- the equipment had a fair value-carrying amount difference of NZ$80, with an expected remaining useful life of 25%
- the NZ tax rate is 25%
- the direct exchange rates for the NZ dollar were:

1 January 2016	1.20
1 July 2016	1.25
1 November 2016	1.35
31 December 2016	1.40
Average for the year	1.30

The business combination valuation entries are then:

The goodwill balance is translated at the historical rate:

Goodwill (96/1.20)	Dr	80
Business Combination Valuation Reserve (96/1.20)	Cr	80

The land is translated at the historical rate, but the deferred tax liability is translated at the closing rate. As the net monetary assets held at the beginning of the period are affected by changes in the exchange rate, an exchange gain is recognised:

Land (200/1.20)	Dr	167
Foreign Exchange Gain	Cr	6
Business Combination Valuation Reserve (150/1.20)	Cr	125
Deferred Tax Liability (50/1.40)	Cr	36

The equipment and related accumulated depreciation are translated at the historical rate, while the deferred tax liability is translated at the closing rate, giving rise to a foreign exchange gain.

Subsequent depreciation is based on the historical rate:

Accumulated Depreciation (200/1.20)	Dr	167
Equipment (120/1.20)	Cr	100
Foreign Exchange Gain	Cr	3
Deferred Tax Liability ([25% × 80]/1.40)	Cr	14
Business Combination Valuation Reserve (60/1.20)	Cr	50
Depreciation Expense ([1/4 × 80]/1.20)	Dr	17
Accumulated Depreciation ([1/4 × 80]/1.20)	Cr	17
Deferred Tax Liability ([25% × 20]/1.40)	Dr	3.5
Foreign Currency Exchange Loss	Dr	0.3
Income Tax Expense ([25% × 20]/1.30)	Cr	3.8

(At acquisition the deferred tax liability was NZ$20 = 25% × NZ$80)

24.10 NET INVESTMENT IN A FOREIGN OPERATION

Paragraph 15 of IAS 21 notes that the investment in a foreign operation may consist of more than just the ownership of shares in that operation. An entity may have a monetary item that is receivable or payable to the foreign subsidiary. According to paragraph 15, where there is an item for which settlement is neither planned nor likely to occur in the foreseeable future, it is in substance a part of the entity's net investment in that foreign operation. These items include long-term receivables and payables but not trade receivables or payables.

Consider the situation where an Australian parent entity has made a long-term loan of 100 000 yen to a Japanese subsidiary when the exchange rate is $2 = ¥1. The parent entity records a receivable of $200 000, while the subsidiary records a payable of ¥100 000. If during the following financial period the exchange rate changes to $3 = ¥1, in accordance with paragraph 28 of IAS 21 the Australian parent passes the following entry in its own records:

Loan Receivable	Dr	100 000
Exchange Gain	Cr	100 000

This results in the receivable being recorded at $300 000. The subsidiary does not pass any entry because it still owes ¥100 000. On translation of the subsidiary into the presentation currency (the Australian dollar), the payable is translated into $300 000. On consolidation of the subsidiary, both the payable and the receivable are eliminated. However, because the receivable is regarded as part of the parent's net investment in the subsidiary, the accounting for the exchange gain is in accord with paragraph 32 of IAS 21:

> Exchange differences arising on a monetary item that forms part of a reporting entity's net investment in a foreign operation (see paragraph 15) shall be recognised in profit or loss in the separate financial statements of the reporting entity or the individual financial statements of the foreign operation, as appropriate. In the financial statements that include the foreign operation and the reporting entity (e.g. consolidated financial statements where the foreign operation is a subsidiary), such exchange differences shall be recognised initially in a separate component of equity and recognised in profit or loss on disposal of the net investment in accordance with paragraph 48.

Hence, the exchange gain of $100 000 recognised as income by the parent must, on consolidation, be reclassified to the foreign currency translation reserve raised as part of the translation process. Hence, in the consolidation worksheet the adjustment entry is:

Exchange Gain	Dr	100 000
Foreign Currency Translation Reserve	Cr	100 000

24.11 DISCLOSURE

Paragraphs 51–57 contain the disclosure requirements under IAS 21. In particular, an entity must disclose:
- the amount of exchange differences included in profit or loss for the period
- net exchange differences classified in a separate component of equity, and a reconciliation of the amount of such exchange differences at the beginning and end of the period
- when the presentation currency of the parent entity is different from the functional currency:
  - the fact that they are different
  - the functional currency
  - the reason for using a different presentation currency
- when there is a change in the functional currency, the fact that such a change has occurred.
  Illustrative disclosures relating to paragraph 52 of IAS 21 are given in figure 24.4.

NOTE			IAS 21 paragraph
Movements in reserves			
Foreign Currency Translation Reserve	**2013**	**2012**	_52(b)_
Balance at beginning of period	(2 420)	(3 020)	
Exchange differences arising on translation of overseas operations	(540)	600	
Balance at end of period	(2 960)	(2 420)	
Profit from operations			
	2010	**2009**	
Profit from operations has been arrived at after charging:			
Amortisation	x	x	
Research and development costs	x	x	
Net foreign exchange losses/(gains)	765	(346)	_52(a)_

FIGURE 24.4 Disclosures required by paragraph 50 of IAS 21

SUMMARY

A parent entity may have investments in subsidiaries that are incorporated in countries other than that of the parent. The foreign operation will record its transactions generally in the local currency. However, the local currency may not be that of the economy that determines the pricing of those transactions. To this end, IAS 21 requires the financial statements of a foreign operation to be translated into its functional currency, being the currency of the primary economic environment in which the entity operates. Determination of the functional currency is a matter of judgement, and the choice of the appropriate currency requires an analysis of the underlying economics of the foreign operation. A further problem addressed by IAS 21 is where the financial statements of the foreign operation need to be presented in a currency different from the functional currency. IAS 21 then provides principles relating to the translation of a set of financial statements into the presentation currency. Whenever a translation process is undertaken, foreign exchange translation adjustments arise. It is necessary to determine whether these adjustments are taken to profit or loss or to other comprehensive income.

Where the foreign operation is a subsidiary, having translated the financial statements of the foreign operation into the currency in which the consolidated financial statements are to be presented, consolidation worksheet adjustments are required as a part of the normal consolidation process. In assessing the assets and liabilities held by the subsidiary at acquisition date, as well as any goodwill or gain on bargain purchase arising as a result of the acquisition, the effects of movements in exchange rates on these assets and liabilities must be taken into consideration. The consolidation adjustments are affected by the process of translation used to translate the foreign entity's financial statements from the local currency into either the functional currency or the presentation currency.

Discussion questions

1. What is the purpose of translating financial statements from one currency to another?
2. What is meant by 'functional currency'?
3. What is the rationale behind the choice of an exchange rate as an entity's functional currency?
4. What guidelines are used to determine the functional currency of an entity?
5. How are statement of profit or loss and other comprehensive income items translated from the local currency into the functional currency?
6. How are statement of financial position items translated from the local currency into the functional currency?
7. How are foreign exchange gains and losses calculated when translating from local currency to functional currency?
8. What is meant by 'presentation currency'?
9. How are statement of profit or loss and other comprehensive income items translated from functional currency to presentation currency?
10. How are statement of financial position items translated from functional currency to presentation currency?
11. What causes a foreign currency translation reserve to arise?
12. Why are gains/losses on translation taken to a foreign currency translation reserve rather than to profit or loss for the period?

References

AASB 2003, *Presentation Currency of Australia Financial Reports* (Agenda paper 12.2), collation of submissions on the invitation to comment meeting of the Australian Accounting Standards Board, 15–16 October, Glenelg, South Australia.

FASB 1981, *Foreign currency translation: Statement of Financial Accounting Standards No. 52*, Norwalk, CT: Financial Accounting Standards Board.

Jeter, D.C. and Chaney, P.K. 2003, *Advanced accounting*, 2nd edn, John Wiley & Sons Inc.

Radford, J. 1996, *Foreign currency translation: clarity or confusion?*, project written as part of a Masters of Commerce degree, Curtin University of Technology, Perth, Western Australia.

Revsine, L. 1984, 'The rationale underlying the functional currency choice', *The Accounting Review*, 59(3), 505–514.

Exercises

STAR RATING ★ BASIC ★★ MODERATE ★★★ DIFFICULT

Exercise 24.1	TRANSLATION INTO FUNCTIONAL CURRENCY

★ Auckland Ltd is a manufacturer of sheepskin products in New Zealand. It is a fully owned subsidiary of a Hong Kong company, China Ltd. The following assets are held by Auckland Ltd at 30 June 2016:

Plant	Cost NZ$	Useful life (years)	Acquisition date	Exchange rate on acquisition date (NZ$1 = HK$)
Tanner	40 000	5	10/8/2012	5.4
Benches	20 000	8	8/3/2014	5.8
Presses	70 000	7	6/10/2015	6.2

Plant is depreciated on a straight-line basis, with zero residual values. All assets acquired in the first half of a month are allocated a full month's depreciation.

Inventory:
- At 1 July 2015, the inventory on hand of $25 000 was acquired during the last month of the 2014–15 period.
- Inventory acquired during the 2015–16 period was acquired evenly throughout the period. Total purchases of $420 000 was acquired during that period.
- The inventory of $30 000 on hand at 30 June 2016 was acquired during June 2016.

Relevant exchange rates (quoted as NZ$1 = HK$) are as follows:

Average for June 2015	7.2
1 July 2016	7.0
Average for 2015–16	7.5
Average for June 2016	7.7
30 June 2016	7.8

Required

1. Assuming the functional currency for Auckland Ltd is the NZ$, calculate:
   (a) the balances for the plant items and inventory in HK$ at 30 June 2016
   (b) the depreciation and cost of sales amounts in the statement of profit or loss and other comprehensive income for 2015–16.
2. Assuming the functional currency is the HK$, calculate:
   (a) the balances for the plant items and inventory in HK$ at 30 June 2016
   (b) the depreciation and cost of sales amounts in the statement of profit or loss and other comprehensive income for 2015–16.
3. Discuss the differences in the results achieved in requirements 1 and 2 above, and why the choice of the functional currency gives a different set of accounting numbers

---

Exercise 24.2   TRANSLATION OF FINANCIAL STATEMENTS INTO FUNCTIONAL CURRENCY

★★   Faber Ltd, a company incorporated in Singapore, acquired all the issued shares of Lantau Ltd, a Hong Kong company, on 1 July 2015. The trial balance of Lantau Ltd at 30 June 2016 was:

	HK$ Dr	HK$ Cr
Share capital		800 000
Retained earnings (1/7/15)		240 000
General reserve		100 000
Payables		160 000
Deferred tax liability		120 000
Current tax liability		20 000
Provisions		80 000
Sales		610 000
Proceeds on sale of land		250 000
Accumulated depreciation — plant		340 000
Plant	920 000	
Land	400 000	
Cash	240 000	
Accounts receivable	300 000	
Inventory at 1 July 2015	60 000	
Purchases	260 000	
Depreciation — plant	156 000	
Carrying amount of land sold	200 000	
Income tax expense	50 000	
Other expenses	134 000	
	2 720 000	2 720 000

Additional information
1. Exchange rates based on equivalence to HK$1 were:

	S$
1 July 2015	0.2
8 October 2015	0.25
1 December 2015	0.28
1 January 2016	0.3
2 April 2016	0.27
30 June 2016	0.22
Average during last quarter 2015–16	0.24
Average 2015–16	0.26

2. Inventory was acquired evenly throughout the year. The closing inventory of HK$60 000 was acquired during the last quarter of the year.
3. Sales and other expenses occurred evenly throughout the year.
4. The Hong Kong tax rate is 20%.
5. The land on hand at the beginning of the year was sold on 8 October 2015. The land on hand at the end of the year was acquired on 1 December 2015.

6. Movements in plant over 2015–16 were:

Plant at 1 July 2012	HK$600 000
Acquisitions — 8 October 2015	200 000
— 2 April 2016	120 000
Plant at 30 June 2016	920 000

Depreciation on plant is measured at 20% per annum on cost. Where assets are acquired during a month, a full month's depreciation is charged.

7. The functional currency of the Hong Kong operation is the Singaporean dollar.

Required

1. Prepare the financial statements of Lantau Ltd in Singaporean dollars at 30 June 2016.
2. Verify the translation adjustment.

Exercise 24.3 **TRANSLATION INTO PRESENTATION CURRENCY, CONSOLIDATION ADJUSTMENTS**

★★★ Dragon Ltd is an international company resident in Singapore. It acquired 80% of the issued shares of an Australian company, Swan Ltd, on 1 July 2015 for A$560 000. All the identifiable assets and liabilities of Swan Ltd were recorded at fair value except for the following:

	Carrying amount A$	Fair value A$
Plant (net)	180 000	240 000
Inventory	68 000	90 000
Brand names	0	140 000

The plant is considered to have a remaining life of 5 years, with depreciation being calculated on a straight-line basis. All inventory on hand at acquisition date was sold within the following 12-month period. The brand names are considered to have an indefinite life, and are adjusted only if impaired.

At 30 June 2016, the following information was available about the two companies:

	Dragon Ltd S$	Swan Ltd A$
Share capital	560 000	350 000
Retained earnings as at 1/7/15	330 000	170 000
Provisions	45 000	30 000
Payables	14 000	40 000
Sales	620 000	310 000
Dividend revenue	6 400	0
Accumulated depreciation — plant	210 000	160 000
	1 785 400	1 060 000
Cash	92 100	30 000
Accounts receivable	145 300	115 000
Inventory	110 000	80 000
Shares in Swan Ltd	336 000	0
Buildings (net)	84 000	220 000
Plant	420 000	400 000
Cost of sales	390 000	120 000
Depreciation — plant	85 000	40 000
Tax expense	23 000	15 000
Other expenses	50 000	10 000
Dividend paid	20 000	10 000
Dividend provided	30 000	20 000
	1 785 400	1 060 000

Additional information

1. Sales, purchases and other expenses were incurred evenly throughout the 2015–16 period. The dividend was paid by Swan Ltd on 1 January 2016, while the dividend was declared on 30 June 2016.
2. The tax rate in Australia is 30% and the tax rate in Singapore is 20%.
3. Swan Ltd acquired A$100 000 of additional new plant on 1 January 2016. Of the depreciation charged in the 2015–16 period, A$8000 related to the new plant.

4. The rates of exchange between the Australian dollar and the Singapore dollar were (expressed as A$1 = S$):

1 July 2015	0.60
1 December 2015	0.64
1 January 2016	0.68
30 June 2016	0.7
Average for the 2015–16 period	0.65

5. The functional currency of the Australian subsidiary is the Australian dollar.
6. On 1 January 2016, Swan Ltd sold some inventory to Dragon Ltd for A$20 000. The inventory had cost the subsidiary $18 000. Only 10% of this inventory remained unsold by the parent entity at 30 June 2016.

Required

1. Translate the financial statements of Swan Ltd into Singapore dollars for inclusion in the consolidated financial statements of Dragon Ltd.
2. Verify the translation adjustment.
3. Prepare the consolidation worksheet entries necessary for the preparation of the consolidated financial statements at 30 June 2016, assuming the use of the partial goodwill method.

Exercise 24.4 TRANSLATION INTO PRESENTATION CURRENCY, CONSOLIDATION ENTRIES

★★★ On 1 July 2015, Cricket Ltd, an Australian company, acquired 80% of the issued shares of Baseball Ltd, a company incorporated in the United States, for US$789 600 (= A$1 579 200). The draft statement of profit or loss and other comprehensive income and statement of financial position of Baseball Ltd at 30 June 2016 are shown below.

	US$	US$
Sales revenues		1 600 000
Cost of sales:		
Opening inventory	140 000	
Purchases	840 000	
	980 000	700 000
Closing inventory	280 000	900 000
Gross profit		
Expenses:		
Depreciation	90 000	
Other	270 000	360 000
Profit before income tax		540 000
Income tax expense		200 000
Profit		340 000
Retained earnings as at 1 July 2015		200 000
		540 000
Dividend paid	120 000	
Dividend declared	200 000	320 000
Retained earnings as at 30 June 2016		220 000

	2016 US$	2015 US$
Current assets:		
Inventory	280 000	140 000
Accounts receivable	20 000	130 000
Cash	20 000	570 000
Total current assets	320 000	840 000
Non-current assets:		
Patent	80 000	80 000
Plant	720 000	600 000
Accumulated depreciation	(130 000)	(80 000)
Land	500 000	300 000
Buildings	920 000	820 000
Accumulated depreciation	(120 000)	(80 000)
Total non-current assets	1 970 000	1 640 000

	2016 US$	2015 US$
Total assets	2 290 000	2 480 000
Current liabilities:		
Provisions	500 000	620 000
Accounts payable	320 000	940 000
Total current liabilities	820 000	1 560 000
Non-current liabilities:		
Loan from Cricket Ltd	530 000	—
Total liabilities	1 350 000	1 560 000
Net assets	940 000	920 000
Equity:		
Share capital	720 000	720 000
Retained earnings	220 000	200 000
Total equity	940 000	920 000

Additional information

1. At acquisition date, all the assets and liabilities of Baseball Ltd were recorded at fair value except for:

	Fair value US$
Plant	540 000
Land	324 000
Inventory	182 000

The plant was expected to have a further 5-year life. The inventory was all sold by July 2016. The US tax rate is 25%.

2. On 1 January 2016, Baseball Ltd acquired new plant for US$120 000. This plant is depreciated over a 5-year period.

3. On 1 April 2016, Baseball Ltd acquired US$200 000 worth of land.

4. On 1 October 2015, Baseball Ltd acquired US$100 000 worth of new buildings. These buildings are depreciated evenly over a 10-year period.

5. The interim dividend was paid on 1 January 2016, half of which was from profits earned prior to 1 July 2015, while the dividend payable was declared on 30 June 2016.

6. Sales, purchases and expenses occurred evenly throughout the period. The inventory on hand at 30 June 2016 was acquired during June 2016.

7. The loan of US$530 000 from Cricket Ltd was granted on 1 July 2015. The interest rate is 8% per annum. Interest is paid on 30 June and 1 January each year.

8. Cricket Ltd sold raw materials to Baseball Ltd at 20% mark-up on cost. During the 2015–16 period there were three shipments of raw materials, costing Baseball Ltd:

1 October 2015	US$120 000
1 January 2016	US$ 96 000
1 April 2016	US$132 000

At 30 June 2016, 20% of the shipment in April remains on hand in Baseball Ltd. The Australian tax rate is 30%.

9. On consolidation, the partial goodwill method is used.

10. The exchange rates for the financial year were as follows:

	US$1 = A$
1 July 2015	2.00
1 October 2015	1.80
1 January 2016	1.70
1 April 2016	1.60
30 June 2016	1.50
Average June 2016	1.52
Average for 2015–16	1.75

Required

1. If the functional currency for Baseball Ltd is the US dollar, prepare the financial statements of Baseball Ltd at 30 June 2016 in the presentation currency of the Australian dollar.
2. Verify the foreign currency translation adjustment.
3. Prepare the consolidation worksheet entries to consolidate the translated financial statements of Baseball Ltd with its parent entity at 30 June 2016.

| Exercise 24.5 | **TRANSLATION INTO FOREIGN CURRENCY, CONSOLIDATION EFFECTS** |

★★★ Use the information in problem 24.4.

Required

1. If the functional currency for Baseball Ltd is the Australian dollar, prepare the financial statements of Baseball Ltd at 30 June 2016 in the functional currency.
2. Verify the foreign currency translation adjustment.
3. Prepare the consolidation worksheet entries to consolidate the translated financial statements of Baseball Ltd with its parent entity at 30 June 2016.
4. Assume on 1 January 2016, Baseball Ltd sold the patent to Cricket Ltd for US$100 000 and that Cricket Ltd depreciates this asset evenly over a 20-year period. Prepare the consolidation worksheet adjustment entries at 30 June 2016.

GLOSSARY

Accounting estimates: Measurement judgements applied in preparing the financial statements.

Accounting policies: The specific principles, bases, conventions, rules and practices applied by an entity in preparing and presenting financial statements.

Accounting profit: Profit for a period (determined in accordance with accounting standards) before deducting tax expense.

Accrual basis: Recognising the effects of transactions and other events when they occur, rather than when cash or its equivalent is received or paid.

Acquirer: The entity that obtains control of the acquiree.

Acquisition date: The date on which the acquirer obtains control of the acquiree.

Active market: A market in which all the following conditions exist: (a) the items traded in the market are homogeneous; (b) willing buyers and sellers can normally be found at any time; and (c) prices are available to the public. A market in which transactions for the asset or liability take place with sufficient frequency and volume to provide pricing information on an ongoing basis (IFRS 13 *Fair Value Measurement*).

Adjusting event after the reporting period: An event that provides evidence of conditions that existed at the end of the reporting period.

Agreement date: The date that a substantive agreement between the combining parties is reached.

Agricultural produce: The harvested product of an entity's biological assets.

Allotment: The process whereby directors of the company allocate shares to applicants. Alternatively, an account recording an amount of money receivable from successful applicants once shares are allotted.

Amortisation: The systematic allocation of the depreciable amount of an intangible asset over its useful life. *See* depreciation.

Amortised cost: The amount at which the financial asset or financial liability is measured at initial recognition minus principal repayments, plus or minus the cumulative amortisation using the effective interest method of any difference between that initial amount and the maturity amount, and minus any reduction (directly or through the use of an allowance account) for impairment or uncollectability.

Application: The process whereby prospective shareholders apply to the company for an allotment of shares. Alternatively, an account used to record the amount of money receivable by the company from applicants for shares.

Asset: A resource controlled by an entity as a result of past events and from which future economic benefits are expected to flow to the entity.

Associate: An entity over which the investor has significant influence and that is neither a subsidiary nor an interest in a joint venture.

Available-for-sale financial assets: Those non-derivative financial assets that are designated as available for sale or that are not classified as (a) loans and receivables, (b) held-to-maturity investments or (c) financial assets at fair value through profit or loss.

Bargain purchase option: A clause in the lease agreement allowing the lessee to purchase the asset at the end of the lease for a preset amount, significantly less than the expected residual value at the end of the lease term.

Bargain renewal option

Biological asset: A living animal or plant.

Bonus issue or bonus shares: An issue of shares to existing owners as a substitute for the payment of cash, particularly as a substitute for a cash dividend.

Business: An integrated set of activities and assets that is capable of being conducted and managed for the purpose of providing a return in the form of dividends, lower costs or other economic benefits directly to investors or other owners, members or participants.

Business combination: A transaction or other event in which an acquirer obtains control of one or more businesses.

Business segment: A distinguishable component of an entity that is engaged in providing an individual product or service or a group of related products or services and that is subject to risks and returns that are different from those of other business segments.

Call: An account used to record amounts of money receivable on shares that have been allotted by shareholders whose shares were forfeited.

Carrying amount: The amount at which an asset is recognised after deducting any accumulated depreciation (amortisation) and accumulated impairment losses thereon.

Cash: Includes cash on hand, currency, cheques, money orders or electronic transfer that a bank will accept as a deposit.

Cash basis: Recognising the effects of transactions and other events when cash or its equivalent is received or paid, rather than when the transactions or other events occur.

Cash dividends

Cash equivalents: Short-term, highly liquid investments that are readily convertible to known amounts of cash and which are subject to an insignificant risk of changes in value.

Cash flow statement: Provides information about the cash payments and cash receipts of an entity during a period.

Cash or settlement discount: An incentive for early payment of amounts owing on credit transactions, normally quoted as a percentage.

Cash-generating unit: The smallest identifiable group of assets that generates cash inflows that are largely independent of the cash inflows from other assets or groups of assets.

Cash-settled share-based payment transaction: A share-based payment transaction in which the entity acquires goods or services by incurring a liability to transfer cash or other assets to the supplier of those goods or services for amounts that are based on the price (or value) of the entity's shares or other equity instruments of the entity.

Class of assets: A category of assets having a similar nature or function in the operations of an entity, and which, for the purposes of disclosure, is shown as a single item without supplementary disclosure.

Closing rate: The spot exchange rate at the end of the reporting period.

Comparability: The quality of accounting information that results from similar accounting recognition, measurement, disclosure, and presentation standards being used by all entities.

Compensation: All employee benefits including share-based payments. This includes all forms of consideration provided by the entity, or on its behalf, in exchange for services rendered to the entity.

Component of an entity: Operations and cash flows that can be clearly distinguished, operationally and for financial reporting purposes, from the rest of the entity.

Conceptual Framework for Financial Reporting: The pronouncement of the International Accounting Standards Board that sets out the concepts underlying the preparation and presentation of financial statements for external users.

Consolidated financial statements: The financial statements of a group in which the assets, liabilities, equity, income, expenses and cash flows of the parent and its subsidiaries are presented as those of a single economic entity.

Constructive obligation: An obligation that derives from an entity's actions where: (a) by an established pattern of past practice, published policies or a sufficiently specific current statement, the entity has indicated to other parties that it will accept certain responsibilities; and (b) as a result, the entity has created a valid expectation on the part of those other parties that it will discharge those responsibilities.

Contingency: A condition arising from past events that exists at reporting date and gives rise to either a possible asset or a possible liability, the outcome of which will be confirmed only on the occurrence of one or more uncertain future events that are outside the control of the entity.

Contingent asset: A possible asset that arises from past events and whose existence will be confirmed only by the occurrence or non-occurrence of one or more uncertain future events not wholly within the control of the entity.

Contingent consideration: Usually, an obligation of the acquirer to transfer additional assets or equity interests to the former owners of an acquiree as part of the exchange for control of the acquiree if specified future events occur or conditions are met. However, contingent consideration also may give the acquirer the right to the return of previously transferred consideration if specified conditions are met.

Contingent liability: (a) A possible obligation that arises from past events and whose existence will be confirmed only by the occurrence or non-occurrence of one or more uncertain future events not wholly within the control of the entity, or (b) a present obligation that arises from past events but is not recognised because (i) it is not probable that an outflow of resources embodying economic events will be required to settle the obligation, or (ii) the amount of the obligation cannot be measured with sufficient reliability.

Contingent rent: The part of the lease payments that is not fixed in amount but is based on the future amount of a factor that changes other than with the passage of time.

Contributed capital

Control: An investor controls an investee when the investor is exposed, or has rights, to variable returns from its involvement with the investee and has the ability to affect those returns through its power over the investee.

Corporate assets: Assets other than goodwill that contribute to the future cash flows of both the cash-generating unit under review and other cash-generating units.

Corporate governance: The system by which companies are directed and managed. It influences how the objectives of the company are set and achieved, how risk is monitored and assessed, and how performance is optimised. Good corporate governance structures encourage companies to create value (through entrepreneurialism, innovation, development and exploration) and provide accountability and control systems commensurate with the risks involved.

Cost: The amount of cash or cash equivalents paid or the fair value of the other consideration given to acquire an asset at the time of its acquisition or construction or, where applicable, the amount attributed to that asset when initially recognised in accordance with the specific requirements of other accounting standards, e.g. IFRS 2 *Share-based Payment.*

Cost approach: A valuation technique that reflects the amount that would be required currently to replace the service capacity of an asset (often referred to as current replacement cost).

Costs of conversion: Costs directly related to the units of production plus a systematic allocation of fixed and variable overheads that are incurred in converting materials into finished goods.

Costs of disposal: Incremental costs directly attributable to the disposal of an asset or cash-generating unit, excluding finance costs and income tax expense.

Costs of purchase: Costs such as purchase price, import duties and other taxes (other than those subsequently recoverable by the entity from the taxing authorities), transport, handling and other costs directly attributable to the acquisition of finished goods, materials and services.

Costs to sell: The incremental costs directly attributable to the disposal of an asset (or disposal group), excluding finance costs and income tax expense.

Cumulative: In relation to preference shares, shares on which undeclared dividends in one year accumulate to the following year/s until paid.

Current liability: A liability that (a) is expected to be settled in the normal course of the entity's operating cycle, or (b) is at call or due or expected to be settled within 12 months of the reporting date.

Current tax: The amount of income taxes payable in respect of the taxable profit for a period.

Customer options: Customer options are opportunities provided to the customer to purchase additional goods or services. These additional goods and services may be priced at a discount or may even be free of charge. Options to acquire additional goods or services at a discount can come in many forms, including sales incentives, customer award credits (e.g. frequent flyer programmes), contract renewal options (e.g. waiver of certain fees, reduced future rates) or other discounts on future goods or services.

Date of exchange: The date when each individual investment is recognised in the financial report of the acquirer.

Deductible temporary differences: Temporary differences that will result in amounts that are deductible in determining taxable profit of future periods when the carrying amount of the asset or liability is recovered or settled.

Deferred tax asset: Amounts of income taxes recoverable in future periods in respect of deferred temporary differences; the carry forward of unused tax losses and the carry forward of unused tax credits.

Deferred tax liability: Amounts of income taxes payable in future periods in respect of taxable temporary differences.

Defined benefit post-employment plans: A defined benefit post-employment plan is an arrangement to provide benefits after completion of employment that does not satisfy the definition of a defined contribution post employment plan (refer defined contribution post-employment plan)

Defined contribution post-employment plans: A define contribution post-employment plan is an arrangement to provide benefits after completion of employment, in which the entity pays predetermined contributions to a separate entity which, in turn, pays post-employment benefits to former employees of the first-mentioned entity.

Depreciable amount: The cost of an asset, or other amount substituted for cost, less its residual value.

Depreciation (amortisation): The systematic allocation of the depreciable amount of an asset over its useful life.

Derivatives: A financial instrument that derives its value from another underlying item, such as a share price or an interest rate. The definition requires all of the following three characteristics to be met: (a) its value must change in response to a change in an underlying variable such as a specified interest rate, price, or foreign exchange rate; (b) it must require no initial net investment or an initial net investment that is smaller than would be required for other types of contracts with similar responses to changes in market factors; and (c) it is settled at a future date.

Development: The application of research findings or other knowledge to a plan or design for the production of new or substantially improved materials, devices, products, processes, systems or services before the start of commercial production or use.

Direct non-controlling interest (DNCI): An NCI that holds shares directly in a subsidiary.

Discontinued operation: A component of an entity that either has been disposed of or is classified as held for sale and (a) represents a separate major line of business or geographical area of operations; (b) is part of a single coordinated plan to dispose of a separate major line of business or geographical area of operations; or (c) is a subsidiary acquired exclusively with a view to resale.

Disposal group: A group of assets to be disposed of, by sale or otherwise, together as a group in a single transaction, and liabilities directly associated with those assets that will be transferred in the transaction.

Dividends: A distribution of profit to the equity holders of a company.

Economic life: Either the period over which an asset is expected to be economically usable by one or more users, or the number of production or similar units expected to be obtained from the asset by one or more users.

Effective interest method: A method of calculating the amortised cost of a financial asset or a financial liability, and of allocating the interest income or interest expense over the relevant period.

Effective interest rate: The rate that exactly discounts estimated future cash payments or receipts through the expected life of the financial instrument (or, when appropriate, a shorter period) to the net carrying amount of the financial asset or financial liability.

Embedded derivative: A component of a combined (or 'hybrid') instrument that also includes a non-derivative host contract, with the effect that some of the cash flows of the combined instrument vary in a way similar to a stand-alone instrument.

Employee benefits: All forms of consideration given by an entity in exchange for services rendered by employees.

Employees and others providing similar services: Individuals who render personal services to the entity and either (a) the individuals are regarded as employees for legal or tax purposes, (b) the individuals work for the entity under its direction in the same way as individuals who are regarded as employees for legal or tax purposes, or (c) the services rendered are similar to those rendered by employees. For example, the term encompasses all management personnel, that is, those persons having authority and responsibility for planning, directing and controlling the activities of the entity, including non-executive directors.

Entity-specific value: The present value of the cash flows an entity (1) expects to arise from the continuing use of an asset and from its disposal at the end of its useful life, or (2) expects to incur when settling a liability.

Entry price: The price paid to acquire an asset or received to assume a liability in an exchange transaction.

Equitable obligation

Equity: The residual interest in the assets of the entity after deducting all its liabilities.

Equity instrument granted: The right (conditional or unconditional) to an equity instrument of the entity conferred by the entity on another party, under a share-based payment arrangement.

Equity instrument: Any contract that evidences a residual interest in the assets of an entity after deducting all of its liabilities.

Equity method: The method of accounting whereby the investment is initially recognised at cost and subsequently adjusted for the post-acquisition change in the investor's share of net assets of the associate. The profit or loss of the investor includes the investor's share of the profit or loss of the investee.

Equity-settled share-based payment transaction: A share-based payment transaction in which the entity receives goods or services as consideration for equity instruments of the entity (including shares or share options).

Errors: Omissions from or misstatements in the financial statements.

Exchange difference: The difference resulting from translating a given number of units of one currency into another currency at different exchange rates.

Exchange rate: The ratio of exchange for two currencies.

Executory contracts: Contracts under which neither party has performed any of its obligations or both parties have partially performed their obligations to an equal extent.

Executory costs: Operating amounts (including insurance, maintenance, consumable supplies, replacement parts and rates) that are paid by the lessor on behalf of the lessee.

Exit price: The price that would be received to sell an asset or paid to transfer a liability.

Expenses: Decreases in economic benefits during the accounting period in the form of outflows or depletions of assets or incurrences of liabilities that result in decreases in equity, other than those relating to distributions to equity participants.

Fair value: The price that would be received to sell an asset or paid to transfer a liability in an orderly transaction between market participants at the measurement date (IFRS 13 *Fair Value Measurement*).

Fair value (of a leased asset): The amount for which an asset could be exchanged or a liability settled between knowledgeable, willing parties in an arm's length transaction.

Faithful representation

Final dividends

Finance lease: A lease that transfers substantially all the risks and benefits incidental to ownership of an asset; title may or may not eventually be transferred.

Financial asset: Any asset that is: (a) cash; (b) an equity instrument of another entity; (c) a contractual right: (i) to receive cash or another financial asset from another entity, or (ii) to exchange financial assets or financial liabilities with another entity under conditions that are potentially favourable to the entity; or (d) a contract that will or may be settled in the entity's own equity instruments that is: (i) a non-derivative for which the entity is or may be obliged to receive a variable number of the entity's own equity instruments, or (ii) a derivative that will or may be settled other than by the exchange of a fixed amount of cash or another financial asset for a fixed number of the entity's own equity instruments (for this purpose the entity's own equity instruments do not include instruments that are themselves contracts for the future receipt or delivery of the entity's own equity instruments).

Financial assets at fair value through profit or loss: Financial assets held for trading and measured at fair value with any gain or loss from a change in fair value recognised in profit or loss, or financial assets that upon initial recognition are designated by the entity as at fair value through profit or loss.

Financial instrument: Any contract that gives rise to a financial asset of one entity and a financial liability or equity instrument of another.

Financial liability: Any liability that is: (a) a contractual obligation: (i) to deliver cash or another financial asset to another entity, or (ii) to exchange financial assets or financial liabilities with another entity under conditions that are potentially unfavourable to the entity; or (b) a contract that will or may be settled in the entity's

own equity instruments and is: (i) a non-derivative for which the entity is or may be obliged to deliver a variable number of the entity's own equity instruments, or (ii) a derivative that will or may be settled other than by the exchange of a fixed amount of cash or another financial asset for a fixed number of the entity's own equity instruments (for this purpose the entity's own equity instruments do not include instruments that are themselves contracts for the future receipt or delivery of the entity's own equity instruments).

Financial position: The assets, liabilities, and residual equity interest of an entity at a given point in time.

Financing activities: Those activities that result in changes in the size and composition of the equity capital and borrowings of the entity.

Firm commitment: A binding agreement for the exchange of a specified quantity of resources at a specified price on a specified future date or dates.

First-in, first-out (FIFO): A method of allocating cost to inventory items that assumes that the items first purchased will be the items first sold.

FOB destination: A condition of sale under which the seller pays all freight costs (FOB means 'free on board').

FOB shipping: A condition of sale under which freight costs incurred from the point of shipment are paid by the buyer (FOB means 'free on board').

Forecast transaction: An uncommitted but anticipated future transaction.

Foreign currency: A currency other than the functional currency of the entity.

Foreign operation: An entity that is a subsidiary, associate, joint venture or branch of a reporting entity, the activities of which are based or conducted in a country or currency other than those of the reporting entity.

Forfeited shares account: An account initially recording the amount of funds supplied by shareholders whose shares were forfeited.

***Framework for the Preparation and Presentation of Financial Statements*:** The pronouncement of the International Accounting Standards Board that sets out the concepts underlying the preparation and presentation of financial statements for external users. This has been superseded by the *Conceptual Framework for Financial Reporting*.

Functional currency: The currency of the primary economic environment in which the entity operates.

Gains

General purpose financial statements: The financial statements that a business entity prepares and presents at least annually to meet the common information needs of a wide range of users external to the entity.

Geographical segment: A distinguishable component of an entity that is engaged in providing products or services within a particular economic environment and that is subject to risks and returns that are different from those of components operating in other economic environments.

Going concern: An entity that is expected to continue in operation for the foreseeable future.

Goodwill: An asset representing the future economic benefits arising from other assets acquired in a business combination that are not individually identified and separately recognised.

Grant date: The date at which the entity and another party (including an employee) agree to a share-based payment arrangement, being when the entity and the counterparty have a shared understanding of the terms and conditions of the arrangement. At grant date the entity confers on the counterparty the right to cash, other assets, or equity instruments of the entity, provided the specified vesting conditions, if any, are met. If that agreement is subject to an approval process (e.g. by shareholders), grant date is the date when that approval is obtained.

Gross investment: The aggregate of the minimum lease payments receivable by the lessor under a finance lease and any unguaranteed residual value accruing to the lessor.

Group: A parent and its subsidiaries.

Guaranteed residual value: That part of the residual value of the leased asset guaranteed by the lessee or a third party related to the lessee.

Hedge effectiveness: The degree to which changes in the fair value or cash flows of the hedged item that are attributable to a hedged risk are offset by changes in the fair value or cash flows of the hedging instrument.

Hedged item: An asset, liability, firm commitment, highly probable forecast transaction or net investment in a foreign operation that (a) exposes the entity to risk of changes in fair value or future cash flows and (b) is designated as being hedged.

Hedging instrument: A designated derivative or (for a hedge of the risk of changes in foreign currency exchange rates only) a designated non-derivative financial asset or non-derivative financial liability whose fair value or cash flows are expected to offset changes in the fair value or cash flows of a designated hedged item.

Held-to-maturity investments: Investments that the entity has the positive intention and ability to hold to maturity (e.g. debt instruments, such as debentures held in another entity or redeemable preference shares) other than: (a) those that the entity upon initial recognition designates as at fair value through profit or loss; (b) those that the entity designates as available for sale; and (c) those that meet the definition of loans and receivables.

Highest and best use: The use of a non-financial asset by market participants that would maximise the value of the asset or the group of assets and liabilities (e.g. a business) within which the asset would be used.

Highly probable: Significantly more likely than probable.

Impairment loss: The amount by which the carrying amount of an asset or a cash-generating unit exceeds its recoverable amount (which is the higher of the asset's net selling price and its value in use).

Inception of the lease: The earlier of the date of the lease agreement and the date of commitment by the parties to the principal provisions of the lease.

Income: An increase in an asset or a decrease in a liability will result in income, unless the increase or decrease results from an equity contribution (such as cash raised through share capital). Because of this broad definition, income is further dissected into revenue and gains.

Income approach: Valuation techniques that convert future amounts (e.g. cash flows or income and expenses) to a single current (i.e. discounted) amount; the fair value measurement is determined on the basis of the value indicated by current market expectations about those future amounts.

Incremental borrowing rate: The rate of interest the lessee would have to pay on a similar lease or, if that is not determinable, the rate that (at the inception of the lease) the lessee would incur to borrow over a similar term, and with a similar security, the funds necessary to purchase the asset.

Indirect non-controlling interest (INCI): An NCI that has an interest in a subsidiary as a result of having an interest in the parent of that subsidiary.

Initial direct costs: Incremental costs that are directly attributable to negotiating and arranging a lease, except for such costs incurred by manufacturer or dealer lessors.

Initial public offering

Inputs: The assumptions that market participants would use when pricing the asset or liability, including assumptions about risk, such as the following: (a) the risk inherent in a particular valuation technique used to measure fair value (such as a pricing model); and (b) the risk inherent in the inputs to the valuation technique. Inputs may be observable or unobservable.

Intangible asset: An identifiable non-monetary asset without physical substance.

Interest rate implicit in the lease rate: The rate that, at the inception of the lease, causes the aggregate present value of the minimum lease payments and the unguaranteed residual value to be equal to the sum of the fair value of the leased asset and any initial direct costs of the lessor.

Interim dividends

Intrinsic value: The difference between the fair value of the shares to which the counterparty has the (conditional or unconditional) right to subscribe or which it has the right to receive, and the price (if any) the counterparty is (or will be) required to pay for those shares. For example, a share option with an exercise price of CU15 (currency units) on a share with a fair value of CU20, has an intrinsic value of CU5.

Inventories: Assets held for sale in the ordinary course of business, in the process of production for such sale, or in the form of materials or supplies to be consumed in the production process or in the rendering of services.

Investee: An entity in which funds have been invested.

Investing activities: Those activities which relate to the acquisition and disposal of long-term assets and other investments not included in cash equivalents.

Investment property: Property (land or a building, or part of a building, or both) held to earn rentals or for capital appreciation or both, rather than for (a) use in the production or supply of goods or services or for administrative purposes, or (b) sale in the ordinary course of business.

Investor: An entity which invests funds in an investee.

Joint control: The contractually agreed sharing of control over an economic activity that exists only when the strategic financial and operating decisions relating to the activity require the unanimous consent of the parties sharing the control (the venturers).

Joint venture: A contractual arrangement whereby two or more parties undertake an economic activity that is subject to joint control.

Key management personnel: Those persons having authority and responsibility for planning, directing and controlling the activities of the entity, directly or indirectly, including any director (whether executive or otherwise) of that entity.

Lease: An agreement whereby the lessor conveys to the lessee in return for a payment or series of payments the right to use an asset for an agreed period of time.

Lease payments: The total amounts payable under the lease agreement.

Lease term: The non-cancellable period for which the lessee has contracted to lease the asset together with any further terms for which the lessee has the option to continue to lease the asset, with or without further payment, when at the inception of the lease it is reasonably certain that the lessee will exercise the option.

Level 1 inputs: Quoted prices (unadjusted) in active markets for identical assets or liabilities that the entity can access at the measurement date.

Level 2 inputs: Inputs other than quoted prices included within Level 1 that are observable for the asset or liability, either directly or indirectly.

Level 3 inputs: Unobservable inputs for the asset or liability.

Liability: A present obligation of the entity arising from past events, the settlement of which is expected to result in an outflow from the entity of resources embodying economic benefits.

Loans and receivables: Non-derivative financial assets with fixed or determinable payments that are not quoted in an active market and which the entity has no intention of trading, e.g. loan to a subsidiary.

Market approach: A valuation technique that uses prices and other relevant information generated by market transactions involving identical or comparable (i.e. similar) assets, liabilities or a group of assets and liabilities, such as a business.

Market condition: A condition upon which the exercise price, vesting or exercisability of an equity instrument depends that is related to the market price of the entity's equity instruments, such as attaining a specified share price or a specified amount of intrinsic value of a share option, or achieving a specified target that is based on the market price of the entity's equity instruments relative to an index of market prices of equity instruments of other entities.

Market participants: Buyers and sellers in the principal (or most advantageous) market for the asset or liability that have all of the following characteristics: (a) they are independent of each other, i.e. they are not related parties as defined in IAS 24, although the price in a related party transaction may be used as an input to a fair value measurement if the entity has evidence that the transaction was entered into at market terms; (b) they are knowledgeable, having a reasonable understanding about the asset or liability and the transaction using all available information, including information that might be obtained through due diligence efforts that are usual and customary; (c) they are able to enter into a transaction for the asset or liability; (d) they are willing to enter into a transaction for the asset or liability, i.e. they are motivated but not forced or otherwise compelled to do so.

Materiality: The notion of materiality guides the margin of error acceptable, the degree of precision required and the extent of the disclosure required when preparing general purpose financial reports.

Measurement: The process of determining the monetary amount at which an asset, liability, income or expense is reported in the financial statements.

Measurement date: The date at which the fair value of the equity instruments granted is measured for the purposes of IFRS 2. For transactions with employees and others providing similar services, the measurement date is the grant date. For transactions with parties other than employees (and those providing similar services), the measurement date is the date the entity obtains the goods or the counterparty renders service.

Minimum lease payments: The payments over the lease term that the lessee is or can be required to make, excluding contingent rent, costs for services and taxes to be paid by and reimbursed to the lessor, together with (a) for a lessee, any amounts guaranteed by the lessee or by a party related to the lessee, and (b) for a lessor, any residual value guaranteed to the lessor.

Monetary assets: Money held and assets to be received in fixed or determinable amounts of money.

Monetary items: Units of currency held and assets and liabilities to be received or paid in a fixed or determinable number of units of currency.

Most advantageous market: The market that maximises the amount that would be received to sell the asset or minimises the amount that would be paid to transfer the liability, after taking into account transaction costs and transport costs.

Net assets: Total assets minus total liabilities.

Net investment in a foreign operation: The amount of the reporting entity's interest in the net assets of that operation.

Net realisable value: The estimated selling price in the ordinary course of business less the estimated costs of completion and the estimated costs necessary to make the sale.

Non-adjusting event after the end of the reporting period: An event that is indicative of conditions that arose after the end of the reporting period.

Non-cancellable lease: A lease that is cancellable only (a) upon the occurrence of some remote contingency, (b) with the permission of the lessor, (c) if the lessee enters into a new lease for the same or an equivalent asset with the same lessor, or (d) upon payment by the lessee of an additional amount such that, at inception of the lease, continuation of the lease is reasonably certain.

Non-controlling interest (NCI): The equity in a subsidiary not attributable, directly or indirectly, to a parent.

Non-performance risk: The risk that an entity will not fulfil an obligation. Non-performance risk includes, but may not be limited to, the entity's own credit risk.

Non-sequential acquisition: Where a parent acquires its shares in a subsidiary after that subsidiary has acquired shares in its subsidiary.

Notes: Notes are prepared in accordance with IAS 1 and form part of a set of general purpose financial statements. They contain information in addition to that presented in the balance sheet, income statement, statement of changes in equity and cash flow statement. They provide narrative descriptions of the basis of preparation of the financial statements and accounting policies adopted, as well as disaggregations of items disclosed in the financial statements and information about items that do not qualify for recognition in those statements.

Obligating event: An event that creates a legal or constructive obligation that results in an entity having no realistic alternative to settling that obligation.

Observable inputs: Inputs that are developed using market data, such as publicly available information about actual events or transactions, and that reflect the assumptions that market participants would use when pricing the asset or liability.

Offsetting: Offsetting refers to the presentation of different elements of financial statements on a net basis, such as the offsetting of income and expense items to present a net gain or loss, or the offsetting of liabilities and assets, so as to report them as a single item, being a net asset or a net liability.

Onerous contract: A contract in which the unavoidable costs of meeting the obligations under the contract exceed the economic benefits expected to be received under it.

Operating activities: Those activities which relate to the main revenue-producing activities of the entity and other activities that are not investing or financing activities.

Operating lease: A lease other than a finance lease.

Operating segment: An operating segment is defined as a component of an entity: (a) that engages in business activities from which it may earn revenues and incur expenses (including revenues and expenses relating to transactions with other components of the same entity); (b) whose operating results are regularly reviewed by the entity's chief operating decision maker to make decisions about resources to be allocated to the segment and assess its performance; and (c) for which discrete financial information is available.

Ordinary shares

Orderly transaction: A transaction that assumes exposure to the market for a period before the measurement date to allow for marketing activities that are usual and customary for transactions involving such assets or liabilities; it is not a forced transaction (e.g. a forced liquidation or distress sale).

Parent: An entity that controls one or more entities.

Participating: In relation to preference shares, shares that receive extra dividends above a fixed rate once a certain level of dividends has been paid on ordinary shares.

Performance: The ability of an entity to earn a profit on the resources that have been invested in it.

Periodic method: A system of recording inventory whereby the value of inventory is determined and recorded on a periodic basis (normally annually).

Perpetual method: A system of recording inventory whereby inventory records are updated each time a transaction involving inventory takes place.

Power: Existing rights that give the current ability to direct the relevant activities.

Pre-acquisition equity: The equity of the subsidiary at acquisition date. It is not just the equity recorded by the subsidiary, but is determined by reference to the cost of the business combination.

Preference shares

Presentation currency: The currency in which the financial report is presented.

Principal market: The market with the greatest volume and level of activity for the asset or liability.

Private placement: An issue of shares usually to a large institutional investor such as a finance company, superannuation fund or life insurance company.

Probable: More likely than not.

Property, plant and equipment: Tangible items that (a) are held for use in the production or supply of goods or services, for rental to others, or for administrative purposes, and (b) are expected to be used during more than one period.

Prospective application: Applying the change to transactions, events or other conditions occurring after the date of the change and recognising the effect in the current and future periods.

Protective rights: Rights designed to protect the interest of the party holding those rights without giving that party power over the entity to which those rights relate.

Provision: A liability of uncertain timing or amount.

Public company: A company entitled to raise funds from the public by lodging a disclosure document with ASIC and have its shares or other ownership documents traded on the stock exchange. It may be a limited company, unlimited company or no-liability company.

Reciprocal shareholdings: Where two entities hold shares in each other.

Recognition: The process of incorporating in the financial statements an item that meets the definition of an asset, liability, income or expense.

Recoverable amount: For an asset or a cash-generating unit, the higher of its fair value less costs of disposal and its value in use.

Related party: A person or entity that is related to the entity that is preparing its financial statements.

Related party transaction: A transfer of resources, services or obligations between a reporting entity and a related party, regardless of whether a price is charged.

Relevance: That quality of information that exists when the information influences economic decisions made by users.

Relevant activities: For the purpose of IFRS 10, the activities of the investee that significantly affect the investee's returns.

Reliability: Information has the quality of reliability when it is free from material error and bias and can be depended on by users to represent faithfully that which it either purports to represent or could reasonably be expected to represent.

Reload feature: A feature that provides for an automatic grant of additional share options whenever the option holder exercises previously granted options using the entity's shares, rather than cash, to satisfy the exercise price.

Reload option: A new share option granted when a share is used to satisfy the exercise price of a previous share option.

Remuneration: *See* compensation.

Reportable segment: A business segment or a geographical segment identified based on the definitions for either a business segment or geographical segment.

Reporting entity: An entity in respect of which it is reasonable to expect the existence of users who rely on the entity's general purpose financial statements for information that will be useful to them for making and evaluating decisions about the allocation of scarce resources. A reporting entity can be a single entity or a group comprising a parent and all of its subsidiaries.

Research: Original and planned investigation undertaken with the prospect of gaining new scientific or technical knowledge and understanding.

Reserve: A category of equity that is not contributed capital.

Residual value: The estimated amount that an entity would currently obtain from disposal of the asset, after deducting the estimated costs of disposal, if the asset were already of the age and in the condition expected at the end of its useful life.

Retained earnings

Retrospective application: Means applying a new accounting policy to transactions, other events and conditions as if that policy had always been applied.

Revaluation decrease (increase): The amount by which the revalued carrying amount of a non-current asset as at the revaluation date is less than (exceeds) its previous carrying amount.

Revenue: The gross inflow of economic benefits during the period arising in the course of the ordinary activities of an entity when those inflows result in increases in equity, other than increases relating to contributions from equity participants.

Reverse acquisition

Rights issue: An issue of new shares giving existing shareholders the right to an additional number of shares in proportion to their current shareholdings.

Sale and leaseback

Scrip dividends

Segment accounting policies: Accounting policies adopted for preparing and presenting the financial statements of the consolidated group or entity as well as those accounting policies that relate specifically to a segment.

Segment assets: Operating assets that are employed by a segment in its operating activities and that either are directly attributable to the segment or can be allocated to the segment on a reasonable basis.

Segment expense: Expense resulting from the operating activities of a segment that is directly attributable to the segment and the relevant portion of an expense that can be allocated on a reasonable basis to the segment, including expenses relating to sales to external customers and expenses relating to transactions with other segments of the same entity.

Segment liabilities: Operating liabilities that result from the operating activities of a segment and that either are directly attributable to the segment or can be allocated to the segment on a reasonable basis.

Segment result: Segment revenue less segment expense. Segment result is determined before any adjustments for minority interest.

Segment revenue: Revenue reported in the entity's income statement that is directly attributable to a segment and the relevant portion of entity revenue that can be allocated on a reasonable basis to a segment, whether from sales to external customers or from transactions with other segments of the same entity.

Separate financial statements: Financial statements presented by a parent (i.e. an investor with control of a subsidiary) or an investor with joint control of, or significant influence over, an investee, in which the investments are accounted for at cost or in accordance

with IAS 39 *Financial Instruments: Recognition and Measurement.*

Sequential acquisition: where a parent acquires its shares in a subsidiary before or on the same date that the subsidiary acquires shares in its subsidiary.

Share buy-back: The repurchase of a company's shares by the company from its shareholders.

Share issue costs: Costs incurred on the issue of equity instruments. These include underwriting costs, stamp duties and taxes, professional advisers' fees and brokerage.

Share option: A contract that gives the holder the right, but not the obligation, to subscribe to the entity's shares at a fixed or determinable price for a specified period of time.

Share split

Share-based payment arrangement: An agreement between the entity and another party (including an employee) to enter into a share-based payment transaction, which thereby entitles the other party to receive cash or other assets of the entity for amounts that are based on the price of the entity's shares or other equity instruments of the entity, or to receive equity instruments of the entity, provided the specified vesting conditions, if any, are met.

Share-based payment transaction: A transaction in which the entity receives goods or services as consideration for equity instruments of the entity (including shares or share options), or acquires goods or services by incurring liabilities to the supplier of those goods or services for amounts that are based on the price of the entity's shares or other equity instruments of the entity.

Significant influence: The power to participate in the financial and operating policies of the investee without having control or joint control over those policies.

Specific identification: A method of allocating cost to inventory based on identifying and aggregating all costs directly related to each individual inventory item.

Spot exchange rate: The exchange rate for immediate delivery.

Statement of changes in equity: A financial statement prepared in accordance with IAS 1 for inclusion in general purpose financial reports. The statement reports on the changes in the entity's equity for the reporting period. Changes in equity disclosed may include movements in retained earnings for the period, items of income and expense recognised directly in equity, and movements in each class of share and each reserve.

Statement of financial position: A financial statement that presents assets, liabilities and equity of an entity at a given point in time.

Statement of profit or loss and other comprehensive income: A financial statement prepared in accordance with the requirements of IAS 1 for inclusion in general purpose financial statements. The statement reports the entity's income, expenses, profit or loss, other comprehensive income and total comprehensive income for the reporting period.

Structured entity: An entity that has been designed so that voting or similar rights are not the dominant factor in deciding who controls the entity, such as when any voting rights relate to administrative tasks only and the relevant activities are directed by means of contractual arrangements.

Subsidiary: An entity, including an unincorporated entity such as a partnership, that is controlled by another entity (known as the parent).

Substance over form: The accounts will reflect the underlying economic reality of transactions and not their legal form.

Tax base: Of an asset or liability, the amount attributed to that asset or liability for tax purposes.

Tax expense: The aggregate amount included in the determination of profit or loss for the period in respect of current tax and deferred tax.

Taxable profit: The profit for a period, determined in accordance with the rules established by the taxation authorities, upon which income taxes are payable.

Taxable temporary differences: Temporary differences that will result in taxable amounts in determining taxable profit of future periods when the carrying amount of the asset and liability is recovered or settled.

Temporary difference: The difference between the carrying amount of an asset or liability and the tax base of that asset or liability.

Timeliness

Trade discount: A reduction in selling prices granted to customers.

Transaction costs: The costs to sell an asset or transfer a liability in the principal (or most advantageous) market for the asset or liability that are directly attributable to the disposal of the asset or the transfer of the liability and meet both of the following criteria: (a) They result directly from and are essential to that transaction. (b) They would not have been incurred by the entity had the decision to sell the asset or transfer the liability not been made (similar to costs to sell, as defined in IFRS 5).

Transport costs: The costs that would be incurred to transport an asset from its current location to its principal (or most advantageous) market.

Understandability: The ability of financial information to be comprehended by financial statement users who have a reasonable knowledge of business and economic activities and accounting, and a willingness to study the information with reasonable diligence.

Underwriter: An entity which, for a fee, undertakes to subscribe for any shares not allotted to applicants as a result of an undersubscription.

Unguaranteed residual value: That part of the residual value of the leased asset, the realisation of which by the lessor is not assured or is guaranteed solely by a party related to the lessor.

Unit of account: The level at which an asset or a liability is aggregated or disaggregated in an IFRS for recognition purposes.

Unobservable inputs: Inputs for which market data are not available and that are developed using the best information available about the assumptions that market participants would use when pricing the asset or liability.

Useful life: (a) The period over which an asset is expected to be available for use by an entity, or (b) the number of production or similar units expected to be obtained from the asset by an entity.

Value in use: The present value of future cash flows expected to be derived from an asset or cash-generating unit.

Venturer: A party to a joint venture that has joint control over that joint venture.

Verifiability

Vest: To become an entitlement. Under a share-based payment arrangement, a counterparty's right to receive cash, other assets or equity instruments of the entity vests when the counterparty's entitlement is no longer conditional on the satisfaction of any vesting conditions.

Vesting conditions: The conditions that must be satisfied for the counterparty to become entitled to receive cash, other assets or equity instruments of the entity, under a share-based payment arrangement. Vesting conditions include service conditions, which require the other party to complete a specified period of service, and performance conditions, which require specified performance targets to be met (such as a specified increase in the entity's profit over a specified period of time).

Vesting period: The period during which all the specified vesting conditions of a share-based payment arrangement are to be satisfied.

Warrants [or Share warrants]

Weighted average: A method of allocating cost to inventory items based on the weighted average of the cost of similar items at the beginning of a period and the cost of similar items purchased or produced during the period.

accounting book value compared with
    market capitalisation 356
accounting estimates 468, 473
accounting policies 468
    retrospective application 469–72
    selecting and changing 468–73
accounting profit
    difference from taxable profit 124–6
    permanent differences 124
    temporary differences 124–6, 133
Accounting Standards Codification (ASC)
    820: 50
accounts receivable inputs 59
accrual basis of accounting 451
accruals 97
accumulated depreciation 423
accumulated profit or loss 34
acquisition method for business
    combination 381–3
active markets 58, 365
actuarial gains and losses 260
actuaries 258, 263
adjusted market assessment approach,
    stand-alone selling price
    determination 81
adjusting event 474
advantageous markets 54–5
agents 569
    revenue from contracts with
        customers 87
aggregation 451
airline industry
    lease accounting policy
        disclosures 333–5
    reserves disclosure notes 37
alcoholic beverages industry
    statement of changes in equity note
        disclosures 39
amortisation of contract costs 85
amortised cost
    calculating 172–3
    financial liabilities 174–5
    intangible assets 366–7
ancillary services 304
annual leave 246, 249, 250–1
ASC see Accounting Standards
    Codification
ask prices, inputs based on 57
asset revaluation reserve 36
assets 11
    current 453, 454
    definition 10, 360
    disposals of 301
    identifiable concepts 358–9
    physical and non-physical 359
    recognition 12
    significant parts approach 278
    tax bases 134
    usefulness of definitions 360
    see also intangible assets
assets held for sale 276
Association of German Banks 519
automobile industry
    accounting policy notes and segment
        information 527–31

balance sheet see statement of financial
    position
bank borrowings 486
bank overdrafts 486
banking industry
    consolidated assets 455
    employee benefits 246
    scrip dividends 35
bargain purchase 281, 326, 327
    business combination 391–2
bargain renewal 328
benefit/years of service method 256
best estimate measurement 100–1
bid prices, inputs based on 57
Black–Scholes–Merton formula 203
bonus issue 31
borrowing cost 103, 281–2
brands 364, 365
broadcasting licence 366
building held and used inputs 58
business combination 385, 388–91
    accounting in records of acquiree 392–5
    accounting in records of acquirer 383
    acquiree does not liquidate 392–3
    acquiree liquidates 393–5
    acquirer buys only shares in
        acquiree 395
    acquisition accounting method 381–3
    acquisition analysis by acquirer 390–1
    acquisition analysis example 396–8
    acquisition-related costs 387–8
    cash and monetary assets 385
    consideration transferred 385–8
    and consolidation 570–2
    contingent consideration 386–7
    contingent liabilities 113–15
    cost of issuing debt and equity
        instruments 386
    deferred tax arising from 143
    determining acquisition date 382–3
    disclosure 398–400, 596–7
    equity instruments 386
    gain on bargain purchase 391–2
    general forms of 381
    goodwill 385
    identifying 380
    identifying acquirer 381–2
    intangible assets 384
    liabilities assumed 386
    measurement 385
    nature of 380–1
    non-monetary assets 386
    recognition 383–4
    subsequent adjustments to contingent
        consideration 395–6
    subsequent adjustments to contingent
        liabilities 395
    subsequent adjustments to
        goodwill 395
    worksheet entries subsequent to
        acquisition date 588–95
business combination valuation entries
    578, 640
    worksheet entries at acquisition date
        583–4

business combination valuation reserve
    (BCVR) 582
business models 169–70
capital 14
capital returns 158
carry-forward tax losses, creating and
    recouping 132–3
cash 159, 486–7
cash dividends 34
cash equivalents 486–7
cash flow characteristics 170
cash flow hedge 183
    of a firm commitment 185–7
    main requirements of 184
cash-generating units
    inputs 58, 59
    reversal of impairment loss 432
cash-settled share-based payments 201,
    209–12
    accounting 202, 209–10
    disclosure 212–13
    grant of shares with cash alternative
        subsequently added 211
    transaction where counterparty has
        settlement choice 210–11
    transaction where entity has settlement
        choice 212
combination goodwill 389
commercial obsolescence 286–7
commercial substance 279–80
commodity contracts 158
common stock 24
    see also ordinary shares
companies 22
    features of corporate
        structure 23–4
    for-profit 23
    limited liability 24
    ordinary share issue 24–5
    returns to shareholders 25
comparability of information 8–9
compound financial instruments 163–4
    measurement approaches 211
compound securities 31
Conceptual Framework see Conceptual
    Framework for Financial Reporting
Conceptual Framework for Financial
    Reporting 4
    assets 10, 349
    assumptions of underlying financial
        statements 9
    equity 11, 22
    expenses 12
    expensing of outlays 278
    income 11
    liabilities 10, 96, 97, 349
    measurement of elements 13
    objective of general purpose financial
        reporting 7
    physical substance characteristic 359
    purpose of 6–7
    qualitative characteristics of financial
        information 7–9
    reporting entity 7
    stewardship and prudence 14–15

consideration paid or payable to a customer, transaction price determination 80–1
consignment inventories 229
consolidated financial statements 569–70
 consolidation process 562–4
 income tax notes 146–7
 multiple groups 564
 reasons for consolidation 563–4
consolidation for business combination 570–2
 formation of new entity 570–1
 reverse acquisitions 571–2
consolidation for controlled entities 562–74
 ability to use power to affect returns 568
 agents or principals 569
 business combination 570–2
 consolidated financial statements 562–4
 disclosure 572–4
 exposure or rights to variable returns 568
 group of entities 563
 level of share ownership 566–7
 potential voting rights 567–8
 power 565–8
 preparing consolidated financial statements 569–70
consolidation for foreign subsidiary
 disclosure 700
 functional currency of parent entity 698–9
 local currency is functional currency 691–8
 net investment in foreign operation 699–700
consolidation for intragroup transactions 606–25
 dividends declared and paid in current period 615–16
 dividends declared in current period but not paid 614–15
 intragroup borrowings 616
 intragroup dividends 614–16
 intragroup services 613–14
 intragroup services realisation of profits or losses 614
 profits in ending inventory 608–11
 profits in opening inventory 611–13
 realisation of profit and loss 608
 reasons for adjusting 606–7
 sales of inventory 607–8
 transfers of inventory 607–13
consolidation for non-controlling interest (NCI) 636–71
 calculating share of equity 636
 comparing full goodwill and partial goodwill methods 642
 consolidated worksheet 643
 effects of NCI on process 638–43
 full goodwill method 639–40
 intragroup transactions 642
 partial goodwill method 640–2
consolidation for non-controlling interest (NCI) share of equity 644–55
 accounting at acquisition date 645–50
 accounting subsequent to acquisition date 651–5
 adjusting for effects of intragroup transactions 656–8, 659–60
 consolidation worksheet 655
 full goodwill method 646–8
 gain on bargain purchase 658–60
 NCI share of recorded equity of subsidiary 644–5

partial goodwill method 648–50
realisation of profits or losses 657–8
realisation of profits or losses for intragroup transfer for services and interest 657–8
realisation of profits or losses for inventory 657
consolidation for wholly owned subsidiaries 578–98
 acquisition analysis 580–3
 acquisition analysis for parent with no previously held equity interest in subsidiary 581–2
 adjustments 578–9
 bonus share dividends 593
 business combination valuation entries 588–91
 business combination valuation entries at acquisition date 583–4
 consolidation process 578–9
 consolidation worksheets 579–80, 585–6
 contingent liability valuation subsequent to acquisition date 590–1
 disclosure 595–7
 dividends paid/payable from subsidiary equity 591–3
 equipment valuation entry subsequent to acquisition date 589
 gain on bargain purchase 587–8
 goodwill valuation entry subsequent to acquisition date 591
 information at acquisition date 581
 inventory valuation entry subsequent to acquisition date 590
 land valuation entry subsequent to acquisition date 590
 parent has previously held equity interest in subsidiary 583
 patent valuation entry subsequent to acquisition date 589–90
 pre-acquisition entries 591
 pre-acquisition entries at acquisition date 584–5
 pre-acquisition reserve transfers 593–5
 revaluations in records of the subsidiary at acquisition date 595
 subsidiary recorded dividends at acquisition date 586–7
 transfers from retained earnings to other reserves 594
 transfers to retained earnings from other reserves 594–5
 worksheet entries at acquisition date 583–8
 worksheet entries subsequent to acquisition date 588–95
construction industry, financial statements 499–506
constructive obligation 97, 99, 106, 109, 246
contingent assets 111
contingent liabilities 97–8
 business combination 113–15
 comparisons between IFRS 3 and IAS 37: 113–15
 difference from provision 98
 disclosure 98, 99, 111
contingent rent 327, 331
contingent settlement provisions 162–3
continuity assumption 9
 see also going-concern assumption

contracts
 amortisation and impairment of costs 85
 assets 87
 combined 75–6
 costs 84–5, 89
 definition 75
 disclosures 88–9
 identification 75–6
 liabilities 87
 modifications 85–6
 own use 165, 188
 see also revenue from contracts with customers
contracts, rights and obligations approach 165
contractual right 159
contributed equity
 share capital issue 26–8
 subsequent movements in share capital 28–32
control criterion for consolidation 564–9
controlled entities 564
controlling entities 563
convertible bonds 163
convertible notes 163–4
core goodwill 389, 398, 639
corporate accounting scandals 356
corporate assets 428–30
corporate social responsibility 450
cost approach valuation 56, 59, 289
cost model
 factors influencing choice 299
 impaired asset 423, 424
 intangible assets 365
 investment properties 304
 property, plant and equipment 283–8
cost of purchase
 deferred payment terms 222
 trade and cash discounts 221–2
 transaction taxes 221
costs of conversion 222
credit default swaps 188
credit-impaired financial assets 177
credit risk 188, 189, 192
currency see functional currency; local currency; presentation currency
currency risk 189
current cost measurement 13
current tax 127–31
 completed worksheet 130
 determining tax rates worksheet 128–30
 items recognised outside profit or loss 143
 offsetting 143
 recognition 131
current value system 14
customer options for additional goods or services 77
cut-off procedures 227, 228
debt instruments
 amortised cost 168, 169, 178–9, 180
 fair value through other comprehensive income 168, 169, 178, 179–80
 fair value through profit or loss 168, 169, 180
decommissioning liability 64
decommissioning provisions 107–8
deductible temporary differences 125, 126, 132
deferred revenue 96
deferred tax 133–9

adjustments 138
from business combination 143
calculating temporary differences 135–6
determining carrying amounts 133
determining tax bases for assets 133–5
determining tax bases for liabilities 134–5
excluded differences 136–7
initial recognition of asset or liability 137
items recognised outside profit or loss 143
recognition 291
recognition of adjustments 141
worksheet 137–9
deferred tax asset
amendments 142–3
calculating 136
recognition 139–41
deferred tax liability
amendments 142–3
calculating 136
recognition 139–40
defined benefit plans 253
accounting for 255–63
alternative approaches to 255
amount of asset/liability 258
modifications to 259–60
present value using projected unit credit
method 256–7
recognised amounts in profit or loss
258–60
remeasurements of liability/asset to be
recognised in other comprehensive
income 260–3
worksheet 262–3
defined contribution plans 253, 254
depreciation
leased assets 342
methods of 285–6
process of allocation 284–5
property, plant and equipment 284–8
revalued assets 298–9
significant parts 288
subsequent measurement 331
derivatives 158, 163, 166–8
embedded 167–8
fair value through profit or loss 168,
169, 180
required characteristics 167
detailed formal plans 106, 107
development costs, criteria for capital
classification 362–3
diminishing-balance method of depreciation
285–6
direct method 489, 492–6
directly attributable costs
acquisition for zero or nominal cost 282
business combination 387
costs not to be included 282
costs to be included 281–2
income earned 282
directors' reports 450
disclosure
consolidation for wholly owned
subsidiaries 595–7
contingent liabilities 98, 99
finance lease by lessees 333–6
foreign subsidiaries 700
income tax 144–7
intangible assets 357–8, 367–70
revenue from contracts with customers
87–9

share-based transactions 212–13
specific 38
statement of changes in equity 38–9
voluntary 518
disclosure notes 9
discount rate
impairment of assets 422–3
lease 327–8
long-service leave 264, 265
provision 101–2
discussion papers 284–5, 336, 348
dividends 34–5
cash 34
consolidation worksheets 586–7
declared and paid in current period
615–16
declared in current period but not paid
614–15
final 35–6
interim 35–6
intragroup 614–16
preference 545
scrip 34–5
wholly owned subsidiaries 593
earnings per share 543–53
basic earnings per share 545–8
bonus issues and share splits 547
calculation to include tax expense and
preference dividends 545
contingently issuable shares 547
determining weighted average number of
shares 547
diluted 549–52
diluted warrants 550
dilutive contingently issuable shares 551
dilutive convertible securities 551
dilutive options 550–1
dilutive potential of contracts 551–2
dilutive potential ordinary shares 550
dilutive shares 550–2
disclosure 553
earnings 545
repurchases and conversion of preference
shares 545–6
retrospective adjustments 553
rights issues 548
share consolidation 546–7
share repurchase 546–7
shares 546
weighted average number when one
than one issue of potentially dilutive
securities 552
earnings per share ratio 543–4
effective interest method 172
effective interest rate 172
embedded derivatives 167–8
employee benefits 246
bonus plans 252–3
definitions 246
non-monetary benefits 246
payroll 247
profit-sharing arrangements 252–3
relationships between employer, pension
plan and employees 253
short-term 246–53
short-term paid absences 249–52
termination benefits 266–7
see also long-term employee benefits; post-
employment benefits
employee retirement plans 253

end-of-period accounting
control account/subsidiary ledger
reconciliations 229–30
inventories 227–30
entity-specific value 280
entry price 51–2
equity 11
equity distributions classification 164
equity instruments 159
business combination 386
definition 157, 162
difference from financial liabilities 160–3
disclosure 213
fair value through other comprehensive
income 168, 169, 180
fair value through profit or loss 168, 169,
180
intrinsic value 207
modifications to terms and conditions
208–9
subsequent measurement 172
equity investments 486
equity method of accounting
accounting for 202–4
transactions in which services are received
203
transactions measured by reference to fair
value of equity instruments granted
203–4
equity-settled share-based payments 201
errors 468, 473
correction of 473
cut-off 228
estimation, reliable 99
European Financial Reporting Advisory
Group (EFRAG) 519
European opinion about IFRS 8: 519
executive remuneration
related party disclosures 542–3
use of earnings per share 544
executory contracts 323
executory costs 327, 331
exit price 51–2, 61
expected cost plus margin approach, stand-
alone selling price determination 81
expected credit loss model 176, 177–80
expected value approach, variable
consideration estimation 78, 79–80
expenses
classification 164
definition 12
recognition 13
exposure drafts 7, 14, 50, 115, 336, 348,
518–19
extraordinary items 459
fair value
definitions 50, 51–3
differences 37
fair value hedge 183
main requirements 184
simple 184–5
fair value measurement
appropriate valuation techniques 56–7
blockage factors 54
calculating less costs of disposal 421
criticisms about 156
disclosure 65–7
equity application 65
equity instruments granted 203–4
fair value definitions 51–3

fair value measurement *(continued)*
  financial instruments with offsetting
      positions application 65
  framework 53–9
  how transaction and transport costs are
      used 53
  incremental 208
  inputs 57–9
  key principles in determining assets or
      liabilities 53–4
  lease assets 326
  liabilities applications 62–4
  market participants 55–6
  non-financial assets applications 59–62
  prioritising inputs 57–8
  property, plant and equipment 279–80
  recurring 66
fair value model, investment properties 304
faithful representation of financial
      information 8
FASB/IASB joint projects *see* IASB/FASB joint
      projects
finance lease 323, 324
  classification guidance 324, 325, 326, 328,
      329, 330
  sale and leaseback transactions 346–7
finance lease by lessees 330–6
  disclosure 333–6
  initial recognition of 330
  lease payment schedules 331–3
  reimbursement of lessor costs and
      contingent rent 331
  subsequent measurement for assets 331
  subsequent measurement for liability 331
finance lease by lessors 336–41
  disclosure 340–1
  executory cost and contingent rent 337–9
  initial direct costs (IDC) 339–40
  initial recognition of 336–7
  lease receipts schedule 338–9
  subsequent measurement 337–9
finance lease by manufacturer/dealer
      lessors 341
  calculating and recognising profit on sale
      with initial direct costs 341
Financial Accounting Standards Board
      (FASB) 5
  fair value 50, 60
  FAS 158 *Defined Benefit Pension and other
      Post-retirement Pension Plans* 256
  functional currency indicators 683
  SFAS No. 52 *Foreign Currency
      Translation* 680
  SFAS No. 131 *Disclosures about Segments of
      an Enterprise and Related Information* 519
  SFAS No. 133 *Accounting for Derivative
      Instruments and Hedging Activities* 157
financial assets
  amortised cost 168, 169
  categories 168–70
  credit-impaired 177
  definition 159
  fair value through other comprehensive
      income 168, 169
  fair value through profit or loss 168, 169
  IFRS 9 requirements 164–5
  impaired and uncollectable 176–80
  measurement rules 180
  offsetting 65, 181
  scope 164–5

subsequent measurement 172–3
financial capital 14
Financial Crisis Advisory Group report about
      accounting for financial instruments
      during GFC 156–7
financial guarantee contracts 165, 174
financial information characteristics 7–8
financial instruments
  categories 168–71
  classification of liability and equity
      components 163–4
  common 159
  definition 158
  disclosure 188–93
  disclosure of risk 191–3
  gains and losses 175–6
  hybrid 167
  initial measurement 171–2
  measurements 171–80
  other disclosures 191
  reclassification 175
  recognition criteria 171
  risks pertaining to 188–93
  settlement options 163
  subsequent measurement 172–5
  transfers of financial assets 193
financial liabilities
  amortised cost 170, 174–5
  categories 170–1
  definition 159
  difference from equity instruments 160–3
  fair value through profit or loss 170, 171
  IFRS 9 requirements 164–5
  measurement rules 180
  offsetting 65, 181
  scope 164–5
  subsequent measurement 174–5
financial liabilities versus equity instruments
  equity/liability test for ordinary shares
      160–1
  equity/liability test for preference
      shares 161
  equity/liability test for settlement in
      entity's own equity instruments 162
financial reporting
  cost constraints of 9
  objective of 7
  by segments 518
financial statements
  adjusting after reporting period 474
  assets definition 10
  assets recognition 12
  assumption underlying 9
  common types of 158
  components of 450
  consistency of presentation 452
  disclosure of comparative information 452
  disclosure of risk 191–3
  equity definition 11
  expenses definition 12
  expenses recognition 13
  fair presentation and compliance 451
  frequency of reporting 452
  general principles 451–2
  going-concern assumption 451
  income definition 11–12
  income recognition 13
  items outside scope of 158
  key users of 7
  liabilities definition 10–11

liabilities recognition 12
  liquidation basis 451
  measurement of elements 13–14
  non-adjusting events after reporting
      period 474–5
financial statements notes 466–7
  accounting policies and sources of
      estimation uncertainty 467
  disclosure 466, 467
  information about capital 467
financing activities 487, 488, 498–9
finished goods inventory at retail outlet 58
finite useful life 366, 367
firm commitment 182
first-in, first-out (FIFO) cost formula 231,
      232–3, 234
food and beverage industry, earnings per
      share 545
forecast transaction 182, 183
foreign currency hedge 183
foreign currency translation differences 36–7
foreign subsidiaries
  acquisition analysis 692
  business combination valuation entries
      692–3
  consolidating functional currency is that
      of parent entity 698–9
  consolidating where local currency is
      functional currency 691–8
  elimination of investment 693
  intragroup transactions 693–4
  non-controlling interest (NCI) 693
  translating statements of 680
formal agreements 246
for-profit companies 23
forward contracts 171, 186
forward derivatives 167
*Framework for the Preparation and
      Presentation of Financial Statements*
      (the Framework) 6
fringe benefits 246
full goodwill method 639–40
  compared with partial goodwill 642
  consolidation worksheet at acquisition
      date 646–8
functional currency
  changing 689
  identifying 683–4
  rationale behind using 680–2
  statement of financial position 685
  statement of profit or loss and other
      comprehensive income 685
  translating into 684–8
  translation from local currency into 686–8
future cash flow, measuring 422
futures derivatives 167
gain on bargain purchase
  consolidation worksheets 587–8
  NCI 658–60
gains 12
  expected disposal of assets 102
general price level accounting system 14
generally accepted accounting principles
      (GAAP) *see* US GAAP
global financial crisis (GFC)
  impact on IAS 39: 156, 162
  report on financial instruments during
      156–7
going-concern assumption 9–10
  financial statements 451

going-concern goodwill 389
goods in transit 228–9
goodwill 385, 388–91
  accounting for 390–1
  acquisition analysis 581–2
  allocation to cash-generating units 427
  cash-generating units 427, 430–2
  components 389
  deferred tax liability 136–7
  difference from identifiable net assets 390
  disclosure of unallocated 434
  foreign subsidiaries 692
  impairment test 419, 430–2
  internally generated 364
  reversal of impairment loss 432–3
guaranteed residual value 328
hedge accounting 181–8
  alternatives 188
  conditions for application 182–7
  discontinuing 187–8
  effectiveness 183, 187
  fair value and cash flow hedges 184–7
  hedge ratio 187–8
  hedged item 182
  hedging instrument 182
  rebalancing 187–8
  types of hedging relationships 182–7
highest and best use of a non-financial asset
  60, 61–2
hire purchase agreements 322
historical cost measurement 13
hold to collect and sell business model 169
hold to collect business model 169
IAS® standards see International Accounting
  Standards
IASB® see International Accounting Standards
  Board
IASB and IFRS Interpretations Committee Due
  Process Handbook 5
IASB and the IASC Foundation: Who We Are
  and What We Do 4
IASB®/FASB joint projects
  on leasing 322, 348
  on post-employment benefits 256
  on revenue recognition 74
IFRIC® 4–5, 6
IFRIC® Interpretations
  IFRIC 1 Changes in Existing
    Decommissioning, Restoration and Similar
    Liabilities 108
  IFRIC 4 Determining whether an
    Arrangement contains a Lease 322–3
  IFRIC 13 Customer Loyalty Programmes 74
  IFRIC 15 Agreements for the Construction of
    Real Estate 74
  IFRIC 18 Transfers of Assets from
    Customers 74
  IFRIC 21 Levies 108–9
IFRS® see International Financial Reporting
  Standards
IFRS® Advisory Council 5, 6
IFRS® Foundation Trustees 5
IFRS® Interpretations Committee
  4–5, 6, 222
impairment loss 418
  corporate assets 428–30
  reversal 432–3
impairment of assets
  cash-generating units reversal of
    impairment 432

disclosure 433–4
discount rate 422–3
other issues relating to goodwill 431–2
scope of 418
when to undertake impairment test
  418–20
write-downs 423, 431
impairment of assets (cash-generating units
  and goodwill) 430–2
  impairment test 430–2
  reversal of previous impairment loss
    432–3
impairment of assets (cash-generating units
  excluding goodwill) 426–30
  cash flows and individual assets 426
  identifying 426–7
impairment of contract costs 85
impairment test 363, 418
  representation diagram 420
  sources of information 419–20
  timing 431
  when to undertake 418–20
impairment test for individual asset 420–6
  calculating fair value less costs of disposal
    421
  calculating value in use 421–3
  calculating value in use for discount rate
    422
  calculating value in use for future cash
    flows 422
  recognition and measurement of loss
    423–6
  reversal of loss 432
impairment test of goodwill 419, 430–2
  carrying amount exceeds recoverable
    amount 431
  recoverable amount exceeds carrying
    amount 430–1
in-combination valuation premise 60–1
income
  definition 11–12
  recognition 13
income approach valuation 56, 57, 59, 289
  non-financial assets 56
income tax 124
  acknowledging current and future
    consequences of items 126
  amended prior year tax figures 142–3
  annual payment 131
  classification in statement of cash flows
    488–9
  disclosure 144–7
  payment by instalment 131–2
  payment options for 131–2
  presentation in financial statements 143–4
  tax losses 132–3
  see also current tax; deferred tax
incremental fair value 208
incurred loss model 176
indefinite useful life 366, 367
  impairment test for intangible asset 421
indirect method 489, 490, 497, 499
information
  disclosure 467
  relevancy and reliability 8
  segment 518
  use in selecting accounting policies 468
initial direct costs (IDC) 339–40, 341, 342
initial measurement
  financial instruments 171–2

interest-free loan 172
initial public offering (IPO) 26
input methods, revenue recognition 83
inputs
  bid and ask prices 57
  disclosure 65, 66
  level 1: 58, 289
  level 2: 58, 59, 289
  level 3: 59, 67, 289
  prioritising 57–8
  selecting 57
intangible assets 10, 360
  acquisition as part of business
    combination 361–2
  acquisition by way of government grant
    362, 369
  amortisation 366–7
  business combination 384
  cost model 365
  differences between physical and non-
    physical 359
  disclosures 357–8, 367–70
  finite useful life 366, 367
  group classifications 367
  identifiable characteristics 358–9, 389
  impairment test 419, 421
  indefinite useful life 366, 367
  internally generated 362–3
  internally generated goodwill 364
  lack of physical substance characteristic
    359
  measurement subsequent to initial
    recognition 364–7
  monetary assets 358
  nature of 358–60
  non-recognised internally generated 363–4
  probability test 361
  recognising expense 364
  recognition and initial measurement
    criteria 360–3
  research and development disclosure 369
  retirements and disposals 367
  revaluation model 365
  separability tests 358–9
  separate acquisition 361
  subsequent expenditures 365
intellectual property, licences from 86–7
interest rate
  hedge 183
  risk 189
  risk-free 204
International Accounting Standards (IAS®) 4
  Application Guidance (AG) 157
  Basis for Conclusions 7, 8
  IAS 1 Presentation of Financial Statements
    10, 34, 38, 89, 143, 220, 279, 300,
    450–75, 636–7
  IAS 2 Inventories 84, 220–37
  IAS 7 Statement of Cash Flows 486–509
  IAS 8 Accounting Policies, Changes in
    Accounting Estimates and Errors 6, 9, 83,
    234, 283, 304, 468–73
  IAS 10 Events after the Reporting Period 35,
    136, 467, 473–5
  IAS 11 Construction Contracts 74
  IAS 12 Income Taxes 124–48, 607
  IAS 14 Segment Reporting 518
  IAS 16 Property, Plant and Equipment 36,
    50, 84, 220, 276–312, 433, 458
  IAS 17 Leases 74, 322–49

International Accounting Standards
(IAS®) (continued)
IAS 18 Revenue 11, 13, 74
IAS 19 Employee Benefits 97, 102, 246–68
IAS 20 Accounting for Government Grants and
Disclosure of Government Assistance 362
IAS 21 The Effects of Changes in Foreign
Exchange Rates 680–700
IAS 23 Borrowing Costs 222
IAS 24 Related Party Disclosures 538–43
IAS 27 Consolidated and Separate Financial
Statements 74, 164–5, 573–4, 591
IAS 27 Separate Financial Statements 592–3
IAS 28 Investments in Associates and Joint
Ventures 74, 164–5
IAS 30 Disclosures in the Financial
Statements of Banks and Similar Financial
Institutions 157
IAS 32 Financial Instruments: Presentation
26, 33, 65, 157–66, 181, 190, 194
IAS 33 Earnings per Share 543–53
IAS 36 Impairment of Assets 53, 61, 418–38,
593
IAS 37 Provisions, Contingent Liabilities and
Contingent Assets 50, 96–115, 384
IAS 38 Intangible Assets 50, 84, 356–72
IAS 39 Financial Instruments: Recognition
and Measurement 38, 50, 74, 87, 156–7,
176, 181, 183
IAS 40 Investment Property 50
IAS 41 Agriculture 50
International Financial Reporting
Interpretations Committee (IFRIC)
4–5, 6
International Accounting Standards Board
(IASB®) 4–6, 50
advisory bodies 6
corporate responses to exposure drafts
51–2, 56
discussion paper Leases — Preliminary
Views 322
discussion paper Measurement of Tangible
Fixed Assets 284–5
Exposure Draft ED/2010/2 Conceptual
Framework for Financial Reporting — The
Reporting Entity 7
exposure draft Fair Value Measurement 50
formation of 4
highest and best use 60
IASB and IFRS Interpretations Committee
Due Process Handbook 5
IASB Update 6
post-implementation review of IFRS 8:
531–2
standard-setting structure 4–6
International Accounting Standards
Committee (IASC) 4, 6, 96
Framework for the Preparation and
Presentation of Financial Statements (the
Framework) 6
International Accounting Standards
Committee Foundation 4
International Financial Reporting Standards
(IFRS®)
applying professional judgement 4
bundle of assets 280–1
compliance 466
due process for issuing 5–6
fair presentation and compliance 451
IFRS 2 Share-based Payment 200–14

IFRS 3 Business Combinations 53, 96, 105,
113–15, 361, 380–406, 581, 638–9
IFRS 4 Insurance Contracts 74
IFRS 5 Non-current Assets Held for Sale and
Discontinued Operations 220, 545
IFRS 7 Financial Instruments: Disclosures
157, 188–93
IFRS 8 Operating Segments 427, 434,
518–32
reasons for controversy 519
IFRS 9 Financial Instruments 37, 74, 87,
156, 164, 168–71, 172–3, 176–88
IFRS 10 Consolidated Financial Statements
74, 164–5, 381, 562–74, 580, 581,
606–8, 636
IFRS 11 Joint Arrangements 74
IFRS 12 Disclosure of Interests in Other
Entities 572–4, 596, 638
IFRS 13 Fair Value Measurement 50–68,
80, 362
IFRS 15 Revenue from Contracts with
Customers 74–89, 96
IFRS 16 Leases 336, 349
International Organization of Securities
Commissions (IOSCO) 5
intragroup borrowings 616
intragroup dividends 614–16
intragroup services 613–14
realisation of profit or losses 657–8
intragroup transactions 578, 656–8
foreign subsidiaries 693–4
intrinsic value method 207
inventories 232–3
accounting methods 224–7
applying cost formulas 232–4
applying net realisable value rule 236
assigning cost to inventory items
sold 231–4
choice of cost formula 234
consignment 229
consistency in applying costing
methods 234
cost of agricultural produce harvested from
biological assets 238
cost of service providers 222–4
costs of conversion 222
costs of purchase 221–2
cut-off procedures 228
definition 220–1
disclosure 236–7, 457
end-of-period accounting 227–30
excluded costs 222
first-in, first-out (FIFO) cost formula 231,
232–3, 234
goods in transit 228–9
initial recognition of 221
moving average method 231, 232, 233
net realisable value 234–6
other costs 222
periodic method 224–5
perpetual method 225
physical count 227–8
realisation of profits or losses 657
recognition as expense 236
settlement discounts 222
techniques for measuring cost 224
transfers of 607–13
write-downs to net realisable value 235–6
investing activities 487, 496–8
investment properties 303

ancillary services 304
definition and classification 303
disclosure 304–5
joint use 303–4
measurement of 304
transfers in and out of 303
joint use properties 303–4
journal entries
acquiree on liquidation after sale of net
assets 393–4
acquiree on sale of business 393
acquisition of machinery 279
adjusting to net realisable value 236
bonus issue 31
business combination 388
business combination by acquirer 397–8
change of tax rate 142
consolidation for wholly owned
subsidiaries 583, 585–6
convertible notes 164
depreciation 285
depreciation of revalued assets 298, 299
dividends 35, 36
end-of-period adjustments 230
finance lease by lessees 330, 332–3
gain on bargain purchase 392
impairment loss 423–4, 428
income tax owing 131, 132
liquidation of acquiree 394–5
options 30
options lapse 30
payroll 248
placement of shares 29
recognition of goodwill at acquisition
date 391
recouping tax losses 133
revaluation decrease 294
revaluation decrease reversing previous
increase 294, 295
revaluation increases 290
revaluation with associated tax effect
291, 292
rights issues 29
share-based transactions 202
tax effect on gain 291
tax losses 132
treasury share cancellation 33
treasury share reissue 33
write-downs to net realisable value 235
judgement and use in best estimate
assessments 101
lease
bargain purchase option 326, 327
bargain renewal 328
cancellability 324–5
changes to standards for 348–9
classification 323–4
classification guidance 324–30
definitions 322–3, 348
discount rate 327–8
extent of asset's economic life transferred
to lessee 326
gains/losses from fair value fluctuation
328
guaranteed residual value 327
incremental borrowing rate 328
initial direct costs (IDC) 327
minimum lease payments 327
present value of minimum lease
payments 327

residual value risk 328
rewards of ownership 323–4
risk of ownership 323–4
sale and leaseback disclosure 348
sale and leaseback transactions 346–8
specialised asset 328
substantial transfer 328
term 324–6
legal obligation 99, 109
levies 108–9
liabilities
  current 453, 454
  decommissioning 64
  definition 10–11
  fair value measurement 62–4
  held as assets 63–4
  non-performance risk 62–3
  recognition 12
  settlement versus transfer 62
  tax bases 134–5
licences from intellectual property 86–7
limited by guarantee 23
limited liability companies 24
liquidity risk 189, 192–3
listed companies 23
local currency, translating into functional
  currency 686–8
long service leave obligations 263–6
long-term employee benefits 263–6
loss see impairment loss
market approach valuation 56, 57, 59, 289
market capitalisation compared with
  accounting book value 356
market participants 55–6
market risk 189, 193
mark-to-market accounting 156
materiality 8, 451
materials and measures of net realisable
  value 235
measurement bases for financial statements
  13–14
mining industry
  cash and cash equivalents
    disclosures 507
  cash flows from operating activities 488
  current and non-current assets and
    liabilities 454
  disclosures 456, 457
  executive remuneration 252
  non-cash investing and financing
    activities 508
  statement of changes in equity 464–5
monetary assets, translating into functional
  currency 684
most likely amount approach, variable
  consideration estimation 78, 80
moving average method 231, 232, 233
multi-employer plans 253
NCI see non-controlling interest (NCI)
net capitalisation 263
  pension plan 255, 256
net realisable value 234–6, 418
  estimating 235
  reasons for falling below cost 235
no-liability companies 23
non-adjusting events 474–5
non-cancellable lease 324–5, 345
non-cancellable service agreements 323
non-cash consideration, transaction price
  determination 80

non-controlling interest (NCI) 383, 565
  disclosure 572–3, 636–8
  foreign subsidiaries 693
  nature of 636
  see also consolidation for non-controlling
    interest (NCI)
non-current assets held for sale 66
non-derivative financial instruments 163
non-monetary assets
  fair value measurement 59–62
  highest and best use 60
  translating into functional currency
    684–5, 698
non-performance risk liabilities 62–3
non-tradeable rights 29
obligating event 99, 110
obligation 97
  constructive 97, 99, 106, 109
  legal 99, 109
  possible 97–8
  present 97–8, 99, 106
observable inputs 57, 421
off balance sheet 255, 256, 322
offsetting
  financial assets and liabilities 65, 181, 452
  hedge accounting 182
  manufactured 181
  tax assets and liabilities 143
onerous contracts 104–5, 110
operating activities 487, 488
operating cycle 220, 454–5
operating lease 323, 342–6
  accounting for 342–3
  accounting for lease incentives 345–6
  accounting for lessees 342
  accounting for lessors 342
  classification guidance 324, 325, 329
  depreciation of leased assets 342
  disclosure for lessees 344
  disclosure for lessors 344–5
  initial direct costs (IDC) 341
  provision requirements 110
  sale and leaseback transactions 347–8
operating segments 518–32
  75% threshold 522
  aggregation criteria 522–3
  applying definition of reportable
    segments 524
  applying disclosures in practice 527–31
  automobile industry 527–31
  basic criteria 522
  chief operating decision maker
    (CODM) 520
  comparative information disclosure 527
  disclosure 524–7
  entity-wide disclosures 526–7
  four steps in identifying segments 521
  general information disclosure 525
  identifying 520–2
  identifying reportable segments 522–3
  identifying segments using matrix
    structure 521–2
  maximum number of reportable
    segments 523
  measurement disclosure 525–6
  non-reportable segments 522
  profit or loss, assets and liabilities
    disclosure 525
  quantitative thresholds 522, 524
  reconciliations disclosure 526

results of post-implementation review of
  IFRS 8: 531–2
segment managers 520
vertically integrated businesses 522
option contracts 166, 167
option-pricing models 203–4, 213
options 29–30, 550–1
orderly transactions 52
ordinary shares 24–5, 158
  dilutive potential 550
  equity/liability test 160–1
other comprehensive income (OCI) 34
  revaluation increases 290
  see also statement of profit or loss and
    other comprehensive income
output methods, revenue recognition 83
owners 23, 24, 29, 31, 566–7
owners' equity 22
parent entities 564, 569
partial capitalisation methods 255
partial goodwill method 640–2
  compared with full goodwill 642
  consolidation worksheet at acquisition
    date 648–50
partnerships 22
patents 55
payroll 247
  accounting 247–8
  accrual of wages and salaries 248–9
pension plans 253
  accounting for defined benefit 255
  determining deficit or surplus 256–8
  modifications to defined benefit 259–60
performance obligations
  disclosure 89
  identification 76–7
  satisfaction 82–4
  separate 76–7
periodic method 224–5
  compared with perpetual method 225–7
  cost of inventory items 231
  cut-off procedures 228
  physical count 227–8
periodic returns 158
perpetual method 225
  compared with periodic method 225–7
  cost of inventory items 231
  cut-off procedures 228
  end-of-period adjustments 229–30
  physical count 227–8
pharmaceutical industry
  disclosure 111–13
  intangible assets 369–70
physical capital 14
plant, foreign subsidiaries 692–3
possible obligation 97–8
post-employment benefits 253–4
  defined benefit plans 253, 255–63
  defined contribution plans 253, 254
potential voting rights
  convertible debt instruments 568
  exercisable options 568
pre-acquisition entries 578
  gain on bargain purchase at acquisition
    date 588
  worksheet entries at acquisition date
    584–5
pre-emptive rights 23
preference shares 25–6, 161, 163, 545–6
present obligation 97–8, 99, 106

present value measurement 14
  decommissioning liability 64
  expected cash flow approach 422
  provision 101–2
presentation currency 680
  statement of financial position 689–90
  statement of profit or loss and other
    comprehensive income 690–1
  translating into 689–91
principal markets 54–5
principals 569
  revenue from contracts with customers 87
probability 99
probability test 361
product warranties 99
projected unit credit method 256–7, 263,
  264–6
property, plant and equipment
  accounting for depreciable 291–2
  acquisition date 280
  acquisition for zero or nominal cost 282
  acquisition of multiple assets 280–1
  capitalisation of outlays 284
  choosing between cost and revaluation
    models 299–300
  costs not to be included 281–2
  costs of dismantling, removal or
    restoration 282–3
  costs to be included 281–2
  definitions 276
  depreciation 284–8
  derecognition reasons 300–1
  directly attributable costs 281–2
  disclosure 301–2, 304–5
  disposals of assets 301
  division into classes 276, 289
  effects of accounting on asset-by-asset
    basis 296–7
  expensing of outlays 278
  generation of future benefits 278
  income earned 282
  initial measurement of 278–83
  initial recognition of 277–8
  investment properties 303–5
  measurement subsequent to initial
    recognition 283
  purchase price measurement 279–81
  recording at cost 281
  residual value 287–8
  revaluation by asset or class of asset 297
  revaluation model 289–99
  significant parts approach to asset
    recognition 278
  useful life 284, 286–7
prospectus 26
protective rights 565
provision 96
  accounting where discounting is applied
    103–4
  binding sales agreements 107
  changes and use of 103–4
  contaminated land 109
  contaminated land and constructive
    obligation 109
  costs that do not qualify as
    restructuring 107
  decision tree for 100
  decommissioning 107–8
  definitions 97

difference from contingent liability 98
disclosure 111–13
distinguishing from other liabilities 97
expected disposal of assets 102
future events 102
future operating losses 104
legal obligation 109
levies 108–9
offshore oilfields 109
onerous contracts 110
present value measurement 101–2
qualifying costs 107
recognition criteria 98–100
recording restructuring provisions 106–7
reimbursements 102–3
repairs and maintenance 111
restructuring 96, 105–7
risk-adjusted rate 101–2
risk and uncertainties 101
smoke filters 110
warranties 109, 112
public companies
  initial public offering (IPO) 26
  no-par shares issue 26–7
  oversubscription 27–8
  par value shares issue 24, 27
purchase price measurement 279–81
  acquisition date 280
put option 167
puttable instruments 161
  see also financial liabilities
quantitative disclosures 467
realisable or settlement value
    measurement 14
reclassification adjustments 462–3
reimbursements 102–3
related party relationship 538–43
  close family members with control or
    significant influence 540
  definitions 538, 539
  exemption from disclosure for
    government-related entities 543
  identifying a joint venture 542
  identifying associate of entity 541
  identifying close member of family 538
  identifying control, joint control and
    significant influence 539–40
  identifying key management personnel
    540–1
  identifying post-employment benefit
    plans 542
  key management personnel
    remuneration 543
  non-related relationships 542
  related party transactions and related party
    relationships disclosures 542–3
relative stand-alone selling price method 81
  application 82
relevancy of financial information 8
reporting entity 7
research costs 135, 362
reserves 22, 34–8
  disclosure notes 37
  transfers 37–8
residual approach, stand-alone selling price
    determination 81
residual value of property, plant and
    equipment 287–8
residual value risk 328

restructuring provisions 96, 105–7
retail cost method 222
retail industry
  disclosures 213, 398–400, 540–1
  executive remuneration 544
  key management personnel 540–1
  key management personnel compensation
    543
  potential dilutive ordinary shares 549
  property, plant and equipment 276–7
  transactions with directors and key
    management personnel 543
retained earnings 34–6
revaluation model 291
  asset-by-asset basis accounting 289–93
  class-by-class basis 297
  cost associated with 299
  decrease reversing previous increase 294–5
  depreciation of revalued assets 298–9
  impaired asset 423–4
  intangible assets 365
  net revaluation increase reversing previous
    decrease 295–6
  property, plant and equipment 283,
    289–99
  reasons for adopting 299–300
  revaluation decrease 293–6
  revaluation decrease worksheet 295
  revaluation increase reversing previous
    decrease 293
  revaluation increases 289–93
  revaluation increases and depreciable
    assets 291–2
  revaluation increases and tax-effect
    worksheet 292–3
  transferring surplus to retained
    earnings 297
revenue, classification of 164
revenue from contracts with customers 74
  contract costs 84–5
  contract identification 75–6
  contract modifications 85–6
  licences of intellectual property 86–7
  performance obligations identification
    76–7
  performance obligations
    satisfaction 82–4
  presentation and disclosures 87–9
  principal versus agent considerations 87
  scope 74
  transaction price allocation 81–2
  transaction price determination 78–81
reverse acquisitions in business combination
    571–2
rights see protective rights; substantive rights
rights issues 29
  adjustment factor containing a bonus
    element 548
  theoretical ex-rights value per share 548
royalties on licences of intellectual
    property 87
sales-based royalties on licences of
    intellectual property 87
scrip dividends 34–5
service agreements 323
settlement 134, 162–3
  versus transfer 62
share-based transactions 32, 200–1, 213
  form and features of 201

grant of equity instruments that are repriced 208–9
grant of equity instruments where exercise price varies 206
grant where number of equity instruments expected varies 204–5
grant with market condition 206
grant with performance condition linked to earnings 205
modifications to terms and conditions 208–9
recognition criteria 201–2
repurchases 209
treatment of non-vesting conditions 207
treatment of reload features 207–8
treatment of vesting conditions 204–7
share capital 23
authorisation to increase 28
issue of 26–8
subsequent decreases 32–4
subsequent movements 28–32
share investments 159
share options
accounting for repriced 208–9
disclosure 212–13
recognition as services are rendered across vesting period 203
reload features 207–8
share split 31–2
share warrants 31
shareholders see owners
shares
buy-back 32, 34
cost of issuing 26
issued at discount 27
issued at premium 27
level of ownership 566–7
oversubscription 27–8
placement of 28–9
returns to shareholders 25
rights issues 29
see also public companies
short-term paid absences 249–52
SIC® see Standing Interpretations Committee
sick leave 246, 249, 251–2
significant financing component, transaction price determination 80
significant judgements 89
significant parts depreciation 288
sole proprietors 22
solely payments of principal and interest (SPPI) test 170
stand-alone selling prices 81–2
stand-alone valuation premise 60
standard cost methods 222
Standards Advisory Council (SAC) 4
Standing Interpretations Committee (SIC®)
SIC Interpretation 15 Operating Leases — Incentives 345, 346
SIC Interpretation 31 Revenue — Barter Transaction Involving Advertising Services 74
statement of cash flows
accounts payable explanation 503
accrued liabilities explanation 503
cash and cash equivalents 486–7
cash flows from financing activities 498–9
cash flows from investing activities 496–8
cash flows from operating activities 492–6

changes in ownership interest of subsidiaries and other businesses 506–8
classifying cash flow activities 487–9
classifying interest and dividends received and paid 488
classifying taxes on income 488–9
components of cash and cash equivalents disclosure 506
depreciation of plant and impairment of intangibles explanation 504
determining cash paid to suppliers and employees 493–5
determining cash receipts from customers 492–3
determining income tax paid 495–6
determining interest paid 495
determining interest recovered 493
disclosures that are encouraged but not required 509
explanations for reconciling adjustments in worksheet 503–5
financial statements 499
financial statements and additional accounting information 491–2
gain on sale of plant explanation 504
income tax paid explanation 504
increase in cash and short-term deposits explanation 505
increase in net accounts receivable explanation 503
interest expense explanation 504
interest income explanation 504
inventory increase explanation 503
non-cash transaction disclosures 508–9
preparing 491–506
prepayments explanation 503
proceeds from borrowings explanation 505
proceeds from share issue and payment of cash dividends explanation 505
profit before tax adjustments explanation 503
purchase of land and plant explanation 505
purpose of 486
reporting from investing and financing activities 490
reporting from operating activities 489–90
reporting on net basis 490
share of profits of associate explanation 503–4
summarising cash flows from operating activities 496
worksheet 501–2
worksheet approach 499–506
statement of changes in equity 38–9, 463–5
information for presentation 463–5
NCI disclosure 637
statement of financial position 452–7
asset revaluation surplus disclosure 291
classifications 453–5
disclosure 189–90, 638
functional currency translation 685
information required for notes 456–7
information required for presentation 455–7
limitations 453
presentation currency translation 689–90

statement of profit or loss and other comprehensive income 457–63
additional line items and labelling 459–60
functional currency translation 685
information required for presentation 458–63
items of comprehensive income 458
limitations 457
NCI disclosure 637
presentation currency translation 690–1
revaluation increases 290
tax expense 144
stock dividend 31
straight-line method of depreciation 285, 301
structured entities 573
subsequent measurement
exceptions to rule 174
finance lease by lessors 337–9
financial instruments 172–5
lease liability 331
leased assets 331
subsidiaries 564
see also controlled entities; foreign subsidiaries; wholly-owned subsidiaries
subsidiary ledgers 225
substantive rights 565
superannuation see pension plans
supermarket industry
option pricing models 204
owners' equity 22
sustainability reports 450
swap contracts 167
swaps, credit default 188
tangible assets 276
tax expense 124, 144
tax rates
calculating deferred tax 136
change in 142
taxable profit
circumstances for 125–6
difference from accounting profit 124–6
permanent differences 124
temporary differences 124–6, 133
taxable temporary differences 135, 140
tax-effect worksheets 292–3, 295
technical obsolescence 286–7
telecommunications industry 23
calculating fair value less costs of disposal 421
impairment of assets 420, 424–6
inventories 221
share capital 24–5
treasury shares 34
time value of money 177–8
timeliness of information 8–9
trade payables 97
tradeable rights 29
trademarks 55, 59, 60, 366, 367
transaction and transport costs 52–3, 54–5
transaction price
allocation 81–2
determination 78–81
transfer versus settlement 62
treasury shares 546
cancelled 33–4
kept in the company 32
reissued 33
UK Accounting Standards Board 284–5

understandability of information 8–9
unit holder funds 161
unit of account 53
unit trusts 161
units-of-production method 286
unlimited companies 23
unlisted companies 23
unobservable inputs 57, 59, 421
   disclosure 67
unrealised profits 608, 657
US GAAP 50, 74, 299, 324, 348, 519

usage-based royalties on licences of
   intellectual property 87
useful life 284, 286–7, 331
   assessment of 287
   finite and indefinite 366, 367
   intangible assets 366–7
valid expectation test 107
valuation premise 60–2
valuation techniques disclosure 66
value in use 61
variable consideration 78–80

estimating 78, 79
verifiability of information 8–9
vesting conditions
   distinguishing between non-vesting and
   207
   share-based transactions 204–7
warrants 31, 550
weighted average cost formula 231–4
weighted average exercise prices 212–13
wholly-owned subsidiaries 578–98
write-downs 235–6, 423, 431

Printed and bound by CPI Group (UK) Ltd, Croydon, CR0 4YY
04/08/2021
03078290-0001